Songs of the American Theater

Songs of the American Theater

A comprehensive listing of more than 12,000 songs, including selected titles from film and television productions

RICHARD LEWINE
AND
ALFRED SIMON

Introduction by Stephen Sondheim

DODD, MEAD & COMPANY · NEW YORK

144606

ISBN: 0–396–06657–7
Library of Congress Catalog Card Number: 72–3931

Printed in the United States of America
by The Haddon Craftsmen, Inc., Scranton, Penna.

Contents

Authors' Notes

THIS BOOK contains a listing of songs from all Broadway and off-Broadway theater productions from 1925 through 1971. Also included are more than three hundred songs from productions prior to 1925, some going back to the turn of the century. These are songs by masters of operetta—Herbert, Friml, and Romberg—as well as early works by such writers as Berlin, Kern, Porter, and Gershwin.

There are also songs written for the films by theater composers and lyricists in the unmistakable style and texture of the theater. They are designated by (F) following the title of the production. Songs for television by such writers are also listed, with the designation (TV) after the production's title.

In the first section of the book, the songs are arranged alphabetically with the name of the composer on the line below the title. Lyric authorship is on the next line, and the production, with the year of its New York premiere, appears on the last line. Songs with music and lyrics by the same writer or writers have their authorship credited on the line following the title. Shows produced off-Broadway are indicated by (OB).

In the second section, there is an alphabetical listing of the productions that includes, in addition to song titles and authorship credits, the dates of the New York opening, the length of the New York run, and information about record albums, complete vocal scores, and what are known as vocal selections—paper-bound folios containing the show's principal songs.

For further cross-reference, there is a chronological year-by-year list of productions and an index of the composers and lyricists.

Happily for those who undertake projects such as this, there exists a large and well-informed body of authorities on the American theater song. We are particularly grateful to Paul Myers, Curator of the New York Public Library's Theatre Collection at Lincoln Center; to Charles Gaynor, Stanley Green, Daniel Langan, Robert E. Kimball, and Haskel Frankel; to both ASCAP and the Shubert Theatre Enterprises; and, finally, to Cornelia M. Lewine for her dedicated and knowledgeable assistance.

RICHARD LEWINE
ALFRED SIMON

Introduction:
What Is That From?

by STEPHEN SONDHEIM

THE QUESTION most often muttered among show-tune buffs is neither "Did you see—?" nor "Have you heard—?" but "What is that from?" Whether it's the friendly neighborhood piano-player at a party, or Bobby Short in a boite, or the song on the record in the background, the inevitable and forever accompaniment is "What is that from?" Well, this book is the permanent definitive answer for every frustrated musical-comedy fan (and, I'm happy to say, there are still thousands) who's ever asked, "What is that from?" Sure, they (we) all know that "Just One of Those Things" is from *Jubilee*—or is it? Turn these pages to the listing of titles for an earlier Cole Porter show, *The New Yorkers* (handily cross-referenced). Different tune but same title, which demonstrates that Mr. Porter never let a good idea go.

Second question: Who cares? (There are four theater songs called "I Love You.") Such information comes readily under the heading of Trivia and, even if this *is* the age of Trivia—accessories in fashion, minute nostalgic reportage in everything else—why should anyone, no matter how fanatical, need or bother to own this book? (Gershwin wrote with Hammerstein?) These questions breed another: What is the difference between Trivia and Information? Answer: Accumulate enough Trivia and you have, respectably, a Reference Book. The *Encyclopedia Britannica* is a compendium of Trivia, as are Webster's Unabridged, the *Farmer's Almanac*, Brewer's *Dictionary of Phrase and Fable*, and a Shakespeare concordance—five of the world's most entertaining objects. Reference books can be the best of browsing, as Trivia can be the best of conversation.

The codifying of any cultural phenomenon is not only pleasure-giving but also necessary—and always a labor of love. The scrupulous work herein of Richard Lewine and Alfred Simon will not make them rich, or even famous. It will be outdated by the time this page is in print: How will we know what songs were deleted from *Sugar?* We can only hope for yearly supplements. But let us be grateful that the record of an enormous minor American art-form has finally been written down—the first and only accurate and blessedly unopinionated catalogue of songs composed for one of the most popular and influential cultural outcroppings of this century: Broadway musical comedy.

Considering *how* popular and *how* influential, it seems astonishing that no one before Lewine and Simon has bothered to research the material in detail. Every other creative effort from painting to playwriting has been exhaustively accounted for: You can easily look up the author of *Sanctuary,* but just try to do the same for "Brother, Can You Spare a Dime?" (shorter but not smaller, and just as significant).

With this book, Lewine and Simon have supported the dignity of what is still considered a stepsister craft. ("Of course, our only original and indigenous art-forms are jazz and musical comedy.") Regrettably, it lacks one thing: The sound of the songs themselves, although there is a discography calculated to make you weep over the recordings you don't have which are no longer available. Perhaps Dick Lewine will devote the next twenty years of his life to an aural *Songs of the American Theater.* As one who has stood by his piano till three in the morning listening to him play obscure choruses and even more obscure verses and asking over and over, "What is that from?" I can assure you it's a consummation devoutly to be wished.

Theater Songs

Theater Songs

A + B= C
Edwin Greenberg
Pilgrim's Progress (OB) (1962)

A-B-C
Elmer Bernstein
Carolyn Leigh
How Now, Dow Jones (1967)

A. B. C's
Mark Bucci
David Rogers
New Faces (1962)

A.B.C. Song, The
Leslie Bricusse and Anthony Newley
Stop the World—I Want to Get Off
   (1962)

ABC's of Success, The
David Baker
Fred Ebb
Smiling, the Boy Fell Dead (OB)
(1961)

A la Pimpernel
Mimi Stone
William Kaye
Pimpernel! (OB) (1964)

A la Viennese
H. Maurice Jacquet
William Brady
The Silver Swan (1929)

A Toujours
Frederick Loewe
Alan Jay Lerner
Gigi (F) (1957)

Abandon
Ida Hoyt Chamberlain
Enchanted Isle (1927)

Abbondanza
Frank Loesser
The Most Happy Fella (1956)

Abe Lincoln
Earl Robinson and Alfred Hayes
Hellzapoppin' (1938)

Abie Baby
Galt MacDermot
Gerome Ragni and James Rado
Hair (1968)

Abou Ben Adhem
Ray Golden
Alive and Kicking (1950)

About Face
Gerald Marks
Sam Lerner
Hold It! (1948)

Abracadabra
Cole Porter
Mexican Hayride (1944)

Abraham
Irving Berlin
Holiday Inn (F) (1942)

Absinthe Frappe
Victor Herbert
Glen MacDonough
It Happened in Nordland (1904)

ACADEMIC FUGUE
Bob Merrill
Henry, Sweet Henry (1967)

ACCENT-CHU-ATE THE POSITIVE
Harold Arlen
Johnny Mercer
Here Come the Waves (F) (1944)

ACCORDING TO MR. GRIMES
George Gershwin
Ira Gershwin
Treasure Girl (1928)

ACCORDING TO PLOTNIK
Sol Berkowitz
James Lipton
Miss Emily Adam (OB) (1960)

ACE IN THE HOLE
Cole Porter
Let's Face It! (1941)

ACE OF SPADES
Frank Marcus and Bernard Maltin
Bamboola (1929)

ACES UP
William Heagney
William Heagney and Tom Connell
There You Are (1932)

ACORN IN THE MEADOW
Richard Adler and Jerry Ross
John Murray Anderson's Almanac
  (1953)

ACT LIKE A LADY
Robert Waldman
Alfred Uhry
Here's Where I Belong (1968)

ADD A LITTLE WIGGLE
Milton Ager
Jack Yellen
Rain or Shine (1928)

ADDIE'S AT IT AGAIN
Jack Lawrence and Stan Freeman
I Had a Ball (1964)

ADELAIDE
Frank Loesser
Guys and Dolls (F) (1955)

ADELAIDE'S LAMENT
Frank Loesser
Guys and Dolls (1950)

ADORABLE
Tom Ford and Ray Wynburn
Earl Carroll's Vanities (1926)

ADORABLE JULIE
Lewis E. Gensler
Owen Murphy and Robert A. Simon
The Gang's All Here (1931)

ADORABLE YOU
Karl Hajos (based on Chopin)
Harry B. Smith
White Lilacs (1928)

ADRIFT
John Addison
John Cranko
Cranks (1956)

ADRIFT ON A STAR
Jacques Offenbach
E. Y. Harburg
The Happiest Girl in the World (1961)

ADVENTURE
Jule Styne
Betty Comden and Adolph Green
Do Re Mi (1960)

ADVICE
Coleman Dowell
The Tattooed Countess (OB) (1961)

ADVICE TO HUSBANDS
Erich Wolfgang Korngold (based on
  Offenbach)
Herbert Baker
Helen Goes to Troy (1944)

AFFABLE, BALDING ME
Robert Emmett Dolan
Johnny Mercer
Texas, Li'l Darlin' (1949)

AFFERDYTIE
Jerry Herman
Madame Aphrodite (OB) (1961)

AFRAID OF LOVE
Alice Clark and David Morton
Vintage '60 (OB) (1960)

AFRAID TO FALL IN LOVE
William Dyer
Don Parks and William Dyer
Jo! (OB) (1964)

AFFLUENT SOCIETY, THE
Jack Lawrence and Stan Freeman
I Had a Ball (1964)

AFRICA
Emmerich Kalman and Herbert Stothart
Otto Harbach and Oscar Hammerstein II
Golden Dawn (1927)

AFRICAN SEQUENCE
Voices, Inc.
The Believers (OB) (1968)

AFRICAN SHRIEKS
Ned Lehak
Edward Eliscu
The Third Little Show (1931)

AFRICAN WHOOPEE
Frank Marcus and Bernard Maltin
Bamboola (1929)

AFRICANA STOMP, THE
Donald Heywood
Africana (1927)

AFRO BLUE
Oscar Brown, Jr. and Mongo Santamaria
Joy (OB) (1970)

AFTER ALL, IT'S SPRING
Walter Kent
Kim Gannon
Seventeen (1951)

AFTER ALL, YOU'RE ALL I'M AFTER
Arthur Schwartz
Edward Heyman
She Loves Me Not (1933)

AFTER GRADUATION
Sidney Lippman
Sylvia Dee
Barefoot Boy with Cheek (1947)

AFTER HOURS
Charles Gaynor
Lend an Ear (1948)

AFTER LOVE
Manos Hadjidakis
Joe Darion
Illya Darling (1967)

AFTER TONIGHT
Al Moss
Alfred Hayes
Tis of Thee (1940)

AFTER YOU
Cole Porter
Gay Divorce (1932)

AFTERNOON OF A PHONEY, THE
John Green
George Marion, Jr.
Beat the Band (1942)

AFTERWARD
Hal Jordan
Jerry Douglas
Rondelay (OB) (1969)

AGE OF MIRACLES
Alyn Heim
Malcolm L. LaPrade
Will the Mail Train Run Tonight?
(OB) (1964)

AGENT'S BLOOD, AN
Willard Straight
David Eddy
The Athenian Touch (OB) (1964)

AGES AGO
Vernon Duke
Time Remembered (1957)

AGGIE
Leon Carr
Earl Shuman
The Secret Life of Walter Mitty (OB)
  (1964)

AGGIE, OH AGGIE
Mitch Leigh
William Alfred and Phyllis Robinson
Cry for Us All (1970)

AGGIE'S SEWING MACHINE SONG
Kurt Weill
Paul Green
Johnny Johnson (1936)

AGNES AND ME
Baldwin Bergersen
William Archibald
The Crystal Heart (OB) (1960)

AGUA SINCOPADA
Cole Porter
Wake Up and Dream (1929)

AH! CAMMINARE
Milton Schafer
Ronny Graham
Bravo Giovanni (1962)

AH, HUM; OH, HUM
Frank Fields
Armand Aulicino
The Shoemaker and the Peddler (OB)
  (1960)

AH, PARIS!
Stephen Sondheim
Follies (1971)

AH STILL SUITS ME
Jerome Kern
Oscar Hammerstein II
Show Boat (F) (1936)

AH, SWEET MYSTERY OF LIFE
Victor Herbert
Rida Johnson Young
Naughty Marietta (1910)

AI YI YI
Manning Sherwin
Harold Purcell
Under the Counter (1947)

AIN'T GOT NO
Galt MacDermot
Gerome Ragni and James Rado
Hair (1968)

AIN'T HE A JOY?
Michael Leonard
Herbert Martin
The Yearling (1965)

AIN'T IT A SHAME?
Jack Urbont
Bruce Geller
Livin' the Life (OB) (1957)

AIN'T IT AWFUL, THE HEAT?
Kurt Weill
Langston Hughes
Street Scene (1947)

AIN'T IT FUNNY?
Stefan Kanfer, Jess J. Gorman, and Jo-
  seph Grayhon
I Want You (OB) (1961)

AIN'T IT THE TRUTH
Harold Arlen
E. Y. Harburg
Jamaica (1957)

AIN'T LOVE GRAND
Joseph Meyer and Philip Charig
Leo Robin
Just Fancy (1927)

AIN'T LOVE WONDERFUL?
Lewis E. Gensler
B. G. DeSylva
Captain Jinks (1925)

AIN'T MISBEHAVIN'
Thomas (Fats) Waller and Harry
  Brooks
Andy Razaf
Hot Chocolates (1929)

AIN'T PUTTIN' OUT NOTHIN'
J. C. Johnson
Change Your Luck (1930)

AIN'T WE GOT LOVE
Eubie Blake
J. Milton Reddie and Cecil Mack
Swing It (1937)

AIN'T YOU ASHAMED?
Sol Berkowitz
James Lipton
Nowhere to Go but Up (1962)

AIN'T YOU NEVER BEEN AFRAID?
Jerry Bock
Sheldon Harnick
Man in the Moon (1963)

AIN'TCHA GLAD YOU GOT MUSIC
Alexander Hill
Hummin' Sam (1933)

AIR
Galt MacDermot
Gerome Ragni and James Rado
Hair (1968)

AIR MINDED
Ray Henderson
B. G. DeSylva and Lew Brown
Flying High (1930)

A. J.
Harry Archer
Will B. Johnstone
Entre-Nous (OB) (1935)

ALABAMA STOMP
James P. Johnson
Henry Creamer
Earl Carroll's Vanities (1926)

ALADDIN
Cole Porter
Aladdin (TV) (1958)

ALADDIN'S DAUGHTER
Jimmy Van Heusen
Johnny Burke
Nellie Bly (1946)

ALAS FOR YOU
Stephen Schwartz
Godspell (OB) (1971)

ALAS, THE TIME IS PAST
Noël Coward
Bitter Sweet (1929)

ALDONZA
Mitch Leigh
Joe Darion
Man of La Mancha (1965)

ALE HOUSE SONG
Robert Kessler
Lola Permagent
O Marry Me! (OB) (1961)

ALESSANDRO THE WISE
Kurt Weill
Ira Gershwin
The Firebrand of Florence (1945)

ALEXANDER'S RAGTIME WEDDING DAY
Porter Grainger and Freddie Johnson
Lucky Sambo (1925)

ALI BABA BABIES, THE
Jerome Kern
Anne Caldwell and Otto Harbach
Criss-Cross (1926)

ALICE BLUE GOWN
Harry Tierney
Joseph McCarthy
Irene (1919)

ALICE IN BOOGIELAND
Sidney Lippman
Sylvia Dee
Barefoot Boy with Cheek (1947)

ALICE IN WONDERLAND
Irving Berlin
The Century Girl (1916)

ALIEN SONG
Sam Shepard
Operation Sidewinder (1970)

ALISON DEAR
Paul Hoffert
David Secter
Get Thee to Canterbury (OB) (1969)

ALIVE AND KICKING
Hal Borne
Ray Golden and Sid Kuller
Alive and Kicking (1950)

ALIVE AND KICKING
Hugh Martin and Ralph Blane
Best Foot Forward (OB) (1963)

ALL ABOARD
Sol Berkowitz
James Lipton
Miss Emily Adam (OB) (1960)

ALL ABOARD FOR PARIS
Edward Kunneke (based on Offenbach)
Harry B. Smith
The Love Song (1925)

ALL ABOARD FOR TIMES SQUARE
Dave Stamper
Gene Buck
Take the Air (1927)

ALL ABOUT EVELYN
Jane Douglas
Tom O'Malley
Bella (OB) (1961)

ALL ABOUT ME
Bruce Montgomery
The Amorous Flea (OB) (1964)

ALL ALONE
Nancy Ford
Gretchen Cryer
Now Is the Time for All Good Men (OB) (1967)

ALL ALONE MONDAY
Harry Ruby
Bert Kalmar
The Ramblers (1926)

ALL AMERICAN
David Baker
Sheldon Harnick
Vintage '60 (OB) (1960)

ALL AMERICAN
Leslie Bricusse and Anthony Newley
Stop the World—I Want to Get Off (1962)

ALL AMERICAN
Paul Nassau and Oscar Brand
The Education of Hyman Kaplan (1968)

ALL AMERICAN MAN
Sammy Fain
George Marion, Jr.
Toplitzky of Notre Dame (1946)

ALL-AMERICAN TWO-STEP, THE
Will Holt
That 5 A.M. Jazz (OB) (1964)

ALL AROUND THE WORLD
Jimmy Van Heusen
Johnny Burke
Nellie Bly (1946)

ALL AROUND THE WORLD
David Baker
David Craig
Phoenix '55 (OB) (1955)

ALL AT ONCE
Richard Rodgers
Lorenz Hart
Babes in Arms (1937)

ALL AT ONCE
Kurt Weill
Ira Gershwin
Where Do We Go from Here? (F) (1945)

ALL AT ONCE YOU LOVE HER
Richard Rodgers
Oscar Hammerstein II
Pipe Dream (1955)

ALL DARK PEOPLE
Richard Rodgers
Lorenz Hart
Babes in Arms (1937)

ALL DRESSED UP
Ernest G. Schweikert
Frank Reardon
Rumple (1957)

ALL ER NOTHIN'
Richard Rodgers
Oscar Hammerstein II
Oklahoma! (1943)

ALL FOR HIM
Frederick Loewe
Alan Jay Lerner
Paint Your Wagon (1951)

ALL FOR LOVE
Allan Roberts
Lester Lee
All for Love (1949)

ALL FOR ONE AND ONE FOR ALL
Rudolf Friml
P. G. Wodehouse and Clifford Grey
The Three Musketeers (1928)

ALL FOR THE BEST
Stephen Schwartz
Godspell (OB) (1971)

ALL FOR YOU
Lee Pockriss
Anne Croswell
Tovarich (1963)

ALL GALL
Donald Swann
Michael Flanders
At the Drop of Another Hat (1966)

ALL-GIRL BAND, THE
Morgan Lewis
Nancy Hamilton
Two for the Show (1940)

ALL GOOD GIFTS
Stephen Schwartz
Godspell (OB) (1971)

ALL HAIL THE EMPRESS
Robert Wright and George Forrest
(based on Rachmaninoff)
Anya (1965)

ALL I NEED IS ONE GOOD BREAK
John Kander
Fred Ebb
Flora, the Red Menace (1965)

ALL I NEED IS SOMEONE LIKE YOU
Harry Archer
Charles Tobias
Keep It Clean (1929)

ALL I NEED IS THE GIRL
Jule Styne
Stephen Sondheim
Gypsy (1959)

ALL I OWE IOWAY
Richard Rodgers
Oscar Hammerstein II
State Fair (F) (1945)

ALL I WANT IS LOVE
Hal Dyson
James Kendis
June Days (1925)

ALL IN FUN
Jerome Kern
Oscar Hammerstein II
Very Warm For May (1939)

ALL IN FUN
Walter Marks
Golden Rainbow (1968)

ALL IN LOVE
Jacques Urbont
Bruce Geller
All in Love (OB) (1961)

ALL IN THE CAUSE OF ECONOMY
David Heneker
Half a Sixpence (1965)

ALL IS VANITY
Morris Hamilton
Grace Henry
Earl Carroll's Vanities (1926)

ALL IS WELL IN LARCHMONT
Albert Hague
Allen Sherman
The Fig Leaves Are Falling (1969)

ALL IS WELL IN THE CITY
Al Carmines
Maria Irene Fornes
Promenade (OB) (1969)

ALL I'VE GOT TO GET NOW IS MY MAN
Cole Porter
Panama Hattie (1940)

ALL KINDS OF GIANTS
Sam Pottle
Tom Whedon
All Kinds of Giants (OB) (1961)

ALL KINDS OF PEOPLE
Richard Rodgers
Oscar Hammerstein II
Pipe Dream (1955)

ALL LANES MUST REACH A TURNING
Jerome Kern
Howard Dietz
Dear Sir (1924)

ALL OF 'EM SAY
Jack Urbont
Bruce Geller
Livin' the Life (OB) (1957)

ALL OF MY LAUGHTER
Albert Hague
Allen Sherman
The Fig Leaves Are Falling (1969)

ALL OF MY LIFE
Jule Styne
Betty Comden and Adolph Green
Do Re Mi (1960)

ALL OF THESE AND MORE
Jerry Bock
Sheldon Harnick
The Body Beautiful (1958)

ALL OF YOU
Cole Porter
Silk Stockings (1955)

ALL OUT BUGLE CALL
Ann Ronell
Count Me In (1942)

ALL OVER MY MIND
Mike Brandt, Michael Knight, and Robert J. Lowery
Exchange (OB) (1970)

ALL THE DEARLY BELOVED
Harvey Schmidt
Tom Jones
I Do! I Do! (1966)

ALL THE ELKS AND MASONS
Harold Arlen
Ira Gershwin and E. Y. Harburg
Life Begins at 8:40 (1934)

ALL THE GIRLS WERE PRETTY
Sandy Wilson
Valmouth (OB) (1960)

ALL THE KING'S HORSES
Alec Wilder, Eddie Brandt, and Howard Dietz
Three's a Crowd (1930)

ALL THE LITTLE THINGS IN THE WORLD ARE WAITING
Lance Mulcahy
Paul Cherry
Park (1970)

ALL THE PRETTY LITTLE HORSES
Paul Klein
Fred Ebb
Morning Sun (OB) (1963)

ALL THE THINGS YOU ARE
Jerome Kern
Oscar Hammerstein II
Very Warm for May (1939)

ALL THE TIME
Arthur Schwartz
Dorothy Fields
Stars in Your Eyes (1939)

ALL THE TIME
Jay Livingston and Ray Evans
Oh Captain! (1958)

ALL THE WAY DOWN
Susan Hulsman Bingham
Myrna Lamb
Mod Donna (OB) (1970)

ALL THE WORLD LOVES A LOVER
Jean Gilbert
Harry Graham
Katja (1926)

ALL THE YOUNG MEN
Jay Thompson
Double Entry (OB) (1961)

ALL THOSE YEARS
Albert Hague
Marty Brill
Café Crown (1964)

ALL THROUGH THE DAY
Jerome Kern
Oscar Hammerstein II
Centennial Summer (F) (1946)

ALL THROUGH THE NIGHT
Cole Porter
Anything Goes (1934)

ALL WE NEED TO KNOW
Willard Straight
David Eddy
The Athenian Touch (OB) (1964)

ALL WORK AND NO PLAY
Tom Johnstone
Phil Cook
When You Smile (1925)

ALL WRAPPED UP IN YOU
Harry Revel
Mack Gordon and Harold Adamson
Everybody's Welcome (1931)

ALL YOU HAVE TO DO IS STAND THERE
Leo Edwards
Herman Timberg
You'll See Stars (1942)

ALL YOU NEED IS A LITTLE LOVE
William Klenosky
Utopia! (OB) (1960)

ALL YOU NEED IS A QUARTER
Jule Styne
Betty Comden and Adolph Green
Do Re Mi (1960)

ALLAH BE PRAISED
Don Walker
George Marion, Jr.
Allah Be Praised (1944)

ALLAH'S HOLIDAY
Rudolf Friml
Otto Harbach
Katinka (1915)

ALLEGHANY AL
Jerome Kern
Oscar Hammerstein II
High, Wide and Handsome (F) (1937)

ALLEGRO
Richard Rodgers
Oscar Hammerstein II
Allegro (1947)

ALLEZ-OOP
Richard Rodgers
Lorenz Hart
The Garrick Gaieties (1926)

ALLEZ-VOUS EN
Cole Porter
Can-Can (1953)

ALLIED HIGH COMMAND, THE
Kurt Weill
Paul Green
Johnny Johnson (1936)

ALLONS
Jerry Bock
Sheldon Harnick
The Rothschilds (1970)

ALL'S FAIR IN LOVE AND WAR
Jean Gilbert
Harry B. Smith
Marching By (1932)

ALL'S WELL
Arthur Schwartz
Howard Dietz
Flying Colors (1932)

ALMANAC COVERS, THE
Henry Sullivan
Edward Eliscu
John Murray Anderson's Almanac
  (1929)

ALMOST
Jack Lawrence and Stan Freeman
I Had a Ball (1964)

ALMOST, BUT NOT QUITE
John Jennings
Riverwind (OB) (1962)

ALMOST LIKE BEING IN LOVE
Frederick Loewe
Alan Jay Lerner
Brigadoon (1947)

ALMOST TOO GOOD TO BE TRUE
James Bredt
Edward Eager
The Happy Hypocrite (OB) (1968)

ALOHA
Rudolf Friml
J. Keirn Brennan
Luana (1930)

ALONE
Giuseppe Verdi
Charles Friedman
My Darlin' Aïda (1952)

ALONE
Jacques Brel
Eric Blau and Mort Shuman
*Jacques Brel Is Alive and Well and
  Living in Paris* (OB) (1968)

ALONE (MY LOVER)
Rudolf Friml
Brian Hooker
The White Eagle (1927)

ALONE TOGETHER
Arthur Schwartz
Howard Dietz
Flying Colors (1932)

ALONE TOO LONG
Arthur Schwartz
Dorothy Fields
By the Beautiful Sea (1954)

ALONE WITH YOU
G. Romilli
Grace Henry and Jo Trent
Fioretta (1929)

ALONG CAME LOVE
Henry Tobias
Charles Tobias and Haven Gillespie
Earl Carroll's Vanities (1932)

ALONG THE WINDING ROAD
Sigmund Romberg
Oscar Hammerstein II
Sunny River (1941)

ALONG WITH ME
Harold Rome
Call Me Mister (1946)

ALPHA, BETA, PI
Jerome Kern
Otto Harbach
Roberta (1933)

ALPHABET SONG
Eaton Magoon, Jr.
13 Daughters (1961)

ALPHABET SONG, THE
Rick Besoyan
Babes in the Wood (OB) (1964)

ALPHABET SONG, THE
Walt Smith
Leon Uris
Ari (1971)

ALPHAGENESIS
Kenn Long and Jim Crozier
Kenn Long
Touch (OB) (1970)

ALTERNATE PARKING
Janet Gari
Toby Garson
Lyle (OB) (1970)

ALWAYS ALWAYS YOU
Bob Merrill
Carnival (1961)

ALWAYS ANOTHER GIRL
Winthrop Cortelyou
Derick Wulff
Kiss Me (1927)

ALWAYS BE A GENTLEMAN
Sigmund Romberg
Oscar Hammerstein II
May Wine (1935)

ALWAYS IN MY HEART
Ralph Benatzky
Meet My Sister (1930)

ALWAYS LEAVE 'EM WANTING MORE
Janet Gari
Toby Garson
Lyle (OB) (1970)

ALWAYS MADEMOISELLE
André Previn
Alan Jay Lerner
Coco (1969)

ALWAYS ON THE JOB
Porter Grainger and Freddie Johnson
Lucky Sambo (1925)

ALWAYS ONE DAY MORE
Philip Springer
Carolyn Leigh
Shoestring Revue (OB) (1957)

ALWAYS TRUE TO YOU IN MY FASHION
Cole Porter
Kiss Me, Kate (1948)

ALWAYS YOU
Gerald Marks
Sam Lerner
Hold It! (1948)

AM I?
Harry Archer
Will B. Johnstone
Entre-Nous (OB) (1935)

AM I A MAN OR A MOUSE?
David Raksin
June Carroll
If the Shoe Fits (1946)

AM I ENCHANTED?
Franz Steininger (adapted from Tchaikovsky)
Forman Brown
Music in My Heart (1947)

AMAPU
Melville Gideon
Edward Knoblock
The Optimists (1928)

AMARILLO
Richard Rodgers
Lorenz Hart
They Met in Argentina (F) (1941)

AMBITION
Jule Styne
Betty Comden and Adolph Green
Do Re Mi (1960)

AMERICA
Leonard Bernstein
Stephen Sondheim
West Side Story (1957)

AMERICA LOVES A BAND
John Green
George Marion, Jr.
Beat the Band (1942)

AMERI-CAN-CAN
Roger Wolfe Kahn
Irving Caesar
Americana (1928)

AMERICAN CANNES
Jimmy McHugh
Harold Adamson
As the Girls Go (1948)

AMERICAN EAGLES
Irving Berlin
This Is the Army (1942)

AMERICAN EXPRESS, THE
Cole Porter
Fifty Million Frenchmen (1929)

AMERICAN FAMILY
Cole Porter
Panama Hattie (1940)

AMERICAN FAMILY PLAN
John Jennings
Riverwind (OB) (1962)

AMERICAN PLAN
Jay Gorney
Henry Myers
Meet the People (1940)

AMERICAN PRIMITIVE
Jay Gorney
Jean and Walter Kerr
Touch and Go (1949)

AMERICAN REVUE GIRLS
Con Conrad
J. P. McEvoy
Americana (1926)

AMERICANS ARE COMING, THE
Sigmund Romberg
Oscar Hammerstein II
East Wind (1931)

AMERICANS ARE HERE, THE
Ray Henderson
B. G. DeSylva
Three Cheers (1928)

AMISHMAN, AN
Howard Blankman
By Hex (OB) (1956)

AMOEBA'S LAMENT, THE
Arthur Schwartz
Agnes Morgan
The Grand Street Follies (1929)

AMONG MY YESTERDAYS
John Kander
Fred Ebb
The Happy Time (1968)

AMOROUS ARROW, THE
James Bredt
Edward Eager
The Happy Hypocrite (OB) (1968)

AMOROUS FLEA, THE
Bruce Montgomery
The Amorous Flea (OB) (1964)

AMSTERDAM
Jacques Brel
Eric Blau and Mort Shuman
*Jacques Brel Is Alive and Well and
    Living in Paris* (OB) (1968)

AMY
Roy Webb
F. Coulon
A Night in Paris (1926)

ANATEVKA
Jerry Bock
Sheldon Harnick
Fiddler on the Roof (1964)

ANATOLE OF PARIS
Sylvia Fine
The Straw Hat Revue (1939)

ANCESTRY
Robert Hood Bowers
Francis DeWitt
Oh, Ernest! (1927)

AND A DROP OF LAVENDAR OIL
Jerry Herman
Madame Aphrodite (OB) (1961)

AND HE FLIPPED
John Rox
New Faces (1956)

AND I AM ALL ALONE
Jerome Kern
Jerome Kern and P. G. Wodehouse
Have a Heart (1917)

AND I WAS BEAUTIFUL
Jerry Herman
Dear World (1969)

AND LOVE WAS BORN
Jerome Kern
Oscar Hammerstein II
Music in the Air (1932)

AND RUSSIA IS HER NAME
Jerome Kern
E. Y. Harburg
And Russia Is Her Name (F) (1944)

AND SO HE DIED
Mischa and Wesley Portnoff
Donagh MacDonagh
Happy As Larry (1950)

AND SO WILL YOU
Frederick Loewe
Earle Crooker
Great Lady (1938)

AND THE MOUNTAINS SING BACK
John Morris
Gerald Freedman
A Time for Singing (1966)

AND THIS IS MY BELOVED
Robert Wright and George Forrest
  (based on Alexander Borodin)
Kismet (1953)

AND WHY NOT I?
Morgan Lewis
Nancy Hamilton
Three to Make Ready (1946)

ANGEL
Peter de Rose
Mitchell Parrish
Earl Carroll's Vanities (1940)

ANGEL FACE
Hal Jordan
Jerry Douglas
Rondelay (OB) (1969)

ANGEL WITHOUT WINGS, AN
Seymour Furth and Lee Edwards
R. F. Carroll
Bringing Up Father (1925)

ANGEL WITHOUT WINGS
Richard Rodgers
Lorenz Hart
I Married an Angel (1938)

ANGELICA
Francis Thorne
Arnold Weinstein
Fortuna (OB) (1962)

ANGRY YOUNG MAN, THE
Julian Stein
Lester Judson
Chic (OB) (1959)

ANIMAL ATTRACTION
Charles Strouse
Lee Adams
All American (1962)

ANIMALS
Jordan Ramin
Frank H. Stanton and Murray Semos
Look Where I'm At! (OB) (1971)

ANIMALS ARE NICE
Lee Wainer
J. B. Rosenberg
New Faces (1943)

ANKLE UP THE ALTAR WITH ME
Richard Myers
Edward Eliscu
The Garrick Gaieties (1930)

ANNA
Frank Marcus and Bernard Maltin
Bamboola (1929)

ANNA LILLA
Bob Merrill
New Girl in Town (1957)

ANNA LOUISE OF LOUISIANA
Will Irwin
Norman Zeno
Earl Carroll's Sketch Book (1935)

ANNE OF GREEN GABLES
Norman Campbell
Donald Campbell and Norman Campbell
Anne of Green Gables (OB) (1971)

ANNETTE
Walter Kollo
Harry B. Smith
Three Little Girls (1930)

ANNIE'S THING
Joseph Martinez Kookoolis and Scott Fagan
Scott Fagan
Soon (1971)

ANOTHER AUTUMN
Frederick Loewe
Alan Jay Lerner
Paint Your Wagon (1951)

ANOTHER CANDLE
Jerry Herman
Parade (OB)(1960)

ANOTHER CASE OF THE BLUES
Richard Myers
Johnny Mercer
Tattle Tales (1933)

ANOTHER DAY
G. Wood
F. Jasmine Addams (OB) (1971)

ANOTHER HOT DAY
Harvey Schmidt
Tom Jones
110 in the Shade (1963)

ANOTHER HUNDRED PEOPLE
Stephen Sondheim
Company (1970)

ANOTHER ONE GONE WRONG
Armand Vecsey
P. G. Wodehouse
The Nightingale (1927)

ANOTHER OP'NIN, ANOTHER SHOW
Cole Porter
Kiss Me, Kate (1948)

ANOTHER TIME, ANOTHER PLACE
Richard Adler
Kwamina (1961)

ANSWER, THE
Hal Jordan
Jerry Douglas
Rondelay (OB) (1969)

ANSWER IS NO, THE
Donald Heywood
Blackberries of 1932

ANSWER MY HEART
Alexander Hill
Hummin' Sam (1933)

ANTHEM
Mike Brandt, Michael Knight, and Robert J. Lowery
Exchange (OB) (1970)

ANTIQUE MAN, THE
Jerry Herman
Parade (OB) (1960)

ANY AFTERNOON ABOUT FIVE
William Roy
Maggie (1953)

ANY DAY NOW
Norman Dean
Autumn's Here (OB) (1966)

ANY LITTLE FISH*
Noël Coward
The Third Little Show (1931)

ANY LITTLE THING
Harry Ruby
Bert Kalmar
The Five O'Clock Girl (1927)

ANY LITTLE TUNE
Harry Ruby
Bert Kalmar
The Ramblers (1926)

---

*Dropped from New York production

ANY MOMENT NOW
Jerome Kern
E. Y. Harburg
Can't Help Singing (F) (1944)

ANY OLD PLACE WITH YOU
Richard Rodgers
Lorenz Hart
A Lonely Romeo (1919)

ANY OTHER WAY
John Clifton
John Clifton and Ben Tarver
Man with a Load of Mischief (OB)
   (1966)

ANY PLACE I HANG MY HAT IS
HOME
Harold Arlen
Johnny Mercer
St. Louis Woman (1946)

ANY SPARE CHANGE?
Ernest McCarty
Jack Ramer and Ernest McCarty
I Dreamt I Dwelt in Bloomingdale's
   (OB) (1970)

ANY STEP
Maury Rubens
Clifford Grey
The Great Temptations (1926)

ANY TIME
Clarence Williams
Joe Jordan
Bottomland (1927)

ANY WAY THE WIND BLOWS
Sam H. Stept
Bud Green
Shady Lady (1933)

ANYA
Robert Wright and George Forrest
(based on Rachmaninoff)
Anya (1965)

ANYBODY'S MAN WILL BE MY MAN
Porter Grainger and Freddie Johnson
Lucky Sambo (1925)

ANYONE CAN MAKE A MISTAKE
Rick Besoyan
Babes in the Wood (OB) (1964)

ANYONE CAN WHISTLE
Stephen Sondheim
Anyone Can Whistle (1964)

ANYONE WOULD LOVE YOU
Harold Rome
Destry Rides Again (1959)

ANYTHING CAN HAPPEN
Ray Henderson
Jack Yellen and Ballard MacDonald
George White's Scandals (1936)

ANYTHING CAN HAPPEN
Jay Gorney
Barry Trivers
Heaven on Earth (1948)

ANYTHING CAN HAPPEN IN NEW
YORK
Richard Lewine
Arnold B. Horwitt
Make Mine Manhattan (1948)

ANYTHING FOR YOU
John Kander
James Goldman, John Kander, and
   William Goldman
A Family Affair (1962)

ANYTHING GOES
Cole Porter
Anything Goes (1934)

ANYTHING IS POSSIBLE
Paul Nassau and Oscar Brand
The Education of Hyman Kaplan
   (1968)

ANYTHING MAY HAPPEN ANY DAY
Jerome Kern
Graham John
Ripples (1930)

ANYTHING YOU CAN DO
Irving Berlin
Annie Get Your Gun (1946)

ANYTHING YOUR HEART DESIRES
Harry Archer
Walter O'Keefe
Just a Minute (1928)

ANYTIME, ANYWHERE, ANYHOW
Richard Rodgers
Lorenz Hart
June Days (1925)

ANYWAY, WE'VE HAD FUN
Vincent Youmans
Ring Lardner
Smiles (1930)

ANYWHERE I WANDER
Frank Loesser
Hans Christian Andersen (F) (1951)

A-1 MARCH
Stephen Sondheim
Anyone Can Whistle (1964)

APACHE
Kenneth Gaburo
Seyril Schochen
The Tiger Rag (OB) (1961)

APHRODITE
Walt Smith
Leon Uris
Ari (1971)

APOLOGY
Robert Wright and George Forrest
Kean (1961)

APOLOGY, THE
Cy Young
That Hat! (OB) (1964)

APPLAUSE
Charles Strouse
Lee Adams
Applause (1970)

APPLAUSE! APPLAUSE!
Burton Lane
Ira Gershwin
Give a Girl a Break (F) (1953)

APPLE JACK
Jay Gorney
Barry Trivers
Heaven on Earth (1948)

APPLE TREE, THE (FORBIDDEN FRUIT)
Jerry Bock
Sheldon Harnick
The Apple Tree (1966)

APPLES AND RAISINS
Lor Crane
John B. Kuntz
Whispers on the Wind (OB) (1970)

APRES VOUS I
Al Carmines
Maria Irene Fornes
Promenade (OB) (1969)

APRIL BLOSSOMS
Vincent Youmans and Herbert Stothart
Otto Harbach and Oscar Hammerstein II
Wildflower (1923)

APRIL FACE
Ralph Blane
Three Wishes for Jamie (1952)

APRIL FOOL
Richard Rodgers
Lorenz Hart
The Garrick Gaieties (1925)

APRIL IN FAIRBANKS
Murray Grand
New Faces (1956)

APRIL IN HARRISBURG
Baldwin Bergersen
Virginia Faulkner
All in Fun (1940)

APRIL IN PARIS
Vernon Duke
E. Y. Harburg
Walk a Little Faster (1932)

APRIL IN SIBERIA
William Klenosky
Utopia! (OB) (1963)

APRIL SHOWERS
Louis Silvers
B. G. DeSylva
Bombo (1921)

APRIL SONG
Richard Hill and John Hawkins
Nevill Coghill
Canterbury Tales (1969)

APRIL SNOW
Sigmund Romberg
Dorothy Fields
Up in Central Park (1945)

AQUARIUS
Galt MacDermot
Gerome Ragni and James Rado
Hair (1968)

ARAB MAID WITH MIDNIGHT EYES
Winthrop Cortelyou
Derick Wulff
Kiss Me (1927)

ARABIAN FOR "GET HAPPY"
Sammy Fain
E. Y. Harburg
Flahooley (1951)

ARABIAN MOON
Eubie Blake
Noble Sissle
Shuffle Along (1933)

ARABIAN NIGHTS
Maury Rubens and Sam Timberg
Moe Jaffe
Broadway Nights (1929)

ARAMINTO TO HERSELF
Jack Lawrence and Don Walker
Courtin' Time (1951)

ARE THERE ANY MORE ROSIE
O'GRADYS?
Robert Dahdah
Curley McDimple (OB) (1967)

ARE WE DOWNHEARTED?
Manning Sherwin
Arthur Herzog, Jr.
Bad Habits of 1926 (OB) (1926)

ARE YOU GOING TO DANCE?
Franz Lehar
Basil Hood
The Count of Luxembourg (1912)

ARE YOU HAVIN' ANY FUN?
Sammy Fain
Jack Yellen
George White's Scandals (1939)

ARE YOU MY LOVE?
Sigmund Romberg
Oscar Hammerstein II
East Wind (1931)

ARE YOU MY LOVE?
Richard Rodgers
Lorenz Hart
Dancing Pirate (F) (1936)

ARE YOU READY, GYP WATSON?
Harold Rome
Destry Rides Again (1959)

ARE YOU SURE?
Meredith Willson
The Unsinkable Molly Brown (1960)

ARE YOU THERE?
Harry Tierney
Joseph McCarthy
Rio Rita (1927)

ARE YOU WITH IT?
Harry Revel
Arnold B. Horwitt
Are You With It? (1945)

AREN'T YOU GLAD?
Frank Loesser
The Most Happy Fella (1956)

AREN'T YOU KIND OF GLAD WE DID
George Gershwin
Ira Gershwin
The Shocking Miss Pilgrim (F) (1946)

AREN'T YOU WARM?
Richard B. Chodosh
Barry Alan Grael
The Streets of New York (OB) (1963)

ARGENTINE
Jean Schwartz
Alfred Bryan
A Night in Spain (1927)

ARGUMENT, THE
Milton Schafer
Ronny Graham
Bravo Giovanni (1962)

ARI'S PROMISE
Walt Smith
Leon Uris
Ari (1971)

ARIES
Ron Steward and Neal Tate
Ron Steward
Sambo (OB) (1969)

ARM IN ARM
Meredith Willson
Here's Love (1963)

ARMADILLO IDYLL
Donald Swann
Michael Flanders
At the Drop of Another Hat (1966)

ARMIES OF THE RIGHT
Dale F. Menten
Dale F. Menten and Frederick Gaines
The House of Leather (OB) (1970)

ARMS FOR THE LOVE OF ME
Richard B. Chodosh
Barry Alan Grael
The Streets of New York (OB) (1963)

ARMY MULE SONG, THE
Ralph Blane
Three Wishes for Jamie (1952)

ARMY OF THE JUST, THE
Jerry Bock
Sheldon Harnick
Tenderloin (1960)

ARMY SONG
Kurt Weill
Marc Blitzstein
The Threepenny Opera (OB) (1954)

ARMY'S MADE A MAN OUT OF ME, THE
Irving Berlin
This Is the Army (1942)

AROUND THE WORLD IN EIGHTY DAYS
Victor Young
Harold Adamson
Around the World in Eighty Days (F) (1956)

ARREST, THE
Andrew Lloyd Webber
Tim Rice
Jesus Christ Superstar (1971)

ARRIVAL OF TOURISTS
Ralph Benatzky
Irving Caesar
White Horse Inn (1936)

ART
Frank Black
Gladys Shelley
The Duchess Misbehaves (1946)

ART FOR ART'S SAKE
Marc Blitzstein
The Cradle Will Rock (1938)

ART OF CONVERSATION, THE
Jerry Bock
Sheldon Harnick
The Body Beautiful (1958)

ARTHUR, SON OF MARTHA
John Addison
John Cranko
Cranks (1956)

ARTIFICIAL FLOWERS
Jerry Bock
Sheldon Harnick
Tenderloin (1960)

ARTY
James Wise
David Bimonte
Put It in Writing (OB) (1963)

ARYANS UNDER THE SKIN
Irving Berlin
This Is The Army (1942)

AS A TROUBADOR
Milton Susskind
Paul Porter and Benjamin Hapgood
  Burt
Florida Girl (1925)

AS ADAM
Stan Harte, Jr.
Walt Whitman
Leaves of Grass (OB) (1971)

AS BUSY AS ANYONE CAN BE
Gordon Duffy
Harry M. Haldane
Happy Town (1959)

AS FAR AS I'M CONCERNED
Richard Rodgers
Martin Charnin
Two by Two (1970)

AS I WENT OVER
Helen Miller
Eve Merriam
Inner City (1971)

AS IF I WEREN'T THERE
Mimi Stone
William Kaye
Pimpernel! (OB) (1964)

AS LONG AS HE NEEDS ME
Lionel Bart
Oliver! (1963)

AS LONG AS I'VE GOT MY MAMMY
Joseph Meyer and James F. Hanley
B. G. DeSylva
Big Boy (1925)

AS LONG AS THERE'S A MOTHER
Glenn Paxton
Robert Goldman and George Weiss
First Impressions (1959)

AS LONG AS WE'RE IN LOVE
Jimmy McHugh
Dorothy Fields
Hello Daddy (1928)

AS OF TODAY
Arthur Schwartz
Dorothy Fields
Stars in Your Eyes (1939)

AS ON THROUGH THE SEASONS WE SAIL
Cole Porter
Silk Stockings (1955)

AS SIMPLE AS THAT
Jerry Herman
Milk and Honey (1961)

AS THE GIRLS GO
Jimmy McHugh
Harold Adamson
As the Girls Go (1948)

AS TIME GOES BY*
Herman Hupfeld
Everybody's Welcome (1931)

ASCOT GAVOTTE
Frederick Loewe
Alan Jay Lerner
My Fair Lady (1956)

ASHES AND FIRE
Frank Harling
Laurence Stallings
Deep River (1926)

ASK AND YOU SHALL RECEIVE
Ron Steward and Neal Tate
Ron Steward
Sambo (OB) (1969)

ASK ME AGAIN
George Lessner
Miriam Battista and Russell Maloney
Sleepy Hollow (1948)

———
*Also in film *Casablanca* (1942)

ASKING FOR YOU
Jule Styne
Betty Comden and Adolph Green
Do Re Mi (1960)

ASTROCIGGY
Susan Hulsman Bingham
Myrna Lamb
Mod Donna (OB) (1970)

ASTROLOGY
Ron Steward and Neal Tate
Ron Steward
Sambo (OB) (1969)

AT CHRISTMASTIME
Robert Wright and George Forrest
(based on Grieg)
Song of Norway (1944)

AT HALF PAST SEVEN
George Gershwin
B. G. DeSylva
Nifties of 1923 (1923)

AT LAST
Henry Tobias
Charles Tobias and Sam Lewis
Earl Carroll's Sketch Book (1935)

AT LAST IT'S LOVE
Morgan Lewis
Nancy Hamilton
Two for the Show (1940)

AT LONG LAST
Lee Wainer
Robert Sour
Sing for Your Supper (1939)

AT LONG LAST LOVE
Cole Porter
You Never Know (1938)

AT LONGCHAMPS TODAY
Cole Porter
Fifty Million Frenchmen (1929)

AT LOVETIME
H. Maurice Jacquet
Preston Sturges
The Well of Romance (1930)

AT THE BALL
Sol Berkowitz
James Lipton
Miss Emily Adam (OB) (1960)

AT THE BARBECUE
Dave Stamper and Harold Levey
Harry A. Steinberg and Eddie Ward
Lovely Lady (1927)

AT THE BARBECUE
Al Wilson, Charles Weinberg, and
  Ken Macomber
Yeah Man (1932)

AT THE CHECK APRON BALL
Bob Merrill
New Girl in Town (1957)

AT THE END OF THE DAY
Johnny Brandon
Billy Noname (OB) (1970)

AT THE GATE OF ROSES
Clarence Gaskill
Earl Carroll's Vanities (1925)

AT THE MARDI GRAS
Arthur Schwartz
Howard Dietz
Inside U.S.A. (1948)

AT THE MATINEE
Frank Grey
McElbert Moore and Frank Grey
The Matinee Girl (1926)

AT THE PARTY
Harry Ruby
Bert Kalmar
Sweetheart Time (1926)

AT THE PLAYLAND JAMBOREE
Robert Dahdah
Curley McDimple (OB) (1967)

AT THE RED ROSE COTILLION
Frank Loesser
Where's Charley? (1948)

AT THE ROUND TABLE
Richard Rodgers
Lorenz Hart
A Connecticut Yankee (1927)

AT THE ROXY MUSIC HALL
Richard Rodgers
Lorenz Hart
I Married an Angel (1938)

AT THE SPOTLIGHT CANTEEN
Philip Charig
Dan Shapiro and Milton Pascal
Follow the Girls (1944)

AT TWENTY-TWO
Harvey Schmidt
Tom Jones
Shoestring Revue (OB) (1957)

AT YE OLDE COFFEE SHOPPE IN CHEYENNE
Cole Porter
Red, Hot and Blue! (1936)

AT YOUR SERVICE
C. Luckey Roberts
Alex C. Rogers
My Magnolia (1926)

ATLANTIC CITY GIRL, THE
Maury Rubens
Clifford Grey
The Great Temptations (1926)

AU REVOIR
Joseph Meyer
William Moll
Jonica (1930)

AU REVOIR
Laurence Rosenthal
James Lipton
Sherry! (1967)

AU REVOIR, CHER BARON
Cole Porter
You Never Know (1938)

AU REVOIR POLAND-HELLO NEW YORK
Albert Hague

Marty Brill
Café Crown (1964)

AU REVOIR, SOLDIER
Frederic Chopin (adapted by Bronislaw Kaper)
John Latouche
Polonaise (1945)

AUF WIEDERSEHN
Sigmund Romberg
Herbert Reynolds
The Blue Paradise (1915)

AUF WIEDERSEHEN
Hal Jordan
Jerry Douglas
Rondelay (OB) (1969)

AUNT JEMIMA
Porter Grainger and Freddie Johnson
Lucky Sambo (1925)

AURORY BORY ALICE
Lily Hyland
Agnes Morgan
The Grand Street Follies (OB) (1926)

AUTOGRAPH CHANT
Jule Styne
Bob Hilliard
Hazel Flagg (1953)

AUTUMN
Coleman Dowell
The Tattooed Countess (OB) (1961)

AUTUMN IN NEW YORK
Vernon Duke
Thumbs Up! (1934)

AUTUMN'S HERE
Norman Dean
Autumn's Here (OB) (1966)

AVONLEA, WE LOVE THEE
Norman Campbell
Donald Campbell and Norman Campbell
Anne of Green Gables (OB) (1971)

AWAY
Giuseppe Verdi
Charles Friedman
My Darlin' Aïda (1952)

AWKWARD LITTLE BOY, AN
Willard Straight
David Eddy
The Athenian Touch (OB) (1964)

AYES OF TEXAS, THE
Norman Martin
Fred Ebb
Put It in Writing (OB) (1963)

BABBITT AND THE BROMIDE, THE*
George Gershwin
Ira Gershwin
Funny Face (1927)

BABES IN ARMS
Richard Rodgers
Lorenz Hart
Babes in Arms (1937)

BABES IN THE WOOD
Jerome Kern
Schuyler Greene
Very Good Eddie (1915)

BABES IN THE WOOD
Cole Porter
Paris (1928)

BABES IN THE WOOD
Rick Besoyan
Babes in the Wood (OB) (1964)

BABY!
George Gershwin
B. G. DeSylva and Ira Gershwin
Tell Me More (1925)

BABY
Percy Wenrich
Raymond Peck
Castles in the Air (1926)

BABY!†
Jimmy McHugh
Dorothy Fields
Blackbirds (1928)

BABY, A
George Fischoff
Carole Bayer
Georgy (1970)

BABY, BABY
Sol Berkowitz
James Lipton
Nowhere to Go but Up (1962)

BABY! BABY!
Hal Hester and Danny Apolinar
Your Own Thing (1968)

BABY BOND, A
Richard Rodgers
Lorenz Hart
I'd Rather Be Right (1937)

BABY COULDN'T DANCE
Vernon Duke
Ogden Nash
Two's Company (1952)

BABY-DOLL DANCE
Maury Rubens and Phil Svigals
J. Keirn Brennan and Moe Jaffe
Broadway Nights (1929)

BABY, DON'T COUNT ON ME
Clay Warnick
Edward Eager
Dream with Music (1944)

BABY DREAM YOUR DREAM
Cy Coleman
Dorothy Fields
Sweet Charity (1966)

BABY, I COULD DO IT FOR YOU
Al Wilson, Charles Weinberg, and Ken Macomber
Yeah Man (1932)

BABY, IT'S COLD OUTSIDE
Frank Loesser
Neptune's Daughter (F) (1949)

---

*Also in film *Ziegfeld Follies* (1946)
†Dropped from N. Y. production

BABY, LET'S FACE IT
Sammy Fain
George Marion, Jr.
Toplitzky of Notre Dame (1946)

BABY MINE
C. Luckey Roberts
Alex C. Rogers
My Magnolia (1926)

BABY RUE
Patrick Fox
Avra Petrides
Blood (OB) 1971

BABY, TALK TO ME
Charles Strouse
Lee Adams
Bye Bye Birdie (1960)

BABY, THAT'S LOVE
G. Wood
F. Jasmine Addams (OB) (1971)

BABY WANNA GO BYE-BYE
Lewis E. Gensler
Owen Murphy and Robert A. Simon
The Gang's All Here (1931)

BABY WANTS
C. Luckey Roberts
Alex C. Rogers
My Magnolia (1926)

BABY! WHAT?
Ray Henderson
B. G. DeSylva and Lew Brown
Good News (1927)

BABY, YOU BORE ME
Jeanne Bargy
Jeanne Bargy, Frank Gehrecke, and
    Herb Corey
Greenwich Village U.S.A. (OB) (1960)

BABY YOU LOVE, THE
Richard Rodgers
Oscar Hammerstein II
Me and Juliet (1953)

BABYKINS
Oscar Levant
Irving Caesar and Graham John
Ripples (1930)

BABY'S AWAKE NOW
Richard Rodgers
Lorenz Hart
Spring Is Here (1929)

BABY'S BABY
David Baker
David Craig
Copper and Brass (1957)

BABY'S BABY GRAND
Al Goodman and J. Fred Coots
Clifford Grey
Gay Paree (1925)

BABY'S BEST FRIEND, A
Richard Rodgers
Lorenz Hart
She's My Baby (1928)

BABY'S BLUE
Herman Hupfeld
A la Carte (1927)

BACCHANALE
Don Elliott
James Costigan
The Beast in Me (1963)

BACHELOR HOEDOWN
Jerry Bock
Larry Holofcener
Catch a Star! (1955)

BACHELOR'S DANCE
Jacques Brel
Eric Blau and Mort Shuman
*Jacques Brel Is Alive and Well and
    Living in Paris* (OB) (1968)

BACK AT THE PALACE
Clay Warnick
Mel Tolkin and Lucille Kallen
Tickets Please (1950)

BACK BAY BEAT
Jerry Livingston
Mack David
Bright Lights of 1944 (1943)

BACK BAY POLKA, THE
George Gershwin
Ira Gershwin
The Shocking Miss Pilgrim (F) (1946)

BACK FROM HOLLYWOOD
Ray Henderson
B. G. DeSylva and Lew Brown
George White's Scandals (1931)

BACK IN THE DAYS OF LONG AGO
Alma Sanders
Monte Carlo
The Houseboat on the Styx (1928)

BACK IN THE KITCHEN
Jule Styne
Betty Comden and Adolph Green
Hallelujah, Baby! (1967)

BACK TO BUNDLING
Lee Wainer
Dorothy Sachs
New Faces (1943)

BACK TO THE FARM
Bud Burtson
Ziegfeld Follies (1943)

BACK TO GENESIS
Peter Link and C. C. Courtney
Salvation (OB) (1969)

BACK TO NATURE
Hal Jordan
Jerry Douglas
Rondelay (OB) (1969)

BACK TO WORK
Harold Rome
Pins and Needles (OB) (1937)

BACKSTAGE BABBLE
Charles Strouse
Lee Adams
Applause (1970)

BAD COMPANIONS
Leroy Anderson
Joan Ford, Walter and Jean Kerr
Goldilocks (1958)

BAD GIRL
Maurice Yvain
Max and Nathaniel Lief
Luckee Girl (1928)

BAD IF HE DOES, WORSE IF HE DON'T
Ray Haney
Alfred Aiken
We're Civilized? (OB) (1962)

BAD IN EVERY MAN, THE
Richard Rodgers
Lorenz Hart
Manhattan Melodrama (F) (1934)

BAD KARMA
Peter Stampfel and Antonia
Operation Sidewinder (1970)

BAD LITTLE BOY WITH DANCING LEGS
Mann Holiner
Alberta Nichols
Gay Paree (1926)

BAD LUCK, I'LL LAUGH AT YOU
Dave Stamper and Harold Levey
Cyrus Wood
Lovely Lady (1927)

BAD MAN NUMBER
Rudolf Friml
Brian Hooker
The White Eagle (1927)

BAD TIMING
Morton Gould
Betty Comden and Adolph Green
Billion Dollar Baby (1945)

BADAROMA
Albert Selden
Burt Shevelove
Small Wonder (1948)

BADDEST MAMMYJAMMY
Ron Steward and Neal Tate
Ron Steward
Sambo (OB) (1969)

BAJOUR
Walter Marks
Bajour (1964)

BAL PETIT BAL
Francis Lemarque
New Faces (1952)

BALALAIKA SERENADE, THE
Franz Steininger (adapted from Tchaikovsky)
Forman Brown
Music in My Heart (1947)

BALI HA'I
Richard Rodgers
Oscar Hammerstein II
South Pacific (1949)

BALLAD FOR A FIRING SQUAD
Edward Thomas
Martin Charnin
Ballad for a Firing Squad (OB) (1968)

BALLAD FOR AMERICANS
Earl Robinson
John Latouche
Sing for Your Supper (1939)

BALLAD FOR BILLIONAIRES
Albert Selden
Burt Shevelove
Small Wonder (1948)

BALLAD FOR BIMSHIRE
Irving Burgie
Ballad for Bimshire (OB) (1963)

BALLAD MAKER
Oscar Brand and Paul Nassau
A Joyful Noise (1966)

BALLAD OF A REDNECK
Don Tucker
Red, White and Maddox (1969)

BALLAD OF BEDFORD GAOL, THE
Edwin Greenberg
Pilgrim's Progress (OB) (1962)

BALLAD OF DEPENDENCY
Kurt Weill
Marc Blitzstein
The Threepenny Opera (OB) (1954)

BALLAD OF DRY DOCK COUNTRY
Ernest McCarty
Jack Ramer and Ernest McCarty
I Dreamt I Dwelt in Bloomingdale's (OB) (1970)

BALLAD OF JOHNNY POT, THE
Clinton Ballard
Carolyn Richter
The Ballad of Johnny Pot (OB) (1971)

BALLAD OF SIR TOPAZ
Paul Hoffert
David Secter
Get Thee to Canterbury (OB) (1969)

BALLAD OF TANCRED
Edward Earle
Yvonne Tarr
The Decameron (OB) (1961)

BALLAD OF THE EASY LIFE
Kurt Weill
Marc Blitzstein
The Threepenny Opera (OB) (1954)

BALLAD OF THE GARMENT TRADE
Harold Rome
I Can Get It for You Wholesale (1962)

BALLAD OF THE GUN
Harold Rome
Destry Rides Again (1959)

BALLAD OF THE ROBBERS
Kurt Weill
Maxwell Anderson
Knickerbocker Holiday (1938)

BALLAD OF THE SAD YOUNG MAN, THE
Tommy Wolf
Fran Landesman
The Nervous Set (1959)

BALLAD OF UTOPIA, THE
William Klenosky
Utopia! (OB) (1963)

BALLAD TO A BRUTE
Moose Charlap
Eddie Lawrence
Kelly (1965)

BALLADE
Charles Gaynor
Lend an Ear (1948)

BALLERINA'S STORY, THE
Franz Steininger (adapted from
    Tchaikovsky)
Forman Brown
Music in My Heart (1947)

BALLIN'
Peter Link and C. C. Courtney
Salvation (OB) (1969)

BALLOON IS ASCENDING, A
Mark Sandrich, Jr.
Sidney Michaels
Ben Franklin In Paris (1964)

BALLOONS
Jack Holmes
From A to Z (1960)

BALLYHUJAH
Lewis E. Gensler
E. Y. Harburg
Ballyhoo (1932)

BALTIMORE
Bill Mahoney
My Wife and I (OB) (1966)

BAMBALINA
Vincent Youmans and Herbert Sto-
    thart
Otto Harbach and Oscar Hammer-
    stein II
Wildflower (1923)

BAMBAZOOLA
Jean Schwartz
Alfred Bryan
A Night in Spain (1927)

BAMBOO BABIES
Joseph Meyer and James F. Hanley
Ballard MacDonald
Gay Paree (1925)

BAMBOOLA
Frank Marcus and Bernard Maltin
Bamboola (1929)

**BAND STARTED SWINGING A SONG,
THE**
Cole Porter
Seven Lively Arts (1944)

BANDANNA BABIES
Jimmy McHugh
Dorothy Fields
Blackbirds (1928)

BANDANNA WAYS
Eubie Blake
Noble Sissle
Shuffle Along (1933)

BANE OF MAN, THE
Franz Lehár
Edward Eliscu
Frederika (1937)

BANG, THE BELL RANG!
Irving Actman
Frank Loesser
The Illustrators' Show (1936)

BANJO EYES
Vernon Duke
John Latouche
Banjo Eyes (1941)

**BANJO THAT MAN JOE PLAYS,
THE**
Cole Porter
Wake Up and Dream (1929)

BANQUET, THE
Max Ewing
Agnes Morgan
The Grand Street Follies (OB) (1927)

BARBARA SONG
Kurt Weill
Marc Blitzstein
The Threepenny Opera (OB) (1954)

BARBARY COAST
George Gershwin
Ira Gershwin
Girl Crazy (1930)

BARBER'S SONG
Mitch Leigh
Joe Darion
Man of La Mancha (1965)

BARCELONA
Stephen Sondheim
Company (1970)

BARD, THE
Alec Wilder
Arnold Sundgaard
Kittiwake Island (OB) (1960)

BAREFOOT BOY
James F. Hanley
Chris Taylor
Ziegfeld Follies (1934)

BAREFOOT GAL
Oscar Brand and Paul Nassau
A Joyful Noise (1966)

BAREFOOT GIRL
Oscar Levant
Irving Caesar and Graham John
Ripples (1930)

BARGAINING
Richard Rodgers
Stephen Sondheim
Do I Hear a Waltz? (1965)

BARKING BABY NEVER BITES, A
Richard Rodgers
Lorenz Hart
Higher and Higher (1940)

BARNABO
Edward Earle
Yvonne Tarr
The Decameron (OB) (1961)

BARNABY BEACH
Morgan Lewis
Nancy Hamilton
Three to Make Ready (1946)

BARON, THE DUCHESS, AND THE COUNT, THE
Alberta Nichols
Mann Holiner
Angela (1928)

BARREL OF BEADS
Vernon Duke
Howard Dietz
Sadie Thompson (1944)

BASIC
Deed Meyer
She Shall Have Music (OB) (1959)

BASKET, MAKE A BASKET
Baldwin Bergersen
William Archibald
Carib Song (1945)

BATTLE OF THE GENIE
Clay Warnick
Edward Eager
Dream with Music (1944)

BAUBLES, BANGLES AND BEADS
Robert Wright and George Forrest
(based on Alexander Borodin)
Kismet (1953)

BAZAAR OF THE CARAVANS
Robert Wright and George Forrest
(based on Alexander Borodin)
Kismet (1953)

BAZOOM
Claude Leveilee
Gladys Shelley
Gogo Loves You (OB) (1964)

BE A CLOWN
Cole Porter
The Pirate (F) (1948)

BE A LITTLE LACKADAISICAL
Herman Hupfeld
Hey Nonny Nonny! (1932)

BE A LOVER
Robert Kessler
Lola Permagent
O Marry Me! (OB) (1961)

BE A MESS
Jay Gorney
Jean and Walter Kerr
Touch and Go (1949)

BE A PERFORMER
Cy Coleman
Carolyn Leigh
Little Me (1962)

BE A PUSSYCAT
George Kleinsinger
Joe Darion
Shinbone Alley (1957)

BE A SANTA
Jule Styne
Betty Comden and Adolph Green
Subways Are for Sleeping (1961)

BE BACK SOON
Lionel Bart
Oliver! (1963)

BE BLACK
Ron Steward and Neal Tate
Ron Steward
Sambo (OB) (1969)

BE CAREFUL, IT'S MY HEART
Irving Berlin
Holiday Inn (F) (1942)

BE GENTLE
Hal Hester and Danny Apolinar
Your Own Thing (1968)

BE GLAD YOU'RE ALIVE
Clay Warnick
Edward Eager
Dream with Music (1944)

BE GOOD, BE GOOD, BE GOOD
James Shelton
Mrs. Patterson (1954)

BE GOOD TO ME
Vincent Youmans
Ring Lardner
Smiles (1930)

BE HAPPY
Larry Grossman
Hal Hackady
Minnie's Boys (1970)

BE KIND TO YOUR PARENTS
Harold Rome
Fanny (1954)

BE LIKE THE BLUEBIRD
Cole Porter
Anything Goes (1934)

BE MY GUEST
Johnny Mercer
Top Banana (1951)

BE MY HOST
Richard Rodgers
No Strings (1962)

BE OH SO CAREFUL, ANN
H. Maurice Jacquet
Preston Sturges
The Well of Romance (1930)

BE THAT WAY
Werner Janssen
Mann Holiner and J. Keirn Brennan
Boom-Boom (1929)

BE VERY CAREFUL
Ann Sternberg
Gertrude Stein
Gertrude Stein's First Reader (OB)
  (1969)

BE YOURSELF
Sam Pottle
Tom Whedon
All Kinds of Giants (OB) (1961)

BEAR HUNT
Michael Leonard
Herbert Martin
The Yearling (1965)

BEARING SILVER PLATTERS
Alberta Nichols
Mann Holiner
Angela (1928)

BEAST IN YOU, THE
Leroy Anderson
Joan Ford, Walter and Jean Kerr
Goldilocks (1958)

BEAT, LITTLE PULSE
Dead Meyer
Toinette (OB) (1961)

BEAT OF A HEART, THE
Gordon Duffy
Harry M. Haldane
Happy Town (1959)

BEAT OF THE CITY, THE
Mildred Kayden
Frank Gagliano
Paradise Gardens East (OB) (1969)

BEAT OUT DAT RHYTHM ON A DRUM
Georges Bizet
Oscar Hammerstein II
Carmen Jones (1943)

BEAT THE WORLD
Jerry Herman
Madame Aphrodite (OB) (1961)

BEATNIK LOVE AFFAIR
Noël Coward
Sail Away (1961)

BEATRICE LILLIE BALLAD
Randall Thompson
Agnes Morgan
The Grand Street Follies (OB) (1926)

BEAUTEOUS IS THE BRIDE
Deed Meyer
Stones of Jehoshaphat (OB) (1963)

BEAUTIFUL
Jerry Herman
Madame Aphrodite (OB) (1961)

BEAUTIFUL
John Kander
James Goldman, John Kander, and
    William Goldman
A Family Affair (1962)

BEAUTIFUL ALLELUJAH DAYS
Oscar Brown, Jr.
Buck White (1969)

BEAUTIFUL BABY
Con Conrad
William B. Friedlander
Mercenary Mary (1925)

BEAUTIFUL BABY
James F. Hanley
B. G. DeSylva
Queen High (1926)

BEAUTIFUL, BEAUTIFUL WORLD
Jerry Bock
Sheldon Harnick
The Apple Tree (1966)

BEAUTIFUL CANDY
Bob Merrill
Carnival (1961)

BEAUTIFUL GIRLS
Joseph Meyer
William Moll
Jonica (1930)

BEAUTIFUL GIRLS
Stephen Sondheim
Follies (1971)

BEAUTIFUL GYPSY*
George Gershwin
Ira Gershwin
Rosalie (1928)

BEAUTIFUL HEAVEN
Coleridge-Taylor Perkinson
Errol Hill
Man Better Man (OB) (1969)

---

*Dropped from New York production

BEAUTIFUL LADIES OF THE NIGHT
Clarence Gaskill
Earl Carroll's Vanities (1925)

BEAUTIFUL LAND, THE
Leslie Bricusse and Anthony Newley
*The Roar of the Greasepaint - The
    Smell of the Crowd* (1965)

BEAUTIFUL MAN
Susan Hulsman Bingham
Myrna Lamb
Mod Donna (OB) (1970)

BEAUTIFUL NIGHT
Ballard MacDonald, Karl Stark, and
    James F. Hanley
Thumbs Up! (1934)

BEAUTIFUL PEOPLE, THE
Tom Sankey
The Golden Screw (OB) (1967)

BEAUTIFUL PEOPLE OF DENVER
Meredith Willson
The Unsinkable Molly Brown (1960)

BEAUTY
Ned Lehak
Allen Boretz
The Garrick Gaieties (1930)

BEAUTY
Carl Millöcker (revised by Theo Mack-
    eben)
Rowland Leigh
The Dubarry (1932)

BEAUTY IN THE MOVIES
Joseph Meyer and Roger Wolfe Kahn
Irving Caesar
Here's Howe (1928)

BEAUTY IS VANITY
Maury Rubens
Clifford Grey
The Great Temptations (1926)

BEAUTY OF BATH, THE
Vivian Ellis
Graham John
By the Way (1925)

BECAUSE, BECAUSE
George Gershwin
Ira Gershwin
Of Thee I Sing (1931)

BECAUSE YOU'RE BEAUTIFUL
Ray Henderson
B. G. DeSylva
Three Cheers (1928)

BECAUSE YOU'RE YOU
Victor Herbert
Henry Blossom
The Red Mill (1906)

BED, THE
Galt MacDermot
Gerome Ragni and James Rado
Hair (1968)

BEDTIME STORY, A
Max Ewing
Agnes Morgan
The Grand Street Follies (OB) (1927)

BEEN A LONG DAY
Frank Loesser
*How to Succeed in Business without
    Really Trying* (1961)

BEER IS BEST
Richard Hill and John Hawkins
Nevill Coghill
Canterbury Tales (1969)

BEETLE RACE, THE
Harry Warren
Jerome Lawrence and Robert E. Lee
Shangri-La (1956)

BEFORE AND AFTER
Billy Barnes
The Billy Barnes People (1961)

BEFORE BREAKFAST
Hal Jordan
Jerry Douglas
Rondelay (OB) (1969)

BEFORE I GAZE AT YOU AGAIN
Frederick Loewe

Alan Jay Lerner
Camelot (1960)

BEFORE I KISS THE WORLD GOOD-BYE
Arthur Schwartz
Howard Dietz
Jennie (1963)

BEFORE THE PARADE PASSES BY
Jerry Herman
Hello, Dolly! (1964)

BEFORE THE WORLD WAS MADE
John Duffy
Rocco Bufano and John Duffy (based
  on W. B. Yeats)
Horseman, Pass By (OB) (1969)

BEFORE YOU KNEW I LOVED YOU
Maggie Hyatt
Doug Dyer
Blood (OB) (1971)

BEG, BORROW OR STEAL
Leon Pober
Bud Freeman
Beg, Borrow or Steal (1960)

BEGAT, THE
Burton Lane
E. Y. Harburg
Finian's Rainbow (1947)

BEGGAR WALTZ, THE
Arthur Schwartz
Howard Dietz
The Band Wagon (1931)

BEGGING FOR LOVE
Irving Berlin
Shoot the Works (1931)

BEGIN THE BEGUINE
Cole Porter
Jubilee (1935)

BEGINNER'S LUCK
George Gershwin
Ira Gershwin
Shall We Dance (F) (1937)

BEGINNING, THE
Wally Harper
Paul Zakrzewski
Sensations (OB) (1970)

BEGINNING, THE
Charles Strouse
Six (OB) (1971)

BEGINNING OF LOVE
Ray Henderson
B. G. DeSylva and Lew Brown
George White's Scandals (1931)

BEGUINE, THE
Jim Wise
George Haimsohn and Robin Miller
Dames at Sea (OB) (1968)

BEHAVE YOURSELF
Albert Hague
Dorothy Fields
Redhead (1959)

BEHIND THE MASK
George M. Cohan
The Merry Malones (1927)

BEIN' A KID
Lance Mulcahy
Paul Cherry
Park (1970)

BEING ALIVE
John Kander
Fred Ebb
The Happy Time (1968)

BEING ALIVE
Stephen Sondheim
Company (1970)

BEING GOOD ISN'T ENOUGH
Jule Styne
Betty Comden and Adolph Green
Hallelujah, Baby! (1967)

BELIEVE
John Kander
Fred Ebb
70, Girls, 70 (1971)

BELIEVE IN ME
Arthur Schwartz
Harry B. Smith
The Red Rose (1928)

BELIEVE IT OR NOT
Percy Wenrich
Harry Clarke
Who Cares? (1930)

BELIEVERS' CHANTS
Voices, Inc.
The Believers (OB) (1968)

BELIEVERS' LAMENTS
Voices, Inc.
The Believers (OB) (1968)

BELLA
Michael Valenti
Just for Love (OB) (1968)

BELLA DONNA
Sigmund Romberg
Rowland Leigh
My Romance (1948)

BELLE, A BEAU AND A BOUTON-NIÈRE, A
Jean Schwartz
Clifford Grey and William Cary Duncan
Sunny Days (1928)

BELLE PLAIN
Irving Burgie
Ballad for Bimshire (OB) (1963)

BELLHOPS, THE
Irving Berlin
The Cocoanuts (1925)

BELLS ARE RINGING
Jule Styne
Betty Comden and Adolph Green
Bells Are Ringing (1956)

BELLY UP TO THE BAR, BOYS
Meredith Willson
The Unsinkable Molly Brown (1960)

BELONGING
Lionel Bart
La Strada (1969)

BENCH IN THE PARK
Jay Gorney
Barry Trivers
Heaven on Earth (1948)

BENVENUTA
Frank Loesser
The Most Happy Fella (1956)

BESIDE THE STAR OF GLORY
Karl Hajos (based on Tchaikovsky)
Harry B. Smith
Natja (1925)

BESS, YOU IS MY WOMAN NOW
George Gershwin
DuBose Heyward and Ira Gershwin
Porgy and Bess (1935)

BEST DANCE OF ALL, THE
Lehman Engel
Agnes Morgan
A Hero Is Born (1937)

BEST GOLD
Jerry Herman
From A to Z (1960)

BEST LITTLE LOVER IN TOWN, THE
Harry Tierney
Joseph McCarthy
Rio Rita (1927)

BEST LOVED GIRLS
David Baker
Sheldon Harnick
Shoestring Revue (OB) (1957)

BEST NIGHT OF MY LIFE, THE
Charles Strouse
Lee Adams
Applause (1970)

BEST OF ALL POSSIBLE WORLDS, THE
Leonard Bernstein
Richard Wilbur
Candide (1956)

BEST OF WHAT THE COUNTRY'S
GOT, THE
Moose Charlap
Norman Gimbel
Whoop-Up (1958)

BEST SONGS OF ALL, THE
Carlton Kelsey and Maury Rubens
Clifford Grey
Sky High (1925)

BEST THING FOR YOU, THE
Irving Berlin
Call Me Madam (1950)

BEST THINGS IN LIFE ARE DIRTY,
THE
Andre Previn
Alan Jay Lerner
Paint Your Wagon (F) (1969)

BEST THINGS IN LIFE ARE FREE,
THE
Ray Henderson
B. G. DeSylva and Lew Brown
Good News (1927)

BEST THINGS OF ALL, THE
Marc Blitzstein
Regina (1949)

BEST TIME OF DAY, THE
Gordon Jenkins
Tom Adair
Along Fifth Avenue (1949)

BEST YEARS OF HIS LIFE, THE
Kurt Weill
Ira Gershwin
Lady in the Dark (1941)

BETCHA I MAKE GOOD
Leo Edwards
Herman Timberg
You'll See Stars (1942)

BETRAYED
Robert Kessler
Lola Permagent
O Marry Me! (OB) (1961)

BETTER ALL THE TIME
Sammy Fain
Marilyn and Alan Bergman
Something More! (1964)

BETTER BE GOOD TO ME
Richard Rodgers
Lorenz Hart
Chee-Chee (1928)

BETTER DAYS
Dov Seltzer
David Paulsen
To Live Another Summer (1971)

BETTER FAR
Oscar Brown, Jr.
Buck White (1969)

BETTER GET OUT OF HERE
Frank Loesser
Where's Charley? (1948)

BETTER LUCK NEXT TIME
Irving Berlin
Easter Parade (F) (1948)

BETTER NOT TRY IT
Michael H. Cleary, Herb Magidson,
   and Ned Washington
The Vanderbilt Revue (1930)

BETTER TIMES ARE COMING
Jimmie Steiger
Dolph Singer
White Lights (1927)

BETTY LOU
Joe Jordan
Rosamond Johnson
Brown Buddies (1930)

BETWEEN YOU AND ME
Cole Porter
Broadway Melody (F) (1940)

BEWARE AS YOU RIDE THROUGH
THE HOLLOW
Norman Dean
Autumn's Here (OB) (1966)

BEWARE OF THE GIRL WITH THE FAN
Ray Henderson
B. G. DeSylva and Lew Brown
George White's Scandals (1925)

BEWARE OF LIPS THAT SAY "CHÉRIE"
Alma Sanders
Monte Carlo
Louisiana Lady (1947)

BEWITCHED, BOTHERED AND BEWILDERED
Richard Rodgers
Lorenz Hart
Pal Joey (1940)

B. G. BIGELOW, INC.
Sammy Fain
E. Y. Harburg
Flahooley (1951)

BHARATHA NATYAN
Sammy Fain
Paul Francis Webster
Christine (1960)

BIANCA
Cole Porter
Kiss Me, Kate (1948)

BICYCLE SONG, THE
Hugh Martin and Timothy Gray
High Spirits (1964)

BIDE-A-WEE IN SOHO, THE
Kurt Weill
Marc Blitzstein
The Threepenny Opera (OB) (1954)

BIDIN' MY TIME
George Gershwin
Ira Gershwin
Girl Crazy (1930)

BIG BACK YARD, THE
Sigmund Romberg
Dorothy Fields
Up in Central Park (1945)

BIG BEST SHOES
Sandy Wilson
Valmouth (OB) (1960)

BIG BETTY'S SONG
C. Jackson and James Hatch
Fly Blackbird (OB) (1962)

BIG, BIG
Jane Douglas
Tom O'Malley
Bella (OB) (1961)

BIG BILL
George Kleinsinger
Joe Darion
Shinbone Alley (1957)

BIG BIRD
Ann Sternberg
Gertrude Stein
Gertrude Stein's First Reader (OB) (1969)

BIG BLACK GIANT, THE
Richard Rodgers
Oscar Hammerstein II
Me and Juliet (1953)

BIG BRASS BAND FROM BRAZIL, THE
Carl Sigman
Bob Hilliard
Angel in the Wings (1947)

BIG BROTHER
Richard Rodgers
Lorenz Hart
The Boys from Syracuse (1938)

BIG CLOWN BALLOONS, THE
Meredith Willson
Here's Love (1963)

BIG "D"
Frank Loesser
The Most Happy Fella (1956)

BIG FISH, LITTLE FISH
Gary Geld
Peter Udell
Purlie (1970)

BIG FOUR, THE
Peter Howard Weiss
All for Love (1949)

BIG GUITAR, THE
Oscar Brand and Paul Nassau
A Joyful Noise (1966)

BIG MEETING TONIGHT
Mary Rodgers
Martin Charnin
Hot Spot (1963)

BIG MOLE
Kurt Weill
Maxwell Anderson
Lost in the Stars (1949)

BIG MOVIE SHOW IN THE SKY, THE
Robert Emmett Dolan
Johnny Mercer
Texas, Li'l Darlin' (1949)

BIG OLD RIVER
Don Walker
Clay Warnick
Memphis Bound (1945)

BIG ONE, A
Gerard Calvi
Harold Rome
La Grosse Valise (1965)

BIG PAPOOSE IS ON THE LOOSE
Jimmy McHugh
Dorothy Fields
Lew Leslie's International Revue (1930)

BIG PARADE, THE
Cole Porter
Seven Lively Arts, (1944)

BIG SPENDER
Cy Coleman
Dorothy Fields
Sweet Charity (1966)

BIG TIME
Jerry Bock, George Weiss, and Larry Holofcener
Mr. Wonderful (1956)

BIG TIME BUCK WHITE CHANT
Oscar Brown, Jr.
Buck White (1969)

BIG TOWN
Cole Porter
Seven Lively Arts (1944)

BIG TROUBLE
Elmer Bernstein
Carolyn Leigh
How Now, Dow Jones (1967)

BIGGER AND BETTER THAN EVER
Cliff Friend and George White
George White's Scandals (1929)

BIGGEST THING IN MY LIFE, THE
Frank Grey
McElbert Moore and Frank Grey
The Matinee Girl (1926)

BILBO'S SONG
Donald Swann
Michael Flanders
At the Drop of Another Hat (1966)

BILL
Jerome Kern
P.G. Wodehouse and Oscar Hammerstein II
Show Boat (1927)

BILL OF RIGHTS, THE
Jay Gorney
Henry Myers
Meet the People (1940)

BILLIE
George M. Cohan
Billie (1928)

BILLY
Ron Dante and Gene Allan
Billy (1969)

BILLY JO JU
Don Tucker
Red, White and Maddox (1969)

BILLY NONAME
Johnny Brandon
Billy Noname (OB) (1970)

BIRD OF PASSAGE
Kurt Weill
Maxwell Anderson
Lost in the Stars (1949)

BIRD UPON THE TREE
Marc Blitzstein
Juno (1959)

BIRD WATCHER'S SONG
Jule Styne
Sammy Cahn
High Button Shoes (1947)

BIRDIES
Maury Rubens
Clifford Grey
The Madcap (1928)

BIRDIES
Al Carmines
Rosalyn Drexler
Home Movies (OB) (1964)

BIRDS AND THE BEES, THE
Sigmund Romberg
Dorothy Fields
Up in Central Park (1945)

BIRDS IN THE SPRING
Ralph Benatzky
Meet My Sister (1930)

BIRDS OF A FEATHER
Carmen Lombardo
Irving Caesar
George White's Music Hall Varieties
  (1932)

BIRDS ON HIGH
Richard Rodgers
Lorenz Hart
Betsy (1926)

BIRTH OF THE BLUES, THE
Ray Henderson
B. G. DeSylva and Lew Brown
George White's Scandals (1926)

BIRTHDAY, A
Michael Valenti
Just for Love (OB) (1968)

BIRTHDAY PARTY
George Gershwin
Ira Gershwin
Funny Face (1927)

BIRTHDAY PARTY
Cy Coleman
Carolyn Leigh
Little Me (1962)

BIRTHDAY SONG
Harold Rome
Fanny (1954)

BIRTHDAY SONG
Manos Hadjidakis
Joe Darion
Illya Darling (1967)

BIT OF A CHARACTER, A
Cyril Ornadel
Leslie Bricusse
Pickwick (1965)

BITTEN BY LOVE
Joseph Meyer
Floyd Huddleston
Shuffle Along (1952)

BITTER HARVEST
Raymond Scott
Bernard Hanighen
Lute Song (1946)

BITTER TEARS
Alyn Heim
Malcolm L. LaPrade
Will the Mail Train Run Tonight?
  (OB) (1964)

BLACK
Gary William Friedman
Will Holt
The Me Nobody Knows (OB) (1970)

BLACK AND BLUE
Thomas (Fats) Waller and Harry
  Brooks

Andy Razaf
Hot Chocolates (1929)

BLACK AND BLUE PUMPS
Mildred Kayden
Frank Gagliano
Paradise Gardens East (OB) (1969)

BLACK AND WHITE
Richard Rodgers
Lorenz Hart
The Garrick Gaieties (1925)

BLACK AND WHITE
George Gershwin
Gus Kahn and Ira Gershwin
Show Girl (1929)

BLACK BALLOONS
Oscar Brown, Jr.
Buck White (1969)

BLACK-BLACK SONG, THE
Coleridge-Taylor Perkinson
Ray McIver
God Is a (Guess What?) (OB) (1968)

BLACK BOTTOM
Ray Henderson
B. G. DeSylva and Lew Brown
George White's Scandals (1926)

BLACK BOY
Johnny Brandon
Billy Noname (OB) (1970)

BLACK BOYS
Galt MacDermot
Gerome Ragni and James Rado
Hair (1968)

BLACK DOG RUM
Michael Valenti
John Lewin
Blood Red Roses (1970)

BLACK HORSE TAVERN
Frank D'Armond
Will Morrissey
Saluta (1934)

BLACK MAN
Ron Steward and Neal Tate
Ron Steward
Sambo (OB) (1969)

BLACK MASK, THE (TEMPTATION)
J. J. Shubert, Jr.
Clifford Grey and McElbert Moore
A Night in Paris (1926)

BLACK PEARLS
Ed Tyler
Sweet Miani (OB) (1962)

BLACKBERRIES
Donald Heywood
Blackberries of 1932

BLACK RHYTHM
Donald Heywood
Black Rhythm (1936)

BLACKBERRY VINE, THE
Ann Sternberg
Gertrude Stein
Gertrude Stein's First Reader (OB) (1969)

BLACKEST OF TRESSES
Edwin Greenberg
Pilgrim's Progress (OB) (1962)

BLACKSHEEP
Frank Grey
Earle Crooker and McElbert Moore
Happy (1927)

BLADE OF MINE
George Bagby
Grace Henry
Fioretta (1929)

BLAH, BLAH, BLAH
George Gershwin
Ira Gershwin
Delicious (F) (1931)

BLAH! BUT NOT BLUE
Abel Baer
Sam Lewis and Joe Young
Lady Do (1927)

BLAME IT ALL ON THE NIGHT
Sigmund Romberg
Otto Harbach
Forbidden Melody (1936)

BLASÉ
Berenice Kazounoff
John Latouche
Two for Tonight (OB) (1939)

BLEECKER STREET
John Dooley
Hobo (OB) (1961)

BLESS THE LORD
Stephen Schwartz
Godspell (OB) (1971)

BLESS THIS LAND
Jerry Bock
Sheldon Harnick
Tenderloin (1960)

BLESS YOU ALL
Harold Rome
Bless You All (1950)

BLIND DATE
Vernon Duke
Howard Dietz
Jackpot (1944)

BLIND MAN'S BUFF
Deed Meyer
She Shall Have Music (OB) (1959)

BLISS
Al Carmines
Maria Irene Fornes
Promenade (OB) (1969)

BLOCKS
Billy Barnes
The Billy Barnes Revue (1959)

BLONDE BLUES
Jerry Bock
Sheldon Harnick
The Body Beautiful (1958)

BLOOD RED ROSES
Michael Valenti
John Lewin
Blood Red Roses (1970)

BLOODY MARY
Richard Rodgers
Oscar Hammerstein II
South Pacific (1949)

BLOOM IS OFF THE ROSE, THE
Arthur Schwartz
Howard Dietz
The Gay Life (1961)

BLOW A BALLOON UP TO THE MOON
Sammy Fain
Charles Tobias
Hellzapoppin' (1938)

BLOW, GABRIEL
Henry Sullivan
Edward Eliscu
A Little Racketeer (1932)

BLOW, GABRIEL, BLOW
Cole Porter
Anything Goes (1934)

BLOW HIGH, BLOW LOW
Richard Rodgers
Oscar Hammerstein II
Carousel (1945)

BLOW HOT AND HEAVY
Philip Charig and Richard Myers
Leo Robin
Allez-Oop (1927)

BLOW HOT-BLOW COLD
Louis Alter
Harry Ruskin and Leighton K. Brill
Ballyhoo (1930)

BLOW THE BLUES AWAY
Werner Janssen
Mann Holiner and J. Keirn Brennan
Boom-Boom (1929)

BLOWIN' THE BLUES AWAY
Philip Charig

Ira Gershwin
Americana (1926)

BLOWING THE TOP
Philip Charig
Dan Shapiro and Milton Pascal
Artists and Models (1943)

BLUE AGAIN
Jimmy McHugh
Dorothy Fields
The Vanderbilt Revue (1930)

BLUE AND TROUBLED
Walter Cool
Mackey of Appalachia (OB) (1965)

BLUE, BLUE, BLUE
George Gershwin
Ira Gershwin
Let 'Em Eat Cake (1933)

BLUE DANUBE BLUES
Jerome Kern
Anne Caldwell
Good Morning, Dearie (1921)

BLUE DAY
Abraham Ellstein
Walter Bullock
Great to Be Alive (1950)

BLUE EYES
Robert Stolz
Irving Caesar
White Horse Inn (1936)

BLUE GRASS
Arthur Schwartz
Howard Dietz
Inside U.S.A. (1948)

BLUE MONDAY
Richard Rodgers
Lorenz Hart
Higher and Higher (1940)

BLUE MOON*
Richard Rodgers
Lorenz Hart

BLUE NIGHT
Bhumibol-Chakraband and N. Tong
  Yai
Michael Todd's Peep Show (1950)

BLUE OCEAN BLUES
Richard Rodgers
Lorenz Hart
Present Arms (1928)

BLUE ROOM, THE
Richard Rodgers
Lorenz Hart
The Girl Friend (1926)

BLUE SHADOWS
Louis Alter
Raymond Klages
Earl Carroll's Vanities (1928)

BLUE SIERRAS
Frederico Valerio
Elizabeth Miele
Hit the Trail (1954)

BLUE SKIES
Irving Berlin
Betsy (1926)

BLUE SKIES, GRAY SKIES
George M. Cohan
The Merry Malones (1927)

BLUEBIRD
Baldwin Bergersen
William Archibald
The Crystal Heart (OB) (1960)

BLUES
John Latouche
Two for Tonight (OB) (1939)

BLUES
Marc Blitzstein
Regina (1949)

BLUES IN THE NIGHT
Harold Arlen
Johnny Mercer
Blues in the Night (F) (1941)

————
*Originally written as "Prayer" for *Hollywood Revue* (F) (1933)

BLUFF
George M. Cohan
Billie (1928)

BOASTING SONG
Al Carmines
Rosalyn Drexler
Home Movies (OB) (1964)

BOBBED HAIRED BABY
J. Fred Coots and Maury Rubens
McElbert Moore
A Night in Paris (1926)

BOBBY AND ME
Ray Henderson
B. G. DeSylva
Three Cheers (1928)

BODY AND SOUL
John Green
Edward Heyman, Robert Sour, and
  Frank Eyton
Three's a Crowd (1930)

BODY BEAUTIFUL, THE
Jerry Bock
Sheldon Harnick
The Body Beautiful (1958)

BOFFOLA
Philip Charig
Danny Shapiro, Milton Pascal, and
  Ray Golden
Catch a Star! (1955)

BOJANGLES OF HARLEM
Jerome Kern
Dorothy Fields
Swing Time (F) (1936)

BOLERO D'AMOUR
Stephen Sondheim
Follies (1971)

BON JOUR
Rudolf Friml
Johnny Burke
The Vagabond King (F) (1956)

BON JOUR
Meredith Willson
The Unsinkable Molly Brown (1960)

BONJOUR
Deed Meyer
'Toinette (OB) (1961)

BON SOIR, PARIS
Heitor Villa-Lobos
Robert Wright and George Forrest
Magdalena (1948)

BON VIVANT
Robert Wright and George Forrest
  (based on Grieg)
Song of Norway (1944)

BON VIVANT
Robert Emmett Dolan
Johnny Mercer
Foxy (1964)

BON VOYAGE
Cole Porter
Anything Goes (1934)

BON VOYAGE
Jerome Moross
Kyle Crichton
Parade (1935)

BON VOYAGE
Leonard Bernstein
Richard Wilbur
Candide (1956)

BONDS
Jerry Bock
Sheldon Harnick
The Rothschilds (1970)

BONGO-BOOLA
Eubie Blake
Noble Sissle
Shuffle Along (1952)

BONITA
Sigmund Romberg
Harry B. Smith
The Love Call (1927)

BONNE NUIT, MERCI
Noël Coward
Bitter Sweet (1929)

BONNIE BANKS
Lee Wainer
Robert Sour
Sing for Your Supper (1939)

BONNIE BLUE FLAG
Sigmund Romberg
Dorothy Donnelly
My Maryland (1927)

BOOK REPORT
Clark Gesner
You're a Good Man, Charlie Brown
  (OB) (1967)

BOOM-BOOM
Cy Coleman
Carolyn Leigh
Little Me (1962)

BOOM DITTY BOOM
John Kander
Fred Ebb
70, Girls, 70 (1971)

BOOMERANG
Joe Jordan
Rosamund Johnson
Fast and Furious (1931)

BOOMPS-A-DAISY
Annette Mills
Hellzapoppin' (1938)

BOONDOGGLING
Ray Henderson
Jack Yellen
George White's Scandals (1936)

**BOOSTERS' SONG OF THE FAR
NORTH, THE**
Randall Thompson
Agnes Morgan
The Grand Street Follies (OB) (1926)

BORED
Harvey Schmidt

Tom Jones
Celebration (1969)

BORN AGAIN
Arthur Schwartz
Howard Dietz
Jennie (1963)

BORN ALL OVER AGAIN
Vernon Duke
Howard Dietz
Sadie Thompson (1944)

BORN AND BRED IN OLD KENTUCKY
Joseph Meyer and James F. Hanley
B. G. DeSylva
Big Boy (1925)

BORN IN AMERICA
Robert Holton
June Carroll
Hi, Paisano! (OB) (1961)

BORN TOO LATE
Vernon Duke
Ogden Nash
The Littlest Revue (OB) (1956)

BOSOM BUDDIES
Jerry Herman
Mame (1966)

BOSS TWEED
Sigmund Romberg
Dorothy Fields
Up in Central Park (1945)

BOSTON
James P. Johnson
Flournoy Miller
Sugar Hill (1931)

BOSTON BEGUINE
Sheldon Harnick
New Faces (1952)

BOSTON IN THE SPRING
Richard Lewine
Ted Fetter
The Girl from Wyoming (OB) (1938)

BOSTON POST ROAD
Joseph Meyer and Roger Wolfe Kahn
Irving Caesar
Here's Howe (1928)

BOTH ENDS AGAINST THE MIDDLE
Sol Kaplan
Edward Eliscu
The Banker's Daughter (OB) (1962)

BOTTLE AND A BIRD, A
Irving Caesar
George White's Music Hall Varieties
  (1932)

BOTTLENECK
Harold Rome
Destry Rides Again (1959)

BOTTOM END OF BLEECKER STREET
Tom Sankey
The Golden Screw (OB) (1967)

BOTTOMLAND
Clarence Williams
Jo Trent
Bottomland (1927)

BOTTOMS UP
Cliff Friend and George White
George White's Scandals (1929)

BOTTOMS UP
Richard Rodgers
Lorenz Hart
By Jupiter (1942)

BOTTOM'S UP
Paul Hoffert
David Secter
Get Thee to Canterbury (OB) (1969)

BOUDOIR DOLLS
Ned Lehak
Edward Eliscu
Nine-Fifteen Revue (1930)

BOUILLOUX GIRLS, THE
Harvey Schmidt
Tom Jones
Colette (OB) (1970)

BOUKRA FILL MISH MISH
Jacques Belasco
Kay Twomey
The Girl from Nantucket (1945)

BOUNCE ME
Con Conrad
Gus Kahn
Kitty's Kisses (1926)

BOUQUET OF FOND MEMORIES, A
Maceo Pinkard
Pansy (1929)

BOY BLUE
Ron Steward and Neal Tate
Ron Steward
Sambo (OB) (1969)

BOW DOWN, SINNERS
Donald Heywood
Black Rhythm (1936)

BOW-LEGGED SAL
Sigmund Romberg
Oscar Hammerstein II
Sunny River (1941)

BOWERY, THE
Vincent Youmans
Harold Adamson and Clifford Grey
Smiles (1930)

BOY AND MAN
Armando Trovaioli
Pietro Garinei and Sandro Giovannini
Rugantino (1964)

BOY, DO I HATE HORSE RACES
Norman Dean
Autumn's Here (OB) (1966)

BOY FOR SALE
Lionel Bart
Oliver! (1963)

BOY FRIEND, THE
Sandy Wilson
The Boy Friend (1954)

BOY FRIEND BACK HOME, THE
Cole Porter
Fifty Million Frenchmen (1929)

BOY FRIENDS
Dave Stamper and Harold Levey
Cyrus Wood
Lovely Lady (1927)

BOY FROM, THE
Mary Rodgers
Esteban Ria Nido
The Mad Show (OB) (1966)

BOY, GIRL, MOON
Dave Stamper
Fred Herendeen
Orchids Preferred (1937)

BOY I LEFT BEHIND ME, THE
Richard Rodgers
Lorenz Hart
By Jupiter (1942)

BOY IN THE BLUE UNIFORM, THE
Emil Gerstenberger and Carle Carlton
Howard Johnson
The Lace Petticoat (1927)

BOY LIKE THAT, A
Leonard Bernstein
Stephen Sondheim
West Side Story (1957)

BOY LIKE YOU, A
Kurt Weill
Langston Hughes
Street Scene (1947)

BOY MOST LIKELY TO SUCCEED
Arthur Siegel
June Carroll
New Faces (1956)

BOY NAMED LEM, A
Sam Stept
Lew Brown and Charles Tobias
Yokel Boy (1939)

BOY NEXT DOOR, THE
Hugh Martin and Ralph Blane
Meet Me in St. Louis (F) (1944)

BOY TALK
Michael Leonard
Herbert Martin
The Yearling (1965)

BOY! WHAT LOVE HAS DONE TO ME!
George Gershwin
Ira Gershwin
Girl Crazy (1930)

BOY WITH THE FIDDLE, THE
Alexander Argov
David Paulsen
To Live Another Summer (1971)

BOYCHILD
Johnny Brandon
Billy Noname (OB) (1970)

BOYS AND GIRLS COME OUT TO PLAY
Helen Miller
Eve Merriam
Inner City (1971)

BOYS AND GIRLS LIKE YOU AND ME*
Richard Rodgers
Oscar Hammerstein II
Oklahoma! (1943)

BOYS, BOYS, BOYS
Jack Lawrence and Stan Freeman
I Had a Ball (1964)

BOYS IN BLUE
Jerome Moross
Paul Peters and George Sklar
Parade (1935)

BOYS IN GRAY
Sigmund Romberg
Dorothy Donnelly
My Maryland (1927)

---

*Dropped before New York opening

BOYS IN THE BACK ROOM, THE
Frederick Hollander
Frank Loesser
Destry Rides Again (F) (1939)

BRAGGART SONG, THE
Robert Kessler
Lola Permagent
O Marry Me! (OB) (1961)

BRAND NEW DRESS, A
André Previn
Alan Jay Lerner
Coco (1969)

BRANDY IN YOUR CHAMPAGNE
Don McAfee
Nancy Leeds
Great Scot! (1965)

BRAVE DESERVE THE FAIR, THE
H. Maurice Jacquet
William Brady
The Silver Swan (1929)

BRAVE OLD CITY OF NEW YORK, THE
Helen Miller
Eve Merriam
Inner City (1971)

BRAVO, BRAVO
Emmerich Kalman
Harry B. Smith
The Circus Princess (1927)

BRAVO, BRAVO, NOVELISTO
Sammy Fain
Marilyn and Alan Bergman
Something More! (1964)

BRAVO, GIOVANNI
Milton Schafer
Ronny Graham
Bravo Giovanni (1962)

BRAZILIAN NUTS
Dorival Caymmi
Al Stillman
Star and Garter (1942)

BREACHY'S LAW
Milton Schafer
Ronny Graham
Bravo Giovanni (1962)

BREAD AND BUTTER
Jerome Kern
Anne Caldwell and Otto Harbach
Criss-Cross (1926)

BREAD AND BUTTER AND SUGAR
William B. Kernell
Dorothy Donnelly
Hello, Lola (1926)

BREAK IT UP
John Green
George Marion, Jr.
Beat the Band (1942)

BREAK IT UP, CINDERELLA
Hoagy Carmichael
Johnny Mercer
Walk with Music (1940)

BREAK-ME-DOWN, THE
Harry Archer
Walter O'Keefe
Just a Minute (1928)

BREAKFAST DANCE
Ralph Rainger
Edward Eliscu
Nine-Fifteen Revue (1930)

BREAKFAST IN BED
Armand Vecsey
P. G. Wodehouse
The Nightingale (1927)

BREAKFAST IN BED
Dave Stamper and Harold Levey
Cyrus Wood
Lovely Lady (1927)

BREAKFAST WITH YOU
Milton Ager
Jack Yellen
Rain or Shine (1928)

BREAKIN' 'EM IN
Eubie Blake
Noble Sissle
Shuffle Along (1933)

BREAKIN' THE RHYTHM
Maceo Pinkard
Pansy (1929)

BREEZE KISSED YOUR HAIR, THE
Jerome Kern
Otto Harbach
The Cat and the Fiddle (1931)

BREEZY
Carl Sigman
Bob Hilliard
Angel in the Wings (1947)

BREWING THE LOVE POTION
Ray Haney
Alfred Aiken
We're Civilized? (OB) (1962)

BRIDE AND GROOM
George Gershwin
Ira Gershwin
Oh, Kay! (1926)

BRIDE WAS DRESSED IN WHITE, THE
Vincent Youmans
Oscar Hammerstein II
Rainbow (1928)

BRIDGE OF CAULAINCOURT, THE
Marguerite Monnot
Julian More, David Heneker, and
    Monte Norman
Irma La Douce (1960)

BRIDGE TO NOWHERE, THE
Ron Dante and Gene Allan
Billy (1969)

BRIEF DISSERTATION ON THE RELE-
VANCY OF A LIBERAL EDUCATION IN
A CONTEMPORARY SOCIETY, A
Earl Wilson, Jr.
*A Day in the Life of Just About Every-
    one* (OB) (1971)

BRIGADOON
Frederick Loewe
Alan Jay Lerner
Brigadoon (1947)

BRIGHT COLLEGE DAYS
Harold Rome
Wish You Were Here (1952)

BRIGHTEN UP AND BE A LITTLE
SUNBEAM
Jimmy McHugh
Harold Adamson
As the Girls Go (1948)

BRING ALL THE BOYS BACK HOME
Galt MacDermot
John Guare
Two Gentlemen of Verona (1971)

BRING BACK THOSE MINSTREL DAYS
Martin Broones
Ballard MacDonald
Rufus Lemaire's Affairs (1927)

BRING ME A ROSE
Lionel Monckton
Arthur Wimperis and Lionel Monck-
    ton
The Arcadians (1910)

BRING ME MY BRIDE
Stephen Sondheim
*A Funny Thing Happened on the Way
    to the Forum* (1962)

BRING ON THE CONCUBINES
Erich Wolfgang Korngold (based on
    Offenbach)
Herbert Baker
Helen Goes to Troy (1944)

BRING ON THE FOLLIES GIRLS
Dave Stamper
Gene Buck
Ziegfeld Follies (1931)

BRING ON THE GIRLS
Richard Myers and Jack Lawrence
Ziegfeld Follies (1957)

BRING YOUR DARLING DAUGHTER
Arthur Schwartz
Howard Dietz
The Gay Life (1961)

BRINGING UP DAUGHTER
David Baker
David Craig
Copper and Brass (1957)

BRINY BLUES, THE
Serge Walter
Agnes Morgan
The Grand Street Follies (1928)

BRISCOE, THE HERO
Coleridge-Taylor Perkinson
Errol Hill
Man Better Man (OB) (1969)

BRITANNIA RULES THE WAVES
Noël Coward
This Year of Grace (1928)

BRITISH MAIDENS
Max Ewing
Agnes Morgan
The Grand Street Follies (1929)

BRITTANIA WAIVES THE RULES
Bernece Kazunoff
Arnold Horwitt and John Latouche
Pins and Needles (OB) (1937)

BROADMINDED
Frank Black
Gladys Shelley
The Duchess Misbehaves (1946)

BROADS AIN'T PEOPLE
Jay Livingston and Ray Evans
Let It Ride (1961)

BROADS OF BROADWAY
Gitz Rice
Paul Porter
Nic-Nax (1926)

BROADWAY
Ray Henderson
B. G. DeSylva and Lew Brown
Manhattan Mary (1927)

BROADWAY
Percy Wenrich
Harry Clarke
Who Cares? (1930)

BROADWAY
Jule Styne
Stephen Sondheim
Gypsy (1959)

BROADWAY BABY
Jim Wise
George Haimsohn and Robin Miller
Dames at Sea (OB) (1968)

BROADWAY BABY
Stephen Sondheim
Follies (1971)

BROADWAY BLOSSOM
Morton Gould
Betty Comden and Adolph Green
Billion Dollar Baby (1945)

BROADWAY LOVE SONG
Jay Gorney
Jean and Walter Kerr
Touch and Go (1949)

BROADWAY MAMMY
Clarence Gaskill and Jimmy Duffy
Keep It Clean (1929)

BROADWAY, MY STREET
John Kander
Fred Ebb
70, Girls, 70 (1971)

BROADWAY OF MY HEART, THE
Skip Redwine and Larry Frank
Frank Merriwell, or Honor Challenged (1971)

BROADWAY REVERIE
Dave Stamper
Gene Buck
Ziegfeld Follies (1931)

BROADWAY TO MADRID
Morris Hamilton
Grace Henry
Earl Carroll's Vanities (1926)

BROKEN BUS, THE
Heitor Villa-Lobos
Robert Wright and George Forrest
Magdalena (1948)

BROKEN HEART, OR THE WAGES OF
SIN, THE
Mitch Leigh
William Alfred and Phyllis Robinson
Cry for Us All (1970)

BROKEN-HEARTED ROMEO
Maria Grever
Raymond Leveen
Viva O'Brien (1941)

BROKEN KIMONA, THE
Robert Stringer
Richard Maury
New Faces (1956)

BROKEN PIANOLITA, THE
Heitor Villa-Lobos
Robert Wright and George Forrest
Magdalena (1948)

BROKEN RHYTHM
Mann Holiner
Alberta Nichols
Gay Paree (1926)

BROKEN STRING BLUES
David Martin
Langston Hughes
Simply Heavenly (1957)

BROM AND KATRINA
Norman Dean
Autumn's Here (OB) (1966)

BRONCHO BUSTERS
George Gershwin
Ira Gershwin
Girl Crazy (1930)

BROOKLYN CANTATA*
George Kleinsinger
Mike Stratton
'Tis of Thee (1940)

BROTHER, CAN YOU SPARE A DIME?
Jay Gorney
E. Y. Harburg
Americana (1932)

BROTHER, WHERE ARE YOU?
Oscar Brown, Jr.
Joy (OB) (1970)

BROTHERHOOD OF MAN
Frank Loesser
*How to Succeed in Business without
 Really Trying* (1961)

BROWN
Ford Dabney
Jo Trent
Rang-Tang (1927)

BROWN BABY
Oscar Brown, Jr.
Joy (OB) (1970)

BROWN EYES
Rudolf Friml
Otto Harbach and Oscar Hammer-
stein II
The Wild Rose (1926)

BROWN PAPER BAG
Ernest McCarty
Jack Ramer and Ernest McCarty
I Dreamt I Dwelt in Bloomingdale's
 (OB) (1970)

BROWN PENNY
Duke Ellington
John Latouche
Beggar's Holiday (1946)

BROWN PENNY
John Duffy
Rocco Bufano and John Duffy (based
 on W.B. Yeats)
Horseman, Pass By (OB) (1969)

BROWN-EYED GIRL
Emmerich Kalman
Harry B. Smith
Countess Maritza (1926)

———
*Also in *Of V We Sing* (1942)

BROWN SUGAR
Donald Heywood
Blackberries of 1932

BRUSH UP YOUR SHAKESPEARE
Cole Porter
Kiss Me, Kate (1948)

BRUSHING STONE, THE
Coleman Dowell
The Tattooed Countess (OB) (1961)

BRUSSELS
Jacques Brel
Eric Blau and Mort Shuman
*Jacques Brel Is Alive and Well and
    Living in Paris* (OB) (1968)

BUBBLE, THE
Rudolf Friml
Otto Harbach
High Jinks (1913)

BUBBLES OF BLISS
Jerome Kern
Anne Caldwell
The City Chap (1925)

BUCHAREST
Sigmund Romberg
Otto Harbach
Forbidden Melody (1936)

BUCK IN THE BANK
Gerald Marks
Sam Lerner
Hold It! (1948)

BUCKIN' BARLEY
Alfred Brooks
Ira J. Bilowit
Of Mice and Men (OB) (1958)

BUCKLE DOWN, WINSOCKI
Hugh Martin and Ralph Blane
Best Foot Forward (1941)

BUDDY, BEWARE
Cole Porter
Anything Goes (1934)

BUDDY ROSE
Abel Baer
Sam Lewis and Joe Young
Lady Do (1927)

BUFFALO BILL
Irving Berlin
Annie Get Your Gun (1946)

BUGLE, THE
Meredith Willson
Here's Love (1963)

BUGLE BLOW
Richard Rodgers
Lorenz Hart
Betsy (1926)

BUILDERS OF DREAMS
Henry Sullivan
John Murray Anderson
John Murray Anderson's Almanac
    (1929)

BUILDING UP TO A LET-DOWN
Will Irwin
Norman Zeno and Lee Brody
Fools Rush In (1934)

BULL BLOOD AND BRANDY
Richard Freitas
Morty Neff and George Mysels
The Difficult Woman (OB) (1962)

BULLS, THE
Jacques Brel
Eric Blau and Mort Shuman
*Jacques Brel Is Alive and Well and
    Living in Paris* (OB) (1968)

BUM WON, THE
Jerry Bock
Sheldon Harnick
Fiorello (1959)

BUMS' OPERA
Richard Rodgers
Oscar Hammerstein II
Pipe Dream (1955)

BUNDLE OF LOVE
Alberta Nichols
Mann Holiner
Angela (1928)

BUNDLING
Sigmund Romberg
Oscar Hammerstein II
Sunny River (1941)

BUNK
Gene Lockhart
Bunk of 1926 (1926)

BUNNY, BUNNY, BUNNY
Harold Rome
Star and Garter (1942)

BURMA MOON
Gitz Rice
Paul Porter
Nic-Nax (1926)

BURN, BABY, BURN
Johnny Brandon
Billy Noname (OB) (1970)

BURN 'EM UP
Edgar Fairchild
Henry Myers
The New Yorkers (1927)

BURN THIS TOWN
Voices, Inc.
The Believers (OB) (1968)

BUSHEL AND A PECK, A
Frank Loesser
Guys and Dolls (1950)

BUSINESS IS BAD
Joseph Raposo
Erich Segal
Sing Muse! (OB) (1961)

BUSINESS IS BUSINESS
Ida Hoyt Chamberlain
Enchanted Isle (1927)

BUSY, BUSY DAY
Bill Mahoney
My Wife and I (OB) (1966)

BUSY EVENING, A
J. Fred Coots
Clifford Grey
June Days (1925)

BUSY LITTLE CENTER, A
George M. Cohan
The Merry Malones (1927)

BUT
Marguerite Monnot
Julian More, David Heneker, and
    Monte Norman
Irma La Douce (1960)

BUT ALIVE
Charles Strouse
Lee Adams
Applause (1970)

BUT IN THE MORNING, NO!
Cole Porter
Du Barry Was a Lady (1939)

BUT, MRS. ADAMS
Sherman Edwards
1776 (1969)

BUT NOT FOR ME
George Gershwin
Ira Gershwin
Girl Crazy (1930)

BUT THAT'S THE WAY YOU ARE
André Previn
Alan Jay Lerner
Coco (1969)

BUT WHO CARES?
Emmerich Kalman
Harry B. Smith
The Circus Princess (1927)

BUT YOURS
Bob Merrill
Take Me Along (1959)

BUTCHER, BAKER, CANDLESTICK-MAKER
Mana-Zucca
Benjamin M. Kaye
The Garrick Gaieties (1925)

BUTLER IN THE ABBEY
Jule Styne
E. Y. Harburg
Darling of the Day (1968)

BUTTER AND EGG BABY
Alma Sanders
Monte Carlo
Oh! Oh! Nurse (1925)

BUTTERFLIES AND THE BEES, THE
Sigmund Romberg
Oscar Hammerstein II
Sunny River (1941)

BUTTERFLY, THE
John Kander
Fred Ebb
Zorbá (1968)

BUTTON UP YOUR HEART
Jimmy McHugh
Dorothy Fields
The Vanderbilt Revue (1930)

BUTTON UP YOUR OVERCOAT
Ray Henderson
B. G. DeSylva and Lew Brown
Follow Thru (1929)

BUY AN EXTRA
Tom Johnstone
Phil Cook
When You Smile (1925)

BUY BONDS, BUSTER, BUY BONDS
Jack Holmes
Bill Conklin and Bob Miller
O Say Can You See! (OB) (1962)

BUY MY PARDONS
Paul Hoffert
David Secter
Get Thee to Canterbury (OB) (1969)

BUY YOUR WAY
Maury Rubens
Clifford Grey
The Madcap (1928)

BUY YOURSELF A BALLOON
Herman Hupfeld
The Show Is On (1926)

BY CANDLELIGHT
Robert Katscher
Rowland Leigh
You Never Know (1938)

BY MY SIDE
Peggy Gordon
Jay Hamburger
Godspell (OB) (1971)

BY MYSELF
Arthur Schwartz
Howard Dietz
Between the Devil (1937)

BY SPECIAL PERMISSION OF THE COPYWRIGHT OWNERS, I LOVE YOU
Lewis E. Gensler
Owen Murphy and Robert A. Simon
The Gang's All Here (1931)

BY STRAUSS
George Gershwin
Ira Gershwin
The Show Is On (1936)

BY THE GLENSIDE
Earl Robinson
Waldo Salt
Sandhog (OB) (1954)

BY THE MISSISSINEWAH
Cole Porter
Something for the Boys (1943)

BY THE SASKATCHEWAN
Ivan Caryll
C. M. S. McLellan
The Pink Lady (1911)

BY THE SEA
Clark Gesner
New Faces (1968)

BY THE SWEAT OF YOUR BROW
Eubie Blake
J. Milton Reddie and Cecil Mack
Swing It (1937)

BY THE WAY
Vivian Ellis
Graham John
By the Way (1925)

BY THIS TOKEN
Sigmund Romberg
Harry B. Smith
Princess Flavia (1925)

BY WELAWELA
Rudolf Friml
J. Keirn Brennan
Luana (1930)

BYE AND BYE
Richard Rodgers
Lorenz Hart
Dearest Enemy (1925)

BYE AND BYE
Steven Metcalf
Fred Bluth
Drat! (OB) (1971)

BYE-BYE BABE
Leon DeCosta
The Blonde Sinner (1926)

BYE BYE BABY
Jule Styne
Leo Robin
Gentlemen Prefer Blondes (1949)

BYE BYE, BONNIE
Albert Von Tilzer
Neville Fleeson
Bye Bye, Bonnie (1927)

BYE-BYE BUTTERFLY LOVER
Arthur Schwartz
Howard Dietz
Between the Devil (1937)

CA C'EST L'AMOUR
Cole Porter
Les Girls (F) (1957)

CA, C'EST SIXTH AVENUE
Lee Brody and Richard Jones
Fools Rush In (1934)

CAB SONG
Emmerich Kalman
George Marion, Jr.
Marinka (1945)

CABALLERO
Noël Coward
This Year of Grace (1928)

CABARET
John Kander
Fred Ebb
Cabaret (1966)

CABARETS
Richard Rodgers
Lorenz Hart
The Girl Friend (1926)

CABBY'S SERENADE, THE
Jimmy McHugh
Al Dubin
Keep Off the Grass (1940)

CABIN DOOR
Eubie Blake
Andy Razaf
Blackbirds (1930)

CABIN IN THE COTTON
Harold Arlen
Irving Caesar and George White
George White's Music Hall Varieties
(1932)

CABIN IN THE SKY
Vernon Duke
John Latouche
Cabin in the Sky (1940)

CAESAR IS WRONG
Ervin Drake
Her First Roman (1968)

CAFÉ ROYALE RAG TIME
Kenneth Jacobson
Rhoda Roberts
Show Me Where the Good Times Are
(OB) (1970)

144604

CAKE WALK YOUR LADY
Harold Arlen
Johnny Mercer
St. Louis Woman (1946)

CAL GETS BY
Robert Waldman
Alfred Uhry
Here's Where I Belong (1968)

CALCUTTA
Gerald Dolin
Edward J. Lambert
Smile at Me (1935)

CALIFORNIA
Ida Hoyt Chamberlain
Enchanted Isle (1927)

CALIFORNIA
Richard B. Chodosh
Barry Alan Grael
The Streets of New York (OB) (1963)

CALIFORNIA SKIES
Harry Ruby
Bert Kalmar
The Ramblers (1926)

CALIFORNI-AY
Jerome Kern
E. Y. Harburg
Can't Help Singing (F) (1944)

CALINDA, THE
Herman Hupfeld
A la Carte (1927)

CALL FROM THE GRAVE
Kurt Weill
Marc Blitzstein
The Threepenny Opera (OB) (1954)

CALL HIM PAPA
Francis Thorne
Arnold Weinstein
Fortuna (OB) (1962)

CALL IN TO HER
Mitch Leigh
William Alfred and Phyllis Robinson
Cry for Us All (1970)

CALL IT A DREAM
Sigmund Romberg
Oscar Hammerstein II
Sunny River (1941)

CALL IT APPLEFRITTERS
Richard Stutz
Milton Pascal
Along Fifth Avenue (1949)

CALL IT LOVE
Abraham Ellstein
Walter Bullock
Great to Be Alive (1950)

CALL ME BABYLOVE
Claibe Richardson
Kenward Elmslie
The Grass Harp (1971)

CALL ME BACK
Stan Freeman and Franklin Underwood
Lovely Ladies, Kind Gentlemen (1970)

CALL ME LUCKY
Johnny Brandon
Cindy (OB) (1964)

CALL ME MISTER
Harold Rome
Call Me Mister (1946)

CALL ME SAVAGE
Jule Styne
Betty Comden and Adolph Green
Fade Out—Fade In (1964)

CALL OF BROADWAY, THE
Maury Rubens
Jack Osterman and Ted Lewis
Artists and Models (1927)

CALL OF LIFE, THE
Noël Coward
Bitter Sweet (1929)

CALL OF THE SEA, THE
Vincent Youmans
Otto Harbach
No, No, Nanette (1925)

CALL OF THE WILD
Berenice Kazounoff
Sylvia Marks
Two for Tonight (OB) (1939)

CALL THE POLICE
David Baker
David Craig
Copper and Brass (1957)

CALLA LILY LADY
Galt MacDermot
John Guare
Two Gentlemen of Verona (1971)

CALLING ALL STARS
Harry Akst
Lew Brown
Calling All Stars (1934)

CALLING YOU MY OWN
A. Baldwin Sloane
Harry Cort and George E. Stoddard
China Rose (1925)

CALLIOPE
Kay Swift
Paris '90 (1952)

CALYPSO JOE
Morgan Lewis
Nancy Hamilton
Two for the Show (1940)

CALYPSO KITTY
Don Elliott
James Costigan
The Beast in Me (1963)

CALYPSO PETE
Charles Gaynor
Show Girl (1961)

CAMELOT
Frederick Loewe
Alan Jay Lerner
Camelot (1960)

CAMELOT SAMBA, THE
Richard Rodgers
Lorenz Hart
A Connecticut Yankee (1943)

CAMERA SHOOT
Richard Rodgers
Lorenz Hart
She's My Baby (1928)

CAMILLE, COLETTE, FIFI
Victor Young
Stella Unger
Seventh Heaven (1955)

CAMP KAREFREE
Harold Rome
Wish You Were Here (1952)

CAMPAIGN, THE
Moose Charlap
Norman Gimbel
The Conquering Hero (1961)

CAMPAIGN SONG
Will Holt
That 5 A.M. Jazz (OB) (1964)

CAMPUS WALK
Maceo Pinkard
Pansy (1929)

CAN ANYONE SEE?
Robert Stolz
Robert Sour
Mr. Strauss Goes to Boston (1945)

CAN-CAN
Cole Porter
Can-Can (1953)

CAN-CANOLA, THE
J. Fred Coots
Arthur Swanstrom and Benny Davis
Sons O' Guns (1929)

CAN I FORGET YOU?
Jerome Kern
Oscar Hammerstein II
High, Wide and Handsome (F) (1937)

CAN I TOUCH YOU?
Tom Sankey
The Golden Screw (OB) (1967)

CAN IT BE POSSIBLE?
Jack Lawrence and Stan Freeman
I Had a Ball (1964)

CAN THE CAN-CAN
Dorcas Cochran and Charles Rosoff
Earl Carroll's Vanities (1940)

CAN THIS BE A TOE PRINT?
Alec Wilder
Arnold Sundgaard
Kittiwake Island (OB) (1960)

CAN THIS BE LOVE?
Kay Swift
Paul James
Fine and Dandy (1930)

CAN YOU HEAR MY VOICE?
Samuel Kraus
George Sherman
To Live Another Summer (1971)

CAN YOU SEE A GIRL LIKE ME IN
THE ROLE?
William Howe
Max Showalter
Shoestring Revue (OB) (1957)

CAN YOU SING?
Sigmund Romberg
Oscar Hammerstein II
Sunny River (1941)

CANARY
Stan Davis
Giles O'Connor
Wet Paint (OB) (1965)

CANDY'S LAMENT
Alfred Brooks
Ira J. Bilowit
Of Mice and Men (OB) (1958)

CAN'T BE BOTHERED NOW
J. C. Johnson
Change Your Luck (1930)

CAN'T GET RID OF ME
Harry Revel
Mack Gordon
Smiling Faces (1932)

CAN'T HELP LOVIN' DAT MAN
Jerome Kern
Oscar Hammerstein II
Show Boat (1927)

CAN'T HELP SINGING
Jerome Kern
E. Y. Harburg
Can't Help Singing (F) (1944)

CAN'T STOP THE SEA
Baldwin Bergersen
William Archibald
Carib Song (1945)

CAN'T WE BE FRIENDS?
Kay Swift
Paul James
The Little Show (1929)

CAN'T WE GET TOGETHER
Thomas (Fats) Waller and Harry
  Brooks
Andy Razaf
Hot Chocolates (1929)

CAN'T YOU DO A FRIEND A FAVOR?
Richard Rodgers
Lorenz Hart
A Connecticut Yankee (1943)

CAN'T YOU JUST SEE YOURSELF?
Jule Styne
Sammy Cahn
High Button Shoes (1947)

CAN'T YOU SEE IT?
Charles Strouse
Lee Adams
Golden Boy (1964)

CANTATA
Gerald Alters
Herbert Hartig
Wet Paint (OB) (1965)

CANTEEN SERENADE
Jack Holmes
Bill Conklin and Bob Miller
O Say Can You See! (OB) (1962)

Canter Banter
Paul Hoffert
David Secter
Get Thee to Canterbury (OB) (1969)

Canterbury Day
Richard Hill and John Hawkins
Nevill Coghill
Canterbury Tales (1969)

Canticle to the Wind
Ed Tyler
Sweet Miani (OB) (1962)

Can You Use Any Money Today?
Irving Berlin
Call Me Madam (1950)

Capital of the World
Edwin Greenberg
Pilgrim's Progress (OB) (1962)

Capricious and Fickle
Al Carmines
Maria Irene Fornes
Promenade (OB) (1969)

Captain Henry St. James
Jay Livingston and Ray Evans
Oh Captain! (1958)

Captain Hook's Tango
Mark Charlap
Carolyn Leigh
Peter Pan (1954)

Captain Hook's Waltz
Jule Styne
Betty Comden and Adolph Green
Peter Pan (1954)

Captain Lincoln March, The
Victor Ziskin
Joan Javits
Young Abe Lincoln (1961)

Captain, Mate and Crew
Eubie Blake
J. Milton Reddie and Cecil Mack
Swing It (1937)

Captain Valentine's Tango
Kurt Weill
Paul Green
Johnny Johnson (1936)

Cardinal's Guard Are We, The
Sigmund Romberg (developed by
    Don Walker)
Leo Robin
The Girl in Pink Tights (1954)

Career Guidance
David Baker
David Craig
Copper and Brass (1957)

Carefully Taught
Richard Rodgers
Oscar Hammerstein II
South Pacific (1949)

Careless Rhapsody
Richard Rodgers
Lorenz Hart
By Jupiter (1942)

Caress Me, Possess Me, Perfume
Moose Charlap
Norman Gimbel
Whoop-Up (1958)

Caribbeana
Gerald Dolin
Edward J. Lambert
Smile at Me (1935)

Carinito
Maria Grever
Raymond Leveen
Viva O'Brien (1941)

Carino Mio
Frederick Loewe
Alan Jay Lerner
Paint Your Wagon (1951)

Carioca, The
Vincent Youmans
Edward Eliscu and Gus Kahn
Flying Down to Rio (F) (1933)

CARISSIMA
G. Romilli
Grace Henry
Fioretta (1929)

CARLOTTA
Cole Porter
Mexican Hayride (1944)

CARMELA
Dave Stamper
Gene Buck
Take the Air (1927)

CARMEN HAS NOTHING ON ME
Dave Stamper
Gene Buck
Take the Air (1927)

CARMEN JONES IS GOIN' TO JAIL
Georges Bizet
Oscar Hammerstein II
Carmen Jones (1943)

CARMEN VISCENZO
Lor Crane
John B. Kuntz
Whispers on the Wind (OB) (1970)

CARNIVAL IN COURT
Jay Navarre
Ray Golden and I. A. L. Diamond
Catch a Star! (1955)

CARNIVAL SONG, THE
Jule Styne
Betty Comden and Adolph Green
Say, Darling (1958)

CARNIVAL THEME (LOVE MAKES THE WORLD GO ROUND)
Bob Merrill
Carnival (1961)

CAROL, A
Clinton Ballard
Carolyn Richter
The Ballad of Johnny Pot (OB) (1971)

CAROLITA
William Heagney

William Heagney and Tom Connell
There You Are (1932)

CAROUSEL
Robert Holton
June Carroll
Hi, Paisano! (OB) (1961)

CAROUSEL
Jacques Brel
Eric Blau and Mort Shuman
Jacques Brel Is Alive and Well and Living in Paris (OB) (1968)

CAROUSEL IN THE PARK
Sigmund Romberg
Dorothy Fields
Up in Central Park (1945)

CAROUSEL WALTZ
Richard Rodgers
Carousel (1945)

CARRIAGE FOR ALIDA, A
Sol Kaplan
Edward Eliscu
The Banker's Daughter (OB) (1962)

CARRIE
Noël Coward
Charlot's Revue (1926)

CARRIED AWAY
Leonard Bernstein
Betty Comden and Adolph Green
On the Town (1944)

CARRIED AWAY
Darwin Venneri
Darwin's Theories (OB) (1960)

CARRION TRAIN
Mike Brandt, Michael Knight, and Robert J. Lowery
Exchange (OB) (1970)

CARRY On
Cole Porter
Red, Hot and Blue! (1936)

CARRY ON, KEEP SMILING*
Vincent Youmans
Harold Adamson
Smiles (1930)

CASAMAGORDO, NEW MEXICO
Jule Styne
Sammy Cahn
Look to the Lilies (1970)

CASANOVA
Vernon Duke
Ted Fetter
The Show Is On (1936)

CASE OF RAPE, A
Robert Emmett Dolan
Johnny Mercer
Foxy (1964)

CASTLE IN INDIA, A
Hal Jordan
Jerry Douglas
Rondelay (OB) (1969)

CASTLE OF DREAMS
Harry Tierney
Joseph McCarthy
Irene (1919)

CASTLE OF LOVE
Karl Hajos (based on Chopin)
Harry B. Smith
White Lilacs (1928)

CASTLES IN THE AIR
William Dyer
Don Parks and William Dyer
Jo! (OB) (1964)

CATALINA
Michael Cleary
Arthur Swanstrom
Sea Legs (1937)

CATCH A STAR!
Sammy Fain
Paul Webster
Catch a Star! (1955)

CATCH HATCH
Kurt Weill

Ogden Nash
One Touch of Venus (1943)

CATCH ME
Sam Shepard
Operation Sidewinder (1970)

CATCH ME IF YOU CAN
Kurt Weill
Langston Hughes
Street Scene (1947)

CATCH MY GARTER
John Kander
Fred Ebb
The Happy Time (1968)

CATCH OUR ACT AT THE MET
Jule Styne
Betty Comden and Adolph Green
Two on the Aisle (1951)

CATCH THAT ON THE CORNER
Melvin Van Peebles
Ain't Supposed to Die a Natural Death (1971)

CATHEDRAL OF CLEMENZA, THE
Sandy Wilson
Valmouth (OB) (1960)

CATHERINE THE GREAT
Sam Stept
Lew Brown and Charles Tobias
Yokel Boy (1939)

CAUGHT IN THE RAIN
Henry Sullivan
Howard Dietz
The Little Show (1929)

CAUSE OF THE SITUATION, THE
George M. Cohan
Billie (1928)

'CAUSE WE GOT CAKE
Richard Rodgers
Lorenz Hart
Too Many Girls (1939)

---

*Dropped from New York production

'CAUSE YOU WON'T PLAY HOUSE
Morgan Lewis
E. Y. Harburg
New Faces (1934)

CAVALIERS
Rudolf Friml
Rowland Leigh and John Shubert
Music Hath Charms (1934)

CAVORTING
Rick Besoyan
Babes in the Wood (OB) (1964)

CECILY
Robert Hood Bowers
Francis DeWitt
Oh, Ernest! (1927)

CELEBRATION!
Gordon Duffy
Harry M. Haldane
Happy Town (1959)

CELEBRATION
Harvey Schmidt
Tom Jones
Celebration (1969)

CELINA COULDN'T SAY "NO"
Arthur Schwartz
Howard Dietz
Between the Devil (1937)

CELLINI'S DREAM
Alfred Goodman, Maury Rubens, and
J. Fred Coots
Clifford Grey
Artists and Models (1925)

CERTAIN GIRL, A
John Kander
Fred Ebb
The Happy Time (1968)

CERTAIN INDIVIDUALS
Harold Rome
Wish You Were Here (1952)

C'EST COMME ÇA
Duke Ellington

Marshall Barer and Fred Tobias
Pousse-Café (1966)

C'EST DEFENDU
Gerard Calvi
Harold Rome
La Grosse Valise (1965)

C'EST LA VIE
Harold Arlen
Ira Gershwin and E. Y. Harburg
Life Begins at 8:40 (1934)

C'EST LA VIE
Victor Young
Stella Unger
Seventh Heaven (1955)

C'EST MAGNIFIQUE
Cole Porter
Can-Can (1953)

C'EST MOI
Frederick Loewe
Alan Jay Lerner
Camelot (1960)

CHAIN STORE DAISY
Harold Rome
Pins and Needles (OB) (1937)

CHAMPAGNE
Hal Jordan
Jerry Douglas
Rondelay (OB) (1969)

CHANCES
Bob Goodman
Wild and Wonderful (1971)

CHANGE PARTNERS
Irving Berlin
Carefree (F) (1938)

CHANGE YOUR LUCK
J. C. Johnson
Change Your Luck (1930)

CHANGE YOUR MIND ABOUT ME
Alexander Hill
Hummin' Sam (1933)

CHANGING MY TUNE
George Gershwin
Ira Gershwin
The Shocking Miss Pilgrim (F) (1946)

CHANGING OF THE GUARDS
Ben Oakland
Jack Murray and Barry Trivers
Ziegfeld Follies (1931)

CHANSON IN THE PRATER, A
Sigmund Romberg
Oscar Hammerstein II
May Wine (1935)

CHANT
Irving Burgie
Ballad for Bimshire (OB) (1963)

CHANT D'AMOUR
Gordon Jenkins
Nat Hiken
Along Fifth Avenue (1949)

CHANTY
Ron Dante and Gene Allan
Billy (1969)

CHAPTER ONE
Jerry Blatt
Jerry Blatt and Lonnie Burstein
Have I Got One for You (OB) (1968)

CHARISMA
Oscar Brand
How to Steal an Election (OB) (1968)

CHARITY
Nacio Herb Brown and Richard Whiting
B. G. DeSylva
Take a Chance (1932)

CHARITY
Murray Grand
Lester Judson and Robin Miller
Chic (OB) (1959)

CHARITY'S SOLILOQUY
Cy Coleman
Dorothy Fields
Sweet Charity (1966)

CHARLESTON
James Johnson
Cecil Mack
Runnin' Wild (1923)

CHARLESTON
Morton Gould
Betty Comden and Adolph Green
Billion Dollar Baby (1945)

CHARLESTON MAD
Con Conrad
William B. Friedlander
Mercenary Mary (1925)

CHARLEY FROM THAT CHARLESTON DANCIN' SCHOOL
Porter Grainger and Freddie Johnson
Lucky Sambo (1925)

CHARLIE
Fred Ebb and Norman Martin
From A to Z (1960)

CHARLIE, MY BACK DOOR MAN
Clarence Todd
Henry Creamer and Con Conrad
Keep Shufflin' (1928)

CHARLIE WELCH
Jerry Bock, George Weiss, and Larry Holofcener
Mr. Wonderful (1956)

CHARLIE'S PLAINT
Susan Hulsman Bingham
Myrna Lamb
Mod Donna (OB) (1970)

CHARLIE'S SONGS
Gary Geld
Peter Udell
Purlie (1970)

CHARM
William Roy
Maggie (1953)

CHARMED LIFE
David Shire
Richard Maltby, Jr.
The Sap of Life (OB) (1961)

CHARMIN' SON-OF-A-BITCH, THE
Bill and Patti Jacob
Jimmy (1969)

CHARMING
George M. Cohan
The Merry Malones (1927)

CHARMING
Edward A. Horan
Frederick Herendeen
All the King's Horses (1934)

CHARMING
Dorcas Cochran and Charles Rosoff
Earl Carroll's Vanities (1940)

CHARMING, CHARMING
Richard Rodgers
Lorenz Hart
Peggy-Ann (1926)

CHARMING, CHARMING
Noël Coward
Conversation Piece (1934)

CHARMING WEATHER
Lionel Monckton and Arthur Wimperis
Lionel Monckton
The Arcadians (1910)

CHARMING WOMEN
J. Fred Coots
Clifford Grey
June Days (1925)

CHASE, THE
Frederick Loewe
Alan Jay Lerner
Brigadoon (1947)

CHASE, THE
Steven Metcalf
Fred Bluth
Drat! (OB) (1971)

CHASING HENRY
Michael Cleary
Arthur Swanstrom
Sea Legs (1937)

CHASTE WOMAN
Con Conrad
William B. Friedlander
Mercenary Mary (1925)

CHATTER
Gene Lockhart
Bunk of 1926 (1926)

CHATTERBOX, THE
Sam Morrison
Dolph Singer
Summer Wives (1936)

CHAUVE SOURIS
Noël Coward
This Year of Grace (1928)

CHAYA
Stan Freeman and Franklin Underwood
Lovely Ladies, Kind Gentlemen (1970)

CHECK YOUR TROUBLES
Frank Grey
Erle Crooker and McElbert Moore
Happy (1927)

CHECKING THE FACTS
Francis Thorne
Arnold Weinstein
Fortuna (OB) (1962)

CHEEK TO CHEEK
Irving Berlin
Top Hat (F) (1935)

CHEER UP!
Victor Ziskin
Joan Javits
Young Abe Lincoln (1961)

CHEERFUL LITTLE EARFUL
Harry Warren
Ira Gershwin and Billy Rose
Sweet and Low (1930)

CHEERIO
Richard Rodgers
Lorenz Hart
Dearest Enemy (1925)

CHEERIO
Jesse Greer
James J. Walker*
Say When (1928)

CHEERIO, OLD BOYS
Kenneth Gaburo
Seyril Schochen
The Tiger Rag (OB) (1961)

CHEERS FOR THE HERO
Jacques Offenbach
E. Y. Harburg
The Happiest Girl in the World (1961)

CHERCHEZ LA FEMME
Con Conrad
William B. Friedlander
Mercenary Mary (1925)

CHEROKEE ROSE
Frank Harling
Laurence Stallings
Deep River (1926)

CHERRY PIES OUGHT TO BE YOU
Cole Porter
Out of This World (1950)

CHESS AND CHECKERS
Bob Merrill
New Girl in Town (1957)

CHEVALIER OF THE HIGHWAY, THE
Maury Rubens
Clifford Grey
The Great Temptations (1926)

CHI-CHI
Irvin Graham
June Sillman
New Faces (1936)

CHIC
Julian Stein
Lester Judson
Chic (OB) (1959)

CHICAGO
Richard Rodgers
Lorenz Hart
Pal Joey (1940)

CHICAGO THAT I KNOW, THE
George Harwell
What a Killing (OB) (1961)

CHICK-A-PEN
Meredith Willson
The Unsinkable Molly Brown (1960)

CHICKEN IS HE
Al Carmines
Maria Irene Fornes
Promenade (OB) (1969)

CHICKEN SONG, THE
Jerry Blatt
Jerry Blatt and Lonnie Burstein
Have I Got One for You (OB) (1968)

CHICKEN'S A POPULAR BIRD
Irving Burgie
Ballad for Bimshire (OB) (1963)

CHICKENS COME HOME TO ROOST
Eubie Blake
Noble Sissle
Shuffle Along (1933)

CHICO-CHICO CHICO-LAYO
Jack Holmes
Bill Conklin and Bob Miller
O Say Can You See! (OB) (1958)

CHIEF OF LOVE
Jule Styne
Betty Comden and Adolph Green
Say, Darling (1958)

CHIFFON
Maurice Yvain
Max and Nathaniel Lief
Luckee Girl (1928)

CHILD OF ERIN
Franklin Hauser
Russell Janney
The O'Flynn (1934)

---

*Then Mayor of New York

CHILD OF SYMPATHY
Joseph Martinez Kookoolis and Scott
  Fagan
Scott Fagan
Soon (1971)

CHILD YOU ARE
Michael Leonard
Herbert Martin
How to Be a Jewish Mother (1967)

CHILDHOOD LULLABY
Frank Fields
Armand Aulicino
The Shoemaker and the Peddler (OB)
  (1960)

CHILDREN HAVE IT EASY
David Shire
Richard Maltby, Jr.
The Sap of Life (OB) (1961)

CHILDREN OF THE RITZ
Noël Coward
Set to Music (1939)

CHILDRENS' GAMES
Voices, Inc.
The Believers (OB) (1968)

CHILDREN'S GAMES
Lor Crane
John B. Kuntz
Whispers on the Wind (OB) (1970)

CHILDREN'S LAMENT
Walt Smith
Leon Uris
Ari (1971)

**CHILDREN'S SONG (RECESS WITH
MRS. GRIMM)**
Dale F. Menten
Dale F. Menten and Frederick Gaines
The House of Leather (OB) (1970)

CHILD'S SONG, THE
Alex Fry
Lyon Phelps
Do You Know the Milky Way? (1961)

CHIME IN!
Robert Wright and George Forrest
Kean (1961)

CHIN UP, LADIES
Jerry Herman
Milk and Honey (1961)

CHINA BOGIE MAN
A. Baldwin Sloane
Harry Cort and George E. Stoddard
China Rose (1925)

CHINA ROSE
A. Baldwin Sloane
Harry Cort and George E. Stoddard
China Rose (1925)

CHINESE IDOL, THE
Berton Braley, M. de Jari, and Alex
  James
Earl Carroll's Vanities (1926)

CHINESE LANTERN MAN
A. Baldwin Sloane
Harry Cort and George E. Stoddard
China Rose (1925)

CHINESE LULLABY
Robert Hood Bowers
East Is West (1918)

CHINESE MARKET PLACE
Raymond Scott
Bernard Hanighen
Lute Song (1946)

CHINESE MELODY
Franz Lehár
Harry Graham
Yours Is My Heart (1946)

CHINESE POTENTATE
A. Baldwin Sloane
Harry Cort and George E. Stoddard
China Rose (1925)

CHINGO-PINGO
Franz Lehár
Harry Graham
Yours Is My Heart (1946)

CHINKY CHINA CHARLESTON
Milton Susskind
Paul Porter and Benjamin Hapgood
  Burt
Florida Girl (1925)

CHINKYPIN
Marc Blitzstein
Regina (1949)

CHINQUAPIN BUSH
Harold Arlen
Johnny Mercer
St. Louis Woman (1946)

CHIQUITIN TRIO
Robert Stolz
Rowland Leigh
Night of Love (1941)

CHIROMANCY
John Addison
John Cranko
Cranks (1956)

CHOCOLATE BAR
Thomas (Fats) Waller
Andy Razaf
Keep Shufflin' (1928)

CHOCOLATE PAS DE TROIS
Robert Wright and George Forrest
  (based on Grieg)
Song of Norway (1944)

CHOCOLATE TURKEY
Al Carmines
Rosalyn Drexler
Home Movies (OB) (1964)

CHOICE IS YOURS, THE
Edward Thomas
Martin Charnin
Ballad for a Firing Squad (OB) (1968)

CHOO-CHOO HONEYMOON
Jim Wise
George Haimsohn and Robin Miller
Dames at Sea (OB) (1968)

CHOO CHOO LOVE
Con Conrad
Gus Kahn
Kitty's Kisses (1926)

CHOOSE YOUR FLOWERS
Lucien Denni
Helena Evans
Happy Go Lucky (1926)

CHOP SUEY
Richard Rodgers
Oscar Hammerstein II
Flower Drum Song (1958)

CHORUS GIRL BLUES
Manning Sherwin
Arthur Herzog, Jr.
Bad Habits of 1926 (OB) (1926)

CHOW MEIN GIRLS, THE
Clarence Gaskill
Earl Carroll's Vanities (1925)

CHRISTINE
Sammy Fain
Paul Francis Webster
Christine (1960)

CHRISTMAS CAROL
Richard B. Chodosh
Barry Alan Grael
The Streets of New York (OB) (1963)

CHRISTMAS CHILD
Marguerite Monnot
Julian More, David Heneker, and
  Monte Norman
Irma La Douce (1960)

CHRISTMAS EVE BROADCAST
Laurence Rosenthal
James Lipton
Sherry! (1967)

CHRISTMAS IS COMING
Helen Miller
Eve Merriam
Inner City (1971)

CHRISTOPHER STREET
Leonard Bernstein
Betty Comden and Adolph Green
Wonderful Town (1953)

CHUCK IT!
Richard Rodgers
Lorenz Hart
Peggy-Ann (1926)

**CHURCH AROUND THE CORNER,
THE**
Walter G. Samuels
Morrie Ryskind
Ned Wayburn's Gambols (1929)

CHURCH OF MY CHOICE
Sammy Fain
Marilyn and Alan Bergman
Something More! (1964)

C.I.A. MAN
Tuli Kupferberg, Peter Stampfel, and
Antonia
Operation Sidewinder (1970)

CIDER ELLA
Henry Souvaine and Jay Gorney
Morrie Ryskind and Howard Dietz
Merry-Go-Round (1927)

CIGARETTE
H. Maurice Jacquet
William Brady
The Silver Swan (1929)

CIGARETTE
Ray Henderson
Jack Yellen
George White's Scandals (1936)

CIGARETTE SONG
Sigmund Romberg
Harry B. Smith
Cherry Blossoms (1927)

CIGARETTE SONG, THE
Al Carmines
Maria Irene Fornes
Promenade (OB) (1969)

CIGARETTES
Harry Ruby
Bert Kalmar
High Kickers (1941)

CIGARETTES, CIGARS!
Harry Revel
Mack Gordon
Ziegfeld Follies (1931)

CINDERELLA
Charles Rosoff
Leo Robin
Judy (1927)

CINDERELLA BROWN
Jimmy McHugh
Dorothy Fields
Lew Leslie's International Revue
(1930)

CINDERELLA, DARLING
Frank Loesser
*How to Succeed in Business without
Really Trying* (1961)

CINDERELLA GIRL
Jerome Kern
Anne Caldwell and Otto Harbach
Criss-Cross (1926)

CINDERELLA OF OUR BLOCK
Manning Sherwin
Arthur Herzog, Jr.
Bad Habits of 1926 (OB) (1926)

CINDY
John Dooley
Hobo (OB) (1961)

CINDY
Johnny Brandon
Cindy (OB) (1964)

CINEMA BLUES
Arthur Brander
The Seventh Heart (1927)

CINEMA LORELEI
Ned Lehak
Edward Eliscu
The Third Little Show (1931)

CINGALESE GIRLS
Harry Ruby
Bert Kalmar and Otto Harbach
Lucky (1927)

CIRCE, CIRCE
Jerome Moross
John Latouche
The Golden Apple (1954)

CIRCUS DAYS
Milton Ager
Jack Yellen
Rain or Shine (1928)

CIRCUS IS ON PARADE, THE
Richard Rodgers
Lorenz Hart
Jumbo (1935)

CIRCUS WEDDING, THE
Richard Rodgers
Lorenz Hart
Jumbo (1935)

CITATION, THE
Ernest Gold
Anne Croswell
I'm Solomon (1968)

CITY CALLED HEAVEN
Eubie Blake
Noble Sissle
Shuffle Along (1952)

CITY CHAP, THE
Jerome Kern
Anne Caldwell
The City Chap (1925)

CITY BLUES
Voices, Inc.
The Believers (OB) (1968)

CITY LIFE
Don Tucker
Red, White and Maddox (1969)

CITY LIFE
Helen Miller
Eve Merriam
Inner City (1971)

CITY MOUSE, COUNTRY MOUSE
Albert Hague
Arnold B. Horwitt
Plain and Fancy (1955)

CITY OF THE ANGELS
Billy Barnes
The Billy Barnes Revue (1959)

CITY SONG
Kenn Long and Jim Crozier
Kenn Long
Touch (OB) (1970)

CIUMACHELLA
Armando Trovaioli
Pietro Garinei and Sandro Giovannini
Rugantino (1964)

CIVILIZATION
Carl Sigman
Bob Hilliard
Angel in the Wings (1947)

CIVILIZED PEOPLE, THE
Heitor Villa-Lobos
Robert Wright and George Forrest
Magdalena (1948)

CIVILIZED PEOPLE
Robert Wright and George Forrest
Kean (1961)

CLANDESTINE
Robert Kessler
Martin Charnin
Fallout (OB) (1959)

CLANG DANG THE BELL
Frank Loesser
Greenwillow (1960)

CLAP YO' HANDS
George Gershwin
Ira Gershwin
Oh, Kay! (1926)

CLARA
Leon Pober
Bud Freeman
Beg, Borrow or Steal (1960)

CLARA, DON'T YOU BE DOWN-HEARTED
George Gershwin
DuBose Heyward
Porgy and Bess (1935)

CLAY AND FRELINGHUYSEN
Oscar Brand
How to Steal an Election (OB) (1968)

CLEAN OUT THE CORNER
Alma Sanders
Monte Carlo
Mystery Moon (1930)

CLEAN UP YOUR OWN BACKYARD
Norman Curtis
Patricia Taylor Curtis
Walk Down Mah Street! (OB) (1968)

CLEAR OUT OF THIS WORLD
Jimmy McHugh
Al Dubin
Keep Off the Grass (1940)

CLEOPATRA
Alma Sanders
Monte Carlo
Oh! Oh! Nurse (1925)

CLEOPATRA
Julian Slade
Dorothy Reynolds and Julian Slade
Salad Days (OB) (1958)

CLEOPATRA, WE'RE FOND OF YOU
Alma Sanders
Monte Carlo
The Houseboat on the Styx (1928)

CLEOPATTERER
Jerome Kern
P.G. Wodehouse
Leave It to Jane (1917)

CLEVER, THOSE CHINESE
Vincent Youmans
Harold Adamson and Clifford Grey
Smiles (1930)

CLICKETY-CLACK
Kurt Weill
Maxwell Anderson
Knickerbocker Holiday (1938)

CLIMB EV'RY MOUNTAIN
Richard Rodgers
Oscar Hammerstein II
The Sound of Music (1959)

CLIMB UP THE MOUNTAIN
Cole Porter
Out of This World (1950)

CLIMB UP THE SOCIAL LADDER
George Gershwin
Ira Gershwin
Let 'Em Eat Cake (1933)

CLIMBING UP THE LADDER OF LOVE
Jesse Greer
Raymond Klages
Earl Carroll's Vanities (1926)

CLOG AND GROG
Jimmy Van Heusen
Sammy Cahn
Walking Happy (1966)

CLOISTERED FROM THE NOISY CITY
George Gershwin
Ira Gershwin
Let 'Em Eat Cake (1933)

CLORINDA
Donald Heywood
Africana (1927)

CLOSE
Cole Porter
Rosalie (F) (1937)

CLOSE AS PAGES IN A BOOK
Sigmund Romberg
Dorothy Fields
Up in Central Park (1945)

CLOSE HARMONY
Jule Styne
Betty Comden and Adolph Green
Fade Out - Fade In (1964)

CLOSE IN YOUR ARMS
Ida Hoyt Chamberlain
Enchanted Isle (1927)

CLOSE YOUR EYES
Alfred Nathan
George Oppenheimer
The Manhatters (1927)

CLOSE YOUR EYES
Richard B. Chodosh
Barry Alan Grael
The Streets of New York (OB) (1963)

CLOSENESS BEGETS CLOSENESS
Bruce Montgomery
The Amorous Flea (OB) (1964)

CLOSER
Hal Jordan
Jerry Douglas
Rondelay (OB) (1969)

CLOTHES MAKE THE MAN, THE
Al Carmines
Maria Irene Fornes
Promenade (OB) (1969)

CLOWN OF LONDON
Robert Wright and George Forrest
Kean (1961)

CLUB SONG
Alma Sanders
Monte Carlo
The Houseboat on the Styx (1928)

CLUTCHING AT SHADOWS
Alexander Fogarty
Seymour Morris
Cape Cod Follies (1929)

COCKEYED OPTIMIST, A
Richard Rodgers
Oscar Hammerstein II
South Pacific (1949)

COAL OIL
Porter Grainger and Freddie Johnson
Lucky Sambo (1925)

COAX ME
Ernest G. Schweikert
Frank Reardon
Rumple (1957)

COCKTAIL MELODY
Walter Donaldson
Ballard MacDonald
Sweetheart Time (1926)

COCO
Andre Previn
Alan Jay Lerner
Coco (1969)

COCOA BEAN SONG, THE
Richard Adler
Kwamina (1961)

COCOANUT SWEET
Harold Arlen
E. Y. Harburg
Jamaica (1957)

COCONUT GIRL, THE
Noël Coward
The Girl Who Came to Supper (1963)

CODE, THE
Sammy Fain
Dan Shapiro
Ankles Aweigh (1955)

CODE OF THE LICENSED PILOT
Ed Tyler
Sweet Miani (OB) (1962)

COFFEE BREAK
Frank Loesser
*How to Succeed in Business without
  Really Trying* (1961)

COFFEE IN A CARDBOARD CUP
John Kander
Fred Ebb
70, Girls, 70 (1971)

COLD CLEAR WORLD
Marian Grudeff and Raymond Jessel
Baker Street (1965)

COLD, COLD ROOM
Harold Rome
The Zulu and the Zayda (1965)

COLD COMFORT
John Addison
John Cranko
Cranks (1956)

COLD CREAM JAR SONG
Harold Rome
Fanny (1954)

COLD STEEL
Horald Griffiths
Doug Dyer
Blood (OB) (1971)

COLD'S THE WIND
Mel Marvin
Ted Berger
Shoemaker's Holiday (OB) (1967)

COLIE GONE
Coleridge-Taylor Perkinson
Errol Hill
Man Better Man (OB) (1969)

COLLECTIVE BEAUTY
William Roy
Michael McWhinney
New Faces (1962)

COLLEGE DAYS
Mann Holiner
Alberta Nichols
Gay Paree (1926)

COLLEGE OF L'AMOUR
Claude Leveilee
Gladys Shelley
Gogo Loves You (OB) (1964)

COLONEL AND THE MAJOR, THE
Rudolf Friml
P. G. Wodehouse and Clifford Grey
The Three Musketeers (1928)

COLOR BLIND
Henry Sullivan
Earle Crooker
Thumbs Up! (1934)

COLOR ME WHITE
Johnny Brandon
Billy Noname (OB) (1970)

COLORADO LOVE CALL
Rick Besoyan
Little Mary Sunshine (OB) (1959)

COLORED SPADE
Galt MacDermot
Gerome Ragni and James Rado
Hair (1968)

COLORFUL
Charles Strouse
Lee Adams
Golden Boy (1964)

COMBAT, THE
Mitch Leigh
Joe Darion
Man of La Mancha (1965)

COME A LITTLE CLOSER
Bob Goodman
Wild and Wonderful (1971)

COME ALONG
Louis Bellson and Will Irwin
Richard Ney
Portofino (1958)

COME-ALONG-A-ME, BABE
Johnny Brandon
Who's Who, Baby? (OB) (1968)

COME ALONG, BOYS
Jerome Moross
John Latouche
The Golden Apple (1954)

COME ALONG, SUNSHINE
Harry Tierney
Joseph McCarthy
Cross My Heart (1928)

COME ALONG WITH ME
Cole Porter
Can-Can (1953)

COME AND BE MARRIED
Earl Robinson
Waldo Salt
Sandhog (OB) (1954)

COME AND BRING YOUR INSTRU-MENTS
David Raksin
June Carroll
If the Shoe Fits (1946)

COME AND TELL ME*
Richard Rodgers
Lorenz Hart
Betsy (1926)

COME A-WANDERING WITH ME
Arthur Schwartz
Howard Dietz
The Gay Life (1961)

COME AWAY, DEATH
Hal Hester and Danny Apolinar
Your Own Thing (1968)

COME BACK TO ME
Burton Lane
Alan Jay Lerner
On a Clear Day You Can See Forever
   (1965)

COME DOWN
Earl Robinson
Waldo Salt
Sandhog (OB) (1954)

COME HIT YOUR BABY
Maury Rubens and Sam Timberg
Moe Jaffe
Broadway Nights (1929)

COME HOME
Richard Rodgers
Oscar Hammerstein II
Allegro (1947)

COME LIVE WITH ME
Michael Valenti
Just for Love (OB) (1968)

COME ON ALONG
Con Conrad
William B. Friedlander
Mercenary Mary (1925)

COME ON AND MAKE WHOOPEE
Werner Janssen
Mann Holiner
Luckee Girl (1928)

COME ON AND MARRY ME HONEY
Richard Hill and John Hawkins

Nevill Coghill
Canterbury Tales (1969)

COME ON AND PLAY
Joseph Meyer and James F. Hanley
B. G. DeSylva
Big Boy (1925)

COME ON FEET, DO YOUR THING
Melvin Van Peebles
*Ain't Supposed to Die a Natural
   Death* (1971)

COME ON HOME
Donald Heywood
Bottomland (1927)

COME ON HOME
Ron Steward and Neal Tate
Ron Steward
Sambo (OB) (1969)

COME ON IN
Cole Porter
Du Barry Was a Lady (1939)

COME ON, L'IL AUGIE
Harold Arlen
Johnny Mercer
St. Louis Woman (1946)

**COME ON OUTSIDE AND GET SOME
AIR**
Deed Meyer
'Toinette (OB) (1961)

COME ON STRONG
Jimmy Van Heusen
Sammy Cahn
Come On Strong (1962)

COME ON TRAIN
Mike Brandt, Michael Knight, and
   Robert J. Lowery
Exchange (OB) (1970)

COME PLAY WIZ ME
Stephen Sondheim
Anyone Can Whistle (1964)

———
*Dropped from New York production

COME RAIN OR COME SHINE
Harold Arlen
Johnny Mercer
St. Louis Woman (1946)

COME RAISE YOUR CUP
Lee Pockriss
Anne Croswell
Ernest in Love (OB) (1960)

COME RAISING YOUR LEG ON ME
Melvin Van Peebles
*Ain't Supposed to Die a Natural
Death* (1971)

COME, SAID MY SOUL
Stan Harte, Jr.
Walt Whitman
Leaves of Grass (OB) (1971)

COME STA
Sammy Fain
Marilyn and Alan Bergman
Something More! (1964)

COME SUMMER
David Baker
Will Holt
Come Summer (1969)

COME, SWEET LOVE
Edward Earle
Yvonne Tarr
The Decameron (OB) (1961)

COME TO AFRICA
Ford Dabney
Jo Trent
Rang-Tang (1927)

COME TO COLOMBIA
Heitor Villa-Lobos
Robert Wright and George Forrest
Magdalena (1948)

COME TO FLORENCE
Kurt Weill
Ira Gershwin
The Firebrand of Florence (1945)

COME TO HARLEM
Al Wilson, Charles Weinberg, and
Ken Macomber
Yeah Man (1932)

COME TO LOWER FALLS
Harold Orlob
Irving Caesar
Talk About Girls (1927)

COME TO ME
Noël Coward
Sail Away (1961)

COME TO ME, BEND TO ME
Frederick Loewe
Alan Jay Lerner
Brigadoon (1947)

COME TO MEE-OW
George Kleinsinger
Joe Darion
Shinbone Alley (1957)

COME TO PARIS
Kurt Weill
Ira Gershwin
The Firebrand of Florence (1945)

COME TO ST. THOMAS'S
George M. Cohan
Billie (1928)

COME TO THE BALL
Lionel Monckton
Adrian Ross
The Quaker Girl (1911)

COME TO THE ROAD
Kenn Long and Jim Crozier
Kenn Long
Touch (OB) (1970)

COME TO THE SACRIFICE
Erich Wolfgang Korngold (based on
Offenbach)
Herbert Baker
Helen Goes to Troy (1944)

COME TO THE SUPERMARKET
Cole Porter
Aladdin (TV) (1958)

COME UP AND HAVE A CUP OF COF-
FEE
Ray Henderson
Jack Yellen
Ziegfeld Follies (1943)

COME UP TO MY PLACE
Leonard Bernstein
Betty Comden and Adolph Green
On the Town (1944)

COME WEST, LITTLE GIRL, COME
WEST
Walter Donaldson
Gus Kahn
Whoopee (1928)

COME WITH ME
Richard Rodgers
Lorenz Hart
The Boys from Syracuse (1938)

COME WITH ME
Erich Wolfgang Korngold (based on
  Offenbach)
Herbert Baker
Helen Goes to Troy (1944)

COME WITH ME
Clay Warnick
Edward Eager
Dream with Music (1944)

COME YOU MEN
John Morris
Gerald Freedman
A Time for Singing (1966)

COMEDY TONIGHT
Stephen Sondheim
*A Funny Thing Happened on the Way
  to the Forum* (1962)

COMES LOVE
Sam Stept
Lew Brown and Charles Tobias
Yokel Boy (1939)

COMES ONCE IN A LIFETIME
Jule Styne
Betty Comden and Adolph Green
Subways Are for Sleeping (1961)

COMES THE DAWN
Alyn Heim
Malcolm L. LaPrade
Will the Mail Train Run Tonight?
(OB) (1964)

COMES THE REVOLUTION
George Gershwin
Ira Gershwin
Let 'Em Eat Cake (1933)

COMING ATTRACTIONS
Charles Strouse
Six (OB) (1971)

COMING OUT OF THE GARDEN
Harry Archer
Walter O'Keefe
Just a Minute (1928)

COMMAND TO LOVE
Serge Walter
Agnes Morgan
The Grand Street Follies (1928)

COMMAND TO LOVE
Henry Sullivan
Jack Scholl
Keep Moving (1934)

COMME CI, COMME ÇA
Philip Charig
Irving Caesar
Polly (1929)

COMMON Sense
Sammy Fain
George Marion, Jr.
Toplitzky of Notre Dame (1946)

COMMUNICATE
Maury Laws
Jules Bass
Month of Sundays (OB) (1968)

COMMUTERS' SONG, THE
Baldwin Bergersen
Phyllis McGinley
Small Wonder (1948)

COMPANIONSHIP
Robert Colby
Robert Colby and Nita Jonas
Half-Past Wednesday (OB) (1962)

COMPANY
Stephen Sondheim
Company (1970)

COMPANY MANNERS
Will Morrisey
Edmund Joseph
Polly of Hollywood (1927)

COMPANY OF MEN
Jordan Ramin
Frank H. Stanton and Murray Semos
Look Where I'm At! (OB) (1971)

COMPANY WAY, THE
Frank Loesser
*How to Succeed in Business without
  Really Trying* (1961)

COMPROMISE
Lance Mulcahy
Paul Cherry
Park (1970)

COMRADE ALONZO
Cole Porter
Leave It to Me (1938)

**COMRADE, YOU HAVE A CHANCE
HERE**
Karl Hajos (based on Tchaikovsky)
Harry B. Smith
Natja (1925)

CONCERT ENCORE
Sheldon Harnick
Wet Paint (OB) (1965)

CONCHITA
Ray Henderson
Lew Brown
Hot-Cha! (1932)

CONEY BY THE SEA
Richard Lewine
Ted Fetter
Naughty-Naught (OB) (1937)

CONEY ISLAND
Richard Rodgers
Lorenz Hart
Simple Simon (1930)

CONEY ISLAND BOAT
Arthur Schwartz
Dorothy Fields
By the Beautiful Sea (1954)

CONEY ISLAND, U.S.A.
Jack Lawrence and Stan Freeman
I Had a Ball (1964)

CONFESSION
Arthur Schwartz
Howard Dietz
The Band Wagon (1931)

**CONFESSION TO A PARK AVENUE
MOTHER (I'M IN LOVE WITH A WEST
SIDE GIRL)**
Jerry Herman
Parade (OB) (1960)

CONFESSIONAL, THE
Mitch Leigh
William Alfred and Phyllis Robinson
Cry for Us All (1970)

CONFIDENCE
Leon Carr
Earl Shuman
The Secret Life of Walter Mitty (OB)
  (1964)

CONFRONTATION SONG
Kenn Long and Jim Crozier
Kenn Long
Touch (OB) (1970)

CONFUSION
Bill Mahoney
My Wife and I (OB) (1966)

CONGA!
Leonard Bernstein
Betty Comden and Adolph Green
Wonderful Town (1953)

CONGRATULATIONS
Jean Gilbert
Harry Graham
Katja (1926)

CONSIDER YOURSELF
Lionel Bart
Oliver! (1963)

CONSOLATION
Emmerich Kalman and Herbert Sto-thart
Otto Harbach and Oscar Hammerstein II
Golden Dawn (1927)

CONSOLATION
John Duffy
Rocco Bufano and John Duffy (based on W.B. Yeats)
Horseman, Pass By (OB) (1969)

CONTINENTAL, THE*
Con Conrad
Herb Magidson
The Gay Divorcee (F) (1934)

CONTINENTAL HONEYMOON
James F. Hanley
Ballard MacDonald and James F. Hanley
Thumbs Up! (1934)

CONVENT BELLS ARE RINGING
Sigmund Romberg
Harry B. Smith
Princess Flavia (1925)

CONVENTION BOUND
Ronny Graham
New Faces (1952)

CONVERSATION PIECE
Leonard Bernstein
Betty Comden and Adolph Green
Wonderful Town (1953)

COO-COO
Joseph Meyer and Philip Charig
Leo Robin
Just Fancy (1927)

COO-COO
Rick Besoyan
Little Mary Sunshine (OB) (1959)

COOKIES AND BOOKIES
Joseph Meyer and James F. Hanley
B. G. DeSylva
Big Boy (1925)

COOL
Leonard Bernstein
Stephen Sondheim
West Side Story (1957)

COOL COMBO MAMBO
David Baker
David Craig
Copper and Brass (1957)

COOL, COOL, CONSIDERATE MEN
Sherman Edwards
1776 (1969)

COOL CREDO
David Baker
David Craig
Copper and Brass (1957)

COOL 'EM OFF
Morris Hamilton
Grace Henry
Earl Carroll's Vanities (1926)

COOL OFF
Harry Ruby
Bert Kalmar
Animal Crackers (1928)

COOLEST PLACE IN TOWN
Melvin Van Peebles
Ain't Supposed to Die a Natural Death (1971)

COONSKIN CAP
Mike Brandt, Michael Knight, and Robert J. Lowery
Exchange (OB) (1970)

———
*Academy Award Winner

COPPER'S CREED
Dale F. Menten
Dale F. Menten and Frederick Gaines
The House of Leather (OB) (1970)

CORDUROY ROAD
Cy Coleman
Carolyn Leigh
Wildcat (1960)

CORNET MAN
Jule Styne
Bob Merrill
Funny Girl (1964)

CORONATION, THE
Rudolf Friml
Otto Harbach and Oscar Hammerstein II
The Wild Rose (1926)

CORONATION CHORALE
Noël Coward
The Girl Who Came to Supper (1963)

CORONATION SONG
George Fischoff
Verna Tomasson
The Prince and the Pauper (OB) (1963)

COSSACK LOVE SONG (DON'T FORGET ME)
George Gershwin and Herbert Stothart
Otto Harbach and Oscar Hammerstein II
Song of the Flame (1925)

COTTAGE IN THE COUNTRY
Richard Rodgers
Lorenz Hart
Simple Simon (1930)

COTTAGE IN THE COUNTRY
Walter Kollo
Harry B. Smith
Three Little Girls (1930)

COULD BE
Harold Rome
Wish You Were Here (1952)

COULD BE
Jane Douglas
Tom O'Malley
Bella (OB) (1961)

COULD I FORGET
Ida Hoyt Chamberlain
Enchanted Isle (1927)

COULD I LEAVE YOU?
Stephen Sondheim
Follies (1971)

COULD IT BE YOU?
Cole Porter
Something for the Boys (1943)

COULD WE START AGAIN, PLEASE
Andrew Lloyd Webber
Tim Rice
Jesus Christ Superstar (1971)

COULD YOU USE A NEW FRIEND?
Eugene and Ralph Berton
Two for Tonight (OB) (1939)

COULD YOU USE ME?
George Gershwin
Ira Gershwin
Girl Crazy (1930)

COULDN'T BE MORE IN LOVE
Frank Black
Gladys Shelley
The Duchess Misbehaves (1946)

COULDN'T WE
C. Jackson and James Hatch
Fly Blackbird (OB) (1962)

COULD'VE BEEN A RING
Frank Loesser
Greenwillow (1960)

COUNT YOUR BLESSINGS
Cole Porter
Mexican Hayride (1944)

COUNT YOUR BLESSINGS
Baldwin Bergersen
Phyllis McGinley
Small Wonder (1948)

COUNTERMELODY
Mary Rodgers and Jay Thompson
Marshall Barer
From A to Z (1960)

COUNTESS DUBINSKY
Joseph Meyer
Billy Rose and Ballard MacDonald
Ziegfeld Follies (1934)

COUNTIN' OUR CHICKENS
Harold Arlen
Johnny Mercer
Saratoga (1959)

COUNTRY GENTLEMAN, A
Tommy Wolf
Fran Landesman
The Nervous Set (1959)

COUNTRY STORE LIVING
Joseph Martinez Kookoolis and Scott
    Fagan
Scott Fagan
Soon (1971)

**COUNTRY'S IN THE VERY BEST OF
HANDS, THE**
Gene de Paul
Johnny Mercer
Li'l Abner (1956)

COUPLE OF SWELLS, A
Irving Berlin
Easter Parade (F) (1948)

COVENANT, THE
Richard Rodgers
Martin Charnin
Two by Two (1970)

COVER GIRL
Jerome Kern
Ira Gershwin
Cover Girl (F) (1944)

COW AND A PLOUGH AND A FRAU, A
Morton Gould
Dorothy Fields
Arms and the Girl (1950)

COW JUMPED OVER THE MOON, THE
Helen Miller
Eve Merriam
Inner City (1971)

COWBOY POTENTATE
Ida Hoyt Chamberlain
Enchanted Isle (1927)

**COWBOY SONG (OH, THE RIO
GRANDE)**
Kurt Weill
Paul Green
Johnny Johnson (1936)

CRADLE OF THE DEEP
Richard Rodgers
Lorenz Hart
Betsy (1926)

CRADLE SONG
Charles M. Schwab
Henry Myers
Bare Facts of 1926 (1926)

CRAP GAME FUGUE
George Gershwin
DuBose Heyward
Porgy and Bess (1935)

CRASHING THE GOLDEN GATE
Jay Gorney and Phil Cohan
E. Y. Harburg
Earl Carroll's Sketch Book (1929)

CRASHING THRU
Sylvia Fine
The Straw Hat Revue (1939)

CRAZY
Clinton Ballard
Carolyn Richter
The Ballad of Johnny Pot (OB) (1971)

CRAZY AS A LOON
Jimmy McHugh
Al Dubin
Keep Off the Grass (1940)

CRAZY ELBOWS
Richard Rodgers
Lorenz Hart
Present Arms (1928)

CRAZY IDEA OF LOVE
Al Wilson, Charles Weinberg, and
Ken Macomber
Yeah Man (1932)

**CRAZY JANE ON THE DAY OF JUDGE-
MENT**
John Duffy
Rocco Bufano and John Duffy (based
on W. B. Yeats)
Horseman, Pass By (OB) (1969)

CRAZY QUILT
Harry Warren
Bud Green
Crazy Quilt (1931)

CRAZY RHYTHM
Joseph Meyer and Roger Wolfe Kahn
Irving Caesar
Here's Howe (1928)

CRAZY WITH THE HEAT
Rudi Revil
Irvin Graham
Crazy with the Heat (1941)

CREAM IN MY COFFEE
Ed Scott
Anne Croswell
Wet Paint (OB) (1965)

CREAM OF ENGLISH YOUTH, THE
Michael Valenti
John Lewin
Blood Red Roses (1970)

CREDO
Elmer Bernstein
Carolyn Leigh
How Now, Dow Jones (1967)

CREOLE CROONING SONG
Richard Rodgers
Lorenz Hart
The Girl Friend (1926)

CREON
Susan Hulsman Bingham
Myrna Lamb
Mod Donna (OB) (1970)

CRESCENT MOON
Walter G. Samuels
Morrie Ryskind
Ned Wayburn's Gambols (1929)

CRICKETS ARE CALLING, THE
Jerome Kern
P. G. Wodehouse
Leave It to Jane (1917)

CRIME
Harry Archer
Harlan Thompson
Twinkle Twinkle (1926)

CRINOLINE DAYS
Irving Berlin
Music Box Revue (1922)

CRITIC, THE
Charles Strouse
Six (OB) (1971)

CRITICS
Robert Swerdlow
Love Me, Love My Children (OB)
(1971)

CROCODILE WIFE
Harold Rome
The Zulu and the Zayda (1965)

CROCODILES CRY
Janet Gari
Toby Garson
Lyle (OB) (1970)

CROON-SPOON
Marc Blitzstein
The Cradle Will Rock (1938)

CROSS WORD PUZZLES
Muriel Pollock
Max and Nathaniel Lief and Harold
Atteridge
Pleasure Bound (1929)

CROSS YOUR FINGERS
J. Fred Coots
Arthur Swanstrom and Benny Davis
Sons o' Guns (1929)

CROSS YOUR HEART
Lewis E. Gensler
B. G. DeSylva
Queen High (1926)

CROUPIER
Baldwin Bergersen
June Sillman
Who's Who (1938)

CROW, THE
John Kander
Fred Ebb
Zorbá (1968)

CROWN ME
Al Carmines
Maria Irene Fornes
Promenade (OB) (1969)

CRUCIFIXION, THE
Andrew Lloyd Webber
Tim Rice
Jesus Christ Superstar (1971)

CRUEL CHIEF
Jean Gilbert
Harry Graham
Katja (1926)

CRUELTY MAN, THE
Mitch Leigh
William Alfred and Phyllis
Robinson
Cry for Us All (1970)

CRY, BABY, CRY
Harold Rome
Alive and Kicking (1950)

CRY FOR US ALL
Mitch Leigh
William Alfred and Phyllis
Robinson
Cry for Us All (1970)

CRY LIKE THE WIND
Jule Styne
Betty Comden and Adolph Green
Do Re Mi (1960)

CRY OF THE PEACOCK
Sandy Wilson
Valmouth (OB) (1960)

CRY, THE BELOVED COUNTRY
Kurt Weill
Maxwell Anderson
Lost in the Stars (1949)

CUBES AND ABSTRACTS
Robert Holton
June Carroll
Hi, Paisano! (OB) (1961)

CUCKOLD'S DELIGHT
Edward Earle
Yvonne Tarr
The Decameron (OB) (1961)

CUCKOO-CHEENA, THE
Alma Sanders
Monte Carlo
Louisiana Lady (1947)

CUDDLE Up
Gene Lockhart
Bunk of 1926 (1926)

CUDDLE UP A LITTLE CLOSER, LOVEY MINE
Karl Hoschna
Otto Harbach
Three Twins (1908)

CUP OF CHINA TEA, A
Franz Lehár
Harry Graham
Yours Is My Heart (1946)

CUP OF COFFEE, A
Robert Dahdah
Curley McDimple (OB) (1967)

CUP OF COFFEE, A SANDWICH AND YOU, A
Joseph Meyer
Billy Rose and Al Dubin
Charlot's Revue (1926)

CUP OF TEA, A
Mischa and Wesley Portnoff
Happy As Larry (1950)

CUPID'S COLLEGE
Robert Hood Bowers
Francis DeWitt
Oh, Ernest! (1927)

CURE, THE
Harold Arlen
Johnny Mercer
Saratoga (1959)

CURFEW SHALL NOT RING TO-NIGHT, THE
Charles Rosoff
Leo Robin
Judy (1927)

CURFEW WALK, THE
Jean Schwartz
Alfred Bryan
A Night in Spain (1927)

CURLEY McDIMPLE
Robert Dahdah
Curley McDimple (OB) (1967)

CURLEY'S WIFE
Alfred Brooks
Ira J. Bilowit
Of Mice and Men (OB) (1958)

CURRIER AND IVES
Sigmund Romberg
Dorothy Fields
Up in Central Park (1945)

CURT, CLEAR AND CONCISE
Noël Coward
The Girl Who Came to Supper (1963)

CUSTOMER IS ALWAYS RIGHT, THE
George Harwell
What a Killing (OB) (1961)

CUT IN
Jimmy McHugh
Dorothy Fields
The Vanderbilt Revue (1930)

CYMBALS AND TAMBOURINES
Arthur Siegel
New Faces (1968)

CZARDAS
Al Carmines
Maria Irene Fornes
Promenade (OB) (1969)

DAARLING MAN
Marc Blitzstein
Juno (1959)

DAD GOT GIRLS
Bill Mahoney
My Wife and I (OB) (1966)

DAILY BUZZ
Voices, Inc.
The Believers (OB) (1968)

DAILY DOZEN
Richard Myers
Leo Robin
Hello, Yourself! (1928)

DAISIES
Al Carmines
Rosalyn Drexler
Home Movies (OB) (1964)

DAISY
G. Wood
Put It in Writing (OB) (1963)

DAMAGES
Cyril Ornadel
Leslie Bricusse
Pickwick (1965)

DAMES AT SEA
Jim Wise
George Haimsohn and Robin Miller
Dames at Sea (OB) (1968)

DAMN-ALOT
Billy Barnes
The Billy Barnes People (1961)

DAMNED FOR ALL TIME
Andrew Lloyd Webber
Tim Rice
Jesus Christ Superstar (1971)

DAMSEL WHO DONE ALL THE DIRT, THE
Richard Rodgers
Lorenz Hart
The Girl Friend (1926)

DANCE ALONE WITH YOU*
George Gershwin
Ira Gershwin
Funny Face (1927)

DANCE AWAY THE NIGHT†
Jerome Kern
Oscar Hammerstein II
Show Boat (1928)

DANCE, DANCE, DANCE
Rudolf Friml
Brian Hooker
The White Eagle (1927)

DANCE FOR THE GENTLEMEN
Carl Millöcker (revised by Theo Mackeben)
Rowland Leigh
The Dubarry (1932)

DANCE FROM DOWN YONDER, THE
Joseph Meyer and James F. Hanley
B. G. DeSylva
Big Boy (1925)

DANCE, LITTLE LADY
Noël Coward
This Year of Grace (1928)

DANCE ME A SONG
James Shelton
Dance Me a Song (1950)

DANCE, MY DARLINGS
Sigmund Romberg
Oscar Hammerstein II
May Wine (1935)

DANCE OF DISTRACTION
Clinton Ballard
Carolyn Richter
The Ballad of Johnny Pot (OB) (1971)

DANCE OF THE FAN
Percy Wenrich
Harry Clarke
Who Cares? (1930)

DANCE ONLY WITH ME
Jule Styne
Betty Comden and Adolph Green
Say, Darling (1958)

DANCE WITH ME
Sigmund Romberg
Harry B. Smith
Princess Flavia (1925)

DANCE WITH YOU
Jean Gilbert
Harry Graham
Katja (1926)

DANCIN' TO A JUNGLE DRUM
Cole Porter
Seven Lively Arts (1944)

DANCIN' 'WAY YOUR SIN
J. C. Johnson
Brown Buddies (1930)

DANCING
Jerry Herman
Hello, Dolly! (1964)

DANCING ALONE
Ralph and Eugene Berton
Two for Tonight (OB) (1939)

DANCING, AND I MEAN DANCING
Alexander Hill
Hummin' Sam (1933)

DANCING BY MOONLIGHT
Martin Broones
Ballard MacDonald
Rufus Lemaire's Affairs (1927)

---

*Dropped from New York production; rewritten as "Everybody Knows I Love Somebody" for *Rosalie* (1928)
†Added to London production (1928)

DANCING FOOL
Al Wilson, Charles Weinberg, and Ken Macomber
Yeah Man (1932)

DANCING GIRL
Clarence Williams
Spencer Williams
Bottomland (1927)

DANCING IN THE DARK
Arthur Schwartz
Howard Dietz
The Band Wagon (1931)

DANCING IN THE RAIN
Robert Dahdah
Curley McDimple (OB) (1967)

DANCING IN THE STREETS
George Gershwin
Ira Gershwin
Pardon My English (1933)

DANCING JIM
Marc Anthony
Donovan Parsons
The Merry World (1926)

DANCING ON A RAINBOW
Leo Edwards
Herman Timberg
You'll See Stars (1942)

DANCING ON THE CEILING*
Richard Rodgers
Lorenz Hart
Simple Simon (1930)

DANCING ROGUE, THE
Stanley Jay Gelber
John Lollos and Don Christopher
Love and Let Love (OB) (1968)

DANCING THE DEVIL AWAY
Harry Ruby
Bert Kalmar and Otto Harbach
Lucky (1927)

DANCING THROUGH LIFETIMES
Mike Brandt, Michael Knight, and

Robert J. Lowery
Exchange (OB) (1970)

DANCING TO OUR SCORE
Vernon Duke
Ira Gershwin
Ziegfeld Follies (1936)

DANCING TO THE RHYTHM OF THE RAINDROPS
Ruth Cleary Patterson
Gladys Shelley
Russell Patterson's Sketch Book (OB) (1960)

DANCING TOES
Leon Decosta
Kosher Kitty Kelly (1925)

DANCING TOWN
Maury Rubens
Clifford Grey
The Great Temptations (1926)

DANCING WEDDING
Vincent Youmans
Harold Adamson and Clifford Grey
Smiles (1930)

DANCING WITH ALICE
Milton Schafer
Ira Levin
Drat! The Cat! (1965)

DANCING WITH TEARS IN THEIR EYES
Will Irwin
Billy Rose and Mort Dixon
Sweet and Low (1930)

DANDY DAN
Porter Grainger and Freddie Johnson
Lucky Sambo (1925)

DANGER IF I LOVE YOU
Henry Sullivan
Edward Eliscu
A Little Racketeer (1932)

---

*Dropped before New York opening

DANGER IN THE DARK
Jimmy McHugh
Al Dubin
The Streets of Paris (1939)

DANGER OF PEACE IS OVER, THE
Menachem Zur
Herbert Appleman
Unfair to Goliath (OB) (1970)

DANGEROUS AGE, THE
Jule Styne
Betty Comden and Adolph Green
Fade Out—Fade In (1964)

DANGEROUS AGE, THE
Ervin Drake
Her First Roman (1968)

DANGEROUS GAME
Mimi Stone
William Kaye
Pimpernel! (OB) (1964)

DANUBE SO BLUE
Johann Strauss
Desmond Carter
The Great Waltz (1934)

DAPHNE
Milton Susskind
Paul Porter and Benjamin Hapgood
  Burt
Florida Girl (1925)

DARING GIBSON GIRL, THE
Ray Henderson
B. G. DeSylva and Lew Brown
Follow Thru (1929)

DARK NEW ENGLAND NIGHT
Norman Dean
Autumn's Here (OB) (1966)

DARK STRANGER, A
Michael Cleary
Arthur Swanstrom
Sea Legs (1937)

DARKIES SONG, THE
Coleridge-Taylor Perkinson

Ray McIver
God Is a (Guess What?) (OB) (1968)

DARKNESS SONG
Al Carmines
Rosalyn Drexler
Home Movies (OB) (1964)

DARKY RHYTHM
Peter Tinturin
Joe Young
Brown Buddies (1930)

DARLIN' OF NEW YORK, THE
Bill and Patti Jacob
Jimmy (1969)

**DARLING, LET ME TEACH YOU HOW
TO KISS**
Richard Hill and John Hawkins
Nevill Coghill
Canterbury Tales (1969)

DARN IT, BABY, THAT'S LOVE
Joan Edwards and Lyn Duddy
Tickets Please (1950)

DARN NICE CAMPUS, A
Richard Rodgers
Oscar Hammerstein II
Allegro (1947)

DARN THAT DREAM
Jimmy Van Heusen
Eddie De Lange
Swingin' the Dream (1939)

DAS CHICAGO SONG
Michael Cohen
Tony Geiss
New Faces (1968)

DAT OL' BOY
Georges Bizet
Oscar Hammerstein II
Carmen Jones (1943)

DAT'S LOVE
Georges Bizet
Oscar Hammerstein II
Carmen Jones (1943)

DAT'S OUR MAN
Georges Bizet
Oscar Hammerstein II
Carmen Jones (1943)

DAVID AND BATHSHEBA
Ernest Gold
Anne Croswell
I'm Solomon (1968)

DAVID AND LENORE
Ray Henderson
B. G. DeSylva and Lew Brown
George White's Scandals (1926)

DAWN
Ray Henderson
B. G. DeSylva and Lew Brown
Manhattan Mary (1927)

DAWN
Robert Stolz and Herbert Stothart
Otto Harbach and Oscar Hammerstein II
Golden Dawn (1927)

DAWN OF DREAMS
Raymond Hubbell
Anne Caldwell
Yours Truly (1927)

DAY AFTER DAY
Arthur Schwartz
Howard Dietz
Flying Colors (1932)

DAY AFTER DAY
Meyer Kupferman
Paul Goodman
Jonah (OB) (1966)

DAY BEFORE SPRING, THE
Frederick Loewe
Alan Jay Lerner
The Day Before Spring (1945)

DAY BORROWED FROM HEAVEN, A
Frank Loesser
Greenwillow (1960)

DAY BY DAY
Stephen Schwartz
Godspell (OB) (1971)

DAY DREAMS
Heinrich Reinhardt
Harry B. and Robert B. Smith
The Spring Maid (1910)

DAY DREAMS
Jacques Urbont
Bruce Geller
All in Love (OB) (1961)

DAY I MET YOUR FATHER, THE
Paul Nassau and Oscar Brand
The Education of Hyman Kaplan (1968)

DAY I RODE HALF FARE, THE
Joseph Meyer and James F. Hanley
B. G. DeSylva
Big Boy (1925)

DAY OF JUDGEMENT
Paul Hoffert
David Secter
Get Thee to Canterbury (OB) (1969)

DAY THE SNOW IS MELTIN', THE
Johnny Burke
Donnybrook! (1961)

DAYDREAMS
David Baker
Fred Ebb
Smiling, the Boy Fell Dead (OB) (1961)

DAYS GONE BY
Jerry Bock
Sheldon Harnick
She Loves Me (1963)

DAYS OF MY YOUTH, THE
Hal Jordan
Jerry Douglas
Rondelay (OB) (1969)

DAYS OF OLD, THE
Oscar Straus

Clare Kummer
Three Waltzes (1937)

DE CARDS DON'T LIE
Georges Bizet
Oscar Hammerstein II
Carmen Jones (1943)

DE-DUM-DUM
Jean Schwartz
Alfred Bryan
A Night in Spain (1927)

DE OLD CLAY ROAD
Frank Harling
Laurence Stallings
Deep River (1926)

DEADALUS
Peter Link and C. C. Courtney
Salvation (OB) (1969)

DEAL, A
Francis Thorne
Arnold Weinstein
Fortuna (OB) (1962)

DEAL, THE
Susan Hulsman Bingham
Myrna Lamb
Mod Donna (OB) (1970)

DEALER, THE
Helen Miller
Eve Merriam
Inner City (1971)

DEAR, DEAR DEPARTED
Emil Gerstenberger and Carle Carlton
Howard Johnson
The Lace Petticoat (1927)

DEAR EYES THAT HAUNT ME
Emmerich Kalman
Harry B. Smith
The Circus Princess (1927)

DEAR FRIEND
Jerry Bock
Sheldon Harnick
Tenderloin (1960)

DEAR FRIEND
Jerry Bock
Sheldon Harnick
She Loves Me (1963)

DEAR HOME OF MINE, GOODBYE
Emmerich Kalman
Harry B. Smith
Countess Maritza (1926)

DEAR LITTLE CAFÉ
Noël Coward
Bitter Sweet (1929)

DEAR LITTLE GIRL
George Gershwin
Ira Gershwin
Oh, Kay! (1926)

DEAR GIRLS, GOODBYE
Sigmund Romberg
Dorothy Donnelly
My Princess (1927)

DEAR LITTLE SOLDIERS
Noël Coward
Conversation Piece (1934)

DEAR LOVE
John Kander
Fred Ebb
Flora, the Red Menace (1965)

DEAR MADAME SCARLATINA
Jay Thompson
Double Entry (OB) (1961)

DEAR MOM
Sol Berkowitz
James Lipton
Nowhere to Go But Up (1962)

DEAR MR. SCHUBERT
Manos Hadjidakis
Joe Darion
Illya Darling (1967)

DEAR, OH DEAR
Richard Rodgers
Lorenz Hart
Chee-Chee (1928)

DEAR OLD CRINOLINE DAYS
Irving Berlin
Face the Music (1932)

DEAR OLD DAD
David Baker
Fred Ebb
Smiling, the Boy Fell Dead (OB) (1961)

DEAR OLD FRIEND
Sol Berkowitz
James Lipton
Miss Emily Adam (OB) (1960)

DEAR OLD SYRACUSE
Richard Rodgers
Lorenz Hart
The Boys from Syracuse (1938)

DEAR WORLD
Jerry Herman
Dear World (1969)

DEARER TO ME
Alyn Heim
Malcolm L. LaPrade
Will the Mail Train Run Tonight? (OB) (1964)

DEARLY BELOVED
Jerome Kern
Johnny Mercer
You Were Never Lovelier (F) (1942)

DEATH AND REALITY
Dale F. Menten
Dale F. Menten and Frederick Gaines
The House of Leather (OB) (1970)

DEATH BEWARE
Paul Hoffert
David Secter
Get Thee to Canterbury (OB) (1969)

DEATH DANCE
William S. Fischer
Maxine Klein
Kiss Now (OB) (1971)

DEATH MESSAGE
Kurt Weill
Marc Blitzstein
The Threepenny Opera (OB) (1954)

DEAUVILLE
Herman Hupfeld
The Merry World (1926)

DEBUTANTE
Sigmund Romberg
Rowland Leigh
My Romance (1948)

DECEIVE ME
Edward Earle
Yvonne Tarr
The Decameron (OB) (1961)

DECEIVING BLUE BIRD
J. Fred Coots
Al Dubin
White Lights (1927)

DECLARATION
Kenn Long and Jim Crozier
Kenn Long
Touch (OB) (1970)

DECLARATION DAY
Ray Henderson
Ted Koehler
Say When (1934)

DEDICATED TEACHER, A
Paul Nassau and Oscar Brand
The Education of Hyman Kaplan (1968)

DEE-LIGHTFUL IS THE WORD
Johnny Burke
Donnybrook! (1961)

DEEP DOWN INSIDE
Cy Coleman
Carolyn Leigh
Little Me (1962)

DEEP HARLEM
Joe Jordan
Homer Tutt and Henry Creamer
Deep Harlem (1929)

DEEP IN ME
James Bredt
Edward Eager
The Happy Hypocrite (OB) (1968)

DEEP IN MY HEART
Irving Bugie
Ballad for Bimshire (OB) (1963)

DEEP IN MY HEART, DEAR
Sigmund Romberg
Dorothy Donnelly
The Student Prince (1924)

DEEP IN THE BOSOM OF THE FAMILY
William Dyer
Don Parks and William Dyer
Jo! (OB) (1964)

DEEP IN THE NIGHT
Helen Miller
Eve Merriam
Inner City (1971)

DEEP IN YOUR HEART
Milton Schafer
Ira Levin
Drat! The Cat! (1965)

DEEP PARADISE
Russell Tarbox
Charles O. Locke
Hello, Paris (1930)

DELILAH DONE ME WRONG
Gerard Calvi
Harold Rome
La Grosse Valise (1965)

DELISHIOUS
George Gershwin
Ira Gershwin
Delicious (F) (1931)

DELIVER
Joe Jordan
Homer Tutt and Henry Creamer
Deep Harlem (1929)

DEMOCRACY'S CALL
Kurt Weill
Paul Green
Johnny Johnson (1936)

DENVER POLICE, THE
Meredith Willson
The Unsinkable Molly Brown (1960)

DERE'S A CAFE ON DE CORNER
Georges Bizet
Oscar Hammerstein II
Carmen Jones (1943)

DESERT FLAME, THE
Harold Rome
Bless You All (1950)

DESERT MOON
Walter Marks
Golden Rainbow (1968)

DESERT SONG, THE
Sigmund Romberg
Otto Harbach and Oscar Hammerstein II
The Desert Song (1926)

DESIGN FOR LIVING
Donald Swann
Michael Flanders
At the Drop of a Hat (1959)

DESIRE
Sigmund Romberg
Rowland Leigh
My Romance (1948)

DESMOND'S DILEMMA
Bob Goodman
Wild and Wonderful (1971)

DESPERATE
Baldwin Bergersen
William Archibald
The Crystal Heart (OB) (1960)

DESPERATE ONES
Jacques Brel
Eric Blau and Mort Shuman
Jacques Brel Is Alive and Well and Living in Paris (OB) (1968)

DESPERATION QUINTET
Steven Metcalf
Fred Bluth
Drat! (OB) (1971)

DESSERT
Hal Jordan
Jerry Douglas
Rondelay (OB) (1969)

DESTRUCTION
Jim Turner
Doug Dyer
Blood (OB) (1971)

DEUTERONOMY XVII VERSE 2
Peter Link and C. C. Courtney
Salvation (OB) (1969)

DEVIL MAY CARE, THE
Ralph Benatzky
Meet My Sister (1930)

DEW WAS ON THE ROSE, THE
Arthur Schwartz
Ira Gershwin
Park Avenue (1946)

DIAGNOSTICIAN, THE
William Roy
The Penny Friend (OB) (1966)

DIALOGUE ON DALLIANCE
Bruce Montgomery
The Amorous Flea (OB) (1964)

DIAMOND IN THE ROUGH
Vincent Youmans
Oscar Hammerstein II
Rainbow (1928)

DIAMONDS ARE A GIRL'S BEST FRIEND
Jule Styne
Leo Robin
Gentlemen Prefer Blondes (1949)

DIANE IS
Mark Sandrich, Jr.
Sidney Michaels
Ben Franklin in Paris (1964)

DIANNA LEE
Eubie Blake
Andy Razaf
Blackbirds (1930)

DIAVALO
Richard Rodgers
Lorenz Hart
Jumbo (1935)

DID I EVER REALLY LIVE?
Albert Hague
Allen Sherman
The Fig Leaves Are Falling (1969)

DID I MAKE A GOOD IMPRESSION?
G. Wood
F. Jasmine Addams (OB) (1971)

DID NOT
Michael Valenti
Just for Love (OB) (1968)

DID YOU CLOSE YOUR EYES?
Bob Merrill
New Girl in Town (1957)

DID YOU EVER GET STUNG?
Richard Rodgers
Lorenz Hart
I Married an Angel (1938)

DID YOU EVER HEAR THE BLUES?
David Martin
Langston Hughes
Simply Heavenly (1957)

DID YOU HEAR?
Norman Campbell
Donald Campbell and Norman Campbell
Anne of Green Gables (OB) (1971)

DID YOU HEAR THAT?
Richard Adler
Kwamina (1961)

DIDDLE DIDDLE DUMPLING
Helen Miller
Eve Merriam
Inner City (1971)

DIDN'T IT
Cliff Friend
Lew Brown
Piggy (1927)

DIDN'T YOUR MOTHER TELL YOU NOTHING?
Harry Ruby
Bert Kalmar
High Kickers (1941)

DIDOES
Robert Hood Bowers
Francis DeWitt
Oh, Ernest! (1927)

DIE ZUSAMMENFUGUNG
Sam Pottle
David Axelrod
New Faces (1968)

DIFFERENT DRUMMER, A
Johnny Brandon
Billy Noname (OB) (1970)

DIFFERENT KIND OF WORLD, A
Bob Goodman
Wild and Wonderful (1971)

DIG, DIG, DIG
Al Carmines
Maria Irene Fornes
Promenade (OB) (1969)

DIGGA DIGGA DO
Jimmy McHugh
Dorothy Fields
Blackbirds (1928)

DIMPLE ON MY KNEE, THE
George Gershwin
Ira Gershwin
Of Thee I Sing (1931)

DIMPLES
Cy Coleman
Carolyn Leigh
Little Me (1962)

DING DONG BELL
Helen Miller

Eve Merriam
Inner City (1971)

DING, DONG, DELL
Cliff Friend
Lew Brown
Piggy (1927)

DING DONG! THE WITCH IS DEAD
Harold Arlen
E. Y. Harburg
The Wizard of Oz (F) (1939)

DINO REPETTI
Robert Holton
June Carroll
Hi, Paisano! (OB) (1961)

DINO'S IN LOVE
Robert Holton
June Carroll
Hi, Paisano! (OB) (1961)

DIOR, DIOR
Jerry Herman
I Feel Wonderful (OB) (1954)

DIRECT FROM VIENNA
Bob Merrill
Carnival (1961)

DIRGE
John Addison
John Cranko
Cranks (1956)

DIRGE FOR A SOLDIER
Kurt Weill
Maxwell Anderson
Knickerbocker Holiday (1938)

DIRGE FOR TWO VETERANS
Stan Harte, Jr.
Walt Whitman
Leaves of Grass (OB) (1971)

DIRTY DOG, THE
Mischa and Wesley Portnoff
Donagh MacDonagh
Happy As Larry (1950)

DIS-DONC, DIS-DONC
Marguerite Monnot
Julian More, David Heneker and
  Monte Norman
Irma La Douce (1960)

DIS FLOWER
Georges Bizet
Oscar Hammerstein II
Carmen Jones (1943)

DIS IS DE DAY
Frank Harling
Laurence Stallings
Deep River (1926)

DISCARDED BLUES
Clinton Ballard
Carolyn Richter
The Ballad of Johnny Pot (OB) (1971)

DISCONTENTED BANDITS, THE
Lily Hyland
Agnes Morgan
The Grand Street Follies (OB) (1926)

DISGUSTINGLY RICH
Richard Rodgers
Lorenz Hart
Higher and Higher (1940)

DISSERTATION ON THE STATE OF BLISS
Harold Arlen
Ira Gershwin
The Country Girl (F) (1954)

DISTANT MELODY
Jule Styne
Betty Comden and Adolph Green
Peter Pan (1954)

DITES-MOI POURQUOI
Richard Rodgers
Oscar Hammerstein II
South Pacific (1949)

DIXIE
Jimmy McHugh
Dorothy Fields
Blackbirds (1928)

DIXIE CINDERELLA
Thomas (Fats) Waller and Harry
  Brooks
Andy Razaf
Hot Chocolates (1929)

DIXIE PRELUDE (CIVIL WAR)
Dale F. Menten
Dale F. Menten and Frederick Gaines
The House of Leather (OB) (1970)

DIXIE VAGABOND
Frank Marcus and Bernard Maltin
Bamboola (1929)

DIXIELAND
Percy Wenrich
Harry Clarke
Who Cares? (1930)

DIZZILY, BUSILY
Kurt Weill
Ira Gershwin
The Firebrand of Florence (1945)

DIZZY FEET
Harry Ruby
Bert Kalmar
Top Speed (1929)

DO A LITTLE EXERCISE
Cy Young
That Hat! (OB) (1964)

DO A REVUE
Billy Barnes
The Billy Barnes Revue (1959)

DO DO DO
George Gershwin
Ira Gershwin
Oh, Kay! (1926)

DO I DEAR, I DO
McElbert Moore
The Matinee Girl (1926)

DO I HEAR A WALTZ?
Richard Rodgers
Stephen Sondheim
Do I Hear a Waltz? (1965)

Do I Hear You Saying "I Love You"?
Richard Rodgers
Lorenz Hart
Present Arms (1928)

Do I Love You?
Henri Christine and E. Ray Goetz
E. Ray Goetz
Naughty Cinderella (1925)

Do I Love You?
Cole Porter
Du Barry Was a Lady (1939)

Do I Love You Because You're Beautiful?
Richard Rodgers
Oscar Hammerstein II
Cinderella (TV) (1957)

Do It Again!
George Gershwin
B. G. DeSylva
The French Doll (1922)

Do It Girl
Peter Stampfel and Antonia
Operation Sidewinder (1970)

Do It in Two
Jack Wilson and Alan Jeffreys
Vintage '60 (OB) (1960)

Do It the Hard Way
Richard Rodgers
Lorenz Hart
Pal Joey (1940)

Do Me a Favor
G. Wood
F. Jasmine Addams (OB) (1971)

Do My Eyes Deceive Me?
Richard Lewine
Ted Fetter
The Fireman's Flame (OB) (1937)

Do Not Bruise the Fruit
Al Carmines
Rosalyn Drexler
Home Movies (OB) (1964)

Do-Re-Mi
Richard Rodgers
Oscar Hammerstein II
The Sound of Music (1959)

Do Tell
Charles M. Schwab
Henry Myers
The Garrick Gaieties (1930)

Do That Doo-Da
Maury Rubens
J. Keirn Brennan
Gay Paree (1926)

Do the Least You Can
Robert Swerdlow
Love Me, Love My Children (OB) (1971)

Do the New York
Ben Oakland
Jack Murray and Barry Trivers
Ziegfeld Follies (1931)

Do This, Do That
George Fischoff
Verna Tomasson
The Prince and the Pauper (OB) (1963)

Do We?
John Kander
Fred Ebb
70, Girls, 70 (1971)

Do What You Do!
George Gershwin
Gus Kahn and Ira Gershwin
Show Girl (1929)

Do What You Like
Philip Charig
Leo Robin
Shoot the Works (1931)

Do You?
Robert Russell Bennett
Owen Murphy and Robert A. Simon
Hold Your Horses (1933)

Do You Care Too Much?
Ron Steward and Neal Tate
Ron Steward
Sambo (OB) (1969)

Do You Do the Charleston?
Gene Lockhart
Bunk of 1926 (1926)

Do You Ever Dream of Vienna?
Rick Besoyan
Little Mary Sunshine (OB) (1959)

Do You Ever Go to Boston
Bob Merrill
Henry, Sweet Henry (1967)

Do You Know a Better Way to Make a Living?
Harold Rome
Bless You All (1950)

Do You Know the Milky Way?
Alex Fry
Lyon Phelps
Do You Know the Milky Way? (1961)

Do You Love as I Love?
Joseph Meyer
Irving Caesar
Yes, Yes, Yvette (1927)

Do You Love Me?
Richard Rodgers
Lorenz Hart
The Garrick Gaieties (1925)

Do You Love Me?
Jerry Bock
Sheldon Harnick
Fiddler on the Roof (1964)

Do You Recall?
Johann Strauss I, adapted by Oscar Straus
Clare Kummer
Three Waltzes (1937)

Do You Recall the House of Leather?
Dale F. Menten
Dale F. Menten and Frederick Gaines
The House of Leather (OB) (1970)

Do You Suppose
Stan Harte, Jr.
Walt Whitman
Leaves of Grass (OB) (1971)

Do You Think I'm Pretty?
Norman Dean
Autumn's Here (OB) (1966)

Do You Want to See Paris?
Cole Porter
Fifty Million Frenchmen (1929)

Do Your Own Thing
Hal Hester and Danny Apolinar
Your Own Thing (1968)

Do What You Wanna Do
Vernon Duke
John Latouche
Cabin in the Sky (1940)

Doctor and Ella
Marc Blitzstein
The Cradle Will Rock (1938)

Doctor's Soliloquy, A
Sammy Fain
Paul Francis Webster
Christine (1960)

Does It Pay to Be a Lady?
Vincent Youmans
Billy Rose and Edward Eliscu
Great Day! (1929)

Does It Really Matter?
Jule Styne
Sammy Cahn
Look to the Lilies (1970)

D-o-g
Baldwin Bergersen
William Archibald
The Crystal Heart (1960)

Dog, A
Ann Sternberg
Gertrude Stein
Gertrude Stein's First Reader (OB) (1969)

DOG EAT DOG
Harold Arlen
Johnny Mercer
Saratoga (1959)

**DOG IS A MAN'S BEST FRIEND,
A**
Johnny Mercer
Top Banana (1951)

DOGFACE JIVE
Jack Holmes
Bill Conklin and Bob Miller
O Say Can You See! (OB) (1962)

DOGGONE
Harry Archer
Walter O'Keefe
Just a Minute (1928)

DOIN' THE CHAMBERLAIN
Jimmy McHugh
Al Dubin
The Streets of Paris (1939)

DOIN' THE GORILLA
Philip Charig and Richard Myers
Leo Robin
Allez-Oop (1927)

DOING THE HIGH
Joseph Martinez Kookoolis and Scott
    Fagan
Scott Fagan
Soon (1971)

DOIN' THE HOT-CHA-CHA
Lester Lee
Keep It Clean (1929)

DOIN' THE NEW LOW-DOWN
Jimmy McHugh
Dorothy Fields
Blackbirds (1928)

DOIN' THE REACTIONARY
Harold Rome
Pins and Needles (OB) (1937)

DOIN' THE SHIM SHAM
Alberta Nichols
Mann Holiner
Blackbirds of 1934 (1933)

DOIN' THE TOLEDO
Donald Heywood
Black Rhythm (1936)

DOIN' THE WALTZ
Richard Lewine
Ted Fetter
The Fireman's Flame (OB) (1937)

DOIN' WHAT COMES NATURALLY
Irving Berlin
Annie Get Your Gun (1946)

DOING GOOD
Charles Strouse
Lee Adams
(It's a Bird, It's a Plane) It's Superman
    (1966)

DOING THE DUMBBELL
Harry Revel
Mack Gordon
Fast and Furious (1931)

DOLCE FAR NIENTE
Meredith Willson
The Unsinkable Molly Brown (1960)

DOLL FANTASY, A
Sigmund Romberg
Oscar Hammerstein II
May Wine (1935)

DOLL SONG
Walter Kollo
Harry B. Smith
Three Little Girls (1930)

DOLLS
Billy Barnes
The Billy Barnes People (1961)

DOLL'S HOUSE, A
Arthur Siegel
June Carroll
New Faces (1956)

**DOLLY FROM THE FOLLIES BER-
GÈRE**
Victor Young
Edward Heyman
Pardon Our French (1950)

DOMESTICITY
Robert Wright and George Forrest
Kean (1961)

DON JOSE OF FAR ROCKAWAY
Harold Rome
Wish You Were Here (1952)

DON JOSE O'BRIEN
Maria Grever
Raymond Leveen
Viva O'Brien (1941)

DON' SHAKE MY TREE
Raymond Hubbell
Anne Caldwell
Yours Truly (1927)

DONKEY SERENADE, THE*
Rudolf Friml and Herbert Stothart
Robert Wright and George Forrest
The Firefly (F) (1937)

DONNA
Galt MacDermot
Gerome Ragni and James Rado
Hair (1968)

DONNYBROOK
Johnny Burke
Donnybrook! (1961)

DONS' CHORUS, THE
Julian Slade
Dorothy Reynolds and Julian Slade
Salad Days (OB) (1958)

DON'T!
Philip Springer
Joan Javits
Hotel Passionato (OB) (1965)

DON'T ASK!
George Gershwin
Ira Gershwin
Oh, Kay! (1926)

DON'T ASK HER ANOTHER
Max Ewing
Agnes Morgan
The Grand Street Follies (OB) (1927)

DON'T ASK ME
Jacques Urbont
Bruce Geller
All in Love (OB) (1961)

DON'T ASK ME NOT TO SING
Jerome Kern
Otto Harbach
Roberta (1933)

DON'T BE A MIRACLE
Robert Swerdlow
Love Me, Love My Children (OB)
   (1971)

DON'T BE A WOMAN IF YOU CAN
Arthur Schwartz
Ira Gershwin
Park Avenue (1946)

DON'T BE AFRAID
Arthur Schwartz
Dorothy Fields
A Tree Grows in Brooklyn (1951)

DON'T BE AFRAID OF ROMANCE
Irving Berlin
Mr. President (1962)

DON'T BOTHER
Billy Barnes
The Billy Barnes People (1961)

DON'T CALL US
Jim Turner
Mary Boylan
Blood (OB) (1971)

DON'T CRY
Frank Loesser
The Most Happy Fella (1956)

DON'T DESTROY THE WORLD
Dov Seltzer
David Paulsen
To Live Another Summer (1971)

---

*Based on Friml's "Chanson"

DON'T DO IT
Arthur Schwartz
Agnes Morgan
The Grand Street Follies (1929)

DON'T DO THE CHARLESTON
James F. Hanley
Gene Buck
No Foolin' (1926)

DON'T EAT IT
Al Carmines
Maria Irene Fornes
Promenade (OB) (1969)

DON'T EVER LEAVE ME
Jerome Kern
Oscar Hammerstein II
Sweet Adeline (1929)

DON'T FALL ASLEEP
Ronny Graham
New Faces (1952)

DON'T FALL IN LOVE WITH ME
Herman Hupfeld
The Merry World (1926)

DON'T FENCE ME IN
Cole Porter
Hollywood Canteen (F) (1944)

DON'T FORGET
James F. Hanley
B. G. DeSylva
Queen High (1926)

DON'T FORGET
Leon Carr
Earl Shuman
The Secret Life of Walter Mitty (OB)
   (1964)

DON'T FORGET BANDANNA DAYS
Porter Grainger and Freddie Johnson
Lucky Sambo (1925)

DON'T FORGET 127TH STREET
Charles Strouse
Lee Adams
Golden Boy (1964)

DON'T FORGET THE GIRL FROM PUNXSUTAWNEY
Jerry Livingston
Mack David
Bright Lights of 1944 (1943)

DON'T FORGET THE LILAC BUSH
Kurt Weill
Langston Hughes
Street Scene (1947)

DON'T FORGET TO DREAM
Jay Gorney
Barry Trivers
Heaven on Earth (1948)

DON'T FORGET YOUR ETIQUETTE
Alberta Nichols
Mann Holiner
Angela (1928)

DON'T GIVE UP THE HUNT, DR. PUFFIN
Alec Wilder
Arnold Sundgaard
Kittiwake Island (OB) (1960)

DON'T GO AWAY, MONSIEUR
Arthur Schwartz
Howard Dietz
Between the Devil (1937)

DON'T HANG YOUR DREAMS ON A RAINBOW
Arnold Johnson
Irving Kahal
Earl Carroll's Sketch Book (1929)

DON'T HAVE THE BABY
Galt MacDermot
John Guare
Two Gentlemen of Verona (1971)

DON'T HAVE TO TAKE IT ANY MORE
Norman Curtis
Patricia Taylor Curtis
Walk Down Mah Street! (OB)
   (1968)

DON'T HOLD EVERYTHING
Ray Henderson
B. G. DeSylva and Lew Brown
Hold Everything! (1928)

DON'T LAUGH
Mary Rodgers
Martin Charnin
Hot Spot (1963)

DON'T LEAVE ME
Hal Hester and Danny Apolinar
Your Own Thing (1968)

DON'T LEAVE ME DANGLING IN THE DUST
Robin Remaily
Operation Sidewinder (1970)

DON'T LEAVE YOUR LITTLE BLACK-BIRD BLUE
Joe Jordan, Porter Grainger, and
    Shelton Brooks
Brown Buddies (1930)

DON'T LET HIM KNOW YOU
John Addison
John Cranko
Cranks (1956)

DON'T LET IT GET YOU DOWN
Cole Porter
You Never Know (1938)

DON'T LET IT GET YOU DOWN
Burton Lane
E. Y. Harburg
Hold On to Your Hats (1940)

DON'T LIKE GOODBYES
Harold Arlen
Harold Arlen and Truman Capote
House of Flowers (1954)

DON'T LISTEN TO YOUR HEART
Bradford Greene
Marianne Brown Waters
Right This Way (1938)

DON'T LOOK AT ME
Stephen Sondheim
Follies (1971)

DON'T LOOK AT ME THAT WAY
Cole Porter
Paris (1928)

DON'T LOOK BACK
Steve Allen
Sophie (1963)

DON'T LOOK NOW
David Baker
David Craig
Copper and Brass (1957)

DON'T MAKE A MOVE
Sammy Fain
Marilyn and Alan Bergman
Something More! (1964)

DON'T MARRY ME
Richard Rodgers
Oscar Hammerstein II
Flower Drum Song (1958)

DON'T P-P-POINT THEM GUNS AT ME
Victor Ziskin
Joan Javits
Young Abe Lincoln (1961)

DON'T PUT IT DOWN
Galt MacDermot
Gerome Ragni and James Rado
Hair (1968)

DON'T RAIN ON MY PARADE
Jule Styne
Bob Merrill
Funny Girl (1964)

DON'T SAY YOU LIKE TCHAIKOWSKY
Claibe Richardson
Paul Rosner
Shoestring Revue (OB) (1957)

DON'T SCOLD
Robert Hood Bowers
Francis DeWitt
Oh, Ernest! (1927)

DON'T SELL THE NIGHT SHORT
Hugh Martin and Ralph Blane
Best Foot Forward (1941)

DON'T SING SOLO
George Kleinsinger
Roslyn Harvey
Of V We Sing (1942)

DON'T STAND TOO CLOSE TO THE
PICTURE
Leon Pober
Bud Freeman
Beg, Borrow or Steal (1960)

DON'T STOP
William B. Kernell
Dorothy Donnelly
Hello, Lola (1926)

DON'T TAKE OUR CHARLIE FOR THE
ARMY
Noël Coward
The Girl Who Came to Supper (1963)

DON'T TAKE SIDES
James Bredt
Edward Eager
The Happy Hypocrite (OB) (1968)

DON'T TALK
Morton Gould
Dorothy Fields
Arms and the Girl (1950)

DON'T TALK ABOUT GOD
Jule Styne
Sammy Cahn
Look to the Lilies (1970)

DON'T TAMPER WITH MY SISTER
Burton Lane
Alan Jay Lerner
On a Clear Day You Can See Forever
(1965)

DON'T TEAR UP THE HORSE SLIPS
Robert Larimer
King of the Whole Damn World! (OB)
(1962)

DON'T TELL MAMA
John Kander
Fred Ebb
Cabaret (1966)

DON'T TELL ME
Harold Karr
Matt Dubey
Happy Hunting (1956)

DON'T TELL ME
Jack Urbont
Bruce Geller
Livin' the Life (OB) (1957)

DON'T TELL ME IT'S BAD
Ray Henderson
Ted Koehler
Say When (1934)

DON'T TELL YOUR FOLKS
Richard Rodgers
Lorenz Hart
Simple Simon (1930)

DON'T TEMPT ME
Emmerich Kalman
Harry B. Smith
Countess Maritza (1926)

DON'T THROW ME DOWN
J. Fred Coots
Al Dubin
White Lights (1927)

DON'T TURN AWAY FROM LOVE
Noël Coward
Sail Away (1961)

DON'T TURN HIS PICTURE TO THE
WALL
Skip Redwine and Larry Frank
*Frank Merriwell, or Honor Chal-
lenged* (1971)

DON'T TURN US OUT OF THE HOUSE
Richard Lewine
John Latouche
Murder in the Old Red Barn (OB)
(1936)

DON'T TWIST MY MIND
Robert Swerdlow
Love Me, Love My Children (OB)
(1971)

DON'T WAIT TILL IT'S TOO LATE TO
SEE PARIS
Arthur Siegel
June Carroll
New Faces (1956)

DON'T WAKE THEM UP TOO SOON
Fred Spielman and Arthur Gershwin
Stanley Adams
A Lady Says Yes (1945)

DON'T WANNA WRITE ABOUT THE
SOUTH
Harold Rome
Bless You All (1950)

DON'T WORRY
Jimmy Van Heusen
Sammy Cahn
Skyscraper (1965)

DON'T YOU CHEAT
Leon DeCosta
The Blonde Sinner (1926)

DON'T YOU THINK IT'S VERY NICE?
Hugo Peretti, Luigi Creatore, and
    George David Weiss
Maggie Flynn (1968)

DOO-DAB
Harry Ruby
Bert Kalmar
Puzzles of 1925 (1925)

DOOMED, DOOMED, DOOMED
Jerome Moross
John Latouche
The Golden Apple (1954)

DOOR OF MY DREAMS, THE
Rudolf Friml
Otto Harbach and Oscar Hammer-
    stein II
Rose Marie (1924)

DOROTHY
Clarence Gaskill
Earl Carroll's Vanities (1925)

DORRIE'S WISH
Frank Loesser
Greenwillow (1960)

DOU, DOU
Henry Sullivan
Edward Eliscu
A Little Racketeer (1932)

DOUBLE DUMMY DRILL
George Gershwin
Ira Gershwin
Let 'Em Eat Cake (1933)

DOUBLE MURDER, DOUBLE DEATH
Mischa and Wesley Portnoff
Donagh MacDonagh
Happy As Larry (1950)

DOUBLE SOLILOQUY
Jule Styne
E. Y. Harburg
Darling of the Day (1968)

DOUBLE STANDARD, THE
Arthur Schwartz
Agnes Morgan
The Grand Street Follies (1929)

DOUBLE STANDARD
Jay Livingston and Ray Evans
Oh Captain! (1958)

DOUGHNUTS AND COFFEE
Sammy Fain
Irving Kahal
Right This Way (1938)

DOUGHNUTS FOR DEFENSE
Jack Holmes
Bill Conklin and Bob Miller
O Say Can You See! (OB) (1962)

DOV'S NIGHTMARE
Walt Smith
Leon Uris
Ari (1971)

DOWN A DOWN DOWN DERRY
Mel Marvin
Ted Berger
Shoemaker's Holiday (OB) (1967)

DOWN AMONG THE GRASS ROOTS
Oscar Brand
How to Steal an Election (OB) (1968)

DOWN AT THE VILLAGE
Ray Perkins
Max and Nathaniel Lief
The Greenwich Village Follies (1928)

DOWN BY THE RIVER
Richard Rodgers
Lorenz Hart
Mississippi (F) (1935)

DOWN BY THE SEA
Richard Rodgers
Lorenz Hart
Present Arms (1928)

DOWN HOME
Gary Geld
Peter Udell
Purlie (1970)

DOWN IN THE DEPTHS, ON THE 90TH FLOOR
Cole Porter
Red, Hot and Blue! (1936)

DOWN IN THE STREETS
Tommy Garlock and Alan Jeffreys
Vintage '60 (OB) (1960)

DOWN IN THE VALLEY
Robert Emmett Dolan
Johnny Mercer
Texas, Li'l Darlin' (1949)

DOWN ON MacCONNACHY SQUARE
Frederick Loewe
Alan Jay Lerner
Brigadoon (1947)

DOWN ON THE DUDE RANCH
Burton Lane
E. Y. Harburg
Hold On to Your Hats (1940)

DOWN THE WELL
Gerald Marks
Sam Lerner
Hold It! (1948)

DOWN THROUGH THE AGENTS
John Green
George Marion, Jr.
Beat the Band (1942)

DOWN TO THE SEA
Ida Hoyt Chamberlain
Enchanted Isle (1927)

DOWN TO THE SEA
David Baker
David Craig
Phoenix '55 (OB) (1955)

DOWN WITH LOVE
Harold Arlen
E. Y. Harburg
Hooray for What! (1937)

DOWN WITH SIN
Robert Stolz
Robert Sour
Mr. Strauss Goes to Boston (1945)

DOWN YOUR TEA
Robert Wright and George Forrest
    (based on Grieg)
Song of Norway (1944)

DOZEN HUSBANDS
Robert Holton
June Carroll
Hi, Paisano! (OB) (1961)

DOZENS, THE
Melvin Van Peebles
Ain't Supposed to Die a Natural Death (1971)

DR. BROCK
Jerry Bock
Sheldon Harnick
Tenderloin (1960)

DR. CRIPPEN
Kurt Weill
Ogden Nash
One Touch of Venus (1943)

DR. IATRO
Deed Meyer
'Toinette (OB) (1961)

DR. LUCY (THE DOCTOR IS IN)
Clark Gesner
You're a Good Man, Charlie Brown
  (OB) (1967)

DRAT!
Steven Metcalf
Fred Bluth
Drat! (OB) (1971)

DRAT! THE CAT!
Milton Schafer
Ira Levin
Drat! The Cat! (1965)

DRAW ME A CIRCLE
Cy Young
That Hat! (OB) (1964)

DREAM, THE
Johnny Brandon
Billy Noname (OB) (1970)

DREAM, THE
Charles Strouse
Six (OB) (1971)

DREAM A DREAM*
Jerome Kern
Otto Harbach and Oscar Hammer-
  stein II
Sunny (1925)

DREAM BABIES
Gary William Friedman
Will Holt
The Me Nobody Knows (OB) (1970)

DREAM BOAT
Ida Hoyt Chamberlain
Enchanted Isle (1927)

DREAM BOAT
George Bagby
Grace Henry and Jo Trent
Fioretta (1929)

DREAM DANCING
Cole Porter
You'll Never Get Rich (F) (1941)

DREAM FOR ANGELA, A
Louis Bellson and Will Irwin
Richard Ney
Portofino (1958)

DREAM GIRL
Ida Hoyt Chamberlain
Enchanted Isle (1927)

DREAM KINGDOM
Harden Church
Edward Heyman
Caviar (1934)

DREAM OF DREAMS
H. Maurice Jacquet
Preston Sturges
The Well of Romance (1930)

DREAM SWEETHEART
Harry Tierney
Joseph McCarthy
Cross My Heart (1928)

DREAMBOAT FROM DREAMLAND
Jack Holmes
Bill Conklin and Bob Miller
O Say Can You See! (OB) (1962)

DREAMER, THE
Arthur Schwartz
Frank Loesser
Thank Your Lucky Stars (F) (1943)

DREAMER WITH A PENNY
Allan Roberts
Lester Lee
All for Love (1949)

DREAMING
Con Conrad and Henry Souvaine
J. P. McEvoy
Americana (1926)

DREAMS
Harold Levey
Owen Murphy
Rainbow Rose (1926)

———
*Dropped from New York production

DREAMS
Rudolf Friml
P. G. Wodehouse and Clifford Grey
The Three Musketeers (1928)

DREAMS
Paul Hoffert
David Secter
Get Thee to Canterbury (OB) (1969)

DREAMS AGO
Abraham Ellstein
Walter Bullock
Great to Be Alive (1950)

DREAMS COME TRUE
Morton Gould
Betty Comden and Adolph Green
Billion Dollar Baby (1945)

DREAMS FOR SALE
James F. Hanley
Eddie Dowling
Honeymoon Lane (1926)

DREAMY MONTMARTRE
Abel Baer
Sam Lewis and Joe Young
Lady Do (1927)

DREARY, DREARY, RAINY DAYS
Porter Grainger and Freddie Johnson
Lucky Sambo (1925)

DRESDEN NORTHWEST MOUNTED, THE
George Gershwin
Ira Gershwin
Pardon My English (1933)

DRESSED UP FOR YOUR SUNDAY BEAU
Joseph Meyer and Philip Charig
Leo Robin
Just Fancy (1927)

DRIFTING ALONG WITH THE TIDE
George Gershwin
Arthur Jackson
George White's Scandals (1921)

DRINK
Cole Porter
Seven Lively Arts (1944)

DRINKING SONG
Sigmund Romberg
Dorothy Donnelly
The Student Prince (1924)

DRINKING SONG
Rudolf Friml
Brian Hooker
The Vagabond King (1925)

DRINKING SONG
Irving Berlin
Face the Music (1932)

DRINKING SONG, THE
Rick Besoyan
The Student Gypsy (OB) (1963)

DRIP, DROP, TAPOKETA
Leon Carr
Earl Shuman
The Secret Life of Walter Mitty (OB) (1964)

DROP THAT NAME
Jule Styne
Betty Comden and Adolph Green
Bells Are Ringing (1956)

DROP YOUR KERCHIEF
Cliff Friend and George White
George White's Scandals (1929)

DROPSY CURE WEATHER
Claibe Richardson
Kenward Elmslie
The Grass Harp (1971)

DRUG STORE SONG, THE
Harold Rome
Call Me Mister (1946)

DRUGSTORE SCENE
Marc Blitzstein
The Cradle Will Rock (1938)

DRUMS
Johnny Brandon
Who's Who, Baby? (OB) (1968)

DRUMS IN MY HEART
Vincent Youmans
Edward Heyman
Through the Years (1932)

DRUMS OF KANE
Rudolf Friml
J. Keirn Brennan
Luana (1930)

DUBARRY, THE
Carl Millöcker (revised by Theo Mackeben)
Rowland Leigh
The Dubarry (1932)

DU BARRY WAS A LADY
Cole Porter
Du Barry Was a Lady (1939)

DUBLIN TOWN
Fred Ebb, Paul Klein, and Lee Goldsmith
Vintage '60 (OB) (1960)

DUDIN' UP
Alfred Brooks
Ira J. Bilowit
Of Mice and Men (OB) (1958)

DUELLO, THE
Sigmund Romberg
Oscar Hammerstein II
Sunny River (1941)

DULCINEA
Mitch Leigh
Joe Darion
Man of La Mancha (1965)

DULL AND GAY
Richard Rodgers
Lorenz Hart
Simple Simon (1930)

DUMB GIRL
Lewis E. Gensler
Owen Murphy and Robert A. Simon
The Gang's All Here (1931)

DUSKY DEBUTANTE
Baldwin Bergersen
June Sillman
Who's Who (1938)

DUSKY LOVE
Will Vodery
Henry Creamer
Keep Shufflin' (1928)

DUST IN YOUR EYES
Irving and Lionel Newman
Murder at the Vanities (1933)

DUSTERS, GOGGLES AND HATS
Coleman Dowell
The Tattooed Countess (OB) (1961)

DUSTING AROUND
Eubie Blake
Noble Sissle
Shuffle Along (1933)

DUTCH COUNTRY TABLE
Norman Dean
Autumn's Here (OB) (1966)

DWARF'S SONG
Robert Dahdah
Curley McDimple (OB) (1967)

D'YE LOVE ME?
Jerome Kern
Oscar Hammerstein II
Sunny (1925)

DYING COWBOY, THE
Richard Lewine
Ted Fetter
The Girl from Wyoming (OB) (1938)

DYING SWAN, THE
Dave Stamper
Fred Herendeen
Orchids Preferred (1937)

DYNAMIC
Frederico Valerio
Elizabeth Miele
Hit the Trail (1954)

EACH TOMORROW MORNING
Jerry Herman
Dear World (1969)

EADIE WAS A LADY
Nacio Herb Brown and Richard Whit-
ing
B. G. DeSylva
Take a Chance (1932)

EAGLE AND ME, THE
Harold Arlen
E. Y. Harburg
Bloomer Girl (1944)

EAGER BEAVER
Richard Rodgers
No Strings (1962)

EARL IS CRAZY
Peter Link
C. C. Courtney and Ragan Courtney
Earl of Ruston (1971)

EARL WAS AHEAD
Peter Link
C. C. Courtney and Ragan Courtney
Earl of Ruston (1971)

EARLY BIRD EDDY
Steven Metcalf
Fred Bluth
Drat! (OB) (1971)

EARLY IN THE MORNING
Con Conrad
Gus Kahn
Kitty's Kisses (1926)

EARLY ONE MORNING BLUES
Voices, Inc.
The Believers (OB) (1968)

EARLY TO BED
Thomas (Fats) Waller
George Marion, Jr.
Early to Bed (1943)

EARTH AND THE SKY, THE
John Rox
John Murray Anderson's Almanac
(1953)

EARTH DANCE
Susan Hulsman Bingham
Myrna Lamb
Mod Donna (OB) (1970)

EARTHLY PARADISE
Harvey Schmidt
Tom Jones
Colette (OB) (1970)

EARTHWORMS
Susan Hulsman Bingham
Myrna Lamb
Mod Donna (OB) (1970)

EAST SIDE STORY
Julian Stein
Lester Judson
Chic (OB) (1959)

EAST WIND
Sigmund Romberg
Oscar Hammerstein II
East Wind (1931)

EASTER PARADE
Irving Berlin
As Thousands Cheer (1933)

EASTER SUNDAY PARADE, THE
George M. Cohan
The Merry Malones (1927)

EASY
Hal Jordan
Jerry Douglas
Rondelay (OB) (1969)

EASY DOES IT
Jay Gorney
Jean and Walter Kerr
Touch and Go (1949)

EASY TO BE HARD
Galt MacDermot
Gerome Ragni and James Rado
Hair (1968)

EASY TO BE LONELY
Peter Link
C. C. Courtney and Ragan Courtney
Earl of Ruston (1971)

EASY TO LOVE
Cole Porter
Born to Dance (F) (1936)

EASY TO TAKE
Duke Ellington
Marshall Barer and Fred Tobias
Pousse-Café (1966)

EAT A LITTLE SOMETHING
Harold Rome
I Can Get It for You Wholesale (1962)

EAT YOUR BREAKFAST
Don Elliott
James Costigan
The Beast in Me (1963)

EAT YOUR NICE LILY, UNICORN
Don Elliott
James Costigan
The Beast in Me (1963)

EBENEZER MCAFEE III
Robert Emmett Dolan
Johnny Mercer
Foxy (1964)

ECCCH
Mary Rodgers
Marshall Barer
The Mad Show (OB) (1966)

ECCENTRICITY
Alberta Nichols
Mann Holiner
Rhapsody in Black (1931)

ECHO
Michael Valenti
Just for Love (OB) (1968)

ECHO OF A SONG, THE
Dave Stamper
Fred Herendeen
Orchids Preferred (1937)

ECHO SONG
James Bredt
Edward Eager
The Happy Hypocrite (OB) (1968)

ECHO WALTZ, THE
Jim Wise
George Haimsohn
Dames at Sea (OB) (1968)

ECONOMIC SITUATION, THE
Vernon Duke
Ira Gershwin
Ziegfeld Follies (1936)

ECONOMICS
Kurt Weill
Alan Jay Lerner
Love Life (1948)

ECONOMICS 1
Harold Rome
Pins and Needles (OB) (1937)

EDELWEISS
Sigmund Romberg
Clifford Grey
Louie the 14th (1925)

EDELWEISS
Richard Rodgers
Oscar Hammerstein II
The Sound of Music (1959)

EDDY-MAC
Dave Stamper
Fred Herendeen
Orchids Preferred (1937)

EDUCATE YOUR FEET
Milton Ager
Jack Yellen
John Murray Anderson's Almanac
(1929)

EENIE, MEENIE, MINEE, MO
Vernon Duke
John Latouche
The Lady Comes Across (1942)

EGG, THE
Sherman Edwards
1776 (1969)

18 DAYS AGO
Cliff Friend and George White
George White's Scandals (1929)

1898
Sigmund Romberg
Rowland Leigh
My Romance (1948)

EILEEN AVOURNEEN
Henry Sullivan
John Murray Anderson
Thumbs Up! (1934)

EL MATADOR TERRIFICO
Maria Grever
Raymond Leveen
Viva O'Brien (1941)

ELBOW ROOM
Maury Laws
Jules Bass
Month of Sundays (OB) (1968)

ELDORADO
Leonard Bernstein
Lillian Hellman
Candide (1956)

ELECTRIC BLUES
Galt MacDermot
Gerome Ragni and James Rado
Hair (1968)

ELEGANCE
Jerry Herman
Hello, Dolly! (1964)

ELELEU!
Willard Straight
David Eddy
The Athenian Touch (OB) (1964)

ELEMENT OF DOUBT, AN
Sammy Fain
Howard Dietz
Ziegfeld Follies (1957)

ELENA
Robert Wright and George Forrest
Kean (1961)

ELEPHANT SONG, THE
John Kander
Fred Ebb
70, Girls, 70 (1971)

ELEVATOR SONG
Johnny Mercer
Top Banana (1951)

ELEVEN O'CLOCK SONG
Sammy Fain
Dan Shapiro
Ankles Aweigh (1955)

ELEVENTH COMMANDMENT, THE
Duke Ellington
Marshall Barer and Fred Tobias
Pousse-Café (1966)

ELGAMOUR
Galt MacDermot
John Guare
Two Gentlemen of Verona (1971)

ELIZABETH
Robert Katscher
Irving Caesar
The Wonder Bar (1931)

ELIZABETH
Lance Mulcahy
Paul Cherry
Park (1970)

ELLEN ROE
Johnny Burke
Donnybrook! (1961)

EMALINE
Donald Heywood
Black Rhythm (1936)

EMBASSY WALTZ
Frederick Loewe
Alan Jay Lerner
My Fair Lady (1956)

EMBRACE ME
Sigmund Romberg
Oscar Hammerstein II
East Wind (1931)

EMBRACEABLE YOU
George Gershwin
Ira Gershwin
Girl Crazy (1930)

EMERALD
Heitor Villa-Lobos
Robert Wright and George Forrest
Magdalena (1948)

EMMY LOU
Norman Martin
Fred Ebb
Put It in Writing (OB) (1963)

EMPTY POCKETS FILLED WITH LOVE
Irving Berlin
Mr. President (1962)

ENCHANTED CASTLE
Ida Hoyt Chamberlain
Enchanted Isle (1927)

ENCHANTED ISLE
Ida Hoyt Chamberlain
Enchanted Isle (1927)

ENCHANTED TRAIN, THE
Jerome Kern
P. G. Wodehouse
Sitting Pretty (1924)

END?, THE
Billy Barnes
The Billy Barnes People (1961)

END OF A PERFECT NIGHT
Vernon Duke
E. Y. Harburg
Walk a Little Faster (1932)

END OF MY RACE, THE
Mitch Leigh
William Alfred and Phyllis Robinson
Cry for Us All (1970)

ENGAGEMENT RING
Emil Gerstenberger and Carle Carlton
Howard Johnson
The Lace Petticoat (1927)

ENGLISH LESSON
Noël Coward
Conversation Piece (1934)

ENGLISH LIDO
Noël Coward
This Year of Grace (1928)

ENGLISH ROSE, THE
Michael Valenti
John Lewin
Blood Red Roses (1970)

ENGLISH TEACHER, AN
Charles Strouse
Lee Adams
Bye Bye Birdie (1960)

ENGLISHMAN'S HEAD, THE
George Lessner
Miriam Battista and Russell Maloney
Sleepy Hollow (1948)

ENOUGH
Stan Harte, Jr.
Walt Whitman
Leaves of Grass (OB) (1971)

ENTIRE HISTORY OF THE WORLD IN TWO MINUTES AND THIRTY-TWO SECONDS
Charles Strouse
Mike Stewart
Shoestring Revue (OB) (1955)

ENTRE-NOUS
Richard Lewine
Will B. Johnstone
Entre-Nous (OB) (1935)

ENTRE-NOUS
Harold Rome
Sing Out the News (1938)

EPILOGUE
Vernon Duke
Ted Fetter
The Show Is On (1936)

EPILOGUE
Jerry Bock
Sheldon Harnick
Fiddler on the Roof (1964)

EPISTLE OF LOVE
Stanley Jay Gelber
John Lollos and Don Christopher
Love and Let Love (OB) (1968)

EQUIPMENT SONG
Al Carmines
Rosalyn Drexler
Home Movies (OB) (1964)

ERBIE FITCH'S TWITCH
Albert Hague
Dorothy Fields
Redhead (1959)

ESTHER
Vernon Duke
Sammy Cahn
Two's Company (1952)

ETERNAL VIRGIN, THE
Ron Steward and Neal Tate
Ron Steward
Sambo (OB) (1969)

ETHEL, BABY
Jerry Bock, George Weiss, and Larry
   Holofcener
Mr. Wonderful (1956)

EUPHORIA
Robin Remaily
Operation Sidewinder (1970)

EUPHORIA
Jordan Ramin
Frank H. Stanton and Murray Semos
Look Where I'm At! (OB) (1971)

EUREKA
Jacques Offenbach
E. Y. Harburg
The Happiest Girl in the World (1961)

EVE
Jerry Bock
Sheldon Harnick
The Apple Tree (1966)

EVELINA
Harold Arlen

E. Y. Harburg
Bloomer Girl (1944)

EVELYN, WHAT DO YOU SAY?
Richard Rodgers
Lorenz Hart
A Connecticut Yankee (1927)

**EVEN A DOCTOR CAN MAKE A MIS-
TAKE**
Deed Meyer
'Toinette (OB) (1961)

EVEN AS YOU AND I
Ray Henderson
B. G. DeSylva and Lew Brown
George White's Scandals (1925)

EVEN AS YOU AND I
Sammy Fain
Irving Kahal
Everybody's Welcome (1931)

EVEN IF I SAY IT MYSELF
Hoagy Carmichael
Johnny Mercer
Walk with Music (1940)

EVENIN'
Frank Marcus and Bernard Maltin
Bamboola (1929)

EVENING STAR
Edward A. Horan
Frederick Herendeen
All the King's Horses (1934)

EVERLASTING
Jule Styne
Betty Comden and Adolph Green
Two on the Aisle (1951)

EVERMORE AND A DAY
Noël Coward
Bitter Sweet (1929)

EVERY ANIMAL HAS ITS MATE
Alfred Nathan
George Oppenheimer
The Manhatters (1927)

EVERY BIT OF YOU
Kenneth Friede and Adrian Samish
Hello, Paris (1930)

EVERY DAY IS A HOLIDAY
Fred Stamer
Gen Genovese
Buttrio Square (1952)

EVERY DAY IS LADIES' DAY WITH ME
Victor Herbert
Henry Blossom
The Red Mill (1906)

EVERY EVE
David Raksin
June Carroll
If the Shoe Fits (1946)

EVERY FATHER
Linda Swenson and Patrick Fox
Doug Dyer and Horald Griffiths
Blood (OB) (1971)

EVERY GIRL MUST HAVE A LITTLE BULL
Al Goodman and J. Fred Coots
Clifford Grey
Gay Paree (1925)

EVERY GIRL WANTS TO GET MARRIED
John Kander
James Goldman, John Kander, and
  William Goldman
A Family Affair (1962)

EVERY LITTLE MOVEMENT
Karl Hoschna
Otto Harbach
Madame Sherry (1910)

EVERY LITTLE NOTE
Harry Archer
Harlan Thompson
Merry-Merry (1925)

EVERY LITTLE NOTHING
Rick Besoyan
Little Mary Sunshine (OB) (1959)

EVERY LITTLE THING YOU DO
James F. Hanley
Gene Buck
No Foolin' (1926)

EVERY MAN IS A STUPID MAN
Cole Porter
Can-Can (1953)

EVERY NIGHT AT SEVEN
Burton Lane
Alan Jay Lerner
Royal Wedding (F) (1951)

EVERY ONCE IN A WHILE
Harold Rome
Destry Rides Again (1959)

EVERY TIME YOU DANCED WITH ME
Harry Warren
Jerome Lawrence and Robert E. Lee
Shangri-La (1956)

EVERY STREET'S A BOULEVARD IN OLD NEW YORK
Jule Styne
Bob Hilliard
Hazel Flagg (1953)

EVERYBOD-EE WHO'S ANYBOD-EE
Cole Porter
Jubilee (1935)

EVERYBODY GETS IT IN THE END
Paul Hoffert
David Secter
Get Thee to Canterbury (OB) (1969)

EVERYBODY HAS A RIGHT TO BE WRONG
Jimmy Van Heusen
Sammy Cahn
Skyscraper (1965)

EVERYBODY LIKES YOU
Bob Merrill
Carnival (1961)

EVERYBODY LOVES A SINGLE GIRL
Earl Wilson, Jr.
A Day in the Life of Just About Everyone (OB) (1971)

EVERYBODY LOVES A TREE
Walter Cool
Mackey of Appalachia (OB) (1965)

EVERYBODY LOVES SOMEBODY
Harold Rome
Wish You Were Here (1952)

EVERYBODY OUGHT TO HAVE A MAID
Stephen Sondheim
A Funny Thing Happened on the Way to the Forum (1962)

EVERYBODY SAYS DON'T
Stephen Sondheim
Anyone Can Whistle (1964)

EVERYBODY SHOUT
Ford Dabney
Jo Trent
Rang-Tang (1927)

EVERYBODY STEP
Irving Berlin
Music Box Revue (1921)

EVERYBODY WANTS TO BE IN SHOW BUSINESS
Ray Golden, Bud Burtson, and Philip Charig
Catch a Star! (1955)

EVERYBODY WANTS TO BE REMEMBERED
Janet Gari
Toby Garson
Lyle (OB) (1970)

EVERYBODY'S HAPPY IN JIMTOWN
Thomas (Fats) Waller
Andy Razaf
Keep Shufflin' (1928)

EVERYBODY'S RUNNING
Joseph Martinez Kookoolis and Scott Fagan
Scott Fagan
Soon (1971)

EVERYONE HAS SOMETHING TO HIDE
Edward Thomas
Martin Charnin
Ballad for a Firing Squad (OB) (1968)

EVERYONE HERE LOVES KELLY
Moose Charlap
Eddie Lawrence
Kelly (1965)

EVERYONE WHO'S "WHO'S WHO"
Harold Karr
Matt Dubey
Happy Hunting (1956)

EVERYTHIN' IS TINGLIN'
Mel Marvin
Ted Berger
Shoemaker's Holiday (OB) (1967)

EVERYTHING
Jerry Bock
Sheldon Harnick
The Rothschilds (1970)

EVERYTHING BEAUTIFUL
Jay Livingston and Ray Evans
Let It Ride (1961)

EVERYTHING BEAUTIFUL
Michael Leonard
Herbert Martin
The Yearling (1965)

EVERYTHING BEAUTIFUL HAPPENS AT NIGHT
Harvey Schmidt
Tom Jones
110 in the Shade (1963)

EVERYTHING BUT MY MAN
Serge Walter
Shady Lady (1933)

EVERYTHING COMES TO THOSE WHO WAIT
C. Jackson and James Hatch
Fly Blackbird (OB) (1962)

EVERYTHING HAPPENS TO ME
Hoagy Carmichael
Johnny Mercer
Walk with Music (1940)

EVERYTHING I HAVE IS YOURS
Burton Lane
Harold Adamson
Dancing Lady (F) (1933)

EVERYTHING IN THE WORLD I LOVE
Michael Leonard
Herbert Martin
The Yearling (1965)

EVERYTHING IS HIGH YELLOW NOW
Gitz Rice
Paul Porter
Nic-Nax (1926)

EVERYTHING IS POSSIBLE IN LIFE
Murray Rumshinsky
Jacob Jacobs
The President's Daughter (1970)

EVERYTHING IS WONDERFUL
Ray Haney
Alfred Aiken
We're Civilized? (OB) (1962)

EVERYTHING LEADS RIGHT BACK TO LOVE
Sidney Lippman
Sylvia Dee
Barefoot Boy with Cheek (1947)

EVERYTHING NEEDS SOMETHING
Lionel Bart
La Strada (1969)

EVERYTHING WILL HAPPEN FOR THE BEST
Lewis E. Gensler
B. G. DeSylva
Queen High (1926)

EVERYTHING'S ALRIGHT
Andrew Lloyd Webber
Tim Rice
Jesus Christ Superstar (1971)

EVERYTHING'S COMING UP ROSES
Jule Styne
Stephen Sondheim
Gypsy (1959)

EVERYTHING'S EASY WHEN YOU KNOW HOW
Charles Strouse
Lee Adams
(It's a Bird, It's a Plane) It's Superman (1966)

EVERYTHING'S GOING TO BE ALL RIGHT
Con Conrad
William B. Friedlander
Mercenary Mary (1925)

EVERYTHING'S GREAT
Charles Strouse
Lee Adams
Golden Boy (1964)

EVERYTHING'S JUST DIVINE
Mimi Stone
William Kaye
Pimpernel! (OB) (1964)

EVERYWHERE
Manning Sherwin
Harold Purcell
Under the Counter (1947)

EVIL
Sidney Shaw
New Faces (1968)

EVIVA
Sigmund Romberg
Dorothy Donnelly
My Princess (1927)

EVOCATION
Meyer Kupferman
Paul Goodman
Jonah (OB) (1966)

EV'RY BOY IN TOWN'S MY SWEETHEART
George M. Cohan
Billie (1928)

EV'RY DAY A HOLIDAY
Cole Porter
Du Barry Was a Lady (1939)

EV'RY LITTLE WHILE
Rudolf Friml
P. G. Wodehouse and Clifford Grey
The Three Musketeers (1928)

EV'RY OTHER HEARTBEAT
John Green
George Marion, Jr.
Beat the Band (1942)

EV'RY SUNDAY AFTERNOON
Richard Rodgers
Lorenz Hart
Higher and Higher (1940)

EV'RY TIME
Hugh Martin and Ralph Blane
Best Foot Forward (1941)

EV'RY TIME WE SAY GOODBYE
Cole Porter
Seven Lively Arts (1944)

EV'RYBODY KNOWS I LOVE SOMEBODY*
George Gershwin
Ira Gershwin
Rosalie (1928)

EV'RYBODY LOVES YOU†
Richard Rodgers
Lorenz Hart
I'd Rather Be Right (1937)

EV'RYBODY NEEDS SOMEBODY TO LOVE
George Fischoff
Verna Tomasson
The Prince and the Pauper (OB) (1963)

EV'RYBODY'S GOT A HOME BUT ME
Richard Rodgers
Oscar Hammerstein II
Pipe Dream (1955)

EV'RYTHING I LOVE
Cole Porter
Let's Face It! (1941)

EV'RYTHING I'VE GOT
Richard Rodgers
Lorenz Hart
By Jupiter (1942)

EXACTLY LIKE YOU
Jimmy McHugh
Dorothy Fields
Lew Leslie's International Revue (1930)

EXCELSIOR
Stan Harte, Jr.
Walt Whitman
Leaves of Grass (OB) (1971)

EXCHANGE OF LOVERS
Frederic Chopin (adapted by Bronislaw Kaper)
John Latouche
Polonaise (1945)

EXCUSE FOR SONG AND DANCE
Harry Warren
Mort Dixon and Joe Young
The Laugh Parade (1931)

EX-GIGOLO
Mario Braggiotti
E. Y. Harburg
The Vanderbilt Revue (1930)

EXODUS, THE
Walt Smith
Leon Uris
Ari (1971)

EXORCISM, THE
Hugh Martin and Timothy Gray
High Spirits (1964)

EXPECT THINGS TO HAPPEN
Meredith Willson
Here's Love (1963)

———
*Same music as "Dance Alone with You" from *Funny Face*
†Dropped from New York production

EXPERIENCE
Arthur Schwartz
Howard Dietz
Between the Devil (1937)

EXPOSITION
Cy Young
That Hat! (OB) (1964)

EXPRESS YOURSELF
John Kander
Fred Ebb
Flora, the Red Menace (1965)

EXQUISITE MOMENT
Rudolf Friml
Rowland Leigh and John Shubert
Music Hath Charms (1934)

EXTRA! EXTRA!
Erich Wolfgang Korngold (based on Offenbach)
Herbert Baker
Helen Goes to Troy (1944)

EXTRA, EXTRA!
Irving Berlin
Miss Liberty (1949)

EYEFUL OF YOU
J. Fred Coots
Al Dubin
White Lights (1927)

EYES THAT HAUNT ME
Karl Hajos (based on Tchaikovsky)
Harry B. Smith
Natja (1925)

EYES THAT LOVE
Sigmund Romberg
Harry B. Smith
The Love Call (1927)

FACE IN THE CROWD, A
Victor Young
Edward Heyman
Pardon Our French (1950)

FACE OF LOVE, THE
James Bredt
Edward Eager
The Happy Hypocrite (OB) (1968)

FACE ON THE DIME, THE
Harold Rome
Call Me Mister (1946)

FACE THE FACTS
George Harwell
What a Killing (OB) (1961)

FACE TO FACE
Robert Swerdlow
Love Me, Love My Children (OB) (1971)

FACES, NAMES AND PLACES
Joseph Martinez Kookoolis and Scott Fagan
Scott Fagan
Soon (1971)

FACES WITHOUT NAMES
Earl Wilson, Jr.
A Day in the Life of Just About Everyone (OB) (1971)

FACT CAN BE A BEAUTIFUL THING, A
Burt Bacharach
Hal David
Promises, Promises (1968)

FACTS, THE
Norman Campbell
Donald Campbell and Norman Campbell
Anne of Green Gables (OB) (1971)

FACTS OF LIFE
Maurice Yvain
Max and Nathaniel Lief
Luckee Girl (1928)

FADE OUT - FADE IN
Jule Styne
Betty Comden and Adolph Green
Fade Out - Fade In (1964)

FAILURE
Hal Jordan
Jerry Douglas
Rondelay (OB) (1969)

FAIR LAND OF DREAMING
Edward Kunneke (based on Offenbach)
Harry B. Smith
The Love Song (1925)

FAIR WARNING
Jerry Bock
Sheldon Harnick
The Body Beautiful (1958)

FAIR WARNING
Harold Rome
Destry Rides Again (1959)

FAIR WEATHER
Edward Pola
Eddie Brandt
Woof, Woof (1929)

FAIR WEATHER FRIENDS
Frank Black
Gladys Shelley
The Duchess Misbehaves (1946)

FAITH
Robert Holton
June Carroll
Hi, Paisano! (OB) (1961)

FAITH
Jack Lawrence and Stan Freeman
I Had a Ball (1964)

FAITHLESS
Morton Gould
Betty Comden and Adolph Green
Billion Dollar Baby (1945)

FALL OF VALOR, THE
Alyn Heim
Malcolm L. LaPrade
Will the Mail Train Run Tonight?
  (OB) (1964)

FALLEN ANGELS
Bob Goodman
Wild and Wonderful (1971)

FALLIN'-OUT-OF-LOVE RAG, THE
Skip Redwine and Larry Frank

Frank Merriwell, or Honor Challenged (1971)

FALLING
Eubie Blake
Noble Sissle
Shuffle Along (1952)

FALLING IN LOVE
Henry Sullivan
Earle Crooker
The Third Little Show (1931)

FALLING IN LOVE
Eubie Blake
Noble Sissle
Shuffle Along (1933)

FALLING IN LOVE WITH LOVE
Richard Rodgers
Lorenz Hart
The Boys from Syracuse (1938)

FALLING OFF THE WAGON
Lewis E. Gensler
E. Y. Harburg
Ballyhoo (1932)

FALLING OUT OF LOVE CAN BE FUN
Irving Berlin
Miss Liberty (1949)

FALLING STAR
Milton Ager
Jack Yellen
Rain or Shine (1928)

FAME!
Joseph Raposo
Erich Segal
Sing Muse ! (OB) (1961)

FAME IS A PHONEY
Edward A. Horan
Frederick Herendeen
All the King's Horses (1934)

FAMILY FUGUE
Leslie Bricusse and Anthony Newley
Stop the World - I Want to Get Off
  (1962)

FAMILY REPUTATION
Irving Berlin
The Cocoanuts (1925)

FAMILY TREE
Bill Mahoney
My Wife and I (OB) (1966)

FAMILY TROUBLE
Leopold Antelme
Anthony Chalmers
Shoestring Revue (OB) (1957)

FAMILY WAY, THE
Harold Rome
I Can Get It for You Wholesale (1962)

FAMOUS RABBI, THE
Menachem Zur
Herbert Appleman
Unfair to Goliath (OB) (1970)

FAN CLUB CHANT
James Mundy
John Latouche
The Vamp (1955)

FAN TAN FANNIE
Richard Rodgers
Oscar Hammerstein II
Flower Drum Song (1958)

FAN THE FLAME
Leon Carr
Earl Shuman
The Secret Life of Walter Mitty (OB) (1964)

FANCY, FANCY
Vernon Duke
Ira Gershwin
Ziegfeld Follies (1936)

FANCY FORGETTING
Sandy Wilson
The Boy Friend (1954)

FANCY FREE
Harold Arlen
Johnny Mercer
The Petty Girl (F) (1950)

FANCY OUR MEETING
Joseph Meyer and Philip Charig
Douglas Furber
Wake Up and Dream (1929)

FANNETTE
Jacques Brel
Eric Blau and Mort Shuman
Jacques Brel Is Alive and Well and Living in Paris (OB) (1968)

FANNY
Harold Rome
Fanny (1954)

FAR AWAY
George Gershwin and Herbert Stothart
Otto Harbach and Oscar Hammerstein II
Song of the Flame (1925)

FAR AWAY AND LONG AGO
Karl Hajos (based on Chopin)
Harry B. Smith
White Lilacs (1928)

FAR AWAY ISLAND
Ed Tyler
Sweet Miani (OB) (1962)

FAR FAR AWAY
Cole Porter
Leave It to Me (1938)

FAR, FAR BETTER WAY, A
Mary Rodgers
Martin Charnin
Hot Spot (1963)

FAR FROM HOME
John Morris
Gerald Freedman
A Time for Singing (1966)

FAR FROM THE HOME I LOVE
Jerry Bock
Sheldon Harnick
Fiddler on the Roof (1964)

FAR ROCKAWAY
Robert Larimer
King of the Whole Damn World! (OB)
(1962)

FARAWAY BOY
Frank Loesser
Greenwillow (1960)

FARE THEE WELL
H. Maurice Jacquet
Preston Sturges
The Well of Romance (1930)

FARE THEE WELL
Earl Wilson, Jr.
A Day in the Life of Just About Everyone (OB) (1971)

FAREWELL
Sigmund Romberg
Otto Harbach and Oscar Hammerstein II
The Desert Song (1926)

FAREWELL, AMANDA
Cole Porter
Adam's Rib (F) (1949)

FAREWELL, FAMILY
David Shire
Richard Maltby, Jr.
The Sap of Life (OB) (1961)

FAREWELL, FAREWELL
Jule Styne
Betty Comden and Adolph Green
Hallelujah, Baby! (1967)

FAREWELL, MY LOVELY
Arthur Schwartz
Howard Dietz
At Home Abroad (1935)

FAREWELL WITH LOVE
Eubie Blake
Noble Sissle
Shuffle Along (1952)

FAREWELLS, THE
Stefan Kanfer, Jess J. Korman, and Joseph Grayhon
I Want You (OB) (1961)

FARMER AND THE COWMAN, THE
Richard Rodgers
Oscar Hammerstein II
Oklahoma! (1943)

FARMER'S DAUGHTER
Harold Arlen
E. Y. Harburg
Bloomer Girl (1944)

FARMER'S LIFE, A
Edward Kunneke (based on Offenbach)
Harry B. Smith
The Love Song (1925)

FARMING
Cole Porter
Let's Face It! (1941)

FARRELL GIRL, THE
Allan Roberts
Lester Lee
All for Love (1949)

FASCINATING RHYTHM
George Gershwin
Ira Gershwin
Lady, Be Good (1924)

FASCINATING YOU
Benee Russell, Vincent Rose, Charles and Harry Tobias
Earl Carroll's Sketch Book (1929)

FASHION GIRL, A
Harold Arlen
E. Y. Harburg
Hooray for What! (1937)

FASHIONS
Robert Kessler
Lola Permagent
O Marry Me! (OB) (1961)

FAST AND FURIOUS
Harry Revel
Mack Gordon
Fast and Furious (1931)

FAST CARS AND FIGHTIN' WOMEN
Steve Allen
Sophie (1963)

FASTEN YOUR SEAT BELTS
Charles Strouse
Lee Adams
Applause (1970)

FASTER THAN SOUND
Hugh Martin and Timothy Gray
High Spirits (1964)

FAT CITY
Robert Swerdlow
Love Me, Love My Children (OB)
   (1971)

FATAL FASCINATION
Arthur Schwartz
Howard Dietz
Flying Colors (1932)

FATE
Robert Wright and George Forrest
   (based on Alexander Borodin)
Kismet (1953)

FATED TO BE MATED
Cole Porter
Silk Stockings (F) (1957)

FATHER, FATHER
Patrick Fox
Blood (OB) (1971)

FATHER OF THE BRIDE, THE
Harvey Schmidt
Tom Jones
I Do! I Do! (1966)

FATHER SPEAKS, A
Deed Meyer
'Toinette (OB) (1961)

FATHER'S DAUGHTER
Sol Kaplan
Edward Eliscu
The Banker's Daughter (OB) (1962)

FATHER'S DAY
Jimmy McHugh
Harold Adamson
As the Girls Go (1948)

FAUCETT FALLS FANCY
David Baker
Will Holt
Come Summer (1969)

FEAR
Kurt Weill
Maxwell Anderson
Lost in the Stars (1949)

FEAR
Jule Styne
Betty Comden and Adolph Green
Fade Out - Fade In (1964)

FEAR IN MY HEART
Jerome Moross
Paul Peters and George Sklar
Parade (1935)

FEAST OF THE LANTERNS
Sigmund Romberg
Harry B. Smith
Cherry Blossoms (1927)

FEATHER IN A BREEZE
Sammy Fain
Irving Kahal
Everybody's Welcome (1931)

FEATHER IN MY SHOE
David Baker
Will Holt
Come Summer (1969)

FEBRUARY
Danny Shapiro, Jerry Seelen, and
   Lester Lee
The Lady Comes Across (1942)

FEE FI FO FUM
Helen Miller
Eve Merriam
Inner City (1971)

FEE-FIE-FO-FUM
Arthur Schwartz
Albert Stillman
Virginia (1937)

FEELIN' GOOD
Owen Murphy
Jack Yellen
Rain or Shine (1928)

FEELING GOOD
Leslie Bricusse and Anthony Newley
The Roar of the Greasepaint - The Smell of the Crowd (1965)

FEELING I'M FALLING
George Gershwin
Ira Gershwin
Treasure Girl (1928)

FEELING IN YOUR HEART, A
George M. Cohan
The Merry Malones (1927)

FEELING SENTIMENTAL*
George Gershwin
Gus Kahn and Ira Gershwin
Show Girl (1929)

FEELINGS
Jerry Bock
Sheldon Harnick
The Apple Tree (1966)

FEET
William Roy
The Penny Friend (OB) (1966)

FEET DO YO' STUFF
Jule Styne
Betty Comden and Adolph Green
Hallelujah, Baby! (1967)

FEET ON THE SIDEWALK (HEAD IN THE SKY)
Sam Lerner and Gerald Marks
My Dear Public (1943)

FELLA WITH AN UMBRELLA, A
Irving Berlin
Easter Parade (F) (1948)

FELLOW AND A GIRL, A
Jay Gorney
Edward Eliscu
Meet the People (1940)

FELLOW NEEDS A GIRL, A
Richard Rodgers
Oscar Hammerstein II
Allegro (1947)

FEMININE-INITY
Johnny Brandon
Who's Who, Baby? (OB) (1968)

FEMININITY
Jay Livingston and Ray Evans
Oh Captain! (1958)

FEMME DU MONDE
Harvey Schmidt
Tom Jones
Colette (OB) (1970)

FERHUDDLED AND FERHEXED
Howard Blankman
By Hex (OB) (1956)

FETISH
Richard Adler
Kwamina (1961)

FEUDIN' AND FIGHTIN'
Burton Lane
Al Dubin and Burton Lane
Laffing Room Only (1944)

FIASCO
André Previn
Alan Jay Lerner
Coco (1969)

FICKLE FINGER OF FATE
Jack Lawrence and Stan Freeman
I Had a Ball (1964)

FIDDLE DEE DEE
Lehman Engel
Agnes Morgan
A Hero Is Born (1937)

---

*Dropped from New York production

FIDDLER AND THE FIGHTER, THE
Jule Styne
Betty Comden and Adolph Green
Fade Out - Fade In (1964)

FIDDLERS' GREEN, THE
Ron Dante and Gene Allan
Billy (1969)

FIDGETY FEET
George Gershwin
Ira Gershwin
Oh, Kay! (1926)

FIE ON GOODNESS
Frederick Loewe
Alan Jay Lerner
Camelot (1960)

FIESTA
Sigmund Romberg
Harry B. Smith
The Love Call (1927)

FIESTA
Ray Henderson
Lew Brown
Hot-Cha! (1932)

FIESTA IN MADRID
Gerald Dolin
Edward J. Lambert
Smile at Me (1935)

FIFTEEN MINUTES A DAY
Alexander Hill
Hummin' Sam (1933)

FIFTH AVENUE
Gordon Jenkins
Tom Adair
Along Fifth Avenue (1949)

FIFTY MILLION YEARS AGO
Harvey Schmidt
Tom Jones
Celebration (1969)

FIG LEAVES ARE FALLING, THE
Albert Hague
Allen Sherman
The Fig Leaves Are Falling (1969)

FIGHT, THE
Charles Strouse
Lee Adams
Golden Boy (1964)

FIGHT OVER ME
Vincent Youmans
Otto Harbach
No, No, Nanette (1925)

FIGHT SONG, THE
Charles Strouse
Lee Adams
All American (1962)

FILL UP YOUR LIFE WITH SUN-SHINE
David Shire
Richard Maltby, Jr.
The Sap of Life (OB) (1961)

FIN DE SICKLE
Coleman Dowell
The Tattooed Countess (OB) (1961)

FIND A GOOD TIME
Carlton Kelsey and Maury Rubens
Clifford Grey
Sky High (1925)

FIND ME A PRIMITIVE MAN
Cole Porter
Fifty Million Frenchmen (1929)

FIND MY WAY ALONE
Clinton Ballard
Carolyn Richter
The Ballad of Johnny Pot (OB) (1971)

FIND YOUR OWN CRICKET
Stan Freeman and Franklin Underwood
Lovely Ladies, Kind Gentlemen (1970)

FIND YOURSELF A MAN
Jule Styne
Bob Merrill
Funny Girl (1964)

FIND YOURSELF SOMETHING TO DO
Julian Slade
Dorothy Reynolds and Julian Slade
Salad Days (OB) (1958)

FINDING WORDS FOR SPRING
Marian Grudeff and Raymond Jessel
Baker Street (1965)

FINE AND DANDY
Kay Swift
Paul James
Fine and Dandy (1930)

FINE FEATHERS
Mann Holiner
Alberta Nichols
Gay Paree (1926)

FINE ROMANCE, A
Jerome Kern
Dorothy Fields
Swing Time (F) (1936)

FINE, THANK YOU, FINE
David Baker
Will Holt
Come Summer (1969)

FINE WORDS AND FANCY PHRASES
Norman Dean
Autumn's Here (OB) (1966)

FINGER SONG, THE
Al Carmines
Maria Irene Fornes
Promenade (OB) (1969)

FINI
Richard Adler and Jerry Ross
John Murray Anderson's Almanac
(1953)

FIORETTA
G. Romilli
Fioretta (1929)

FIRE BELLES GALLOP
Richard Lewine
Ted Fetter
The Fireman's Flame (OB) (1937)

FIREFLIES
Baldwin Bergersen
William Archibald
The Crystal Heart (OB) (1960)

FIREMAN'S BRIDE, THE
Sigmund Romberg
Dorothy Fields
Up in Central Park (1945)

FIREMAN'S FLAME, THE
Richard Lewine
Ted Fetter
The Fireman's Flame (OB) (1937)

FIREWORKS
Harry Ruby
Bert Kalmar
Top Speed (1929)

FIREWORKS
Jule Styne
Betty Comden and Adolph Green
Do Re Mi (1960)

FIRST ACT CRISIS
Susan Hulsman Bingham
Myrna Lamb
Mod Donna (OB) (1970)

FIRST CAMPAIGN SONG
Don Tucker
Red, White and Maddox (1969)

FIRST CLASS NUMBER ONE BUM
Jule Styne
Sammy Cahn
Look to the Lilies (1970)

FIRST IMPRESSION
Harold Rome
Harold Rome and Charles Friedman
Pins and Needles (OB) (1937)

FIRST KISS, THE
Hal Jordan
Jerry Douglas
Rondelay (OB) (1969)

FIRST LADY, THE
Irving Berlin
Mr. President (1962)

FIRST LADY OF THE LAND, THE
Michael H. Cleary
Max and Nathaniel Lief
Shoot the Works (1931)

FIRST, LAST AND ONLY
Harold Levey
Owen Murphy
Rainbow Rose (1926)

FIRST MATE MARTIN
Jerome Kern
Oscar Hammerstein II
Sweet Adeline (1929)

FIRST PRIZE AT THE FAIR
Arthur Schwartz
Howard Dietz
Inside U.S.A. (1948)

FIRST ROSE OF SUMMER, THE
Jerome Kern
Anne Caldwell
She's a Good Fellow (1919)

FIRST SPRING DAY, THE
Howard Jackson
Edward Eliscu
Tattle Tales (1933)

FIRST THING IN THE MORNING
Donald Heywood
Blackberries of 1932

FIRST THING MONDAY MORNIN'
Gary Geld
Peter Udell
Purlie (1970)

FIRST THING YOU KNOW, THE
Andre Previn
Alan Jay Lerner
Paint Your Wagon (F) (1969)

FIRST TIME, THE
John Kander
Fred Ebb
Zorbá (1968)

FIRST TIME FOR ME, THE
Ray Henderson

B. G. DeSylva and Lew Brown
Flying High (1930)

FIRST TIME I SPOKE OF YOU, THE
Ernest G. Schweikert
Frank Reardon
Rumple (1957)

FISH SONG
Frank Fields
Armand Aulicino
The Shoemaker and the Peddler (OB)
   (1960)

FISHERMAN'S WHARF
Vernon Duke
Howard Dietz
Sadie Thompson (1944)

FIVE A.M.
Vernon Duke
Ira Gershwin
Ziegfeld Follies (1936)

FIVE DAUGHTERS
Glenn Paxton
Robert Goldman and George Weiss
First Impressions (1959)

FIVE FOOT-TWO
William B. Kernell
Dorothy Donnelly
Hello, Lola (1926)

FIVE GROWING BOYS
Larry Grossman
Hal Hackady
Minnie's Boys (1970)

FIVE HUNDRED MILLION
Cole Porter
Red, Hot and Blue! (1936)

FIVE LOVELY LADIES
Bill and Patti Jacob
Jimmy (1969)

FIVE MINUTES OF SPRING
Jay Gorney
E. Y. Harburg
Americana (1932)

FIVE MINUTES OF SPRING
Jacques Offenbach
E. Y. Harburg
The Happiest Girl in the World (1961)

FIVE MORE MINUTES IN BED
Harry Revel
Arnold B. Horwitt
Are You With It? (1945)

FIVE O'CLOCK
Arthur Schwartz
Howard Dietz
Between the Devil (1937)

FIVE O'CLOCK
Bernie Wayne
Ben Raleigh
Two for Tonight (OB) (1939)

FIVE O'CLOCK TEA
Irving Berlin
The Cocoanuts (1925)

FIVE SHOTS OF WHISKEY
Moose Charlap
Norman Gimbel
The Conquering Hero (1961)

FIVE-STEP, THE
Ray Henderson
B. G. DeSylva and Lew Brown
Manhattan Mary (1927)

FIVE THOUSAND FRANCS
Ralph Benatzky
Meet My Sister (1930)

FIXED FOR LIFE
Randall Thompson
Agnes Morgan
The Grand Street Follies (OB) (1926)

FIXIN' FOR A LONG COLD WINTER
Jack Lawrence and Don Walker
Courtin' Time (1951)

FIZKIN AND PICKWICK
Cyril Ornadel
Leslie Bricusse
Pickwick (1965)

F. JASMINE ADDAMS
G. Wood
F. Jasmine Addams (OB) (1971)

FLAHOOLEY
Sammy Fain
E. Y. Harburg
Flahooley (1951)

FLAME, THE
John Kander
Fred Ebb
Flora, the Red Menace (1965)

FIAMENCO
Arthur Schwartz
Howard Dietz
Revenge with Music (1934)

FLAMENCO
Henry Sullivan
Earle Crooker
Thumbs Up! (1934)

FLAMING AGNES
Harvey Schmidt
Tom Jones
I Do! I Do! (1966)

FLAMING YOUTH
Ray Henderson
B. G. DeSylva and Lew Brown
Good News (1927)

FLAMING YOUTH
Albert Selden
Burt Shevelove
Small Wonder (1948)

FLAP-A-DOODLE
Jerome Kern
Anne Caldwell and Otto Harbach
Criss-Cross (1926)

FLASH BANG WALLOP
David Heneker
Half a Sixpence (1965)

FLAT IN MONTMARTRE, A
Maurice Yvain
Max and Nathaniel Lief
Luckee Girl (1928)

FLATTERY
Harold Rome
Wish You Were Here (1952)

FLATTERY
Moose Charlap
Norman Gimbel
Whoop-Up (1958)

FLATTERY
Edward C. Redding
Lester Judson
Chic (OB) (1959)

FLATULENT BALLAD, THE
Mischa and Wesley Portnoff
Donagh MacDonagh
Happy As Larry (1950)

FLESH FAILURES, THE
Galt MacDermot
Gerome Ragni and James Rado
Hair (1968)

FLEXATONE
Alfred Goodman, Maury Rubens, and
    J. Fred Coots
Clifford Grey
Artists and Models (1925)

FLICKERS, THE
James Mundy
John Latouche
The Vamp (1955)

FLIM FLAM FLOOEY
Jack Holmes
Bill Conklin and Bob Miller
O Say Can You See! (OB) (1962)

FLINGS
Bob Merrill
New Girl in Town (1957)

FLIPPIN' OUT
Tom Sankey
The Golden Screw (OB) (1967)

FLIRTATION WALTZ
Kenneth Gaburo
Seyril Schochen
The Tiger Rag (OB) (1961)

FLOAT ME DOWN YOUR PIPELINE
Antonia
Operation Sidewinder (1970)

FLOATING THRU THE AIR
Arthur Schwartz
Henry Myers
The New Yorkers (1927)

FLOOZIES
Claibe Richardson
Kenward Elmslie
The Grass Harp (1971)

FLORIDA BY THE SEA
Irving Berlin
The Cocoanuts (1925)

FLORIDA, THE MOON AND YOU
Rudolf Friml
Gene Buck
No Foolin' (1926)

FLOTSAM AND JETSAM
George Kleinsinger
Joe Darion
Shinbone Alley (1957)

FLOWER, A
Al Carmines
Maria Irene Fornes
Promenade (OB) (1969)

FLOWER CHILD
Norman Curtis
Patricia Taylor Curtis
Walk Down Mah Street! (OB) (1968)

**FLOWER GARDEN OF MY HEART,
THE**
Richard Rodgers
Lorenz Hart
Pal Joey (1940)

**FLOWER, I DON'T NEED YOU ANY-
MORE**
Maury Laws
Jules Bass
Month of Sundays (OB) (1968)

FLOWER SONG, THE
Victor Young
Edward Heyman
Pardon Our French (1950)

FLOWER SONG, THE
Mike Brandt, Michael Knight, and
Robert J. Lowery
Exchange (OB) (1970)

FLOWERS, THE
Hal Hester and Danny Apolinar
Your Own Thing (1968)

FLOWING TO THE SEA
Oscar Brown, Jr.
Joy (OB) (1970)

FLUTTERBY BABY
Morris Hamilton
Grace Henry
Earl Carroll's Vanities (1928)

FLY AWAY
Deed Meyer
'Toniette (OB) (1961)

FLY AWAY
Jerry Blatt
Jerry Blatt and Lonnie Burstein
Have I Got One for You (OB) (1968)

FLY BLACKBIRD
C. Jackson and James Hatch
Fly Blackbird (OB) (1962)

FLY, BUTTERFLY
Ray Henderson
B. G. DeSylva and Lew Brown
George White's Scandals (1925)

FLY BY NIGHT
Arthur Schwartz
Howard Dietz
Between the Devil (1937)

FLY, LITTLE HEART
Jerry Bock
Larry Holofcener
Catch a Star! (1955)

FLY NOW, PAY LATER
Vernon Duke
Ogden Nash
The Littlest Revue (OB) (1956)

FLYING DOWN TO RIO
Vincent Youmans
Edward Eliscu and Gus Kahn
Flying Down to Rio (F) (1933)

FLYING HIGH
Ray Henderson
B. G. DeSylva and Lew Brown
Flying High (1930)

**FLYING MILK AND RUNAWAY
PLATES**
Gary William Friedman
Will Holt
The Me Nobody Knows (OB) (1970)

FLYING SOMEHOW
Mike Brandt, Michael Knight, and
Robert J. Lowery
Exchange (OB) (1970)

FOG AND THE GROG, THE
Robert Wright and George Forrest
Kean (1961)

FOGARTY THE GREAT
Jimmy Van Heusen
Johnny Burke
Nellie Bly (1946)

FOGGY DAY, A
George Gershwin
Ira Gershwin
A Damsel in Distress (F) (1937)

FOLKS WHO LIVE ON THE HILL, THE
Jerome Kern
Oscar Hammerstein II
High, Wide and Handsome (F) (1937)

FOLLOW HIM
Paul Klein
Fred Ebb
Morning Sun (OB) (1963)

FOLLOW MASTER
Joseph Meyer
Edward Eliscu
Lady Fingers (1929)

FOLLOW ME
Frederick Loewe
Alan Jay Lerner
Camelot (1960)

FOLLOW ME UP THE STAIRS
Duke Ellington
Marshall Barer and Fred Tobias
Pousse-Café (1966)

FOLLOW ON
Richard Rodgers
Lorenz Hart
Betsy (1926)

FOLLOW THE FOLD
Frank Loesser
Guys and Dolls (1950)

FOLLOW THE GIRLS
Philip Charig
Dan Shapiro and Milton Pascal
Follow the Girls (1944)

FOLLOW THE GUIDE
Raymond Hubbell
Anne Caldwell
Yours Truly (1927)

FOLLOW THE LAMB
Jule Styne
Sammy Cahn
Look to the Lilies (1970)

FOLLOW THE LEADER JIG
Irving Berlin
Miss Liberty (1949)

FOLLOW THE LEADER SEPTET
Sol Berkowitz
James Lipton
Nowhere to Go but Up (1962)

FOLLOW THE MINSTREL BAND
George Gershwin
Gus Kahn and Ira Gershwin
Show Girl (1929)

FOLLOW THE RAINBOW
Galt MacDermot
John Guare
Two Gentlemen of Verona (1971)

FOLLOW THE RAJAH
Sigmund Romberg
Arthur Wimperis
Louie the 14th (1925)

FOLLOW THE SUN TO THE SOUTH
Sigmund Romberg
Dorothy Donnelly
My Princess (1927)

FOLLOW THRU
Ray Henderson
B. G. DeSylva and Lew Brown
Follow Thru (1929)

FOLLOW YOUR HEART
Albert Hague
Arnold B. Horwitt
Plain and Fancy (1955)

FOLLOW YOUR HEART
Kenneth Jacobson
Rhoda Roberts
Show Me Where the Good Times Are
(OB) (1970)

FOLLOW YOUR STAR
Alfred Goodman, Maury Rubens, and
J. Fred Coots
Clifford Grey
Artists and Models (1925)

FOLLOWING IN FATHER'S FOOT-STEPS
Harry Ruby
Bert Kalmar
The Five O'Clock Girl (1927)

FOLLOWING THE SUN AROUND
Harry Tierney
Joseph McCarthy
Rio Rita (1927)

FOND OF YOU
Lewis E. Gensler
B. G. DeSylva
Captain Jinks (1925)

FOOD FOR THOUGHT
Heitor Villa-Lobos
Robert Wright and George Forrest
Magdalena (1948)

FOOD FOR THOUGHT
Donald Swann
Michael Flanders
At the Drop of Another Hat (1966)

FOOD, GLORIOUS FOOD
Lionel Bart
Oliver! (1963)

FOOD IS LOVE
Susan Hulsman Bingham
Myrna Lamb
Mod Donna (OB) (1970)

FOOL FOR LUCK
Morgan Lewis
Nancy Hamilton
Two for the Show (1940)

FOOLIN' OURSELVES
Billy Barnes
The Billy Barnes Revue (1959)

FOOLING AROUND WITH LOVE
James P. Johnson
Flournoy Miller
Sugar Hill (1931)

FOOLISH FACE
Arthur Schwartz
Howard Dietz
The Second Little Show (1930)

FOOLISH HEART
Kurt Weill
Ogden Nash
One Touch of Venus (1943)

FOOLISH WIVES
Edward Kunneke
Clifford Grey
Mayflowers (1925)

FOOLS COME AND FOOLS GO
George Harwell
What a Killing (OB) 1961)

FOOLS FALL IN LOVE
Irving Berlin
Louisiana Purchase (1940)

FOOL'S GOLD
Oscar Brand and Paul Nassau
A Joyful Noise (1966)

FOOTLIGHT WALK
Harry Denny
Footlights (1927)

FOOTLOOSE YOUTH AND FANCY
FREE
Peter Link and C. C. Courtney
Salvation (OB) (1969)

FOOTWORK
Ray Henderson
B. G. DeSylva and Lew Brown
Hold Everything! (1928)

FOR A GIRL LIKE YOU
Gitz Rice
Joe Goodwin
Nic-Nax (1926)

FOR A QUARTER
Lester Lee
Jerry Seelen
Star and Garter (1942)

FOR BETTER OR WORSE
Arthur Schwartz
Howard Dietz
Jennie (1963)

FOR CRITICS ONLY
Shelley Mowell
Mike Stewart
Shoestring Revue (OB) (1957)

FOR EVER
Peter Link and C. C. Courtney
Salvation (OB) (1969)

FOR EVERY FISH
Harold Arlen
E. Y. Harburg
Jamaica (1957)

FOR EVERY MAN THERE'S A WOMAN
Harold Arlen
Leo Robin
Casbah (F) (1948)

FOR FOUR HUNDRED YEARS
Norman Curtis
Patricia Taylor Curtis
Walk Down Mah Street! (OB) (1968)

FOR I'M IN LOVE
Arthur Brander
The Seventh Heart (1927)

FOR I'M IN LOVE AGAIN
Mischa Spoliansky
Billy Rose and Mort Dixon
Sweet and Low (1930)

FOR JUPITER AND GREECE
Richard Rodgers
Lorenz Hart
By Jupiter (1942)

FOR LOVE
Marc Blitzstein
Juno (1959)

FOR LOVE OR MONEY
Harold Karr
Matt Dubey
Happy Hunting (1956)

FOR LOVE OR MONEY
Jane Douglas
Tom O'Malley
Bella (OB) (1961)

FOR MY OWN
Johnny Burke
Donnybrook! (1961)

FOR NO RHYME OR REASON
Cole Porter
You Never Know (1938)

FOR ONCE IN MY LIFE
Paul Klein
Fred Ebb
Morning Sun (OB) (1963)

FOR ONCE IN YOUR LIFE
Walter Marks
Golden Rainbow (1968)

FOR OUR SAKE
Albert Hague
Allen Sherman
The Fig Leaves Are Falling (1969)

FOR SOMEONE I LOVE
Ted Snyder
Benny Davis
Earl Carroll's Sketch Book (1929)

FOR SWEET CHARITY
Bob Merrill
Take Me Along (1959)

FOR SWEET CHARITY'S SAKE
Ray Henderson
B. G. DeSylva and Lew Brown
Hold Everything! (1928)

FOR THE FIRST TIME
Arthur Schwartz
Howard Dietz
The Gay Life (1961)

**FOR THE HARVEST SAFELY GATH-
ERED**
Norman Dean
Autumn's Here (OB) (1966)

FOR THE LIFE OF ME
Arthur Schwartz
Ira Gershwin
Park Avenue (1946)

FOR THE PAPA
Emile Berté and Maury Rubens
J. Keirn Brennan
Music in May (1929)

FOR THE REST OF MY LIFE
Albert Hague
Allen Sherman
The Fig Leaves Are Falling (1969)

FOR THE SAKE OF ART
Robert Stolz
Robert Sour
Mr. Strauss Goes to Boston (1945)

FOR THE SAKE OF LEXINGTON
Sam Stept
Lew Brown and Charles Tobias
Yokel Boy (1939)

FOR WE LOVE YOU STILL
Johann Strauss
Desmond Carter
The Great Waltz (1934)

FOR YOU
Gerard Calvi
Harold Rome
La Grosse Valise (1965)

FOR YOU AND FOR ME
H. Maurice Jacquet
Preston Sturges
The Well of Romance (1930)

FOR YOU, FOR ME, FOR EVERMORE
George Gershwin
Ira Gershwin
The Shocking Miss Pilgrim (F) (1946)

FORBIDDEN LOVE (IN GAUL)
Jerry Bock
Sheldon Harnick
The Apple Tree (1966)

FORBIDDEN ORCHID, THE
Heitor Villa-Lobos
Robert Wright and George Forrest
Magdalena (1948)

FORE DAY NOON IN THE MORNIN'
Irving Burgie
Ballad for Bimshire (OB) (1963)

FOREIGN CARS
Norman Martin
Catch a Star! (1955)

FORESIGHT
Stanley Lebowsky
Fred Tobias
Gantry (1970)

FOREST RANGERS, THE
Rick Besoyan
Little Mary Sunshine (OB) (1959)

FOREVER
Bob Merrill
Henry, Sweet Henry (1967)

FOREVER AND A DAY
Hugh Martin and Timothy Gray
High Spirits (1964)

FOREVER AND ALWAYS
Ed Tyler
Sweet Miani (OB) (1962)

FOREVER AND EVER
Milton Ager
Jack Yellen
Rain or Shine (1928)

FORGET
John Clifton
John Clifton and Ben Tarver
Man with a Load of Mischief (OB)
  (1966)

FORGET ALL YOUR BOOKS
Burton Lane
Howard Dietz
Three's a Crowd (1930)

FORGET ME
David Baker
Sheldon Harnick
Vintage '60 (OB) (1960)

FORSAKEN
Richard Myers
Edward Heyman
Earl Carroll's Vanities (1932)

FORTUNE, THE
Jay Thompson
Double Entry (OB) (1961)

FORTY DAYS
Meyer Kupferman
Paul Goodman
Jonah (OB) (1966)

FORTY-FIVE MINUTES FROM BROAD-
WAY
George M. Cohan
Forty-Five Minutes from Broadway
  (1906)

FORTY-SECOND STREET
Harry Warren
Al Dubin
Forty-Second Street (F) (1933)

FOUNTAIN OF YOUTH, THE
Jerome Kern
Anne Caldwell
The City Chap (1925)

FOUNTAIN OF YOUTH, THE
Alma Sanders
Monte Carlo
The Houseboat on the Styx (1928)

FOUR
Al Carmines
Maria Irene Fornes
Promenade (OB) (1969)

FOUR FOR THE ROAD
Paul Klein
Lee Goldsmith and Fred Ebb
From A to Z (1960)

FOUR FREEDOMS - CALYPSO, THE
John Green
George Marion, Jr.
Beat the Band (1942)

FOUR LITTLE ANGELS OF PEACE
Harold Rome
Pins and Needles (OB) (1937)

FOUR LITTLE MISFITS
James Mundy
John Latouche
The Vamp (1955)

FOUR LITTLE SONG PLUGGERS
Richard Rodgers
Lorenz Hart
The Garrick Gaieties (1926)

FOUR NIGHTINGALES
Larry Grossman
Hal Hackady
Minnie's Boys (1970)

FOUR THOUSAND YEARS
Patrick Fox
Doug Dyer
Blood (OB) (1971)

FOUR YOUNG PEOPLE
James Shelton
The Straw Hat Revue (1939)

FOURTH LIGHT DRAGOONS, THE
Michael Valenti
John Lewin
Blood Red Roses (1970)

FOX HAS LEFT HIS LAIR, THE
Peggy Connor
Douglas Furber
Charlot's Revue (1926)

FOX HUNT, THE
Jerry Herman
Mame (1966)

FRAGRANT FLOWER
Glenn Paxton
Robert Goldman and George Weiss
First Impressions (1959)

FRAHNGEE-PAHNEE
Cole Porter
Seven Lively Arts (1944)

FRANCE WILL NOT FORGET
Geoffrey O'Hara and Gordon Johnstone
Half a Widow (1927)

FRANK, FRANK, FRANK
Skip Redwine and Larry Frank
Frank Merriwell, or Honor Challenged (1971)

FRANK MILLS
Galt MacDermot
Gerome Ragni and James Rado
Hair (1968)

FREDDY AND HIS FIDDLE
Robert Wright and George Forrest
(based on Grieg)
Song of Norway (1944)

FREE
Stephen Sondheim
A Funny Thing Happened on the Way to the Forum (1962)

FREE AS THE AIR
Franz Lehár
Harry Graham
Yours Is my Heart (1946)

FREE, CUTE AND SIZE FOURTEEN
John Green
George Marion, Jr.
Beat the Band (1942)

FREE FOR ALL
Richard A. Whiting
Oscar Hammerstein II
Free for All (1931)

FREE, FREE, FREE
Lucien Denni
Helena Evans
Happy Go Lucky (1926)

FREEDOM
Heitor Villa-Lobos
Robert Wright and George Forrest
Magdalena (1948)

FREEDOM CAN BE A MOST UNCOM-
FORTABLE THING
Sammy Fain
Paul Francis Webster
Christine (1960)

FREEDOM CHOO CHOO IS LEAVING
TODAY, THE
Jack Holmes
Bill Conklin and Bob Miller
O Say Can You See! (OB) (1962)

FREEDOM OF THE PRESS, THE
Marc Blitzstein
The Cradle Will Rock (1938)

FREEDOM ROAD
Toby Sacher
Lewis Allen
Of V We Sing (1942)

FREEDOMLAND
Jack Holmes
New Faces (1962)

FRENCH HAVE A WORD FOR IT, THE
Jimmy McHugh
Al Dubin
The Streets of Paris (1939)

FRENCH LESSON, THE
Roger Edens
Betty Comden and Adolph Green
Good News (F) (1947)

FRENCH MARCHING SONG
Sigmund Romberg
Otto Harbach and Oscar Hammer-
stein II
The Desert Song (1926)

FRENCH THING TANGO
William S. Fischer
Maxine Klein
Kiss Now (OB) (1971)

FRENCH WITH TEARS
Harold Rome
Alive and Kicking (1950)

FRESH AS A DAISY
Cole Porter
Panama Hattie (1940)

FRESNO   BEAUTIES   (COLD   AND
DEAD)
Frank Loesser
The Most Happy Fella (1956)

FREUD
Jack Lawrence and Stan Freeman
I Had a Ball (1964)

FRIAR'S TUNE
Wally Harper
Paul Zakrzewski
Sensations (OB) (1970)

FRIDAY DANCING CLASS
Charles Gaynor
Lend an Ear (1948)

FRIDAY, FRIDAY
Steven Metcalf
Fred Bluth
Drat! (OB) (1971)

FRIEND LIKE YOU, A
John Clifton
John Clifton and Ben Tarver
Man with a Load of Mischief (OB) (1966)

FRIEND OF THE FAMILY
Hoagy Carmichael
Johnny Mercer
Walk with Music (1940)

FRIENDLIEST THING, THE
Ervin Drake
What Makes Sammy Run? (1964)

FRIENDLY ENEMY
Gerald Marks
Sam Lerner
Hold It! (1948)

FRIENDS
George M. Cohan
Billie (1928)

FRIENDS
Sam Pottle
Tom Whedon
All Kinds of Giants (OB) (1961)

FRIENDS
Jerry Bock
Sheldon Harnick
The Apple Tree (1966)

FRIENDS AND LOVERS
Maurice Yvain
Max and Nathaniel Lief
Luckee Girl (1928)

FRIENDS TO THE END
Frederick Loewe
Alan Jay Lerner
The Day Before Spring (1945)

FRIENDSHIP
Ralph Benatzky
Meet My Sister (1930)

FRIENDSHIP
Cole Porter
Du Barry Was a Lady (1939)

FRIGHTENED OF THE DARK
Steven Metcalf
Fred Bluth
Drat! (OB) (1971)

FRISCO FANNY
Henry Sullivan
Earl Crooker
Walk a Little Faster (1932)

FRITZIE
Edward Thomas
Martin Charnin
Ballad for a Firing Squad (OB) (1968)

FROM A PRISON CELL
Marguerite Monnot
Julian More, David Heneker, and
    Monte Norman
Irma La Douce (1960)

FROM A TO Z
Albert Selden
Burt Shevelove
Small Wonder (1948)

FROM ALPHA TO OMEGA
Cole Porter
You Never Know (1938)

FROM ANOTHER WORLD
Richard Rodgers
Lorenz Hart
Higher and Higher (1940)

FROM MORNING TILL NIGHT
Jacques Belasco
Kay Twomey
The Girl from Nantucket (1945)

FROM NOW ON
Richard Myers
Edward Eliscu
The Street Singer (1929)

FROM NOW ON
Cole Porter
Leave It to Me (1938)

FROM NOW ONWARD
Sigmund Romberg

Rowland Leigh
My Romance (1948)

FROM OUR BESTIARY
Donald Swann
Michael Flanders
At the Drop of Another Hat (1966)

FROM THE CHIMNEY TO THE CELLAR
Frederick Loewe
Alan Jay Lerner
What's Up? (1943)

FROM THE MOMENT
John Dooley
Hobo (OB) (1961)

FROM THE U.S.A. TO THE U.S.S.R.
Cole Porter
Leave It to Me (1938)

FROM THIS DAY ON
Frederick Loewe
Alan Jay Lerner
Brigadoon (1947)

FROM THIS DAY ON
Abraham Ellstein
Walter Bullock
Great to Be Alive (1950)

FROM THIS MOMENT ON*
Cole Porter
Out of This World (1950)

FRONT PAGE NEWS
Arthur Schwartz
Howard Dietz
Between the Devil (1937)

FRONTIER POLITICS
Victor Ziskin
Joan Javits
Young Abe Lincoln (1961)

FROWNS
Harry Revel
Mack Gordon
Fast and Furious (1931)

FRUSTRATION
Joseph Martinez Kookoolis and Scott Fagan
Scott Fagan
Soon (1971)

FUDDLE-DEE-DUDDLE
Sammy Fain
Charles Tobias
Hellzapoppin' (1938)

FUGITIVE FROM ESQUIRE, A
Jimmy McHugh
Howard Dietz
Keep Off the Grass (1940)

FUGITIVE FROM FIFTH AVENUE, THE
Richard Stutz
Nat Hiken
Along Fifth Avenue (1949)

FUGUE FOR FOUR GIRLS
Gary William Friedman
Will Holt
The Me Nobody Knows (OB) (1970)

FUGUE FOR TINHORNS
Frank Loesser
Guys and Dolls (1950)

FUGUE ON A HOT AFTERNOON IN A SMALL FLAT
Earl Robinson
Waldo Salt
Sandhog (OB) (1954)

FULL BLOWN ROSES
Richard Rodgers
Lorenz Hart
Dearest Enemy (1925)

FUN
Sol Berkowitz
James Lipton
Miss Emily Adam (OB) (1960)

FUN IN THE COUNTRY
William Roy
Maggie (1953)

_____
*Dropped from New York production

FUN LIFE
Tommy Wolf
Fran Landesman
The Nervous Set (1959)

FUN TO BE FOOLED
Harold Arlen
Ira Gershwin and E. Y. Harburg
Life Begins at 8:40 (1934)

FUNDAMENTAL CHARACTER
Gerald Marks
Sam Lerner
Hold It! (1948)

FUNERAL OF CHARLESTON
Manning Sherwin
Arthur Herzog, Jr.
Bad Habits of 1926 (OB) (1926)

FUNERAL SEQUENCE
Stephen Sondheim
*A Funny Thing Happened on the Way
to the Forum* (1962)

FUNERAL TANGO
Jacques Brel
Eric Blau and Mort Shuman
*Jacques Brel Is Alive and Well and
Living in Paris* (OB) (1968)

**FUNKY GIRL ON MOTHERLESS
BROADWAY**
Melvin Van Peebles
*Ain't Supposed to Die a Natural
Death* (1971)

FUNKY WORLD
Oscar Brown, Jr.
Joy (OB) (1970)

FUNNIES, THE
Irving Berlin
As Thousands Cheer (1933)

FUNNY FACE
George Gershwin
Ira Gershwin
Funny Face (1927)

FUNNY FEELIN'
Oscar Brown, Jr. and Luis Henrique
Joy (OB) (1970)

FUNNY FUNERAL
Leslie Bricusse and Anthony Newley
*The Roar of the Greasepaint - The
Smell of the Crowd* (1965)

FUNNY GIRL
Jule Styne
Bob Merrill
Funny Girl (F) (1968)

FUNNY HEART, A
David Baker
David Craig
Phoenix '55 (OB) (1955)

FUNNY LITTLE SAILOR MAN
Sigmund Romberg
Oscar Hammerstein II
The New Moon (1928)

FUNNY THING HAPPENED, A
Harold Rome
I Can Get It for You Wholesale (1962)

FUTURE STARS
Leo Edwards
Herman Timberg
You'll See Stars (1942)

FUTURISTIC RHYTHM
Jimmy McHugh
Dorothy Fields
Hello Daddy (1928)

GABIE
Mary Rodgers
Martin Charnin
Hot Spot (1963)

GABRIEL
Henry Souvaine and Jay Gorney
Morrie Ryskind and Howard Dietz
Merry-Go-Round (1927)

GABRIELLE
André Previn
Alan Jay Lerner
Coco (1969)

GA-GA!
Joseph Meyer
Edward Eliscu
Lady Fingers (1929)

GA-GA
Carl Millöcker (revised by Theo Mack-
   eben)
Rowland Leigh
The Dubarry (1932)

GAINESBORO GLIDE, THE
Seymour Furth and Lee Edwards
R. F. Carroll
Bringing Up Father (1925)

GAL IN CALICO, A
Arthur Schwartz
Leo Robin
The Time, The Place, and the Girl (F)
   (1946)

GALLIVANTIN' AROUND
Jerome Kern
Oscar Hammerstein II
Show Boat (F) (1936)

GALLOPIN' DOMINOES
C. Luckey Roberts
Alex C. Rogers
My Magnolia (1926)

GALLOPING THROUGH THE PARK
Robert Russell Bennett
Owen Murphy and Robert A. Simon
Hold Your Horses (1933)

GAMBLERS, THE
Harold Arlen
Johnny Mercer
Saratoga (1959)

GAME, THE
Richard Adler and Jerry Ross
Damn Yankees (1955)

GAME OF LOVE, THE
Harold Karr
Matt Dubey
Happy Hunting (1956)

GAME OF MORRA, THE
Armando Trovaioli
Pietro Garinei and Sandro Giovannini
Rugantino (1964)

GAME OF POKER, A
Harold Arlen
Johnny Mercer
Saratoga (1959)

GANG'S ALL HERE, THE
Lewis E. Gensler
Owen Murphy and Robert A. Simon
The Gang's All Here (1931)

GARBAGE
Sheldon Harnick
Shoestring Revue (OB) (1955)

GARBAGE
Jerry Herman
Dear World (1969)

GARBAGE COURT ROUND
George Fischoff
Verna Tomasson
The Prince and the Pauper (OB)
   (1963)

GARCON, S'IL VOUS PLAIT
George Gershwin
Ira Gershwin
Of Thee I Sing (1931)

GARDEN, THE
Charles Strouse
Six (OB) (1971)

GARDEN GUARACHA
Stan Freeman and Franklin Underwood
Lovely Ladies, Kind Gentlemen
   (1970)

GARDEN IN THE SKY
Vernon Duke
Howard Dietz
Sadie Thompson (1944)

GARDEN IN THE SUN, A
Michael Valenti
John Lewin
Blood Red Roses (1970)

GARDEN OF MEMORIES, A
Maury Rubens
Clifford Grey
The Great Temptations (1926)

GARDEN SONG
Kenn Long and Jim Crozier
Kenn Long
Touch (OB) (1970)

GARY, INDIANA
Meredith Willson
The Music Man (1957)

GAS CAN
Patrick Fox
Doug Dyer
Blood (OB) (1971)

GAS MAN COMETH, THE
Donald Swann
Michael Flanders
At the Drop of Another Hat (1966)

GATEWAY OF THE TEMPLE OF MINERVA, THE
Richard Rodgers
Lorenz Hart
By Jupiter (1942)

GATHER ROSES WHILE YOU MAY
Vivian Ellis
Graham John
By the Way (1925)

GATHER THE ROSE
Rudolf Friml
Brian Hooker
The White Eagle (1927)

GATHER YE AUTOGRAPHS WHILE YE MAY
Cole Porter
Jubilee (1935)

GATHER YE ROSEBUDS
Mel Marvin
Ted Berger
Shoemaker's Holiday (OB) (1967)

GATSBY BRIDGE MARCH, THE
David Baker
Fred Ebb
Smiling, the Boy Fell Dead (OB) (1961)

GAUCHO LOVE SONG, A
Sigmund Romberg
Irving Caesar
Nina Rosa (1930)

GAVOTTE
Richard Rodgers
Lorenz Hart
Dearest Enemy (1925)

GAVOTTE
Leonard Bernstein
Dorothy Parker
Candide (1956)

GAY LITTLE WIVES
Cole Porter
Jubilee (1935)

GAZOOKA, THE
Vernon Duke
Ira Gershwin
Ziegfeld Follies (1936)

GEE, BUT I'D LIKE TO BE BAD
James F. Hanley
Eddie Dowling
Honeymoon Lane (1926)

GEE, BUT IT'S GOOD TO BE HERE
Harold Karr
Matt Dubey
Happy Hunting (1956)

GEE CHEE
C. Luckey Roberts
Alex C. Rogers
My Magnolia (1926)

GEE, I'M GLAD I'M NO ONE ELSE BUT ME
Norman Campbell
Donald Campbell and Norman Campbell
Anne of Green Gables (OB) (1971)

GEE, IT'S GREAT TO BE ALIVE
Ray Henderson
B. G. DeSylva
Three Cheers (1928)

GEE IT'S SO GOOD, IT'S TOO BAD
Harold Arlen
Ted Koehler
Nine-Fifteen Revue (1930)

GEE, OFFICER KRUPKE!
Leonard Bernstein
Stephen Sondheim
West Side Story (1957)

GEE, WE GET ALONG
Tom Johnstone
Phil Cook
When You Smile (1925)

GEISHA
Stan Freeman and Franklin Underwood
Lovely Ladies, Kind Gentlemen (1970)

GEISHA GIRL
Manning Sherwin
Arthur Herzog, Jr.
Bad Habits of 1926 (OB) (1926)

GENDARME, THE
Arthur Schwartz
Howard Dietz
Between the Devil (1937)

GENDARME
Robert Katscher
Rowland Leigh
You Never Know (1938)

GENEALOGY
Ray Henderson
B. G. DeSylva and Lew Brown
Hold Everything! (1928)

GENERALONELY
Steve Weber
Operation Sidewinder (1970)

GENERAL STORE
Norman Campbell
Donald Campbell and Norman Campbell
Anne of Green Gables (OB) (1971)

GENERAL'S SONG, THE
Vernon Duke
John Latouche
Cabin in the Sky (1940)

GENERAL'S SONG, THE
Don Tucker
Red, White and Maddox (1969)

GENERATION GAP
Janet Gari
Toby Garson
Lyle (OB) (1970)

GENIUS BURNS
William Dyer
Don Parks and William Dyer
Jo! (OB) (1964)

GENTEEL
Sol Kaplan
Edward Eliscu
The Banker's Daughter (OB) (1962)

GENTLEMAN FRIEND
Richard Lewine
Arnold B. Horwitt
Make Mine Manhattan (1948)

GENTLEMAN IS A DOPE, THE
Richard Rodgers
Oscar Hammerstein II
Allegro (1947)

GENTLEMAN JIMMY
Jerry Bock
Sheldon Harnick
Fiorello (1959)

GENTLEMAN NEVER FALLS WILDLY
IN LOVE, A
Glenn Paxton
Robert Goldman and George Weiss
First Impressions (1959)

GENTLEMEN OF THE PRESS
Oscar Levant
Irving Caesar and Graham John
Ripples (1930)

GENTLEMEN OF THE PRESS
Ernest G. Schweikert
Frank Reardon
Rumple (1957)

GENTLEMEN PREFER BLONDES
Lewis E. Gensler
B. G. DeSylva
Queen High (1926)

GENTLEMEN PREFER BLONDES
Jule Styne
Leo Robin
Gentlemen Prefer Blondes (1949)

GENTLEMAN'S GENTLEMAN, A
Cyril Ornadel
Leslie Bricusse
Pickwick (1965)

GENTLEMAN'S GENTLEMAN, A
Jule Styne
E. Y. Harburg
Darling of the Day (1968)

GENTLEMEN'S UNDERSTANDING
Sol Kaplan
Edward Eliscu
The Banker's Daughter (OB) (1962)

GENUINE FEMININE GIRL, A
Johnny Brandon
Cindy (OB) (1964)

GEORGE L.
Jerry Bock
Sheldon Harnick
The Apple Tree (1966)

GEORGY
George Fischoff
Carole Bayer
Georgy (1970)

GERANIUMS IN THE WINDER
Richard Rodgers
Oscar Hammerstein II
Carousel (1945)

GERTIE THE STOOL PIGEON'S DAUGHTER
Ned Lehak
Joe Darion
Of V We Sing (1942)

GESTICULATE
Robert Wright and George Forrest
(based on Alexander Borodin)
Kismet (1953)

GET A LOAD OF THAT
Kurt Weill
Langston Hughes
Street Scene (1947)

GET A LOAD OF THIS
Harry Archer
Harlan Thompson
Twinkle Twinkle (1926)

GET AN EDUCATION
Ron Steward and Neal Tate
Ron Steward
Sambo (OB) (1969)

GET AWAY FOR A DAY IN THE COUNTRY
Jule Styne
Sammy Cahn
High Button Shoes (1947)

GET AWAY FROM IT ALL
Arthur Schwartz
Howard Dietz
At Home Abroad (1935)

GET AWAY FROM THAT WINDOW
Jimmy Johnson
Perry Bradford
Messin' Around (1929)

GET AWAY, YOUNG MAN
Thomas (Fats) Waller
George Marion, Jr.
Early to Bed (1943)

GET DOWN
Oscar Brown, Jr.
Buck White (1969)

GET HAPPY
Harold Arlen
Ted Koehler
Nine-Fifteen Revue (1930)

GET HOT FOOT
Sam H. Stept
Bud Green
Shady Lady (1933)

GET IN LINE
Jacques Urbont
David Newburger
Stag Movie (OB) (1971)

GET ME OUT
Fred Stamer
Gen Genovese
Buttrio Square (1952)

GET ME TO THE CHURCH ON TIME
Frederick Loewe
Alan Jay Lerner
My Fair Lady (1956)

GET ON THE RAFT WITH TAFT
Oscar Brand
How to Steal an Election (OB) (1968)

GET OUT OF TOWN
Cole Porter
Leave It to Me (1938)

GET OUT THE VOTE
Oscar Brand
How to Steal an Election (OB) (1968)

GET THAT SUN INTO YOU
Richard Myers
E. Y. Harburg
Americana (1932)

GET THE NEWS
Eddie Stuart
Harvey Lasker
Old Bucks and New Wings (OB) (1962)

GET THEE BEHIND ME SATAN
Irving Berlin
Follow the Fleet (F) (1936)

GET THEE TO CANTERBURY
Paul Hoffert
David Secter
Get Thee to Canterbury (OB) (1969)

GET UP ON A NEW ROUTINE
Arthur Schwartz
Howard Dietz
The Little Show (1929)

GET YER PROGRAM FOR DE BIG FIGHT
Georges Bizet
Oscar Hammerstein II
Carmen Jones (1943)

GET YOUR MAN
Ray Perkins
Max and Nathaniel Lief
The Greenwich Village Follies (1928)

GET YOUR ROCKS OFF ROCK
Jacques Urbont
David Newburger
Stag Movie (OB) (1971)

GET YOUR SLICE OF CAKE
Johnny Brandon
Billy Noname (OB) (1970)

GET YOURSELF A GEISHA
Arthur Schwartz
Howard Dietz
At Home Abroad (1935)

GET YOURSELF A GIRL
Cole Porter
Let's Face It! (1941)

GETAWAY QUINTET, THE
Jerry Blatt
Jerry Blatt and Lonnie Burstein
Have I Got One for You (OB) (1968)

GETHSEMANE
Andrew Lloyd Webber
Tim Rice
Jesus Christ Superstar (1971)

GETTIN' A MAN
Johnny Mercer
Saratoga (1959)

GETTIN' BACK TO ME
George Fischoff
Carole Bayer
Georgy (1970)

GETTIN' TOGETHER
Maceo Pinkard
Pansy (1929)

GETTING INTO THE TALKIES
Milton Ager
Jack Yellen
John Murray Anderson's Almanac
(1929)

GETTING MARRIED TODAY
Stephen Sondheim
Company (1970)

GETTING ORIENTAL OVER YOU
Don Walker
George Marion, Jr.
Allah Be Praised (1944)

GETTING THE BEAUTIFUL GIRLS
Michael Cleary
Ned Washington
Earl Carroll's Vanities (1928)

GETTING TO KNOW YOU
Richard Rodgers
Oscar Hammerstein II
The King and I (1951)

GHOST OF LITTLE EGYPT, THE
Philip Charig
James Dyrenforth
Nikki (1931)

GHOST OF OLD BLACK JOE, THE
Vincent Valentini
Parisiana (1928)

GHOST TOWN
Will Irwin
Norman Zeno
Fools Rush In (1934)

GIANNINA MIA
Rudolf Friml
Otto Harbach
The Firefly (1912)

GIDEON BRIGGS, I LOVE YOU
Frank Loesser
Greenwillow (1960)

GIFT NUMBER
Jay Gorney
Barry Trivers
Heaven on Earth (1948)

GIFT OF MAGGIE (AND OTHERS), THE
Mary Rodgers
Marshall Barer
The Mad Show (OB) (1966)

GIFT TODAY, A
Harold Rome
I Can Get It for You Wholesale (1962)

GIGI*
Frederick Loewe
Alan Jay Lerner
Gigi (F) (1958)

GIGOLETTE
Franz Lehár
Irving Caesar
Charlot's Revue (1926)

GIGOLO
Richard Rodgers
Lorenz Hart
The Garrick Gaieties (1926)

GIGOLO
Sigmund Romberg
Dorothy Donnelly
My Princess (1927)

GILDING THE GUILD
Richard Rodgers
Lorenz Hart
The Garrick Gaieties (1925)

GIMME SOME
Charles Strouse
Lee Adams
Golden Boy (1964)

———
*Academy Award Winner

GIMME THE SHIMMY
Harold Rome
Michael Todd's Peep Show (1950)

GINA
Peter Link and C. C. Courtney
Salvation (OB) (1969)

GINETTE
Jean Schwartz
Clifford Grey and William Cary Duncan
Sunny Days (1928)

GINGERBREAD GIRL
Robert Swerdlow
Love Me, Love My Children (OB) (1971)

GIP-GIP
George M. Cohan
The Merry Malones (1927)

GIRL FRIEND, THE
Richard Rodgers
Lorenz Hart
The Girl Friend (1926)

GIRL HE ADORES
Robert Holton
June Carroll
Hi, Paisano! (OB) (1961)

GIRL I MIGHT HAVE BEEN, THE
Max Ewing
The Grand Street Follies (1929)

GIRL IN HIS ARMS, THE
Moose Charlap
Norman Gimbel
Whoop-Up (1958)

GIRL IN THE COFFEE
Coleridge-Taylor Perkinson
Errol Hill
Man Better Man (OB) (1969)

GIRL IN THE MIRROR, THE
Fred Hellerman
Fran Minkoff
New Faces (1968)

GIRL IN THE SHOW, THE
Charles Gaynor
Show Girl (1961)

GIRL IN YOUR ARMS, A
Jay Gorney
Irving Caesar
Sweetheart Time (1926)

GIRL IS LIKE A BOOK, A
Frederick Loewe
Alan Jay Lerner
What's Up? (1943)

GIRL IS YOU AND THE BOY IS ME, THE
Ray Henderson
B. G. DeSylva and Lew Brown
George White's Scandals (1926)

GIRL LIKE YOU, A
Edward Pola
Eddie Brandt
Woof, Woof (1929)

GIRL NEXT DOOR, THE
Richard A. Whiting
Oscar Hammerstein II
Free for All (1931)

GIRL OF THE MINUTE, THE
David Shire
Richard Maltby, Jr.
New Faces (1968)

GIRL OF THE MOMENT
Kurt Weill
Ira Gershwin
Lady in the Dark (1941)

GIRL OF THE PI BETA PHI, A
Ray Henderson
B. G. DeSylva and Lew Brown
Good News (1927)

GIRL OF TOMORROW, THE
Ray Henderson
B. G. DeSylva and Lew Brown
George White's Scandals (1925)

GIRL ON THE POLICE GAZETTE
Irving Berlin
On the Avenue (F) (1937)

GIRL ON THE PROW, THE
Sigmund Romberg
Oscar Hammerstein II
The New Moon (1928)

GIRL SHE CAN'T REMAIN, A
Baldwin Bergersen
William Archibald
Carib Song (1945)

GIRL THAT I ADORE, THE
Emil Gerstenberger
Carle Carlton
The Lace Petticoat (1927)

GIRL THAT I COURT IN MY MIND, THE
Ralph Blane
Three Wishes for Jamie (1952)

GIRL THAT I MARRY, THE
Irving Berlin
Annie Get Your Gun (1946)

GIRL THAT I'LL ADORE, THE
Niclas Kempner
Graham John
The Street Singer (1929)

GIRL WHO DOESN'T RIPPLE WHEN SHE BENDS, A
Thomas (Fats) Waller
George Marion, Jr.
Early to Bed (1943)

GIRL WHO LIVED IN MONTPARNASSE, THE
Charles Gaynor
Show Girl (1961)

GIRL WITH A FLAME, A
Morton Gould
Dorothy Fields
Arms and the Girl (1950)

GIRL WITH A RIBBON, A
Baldwin Bergersen

William Archibald
The Crystal Heart (OB) (1960)

GIRL WITH THE PAINT ON HER FACE, THE
Irvin Graham
Who's Who (1938)

GIRLS, THE
Harry Ruby
Bert Kalmar
High Kickers (1941)

GIRLS
Cole Porter
Mexican Hayride (1944)

GIRLS AGAINST THE BOYS, THE
Richard Lewine
Arnold B. Horwitt
The Girls Against the Boys (1959)

GIRLS AND BOYS
Richard Lewine
Arnold B. Horwitt
The Girls Against the Boys (1959)

GIRLS AND DOGS
Jacques Brel
Eric Blau and Mort Shuman
Jacques Brel Is Alive and Well and Living in Paris (OB) (1968)

GIRLS AND THE GIMMIES
Percy Wenrich
Raymond Peck
Castles in the Air (1926)

GIRLS DREAM OF ONE THING
J. Fred Coots
Clifford Grey
June Days (1925)

GIRLS! GIRLS!
Moose Charlap
Norman Gimbel
The Conquering Hero (1961)

GIRLS, I AM TRUE TO ALL OF YOU
Emmerich Kalman
Harry B. Smith
The Circus Princess (1927)

GIRLS LIKE ME
Jule Styne
Betty Comden and Adolph Green
Subways Are for Sleeping (1961)

GIRLS 'N GIRLS 'N GIRLS
Irvin Graham
New Faces (1956)

GIRLS OF LONG AGO
Oscar Levant
Irving Caesar and Graham John
Ripples (1930)

GIRLS OF NEW YORK, THE
Seymour Furth and Lee Edwards
R. F. Carroll
Bringing Up Father (1925)

GIRLS OF SUMMER
Stephen Sondheim
Girls of Summer (1956)

GIRLS OF THE OLD BRIGADE, THE
Vincent Youmans
Anne Caldwell
Oh, Please! (1926)

GIRLS WANT A HERO
Duke Ellington
John Latouche
Beggar's Holiday (1946)

GIRLS WHO SELL ORANGEADE, THE
Edwin Greenberg
Pilgrim's Progress (OB) (1962)

GIRLS WHO SIT AND WAIT, THE
Jerry Herman
Madame Aphrodite (OB) (1961)

GITKA'S SONG, THE
Richard Rodgers
Martin Charnin
Two by Two (1970)

GIVE A GIRL A BREAK
Burton Lane
Ira Gershwin
Give a Girl a Break (F) (1953)

GIVE A LITTLE, GET A LITTLE
Jule Styne
Betty Comden and Adolph Green
Two on the Aisle (1951)

GIVE A LITTLE WHISTLE
Cy Coleman
Carolyn Leigh
Wildcat (1960)

GIVE AND TAKE
Hal Jordan
Jerry Douglas
Rondelay (OB) (1969)

GIVE 'EM A KISS
G. Wood
Put It in Writing (OB) (1963)

GIVE 'EM A LOLLIPOP
Robert Colby
Robert Colby and Nita Jonas
Half-Past Wednesday (OB) (1962)

GIVE ENGLAND STRENGTH
Jerry Bock
Sheldon Harnick
The Rothschilds (1970)

GIVE HER A KISS
Richard Rodgers
Lorenz Hart
The Phantom President (F) (1932)

GIVE HIM THE OO-LA-LA
Cole Porter
Du Barry Was a Lady (1939)

GIVE IT ALL YOU GOT
Jay Livingston and Ray Evans
Oh Captain! (1958)

GIVE IT BACK TO THE INDIANS
Richard Rodgers
Lorenz Hart
Too Many Girls (1939)

GIVE IT LOVE
Joseph Meyer
Floyd Huddleston
Shuffle Along (1952)

GIVE ME
Stan Harte, Jr.
Walt Whitman
Leaves of Grass (OB) (1971)

GIVE ME A CAUSE
Albert Hague
Allen Sherman
The Fig Leaves Are Falling (1969)

GIVE ME A MAN LIKE THAT
George A. Little and Art Sizemore
Brown Buddies (1930)

GIVE ME A NIGHT
Frank E. Harling
Say, Darling (1928)

GIVE ME A PINCH
Cy Young
That Hat! (OB) (1964)

GIVE ME A ROLL ON A DRUM
Sigmund Romberg
Irving Caesar
Melody (1933)

GIVE ME A STAR
David Krivoshei
David Paulsen
To Live Another Summer (1971)

GIVE ME ONE GOOD REASON
Walt Smith
Leon Uris
Ari (1971)

GIVE ME ONE HOUR
Rudolf Friml
Brian Hooker
The White Eagle (1927)

GIVE ME SOMEONE
Robert Hood Bowers
Francis DeWitt
Oh, Ernest! (1927)

GIVE ME THE RAIN
Maury Rubens
Lester Allen and Henry Creamer
Gay Paree (1925)

GIVE ME THE SUNSHINE
Jimmy Johnson
Henry Creamer and Con Conrad
Keep Shufflin' (1928)

GIVE ME THE WILD TRUMPETS
Irving Actman
Frank Loesser
The Illustrators' Show (1936)

GIVE ME YOUR LOVE
Al Wilson, Charles Weinberg, and
    Ken Macomber
Yeah Man (1932)

GIVE ME YOUR TIRED, YOUR POOR
Irving Berlin
Emma Lazarus
Miss Liberty (1949)

GIVE MY REGARDS TO BROADWAY
George M. Cohan
Little Johnny Jones (1904)

GIVE OUR CHILD A NAME
Ring Lardner
June Moon (1929)

GIVE SHALOM AND SABBATH TO JERUSALEM
Dov Seltzer
David Paulsen
To Live Another Summer (1971)

GIVE, SINBAD, GIVE
Clay Warnick
Edward Eager
Dream with Music (1944)

GIVE THE DOCTOR THE BEST IN THE HOUSE
Mischa and Wesley Portnoff
Donagh MacDonagh
Happy As Larry (1950)

GIVE THE LITTLE LADY A GREAT BIG HAND
Leroy Anderson
Joan Ford, Walter and Jean Kerr
Goldilocks (1958)

GIVE THIS LITTLE GIRL A HAND
Richard Rodgers
Lorenz Hart
Peggy-Ann (1926)

GIVE TROUBLE THE AIR
Louis Alter
Leo Robin
A la Carte (1927)

GIVE US THE CHARLESTON
Ray Henderson
B. G. DeSylva and Lew Brown
George White's Scandals (1925)

GIVE US THIS DAY
Earl Wilson, Jr.
A Day in the Life of Just About Every-one (OB) (1971)

GIVE YOUR HEART A CHANCE TO SING
Charles Gaynor
Lend an Ear (1948)

GIVE YOUR HEART IN JUNE-TIME
Victor Herbert
Clifford Grey and Harold Atteridge
Sky High (1925)

GIVERS AND GETTERS
Don Tucker
Red, White and Maddox (1969)

GIZA-ON-THE-NILE
Edwin Greenberg
Pilgrim's Progress (OB) (1962)

GLAD TIDINGS
Milton Ager
Jack Yellen
Rain or Shine (1928)

GLAD TO BE BACK
Richard Lewine
Arnold B. Horwitt
Make Mine Manhattan (1948)

GLAD TO BE HOME
Irving Berlin
Mr. President (1962)

GLAD TO BE UNHAPPY
Richard Rodgers
Lorenz Hart
On Your Toes (1936)

GLAD TO KNOW YA
Joseph Martinez Kookoolis and Scott Fagan
Scott Fagan
Soon (1971)

GLADIOLA GIRL, THE
Charles Gaynor
Lend an Ear (1948)

GLENDA'S PLACE
Moose Charlap
Norman Gimbel
Whoop-Up (1958)

GLIDING THROUGH MY MEMOREE
Richard Rodgers
Oscar Hammerstein II
Flower Drum Song (1958)

GLIMPSE OF LOVE*
Harold Rome
Wish You Were Here (1952)

GLITTER AND BE GAY
Leonard Bernstein
Richard Wilbur
Candide (1956)

GLORIA
Jerry Bock
Sheldon Harnick
The Body Beautiful (1958)

GLORIOUS CHEESE
Don Elliott
James Costigan
The Beast in Me (1963)

GLORIOUS RUSSIAN
Leslie Bricusse and Anthony Newley
Stop the World—I Want to Get Off (1962)

_____

*Dropped from New York production

GLORY OF SPRING, THE
Emile Berté and Maury Rubens
J. Keirn Brennan
Music in May (1929)

GLORY THAT IS GREECE, THE
Jacques Offenbach
E. Y. Harburg
The Happiest Girl in the World (1961)

GNU, A
Donald Swann
Michael Flanders
At the Drop of a Hat (1959)

GO DOWN TO BOSTON HARBOR
Burton Lane
Laffing Room Only (1944)

GO DOWN TO THE RIVER (WASHER WOMAN)
Baldwin Bergersen
William Archibald
Carib Song (1945)

GO GET 'IM
Walter Donaldson
Gus Kahn
Whoopee (1928)

GO-GETTER, THE
Jerome Kern
Anne Caldwell
The City Chap (1925)

GO, GO, GO
Don Elliott
James Costigan
The Beast in Me (1963)

GO HOME EV'RY ONCE IN A WHILE
George M. Cohan
Billie (1928)

GO HOME TRAIN
Jule Styne
Betty Comden and Adolph Green
Fade Out—Fade In (1964)

GO INTO YOUR DANCE
Cole Porter
The New Yorkers (1930)

GO INTO YOUR TRANCE
Hugh Martin and Timothy Gray
High Spirits (1964)

GO, LITTLE BOAT
Jerome Kern
P. G. Wodehouse
Miss 1917 (1917)

GO PLACES AND DO THINGS
Harry Ruby
Bert Kalmar
Animal Crackers (1928)

GO SIT BY THE BODY
Baldwin Bergersen
William Archibald
Carib Song (1945)

GO SLOW, JOHNNY
Noël Coward
Sail Away (1961)

GO SOUTH
Richard Myers
Owen Murphy
The Greenwich Village Follies (1925)

GO TO SLEEP
Burton Lane
Alan Jay Lerner
On a Clear Day You Can See Forever
(F) (1969)

GO TO SLEEP WHATEVER YOU ARE
Jerry Bock
Sheldon Harnick
The Apple Tree (1966)

GO UP TO THE MOUNTAIN
Walter Cool
Mackey of Appalachia (OB) (1965)

GO VISIT
John Kander
Fred Ebb
70, Girls, 70 (1971)

GOD BLESS THE HUMAN ELBOW
Mark Sandrich, Jr.
Sidney Michaels
Ben Franklin in Paris (1964)

GOD BLESS THE WOMEN
Cole Porter
Panama Hattie (1940)

GOD IS AN AMERICAN
Don Tucker
Red, White and Maddox (1969)

GOD IS BLACK
Dale F. Menten
Dale F. Menten and Frederick Gaines
The House of Leather (OB) (1970)

GOD IS GOOD TO THE IRISH
George M. Cohan
The Merry Malones (1927)

GOD-WHY-DON'T-YOU-LOVE-ME BLUES, THE
Stephen Sondheim
Follies (1971)

GOD WILL TAKE CARE
Coleridge-Taylor Perkinson
Ray McIver
God Is a (Guess What?) (OB) (1968)

GODDESS OF RAIN
Thomas (Fats) Waller and Harry Brooks
Andy Razaf
Hot Chocolates (1929)

GOD'S COUNTRY
Harold Arlen
E. Y. Harburg
Hooray for What! (1937)

GOD'S GREEN WORLD
Frederick Loewe
Alan Jay Lerner
The Day Before Spring (1945)

GOGO
Claude Leveilee
Gladys Shelley
Gogo Loves You (OB) (1964)

GOIN' HOME
Earl Wilson, Jr.
A Day in the Life of Just About Everyone (OB) (1971)

GOIN' HOME TRAIN
Harold Rome
Call Me Mister (1946)

GOIN' ON A HAYRIDE
Ralph Blane
Three Wishes for Jamie (1952)

GOING BACK HOME
Robert Stolz
Robert Sour
Mr. Strauss Goes to Boston (1945)

GOING DOWN
Galt MacDermot
Gerome Ragni and James Rado
Hair (1968)

GOING, GOING, GONE!
Henry Sullivan
Edward Eliscu
The Third Little Show (1931)

GOING NATIVE
Ed Tyler
Sweet Miani (OB) (1962)

GOING OVER THE BUMPS
Harold Levey
Owen Murphy
Rainbow Rose (1926)

GOING TO TOWN WITH ME
Burton Lane
Harold Adamson
Earl Carroll's Vanities (1931)

GOING UP
Louis A. Hirsch
Otto Harbach
Going Up (1917)

GOING UP
Jay Gorney
E. Y. Harburg
Earl Carroll's Vanities (1930)

GOLD CANNOT BUY
Frederico Valerio
Elizabeth Miele
Hit the Trail (1954)

GOLD FEVER
Andre Previn
Alan Jay Lerner
Paint Your Wagon (F) (1969)

GOLD, WOMEN AND LAUGHTER
Alma Sanders
Monte Carlo
Louisiana Lady (1947)

GOLDEN BOY
Charles Strouse
Lee Adams
Golden Boy (1964)

GOLDEN DAYS
Sigmund Romberg
Dorothy Donnelly
The Student Prince (1924)

GOLDEN GATE
Ray Perkins
Max and Nathaniel Lief
The Greenwich Village Follies (1928)

GOLDEN GATES OF HAPPINESS
J. Fred Coots
Clifford Grey
The Merry World (1926)

GOLDEN GOBLET
Edward Earle
Yvonne Tarr
The Decameron (OB) (1961)

GOLDEN HELMET
Mitch Leigh
Joe Darion
Man of La Mancha (1965)

GOLDEN LAND
Manos Hadjidakis
Joe Darion
Illya Darling (1967)

GOLDEN MOMENT
Jack Lawrence and Don Walker
Courtin' Time (1951)

GOLDEN RAINBOW
Walter Marks
Golden Rainbow (1968)

GOLDEN RAM, THE
Richard Rodgers
Martin Charnin
Two by Two (1970)

GOLDEN RULE SONG, THE
Coleridge-Taylor Perkinson
Ray McIver
God Is a (Guess What?) (OB) (1968)

GOLDFISH GLIDE
James F. Hanley
Eddie Dowling
Sidewalks of New York (1927)

GOLLIWOG
Vincent Valentini
Parisiana (1928)

GONDOLIER SONG
Rudolf Friml
Rowland Leigh and John Shubert
Music Hath Charms (1934)

GONE AWAY BLUES
Manning Sherwin
Arthur Herzog, Jr.
Bad Habits of 1926 (OB) (1926)

GONE, GONE, GONE!
George Gershwin
DuBose Heyward
Porgy and Bess (1935)

GONE IN SORROW
John Morris
Gerald Freedman
A Time for Singing (1966)

GONG SONG, THE
C. Jackson and James Hatch
Fly Blackbird (OB) (1962)

GONNA BUILD A MOUNTAIN
Leslie Bricusse and Anthony Newley
Stop the World—I Want to Get Off
(1962)

GONNA GET A WOMAN
Will Holt
That 5 A. M. Jazz (OB) (1964)

GOOCH'S SONG
Jerry Herman
Mame (1966)

GOOD AND LUCKY
Arthur Schwartz
Albert Stillman
Virginia (1937)

GOOD AS ANYBODY
Paul Klein
Fred Ebb
Morning Sun (OB) (1963)

GOOD AS ANYBODY
G. Wood
F. Jasmine Addams (OB) (1971)

GOOD BOY
Herbert Stothart, Bert Kalmar, and
Harry Ruby
Good Boy (1928)

GOOD BOY
Robert Waldman
Alfred Uhry
Here's Where I Belong (1968)

GOOD BOY WEDDING MARCH
Herbert Stothart, Bert Kalmar, and
Harry Ruby
Good Boy (1928)

GOOD CLEAN FUN
Jerry Bock
Sheldon Harnick
Tenderloin (1960)

GOOD CLEAN SPORT
Arthur Schwartz
Howard Dietz
The Second Little Show (1930)

GOOD EVENING, FRIENDS
Robert Katscher
Irving Caesar
The Wonder Bar (1931)

GOOD EVENING, MR. MAN IN THE MOON
Robert Russell Bennett

Owen Murphy and Robert A. Simon
Hold Your Horses (1933)

GOOD EVENING, PRINCESS
Cole Porter
You Never Know (1938)

GOOD FELLOW, MINE
Richard Rodgers
Lorenz Hart
The Girl Friend (1926)

GOOD FOR NOTHING
John Dooley
Hobo (OB) (1961)

GOOD FOR YOU—BAD FOR ME
Ray Henderson
B. G. DeSylva and Lew Brown
Flying High (1930)

GOOD FRIENDS
Charles Strouse
Lee Adams
Applause (1970)

GOOD FRIENDS SURROUND ME
Sigmund Romberg
Irving Caesar
Melody (1933)

GOOD GIRLS LOVE BAD MEN
Louis Alter
Harry Ruskin and Leighton K. Brill
Ballyhoo (1930)

GOOD-GOOD-GOOD
Philip Springer
Joan Javits
Hotel Passionato (OB) (1965)

GOOD LITTLE BOY
Wally Harper
Paul Zakrzewski
Sensations (OB) (1970)

GOOD LITTLE GIRLS
Vernon Duke
Sammy Cahn
The Littlest Revue (OB) (1956)

GOOD LUCK
Georges Bizet
Oscar Hammerstein II
Carmen Jones (1943)

GOOD MORNING
David Shire
Richard Maltby, Jr.
The Sap of Life (OB) (1961)

GOOD MORNING, DEARIE!
Jerome Kern
Anne Caldwell
Good Morning, Dearie (1921)

GOOD MORNING, GOOD DAY
Jerry Bock
Sheldon Harnick
She Loves Me (1963)

GOOD MORNING, DR. PUFFIN
Alec Wilder
Arnold Sundgaard
Kittiwake Island (OB) (1960)

GOOD MORNING, MISS STANDING
Cole Porter
Jubilee (1935)

GOOD MORNING STARSHINE
Galt MacDermot
Gerome Ragni and James Rado
Hair (1968)

GOOD NEWS
Ray Henderson
B. G. DeSylva and Lew Brown
Good News (1927)

GOOD NIGHT
George Lessner
Miriam Battista and Russell Maloney
Sleepy Hollow (1948)

GOOD NIGHT
Harvey Schmidt
Tom Jones
I Do! I Do! (1966)

GOOD NIGHT, GOOD NEIGHBOR
Arthur Schwartz
Frank Loesser
Thank Your Lucky Stars (F) (1943)

GOOD NIGHT HYMN
Richard Hill and John Hawkins
Nevill Coghill
Canterbury Tales (1969)

GOOD NIGHT LADIES
Edward Kunneke
Clifford Grey
Mayflowers (1925)

GOOD NIGHT, MY BEAUTIFUL
Sammy Fain
Jack Yellen
George White's Scandals (1939)

GOOD OLD DAYS, THE
Ray Henderson
B. G. DeSylva and Lew Brown
George White's Scandals (1931)

GOOD OLD DAYS, THE
Richard Lewine
Arnold B. Horwitt and Ted Fetter
Make Mine Manhattan (1948)

GOOD OLD DAYS
Earl Robinson
Waldo Salt
Sandhog (OB) (1954)

GOOD OLD DAYS, THE
Duke Ellington
Marshall Barer and Fred Tobias
Pousse-Café (1966)

GOOD OLD EGG, A
Maurice Yvain
Max and Nathaniel Lief
Luckee Girl (1928)

GOOD OLD GIRL
David Martin
Langston Hughes
Simply Heavenly (1957)

GOOD OLD WAYS, THE
Jacques Urbont
Bruce Geller
All in Love (OB) (1961)

GOOD PALS
Sigmund Romberg
Harry B. Smith
The Love Call (1927)

GOOD TIME CHARLIE
Arthur Schwartz
Dorothy Fields
By the Beautiful Sea (1954)

GOOD TIME CHARLIE
David Baker
Will Holt
Come Summer (1969)

GOOD TIMES ARE HERE TO STAY
Jim Wise
George Haimsohn
Dames at Sea (OB) (1968)

GOOD TO BE ALIVE
Harold Rome
The Zulu and the Zayda (1965)

GOOD-WILL MOVEMENT, THE
Cole Porter
Mexican Hayride (1944)

GOODBYE, AU REVOIR, AUF WIEDER-SEHN*
Eric Coates
Irving Caesar
White Horse Inn (1936)

GOODBYE, CANAVARO
John Kander
Fred Ebb
Zorbá (1968)

GOODBYE CHARLIE
Duke Ellington
Marshall Barer and Fred Tobias
Pousse-Café (1966)

GOODBYE, DARLIN'
Frank Loesser
The Most Happy Fella (1956)

GOODBYE, DEAR FRIEND
Jack Lawrence and Don Walker
Courtin' Time (1951)

GOODBYE, FAILURE, GOODBYE
Elmer Bernstein
Carolyn Leigh
How Now, Dow Jones (1967)

GOODBYE GIRLS, HELLO YALE
Richard Lewine
Ted Fetter
Naughty-Naught (OB) (1937)

GOODBYE GIRLS, I'M THROUGH
Ivan Caryll
John Golden
Chin-Chin (1914)

GOODBYE, GEORG
Jerry Bock
Sheldon Harnick
She Loves Me (1963)

GOODBYE, JONAH
Arthur Schwartz
Albert Stillman
Virginia (1937)

GOOD-BYE, LENNY!
Richard Rodgers
Lorenz Hart
The Girl Friend (1926)

GOODBYE, LITTLE DREAM, GOOD-BYE†
Cole Porter
Red, Hot and Blue! (1936)

GOODBYE, MY BACHELOR
David Baker
Will Holt
Come Summer (1969)

GOODBYE, MY CITY
Frank Fields
Armand Aulicino
The Shoemaker and the Peddler (OB) (1960)

---

*Adapted from Coates' *Knightsbridge March*
†Dropped fron New York production

GOODBYE, MY FANCY
Stan Harte, Jr.
Walt Whitman
Leaves of Grass (OB) (1971)

GOODBYE, MY SWEET
John Clifton
John Clifton and Ben Tarver
Man with a Load of Mischief (OB)
(1966)

GOODBYE, OLD GIRL
Richard Adler and Jerry Ross
Damn Yankees (1955)

GOODBYE, PAREE
Franz Lehár
Harry Graham
Yours Is my Heart (1946)

GOODBYE TO ALL THAT
Arthur Schwartz
Ira Gershwin
Park Avenue (1946)

GOODBYES
Kenn Long and Jim Crozier
Kenn Long
Touch (OB) (1970)

GOODNESS GRACIOUS
Harry Ruby
Bert Kalmar
Top Speed (1929)

GOODNIGHT
John Addison
John Cranko
Cranks (1956)

GOODNIGHT MY SOMEONE
Meredith Willson
The Music Man (1957)

GOONA GOONA
Gerald Dolin
Edward J. Lambert
Smile at Me (1935)

GOONA-GOONA
Jerome Moross

John Latouche
The Golden Apple (1954)

GOOSE NEVER BE A PEACOCK
Harold Arlen
Johnny Mercer
Saratoga (1959)

GORGEOUS
Jerry Bock
Sheldon Harnick
The Apple Tree (1966)

GORGEOUS ALEXANDER
Sigmund Romberg
Oscar Hammerstein II
The New Moon (1928)

GOSPEL: GREAT DAY
Vernon Duke
John Latouche
Cabin in the Sky (OB) (1964)

GOSPEL OF NO NAME CITY, THE
Andre Previn
Alan Jay Lerner
Paint Your Wagon (F) (1969)

GOSSIP
Franz Steininger (adapted from
  Tchaikovsky)
Forman Brown
Music in My Heart (1947)

GOSSIP
Coleman Dowell
The Tattooed Countess (OB) (1961)

GOSSIP SONG, THE
Harold Arlen
Johnny Mercer
Saratoga (1959)

GOSSIP SONG, THE
Rick Besoyan
Babes in the Wood (OB) (1964)

GOSSIPS, THE
Frank Loesser
Where's Charley? (1948)

GOT A BRAN' NEW SUIT
Arthur Schwartz
Howard Dietz
At Home Abroad (1935)

GOT A RAINBOW
George Gershwin
Ira Gershwin
Treasure Girl (1928)

GOT THAT GOOD TIME FEELIN'
Burton Lane
Laffing Room Only (1944)

GOT THE WORLD IN THE PALM OF MY HAND
Johnny Brandon
Cindy (OB) (1964)

GOT TO BE A WOMAN NOW
Earl Wilson, Jr.
A Day in the Life of Just About Everyone (OB) (1971)

GOT TO FIND MY WAY
Coleman Dowell
The Tattooed Countess (OB) (1961)

GOT TO GO TO TOWN
Harry Warren
Mort Dixon and Joe Young
The Laugh Parade (1931)

GOT WHAT IT TAKES
Sammy Stept
Dan Shapiro
Michael Todd's Peep Show (1950)

GOTT ISS GUT
Jule Styne
Sammy Cahn
Look to the Lilies (1970)

GOTTA DANCE
Hugh Martin
Look Ma, I'm Dancin'! (1948)

GOTTA FIND A WAY TO DO IT
Roger Wolfe Kahn
Paul James
Nine-Fifteen Revue (1930)

GOTTA GET DE BOAT LOADED
Al Wilson, Charles Weinberg, and Ken Macomber
Yeah Man (1932)

GOTTA GET JOY
Burton Lane
Al Dubin and Burton Lane
Laffing Room Only (1944)

GOTTA HAVE HIPS NOW
Russell Tarbox
Charles O. Locke
Hello, Paris (1930)

GOTTA HAVE ME GO WITH YOU
Harold Arlen
Ira Gershwin
A Star Is Born (F) (1954)

GOTTA LIVE FREE
Giuseppe Verdi
Charles Friedman
My Darlin' Aïda (1952)

GOTTA PAY
Walter Cool
Mackey of Appalachia (OB) (1965)

GRADE POLONAISE
Lee Pockriss
Anne Croswell
Tovarich (1963)

GRADUATES OF MRS. GRIMM'S LEARNING
Dale F. Menten
Dale F. Menten and Frederick Gaines
The House of Leather (OB) (1970)

GRAND AND GLORIOUS FOURTH, THE
Robert Stolz
Robert Sour
Mr. Strauss Goes to Boston (1945)

GRAND IMPERIAL CIRQUE DE PARIS
Bob Merrill
Carnival (1961)

GRAND JURY JUMP
Paul Klein
Fred Ebb
From A to Z (1960)

GRAND KNOWING YOU
Jerry Bock
Sheldon Harnick
She Loves Me (1963)

GRAND OLD IVY
Frank Loesser
*How to Succeed in Business without
    Really Trying* (1961)

GRAND PARADE, THE
William Roy
The Penny Friend (OB) (1966)

GRAND PRIX OF PORTOFINO, THE
Louis Bellson and Will Irwin
Richard Ney
Portofino (1958)

GRANDFATHERS
Robert Colby
Robert Colby and Nita Jonas
Half-Past Wednesday (OB) (1962)

GRANDIOSO
Richard Freitas
Morty Neff and George Mysels
The Difficult Woman (OB) (1962)

GRANDPAPA
John Kander
Fred Ebb
Zorbá (1968)

GRANT
Oscar Brand
How to Steal an Election (OB) (1968)

GRANT AVENUE
Richard Rodgers
Oscar Hammerstein II
Flower Drum Song (1958)

GRASSHOP SONG
Robert Larimer
King of the Whole Damn World! (OB)
    (1962)

GRAY GOOSE, THE
George Lessner
Miriam Battista and Russell Maloney
Sleepy Hollow (1948)

GRAZIE PER NIENTE
Sammy Fain
Marilyn and Alan Bergman
Something More! (1964)

GREAT BIG BEAR
Herbert Stothart
Otto Harbach and Oscar Hammer-
    stein II
Song of the Flame (1925)

GREAT CHANDELIER
Sylvia Fine
The Straw Hat Revue (1939)

GREAT DAY!
Vincent Youmans
Billy Rose and Edward Eliscu
Great Day! (1929)

GREAT DICTATOR AND ME, THE
Frank D'Armond
Will Morrissey
Saluta (1934)

GREAT IF, THE
Helen Miller
Eve Merriam
Inner City (1971)

GREAT INDOORS, THE
Cole Porter
The New Yorkers (1930)

GREAT LITTLE GUY
Lewis E. Gensler
Robert A. Simon
Ups-A-Daisy (1928)

GREAT SCOT!
Don McAfee
Nancy Leeds
Great Scot! (OB) (1965)

GREAT UNKNOWN, THE
William Roy
The Penny Friend (OB) (1966)

GREAT WHITE FATHER
Gary Geld
Peter Udell
Purlie (1970)

GREAT WHITE WAY IN CHINA
A. Baldwin Sloane
Harry Cort and George E. Stoddard
China Rose (1925)

GREAT WORKERS FOR THE CAUSE
Norman Campbell
Donald Campbell and Norman Campbell
Anne of Green Gables (OB) (1971)

GREAT ZAMPANO, THE
Lionel Bart
La Strada (1969)

GREATEST INVENTION, THE
Matt Dubey, Harold Karr, and Sid Silvers
New Faces (1956)

GREATEST SHOW ON EARTH, THE
Kurt Weill
Ira Gershwin
Lady in the Dark (1941)

GREATHEAD SHIELD
Earl Robinson
Waldo Salt
Sandhog (OB) (1954)

GRECIAN BEND, THE
Edward Kunneke
Clifford Grey
Mayflowers (1925)

GREEDY GIRL
Marc Blitzstein
Regina (1949)

GREEK MARINE, THE
Jacques Offenbach
E. Y. Harburg
The Happiest Girl in the World (1961)

GREEN AND BLUE
Eubie Blake
J. Milton Reddie and Cecil Mack
Swing It (1937)

GREEN CARNATIONS
Noël Coward
Bitter Sweet (1929)

GREEN PASTURES
Will Morrissey and Andy Razaf
Blackbirds (1930)

GREEN-UP TIME
Kurt Weill
Alan Jay Lerner
Love Life (1948)

GREENWICH VILLAGE U.S.A.
Jeanne Bargy
Jeanne Bargy, Frank Gehrecke, and Herb Corey
Greenwich Village U.S.A. (OB) (1960)

GREENWILLOW CHRISTMAS
Frank Loesser
Greenwillow (1960)

GREETING
Heitor Villa-Lobos
Robert Wright and George Forrest
Magdalena (1948)

GREETING CARDS, THE
Vernon Duke
John Latouche
Banjo Eyes (1941)

GREETINGS
Rick Besoyan
The Student Gypsy (OB) (1963)

GREETINGS, GATES
Hoagy Carmichael
Johnny Mercer
Walk with Music (1940)

GRENADIERS' MARCHING SONG, THE
Rick Besoyan
The Student Gypsy (OB) (1963)

GRINGOLA
Charles Tobias, Charles Newman, and Murray Mencher
Earl Carroll's Sketch Book (1935)

GROCERY BOY
Jacques Urbont
David Newburger
Stag Movie (OB) (1971)

GROVE OF EUCALYPTUS, THE
Naomi Shemer
George Sherman
To Live Another Summer (1971)

GROWING PAINS
Don Walker
Clay Warnick
Memphis Bound (1945)

GROWING PAINS
Arthur Schwartz
Dorothy Fields
A Tree Grows in Brooklyn (1951)

GRUNTLED
Ray Golden, Sy Kleinman, and Philip
   Charig
Catch a Star! (1955)

GUARANTEE
Walter Marks
Bajour (1964)

GUARDED
Emmerich Kalman
Harry B. Smith
The Circus Princess (1927)

GUARDS OF FANTASY, THE
Maury Rubens
Clifford Grey
The Great Temptations (1926)

GUENEVERE
Frederick Loewe
Alan Jay Lerner
Camelot (1960)

GUESS WHO I SAW TODAY?
Murray Grand
Elisse Boyd
New Faces (1952)

GUESTS, THE
Irving Berlin
The Cocoanuts (1925)

GUILTY!
Frank Fields
Armand Aulicino
The Shoemaker and the Peddler (OB)
   (1960)

GUINESS, WOMAN
Kenn Long and Jim Crozier
Kenn Long
Touch (OB) (1970)

GUITAR SONG
Peter Link
C. C. Courtney and Ragan Courtney
Earl of Ruston (1971)

GUNMAN, THE
Raymond Hubbell
Anne Caldwell
Yours Truly (1927)

GUS AND SADIE LOVE SONG
Marc Blitzstein
The Cradle Will Rock (1938)

GUSSY AND THE BEAUTIFUL PEOPLE
Mildred Kayden
Frank Gagliano
Paradise Gardens East (OB) (1969)

GUSTO
Hal Jordan
Jerry Douglas
Rondelay (OB) (1969)

GUTTER SONG, THE
James Shelton
New Faces (1934)

GUY, A GUY, A GUY, A
Alfred Brooks
Ira J. Bilowit
Of Mice and Men (OB) (1958)

GUY WHO BROUGHT ME, THE
Hugh Martin and Ralph Blane
Best Foot Forward (1941)

GUYS AND DOLLS
Frank Loesser
Guys and Dolls (1950)

GYPSY
Harden Church
Edward Heyman
Caviar (1934)

GYPSY DAYS
Arthur Schwartz
Morrie Ryskind
Ned Wayburn's Gambols (1929)

GYPSY IN ME, THE
Cole Porter
Anything Goes (1934)

GYPSY JOE
Walter Donaldson
Gus Kahn
Whoopee (1928)

GYPSY LIFE, THE
Rick Besoyan
The Student Gypsy (OB) (1963)

GYPSY LOVE
Jimmy McHugh
Dorothy Fields
Lew Leslie's International Revue
(1930)

GYPSY OF LOVE
Rick Besoyan
The Student Gypsy (OB) (1963)

GYPSY ROSE
Lewis E. Gensler
Owen Murphy and Robert A. Simon
The Gang's All Here (1931)

GYPSY SWEETHEART
Irving Kahal, Francis Wheeler, and
    Ted Snyder
Footlights (1927)

HA! CHA! CHA!
Jerome Kern
Otto Harbach
The Cat and the Fiddle (1931)

HACIENDA GARDEN
Ida Hoyt Chamberlain
Enchanted Isle (1927)

HAIL BRITANNIA
Irving Burgie
Ballad for Bimshire (OB) (1963)

HAIL, HAIL, HAIL
Cole Porter
Out of This World (1950)

HAIL SPHINX
Ervin Drake
Her First Roman (1968)

HAIL STONEWALL JACKSON
Sigmund Romberg
Dorothy Donnelly
My Maryland (1927)

HAIL THE BRIDEGROOM
A. Baldwin Sloane
Harry Cort and George B. Stoddard
China Rose (1925)

HAIL, THE CONQUERING HERO!
Moose Charlap
Norman Gimbel
The Conquering Hero (1961)

HAIL THE HAPPY COUPLE
George Gershwin
Ira Gershwin
Pardon My English (1933)

HAIL THE KING
H. Maurice Jacquet
Preston Sturges
The Well of Romance (1930)

HAIL, THE MYTHIC SMEW
Alec Wilder
Arnold Sundgaard
Kittiwake Island (OB) (1960)

HAIL THE SON OF DAVID
Ernest Gold
Anne Croswell
I'm Solomon (1968)

HAIL TO MacCRACKEN'S
Johnny Mercer
Top Banana (1951)

HAIL TO THE BLOOD
Horald Griffiths
Blood (OB) (1971)

HAIR
Galt MacDermot
Gerome Ragni and James Rado
Hair (1968)

HAIR OF THE HEIR, THE
Edward A. Horan
Frederick Herendeen
All the King's Horses (1934)

HAIRPIN HARMONY
Harold Orlob
Hairpin Harmony (1943)

HALF A MOON
James F. Hanley
Eddie Dowling and Herbert Reynolds
Honeymoon Lane (1926)

HALF A SIXPENCE
David Heneker
Half a Sixpence (1965)

HALF ALIVE
Helen Miller
Eve Merriam
Inner City (1971)

HALF AS BIG AS LIFE
Burt Bacharach
Hal David
Promises, Promises (1968)

HALF-CASTE WOMAN
Noël Coward
Ziegfeld Follies (1931)

HALF OF IT, DEARIE, BLUES, THE
George Gershwin
Ira Gershwin
Lady, Be Good (1924)

HALF OF ME
George Fischoff
Carole Bayer
Georgy (1970)

HALF THE BATTLE
Mark Sandrich, Jr.
Sidney Michaels
Ben Franklin in Paris (1964)

HALF WAY TO HEAVEN
Mario Braggiotti
David Sidney
The Vanderbilt Revue (1930)

HALLELUJAH!
Vincent Youmans
Leo Robin and Clifford Grey
Hit the Deck (1927)

HALLELUJAH
Don Elliott
James Costigan
The Beast in Me (1963)

HALLELUJAH, BABY!
Jule Styne
Betty Comden and Adolph Green
Hallelujah, Baby! (1967)

HALLELUJAH, I'M A BUM
Richard Rodgers
Lorenz Hart
Hallelujah, I'm a Bum (F) (1933)

HALLOWEEN HAYRIDE
Nancy Ford
Gretchen Cryer
Now Is the Time for All Good Men
  (OB) (1967)

HALLOWE'EN WHOOPEE BALL
Walter Donaldson
Gus Kahn
Whoopee (1928)

HAM AND EGGS IN THE MORNING
Con Conrad and Abner Silver
Al Dubin
Take the Air (1927)

HAMBURG WALTZ
Gerard Calvi
Harold Rome
La Grosse Valise (1965)

HAMMOCK IN THE BLUE
Jacques Belasco
Kay Twomey
The Girl from Nantucket (1945)

HAND IN HAND
Jane Douglas
Tom O'Malley
Bella (OB) (1961)

HAND IN HAND
Robert Wright and George Forest
(based on Rachmanioff)
Anya(1965)

HAND ME DOWN THAT CAN O' BEANS
Frederick Loewe
Alan Jay Lerner
Paint Your Wagon (1951)

HANDBAG IS NOT A PROPER MOTHER, A
Lee Pockriss
Anne Croswell
Ernest in Love (OB) (1960)

HANDSOME HUSBANDS
Baldwin Bergersen
William Archibald
The Crystal Heart (OB) (1960)

HANG A LITTLE MOOLAH ON THE WASHLINE
Claibe Richardson
Kenward Elmslie
The Grass Harp (1971)

HANG ON TO ME
George Gershwin
Ira Gershwin
Lady, Be Good (1924)

HANG UP!
Arthur Schwartz
Dorothy Fields
By the Beautiful Sea (1954)

HANG UP YOUR HAT ON BROADWAY
Edward Ward
George Waggner, Grossman and
Sylvester
Tattle Tales (1933)

HANG YOUR HAT ON THE MOON
Jean Schwartz
Clifford Grey and William Cary Duncan
Sunny Days (1928)

HANGIN' AROUND WITH YOU
George Gershwin
Ira Gershwin
Strike Up the Band (1930)

HANGING AROUND YO' DOOR
James P. Johnson
Flournoy Miller
Sugar Hill (1931)

HANGING THROTTLEBOTTOM IN THE MORNING
George Gershwin
Ira Gershwin
Let 'Em Eat Cake (1933)

HANGMAN'S PLEA, THE
Richard Freitas
Morty Neff and George Mysels
The Difficult Woman (OB) (1962)

HANNIBAL'S COMIN'
Robert Rosenblum
Robert Rosenblum and Howard Schuman
Up Eden (OB) (1968)

HAPPIEST DAY OF MY LIFE, THE
Burton Lane
Alan Jay Lerner
Royal Wedding (F) (1951)

HAPPIEST GIRL IN THE WORLD, THE
Jacques Offenbach
E. Y. Harburg
The Happiest Girl in the World (1961)

HAPPIEST HOUSE ON THE BLOCK, THE
Richard Rodgers
Oscar Hammerstein II
Pipe Dream (1955)

HAPPILY EVER AFTER
Mary Rodgers
Marshall Barer
Once Upon a Mattress (OB) (1959)

HAPPINESS
Marie Gordon
David Rogers
New Faces (1962)

HAPPINESS
Clark Gesner
You're a Good Man, Charlie Brown
(OB) (1967)

HAPPINESS AND JOY TO THE KING
Albert Sirmay and Arthur Schwartz
Arthur Swanstrom
Princess Charming (1930)

HAPPINESS IS A THING CALLED JOE
Harold Arlen
E. Y. Harburg
Cabin In the Sky (F) (1943)

HAPPY
Porter Grainger and Freddie Johnson
Lucky Sambo (1925)

HAPPY
Frank Grey
Earle Crooker and McElbert Moore
Happy (1927)

HAPPY
George M. Cohan
Billie (1928)

HAPPY
Nat Reed
Bob Joffe
Brown Buddies (1930)

HAPPY BECAUSE I'M IN LOVE
Vincent Youmans
Billy Rose and Edward Eliscu
Great Day! (1929)

HAPPY BIRTHDAY
George Gershwin
Gus Kahn and Ira Gershwin
Show Girl (1929)

HAPPY BIRTHDAY
Jay Livingston and Ray Evans
Let It Ride (1961)

HAPPY BIRTHDAY
John Kander
Fred Ebb
Zorbá (1968)

HAPPY BIRTHDAY, MRS. J. J. BROWN
Meredith Willson
The Unsinkable Molly Brown (1960)

HAPPY BRIDE
A. Baldwin Sloane
Harry Cort and George E. Stoddard
China Rose (1925)

HAPPY DAYS
Ray Henderson
B. G. DeSylva and Lew Brown
Good News (1927)

HAPPY DAZE SALOON, THE
Will Holt
That 5 A. M. Jazz (OB) (1964)

HAPPY ENDING
Harvey Schmidt
Tom Jones
The Fantasticks (OB) (1960)

HAPPY ENDING
Hal Jordan
Jerry Douglas
Rondelay (OB) (1969)

HAPPY GO LUCKY
Lucien Denni
Helena Evans
Happy Go Lucky (1926)

HAPPY GO LUCKY
Harry Ruby
Bert Kalmar
The Five O'Clock Girl (1927)

HAPPY GUY
Jeanne Bargy
Jeanne Bargy, Frank Gehrecke, and
Herb Corey
Greenwich Village U.S.A. (OB) (1960)

HAPPY HABIT
Arthur Schwartz
Dorothy Fields
By the Beautiful Sea (1954)

HAPPY HEAVEN OF HARLEM, THE
Cole Porter
Fifty Million Frenchmen (1929)

HAPPY HOBOES
Ray Henderson
B. G. DeSylva
Three Cheers (1928)

HAPPY HOLIDAY
Irving Berlin
Holiday Inn (F) (1942)

HAPPY HUNTING
Sammy Fain
E. Y. Harburg
Flahooley (1951)

HAPPY HUNTING
Harold Karr
Matt Dubey
Happy Hunting (1956)

HAPPY HUNTING HORN
Richard Rodgers
Lorenz Hart
Pal Joey (1940)

HAPPY IN LOVE
Sammy Fain
Jack Yellen
Sons o' Fun (1941)

HAPPY LANDING
Ray Henderson
B. G. DeSylva and Lew Brown
Flying High (1930)

HAPPY LITTLE CROOK
Victor Young
Stella Unger
Seventh Heaven (1955)

HAPPY LITTLE JEANNE
Carol Millöcker (revised by Theo
   Mackeben)
Rowland Leigh
The Dubarry (1932)

HAPPY LITTLE WEEKEND
Robert Russell Bennett
Owen Murphy and Robert A. Simon
Hold Your Horses (1933)

HAPPY LOVE AFFAIR
Claude Leveilee
Gladys Shelley
Gogo Loves You (OB) (1964)

HAPPY MELODY
Lucien Denni
Helena Evans
Happy Go Lucky (1926)

HAPPY NEW YEAR
Don McAfee
Nancy Leeds
Great Scot! (OB) (1965)

HAPPY RICKSHAW MAN
Sigmund Romberg
Harry B. Smith
Cherry Blossoms (1927)

HAPPY SONG, A
Donald Swann
Michael Flanders
At the Drop of a Hat (1959)

HAPPY SONG
Gerard Calvi
Harold Rome
La Grosse Valise (1965)

HAPPY TALK
Richard Rodgers
Oscar Hammerstein II
South Pacific (1949)

HAPPY THE DAY
Jack Waller and Joseph Tunbridge
R. P. Weston and Bert Lee
Tell Her the Truth (1932)

HAPPY TIME, THE
John Kander
Fred Ebb
The Happy Time (1968)

Happy to Keep His Dinner Warm
Frank Loesser
How to Succeed in Business Without Really Trying (1961)

Happy to Make Your Acquaintance
Frank Loesser
The Most Happy Fella (1956)

Happy Years, The
Raymond Taylor
Lester Judson
Chic (OB) (1959)

Harbor of Dreams
George Gershwin
Ira Gershwin
Tip-Toes (1925)

Harbor of My Heart, The
Vincent Youmans
Leo Robin and Clifford Grey
Hit the Deck (1927)

Hard Hat Stetsons
Clinton Ballard
Carolyn Richter
The Ballad of Johnny Pot (OB) (1971)

Hard Time War Time
The Blood Company
Blood (OB (1971)

Hard Times
C. Luckey Roberts
Alex C. Rogers
My Magnolia (1926)

Hard to Get Along With
Charles Rosoff
Leo Robin
Judy (1927)

Harder They Fall, The
Gary Geld
Peter Udell
Purlie (1970)

Hare Krishna
Galt MacDermot
Gerome Ragni and James Rado
Hair (1968)

Harem, The
Irving Gordon, Alan Roberts, and Jerome Brainin
Star and Garter (1942)

Hark to the Song of the Night
Cole Porter
Out of This World (1950)

Harlem
Ford Dabney
Jo Trent
Rang-Tang (1927)

Harlem Dan
Alexander Hill
Hummin' Sam (1933)

Harlem Lullaby
Willard Robison
Tattle Tales (1933)

Harlem Mania
Donald Heywood
Blackberries of 1932

Harlem Moon
Alberta Nichols
Mann Holiner
Rhapsody in Black (1931)

Harlem Serenade
George Gershwin
Gus Kahn and Ira Gershwin
Show Girl (1929)

Harlequinade
Richard Adler and Jerry Ross
John Murray Anderson's Almanac (1953)

Harmony
Jimmy Van Heusen
Johnny Burke
Nellie Bly (1946)

Harmony
John Kander
James Goldman, John Kander, and William Goldman
A Family Affair (1962)

HARMONY
Mildred Kayden
Frank Gagliano
Paradise Gardens East (OB) (1969)

HARMONY, MASS.
William Dyer
Don Parks and William Dyer
Jo! (OB) (1964)

HARMONY, SWEET HARMONY
Willard Straight
David Eddy
The Athenian Touch (OB) (1964)

HARRIET SEDLEY
Laurence Rosenthal
James Lipton
Sherry! (1967)

HARRIGAN
George M. Cohan
Fifty Miles from Boston (1908)

HAS ANYONE SEEN MY DADDY
Steven Metcalf
Fred Bluth
Drat! (OB) (1971)

HAS ANYBODY HERE SEEN KELLY?
John Charles Moore, C. W. Murphy,
   and William J. McKenna
The Jolly Bachelors (1910)

HAS ANYBODY SEEN OUR SHIP?
Noël Coward
Tonight at 8:30 (Red Peppers) (1936)

HAS I LET YOU DOWN?
Harold Arlen
Harold Arlen and Truman Capote
House of Flowers (1954)

HASHISH
Galt MacDermot
Gerome Ragni and James Rado
Hair (1968)

HASSELTOWN
Kenn Long and Jim Crozier
Kenn Long
Touch (OB) (1970)

HAT, THE
Lee Pockriss
Anne Croswell
Ernest in Love (OB) (1960)

HATE SONG
Mary Rodgers
Steven Vinaver
The Mad Show (OB) (1966)

HATHOR
Peter Stampfel
Operation Sidewinder (1970)

HATS OFF
Richard Lewine
Ted Fetter
The Girl from Wyoming (OB)
(1938)

HAUNTED HEART
Arthur Schwartz
Howard Dietz
Inside U.S.A. (1948)

HAUNTED HOT SPOT
Vernon Duke
Ogden Nash
Two's Company (1952)

HAUNTING REFRAIN
William Heagney
William Heagney and Tom Connell
There You Are (1932)

HAUTE COUTURE
Jimmy Van Heusen
Sammy Cahn
Skyscraper (1965)

HAVANA
Richard Rodgers
Lorenz Hart
Peggy-Ann (1926)

HAVANOLA
Frank Grey
McElbert Moore and Frank Grey
The Matinee Girl (1926)

HAVE A DREAM
Charles Strouse
Lee Adams
All American (1962)

HAVE A HEART
Burton Lane
Harold Adamson
Earl Carroll's Vanities (1931)

HAVE A LITTLE SOOTH ON ME
Willard Straight
David Eddy
The Athenian Touch (OB) (1964)

HAVE I GOT A GIRL FOR YOU
Jerry Blatt
Jerry Blatt and Lonnie Burstein
Have I Got One for You (OB) (1968)

HAVE I GOT A GIRL FOR YOU
Stephen Sondheim
Company (1970)

HAVE I TOLD YOU LATELY?
Harold Rome
I Can Get It for You Wholesale (1962)

HAVE SOME POT
Clinton Ballard
Carolyn Richter
The Ballad of Johnny Pot (OB) (1971)

HAVE YOU EVER BEEN ALONE WITH
A KING BEFORE?
Bill Weeden
David Finkle
I'm Solomon (1968)

HAVE YOU EVER SEEN A PRETTIER
LITTLE CONGRESS?
Jerry Bock
Sheldon Harnick
The Rothschilds (1970)

HAVE YOU FORGOTTEN?
Emil Gerstenberger and Carle Carlton
Howard Johnson
The Lace Petticoat (1927)

HAVE YOU GOT CHARM?
Irving Burgie
Ballad for Bimshire (OB) (1963)

HAVE YOU HEARD?
Ernest Gold
Anne Croswell
I'm Solomon (1968)

HAVE YOU HEARD THE NEWS?
Glenn Paxton
Robert Goldman and George Weiss
First Impressions (1959)

HAVE YOU MET DELILAH?
James Mundy
John Latouche
The Vamp (1955)

HAVE YOU MET MISS JONES?
Richard Rodgers
Lorenz Hart
I'd Rather Be Right (1937)

HAVE YOU SEEN THE COUNTESS
CINDY?
David Raksin
June Carroll
If the Shoe Fits (1946)

HAVE YOU USED SOFT SOAP?
Albert Von Tilzer
Neville Fleeson
Bye Bye, Bonnie (1927)

HAVE YOURSELF A MERRY LITTLE
CHRISTMAS
Hugh Martin and Ralph Blane
Meet Me in St. Louis (F) (1944)

HAVEN'T WE MET BEFORE?
Jerry Livingston
Mack David
Bright Lights of 1944 (1943)

HAVEN'T YOU WONDERED
Robert Rosenblum
Robert Rosenblum and Howard Schuman
Up Eden (OB) (1968)

HAVIN' A TIME
Morton Gould
Betty Comden and Adolph Green
Billion Dollar Baby (1945)

HAVIN' A WONDERFUL TIME
Porter Grainger and Freddie Johnson
Lucky Sambo (1925)

HAWAII
Richard Rodgers
Lorenz Hart
Present Arms (1928)

HAWAII
Gerard Calvi
Harold Rome
La Grosse Valise (1965)

HAY, HAY, HAY
Bronislaw Kaper
John Latouche
Polonaise (1945)

HAY! STRAW!
Vincent Youmans
Oscar Hammerstein II
Rainbow (1928)

HAYWIRE
Edward Heyman
Caviar (1934)

HE AIN'T GOT RHYTHM
Irving Berlin
On the Avenue (F) (1937)

HE AND SHE
Richard Rodgers
Lorenz Hart
The Boys from Syracuse (1938)

HE CAN DANCE
Sammy Fain
Irving Kahal
Right This Way (1938)

HE CAN DO IT
Gary Geld
Peter Udell
Purlie (1970)

HE CAN, I CAN
Claude Leveilee
Gladys Shelley
Gogo Loves You (OB) (1964)

HE COULD SHOW ME
Nancy Ford
Gretchen Cryer
Now Is the Time for All Good Men
   (OB) (1967)

HE DIED GOOD
Frank Loesser
Greenwillow (1960)

HE FOLLOWS ME AROUND
Buster Davis
Steven Vinaver
Diversions (OB) (1958)

"HE" FOR ME, THE
Rudolf Friml
P. G. Wodehouse and Clifford Grey
The Three Musketeers (1928)

HE HAD REFINEMENT
Arthur Schwartz
Dorothy Fields
A Tree Grows in Brooklyn (1951)

HE HASN'T A THING EXCEPT ME
Vernon Duke
Ira Gershwin
Ziegfeld Follies (1936)

HE IS THE TYPE
Jerome Kern
Anne Caldwell
The City Chap (1925)

HE JUST BEATS A TOM-TOM
Harry Akst
Lew Brown
Calling All Stars (1934)

HE KNOWS WHERE THE ROSE IS IN
BLOOM
Robert Hood Bowers
Francis DeWitt
Oh, Ernest! (1927)

HE KNOWS WHERE TO FIND ME
Don McAfee
Nancy Leeds
Great Scot! (OB) (1965)

HE LOVES AND SHE LOVES
George Gershwin
Ira Gershwin
Funny Face (1927)

HE LOVES HER
Sammy Fain
Paul Francis Webster
Christine (1960)

HE LOVES ME
Cliff Allen
Nancy Hamilton
New Faces (1934)

HE MAKES ME FEEL I'M LOVELY
Johnny Burke
Donnybrook! (1961)

HE MAN
Richard Myers
Leo Robin
Hello, Yourself! (1928)

HE NEEDS ME NOW
Walter Marks
Golden Rainbow (1968)

HE NEEDS YOU
Jay Livingston and Ray Evans
Let It Ride (1961)

HE PLAYS THE VIOLIN
Sherman Edwards
1776 (1969)

HE TAKES ME OFF HIS INCOME TAX
Arthur Siegel
June Carroll
New Faces (1952)

HE TALKS TO ME
Lance Mulcahy
Paul Cherry
Park (1970)

HE TOSSED A COIN
Jerry Bock
Sheldon Harnick
The Rothschilds (1970)

HE TRIED TO MAKE A DOLLAR
Jule Styne
Sammy Cahn
High Button Shoes (1947)

HE WAS THERE
Stanley Lebowsky
Fred Tobias
Gantry (1970)

HE WAS TOO GOOD TO ME*
Richard Rodgers
Lorenz Hart
Simple Simon (1930)

HE WILL TONIGHT
Morton Gould
Dorothy Fields
Arms and the Girl (1950)

HEAD DOWN THE ROAD
Clinton Ballard
Carolyn Richter
The Ballad of Johnny Pot (OB) (1971)

HEAD IN THE STARS
Sol Kaplan
Edward Eliscu
The Banker's Daughter (OB) (1962)

HEAD OVER HEELS IN LOVE
James F. Hanley
Eddie Dowling
Honeymoon Lane (1926)

HEADACHE AND A HEARTACHE, A
Walter Kent
Kim Gannon
Seventeen (1951)

HEADIN' FOR A WEDDIN'
Abraham Ellstein
Walter Bullock
Great to Be Alive (1950)

———
*Dropped before New York opening

HEADIN' FOR HARLEM
James F. Hanley
Eddie Dowling
Sidewalks of New York (1927)

HEADIN' FOR THE BOTTOM
Sammy Fain
Dan Shapiro
Ankles Aweigh (1955)

HEADIN' SOUTH
C. Luckey Roberts
Alex C. Rogers
My Magnolia (1926)

HEADLINES
Frank Fields
Armand Aulicino
The Shoemaker and the Peddler (OB)
    (1960)

HEADSMAN AND I, THE
Armando Trovaioli
Pietro Garinei and Sandro Giovannini
Rugantino (1964)

HEAR THE GUNS
Margaret Dorn, Elizabeth Howard,
    and Tom Willis
Doug Dyer
Blood (OB) (1971)

HEAR THE GYPSIES PLAYING
Sigmund Romberg
Otto Harbach
Forbidden Melody (1936)

HEAR THE TRUMPET CALL
Sigmund Romberg
Harry B. Smith
The Love Call (1927)

HEART HAS WON THE GAME, THE
Glenn Paxton
Robert Goldman and George Weiss
First Impressions (1959)

HEART IN HAND
Jack Lawrence and Don Walker
Courtin' Time (1951)

HEART IS FREE, THE
Emil Gerstenberger and Carle Carl-
    ton
Howard Johnson
The Lace Petticoat (1927)

**HEART IS QUICKER THAN THE EYE,
THE**
Richard Rodgers
Lorenz Hart
On Your Toes (1936)

HEART OF A ROSE
Maury Rubens and Sam Timberg
Moe Jaffe
Broadway Nights (1929)

HEART OF MINE
Rudolf Friml
P. G. Wodehouse and Clifford Grey
The Three Musketeers (1928)

HEART OF STONE
Leroy Anderson
Joan Ford, Walter and Jean Kerr
Goldilocks (1958)

HEARTS AND FLOWERS
Noël Coward
Tonight at 8:30 (Family Album)
    (1936)

HEAT WAVE
Irving Berlin
As Thousands Cheer (1933)

HEATHER ON THE HILL, THE
Frederick Loewe
Alan Jay Lerner
Brigadoon (1947)

HEAVEN HOP
Cole Porter
Paris (1928)

**HEAVEN IN MY ARMS (MUSIC IN MY
HEART)**
Jerome Kern
Oscar Hammerstein II
Very Warm for May (1939)

HEAVEN ON EARTH
George Gershwin
Ira Gershwin and Howard Dietz
Oh, Kay! (1926)

HEAVEN ON EARTH
Jay Gorney
Barry Trivers
Heaven on Earth (1948)

HEAVEN ON THEIR MINDS
Andrew Lloyd Webber
Tim Rice
Jesus Christ Superstar (1971)

HEAVEN PROTECT ME!
Gordon Duffy
Harry M. Haldane
Happy Town (1959)

HEAVEN SENT
Gerald Marks
Sam Lerner
Hold It! (1948)

HEAVENLY PARTY, A
Jerome Kern
Dorothy Fields
The Joy of Living (F) (1938)

HEAVYWEIGHT CHAMP OF THE WORLD
Moose Charlap
Eddie Lawrence
Kelly (1965)

HEEBIE-JEEBIE FURIES
Jim Turner
Doug Dyer
Blood (OB) (1971)

HEEL AND TOE
Philip Charig
Irving Caesar
Polly (1929)

HEH HEH GOOD MORNIN' SUNSHINE
Melvin Van Peebles
Ain't Supposed to Die a Natural Death (1971)

HEIDELBERG STEIN SONG
Gustav Luders
Frank Pixley
The Prince of Pilsen (1903)

HEIGH-HO CHEERIO
Harry Archer
Walter O'Keefe
Just a Minute (1928)

HEIGH-HO, LACKADAY!
Richard Rodgers
Lorenz Hart
Dearest Enemy (1925)

HEIGH HO, THE GANG'S ALL HERE
Burton Lane
Harold Adamson
Earl Carroll's Vanities (1931)

HELEN IS ALWAYS WILLING
Jerome Moross
John Latouche
The Golden Apple (1954)

HELEN QUIT YOUR YELLIN'
Joseph Raposo
Erich Segal
Sing Muse! (OB) (1961)

HELENA
Rick Besoyan
Babes in the Wood (OB) (1964)

HELENA'S SOLUTION
Rick Besoyan
Babes in the Wood (OB) (1964)

HE'LL COME TO ME CRAWLING
Richard B. Chodosh
Barry Alan Grael
The Streets of New York (OB) (1963)

HE'LL NEVER BE MINE
Walt Smith
Leon Uris
Ari (1971)

HELL HATH NO FURY
James Bredt
Edward Eager
The Happy Hypocrite (OB) (1968)

HELL OF A HOLE, A
George Gershwin
Ira Gershwin
Let 'Em Eat Cake (1933)

HELLO
Richard Rodgers
Lorenz Hart
Peggy-Ann (1926)

HELLO, COUSIN LOLA
William B. Kernell
Dorothy Donnelly
Hello, Lola (1926)

HELLO, DOLLY!
Jerry Herman
Hello, Dolly! (1964)

HELLO, FRISCO, HELLO
Louis A. Hirsch
Gene Buck
Ziegfeld Follies (1915)

HELLO, HAZEL
Jule Styne
Bob Hilliard
Hazel Flagg (1953)

HELLO, HELLO THERE
Jule Styne
Betty Comden and Adolph Green
Bells Are Ringing (1956)

HELLO, I LOVE YOU, GOODBYE
Leon Carr
Earl Shuman
The Secret Life of Walter Mitty (OB)
(1964)

HELLO IS THE WAY THINGS BEGIN
Lance Mulcahy
Paul Cherry
Park (1970)

HELLO, MA
Michael H. Cleary
Max and Nathaniel Lief
The Illustrators' Show (1936)

HELLO, MY LOVER, GOODBYE
John Green
Edward Heyman
Here Goes the Bride (1931)

HELLO, THE LITTLE BIRDS HAVE FLOWN
Carlton Kelsey and Maury Rubens
Clifford Grey
Sky High (1925)

HELLO, TUCKY
Joseph Meyer and James F. Hanley
B. G. DeSylva
Big Boy (1925)

HELLO, WAVES
John Kander
Fred Ebb
Flora, the Red Menace (1965)

HELLO WORLD
Johnny Brandon
Billy Noname (OB) (1970)

HELLO YANK
Edward Thomas
Martin Charnin
Ballad for a Firing Squad (OB) (1968)

HELLO, YOUNG LOVERS
Richard Rodgers
Oscar Hammerstein II
The King and I (1951)

HELLO, YOURSELF
Richard Myers
Leo Robin
Hello, Yourself! (1928)

HELL'S FINEST
Alma Sanders
Monte Carlo
The Houseboat on the Styx (1928)

HELLZAPOPPIN'
Sammy Fain
Charles Tobias
Hellzapoppin' (1938)

HELP THE SEAMEN
Frank D'Armond
Will Morrissey
Saluta (1934)

HELP US TONIGHT
Vincent Youmans
Billy Rose and Edward Eliscu
Great Day! (1929)

HELP YOURSELF TO HAPPINESS
Harry Revel
Harry Richman and Mack Gordon
Ziegfeld Follies (1931)

HENCE IT DON'T MAKE SENSE
Cole Porter
Seven Lively Arts (1944)

HENRY IS WHERE IT'S AT
Joseph Martinez Kookoolis and Scott
  Fagan
Scott Fagan
Soon (1971)

HENRY STREET
Jule Styne
Bob Merrill
Funny Girl (1964)

HENRY, SWEET HENRY
Bob Merrill
Henry, Sweet Henry (1967)

HER ANXIETY
John Duffy
Rocco Bufano and John Duffy (based
  on W.B. Yeats)
Horseman, Pass By (OB) (1969)

HER FACE
Bob Merrill
Carnival (1961)

HER FIRST ROMAN
Ervin Drake
Her First Roman (1968)

HER IS
Richard Adler and Jerry Ross
The Pajama Game (1954)

HER POP'S A COP
Ned Lehak
Irving Crane and Phil Conwit
Sing for Your Supper (1939)

HERE AM I
Jerome Kern
Oscar Hammerstein II
Sweet Adeline (1929)

HERE AM I—BROKEN HEARTED
Ray Henderson
B. G. DeSylva and Lew Brown
Artists and Models (1927)

HERE AND NOW
George Lessner
Miriam Battista and Russell Maloney
Sleepy Hollow (1948)

HERE AND NOW
Noël Coward
The Girl Who Came to Supper (1963)

HERE AND THERE
Gerald Dolin
Edward J. Lambert
Smile at Me (1935)

HERE ARE WE
Sam Pottle
Tom Whedon
All Kinds of Giants (OB) (1961)

HERE COME YOUR MEN
John Morris
Gerald Freedman
A Time for Singing (1966)

HERE COMES MY BLACKBIRD
Jimmy McHugh
Dorothy Fields
Blackbirds (1928)

HERE COMES THE BALLAD
Buster Davis
Steven Vinaver
Diversions (OB) (1958)

HERE COMES THE PRINCE OF WALES
Arthur Schwartz
Henry Myers
The New Yorkers (1927)

HERE I AM
Bob Merrill
Henry, Sweet Henry (1967)

HERE I AM
Dale F. Menten
Dale F. Menten and Frederick Gaines
The House of Leather (OB) (1970)

HERE I COME
Louis Bellson and Will Irwin
Richard Ney
Portofino (1958)

HERE I COME
George Harwell
What a Killing (OB) (1961)

HERE I GO AGAIN
Harry Revel
Arnold B. Horwitt
Are You With It? (1945)

HERE I'LL STAY
Kurt Weill
Alan Jay Lerner
Love Life (1948)

HERE IN EDEN
Jerry Bock
Sheldon Harnick
The Apple Tree (1966)

HERE IN MY ARMS
Richard Rodgers
Lorenz Hart
Dearest Enemy (1925)

HERE IN MY HEART
Joseph Meyer
William Moll
Jonica (1930)

HERE IN THE DARK
Emmerich Kalman and Herbert Stothart
Otto Harbach and Oscar Hammerstein II
Golden Dawn (1927)

HERE IT IS
Ray Henderson
B. G. DeSylva and Lew Brown
George White's Scandals (1931)

HERE SHE COMES
Richard Rodgers
Lorenz Hart
She's My Baby (1928)

HERE SHE COMES NOW
Jule Styne
Betty Comden and Adolph Green
Two on the Aisle (1951)

HERE THEY COME NOW
Al Carmines
Rosalyn Drexler
Home Movies (OB) (1964)

HERE 'TIS
Eubie Blake
Noble Sissle
Shuffle Along (1933)

HERE 'TIS
Donald Heywood
Black Rhythm (1936)

HERE TONIGHT, TOMORROW WHERE?
Robert Wright and George Forrest (based on Rachmaninoff)
Anya (1965)

HERE WE ARE AGAIN
Richard Rodgers
Stephen Sondheim
Do I Hear a Waltz? (1965)

HERE WE ARE IN LOVE
Ben Oakland
Jack Murray and Barry Trivers
Ziegfeld Follies (1931)

HERE WE ARE IN LOVE
Jean Gilbert
Harry B. Smith
Marching By (1932)

HEREDITY—ENVIRONMENT
David Baker
Fred Ebb
Smiling, the Boy Fell Dead (OB)
(1961)

HERE'S A DAY TO BE HAPPY
Vincent Youmans
Harold Adamson and Clifford Grey
Smiles (1930)

HERE'S A HAND
Richard Rodgers
Lorenz Hart
By Jupiter (1942)

HERE'S A KISS
Richard Rodgers
Lorenz Hart
Dearest Enemy (1925)

HERE'S A KISS FOR CINDERELLA
George Gershwin
Ira Gershwin
Of Thee I Sing (1931)

HERE'S A TOAST
Noël Coward
Tonight at 8:30 (Family Album)
(1936)

HERE'S HOW
Sigmund Romberg
Dorothy Donnelly
My Princess (1927)

HERE'S HOWE
Joseph Meyer and Roger Wolfe Kahn
Irving Caesar
Here's Howe (1928)

HERE'S LOVE
Meredith Willson
Here's Love (1963)

HERE'S THAT RAINY DAY
Jimmy Van Heusen
Johnny Burke
Carnival in Flanders (1953)

HERE'S TO DEAR OLD US
Sammy Fain
Dan Shapiro
Ankles Aweigh (1955)

HERE'S TO NIGHT
Henry Sullivan
Edward Eliscu
A Little Racketeer (1932)

HERE'S TO THE GIRL OF MY HEART
Walter Donaldson
Gus Kahn
Whoopee (1928)

HERE'S TO US
Cy Coleman
Carolyn Leigh
Little Me (1962)

HERE'S TO YOU
Harden Church
Edward Heyman
Caviar (1934)

HERE'S TO YOU, JACK
Frank Grey
Earle Crooker and McElbert Moore
Happy (1927)

HERE'S TO YOUR ILLUSIONS
Sammy Fain
E. Y. Harburg
Flahooley (1951)

HERE'S WHAT A MISTRESS OUGHT
TO BE
Deed Meyer
She Shall Have Music (OB) (1959)

HERE'S WHAT I'M HERE FOR
Harold Arlen
Ira Gershwin
A Star Is Born (F) (1954)

HERE'S WHERE I BELONG
Robert Waldman
Alfred Uhry
Here's Where I Belong (1968)

HERMITS, THE
Richard Rodgers
Lorenz Hart
Dearest Enemy (1925)

HERNANDO'S HIDEAWAY
Richard Adler and Jerry Ross
The Pajama Game (1954)

HEROES IN THE FALL
Richard Rodgers
Lorenz Hart
Too Many Girls (1939)

HEROISM
Alyn Heim
Malcolm L. LaPrade
Will the Mail Train Run Tonight?
   (OB) (1964)

HERO'S LOVE, A
David Shire
Richard Maltby, Jr.
The Sap of Life (OB) (1961)

HE'S A BOLD ROGUE
Mischa and Wesley Portnoff
Donagh MacDonagh
Happy As Larry (1950)

HE'S A GENIUS
Jule Styne
E. Y. Harburg
Darling of the Day (1968)

HE'S A MAN'S MAN
Ray Henderson
B. G. DeSylva and Lew Brown
Follow Thru (1929)

HE'S A RIGHT GUY
Cole Porter
Something for the Boys (1943)

HE'S A WINNER
Richard Rodgers
Lorenz Hart
The Girl Friend (1926)

HE'S BACK
John Kander
Fred Ebb
The Happy Time (1968)

**HE'S BEGINNING TO LOOK A LOT
LIKE ME**
Earl Wilson, Jr.
*A Day in the Life of Just About Every-
one* (OB) (1971)

HE'S GOIN' HOME
Arthur Schwartz
Dorothy Fields
Stars in Your Eyes (1939)

HE'S GOOD FOR NOTHING BUT ME
Vernon Duke
Howard Dietz
Jackpot (1944)

HE'S HERE!
Elmer Bernstein
Carolyn Leigh
How Now, Dow Jones (1967)

HE'S JUST MY IDEAL
Werner Janssen
Mann Holiner and J. Keirn Brennan
Boom-Boom (1929)

HE'S IN LOVE!
Robert Wright and George Forrest
   (based on Alexander Borodin)
Kismet (1953)

HE'S NEVER TOO BUSY
Stanley Lebowsky
Fred Tobias
Gantry (1970)

HE'S NOT FOR ME
Don McAfee
Nancy Leeds
Great Scot! (OB) (1965)

HE'S NOT HIMSELF
George Gershwin
Ira Gershwin
Pardon My English (1933)

HE'S ONLY WONDERFUL
Sammy Fain
E. Y. Harburg
Flahooley (1951)

HE'S THE MAN
William Roy
Maggie (1953)

HE'S WITH MY JOHNNY
Mischa and Wesley Portnoff
Donagh MacDonagh
Happy As Larry (1950)

HE'S WONDERFUL
Kenneth Jacobson
Rhoda Roberts
Show Me Where the Good Times Are
  (OB) (1970)

HEY, BABE, HEY
Cole Porter
Born to Dance (F) (1936)

HEY BOY
Ron Steward and Neal Tate
Ron Steward
Sambo (OB) (1969)

HEY! FELLAH!
Jerome Kern
Oscar Hammerstein II
Show Boat (1927)

HEY, GAL!
Will Irwin
June Carroll
New Faces (1943)

HEY, GIRLIE
Richard Rodgers
Martin Charnin
Two by Two (1970)

HEY, GOOD-LOOKIN'
Cole Porter
Something for the Boys (1943)

HEY! HEY!
Richard Rodgers
Lorenz Hart
The Girl Friend (1926)

HEY, JIMMY, JOE, JOHN, JIM, JACK
Jay Livingston and Ray Evans
Let It Ride (1961)

HEY JOE
Earl Robinson
Waldo Salt
Sandhog (OB) (1954)

HEY, LOOK ME OVER
Cy Coleman
Carolyn Leigh
Wildcat (1960)

HEY, LOVE
Mary Rodgers
Martin Charnin
Hot Spot (1963)

HEY, MADAME
Jay Livingston and Ray Evans
Oh Captain! (1958)

HEY, NONNY, HEY
Max Ewing
Agnes Morgan
The Grand Street Follies (1928)

HEY NONNY NONNY
Will Irwin
Ogden Nash
Hey Nonny Nonny! (1932)

HEY, RUBE
Milton Ager
Jack Yellen
Rain or Shine (1928)

HEY THERE
Richard Adler and Jerry Ross
The Pajama Game (1954)

HEY, WHAT'S THIS?
Meyer Kupferman
Paul Goodman
Jonah (OB) (1966)

HI DE HI DE HI, HI DE HI DE HO
Robert Dahdah
Curley McDimple (OB) (1967)

HI, PAISANO
Robert Holton
June Carroll
Hi, Paisano! (OB) (1961)

HIC HAEC HOC
Mark Sandrich, Jr.
Sidney Michaels
Ben Franklin in Paris (1964)

HICKETY, PICKETY
Helen Miller
Eve Merriam
Inner City (1971)

HICKORY, DICKORY
Alyn Heim
Malcolm L. LaPrade
Will the Mail Train Run Tonight?
(OB) (1964)

HIGH AIR
Earl Robinson
Waldo Salt
Sanghog (OB) (1954)

HIGH AND LOW
Arthur Schwartz
Howard Dietz
The Band Wagon (1931)

HIGH HAT
George Gershwin
Ira Gershwin
Funny Face (1927)

HIGH, HIGH, HIGH
Emile Berté and Maury Rubens
J. Keirn Brennan
Music in May (1929)

HIGH, HIGH UP IN THE CLOUDS
Maury Rubens
Max and Nathaniel Lief
The Greenwich Village Follies (1928)

HIGH IS BETTER THAN LOW
Arthur Schwartz
Howard Dietz
Jennie (1963)

HIGH JINKS (SOMETHING SEEMS
TINGLE-INGLEING)
Rudolf Friml
Otto Harbach
High Jinks (1913)

HIGH LONESOME
Horald Griffiths
Doug Dyer
Blood (OB) (1971)

HIGH SHOES
Robert Russell Bennett
Owen Murphy and Robert A. Simon
Hold Your Horses (1933)

HIGH SOCIETY CALYPSO
Cole Porter
High Society (F) (1956)

HIGH STREET, AFRICA
Vivian Ellis
Graham John
By the Way (1925)

HIGH UP
Coleman Dowell
The Tattooed Countess (OB) (1961)

HIGH UP ON THE HILLS
Ralph Benatzky
Irving Caesar
White Horse Inn (1936)

HIGH, WIDE, AND HANDSOME
Jerome Kern
Oscar Hammerstein II
High, Wide, and Handsome (F) (1937)

HIGHBROW, LOWBROW
Jay Gorney
Jean and Walter Kerr
Touch and Go (1949)

HIGHEST JUDGE OF ALL, THE
Richard Rodgers
Oscar Hammerstein II
Carousel (1945)

HIGHWAY'S CALL, THE
Will Ortman
Gus Kahn and Raymond B. Egan
Holka-Polka (1925)

HIIAKA
Eaton Magoon, Jr.
13 Daughters (1961)

HILL OF DREAMS
Robert Wright and George Forrest
  (based on Grieg)
Song of Norway (1944)

HILLS OF IXOPO, THE
Kurt Weill
Maxwell Anderson
Lost in the Stars (1949)

HIMMLISHER VATER
Jule Styne
Sammy Cahn
Look to the Lilies (1970)

HINDU SERENADE
Ray Henderson
Jack Yellen
Ziegfeld Follies (1943)

HIP-HOORAY FOR WASHINGTON
Don Tucker
Red, White and Maddox (1969)

HIPPOPOTAMUS, THE
Donald Swann
Michael Flanders
At the Drop of a Hat (1959)

HIRE A GUY
Mary Rodgers
Marshall Barer
From A to Z (1960)

HIS AND HERS
Sammy Fain
Dan Shapiro
Ankles Aweigh (1955)

HIS LOVE MAKES ME BEAUTIFUL
Jule Styne
Bob Merrill
Funny Girl (1964)

HIS OLD MAN
Harold Rome
Call Me Mister (1946)

HIS OWN LITTLE ISLAND
Jay Livingston and Ray Evans
Let It Ride (1961)

HIS SPANISH GUITAR
Frank Grey
McElbert Moore and Frank Grey
The Matinee Girl (1926)

HISTORY IS MADE AT NIGHT
Harold Rome
The Streets of Paris (1939)

**HISTORY OF THREE GENERATIONS
OF CHORUS GIRLS, THE**
Oscar Straus
Clare Kummer
Three Waltzes (1937)

HIT IT, LORRAINE
John Kander
Fred Ebb
70, Girls, 70 (1971)

HIT THE RAMP
Vernon Duke
John Latouche
The Lady Comes Across (1942)

HIT THE ROAD TO DREAMLAND
Harold Arlen
Johnny Mercer
Star Spangled Rhythm (F) (1942)

HITCH YOUR WAGON TO A STAR
Richard Lewine
Ted Fetter
Broadway Sho-Window (1936)

HITTING ON HIGH
Frank Grey
Earle Crooker and McElbert Moore
Happy (1927)

HITTIN' THE BOTTLE
Harold Arlen
Ted Koehler
Earl Carroll's Vanities (1930)

HIYA SUCKER
Jesse Greer
Stanley Adams
Shady Lady (1933)

H. N. I. C.
Oscar Brown, Jr.
Buck White (1969)

Ho, Billy O!
Kurt Weill
Alan Jay Lerner
Love Life (1948)

Hobohemia
Charles Rosoff
Leo Robin
Judy (1927)

Hoch, Caroline!
Jack Waller and Joseph Tunbridge
R. P. Weston and Bert Lee
Tell Her the Truth (1932)

Hoe Down
Don Tucker
Red, White and Maddox (1969)

Hoedown!
Gordon Duffy
Harry M. Haldane
Happy Town (1959)

Hog Beneath the Skin, The
Donald Swann
Michael Flanders
At the Drop of a Hat (1959)

Hogan's Alley
Henry Souvaine and Jay Gorney
Morrie Ryskind and Howard Dietz
Merry-Go-Round (1927)

Hoku Loa
Rudolf Friml
J. Keirn Brennan
Luana (1930)

Hola, Follow, Follow Me
Emmerich Kalman
Harry B. Smith
Countess Maritza (1926)

Hold It!
Gerald Marks
Sam Lerner
Hold It! (1948)

Hold Me Closer
Max Rich, Frank Littau, and Jack
  Scholl
George White's Music Hall Varieties
  (1932)

Hold Me—Hold Me—Hold Me
Jule Styne
Betty Comden and Adolph Green
Two on the Aisle (1951)

Hold On to Your Hats
Burton Lane
E. Y. Harburg
Hold On to Your Hats (1940)

Hold On to Your Hats
Steve Allen
Sophie (1963)

Hold That Smile
Ray Henderson
Jack Yellen
Ziegfeld Follies (1943)

Hold Your Horses
Robert Russell Bennett
Owen Murphy and Robert A. Simon
Hold Your Horses (1933)

Holding Hands
Frank Grey
McElbert Moore and Frank Grey
The Matinee Girl (1926)

Hold Your Man
Maurice Yvain
Max and Nathaniel Lief
Luckee Girl (1928)

Holiday in the Country
Jimmy McHugh
Harold Adamson
As the Girls Go (1948)

Holka-Polka
Will Ortman
Gus Kahn and Raymond B. Egan
Holka-Polka (1925)

HOLLER BLUE MURDER
Carl Sigman
Bob Hilliard
Angel in the Wings (1947)

HOLLOW
Susan Hulsman Bingham
Myrna Lamb
Mod Donna (OB) (1970)

HOLLYWOOD AND VINE
Sam Stept
Lew Brown and Charles Tobias
Yokel Boy (1939)

HOLLYWOOD AND VINE
Stephen Sondheim
Twigs (1971)

HOLLYWOOD, PARK AVENUE AND BROADWAY
Ray Henderson
B. G. DeSylva and Lew Brown
Strike Me Pink (1933)

HOLLYWOOD PARTY
Richard Rodgers
Lorenz Hart
Hollywood Party (F) (1934)

HOLLYWOOD STORY
Hugh Martin and Ralph Blane
Best Foot Forward (OB) (1963)

HOLMES AND WATSON
Milton Schafer
Ira Levin
Drat! The Cat! (1965)

HOME
A. Baldwin Sloane
Harry Cort and George E. Stoddard
China Rose (1925)

HOME
Sol Berkowitz
James Lipton
Miss Emily Adam (OB) (1960)

HOME
John Kander

Fred Ebb
70, Girls, 70 (1971)

HOME AGAIN
Jerry Bock
Sheldon Harnick
Fiorello (1959)

HOME BLUES
George Gershwin
Gus Kahn and Ira Gershwin
Show Girl (1929)

HOME FOR YOU, A
Rudolf Friml
Brian Hooker
The White Eagle (1927)

HOME FREE ALL
Mitch Leigh
William Alfred and Phyllis Robinson
Cry for Us All (1970)

HOME IS WHERE THE HEART IS
Jay Gorney
Barry Trivers
Heaven on Earth (1948)

HOME IS WHERE YOU HANG YOUR HAT
Berenice Kazounoff
John Latouche
Two for Tonight (OB) (1939)

HOME O' MINE
Jean Gilbert
Harry B. Smith
The Red Rose (1928)

HOME OF MY HEART
Will Ortman
Gus Kahn and Raymond B. Egan
Holka-Polka (1925)

HOME OF OUR OWN, A
Harold Rome
Call Me Mister (1946)

HOME SWEET HEAVEN
Hugh Martin and Timothy Gray
High Spirits (1964)

HOME TO HARLEM
Ray Henderson
B. G. DeSylva and Lew Brown
Strike Me Pink (1933)

HOME TOWN
Harold Orlob
Irving Caesar
Talk About Girls (1927)

HOME TOWN GIRL
Coleman Dowell
The Tattooed Countess (OB) (1961)

HOMECOMING
Giuseppe Verdi
Charles Friedman
My Darlin' Aïda (1952)

HOMELAND
Sigmund Romberg
Arthur Wimperis
Louie the 14th (1925)

HOMELAND
Armand Vecsey
P. G. Wodehouse
The Nightingale (1927)

HOMELY BUT CLEAN
Vincent Youmans
Anne Caldwell
Oh, Please! (1926)

HOMESICK
Robert Rosenblum
Robert Rosenblum and Howard
  Schuman
Up Eden (OB) (1968)

HOMESICK BLUES
Jule Styne
Leo Robin
Gentlemen Prefer Blondes (1949)

HOMESICK IN OUR HEARTS
Ed Tyler
Sweet Miani (OB) (1962)

HOMEWARD
Sol Berkowitz
James Lipton
Miss Emily Adam (OB) (1960)

HOMEWARD
Robert Wright and George Forrest
  (based on Rachmaninoff)
Anya (1965)

HOMEWORK
Irving Berlin
Miss Liberty (1949)

HOMOGENEOUS CABINET, A
Richard Rodgers
Lorenz Hart
I'd Rather Be Right (1937)

**HONEST CONFESSION IS GOOD FOR
THE SOUL**
Peter Link and C. C. Courtney
Salvation (OB) (1969)

HONEST HONORE
Deed Meyer
'Toinette (OB) (1961)

HONEST MAN
Walter Marks
Bajour (1964)

HONESTLY SINCERE
Charles Strouse
Lee Adams
Bye Bye Birdie (1960)

HONESTY
J. C. Johnson
Change Your Luck (1930)

HONEY, BE MINE
James F. Hanley
Gene Buck
No Foolin' (1926)

HONEY, BE MY HONEY-BEE
Maury Rubens and J. Fred Coots
Clifford Grey
The Madcap (1928)

HONEY BUN
Richard Rodgers
Oscar Hammerstein II
South Pacific (1949)

HONEY GAL O' MINE
Georges Bizet
Oscar Hammerstein II
Carmen Jones (1943)

HONEY, I'M IN LOVE WITH YOU
Con Conrad
William B. Friedlander
Mercenary Mary (1925)

HONEY IN THE HONEYCOMB
Vernon Duke
John Latouche
Cabin in the Sky (1940)

HONEY MAN SONG
Oscar Brown, Jr.
Buck White (1969)

HONEY TO LOVE, A
Ed Tyler
Sweet Miani (OB) (1962)

HONEYMOON
Sammy Fain
Dan Shapiro
Ankles Aweigh (1955)

HONEYMOON CHOO-CHOO
Alyn Heim
Malcolm L. LaPrade
Will the Mail Train Run Tonight?
(OB) (1964)

HONEYMOON IS OVER, THE
Frank Black
Gladys Shelley
The Duchess Misbehaves (1946)

HONEYMOON IS OVER, THE
Jerry Bock
Sheldon Harnick
The Body Beautiful (1958)

HONEYMOON IS OVER, THE
Harvey Schmidt
Tom Jones
I Do! I Do! (1966)

HONEYMOONING BLUES
Maury Rubens
Clifford Grey
The Madcap (1928)

HONEYSUCKLE VINE
Kenneth Gaburo
Seyril Schochen
The Tiger Rag (OB) (1961)

HONG KONG GONG
Stefan Kanfer, Jess J. Korman, and Joseph Grayhon
I Want You (OB) (1961)

HONOLULU
Marc Blitzstein
The Cradle Will Rock (1938)

HONOR
Hal Jordan
Jerry Douglas
Rondelay (OB) (1969)

HONOR AND GLORY
Karl Hajos (based on Tchaikovsky)
Harry B. Smith
Natja (1925)

HONOR OF THE FAMILY
George M. Cohan
The Merry Malones (1927)

HONORABLE MAMBO
Dean Fuller
Marshall Barer
Ziegfeld Follies (1957)

HONORABLE PROFESSION OF THE FOURTH ESTATE, THE*
Irving Berlin
Miss Liberty (1949)

HONOUR
Jacques Urbont
Bruce Geller
All in Love (OB) (1961)

HOOF, HOOF
Philip Charig and Richard Myers
Leo Robin
Allez-Oop (1927)

------

*Dropped from New York production

HOOKER, THE
Helen Miller
Eve Merriam
Inner City (1971)

HOOMALIMALI
Eaton Magoon, Jr.
13 Daughters (1961)

HOOP-DE-DINGLE
Harold Rome
Destry Rides Again (1959)

HOOPS
Arthur Schwartz
Howard Dietz
The Band Wagon (1931)

HOORAY FOR ANYWHERE
Burton Lane
Laffing Room Only (1944)

HOORAY FOR CAPTAIN SPALDING!
Harry Ruby
Bert Kalmar
Animal Crackers (1928)

HOORAY FOR GEORGE THE THIRD
Arthur Schwartz
Dorothy Fields
By the Beautiful Sea (1954)

HOORAY FOR LOVE
Harold Arlen
Leo Robin
Casbah (F) (1948)

HOORAY FOR WHAT!
Harold Arlen
E. Y. Harburg
Hooray for What! (1937)

HOOSIER WAY, THE
Walter Kent
Kim Gannon
Seventeen (1951)

HOOTIN' OWL TRAIL
Robert Emmett Dolan
Johnny Mercer
Texas, Li'l Darlin' (1949)

HOP, A SKIP, A JUMP, A LOOK, A
Fred Spielman and Arthur Gershwin
Stanley Adams
A Lady Says Yes (1945)

HOPE FOR THE BEST
Arthur Schwartz
Ira Gershwin
Park Avenue (1946)

HOPE YOU COME BACK
Richard Adler and Jerry Ross
John Murray Anderson's Almanac
(1953)

HOROSCOPE
Donald Swann
Michael Flanders
At the Drop of Another Hat (1966)

HORRIBLE, HORRIBLE LOVE
Hugh Martin
Look Ma, I'm Dancin'! (1948)

HORRORTORIO
Jack Waller and Joseph Tunbridge
R. P. Weston and Bert Lee
Tell Her the Truth (1932)

HORS D'OEUVRES
Herman Hupfeld
A la Carte (1927)

HORSE, THE
Gary William Friedman
Will Holt
The Me Nobody Knows (OB) (1970)

HORSESHOES ARE LUCKY
Robert Emmett Dolan
Johnny Mercer
Texas, Li'l Darlin' (1949)

HOSANNA
Andrew Lloyd Webber
Tim Rice
Jesus Christ Superstar (1971)

HOSE BOYS
Richard Lewine
Ted Fetter
The Fireman's Flame (OB) (1937)

HOSTESS WITH THE MOSTES' ON THE BALL
Irving Berlin
Call Me Madam (1950)

HOT
Lewis E. Gensler
Robert A. Simon
Ups-A-Daisy (1928)

HOT AND BOTHERED
Harry Ruby
Bert Kalmar
Top Speed (1929)

HOT-CHA CHIQUITA
Max Rich
Jack Scholl
Keep Moving (1934)

HOT FEET
Harry Revel
Mack Gordon
Fast and Furious (1931)

HOT HARLEM
James P. Johnson
Flournoy Miller
Sugar Hill (1931)

HOT HEELS
Lee David
Billy Rose and Ballard MacDonald
Padlocks (1927)

HOT, HOT HONEY
Jean Schwartz
Alfred Bryan
A Night in Spain (1927)

HOT, HOT MAMA
Porter Grainger
Fast and Furious (1931)

HOT LOVER
Galt MacDermot
John Guare
Two Gentlemen of Verona (1971)

HOT MOONLIGHT
Jay Gorney

E. Y. Harburg
Shoot the Works (1931)

HOT PANTS
Roger Wolfe Kahn
Irving Caesar
Americana (1928)

HOT PATOOTIE WEDDING NIGHT
Frank Marcus and Bernard Maltin
Bamboola (1929)

HOT RHYTHM
Porter Grainger
Donald Heywood
Hot Rhythm (1930)

HOT RHYTHM
James P. Johnson
Flournoy Miller
Sugar Hill (1931)

HOT SANDS
Harry Tierney
Joseph McCarthy
Cross My Heart (1928)

HOT SPOT
Jerome Kern
Otto Harbach
Roberta (1933)

HOT WATER BOTTLES
Philip Springer
Joan Javits
Hotel Passionato (OB) (1965)

HOTCHA MA CHOTCH
Vincent Youmans
Harold Adamson and Clifford Grey
Smiles (1930)

HOTEL PASSIONATO
Philip Springer
Joan Javits
Hotel Passionato (OB) (1965)

HOTSY TOTSY HATS
Maury Rubens and Sam Timberg
Moe Jaffe
Broadway Nights (1929)

HOTTENTOT POTENTATE
Arthur Schwartz
Howard Dietz
At Home Abroad (1935)

HOUSE IN TOWN, A
Glenn Paxton
Robert Goldman and George Weiss
First Impressions (1959)

HOUSE IS NOT THE SAME WITHOUT A WOMAN, A
Armando Trovaioli
Pietro Garinei and Sandro Giovannini
Rugantino (1964)

HOUSE OF FLOWERS
Harold Arlen
Harold Arlen and Truman Capote
House of Flowers (1954)

HOUSE OF LEATHER THEME
Dale F. Menten
Dale F. Menten and Frederick Gaines
The House of Leather (OB) (1970)

HOUSE OF MARCUS LYCUS, THE
Stephen Sondheim
A Funny Thing Happened on the Way to the Forum (1962)

HOUSE ON THE HILL
Eaton Magoon, Jr.
13 Daughters (1961)

HOUSE WITH A LITTLE RED BARN, A
Morgan Lewis
Nancy Hamilton
Two for the Show (1940)

HOUSEBOAT ON THE STYX, THE
Alma Sanders
Monte Carlo
The Houseboat on the Styx (1928)

HOW ABOUT A BALL?
Hugo Peretti, Luigi Creatore and George David Weiss
Maggie Flynn (1968)

HOW ABOUT A BOY LIKE ME?
George Gershwin
Ira Gershwin
Strike Up the Band (1930)

HOW ABOUT A CHEER FOR THE NAVY
Irving Berlin
This Is the Army (1942)

HOW ABOUT A DATE?
Jimmy Van Heusen
Johnny Burke
Nellie Bly (1946)

HOW ABOUT IT?
Jesse Greer
Raymond Klages
Say When (1928)

HOW ABOUT IT?
Richard Rodgers
Lorenz Hart
America's Sweetheart (1931)

HOW ABOUT YOU
Burton Lane
Ralph Freed
Babes on Broadway (F) (1941)

HOW ABOUT YOU AND ME?
G. Wood
F. Jasmine Addams (OB) (1971)

HOW ARE THINGS IN GLOCCA MORRA?
Burton Lane
E. Y. Harburg
Finian's Rainbow (1947)

HOW ARE YOU, LADY LOVE?
Lucien Denni
Helena Evans
Happy Go Lucky (1926)

HOW ARE YOU SINCE?
Mitch Leigh
William Alfred and Phyllis Robinson
Cry for Us All (1970)

HOW BEAUTIFUL THE DAYS
Frank Loesser
The Most Happy Fella (1956)

HOW CAN ANYONE SO SWEET
Jeanne Bargy
Jeanne Bargy, Frank Gehrecke, and
  Herb Corey
Greenwich Village U.S.A. (OB) (1960)

HOW CAN I GET RID OF THOSE BLUES?
Lewis E. Gensler
Owen Murphy and Robert A. Simon
The Gang's All Here (1931)

HOW CAN I WAIT?
Frederick Loewe
Alan Jay Lerner
Paint Your Wagon (1951)

HOW CAN I WIN YOU NOW?
George Gershwin
B. G. DeSylva and Ira Gershwin
Tell Me More (1925)

HOW CAN LOVE SURVIVE?
Richard Rodgers
Oscar Hammerstein II
The Sound of Music (1959)

HOW CAN THE NIGHT BE GOOD?
Michael H. Cleary
Max and Nathaniel Lief
Shoot the Works (1931)

HOW CAN WE SWING IT?
Lee Wainer
Robert Sour
Sing for Your Supper (1939)

HOW CAN YOU DESCRIBE A FACE?
Jule Styne
Betty Comden and Adolph Green
Subways Are for Sleeping (1961)

HOW CAN YOU FORGET?
Richard Rodgers
Lorenz Hart
Fools for Scandal (F) (1938)

HOW CAN YOU KISS THOSE TIMES GOODBYE?
Laurence Rosenthal
James Lipton
Sherry! (1967)

HOW CAN YOU TELL?
H. Maurice Jacquet
Preston Sturges
The Well of Romance (1930)

HOW CAN YOU TELL AN AMERICAN?
Kurt Weill
Maxwell Anderson
Knickerbocker Holiday (1938)

HOW COULD A FELLOW WANT MORE?
Sigmund Romberg
Otto Harbach
Forbidden Melody (1936)

HOW COULD I BE SO WRONG
Walter Marks
Golden Rainbow (1968)

HOW COULD I FORGET?
George Gershwin
Gus Kahn and Ira Gershwin
Show Girl (1929)

HOW COULD YOU BELIEVE ME WHEN I SAID I LOVED YOU
Burton Lane
Alan Jay Lerner
Royal Wedding (F) (1951)

HOW DID IT GET SO LATE SO EARLY?
Will Irwin
June Sillman
All in Fun (1940)

HOW DO I FEEL?
Kenneth Jacobson
Rhoda Roberts
Show Me Where the Good Times Are (OB) (1970)

HOW DO I KNOW YOU'RE NOT MAD, SIR?
Stanley Jay Gelber

John Lollos and Don Christopher
Love and Let Love (OB) (1968)

HOW DO THEY EVER GROW UP?
Robert Larimer
King of the Whole Damn World! (OB)
(1962)

HOW DO YOU DO?
Edward Kunneke
Clifford Grey
Mayflowers (1925)

HOW DO YOU DO?
Rick Besoyan
Little Mary Sunshine (OB) (1959)

HOW DO YOU DO IT?
Lewis E. Gensler
E. Y. Harburg
Ballyhoo (1932)

HOW DO YOU DO, MIDDLE AGE?
Noël Coward
The Girl Who Came to Supper (1963)

HOW DO YOU DO, MISS PRATT
Walter Kent
Kim Gannon
Seventeen (1951)

HOW DO YOU DOODLE DO?
J. Fred Coots
Clifford Grey
June Days (1925)

HOW DO YOU FIND THE WORDS?
Lee Pockriss
Anne Croswell
Ernest in Love (OB) (1960)

HOW DO YOU LIKE YOUR LOVE?
Tommy Wolf
Fran Landesman
The Nervous Set (1959)

HOW DO YOU RAISE A BARN?
Albert Hague
Arnold B. Horwitt
Plain and Fancy (1955)

HOW DO YOU SAY GOODBYE?
Ernest G. Schweikert
Frank Reardon
Rumple (1957)

**HOW DO YOU SPEAK TO AN
ANGEL?**
Jule Styne
Bob Hilliard
Hazel Flagg (1953)

HOW DO YOU SPELL AMBASSADOR?
Cole Porter
Leave It to Me (1938)

**HOW DO YOU STOP LOVING SOME-
ONE?**
Johnny Brandon
Who's Who, Baby? (OB) (1968)

**HOW DOTH THE APPLE BUTTER-
FLY?**
William Roy
The Penny Friend (OB) (1966)

HOW D'YA TALK TO A GIRL
Jimmy Van Heusen
Sammy Cahn
Walking Happy (1966)

HOW D'YOU DO
Philip Braham
Eric Blore and Dion Titheradge
Charlot's Revue (1926)

HOW FAR CAN A LADY GO?
Jimmy Van Heusen
Johnny Burke
Carnival in Flanders (1953)

HOW FAR CAN YOU FOLLOW
Maury Laws
Jules Bass
Month of Sundays (OB) (1968)

HOW FLY TIMES
Frederick Loewe
Alan Jay Lerner
What's Up? (1943)

How Fucked Up Things Are
Michael Valenti
John Lewin
Blood Red Roses (1970)

How Green Was My Valley
John Morris
Gerald Freedman
A Time for Singing (1966)

How Happy Is the Bride
Vincent Youmans
Edward Heyman
Through the Years (1932)

How High the Moon
Morgan Lewis
Nancy Hamilton
Two for the Show (1940)

How I Could Go for You
Louis Alter
Harry Ruskin and Leighton K. Brill
Ballyhoo (1930)

How I Feel
Gary William Friedman
Will Holt
The Me Nobody Knows (OB) (1970)

How Jazz Was Born
Thomas (Fats) Waller
Andy Razaf
Keep Shufflin' (1928)

How Laughable It Is
Mark Sandrich, Jr.
Sidney Michaels
Ben Franklin in Paris (1964)

How Little We Know
Hoagy Carmichael
Johnny Mercer
To Have and Have Not (F) (1944)

How Long?
Maria Grever
Raymond Leveen
Viva O'Brien (1941)

How Long?
Richard Rodgers
Oscar Hammerstein II
Pipe Dream (1955)

How Long Can Love Keep Laughing?
Harold Rome
Sing Out the News (1938)

How Long Has This Been Going On?
George Gershwin
Ira Gershwin
Rosalie (1928)

How Lovely, How Lovely
Robert Colby
Robert Colby and Nita Jonas
Half-Past Wednesday (OB) (1962)

How Lovely to Be a Woman
Charles Strouse
Lee Adams
Bye Bye Birdie (1960)

How Much I Love You
Kurt Weill
Ogden Nash
One Touch of Venus (1943)

How Nice for Me
Hoagy Carmichael
Johnny Mercer
Walk with Music (1940)

How Sad
Richard Rodgers
No Strings (1962)

How She Glows
Coleman Dowell
The Tattooed Countess (OB) (1961)

How Solemn
Stan Harte, Jr.
Walt Whitman
Leaves of Grass (OB) (1971)

How Soon, Oh Moon
Jacques Offenbach

E. Y. Harburg
The Happiest Girl in the World (1961)

HOW STRANGE THE SILENCE
Baldwin Bergersen
William Archibald
The Crystal Heart (OB) (1960)

HOW SWEET IS PEACH ICE CREAM
G. Wood
F. Jasmine Addams (OB) (1971)

HOW SWEET YOU ARE
Arthur Schwartz
Frank Loesser
Thank Your Lucky Stars (F) (1943)

HOW SWEETLY FRIENDSHIP BINDS
Kurt Weill
Paul Green
Johnny Johnson (1936)

HOW THE FIRST SONG WAS BORN
Alexander Hill
Hummin' Sam (1933)

HOW THE GIRLS ADORE ME
Jean Gilbert
Harry B. Smith
The Red Rose (1928)

HOW THE MONEY CHANGES HANDS
Jerry Bock
Sheldon Harnick
Tenderloin (1960)

HOW THEY DO, DO
Ann Sternberg
Gertrude Stein
Gertrude Stein's First Reader (OB)
(1969)

HOW TO
Frank Loesser
*How to Succeed in Business without
Really Trying* (1961)

HOW TO HANDLE A WOMAN
Frederick Loewe
Alan Jay Lerner
Camelot (1960)

HOW TO PICK A MAN A WIFE
Sammy Fain
Paul Francis Webster
Christine (1960)

HOW TO STEAL AN ELECTION
Oscar Brand
How to Steal an Election (OB) (1968)

HOW TO SURVIVE
Kurt Weill
Marc Blitzstein
The Threepenny Opera (OB) (1954)

**HOW TO WIN FRIENDS AND INFLU-
ENCE PEOPLE**
Richard Rodgers
Lorenz Hart
I Married an Angel (1938)

HOW VERY LONG AGO
Gene Lockhart
Bunk of 1926 (1926)

HOW WAS I TO KNOW?*
Richard Rodgers
Lorenz Hart
She's My Baby (1928)

HOW WE WOULD LIKE OUR MAN
Walter Cool
Mackey of Appalachia (OB) (1965)

HOW WILL HE KNOW?
Jule Styne
Betty Comden and Adolph Green
Two on the Aisle (1951)

HOW WONDERFUL IT IS
Clinton Ballard
Carolyn Richter
The Ballad of Johnny Pot (OB) (1971)

HOW WOULD A CITY GIRL KNOW?
Kay Swift
Paul James
Nine-Fifteen Revue (1930)

---

*Dropped from New York production; Re-
written as "Why Do You Suppose" for
Heads Up

How Young You Were Tonight
Edward Thomas
Martin Charnin
Ballad for a Firing Squad (OB) (1968)

How'd You Like To
Stephen Jones
Irving Caesar
Yes, Yes, Yvette (1927)

How'd You Like to Spoon with Me?
Jerome Kern
Edward Laska
The Earl and the Girl (1905)

Howdjadoo
George Fischoff
Carole Bayer
Georgy (1970)

Howdy Broadway
Richard Rodgers
Lorenz Hart
Peggy-Ann (1926)

Howdy, Mr. Sunshine
Skip Redwine and Larry Frank
Frank Merriwell, or Honor Challenged (1971)

How 'Ja Like to Take Me Home
Philip Charig
Dan Shapiro and Milton Pascal
Artists and Models (1943)

How's Chances?
Irving Berlin
As Thousands Cheer (1933)

How's Your Health
Richard Rodgers
Lorenz Hart
Higher and Higher (1940)

How's Your Romance?
Cole Porter
Gay Divorce (1932)

How's Your Uncle?
Jimmy McHugh
Dorothy Fields
Shoot the Works (1931)

Hudson Duster
Ray Henderson
B. G. DeSylva and Lew Brown
Manhattan Mary (1927)

Huggin' and Muggin'
Eubie Blake
J. Milton Reddie and Cecil Mack
Swing It (1937)

Hugs and Kisses
Louis Alter
Raymond Klages
Earl Carroll's Vanities (1926)

Huguette Waltz
Rudolf Friml
Brian Hooker
The Vagabond King (1925)

Hula Girl, The
John Green
George Marion, Jr.
Beat the Band (1942)

Hullabaloo at Thebes
Ronny Graham
New Faces (1968)

Hulla-Baloo-Balay
John Clifton
John Clifton and Ben Tarver
Man with a Load of Mischief (OB) (1966)

Hum a Little Tune
Vivian Ellis
Graham John
By the Way (1925)

Humble Pie
Norman Campbell
Donald Campbell and Norman Campbell
Anne of Green Gables (OB) (1971)

Humming
Bob Merrill
Carnival (1961)

HUMPTY-DUMPTY
Joseph Meyer and Philip Charig
Leo Robin
Just Fancy (1927)

HUNCA MUNCA
Hal Hester and Danny Apolinar
Your Own Thing (1968)

HUNDRED MILLION MIRACLES, A
Richard Rodgers
Oscar Hammerstein II
Flower Drum Song (1958)

HUNDRED YEARS FROM TODAY, A
Victor Young
Joseph Young and Ned Washington
Blackbirds (1934)

HUNG
Galt MacDermot
Gerome Ragni and James Rado
Hair (1968)

HUNGRY
Murray Grand
New Faces (1968)

HUNGRY MEN
Harvey Schmidt
Tom Jones
110 in the Shade (1963)

HUNT, THE
Percy Wenrich
Harry Clarke
Who Cares? (1930)

HUNTED, THE
Duke Ellington
John Latouche
Beggar's Holiday (1946)

HUNTING
Rudolf Friml
Brian Hooker
The Vagabond King (1925)

HUNTING THE FOX
Richard Rodgers
Lorenz Hart
Simple Simon (1930)

HURRAY FOR LIFE
Lehman Engel
Agnes Morgan
A Hero Is Born (1937)

HURRY
Murray Grand
Murray Grand and Elisse Boyd
New Faces (1956)

HURRY BACK
Charles Strouse
Lee Adams
Applause (1970)

HURRY HOME
William Dyer
Don Parks and William Dyer
Jo! (OB) (1964)

HURRY! IT'S LOVELY UP HERE
Burton Lane
Alan Jay Lerner
On a Clear Day You Can See Forever
(1965)

HUSBAND, LOVER, AND WIFE
Lewis E. Gensler
Owen Murphy and Robert A. Simon
The Gang's All Here (1931)

HUSBAND OF MINE
Edwin Greenberg
Pilgrim's Progress (OB) (1962)

HUSH-HUSH
Julian Slade
Dorothy Reynolds and Julian Slade
Salad Days (OB) (1958)

HUSHABYE BABY
Helen Miller
Eve Merriam
Inner City (1971)

HUSKING BEE, THE
Jule Styne
Betty Comden and Adolph Green
Say, Darling (1958)

HUSKY, DUSKY ANNABELLE
Max Ewing
Agnes Morgan
The Grand Street Follies (1928)

HUSSARS MARCH
Sigmund Romberg
P. G. Wodehouse
Rosalie (1928)

HUSSAR'S SONG, THE
Emmerich Kalman
Harry B. Smith
The Circus Princess (1927)

HUSTLE, BUSTLE
Harry Archer
Harlan Thompson
Twinkle Twinkle (1926)

HUT IN HOBOKEN
Herman Hupfeld
The Little Show (1929)

HUXLEY
Kurt Weill
Ira Gershwin
Lady in the Dark (1941)

HYMEN, HYMEN
Richard Hill and John Hawkins
Nevill Coghill
Canterbury Tales (1969)

HYMN FOR A SUNDAY EVENING
Charles Strouse
Lee Adams
Bye Bye Birdie (1960)

HYMN OF BETROTHAL
Robert Wright and George Forrest
(based on Grieg)
Song of Norway (1944)

HYMN TO HIM, A
Frederick Loewe
Alan Jay Lerner
My Fair Lady (1956)

HYMN TO HYMEN
Cole Porter
Red, Hot and Blue! (1936)

HYMN TO HYMIE
Jerry Herman
Milk and Honey (1961)

HYMN TO PEACE
Kurt Weill
Paul Green
Johnny Johnson (1936)

I ADMIRE YOU VERY MUCH, MR. SCHMIDT
Jule Styne
Sammy Cahn
Look to the Lilies (1970)

I ADMIT
Emmerich Kalman
George Marion, Jr.
Marinka (1945)

I ADORE YOU
Ballard MacDonald, Sam Coslow, and
    Rene Mercier
Footlights (1927)

I ADORE YOU
Cole Porter
Aladdin (TV) (1958)

I AIN'T DOWN YET
Meredith Willson
The Unsinkable Molly Brown (1960)

I AM
Niclas Kempner
Graham John
The Street Singer (1929)

I AM A LITTLE WORM
Meyer Kupferman
Paul Goodman
Jonah (OB) (1966)

I AM A TRAVELLING POET
Joseph Raposo
Erich Segal
Sing Muse! (OB) (1961)

I AM A WITCH
Richard Rodgers
Oscar Hammerstein II
Pipe Dream (1955)

I AM ALL A-BLAZE
Richard Hill and John Hawkins
Nevill Coghill
Canterbury Tales (1969)

I AM ASHAMED THAT WOMEN ARE
SO SIMPLE
Cole Porter
Kiss Me, Kate (1948)

I AM CAPTURED
Sigmund Romberg
Harry B. Smith
The Love Call (1927)

I AM CHILD
Ron Steward and Neal Tate
Ron Steward
Sambo (OB) (1969)

I AM EASILY ASSIMILATED
Leonard Bernstein
Candide (1956)

I AM FREE
John Kander
Fred Ebb
Zorbá (1968)

I AM GASTON
Cole Porter
You Never Know (1938)

I AM GOING TO DANCE
William Roy
The Penny Friend (OB) (1966)

I AM GOING TO LIKE IT HERE
Richard Rodgers
Oscar Hammerstein II
Flower Drum Song (1958)

I AM HAPPY HERE
Kurt Weill
Ira Gershwin
The Firebrand of Florence (1945)

I AM IN LOVE
Cole Porter
Can-Can (1953)

I AM LOVED
Cole Porter
Out of This World (1950)

I AM NOT INTERESTED IN LOVE
Galt MacDermot
John Guare
Two Gentlemen of Verona (1971)

I AM ONLY HUMAN AFTER ALL
Vernon Duke
Ira Gershwin and E. Y. Harburg
The Garrick Gaieties (1930)

I AM SO EAGER
Jerome Kern
Oscar Hammerstein II
Music in the Air (1932)

I AM WHAT I AM!
Gordon Duffy
Harry M. Haldane
Happy Town (1959)

I ASKED MY HEART
Franz Lehár
Edward Eliscu
Frederika (1937)

I BEG YOUR PARDON
Richard Rodgers
Lorenz Hart
Dearest Enemy (1925)

I BELIEVE IN LOVE
Galt MacDermot
Gerome Ragni and James Rado
Hair (1968)

I BELIEVE IN TAKIN' A CHANCE
Arthur Schwartz
Howard Dietz
Jennie (1963)

I BELIEVE IN YOU
Frank Loesser
*How to Succeed in Business without
    Really Trying* (1961)

I BELONG
Janet Gari
Toby Garson
Lyle (OB) (1970)

I BLUSH*
Richard Rodgers
Lorenz Hart
A Connecticut Yankee (1927)

I BRING A LOVE SONG
Sigmund Romberg
Oscar Hammerstein II
Viennese Nights (F) (1930)

I BRING MY GIRLS ALONG
Walter G. Samuels
Morrie Ryskind
Ned Wayburn's Gambols (1929)

I BUILT A DREAM ONE DAY
Sigmund Romberg
Oscar Hammerstein II
May Wine (1935)

I CAIN'T SAY NO
Richard Rodgers
Oscar Hammerstein II
Oklahoma! (1943)

I CAME TO LIFE
Jay Gorney
E. Y. Harburg
Earl Carroll's Vanities
(1930)

I CAME TO YOUR ROOM
Richard Addinsell
Clemence Dane
Come of Age (1934)

I CAN
Walter Marks
Bajour (1964)

I CAN ALWAYS FIND A LITTLE SUN-
SHINE IN THE Y.M.C.A.
Irving Berlin
Yip! Yip! Yaphank (1918)

I CAN BE LIKE GRANDPA
Harold Orlob
Hairpin Harmony (1943)

I CAN COOK TOO
Leonard Bernstein
Leonard Bernstein, Betty Comden,
   and Adolph Green
On the Town (1944)

I CAN DO WONDERS WITH YOU
Richard Rodgers
Lorenz Hart
Simple Simon (1930)

I CAN DREAM, CAN'T I?
Sammy Fain
Irving Kahal
Right This Way (1938)

I CAN HEAR IT NOW
Harold Rome
Bless You All (1950)

I CAN LEARN
Howard Blankman
By Hex (OB) (1956)

I CAN MAKE IT
Mike Brandt, Michael Knight, and
   Robert J. Lowery
Exchange (OB) (1970)

I CAN SEE
Lance Mulcahy
Paul Cherry
Park (1970)

I CAN SEE IT
Harvey Schmidt
Tom Jones
The Fantasticks (OB) (1960)

I CAN SPEAK ESPAGNOL
Harry Tierney
Joseph McCarthy
Rio Rita (1927)

I CAN TAKE IT
Coleman Dowell
The Tattooed Countess (OB) (1961)

———
*Dropped from New York production

I CAN TEACH THEM
Charles Strouse
Lee Adams
All American (1962)

I CANNOT LIVE WITHOUT YOUR LOVE
Ralph Benatzky
Irving Caesar
White Horse Inn (1936)

I CANNOT MAKE HIM JEALOUS
Ervin Drake
Her First Roman (1968)

I CANNOT TELL HER SO
John Jennings
Riverwind (OB) (1962)

I CANNOT WAIT
Wally Harper
Paul Zakrzewski
Sensations (OB) (1970)

I CAN'T AFFORD TO DREAM
Sam Stept
Lew Brown and Charles Tobias
Yokel Boy (1939)

I CAN'T BE BOTHERED NOW
George Gershwin
Ira Gershwin
A Damsel in Distress (F) (1937)

I CAN'T BE HAPPY
Vincent Youmans
Anne Caldwell
Oh, Please! (1926)

I CAN'T BE IN LOVE
Leroy Anderson
Joan Ford, Walter and Jean Kerr
Goldilocks (1958)

I CAN'T BELIEVE IT'S REAL
Janet Gari
Toby Garson
Lyle (OB) (1970)

I CAN'T BELIEVE IT'S TRUE*
Lewis E. Gensler
Robert A. Simon
Ups-A-Daisy (1928)

I CAN'T BELIEVE IT'S TRUE
Alberta Nichols
Mann Holiner
Angela (1928)

I CAN'T DO THE SUM
Victor Herbert
Glen MacDonough
Babes in Toyland (1903)

I CAN'T GET INTO THE QUOTA
Arthur Schwartz
Henry Myers
The New Yorkers (1927)

I CAN'T GET OVER A GIRL LIKE YOU
Martin Broones
Harry Ruskin
Rufus Lemaire's Affairs (1927)

I CAN'T GET STARTED
Vernon Duke
Ira Gershwin
Ziegfeld Follies (1936)

I CAN'T GIVE YOU ANYTHING BUT LOVE
Jimmy McHugh
Dorothy Fields
Blackbirds (1928)

I CAN'T MAKE IT ANYMORE
Tom Sankey
The Golden Screw (OB) (1967)

I CAN'T PRETEND
William Klenosky
Utopia! (OB) (1963)

I CAN'T REMEMBER
Tom Sankey
The Golden Screw (OB) (1967)

I CAN'T REMEMBER THE WORDS
Milton Ager and Henry Cabot Lodge
Jack Yellen
John Murray Anderson's Almanac (1929)

---

*Dropped from New York production

I CAN'T STOP TALKING
Leon Pober
Bud Freeman
Beg, Borrow or Steal (1960)

I COME OUT OF A DREAM
Richard Addinsell
Clemence Dane
Come of Age (1934)

I CONCENTRATE ON YOU
Cole Porter
Broadway Melody (F) (1940)

I COULD BE HAPPY WITH YOU
Sandy Wilson
The Boy Friend (1954)

I COULD DIG YOU
Ron Steward and Neal Tate
Ron Steward
Sambo (OB) (1969)

I COULD GET MARRIED TODAY
Walter Kent
Kim Gannon
Seventeen (1951)

I COULD GIVE UP ANYTHING BUT YOU
Ray Henderson
B. G. DeSylva and Lew Brown
Follow Thru (1929)

I COULD GO WITH THE WIND
Deed Meyer
Stones of Jehoshaphat (OB) (1963)

I COULD HAVE DANCED ALL NIGHT
Frederick Loewe
Alan Jay Lerner
My Fair Lady (1956)

I COULD WRITE A BOOK
Richard Rodgers
Lorenz Hart
Pal Joey (1940)

I COULDN'T HAVE DONE IT ALONE
Charles Strouse
Lee Adams
All American (1962)

I COULDN'T HOLD MY MAN
Harold Arlen
Ira Gershwin and E. Y. Harburg
Life Begins at 8:40 (1934)

I CRIED FOR MY TROUBLES
Meyer Kupferman
Paul Goodman
Jonah (OB) (1966)

I DANCE ALONE
James Shelton
Who's Who (1938)

I DARE NOT LOVE YOU
Sigmund Romberg
Harry B. Smith
Princess Flavia (1925)

I DARE TO DREAM
Michael Grace and Carl Tucker
Sammy Gallup
John Murray Anderson's Almanac
(1953)

I DARE TO SPEAK OF LOVE TO YOU
Emmerich Kalman
Harry B. Smith
The Circus Princess (1927)

I DELIGHT IN THE SIGHT OF MY LYDIA
Alec Wilder
Arnold Sundgaard
Kittiwake Island (OB) (1960)

I DETEST A FIESTA
Cole Porter
Panama Hattie (1940)

I DID NOT SLEEP LAST NIGHT
Edward Thomas
Martin Charnin
Ballad for a Firing Squad (OB) (1968)

I DIDN'T KNOW THAT IT WAS LOADED
Michael H. Cleary
Max and Nathaniel Lief
Hey Nonny Nonny! (1932)

I DIDN'T KNOW WHAT TIME IT WAS
Richard Rodgers
Lorenz Hart
Too Many Girls (1939)

I DISREMEMBER QUITE WELL
Antonia
Operation Sidewinder (1970)

I DO
Lewis E. Gensler
B. G. DeSylva
Captain Jinks (1925)

I DO! HE DOESN'T!
Jack Lawrence and Don Walker
Courtin' Time (1951)

I DO! I DO!
Harvey Schmidt
Tom Jones
I Do! I Do! (1966)

I DO NOT KNOW A DAY I DID NOT LOVE YOU
Richard Rodgers
Martin Charnin
Two by Two (1970)

I DON'T BLAME 'EM
Percy Wenrich
Raymond Peck
Castles in the Air (1926)

I DON'T CARE
Kenn Long and Jim Crozier
Kenn Long
Touch (OB) (1970)

I DON'T CARE WHAT THEY SAY ABOUT ME
Fred Spielman and Arthur Gershwin
Stanley Adams
A Lady Says Yes (1945)

I DON'T GET IT
Doris Tauber
Sis Wilner
Star and Garter (1942)

I DON'T KNOW HER NAME
Richard Lewine
Arnold B. Horwitt
Make Mine Manhattan (1948)

I DON'T KNOW HIS NAME
Jerry Bock
Sheldon Harnick
She Loves Me (1963)

I DON'T KNOW HOW TO LOVE HIM
Andrew Lloyd Webber
Tim Rice
Jesus Christ Superstar (1971)

I DON'T KNOW WHERE SHE GOT IT
Jule Styne
Betty Comden and Adolph Green
Hallelujah, Baby! (1967)

I DON'T LIKE THIS DAME
Frank Loesser
The Most Happy Fella (1956)

I DON'T LIKE YOU
Lionel Bart
La Strada (1969)

I DON'T LOVE NOBODY BUT YOU
Jimmy Johnson
Perry Bradford
Messin' Around (1929)

I DON'T MIND
Jerry Herman
Madame Aphrodite (OB) (1961)

I DON'T REMEMBER YOU
John Kander
Fred Ebb
The Happy Time (1968)

I DON'T SEE HIM VERY MUCH ANYMORE
Edward Thomas
Martin Charnin
Ballad for a Firing Squad (OB) (1968)

I DON'T THINK I'LL END IT ALL TODAY
Harold Arlen
E. Y. Harburg
Jamaica (1957)

**I DON'T THINK I'LL FALL IN LOVE
TODAY**
George Gershwin
Ira Gershwin
Treasure Girl (1928)

I DON'T THINK I'M IN LOVE
Jimmy Van Heusen
Sammy Cahn
Walking Happy (1966)

I DON'T WANNA ROCK
Colin Romoff
David Rogers
Ziegfeld Follies (1957)

I DON'T WANT A SONG AT TWILIGHT
Alfred Nathan
George Oppenheimer
The Manhatters (1927)

I DON'T WANT HIM
Con Conrad
Gus Kahn
Kitty's Kisses (1926)

I DON'T WANT TO BE MARRIED
Irving Berlin
Face the Music (1932)

I DON'T WANT TO BE PRESIDENT
Harry Akst
Lew Brown
Calling All Stars (1934)

I DON'T WANT TO KNOW
Jerry Herman
Dear World (1969)

I DON'T WANT YOU
Giuseppe Verdi
Charles Friedman
My Darlin' Aïda (1952)

I DREAM OF A GIRL IN A SHAWL
Cole Porter
Wake Up and Dream (1929)

I DREAM TOO MUCH
Jerome Kern
Dorothy Fields
I Dream Too Much (F) (1935)

I DREAMT ABOUT MY HOME
Linda Swenson
Doug Dyer
Blood (OB) (1971)

**I DREAMT I DWELT IN BLOOMING-
DALE'S**
Ernest McCarty
Jack Ramer and Ernest McCarty
I Dreamt I Dwelt in Bloomingdale's
(OB) (1970)

I ENJOY BEING A GIRL
Richard Rodgers
Oscar Hammerstein II
Flower Drum Song (1958)

I FEEL A SONG COMIN' ON
Jimmy McHugh
Dorothy Fields and George Oppen-
heimer
Every Night at Eight (F) (1935)

I FEEL AT HOME WITH YOU
Richard Rodgers
Lorenz Hart
A Connecticut Yankee (1927)

I FEEL HUMBLE
Ervin Drake
What Makes Sammy Run? (1964)

I FEEL LIKE A BROTHER TO YOU
Gordon Duffy
Harry M. Haldane
Happy Town (1959)

**I FEEL LIKE I'M GONNA LIVE
FOREVER**
Jule Styne
Bob Hilliard
Hazel Flagg (1953)

**I FEEL LIKE I'M NOT OUT OF BED
YET**
Leonard Bernstein
Betty Comden and Adolph Green
On the Town (1944)

I FEEL LIKE NEW YEAR'S EVE
Sammy Fain
Marilyn and Alan Bergman
Something More! (1964)

I FEEL MY LUCK COMIN' DOWN
Harold Arlen
Johnny Mercer
St. Louis Woman (1946)

I FEEL PRETTY
Leonard Bernstein
Stephen Sondheim
West Side Story (1957)

I FEEL SORRY FOR THE GIRL
Glenn Paxton
Robert Goldman and George Weiss
First Impressions (1959)

I FEEL SORTA . . .
Harden Church
Edward Heyman
Caviar (1934)

I FEEL WONDERFUL
Jerry Herman
I Feel Wonderful (OB) (1954)

I FELL HEAD OVER HEELS IN LOVE
Pat Thayer
Donovan Parsons
The Merry World (1926)

I FELL HEAD OVER HEELS IN LOVE
Jean Gilbert
Harry Graham
Katja (1926)

I FELL IN LOVE WITH YOU
Richard Lewine
Arnold B. Horwitt
Make Mine Manhattan (1948)

I FOUGHT EVERY STEP OF THE WAY
Johnny Mercer
Top Banana (1951)

I FOUND A FRIEND
Emile Berté and Maury Rubens
J. Keirn Brennan
Music in May (1929)

I FOUND A MILLION DOLLAR BABY
Harry Warren
Billy Rose and Mort Dixon
Crazy Quilt (1931)

I FOUND A SONG
Edward A. Horan
Frederick Herendeen
All the King's Horses (1934)

I FOUND HIM
Jacques Urbont
Bruce Geller
All in Love (OB) (1961)

I FOUND MY TWIN
Stanley Jay Gelber
John Lollos and Don Christopher
Love and Let Love (OB) (1968)

I GET A KICK OUT OF YOU
Cole Porter
Anything Goes (1934)

I GET EMBARRASSED
Bob Merrill
Take Me Along (1959)

I GIVE MY HEART
Carl Millöcker (revised by Theo Mackeben)
Rowland Leigh
The Dubarry (1932)

I GIVE MYSELF AWAY
Jacques Fray
Edward Eliscu
The Vanderbilt Revue (1930)

I GO TO BED
Lee Pockriss
Anne Croswell
Tovarich (1963)

I GOT A MARBLE AND A STAR
Kurt Weill
Langston Hughes
Street Scene (1947)

I Got a Song
Harold Arlen
E. Y. Harburg
Bloomer Girl (1944)

I Got Beauty
Cole Porter
Out of This World (1950)

I Got Everything I Want
Jack Lawrence and Stan Freeman
I Had a Ball (1964)

I Got Life
Galt MacDermot
Gerome Ragni and James Rado
Hair (1968)

I Got Lost in His Arms
Irving Berlin
Annie Get Your Gun (1946)

I Got Love
Jerome Kern
Dorothy Fields
I Dream Too Much (F) (1935)

I Got Love
Gary Geld
Peter Udell
Purlie (1970)

I Got Lucky in the Rain
Jimmy McHugh
Harold Adamson
As the Girls Go (1948)

I Got Plenty o' Nuttin'
George Gershwin
DuBose Heyward and Ira Gershwin
Porgy and Bess (1935)

I Got Religion
Vincent Youmans
B. G. DeSylva
Take a Chance (1932)

I Got Rhythm
George Gershwin
Ira Gershwin
Girl Crazy (1930)

I Got the Blood
Melvin Van Peebles
Ain't Supposed to Die a Natural Death (1971)

I Got the Sun in the Morning
Irving Berlin
Annie Get Your Gun (1946)

I Gotta Be
George Kleinsinger
Joe Darion
Shinbone Alley (1957)

I Gotta Get Back to New York
Richard Rodgers
Lorenz Hart
Hallelujah, I'm a Bum (F) (1933)

I Gotta Have My Moments
Ralph Benatzky
Meet My Sister (1930)

I Gotta Have You
Richard Lewine
Arnold B. Horwitt
The Girls Against the Boys (1959)

I Guess I Love You
Robert Russell Bennett
Owen Murphy and Robert A. Simon
Hold Your Horses (1933)

I Guess I'll Have to Change My Plan
Arthur Schwartz
Howard Dietz
The Little Show (1929)

I Had a Ball
Jack Lawrence and Stan Freeman
I Had a Ball (1964)

I Had a Little Teevee
Helen Miller
Eve Merriam
Inner City (1971)

I Had a Son
Mary Boylan
Blood (OB) (1971)

I HAD TWINS
Richard Rodgers
Lorenz Hart
The Boys from Syracuse (1938)

I HAD TWO DREGS
Mary Rodgers
Martin Charnin
Hot Spot (1963)

I HAPPEN TO LIKE NEW YORK
Cole Porter
The New Yorkers (1930)

I HATE A PARADE
Harold Rome
Michael Todd's Peep Show (1950)

I HATE HIM
Harold Rome
Destry Rides Again (1959)

I HATE HIM
Bob Merrill
Carnival (1961)

I HATE MEN
Cole Porter
Kiss Me, Kate (1948)

I HATE MYSELF (FOR FALLING IN LOVE WITH YOU)
Abner Silver and Dave Oppenheim
Brown Buddies (1930)

I HATE MYSELF IN THE MORNING
Frank Black
Gladys Shelley
The Duchess Misbehaves (1946)

I HATE TO TALK ABOUT MYSELF
Harry Archer
Harlan Thompson
Twinkle Twinkle (1926)

I HATE TO THINK THAT YOU'LL GROW OLD, BABY
Ray Henderson
B. G. DeSylva and Lew Brown
Strike Me Pink (1933)

I HATE YOU
Maurice Yvain
Max and Nathaniel Lief
Luckee Girl (1928)

I HATE YOU
John Dooley
Hobo (OB) (1961)

I HATE YOU, DARLING
Cole Porter
Let's Face It! (1941)

I HAVE A LOVE
Leonard Bernstein
Stephen Sondheim
West Side Story (1957)

I HAVE A NOBLE COCK
Richard Hill and John Hawkins
Nevill Coghill
Canterbury Tales (1969)

I HAVE A RUN IN MY STOCKING
Henry Sullivan
Edward Eliscu
A Little Racketeer (1932)

I HAVE CONFIDENCE IN ME
Richard Rodgers
The Sound of Music (F) (1965)

I HAVE DREAMED
Richard Rodgers
Oscar Hammerstein II
The King and I (1951)

I HAVE FORGOTTEN YOU ALMOST
Gitz Rice
Anna Fitziu
Nic-Nax (1926)

I HAVE LIVED
Howard Blankman
By Hex (OB) (1956)

I HAVE MY MOMENTS
Herbert Stothart, Bert Kalmar, and
  Harry Ruby
Good Boy (1928)

I HAVE MY OWN WAY
Johnny Burke
Donnybrook! (1961)

I HAVE ROOM IN MY HEART
Frederick Loewe
Earle Crooker
Great Lady (1938)

I HAVE SOMETHING NICE FOR
YOU
Winthrop Cortelyou
Derick Wulff
Kiss Me (1927)

I HAVE THE ROOM ABOVE
Jerome Kern
Oscar Hammerstein II
Show Boat (F) (1936)

I HAVE TO TELL YOU
Harold Rome
Fanny (1954)

I HAVE WHAT YOU WANT!
Murray Rumshinsky
Jacob Jacobs
The President's Daughter (1970)

I HAVEN'T GOT A WORRY IN THE
WORLD
Richard Rodgers
Oscar Hammerstein II
Happy Birthday (1946)

I HEAR
Cy Coleman
Carolyn Leigh
Wildcat (1960)

I HEAR AMERICA SINGING
Stan Harte, Jr.
Walt Whitman
Leaves of Grass (OB) (1971)

I HEAR LOVE CALL ME
Karl Hajos (based on Tchaikovsky)
Harry B. Smith
Natja (1925)

I HEARD MY MOTHER CRYING
Tom Sankey
The Golden Screw (OB) (1967)

I HOPE YOU'RE HAPPY
Norman Martin
Fred Ebb
Put It in Writing (OB) (1963)

I INVENTED MYSELF
Mark Sandrich, Jr.
Sidney Michaels
Ben Franklin in Paris (1964)

I JUPITER, I REX
Cole Porter
Out of This World (1950)

I JUST CAN'T WAIT
Jule Styne
Betty Comden and Adolph Green
Subways Are for Sleeping (1961)

I JUST COULDN'T TAKE IT, BABY
Alberta Nichols
Mann Holiner
Blackbirds of 1934 (1933)

I JUST GOT IN THE CITY
Voices, Inc.
The Believers (OB) (1968)

I JUST HEARD
Jerry Bock
Sheldon Harnick
Fiddler on the Roof (1964)

I KEEP TELLING MYSELF
Arthur Jones
Gen Genovese
Buttrio Square (1952)

I KISS YOUR HAND, MADAME
Ralph Erwin
Samuel Lewis and Joseph Young
Lady Fingers (1929)

I KISSED MY GIRL GOODBYE
Vernon Duke
Howard Dietz
Jackpot (1944)

I KNEW HIM BEFORE HE WAS SPAN-
ISH
Dana Suesse
Billy Rose and Ballard McDonald
Sweet and Low (1930)

I KNEW I'D KNOW
Sidney Lippman
Sylvia Dee
Barefoot Boy with Cheek (1947)

I KNOW A FOUL BALL
George Gershwin
Ira Gershwin
Let 'Em Eat Cake (1933)

I KNOW A SECRET
Robert Colby
Robert Colby and Nita Jonas
Half-Past Wednesday (OB) (1962)

I KNOW ABOUT LOVE
Jule Styne
Betty Comden and Adolph Green
Do Re Mi (1960)

I KNOW HE'LL UNDERSTAND
Johnny Myers
Wet Paint (OB) (1965)

I KNOW HOW IT IS
Frank Loesser
The Most Happy Fella (1956)

I KNOW HOW YOU WONDER
Darwin Venneri
Darwin's Theories (OB) (1960)

I KNOW, I KNOW
Edward Earle
Yvonne Tarr
The Decameron (OB) (1961)

I KNOW I'M NOBODY
Sam Stept
Lew Brown and Charles Tobias
Yokel Boy (1939)

I KNOW IT CAN HAPPEN AGAIN
Richard Rodgers
Oscar Hammerstein II
Allegro (1947)

I KNOW MY LOVE
Howard Blankman
By Hex (OB) (1956)

I KNOW SOMEONE LOVES ME
Vivian Ellis
Graham John
By the Way (1925)

I KNOW SOMETHING
William B. Kernell
Dorothy Donnelly
Hello, Lola (1926)

I KNOW THAT I LOVE YOU
Harry Ruby
Bert Kalmar
Sweetheart Time (1926)

I KNOW THAT YOU KNOW
Vincent Youmans
Anne Caldwell
Oh, Please! (1926)

I KNOW THE FEELING
Lee Pockriss
Anne Croswell
Tovarich (1963)

I KNOW WHAT HE'S UP TO
Robert Holton
June Carroll
Hi, Paisano! (OB) (1961)

I KNOW WHAT I AM
David Heneker
Half a Sixpence (1965)

I KNOW WHERE THERE'S A COZY
NOOK
Kurt Weill
Ira Gershwin
The Firebrand of Florence (1945)

I KNOW YOU BY HEART
Hugh Martin and Ralph Blane
Best Foot Forward (1941)

I KNOW YOU SELL IT
Al Carmines
Rosalyn Drexler
Home Movies (OB) (1964)

I KNOW YOUR HEART
Hugh Martin and Timothy Gray
High Spirits (1964)

I KNOW YOUR KIND
Harold Rome
Destry Rides Again (1959)

I LEFT A DREAM SOMEWHERE
Don McAfee
Nancy Leeds
Great Scot! (OB) (1965)

I LEFT MY HAT IN HAITI
Burton Lane
Alan Jay Lerner
Royal Wedding (F) (1951)

I LEFT MY HEART AT THE STAGE DOOR CANTEEN
Irving Berlin
This Is the Army (1942)

I LIKE
Ray Haney
Alfred Aiken
We're Civilized? (OB) (1962)

I LIKE
William Dyer
Don Parks and William Dyer
Jo! (OB) (1964)

I LIKE EVERYBODY
Frank Loesser
The Most Happy Fella (1956)

I LIKE HIM
Milton Schafer
Ira Levin
Drat! The Cat! (1965)

I LIKE IT
Edward Pola
Eddie Brandt
Woof, Woof (1929)

I LIKE IT
Stanley Jay Gelber
John Lollos and Don Christopher
Love and Let Love (OB) (1968)

I LIKE IT
Albert Hague
Allen Sherman
The Fig Leaves Are Falling (1969)

I LIKE IT HERE
Morton Gould
Dorothy Fields
Arms and the Girl (1950)

I LIKE IT WITH MUSIC
Ray Henderson
Jack Yellen
George White's Scandals (1936)

I LIKE THE BOYS
Emmerich Kalman
Harry B. Smith
The Circus Princess (1927)

I LIKE THE COMPANY OF MEN
Cyril Ornadel
Leslie Bricusse
Pickwick (1965)

I LIKE THE GIRLS
A. Baldwin Sloane
Harry Cort and George E. Stoddard
China Rose (1925)

I LIKE THE LIKES OF YOU
Vernon Duke
E. Y. Harburg
Ziegfeld Follies (1934)

I LIKE THE MILITARY MAN
H. Maurice Jacquet
William Brady
The Silver Swan (1929)

I LIKE THE NOSE ON YOUR FACE
Richard Lewine
Ted Fetter
The Fireman's Flame (OB) (1937)

I LIKE TO BE LIKED
Harry Ruby
Bert Kalmar
Top Speed (1929)

I LIKE TO LOOK MY BEST
Oscar Brand and Paul Nassau
A Joyful Noise (1966)

I LIKE TO MAKE IT COZY
Albert Von Tilzer
Neville Fleeson
Bye Bye, Bonnie (1927)

I LIKE TO RECOGNIZE THE TUNE
Richard Rodgers
Lorenz Hart
Too Many Girls (1939)

I LIKE WHAT YOU LIKE
Vincent Youmans
Billy Rose and Edward Eliscu
Great Day! (1929)

I LIKE YOU
Ralph Benatzky
Meet My Sister (1930)

I LIKE YOU
Harold Rome
Fanny (1954)

I LIKE YOU
Billy Barnes
The Billy Barnes People (1961)

I LIKE YOU AS YOU ARE
Vincent Youmans
Oscar Hammerstein II
Rainbow (1928)

I LIVE, I DIE FOR YOU
Sigmund Romberg
Harry B. Smith
The Love Call (1927)

I LIVE TO LOVE
Deed Meyer
She Shall Have Music (OB) (1959)

I LOST IT
Mitch Leigh
William Alfred and Phyllis Robinson
Cry for Us All (1970)

I LOST THE RHYTHM
Charles Strouse
The Littlest Revue (OB) (1956)

I LOVE A COP
Jerry Bock
Sheldon Harnick
Fiorello (1959)

I LOVE A FOOL
Jacques Urbont
Bruce Geller
All in Love (OB) (1961)

I LOVE A MAN
Cy Young
That Hat! (OB) (1964)

I LOVE A MAN IN UNIFORM
Jimmy Monaco
Billy Rose and Ballard MacDonald
Harry Delmar's Revels (1927)

I LOVE A PIANO
Irving Berlin
Stop! Look! Listen! (1915)

I LOVE A POLKA SO
Berenice Kazounoff
Carl Randall
The Illustrators' Show (1936)

I LOVE EVERYTHING THAT'S OLD
Robert Kessler
Lola Permagent
O Marry Me! (OB) (1961)

I LOVE HIM
Frank Loesser
The Most Happy Fella (1956)

I LOVE HIM
Sammy Fain
Paul Francis Webster
Christine (1960)

I LOVE HIM, THE RAT
Richard A. Whiting
Oscar Hammerstein II
Free for All (1931)

I LOVE LOUISA
Arthur Schwartz
Howard Dietz
The Band Wagon (1931)

I LOVE LOVE
Karl Hajos (based on Chopin)
Harry B. Smith
White Lilacs (1928)

I LOVE LOVE
Robert Emmett Dolan
Walter O'Keefe
Princess Charming (1930)

I LOVE LOVE IN NEW YORK
Gordon Jenkins
Tom Adair
Along Fifth Avenue (1949)

I LOVE MY FATHER
Galt MacDermot
John Guare
Two Gentlemen of Verona (1971)

I LOVE MY WIFE
Harvey Schmidt
Tom Jones
I Do! I Do! (1966)

I LOVE NASHVILLE
Oscar Brand and Paul Nassau
A Joyful Noise (1966)

I LOVE PARIS
Cole Porter
Can-Can (1953)

I LOVE PETITE BELLE
Coleridge-Taylor Perkinson
Errol Hill
Man Better Man (OB) (1969)

I LOVE THAT BOY
Jacques Belasco
Kay Twomey
The Girl from Nantucket (1945)

I LOVE THE LADIES
Mark Sandrich, Jr.
Sidney Michaels
Ben Franklin in Paris (1964)

I LOVE THE WAY WE FELL IN LOVE
Sammy Fain
Irving Kahal
Right This Way (1938)

I LOVE THE WOODS
Richard Rodgers
Lorenz Hart
Simple Simon (1930)

I LOVE THEM ALL
Sigmund Romberg
Harry B. Smith
Princess Flavia (1925)

I LOVE TO CRY AT WEDDINGS
Cy Coleman
Dorothy Fields
Sweet Charity (1966)

I LOVE TO DANCE
Con Conrad
Gus Kahn
Kitty's Kisses (1926)

I LOVE TO FLUTTER
Gerald Dolin
Edward J. Lambert
Smile at Me (1935)

I LOVE TO RHYME
George Gershwin
Ira Gershwin
The Goldwyn Follies (F) (1938)

I LOVE TO SING THE WORDS
Irving Caesar
Gerald Marks and Sam Lerner
My Dear Public (1943)

I LOVE WHAT I'M DOING
Jule Styne
Leo Robin
Gentlemen Prefer Blondes (1949)

I LOVE WHAT THE GIRLS HAVE
Gary William Friedman
Will Holt
The Me Nobody Knows (OB) (1970)

I LOVE YOU
Harry Archer
Harlan Thompson
Little Jessie James (1923)

I LOVE YOU
Cole Porter
Mexican Hayride (1944)

I LOVE YOU
Robert Wright and George Forrest
   (based on Grieg)
Song of Norway (1944)

I LOVE YOU
Cy Coleman
Carolyn Leigh
Little Me (1962)

I LOVE YOU AND I ADORE YOU
Karl Hajos (based on Chopin)
Harry B. Smith
White Lilacs (1928)

I LOVE YOU AND I LIKE YOU
Arthur Schwartz
Max and Nathaniel Lief
The Grand Street Follies (1929)

I LOVE YOU FOR THAT
Sol Berkowitz
James Lipton
Nowhere to Go but Up (1962)

I LOVE YOU, HONEY
James P. Johnson
Flournoy Miller
Sugar Hill (1931)

I LOVE YOU, I ADORE YOU
H. Maurice Jacquet
William Brady
The Silver Swan (1929)

I LOVE YOU MORE THAN YESTERDAY
Richard Rodgers
Lorenz Hart
Lady Fingers (1929)

I LOVE YOU, MY DARLING
Jean Gilbert
George Hirst and Edward Eliscu
Marching By (1932)

I LOVE YOU, SAMANTHA
Cole Porter
High Society (F) (1956)

I LOVE YOU SO
Franz Lehár
Adrian Ross
The Merry Widow (1907)

I LOVE YOU SO
Maurice Yvain
Max and Nathaniel Lief
Luckee Girl (1928)

I LOVE YOU SO MUCH
Harry Ruby
Bert Kalmar
The Cuckoos (F) (1930)

I LOVE YOU THIS MORNING
Frederick Loewe
Alan Jay Lerner
The Day Before Spring (1945)

I LOVE YOU TODAY
Steve Allen
Sophie (1963)

I LOVED
Jacques Brel
Eric Blau and Mort Shuman
*Jacques Brel Is Alive and Well and
   Living in Paris* (OB) (1968)

I LOVED A MAN
Sandy Wilson
Valmouth (OB) (1960)

I LOVED HER, TOO
Kurt Weill
Langston Hughes
Street Scene (1947)

I LOVED HIM BUT HE DIDN'T LOVE ME
Cole Porter
Wake Up and Dream (1929)

I LOVED YOU ONCE IN SILENCE
Frederick Loewe
Alan Jay Lerner
Camelot (1960)

I LOVES YOU, PORGY
George Gershwin
DuBose Heyward and Ira Gershwin
Porgy and Bess (1935)

I MADE A FIST
Frank Loesser
The Most Happy Fella (1956)

I MAKE UP FOR THAT IN OTHER WAYS
Ray Henderson
Lew Brown
Hot-Cha! (1932)

I MARRIED AN ANGEL
Richard Rodgers
Lorenz Hart
I Married an Angel (1938)

I MAY
Maury Rubens and Kendall Burgess
Harry B. Smith
Naughty Riquette (1926)

I MAY BE WRONG (BUT I THINK YOU'RE WONDERFUL)
Henry Sullivan
Harry Ruskin
John Murray Anderson's Almanac (1929)

I MEAN TO SAY
George Gershwin
Ira Gershwin
Strike Up the Band (1930)

I MEAN TO SAY "I LOVE YOU"
Erich Wolfgang Korngold
Oscar Hammerstein II
Give Us This Night (F) (1936)

I MEAN WHAT I SAY
Edward Pola
Eddie Brandt
Woof, Woof (1929)

I MET A GIRL
Jule Styne
Betty Comden and Adolph Green
Bells Are Ringing (1956)

I MIGHT BE YOUR ONCE-IN-A-WHILE
Victor Herbert
Robert B. Smith
Angel Face (1919)

I MIGHT FALL BACK ON YOU
Jerome Kern
Oscar Hammerstein II
Show Boat (1927)

I MUST BE HOME BY TWELVE O'-CLOCK
George Gershwin
Gus Kahn and Ira Gershwin
Show Girl (1929)

I MUST HAVE A DINNER COAT
James Shelton
Who's Who (1938)

I MUST LOVE YOU*
Richard Rodgers
Lorenz Hart
Chee-Chee (1928)

I MUST PAINT
Baldwin Bergersen
William Archibald
The Crystal Heart (OB) (1960)

I MUST SMILE
James Bredt
Edward Eager
The Happy Hypocrite (OB) (1968)

I MUST WALTZ
Baldwin Bergersen

---

*Rewritten as "Send for Me" in *Simple Simon*

Irvin Graham
Who's Who (1938)

I NEED A LITTLE BIT, YOU NEED A LITTLE BIT
Cliff Friend
Lew Brown
Piggy (1927)

I NEED ALL THE HELP I CAN GET
David Baker
David Craig
Copper and Brass (1957)

I NEED SOME COOLING OFF
Richard Rodgers
Lorenz Hart
She's My Baby (1928)

I NEED YOU
Jimmy Johnson
Perry Bradford
Messin' Around (1929)

I NEED YOU SO
Arthur Schwartz
David Goldberg and Howard Dietz
The Grand Street Follies (1929)

I NEVER FELT BETTER IN MY LIFE
Paul Nassau and Oscar Brand
The Education of Hyman Kaplan (1968)

I NEVER HAD A CHANCE
Arthur Schwartz
Howard Dietz
The Gay Life (1961)

I NEVER HAS SEEN SNOW
Harold Arlen
Harold Arlen and Truman Capote
House of Flowers (1954)

I NEVER KNOW WHEN
Leroy Anderson
Joan Ford, Walter and Jean Kerr
Goldilocks (1958)

I NEVER LAUGHED IN MY LIFE
William Roy
Maggie (1953)

I NEVER MEANT TO FALL IN LOVE
Sammy Fain
Paul Francis Webster
Christine (1960)

I NEVER REALIZED
Cole Porter
Buddies (1919)

I NEVER SAW A KING BEFORE
Frederick Loewe
Earle Crooker
Great Lady (1938)

I NEVER WAS BORN
Harold Arlen
E. Y. Harburg
Bloomer Girl (1944)

I ONLY KNOW
Morgan Lewis
Nancy Hamilton
One for the Money (1939)

I ONLY WANNA LAUGH
Bill and Patti Jacob
Jimmy (1969)

I OUGHT TO KNOW MORE ABOUT YOU
Victor Young
Edward Heyman
Pardon Our French (1950)

I OWE OHIO
Don Elliott
James Costigan
The Beast in Me (1963)

I PLEAD, DEAR HEART
Jean Gilbert
Harry B. Smith
The Red Rose (1928)

I PROMISE I'LL BE PRACTICALLY TRUE TO YOU
Melville Gideon
Clifford Grey
The Optimists (1928)

I Promise You
Harold Arlen
Johnny Mercer
Here Come the Waves (F) (1944)

I Promised Their Mothers
Sigmund Romberg (developed by Don Walker)
Leo Robin
The Girl in Pink Tights (1954)

I Put My Hand In
Jerry Herman
Hello, Dolly! (1964)

I Really Like Him
Mitch Leigh
Joe Darion
Man of La Mancha (1965)

I Really Love You
Bill Mahoney
My Wife and I (OB) (1966)

I Remember Her
Mischa and Wesley Portnoff
Donagh MacDonagh
Happy As Larry (1950)

I Remember It Well
Frederick Loewe
Alan Jay Lerner
Gigi (F) (1958)

I Resolve
Jerry Bock
Sheldon Harnick
She Loves Me (1963)

I Said It and I'm Glad
Jule Styne
Betty Comden and Adolph Green
Subways Are for Sleeping (1961)

I Said to Love
Paul Klein
Fred Ebb
From A to Z (1960)

I Saw a Man
Al Carmines
Maria Irene Fornes
Promenade (OB) (1969)

I Saw Your Eyes
Sigmund Romberg
Oscar Hammerstein II
East Wind (1931)

I Say Hello
Harold Rome
Destry Rides Again (1959)

I Say It's Spinach
Irving Berlin
Face the Music (1932)

I Say Yes
Oscar Brand and Paul Nassau
A Joyful Noise (1966)

I See Something
Ervin Drake
What Makes Sammy Run? (1964)

I See the Light/Gentle Sighs
Joseph Martinez Kookoolis and Scott Fagan
Scott Fagan
Soon (1971)

I See What I Choose to See
Walt Smith
Leon Uris
Ari (1971)

I See You but What Do You See in Me?
Lester Lee
Keep It Clean (1929)

I See Your Face Before Me
Arthur Schwartz
Howard Dietz
Between the Devil (1937)

I Seen It with My Very Own Eyes
Paul Klein
Fred Ebb
Morning Sun (OB) (1963)

I Shall Love You
Joe Jordan
Homer Tutt and Henry Creamer
Deep Harlem (1929)

I Shall Miss You
Marian Grudeff and Raymond Jessel
Baker Street (1965)

I Shall Scream
Lionel Bart
Oliver! (1963)

I Shot the Works
Manning Sherwin
Arthur Lippman and Milton Pascal
Everybody's Welcome (1931)

I Should Stay
Jerry Blatt
Jerry Blatt and Lonnie Burstein
Have I Got One for You (OB)
(1968)

I Sing of Love
Cole Porter
Kiss Me, Kate (1948)

I Sit in the Sun
Julian Slade
Dorothy Reynolds and Julian Slade
Salad Days (OB) (1958)

I Sleep Easier Now
Cole Porter
Out of This World (1950)

I Sometimes Wonder
Oscar Straus
Clare Kummer
Three Waltzes (1937)

I Spy
Bob Goodman
Wild and Wonderful (1971)

I Started on a Shoestring
Arthur Schwartz
Howard Dietz
The Second Little Show (1930)

I Still Believe in You
Richard Rodgers
Lorenz Hart
Simple Simon (1930)

I Still Can Dream
Emmerich Kalman
B. G. DeSylva
The Yankee Princess (1921)

I Still Get Jealous
Jule Styne
Sammy Cahn
High Button Shoes (1947)

I Still Have to Learn
George Lessner
Miriam Battista and Russell Maloney
Sleepy Hollow (1948)

I Still Look at You That Way
Arthur Schwartz
Howard Dietz
Jennie (1963)

I Still Love the Red, White and Blue
Cole Porter
Gay Divorce (1932)

I Still See Elisa
Frederick Loewe
Alan Jay Lerner
Paint Your Wagon (1951)

I Stumbled over You
Maury Rubens
Henry Dagand
Hello, Paris (1930)

I Stumbled over You and Fell in Love
Harry Revel
Mack Gordon
Smiling Faces (1932)

I Suddenly Find It Agreeable
Glenn Paxton
Robert Goldman and George Weiss
First Impressions (1959)

I Take after Rip
Oscar Levant
Irving Caesar and Graham John
Ripples (1930)

I TALK TO THE TREES
Frederick Loewe
Alan Jay Lerner
Paint Your Wagon (1951)

I THANK YOU
Clarence Gaskill
Earl Carroll's Vanities (1925)

I THINK I'D LIKE TO FALL IN LOVE
Martin Charnin
Fallout (OB) (1959)

I THINK SHE NEEDS ME
Manos Hadjidakis
Joe Darion
Illya Darling (1967)

I THINK THE WORLD OF YOU
Mary Rodgers
Martin Charnin
Hot Spot (1963)

I TOOK ANOTHER LOOK
David Raksin
June Carroll
If the Shoe Fits (1946)

I TRY
Robert Dahdah
Curley McDimple (OB) (1967)

I USED TO BE COLOR BLIND
Irving Berlin
Carefree (F) (1938)

I WALK WITH MUSIC
Hoagy Carmichael
Johnny Mercer
Walk with Music (1940)

I WANNA BE BAD
Duke Ellington
John Latouche
Beggar's Holiday (1946)

I WANNA BE GOOD 'N BAD
Hugh Martin
Make a Wish (1951)

I WANNA BE LOVED BY YOU
Herbert Stothart, Bert Kalmar, and
  Harry Ruby
Good Boy (1928)

I WANNA GET MARRIED
Philip Charig
Dan Shapiro and Milton Pascal
Follow the Girls (1944)

I WANNA GO TO CITY COLLEGE
Sammy Fain
George Marion, Jr.
Toplitzky of Notre Dame (1946)

I WANNA GO VOOM VOOM
Cliff Friend
Lew Brown
Piggy (1927)

I WANT A KISS
Sigmund Romberg
Otto Harbach and Oscar Hammer-
  stein II
The Desert Song (1926)

I WANT A LOVABLE BABY
Ray Henderson
B. G. DeSylva and Lew Brown
George White's Scandals (1925)

I WANT A MAN
Vincent Youmans
Oscar Hammerstein II
Rainbow (1928)

I WANT A MAN
Richard Rodgers
Lorenz Hart
America's Sweetheart (1931)

I WANT A PAL
Raymond Hubbell
Anne Caldwell
Yours Truly (1927)

I WANT A SURPRISE
John Jennings
Riverwind (OB) (1962)

I WANT ANOTHER PORTION OF THAT
Ray Henderson
Lew Brown
Hot-Cha! (1932)

I WANT IT JUST TO HAPPEN
Lance Mulcahy
Paul Cherry
Park (1970)

I WANT MORE OUT OF LIFE THAN THIS
Jacques Urbont
David Newburger
Stag Movie (OB) (1971)

I WANT MY MAMA
Jararaca and Vincent Paiva
Al Stillman
Earl Carroll's Vanities (1940)

I WANT PLENTY OF YOU
Jimmy McHugh
Dorothy Fields
Hello Daddy (1928)

I WANT SOMEONE
William B. Friedlander
Jonica (1930)

I WANT THE KIND OF A FELLA
Steve Allen
Sophie (1963)

I WANT THE WORLD TO KNOW
Richard Myers
Leo Robin
Hello, Yourself! (1928)

I WANT TO BE A LITTLE FROG IN A LITTLE POND
Victor Ziskin
Joan Javits
Young Abe Lincoln (1961)

I WANT TO BE A WAR BRIDE
George Gershwin
Ira Gershwin
Strike Up the Band (1930)

I WANT TO BE BAD
Ray Henderson
B. G. DeSylva and Lew Brown
Follow Thru (1929)

I WANT TO BE HAPPY
Vincent Youmans
Irving Caesar
No, No, Nanette (1925)

I WANT TO BE RAIDED BY YOU
Cole Porter
Wake Up and Dream (1929)

I WANT TO BE RICH
Leslie Bricusse and Anthony Newley
Stop the World—I Want to Get Off (1962)

I WANT TO BE SEEN WITH YOU TO-NIGHT
Jule Styne
Bob Merrill
Funny Girl (1964)

I WANT TO BE THERE
Sigmund Romberg
Harry B. Smith
Cherry Blossoms (1927)

I WANT TO BE WITH YOU*
Vincent Youmans
B. G. DeSylva
Take a Chance (1932)

I WANT TO BE WITH YOU
Charles Strouse
Lee Adams
Golden Boy (1964)

I WANT TO CHISEL IN ON YOUR HEART
Michael H. Cleary
Max and Nathaniel Lief
Shoot the Works (1931)

I WANT TO DANCE
Will Irwin
Norman Zeno
Fools Rush In (1934)

_____

*Dropped from New York production.

I Want to Dance with You
Leon DeCosta
Kosher Kitty Kelly (1925)

I Want to Do a Number with the Boys
Rowland Wilson
Ned Wever
Crazy Quilt (1931)

I Want to Go Back to the Bottom of the Garden
David Raksin
June Carroll
If the Shoe Fits (1946)

I Want to Go Home
Cole Porter
Leave It to Me (1938)

I Want to Take 'Em Off for Norman Rockwell
Ruth Cleary Patterson
Les Kramer
Russell Patterson's Sketch Book (OB) (1960)

I Want to Live
Sammy Fain
Jack Yellen
Boys and Girls Together (1940)

I Want to Live
Johnny Brandon
Billy Noname (OB) (1970)

I Want to Live—I Want to Love
Alma Sanders
Monte Carlo
Louisiana Lady (1947)

I Want to Play with the Girls
Edgar Fairchild
Milton Pascal
The Illustrators' Show (1936)

I Want to Pray
Giuseppe Verdi
Charles Friedman
My Darlin' Aïda (1952)

I Want to See More of You
Jacques Belasco
Kay Twomey
The Girl from Nantucket (1945)

I Want to Walk to San Francisco
Nancy Ford
Gretchen Cryer
The Last Sweet Days of Isaac (OB) (1970)

I Want What I Want When I Want It
Victor Herbert
Henry Blossom
Mlle Modiste (1905)

I Want You
Stefan Kanfer, Jess J. Korman, and Joseph Grayhon
I Want You (OB) (1961)

I Want You All to Myself
Joseph Meyer
Edward Eliscu
Lady Fingers (1929)

I Want You to Be the First to Know
Arthur Siegel
June Carroll
New Faces (1962)

I Wanted to Change Him
Jule Styne
Betty Comden and Adolph Green
Hallelujah, Baby! (1967)

I Wanted to See the World
Baldwin Bergersen
William Archibald
The Crystal Heart (OB) (1960)

I Was a Shoo-In
Jule Styne
Betty Comden and Adolph Green
Subways Are for Sleeping (1961)

I Was Alone
Jerome Kern

Oscar Hammerstein II and Otto Harbach
Sunny (F) (1930)

I WAS BLUE
Harry Archer
Harlan Thompson
Merry-Merry (1925)

I WAS DOING ALL RIGHT
George Gershwin
Ira Gershwin
The Goldwyn Follies (F) (1938)

I WAS MEANT FOR SOMEONE
James F. Hanley
Ballard MacDonald
Gay Paree (1925)

I WAS SO YOUNG (YOU WERE SO BEAUTIFUL)
George Gershwin
Irving Caesar and Al Bryan
Good Morning, Judge (1919)

I WAS THE MOST BEAUTIFUL BLOSSOM
George Gershwin
Ira Gershwin
Of Thee I Sing (1931)

I WASH MY HANDS
Moose Charlap
Norman Gimbel
Whoop-Up (1958)

I WATCH THE LOVE PARADE
Jerome Kern
Otto Harbach
The Cat and the Fiddle (1931)

I WENT TO A MARVELOUS PARTY
Noël Coward
Set to Music (1939)

I WHISTLE A HAPPY TUNE
Richard Rodgers
Oscar Hammerstein II
The King and I (1951)

I WILL FOLLOW YOU
Jerry Herman
Milk and Honey (1961)

I WILL HAVE HIM
Stanley Jay Gelber
John Lollos and Don Christopher
Love and Let Love (OB) (1968)

I WILL MISS YOU
Sandy Wilson
Valmouth (OB) (1960)

I WISH
David Raksin
June Carroll
If the Shoe Fits (1946)

I WISH I WAS A BUMBLE BEE
James Shelton
Mrs. Patterson (1954)

I WISH I WERE IN LOVE AGAIN
Richard Rodgers
Lorenz Hart
Babes in Arms (1937)

I WISH IT SO
Marc Blitzstein
Juno (1959)

I WOKE UP TODAY
Christopher Cox
Blood (OB) (1971)

I WONDER AS I WANDER
Bronislaw Kaper (based on Chopin)
John Latouche
Polonaise (1945)

I WONDER HOW IT IS TO DANCE WITH A BOY
Bob Merrill
Henry, Sweet Henry (1967)

I WONDER IF
John Morris
Gerald Freedman
A Time for Singing (1966)

I WONDER IF LOVE IS A DREAM
Arthur Brander
The Seventh Heart (1927)

I WONDER IF SHE WILL REMEMBER
Shep Camp
Frank DuPree and Harry B. Smith
Half a Widow (1927)

I WONDER WHAT BECAME OF ME*
Harold Arlen
Johnny Mercer
St. Louis Woman (1946)

I WONDER WHAT IT'S LIKE*
Jerry Bock
Sheldon Harnick
Tenderloin (1960)

I WONDER WHAT THE KING IS DO-ING TONIGHT
Frederick Loewe
Alan Jay Lerner
Camelot (1960)

I WONDER WHETHER
Louis A Hirsch
P. G. Wodehouse
Oh, My Dear! (1918)

I WONDER WHY
Sigmund Romberg
Dorothy Donnelly
My Princess (1927)

I WONDER WHY
Walter Cool
Mackey of Appalchia (OB) (1965)

I WONDER WHY YOU WANDER
Fred Spielman and Arthur Gershwin
Stanley Adams
A Lady Says Yes (1945)

I WON'T DANCE
Jerome Kern
Dorothy Fields, Oscar Hammerstein II, Otto Harbach, and Jimmy McHugh
Roberta (F) (1935)

I WON'T GROW UP
Mark Charlap
Carolyn Leigh
Peter Pan (1954)

I WON'T LET IT HAPPEN AGAIN
Hugo Peretti, Luigi Creatore, and George David Weiss
Maggie Flynn (1968)

I WON'T TAKE NO FOR AN ANSWER
Richard Freitas
Morty Neff and George Mysels
The Difficult Woman (OB) (1962)

I WON'T WORRY
Maury Laws
Jules Bass
Month of Sundays (OB) (1968)

I WORK FOR PRAVDA
William Klenosky
Utopia! (OB) (1963)

I WORSHIP YOU*
Cole Porter
Fifty Million Frenchmen (1929)

I WOULD DIE
Bob Merrill
Take Me Along (1959)

I WOULD LIKE TO FONDLE YOU
Percy Wenrich
Raymond Peck
Castles in the Air (1926)

I WOULD LOVE TO HAVE YOU LOVE ME
Irving Caesar
Norman Zeno
White Horse Inn (1936)

I WOULDN'T BET ONE PENNY
Johnny Burke
Donnybrook! (1961)

I WOULDN'T HAVE HAD TO
Jay Livingston and Ray Evans
Let It Ride (1961)

I WOULDN'T HAVE YOU ANY OTHER WAY
Hugo Peretti, Luigi Creatore, and George David Weiss
Maggie Flynn (1968)

———
*Dropped from New York production

I WOULDN'T MARRY YOU
Arthur Schwartz
Howard Dietz
The Gay Life (1961)

I WROTE A SONG FOR YOU
Sam Morrison
Dolph Singer and William Dunham
Summer Wives (1936)

I, YES ME, THAT'S WHO
Jule Styne
Sammy Cahn
Look to the Lilies (1970)

ICE COLD KATY
Arthur Schwartz
Frank Loesser
Thank Your Lucky Stars (F) (1943)

ICE CREAM
Kurt Weill
Langston Hughes
Street Scene (1947)

ICE CREAM
Jerry Bock
Sheldon Harnick
She Loves Me (1963)

ICE CREAM
Norman Campbell
Donald Campbell and Norman Campbell
Anne of Green Gables (OB) (1971)

ICE HOUSE FIRE, THE
Francis Thorne
Arnold Weinstein
Fortuna (OB) (1962)

ICHABOD
George Lessner
Miriam Battista and Russell Maloney
Sleepy Hollow (1948)

I'D BE A FOOL
Sigmund Romberg
Oscar Hammerstein II
East Wind (1931)

I'D BE CRAZY TO BE CRAZY OVER YOU
Skip Redwine and Larry Frank
Frank Merriwell, or Honor Challenged (1971)

I'D BE HAPPY
Maceo Pinkard
Pansy (1929)

I'D DO ANYTHING
Lionel Bart
Oliver! (1963)

I'D DO IT AGAIN
Richard Rodgers
Lorenz Hart
Hallelujah, I'm a Bum (F) (1933)

I'D DO IT AGAIN
Marian Grudeff and Raymond Jessel
Baker Street (1965)

I'D FORGOTTEN HOW BEAUTIFUL SHE COULD BE
John Jennings
Riverwind (OB) (1962)

I'D GIVE HER TO THE WORLD OF DIAMONDS
Dale F. Menten
Dale F. Menten and Frederick Gaines
The House of Leather (OB) (1970)

I'D GLADLY TRADE
Hugh Martin and Ralph Blane
Best Foot Forward (1941)

I'D GLADLY WALK TO ALASKA
Alec Wilder
Arnold Sundgaard
Kittiwake Island (OB) (1960)

I'D KNOW IT
Steve Allen
Sophie (1963)

I'D LIKE MY PICTURE TOOK
Irving Berlin
Miss Liberty (1949)

I'D LIKE TO BE A ROSE
Galt MacDermot
John Guare
Two Gentlemen of Verona (1971)

**I'D LIKE TO DUNK YOU IN MY COF-
FEE**
Harry Akst
Lew Brown
Calling All Stars (1934)

I'D LIKE TO HIDE IT
Richard Rodgers
Lorenz Hart
Dearest Enemy (1925)

I'D LIKE TO LOVE THEM ALL
Emile Berté and Maury Rubens
J. Keirn Brennan
Music in May (1929)

I'D LIKE TO TAKE YOU HOME
Richard Rodgers
Lorenz Hart
The Girl Friend (1926)

**I'D LIKE TO TAKE YOU HOME TO
MEET MY MOTHER**
Robert Russell Bennett
Owen Murphy and Robert A. Simon
Hold Your Horses (1933)

I'D MARRY YOU AGAIN
Lance Mulcahy
Paul Cherry
Park (1970)

I'D RATHER BE RIGHT
Richard Rodgers
Lorenz Hart
I'd Rather Be Right (1937)

**I'D RATHER DANCE HERE THAN
HEREAFTER**
Joseph Meyer and Roger Wolfe Kahn
Irving Caesar
Here's Howe (1928)

I'D RATHER LEAD A BAND
Irving Berlin
Follow the Fleet (F) (1936)

I'D RATHER WAKE UP BY MYSELF
Arthur Schwartz
Dorothy Fields
By the Beautiful Sea (1954)

I'D STEAL A STAR
Vincent Youmans
Anne Caldwell
Oh, Please! (1926)

I'D SURE LIKE TO GIVE IT A SHOT
Jule Styne
Sammy Cahn
Look to the Lilies (1970)

I'D WRITE A SONG
Sigmund Romberg
Irving Caesar
Melody (1933)

IDLES OF THE KING
Richard Rodgers
Lorenz Hart
The Garrick Gaieties (1926)

IF
George Lessner
Miriam Battista and Russell Maloney
Sleepy Hollow (1948)

IF A GIRL ISN'T PRETTY
Jule Styne
Bob Merrill
Funny Girl (1964)

IF EVER I WOULD LEAVE YOU
Frederick Loewe
Alan Jay Lerner
Camelot (1960)

IF EVERY MONTH WERE JUNE
Henry Sullivan
John Murray Anderson
John Murray Anderson's Almanac
(1953)

IF FLUTTERBY WINS
Jay Livingston and Ray Evans
Let It Ride (1961)

IF HE REALLY LOVES ME
Harold Arlen
Jack Yellen
You Said It (1931)

IF HE WALKED INTO MY LIFE
Jerry Herman
Mame (1966)

IF HE'LL COME BACK TO ME
Vincent Youmans
Leo Robin and Clifford Grey
Hit the Deck (1927)

IF I AM DREAMING
Carl Millöcker (revised by Theo Mack-
eben)
Rowland Leigh
The Dubarry (1932)

IF I AM TO MARRY YOU
Deed Meyer
She Shall Have Music (OB) (1959)

IF I BE YOUR BEST CHANCE
Jimmy Van Heusen
Sammy Cahn
Walking Happy (1966)

IF I BECAME THE PRESIDENT
George Gershwin
Ira Gershwin
Strike Up the Band (1930)

IF I COULD LIVE MY LIFE AGAIN
Earl Wilson, Jr.
*A Day in the Life of Just About Every-
one* (Ob) (1971)

IF I DIDN'T HAVE YOU
Alexander Hill
Hummin' Sam (1933)

IF I FELT ANY YOUNGER TODAY
David Baker
Fred Ebb
Smiling, the Boy Fell Dead (OB)
(1961)

IF I GAVE YOU
Hugh Martin and Timothy Gray
High Spirits (1964)

IF I GAVE YOU A ROSE
Melville Gideon
Granville English
The Optimists (1928)

IF I HAD A . . . .
G. Wood
F. Jasmine Addams (OB) (1971)

IF I HAD A LOVER
Henry Tobias
Billy Rose and Ballard MacDonald
Padlocks (1927)

IF I HAD A MILLION DOLLARS
Gary William Friedman
Will Holt
The Me Nobody Knows (OB) (1970)

IF I HAD A TALKING PICTURE OF
YOU
Ray Henderson
B. G. DeSylva and Lew Brown
Sunny Side Up (F) (1929)

IF I HAD MY DRUTHERS
Gene de Paul
Johnny Mercer
Li'l Abner (1956)

IF I HAD THE ANSWERS
Mike Brandt, Michael Knight, and
Robert J. Lowery
Exchange (OB) (1970)

IF I KNEW
Meredith Willson
The Unsinkable Molly Brown (1960)

IF I LOVE AGAIN
Ben Oakland
J. P. Murray
Hold Your Horses (1933)

IF I LOVED YOU
Richard Rodgers
Oscar Hammerstein II
Carousel (1945)

IF I MAY
Richard B. Chodosh
Barry Alan Grael
The Streets of New York (OB) (1963)

IF I NEVER WALTZ AGAIN
Emmerich Kalman
George Marion, Jr.
Marinka (1945)

IF I ONLY HAD
Oscar Brown, Jr. and Charles Az-
navour
Joy (OB) (1970)

IF I ONLY HAD A BRAIN
Harold Arlen
E. Y. Harburg
The Wizard of Oz (F) (1939)

IF I RULED THE WORLD
Cyril Ornadel
Leslie Bricusse
Pickwick (1965)

IF I WAS A BOY
James Shelton
Mrs. Patterson (1954)

IF I WERE A BELL
Frank Loesser
Guys and Dolls (1950)

IF I WERE A RICH MAN
Jerry Bock
Sheldon Harnick
Fiddler on the Roof (1964)

IF I WERE KING
Newell Chase, Leo Robin, and Sam
Coslow
The Vagabond King (F) (1930)

IF I WERE ONLY SOMEONE
Sam Pottle
Tom Whedon
All Kinds of Giants (OB) (1961)

IF I WERE THE MAN
Milton Schafer
Ronny Graham
Bravo Giovanni (1962)

IF I WERE YOU
Richard Rodgers
Lorenz Hart
Betsy (1926)

IF I WERE YOU
Louis Alter
Harry Ruskin and Leighton K. Brill
Ballyhoo (1930)

IF I WERE YOU
Charles Strouse
Lee Adams
All American (1962)

IF I WERE YOU, LOVE
Vincent Youmans
Ring Lardner
Smiles (1930)

IF-IF-IF-IF
Robert Colby
Robert Colby and Nita Jonas
Half-Past Wednesday (OB) (1962)

IF IT HADN'T BEEN FOR ME
Norman Campbell
Donald Campbell and Norman Camp-
bell
Anne of Green Gables (OB) (1971)

IF IT WASN'T FOR PEOPLE
Billy Barnes
The Billy Barnes People (1961)

IF IT WERE EASY TO DO
Carl Sigman
Bob Hilliard
Angel in the Wings (1947)

IF IT'S A DREAM
Victor Young
Stella Unger
Seventh Heaven (1955)

IF IT'S ANY NEWS TO YOU
Eubie Blake
Noble Sissle
Shuffle Along (1933)

IF IT'S GOOD ENOUGH FOR LADY AS-
TOR
Stan Freeman and Franklin Under-
wood
Lovely Ladies, Kind Gentlemen
(1970)

IF IT'S LOVE
Harry Akst
Lew Brown
Calling All Stars (1934)

IF IT'S LOVE
Morgan Lewis
Nancy Hamilton
Three to Make Ready (1946)

IF IT'S LOVE
Johnny Brandon
Cindy (OB) (1964)

IF LOVE SHOULD COME TO ME
Henry Souvaine and Jay Gorney
Morrie Ryskind and Howard Dietz
Merry-Go-Round (1927)

IF LOVE WERE ALL
Noël Coward
Bitter Sweet (1929)

IF LOVE'S LIKE A LARK
Alec Wilder
Arnold Sundgaard
Kittiwake Island (OB) (1960)

IF MENELAUS ONLY KNEW IT
Erich Wolfgang Korngold (based on
Offenbach)
Herbert Baker
Helen Goes to Troy (1944)

IF MOMMA WAS MARRIED
Jule Styne
Stephen Sondheim
Gypsy (1959)

IF MY FRIENDS COULD SEE ME NOW
Cy Coleman
Dorothy Fields
Sweet Charity (1966)

IF ONLY
Sigmund Romberg
Rowland Leigh
My Romance (1948)

IF ONLY I COULD BE A KID AGAIN
Murray Rumshinsky
Jacob Jacobs
The President's Daughter (1970)

IF SHE COULD ONLY FEEL THE
SAME
Stanley Jay Gelber
John Lollos and Don Christopher
Love and Let Love (OB) (1968)

IF SHE HAS NEVER LOVED BEFORE
Richard Hill and John Hawkins
Nevill Coghill
Canterbury Tales (1969)

IF THAT WAS LOVE
Bob Merrill
New Girl in Town (1957)

IF THAT'S WHAT YOU WANT
Sigmund Romberg
Harry B. Smith
The Love Call (1927)

IF THE BLUES DON'T GET YOU
Maceo Pinkard
Pansy (1929)

IF THE RAIN'S GOT TO FALL
David Heneker
Half a Sixpence (1965)

IF THE SHOE FITS
David Raksin
June Carroll
If the Shoe Fits (1946)

IF THERE IS SOMEONE LOVELIER
THAN YOU
Arthur Schwartz
Howard Dietz
Revenge with Music (1934)

IF THERE'S LOVE ENOUGH
Claibe Richardson
Kenward Elmslie
The Grass Harp (1971)

IF THIS IS GLAMOUR!
Richard Stutz
Rick French
Along Fifth Avenue (1949)

IF THIS IS GOODBYE
Robert Wright and George Forrest
(based on Rachmaninoff)
Anya (1965)

IF THIS ISN'T LOVE
Burton Lane
E. Y. Harburg
Finian's Rainbow (1947)

IF WE ONLY COULD STOP THE OLD TOWN CLOCK
Walter Kent
Kim Gannon
Seventeen (1951)

IF WE ONLY HAVE LOVE
Jacques Brel
Eric Blau and Mort Shuman
Jacques Brel Is Alive and Well and Living in Paris (OB) (1968)

IF WISHES WERE HORSES
Helen Miller
Eve Merriam
Inner City (1971)

IF YOU ARE AS GOOD AS YOU LOOK
Jerome Kern
Anne Caldwell
The City Chap (1925)

IF YOU ARE IN LOVE WITH A GIRL
Percy Wenrich
Raymond Peck
Castles in the Air (1926)

IF YOU CAN FIND A TRUE LOVE
William Dyer
Don Parks and William Dyer
Jo! (OB) (1964)

IF YOU CAN'T BRING IT, YOU'VE GOT TO SEND IT
Porter Grainger and Freddie Johnson
Lucky Sambo (1925)

IF YOU CARED
Jean Gilbert
Harry Graham
Katja (1926)

IF YOU COULD CARE
Herman Darewski
Arthur Wimperis
As You Were (1920)

IF YOU COULD ONLY COME WITH ME
Noël Coward
Bitter Sweet (1929)

IF YOU COULD SEE HER
John Kander
Fred Ebb
Cabaret (1966)

IF YOU DID IT ONCE
Robert Colby
Robert Colby and Nita Jonas
Half-Past Wednesday (OB) (1962)

IF YOU GOT MUSIC
Colin Romoff
David Rogers
Ziegfeld Follies (1957)

IF YOU HADN'T, BUT YOU DID
Jule Styne
Betty Comden and Adolph Green
Two on the Aisle (1951)

IF YOU HAVE TROUBLES LAUGH THEM AWAY
Lester Lee
Harry Delmar's Revels (1927)

IF YOU HAVEN'T GOT A SWEETHEART
Arthur Schwartz
Dorothy Fields
A Tree Grows in Brooklyn (1951)

IF YOU HAVEN'T GOT "IT"
Max Ewing
Agnes Morgan
The Grand Street Follies (OB) (1927)

IF YOU KNOW WHAT I MEAN
Arthur Schwartz
Theodore Goodwin and Albert Carroll
The Grand Street Follies (OB) (1926)

IF YOU KNOW WHAT I THINK
Sigmund Romberg
Harry B. Smith
Cherry Blossoms (1927)

IF YOU LET ME MAKE LOVE TO YOU THEN WHY CAN'T I TOUCH YOU?
Peter Link and C. C. Courtney
Salvation (OB) (1969)

IF YOU LISTEN TO MY SONG
Mike Brandt, Michael Knight, and Robert J. Lowery
Exchange (OB) (1970)

IF YOU LOVED ME TRULY
Cole Porter
Can-Can (1953)

IF YOU SAID WHAT YOU THOUGHT
Leon DeCosta
The Blonde Sinner (1926)

IF YOU SMILE AT ME
Cole Porter
Around the World (1946)

IF YOU WANT TO GET AHEAD
Norman Curtis
Patricia Taylor Curtis
Walk Down Mah Street! (OB) (1968)

IF YOU WERE SOMEONE ELSE
Harold Levey
Owen Murphy
Rainbow Rose (1926)

IF YOU WERE SOMEONE ELSE
Arthur Schwartz
Albert Stillman
Virginia (1937)

IF YOU WERE THE APPLE
Joseph Meyer
William Moll
Jonica (1930)

IF YOU WIND ME UP
Larry Grossman
Hal Hackady
Minnie's Boys (1970)

IF YOU WOULD ONLY COME AWAY
Georges Bizet
Oscar Hammerstein II
Carmen Jones (1943)

IF YOU'D BE HAPPY, DON'T FALL IN LOVE
Maurice Yvain
Max and Nathaniel Lief
Luckee Girl (1928)

IF YOU'LL ALWAYS SAY YES
Winthrop Cortelyou
Derick Wulff
Kiss Me (1927)

IF YOU'LL BE MINE
Hugh Martin
Look Ma, I'm Dancin'! (1948)

IF YOU'LL PUT UP WITH ME
Frank Grey
Earle Crooker and McElbert Moore
Happy (1927)

IF YOU'RE IN LOVE, YOU'LL WALTZ
Harry Tierney
Joseph McCarthy
Rio Rita (1927)

IF YOU'VE GOT IT, YOU'VE GOT IT
Johnny Brandon
Cindy (OB) (1964)

IF'N
Harold Karr
Matt Dubey
Happy Hunting (1956)

I'LL ADMIT
Maury Rubens
Henry Dagand
Hello, Paris (1930)

I'll Always Be in Love
Claibe Richardson
Kenward Elmslie
The Grass Harp (1971)

I'll Applaud You with My Feet
Jimmy McHugh
Al Dubin
Keep Off the Grass (1940)

I'll Ballyhoo You
Dimitri Tiomkin
Edward Eliscu
A Little Racketeer (1932)

I'll Be a Buoyant Girl
Sigmund Romberg
Otto Harbach and Oscar Hammerstein II
The Desert Song (1926)

I'll Be Hard to Handle
Jerome Kern
Bernard Dougall
Roberta (1933)

I'll Be Respectable
Harold Arlen
Johnny Mercer
Saratoga (1959)

I'll Be Seeing You
Sammy Fain
Irving Kahal
Right This Way (1938)

I'll Be Sittin' in de Lap o' de Lord
Arthur Schwartz
Albert Stillman
Virginia (1937)

I'll Be Smiling
Jean Schwartz
Clifford Grey and William Cary Duncan
Sunny Days (1928)

I'll Be There
Albert Sirmay and Arthur Schwartz
Arthur Swanstrom
Princess Charming (1930)

I'll Be True, but I'll Be Blue
Alexander Hill
Hummin' Sam (1933)

I'll Be Waiting
Emmerich Kalman
Harry B. Smith
The Circus Princess (1927)

I'll Bet You're a Cat Girl
Mildred Kayden
Frank Gagliano
Paradise Gardens East (OB) (1969)

I'll Betcha That I'll Getcha
Jesse Greer
Stanley Adams
Shady Lady (1933)

I'll Build a Stairway to Paradise
George Gershwin
B. G. DeSylva and Arthur Francis (Ira Gershwin)
George White's Scandals (1922)

I'll Buy It
Burton Lane
Dorothy Fields
Junior Miss (TV) (1957)

I'll Buy You a Star
Arthur Schwartz
Dorothy Fields
A Tree Grows in Brooklyn (1951)

I'll Can-Can All Day
Johann Strauss II, adapted by Oscar Straus
Clare Kummer
Three Waltzes (1937)

I'll Carry You an Inch
Meyer Kupferman
Paul Goodman
Jonah (OB) (1966)

I'll Come Back to You
Vincent Youmans
Edward Heyman
Through the Years (1932)

I'LL COME BY
Bill Mahoney
My Wife and I (OB) (1966)

I'LL CUDDLE UP TO YOU
Leon DeCosta
Kosher Kitty Kelly (1925)

I'LL FIND A DREAM SOMEWHERE
Don McAfee
Nancy Leeds
Great Scot! (OB) (1965)

I'LL FOLLOW MY SECRET HEART
Noël Coward
Conversation Piece (1934)

I'LL GET MY MAN
Ray Henderson
B. G. DeSylva and Lew Brown
Flying High (1930)

I'LL GIVE MY LOVE A RING
Richard Hill and John Hawkins
Nevill Coghill
Canterbury Tales (1969)

I'LL GIVE THE WORLD TO YOU
Alma Sanders
Monte Carlo
Oh! Oh! Nurse (1925)

I'LL GO HOME WITH BONNIE JEAN
Frederick Loewe
Alan Jay Lerner
Brigadoon (1947)

I'LL HIT A NEW HIGH
Kay Swift
Paul James
Fine and Dandy (1930)

I'LL KEEP ON DREAMING
Emmerich Kalman
Harry B. Smith
Countess Maritza (1926)

I'LL KEEP ON DREAMING OF YOU
J. Fred Coots
Al Dubin
White Lights (1927)

I'LL KNOW
Frank Loesser
Guys and Dolls (1950)

I'LL KNOW AND SHE'LL KNOW
Harry Ruby
Bert Kalmar
Top Speed (1929)

I'LL KNOW HIM
Ray Henderson
B. G. DeSylva and Lew Brown
Flying High (1930)

I'LL LEARN YA
Jay Livingston and Ray Evans
Let It Ride (1961)

I'LL LOVE THEM ALL TO DEATH
Jean Gilbert
Harry B. Smith
The Red Rose (1928)

I'LL MAKE A MAN OF THE MAN
Jimmy Van Heusen
Sammy Cahn
Walking Happy (1966)

I'LL NEVER BE JEALOUS AGAIN
Richard Adler and Jerry Ross
The Pajama Game (1954)

I'LL NEVER BE LONELY AGAIN
Cyril Ornadel
Leslie Bricusse
Pickwick (1965)

I'LL NEVER COMPLAIN
H. Maurice Jacquet
Preston Sturges
The Well of Romance (1930)

I'LL NEVER FALL IN LOVE AGAIN
Burt Bacharach
Hal David
Promises, Promises (1968)

I'LL NEVER FORGET
Max Ewing
Albert Carroll
The Grand Street Follies (1929)

I'LL NEVER LAY DOWN ANY MORE
Manos Hadjidakis
Joe Darion
Illya Darling (1967)

I'LL NEVER LEARN
Morton Gould
Dorothy Fields
Arms and the Girl (1950)

I'LL NEVER LEAVE YOU
Albert Sirmay and Arthur Schwartz
Arthur Swanstrom
Princess Charming (1930)

I'LL NEVER MAKE A FRENCHMAN OUT OF YOU
Hugh Martin
Make a Wish (1951)

I'LL NEVER SAY NO
Meredith Willson
The Unsinkable Molly Brown (1960)

I'LL ONLY MISS HER WHEN I THINK OF HER
Jimmy Van Heusen
Sammy Cahn
Skyscraper (1965)

I'LL PAY THE CHECK
Arthur Schwartz
Dorothy Fields
Stars in Your Eyes (1939)

I'LL PEEK-A-BOO YOU
Sigmund Romberg
Harry B. Smith
Cherry Blossoms (1927)

I'LL PRODUCE FOR YOU
Frank D'Armond
Will Morrissey
Saluta (1934)

I'LL PUTCHA PITCHA IN THE PAPER
Michael H. Cleary
Max and Nathaniel Lief
The Third Little Show (1931)

I'LL REMEMBER HER
Noël Coward
The Girl Who Came to Supper (1963)

I'LL SEE YOU AGAIN
Noël Coward
Bitter Sweet (1929)

I'LL SEE YOU HOME
Harry Archer
Will B. Johnstone
Entre-Nous (OB) (1935)

I'LL SHARE IT ALL WITH YOU
Irving Berlin
Annie Get Your Gun (1946)

I'LL SHOW HIM!
Albert Hague
Arnold B. Horwitt
Plain and Fancy (1955)

I'LL SHOW HIM
Norman Campbell
Donald Campbell and Norman Campbell
Anne of Green Gables (OB) (1971)

I'LL SHOW THEM ALL
Steve Allen
Sophie (1963)

I'LL SHOW YOU THE WORLD TO-NIGHT
Hal Jordan
Jerry Douglas
Rondelay (OB) (1969)

I'LL SING YOU A SONG
Ralph Blane
Three Wishes for Jamie (1952)

I'LL SMILE
Stanley Jay Gelber
John Lollos and Don Christopher
Love and Let Love (OB) (1968)

I'LL STAY, I'LL GO
Wally Harper
Paul Zakrzewski
Sensations (OB) (1970)

I'LL STILL LOVE JEAN
Don McAfee
Nancy Leeds
Great Scot! (OB) (1965)

I'LL TAKE AN OPTION ON YOU
Ralph Rainger
Leo Robin
Tattle Tales (1933)

I'LL TAKE CARE OF YOU
Edward Pola
Eddie Brandt
Woof, Woof (1929)

I'LL TAKE ROMANCE
Ben Oakland
Oscar Hammerstein II
I'll Take Romance (F) (1937)

I'LL TAKE THE CITY
Vernon Duke
John Latouche
Banjo Eyes (1941)

I'LL TAKE THE SOLO
Clay Warnick
Edward Eager
Dream with Music (1944)

I'LL TAKE YOU TO THE COUNTRY
Maurice Yvain
Max and Nathaniel Lief
Luckee Girl (1928)

I'LL TELL THE MAN IN THE STREET
Richard Rodgers
Lorenz Hart
I Married an Angel (1938)

I'LL TELL THE WORLD
Fred Stamer
Gen Genovese
Buttrio Square (1952)

I'LL TELL YOU
Walter Kollo
Harry B. Smith
Three Little Girls (1930)

I'LL TELL YOU A TRUTH
Jerry Bock
Sheldon Harnick
The Apple Tree (1966)

I'LL TELL YOU ALL SOMEDAY
Ben Schwartz
Tales of Rigo (1927)

I'LL TRY
Albert Hague
Dorothy Fields
Redhead (1959)

I'LL TRY TO SMILE
Bill Mahoney
My Wife and I (OB) (1966)

I'LL TURN A LITTLE COG
Sidney Lippman
Sylvia Dee
Barefoot Boy with Cheek (1947)

I'LL WALK ALONE
Jule Styne
Sammy Cahn
Follow the Boys (F) (1944)

I'LL WALK ALONE
Alyn Heim
Malcolm L. LaPrade
Will the Mail Train Run Tonight?
(OB) (1964)

ILL-TEMPERED CLAVICHORD, THE
Frederick Loewe
Alan Jay Lerner
What's Up? (1943)

ILL WIND
Donald Swann
Michael Flanders
At the Drop of Another Hat (1966)

ILLEGITIMATE DAUGHTER, THE
George Gershwin
Ira Gershwin
Of Thee I Sing (1931)

ILLYA DARLING
Manos Hadjidakis
Joe Darion
Illya Darling (1967)

ILONA
Jerry Bock
Sheldon Harnick
She Loves Me (1963)

I'M A BAD, BAD MAN
Irving Berlin
Annie Get Your Gun (1946)

I'M A BRASS BAND
Cy Coleman
Dorothy Fields
Sweet Charity (1966)

I'M A BUTTER HOARDER
Harold Orlob
Hairpin Harmony (1943)

I'M A DANDY
Irving Burgie
Ballad for Bimshire (OB) (1963)

I'M A DREAMER (AREN'T WE ALL)
Ray Henderson
B. G. DeSylva and Lew Brown
Sunny Side Up (F) (1929)

I'M A FOOL, LITTLE ONE
Richard Rodgers
Lorenz Hart
Present Arms (1928)

I'M A FUNNY DAME
Harold Karr
Matt Dubey
Happy Hunting (1956)

I'M A GIGOLO
Cole Porter
Wake Up and Dream (1929)

I'M A HIGHWAY GENTLEMAN
Joseph Meyer and Philip Charig
Leo Robin
Just Fancy (1927)

I'M A LITTLE BIT FONDER OF YOU
Irving Caesar
Ripples (1930)

I'M A ONE GIRL MAN
George M. Cohan
Billie (1928)

I'M A POSITIVE GUY
George Harwell
What a Killing (OB) (1961)

I'M A STRANGER HERE MYSELF
Kurt Weill
Ogden Nash
One Touch of Venus (1943)

I'M ABOUT TO BE A MOTHER (WHO
COULD ASK FOR ANYTHING MORE?)
George Gershwin
Ira Gershwin
Of Thee I Sing (1931)

I'M AFRAID
Albert Sirmay
Irving Caesar and Graham John
Ripples (1930)

I'M AFRAID
Richard Rodgers
Lorenz Hart
Higher and Higher (1940)

I'M AFRAID I'M IN LOVE
Clay Warnick
Edward Eager
Dream with Music (1944)

I'M AFRAID OF THE DARK
Richard Addinsell
Clemence Dane
Come of Age (1934)

I'M AGAINST RHYTHM
Arthur Schwartz
Howard Dietz
Between the Devil (1937)

I'M ALIVE
David Krivoshei
David Paulsen
To Live Another Summer (1971)

I'M ALL ALONE
A. Baldwin Sloane
Harry Cort and George E. Stoddard
China Rose (1925)

I'M ALL I'VE GOT
Milton Schafer
Ronny Graham
Bravo Giovanni (1962)

I'M ALL SMILES
Michael Leonard
Herbert Martin
The Yearling (1965)

I'M ALL YOURS
Leo Schumer
Mike Stuart
Alive and Kicking (1950)

I'M ALONE
Jerome Kern
Oscar Hammerstein II
Music in the Air (1932)

I'M ALWAYS CHASING RAINBOWS
Harry Carroll
Joseph McCarthy
Oh, Look! (1918)

I'M ALWAYS HAPPY WHEN I'M IN
YOUR ARMS
Al Wilson, Charles Weinberg, and
  Ken Macomber
Yeah Man (1932)

I'M ALWAYS WRONG
John Morris
Gerald Freedman
A Time for Singing (1966)

I'M AN INDIAN TOO
Irving Berlin
Annie Get Your Gun (1946)

I'M AN INTERNATIONAL ORPHAN
Jerome Moross
Paul Peters and George Sklar
Parade (1935)

I'M AN ORDINARY MAN
Frederick Loewe
Alan Jay Lerner
My Fair Lady (1956)

I'M A'TINGLE, I'M A'GLOW
Jule Styne
Leo Robin
Gentlemen Prefer Blondes (1949)

I'M BACK IN CIRCULATION
Albert Hague
Dorothy Fields
Redhead (1959)

I'M BACK IN CIRCULATION AGAIN
Michael H. Cleary
Max and Nathaniel Lief
Earl Carroll's Vanities (1931)

I'M BEAUTIFUL
Moose Charlap
Norman Gimbel
The Conquering Hero (1961)

I'M BLUE TOO
Bob Merrill
Henry, Sweet Henry (1967)

I'M BRINGING A RED, RED ROSE
Walter Donaldson
Gus Kahn
Whoopee (1928)

I'M CALM
Stephen Sondheim
*A Funny Thing Happened on the Way
  to the Forum* (1962)

I'M COMIN', VIRGINIA
Donald Heywood
Will Marion Cook and Donald Heywood
Africana (1927)

I'M COMING HOME
Jerome Kern
Oscar Hammerstein II
Music in the Air (1932)

I'M DREAMING WHILE WE'RE
DANCING
Gerald Dolin
Edward J. Lambert
Smile at Me (1935)

I'M EVERYBODY'S BABY
James Mundy
John Latouche
The Vamp (1955)

I'M FALLING IN LOVE
Robert Katscher
Irving Caesar
The Wonder Bar (1931)

**I'M FALLING IN LOVE WITH SOME-
ONE**
Victor Herbert
Rida Johnson Young
Naughty Marietta (1910)

I'M FASCINATING
Charles Strouse
Lee Adams
All American (1962)

I'M FEELING BETTER ALL THE TIME
Edwin Greenberg
Pilgrim's Progress (OB) (1962)

I'M FLYING
Mark Charlap
Carolyn Leigh
Peter Pan (1954)

I'M FLYIN' HIGH
Abner Silver, Jack Le Soir, and Roy
Doll
Earl Carroll's Vanities (1928)

I'M FOR YOU
Lee David
J. Keirn Brennan
A Night in Venice (1929)

I'M FROM GRANADA
Mario Braggiotti
David Sidney
The Vanderbilt Revue (1930)

**I'M GETTING MYSELF READY FOR
YOU**
Cole Porter
The New Yorkers (1930)

I'M GETTING TIRED SO I CAN SLEEP
Irving Berlin
This Is the Army (1942)

I'M GLAD I WAITED
Vincent Youmans
Harold Adamson and Clifford Grey
Smiles (1930)

I'M GLAD I'M LEAVING
Jule Styne
Bob Hilliard
Hazel Flagg (1953)

I'M GLAD I'M NOT A MAN
Vernon Duke
Ogden Nash
The Littlest Revue (OB) (1956)

**I'M GLAD I'M NOT YOUNG ANY
MORE**
Frederick Loewe
Alan Jay Lerner
Gigi (F) (1958)

I'M GLAD I'M SINGLE
Arthur Schwartz
Howard Dietz
The Gay Life (1961)

**I'M GLAD TO SEE YOU'VE GOT WHAT
YOU WANT**
Harvey Schmidt
Tom Jones
Celebration (1969)

I'M GOING BACK
Jule Styne
Betty Comden and Adolph Green
Bells Are Ringing (1956)

I'M GONNA BE A POP
Fred Stamer
Gen Genovese
Buttrio Square (1952)

I'M GONNA BE JOHN HENRY
David Martin
Langston Hughes
Simply Heavenly (1957)

I'M GONNA DO MY THINGS
Voices, Inc.
The Believers (OB) (1968)

I'M GONNA GET HIM
Irving Berlin
Mr. President (1962)

I'M GONNA HANG MY HAT
Philip Charig
Dan Shapiro and Milton Pascal
Follow the Girls (1944)

I'M GONNA HAVE A BABY
Don McAfee
Nancy Leeds
Great Scot! (OB) (1965)

I'M GONNA LEAVE OFF WEARING MY SHOES
Harold Arlen
Harold Arlen and Truman Capote
House of Flowers (1954)

I'M GONNA MAKE A FOOL OUT OF APRIL
Victor Young
Edward Heyman
Pardon Our French (1950)

I'M GONNA MOVE
Albert Hague
Marty Brill
Café Crown (1964)

I'M GONNA WALK RIGHT UP TO HER
Moose Charlap
Eddie Lawrence
Kelly (1965)

I'M GONNA WASH THAT MAN RIGHT OUTA MY HAIR
Richard Rodgers
Oscar Hammerstein II
South Pacific (1949)

I'M GROVER
Vernon Duke
Newman Levy
The Garrick Gaieties (1930)

I'M GWINE LIE DOWN
Al Carmines
Rosalyn Drexler
Home Movies (OB) (1964)

I'M HANS CHRISTIAN ANDERSEN
Frank Loesser
Hans Christian Andersen (F) (1951)

I'M HAPPY
Jane Douglas
Tom O'Malley
Bella (OB) (1961)

I'M HAPPY
Armando Trovaioli
Pietro Garinei and Sandro Giovannini
Rugantino (1964)

I'M HAROLD, I'M HAROLD
Sigmund Romberg
Arthur Wimperis
Louie the 14th (1925)

I'M HIGH, I'M LOW
A. Baldwin Sloane
Harry Cort and George E. Stoddard
China Rose (1925)

I'M HONEST
J. C. Johnson
Change Your Luck (1930)

I'M IN LEAGUE WITH THE DEVIL
Louis Bellson and Will Irwin
Richard Ney
Portofino (1958)

I'M IN LONDON AGAIN
Marian Grudeff and Raymond Jessel
Baker Street (1965)

I'M IN LOVE
Con Conrad
Gus Kahn and Otto Harbach
Kitty's Kisses (1926)

I'M IN LOVE
Cole Porter
Fifty Million Frenchmen (1929)

I'M IN LOVE
Emile Berté and Maury Rubens
J. Keirn Brennan
Music in May (1929)

I'M IN LOVE AGAIN
Cole Porter
Greenwich Village Follies (1924)

I'M IN LOVE! I'M IN LOVE!
Jerry Bock
Sheldon Harnick
The Rothschilds (1970)

I'M IN LOVE WITH A SOLDIER BOY
Cole Porter
Something for the Boys (1943)

I'M IN LOVE WITH A WONDERFUL
GUY
Richard Rodgers
Oscar Hammerstein II
South Pacific (1949)

I'M IN LOVE WITH MISS LOGAN
Ronny Graham
New Faces (1952)

I'M IN THE MOOD FOR LOVE
Jimmy McHugh
Dorothy Fields
Every Night at Eight (F) (1935)

I'M JUST A LITTLE BIT CONFUSED
Harry Warren
Jerome Lawrence and Robert E. Lee
Shangri-La (1956)

I'M JUST A LITTLE SPARROW
Sammy Fain
Paul Francis Webster
Christine (1960)

I'M JUST A STATISTIC
Norman Curtis
Patricia Taylor Curtis
Walk Down Mah Street! (OB) (1968)

I'M JUST TAKING MY TIME
Jule Styne
Betty Comden and Adolph Green
Subways Are for Sleeping (1961)

I'M JUST WILD ABOUT HARRY
Eubie Blake
Noble Sissle
Shuffle Along (1921)

I'M LEAVING THE BAD GIRLS FOR
GOOD
Dave Stamper
Fred Herendeen
Orchids Preferred (1937)

I'M LIKE A NEW BROOM
Arthur Schwartz
Dorothy Fields
A Tree Grows in Brooklyn (1951)

I'M LIKE THE BLUEBIRD
Stephen Sondheim
Anyone Can Whistle (1964)

I'M LOST
George Lessner
Ruth Aarons
Sleepy Hollow (1948)

I'M ME
Glenn Paxton
Robert Goldman and George Weiss
First Impressions (1959)

I'M ME! (I'M NOT AFRAID)
Hal Hester and Danny Apolinar
Your Own Thing (1968)

I'M NINETY POUNDS OF SWEETNESS
Harry Archer
Walter O'Keefe
Just a Minute (1928)

I'M NO BUTTERFLY
A. Baldwin Sloane
Harry Cort and George E. Stoddard
China Rose (1925)

I'M NOT A WELL MAN
Harold Rome
I Can Get it for You Wholesale (1962)

I'M NOT AT ALL IN LOVE
Richard Adler and Jerry Ross
The Pajama Game (1954)

I'M NOT FINISHED YET
Charles Strouse
Lee Adams
(It's a Bird, It's a Plane) It's Superman
(1966)

I'M NOT FOR YOU
Rick Besoyan
Babes in the Wood (OB) (1964)

I'M NOT GETTING ANY YOUNGER
Kenneth Jacobs
Rhoday Roberts
Show Me Where the Good Times Are
(OB) (1970)

I'M NOT IN LOVE
Charles Gaynor
Lend an Ear (1948)

I'M NOT MYSELF TONIGHT
David Raksin
June Carroll
If the Shoe Fits (1946)

I'M NOT SO BRIGHT
Hugh Martin
Look Ma, I'm Dancin'! (1948)

I'M OLD FASHIONED
Jerome Kern
Johnny Mercer
You Were Never Lovelier (F) (1942)

I'M ON MY WAY
George Gershwin
DuBose Heyward
Porgy and Bess (1935)

I'M ON MY WAY
Frederick Loewe
Alan Jay Lerner
Paint Your Wagon (1951)

I'M ON MY WAY TO THE TOP
Hal Hester and Danny Apolinar
Your Own Thing (1968)

I'M ON THE CREST OF A WAVE
Ray Henderson
B. G. DeSylva and Lew Brown
George White's Scandals (1928)

I'M ON THE LOOKOUT
Charles Gaynor
Lend an Ear (1948)

I'M ONE LITTLE PARTY
Harry Ruby
Bert Kalmar
The Five O'Clock Girl (1927)

I'M ONE OF GOD'S CHILDREN
Louis Alter
Oscar Hammerstein II and Harry Ruskin
Ballyhoo (1930)

I'M ONE OF YOUR ADMIRERS
Jimmy Van Heusen
Johnny Burke
Carnival in Flanders (1953)

I'M ONLY THINKING OF HIM
Mitch Leigh
Joe Darion
Man of La Mancha (1965)

I'M PHYSICAL, YOU'RE CULTURED
John Green
George Marion, Jr.
Beat the Band (1942)

I'M PUTTING ALL MY EGGS IN ONE BASKET
Irving Berlin
Follow the Fleet (F) (1936)

I'M READY
Oscar Brand and Paul Nassau
A Joyful Noise (1966)

I'M REALLY NOT THAT WAY
Will Irwin
Malcolm McComb
Hey Nonny Nonny! (1932)

I'M RIDIN' FOR A FALL
Arthur Schwartz
Frank Loesser
Thank Your Lucky Stars (F) (1943)

I'M SAVING MYSELF FOR A SOLDIER
Edward Thomas
Martin Charnin
Ballad for a Firing Squad (OB) (1968)

I'M SEEING THINGS
Mimi Stone
William Kaye
Pimpernel! (OB) (1964)

I'M SICK OF THE WHOLE DAMN
PROBLEM
C. Jackson and James Hatch
Fly Blackbird (OB) (1962)

I'M SO HUMBLE
Richard Rodgers
Lorenz Hart
Peggy-Ann (1926)

I'M SO IN LOVE
Will Irwin
Norman Zeno
Fools Rush In (1934)

I'M SO WEARY OF IT ALL
Noël Coward
Set to Music (1939)

I'M SORRY SAYS THE MACHINE
Helen Miller
Eve Merriam
Inner City (1971)

I'M STEPPING OUT OF THE PICTURE
Harry Akst
Lew Brown
Calling All Stars (1934)

I'M STILL HERE
Stephen Sondheim
Follies (1971)

I'M STUCK WITH LOVE
Gordon Duffy
Harry M. Haldane
Happy Town (1959)

I'M SURE OF YOUR LOVE
Morton Gould
Betty Comden and Adolph Green
Billion Dollar Baby (1945)

I'M TAKING THE STEPS TO RUSSIA
Cole Porter
Leave It to Me (1938)

I'M TELLING YOU, LOUIE
Jerome Moross
Paul Peters and George Sklar
Parade (1935)

I'M THAT WAY OVER YOU
J. Fred Coots
Arthur Swanstrom and Benny Davis
Sons o' Guns (1929)

I'M THE BOY YOU SHOULD SAY "YES"
TO
John Addison
John Cranko
Cranks (1956)

I'M THE BRAVEST INDIVIDUAL
Cy Coleman
Dorothy Fields
Sweet Charity (1966)

I'M THE ECHO, YOU'RE THE SONG
Jerome Kern
Dorothy Fields
I Dream Too Much (F) (1935)

I'M THE FELLOW WHO LOVES YOU
Ray Henderson
Jack Yellen
George White's Scandals (1936)

I'M THE FIRST GIRL
Hugh Martin
Look Ma, I'm Dancin'! (1948)

I'M THE GIRL
James Shelton
Dance Me a Song (1950)

I'M THE GREATEST STAR
Jule Styne
Bob Merrill
Funny Girl (1964)

I'M THINKING OF LOVE
Robert Stolz
Rowland Leigh
Night of Love (1941)

I'M THROUGH WITH WAR
Shep Camp
Frank DuPree and Harry B. Smith
Half a Widow (1927)

I'M THROWING A BALL TONIGHT
Cole Porter
Panama Hattie (1940)

I'M TICKLED PINK
Harold Orlob
Hairpin Harmony (1943)

I'M TIRED OF TEXAS
Hugh Martin
Look Ma, I'm Dancin'! (1948)

I'M TO BLAME
Joseph Raposo
Erich Segal
Sing Muse! (OB) (1961)

I'M UNLUCKY AT GAMBLING
Cole Porter
Fifty Million Frenchmen (1929)

I'M WAITING FOR A WONDERFUL GIRL
Vincent Youmans
Anne Caldwell
Oh, Please! (1926)

I'M WALKIN' THE CHALK LINE
Alberta Nichols
Mann Holiner
Blackbirds of 1934 (1933)

I'M WAY AHEAD OF THE GAME
Robert Emmett Dolan
Johnny Mercer
Foxy (1964)

I'M WITH YOU
Jule Styne
Betty Comden and Adolph Green
Fade Out - Fade In (1964)

I'M WORSE THAN ANYBODY
John Kander
James Goldman, John Kander, and William Goldman
A Family Affair (1962)

I'M YOU
Irving Actman
Frank Loesser
The Illustrators' Show (1936)

I'M YOUR GIRL
Richard Rodgers
Oscar Hammerstein II
Me and Juliet (1953)

I'M YOUR MAN
Kurt Weill
Alan Jay Lerner
Love Life (1948)

I'M YOUR VALENTINE
Sol Berkowitz
James Lipton
Miss Emily Adam (OB) (1960)

IMAGINATION
Joseph Meyer and Roger Wolfe Kahn
Irving Caesar
Here's Howe (1928)

IMAGINE
Richard Rodgers
Lorenz Hart
Babes in Arms (1937)

IMAGINE ME
Jerry Blatt
Jerry Blatt and Lonnie Burstein
Have I Got One for You (OB) (1968)

IMAGINE MY FINDING YOU HERE
Ned Lehak
Robert Sour
Sing for Your Supper (1939)

IMAGINE THAT
Laurence Rosenthal
James Lipton
Sherry! (1967)

IMAGINE YOU'RE ALIVE
Dale F. Menten
Dale F. Menten and Frederick Gaines
The House of Leather (OB) (1970)

IMPEACHMENT WALTZ, THE
Don Tucker
Red, White and Maddox (1969)

IMPERIAL CONFERENCE, AN
Bronislaw Kaper (based on Chopin)
John Latouche
Polonaise (1945)

IMPOSSIBLE
Stephen Sondheim
*A Funny Thing Happened on the Way
  to the Forum* (1962)

IMPOSSIBLE DREAM, THE (THE
QUEST)
Mitch Leigh
Joe Darion
Man of La Mancha (1965)

IMPOSSIBLE SHE, THE
James Mundy
John Latouche
The Vamp (1955)

IN A BROWNSTONE MANSION
Sol Kaplan
Edward Eliscu
The Banker's Daughter (OB) (1962)

IN A GARDEN
Ann Sternberg
Gertrude Stein
Gertrude Stein's First Reader (OB)
  (1969)

IN A GONDOLA WITH YOU
Vincent Valentini
Parisiana (1928)

IN A GREAT BIG WAY
Jimmy McHugh
Dorothy Fields
Hello Daddy (1928)

IN A KINGDOM OF OUR OWN
George M. Cohan
The Royal Vagabond (1919)

IN A LITTLE STUCCO IN THE STICKS
Harry Revel

Mack Gordon
Smiling Faces (1932)

IN A LITTLE SWISS CHALET
Will Irwin
Norman Zeno
White Horse Inn (1936)

IN A LITTLE WHILE
Will Ortman
Gus Kahn and Raymond B. Egan
Holka-Polka (1925)

IN A LITTLE WHILE
Mary Rodgers
Marshall Barer
Once Upon a Mattress (OB) (1959)

IN A STORY BOOK
George Fischoff
Verna Tomasson
The Prince and the Pauper (OB)
  (1963)

IN ARABY WITH YOU
Jerome Kern
Anne Caldwell and Otto Harbach
Criss-Cross (1926)

IN ARMENIA
Oscar Straus
Harry B. Smith
Naughty Riquette (1926)

IN BETWEEN
Frederick Loewe
Alan Jay Lerner
Paint Your Wagon (1951)

IN BETWEEN
Peter Link and C. C. Courtney
Salvation (OB) (1969)

IN BUDDY'S EYES
Stephen Sondheim
Follies (1971)

IN CALIFORN-I-A
Richard Rodgers
Lorenz Hart
America's Sweetheart (1931)

IN CENTRAL PARK
Harold Orlob
Irving Caesar
Talk About Girls (1927)

IN CHICHICASTENANGO
Jay Gorney
Henry Myers
Meet the People (1940)

IN CHINATOWN IN FRISCO
Maurice Yvain
Clifford Grey and McElbert Moore
A Night in Paris (1926)

IN DAHOMEY
Jerome Kern
Oscar Hammerstein II
Show Boat (1927)

IN EGERN ON THE TEGERN SEE
Jerome Kern
Oscar Hammerstein II
Music in the Air (1932)

IN HIS ARMS
Richard Rodgers
Lorenz Hart
Peggy-Ann (1926)

IN IZZENSCHNOOKEN ON THE
LOVELY ESSENZOOK ZEE
Rick Besoyan
Little Mary Sunshine (OB) (1959)

IN JAIL
Jean Gilbert
Harry Graham
Katja (1926)

IN LOVE IN VAIN
Jerome Kern
Leo Robin
Centennial Summer (F) (1946)

IN LOVE WITH A FOOL
Ernest Gold
Anne Croswell
I'm Solomon (1968)

IN LOVE WITH LOVE
Jerome Kern
Anne Caldwell
The Stepping Stones (1923)

IN LOVE WITH ROMANCE
Sigmund Romberg
Rowland Leigh
My Romance (1948)

IN LOVING MEMORY
Robert Emmett Dolan
Johnny Mercer
Foxy (1964)

IN MY ARMS AGAIN
Albert Von Tilzer
Neville Fleeson
Bye Bye, Bonnie (1927)

IN MY CASTLE IN SORRENTO
Abel Baer
Sam Lewis and Joe Young
Lady Do (1927)

IN MY GARDEN
Sigmund Romberg
Irving Caesar
Melody (1933)

IN MY HEART
Francis Thorne
Arnold Weinstein
Fortuna (OB) (1962)

IN MY LOVE BOAT
Ray Perkins
Max and Nathaniel Lief
Say When (1928)

IN MY OWN LIFETIME
Jerry Bock
Sheldon Harnick
The Rothschilds (1970)

IN MY OWN LITTLE CORNER
Richard Rodgers
Oscar Hammerstein II
Cinderella (TV) (1957)

IN NO TIME AT ALL
Sammy Fain
Marilyn and Alan Bergman
Something More! (1964)

IN NOMINE DEI
Wally Harper
Paul Zakrzewski
Sensations (OB) (1970)

IN OTHER WORDS, SEVENTEEN
Jerome Kern
Oscar Hammerstein II
Very Warm for May (1939)

IN OUR COZY LITTLE COTTAGE OF TOMORROW
Harry Revel
Arnold B. Horwitt
Are You With It? (1945)

IN OUR HIDE-AWAY
Irving Berlin
Mr. President (1962)

IN OUR LITTLE DEN OF INIQUITY
Richard Rodgers
Lorenz Hart
Pal Joey (1940)

IN OUR OWN LITTLE SALON
Joseph Raposo
Erich Segal
Sing Muse! (OB) (1961)

IN OUR PARLOR ON THE THIRD FLOOR BACK
Richard Rodgers
Lorenz Hart
Betsy (1926)

IN OUR UNITED STATE
Burton Lane
Ira Gershwin
Give a Girl a Break (F) (1953)

IN PARIS AND IN LOVE
Sigmund Romberg (developed by Don Walker)
Leo Robin
The Girl in Pink Tights (1954)

IN REAL LIFE
Skip Redwine and Larry Frank
Frank Merriwell, or Honor Challenged (1971)

IN ROMANY
Ben Schwartz
Tales of Rigo (1927)

IN RURITANIA
Sigmund Romberg
Harry B. Smith
Princess Flavia (1925)

IN SARDINIA
George Gershwin
B. G. DeSylva and Ira Gershwin
Tell Me More (1925)

IN SOME LITTLE WORLD
Bob Merrill
Henry, Sweet, Henry (1967)

IN SOMEONE ELSE'S SANDALS
Ernest Gold
Anne Croswell
I'm Solomon (1968)

IN THE ARMS OF A STRANGER
Ron Dante and Gene Allan
Billy (1969)

IN THE BACK OF A HACK
Jay Gorney
Barry Trivers
Heaven on Earth (1948)

IN THE BATH
Donald Swann
Michael Flanders
At the Drop of a Hat (1959)

IN THE CAREFREE REALM OF FANCY
Frederick Loewe
Earle Crooker
Great Lady (1938)

IN THE CLOUDS
Rudolf Friml
J. Keirn Brennan
Luana (1930)

IN THE COUNTRY WHERE I COME
FROM
Michael Valenti
John Lewin
Blood Red Roses (1970)

IN THE DARK
William B. Kernell
Dorothy Donnelly
Hello, Lola (1926)

IN THE DAYS GONE BY
Emmerich Kalman
Harry B. Smith
Countess Maritza (1926)

IN THE DAYS GONE BY
Walter G. Samuels
Morrie Ryskind
Ned Wayburn's Gambols (1929)

IN THE DESERT
Donald Swann
Michael Flanders
At the Drop of Another Hat (1966)

IN THE GARDENS OF NOOR-ED-DEEN
Harry Tierney
Joseph McCarthy
Cross My Heart (1928)

IN THE HEART OF SPAIN
Philip Charig and Richard Myers
Leo Robin
Allez-Oop (1927)

IN THE HEART OF THE DARK
Jerome Kern
Oscar Hammerstein II
Very Warm for May (1939)

IN THE LAND OF SUNNY SUNFLOW-
ERS
Eubie Blake
Noble Sissle
Shuffle Along (1933)

IN THE LOBBY
Gordon Jenkins
Tom Adair
Along Fifth Avenue (1949)

IN THE LONG RUN
Abel Baer
Sam Lewis and Joe Young
Lady Do (1927)

IN THE MEANTIME
Ray Henderson
B. G. DeSylva and Lew Brown
Good News (1927)

IN THE MERRY MONTH OF MAYBE
Harry Warren
Ira Gershwin and Billy Rose
Crazy Quilt (1931)

IN THE MIDDLE OF THE NIGHT
Arthur Schwartz
Howard Dietz
Revenge with Music (1934)

IN THE MORNING
David Raksin
June Carroll
If the Shoe Fits (1946)

IN THE MORNING
Ronny Graham
New Faces (1962)

IN THE NOONDAY SUN
Arthur Schwartz
Howard Dietz
Revenge with Music (1934)

IN THE PRISON
Stan Harte, Jr.
Walt Whitman
Leaves of Grass (OB) (1971)

IN THE REIGN OF CHAIM
Menachem Zur
Herbert Appleman
Unfair to Goliath (OB) (1970)

IN THE SAME WAY I LOVE YOU
H. M. Tennent
Eric Little
By the Way (1925)

IN THE SHADE OF THE NEW APPLE
TREE
Harold Arlen
E. Y. Harburg
Hooray for What! (1937)

IN THE STILL OF THE NIGHT
Cole Porter
Rosalie (F) (1937)

IN THE STRETCH
Alexander Hill
Hummin' Sam (1933)

IN THE SUMMER
Harry Ruby
Bert Kalmar
Top Speed (1929)

IN THE SWIM
George Gershwin
Ira Gershwin
Funny Face (1927)

IN THE VERY NEXT MOMENT
Laurence Rosenthal
James Lipton
Sherry! (1967)

IN THOSE GOOD OLD HORSECAR DAYS
Will Irwin
Malcolm McComb
Hey Nonny Nonny! (1932)

IN TIME
Leon Pober
Bud Freeman
Beg, Borrow or Steal (1960)

IN TIMES LIKE THESE
Ernest G. Schweikert
Frank Reardon
Rumple (1957)

IN TIMES OF TUMULT AND WAR
Kurt Weill
Paul Green
Johnny Johnson (1936)

IN TWOS
Harold Orlob
Irving Caesar
Talk About Girls (1927)

IN VAUDEVILLE
Lucien Denni
Helena Evans
Happy Go Lucky (1926)

IN VINO VERITAS
Ervin Drake
Her First Roman (1968)

IN WAIKIKI
Sammy Fain
Jack Yellen
George White's Scandals (1939)

IN YOUR CHAPEAU
Richard Rodgers
Lorenz Hart
Simple Simon (1930)

IN YOUR HANDS
Joseph Martinez Kookoolis and Scott Fagan
Scott Fagan
Soon (1971)

INCANTATION
Susan Hulsman Bingham
Myrna Lamb
Mod Donna (OB) (1970)

INCHWORM, THE
Frank Loesser
Hans Christian Andersen (F) (1951)

INCINERATOR HOUR, THE
Mildred Kayden
Frank Gagliano
Paradise Gardens East (OB) (1969)

INCOMPATIBILITY
Harold Arlen
E. Y. Harburg
Jamaica (1957)

INCORPORATION, THE
Susan Hulsman Bingham
Myrna Lamb
Mod Donna (OB) (1970)

INDEPENDENCE DAY HORA
Jerry Herman
Milk and Honey (1961)

INDEPENDENT
Jule Styne
Betty Comden and Adolph Green
Bells Are Ringing (1956)

INDIAN BLUES
Claibe Richardson
Kenward Elmslie
The Grass Harp (1971)

INDIAN LOVE CALL
Rudolf Friml
Otto Harbach and Oscar Hammerstein II
Rose Marie (1924)

INDIAN LULLABY
Rudolf Friml
Brian Hooker
The White Eagle (1927)

INDIANS
Mark Charlap
Carolyn Leigh
Peter Pan (1954)

INDIVIDUALS
Jerry Alters
Herb Hartig
Fallout (OB) (1959)

INEVITABLY ME
Ken Welch
Shoestring Revue (OB) (1955)

INFATUATION
Michael Cleary
Arthur Swanstrom
Sea Legs (1937)

INITIALS
Galt MacDermot
Gerome Ragni and James Rado
Hair (1968)

INNER THOUGHTS
Charles Strouse
Lee Adams
Applause (1970)

INNOCENT CHORUS GIRLS OF YES-TERDAY
Richard Rodgers
Lorenz Hart
America's Sweetheart (1931)

INNOCENT INGENUE BABY
George Gershwin and William Daly
Brian Hooker
Our Nell (1922)

INSANE POONTANG
C. C. Courtney and Ragan Courtney
Earl of Ruston (1971)

INSIDE STORY, THE
John Green
Edward Heyman
Here Goes the Bride (1931)

INSIDE U.S.A
Arthur Schwartz
Howard Dietz
Inside U.S.A (1948)

INSTEAD-OF SONG
Kurt Weill
Marc Blitzstein
The Threepenny Opera (OB) (1954)

INTERMISSION TALK
Richard Rodgers
Oscar Hammerstein II
Me and Juliet (1953)

INTERNATIONAL REVUE
Jimmy McHugh
Dorothy Fields
Lew Leslie's International Revue (1930)

INTERNATIONAL VAMP
Jean Schwartz
Alfred Bryan
A Night in Spain (1927)

INTERRUPTED LOVE SONG, AN
Sigmund Romberg
Oscar Hammerstein II
The New Moon (1928)

INTO SOCIETY
Milton Susskind
Paul Porter and Benjamin Hapgood
  Burt
Florida Girl (1925)

INTO THE NIGHT
Robert Stolz
Robert Sour
Mr. Strauss Goes to Boston (1945)

INTOXICATION
Dean Fuller
Marshall Barer
Ziegfeld Follies (1957)

INTRODUCIN' MR. PARIS
Jerome Moross
John Latouche
The Golden Apple (1954)

INVISIBLE MAN, THE
Charles Strouse
Six (OB) (1971)

INVITATION
Susan Hulsman Bingham
Myrna Lamb
Mod Donna (OB) (1970)

INZA
Skip Redwine and Larry Frank
*Frank Merriwell, or Honor Chal-
  lenged* (1971)

IOWA STUBBORN
Meredith Willson
The Music Man (1957)

IRATE PIRATE AM I, AN
Alma Sanders
Monte Carlo
The Houseboat on the Styx (1928)

IRELAND WAS NEVER LIKE THIS
Sammy Fain
Paul Francis Webster
Christine (1960)

IRENE
Harry Tierney
Joseph McCarthy
Irene (1919)

IRISH HAVE A GREAT DAY TONIGHT,
THE
Victor Herbert
Henry Blossom
Eileen (1917)

IRISH WASHERWOMAN'S LAMENT
Kenneth Gaburo
Seyril Schochen
The Tiger Rag (OB) (1961)

IRMA LA DOUCE
Marguerite Monnot
Julian More, David Heneker, and
  Monte Norman
Irma La Douce (1960)

IRRESISTIBLE YOU
Jimmy Monaco
Billy Rose and Ballard MacDonald
Harry Delmar's Revels (1927)

IS ANYBODY THERE?
Sherman Edwards
1776 (1969)

IS EVERYBODY HAPPY NOW?
Maury Rubens
Jack Osterman and Ted Lewis
Artists and Models (1927)

IS HE THE ONLY MAN IN THE
WORLD?
Irving Berlin
Mr. President (1962)

IS IT A CRIME?
Jule Styne
Betty Comden and Adolph Green
Bells Are Ringing (1956)

IS IT A DREAM?
Erich Wolfgang Korngold (based on
  Offenbach)
Herbert Baker
Helen Goes to Troy (1944)

IS IT ANY WONDER?
Alma Sanders
Monte Carlo
Oh! Oh! Nurse (1925)

IS IT HIM OR IS IT ME?
Kurt Weill
Alan Jay Lerner
Love Life (1948)

IS IT LOVE?
Oscar Levant
Irving Caesar
Ripples (1930)

IS IT POSSIBLE?
Jimmy McHugh
Al Dubin
The Streets of Paris (1939)

IS IT REALLY ME?
Harvey Schmidt
Tom Jones
110 in the Shade (1963)

IS IT THE GIRL?
Cole Porter
Seven Lively Arts (1944)

IS IT THE UNIFORM?
Richard Rodgers
Lorenz Hart
Present Arms (1928)

IS IZZY AZZY WOZ?
Cliff Friend and George White
George White's Scandals (1929)

IS RHYTHM NECESSARY?
Sammy Fain
Irving Kahal
Everybody's Welcome (1931)

IS THAT MY PRINCE?
Arthur Schwartz
Dorothy Fields
A Tree Grows in Brooklyn (1951)

IS THERE A CITY?
Lor Crane
John B. Kuntz
Whispers on the Wind (OB) (1970)

IS THERE SOME PLACE FOR ME
Alfred Brooks
Ira J. Bilowit
Of Mice and Men (OB) (1958)

IS THERE SOMETHING TO WHAT HE SAID?
Johnny Brandon
Cindy (OB) (1964)

IS THIS A FACT?
Edward Thomas
Martin Charnin
Ballad for a Firing Squad (OB) (1968)

IS THIS MY TOWN?
Bob Goodman
Wild and Wonderful (1971)

IS THIS THE WAY?
Frank Fields
Armand Aulicino
The Shoemaker and the Peddler (OB) (1960)

ISLAND IN THE WEST INDIES
Vernon Duke
Ira Gershwin
Ziegfeld Follies (1936)

ISLAND OF HAPPINESS
Johnny Brandon
Who's Who, Baby? (OB) (1968)

ISN'T IT A FUNNY THING?
Max Rich
Jack Scholl
Keep Moving (1934)

ISN'T IT A LOVELY VIEW?
Jacques Belasco
Kay Twomey
The Girl from Nantucket (1945)

ISN'T IT A PITY?
George Gershwin
Ira Gershwin
Pardon My English (1933)

ISN'T IT JUNE?
Ray Henderson
Ted Koehler
Say When (1934)

ISN'T IT KINDA FUN?
Richard Rodgers
Oscar Hammerstein II
State Fair (F) (1945)

ISN'T IT REMARKABLE?
Jesse Greer
Stanley Adams
Shady Lady (1933)

ISN'T IT ROMANTIC?
Richard Rodgers
Lorenz Hart
Love Me Tonight (F) (1932)

ISN'T IT SWELL TO DREAM?
Sam H. Stept
Bud Green
Shady Lady (1933)

ISN'T IT WONDERFUL
Louis Bellson and Will Irwin
Richard Ney
Portofino (1958)

ISN'T SHE LOVELY?
Dean Fuller
Marshall Barer
New Faces (1956)

ISN'T THAT CLEAR?
Al Carmines
Maria Irene Fornes
Promenade (OB) (1969)

ISN'T THAT WHAT MAKES LIFE WORTHWHILE?
Earl Wilson, Jr.
A Day in the Life of Just About Everyone (OB) (1971)

ISN'T THIS A LOVELY DAY
Irving Berlin
Top Hat (F) (1935)

"IT"
Sigmund Romberg
Otto Harbach and Oscar Hammerstein II
The Desert Song (1926)

IT AIN'T ETIQUETTE
Cole Porter
Du Barry Was a Lady (1939)

IT AIN'T NECESSARILY SO
George Gershwin
Ira Gershwin
Porgy and Bess (1935)

IT AIN'T US WHO MAKE THE WARS
Ron Dante and Gene Allan
Billy (1969)

IT ALL BELONGS TO ME
Irving Berlin
Ziegfeld Follies (1927)

IT ALWAYS TAKES TWO
Lewis E. Gensler
Owen Murphy and Robert A. Simon
The Gang's All Here (1931)

IT BETTER BE GOOD
Arthur Schwartz
Howard Dietz
The Band Wagon (1931)

IT CAN HAPPEN TO ANYONE
Sigmund Romberg
Oscar Hammerstein II
Sunny River (1941)

IT COULD BE CALAIS
Eddie Stuart
Harvey Lasker
Old Bucks and New Wings (OB) (1962)

IT COULD ONLY HAPPEN IN THE MOVIES
Vernon Duke
Harold Adamson
Banjo Eyes (1941)

IT COULDN'T BE DONE (BUT WE DID IT)
Sidney Lippman
Sylvia Dee
Barefoot Boy with Cheek (1947)

IT COULDN'T PLEASE ME MORE
John Kander
Fred Ebb
Cabaret (1966)

IT DEPENDS ON HOW YOU LOOK AT THINGS
Arthur Siegel
June Carroll
New Faces (1962)

IT DEPENDS ON WHAT YOU PAY
Harvey Schmidt
Tom Jones
The Fantasticks (OB) (1960)

IT DEPENDS ON WHAT YOU'RE AT
Richard Hill and John Hawkins
Nevill Coghill
Canterbury Tales (1969)

IT DOESN'T COST YOU ANYTHING TO DREAM
Sigmund Romberg
Dorothy Fields
Up in Central Park (1945)

IT DOESN'T LOOK DESERTED
Alec Wilder
Arnold Sundgaard
Kittiwake Island (OB) (1960)

IT FEELS GOOD
Richard Rodgers
Oscar Hammerstein II
Me and Juliet (1953)

IT GETS LONELY IN THE WHITE HOUSE
Irving Berlin
Mr. President (1962)

IT HAPPENED
Rudolf Friml
Rowland Leigh and John Shubert
Music Hath Charms (1934)

IT HAPPENS EVERY DAY
Robert Holton
June Carroll
Hi, Paisano! (OB) (1961)

IT ISN'T DONE
Cole Porter
Fifty Million Frenchmen (1929)

IT ISN'T EASY
Gordon Duffy
Harry M. Haldane
Happy Town (1959)

IT ISN'T ENOUGH
Leslie Brieusse and Anthony Newley
The Roar of the Greasepaint - The Smell of the Crowd (1965)

IT ISN'T THE SAME
Jane Douglas
Tom O'Malley
Bella (OB) (1961)

IT JUST HAD TO HAPPEN
Cliff Friend
Lew Brown
Piggy (1927)

IT JUST OCCURRED TO ME
Vernon Duke
Sammy Cahn
Two's Company (1952)

IT MAY BE A GOOD IDEA
Richard Rodgers
Oscar Hammerstein II
Allegro (1947)

IT MEANS SO LITTLE TO YOU
Richard Myers
Edward Heyman
Here Goes the Bride (1931)

IT MIGHT AS WELL BE HER
Jimmy Van Heusen
Sammy Cahn
Walking Happy (1966)

IT MIGHT AS WELL BE SPRING*
Richard Rodgers
Oscar Hammerstein II
State Fair (F) (1945)

---

*Academy Award Winner

IT MIGHT BE LOVE
Louis Bellson and Will Irwin
Richard Ney
Portofino (1958)

IT MIGHT HAVE BEEN
Gus Arnheim, George Waggner, and
    Neil Moret
Marching By (1932)

IT MUST BE HEAVEN
Richard Rodgers
Lorenz Hart
Heads Up! (1929)

IT MUST BE LOVE
Harry Archer
Harlan Thompson
Merry-Merry (1925)

IT MUST BE ME
Leonard Bernstein
Richard Wilbur
Candide (1956)

IT MUST BE SO
Leonard Bernstein
Richard Wilbur
Candide (1956)

IT MUST BE SPRING
Ralph Blane
Three Wishes for Jamie (1952)

IT MUST HAVE BEEN THE NIGHT
Ray Henderson
Ted Koehler
Say When (1934)

IT NEVER ENTERED MY MIND
Richard Rodgers
Lorenz Hart
Higher and Higher (1940)

IT NEVER WAS YOU
Kurt Weill
Maxwell Anderson
Knickerbocker Holiday (1938)

IT ONLY HAPPENS WHEN I DANCE WITH YOU
Irving Berlin
Easter Parade (F) (1948)

IT ONLY TAKES A MOMENT
Jerry Herman
Hello, Dolly! (1964)

IT PAYS TO ADVERTISE
Lewis E. Gensler
B. G. DeSylva
Queen High (1926)

IT SAYS HERE
David Baker
David Craig
Phoenix '55 (OB) (1955)

IT TAKE A LONG PULL TO GET THERE
George Gershwin
DuBose Heyward
Porgy and Bess (1935)

IT TAKES A WOMAN
Jerry Herman
Hello, Dolly! (1964)

IT TAKES A WOMAN TO TAKE A MAN
Jimmy McHugh
Harold Adamson
As the Girls Go (1948)

IT TAKES TIME
Howard Blankman
By Hex (OB) (1956)

IT TOOK THEM
Baldwin Bergersen
William Archibald
The Crystal Heart (OB) (1960)

IT USED TO BE
Lee Pockriss
Anne Croswell
Tovarich (1963)

IT WAS A GLAD ADVENTURE
Jerome Moross
John Latouche
The Golden Apple (1954)

IT WAS DESTINY
Frederico Valerio
Elizabeth Miele
Hit the Trail (1954)

IT WAS FATE
Rudolf Friml
Otto Harbach and Oscar Hammerstein II
The Wild Rose (1926)

IT WAS GOOD ENOUGH FOR GRANDMA
Harold Arlen
E. Y. Harburg
Bloomer Girl (1944)

IT WAS GOOD ENOUGH FOR GRANDPA
Nancy Ford
Gretchen Cryer
Now Is the Time for All Good Men (OB) (1967)

IT WAS LONG AGO
Harold Arlen
Ira Gershwin and E. Y. Harburg
Life Begins at 8:40 (1934)

IT WAS NEVER LIKE THIS
Arthur Schwartz
Howard Dietz
Flying Colors (1932)

IT WASN'T YOUR FAULT
Jerome Kern
Herbert Reynolds
Love o' Mike (1917)

IT WAS NICE KNOWING YOU
Vernon Duke
Howard Dietz
Jackpot (1944)

IT WAS SO NICE HAVING YOU
Gerald Marks
Sam Lerner
Hold It! (1948)

IT WAS WRITTEN IN THE STARS
Cole Porter
Du Barry Was a Lady (1939)

IT WONDERS ME
Albert Hague
Arnold B. Horwitt
Plain and Fancy (1955)

IT WON'T BE LONG
Lor Crane
John B. Kuntz
Whispers on the Wind (OB) (1970)

IT WON'T BE LONG
Joseph Martinez Kookoolis and Scott Fagan
Scott Fagan
Soon (1971)

IT WON'T BE LONG NOW
Ray Henderson
B. G. DeSylva and Lew Brown
Manhattan Mary (1927)

ITALIAN STRAW HAT
Cy Young
That Hat! (OB) (1964)

ITALIAN STREET SONG
Victor Herbert
Rida Johnson Young
Naughty Marietta (1910)

ITALY
Sammy Fain
Dan Shapiro
Ankles Aweigh (1955)

ITCH TO BE RICH
Jerry Bock
Sheldon Harnick
Man in the Moon (1963)

IT'LL BE ALL RIGHT IN A HUNDRED YEARS
Jay Gorney
Jean and Walter Kerr
Touch and Go (1949)

IT'S A BEAUTIFUL DAY TODAY
Walter Donaldson
Gus Kahn
Whoopee (1928)

IT'S A BIG, WIDE, WONDERFUL
WORLD
John Rox
All in Fun (1940)

IT'S A CHEMICAL REACTION
Cole Porter
Silk Stockings (1955)

IT'S A FINE LIFE
Lionel Bart
Oliver! (1963)

IT'S A FINE OLD INSTITUTION
Jimmy Van Heusen
Johnny Burke
Carnival in Flanders (1953)

IT'S A FISH
Jerry Bock
Sheldon Harnick
The Apple Tree (1966)

IT'S A GRAND NIGHT FOR SINGING
Richard Rodgers
Oscar Hammerstein II
State Fair (F) (1945)

IT'S A GREAT LIFE
Cole Porter
Red, Hot and Blue! (1936)

IT'S A GREAT LITTLE WORLD
George Gershwin
Ira Gershwin
Tip-Toes (1925)

IT'S A GREAT SPORT
Ray Henderson
B. G. DeSylva and Lew Brown
Follow Thru (1929)

IT'S A HELLUVA WAY TO RUN A
LOVE AFFAIR
Albert Hague
Arnold B. Horwitt
Plain and Fancy (1955)

IT'S A LAW
Kurt Weill
Maxwell Anderson
Knickerbocker Holiday (1938)

IT'S A LIE
Paul Klein
Fred Ebb
Morning Sun (OB) (1963)

IT'S A LIVING
Allan Roberts
Lester Lee
All for Love (1949)

IT'S A LONG ROAD HOME
Norman Dean
Autumn's Here (OB) (1966)

IT'S A LONG TIME TILL TOMORROW
Abraham Ellstein
Walter Bullock
Great to Be Alive (1950)

IT'S A LOVELY DAY TODAY
Irving Berlin
Call Me Madam (1950)

IT'S A LOVELY NIGHT ON THE HUD-
SON RIVER
Richard Lewine
Ted Fetter
The Fireman's Flame (OB) (1937)

IT'S A MIGHTY FINE COUNTRY WE
HAVE HERE
Sammy Fain
Jack Yellen
Sons o' Fun (1941)

IT'S A MOST UNUSUAL DAY
Jimmy McHugh
Harold Adamson
A Date with Judy (F) (1948)

IT'S A NEW KIND OF THING
Sammy Fain
Jack Yellen
Sons o' Fun (1941)

IT'S A NEW WORLD
Harold Arlen
Ira Gershwin
A Star Is Born (F) (1954)

It's a Nice Cold Morning
Hugo Peretti, Luigi Creatore, and
  George David Weiss
Maggie Flynn (1968)

It's a Nice Face
Cy Coleman
Dorothy Fields
Sweet Charity (F) (1970)

It's a Nice Night for It
Morgan Lewis
Nancy Hamilton
Three to Make Ready (1946)

It's a Nice Place to Visit
Bill and Patti Jacob
Jimmy (1969)

It's a Perfect Relationship
Jule Styne
Betty Comden and Adolph Green
Bells Are Ringing (1956)

It's a Scandal! It's an Outrage!
Richard Rodgers
Oscar Hammerstein II
Oklahoma! (1943)

It's a Simple Little System
Jule Styne
Betty Comden and Adolph Green
Bells Are Ringing (1956)

It's a Stretchy Day
Bruce Montgomery
The Amorous Flea (OB) (1964)

It's a Typical Day
Gene de Paul
Johnny Mercer
Li'l Abner (1956)

It's a Wishing World
Ralph Blane
Three Wishes for Jamie (1952)

It's a Wonderful Day to Do
Nothing
Rick Besoyan
The Student Gypsy (OB) (1963)

It's a Wonderful Thing for a
King
Albert Sirmay and Arthur Schwartz
Arthur Swanstrom
Princess Charming (1930)

It's a Wonderful World
Sigmund Romberg
Oscar Hammerstein II
East Wind (1931)

It's All in Fun
Baldwin Bergersen
S. K. Russell
All in Fun (1940)

It's All in Your Mind
Leon Pober
Bud Freeman
Beg, Borrow or Steal (1960)

It's All Off
Cy Young
That Hat! (OB) (1964)

It's All O. K.
Alma Sanders
Monte Carlo
Mystery Moon (1930)

It's All Over but the Shoutin'
Ray Henderson
B. G. DeSylva and Lew Brown
Hold Everything! (1928)

It's All Right with Me
Cole Porter
Can-Can (1953)

It's All the Same
Mitch Leigh
Joe Darion
Man of La Mancha (1965)

It's All Yours
Arthur Schwartz
Dorothy Fields
Stars in Your Eyes (1939)

IT'S ALWAYS THE WAY
Emmerich Kalman and Herbert Sto-
thart
Otto Harbach and Oscar Hammer-
stein II
Golden Dawn (1927)

IT'S AN OLD SPANISH CUSTOM
Ray Henderson
B. G. DeSylva
Three Cheers (1928)

IT'S AN OLD SPANISH CUSTOM
Jimmy Van Heusen
Johnny Burke
Carnival in Flanders (1953)

IT'S BETTER WITH A UNION MAN
Harold Rome
Pins and Needles (OB) (1937)

IT'S CHRISTMAS TODAY
Jerry Herman
I Feel Wonderful (OB) (1954)

IT'S COMIN' TRUE
Jerry Blatt
Jerry Blatt and Lonnie Burstein
Have I Got One for You (OB) (1968)

IT'S COMMENCEMENT DAY
Maceo Pinkard
Pansy (1929)

IT'S DELIGHTFUL DOWN IN CHILE
Jule Styne
Leo Robin
Gentlemen Prefer Blondes (1949)

IT'S DELIGHTFUL TO BE MARRIED
Vincent Scotto
Anna Held
The Parisian Model (1906)

IT'S DE-LOVELY
Cole Porter
Red, Hot and Blue! (1936)

IT'S DIFFERENT WITH ME
Harold Arlen
Jack Yellen
You Said It (1931)

IT'S DOOM
Jule Styne
Betty Comden and Adolph Green
Say, Darling (1958)

IT'S EASY TO REMEMBER
Richard Rodgers
Lorenz Hart
Mississippi (F) (1935)

IT'S EASY TO SAY HELLO
Cliff Friend
Lew Brown
Piggy (1927)

IT'S EASY TO SING
Julian Slade
Dorothy Reynolds and Julian Slade
Salad Days (OB) (1958)

IT'S EASY WHEN YOU KNOW HOW
Robert Emmett Dolan
Johnny Mercer
Foxy (1964)

IT'S ENOUGH TO MAKE A LADY FALL
IN LOVE
Jule Styne
E. Y. Harburg
Darling of the Day (1968)

IT'S EVERY GIRL'S AMBITION
Vincent Youmans
Edward Heyman
Through the Years (1932)

IT'S FUN TO THINK
Charles Strouse
Lee Adams
All American (1962)

IT'S GOOD TO BE ALIVE
Bob Merrill
New Girl in Town (1957)

IT'S GOOD TO BE BACK HOME
Jule Styne
Betty Comden and Adolph Green
Fade Out—Fade In (1964)

IT'S GOT TO BE LOVE
Richard Rodgers
Lorenz Hart
On Your Toes (1936)

IT'S GREAT TO BE A DOUGHBOY
Shep Camp
Frank DuPree
Half a Widow (1927)

IT'S GREAT TO BE ALIVE
Ray Henderson
B. G. DeSylva and Lew Brown
Strike Me Pink (1933)

IT'S GREAT TO BE ALIVE
Robert Emmett Dolan
Johnny Mercer
Texas, Li'l Darlin' (1949)

IT'S GREAT TO BE HOME AGAIN
Sammy Fain
Irving Kahal
Right This Way (1938)

IT'S GREAT TO BE IN LOVE
Cliff Friend
Earl Carroll's Vanities (1931)

IT'S HIGH TIME
Jule Styne
Leo Robin
Gentlemen Prefer Blondes (1949)

IT'S IN, IT'S OUT
Lucien Denni
Helena Evans
Happy Go Lucky (1926)

IT'S IN THE STARS
Michael H. Cleary
Max and Nathaniel Lief
Shoot the Works (1931)

IT'S LEGITIMATE
Jule Styne
Betty Comden and Adolph Green
Do Re Mi (1960)

IT'S LIKE A BEAUTIFUL WOMAN
Harold Karr

Matt Dubey
Happy Hunting (1956)

IT'S LOVE
Leonard Bernstein
Betty Comden and Adolph Green
Wonderful Town (1953)

IT'S MAGIC
Jule Styne
Sammy Cahn
Romance on the High Seas (F) (1948)

IT'S MARDI GRAS
Alma Sanders
Monte Carlo
Louisiana Lady (1947)

IT'S ME
Richard Rodgers
Oscar Hammerstein II
Me and Juliet (1953)

IT'S ME AGAIN
Sam Stept
Lew Brown and Charles Tobias
Yokel Boy (1939)

IT'S MONEY—IT'S FAME—IT'S LOVE
Ralph Benatzky
Meet My Sister (1930)

IT'S MORE FUN THAN A PICNIC
Jimmy McHugh
Harold Adamson
As the Girls Go (1948)

IT'S MY BELIEF
Helen Miller
Eve Merriam
Inner City (1971)

IT'S MY NATURE
John Green
Edward Heyman
Here Goes the Bride (1931)

IT'S NEVER QUITE THE SAME
Jay Livingston and Ray Evans
Oh Captain! (1958)

IT'S NEVER TOO LATE TO FALL IN
LOVE
Sandy Wilson
The Boy Friend (1954)

IT'S NOT CRICKET TO PICKET
Harold Rome
Pins and Needles (OB) (1937)

IT'S NOT EASY
Billy Barnes
The Billy Barnes People (1961)

IT'S NOT IRISH
Marc Blitzstein
Juno (1959)

IT'S ONLY A PAPER MOON*
Harold Arlen
Billy Rose and E. Y. Harburg
The Great Magoo (1932)

IT'S ONLY THIRTY YEARS
William Roy
Maggie (1953)

IT'S OUR DUTY TO THE KING
Arthur Schwartz
Albert Stillman
Virginia (1937)

IT'S OUR TIME NOW
Johnny Brandon
Billy Noname (OB) (1970)

IT'S OUT OF MY HANDS
Maury Laws
Jules Bass
Month of Sundays (OB) (1968)

IT'S PLEASANT AND DELIGHTFUL
Mischa and Wesley Portnoff
Donagh MacDonagh
Happy As Larry (1950)

IT'S POSITIVELY YOU
Sol Berkowitz
James Lipton
Miss Emily Adam (OB) (1960)

IT'S POURING
Bill Mahoney
My Wife and I (OB) (1966)

IT'S QUICK AND EASY
Armando Trovaioli
Pietro Garinei and Sandro Giovannini
Rugantino (1964)

IT'S SAD TO BE LONESOME
Walter Cool
Mackey of Appalachia (OB) (1965)

IT'S SO EASY TO SAY
Alec Wilder
Arnold Sundgaard
Kittiwake Island (OB) (1960)

IT'S SO GOOD
Jacques Urbont
David Newburger
Stag Movie (OB) (1971)

IT'S SO HEART-WARMING
Sol Kaplan
Edward Eliscu
The Banker's Daughter (OB) (1962)

IT'S SO SIMPLE
Marian Grudeff and Raymond Jessel
Baker Street (1965)

IT'S SUPER NICE
Charles Strouse
Lee Adams
(It's a Bird, It's a Plane) It's Superman
(1966)

IT'S SUPERMAN
Charles Strouse
Lee Adams
(It's a Bird, It's a Plane) It's Superman
(1966)

IT'S THE DARNDEST THING
Jimmy McHugh
Dorothy Fields
Singin' the Blues (1931)

---

*Also in film *Take a Chance* (1933)

IT's THE GIRL EVERYTIME, IT's THE GIRL
Fred Spielman and Arthur Gershwin
Stanley Adams
A Lady Says Yes (1945)

IT's THE GOING HOME TOGETHER
Jerome Moross
John Latouche
The Golden Apple (1954)

IT's THE GOWN THAT MAKES THE GAL THAT MAKES THE GUY
Eubie Blake
Joan Javits
Shuffle Along (1952)

IT's THE LITTLE THINGS IN TEXAS
Richard Rodgers
State Fair (F) (remake) (1962)

IT's THE SECOND TIME YOU MEET THAT MATTERS
Jule Styne
Betty Comden and Adolph Green
Say, Darling (1958)

IT's THE WEATHER
James Shelton
Dance Me a Song (1950)

IT's THE YOUTH IN ME
Eubie Blake
J. Milton Reddie and Cecil Mack
Swing It (1937)

IT's THREE O'CLOCK
Rudolf Friml
Rowland Leigh and John Shubert
Music Hath Charms (1934)

IT's TIME TO SAY "ALOHA"
Sammy Fain
Charles Tobias
Hellzapoppin' (1938)

IT's TODAY
Jerry Herman
Mame (1966)

IT's UP TO ME
Charles Strouse
Lee Adams
All American (1962)

IT's UP TO THE BAND
Irving Berlin
Ziegfeld Follies (1927)

IT's WONDERFUL
Lucien Denni
Helena Evans
Happy Go Lucky (1926)

IT's YOU
Meredith Willson
The Music Man (1957)

IT's YOU
Jim Wise
George Haimsohn and Robin Miller
Dames at Sea (OB) (1968)

IT's YOU AGAIN
Walter Marks
Golden Rainbow (1968)

IT's YOU FOR ME
Ernest G. Schweikert
Frank Reardon
Rumple (1957)

IT's YOU I LOVE
J. Fred Coots
Arthur Swanstrom and Benny Davis
Sons o' Guns (1929)

IT's YOU I WANT
Paul McGrane
Al Stillman
Who's Who (1938)

IT's YOU I WANT TO LOVE TONIGHT
Rudolf Friml
Rowland Leigh and John Shubert
Music Hath Charms (1934)

IT's YOU WHO MAKES ME YOUNG
Harvey Schmidt
Tom Jones
Celebration (1969)

IT'S YOUR FAULT
Milton Schafer
Ira Levin
Drat! The Cat! (1965)

I'VE A SHOOTING BOX IN SCOTLAND
Cole Porter
Cole Porter and T. Lawrason Riggs
See America First (1916)

I'VE ALWAYS LOVED YOU
James Mundy
John Latouche
The Vamp (1955)

I'VE A'READY STARTED IN
Meredith Willson
The Unsinkable Molly Brown (1960)

I'VE BEEN A-BEGGING
George Fischoff
Verna Tomasson
The Prince and the Pauper (OB)
(1963)

I'VE BEEN INVITED TO A PARTY
Noël Coward
The Girl Who Came to Supper (1963)

I'VE BEEN SENT BACK TO THE FIRST
GRADE
C. C. Courtney
C. C. Courtney and Ragan Courtney
Earl of Ruston (1971)

I'VE BEEN THERE AND I'M BACK
Jay Livingston and Ray Evans
Oh Captain! (1958)

I'VE BEEN TOO BUSY
Jerry Bock, George Weiss, and Larry
  Holofcener
Mr. Wonderful (1956)

I'VE COME TO WIVE IT WEALTHILY
IN PADUA
Cole Porter
Kiss Me, Kate (1948)

I'VE CONFESSED TO THE BREEZE*
Vincent Youmans

Otto Harbach
No, No, Nanette (1925)

I'VE FALLEN OUT OF LOVE
Harry Revel
Mack Gordon
Smiling Faces (1932)

I'VE GONE NUTS OVER YOU
Edward A. Horan
Frederick Herendeen
All the King's Horses (1934)

I'VE GONE ROMANTIC ON YOU
Harold Arlen
E. Y. Harburg
Hooray for What! (1937)

I'VE GOT A BABY
Lewis E. Gensler
Robert A. Simon
Ups-A-Daisy (1928)

I'VE GOT A COOKIE JAR BUT NO
COOKIES
Harry Archer
Walter O'Keefe
Just a Minute (1928)

I'VE GOT A CRUSH ON YOU†
George Gershwin
Ira Gershwin
Treasure Girl (1928)

I'VE GOT A GOOSE
Robert Colby
Robert Colby and Nita Jonas
Half-Past Wednesday (OB) (1962)

I'VE GOT A LITTLE SECRET
Robert Dahdah
Curley McDimple (OB) (1967)

I'VE GOT A LOT TO LEARN ABOUT
LIFE
Tommy Wolf
Fran Landesman
The Nervous Set (1959)

---

*Added to 1971 revival
†Also in *Strike Up the Band*

I'VE GOT A ONE TRACK MIND
Vernon Duke
Howard Dietz
Jackpot (1944)

I'VE GOT A PAIN
Stanley Jay Gelber
John Lollos and Don Christopher
Love and Let Love (OB) (1968)

I'VE GOT A PROBLEM
Bill Mahoney
My Wife and I (OB) (1966)

I'VE GOT A RAINBOW WORKING FOR ME
Jule Styne
E. Y. Harburg
Darling of the Day (1968)

I'VE GOT A RIGHT TO SING THE BLUES
Harold Arlen
Ted Koehler
Earl Carroll's Vanities (1932)

I'VE GOT A SURPRISE FOR YOU
Hal Jordan
Jerry Douglas
Rondelay (OB) (1969)

I'VE GOT A WONDERFUL FUTURE
David Baker
Fred Ebb
Smiling, the Boy Fell Dead (OB) (1961)

I'VE GOT A YES GIRL
Henry Souvaine and Jay Gorney
Morrie Ryskind and Howard Dietz
Merry-Go-Round (1927)

I'VE GOT 'EM STANDING IN LINE
Steve Allen
Sophie (1963)

I'VE GOT FIVE DOLLARS
Richard Rodgers
Lorenz Hart
America's Sweetheart (1931)

I'VE GOT HARLEM ON MY MIND
Irving Berlin
As Thousands Cheer (1933)

I'VE GOT IT
Alberta Nichols
Mann Holiner
The Red Rose (1928)

I'VE GOT IT AGAIN
Ned Lehak
Allen Boretz
The Garrick Gaieties (1930)

I'VE GOT ME
Jerome Moross
John Latouche
Ballet Ballads (1948)

I'VE GOT MY EYES ON YOU
Cole Porter
Broadway Melody (F) (1940)

I'VE GOT MY LOVE TO KEEP ME WARM
Irving Berlin
On the Avenue (F) (1937)

I'VE GOT NOTHIN' TO DO
Sammy Fain
Marilyn and Alan Bergman
Something More! (1964)

I'VE GOT RINGS ON MY FINGERS
Maurice Scott
F. J. Barnes and R. P. Weston
The Yankee Girl (1910)

I'VE GOT SOME UNFINISHED BUSINESS WITH YOU
Cole Porter
Let's Face It! (1941)

I'VE GOT SOMETHING
Harry Ruby
Bert Kalmar
High Kickers (1941)

I'VE GOT THE NERVE TO BE IN LOVE
Harold Rome
Pins and Needles (OB) (1937)

I'VE GOT THE PRESIDENT'S EAR
Jimmy McHugh
Harold Adamson
As the Girls Go (1948)

I'VE GOT TO BE AROUND
Irving Berlin
Mr. President (1962)

I'VE GOT TO BE GOOD
Jean Schwartz
Clifford Grey and William Cary Duncan
Sunny Days (1928)

I'VE GOT TO BE ME
Walter Marks
Golden Rainbow (1968)

I'VE GOT TO BE THERE
George Gershwin
Ira Gershwin
Pardon My English (1933)

I'VE GOT TO FIND A REASON
Bob Merrill
Carnival (1961)

I'VE GOT TO GET HOT
Ray Henderson
Jack Yellen
George White's Scandals (1936)

I'VE GOT TO HAND IT TO YOU
Vernon Duke
John Latouche
Banjo Eyes (1941)

I'VE GOT WHAT IT TAKES
Al Wilson, Charles Weinberg, and Ken Macomber
Yeah Man (1932)

I'VE GOT WHAT YOU WANT
Jerry Bock
Sheldon Harnick
The Apple Tree (1966)

I'VE GOT YOU ON MY MIND
Max Ewing
The Grand Street Follies (1929)

I'VE GOT YOU ON MY MIND
Cole Porter
Gay Divorce (1932)

I'VE GOT YOU TO LEAN ON
Stephen Sondheim
Anyone Can Whistle (1964)

I'VE GOT YOU UNDER MY SKIN
Cole Porter
Born to Dance (F) (1936)

I'VE GOT YOUR NUMBER
Cy Coleman
Carolyn Leigh
Little Me (1962)

I'VE GOTTA CROW
Mark Charlap
Carolyn Leigh
Peter Pan (1954)

I'VE GOTTA KEEP MY EYE ON YOU
Harry Revel
Mack Gordon
Marching By (1932)

I'VE GOTTA SEE A MAN ABOUT HIS DAUGHTER
Jean Herbert, Karl Stark and James F. Hanley
Thumbs Up! (1934)

I'VE GROWN ACCUSTOMED TO HER FACE
Frederick Loewe
Alan Jay Lerner
My Fair Lady (1956)

I'VE JUST SEEN HER
Charles Strouse
Lee Adams
All American (1962)

I'VE LOST MY HEART
Morris Hamilton
Grace Henry
The Third Little Show (1931)

I'VE MADE A HABIT OF YOU
Arthur Schwartz

Howard Dietz
The Little Show (1929)

I'VE MADE UP MY MIND
Arthur Schwartz
Howard Dietz
Between the Devil (1937)

I'VE NEVER BEEN IN LOVE BEFORE
Frank Loesser
Guys and Dolls (1950)

I'VE NEVER SAID I LOVE YOU
Jerry Herman
Dear World (1969)

I'VE NOTHING TO OFFER
Harry Akst
Lew Brown
Calling All Stars (1934)

I'VE STILL GOT MY HEALTH
Cole Porter
Panama Hattie (1940)

I'VE TOLD EVERY LITTLE STAR
Jerome Kern
Oscar Hammerstein II
Music in the Air (1932)

I'VE WALKED IN THE MOONLIGHT
Edgar Fairchild
Milton Pascal
The Illustrators' Show (1936)

JACK BE NIMBLE
Helen Miller
Eve Merriam
Inner City (1971)

JACKIE
Jacques Brel
Eric Blau and Mort Shuman
Jacques Brel Is Alive and Well and Living in Paris (OB) (1968)

JACQUES D'IRAQ
Jerry Bock, George Weiss, and Larry Holofcener
Mr. Wonderful (1956)

JADED, DEGRADED AM I
Sammy Fain
Marilyn and Alan Bergman
Something More! (1964)

J'AI
Don Elliott
James Costigan
The Beast in Me (1963)

J'AI DEUX AMANTS
Andre Messager
Sacha Guitry
Naughty Cinderella (1925)

JAIL-LIFE WALK
Gary William Friedman
Will Holt
The Me Nobody Knows (OB) (1970)

JAILHOUSE BLUES
Jerry Herman
I Feel Wonderful (OB) (1954)

JAMIE
Lance Mulcahy
Paul Cherry
Park (1970)

JAPANESE MOON
Dave Stamper
Gene Buck
Take the Air (1927)

JAPANESE SERENADE
Sigmund Romberg
Harry B. Smith
Cherry Blossoms (1927)

JAZZ
Ida Hoyt Chamberlain
Enchanted Isle (1927)

JAZZ CITY
Henry Souvaine
J. P. McEvoy
Americana (1928)

J. B. PICTURES, INC.
Ray Haney
Alfred Aiken
We're Civilized? (OB) (1962)

JE M'EN FICHE
Coleman Dowell
The Tattooed Countess (OB) (1961)

JE T'AIME
Arthur Schwartz
Howard Dietz
Three's a Crowd (1930)

"JE T'AIME" MEANS I LOVE YOU
Powers Gouraud
Gay Paree (1926)

JE VOUS AIME
Arthur L. Beiner
Puzzles of 1925 (1925)

JEALOUS
Harold Levey
Owen Murphy
Rainbow Rose (1926)

JEALOUSY BEGINS AT HOME
Franz Lehár
Edward Eliscu
Frederika (1937)

JEALOUSY DUET
Kurt Weill
Marc Blitzstein
The Threepenny Opera (OB) (1954)

JEANNETTE AND HER LITTLE WOODEN SHOES
Victor Herbert
Robert B. Smith
Sweethearts (1913)

JEANNIE'S PACKIN' UP
Frederick Loewe
Alan Jay Lerner
Brigadoon (1947)

JEFF'S PLAINTS
Susan Hulsman Bingham
Myrna Lamb
Mod Donna (OB) (1970)

JEHOSHAPHAT MAKES UP HIS MIND
Deed Meyer
Stones of Jehoshaphat (OB) (1963)

JENNY
Ann Sternberg
Gertrude Stein
Gertrude Stein's First Reader (OB) (1969)

JENNY
Bob Goodman
Wild and Wonderful (1971)

JENNY KISSED ME
Michael Valenti
Just for Love (OB) (1968)

JENNY (THE SAGA OF)
Kurt Weill
Ira Gershwin
Lady in the Dark (1941)

JEREMIAH OBADIAH
Helen Miller
Eve Merriam
Inner City (1971)

JERICHO
Richard Myers
Leo Robin
Hello, Yourself! (1928)

JERRY, MY SOLDIER BOY
Cole Porter
Let's Face It! (1941)

JERSEY WALK
James F. Hanley
Eddie Dowling
Honeymoon Lane (1926)

JESTER AND I, THE
Mary Rodgers
Marshall Barer
Once Upon a Mattress (OB) (1959)

JESTER'S TALE, THE
Deed Meyer
Stones of Jehoshaphat (OB) (1963)

JESUS COME DOWN
Tom Sankey
The Golden Screw (OB) (1967)

JET SONG
Leonard Bernstein
Stephen Sondheim
West Side Story (1957)

JEWEL OF A DUEL, A
John Mundy
Edward Eager
The Liar (1950)

JEWELRY
Marian Grudeff and Raymond Jessel
Baker Street (1965)

JIG, THE
Arthur Schwartz
Howard Dietz
Jennie (1963)

JIG HOP, THE
Kay Swift
Paul James
Fine and Dandy (1930)

JIG SAW JAMBOREE
Eddie Bienbryer
William Walsh
Tattle Tales (1933)

JIGGLE YOUR FEET
Abel Baer
Sam Lewis and Joe Young
Lady Do (1927)

JILTED
George Gershwin
Ira Gershwin
Of Thee I Sing (1931)

JIM DANDY
Will Irwin
Norman Zeno
Fools Rush In (1934)

JIMMY
Irving Berlin
Ziegfeld Follies (1927)

JIMMY
Bill and Patti Jacob
Jimmy (1969)

JITTERS
Alexander Hill
Hummin' Sam (1933)

JOCKEY ON THE CAROUSEL, THE
Jerome Kern
Dorothy Fields
I Dream Too Much (F) (1935)

JOE WORKER
Marc Blitzstein
The Cradle Will Rock (1938)

JOEY, JOEY, JOEY
Frank Loesser
The Most Happy Fella (1956)

JOHN 19:41
Andrew Lloyd Webber
Tim Rice
Jesus Christ Superstar (1971)

JOHN PAUL JONES
Philip Charig
Dan Shapiro and Milton Pascal
Follow the Girls (1944)

JOHNNY
Marc Blitzstein
Juno (1959)

JOHNNY MISHUGA
Mark Bucci
David Rogers and Mark Bucci
New Faces (1962)

JOHNNY O
Earl Robinson
Waldo Salt
Sandhog (OB) (1954)

JOHNNY ONE NOTE
Richard Rodgers
Lorenz Hart
Babes in Arms (1937)

JOHNNY RIDE THE SKY
Jack Lawrence and Don Walker
Courtin' Time (1951)

JOHNNY WANAMAKER
Kay Swift
Paul James
The Garrick Gaieties (1930)

JOHNNY'S ARREST AND HOMECOM-ING
Kurt Weill
Paul Green
Johnny Johnson (1936)

JOHNNY'S CREED
Clinton Ballard
Carolyn Richter
The Ballad of Johnny Pot (OB) (1971)

JOHNNY'S CURSING SONG
Earl Robinson
Waldo Salt
Sandhog (OB) (1954)

JOHNNY'S MELODY
Kurt Weill
Paul Green
Johnny Johnson (1936)

JOHNNY'S SONG (LISTEN TO MY SONG)*
Kurt Weill
Paul Green
Johnny Johnson (1936)

JOIN IT RIGHT AWAY
Cole Porter
Panama Hattie (1940)

JOIN OUR RANKS
Jerome Moross
Paul Peters and George Sklar
Parade (1935)

JOIN THE NAVY
Vincent Youmans
Leo Robin and Clifford Grey
Hit the Deck (1927)

JOIN US IN A CUP OF TEA†
Charles Gaynor
Lend an Ear (1948)

JOKER, THE
Leslie Bricusse and Anthony Newley
The Roar of the Greasepaint—The Smell of the Crowd (1965)

JOLLY TAR AND THE MILKMAID, THE
George Gershwin
Ira Gershwin
A Damsel in Distress (F) (1937)

JOLLY THEATRICAL SEASON
Jerry Herman
Parade (OB) (1960)

JONAH'S MELODRAMA
Meyer Kupferman
Paul Goodman
Jonah (OB) (1966)

JONAH'S WAIL
John Dooley
Hobo (OB) (1961)

JONES' FAMILY FRIENDS, THE
George M. Cohan
Billie (1928)

JOSE, CAN'T YOU SEE!
Ray Henderson
Lew Brown
Hot-Cha! (1932)

JOSEPH TAYLOR, JR.
Richard Rodgers
Oscar Hammerstein II
Allegro (1947)

JOSEPHINE
Armand Vecsey
Clifford Grey
The Nightingale (1927)

JOSEPHINE
Cole Porter
Silk Stockings (1955)

---

*Later published as "To Love You and to Lose You," with lyrics by Edward Heyman
†Also in *Show Girl* (1961)

JOSEPHINE WATERS
Harold Arlen
E. Y. Harburg
The Show Is On (1936)

JOSHUA
Frederick Loewe
Alan Jay Lerner
What's Up? (1943)

JOURNEY, THE
Paul Hoffert
David Secter
Get Thee to Canterbury (OB) (1969)

JOURNEY HOME
Robert Swerdlow
Love Me, Love My Children (OB)
(1971)

JOURNEY'S END
Harry Tierney
Joseph McCarthy
Up She Goes (1922)

JOURNEY'S END
Jerome Kern
P. G. Wodehouse
The City Chap (1925)

JOUSTS, THE
Frederick Loewe
Alan Jay Lerner
Camelot (1960)

JOY BELLS
Emmerich Kalman
Harry B. Smith
The Circus Princess (1927)

JOY OR STRIFE
Jean Gilbert
Harry B. Smith
The Red Rose (1928)

JOY RIDE
Frank Grey and McElbert Moore
McElbert Moore and Frank Grey
The Matinee Girl (1926)

JOY SPREADER, THE
Richard Rodgers
Lorenz Hart
The Garrick Gaieties (1925)

JOYFUL NOISE, A
Oscar Brand and Paul Nassau
A Joyful Noise (1966)

JOYFUL THING, A
Jimmy Van Heusen
Sammy Cahn
Walking Happy (1966)

JUBILATION T. CORNPONE
Gene de Paul
Johnny Mercer
Li'l Abner (1956)

JUBILEE
Alexander Hill
Hummin' Sam (1933)

JUBILEE JOE
Don Tucker
Red, White and Maddox (1969)

JUDAS' DEATH
Andrew Lloyd Webber
Tim Rice
Jesus Christ Superstar (1971)

JUDE'S HOLLER
David Baker
Will Holt
Come Summer (1969)

JUDGEMENT OF PARIS, THE
Erich Wolfgang Korngold (based on
    Offenbach)
Herbert Baker
Helen Goes to Troy (1944)

JUDGEMENT OF PARIS
Donald Swann
Michael Flanders
At the Drop of a Hat (1959)

JUDGING SONG
Walter Cool
Mackey of Appalachia (OB) (1965)

JUDY, WHO D'YA LOVE?
Charles Rosoff
Leo Robin
Judy (1927)

JUG OF WINE, A
Frederick Loewe
Alan Jay Lerner
The Day Before Spring (1945)

JUKE BOX
Alex North
Alfred Hayes
Of V We Sing (1942)

JUKE BOX HOP, THE
Jule Styne
Betty Comden and Adolph Green
Do Re Mi (1960)

JULIANNE
Ida Hoyt Chamberlain
Enchanted Isle (1927)

JULIE
John Dooley
Hobo (OB) (1961)

JULIE IS MINE
Raymond Taylor
Lester Judson
Chic (OB) (1959)

JULIUS CAESAR
Paul Nassau and Oscar Brand
The Education of Hyman Kaplan
  (1968)

JUMP IN
Milton Schafer
Ronny Graham
Bravo Giovanni (1962)

JUMP, LITTLE CHILLUN
Sammy Fain
E. Y. Harburg
Flahooley (1951)

JUMPIN' JEHOSEPHAT
Robert Colby
Robert Colby and Nita Jonas
Half-Past Wednesday (OB) (1962)

JUMPING JACK
Frank Grey
McElbert Moore and Frank Grey
The Matinee Girl (1926)

JUNE
Porter Grainger and Freddie Johnson
Lucky Sambo (1925)

JUNE
Tom Johnstone
Phil Cook
When You Smile (1925)

JUNE DAYS
Stephen Jones
Clifford Grey and Cyrus Wood
June Days (1925)

JUNE IS BUSTIN' OUT ALL OVER
Richard Rodgers
Oscar Hammerstein II
Carousel (1945)

JUNE MOON
Ring Lardner
June Moon (1929)

JUNE TAYLOR, THE
William S. Fischer
Maxine Klein
Kiss Now (OB) (1971)

JUNGLE JINGLE
Irving Berlin
Ziegfeld Follies (1927)

JUNGLE ROSE
Ford Dabney
Jo Trent
Rang-Tang (1927)

JUNGLE SHADOWS
Emmerich Kalman and Herbert Sto-
  thart
Otto Harbach and Oscar Hammer-
  stein II
Golden Dawn (1927)

JUNIOR MISS
Burton Lane
Dorothy Fields
Junior Miss (TV) (1957)

JUPITER FORBID
Richard Rodgers
Lorenz Hart
By Jupiter (1942)

JUST A BIG-HEARTED MAN
Werner Janssen
Mann Holiner and J. Keirn Brennan
Boom-Boom (1929)

JUST A BIT NAïVE
Alma Sanders
Monte Carlo
Louisiana Lady (1947)

JUST A KISS
A. Baldwin Sloane
Harry Cort and George E. Stoddard
China Rose (1925)

JUST A KISS APART
Jule Styne
Leo Robin
Gentlemen Prefer Blondes (1949)

JUST A LITTLE BIT
Horald Griffiths
Blood (OB) (1971)

JUST A LITTLE BIT MORE
Arthur Schwartz
Dorothy Fields
Stars in Your Eyes (1939)

JUST A LITTLE BLUE FOR YOU
James F. Hanley
Keep It Clean (1929)

JUST A LITTLE JOINT WITH A JUKE
BOX
Hugh Martin and Ralph Blane
Best Foot Forward (1941)

JUST A LITTLE LOVE SONG
Max Ewing
The Grand Street Follies (1928)

JUST A LITTLE PENTHOUSE AND YOU
William Heagney
William Heagney and Tom Connell
There You Are (1932)

JUST A LITTLE SMILE FROM YOU
James F. Hanley
Eddie Dowling
Sidewalks of New York (1927)

JUST A MINUTE
Harry Archer
Walter O'Keefe
Just a Minute (1928)

JUST A SENTIMENTAL TUNE
Louis Alter
Max and Nathaniel Lief
Tattle Tales (1933)

JUST A SISTER
Thomas McKnight
The Garrick Gaieties (1930)

JUST A VOICE TO CALL ME, DEAR
Emmerich Kalman
P. G. Wodehouse
The Riviera Girl (1917)

JUST A WONDERFUL TIME
Frederico Vallerio
Elizabeth Miele
Hit the Trail (1954)

JUST AN HONEST MISTAKE
Jay Livingston and Ray Evans
Let It Ride (1961)

JUST AN ORDINARY GUY
Albert Selden
Phyllis McGinley and Burt Sheve-
love
Small Wonder (1948)

JUST ANOTHER GUY
Harold Karr
Matt Dubey
Happy Hunting (1956)

JUST BEYOND THE RAINBOW
Harry Revel
Arnold B. Horwitt
Are You With It? (1945)

JUST CROSS THE RIVER FROM
QUEENS
Albert Von Tilzer

Neville Fleeson
Bye Bye, Bonnie (1927)

JUST DON'T MAKE NO SENSE
Melvin Van Peebles
Ain't Supposed to Die a Natural Death (1971)

JUST EIGHTEEN
Richard A. Whiting
Oscar Hammerstein II
Free for All (1931)

JUST FOR LOVE
Michael Valenti
Just for Love (OB) (1968)

JUST FOR ONCE
Albert Hague
Dorothy Fields
Redhead (1959)

JUST FOR THE RIDE
George Fischoff
Carole Bayer
Georgy (1970)

JUST FOR TODAY
Ervin Drake
Her First Roman (1968)

JUST FOR TONIGHT
Maury Rubens
Clifford Grey
Katja (1926)

JUST FOR TONIGHT
Charlotte Kent
The Illustrators' Show (1936)

JUST FOR TONIGHT
Bronislaw Kaper (based on Chopin)
John Latouche
Polonaise (1945)

JUST HELLO
Sigmund Romberg
Otto Harbach
Forbidden Melody (1936)

JUST HIM
David Baker
David Craig
Phoenix '55 (OB) (1955)

JUST IMAGINE
Ray Henderson
B. G. DeSylva and Lew Brown
Good News (1927)

JUST IN CASE
Kurt Weill
Ira Gershwin
The Firebrand of Florence (1945)

JUST IN TIME
Jule Styne
Betty Comden and Adolph Green
Bells Are Ringing (1956)

JUST LET ME LOOK AT YOU
Jerome Kern
Dorothy Fields
The Joy of Living (F) (1938)

JUST LIKE A MAN
Vernon Duke
Ogden Nash
Two's Company (1952)

JUST LOOK!
Armando Trovaioli
Pietro Garinei and Sandro Giovannini
Rugantino (1964)

JUST MENTION JOE
Harry Akst
Lew Brown
Calling All Stars (1934)

JUST MY LUCK
Jimmy Van Heusen
Johnny Burke
Nellie Bly (1946)

JUST MY LUCK
Jerry Bock
Sheldon Harnick
The Body Beautiful (1958)

JUST ONCE AROUND THE CLOCK
Sigmund Romberg
Oscar Hammerstein II
May Wine (1935)

JUST ONCE MORE
Sandy Wilson
Valmouth (OB) (1960)

JUST ONE KISS
Harry Ruby
Bert Kalmar
The Ramblers (1926)

JUST ONE OF THOSE THINGS*
Cole Porter
The New Yorkers (1930)

JUST ONE OF THOSE THINGS
Cole Porter
Jubilee (1935)

JUST ONE MORE TIME
Norman Curtis
Patricia Taylor Curtis
Walk Down Mah Street! (OB) (1968)

JUST ONE WAY TO SAY I LOVE YOU
Irving Berlin
Miss Liberty (1949)

JUST PLAIN FOLKS
Jerry Herman
Parade (OB) (1960)

JUST SAY THE WORD
Frank D'Armond
Milton Berle
Saluta (1934)

JUST SIT BACK AND RELAX
Ed Tyler
Sweet Miani (OB) (1962)

JUST SOMEONE TO TALK TO
Alfred Brooks
Ira J. Bilowit
Of Mice and Men (OB) (1958)

JUST STAY ALIVE
Armando Trovaioli

Pietro Garinei and Sandro Giovannini
Rugantino (1964)

JUST SUPPOSE
Phil Baker and Maury Rubens
Sid Silvers and Moe Jaffe
Pleasure Bound (1929)

JUST THE CRUST
Jimmy Van Heusen
Sammy Cahn
Skyscraper (1965)

JUST THE WAY YOU ARE
Jack Holmes
Bill Conklin and Bob Miller
O Say Can You See! (OB) (1962)

**JUST WHEN I THOUGHT I HAD YOU
ALL TO MYSELF**
Harry Denny and Joe Fletcher
Footlights (1927)

JUST YOU AND I AND THE BABY
Con Conrad
William B. Friedlander
Mercenary Mary (1925)

JUST YOU WAIT
Frederick Loewe
Alan Jay Lerner
My Fair Lady (1956)

JUST YOUR OLD FRIEND
Peter Link
C. C. Courtney and Ragan Courtney
Earl of Ruston (1971)

JUSTICE TRIUMPHANT
Milton Schafer
Ira Levin
Drat! The Cat! (1965)

KA-LU-A
Jerome Kern
Anne Caldwell
Good Morning, Dearie (1921)

---

*Dropped from New York production; title
re-used for new song in *Jubilee*

KA WAHINE AKAMAI
Eaton Magoon, Jr.
13 Daughters (1961)

KABUKI ROCK
William S. Fischer
Maxine Klein
Kiss Now (OB) (1971)

KALUA BAY
John Kander
James Goldman, John Kander, and
    William Goldman
A Family Affair (1962)

KANDAHAR ISLE
Mann Holiner
Alberta Nichols
Gay Paree (1926)

KANGAROO
James P. Johnson
Henry Creamer
A la Carte (1927)

KANGAROO, THE
Milton Schafer
Ronny Graham
Bravo Giovanni (1962)

KANSAS CITY
Richard Rodgers
Oscar Hammerstein II
Oklahoma! (1943)

KAREN'S LULLABY
Walt Smith
Leon Uris
Ari (1971)

KATHAKALI
Sammy Fain
Paul Francis Webster
Christine (1960)

KATHLEEN, MINE
Vincent Youmans
Edward Heyman
Through the Years (1932)

KATIE DID IN MADRID
Frank Black
Gladys Shelley
The Duchess Misbehaves (1946)

KATIE JONAS
Stanley Lebowsky
Fred Tobias
Gantry (1970)

KATIE O'SULLIVAN
Earl Robinson
Waldo Salt
Sandhog (OB) (1954)

KATIE WENT TO HAITI
Cole Porter
Du Barry Was a Lady (1939)

KATINKA TO EVA TO FRANCES
Don Walker
George Marion, Jr.
Allah Be Praised (1944)

KEEP A-DIGGIN'
Porter Grainger and Freddie Johnson
Lucky Sambo (1925)

KEEP-A-HOPPIN'
Meredith Willson
The Unsinkable Molly Brown (1960)

KEEP A KISS FOR ME
Alma Sanders
Monte Carlo
Oh! Oh! Nurse (1925)

KEEP BUILDING YOUR CASTLES
Tom Johnstone
Phil Cook
When You Smile (1925)

KEEP 'EM BUSY, KEEP 'EM QUIET
Nancy Ford
Gretchen Cryer
Now Is the Time for All Good Men
    (OB) (1967)

KEEP IN TOUCH
Claude Leveilee
Gladys Shelley
Gogo Loves You (OB) (1964)

KEEP IT CASUAL
John Green
George Marion, Jr.
Beat the Band (1942)

KEEP IT GAY
Richard Rodgers
Oscar Hammerstein II
Me and Juliet (1953)

KEEP IT SIMPLE
Jay Livingston and Ray Evans
Oh Captain! (1958)

KEEP IT UNDER YOUR HAT
Vincent Valentini
Parisiana (1928)

KEEP IT UP
William B. Kernell
Dorothy Donnelly
Hello, Lola (1926)

KEEP ON DANCING
Vincent Valentini
Parisiana (1928)

KEEP SHUFFLIN'
Thomas (Fats) Waller
Andy Razaf
Keep Shufflin' (1928)

KEEP THEM GUESSING
Tom Johnstone
Phil Cook
When You Smile (1925)

KEEP YOUR CHIN UP
Eubie Blake
Noble Sissle
Shuffle Along (1933)

KEEP YOUR HAND ON YOUR HEART
Frederick Loewe
Earle Crooker
Great Lady (1938)

KEEP YOUR NOSE TO THE GRIND-
STONE
James Mundy
John Latouche
The Vamp (1955)

KEEP YOUR SHIRT ON
Manning Sherwin
Arthur Herzog, Jr.
Bad Habits of 1926 (OB) (1926)

KEEP YOUR UNDERSHIRT ON
Harry Ruby
Bert Kalmar
Top Speed (1929)

KEEPIN' MYSELF FOR YOU
Vincent Youmans
Sidney Clare
Hit the Deck (F) (1929)

KEEPING COOL WITH COOLIDGE
Jule Styne
Leo Robin
Gentlemen Prefer Blondes (1949)

KEEPING PRIGIO COMPANY
Lehman Engel
Agnes Morgan
A Hero Is Born (1937)

KEITH'S, PANTAGES AND LOEWS
Eddie Stuart
Harvey Lasker
Old Bucks and New Wings (OB)
(1962)

KENOSHA CANOE
Morgan Lewis
Nancy Hamilton
Three to Make Ready (1946)

KENTUCKY
Joe Jordan
Homer Tutt and Henry Creamer
Deep Harlem (1929)

KEPT IN SUSPENSE
Carroll Gibbons
Billy Rose and James Dyrenforth
Crazy Quilt (1931)

KER-CHOO!
Sigmund Romberg
Dorothy Donnelly
My Maryland (1927)

KEY TO MY HEART, THE
Lou Alter
Ira Gershwin
The Social Register (1931)

KEYS TO HEAVEN
Richard Rodgers
Lorenz Hart
The Garrick Gaieties (1926)

KEYS TO YOUR HEART
Jimmy McHugh
Dorothy Fields
Lew Leslie's International Revue
(1930)

KICK IN THE PANTS
Harry Archer
Will B. Johnstone
Entre-Nous (OB) (1935)

KICK IT AROUND
Steven Metcalf
Fred Bluth
Drat! (OB) (1971)

KICKIN' THE CLOUDS AWAY
George Gershwin
B. G. DeSylva and Ira Gershwin
Tell Me More (1925)

KICKIN' THE CORN AROUND
Richard Lewine
Ted Fetter
The Girl from Wyoming (OB) (1938)

KID
Walter Marks
Golden Rainbow (1968)

KIDNAPPED
Galt MacDermot
John Guare
Two Gentlemen of Verona (1971)

KIDS
Charles Strouse
Lee Adams
Bye Bye Birdie (1960)

KIKI
Lewis E. Gensler
B. G. DeSylva
Captain Jinks (1925)

KILL, THE
Wally Harper
Paul Zakrzewski
Sensations (OB) (1970)

KIND OF MAN, THE
Robert Kessler
Lola Permagent
O Marry Me! (OB) (1961)

KIND OF MAN A WOMAN NEEDS, THE
Michael Leonard
Herbert Martin
The Yearling (1965)

KIND OLD GENTLEMAN
Ervin Drake
Her First Roman (1968)

KINDA CUTE
Jay Gorney
E. Y. Harburg
Earl Carroll's Sketch Book (1929)

KINDA LIKE YOU
Vincent Youmans
Edward Heyman
Through the Years (1932)

KINDA SORTA DOIN' NOTHING
Jay Thompson
Double Entry (OB) (1961)

KINDNESS
Helen Miller
Eve Merriam
Inner City (1971)

KINDRED SPIRITS
Norman Campbell
Donald Campbell and Norman Campbell
Anne of Green Gables (OB) (1971)

KING
Mike Brandt, Michael Knight, and
  Robert J. Lowery
Exchange (OB) (1970)

KING COTTON
Giuseppe Verdi
Charles Friedman
My Darlin' Aïda (1952)

KING FOO-FOO THE FIRST
George Fischoff
Verna Tomasson
The Prince and the Pauper (OB)
  (1963)

KING HEROD'S SONG
Andrew Lloyd Webber
Tim Rice
Jesus Christ Superstar (1971)

KING JOE
Johnny Brandon
Billy Noname (OB) (1970)

KING OF LONDON
Robert Wright and George Forrest
Kean (1961)

KING OF THE SWORD
Robert Stolz and Maury Rubens
J. Keirn Brennan
The Red Rose (1928)

KING OF THE WORLD
Robert Larimer
King of the Whole Damn World! (OB)
  (1962)

KINGS AND QUEENS
Arthur Siegel
June Carroll
Shoestring Revue (OB) (1955)

KING'S SONG, THE
Richard Rodgers
Oscar Hammerstein II
The King and I (1951)

KINKAJOU, THE
Harry Tierney
Joseph McCarthy
Rio Rita (1927)

KISS A FOUR LEAF CLOVER
Jerome Kern
Anne Caldwell and Otto Harbach
Criss-Cross (1926)

KISS BEFORE I GO, A
Rudolf Friml
P. G. Wodehouse and Clifford Grey
The Three Musketeers (1928)

KISS FOR CINDERELLA, A
Richard Rodgers
Lorenz Hart
Present Arms (1928)

KISS HER NOW
Jerry Herman
Dear World (1969)

KISS I MUST REFUSE YOU, A
Sigmund Romberg
Irving Caesar
Nina Rosa (1930)

KISS IN THE DARK, A
Victor Herbert
B. G. DeSylva
Orange Blossoms (1922)

KISS IN THE MOONLIGHT, A
Clarence Gaskill
Earl Carroll's Vanities (1925)

KISS ME
Winthrop Cortelyou
Derick Wulff
Kiss Me (1927)

KISS ME
Noël Coward
Bitter Sweet (1929)

KISS ME
Jane Douglas
Tom O'Malley
Bella (OB) (1961)

KISS ME
Rick Besoyan
The Student Gypsy (OB) (1963)

KISS ME AGAIN
Victor Herbert
Henry Blossom
Mlle Modiste (1905)

KISS ME AND KILL ME WITH LOVE
Sammy Fain
Dan Shapiro
Ankles Aweigh (1955)

KISS ME AND WE'LL BOTH GO HOME
Morgan Lewis
Nancy Hamilton
One for the Money (1939)

KISS ME NO KISSES
Ervin Drake
What Makes Sammy Run? (1964)

KISS NOW
William S. Fischer
Maxine Klein
Kiss Now (OB) (1971)

KISS TO REMIND YOU, A
Franz Lehár
Edward Eliscu
Frederika (1937)

KISS WITH A KICK, A
Philip Charig and Richard Myers
Leo Robin
Allez-Oop (1927)

KITE
Clark Gesner
You're a Good Man, Charlie Brown (OB) (1967)

KITTY'S KISSES
Con Conrad
Gus Kahn
Kitty's Kisses (1926)

KITZEL ENGAGEMENT, THE
Richard Rodgers
Lorenz Hart
Betsy (1926)

KLING-KLING BIRD ON THE DIVI-DIVI TREE, THE
Cole Porter
Jubilee (1935)

KNEE DEEP IN JUNE
Jay Gorney
E. Y. Harburg
Earl Carroll's Vanities (1930)

KNEES
Richard Rodgers
Lorenz Hart
Heads Up! (1929)

KNIGHT OF THE MIRRORS, THE
Mitch Leigh
Joe Darion
Man of La Mancha (1965)

KNIGHT OF THE WOEFUL COUNTENANCE
Mitch Leigh
Joe Darion
Man of La Mancha (1965)

KNIGHTS OF THE WHITE CROSS
Giuseppe Verdi
Charles Friedman
My Darlin' Aida (1952)

KNOCK, KNOCK
John Kander
Fred Ebb
Flora, the Red Menace (1965)

KNOCK ON WOOD
Richard Myers
Edward Eliscu
Nine-Fifteen Revue (1930)

KNOCKING ON WOOD
Niclas Kempner
Graham John
The Street Singer (1929)

KNOW WHEN TO SMILE
Karl Hajos (based on Chopin)
Harry B. Smith
White Lilacs (1928)

KNOWING WHEN TO LEAVE
Burt Bacharach
Hal David
Promises, Promises (1968)

KOHALA, WELCOME
Richard Rodgers
Lorenz Hart
Present Arms (1928)

KOKORAKI
Donald Swann
Michael Flanders
At the Drop of a Hat (1959)

KOSHER KITTY KELLY
Leon DeCosta
Kosher Kitty Kelly (1925)

KOSHER KLEAGLE
Philip Charig
J. P. McEvoy
Americana (1926)

K-RA-ZY FOR YOU
George Gershwin
Ira Gershwin
Treasure Girl (1928)

KUKLA KATUSHA
Lee Pockriss
Anne Croswell
Tovarich (1963)

KULI, KULI
Eaton Magoon, Jr.
13 Daughters (1961)

LA CALINDA
Ruth Cleary Patterson
Gladys Shelley
Russell Patterson's Sketch Book (OB)
   (1960)

LA FIESTA
Sammy Fain
Dan Shapiro
Ankles Aweigh (1955)

L. A. INCIDENT
Mike Brandt, Michael Knight, and
   Robert J. Lowery
Exchange (OB) (1970)

LA GROSSE VALISE
Gerard Calvi

Harold Rome
La Grosse Valise (1965)

LA JAVA
Gerard Calvi
Harold Rome
La Grosse Valise (1965)

LA LA LA
Richard Rodgers
No Strings (1962)

LA MARSEILLES
Vincent Youmans
Harold Adamson and Clifford Grey
Smiles (1930)

LA PRINCESSE ZENOBIA (BALLET)
Richard Rodgers
On Your Toes (1936)

LA PRISONNIÈRE
Max Ewing
Agnes Morgan
The Grand Street Follies (OB) (1927)

LABEL ON THE BOTTLE, THE
Arthur Schwartz
Howard Dietz
The Gay Life (1961)

LABOR DAY PARADE
Clarence Todd
Andy Razaf
Keep Shufflin' (1928)

LABOR DAY PARADE
Eubie Blake
Noble Sissle
Shuffle Along (1933)

LABOR IS THE THING
Richard Rodgers
Lorenz Hart
I'd Rather Be Right (1937)

LACK-A-DAY
John Mundy
Edward Eager
The Liar (1950)

LACKAWANNA
Joseph Meyer and James F. Hanley
B. G. DeSylva
Big Boy (1925)

LADIES
Harold Rome
Destry Rides Again (1959)

LADIES AND GENTLEMEN, THAT'S LOVE
Ray Henderson
B. G. DeSylva and Lew Brown
George White's Scandals (1931)

LADIES, BEWARE
Rudolf Friml
Rowland Leigh and John Shubert
Music Hath Charms (1934)

LADIES' HOME COMPANION, A
Richard Rodgers
Lorenz Hart
A Connecticut Yankee (1927)

LADIES IN WAITING
Cole Porter
Les Girls (F) (1957)

LADIES IN WAITING
Robert Colby
Robert Colby and Nita Jonas
Half-Past Wednesday (OB) (1962)

LADIES' MAN
Ray Henderson
B. G. DeSylva and Lew Brown
Good News (1927)

LADIES OF THE BOX OFFICE
Richard Rodgers
Lorenz Hart
The Garrick Gaieties (1925)

LADIES OF THE EVENING
Richard Rodgers
Lorenz Hart
The Boys from Syracuse (1938)

LADIES OF THE JURY
Sigmund Romberg
Oscar Hammerstein II
The New Moon (1928)

LADIES OF THE TOWN
Noël Coward
Bitter Sweet (1929)

LADIES' OPINION
John Mundy
Edward Eager
The Liar (1950)

LADIES ROOM
Alex Fogarty
Edwin Gilbert
You Never Know (1938)

LADIES WHO LUNCH, THE
Stephen Sondheim
Company (1970)

LADIES WHO SING WITH A BAND, THE
Thomas (Fats) Waller
George Marion, Jr.
Early to Bed (1943)

LADY, THE
Elsie Peters
Alfred Hayes
Tis of Thee (1940)

LADY BRED IN THE PURPLE, A
Seymour Furth and Lee Edwards
R. F. Carroll
Bringing Up Father (1925)

LADY BUG SONG, THE
George Kleinsinger
Joe Darion
Shinbone Alley (1957)

LADY DO
Abel Baer
Sam Lewis and Joe Young
Lady Do (1927)

LADY FAIR
Ray Henderson
B. G. DeSylva and Lew Brown
George White's Scandals (1926)

LADY HAS OOMPH, THE
Dorcas Cochran and Charles Rosoff
Earl Carroll's Vanities (1940)

LADY IN THE WINDOW
Sigmund Romberg
Otto Harbach
Forbidden Melody (1936)

LADY IN WAITING
Alberta Nichols
Mann Holiner
Hey Nonny Nonny! (1932)

LADY IN WAITING
Leroy Anderson
Joan Ford, Walter and Jean Kerr
Goldilocks (1958)

LADY IS A TRAMP, THE
Richard Rodgers
Lorenz Hart
Babes in Arms (1937)

LADY LUCK
George Gershwin
Ira Gershwin
Tip-Toes (1925)

LADY LUCK
Ray Henderson
B. G. DeSylva
Three Cheers (1928)

LADY MUST LIVE, A
Richard Rodgers
Lorenz Hart
America's Sweetheart (1931)

LADY NEEDS A CHANGE, THE
Arthur Schwartz
Dorothy Fields
Stars in Your Eyes (1939)

LADY NEEDS A REST, A
Cole Porter
Let's Face It! (1941)

LADY OF LEISURE, A
Willard Straight
David Eddy
The Athenian Touch (OB) (1964)

LADY OF MY HEART
Milton Susskind
Paul Porter and Benjamin Hapgood
  Burt
Florida Girl (1925)

LADY OF THE EVENING
Irving Berlin
Music Box Revue (1922)

LADY OF THE MANOR
Sandy Wilson
Valmouth (OB) (1960)

LADY OF THE ROSE
Rudolf Friml
Otto Harbach and Oscar Hammer-
  stein II
The Wild Rose (1926)

LADY OF THE SNOW, THE
Harold Levey
Owen Murphy
The Greenwich Village Follies (1925)

LADY WAS MADE TO BE LOVED, THE
Jacques Urbont
Bruce Geller
All in Love (OB) (1961)

LADY WHIPPOORWILL
Harry Tierney
Joseph McCarthy
Cross My Heart (1928)

LADY WITH THE TAP, THE
Arthur Schwartz
Howard Dietz
At Home Abroad (1935)

LADY'S IN LOVE WITH YOU, THE
Burton Lane
Frank Loesser
Some Like it Hot (F) (1939)

LAMENT OF SHAKESPEARE, THE
Morris Hamilton
Grace Henry
Earl Carroll's Vanities (1926)

LAMENT ON FIFTH AVENUE
Claibe Richardson
Paul Rosner
Shoestring Revue (OB) (1957)

LAMPLIGHT
James Shelton
New Faces (1934)

LAND OF BETRAYAL
Galt MacDermot
John Guare
Two Gentlemen of Verona (1971)

LAND OF BROKEN DREAMS
Martin Broones
Ballard MacDonald
Rufus Lemaire's Affairs (1927)

LAND OF GOING TO BE, THE
E. Ray Goetz and Walter Kollo
Paris (1928)

LAND OF "LET'S PRETEND," THE
Jerome Kern
Harry B. Smith
The Girl from Utah (1914)

LAND OF MINE
Giuseppe Verdi
Charles Friedman
My Darlin' Aïda (1952)

LAND OF OPPORTUNITEE, THE
Arthur Schwartz
Ira Gershwin
Park Avenue (1946)

LAND OF ROCKEFELLERA
Lee Wainer
John Lund
New Faces (1943)

LAND OF ROMANCE
Percy Wenrich
Raymond Peck
Castles in the Air (1926)

LAND OF THE GAY CABALLERO
George Gershwin
Ira Gershwin
Girl Crazy (1930)

LAND WHERE THE GOOD SONGS GO, THE
Jerome Kern
P.G. Wodehouse
Miss 1917 (1917)

LANGENSTEIN IN SPRING
Edward A. Horan
Frederick Herendeen
All the King's Horses (1934)

LANTERN NIGHT
Armando Trovaioli
Pietro Garinei and Sandro Giovannini
Rugantino (1964)

LANTERN OF LOVE
Percy Wenrich
Raymond Peck
Castles in the Air (1926)

L'APRÈS-MIDI D'UN BOEUF
Cole Porter
Du Barry Was a Lady (1939)

LARCENY AND LOVE
Robert Emmett Dolan
Johnny Mercer
Foxy (1964)

LARK, THE
Sigmund Romberg
Harry B. Smith
The Love Call (1927)

LAS VEGAS
Ray Golden, Sy Kleinman, and Lee Adams
Catch a Star! (1955)

LAS VEGAS
Billy Barnes
The Billy Barnes Revue (1959)

LASS WHO LOVED A SAILOR, THE
Richard Rodgers
Lorenz Hart
Heads Up! (1929)

LAST CONFESSION
John Duffy
Rocco Bufano and John Duffy (based

on W.B. Yeats)
Horseman, Pass By (OB) (1969)

LAST DANCE, THE
Noël Coward
Bitter Sweet (1929)

LAST LONG MILE, THE
Vernon Duke
Howard Dietz
Jackpot (1944)

LAST SUPPER, THE
Andrew Lloyd Webber
Tim Rice
Jesus Christ Superstar (1971)

LAST SWEET DAYS OF ISAAC, THE
Nancy Ford
Gretchen Cryer
The Last Sweet Days of Isaac (OB)
(1970)

LAST TIME I SAW PARIS, THE*
Jerome Kern
Oscar Hammerstein II
Lady, Be Good (F) (1941)

LAST WALTZ, THE
Oscar Straus
Edward Delaney Dunn
The Last Waltz (1921)

LAST WORD, THE
Lehman Engel
Agnes Morgan
A Hero Is Born (1937)

LATAVIA
Percy Wenrich
Raymond Peck
Castles in the Air (1926)

LATAVIAN CHANT, THE
Percy Wenrich
Raymond Peck
Castles in the Air (1926)

LATE, LATE SHOW, THE
Jule Styne
Betty Comden and Adolph Green
Do Re Mi (1960)

LATE LOVE
Jack Urbont
Bruce Geller
Livin' the Life (OB) (1957)

LATELY I'VE BEEN FEELING SO STRANGE
Irving Burgie
Ballad for Bimshire (OB) (1963)

LATER THAN SPRING
Noël Coward
Sail Away (1961)

LATIGO
Sigmund Romberg
Irving Caesar
Nina Rosa (1930)

LATIN IN ME, THE
Sammy Fain
Irving Kahal and Jack Yellen
Boys and Girls Together (1940)

LATIN TUNE, A MANHATTAN MOON AND YOU, A
Jimmy McHugh
Al Dubin
Keep Off the Grass (1940)

LATINS KNOW HOW
Irving Berlin
Louisiana Purchase (1940)

LAUGH
Richard Rodgers
Lorenz Hart
Jumbo (1935)

LAUGH A LITTLE
Michael Leonard
Herbert Martin
How to Be a Jewish Mother (1967)

LAUGH AFTER LAUGH
Richard B. Chodosh
Barry Alan Grael
The Streets of New York (OB) (1963)

———
*Academy Award Winner

LAUGH AT LIFE
Maury Rubens
J. Delany Dunn
The Red Rose (1928)

LAUGH, I THOUGHT I'D DIE
Tommy Wolf
Fran Landesman
The Nervous Set (1959)

LAUGH IT UP
Irving Berlin
Mr. President (1962)

LAUGH IT UP
Johnny Brandon
Cindy (OB) (1964)

LAUGH PARADE, THE
Harry Warren
Mort Dixon and Joe Young
The Laugh Parade (1931)

LAUGH YOUR BLUES AWAY
C. Luckey Roberts
Alex C. Rogers
My Magnolia (1926)

LAUGHING BELLS
Bronislaw Kaper (based on Chopin)
John Latouche
Polonaise (1945)

LAUGHING FACE
John Jennings
Riverwind (OB) (1962)

LAUGHING OUT LOUD
George Harwell
What a Killing (OB) (1961)

LAUGHING SONG, THE
Al Carmines
Maria Irene Fornes
Promenade (OB) (1969)

LAUGHING WALTZ*
Robert Stolz
Robert Sour
Mr. Strauss Goes to Boston (1945)

LAUGHTER IN THE AIR
Erich Korngold
Oscar Hammerstein II
Give Us This Night (F) (1936)

LAURA DE MAUPASSANT
Jule Styne
Bob Hilliard
Hazel Flagg (1953)

LAW AND ORDER
Oscar Brand
How to Steal an Election (OB) (1968)

LAW AND ORDER
Helen Miller
Eve Merriam
Inner City (1971)

LAY YOUR BETS
Edward Pola
Eddie Brandt
Woof, Woof (1929)

LAZY AFTERNOON
Jerome Moross
John Latouche
The Golden Apple (1954)

LAZY LEVEE LOUNGERS
Willard Robison
The Garrick Gaieties (1930)

LAZY MOON
Leroy Anderson
Joan Ford, Walter and Jean Kerr
Goldilocks (1958)

L'CHAYIM
Harold Rome
The Zulu and the Zayda (1965)

LE BON MOT
Mimi Stone
William Kaye
Pimpernel! (OB) (1964)

---

*Adaptation of Johann Strauss melody

LE CROISSANT
Mimi Stone
William Kaye
Pimpernel! (OB) (1964)

LE FIVE O'CLOCK
Will Irwin
Carl Randall
The Third Little Show (1931)

LE GRISBI IS LE ROOT OF LE EVIL IN MAN
Marguerite Monnot
Julian More, David Heneker, and Monte Norman
Irma La Douce (1960)

LEAD 'EM ON
Joseph Meyer and James F. Hanley
B. G. DeSylva
Big Boy (1925)

LEADER OF A BIG-TIME BAND, THE
Cole Porter
Something for the Boys (1943)

LEAF IN THE WIND
Baldwin Bergersen
George Marion, Jr.
Allah Be Praised (1944)

LEAFLETS
Marc Blitzstein
The Cradle Will Rock (1938)

LEAN ON ME
Steven Metcalf
Fred Bluth
Drat! (OB) (1971)

LEANDER
Jean Gilbert
Harry Graham
Katja (1926)

LEANING ON A SHOVEL
Lee Wainer
John Latouche
Sing for Your Supper (1939)

LEARN HOW TO LAUGH
Hugo Peretti, Luigi Creatore, and George David Weiss
Maggie Flynn (1968)

LEARN TO CROON
Harold Arlen
Jack Yellen
You Said It (1931)

LEARN TO LOVE
Voices, Inc.
The Believers (OB) (1968)

LEARN TO SING A LOVE SONG
Irving Berlin
Ziegfeld Follies (1927)

LEARN TO SMILE
Louis A. Hirsch
Otto Harbach
The O'Brien Girl (1921)

LEARN YOUR LESSONS WELL
Stephen Schwartz
Godspell (OB) (1971)

LEARNING LOVE
Bruce Montgomery
The Amorous Flea (OB) (1964)

LEAST THAT'S MY OPINION
Harold Arlen
Johnny Mercer
St. Louis Woman (1946)

LEAVE IT ALL TO YOUR FAITHFUL AMBASSADOR
Albert Sirmay and Arthur Schwartz
Arthur Swanstrom
Princess Charming (1930)

LEAVE IT TO JANE
Jerome Kern
P. G. Wodehouse
Leave It to Jane (1917)

LEAVE IT TO KATARINA
Jara Benes
Irving Caesar
White Horse Inn (1936)

LEAVE IT TO LEVY
Irving Caesar
Betsy (1926)

LEAVE IT TO US, GOV
Marian Grudeff and Raymond Jessel
Baker Street (1965)

LEAVE THE ATOM ALONE
Harold Arlen
E. Y. Harburg
Jamaica (1957)

LEAVE THE WORLD BEHIND
Robert Swerdlow
Love Me, Love My Children (OB)
   (1971)

LEAVE WELL ENOUGH ALONE
Jerry Bock
Sheldon Harnick
The Body Beautiful (1958)

LEAVIN' FO' DE PROMIS' LAN'
George Gershwin
DuBose Heyward
Porgy and Bess (1935)

LEAVIN' TIME
Harold Arlen
Johnny Mercer
St. Louis Woman (1946)

LEBEN SIE WOHL
Robert Wright and George Forrest
   (based on Rachmaninoff)
Anya (1965)

LEES OF OLD VIRGINIA, THE
Sherman Edwards
1776 (1969)

LEFT ALL ALONE AGAIN BLUES
Jerome Kern
Anne Caldwell
The Night Boat (1920)

LEG IT
Clarence Todd
Henry Creamer and Con Conrad
Keep Shufflin' (1928)

LEG OF THE DUCK, THE
Mitch Leigh
William Alfred and Phyllis Robinson
Cry for Us All (1970)

LEGALIZE MY NAME
Harold Arlen
Johnny Mercer
St. Louis Woman (1946)

LEGEND, THE
Robert Wright and George Forrest
   (based on Grieg)
Song of Norway (1944)

LEGEND OF BLACK-EYED SUSAN GREY, THE
Gordon Duffy
Harry M. Haldane
Happy Town (1959)

LEGEND OF THE ISLANDS
Ed Tyler
Sweet Miani (OB) (1962)

LEGEND OF THE MISSION BELLS
William Heagney
William Heagney and Tom Connell
There You Are (1932)

LEGEND SONG
Sigmund Romberg
Harry B. Smith
Cherry Blossoms (1927)

LEGENDARY EINO FFLLIIKKIIN-NENN, THE
Sidney Lippman
Sylvia Dee
Barefoot Boy with Cheek (1947)

LEGITIMATE
Lee Wainer
John Latouche
Sing for Your Supper (1939)

LEGS, LEGS, LEGS
Jay Gorney
E. Y. Harburg
Earl Carroll's Sketch Book (1929)

LEMME TELL YA
Alfred Brooks
Ira J. Bilowit
Of Mice and Men (OB) (1958)

LEND ME A BOB TILL MONDAY
Kay Swift
Paris '90 (1952)

LENNIE
George Harwell
What a Killing (OB) (1961)

LES GIRLS
Cole Porter
Les Girls (F) (1957)

LES SYLPHIDES AVEC LA BUMPE
Irving Gordon, Alan Roberts, and
   Jerome Brainin
Star and Garter (1942)

LESSON, THE
Manos Hadjidakis
Joe Darion
Illya Darling (1967)

LESSON IN YIDDISH, A
Murray Rumshinsky
Jacob Jacobs
The President's Daughter (1970)

LESSONS ON LIFE
Bruce Montgomery
The Amorous Flea (Ob) (1964)

LET-A-GO YOUR HEART
Eaton Magoon, Jr.
13 Daughters (1961)

LET ANTIPHOLUS IN
Richard Rodgers
Lorenz Hart
The Boys from Syracuse (1938)

LET 'EM EAT CAKE
George Gershwin
Ira Gershwin
Let 'Em Eat Cake (1933)

LET 'EM EAT CAVIAR
George Gershwin
Ira Gershwin
Let 'Em Eat Cake (1933)

LET FATE DECIDE
Maury Rubens
Harry B. Smith
Marching By (1932)

LET HIM KICK UP HIS HEELS
Michael Leonard
Herbert Martin
The Yearling (1965)

LET IT RAIN
James Kendis and Hal Dyson
Sky High (1925)

LET IT RIDE
Jay Livingston and Ray Evans
Let It Ride (1961)

LET LOVE GO
Sigmund Romberg
Otto Harbach and Oscar Hammer-
   stein II
The Desert Song (1926)

LET ME BE
David Baker
Will Holt
Come Summer (1969)

LET ME BE A FRIEND TO YOU
George Gershwin
Ira Gershwin
Rosalie (1928)

LET ME BE BORN AGAIN
Victor Young
Joseph Young and Ned Washington
Blackbirds of 1934 (1933)

LET ME BE FREE
Rudolf Friml
Rowland Leigh and John Shubert
Music Hath Charms (1934)

LET ME BE MYSELF
Manning Sherwin
Arthur Herzog, Jr.
Bad Habits of 1926 (OB) (1926)

LET ME COME IN
Gary William Friedman
Will Holt
The Me Nobody Knows (OB) (1970)

LET ME DANCE
Alfred Goodman, Maury Rubens, and
 J. Fred Coots
Clifford Grey
Artists and Models (1925)

LET ME DOWN WALKING IN THE
WORLD
Robert Swerdlow
Love Me, Love My Children (OB)
 (1971)

LET ME DROWN
Robert Holton
June Carroll
Hi, Paisano! (OB) (1961)

LET ME ENTERTAIN YOU
Jule Styne
Stephen Sondheim
Gypsy (1959)

LET ME GIVE ALL MY LOVE TO
THEE
Vincent Youmans
Oscar Hammerstein II
Rainbow (1928)

LET ME HOLD YOU IN MY ARMS
Clarence Gaskill
Keep It Clean (1929)

LET ME LIVE TODAY
Sigmund Romberg
Oscar Hammerstein II
Sunny River (1941)

LET ME LOVE YOU
John Morris
Gerald Freedman
A Time for Singing (1966)

LET ME MATCH MY PRIVATE LIFE
WITH YOURS
Vernon Duke
E. Y. Harburg
Americana (1932)

LET ME SHOW YOU THE WORLD
Robert Rosenblum
Robert Rosenblum, Howard Schuman
Up Eden (OB) (1968)

LET ME TAKE YOU FOR A RIDE
David Martin
Langston Hughes
Simply Heavenly (1957)

LET ME WEEP ON YOUR SHOULDER
Joseph Meyer
Edward Eliscu
Lady Fingers (1929)

LET THE MAN WHO MAKES THE
GUN
Gerald Marks
Raymond B. Egan
Earl Carroll's Sketch Book (1935)

LET THE MOMENT SLIP BY
Peter Link and C. C. Courtney
Salvation (OB) (1969)

LET THE WORLD BEGIN AGAIN
Joseph Martinez Kookoolis and Scott
 Fagan
Scott Fagan
Soon (1971)

LET THINGS BE LIKE THEY ALWAYS
WAS
Kurt Weill
Langston Hughes
Street Scene (1947)

LET US GATHER AT THE GOAL LINE
Sammy Fain
George Marion, Jr.
Toplitzky of Notre Dame (1946)

LET YOUR HAIR DOWN WITH A
BANG
Baldwin Bergersen
June Sillman
Who's Who (1938)

LET YOURSELF GO
Irving Berlin
Follow the Fleet (F) (1936)

LET'S
Duke Ellington
Marshall Barer and Fred Tobias
Pousse-Café (1966)

LET'S ALL GO RAVING MAD
Philip Braham
Hugh E. Wright
Charlot's Revue (1926)

LET'S ALL BE EXACTLY AND PRECISELY WHAT WE ARE
Robert Kessler
Lola Permagent
O Marry Me! (OB) (1961)

LET'S ALL SING THE LARD SONG
Leslie Sarony
Anne Caldwell
Three Cheers (1928)

LET'S BALL AWHILE
David Martin
Langston Hughes
Simply Heavenly (1957)

LET'S BE BUDDIES
Cole Porter
Panama Hattie (1940)

LET'S BE ELEGANT OR DIE!
William Dyer
Don Parks and William Dyer
Jo! (OB) (1964)

LET'S BE HAPPY NOW
Henry Souvaine and Jay Gorney
Morrie Ryskind and Howard Dietz
Merry-Go-Round (1927)

LET'S BE STRANGERS AGAIN
Leon Pober
Bud Freeman
Beg, Borrow or Steal (1960)

LET'S BEGIN
Jerome Kern
Otto Harbach
Roberta (1933)

LET'S BRING BACK SHOWBUSINESS
Eddie Stuart
Harvey Lasker
Old Bucks and New Wings (OB) (1962)

LET'S CALL IT A DAY
Ray Henderson
B. G. DeSylva and Lew Brown
Strike Me Pink (1933)

LET'S CALL THE WHOLE THING OFF
George Gershwin
Ira Gershwin
Shall We Dance (F) (1937)

LET'S COMB BEACHES
John Green
George Marion, Jr.
Beat the Band (1942)

LET'S DANCE AND MAKE UP
Tom Johnstone
Phil Cook
When You Smile (1925)

LET'S DO AND SAY WE DIDN'T
Hughie Prince and Dick Rogers
The Girl from Nantucket (1945)

LET'S DO IT (LET'S FALL IN LOVE)
Cole Porter
Paris (1928)

LET'S EVOLVE
David Baker
Fred Ebb
Smiling, the Boy Fell Dead (OB) (1961)

LET'S FACE IT
Cole Porter
Let's Face It! (1941)

LET'S FACE THE MUSIC AND DANCE
Irving Berlin
Follow the Fleet (F) (1936)

LET'S FALL IN LOVE
Harold Arlen
Ted Koehler
Let's Fall in Love (F) (1934)

LET'S FETCH THE CARRIAGE
Glenn Paxton
Robert Goldman and George Weiss
First Impressions (1959)

LET'S FLY AWAY
Cole Porter
The New Yorkers (1930)

LET'S GET BACK TO GLAMOUR
Manning Sherwin
Harold Purcell
Under the Counter (1947)

LET'S GET DRUNK
Billy Barnes
The Billy Barnes People (1961)

LET'S GET LOST IN NOW
Peter Link and C. C. Courtney
Salvation (OB) (1969)

LET'S GET MARRIED OR SOMETHING
Richard Lewine
Ted Fetter
Entre-Nous (OB) (1935)

LET'S GO
Milton Schafer
Ira Levin
Drat! The Cat! (1965)

LET'S GO BACK TO THE WALTZ
Irving Berlin
Mr. President (1962)

LET'S GO DOWN
Ron Steward and Neal Tate
Ron Steward
Sambo (OB) (1969)

LET'S GO EAT WORMS IN THE GAR-
DEN
Kay Swift
Paul James
Fine and Dandy (1930)

LET'S GO HIGH HAT
Richard Lewine
Will B. Johnstone
Entre-Nous (OB) (1935)

LET'S GO HOME
André Previn
Alan Jay Lerner
Coco (1969)

LET'S GO LOVIN'
Herman Hupfeld
Hey Nonny Nonny! (1932)

LET'S GO OUT IN THE OPEN AIR
Ann Ronell
Shoot the Works (1931)

LET'S GO TOO FAR
Don Walker
George Marion, Jr.
Allah Be Praised (1944)

LET'S HAVE A GOOD TIME
Tom Johnstone
Phil Cook
When You Smile (1925)

LET'S HAVE A LOVE AFFAIR
Sigmund Romberg
Otto Harbach and Oscar Hammer-
stein II
The Desert Song (1926)

LET'S HAVE A SIMPLE WEDDING
Jim Wise
George Haimsohn and Robin Miller
Dames at Sea (OB) (1968)

LET'S HAVE ANOTHER CUP OF COF-
FEE
Irving Berlin
Face the Music (1932)

LET'S HOLD HANDS
Richard Lewine
June Sillman
Fools Rush In (1934)

LET'S IMPROVISE
Robert Wright and George Forrest
Kean (1961)

LET'S KISS AND MAKE UP
George Gershwin
Ira Gershwin
Funny Face (1927)

LET'S LAUGH AND BE MERRY
Shep Camp
Frank DuPree and Harry B. Smith
Half a Widow (1927)

LET'S MAKE IT FOREVER
Fred Stamer
Gen Genovese
Buttrio Square (1952)

LET'S MAKE MEMORIES TONIGHT
Sam Stept
Lew Brown and Charles Tobias
Yokel Boy (1939)

LET'S MERGE
J. Fred Coots
Arthur Swanstrom and Benny Davis
Sons o' Guns (1929)

LET'S MISBEHAVE*
Cole Porter
Paris (1928)

LET'S NOT GET MARRIED
Ruth Cleary Patterson
George Blake and Les Kramer
Russell Patterson's Sketch Book (OB)
(1960)

LET'S NOT TALK ABOUT LOVE
Cole Porter
Let's Face It! (1941)

LET'S NOT WASTE A MOMENT
Jerry Herman
Milk and Honey (1961)

LET'S PLAY A TUNE ON THE MUSIC BOX
Noël Coward
Tonight at 8:30 (Family Album)
(1936)

LET'S PRETEND
Robert Hood Bowers
Francis DeWitt
Oh, Ernest! (1927)

LET'S PRETEND
Johnny Brandon
Cindy (OB) (1964)

LET'S PUT IT TO MUSIC
Alex Fogarty
Edwin Gilbert
You Never Know (1938)

LET'S RAISE HELL
Porter Grainger
Fast and Furious (1931)

LET'S RUN AWAY AND GET MARRIED
Harold Levey
Owen Murphy
Rainbow Rose (1926)

LET'S SAY GOOD NIGHT TILL IT'S MORNING
Jerome Kern
Oscar Hammerstein II
Sunny (1925)

LET'S SAY GOODNIGHT WITH A DANCE
Sammy Fain
Jack Yellen
Sons o' Fun (1941)

LET'S SEE WHAT HAPPENS
Jule Styne
E. Y. Harburg
Darling of the Day (1968)

LET'S SIT AND TALK ABOUT YOU
Jimmy McHugh
Dorothy Fields
Hello Daddy (1928)

LET'S STEAL A TUNE FROM OFFENBACH
Jay Gorney
Henry Myers
Meet the People (1940)

LET'S STEP OUT
Cole Porter
Fifty Million Frenchmen (1929)

———
*Dropped from New York production

LET'S STROLL ALONG AND SING A SONG OF LOVE
Cliff Friend
Lew Brown
Piggy (1927)

LET'S SWING IT
Charles Tobias, Charles Newman, and
  Murray Mencher
Earl Carroll's Sketch Book (1935)

LET'S TAKE A WALK AROUND THE BLOCK
Harold Arlen
Ira Gershwin and E. Y. Harburg
Life Begins at 8:40 (1934)

LET'S TAKE A STROLL THROUGH LONDON
Julian Slade
Dorothy Reynolds and Julian Slade
Salad Days (OB) (1958)

LET'S TAKE ADVANTAGE OF NOW
Ray Henderson
Ted Koehler
Say When (1934)

LET'S TAKE AN OLD-FASHIONED WALK
Irving Berlin
Miss Liberty (1949)

LET'S TAKE THE LONG WAY HOME
Harold Arlen
Johnny Mercer
Here Come the Waves (F) (1944)

LET'S TALK ABOUT THE WEATHER
Charlotte Kent
The Illustrators' Show (1936)

LET'S TURN OUT THE LIGHTS AND GO TO BED
Herman Hupfeld
George White's Music Hall Varieties (1932)

LETTER, THE
Jay Gorney
Barry Trivers
Heaven on Earth (1948)

LETTER, THE
Frank Loesser
The Most Happy Fella (1956)

LETTER, THE
Frank Fields
Armand Aulicino
The Shoemaker and the Peddler (OB) (1960)

LETTER, THE
Clinton Ballard
Carolyn Richter
The Ballad of Johnny Pot (OB) (1971)

LETTER SONG, THE
Carlton Kelsey and Maury Rubens
Clifford Grey
Sky High (1925)

LETTER SONG
Walter Kollo
Harry B. Smith
Three Little Girls (1930)

LETTERS
Marian Grudeff and Raymond Jessel
Baker Street (1965)

LEVIATHAN
Meyer Kupferman
Paul Goodman
Jonah (OB) (1966)

LIABLE TO CATCH ON
Sammy Fain
Irving Kahal and Jack Yellen
Boys and Girls Together (1940)

LIAR'S SONG, THE
John Mundy
Edward Eager
The Liar (1950)

LIBERIA
Susan Hulsman Bingham
Myrna Lamb
Mod Donna (OB) (1970)

LIBERTY, EQUALITY, FRATERNITY
Mimi Stone

William Kaye
Pimpernel! (OB) (1964)

LICHTENBURG
Irving Berlin
Call Me Madam (1950)

**LICK, AND A RIFF, AND A SLOW
BOUNCE, A**
Jerry Livingston
Mack David
Bright Lights of 1944 (1943)

LIDA ROSE
Meredith Willson
The Music Man (1957)

LIDO BEACH, THE
Noël Coward
This Year of Grace (1928)

LIEBEN DICH
PaulNassau and Oscar Brand
The Education of Hyman Kaplan
(1968)

LIF' 'EM UP AND PUT 'EM DOWN
Georges Bizet
Oscar Hammerstein II
Carmen Jones (1943)

LIFE AS A TWOSOME*
Joseph Meyer and Roger Wolfe Kahn
Irving Caesar
Here's Howe (1928)

LIFE BEGINS AT SWEET SIXTEEN
Ray Henderson
Jack Yellen
George White's Scandals (1936)

LIFE CAN BE BEAUTIFUL
Moose Charlap
Eddie Lawrence
Kelly (1965)

LIFE COULD BE SO BEAUTIFUL
Jerome Moross
Paul Peters and George Sklar
Parade (1935)

LIFE DOES A MAN A FAVOR
Jay Livingston and Ray Evans
Oh Captain! (1958)

LIFE IN THE MORNING
Noël Coward
Bitter Sweet (1929)

LIFE IS
John Kander
Fred Ebb
Zorbá (1968)

LIFE IS A GAME
Ring Lardner
June Moon (1929)

LIFE IS A ONE-WAY STREET
Bill and Patti Jacobs
Jimmy (1969)

LIFE IS JUST A BOWL OF CHERRIES
Ray Henderson
B. G. DeSylva and Lew Brown
George White's Scandals (1931)

LIFE IS LIKE A TOY BALLOON
Harold Levey
Owen Murphy
The Greenwich Village Follies (1925)

LIFE IS LOVE
Philip Charig
Irving Caesar
Polly (1929)

LIFE IS LOVELY
Claude Leveilee
Gladys Shelley
Gogo Loves You (OB) (1964)

LIFE IS TOO SHORT
Sammy Fain
Marilyn and Alan Bergman
Something More! (1964)

LIFE OF THE PARTY, THE
Richard Myers
Harry Ruskin
The Greenwich Village Follies (1925)

---

*Also in *Americana* (1928)

LIFE OF THE PARTY, THE
Nacio Herb Brown and Richard Whiting
B. G. DeSylva
Take a Chance (1932)

LIFE OF THE PARTY, THE
John Kander
Fred Ebb
The Happy Time (1968)

LIFE THAT I PLANNED FOR HIM, THE
Johnny Brandon
Cindy (OB) (1964)

LIFE UPON THE WICKED STAGE
Jerome Kern
Oscar Hammerstein II
Show Boat (1927)

LIFE WAS PIE FOR THE PIONEER
Burton Lane
E. Y. Harburg
Hold On to Your Hats (1940)

LIFE WITH FATHER
Richard Rodgers
Lorenz Hart
By Jupiter (1942)

LIFE WITH ROCKY, A
Morton Gould
Betty Comden and Adolph Green
Billion Dollar Baby (1945)

LIFEGUARDS, THE
Manning Sherwin
Arthur Herzog, Jr.
Bad Habits of 1926 (OB) (1926)

LIFE'S A DANCE
Harold Arlen
E. Y. Harburg
Hooray for What! (1937)

LIFE'S A FUNNY PRESENT FROM SOMEONE
Vernon Duke
Howard Dietz
Sadie Thompson (1944)

LIFE'S A HOLIDAY
George Fischoff
Carole Bayer
Georgy (1970)

LIFE'S A TALE
Emmerich Kalman
P. G. Wodehouse
The Riviera Girl (1917)

LIFETIME LOVE, A
Albert Hague
Marty Brill
Café Crown (1964)

LIFFEY WALTZ, THE
Marc Blitzstein
Juno (1959)

LIGHT OF THE WORLD
Stephen Schwartz
Godspell (OB) (1971)

LIGHT ONE CANDLE
Albert Hague
Allen Sherman
The Fig Leaves Are Falling (1969)

LIGHT SINGS
Gary William Friedman
Will Holt
The Me Nobody Knows (OB) (1970)

LIGHTNING BUG SONG, THE
George Kleinsinger
Joe Darion
Shinbone Alley (1957)

LIKE A GOD
Richard Rodgers
Oscar Hammerstein II
Flower Drum Song (1958)

LIKE A LITTLE LADYLIKE LADY LIKE YOU
George M. Cohan
The Merry Malones (1927)

LIKE-A-ME, LIKE A-YOU
Frank Grey and McElbert Moore
The Matinee Girl (1926)

LIKE A STAR IN THE SKY
Johann Strauss
Desmond Carter
The Great Waltz (1934)

LIKE A WOMAN LOVES A MAN
Frank Loesser
The Most Happy Fella (1956)

LIKE A YOUNG MAN
Jerry Herman
Milk and Honey (1961)

LIKE HE LOVES ME
Vincent Youmans
Anne Caldwell
Oh, Please! (1926)

LIKE IT
Clinton Ballard
Carolyn Richter
The Ballad of Johnny Pot (OB) (1971)

LIKE ME LESS, LOVE ME MORE
Jay Gorney
E. Y. Harburg
Earl Carroll's Sketch Book (1929)

LIKE ORDINARY PEOPLE DO
Richard Rodgers
Lorenz Hart
The Hot Heiress (F) (1931)

LIKE THE BREEZE BLOWS
Harold Rome
The Zulu and the Zayda (1965)

LIKE THE NYMPHS OF SPRING
Jerome Kern
Anne Caldwell
The City Chap (1925)

LIKE THE WANDERING MINSTREL
George M. Cohan
The Merry Malones (1927)

LIKE YOU
Emmerich Kalman
Harry B. Smith
The Circus Princess (1927)

LIKE YOU DO
Harry Ruby
Bert Kalmar
The Ramblers (1926)

LIKE YOURS
Albert Hague
Allen Sherman
The Fig Leaves Are Falling (1969)

L'IL AUGIE IS A NATURAL MAN
Harold Arlen
Johnny Mercer
St. Louis Woman (1946)

LILA TREMAINE
Jule Styne
Betty Comden and Adolph Green
Fade Out—Fade In (1964)

LILAC TREE
C. Jackson and James Hatch
Fly Blackbird (OB) (1962)

LILAC WINE
James Shelton
Dance Me a Song (1950)

LILLIAN
Albert Hague
Allen Sherman
The Fig Leaves Are Falling (1969)

LILY BELLE MAY JUNE
Henry Sullivan
Earle Crooker
Thumbs Up! (1934)

LIMEHOUSE BLUES
Philip Braham
Douglas Furber
Charlot's Revue (1924)

LILY HAS DONE THE ZAMPOUGHI EVERY TIME I PULLED HER COAT-TAIL
Melvin Van Peebles
Ain't Supposed to Die a Natural Death (1971)

LINCOLN AND LIBERTY
Oscar Brand
How to Steal an Election (OB) (1968)

LINCOLN AND SODA
Oscar Brand
How to Steal an Election (OB) (1968)

LINGERIE
Dave Stamper and Harold Levey
Cyrus Wood
Lovely Lady (1927)

LION AND THE LAMB, THE
Clay Warnick
Edward Eager
Dream with Music (1944)

LIPS
Leon DeCosta
The Blonde Sinner (1926)

LIPS THAT LAUGH AT LOVE
Emile Berté and Maury Rubens
J. Keirn Brennan
Music in May (1929)

LISBON SEQUENCE
Leonard Bernstein
Candide (1956)

LISTEN, COSETTE
Laurence Rosenthal
James Lipton
Sherry! (1967)

LISTEN, I FEEL
Al Carmines
Maria Irene Fornes
Promenade (OB) (1969)

LISTEN TO THE BEAT!
Billy Barnes
The Billy Barnes Revue (1959)

LITERARY COCKTAIL PARTY
Bud McCreery
Put It in Writing (OB) (1963)

LITES—CAMERA—PLATITUDE
Ervin Drake
What Makes Sammy Run? (1964)

LITTLE BIRD, LITTLE BIRD
Mitch Leigh
Joe Darion
Man of La Mancha (1965)

LITTLE BIRDIE TOLD ME SO, A
Richard Rodgers
Lorenz Hart
Peggy-Ann (1926)

LITTLE BIRDS
John Dooley
Hobo (OB) (1961)

LITTLE BISCUIT
Harold Arlen
E. Y. Harburg
Jamaica (1957)

LITTLE BIT DELIGHTED WITH THE WEATHER, A
Morgan Lewis
Nancy Hamilton
One for the Money (1939)

LITTLE BIT IN LOVE, A
Leonard Bernstein
Betty Comden and Adolph Green
Wonderful Town (1953)

LITTLE BIT OF CONSTITUTIONAL FUN, A
Richard Rodgers
Lorenz Hart
I'd Rather Be Right (1937)

LITTLE BIT OF QUICKSILVER, A
Alexander Hill
Hummin' Sam (1933)

LITTLE BIT OF SPANISH, A
Frank Grey
McElbert Moore and Frank Grey
The Matinee Girl (1926)

LITTLE BLUE PIG, THE
Sigmund Romberg
Arthur Wimperis
Louie the 14th (1925)

LITTLE BO-PEEP
Philip Charig
Irving Caesar
Polly (1929)

LITTLE BOY BLUE
William B. Kernell
Dorothy Donnelly
Hello, Lola (1926)

LITTLE BOY BLUES, THE
Hugh Martin
Look Ma, I'm Dancin'! (1948)

**LITTLE BRAINS—A LITTLE TAL-
ENT, A**
Richard Adler and Jerry Ross
Damn Yankees (1955)

LITTLE BUM
James F. Hanley
Eddie Dowling
Sidewalks of New York (1927)

LITTLE BUNGALOW, A
Irving Berlin
The Cocoanuts (1925)

LITTLE CHANGE OF ATMOSPHERE, A
Cliff Friend
Lew Brown
Piggy (1927)

LITTLE CHAT, A
Erich Wolfgang Korngold (based on
    Offenbach)
Herbert Baker
Helen Goes to Troy (1944)

LITTLE CORPORAL, THE
Frederick Loewe
Earle Crooker
Great Lady (1938)

LITTLE DOG BLUE
Robert Larimer
King of the Whole Damn World! (OB)
    (1962)

**LITTLE DREAM THAT'S COMING
TRUE**
Walter G. Samuels

Morrie Ryskind
Ned Wayburn's Gambols (1929)

LITTLE DROPS OF RAIN
Harold Arlen
E. Y. Harburg
Gay Purr-ee (F) (1961)

LITTLE EMMALINE
Sigmund Romberg
Rowland Leigh
My Romance (1948)

LITTLE FAIRIES
Steven Metcalf
Fred Bluth
Drat! (OB) (1971)

LITTLE FISH IN A BIG POND, A
Irving Berlin
Miss Liberty (1949)

LITTLE FOOL
Al Carmines
Maria Irene Fornes
Promenade (OB) (1969)

LITTLE GEEZER
Michael H. Cleary
Max and Nathaniel Lief and Dave Op-
    penheim
The Third Little Show (1931)

LITTLE GIRL
Harry Archer
Harlan Thompson
Merry-Merry (1925)

LITTLE GIRL BABY
Sandy Wilson
Valmouth (OB) (1960)

LITTLE GIRL BLUE
Richard Rodgers
Lorenz Hart
Jumbo (1935)

LITTLE GIRL FROM LITTLE ROCK, A
Jule Styne
Leo Robin
Gentlemen Prefer Blondes (1949)

LITTLE GIRLS, GOOD BYE
Victor Jacobi
William LeBaron
Apple Blossoms (1919)

LITTLE GOSSIP, A
Mitch Leigh
Joe Darion
Man of La Mancha (1965)

LITTLE GRAY HOUSE, THE
Kurt Weill
Maxwell Anderson
Lost in the Stars (1949)

LITTLE GREEN SNAKE
Bob Merrill
Take Me Along (1959)

LITTLE HANDS
Robert Wright and George Forrest
  (based on Rachmaninoff)
Anya (1965)

LITTLE HOUSE IN SOHO, A
Richard Rodgers
Lorenz Hart
She's My Baby (1928)

LITTLE IGLOO FOR TWO
Arthur Schwartz
Agnes Morgan
The Grand Street Follies (OB) (1926)

LITTLE INVESTIGATION, A
Elmer Bernstein
Carolyn Leigh
How Now, Dow Jones (1967)

LITTLE JACK HORNER
Helen Miller
Eve Merriam
Inner City (1971)

LITTLE JAZZ BIRD
George Gershwin
Ira Gershwin
Lady, Be Good (1924)

LITTLE KNOWN FACTS
Clark Gesner
You're a Good Man, Charlie Brown
  (OB) (1967)

LITTLE LACE PETTICOAT
Emil Gerstenberger and Carle Carl-
  ton
Carle Carlton
The Lace Petticoat (1927)

LITTLE LACQUER LADY
Melville Gideon
Clifford Seyler
The Optimists (1928)

LITTLE LAMB
Jule Styne
Stephen Sondheim
Gypsy (1959)

LITTLE LOVE, A LITTLE MONEY, A
Vernon Duke
Ogden Nash
The Littlest Revue (OB) (1956)

LITTLE MARY SUE
Don Tucker
Red, White and Maddox (1969)

LITTLE MARY SUNSHINE
Rick Besoyan
Little Mary Sunshine (OB) (1959)

LITTLE ME
Cy Coleman
Carolyn Leigh
Little Me (1962)

LITTLE MISS SMALL TOWN
Abel Baer
Sam Lewis and Joe Young
Lady Do (1927)

LITTLE MORE HEART, A
Jule Styne
Bob Hilliard
Hazel Flagg (1953)

LITTLE MORE LIKE YOU, A
Robert Rosenblum
Robert Rosenblum and Howard Schu-
  man
Up Eden (OB) (1968)

LITTLE NAKED BOY, THE
Kurt Weill
Ira Gershwin
The Firebrand of Florence (1945)

LITTLE OLD LADY
Hoagy Carmichael
Stanley Adams
The Show Is On (1936)

LITTLE OLD NEW HAMPSHIRE
James F. Hanley
Eddie Dowling
Honeymoon Lane (1926)

LITTLE OLD NEW YORK
Arthur Schwartz
Howard Dietz
The Little Show (1929)

LITTLE OLD NEW YORK
Jerry Bock
Sheldon Harnick
Tenderloin (1960)

LITTLE ONE
Cole Porter
High Society (F) (1956)

LITTLE ONES' ABC, THE
Noël Coward
Sail Away (1961)

LITTLE PEACH
Sigmund Romberg
Arthur Wimperis
Louie the 14th (1925)

LITTLE PEOPLE
Leon Pober
Bud Freeman
Beg, Borrow or Steal (1960)

LITTLE PRINCESS
Ben Schwartz
Tales of Rigo (1927)

LITTLE RAG DOLL
John Clifton
John Clifton and Ben Tarver
Man with a Load of Mischief (OB)
   (1966)

LITTLE RED HAT
Harvey Schmidt
Tom Jones
110 in the Shade (1963)

LITTLE RUMBA NUMBA, A
Cole Porter
Let's Face It! (1941)

LITTLE SKIPPER FROM HEAVEN
ABOVE, A
Cole Porter
Red, Hot and Blue! (1936)

LITTLE SMILE, A LITTLE SIGH, A
James F. Hanley
Eddie Dowling
Honeymoon Lane (1926)

LITTLE SPARROW
Jordan Ramin
Frank H. Stanton and Murray Semos
Look Where I'm At (OB) (1971)

LITTLE SPARROWS
Clinton Ballard
Carolyn Richter
The Ballad of Johnny Pot (OB) (1971)

LITTLE STRANGER
Robert Hood Bowers
Francis DeWitt
Oh, Ernest! (1927)

LITTLE TEAR
Rick Besoyan
Babes in the Wood (OB) (1964)

LITTLE THINGS MEANT SO MUCH TO
ME
Harold Rome
Bless You All (1950)

LITTLE THINGS YOU DO TOGETHER,
THE
Stephen Sondheim
Company (1970)

LITTLE TIN BOX
Jerry Bock
Sheldon Harnick
Fiorello (1959)

LITTLE TRAVELING MUSIC, A
Hal Borne
Paul Webster and Ray Golden
Catch a Star! (1955)

LITTLE TROUBLE, A
Mary Rodgers
Martin Charnin
Hot Spot (1963)

LITTLE WHITE DOG
Tom Sankey
The Golden Screw (OB) (1967)

LITTLE WHITE HOUSE
James F. Hanley
Eddie Dowling
Honeymoon Lane (1926)

LITTLE WOMAN
Noël Coward
This Year of Grace (1928)

LITTLE WOMAN
David Daker
David Craig
Copper and Brass (1957)

LITTLE WOMAN, THE
Bill and Patti Jacob
Jimmy (1969)

LITTLE YETTA'S GONNA GET A MAN
Sidney Lippman
Sylvia Dee
Barefoot Boy with Cheek (1947)

LIVE A LITTLE
Sol Berkowitz
James Lipton
Nowhere to Go but Up (1962)

LIVE A LITTLE
Elmer Bernstein
Carolyn Leigh
How Now, Dow Jones (1967)

LIVE AND LET LIVE
Cole Porter
Can-Can (1953)

LIVE, LAUGH AND LOVE
Sam H. Stept
Bud Green
Shady Lady (1933)

LIVE, LAUGH, LOVE
Stephen Sondheim
Follies (1971)

LIVE TODAY
Abel Baer
Sam Lewis and Joe Young
Lady Do (1927)

LIVIN' IN A HOLE
Jerry Blatt
Jerry Blatt and Lonnie Burstein
Have I Got One for You (OB) (1968)

LIVIN' THE LIFE
Jack Urbont
Bruce Geller
Livin' the Life (OB) (1957)

LIVING IN SIN
Richard A. Whiting
Oscar Hammerstein II
Free for All (1931)

LIVING IT UP
Vernon Duke
Cabin in the Sky (OB) (1964)

LIVING SIMPLY
Walter Marks
Bajour (1964)

LIZA (ALL THE CLOUDS'LL ROLL AWAY)
George Gershwin
Gus Kahn and Ira Gershwin
Show Girl (1929)

LIZZIE BORDEN
Michael Brown
New Faces (1952)

LIZZIE'S COMING HOME
Harvey Schmidt
Tom Jones
110 in the Shade (1963)

LOADS OF LOVE
Richard Rodgers
No Strings (1962)

LOBSTER CRAWL, THE
Harry Akst
Benny Davis
Artists and Models (1927)

LOCAL 403
Jimmy Van Heusen
Sammy Cahn
Skyscraper (1965)

LOCKS
Helen Miller
Eve Merriam
Inner City (1971)

LOGGER'S SONG, THE
David Baker
Will Holt
Come Summer (1969)

LOGIC!
Sam Pottle
Tom Whedon
All Kinds of Giants (OB) (1961)

LOLITA
George Gershwin
Gus Kahn and Ira Gershwin
Show Girl (1929)

LOLITA
Richard Lewine
Arnold B. Horwitt
The Girls Against the Boys (1959)

LONDON IS A LITTLE BIT OF ALL RIGHT
Noël Coward
The Girl Who Came to Supper (1963)

LONDON UNDERWORLD
Marian Grudeff and Raymond Jessel
Baker Street (1965)

LONELINESS OF EVENING*
Richard Rodgers
Oscar Hammerstein II
Cinderella (TV—1965 version)

LONELY
Noël Coward
The Girl Who Came to Supper (1963)

LONELY CHILDREN
Wally Harper
Paul Zakrzewski
Sensations (OB) (1970)

LONELY CLEARING
Michael Leonard
Herbert Martin
The Yearling (1965)

LONELY FEET
Jerome Kern
Oscar Hammerstein II
Sweet Adeline (F) (1935)

LONELY GIRL, A
Harold Orlob
Irving Caesar
Talk About Girls (1927)

LONELY GIRL
Norman Curtis
Patricia Taylor Curtis
Walk Down Mah Street! (OB) (1968)

LONELY GOATHERD, THE
Richard Rodgers
Oscar Hammerstein II
The Sound of Music (1959)

LONELY HEART
Irving Berlin
As Thousands Cheer (1933)

LONELY HOUSE
Kurt Weill
Langston Hughes
Street Scene (1947)

---

*Written for *South Pacific*, but dropped from New York production

LONELY IS THE LIFE
Clinton Ballard
Carolyn Richter
The Ballad of Johnny Pot (OB) (1971)

LONELY NIGHTS
Arthur Schwartz
Howard Dietz
Jennie (1963)

LONELY ONES
Leon Carr
Earl Shuman
The Secret Life of Walter Mitty (OB)
   (1964)

LONELY ROAD, THE
H. Maurice Jacquet
William Brady
The Silver Swan (1929)

LONELY ROOM
Richard Rodgers
Oscar Hammerstein II
Oklahoma! (1943)

LONELY TOWN
Leonard Bernstein
Betty Comden and Adolph Green
On the Town (1944)

LONELY VOICE
Walter Cool
Mackey of Appalachia (OB) (1965)

LONESOME COWBOY, THE
George Gershwin
Ira Gershwin
Girl Crazy (1930)

LONESOME IN NEW YORK
Jerry Herman
I Feel Wonderful (OB) (1954)

LONESOME MAN
Eubie Blake
Noble Sissle
Shuffle Along (1933)

LONESOME ROMEOS
Harry Ruby
Bert Kalmar
The Five O'Clock Girl (1927)

LONESOME WALLS
Jerome Kern
DuBose Heyward
Mamba's Daughters (1939)

LONG AGO
David Heneker
Half a Sixpence (1965)

LONG AGO AND FAR AWAY
Jerome Kern
Ira Gershwin
Cover Girl (F) (1944)

LONG AND WEARY WAIT
William Roy
Maggie (1953)

LONG AS YOU'VE GOT YOUR HEALTH
Will Irwin
E. Y. Harburg and Norman Zeno
The Show Is On (1936)

LONG BEFORE I KNEW YOU
Jule Styne
Betty Comden and Adolph Green
Bells Are Ringing (1956)

LONG BEFORE YOU CAME ALONG
Harold Arlen
E. Y. Harburg
Rio Rita (F) (1942)

LONG GREEN BLUES
Carl Sigman
Bob Hilliard
Angel in the Wings (1947)

LONG ISLAND LOW DOWN, THE
Harry Ruby
Bert Kalmar
Animal Crackers (1928)

LONG LIVE THE GREEDY
Deed Meyer
Stones of Jehoshaphat (OB) (1963)

LONG TIME NO SONG
Thomas (Fats) Waller
George Marion, Jr.
Early to Bed (1943)

LONGING FOR YOU
Shep Camp
Frank DuPree
Half a Widow (1927)

LONGTIME TRAVELIN'
Oscar Brand and Paul Nassau
A Joyful Noise (1966)

LOO LOO
Vincent Youmans
Leo Robin and Clifford Grey
Hit the Deck (1927)

LOOK
Robert Kessler
Martin Charnin
Fallout (OB) (1959)

LOOK AND LOVE IS HERE
Ralph Benatzky
Meet My Sister (1930)

LOOK AROUND YOUR LITTLE
WORLD
Hugo Peretti, Luigi Creatore, and
George David Weiss
Maggie Flynn (1968)

LOOK AT 'ER
Bob Merrill
New Girl in Town (1957)

LOOK AT ME
Janet Gari
Toby Garson
Lyle (OB) (1970)

LOOK AT MY SISTER
Mildred Kayden
Frank Gagliano
Paradise Gardens East (OB) (1969)

LOOK AT THAT FACE
Leslie Bricusse and Anthony Newley
*The Roar of the Greasepaint—The
Smell of the Crowd* (1965)

LOOK AT THE WORLD AND SMILE
Raymond Hubbell
Anne Caldwell
Yours Truly (1927)

LOOK AT THEM
Oscar Brown, Jr.
Buck White (1969)

LOOK AT WHAT IT'S DONE
George Harwell
What a Killing (OB) (1961)

LOOK AWAY
Willard Straight
David Eddy
The Athenian Touch (OB) (1964)

LOOK BEFORE YOU LEAP
Johann Strauss
Desmond Carter
The Great Waltz (1934)

LOOK FOR A SKY OF BLUE
Rick Besoyan
Little Mary Sunshine (OB) (1959)

LOOK FOR SMALL PLEASURES
Mark Sandrich, Jr.
Sidney Michaels
Ben Franklin in Paris (1964)

LOOK FOR THE HAPPINESS AHEAD
Skip Redwine and Larry Frank
*Frank Merriwell, or Honor Chal-
lenged* (1971)

LOOK FOR THE MORNING STAR
David Martin
Langston Hughes
Simply Heavenly (1957)

LOOK FOR THE SILVER LINING
Jerome Kern
B. G. DeSylva
Sally (1920)

LOOK IN YOUR ENGAGEMENT BOOK
Albert Von Tilzer
Neville Fleeson
Bye, Bye, Bonnie (1927)

LOOK, LITTLE GIRL
Meredith Willson
Here's Love (1963)

LOOK NO FURTHER
Richard Rodgers
No Strings (1962)

LOOK OUT
Richard Rodgers
Lorenz Hart
Too Many Girls (1939)

LOOK OUT FOR MY HEART
Jimmy McHugh
Al Dubin
Keep Off the Grass (1940)

LOOK THROUGH THE MOONGATE
Deed Meyer
Stones of Jehoshaphat (OB) (1963)

LOOK THROUGH THE WINDOW
Johnny Brandon
Billy Noname (OB) (1970)

LOOK TO THE LILIES
Jule Styne
Sammy Cahn
Look to the Lilies (1970)

LOOK TO THE RAINBOW
Burton Lane
E. Y. Harburg
Finian's Rainbow (1947)

LOOK UP
Kenneth Jacobson
Rhoda Roberts
Show Me Where the Good Times Are
(OB) (1970)

LOOK WHAT I FOUND
Cole Porter
Around the World (1946)

LOOK WHERE I AM
Jerry Bock
Sheldon Harnick
Man in the Moon (1963)

LOOK WHERE I'M AT!
Jordan Ramin
Frank H. Stanton and Murray Semos
Look Where I'm At! (OB) (1971)

LOOK WHO'S DANCING
Arthur Schwartz
Dorothy Fields
A Tree Grows in Brooklyn (1951)

LOOK WHO'S IN LOVE
Albert Hague
Dorothy Fields
Redhead (1959)

LOOK WHO'S THROWING A PARTY
Kenneth Jacobson
Rhoda Roberts
Show Me Where the Good Times Are
(OB) (1970)

LOOKING AT LIFE THROUGH A RAINBOW
Kenneth Burton
Walter Craig
Cape Cod Follies (1929)

LOOKING AT THE SUN
Jacques Urbont
David Newburger
Stag Movie (OB) (1971)

LOOKING AT YOU
Cole Porter
Wake Up and Dream (1929)

LOOKING FOR A BOY
George Gershwin
Ira Gershwin
Tip-Toes (1925)

LOOKING FOR A THRILL
Charles Rosoff
Leo Robin
Judy (1927)

LOOKING FOR SOMEONE
Mary Rodgers
Marshall Barer
The Mad Show (OB) (1966)

LOOKS LIKE LOVE IS HERE TO STAY
Michael Cleary
Arthur Swanstrom
Sea Legs (1937)

LOOSE ANKLES
Moe Jaffe, Clay Boland, and Maury
  Rubens
A Night in Venice (1929)

LOOSEN UP
Robert Stolz
Rowland Leigh
Night of Love (1941)

LOPSIDED BUS, A
Richard Rodgers
Oscar Hammerstein II
Pipe Dream (1955)

**LORD DONE FIXED UP MY SOUL,
THE**
Irving Berlin
Louisiana Purchase (1940)

**LORD HELPS THOSE WHO HELP
THEMSELVES, THE**
Walt Smith
Leon Uris
Ari (1971)

LORD I AM BUT A LITTLE CHILD
Ernest Gold
Anne Croswell
I'm Solomon (1968)

**LORD, YOU SURE KNOW HOW TO
MAKE A NEW DAY**
Oscar Brand and Paul Nassau
A Joyful Noise (1966)

LORELEI
Frank Grey
Earle Crooker and McElbert Moore
Happy (1927)

LORELEI
Noël Coward
This Year of Grace (1928)

LORELEI
George Gershwin
Ira Gershwin
Pardon My English (1933)

LORELEI ON THE ROCKS
Berenice Kazounoff
John Latouche
Pins and Needles (OB) (1937)

LORETTA
Janet Gari
Toby Garson
Lyle (OB) (1970)

LORNA'S HERE
Charles Strouse
Lee Adams
Golden Boy (1964)

LOS OLIVADOS
Donald Swann
Michael Flanders
At the Drop of Another Hat (1966)

LOSE THAT LONG FACE
Harold Arlen
Ira Gershwin
A Star Is Born (F) (1954)

LOSING MY MIND
Stephen Sondheim
Follies (1971)

LOST
Frank Black
Gladys Shelley
The Duchess Misbehaves (1946)

LOST
Heitor Villa-Lobos
Robert Wright and George Forrest
Magdalena (1948)

LOST
Lee Pockriss
Anne Croswell
Ernest in Love (OB) (1960)

LOST HORIZON
Harry Warren
Jerome Lawrence and Robert E. Lee
Shangri-La (1956)

LOST IN LOVELINESS
Sigmund Romberg (developed by Don Walker)
Leo Robin
The Girl in Pink Tights (1954)

LOST IN THE STARS
Kurt Weill
Maxwell Anderson
Lost in the Stars (1949)

LOST STEP, THE
David Stamper and Harold Levey
Cyrus Wood
Lovely Lady (1927)

LOT OF LIVIN' TO DO, A
Charles Strouse
Lee Adams
Bye Bye Birdie (1960)

LOTTIE OF THE LITERATI
Alex Fogarty
Edwin Gilbert
New Faces (1936)

LOTS OF TIME FOR SUE
Philip Charig
Irving Caesar
Polly (1929)

LOTUS FLOWER
Raymond Hubbell
Anne Caldwell
Yours Truly (1927)

LOUISIANA
J. Fred Coots and Maury Rubens
McElbert Moore
A Night in Paris (1926)

LOUISIANA HAYRIDE
Arthur Schwartz
Howard Dietz
Flying Colors (1932)

LOUISIANA PURCHASE
Irving Berlin
Louisiana Purchase (1940)

LOUISIANA'S HOLIDAY
Alma Sanders
Monte Carlo
Louisiana Lady (1947)

LOVE
Hugh Martin and Ralph Blane
Ziegfeld Follies (F) (1946)

LOVE
James Shelton
Dance Me a Song (1950)

LOVE AFFAIR
Bob Kessler
Martin Charnin
Wet Paint (OB) (1965)

LOVE AND I
Baldwin Bergersen
Irvin Graham and June Sillman
All in Fun (1940)

LOVE AND KINDNESS
Frank Loesser
The Most Happy Fella (1956)

LOVE AND LAUGHTER
Sigmund Romberg
Rowland Leigh
My Romance (1948)

LOVE AND THE MOON
Jerome Kern
Booth Tarkington
Rose Briar (1922)

LOVE AND RHYTHM
Ray Henderson
B. G. DeSylva and Lew Brown
Strike Me Pink (1933)

LOVE AND WAR
Johann Strauss
Desmond Carter
The Great Waltz (1934)

LOVE, ARE YOU RAISING YOUR HEAD?
Lee Wainer
June Carroll
New Faces (1943)

LOVE AT GOLDEN YEARS
Murray Rumshinsky
Jacob Jacobs
The President's Daughter (1970)

LOVE AT LAST
Erich Wolfgang Korngold (based on
Offenbach)
Herbert Baker
Helen Goes to Troy (1944)

LOVE AT SECOND SIGHT
Clay Warnick
Edward Eager
Dream with Music (1944)

LOVE BIRDS
Cliff Friend and George White
George White's Scandals (1929)

LOVE BOATS
Jay Gorney
E. Y. Harburg
Earl Carroll's Vanities (1930)

LOVE CAME INTO MY HEART
Burton Lane
Harold Adamson
Earl Carroll's Vanities (1931)

LOVE CAME TO ME
Doug Dyer, Patrick Fox, and The
Blood Company
Doug Dyer
Blood (OB) (1971)

LOVE, COME TAKE ME
Will Irwin
Norman Zeno
Fools Rush In (1934)

LOVE COMES ONCE IN A LIFETIME
Harold Stern and Harry Perella
Stella Unger
Three Little Girls (1930)

LOVE DOESN'T GROW ON TREES
Jane Douglas
Tom O'Malley
Bella (OB) (1961)

LOVE, DON'T TURN AWAY
Harvey Schmidt
Tom Jones
110 in the Shade (1963)

LOVE ELIXIR, THE
C. Jackson and James Hatch
Fly Blackbird (OB) (1962)

LOVE EYES
Moose Charlap
Norman Gimbel
Whoop-Up (1958)

LOVE FOR SALE
Rudolf Friml
Brian Hooker
The Vagabond King (1925)

LOVE FOR SALE
Cole Porter
The New Yorkers (1930)

LOVE FROM A HEART OF GOLD
Frank Loesser
*How to Succeed in Business without
Really Trying* (1961)

LOVE HAS DRIVEN ME SANE
Galt MacDermot
John Guare
Two Gentlemen of Verona (1971)

LOVE HAS FADED AWAY
Ralph Benatzky
Meet My Sister (1930)

LOVE HAS FOUND MY HEART*
Emmerich Kalman
Harry B. Smith
Countess Maritza (1926)

LOVE HAS NOTHING TO DO WITH
LOOKS
Ralph Blane
Charles Lederer
Three Wishes for Jamie (1952)

LOVE HELD LIGHTLY
Harold Arlen
Johnny Mercer
Saratoga (1959)

---

*Melody revised by Alfred Goodman

LOVE, I HEAR
Stephen Sondheim
*A Funny Thing Happened on the Way
 to the Forum* (1962)

LOVE I LONG FOR, THE
Vernon Duke
Howard Dietz
Sadie Thompson (1944)

LOVE IN A HOME
Gene de Paul
Johnny Mercer
Li'l Abner (1956)

LOVE IN A NEW TEMPO
Ronny Graham
New Faces (1968)

LOVE IS
Martin Charnin
Fallout (OB) (1959)

LOVE IS
Sol Berkowitz
James Lipton
Miss Emily Adam (OB) (1960)

LOVE IS A CHANCE
Walter Marks
Bajour (1964)

LOVE IS A DANCER
Muriel Pollock
Jean Sothern
New Faces (1936)

LOVE IS A DANCING THING
Arthur Schwartz
Howard Dietz
At Home Abroad (1935)

LOVE IS A FEELING
Moose Charlap
Norman Gimbel
Shoestring Revue (OB) (1957)

LOVE IS A GAME FOR SOLDIERS
Franz Steininger (adapted from
 Tchaikovsky)
Forman Brown
Music in My Heart (1947)

LOVE IS A RANDOM THING
Sammy Fain
George Marion, Jr.
Toplitzky of Notre Dame (1946)

LOVE IS A SIMPLE THING
Arthur Siegel
June Carroll
New Faces (1952)

LOVE IS A VERY LIGHT THING
Harold Rome
Fanny (1954)

LOVE IS GOOD FOR YOU
Arthur Siegel
June Carroll
New Faces (1962)

LOVE IS HELL
Jay Livingston and Ray Evans
Oh Captain! (1958)

LOVE IS HERE TO STAY
George Gershwin
Ira Gershwin
The Goldwyn Follies (F) (1938)

LOVE IS IN THE AIR
George Gershwin
B. G. DeSylva and Ira Gershwin
Tell Me More (1925)

LOVE IS IN THE AIR*
Stephen Sondheim
*A Funny Thing Happened on the Way
 to the Forum* (1962)

LOVE IS JUST AROUND THE CORNER
Lewis E. Gensler
Leo Robin
Here Is My Heart (F) (1934)

LOVE IS LIKE A BLUSHING ROSE
Albert Von Tilzer
Neville Fleeson
Bye Bye, Bonnie (1927)

———
*Dropped from New York production

LOVE IS LIKE A SONG
Vincent Youmans
George Waggner and J. Russel Robinson
What a Widow! (F) (1930)

LOVE IS LIKE THAT
Alberta Nichols
Mann Holiner
Angela (1928)

LOVE IS LOVE ANYWHERE
Harold Arlen
Ted Koehler
Let's Fall in Love (F) (1934)

LOVE IS LOVELY
Rick Besoyan
Babes in the Wood (OB) (1964)

LOVE IS MY ENEMY
Kurt Weill
Ira Gershwin
The Firebrand of Florence (1945)

LOVE IS MY FRIEND*
Richard Rodgers
Lorenz Hart
Pal Joey (1940)

LOVE IS MY INSPIRATION
André Renaud
Ted Koehler
Earl Carroll's Vanities (1932)

LOVE IS NOT FOR A DAY
Edward Kunneke (based on Offenbach)
Harry B. Smith
The Love Song (1925)

LOVE IS ONLY WHAT YOU MAKE IT
Rudolf Friml
Rowland Leigh and John Shubert
Music Hath Charms (1934)

LOVE IS PARADISE
Edward Earle
Yvonne Tarr
The Decameron (OB) (1961)

LOVE IS QUITE A SIMPLE THING
Sigmund Romberg
Oscar Hammerstein II
The New Moon (1928)

LOVE IS STILL IN TOWN
Vernon Duke
Ogden Nash
The Littlest Revue (OB) (1956)

LOVE IS STRANGE
Darwin Venneri
Darwin's Theories (OB) (1960)

LOVE IS SUCH A CHEAT
Irving Caesar, Gerald Marks, and Irma Hollander
My Dear Public (1943)

LOVE IS SWEEPING THE COUNTRY
George Gershwin
Ira Gershwin
Of Thee I Sing (1931)

LOVE, IS THAT YOU?
Galt MacDermot
John Guare
Two Gentlemen of Verona (1971)

LOVE IS THE FUNNIEST THING
Sigmund Romberg (developed by Don Walker)
Leo Robin
The Girl in Pink Tights (1954)

LOVE IS THE LOVELIEST LOVE SONG
Robert Dahdah
Curley McDimple (OB) (1967)

LOVE IS THE REASON
Arthur Schwartz
Dorothy Fields
A Tree Grows in Brooklyn (1951)

LOVE IS THE SOVEREIGN OF MY HEART
Franz Steininger (adapted from Tchaikovsky)
Forman Brown
Music in My Heart (1947)

---

*Lyric rewritten as "What Is a Man?" after New York opening

LOVE IS THE SUN
Rudolf Friml
P. G. Wodehouse and Clifford Grey
The Three Musketeers (1928)

LOVE IS TROUBLE
Giuseppe Verdi
Charles Friedman
My Darlin' Aïda (1952)

LOVE IS WHAT I NEVER KNEW
Harry Warren
Jerome Lawrence and Robert E. Lee
Shangri-La (1956)

LOVE ISN'T BORN, IT'S MADE
Arthur Schwartz
Frank Loesser
Thank Your Lucky Stars (F) (1943)

LOVE ISN'T EVERYTHING
Harvey Schmidt
Tom Jones
I Do! I Do! (1966)

LOVE, IT HURTS SO GOOD
Harold Rome
Alive and Kicking (1950)

LOVE LASTS A DAY
Frank Harling
Laurence Stallings
Deep River (1926)

LOVE LESSON
Stanley Jay Gelber
John Lollos and Don Christopher
Love and Let Love (OB) (1968)

LOVE LET ME KNOW
Jay Livingston and Ray Evans
Let It Ride (1961)

LOVE LETTER TO MANHATTAN
Harold Rome
Bless You All (1950)

LOVE LETTERS
H. Maurice Jacquet
William Brady
The Silver Swan (1929)

LOVE LIKE YOURS IS RARE INDEED
Armand Vecsey
P. G. Wodehouse
The Nightingale (1927)

LOVE-LINE
Walter Marks
Bajour (1964)

LOVE LIVES ON
William Heagney
William Heagney and Tom Connell
There You Are (1932)

LOVE, LOOK AWAY
Richard Rodgers
Oscar Hammerstein II
Flower Drum Song (1958)

LOVE, LOOK IN MY WINDOW*
Jerry Herman
Hello, Dolly! (1964)

LOVE-LORN MAID, A
Lehman Engel
Agnes Morgan
A Hero Is Born (1937)

LOVE, LOVE, LOVE
Victor Young
Stella Unger
Seventh Heaven (1955)

LOVE, LOVE, LOVE
Manos Hadjidakis
Joe Darion
Illya Darling (1967)

LOVE MAKES THE WORLD GO
Richard Rodgers
No Strings (1962)

LOVE MAKES THE WORLD GO ROUND
Richard Lewine
Ted Fetter
Naughty-Naught (OB) (1937)

———
*Added in 1970.

LOVE ME
Vincent Youmans
Anne Caldwell
Oh, Please! (1926)

LOVE ME
Jeanne Bargy
Jeanne Bargy, Frank Gehrecke, and
    Herb Corey
Greenwich Village U.S.A. (OB) (1960)

LOVE ME
Galt MacDermot
John Guare
Two Gentlemen of Verona (1971)

LOVE ME, DON'T YOU?
Rudolf Friml
Otto Harbach and Oscar Hammer-
    stein II
The Wild Rose (1926)

LOVE ME FOREVER
Harry Warren
Mort Dixon and Joe Young
The Laugh Parade (1931)

LOVE ME LITTLE
Darwin Venneri
Darwin's Theories (OB) (1960)

LOVE ME, LOVE MY CHILDREN
Robert Swerdlow
Love Me, Love My Children (OB)
    (1971)

LOVE ME, LOVE MY DOG
Robert Emmett Dolan
Johnny Mercer
Texas, Li'l Darlin' (1949)

LOVE ME OR LEAVE ME
Walter Donaldson
Gus Kahn
Whoopee (1928)

LOVE ME MORE—LOVE ME LESS
Tom Peluso
Ben Bernard
Blackberries of 1932

LOVE ME TOMORROW
Vernon Duke
John Latouche
Cabin in the Sky (1940)

LOVE ME TONIGHT
Rudolf Friml
Brian Hooker
The Vagabond King (1925)

LOVE ME TONIGHT
Richard Rodgers
Lorenz Hart
Love Me Tonight (F) (1932)

LOVE ME TOO
Walter Cool
Mackey of Appalachia (OB) (1965)

LOVE ME WHILE YOU'RE GONE
Porter Grainger and Freddie Johnson
Lucky Sambo (1925)

LOVE NEST, THE
Louis A. Hirsch
Otto Harbach
Mary (1920)

LOVE NEVER WENT TO COLLEGE
Richard Rodgers
Lorenz Hart
Too Many Girls (1939)

LOVE, NUTS AND NOODLES
Lewis E. Gensler
E. Y. Harburg
Ballyhoo (1932)

LOVE OF LONG AGO
Mimi Stone
William Kaye
Pimpernel! (OB) (1964)

LOVE OF MY LIFE, THE
Frederick Loewe
Alan Jay Lerner
Brigadoon (1947)

LOVE OF MY LIFE
Cole Porter
The Pirate (F) (1948)

LOVE OF YOUR LIFE, THE
David Shire
Richard Maltby, Jr.
The Sap of Life (OB) (1961)

LOVE POTION, THE
William Heagney
William Heagney and Tom Connell
There You Are (1932)

LOVE RULES THE WORLD
Percy Wenrich
Raymond Peck
Castles in the Air (1926)

LOVE-SICK SERENADE
Jacques Offenbach
E. Y. Harburg
The Happiest Girl in the World (1961)

LOVE SNEAKS UP ON YOU
Victor Young
Stella Unger
Seventh Heaven (1955)

LOVE SONG
Franz Steininger (adapted from Tchaikovsky)
Forman Brown
Music in My Heart (1947)

LOVE SONG
Kurt Weill
Alan Jay Lerner
Love Life (1948)

LOVE SONG
Kurt Weill
Marc Blitzstein
The Threepenny Opera (OB) (1954)

LOVE SONG
Harvey Schmidt
Tom Jones
Celebration (1969)

LOVE SONG
Charles Strouse
Six (OB) (1971)

LOVE SONGS ARE MADE IN THE NIGHT
Ray Henderson
Jack Yellen
Ziegfeld Follies (1943)

LOVE SWEPT LIKE A STORM
Fred Stamer
Gen Genovese
Buttrio Square (1952)

LOVE THOUGHT GARDEN
Ida Hoyt Chamberlain
Enchanted Isle (1927)

LOVE THOUGHTS
Lucien Denni
Helena Evans
Happy Go Lucky (1926)

LOVE TIPTOED THROUGH MY HEART
Frederick Loewe
Irene Alexander
Petticoat Fever (1935)

LOVE TURNED THE LIGHT OUT
Vernon Duke
John Latouche
Cabin in the Sky (1940)

LOVE WALKED IN
George Gershwin
Ira Gershwin
The Goldwyn Follies (F) (1938)

LOVE WAS
Oscar Brand and Paul Nassau
A Joyful Noise (1966)

LOVE, WHAT HAS GIVEN YOU THIS MAGIC POWER?
Franz Lehár
Harry Graham
Yours Is My Heart (1946)

LOVE WILL COME YOUR WAY
Walter Cool
Mackey of Appalachia (OB) (1965)

LOVE WILL CONQUER ALL
Richard Hill and John Hawkins
Nevill Coghill
Canterbury Tales (1969)

LOVE WILL FIND A WAY
Eubie Blake
Noble Sissle
Shuffle Along (1921)

LOVE WILL FIND OUT THE WAY
Glenn Paxton
Robert Goldman and George Weiss
First Impressions (1959)

LOVE WILL FIND YOU
Johann Strauss
Desmond Carter
The Great Waltz (1934)

LOVE WILL FIND YOU SOME DAY
Edward Kunneke (based on Offen-
  bach)
Harry B. Smith
The Love Song (1925)

LOVE WILL KEEP US YOUNG
Alma Sanders
Monte Carlo
Oh! Oh! Nurse (1925)

LOVE WILL SEE US THROUGH
Stephen Sondheim
Follies (1971)

LOVE WINS AGAIN
Richard B. Chodosh
Barry Alan Grael
The Streets of New York (OB) (1963)

LOVE WITH ALL THE TRIMMINGS
Burton Lane
Alan Jay Lerner
On a Clear Day You Can See Forever
  (F) (1969)

LOVE, YOU ARE SO DIFFICULT
Willard Straight
David Eddy
The Athenian Touch (OB) (1964)

LOVE YOU CAME TO ME
Nancy Ford
Gretchen Cryer
The Last Sweet Days of Isaac (OB)
  (1970)

LOVEABLE IRISH, THE
Johnny Burke
Donnybrook! (1961)

LOVELAND
Stephen Sondheim
Follies (1971)

LOVELIER THAN EVER
Frank Loesser
Where's Charley? (1948)

LOVELY
Stephen Sondheim
*A Funny Thing Happened on the Way
to the Forum* (1962)

LOVELY BRIDESMAIDS
Baldwin Bergersen
William Archibald
The Crystal Heart (OB) (1960)

LOVELY DAY FOR A MURDER
Richard Rodgers
Lorenz Hart
Higher and Higher (1940)

LOVELY GIRL, A
Morton Gould
Betty Comden and Adolph Green
Billion Dollar Baby (1945)

LOVELY GIRLS OF AKBARABAD, THE
Sammy Fain
Paul Francis Webster
Christine (1960)

LOVELY ISLAND
Baldwin Bergersen
William Archibald
The Crystal Heart (OB) (1960)

LOVELY LADIES, KIND GENTLEMEN
Stan Freeman and Franklin Underwood
Lovely Ladies, Kind Gentlemen
  (1970)

LOVELY LADY
Rudolf Friml
Otto Harbach and Oscar Hammer-
stein II
The Wild Rose (1926)

LOVELY LADY
Dave Stamper and Harold Levey
Harry A. Steinberg and Eddie Ward
Lovely Lady (1927)

LOVELY LADY, A
Franklin Hauser
Russell Janney
The O'Flynn (1934)

LOVELY LAURIE*
Jerry Bock
Sheldon Harnick
Tenderloin (1960)

LOVELY LAZY KIND OF DAY, A
Morgan Lewis
Nancy Hamilton
Three to Make Ready (1946)

LOVELY, LOVELY DAY
Max Rich and Billy Taylor
Jack Scholl
Keep Moving (1934)

LOVELY NIGHT, A
Richard Rodgers
Oscar Hammerstein II
Cinderella (TV) (1957)

LOVELY TO LOOK AT
Jerome Kern
Dorothy Fields and Jimmy McHugh
Roberta (F) (1935)

**LOVELY WAY TO SPEND AN EVE-
NING, A**
Jimmy McHugh
Harold Adamson
Higher and Higher (F) (1943)

LOVER
Richard Rodgers

Lorenz Hart
Love Me Tonight (F) (1932)

LOVER, COME BACK TO ME
Sigmund Romberg
Oscar Hammerstein II
The New Moon (1928)

LOVER IN ME, THE
Philip Springer
Carolyn Leigh
Ziegfeld Follies (1957)

LOVER LOST
John Clifton
John Clifton and Ben Tarver
Man with a Load of Mischief (OB)
   (1966)

**LOVER OF MY DREAMS (MIRABELLE
WALTZ)†**
Noël Coward
Cavalcade (F) (1932)

LOVER WAITS, A
Rick Besoyan
Babes in the Wood (OB) (1964)

LOVER'S HOLIDAY
William Heagney
William Heagney and Tom Connell
There You Are (1932)

LOVERS OF THE LAMPLIGHT
Hal Jordan
Jerry Douglas
Rondelay (OB) (1969)

LOVE'S A RIDDLE
Jimmy Van Heusen
Eddie De Lange
Swingin' the Dream (1939)

LOVE'S HAPPY DREAM
Walter Kollo
Harry B. Smith
Three Little Girls (1930)

---

*Dropped from New York production
†Originally in London stage production

LOVE'S INTENSE IN TENTS
Richard Rodgers
Lorenz Hart
Poor Little Ritz Girl (1920)

LOVE'S MELODY
Jeanne Bargy
Jeanne Bargy, Frank Gehrecke, and
  Herb Corey
Greenwich Village U.S.A. (OB) (1960)

LOVE'S NEVER LOST
Johann Strauss
Desmond Carter
The Great Waltz (1934)

LOVE'S OLD SWEET SONG
Alfred Nathan
George Oppenheimer
The Manhatters (1927)

LOVE'S OWN SWEET SONG
Emmerich Kalman
C. C. S. Cushing and E. P. Heath
Sari (1914)

LOVE'S REFRAIN
Percy Wenrich
Raymond Peck
Castles in the Air (1926)

LOVE'S REVENGE
Galt MacDermot
John Guare
Two Gentlemen of Verona (1971)

LOVE'S ROUNDELAY
Oscar Straus
Joseph W. Herbert
A Waltz Dream (1908)

LOVEY-DOVEY
Rudolf Friml
Rowland Leigh and John Shubert
Music Hath Charms (1934)

LOVIN' OFF MY MIND
Albert Von Tilzer
Neville Fleeson
Bye Bye, Bonnie (1927)

LOVING YOU
Paul Nassau and Oscar Brand
The Education of Hyman Kaplan
  (1968)

LOVING YOU THE WAY I DO
Eubie Blake
Donald Heywood
Hot Rhythm (1930)

LOWEN-GREEN COUNTRY CLUB, I
LOVE YOU
Sam Morrison
Dolph Singer
Summer Wives (1936)

LOWER THE BOOM
Al Carmines
Rosalyn Drexler
Home Movies (OB) (1964)

LOYAL AMERICAN
Stefan Kanfer, Jess J. Korman, and Jo-
  seph Grayhon
I Want You (OB) (1961)

LOYALIST WIFE, THE
Mischa and Wesley Portnoff
Donagh MacDonagh
Happy As Larry (1950)

LUANA
Rudolf Friml
J. Keirn Brennan
Luana (1930)

LUCITA
Alfred Goodman, Maury Rubens, and
  J. Fred Coots
Clifford Grey
Artists and Models (1925)

LUCK BE A LADY
Frank Loesser
Guys and Dolls (1950)

LUCKIEST MAN IN THE WORLD
George Gershwin
Ira Gershwin
Pardon My English (1933)

LUCKY
J. Fred Coots
Clifford Grey
June Days (1925)

LUCKY
Jerome Kern
Bert Kalmar and Harry Ruby
Lucky (1927)

LUCKY
Lee Wainer
Robert Sour
Sing for Your Supper (1939)

LUCKY BIRD
Vincent Youmans
Leo Robin and Clifford Grey
Hit the Deck (1927)

LUCKY BOY
Irving Berlin
The Cocoanuts (1925)

LUCKY DAY
Ray Henderson
B. G. DeSylva and Lew Brown
George White's Scandals (1926)

LUCKY IN LOVE
Ray Henderson
B. G. DeSylva and Lew Brown
Good News (1927)

LUCKY LINDY
Oscar Brand
How to Steal an Election (OB) (1968)

LUCKY PIERRE
Ronny Graham
New Faces (1952)

LUCKY SEVEN
Arthur Schwartz
Howard Dietz
The Second Little Show (1930)

LUCKY TO BE ME
Leonard Bernstein
Betty Comden and Adolph Green
On the Town (1944)

LUCY LOCKET
Helen Miller
Eve Merriam
Inner City (1971)

LULLABY
Dave Stamper
Gene Buck
Take the Air (1927)

LULLABY
Harold Arlen
Johnny Mercer
St. Louis Woman (1946)

LULLABY
Kurt Weill
Langston Hughes
Street Scene (1947)

LULLABY, THE
George Kleinsinger
Joe Darion
Shinbone Alley (1957)

LULLABY
Mary Rodgers
Marshall Barer
Once Upon a Mattress (OB) (1959)

LULLABY, A
Deed Meyer
'Toinette (OB) (1961)

LULLABY
Patrick Fox
Blood (OB) (1971)

LULLABY FOR JUNIOR
Duke Ellington
John Latouche
Beggar's Holiday (1946)

LULLABY OF THE PLAIN
Richard Lewine
Ted Fetter
The Girl from Wyoming (OB) (1938)

LULLABY WIND
Ray Haney
Alfred Aiken
We're Civilized? (OB) (1962)

LUMBERED
Leslie Bricusse and Anthony Newley
Stop the World—I Want to Get Off
(1962)

LUNCHEON BALLAD
Jerry Powell
Michael McWhinney
New Faces (1968)

LUNCHING AT THE AUTOMAT
Irving Berlin
Face the Music (1932)

LUPE
Alex North
Alfred Hayes
Tis of Thee (1940)

LUSTY MONTH OF MAY, THE
Frederick Loewe
Alan Jay Lerner
Camelot (1960)

LUTE SONG, THE
Raymond Scott
Bernard Hanighen
Lute Song (1946)

LYDIA, THE TATTOOED LADY
Harold Arlen
E. Y. Harburg
At the Circus (F) (1939)

LYING HERE
Wally Harper
Paul Zakrzewski
Sensations (OB) (1970)

LYLE
Janet Gari
Toby Garson
Lyle (OB) (1970)

LYLE'S TURN
Janet Gari
Toby Garson
Lyle (OB) (1970)

LYNCH-HIM SONG, THE
Coleridge-Taylor Perkinson

Ray McIver
God Is a (Guess What?) (OB) (1968)

LYNCHERS' PRAYER, THE
Coleridge-Taylor Perkinson
Ray McIver
God Is a (Guess What?) (OB) (1968)

LYSISTRATA
Willard Straight
David Eddy
The Athenian Touch (OB) (1964)

MA BELLE
Rudolf Friml
P. G. Wodehouse and Clifford Grey
The Three Musketeers (1928)

MA, MA, WHERE'S MY DAD?
Earl Robinson
Waldo Salt
Sandhog (OB) (1954)

MA MÈRE
Harry Warren
Al Jolson and Irving Caesar
The Wonder Bar (1931)

MA PETITE CHÉRIE
Franz Lehár
Harry Graham
Yours Is My Heart (1946)

MACDOUGAL'S CAVE
Jack Urbont
Bruce Geller
Livin' the Life (OB) (1957)

MACK THE BLACK
Cole Porter
The Pirate (F) (1948)

MACK THE KNIFE
Kurt Weill
Marc Blitzstein
The Threepenny Opera (OB) (1954)

MACKEY OF APPALACHIA
Walter Cool
Mackey of Appalachia (OB) (1965)

MACUMBA
Baldwin Bergersen
June Sillman
All in Fun (1940)

MAD ABOUT THE BOY
Noël Coward
Set to Music (1939)

MAD ABOUT YOU
Frank Grey
Earle Crooker and McElbert Moore
Happy (1927)

MAD AS THE MIST AND SNOW
John Duffy
Rocco Bufano and John Duffy (based
   on W. B. Yeats)
Horseman, Pass By (OB) (1969)

MAD DOGS AND ENGLISHMEN
Noël Coward
The Third Little Show (1931)

MAD FOR ART
Jule Styne
E. Y. Harburg
Darling of the Day (1968)

MADAM, I BEG YOU!
Baldwin Bergersen
William Archibald
The Crystal Heart (OB) (1960)

MADAME ARTHUR
Yvette Guilbert
Kay Swift
Paris '90 (1952)

MADAME FROM PAREE
Jane Douglas
Tom O'Malley
Bella (OB) (1961)

MADAME IS AT HOME
Frederick Loewe
Earle Crooker
Great Lady (1938)

MADAME ZUZU
Kurt Weill
Alan Jay Lerner
Love Life (1948)

MADEIRA, M'DEAR?
Donald Swann
Michael Flanders
At the Drop of a Hat (1959)

MADELEINE
Jacques Brel
Eric Blau and Mort Shuman
*Jacques Brel Is Alive and Well and
   Living in Paris* (OB) (1968)

MADELINE
Al Carmines
Maria Irene Fornes
Promenade (OB) (1969)

MADEMOISELLE CLICHÉ DE PARIS
André Previn
Alan Jay Lerner
Coco (1969)

MADEMOISELLE IN NEW ROCHELLE
George Gershwin
Ira Gershwin
Strike Up the Band (1930)

MADLY IN LOVE
Vernon Duke
Ogden Nash
The Littlest Revue (OB) (1956)

MADLY IN LOVE WITH YOU AM I
Deed Meyer
'Toinette (OB) (1961)

MADNESS MURDER
Margaret Dorn
Doug Dyer
Blood (OB) (1971)

MAGDALENA
Heitor Villa-Lobos
Robert Wright and George Forrest
Magdalena (1948)

MADRIGAL, A
Mike Brandt, Michael Knight, and
   Robert J. Lowery
Exchange (OB) (1970)

MAGGIE FLYNN
Hugo Peretti, Luigi Creatore, and
George David Weiss
Maggie Flynn (1968)

MAGGIE'S DATE
Laurence Rosenthal
James Lipton
Sherry! (1967)

MAGIC CARPET
Ervin Drake
Her First Roman (1968)

MAGIC FINGERS
Sandy Wilson
Valmouth (OB) (1960)

MAGIC GARDEN OF LOVE, THE
Alfred Goodman, Maury Rubens, and
J. Fred Coots
Clifford Grey
Artists and Models (1925)

MAGIC GIFTS
Lehman Engel
Agnes Morgan
A Hero Is Born (1937)

MAGIC, MAGIC
Bob Merrill
Carnival (1961)

MAGIC MOMENT
Arthur Schwartz
Howard Dietz
The Gay Life (1961)

MAGIC MOMENTS
Leo Fall
Clare Kummer
Madame Pompadour (1924)

MAGIC MUSIC
Richard Rodgers
Lorenz Hart
Simple Simon (1930)

MAGIC OF MOONLIGHT AND LOVE, THE
Karl Hajos (based on Tchaikovsky)
Harry B. Smith
Natja (1925)

MAGIC SPELL OF LOVE
Rudolf Friml
J. Keirn Brennan
Luana (1930)

MAGICAL THINGS IN LIFE
Albert Hague
Marty Brill
Café Crown (1964)

MAGNIFICENT FAILURE
Hughie Prince and Dick Rogers
The Girl from Nantucket (1945)

MAGNOLIA IN THE WOODS
Jerome Kern
Oscar Hammerstein II
Sunny (1925)

MAGNOLIA'S WEDDING DAY
Jimmy McHugh
Dorothy Fields
Blackbirds (1928)

MAHA ROGER
Clay Warnick
Mel Tolkin and Lucille Kallen
Tickets Please (1950)

MAHARANEE
Vernon Duke
Ira Gershwin
Ziegfeld Follies (1936)

MAHONEYPHONE, THE
Burton Lane
Harold Adamson
Earl Carroll's Vanities (1931)

MAID OF THE MILKY WAY, THE
Alfred Goodman, Maury Rubens, and
J. Fred Coots
Clifford Grey
Artists and Models (1925)

MAIDEN FAIR
A. Baldwin Sloane
Harry Cort and George E. Stoddard
China Rose (1925)

MAIDENS TYPICAL OF FRANCE
Cole Porter
Can-Can (1953)

MAILU
Jay Gorney
E. Y. Harburg
Ziegfeld Follies (1931)

MAINE
Richard Rodgers
No Strings (1962)

MAINE WILL REMEMBER THE
MAINE
Jack Lawrence and Don Walker
Courtin' Time (1951)

MAJESTIC SAILS AT MIDNIGHT
Irving Berlin
As Thousands Cheer (1933)

MAKE A FRIEND
Lee Pockriss
Anne Croswell
Tovarich (1963)

MAKE A MIRACLE
Frank Loesser
Where's Charley? (1948)

MAKE A WISH
Hugh Martin
Make a Wish (1951)

MAKE BELIEVE
Jerome Kern
Oscar Hammerstein II
Show Boat (1927)

MAKE BELIEVE YOU'RE HAPPY
Dave Stamper and Harold Levey
Cyrus Wood
Lovely Lady (1927)

MAKE BELIEVE YOU'RE MINE
Oscar Straus
Harry B. Smith
Naughty Riquette (1926)

MAKE IT ANOTHER OLD-FASH-
IONED, PLEASE
Cole Porter
Panama Hattie (1940)

MAKE IT HAPPEN NOW
George Fischoff
Carole Bayer
Georgy (1970)

MAKE ME
Tony Velone, Larry Spier, and Uhpio
    Minucci
Ziegfeld Follies (1957)

MAKE OUR GARDEN GROW
Leonard Bernstein
Richard Wilbur
Candide (1956)

MAKE SOMEONE HAPPY
Jule Styne
Betty Comden and Adolph Green
Do Re Mi (1960)

MAKE THE MAN LOVE ME
Arthur Schwartz
Dorothy Fields
A Tree Grows in Brooklyn (1951)

MAKE THE MOST OF SPRING
Albert Hague
Marty Brill
Café Crown (1964)

MAKE UP YOUR MIND
Emmerich Kalman
Harry B. Smith
Countess Maritza (1926)

MAKE UP YOUR MIND
Jimmy McHugh
Dorothy Fields
Lew Leslie's International Revue
(1930)

MAKE WAY
Vernon Duke
John Latouche
Cabin in the Sky (OB) (1964)

MAKE WAY
Jerry Bock
Sheldon Harnick
The Apple Tree (1966)

MAKE WAY FOR MY LADY!
John Clifton
John Clifton and Ben Tarver
Man with a Load of Mischief (OB)
  (1966)

MAKE WAY FOR TOMORROW
Jerome Kern
Ira Gershwin
Cover Girl (F) (1944)

MAKE WITH THE FEET
Vernon Duke
Harold Adamson
Banjo Eyes (1941)

MAKIN' BELIEVE
Ernest McCarty
Jack Ramer and Ernest McCarty
I Dreamt I Dwelt in Bloomingdale's
  (OB) (1970)

MAKIN' WHOOPEE
Walter Donaldson
Gus Kahn
Whoopee (1928)

MAKING CONVERSATION
Sigmund Romberg
Oscar Hammerstein II
Sunny River (1941)

MALUAN MOON
Ed Tyler
Sweet Miani (OB) (1962)

MALUMBA
Richard Freitas
Morty Neff and George Mysels
The Difficult Woman (OB) (1962)

MAMA, A RAINBOW
Larry Grossman
Hal Hackady
Minnie's Boys (1970)

MAMA ALWAYS SAID
Ron Steward and Neal Tate
Ron Steward
Sambo (OB) (1969)

MAMA, EARL DONE ATE THE TOOTH PASTE AGAIN
C. C. Courtney and Ragan Courtney
Earl of Ruston (1971)

MAMA, MAMA
Frank Loesser
The Most Happy Fella (1956)

MAMA, MAMA, MAMA
Peter Link
C. C. Courtney and Ragan Courtney
Earl of Ruston (1971)

MAMAN
Edward Thomas
Martin Charnin
Ballad for a Firing Squad (OB) (1968)

MAMAZELLE PAPAZELLE
Edward A. Horan
Frederick Herendeen
All the King's Horses (1934)

MAME
Jerry Herman
Mame (1966)

MAMIE IS MIMI
Jule Styne
Leo Robin
Gentlemen Prefer Blondes (1949)

MAMMY TRADERS
Richard Adler
Kwamina (1961)

MAMMY'S LITTLE BABY
Alma Sanders
Monte Carlo
Louisiana Lady (1947)

MAN ABOUT TOWN
Arthur Schwartz
Howard Dietz
The Little Show (1929)

MAN ABOUT TOWN
Dave Stamper
Fred Herendeen
Orchids Preferred (1937)

MAN ABOUT YONKERS
Lewis E. Gensler
E. Y. Harburg
Ballyhoo (1932)

MAN AND A WOMAN, A
Harvey Schmidt
Tom Jones
110 in the Shade (1963)

MAN AND SHADOW
Robert Wright and George Forrest
Kean (1961)

MAN BETTER MAN
Coleridge-Taylor Perkinson
Errol Hill
Man Better Man (OB) (1969)

MAN CAN HAVE NO CHOICE, A
Richard Adler
Kwamina (1961)

MAN DOESN'T KNOW, A
Richard Adler and Jerry Ross
Damn Yankees (1955)

MAN FOR SALE
Harold Arlen
E. Y. Harburg
Bloomer Girl (1944)

MAN I COULD HAVE BEEN, THE
Earl Wilson, Jr.
*A Day in the Life of Just About Every-
one* (OB) (1971)

MAN I LOVE, THE*
George Gershwin
Ira Gershwin
Lady, Be Good (1924)

MAN I LOVE IS HERE, THE
Franklin Hauser
Brian Hooker
The O'Flynn (1934)

MAN I NEVER MET, THE
Harry Warren
Jerome Lawrence and Robert E. Lee
Shangri-La (1956)

MAN I USED TO BE, THE
Richard Rodgers
Oscar Hammerstein II
Pipe Dream (1955)

MAN IN MY LIFE, THE
Harold Arlen
Johnny Mercer
Saratoga (1959)

MAN IN THE DOORWAY
Helen Miller
Eve Merriam
Inner City (1971)

MAN IN THE MOON, THE
Jerry Herman
Mame (1966)

MAN IS A MAN'S BEST FRIEND
Bruce Montgomery
The Amorous Flea (OB) (1964)

MAN IS A MISTAKE
Leon DeCosta
The Blonde Sinner (1926)

MAN IS FOR WOMAN MADE
Michael Valenti
Just for Love (OB) (1968)

MAN IS MADE FOR WOMAN
Stanley Jay Gelber
John Lollos and Don Christopher
Love and Let Love (OB) (1968)

**MAN MUST HAVE SOMETHING TO
LIVE FOR, A**
Albert Hague
Marty Brill
Café Crown (1964)

———
*Dropped from New York production

MAN O' MY DREAMS
Alfred Goodman
Clifford Grey
Sky High (1925)

MAN OF LA MANCHA
Mitch Leigh
Joe Darion
Man of La Mancha (1965)

MAN OF THE YEAR THIS WEEK, THE
Johnny Mercer
Top Banana (1951)

MAN THAT GOT AWAY, THE
Harold Arlen
Ira Gershwin
A Star Is Born (F) (1954)

MAN TO MAN TALK
Mary Rodgers
Marshall Barer
Once Upon a Mattress (OB) (1959)

MAN UPSTAIRS, THE
Vernon Duke
John Latouche
Cabin in the Sky (OB) (1964)

MAN, WE'RE BEAT
Tommy Wolf
Fran Landesman
The Nervous Set (1959)

MAN WHO HAS EVERYTHING, THE
Richard Rodgers
No Strings (1962)

MAN WHO SPEAKS FOR HIMSELF, A
Deed Meyer
Stones of Jehoshaphat (OB) (1963)

MAN WITH A DREAM, A
Victor Young
Stella Unger
Seventh Heaven (1955)

MAN WITH A LOAD OF MISCHIEF
John Clifton
John Clifton and Ben Tarver
Man with a Load of Mischief (OB)
  (1966)

MANAGED
Lee Pockriss
Anne Croswell
Tovarich (1963)

MANCHESTER
Galt MacDermot
Gerome Ragni and James Rado
Hair (1968)

MANCHILD
Johnny Brandon
Billy Noname (OB) (1970)

MANDY*
Irving Berlin
Yip! Yip! Yaphank (1918)

MANGOES
Dee Libbey and Sid Wayne
Ziegfeld Follies (1957)

MANHATTAN
Richard Rodgers
Lorenz Hart
The Garrick Gaieties (1925)

MANHATTAN LULLABY
Michael H. Cleary
Max and Nathaniel Lief
Hey Nonny Nonny! (1932)

MANHATTAN MADNESS
Irving Berlin
Face the Music (1932)

MANHATTAN MARY
Ray Henderson
B. G. DeSylva and Lew Brown
Manhattan Mary (1927)

MANHATTAN TRANSFER
Manning Sherwin
Arthur Herzog, Jr.
Bad Habits of 1926 (OB) (1926)

MANHATTAN WALK
Herbert Stothart, Bert Kalmar, and
  Harry Ruby
Good Boy (1928)

---

*Also in *Ziegfeld Follies* (1919)

MANIA, A
Al Carmines
Rosalyn Drexler
Home Movies (OB) (1964)

MAN'S HOME, A
Sheldon Harnick
Two's Company (1952)

MAN'S INHUMANITY
Charles Strouse
Mike Stewart
Shoestring Revue (OB) (1955)

MANSION
Galt MacDermot
John Guare
Two Gentlemen of Verona (1971)

MANUEL YOUR FRIEND
Skip Redwine and Larry Frank
Frank Merriwell, or Honor Challenged (1971)

MANUELO
Richard Lewine
Ted Fetter
The Girl from Wyoming (OB) (1938)

MANUELO
Sammy Fain
Jack Yellen
Sons o' Fun (1941)

MANY A NEW DAY
Richard Rodgers
Oscar Hammerstein II
Oklahoma! (1943)

MANY MOONS AGO
Mary Rodgers
Marshall Barer
Once Upon a Mattress (OB) (1959)

MANY WAYS TO SKIN A CAT
Robert Emmett Dolan
Johnny Mercer
Foxy (1964)

MANY YOUNG MEN FROM NOW
Ervin Drake
Her First Roman (1968)

MAPLETON HIGH CHORAL
Kurt Weill
Ira Gershwin
Lady in the Dark (1941)

MARATHON
Jacques Brel
Eric Blau and Mort Shuman
Jacques Brel Is Alive and Well and Living in Paris (OB) (1968)

MARCH OF THE MUSKETEERS
Rudolf Friml
P. G. Wodehouse and Clifford Grey
The Three Musketeers (1928)

MARCH OF THE RICE AND OLD SHOES
Joseph Meyer
William Moll
Jonica (1930)

MARCH OF THE ROYAL SIAMESE CHILDREN
Richard Rodgers
The King and I (1951)

MARCH OF THE TOYS
Victor Herbert
Babes in Toyland (1903)

MARCH OF THE TROLLGERS
Robert Wright and George Forrest
(based on Grieg)
Song of Norway (1944)

MARCH OF THE VIGILANT VASSALS
Bruce Montgomery
The Amorous Flea (OB) (1964)

MARCH OF TIME, THE
Harold Arlen
Ted Koehler
Earl Carroll's Vanities (1930)

MARCH ON
Karl Hajos (based on Tchaikovsky)
Harry B. Smith
Natja (1925)

MARCH ON FOR TENNESSEE
Giuseppe Verdi
Charles Friedman
My Darlin' Aida (1952)

MARCH WITH ME!
Ivor Novello
Douglas Furber
Charlot's Revue (1926)

MARCH YOU OFF IN STYLE
Robert Larimer
King of the Whole Damn World! (OB)
(1962)

MARCHING BY
Gus Edwards
Harry Clarke and Guy Robertson
Marching By (1932)

MARDI GRAS
Harold Arlen
Harold Arlen and Truman Capote
House of Flowers (1954)

MARDI GRAS DAY IN NEW ORLEANS
Will Irwin
Norman Zeno
Earl Carroll's Sketch Book (1935)

MARGINEERS, THE
Jimmy McHugh
Dorothy Fields
Lew Leslie's International Revue
(1930)

MARGOT
Sigmund Romberg
Otto Harbach and Oscar Hammer-
stein II
The Desert Song (1926)

MARIA
Arthur Schwartz
Howard Dietz
Revenge with Music (1934)

MARIA
Rudolf Friml
Rowland Leigh and John Shubert
Music Hath Charms (1934)

MARIA
Cole Porter
You Never Know (1938)

MARIA
Leonard Bernstein
Stephen Sondheim
West Side Story (1957)

MARIA
Richard Rodgers
Oscar Hammerstein II
The Sound of Music (1959)

MARIA IN SPATS
Jerry Herman
Parade (OB) (1960)

MARIAN
Walter Donaldson
Ballard MacDonald
Sweetheart Time (1926)

MARIAN THE LIBRARIAN
Meredith Willson
The Music Man (1957)

MARIANNE
Sigmund Romberg
Oscar Hammerstein II
The New Moon (1928)

MARIEKE
Jacques Brel
Eric Blau and Mort Shuman
*Jacques Brel Is Alive and Well and
Living in Paris* (OB) (1968)

MARIE'S LAW
Jerry Bock
Sheldon Harnick
Fiorello (1959)

MARINE'S HYMN, THE
Cole Porter
Around the World (1946)

MARIONETTES
Sigmund Romberg
Harry B. Smith
Princess Flavia (1925)

MARITAL INFIDELITY
Billy Barnes
The Billy Barnes People (1961)

MARKET DAY
Sigmund Romberg
Arthur Wimperis
Louie the 14th (1925)

MARKET DAY
Howard Blankman
By Hex (OB) (1956)

MARKET DAY IN THE VILLAGE
Ralph Benatzky
Irving Caesar
White Horse Inn (1936)

MARKET SONG
Baldwin Bergersen
William Archibald
Carib Song (1945)

MARKETING, MARKETING
Joseph Martinez Kookoolis and Scott
    Fagan
Scott Fagan
Soon (1971)

MARRIAGE IS FOR OLD FOLKS
Leon Carr
Earl Shuman
The Secret Life of Walter Mitty (OB)
    (1964)

MARRIAGE TYPE LOVE
Richard Rodgers
Oscar Hammerstein II
Me and Juliet (1953)

MARRIED
John Kander
Fred Ebb
Cabaret (1966)

MARRIED MAN, A
Marian Grudeff and Raymond Jessel
Baker Street (1965)

MARRIED MEN AND SINGLE MEN
Ray Henderson
B. G. DeSylva and Lew Brown
Follow Thru (1929)

MARRY ME
Philip Springer
Joan Javits
Hotel Passionato (OB) (1965)

MARRY THE FAMILY
Jerome Moross
Michael Blankfort
Parade (1935)

MARRY THE GIRL MYSELF
Laurence Rosenthal
James Lipton
Sherry! (1967)

MARRY WITH ME
Claibe Richardson
Kenward Elmslie
The Grass Harp (1971)

MARRYING FOR LOVE
Irving Berlin
Call Me Madam (1950)

MARY ANN
Michael Valenti
Just for Love (OB) (1968)

MARY DEAR
James F. Hanley
Eddie Dowling
Honeymoon Lane (1926)

MARY HAS A LITTLE FAIR
Raymond Hubbell
Anne Caldwell
Yours Truly (1927)

MARY MAKE BELIEVE
Noël Coward
This Year of Grace (1928)

MARY, MARY
Helen Miller
Eve Merriam
Inner City (1971)

MARY'S A GRAND OLD NAME
George M. Cohan
Forty-Five Minutes from Broadway
    (1906)

MASCOT OF THE TROOP, THE
Victor Herbert
Henry Blossom
Mlle Modiste (1905)

MASCULINITY
Jack Lawrence and Don Walker
Courtin' Time (1951)

MASH NOTES
Frank Grey and McElbert Moore
The Matinee Girl (1926)

MASQUERADE
Charles Herbert
Two for Tonight (OB) (1939)

MASQUERADE
John Clifton
John Clifton and Ben Tarver
Man with a Load of Mischief (OB)
   (1966)

MASQUERADE
Hal Jordan
Jerry Douglas
Rondelay (OB) (1969)

MASSES ARE ASSES, THE
William Klenosky
Utopia! (OB) (1963)

MASTER OF THE GREATEST ART OF
ALL, THE
Sammy Fain
Marilyn and Alan Bergman
Something More! (1964)

MASTER PLAN, THE
Irving Burgie
Ballad for Bimshire (OB) (1963)

MATA HARI
Rick Besoyan
Little Mary Sunshine (OB) (1959)

MATCHMAKER, MATCHMAKER
Jerry Bock
Sheldon Harnick
Fiddler on the Roof (1964)

MATHILDE
Jacques Brel
Eric Blau and Mort Shuman
*Jacques Brel Is Alive and Well and
   Living in Paris* (OB) (1968)

MATILDA
James Shelton
Dance Me a Song (1950)

MATINEE, THE
Billy Barnes
The Billy Barnes People (1961)

MATRIMONIAL STOMP, THE
Gene de Paul
Johnny Mercer
Li'l Abner (1956)

MATTER OF TIME, A
Mary Rodgers
Martin Charnin
Hot Spot (1963)

MATTERS CULINARY
Lehman Engel
Agnes Morgan
A Hero Is Born (1937)

MAUD, THE BAWD
Deed Meyer
She Shall Have Music (OB) (1959)

MAX THE MILLIONAIRE
Tommy Wolf
Fran Landesman
The Nervous Set (1959)

MAXIM'S
Franz Lehár
Adrian Ross
The Merry Widow (1907)

MAXINE!
Kenn Long and Jim Crozier
Kenn Long
Touch (OB) (1970)

MAY I HAVE MY GLOVES?
Ray Henderson
Jack Yellen
George White's Scandals (1936)

MAY I SAY I LOVE YOU?
J. Fred Coots
Arthur Swanstrom and Benny Davis
Sons o' Guns (1929)

MAY I SUGGEST ROMANCE?
Frederick Loewe
Earle Crooker
Great Lady (1938)

MAY IN MANHATTAN
Ruth Cleary Patterson
Tom Romano
Russell Patterson's Sketch Book (OB)
   (1960)

MAY MOON
Armand Vecsey
P. G. Wodehouse
The Nightingale (1927)

MAY THE BEST MAN WIN
Jimmy Van Heusen
Johnny Burke
Nellie Bly (1946)

MAYBE
George Gershwin
Ira Gershwin
Oh, Kay! (1926)

MAYBE I WILL
Harold Orlob
Irving Caesar
Talk About Girls (1927)

MAYBE I SHOULD CHANGE MY WAYS
Duke Ellington
John Latouche
Beggar's Holiday (1946)

MAYBE I'LL BABY YOU
Dave Stamper
Gene Buck
Take the Air (1927)

MAYBE IT'S ME
Richard Rodgers
Lorenz Hart
Peggy-Ann (1926)

MAYBE IT'S TIME FOR ME
Laurence Rosenthal
James Lipton
Sherry! (1967)

MAYBE MEANS YES
Jimmy McHugh
Dorothy Fields
Hello Daddy (1928)

MAYBE SO
Alberta Nichols
Mann Holiner
Angela (1928)

MAYBE SOME OTHER TIME
Ervin Drake
What Makes Sammy Run? (1964)

MAYBE THIS IS LOVE
Ray Henderson
B. G. DeSylva
Three Cheers (1928)

MAYBE THIS TIME*
John Kander
Fred Ebb
Cabaret (F) (1972)

MAYBE TOMORROW
Mike Brandt, Michael Knight, and
   Robert J. Lowery
Exchange (OB) (1970)

MAYFAIR
Raymond Hubbell
Anne Caldwell
Yours Truly (1927)

MAYFAIR
William Waliter
Rowland Leigh
Walk a Little Faster (1932)

MAYFAIR AFFAIR
Robert Wright and George Forrest
Kean (1961)

———
*Added to Film version

MAYFLOWER
J. Fred Coots, Maury Rubens, and Pat
  Thayer
Clifford Grey
Mayflowers (1925)

MAYOR'S CHAIR, THE
Mitch Leigh
William Alfred and Phyllis Robinson
Cry for Us All (1970)

McINERNEY'S FARM
Sammy Fain
George Marion, Jr.
Toplitzky of Notre Dame (1946)

ME
Johnny Brandon
Who's Who, Baby? (OB) (1968)

ME, A BIG HEAP INDIAN
Rick Besoyan
Little Mary Sunshine (OB) (1959)

ME ALONE
Coleridge-Taylor Perkinson
Errol Hill
Man Better Man (OB) (1969)

ME AND DOROTHEA
David Baker
Fred Ebb
Smiling, the Boy Fell Dead (OB)
  (1961)

ME AND LEE
Giuseppe Verdi
Charles Friedman
My Darlin' Aïda (1952)

ME AND LOVE
David Baker
David Craig
Copper and Brass (1957)

ME AND MARIE
Cole Porter
Jubilee (1935)

ME AN' MY BUNDLE
Irving Berlin
Miss Liberty (1949)

ME AND MY HORSE
Norman Dean
Autumn's Here (OB) (1966)

ME AND MY OLD WORLD CHARM
Thomas (Fats) Waller
George Marion, Jr.
Early to Bed (1943)

ME AND MY TOWN
Stephen Sondheim
Anyone Can Whistle (1964)

ME AND THE ELEMENTS
Moose Charlap
Eddie Lawrence
Kelly (1965)

ME ATAHUALPA
Ray Haney
Alfred Aiken
We're Civilized? (OB) (1962)

ME FOR YOU
Richard Rodgers
Lorenz Hart
Heads Up! (1929)

ME FOR YOU FOREVER
Richard Myers
Edward Heyman
Murder at the Vanities (1933)

ME I WANT TO BE, THE
Jordan Ramin
Frank H. Stanton and Murray Semos
Look Where I'm At! (OB) (1971)

ME, ME, ME
Janet Gari
Toby Garson
Lyle (OB) (1970)

ME, THE MOONLIGHT AND ME
Maury Rubens
Clifford Grey
The Madcap (1928)

MEADOWLARK
Bronislaw Kaper (based on Chopin)
John Latouche
Polonaise (1945)

MEAN
Gordon Duffy
Harry M. Haldane
Happy Town (1959)

MEAN
Walter Marks
Bajour (1964)

MEANEST MAN IN TOWN, THE
Robert Dahdah
Curley McDimple (OB) (1967)

MEAT AND POTATOES
Irving Berlin
Mr. President (1962)

MECHANICAL MAN
Alma Sanders
Monte Carlo
Mystery Moon (1930)

MEDEA IN DISNEYLAND
Lloyd Norlin
Sheldon Harnick
Shoestring Revue (OB) (1955)

MEDEA TANGO
Manos Hadjidakis
Joe Darion
Illya Darling (1967)

MEDIOCRITY
Murray Grand
Lester Judson
Chic (OB) (1959)

MEDITERANEE
Dov Seltzer
David Paulsen
To Live Another Summer (1971)

MEERAHLAH
Cole Porter
Around the World (1946)

MEESKITE
John Kander
Fred Ebb
Cabaret (1966)

MEET ME AT THE FAIR
Arthur Schwartz
Albert Stillman
Virginia (1937)

MEET MISS BLENDO
Johnny Mercer
Top Banana (1951)

MEET MY SEESTER
Jule Styne
Sammy Cahn
Look to the Lilies (1970)

MEET THE PEOPLE
Jay Gorney
Henry Myers
Meet the People (1940)

MEETING, THE
Robert Kessler
Lola Permagent
O Marry Me! (OB) (1961)

MEILINKI MEILCHICK
Leslie Bricusse and Anthony Newley
Stop the World—I Want to Get Off
(1962)

MEIN HERR*
John Kander
Fred Ebb
Cabaret (F) (1972)

MELINDA
Burton Lane
Alan Jay Lerner
On a Clear Day You Can See Forever
(1965)

MELISANDE
Harvey Schmidt
Tom Jones
110 in the Shade (1963)

MELODIES OF MAY†
Jerome Kern
Oscar Hammerstein II
Music in the Air (1932)

---

*Added to film version
†Choral setting of Beethoven Piano Sonata
Op. 2 No. 3

MELODIES WITHIN MY HEART
Karl Hajos (based on Chopin)
Harry B. Smith
White Lilacs (1928)

MELODY
Sigmund Romberg
Irving Caesar
Melody (1933)

MELODY IN FOUR F
Sylvia Fine and Max Liebman
Let's Face It! (1941)

MELT US!
Charles Strouse
Lee Adams
All American (1962)

MEMORIES
Ray Henderson
B. G. DeSylva and Lew Brown
Manhattan Mary (1927)

MEMORIES
Joseph Meyer and Philip Charig
Leo Robin
Just Fancy (1927)

MEMORIES OF MADISON SQUARE GARDEN
Richard Rodgers
Lorenz Hart
Jumbo (1935)

MEMORIES OF YOU
Eubie Blake
Andy Razaf
Blackbirds of 1930 (1930)

MEN
John Green
George Marion, Jr.
Beat the Band (1942)

MEN
Frank Black
Gladys Shelley
The Duchess Misbehaves (1946)

MEN
Moose Charlap
Norman Gimbel
Whoop-Up (1958)

MEN ABOUT TOWN
Noël Coward
Tonight at 8:30 (Red Peppers) (1936)

MEN ABOUT TOWN
Alma Sanders
Monte Carlo
Louisiana Lady (1947)

MEN ARE A PAIN IN THE NECK
Frederico Valerio
Elizabeth Miele
Hit the Trail (1954)

MEN AWAKE
Harold Rome
Pins and Needles (OB) (1937)

MEN IN MY LIFE, THE
David Martin
Langston Hughes
Simply Heavenly (1957)

MEN OF CHINA
Franz Lehár
Harry Graham
Yours Is My Heart (1946)

MEN OF HADES
Alma Sanders
Monte Carlo
The Houseboat on the Styx (1928)

MEN OF THE WATER-MARK
Jay Gorney
Jean and Walter Kerr
Touch and Go (1949)

MEN WHO RUN THE COUNTRY, THE
Johnny Mercer
Saratoga (1959)

MENE, MENE, TEKEL
Harold Rome
Pins and Needles (OB) (1937)

MEIN KLEINE AKROBAT
Arthur Schwartz
Howard Dietz
Flying Colors (1932)

MERCENARY MARY
Con Conrad
William B. Friedlander
Mercenary Mary (1925)

MERELY MARVELOUS
Albert Hague
Dorothy Fields
Redhead (1959)

MERRILL, LYNCH, PIERCE, FENNER AND CLYDE
Earl Wilson, Jr.
A Day in the Life of Just About Everyone (OB) (1971)

MERRILY WE WALTZ ALONG
Henry Sullivan
Earle Crooker
Thumbs Up! (1934)

MERRY CHRISTMAS
C. Luckey Roberts
Alex C. Rogers
My Magnolia (1926)

MERRY GO ROUND, THE
Seymour Furth and Lee Edwards
R. F. Carroll
Bringing Up Father (1925)

MERRY-GO-ROUND
H. Maurce Jacquet
William Brady
The Silver Swan (1929)

MERRY LITTLE MINUET
Sheldon Harnick
John Murray Anderson's Almanac (1953)

MERRY MAY
Rick Besoyan
The Student Gypsy (OB) (1963)

MERRY OLD LAND OF OZ, THE
Harold Arlen
E. Y. Harburg
The Wizard of Oz (F) (1939)

MESDAMES AND MESSIEURS
Cole Porter
Du Barry Was a Lady (1939)

MESSAGE OF THE VIOLET, THE
Gustav Luders
Frank Pixley
The Prince of Pilsen (1903)

MESSIN' AROUND
Jimmy Johnson
Perry Bradford
Messin' Around (1929)

MESSIN' ROUND
Werner Janssen
Mann Holiner and J. Keirn Brennan
Boom-Boom (1929)

METAMORPHOSIS
John Addison
John Cranko
Cranks (1956)

METAPHOR
Harvey Schmidt
Tom Jones
The Fantasticks (OB) (1960)

METAPHORICALLY SPEAKING
Lee Pockriss
Anne Croswell
Ernest in Love (OB) (1960)

MEXICAN BAD MEN
Maria Grever
Raymond Leveen
Viva O'Brien (1941)

MEXICAN BLUES
Joe Jordan
Homer Tutt and Henry Creamer
Deep Harlem (1929)

MEXICO
Martin Broones
Ballard MacDonald
Rufus Lemaire's Affairs (1927)

MEXICO
Sigmund Romberg
Dorothy Donnelly
My Maryland (1927)

MEXICONGA, THE
Sammy Fain
Jack Yellen and Herb Magidson
George White's Scandals (1939)

MI CHIQUITA
Joseph Meyer and Philip Charig
Leo Robin
Just Fancy (1927)

MI! MI!
Frank D'Armond
Will Morrissey
Saluta (1934)

MIA LUNA
Puccini*
E. Ray Goetz
Naughty Cinderella (1925)

MIANI
Ed Tyler
Sweet Miani (OB) (1962)

MICKEY
Sam Morrison
Dolph Singer
Summer Wives (1936)

MICROMANIAC, THE
Harold Rome
Ziegfeld Follies (1943)

MIDAS TOUCH, THE
Jule Styne
Betty Comden and Adolph Green
Bells Are Ringing (1956)

MIDDLE CLASS, THE
Jacques Brel
Eric Blau and Mort Shuman
Jacques Brel Is Alive and Well and Living in Paris (OB) (1968)

MIDDLE CLASS REVOLUTION
Wally Harper
Paul Zakrzewski
Sensations (OB) (1970)

MIDDLE OF THE SEA
Ed Tyler
Sweet Miani (OB) (1962)

MIDDLE YEARS, THE
Hal Hester and Danny Apolinar
Your Own Thing (1968)

MIDNIGHT BELLS
George Gershwin
Otto Harbach and Oscar Hammerstein II
Song of the Flame (1925)

MIDNIGHT CABARET
Porter Grainger and Freddie Johnson
Lucky Sambo (1925)

MIDNIGHT DADDY
Will Morrisey
Edmund Joseph
Polly of Hollywood (1927)

MIDNIGHT MATINEE
Noël Coward
Set to Music (1939)

MIDNIGHT WALTZ†
Robert Stolz
Robert Sour
Mr. Strauss Goes to Boston (1945)

MIDSUMMER NIGHT
Rick Besoyan
Babes in the Wood (OB) (1964)

MIDSUMMER'S EVE
Robert Wright and George Forrest (based on Grieg)
Song of Norway (1944)

---

*Not Giacomo
†Adaptation of Johann Strauss melody

MIDTOWN
Max Rich
Jack Scholl
Keep Moving (1934)

MIDWESTERN SUMMER
Lor Crane
John B. Kuntz
Whispers on the Wind (OB) (1970)

MIGHTY FORTRESS
Coleridge-Taylor Perkinson
Ray McIver
God Is a (Guess What?) (OB) (1968)

MIGHTY WHITEY
Oscar Brown, Jr.
Buck White (1969)

MILITARY DANCING DRILL
George Gershwin
Ira Gershwin
Strike Up the Band (1930)

MILITARY LIFE
Harold Rome
Call Me Mister (1946)

MILITARY MEN I LOVE
Edward Kunneke (based on Offen-
bach)
Harry B. Smith
The Love Song (1925)

MILK AND HONEY
Jerry Herman
Milk and Honey (1961)

MILK, MILK, MILK
Cole Porter
Let's Face It ! (1941)

MILKMAID
Galt MacDermot
John Guare
Two Gentlemen of Verona (1971)

MILKMAIDS OF BROADWAY
Alma Sanders
Monte Carlo
Mystery Moon (1930)

MILKY WAY, THE
Gene Lockhart
Bunk of 1926 (1926)

MILLEFLEURS
Sigmund Romberg
Rowland Leigh
My Romance (1948)

MILLION DOLLAR SMILE
Morton Gould
Betty Comden and Adolph Green
Billion Dollar Baby (1945)

MILLION DOLLARS, A
Dave Stamper
Fred Herendeen
Orchids Preferred (1937)

MILLION EYES, A
Jean Schwartz
Alfred Bryan
A Night in Spain (1927)

MILLION GOES TO MILLION
Francis Thorne
Arnold Weinstein
Fortuna (OB) (1962)

MILLION GOOD REASONS, A
Joseph Meyer
William Moll
Jonica (1930)

**MILLION MILES AWAY BEHIND THE
DOOR, A**
André Previn
Alan Jay Lerner
Paint Your Wagon (F) (1969)

MILLION WINDOWS AND I, A
Alec Wilder
Norman Gimbel
Shoestring Revue (OB) (1955)

MILONGA
Richard Freitas
Morty Neff and George Mysels
The Difficult Woman (OB) (1962)

MIMI
Richard Rodgers
Lorenz Hart
Love Me Tonight (F) (1932)

MIND IF I MAKE LOVE TO YOU
Cole Porter
High Society (F) (1956)

MIND OVER MATTER
David Shire
Richard Maltby, Jr.
The Sap of Life, (OB) (1961)

MINE
George Gershwin
Ira Gershwin
Let 'Em Eat Cake (1933)

MINE 'TIL MONDAY
Arthur Schwartz
Dorothy Fields
A Tree Grows in Brooklyn (1951)

MINEOLA
Sammy Fain
Marilyn and Alan Bergman
Something More! (1964)

MINNIE
Sigmund Romberg
Oscar Hammerstein II
East Wind (1931)

MINNIE'S BOYS
Larry Grossman
Hal Hackady
Minnie's Boys (1970)

MINSKY
Dave Stamper
Fred Herendeen
Orchids Preferred (1937)

MINSKY'S METROPOLITAN GRAND OPERA
Michael H. Cleary
Max and Nathaniel Lief
Hey Nonny Nonny! (1932)

MINSTREL, THE
Mary Rodgers
Marshall Barer
Once Upon a Mattress (OB) (1959)

MINSTREL DAYS
Irving Berlin
The Cocoanuts (1925)

MINSTREL PARADE
Kurt Weill
Alan Jay Lerner
Love Life (1948)

MINUTE BY MINUTE
Patrick Fox
Doug Dyer
Blood (OB) (1971)

MIO FRATELLA
Frank Fields
Armand Aulicino
The Shoemaker and the Peddler (OB) (1960)

MIRA
Bob Merrill
Carnival (1961)

MIRACLE OF MIRACLES
Jerry Bock
Sheldon Harnick
Fiddler on the Roof (1964)

MIRACLE SONG
Stephen Sondheim
Anyone Can Whistle (1964)

MIRANDA
Milton Schafer
Ronny Graham
Bravo Giovanni (1962)

MIRROR, MIRROR ON THE WALL
Melvin Van Peebles
Ain't Supposed to Die a Natural Death (1971)

MISALLIANCE
Donald Swann
Michael Flanders
At the Drop of a Hat (1959)

MISERABLE WITH YOU
Arthur Schwartz
Howard Dietz
The Band Wagon (1931)

MISERERE
Meyer Kupferman
Paul Goodman
Jonah (OB) (1966)

MISERY IS
Mary Rodgers
Marshall Barer
The Mad Show (OB) (1966)

MISS CADWALLADER
Lor Crane
John B. Kuntz
Whispers on the Wind (OB) (1970)

MISS EUCLID AVENUE
Jerry Herman
Madame Aphrodite (OB) (1961)

MISS FOLLIES OF 192–
Herman Hupfeld
Ziegfeld Follies (1957)

MISS LANGLEY'S SCHOOL FOR GIRLS
Frederick Loewe
Alan Jay Lerner
What's Up? (1943)

MISS LIBERTY
Irving Berlin
Miss Liberty (1949)

MISS MARMELSTEIN
Harold Rome
I Can Get It for You Wholesale (1962)

MISS MERE
James Bredt
Edward Eager
The Happy Hypocrite (OB) (1968)

MISS MIMSEY
Irvin Graham
New Faces (1936)

MISS PINHEAD
G. Wood
F. Jasmine Addams (OB) (1971)

MISS PLATT SELECTS MATE
Jay Gorney
Jean and Walter Kerr
Touch and Go (1949)

"MISS YOU" KISS, A
Victor Young
Stella Unger
Seventh Heaven (1955)

MISSED AMERICA
Kenny Solms and Gail Parent
New Faces (1968)

M-I-S-S-I-S-S-I-P-P-I
Harry Tierney
Ben Ryan and Bert Hanlon
Hitchy-Koo (1917)

MISSISSIPPI
Jimmy Johnson
Perry Bradford
Messin' Around (1929)

MISSISSIPPI JOYS
Al Wilson, Charles Weinberg, and
    Ken Macomber
Yeah Man (1932)

MISSOURI
Nat Reed
Brown Buddies (1930)

MISSOURI MULE
Paul Klein
Fred Ebb
Morning Sun (OB) (1963)

MIST IS OVER THE MOON, A
Ben Oakland
Oscar Hammerstein II
The Lady Objects (F) (1938)

MISTER BOY
C. Jackson and James Hatch
Fly Blackbird (OB) (1962)

MISTER WASHINGTON! UNCLE
GEORGE
Morton Gould
Dorothy Fields
Arms and the Girl (1950)

MIX AND MINGLE
Harold Rome
Wish You Were Here (1952)

MOANIN' IN THE MORNIN'
Harold Arlen
E. Y. Harburg
Hooray for What! (1937)

MOANIN' LOW
Ralph Rainger
Howard Dietz
The Little Show (1929)

MOCKING BIRD, THE
Sigmund Romberg
Dorothy Donnely
My Maryland (1927)

MOCKING BIRD
Richard Rodgers
Lorenz Hart
Simple Simon (1930)

MODEL HASN'T CHANGED, THE
Harold Rome
Michael Todd's Peep Show (1950)

MODELS
Ray Henderson
Jack Yellen
George White's Scandals (1936)

MODERN MADRIGAL
Warburton Guilbert
Viola Brothers Shore and June Sillman
New Faces (1934)

MODERNISTIC MOE
Vernon Duke
Ira Gershwin and Billy Rose
Ziegfeld Follies (1936)

MODEST LITTLE THING, A
Gene Lockhart
Bunk of 1926 (1926)

MODISTE, THE
Richard Rodgers
Lorenz Hart
I Married an Angel (1938)

MOI
Deed Meyer
She Shall Have Music (OB) (1959)

MOLASSES TO RUM
Sherman Edwards
1776 (1969)

MOLECULES
Joseph Martinez Kookoolis and Scott
    Fagan
Scott Fagan
Soon (1971)

MOLLIE O'DONAHUE
Jerome Kern
Oscar Hammerstein II
Sweet Adeline (1929)

MOLLY
Ron Dante and Gene Allan
Billy (1969)

MOLLY MALONE
George M. Cohan
The Merry Malones (1927)

MOLLY O'REILLY
Charles Gaynor
Lend an Ear (1948)

MOMENT AGO, A
Moose Charlap
Eddie Lawrence
Kelly (1965)

MOMENT HAS PASSED, THE
Al Carmines
Maria Irene Fornes
Promenade (OB) (1969)

MOMENT I LOOKED IN YOUR EYES,
THE
Joan Edwards and Lyn Duddy
Tickets Please (1950)

MOMENT I SAW YOU, THE
Arthur Schwartz
Howard Dietz
Three's a Crowd (1930)

MOMENT I SAW YOU, THE
Manning Sherwin
Harold Purcell
Under the Counter (1947)

MOMENT IS NOW, THE
Bob Goodman
Wild and Wonderful (1971)

MOMENT OF TRUTH, A
Jack Holmes
New Faces (1962)

MOMENT OF YOUR LOVE, A
Jimmy Van Heusen
Johnny Burke
Carnival in Flanders (1953)

MOMMA LOOK SHARP
Sherman Edwards
1776 (1969)

MOMMA, MOMMA
Harold Rome
I Can Get It for You Wholesale (1962)

MON AMI, MY FRIEND
Kurt Weill
Paul Green
Johnny Johnson (1936)

MONA FROM ARIZONA
Arthur Schwartz
Dorothy Fields
By the Beautiful Sea (1954)

MONEY*
John Kander
Fred Ebb
Cabaret (F) (1972)

MONEY ISN'T EV'RYTHING
Richard Rodgers
Oscar Hammerstein II
Allegro (1947)

MONEY ISN'T EVERYTHING
Robert Emmett Dolan
Johnny Mercer
Foxy (1964)

**MONEY ISN'T EVERYTHING,
BUT . . .**
Jordan Ramin
Frank H. Stanton and Murray Semos
Look Where I'm At! (OB) (1971)

MONEY, MONEY, MONEY
Jule Styne
E. Y. Harburg
Darling of the Day (1968)

MONEY, MONEY, MONEY
Oscar Brown, Jr.
Buck White (1969)

**MONEY RINGS OUT LIKE FREEDOM,
THE**
André Previn
Alan Jay Lerner
Coco (1969)

MONEY SONG, THE
John Kander
Fred Ebb
Cabaret (1966)

MONEY TO BURN
David Heneker
Half a Sixpence (1965)

MONKEY DOODLE-DOO, THE
Irving Berlin
The Cocoanuts (1925)

MONKEY IN A TREE
David Cohen
Horald Griffiths
Blood (OB) (1971)

MONKEY IN THE MANGO TREE
Harold Arlen
E. Y. Harburg
Jamaica (1957)

———
*Added to film version

MONKEY LAND
Ford Dabney
Jo Trent
Rang-Tang (1927)

MONKEY WHEN HE LOVES, A
Baldwin Bergersen
William Archibald
The Crystal Heart (OB) (1960)

MONOTONOUS
Arthur Siegel
June Carroll
New Faces (1952)

MONSOON
Ervin Drake
What Makes Sammy Run? (1964)

MONTANA
Moose Charlap
Norman Gimbel
Whoop-Up (1958)

MONTANA MOON
Ring Lardner
June Moon (1929)

MONTE, THE MODEL
Gene Lockhart
Bunk of 1926 (1926)

MONTH OF SUNDAYS, A
Robert Emmett Dolan
Johnny Mercer
Texas, Li'l Darlin' (1949)

MONTMART'
Cole Porter
Can-Can (1953)

MOOD OF THE MOMENT
Maria Grever
Raymond Leveen
Viva O'Brien (1941)

MOON ABOUT TOWN
Dana Suesse
E. Y. Harburg
Ziegfeld Follies (1934)

MOON-FACED, STARRY-EYED
Kurt Weill
Langston Hughes
Street Scene (1947)

MOON FLOWER
Sigmund Romberg
Arthur Wimperis
Louie the 14th (1925)

MOON OF MY DELIGHT
Richard Rodgers
Lorenz Hart
Chee-Chee (1928)

MOON IN MY WINDOW
Richard Rodgers
Stephen Sondheim
Do I Hear a Waltz? (1965)

MOON MADNESS
Rick Besoyan
Babes in the Wood (OB) (1964)

MOON SONG
Jerome Kern
P. G. Wodehouse
Oh, Lady! Lady! (1918)

MOON SONG, THE
Clay Warnick
Edward Eager
Dream with Music (1944)

MOON, THE WIND AND THE SEA, THE
Lewis E. Gensler
Owen Murphy and Robert A. Simon
The Gang's All Here (1931)

MOONBEAMS
Victor Herbert
Henry Blossom
The Red Mill (1906)

MOONGLADE
David Baker
Will Holt
Come Summer (1969)

MOONLAND
Jimmy Van Heusen
Eddie De Lange
Swingin' the Dream (1939)

MOONLIGHT
Seymour Furth and Lee Edwards
R. F. Carroll
Bringing Up Father (1925)

MOONLIGHT AND VIOLINS
Sigmund Romberg
Otto Harbach
Forbidden Melody (1936)

MOONLIGHT SOLILOQUY
Bronislaw Kaper (based on Chopin)
John Latouche
Polonaise (1945)

MOONSHINE LULLABY
Irving Berlin
Annie Get Your Gun (1946)

MORAL REARMAMENT
Jack Holmes
New Faces (1962)

MORALITY
Robert Kessler
Lola Permagent
O Marry Me! (OB) (1961)

MORE AND MORE
William Heagney
William Heagney and Tom Connell
There You Are (1932)

MORE AND MORE
Jerome Kern
E. Y. Harburg
Can't Help Singing (F) (1944)

MORE AND MORE
Fred Stamer
Gen Genovese
Buttrio Square (1952)

MORE I CANNOT WISH YOU
Frank Loesser
Guys and Dolls (1950)

MORE INCREDIBLE HAPPENINGS
Ronald Jeans
Wake Up and Dream (1929)

MORE LOVE THAN YOUR LOVE
Arthur Schwartz
Dorothy Fields
By the Beautiful Sea (1954)

MORE OF THE SAME
Oscar Brand
How to Steal an Election (OB) (1968)

MORE PRECIOUS FAR
Larry Grossman
Hal Hackady
Minnie's Boys (1970)

MORE THAN EVER NOW
David Baker
Fred Ebb
Smiling, the Boy Fell Dead (OB)
(1961)

MORE THAN FRIENDS
William Dyer
Don Parks and William Dyer
Jo! (OB) (1964)

MORE THAN JUST A FRIEND
Richard Rodgers
State Fair (F) (remake) (1962)

MORE THAN ONE MORE DAY
Sol Kaplan
Edward Eliscu
The Banker's Daughter (OB) (1962)

MORE THAN ONE WAY
Jimmy Van Heusen
Sammy Cahn
Skyscraper (1965)

**MORE THAN ORDINARY GLORIOUS
VOCABULARY, A**
Jacques Urbont
Bruce Geller
All in Love (OB) (1961)

MORE THAN YOU KNOW
Vincent Youmans
Billy Rose and Edward Eliscu
Great Day! (1929)

MORNING
Johann Strauss
Desmond Carter
The Great Waltz (1934)

MORNING AFTER, THE
Susan Hulsman Bingham
Myrna Lamb
Mod Donna (OB) (1970)

MORNING ANTHEM
Kurt Weill
Marc Blitzstein
The Threepenny Opera (OB) (1954)

MORNING IN MADRID
Frank Black
Gladys Shelley
The Duchess Misbehaves (1946)

MORNING MUSIC OF MONTMARTRE, THE
Jay Livingston and Ray Evans
Oh Captain! (1958)

MORNING PRAYER
Louis Bellson and Will Irwin
Richard Ney
Portofino (1958)

MORNING SUN
Paul Klein
Fred Ebb
Morning Sun (OB) (1963)

MORNING SUN
Wally Harper
Paul Zakrzewski
Sensations (OB) (1970)

MORNINGS AT SEVEN
Richard Rodgers
Lorenz Hart
Higher and Higher (1940)

MORNINGS AT SEVEN
James Bredt
Edward Eager
The Happy Hypocrite (OB) (1968)

MOST BEAUTIFUL GIRL IN THE WORLD, THE
Richard Rodgers
Lorenz Hart
Jumbo (1935)

MOST EXPENSIVE STATUE IN THE WORLD, THE
Irving Berlin
Miss Liberty (1949)

MOST GENTLEMEN DON'T LIKE LOVE
Cole Porter
Leave It to Me (1938)

MOST HAPPY FELLA, THE
Frank Loesser
The Most Happy Fella (1956)

MOTH SONG, THE
George Kleinsinger
Joe Darion
Shinbone Alley (1957)

MOTHER
Sigmund Romberg
Dorothy Donnelly
My Maryland (1927)

MOTHER
Rick Besoyan
Babes in the Wood (OB) (1964)

MOTHER AFRICA'S DAY
Oscar Brown, Jr. and Sivuca
Joy! (OB) (1970)

MOTHER EARTH
Johnny Brandon
Billy Noname (OB) (1970)

MOTHER GROWS YOUNGER
Richard Rodgers
Lorenz Hart
Heads Up! (1929)

MOTHER ISN'T GETTING ANY YOUNGER
Richard Lewine
Ted Fetter
The Fireman's Flame (OB) (1937)

MOTHER NATURE
Ray Haney
Alfred Aiken
We're Civilized? (OB) (1962)

MOTHER TOLD ME SO
Arthur Schwartz
Howard Dietz
Flying Colors (1932)

MOTHERHOOD
Jerry Herman
Hello, Dolly! (1964)

MOTHERLY LOVE
Robert Kessler
Lola Permagent
O Marry Me! (OB) (1961)

MOTHER'S COMPLAINT
Noël Coward
This Year of Grace (1928)

MOTHER'S GETTING NERVOUS
Kurt Weill
Alan Jay Lerner
Love Life (1948)

MOTHER'S HEART, A
Albert Hague
Marty Brill
Café Crown (1964)

MOTHER'S LOVE, A
Al Carmines
Maria Irene Fornes
Promenade (OB) (1969)

MOTHERS OF THE WORLD
Alfred Goodman, Maury Rubens, and
 J. Fred Coots
Clifford Grey
Artists and Models (1925)

MOTOR PERPETUO
Donald Swann
Michael Flanders
At the Drop of Another Hat (1966)

MOUNTAIN GREENERY
Richard Rodgers
Lorenz Hart
The Garrick Gaieties (1926)

MOUNTAIN HIGH, VALLEY LOW
Raymond Scott
Bernard Hanighen
Lute Song (1946)

MOUNTED MESSENGER, THE
Kurt Weill
Marc Blitzstein
The Threepenny Opera (OB) (1954)

MOUSE, THE
Edward C. Redding
Lester Judson and Edward C. Red-
 ding
Chic (OB) (1959)

MOUSE MEETS GIRL
Clay Warnick
Edward Eager
Dream with Music (1944)

MOVE OVER, NEW YORK
Walter Marks
Bajour (1964)

MOVIE BALL, THE
Harry Ruby
Bert Kalmar
The Ramblers (1926)

MOVIE HOUSE IN MANHATTAN
Richard Lewine
Arnold B. Horwitt
Make Mine Manhattan (1948)

MOVIN'
Frederick Loewe
Alan Jay Lerner
Paint Your Wagon (1951)

MOVIN'
Johnny Brandon
Billy Noname (OB) (1970)

MOVING DAY
James P. Johnson
Flournoy Miller
Sugar Hill (1931)

MOZAMBAMBA
Maria Grever
Raymond Leveen
Viva O'Brien (1941)

MOZAMBIQUE
Eubie Blake
Andy Razaf
Blackbirds (1930)

MR. AND MISSUS FITCH
Cole Porter
Gay Divorce (1932)

MR. AND MRS. SIPKIN
George Gershwin
B. G. DeSylva and Ira Gershwin
Tell Me More (1925)

MR. AND MRS. SMITH
Cole Porter
Jubilee (1935)

MR. AND MRS. WRONG
Clay Warnick
Edward Eager
Dream with Music (1944)

MR. BAIELLO
Sol Berkowitz
James Lipton
Nowhere to Go but Up (1962)

MR. BROWN, MISS DUPREE
Jay Gorney
Jean and Walter Kerr
Touch and Go (1949)

MR. BUNBURY
Lee Pockriss
Anne Croswell
Ernest in Love (OB) (1960)

MR. CHIGGER
Paul Klein
Fred Ebb
Morning Sun (OB) (1963)

MR. CLOWN
Hugo Pretti, Luigi Creatore, and
  George David Weiss
Maggie Flynn (1968)

MR. CUPID
Sigmund Romberg
Dorothy Donnelly
My Maryland (1927)

MR. DOLAN IS PASSING THROUGH
Richard Rodgers
Lorenz Hart
America's Sweetheart (1931)

MR. FLYNN
Johnny Burke
Donnybrook! (1961)

MR. GALLAGHER AND MR. SHEAN
Ed Gallagher and Al Shean
Ziegfeld Follies (1922)

MR. GOLDSTONE
Jule Styne
Stephen Sondheim
Gypsy (1959)

MR. HENRY JONES
Steve Allen
Sophie (1963)

MR. JESSEL
Charlotte Kent
Sweet and Low (1930)

MR. LIVINGSTONE
Harold Karr
Matt Dubey
Happy Hunting (1956)

MR. MAMMY MAN
J. C. Johnson
Change Your Luck (1930)

MR. MIGHT'VE BEEN
Oscar Brand
How to Steal an Election (OB) (1968)

MR. MOON
Lloyd Waner, Lupin Feine, and Moe
  Jaffe
A Little Racketeer (1932)

MR. PHELPS
Al Carmines
Maria Irene Fornes
Promenade (OB) (1969)

MR. RIGHT
Kurt Weill
Alan Jay Lerner
Love Life (1948)

MR. RIGHT
Frederico Valerio
Elizabeth Miele
Hit the Trail (1954)

MR. STRAUSS GOES TO BOSTON
Robert Stolz
Robert Sour
Mr. Strauss Goes to Boston (1945)

MR. WONDERFUL
Jerry Bock, George Weiss, and Larry
  Holofcener
Mr. Wonderful (1956)

MRS. BRODIE
William Roy
The Penny Friend (OB) (1966)

MRS. GRIMM
Dale F. Menten
Dale F. Menten and Frederick Gaines
The House of Leather (OB) (1970)

MRS. KRAUSE'S BLUE-EYED BABY
BOY
Ray Henderson
B. G. DeSylva and Lew Brown
Flying High (1930)

MRS. LARRY, TELL ME THIS
Mischa and Wesley Portnoff
Happy As Larry (1950)

MRS. PATTERSON
James Shelton
Mrs. Patterson (1954)

MRS. SALLY ADAMS
Irving Berlin
Call Me Madam (1950)

MUCHACHA
Vernon Duke and Jay Gorney
E. Y. Harburg
Shoot the Works (1931)

MU-CHA-CHA
Jule Styne
Betty Comden and Adolph Green
Bells Are Ringing (1956)

MUCH AS I LOVE YOU
Oscar Brown, Jr. and Luis Henrique
Joy! (OB) (1970)

MUCH MORE
Harvey Schmidt
Tom Jones
The Fantasticks (OB) (1960)

MUFFIN SONG, THE
Lee Pockriss
Anne Croswell
Ernest in Love (OB) (1960)

MULHANEY'S SONG
Jeanne Bargy
Jeanne Bargy, Frank Gehrecke, and
  Herb Corey
Greenwich Village U.S.A. (OB) (1960)

MULUNGHU TABU
Emmerich Kalman and Herbert Sto-
  thart
Otto Harbach and Oscar Hammer-
  stein II
Golden Dawn (1927)

MUMBLE NOTHING
Mike Brandt, Michael Knight, and
  Robert J. Lowery
Exchange (OB) (1970)

MUMBO JUMBO
Leslie Bricusse and Anthony Newley
Stop the World - I Want to Get Off
  (1962)

MUNCHKINLAND
Harold Arlen
E. Y. Harburg
The Wizard of Oz (F) (1939)

MURDER IN PARKWOLD
Kurt Weill
Maxwell Anderson
Lost in the Stars (1949)

MUSIC CALL, THE
Karl Hajos (based on Chopin)
Harry B. Smith
White Lilacs (1928)

MUSIC FOR MADAME
Jack Lawrence and Richard Myers
Ziegfeld Follies (1957)

MUSIC HATH'NT
Robert Kessler
Martin Charnin
Fallout (OB) (1959)

MUSIC IN MY FINGERS
Richard Myers
Edward Heyman
Here Goes the Bride (1931)

MUSIC IN MY HEART
Warburton Guilbert
June Sillman
New Faces (1934)

MUSIC IN THE AIR
Lehman Engel
Agnes Morgan
A Hero Is Born (1937)

MUSIC IN THE HOUSE
Marc Blitzstein
Juno (1959)

MUSIC IN THE NIGHT
Erich Korngold
Oscar Hammerstein II
Give Us This Night (F) (1936)

MUSIC MAKES ME
Vincent Youmans
Edward Eliscu and Gus Kahn
Flying Down to Rio (F) (1933)

MUSIC, MUSIC
Joseph Martinez Kookoolis and Scott
   Fagan
Scott Fagan
Soon (1971)

MUSIC OF A RIPPLING STREAM, THE
Cliff Friend
Lew Brown
Piggy (1927)

MUSIC OF HOME, THE
Frank Loesser
Greenwillow (1960)

MUSIC THAT MAKES ME DANCE, THE
Jule Styne
Bob Merrill
Funny Girl (1964)

MUSIC THRILLS ME, THE
Emmerich Kalman
Harry B. Smith
Countess Maritza (1926)

MUSICAL LESSON, A
George Lessner
Miriam Battista and Russell Maloney
Sleepy Hollow (1948)

MUSICAL TOUR OF THE CITY
Jay Gorney
Barry Trivers
Heaven on Earth (1948)

MUSKETEERS
Harry Ruby
Bert Kalmar
Animal Crackers (1928)

MUST BE GIVEN TO YOU
Moose Charlap
Norman Gimbel
The Conquering Hero (1961)

MUST IT BE LOVE?
Walter Marks
Bajour (1964)

MUSTAPHA
Sandy Wilson
Valmouth (OB) (1960)

MUSTAPHA ABDULLAH ABU BEN AL RAAJID
Dean Fuller
Marshall Barer
New Faces (1956)

MUTED
Ray Haney
Alfred Aiken
We're Civilized? (OB) (1962)

MUTUAL ADMIRATION SOCIETY
Harold Karr
Matt Dubey
Happy Hunting (1956)

MY ARMS ARE OPEN
Michael Cleary
Ned Washington
Earl Carroll's Vanities (1928)

MY ARAB COMPLEX
Henry Sullivan
Ballard MacDonald
Thumbs Up! (1934)

MY BABY TALK LADY
William B. Kernell
Dorothy Donnelly
Hello, Lola (1926)

MY BABY'S BORED
Allan Roberts
Lester Lee
All For Love (1949)

MY BEAUTIFUL LADY
Ivan Caryll
C. M. S. McLellan
The Pink Lady (1911)

MY BEAUTIFUL RHINESTONE GIRL
Irving Berlin
Face the Music (1932)

MY BEST GIRL
Jerry Herman
Mame (1966)

MY BEST LOVE*
Richard Rodgers
Oscar Hammerstein II
Flower Drum Song (1958)

MY BEST PAL
Maury Rubens
Clifford Grey
The Madcap (1928)

MY BIRD OF PARADISE
Rudolf Friml
J. Keirn Brennan
Luana (1930)

MY BLANKET AND ME
Clark Gesner
You're a Good Man, Charlie Brown
   (OB) (1967)

MY BLUE BIRD'S HOME AGAIN
Ray Henderson
B. G. DeSylva and Lew Brown
Manhattan Mary (1927)

MY BRIDAL GOWN
Arthur Schwartz
Albert Stillman and Laurence Stall-
   ings
Virginia (1937)

MY BROTHER WILLIE
William B. Kernell
Dorothy Donnelly
Hello, Lola (1926)

MY BROTHER'S KEEPER
Walt Smith
Leon Uris
Ari (1971)

MY BRUDDER AND ME
Richard Lewine
|Arnold B. Horwitt
Make Mine Manhattan (1948)

MY BUS AND I
Heitor Villa-Lobos
Robert Wright and George Forrest
Magdalena (1948)

MY BUSINESS MAN
David Raksin
June Carroll
If the Shoe Fits (1946)

---

*Dropped from New York production

MY BWANNA
Emmerich Kalman and Herbert Stothart
Otto Harbach and Oscar Hammerstein II
Golden Dawn (1927)

MY CAPTAIN
Ron Dante and Gene Allan
Billy (1969)

MY CARD
Jane Douglas
Tom O'Malley
Bella (OB) (1961)

MY CASTLE IN SPAIN
Isham Jones
By the Way (1925)

MY CONVICTION
Galt MacDermot
Gerome Ragni and James Rado
Hair (1968)

MY COUSIN IN MILWAUKEE
George Gershwin
Ira Gershwin
Pardon My English (1933)

MY CUP RUNNETH OVER
Harvey Schmidt
Tom Jones
I Do! I Do! (1966)

MY DADDY IS A DANDY
James Shelton
Mrs. Patterson (1954)

MY DADDY WAS RIGHT
Stefan Kanfer, Jess J. Korman, and Joseph Grayhon
I Want You (OB) (1961)

MY DANCING LADY
Jimmy McHugh
Dorothy Fields
Dancing Lady (F) (1933)

MY DARLIN' AÏDA
Giuseppe Verdi
Charles Friedman
My Darlin' Aïda (1952)

MY DARLIN' EILEEN
Leonard Bernstein
Betty Comden and Adolph Green
Wonderful Town (1953)

MY DARLING
Richard Myers
Edward Heyman
Earl Carroll's Vanities (1932)

MY DARLING, MY DARLING
Frank Loesser
Where's Charley? (1948)

MY DAUGHTER, MY ANGEL
Edwin Greenberg
Pilgrim's Progress (OB) (1962)

MY DAY
Joseph Meyer
Floyd Huddleston
Shuffle Along (1952)

MY DEAR BENVENUTO
Kurt Weill
Ira Gershwin
The Firebrand of Florence
(1945)

MY DEATH
Jacques Brel
Eric Blau and Mort Shuman
Jacques Brel Is Alive and Well and Living in Paris (OB) (1968)

MY DEFENSES ARE DOWN
Irving Berlin
Annie Get Your Gun (1946)

MY DOCTOR
Vincent Youmans
Otto Harbach
No, No, Nanette (1925)

MY DREAM BOOK OF MEMORIES
David Rose
Winged Victory (1943)

MY DREAM GIRL
Victor Herbert
Rida Johnson Young
The Dream Girl (1924)

MY DREAM IS THROUGH
Jerry Blatt
Jerry Blatt and Lonnie Burstein
Have I Got One for You (OB) (1968)

MY DYNAMO
Arthur Schwartz
Agnes Morgan
The Grand Street Follies (1929)

MY ETERNAL DEVOTION
Lee Pockriss
Anne Croswell
Ernest in Love (OB) (1960)

MY FAIR LADY
George Gershwin
B. G. DeSylva and Ira Gershwin
Tell Me More (1925)

MY FAITHFUL STRADIVARI
Emmerich Kalman
C. C. S. Cushing and E. P. Heath
Sari (1914)

MY FAMILY TREE
Noël Coward
The Girl Who Came to Supper (1963)

MY FATAL CHARM
Frederico Valerio
Elizabeth Miele
Hit the Trail (1954)

MY FATHER SAID
Arthur Schwartz
Howard Dietz
Revenge with Music (1934)

MY FATHER WAS A PECULIAR MAN
Kenneth Gaburo

Seyril Schochen
The Tiger Rag (OB) (1961)

MY FAVORITE THINGS
Richard Rodgers
Oscar Hammerstein II
The Sound of Music (1959)

MY FEET ARE FIRMLY PLANTED ON THE GROUND
Jerome Moross
Emanuel Eisenberg
Parade (1935)

MY FIRST GIRL
Maury Laws
Jules Bass
Month of Sundays (OB) (1968)

MY FIRST LOVE
Ruth Cleary Patterson
Fred Heider
Russell Patterson's Sketch Book (OB) (1960)

MY FIRST LOVE, MY LAST LOVE
Sigmund Romberg
Irving Caesar and Otto Harbach
Nina Rosa (1930)

MY FIRST LOVE SONG
Leslie Bricusse and Anthony Newley
The Roar of the Greasepaint - The Smell of the Crowd (1965)

MY FIRST MOMENT
Bob Goodman
Wild and Wonderful (1971)

MY FIRST PROMISE
Hugh Martin and Ralph Blane
Best Foot Forward (1941)

MY FORTUNE IS MY FACE
Jule Styne
Betty Comden and Adolph Green
Fade Out - Fade In (1964)

MY FUNNY VALENTINE
Richard Rodgers
Lorenz Hart
Babes in Arms (1937)

MY GAL IS MINE ONCE MORE
Arthur Schwartz
Howard Dietz
Inside U.S.A. (1948)

MY GALILEE
Walt Smith
Leon Uris
Ari (1971)

MY GARDEN
Harvey Schmidt
Tom Jones
Celebration (1969)

MY GENTLE YOUNG JOHNNY
Jerry Bock
Sheldon Harnick
Tenderloin (1960)

MY GERANIUM
Steven Metcalf
Fred Bluth
Drat! (OB) (1971)

MY G.I. JOEY
Jack Holmes
Bill Conklin and Bob Miller
O Say Can You See! (OB) (1962)

MY GIRL AND I
Sigmund Romberg
Oscar Hammerstein II
Sunny River (1941)

MY GIRL BACK HOME*
Richard Rodgers
Oscar Hammerstein II
South Pacific (1949)

MY GIRL IS JUST ENOUGH WOMAN
FOR ME
Albert Hague
Dorothy Fields
Redhead (1959)

MY GOD, WHY HAST THOU FOR-
SAKEN ME?
Meyer Kupferman
Paul Goodman
Jonah (OB) (1966)

MY HANDY MAN AIN'T HANDY NO
MORE
Eubie Blake
Andy Razaf
Blackbirds (1930)

MY HAWAII
Eaton Magoon, Jr.
13 Daughters (1961)

MY HEART BEGINS TO THUMP!
THUMP!
Morgan Lewis
Ted Fetter
The Second Little Show (1930)

MY HEART BELONGS TO DADDY
Cole Porter
Leave It to Me (1938)

MY HEART CONTROLS MY HEAD
Johann Strauss I, adapted by Oscar
Straus
Clare Kummer
Three Waltzes (1937)

MY HEART IS CALLING
Philip Charig
James Dyrenforth
Nikki (1931)

MY HEART IS DANCING
Arthur Schwartz
Albert Stillman
Virginia (1937)

MY HEART IS ON A BINGE
Philip Charig
Dan Shapiro and Milton Pascal
Artists and Models (1943)

MY HEART IS PART OF YOU
Arthur Schwartz
Howard Dietz
Flying Colors (1932)

MY HEART IS SO FULL OF YOU
Frank Loesser
The Most Happy Fella (1956)

---

*Dropped from New York production;
used in film version (1958)

MY HEART IS UNEMPLOYED
Harold Rome
Sing Out the News (1938)

MY HEART STOOD STILL
Richard Rodgers
Lorenz Hart
A Connecticut Yankee (1927)

MY HEART WON'T LEARN
Baldwin Bergersen
William Archibald
The Crystal Heart (OB) (1960)

MY HEART WON'T SAY GOODBYE
Sigmund Romberg (developed by Don Walker)
Leo Robin
The Girl in Pink Tights (1954)

MY HEART'S A BANJO
Jay Gorney
E. Y. Harburg
Shoot the Works (1931)

MY HEART'S AN OPEN BOOK
Harden Church
Edward Heyman
Caviar (1934)

MY HEART'S DARLIN'
Ralph Blane
Three Wishes for Jamie (1952)

MY HEART'S IN THE MIDDLE OF JULY
Allan Roberts
Lester Lee
All for Love (1949)

MY HEAVEN
Alma Sanders
Monte Carlo
The Houseboat on the Styx (1928)

MY HEAVEN WITH YOU
Rudolf Friml
Brian Hooker
The White Eagle (1927)

MY HERO
Oscar Straus
Stanislaus Stange
The Chocolate Soldier (1909)

MY HOLIDAY
Nancy Ford
Gretchen Cryer
Now Is the Time for All Good Men (OB) (1967)

MY HOME IS IN MY SHOES
Johnny Mercer
Top Banana (1951)

MY HOME'S A HIGHWAY
Ralph Blane
Three Wishes for Jamie (1952)

MY HOMETOWN
Ervin Drake
What Makes Sammy Run? (1964)

MY HOUSE
Leonard Bernstein
Peter Pan (1950)

MY HUSBAND
Cy Young
That Hat! (OB) (1964)

MY HUSBAND'S FIRST WIFE
Jerome Kern
Oscar Hammerstein II
Sweet Adeline (1929)

MY ICY FLOE
Randall Thompson
Agnes Morgan
The Grand Street Follies (OB) (1926)

MY INDIAN FAMILY
Sammy Fain
Paul Francis Webster
Christine (1960)

MY INTUITION
Arthur Schwartz
Howard Dietz
The Second Little Show (1930)

MY, IT'S BEEN GRAND
Cy Young
That Hat! (OB) (1964)

MY JEWELS
Ray Henderson
B. G. DeSylva and Lew Brown
George White's Scandals (1926)

MY JOE
Georges Bizet
Oscar Hammerstein II
Carmen Jones (1943)

MY KIND OF LOVE
Charles Gaynor
Show Girl (1961)

MY KIND OF NIGHT
Kurt Weill
Alan Jay Lerner
Love Life (1948)

MY LADY
Frank Crumit and Ben Jerome
Yes, Yes, Yvette (1927)

MY LADY LOVE
Alma Sanders
Monte Carlo
Oh! Oh! Nurse (1925)

MY LADY'S FAN
Seymour Furth and Lee Edwards
R. F. Carroll
Bringing Up Father (1925)

MY LADY'S HAND
Dave Stamper
Fred Herendeen
Orchids Preferred (1937)

MY LAST AFFAIR
Haven Johnson
New Faces (1934)

MY LAST LOVE
Frederick Loewe
Alan Jay Lerner
What's Up? (1943)

MY LATE, LATE LADY
Dean Fuller
Marshall Barer
Ziegfeld Follies (1957)

MY LIFE IS YOURS
Rick Besoyan
The Student Gypsy (OB) (1963)

MY LIPS, MY LOVE, MY SOUL
Percy Wenrich
Raymond Peck
Castles in the Air (1926)

MY LITTLE DOG HAS EGO
Herman Hupfeld
Dance Me a Song (1950)

MY LITTLE GIRL
Walter Cool
Mackey of Appalachia (OB) (1965)

MY LITTLE LOST GIRL
Sammy Fain
Paul Francis Webster
Christine (1960)

MY LORD AND MASTER
Richard Rodgers
Oscar Hammerstein II
The King and I (1951)

MY LORDS AND LADIES
Kurt Weill
Ira Gershwin
The Firebrand of Florence (1945)

MY LOULOU
Cole Porter
Jubilee (1935)

MY LOVE
Leonard Bernstein
John Latouche and Richard Wilbur
Candide (1956)

MY LOVE AND I
Erich Korngold
Oscar Hammerstein II
Give Us This Night (F) (1936)

MY LOVE CARRIES ON
Sam Morrison
Dolph Singer
Summer Wives (1936)

MY LOVE IS A MARRIED MAN
Frederick Loewe
Alan Jay Lerner
The Day Before Spring (1945)

MY LOVE IS A WANDERER
Bart Howard
John Murray Anderson's Almanac
  (1953)

MY LOVE IS ON THE WAY
Jerome Moross
John Latouche
The Golden Apple (1954)

MY LOVE IS YOUNG
Irvin Graham
Bickley Reichner
New Faces (1936)

MY LOVE, MY LOVE
Walter Cool
Mackey of Appalachia (OB) (1965)

MY LOVE WILL COME BY
Irving Burgie
Ballad for Bimshire (OB) (1963)

MY LOVED ONE
Robert Stolz
Rowland Leigh
Night of Love (1941)

MY LOVELY LAD
Mel Marvin
Ted Berger
Shoemaker's Holiday (OB) (1967)

MY LOVER*
Vincent Youmans
B.G. DeSylva
Take a Chance (1932)

MY LUCKY LOVER
George Lessner
Miriam Battista and Russell Maloney
Sleepy Hollow (1948)

MY LUCKY STAR
Richard Rodgers
Lorenz Hart
She's My Baby (1928)

MY LUCKY STAR
Ray Henderson
B. G. DeSylva and Lew Brown
Follow Thru (1929)

MY MAGNOLIA
C. Luckey Roberts
Alex C. Rogers
My Magnolia (1926)

MY MAN
Maurice Yvain
Channing Pollock
Ziegfeld Follies (1921)

MY MAN IS ON THE MAKE
Richard Rodgers
Lorenz Hart
Heads Up! (1929)

MY MAN'S GONE NOW
George Gershwin
DuBose Heyward
Porgy and Bess (1935)

MY MELODY MAN
Peter DeRose
Charles Tobias and Henry Clare
Pleasure Bound (1929)

MY MEMORIES STARTED WITH YOU
Baldwin Bergersen
June Sillman
All in Fun (1940)

MY MIMOSA
Sigmund Romberg
Dorothy Donnelly
My Princess (1927)

MY MISS MARY
Jerry Bock
Sheldon Harnick
Tenderloin (1960)

---

*Dropped from New York production

MY MISSUS
Richard Rodgers
Lorenz Hart
Betsy (1926)

MY MOST IMPORTANT MOMENTS GO
BY
Nancy Ford
Gretchen Cryer
The Last Sweet Days of Isaac (OB)
(1970)

MY MOST INTIMATE FRIEND
Cole Porter
Jubilee (1935)

MY MOTHER SAID
Helen Miller
Eve Merriam
Inner City (1971)

MY MOTHER TOLD ME NOT TO
TRUST A SOLDIER
Vincent Youmans
Oscar Hammerstein II
Rainbow (1928)

MY MOTHER WOULD LOVE YOU
Cole Porter
Panama Hattie (1940)

MY MOTHER'S WEDDING DAY
Frederick Loewe
Alan Jay Lerner
Brigadoon (1947)

MY NAME
Lionel Bart
Oliver! (1963)

MY NAME IS LEDA PEARL
C. C. Courtney
C. C. Courtney and Ragan Courtney
Earl of Ruston (1971)

MY NAME IS SAMUEL COOPER
Kurt Weill
Alan Jay Lerner
Love Life (1948)

MY NUMBER IS ELEVEN
Al Carmines
Rosalyn Drexler
Home Movies (OB) (1964)

MY OLD HOSS
Harry Akst
Lew Brown
Calling All Stars (1934)

MY OLD VIRGINIA HOME (ON THE
RIVER NILE)
Vernon Duke
John Latouche
Cabin in the Sky (1940)

MY ONE AND ONLY
George Gershwin
Ira Gershwin
Funny Face (1927)

MY ONE AND ONLY HIGHLAND
FLING
Harry Warren
Ira Gershwin
The Barkleys of Broadway (F) (1949)

MY ONE GIRL
Frank E. Harling
Say When (1928)

MY ONLY ROMANCE
Frank Black
Gladys Shelley
The Duchess Misbehaves (1946)

MY OWN
Harry Archer
Harlan Thompson
Merry-Merry (1925)

MY OWN BRASS BED
Meredith Willson
The Unsinkable Molly Brown (1960)

MY OWN MORNING
Jule Styne
Betty Comden and Adolph Green
Hallelujah, Baby! (1967)

MY PALACE OF DREAMS
Rudolf Friml
Rowland Leigh and John Shubert
Music Hath Charms (1934)

MY PARAMOUNT-PUBLIX-ROXY ROSE
Harold Arlen
Ira Gershwin and E. Y. Harburg
Life Begins at 8:40 (1934)

MY PASSION FLOWER
Sigmund Romberg
Dorothy Donnelly
My Princess (1927)

MY PERSONAL PROPERTY
Cy Coleman
Dorothy Fields
Sweet Charity (F) (1970)

MY PICTURE IN THE PAPERS
Jerome Moross
John Latouche
The Golden Apple (1954)

MY PLEASURE
Eaton Magoon, Jr.
13 Daughters (1961)

MY PRINCE
Richard Rodgers
Lorenz Hart
Too Many Girls (1939)

MY PRINCE
Sam Pottle
Tom Whedon
All Kinds of Giants (OB) (1961)

MY PRINCE CAME RIDING
Emmerich Kalman
George Marion, Jr.
Marinka (1945)

MY RAINBOW
Jeanne Hackett
Lester Lee
Harry Delmar's Revels (1927)

MY REAL IDEAL
Burton Lane
Samuel Lerner
Artists and Models (1930)

MY RED-LETTER DAY
Vernon Duke
Ira Gershwin
Ziegfeld Follies (1936)

MY RED RIDING HOOD
Jule Styne
Bob Merrill
Dangerous Christmas of Red Riding Hood (TV) (1965)

MY REGULAR MAN
J. C. Johnson
Change Your Luck (1930)

MY ROMANCE
Richard Rodgers
Lorenz Hart
Jumbo (1935)

MY ROSE OF SPAIN
Jean Schwartz
Alfred Bryan
A Night in Spain (1927)

MY SERGEANT AND I ARE BUDDIES
Irving Berlin
This Is the Army (1942)

MY SHINING HOUR
Harold Arlen
Johnny Mercer
The Sky's the Limit (F) (1943)

MY SHIP
Kurt Weill
Ira Gershwin
Lady in the Dark (1941)

MY SILVER TREE
Raymond Hubbell
Anne Caldwell
Three Cheers (1928)

MY SISTER-IN-LAW
Paul Klein
Fred Ebb
Morning Sun (OB) (1963)

MY SON-IN-LAW
Arthur Schwartz
Ira Gershwin
Park Avenue (1946)

MY SON, THE LAWYER
John Kander
James Goldman, John Kander, and
  William Goldman
A Family Affair (1962)

MY SON, UPHOLD THE LAW
Milton Schafer
Ira Levin
Drat! The Cat! (1965)

MY SONG
Ray Henderson
B. G. DeSylva and Lew Brown
George White's Scandals (1931)

**MY SPIES TELL ME (YOU LOVE NO-
BODY BUT ME)**
Gerald Marks
Irving Caesar and Sam Lerner
My Dear Public (1943)

MY STAR
Sam Pottle
Tom Whedon
All Kinds of Giants (OB) (1961)

MY STATE
Meredith Willson
Here's Love (1963)

MY SUGAR PLUM
Joseph Meyer and J. Fred Coots
B. G. DeSylva
Gay Paree (1925)

MY SUNDAY FELLA
George Gershwin
Gus Kahn and Ira Gershwin
Show Girl (1929)

MY SUNNY SOUTH
Abner Silver
Earl Carroll's Sketch Book (1929)

MY SWEET
Richard Rodgers
Lorenz Hart
America's Sweetheart (1931)

MY SWEETHEART MAMIE
Harry Ruby
Bert Kalmar
High Kickers (1941)

MY SWEETHEART 'TIS OF THEE
John Green
Edward Heyman
Here Goes the Bride (1931)

MY SWORD
Rudolf Friml
P. G. Wodehouse and Clifford Grey
The Three Musketeers (1928)

MY TALKING DAY
Sandy Wilson
Valmouth (OB) (1960)

MY TIME OF DAY
Frank Loesser
Guys and Dolls (1950)

MY TOP SERGEANT
Vernon Duke
Howard Dietz
Jackpot (1944)

MY TRUE HEART
Marc Blitzstein
Juno (1959)

MY UNCLE'S MISTRESS
Claude Leveilee
Gladys Shelley
Gogo Loves You (OB) (1964)

MY VERY FIRST IMPRESSION
Lee Pockriss
Anne Croswell
Ernest in Love (OB) (1960)

MY WALKING STICK
Irving Berlin
Alexander's Ragtime Band (F) (1938)

MY WAY
Leslie Bricusse and Anthony Newley
*The Roar of the Greasepaint - The
Smell of the Crowd* (1965)

MY WEDDING
Joseph Meyer
Edward Eliscu
Lady Fingers (1929)

MY WEIGHT IN GOLD
Robert Emmett Dolan
Johnny Mercer
Foxy (1964)

MY WHITE KNIGHT
Meredith Willson
The Music Man (1957)

MY WIFE AND I
Bill Mahoney
My Wife and I (OB) (1966)

MY WISH
Meredith Willson
Here's Love (1963)

MY YELLOW FLOWER
Jerome Moross
John Latouche
Ballet Ballads (1948)

MYSTERIOUS LADY
Jule Styne
Betty Comden and Adolph Green
Peter Pan (1954)

MYSTERY MOON
Alma Sanders
Monte Carlo
Mystery Moon (1930)

NAG! NAG! NAG!
Leslie Bricusse and Anthony Newley
Stop the World - I Want to Get Off
(1962)

NAJLA'S SONG
Sammy Fain
E. Y. Harburg
Flahooley (1951)

NAME: EMILY ADAM
Sol Berkowitz
James Lipton
Miss Emily Adam (OB) (1960)

NAMELY YOU
Gene de Paul
Johnny Mercer
Li'l Abner (1956)

NAME'S LAGUARDIA, THE
Jerry Bock
Sheldon Harnick
Fiorello (1959)

NANTY PUTS HER HAIR UP
Arthur Siegel
Herbert Farjeon
New Faces (1952)

NAOMI
Ernest McCarty
Jack Ramer and Ernest McCarty
I Dreamt I Dwelt in Bloomingdale's
(OB) (1970)

NAPOLEON
Will Irwin
Norman Zeno
Fools Rush In (1934)

NAPOLEON
Harold Arlen
E. Y. Harburg
Jamaica (1957)

NAPOLEON'S A PASTRY
Harold Arlen
E. Y. Harburg
Hooray for What! (1937)

NATACHA
Berton Braley, M. de Jari, and Alex
James
Earl Carroll's Vanities (1926)

NASHVILLE NIGHTINGALE
George Gershwin
Irving Caesar
Nifties of 1923 (1923)

NATCHITOCHES, LOUISIANA
C. Jackson and James Hatch
Fly Blackbird (OB) (1962)

NATIONAL ANTHEM OF UTOPIA,
THE
William Klenosky
Utopia! (OB) (1963)

NATURE PLAYED A DIRTY TRICK ON
YOU
Manning Sherwin
Arthur Lippman and Milton Pascal
Everybody's Welcome (1931)

NATURE'S SERENADE
Alyn Heim
Malcolm L. LaPrade
Will the Mail Train Run Tonight?
  (OB) (1964)

NATUSCHA
Franz Steininger (adapted from
Tchaikovsky)
Forman Brown
Music in My Heart (1947)

NAUGHTY BIRD TARANTELLA
Frank Fields
Armand Aulicino
The Shoemaker and the Peddler (OB)
  (1960)

NAUGHTY BOY
Joseph Meyer and Philip Charig
Leo Robin
Just Fancy (1927)

NAUGHTY BOY
Jerome Kern
Oscar Hammerstein II
Sweet Adeline (1929)

NAUGHTY EYES
Tom Johnstone
Phil Cook
When You Smile (1925)

NAUGHTY LITTLE STEP
J. Fred Coots
Clifford Grey
June Days (1925)

NAUGHTY-NAUGHT
Richard Lewine
Ted Fetter
Naughty-Naught (OB) (1937)

NAUGHTY, NAUGHTY NANCY
Rick Besoyan
Little Mary Sunshine (OB) (1959)

NAUGHTY NINETIES, THE
Max Ewing
Agnes Morgan
The Grand Street Follies (OB) (1927)

NAUGHTY RIQUETTE
Maury Rubens and Kendall Burgess
Harry B. Smith
Naughty Riquette (1926)

NEAPOLITAN LOVE SONG
Victor Herbert
Henry Blossom
The Princess Pat (1915)

NEAR TO YOU
Richard Adler and Jerry Ross
Damn Yankees (1955)

NECESSITY
Burton Lane
E. Y. Harburg
Finian's Rainbow (1947)

NEEDLES
Con Conrad
Gus Kahn
Kitty's Kisses (1926)

NEIGHBORHOOD SONG, THE
Jack Lawrence and Stan Freeman
I Had a Ball (1964)

NEIGHBORS
Lor Crane
John B. Kuntz
Whispers on the Wind (OB) (1970)

NELLIE BLY
Jimmy Van Heusen
Johnny Burke
Nellie Bly (1946)

NELLIE KELLY, I LOVE YOU
George M. Cohan
Little Nellie Kelly (1922)

NERO, CAESAR, NAPOLEON
Sol Kaplan
Edward Eliscu
The Banker's Daughter (OB) (1962)

NESTING TIME IN FLATBUSH
Jerome Kern
P. G. Wodehouse
Oh, Boy! (1917)

NEUROTIC YOU AND PSYCHOPATHIC ME
Charles Gaynor
Lend an Ear (1948)

NEVADA
Arthur Schwartz
Ira Gershwin
Park Avenue (1946)

NEVADA HOE DOWN
Frederico Valerio
Elizabeth Miele
Hit the Trail (1954)

NEVADA MOONLIGHT
Richard A. Whiting
Oscar Hammerstein II
Free for All (1931)

NEVER A DULL MOMENT
Arthur Schwartz
Dorothy Fields
Stars in Your Eyes (1939)

NEVER AGAIN
Norman Gregg
A la Carte (1927)

NEVER AGAIN
Noël Coward
Set to Music (1939)

NEVER BE-DEVIL THE DEVIL
Jacques Offenbach
E. Y. Harburg
The Happiest Girl in the World (1961)

NEVER BEFORE
Moose Charlap
Norman Gimbel
Whoop-Up (1958)

NEVER DO A BAD THING
Alfred Brooks
Ira J. Bilowit
Of Mice and Men (OB) (1958)

NEVER EVER LAND
Mike Brandt, Michael Knight, and Robert J. Lowery
Exchange (OB) (1970)

NEVER GIVE ANYTHING AWAY
Cole Porter
Can-Can (1953)

NEVER GO THERE ANYMORE
Moose Charlap
Eddie Lawrence
Kelly (1965)

NEVER GONNA DANCE
Jerome Kern
Dorothy Fields
Swing Time (F) (1936)

NEVER GONNA MAKE ME FIGHT
Hugo Peretti, Luigi Creatore, and George David Weiss
Maggie Flynn (1968)

NEVER HAD AN EDUCATION
Sigmund Romberg
Irving Caesar
Melody (1933)

NEVER LAND
Leonard Bernstein
Peter Pan (1950)

NEVER LET HER GO
George Lessner
Miriam Battista and Russell Maloney
Sleepy Hollow (1948)

NEVER MARRY A DANCER
Arthur Schwartz
Howard Dietz
Revenge with Music (1934)

NEVER, NEVER BE AN ARTIST
Cole Porter
Can-Can (1953)

NEVER NEVER LAND
Jule Styne
Betty Comden and Adolph Green
Peter Pan (1954)

NEVER, NEVER LEAVE ME
Jordan Ramin
Frank H. Stanton and Murray Semos
Look Where I'm At! (OB) (1971)

NEVER ON SUNDAY
Manos Hadjidakis
Joe Darion
Illya Darling (1967)

NEVER SAY NO
Harvey Schmidt
Tom Jones
The Fantasticks (OB) (1960)

NEVER SAY "NO"
Richard Rodgers
State Fair (F) (1962)

NEVER SAY THE WORLD WAS MADE
TO CRY
Maury Rubens
Clifford Grey
The Great Temptations (1926)

NEVER TOO LATE CHA-CHA
Jerry Bock
Sheldon Harnick
Never Too Late (1962)

NEVER TOO LATE FOR LOVE
Harold Rome
Fanny (1954)

NEVER TROUBLE TROUBLE
Robert Hood Bowers
Francis DeWitt
Oh, Ernest! (1927)

NEVER TRUST A VIRGIN
Jacques Offenbach
E. Y. Harburg
The Happiest Girl in the World (1961)

NEVER TRY TOO HARD
Alec Wilder
Arnold Sundgaard
Kittiwake Island (OB) (1960)

NEVER WAIT FOR LOVE
David Baker
David Craig
Phoenix '55 (OB) (1955)

NEVER WAS THERE A GIRL SO FAIR
George Gershwin
Ira Gershwin
Of Thee I Sing (1931)

NEVER WILL I MARRY
Frank Loesser
Greenwillow (1960)

NEVERMORE
Noël Coward
Conversation Piece (1934)

NEVERMORE
Gerald Marks
Sam Lerner
Hold It! (1948)

NEVILLE
Tony Geiss
Wet Paint (OB) (1965)

NEW ART IS TRUE ART
Kurt Weill
Ogden Nash
One Touch of Venus (1943)

NEW ASHMOLEAN MARCHING SO-
CIETY AND STUDENTS' CONSERVA-
TORY BAND, THE
Frank Loesser
Where's Charley? (1948)

NEW BLUE
John Addison
John Cranko
Cranks (1956)

NEW BOY IN TOWN
Paul Klein
Fred Ebb
Morning Sun (OB) (1963)

NEW DREAMS FOR OLD
Louis Bellson and Will Irwin
Richard Ney
Portofino (1958)

NEW EVALINE
Tom Sankey
The Golden Screw (OB) (1967)

NEW FACES
Martha Caples
Nancy Hamilton
New Faces (1934)

NEW FACES
Alex Fogarty
Edwin Gilbert
New Faces (1936)

NEW FANGLED PREACHER MAN
Gary Geld
Peter Udell
Purlie (1970)

NEW-FANGLED TANGO, A
Harold Karr
Matt Dubey
Happy Hunting (1956)

NEW GENERATION, A
Oscar Brown, Jr. and Luis Henrique
Joy (1970)

NEW HOLLYWOOD PLOTS
Sammy Fain
Paul Webster
Catch a Star! (1955)

NEW KIND OF RHYTHM
Will Morrisey
Edmund Joseph
Polly of Hollywood (1927)

NEW LOOK, THE
Hugh Martin
Look Ma, I'm Dancin'! (1948)

NEW LOOK FEELING
Frederico Valerio
Elizabeth Miele
Hit the Trail (1954)

NEW LOVE
Lewis E. Gensler
B. G. DeSylva
Captain Jinks (1925)

NEW LOVE IS OLD, A
Jerome Kern
Otto Harbach
The Cat and the Fiddle (1931)

NEW ME, THE
William Roy
Maggie (1953)

NEW NEW YORK
Arthur Schwartz
Howard Dietz
The Second Little Show (1930)

NEW PAIR OF SHOES, A
Ervin Drake
What Makes Sammy Run? (1964)

NEW SENSATION
Will Irwin
Norman Zeno
Fools Rush In (1934)

NEW SNOW
Margaret Dorn
Doug Dyer
Blood (OB) (1971)

NEW SUN IN THE SKY
Arthur Schwartz
Howard Dietz
The Band Wagon (1931)

NEW TO ME
Ken Welch
Bud McCreery
Shoestring Revue (OB) (1955)

NEW TOWN IS A BLUE TOWN, A
Richard Adler and Jerry Ross
The Pajama Game (1954)

NEW WALTZ, A
Fred Hellerman
Fran Minkoff
New Faces (1968)

NEW WORDS FOR AN OLD LOVE
SONG
Dave Stamper
Frederick Herendeen
Provincetown Follies (OB) (1935)

NEW WORLD
Ann Sternberg
Gertrude Stein
Gertrude Stein's First Reader (OB)
(1969)

NEW YORK
George M. Cohan
Billie (1928)

NEW YORK
Tommy Wolf
Fran Landesman
The Nervous Set (1959)

NEW YORK, NEW YORK
Leonard Bernstein
Betty Comden and Adolph Green
On the Town (1944)

NEW YORK SERENADE
George Gershwin
Ira Gershwin and P. G. Wodehouse
Rosalie (1928)

NEW YORK TOWN
Henry Souvaine and Jay Gorney
Morrie Ryskind and Howard Dietz
Merry-Go-Round (1927)

NEW YORKER, THE
Milton Ager
Jack Yellen
John Murray Anderson's Almanac
(1929)

NEWLYWED EXPRESS
Alma Sanders
Monte Carlo
Oh! Oh! Nurse (1925)

NEWS
Harry Ruby
Bert Kalmar
Animal Crackers (1928)

NEXT
Jacques Brel
Eric Blau and Mort Shuman
*Jacques Brel Is Alive and Well and
  Living in Paris* (OB) (1968)

NEXT TIME I CARE, THE
Bronislaw Kaper
John Latouche
Polonaise (1945)

NEXT TIME I LOVE, THE
Jerry Herman
Parade (OB) (1960)

NEXT TIME IT HAPPENS, THE
Richard Rodgers
Oscar Hammerstein II
Pipe Dream (1955)

NEXT TO TEXAS, I LOVE YOU
Jule Styne
Sammy Cahn
High Button Shoes (1947)

NICE AS ANY MAN CAN BE
William Dyer
Don Parks and William Dyer
Jo! (OB) (1964)

NICE BABY! (COME TO PAPA!)
George Gershwin
Ira Gershwin
Tip-Toes (1925)

NICE FELLA
Alfred Brooks
Ira J. Bilowit
Of Mice and Men (OB) (1958)

NICE GIRL
Charles M. Schwab
Henry Myers
Bare Facts of 1926 (1926)

NICE GIRL LIKE YOU, A
Jerry Blatt
Jerry Blatt and Lonnie Burstein
Have I Got One for You (OB) (1968)

NICE HOUSE WE GOT HERE
Alfred Brooks
Ira J. Bilowit
Of Mice and Men (OB) (1958)

NICE WORK IF YOU CAN GET IT
George Gershwin
Ira Gershwin
A Damsel in Distress (F) (1937)

NICEST THING, THE
Jay Livingston and Ray Evans
Let It Ride (1961)

NICKEL TO MY NAME, A
Vernon Duke
John Latouche
Banjo Eyes (1941)

NICKEL UNDER THE FOOT
Marc Blitzstein
The Cradle Will Rock (1938)

NICODEMUS
Vincent Youmans
Anne Caldwell
Oh, Please! (1926)

NIGGER HEAVEN BLUES
Alfred Nathan
George Oppenheimer
The Manhatters (1927)

NIGHT
Frank D'Armond
Will Morrissey
Saluta (1934)

NIGHT
Johann Strauss
Desmond Carter
The Great Waltz (1934)

NIGHT AFTER NIGHT
Arthur Schwartz
Howard Dietz
Three's a Crowd (1930)

NIGHT AFTER NIGHT
David Raksin
June Carroll
If the Shoe Fits (1946)

NIGHT AND DAY
Cole Porter
Gay Divorce (1932)

NIGHT AND THE SEA, THE
Ron Dante and Gene Allan
Billy (1969)

NIGHT BEFORE THE MORNING AFTER, THE
Arthur Schwartz
Howard Dietz
Between the Devil (1937)

NIGHT BIRDS
Jean Gilbert
Harry Graham
Katja (1926)

NIGHT CLUB NIGHTS
Henry Sullivan
Edward Eliscu
A Little Racketeer (1932)

NIGHT FLIES BY
Jerome Kern
Oscar Hammerstein II
Music in the Air (1932)

NIGHT GONDOLFI GOT MARRIED, THE
Robert Larimer
King of the Whole Damn World! (OB) (1962)

NIGHT IS YOUNG, THE
Sigmund Romberg
Oscar Hammerstein II
The Night Is Young (F) (1935)

NIGHT IT HAPPENED, THE
Joseph Meyer
William Moll
Jonica (1930)

NIGHT LETTER
Galt MacDermot
John Guare
Two Gentlemen of Verona (1971)

NIGHT MAY BE DARK, THE
Arthur Schwartz
Howard Dietz
Jennie (1963)

NIGHT OF MASQUERADE, A
George M. Cohan
The Merry Malones (1927)

NIGHT OF MY NIGHTS
Robert Wright and George Forrest
   (based on Alexander Borodin)
Kismet (1953)

NIGHT OF THE EMBASSY BALL, THE
Harold Arlen
E. Y. Harburg
Hooray for What! (1937)

NIGHT PEOPLE
Tommy Wolf
Fran Landesman
The Nervous Set (1959)

NIGHT SONG
Charles Strouse
Lee Adams
Golden Boy (1964)

NIGHT THEY INVENTED CHAM-
PAGNE, THE
Frederick Loewe
Alan Jay Lerner
Gigi (F) (1958)

NIGHT WAS ALL TO BLAME, THE
Alma Sanders
Monte Carlo
Louisiana Lady (1947)

NIGHT WAS MADE FOR LOVE, THE
Jerome Kern
Otto Harbach
The Cat and the Fiddle (1931)

NIGHTIE-NIGHT
George Gershwin
Ira Gershwin
Tip-Toes (1925)

NIGHTINGALE
Edward Earle
Yvonne Tarr
The Decameron (OB) (1961)

NIGHTINGALE, BRING ME A ROSE
Henry Sullivan
John Murray Anderson
John Murray Anderson's Almanac
   (1953)

NIGHTINGALE SONG, THE
Milton Ager
Jack Yellen
John Murray Anderson's Almanac
   (1929)

NIGHTLIFE
Charles Strouse
Lee Adams
All American (1962)

NIGHTMARE, THE
Frank Black
Gladys Shelley
The Duchess Misbehaves (1946)

NIGHTMARE, THE
Frank Fields
Armand Aulicino
The Shoemaker and the Peddler (OB)
   (1960)

NIGHTTIME IS NO TIME FOR THINK-
ING, THE
Kurt Weill
Ira Gershwin
The Firebrand of Florence (1945)

NIGHTWIND
Harden Church
Edward Heyman
Caviar (1934)

NILE, THE
Xaver Leroux
A Night in Paris (1926)

NINA
Herbert Stothart, Bert Kalmar, and
   Harry Ruby
Good Boy (1928)

NINA
Werner Janssen
Mann Holiner and J. Keirn Brennan
Boom-Boom (1929)

NINA
Cole Porter
The Pirate (F) (1948)

NINA ROSA
Sigmund Romberg
Irving Caesar
Nina Rosa (1930)

NINA, THE PINTA, THE SANTA
MARIA, THE
Kurt Weill
Ira Gershwin
Where Do We Go from Here? (F)
(1945)

NINE O'CLOCK
Bob Merrill
Take Me Along (1959)

1908 LIFE, THE
Ray Henderson
B. G. DeSylva and Lew Brown
Follow Thru (1929)

NINETEEN TWENTY-SEVEN
Harold Orlob
Irving Caesar
Talk About Girls (1927)

NINETY AGAIN!
Richard Rodgers
Martin Charnin
Two by Two (1970)

NINETY MINUTES IS A LONG, LONG
TIME
Noël Coward
Together with Music (TV) (1955)

99 PER CENT PURE
Arthur Schwartz
Henry Myers
The New Yorkers (1927)

NIPPY
Vivian Ellis
Graham John
By the Way (1925)

NIRI-ESTHER
Sandy Wilson
Valmouth (OB) (1960)

NITCHEVO
Lee Pockriss
Anne Croswell
Tovarich (1963)

NIZE BABY
James F. Hanley
Ballard MacDonald
No Foolin' (1926)

NO
David Baker
Will Holt
Come Summer (1969)

NO BETTER WAY TO START A CASE
George Gershwin
Ira Gershwin
Let 'Em Eat Cake (1933)

NO BOOM BOOM
John Kander
Fred Ebb
Zorbá (1968)

NO CHAMPAGNE
Joseph Raposo
Erich Segal
Sing Muse! (OB) (1961)

NO COMPRENEZ, NO CAPISH, NO
VERSTEH!
George Gershwin
Ira Gershwin
Let 'Em Eat Cake (1933)

NO FOOLIN'
James F. Hanley
Gene Buck
No Foolin' (1926)

No GARLIC TONIGHT
Willard Straight
David Eddy
The Athenian Touch (OB) (1964)

No HEARTS FOR SALE
Alma Sanders
Monte Carlo
Oh! Oh! Nurse (1925)

No, I WON'T
Alma Sanders
Monte Carlo
Oh! Oh! Nurse (1925)

No KETCHUP
Alfred Brooks
Ira J. Bilowit
Of Mice and Men (OB) (1958)

No LOOKIN' BACK
Jay Gorney
Henry Myers and Edward Eliscu
Meet the People (1940)

No LOVER FOR ME
Cole Porter
Out of This World (1950)

No MORE
Charles Strouse
Lee Adams
Golden Boy (1964)

No MORE CANDY
Jerry Bock
Sheldon Harnick
She Loves Me (1963)

No MORE EDENS
Robert Rosenblum
Robert Rosenblum and Howard Schuman
Up Eden (OB) (1968)

No MORE YOU
Ray Henderson
B. G. DeSylva and Lew Brown
Follow Thru (1929)

No MORE WAITING
Richard Rodgers
Androcles and the Lion (TV) (1967)

No, MOTHER, No
Richard Rodgers
Lorenz Hart
By Jupiter (1942)

No NEWS TODAY
Jimmy Van Heusen
Johnny Burke
Nellie Bly (1946)

No, No, MAMSELLE
Alma Sanders
Monte Carlo
Louisiana Lady (1947)

No, No, NANETTE
Vincent Youmans
Otto Harbach
No, No, Nanette (1925)

No! No! No!
Franz Steininger (adapted from Tchaikovsky)
Forman Brown
Music in My Heart (1947)

No! No! No!
Frederico Valerio
Elizabeth Miele
Hit the Trail (1954)

No! No! No!
Lee Pockriss
Anne Croswell
Tovarich (1963)

No ONE CARES FOR DREAMS
Alma Sanders
Monte Carlo
Louisiana Lady (1947)

No ONE KNOWS
Jerome Kern
Anne Caldwell
The City Chap (1925)

NO ONE KNOWS ME
Leon Pober
Bud Freeman
Beg, Borrow or Steal (1960)

NO ONE LOVES ME
Mischa and Wesley Portnoff
Donagh MacDonagh
Happy As Larry (1950)

NO ONE'LL EVER LOVE YOU
Leroy Anderson
Joan Ford, Walter and Jean Kerr
Goldilocks (1958)

NO ONE'S EVER KISSED ME
Vivian Ellis
Graham John
By the Way (1925)

NO ONE'S PERFECT, DEAR
Hal Hester and Danny Apolinar
Your Own Thing (1968)

NO ONE'S TRIED TO KISS ME
Manning Sherwin
Harold Purcell
Under the Counter

NO OTHER LOVE
Emile Berté and Maury Rubens
J. Keirn Brennan
Music in May (1929)

NO OTHER LOVE
Richard Rodgers
Oscar Hammerstein II
Me and Juliet (1953)

NO PLACE FOR ME
Wally Harper
Paul Zakrzewski
Sensations (OB) (1970)

NO PLACE LIKE HOME
Roger Wolfe Kahn
Irving Caesar
Americana (1928)

NO PLACE TO GO
Ray Haney

Alfred Aiken
We're Civilized? (OB) (1962)

NO QUESTIONS
Sammy Fain
Marilyn and Alan Bergman
Something More! (1964)

NO ROOM IN MY HEART
Ray Perkins
Max and Nathaniel Lief
Say When (1928)

NO SACRIFICE
Alyn Heim
Malcolm L. LaPrade
Will the Mail Train Run Tonight?
(OB) (1964)

NO STRINGS
Irving Berlin
Top Hat (F) (1935)

NO STRINGS
Richard Rodgers
No Strings (1962)

NO TALENT
Oscar Brand and Paul Nassau
A Joyful Noise (1966)

NO TIME
Baldwin Bergersen
Phyllis McGinley
Small Wonder (1948)

NO TIME
Robert Waldman
Alfred Uhry
Here's Where I Belong (1968)

NO TIME FOR NOTHIN' BUT LOVE
Allan Roberts
Lester Lee
All for Love (1949)

NO TOUCH MINE
William S. Fischer
Maxine Klein
Kiss Now (OB) (1971)

NO TRUE LOVE
Deed Meyer
She Shall Have Music (OB) (1959)

NO TWO PEOPLE
Frank Loesser
Hans Christian Andersen (F) (1951)

NO UNDERSTAND
Richard Rodgers
Stephen Sondheim
Do I Hear a Waltz? (1965)

NO USE PRETENDING
Sigmund Romberg
Otto Harbach
Forbidden Melody (1936)

NO WAY TO STOP IT
Richard Rodgers
Oscar Hammerstein II
The Sound of Music (1959)

NO WEDDING BELLS FOR ME
Louis Bellson and Will Irwin
Richard Ney
Portofino (1958)

NO WONDER I'M BLUE
Louis Alter
Oscar Hammerstein II
Ballyhoo (1930)

NO (YOU CAN'T HAVE MY HEART)
Dana Suesse
You Never Know (1938)

NOAH'S ARK
Naomi Shemer
David Paulsen
To Live Another Summer (1971)

NOBILITY
Jerry Bock
Sheldon Harnick
The Body Beautiful (1958)

NOBODY BREAKS MY HEART
Kay Swift
Paul James
Fine and Dandy (1930)

NOBODY BUT YOU
George Gershwin
B. G. DeSylva
La La Lucille (1919)

NOBODY CHEATS BIG MIKE
George Harwell
What a Killing (OB) (1961)

NOBODY DOES MY THING
Oscar Brown, Jr.
Buck White (1936)

NOBODY ELSE BUT ME*
Jerome Kern
Oscar Hammerstein II
Show Boat (1946)

NOBODY ELSE BUT YOU
Albert Hague
Arnold B. Horwitt
The Girls Against the Boys (1959)

NOBODY EVER DIED FOR DEAR OLD
RUTGERS
Jule Styne
Sammy Cahn
High Button Shoes (1947)

NOBODY EVER PINS ME UP
Vernon Duke
Howard Dietz
Jackpot (1944)

NOBODY MAKES A PASS AT ME
Harold Rome
Pins and Needles (OB) (1937)

NOBODY STEPS ON KAFRITZ
Bob Merrill
Henry, Sweet Henry (1967)

NOBODY THROW THOSE BULL
Moose Charlap
Norman Gimbel
Whoop-Up (1958)

NOBODY TO CRY TO
Johnny Brandon
Who's Who, Baby? (OB) (1968)

---

*Added to 1946 revival

NOBODY TOLD ME
Baldwin Bergersen
Phyllis McGinley
Small Wonder (1948)

NOBODY TOLD ME
Richard Rodgers
No Strings (1962)

NOBODY WANTS ME
Philip Charig
Irving Caesar
Polly (1929)

NOBODY'S CHASING ME
Cole Porter
Out of This World (1950)

NOBODY'S FAULT
Alex Ander
Blood (OB) (1971)

NOBODY'S HEART
Richard Rodgers
Lorenz Hart
By Jupiter (1942)

NOBODY'S HEART BUT MINE
Jimmy McHugh
Harold Adamsom
As the Girls Go (1948)

NOBODY'S LISTENING
Oscar Brand
How to Steal an Election (OB) (1968)

NOBODY'S PERFECT
Harvey Schmidt
Tom Jones
I Do! I Do! (1966)

NOCTURNE
Rudolf Friml
Brian Hooker
The Vagabond King (1925)

NOISES IN THE STREET
Richard Lewine
Peter Barry, David Greggory, and Arnold B. Horwitt
Make Mine Manhattan (1948)

NOISY NEIGHBORS
James P. Johnson
Flournoy Miller
Sugar Hill (1931)

NORDRAAK'S FAREWELL
Robert Wright and George Forrest
(based on Grieg)
Song of Norway (1944)

NORMAL AMERICAN BOY
Charles Strouse
Lee Adams
Bye Bye Birdie (1960)

NORMANDY
Mary Rodgers
Marshall Barer
Once Upon a Mattress (OB) (1959)

NORTH AMERICAN SHMEAR
Robert Swerdlow
Love Me, Love My Children (OB)
(1971)

NORTHERN BLUES
Walter (Gustave) Haenschen
Robert A. Simon
The Grand Street Follies (OB) (1926)

NOSE AHEAD
Mimi Stone
William Kaye
Pimpernel! (OB) (1964)

NOT EVERY DAY OF THE WEEK
John Kander
Fred Ebb
Flora, the Red Menace (1965)

NOT FOR ALL THE RICE IN CHINA
Irving Berlin
As Thousands Cheer (1933)

NOT GETTING ANY YOUNGER
Philip Springer
Joan Javits
Hotel Passionato (OB) (1965)

NOT GUILTY
Harold Rome
Destry Rides Again (1959)

NOT ME
Oscar Brand and Paul Nassau
A Joyful Noise (1966)

NOT MINE
Jule Styne
Betty Comden and Adolph Green
Hallelujah, Baby! (1967)

NOT MY PROBLEM
Harvey Schmidt
Tom Jones
Celebration (1969)

NOT NOW, NOT HERE
Edward Thomas
Martin Charnin
Ballad for a Firing Squad (OB) (1968)

NOT ON YOUR NELLIE
Jule Styne
E. Y. Harburg
Darling of the Day (1968)

NOT ON YOUR TINTYPE
Richard Lewine
John Latouche
Murder in the Old Red Barn (OB) (1936)

NOT SINCE NINEVEH
Robert Wright and George Forrest
  (based on Alexander Borodin)
Kismet (1953)

NOT SO BAD TO BE GOOD
Vernon Duke
John Latouche
Cabin in the Sky (OB) (1964)

NOT SO LONG AGO
Porter Grainger and Freddie Johnson
Lucky Sambo (1925)

NOT SO YOUNG LOVE
Hal Jordan
Jerry Douglas
Rondelay (OB) (1969)

NOT TABU
Ed Tyler
Sweet Miani (OB) (1962)

NOT THAT I CARE
Richard A. Whiting
Oscar Hammerstein II
Free for All (1931)

NOTHIN' FOR NOTHIN'
Morton Gould
Dorothy Fields
Arms and the Girl (1950)

NOTHING AT ALL
Sammy Fain
Dan Shapiro
Ankles Aweigh (1955)

NOTHING BUT A FOOL
Oscar Brown, Jr. and Luis Henrique
Joy (OB) (1970)

NOTHING BUT LOVE
Ray Henderson
B. G. DeSylva and Lew Brown
Manhattan Mary (1927)

NOTHING BUT "YES" IN MY EYES
E. Ray Goetz
Naughty Cinderella (1925)

NOTHING BUT YOU
Richard Rodgers
Lorenz Hart
Higher and Higher (1940)

NOTHING CAN EVER HAPPEN IN NEW YORK
James F. Hanley
Eddie Dowling
Sidewalks of New York (1927)

NOTHING CAN REPLACE A MAN
Sammy Fain
Dan Shapiro
Ankles Aweigh (1955)

NOTHING CAN STOP ME NOW!
Leslie Bricusse and Anthony Newley
The Roar of the Greasepaint—The Smell of the Crowd (1965)

NOTHING COULD BE SWEETER*
Vincent Youmans
Leo Robin and Clifford Grey
Hit the Deck (1927)

NOTHING EVER HAPPENS IN ANGEL'S ROOST
Jerome Moross
John Latouche
The Golden Apple (1954)

NOTHING EVER HAPPENS TILL 2 A.M.
Robert Rosenblum
Robert Rosenblum, Howard Schuman
Up Eden (OB) (1968)

NOTHING IN COMMON
Gordon Duffy
Harry M. Haldane
Happy Town (1959)

NOTHING IN COMMON
Meredith Willson
Here's Love (1963)

NOTHING IS WORKING QUITE RIGHT
Alec Wilder
Arnold Sundgaard
Kittiwake Island (OB) (1960)

NOTHING LEFT BUT DREAMS
Edgar Fairchild
Henry Myers
The New Yorkers (1927)

NOTHING MAN CANNOT DO
Eaton Magoon, Jr.
13 Daughters (1961)

NOTHING MATTERS
Jacques Belasco
Kay Twomey
The Girl from Nantucket (1945)

NOTHING MORE
Michael Leonard
Herbert Martin
The Yearling (1965)

NOTHING MORE TO LOOK FORWARD TO
Richard Adler
Kwamina (1961)

NOTHING TO DO
Armando Trovaioli
Pietro Garinei and Sandro Giovannini
Rugantino (1964)

NOTHING'S WRONG
Richard Rodgers
Lornez Hart
A Connecticut Yankee (1927)

NOTHIN'S GONNA CHANGE
Johnny Brandon
Who's Who, Baby? (OB) (1968)

NOW
Vernon Duke
Ted Fetter
The Show Is On (1936)

NOW
Robert Wright and George Forrest
(based on Grieg)
Song of Norway (1944)

NOW
C. Jackson and James Hatch
Fly Blackbird (OB) (1962)

NOW!
Susan Hulsman Bingham
Myrna Lamb
Mod Donna (OB) (1970)

NOW AND THEN
Mischa and Wesley Portnoff
Donagh MacDonagh
Happy As Larry (1950)

NOW GENERATION, THE
Hal Hester and Danny Apolinar
Your Own Thing (1968)

NOW I HAVE EVERYTHING
Jerry Bock
Sheldon Harnick
Fiddler on the Roof (1964)

NOW I KNOW
Philip Charig

---

*Later published as "Why, Oh Why?"

James Dyrenforth
Nikki (1931)

NOW I KNOW
Harold Arlen
Ted Koehler
Up In Arms (F) (1944)

NOW I KNOW YOUR FACE BY HEART
Bronislaw Kaper (based on Chopin)
John Latouche
Polonaise (1945)

NOW I LAY ME
Helen Miller
Eve Merriam
Inner City (1971)

NOW I'M READY FOR A FRAU
Arthur Schwartz
Howard Dietz
The Gay Life (1961)

NOW IS THE TIME
Max Rich
Jack Scholl
Keep Moving (1934)

NOW IT CAN BE TOLD
Irving Berlin
Alexander's Ragtime Band (F) (1938)

NOW IT'S FALL
Skip Redwine and Larry Frank
Frank Merriwell, or Honor Challenged (1971)

NOW IT'S GONE, GONE, GONE
Dale F. Menten
Dale F. Menten and Frederick Gaines
The House of Leather (OB) (1970)

NOW, MORRIS
John Kander
James Goldman, John Kander, and William Goldman
A Family Affair (1962)

NOW THAT I AM FORTY
Leon Carr
Earl Shuman
The Secret Life of Walter Mitty (OB) (1964)

NOW THAT I'M FREE
Irving Caesar
Irma Hollander
My Dear Public (1943)

NOW THAT I'VE GOT MY STRENGTH
Richard Rodgers
Lorenz Hart
By Jupiter (1942)

NOW YOU HAS JAZZ
Cole Porter
High Society (F) (1956)

NOWHERE TO GO BUT UP
Sol Berkowitz
James Lipton
Nowhere to Go but Up (1962)

NOW'S THE TIME
Jule Styne
Betty Comden and Adolph Green
Hallelujah, Baby! (1967)

NUB OF THE NATION, THE
Helen Miller
Eve Merriam
Inner City (1971)

NUEVO LAREDO
Will Holt
That 5 A.M. Jazz (OB) (1964)

NUMBERS
Gary William Friedman
Will Holt
The Me Nobody Knows (OB) (1970)

NUMBERS
Helen Miller
Eve Merriam
Inner City (1971)

NURSERY
Charles Herbert
Two for Tonight (OB) (1939)

NUTHIN' FOR NUTHIN'
John Dooley
Hobo (OB) (1961)

NUTMEG INSURANCE
Harry Revel
Arnold B. Horwitt
Are You With It? (1945)

O, HEART OF LOVE
Kurt Weill
Paul Green
Johnny Johnson (1936)

O HEART OF MY COUNTRY
Frederic Chopin (adapted by Bronis-
  law Kaper)
John Latouche
Polonaise (1945)

O LEO
Arthur Schwartz
Howard Dietz
At Home Abroad (1935)

O MARRY ME!
Robert Kessler
Lola Permagent
O Marry Me! (OB) (1961)

O PALLAS ATHENE
Joseph Raposo
Erich Segal
Sing Muse! (OB) (1961)

O ROCK ETERNAL
Michael Valenti
John Lewin
Blood Red Roses (1970)

O SAY CAN YOU SEE!
Jack Holmes
Bill Conklin and Bob Miller
O Say Can You See! (OB) (1962)

O SOLE MI—WHOSE SOUL ARE YOU?
Abel Baer
Sam Lewis and Joe Young
Lady Do (1927)

O STOMACH OF MINE, WE EAT!
Francis Thorne
Arnold Weinstein
Fortuna (OB) (1962)

O TIXO, TIXO, HELP ME
Kurt Weill
Maxwell Anderson
Lost in the Stars (1949)

OBEDIAN MARCH
Sol Berkowitz
James Lipton
Miss Emily Adam (OB) (1960)

OBLIVIA
Ernest G. Schweikert
Frank Reardon
Rumple (1957)

OCARINA, THE
Irving Berlin
Call Me Madam (1950)

OCCASIONAL FLIGHT OF FANCY
Jimmy Van Heusen
Sammy Cahn
Skyscraper (1965)

OCCASIONAL MAN, AN
Hugh Martin
Ralph Blane
Girl Rush (F) (1955)

**OCEANOGRAPHY AND OLD AS-
TRONOMY**
Alec Wilder
Arnold Sundgaard
Kittiwake Island (OB) (1960)

OCTOBER
Mischa and Wesley Portnoff
Happy As Larry (1950)

OCTOPUS SONG
Harold Rome
Fanny (1954)

ODE TO A KEY
Sammy Fain
Marilyn and Alan Bergman
Something More! (1964)

ODE TO LOLA
Walter Kent
Kim Gannon
Seventeen (1951)

ODE TO THE BRIDGE
Moose Charlap
Eddie Lawrence
Kelly (1965)

ODDS
Jacques Urbont
Bruce Geller
All in Love (OB) (1961)

ODDS AND ENDS OF LOVE, THE
Sol Berkowitz
James Lipton
Nowhere to Go but Up (1962)

ODE TO MARCELLO
Jerry Blatt
Jerry Blatt and Lonnie Burstein
Have I Got One for You (OB) (1968)

ODE TO THE STYX
Alma Sanders
Monte Carlo
The Houseboat on the Styx (1928)

ODLE-DE-O
Maury Rubens
Clifford Grey
The Madcap (1928)

OF THEE I SING
George Gershwin
Ira Gershwin
Of Thee I Sing (1931)

OF V WE SING
Lou Cooper
Arthur Zipser
Of V We Sing (1942)

OFF AGAIN, ON AGAIN
Vernon Duke
E. Y. Harburg
Walk a Little Faster (1932)

OFF ON A WEEKEND CRUISE
Michael Cleary
Arthur Swanstrom
Sea Legs (1937)

OFF TO GLUCKSTEIN
Lehman Engel
Agnes Morgan
A Hero Is Born (1937)

OFF THE RECORD
Richard Rodgers
Lorenz Hart
I'd Rather Be Right (1937)

OFF TIME
Thomas (Fats) Waller and Harry
  Brooks
Andy Razaf
Hot Chocolates (1929)

OFF TO SEE NEW YORK
Alfred Nathan
George Oppenheimer
The Manhatters (1927)

OFFICE UNDER THE SKY
Robert Holton
June Carroll
Hi, Paisano! (OB) (1961)

OH, BABY
Cliff Friend
Lew Brown
Piggy (1927)

OH, BABY!
Owen Murphy
Rain or Shine (1928)

OH, BESS, OH WHERE'S MY BESS
George Gershwin
Ira Gershwin
Porgy and Bess (1935)

OH, BOY
Albert Hague
Allen Sherman
The Fig Leaves Are Falling (1969)

OH BOY, CAN WE DEDUCT
Lee Wainer
Robert Sour
Sing for Your Supper (1939)

OH, BUT I DO
Arthur Schwartz
Leo Robin
The Time, the Place and the Girl (F)
(1946)

OH, CAPTAIN, MY CAPTAIN
Stan Harte, Jr.
Walt Whitman
Leaves of Grass (OB) (1971)

OH, DE LAWD SHAKE DE HEAVEN
George Gershwin
DuBose Heyward
Porgy and Bess (1935)

OH, DIOGENES
Richard Rodgers
Lorenz Hart
The Boys from Syracuse (1938)

OH, DOCTOR JESUS
George Gershwin
DuBose Heyward and Ira Gershwin
Porgy and Bess (1935)

OH, DONNA CLARA
J. Petersburski
Irving Caesar
The Wonder Bar (1931)

OH, FABULOUS ONE
Kurt Weill
Ira Gershwin
Lady in the Dark (1941)

OH, FOR THE LIFE OF A COWBOY
James F. Hanley
Eddie Dowling
Sidewalks of New York (1927)

OH, GEE!
Bill and Patti Jacob
Jimmy (1969)

OH, GEE! OH JOY!
George Gershwin
Ira Gershwin and P. G. Wodehouse
Rosalie (1928)

OH, GIVE ME THE GOOD OLD DAYS
Harold Rome
Pins and Needles (OB) (1937)

OH, GOSH
Ray Henderson
B.G. DeSylva and Lew Brown
Hold Everything! (1928)

OH, HAPPY DAY
Gene de Paul
Johnny Mercer
Li'l Abner (1956)

OH, HAPPY WE
Leonard Bernstein
Richard Wilbur
Candide (1956)

OH, HOW HAPPY WE'LL BE
Lewis E. Gensler
Robert A. Simon and Clifford Grey
Ups-A-Daisy (1928)

OH, HOW I ADORE YOUR NAME
John Morris
Gerald Freedman
A Time for Singing (1966)

OH, HOW I HATE TO GET UP IN THE MORNING*
Irving Berlin
Yip! Yip! Yaphank (1918)

OH, HOW I LONG TO BELONG TO YOU
Vincent Youmans
B. G. DeSylva
Take a Chance (1932)

OH, HOW I LOVE YOU
George Harwell
What a Killing (OB) (1961)

OH, HOW I MISS YOU BLUES
Lewis E. Gensler
Robert A. Simon and Clifford Grey
Ups-A-Daisy (1928)

---

*Also in *This Is the Army* (1942)

OH, HOW THAT MAN CAN LOVE
Lillian Roth and Herb Magidson
Earl Carroll's Vanities (1928)

OH, HOW UNFORTUNATE YOU MOR-
TALS Be
Allan Roberts
Lester Lee
All for Love (1949)

OH! HOW WE LOVE OUR ALMA MA-
TER
Harry Ruby
Bert Kalmar
The Ramblers (1926)

OH, I CAN'T SIT DOWN
George Gershwin
Ira Gershwin
Porgy and Bess (1935)

OH, KAY
George Gershwin
Ira Gershwin and Howard Dietz
Oh, Kay! (1926)

OH, LADY
Sam Stept
Herb Magidson
George White's Music Hall Varieties
(1932)

OH, LADY BE GOOD!
George Gershwin
Ira Gershwin
Lady, Be Good (1924)

OH, LONELY ONE
Baldwin Bergersen
William Archibald
Carib Song (1945)

OH, LOOK AT ME!
Julian Slade
Dorothy Reynolds and Julian Slade
Salad Days (OB) (1958)

OH ME! OH MY!
Vincent Youmans
Arthur Francis (Ira Gershwin)
Two Little Girls in Blue (1921)

OH, MEIN LIEBCHEN
Arthur Schwartz
Howard Dietz
The Gay Life (1961)

OH, MRS. LARRY
Mischa and Wesley Portnoff
Donagh MacDonagh
Happy As Larry (1950)

OH, MRS. LYNDE
Norman Campbell
Donald Campbell and Norman Camp-
bell
Anne of Green Gables (OB) (1971)

OH, MY AGE
Wally Harper
Paul Zakrzewski
Sensations (OB) (1970)

OH, OH, OH, O'SULLIVAN
Earl Robinson
Waldo Salt
Sandhog (OB) (1954)

OH, PEGGY
Harry Akst
Benny Davis
Artists and Models (1927)

OH, PITY THE MAN
George Fischoff
Verna Tomasson
The Prince and the Pauper (OB)
(1963)

OH, PLEASE
Bob Merrill
Take Me Along (1959)

OH! SAM
J. Fred Coots and Maury Rubens
Clifford Grey
Mayflowers (1925)

OH, SAY, CAN YOU SEE?
Robert Kessler
Martin Charnin
Fallout (OB) (1959)

OH, SKY, GOODBYE
Giuseppe Verdi
Charles Friedman
My Darlin' Aïda (1952)

OH, SO NICE
George Gershwin
Ira Gershwin
Treasure Girl (1928)

OH, THE SHAME
Sol Berkowitz
James Lipton
Miss Emily Adam (OB) (1960)

OH, THEOBOLD, OH, ELMER
Niclas Kempner
Graham John
The Street Singer (1929)

OH, TO BE A MOVIE STAR
Jerry Bock
Sheldon Harnick
The Apple Tree (1966)

OH, WASN'T IT LOVELY?
Harry Archer
Harlan Thompson
Merry-Merry (1925)

OH, WHAT A BEAUTIFUL MORNIN'
Richard Rodgers
Oscar Hammerstein II
Oklahoma! (1943)

OH, WHAT A GIRL
Tom Johnstone
Phil Cook
When You Smile (1925)

OH, WHAT A MAN
Herbert Stothart, Bert Kalmar, and
   Harry Ruby
Good Boy (1928)

OH, WHAT A PLAYMATE YOU COULD MAKE
Leon DeCosta
The Blonde Sinner (1926)

OH, WOE IS ME
Jean Gilbert
Harry Graham
Katja (1926)

OH, YOU!
Milton Susskind
Paul Porter and Benjamin Hapgood
   Burt
Florida Girl (1925)

OH, YOU'RE A WONDERFUL PERSON
Morgan Lewis
Nancy Hamilton
Three to Make Ready (1946)

OHHH! AHHH!
John Green
Edward Heyman
Here Goes the Bride (1931)

OHIO
Leonard Bernstein
Betty Comden and Adolph Green
Wonderful Town (1953)

OHRBACH'S, BLOOMINGDALE'S, BEST AND SAKS
André Previn
Alan Jay Lerner
Coco (1969)

OISGETZAYCHNET
Harold Rome
The Zulu and the Zayda (1965)

O.K. FOR T.V.
Johnny Mercer
Top Banana (1951)

OKAY FOR SOUND
Arthur Schwartz
Dorothy Fields
Stars in Your Eyes (1939)

OKLAHOMA
Richard Rodgers
Oscar Hammerstein II
Oklahoma! (1943)

OL' MAN RIVER
Jerome Kern
Oscar Hammerstein II
Show Boat (1927)

OL' PEASE PUDDIN'
George Fischoff
Carole Bayer
Georgy (1970)

OLD DEVIL MOON
Burton Lane
E. Y. Harburg
Finian's Rainbow (1947)

OLD ENOUGH TO LOVE
Richard Rodgers
Lorenz Hart
Dearest Enemy (1925)

OLD ENOUGH TO LOVE
Arthur Schwartz
Dorothy Fields
By the Beautiful Sea (1954)

OLD ENOUGH TO MARRY
Maury Rubens
Clifford Grey
The Madcap (1928)

OLD-FASHIONED CAKEWALK, THE
Donald Heywood
Africana (1927)

OLD-FASHIONED GARDEN
Cole Porter
Hitchy-Koo (1919)

OLD-FASHIONED GIRL, AN
Richard Rodgers
Edith Meiser
The Garrick Gaieties (1925)

OLD FASHIONED GIRL, AN
Ray Henderson
B. G. DeSylva and Lew Brown
George White's Scandals (1928)

OLD FASHIONED GIRL
Richard Lewine
Arnold B. Horwitt
The Girls Against the Boys (1959)

OLD FASHIONED GIRL
Rick Besoyan
Babes in the Wood (OB) (1964)

OLD-FASHIONED GLIMMER IN YOUR EYE, AN
Jack Lawrence and Don Walker
Courtin' Time (1951)

OLD FASHIONED HUSBAND
Paul Nassau and Oscar Brand
The Education of Hyman Kaplan (1968)

OLD-FASHIONED LOVE
James Johnson
Cecil Mack
Runnin' Wild (1923)

OLD FASHIONED MOTHERS
Sammy Fain
Dan Shapiro
Ankles Aweigh (1955)

OLD FASHIONED SONG
Albert Hague
Allen Sherman
The Fig Leaves Are Falling (1969)

OLD-FASHIONED WEDDING
Lewis E. Gensler
E. Y. Harburg
Ballyhoo (1932)

OLD-FASHIONED WEDDING, AN*
Irving Berlin
Annie Get Your Gun (1966)

OLD-FASHIONED WIFE, AN
Jerome Kern
P. G. Wodehouse
Oh, Boy! (1917)

OLD FLAME NEVER DIES, AN
Arthur Schwartz
Albert Stillman and Laurence Stallings
Virginia (1937)

---

*Added to 1966 revival

OLD FOLKS
Jacques Brel
Eric Blau and Mort Shuman
Jacques Brel Is Alive and Well and Living in Paris (OB) (1968)

OLD FOLKS
John Kander
Fred Ebb
70, Girls, 70 (1971)

OLD JITTERBUG
Jimmy McHugh
Al Dubin
Keep Off the Grass (1940)

OLD JOHN BARLEYCORN
Sigmund Romberg
Dorothy Donnelly
My Maryland (1927)

OLD LONG JOHN
John Morris
Gerald Freedman
A Time for Singing (1966)

OLD LOVE AND BRAND NEW LOVE
Don Walker
Clay Warnick
Memphis Bound (1945)

OLD MAID
Harvey Schmidt
Tom Jones
110 in the Shade (1963)

OLD MAN, AN
Richard Rodgers
Martin Charnin
Two by Two (1970)

OLD MAN DANUBE
Emmerich Kalman
George Marion, Jr.
Marinka (1945)

OLD MAN SHOULDN'T BE BORN, AN
Murray Rumshinsky
Jacob Jacobs
The President's Daughter (1970)

OLD MAN SUBWAY
Robert Russell Bennett
Owen Murphy and Robert A. Simon
Hold Your Horses (1933)

OLD MAN'S DARLING—YOUNG MAN'S SLAVE
Irving Berlin
Louisiana Purchase (1940)

OLD MILITARY CANAL, THE
David Heneker
Half a Sixpence (1965)

OLD PARK BENCH, THE
Jimmy McHugh
Howard Dietz
Keep Off the Grass (1940)

OLD SAYIN'S
Marc Blitzstein
Juno (1959)

OLD SOFT SHOE, THE
Morgan Lewis
Nancy Hamilton
Three to Make Ready (1946)

OLD SPANISH CUSTOM
Harry Revel
Mack Gordon
Smiling Faces (1932)

OLD TIME SWING
Eubie Blake
J. Milton Reddie and Cecil Mack
Swing It (1937)

OLD TIMER
Burton Lane
E. Y. Harburg
Hold On to Your Hats (1940)

OLD WHITE TOM
C. Jackson and James Hatch
Fly Blackbird (OB) (1962)

OLD WORLD CHARM
Duke Ellington
Marshall Barer and Fred Tobias
Pousse-Café (1966)

OLDEST ESTABLISHED, THE
Frank Loesser
Guys and Dolls (1950)

OLDEST TRICK IN THE WORLD, THE
Jay Thompson
Double Entry (OB) (1961)

OLE OLE
Frank Black
Gladys Shelley
The Duchess Misbehaves (1946)

OLIVE TREE, THE
Robert Wright and George Forrest
  (based on Alexander Borodin)
Kismet (1953)

OLIVER!
Lionel Bart
Oliver! (1963)

OLYMPICS, THE
Jacques Offenbach
E. Y. Harburg
The Happiest Girl in the World (1961)

OM MANI PADME HUM
Harry Warren
Jerome Lawrence and Robert E. Lee
Shangri-La (1956)

OMEN BIRD, THE
Heitor Villa-Lobos
Robert Wright and George Forrest
Magdalena (1948)

ON A CLEAR DAY YOU CAN SEE FOREVER
Burton Lane
Alan Jay Lerner
On a Clear Day You Can See Forever (1965)

ON A DAY LIKE THIS
Marc Blitzstein
Juno (1959)

ON A DESERT ISLAND WITH THEE
Richard Rodgers
Lorenz Hart
A Connecticut Yankee (1927)

ON A PONY FOR TWO
James F. Hanley

Gene Buck
Take the Air (1927)

ON A ROOF IN MANHATTAN
Irving Berlin
Face the Music (1932)

ON A SUNDAY BY THE SEA
Jule Styne
Sammy Cahn
High Button Shoes (1947)

ON ACCOUNT OF I LOVE YOU
Philip Charig
James Dyrenforth
Nikki (1931)

ON AND ON AND ON
George Gershwin
Ira Gershwin
Let 'Em Eat Cake (1933)

ON ANY STREET
Ray Henderson
B. G. DeSylva and Lew Brown
Strike Me Pink (1933)

ON, COMRADES
Sigmund Romberg
Harry B. Smith
Princess Flavia (1925)

ON DOUBLE FIFTH AVENUE
Abel Baer
Sam Lewis and Joe Young
Lady Do (1927)

ON LEAVE FOR LOVE
Ann Ronell
Count Me In (1942)

ON LOVE ALONE
Johann Strauss
Desmond Carter
The Great Waltz (1934)

ON MY MIND A NEW LOVE
Joseph Myer and Roger Wolfe Kahn
Irving Caesar
Here's Howe (1928)

ON MY NUDE RANCH WITH YOU
Michael H. Cleary
Max and Nathaniel Lief
Hey Nonny Nonny! (1932)

ON MY OWN
Jule Styne
Betty Comden and Adolph Green
Bells Are Ringing (1956)

ON MY OWN
Nancy Ford
Gretchen Cryer
Now Is the Time for All Good Men
  (OB) (1967)

ON PARADE
Jerome Moross
Paul Peters and George Sklar
Parade (1935)

ON THAT DAY
Robert Wright and George Forrest
(Based on Rachmaninoff)
Anya (1965)

**ON THE ATCHISON, TOPEKA, AND
SANTA FE**
Harry Warren
Johnny Mercer
The Harvey Girls (F) (1946)

ON THE BEACH
Robert Hood Bowers
Francis DeWitt
Oh, Ernest! (1927)

ON THE BORDER LINE
Harry Ruby
Bert Kalmar
Top Speed (1929)

ON THE CAMPUS
Ray Henderson
B. G. DeSylva and Lew Brown
Good News (1927)

ON THE CHARTS
Joseph Martinez Kookoolis and Scott
  Fagan
Scott Fagan
Soon (1971)

**ON THE CORNER OF THE RUE CAM-
BON**
André Previn
Alan Jay Lerner
Coco (1969)

**ON THE DAY WHEN THE WORLD
GOES BOOM**
John Dooley
Hobo (OB) (1961)

ON THE FARM
Bob Merrill
New Girl in Town (1957)

ON THE GOLDEN TRAIL
Vincent Youmans
Oscar Hammerstein II
Rainbow (1928)

ON THE LEVEE
Jimmy Johnson
Henry Creamer
Keep Shufflin' (1928)

ON THE OTHER HAND
Martha Caples
Nancy Hamilton
New Faces (1934)

**ON THE RELATIVE MERITS OF EDU-
CATION AND EXPERIENCE**
Paul Hoffert
David Secter
Get Thee to Canterbury (OB) (1969)

ON THE ROAD
Janet Gari
Toby Garson
Lyle (OB) (1970)

ON THE SEASHORE BY THE SEA
Jane Douglas
Tom O'Malley
Bella (OB) (1961)

ON THE SIDE OF THE ANGELS
Jerry Bock
Sheldon Harnick
Fiorello (1959)

ON THE S.S. BERNARD COHN
Burton Lane
Alan Jay Lerner
On a Clear Day You Can See Forever
(1965)

ON THE STAGE
Carl Millöcker (revised by Theo Mack-
eben)
Rowland Leigh
The Dubarry (1932)

ON THE STREET WHERE YOU LIVE
Frederick Loewe
Alan Jay Lerner
My Fair Lady (1956)

ON THE SUNNY SIDE OF THE STREET
Jimmy McHugh
Dorothy Fields
Lew Leslie's International Revue
(1930)

ON THE WILLOWS
Stephen Schwartz
Godspell (OB) (1971)

ON THE WRONG SIDE OF THE RAIL-
ROAD TRACKS
Duke Ellington
John Latouche
Beggar's Holiday (1946)

ON THIS ROCK
Helen Miller
Eve Merriam
Inner City (1971)

ON THIS WEDDING DAY
Albert Hague
Marty Brill
Café Crown (1964)

ON TO AFRICA!
Sigmund Romberg
Irving Caesar
Melody (1933)

ON TO HOLLYWOOD
James F. Hanley
Eddie Dowling
Honeymoon Lane (1926)

ON TOP
Werner Janssen
Mann Holiner and J. Keirn Brennan
Boom-Boom (1929)

ON WITH THE DANCE
Richard Rodgers
Lorenz Hart
The Garrick Gaieties (1925)

ON WITH THE DANCE
Philip Charig
Irving Caesar
Polly (1929)

ON WITH THE DANCE
Richard Rodgers
Lorenz Hart
Simple Simon (1930)

ON WITH THE SHOW
Frederico Valerio
Elizabeth Miele
Hit the Trail (1954)

ON YOUR TOES
Richard Rodgers
Lorenz Hart
On Your Toes (1936)

ONCE
George Gershwin
Ira Gershwin
Funny Face (1927)

ONCE A YEAR DAY
Richard Adler and Jerry Ross
The Pajama Game (1954)

ONCE IN A BLUE MOON
Jerome Kern
Anne Caldwell
The Stepping Stones (1923)

ONCE IN A BLUE MOON
Rick Besoyan
Little Mary Sunshine (OB) (1959)

ONCE IN A LIFETIME
Jesse Greer
Raymond Klages
Earl Carroll's Vanities (1928)

ONCE IN A LIFETIME
Leslie Bricusse and Anthony Newley
Stop the World—I Want to Get Off
(1962)

ONCE IN A MILLION MOONS*
Jerome Kern
E. Y. Harburg
Can't Help Singing (F) (1944)

ONCE-IN-A-WHILE
Arthur Schwartz
Howard Dietz
Revenge with Music (1934)

ONCE IN LOVE WITH AMY
Frank Loesser
Where's Charley? (1948)

ONCE IN SEPTEMBER
Armand Vecsey
Clifford Grey
The Nightingale (1927)

ONCE IN THE HIGHLANDS
Frederick Loewe
Alan Jay Lerner
Brigadoon (1947)

ONCE IN 2.7 YEARS
Ernest Gold
Anne Croswell
I'm Solomon (1968)

ONCE KNEW A FELLA
Harold Rome
Destry Rides Again (1959)

ONCE, ONLY ONCE
James Bredt
Edward Eager
The Happy Hypocrite (OB) (1968)

ONCE THE MAN YOU LAUGHED AT
Michael Leonard
Herbert Martin
How to Be a Jewish Mother (1967)

ONCE UPON A TIME
Morgan Lewis
Nancy Hamilton
One for the Money (1939)

ONCE UPON A TIME
Franz Steininger (adapted from
  Tchaikovsky)
Forman Brown
Music in My Heart (1947)

ONCE UPON A TIME
Sol Berkowitz
James Lipton
Miss Emily Adam (OB) (1960)

ONCE UPON A TIME
Charles Strouse
Lee Adams
All American (1962)

ONCE UPON A TIME
Johnny Brandon
Cindy (OB) (1964)

ONCE UPON A TIME TODAY
Irving Berlin
Call Me Madam (1950)

ONCE YOU'VE HAD A LITTLE TASTE
John Clifton
John Clifton and Ben Tarver
Man with a Load of Mischief (OB)
  (1966)

ONCE YOU'VE SEEN EVERYTHING
Al Carmines
Rosalyn Drexler
Home Movies (OB) (1964)

ONE
Franz Lehár
Edward Eliscu
Frederika (1937)

ONE ALONE
Sigmund Romberg
Otto Harbach and Oscar Hammer-
  stein II
The Desert Song (1926)

ONE AND TWENTY
Michael Valenti
Just for Love (OB) (1968)

---

*Dropped from film

ONE BABY
Charles Rosoff
Leo Robin
Judy (1927)

ONE BIG HAPPY FAMILY
Kenneth Jacobson
Rhoda Roberts
Show Me Where the Good Times Are
(OB) (1970)

ONE BIG UNION FOR TWO
Harold Rome
Pins and Needles (OB) (1937)

ONE BOY
Charles Strouse
Lee Adams
Bye Bye Birdie (1960)

ONE BOY'S ENOUGH FOR ME
Harold Orlob
Irving Caesar
Talk About Girls (1927)

ONE BRIEF MOMENT
Arthur Schwartz
Dorothy Fields
Stars in Your Eyes (1939)

ONE DAY, ONE DAY, CONGOTAY
Coleridge-Taylor Perkinson
Errol Hill
Man Better Man (OB) (1969)

ONE DAY WE DANCE
Cy Coleman
Carolyn Leigh
Wildcat (1960)

ONE FLAG
Walt Smith
Leon Uris
Ari (1971)

ONE FLOWER GROWS ALONE IN YOUR GARDEN
Sigmund Romberg
Otto Harbach and Oscar Hammerstein II
The Desert Song (1926)

ONE FOOT, OTHER FOOT
Richard Rodgers
Oscar Hammerstein II
Allegro (1947)

ONE FOR ALL
Albert Sirmay and Arthur Schwartz
Arthur Swanstrom
Princess Charming (1930)

ONE FOR MY BABY
Harold Arlen
Johnny Mercer
The Sky's the Limit (F) (1943)

ONE GIRL, THE
Vincent Youmans
Oscar Hammerstein II
Rainbow (1928)

ONE GOLDEN HOUR
Rudolf Friml
Otto Harbach and Oscar Hammerstein II
The Wild Rose (1926)

ONE GOOD FRIEND
Frank Grey
Earle Crooker and McElbert Moore
Happy (1927)

ONE GOOD MAN GONE WRONG
Sigmund Romberg
Otto Harbach and Oscar Hammerstein II
The Desert Song (1926)

ONE HALLOWE'EN
Charles Strouse
Lee Adams
Applause (1970)

ONE HAND, ONE HEART
Leonard Bernstein
Stephen Sondheim
West Side Story (1957)

ONE HEART
Sam H. Stept
Bud Green
Shady Lady (1933)

ONE HOUR AHEAD OF THE POSSE
Philip Charig
Ray Golden and Dave Ormont
Catch a Star! (1955)

ONE HUNDRED EASY WAYS
Leonard Bernstein
Betty Comden and Adolph Green
Wonderful Town (1953)

ONE HUNDRED VIRGINS
Hal Jordan
Jerry Douglas
Rondelay (OB) (1969)

ONE I'M LOOKING FOR, THE
Emmerich Kalman
Harry B. Smith
Countess Maritza (1926)

ONE IN A MILLION
Harry Revel
Mack Gordon
Everybody's Welcome (1931)

ONE IN A MILLION
Harden Church
Edward Heyman
Caviar (1934)

ONE IN A MILLION
Bill and Patti Jacob
Jimmy (1969)

ONE IN MY POSITION
Richard Freitas
Morty Neff and George Mysels
The Difficult Woman (OB) (1962)

ONE INDISPENSABLE MAN, THE
Kurt Weill
Maxwell Anderson
Knickerbocker Holiday (1938)

ONE IS A LONELY NUMBER
Albert Hague
Maurice Valency
Dance Me a Song (1950)

ONE IS A LONELY NUMBER
Fred Samer

Gen Genovese
Buttrio Square (1952)

ONE KIND WORD
Marc Blitzstein
Juno (1959)

ONE KISS
Sigmund Romberg
Oscar Hammerstein II
The New Moon (1928)

ONE LAST KISS
Charles Strouse
Lee Adams
Bye Bye Birdie (1960)

ONE LAST LOVE SONG
Emmerich Kalman
George Marion, Jr.
Marinka (1945)

ONE LIFE TO LIVE
Kurt Weill
Ira Gershwin
Lady in the Dark (1941)

ONE LITTLE BRICK AT A TIME
Jule Styne
Sammy Cahn
Look to the Lilies (1970)

ONE LITTLE GIRL
Tom Johnstone
Phil Cook
When You Smile (1925)

ONE LITTLE WORLD APART
Milton Schafer
Ronny Graham
Bravo Giovanni (1962)

ONE LONG LAST LOOK
Sammy Fain
Marilyn and Alan Bergman
Something More! (1964)

ONE LOVE
Vincent Youmans
Billy Rose and Edward Eliscu
Great Day! (1929)

ONE LOVE
Harold Arlen
Ted Koehler
Earl Carroll's Vanities (1930)

ONE MAN
George Gershwin
Gus Kahn and Ira Gershwin
Show Girl (1929)

ONE MAN
Lance Mulcahy
Paul Cherry
Park (1970)

ONE MAN
Helen Miller
Eve Merriam
Inner City (1971)

ONE MAN AIN'T QUITE ENOUGH
Harold Arlen
Harold Arlen and Truman Capote
House of Flowers (1954)

ONE MAN I NEED, THE
Robert Stolz
Rowland Leigh
Night of Love (1941)

ONE MAN'S DEATH IS ANOTHER
MAN'S LIVING
Kurt Weill
Ira Gershwin
The Firebrand of Florence (1945)

ONE MISTY, MOISTY MORNING
Helen Miller
Eve Merriam
Inner City (1971)

ONE MOMENT ALONE
Jerome Kern
Otto Harbach
The Cat and the Fiddle (1931)

ONE MORE DANCE
Jerome Kern
Oscar Hammerstein II
Music in the Air (1932)

ONE MORE DAY
Sol Kaplan
Edward Eliscu
The Banker's Daughter (OB) (1962)

ONE MORE FOR THE LAST ONE
Stan Freeman and Franklin Underwood
Lovely   Ladies,   Kind   Gentlemen
(1970)

ONE MORE KISS
Stephen Sondheim
Follies (1971)

ONE MORE TIME
Joseph Martinez Kookoolis and Scott
Fagan
Scott Fagan
Soon (1971)

ONE MOTHER EACH
Moose Charlap
Norman Gimbel
The Conquering Hero (1961)

ONE NIGHT
H. Maurice Jacquet
Preston Sturges
The Well of Romance (1930)

ONE NIGHT IN THE RAIN
Alma Sanders
Monte Carlo
Mystery Moon (1930)

ONE NIGHT OF LOVE
Maury Rubens
J. Keirn Brennan
A Night in Venice (1929)

ONE OF A KIND
Charles Strouse
Lee Adams
Applause (1970)

ONE OF THESE FINE DAYS
Harold Rome
Sing Out the News (1938)

ONE OF THOSE DAYS
Billy Barnes
The Billy Barnes Revue (1959)

ONE OF THOSE MOMENTS
Elmer Bernstein
Carolyn Leigh
How Now, Dow Jones (1967)

ONE OF US SHOULD BE TWO
Richard Rodgers
Lorenz Hart
Betsy (1926)

ONE PERFECT MOMENT
Marshall Barer, Dean Fuller, and Leslie Julian-Jones
New Faces (1956)

ONE PERSON
Jerry Herman
Dear World (1969)

ONE PROMISE
Michael Leonard
Herbert Martin
The Yearling (1965)

ONE ROOM
Jerry Bock
Sheldon Harnick
The Rothschilds (1970)

ONE SECOND OF SEX
John Green
Edward Heyman
Here Goes the Bride (1931)

ONE SIDE OF WORLD
Stan Freeman and Franklin Underwood
Lovely Ladies, Kind Gentlemen (1970)

ONE STEP NEARER THE MOON
Joseph Meyer
William Moll
Jonica (1930)

ONE STEP TO HEAVEN
Jesse Greer

Raymond Klages
Say When (1928)

ONE STEP—TWO STEP
Harold Arlen
Johnny Mercer
Saratoga (1959)

ONE SUNNY DAY
Jean Schwartz
Clifford Grey and William Cary Duncan
Sunny Days (1928)

ONE SWEET MOMENT
Deed Meyer
She Shall Have Music (OB) (1959)

1001
Peter Link and C.C. Courtney
Salvation (OB) (1969)

ONE TOUCH OF ALCHEMY
Kurt Weill
Maxwell Anderson
Knickerbocker Holiday (1938)

ONE TOUCH OF VENUS
Kurt Weill
Ogden Nash
One Touch of Venus (1943)

ONE TOUCH OF VIENNA
Emmerich Kalman
George Marion, Jr.
Marinka (1945)

ONE TRACK MIND
Morton Gould
Betty Comden and Adolph Green
Billion Dollar Baby (1945)

ONE, TWO
Helen Miller
Eve Merriam
Inner City (1971)

ONE! TWO! THREE!
Sonny Burke
Paul Francis Webster and Ray Golden
Alive and Kicking (1950)

ONE, TWO, THREE
Coleridge-Taylor Perkinson
Errol Hill
Man Better Man (OB) (1969)

ONE WAY STREET
Walter Donaldson
Ballard MacDonald
Sweetheart Time (1926)

ONE WIFE
Richard Adler
Kwamina (1961)

ONE WORD LED TO ANOTHER
Hal Borne
Ray Golden
Alive and Kicking (1950)

ONE YOU LOVE, THE
Frank Grey
McElbert Moore and Frank Grey
The Matinee Girl (1926)

ONGSAY AND ANCEDAY
Richard Rodgers
Lorenz Hart
Heads Up! (1929)

ONLY A DAY DREAM
Walter Cool
Mackey of Appalachia (OB) (1965)

ONLY A DREAM
Edward Kunneke (based on Offen-
bach)
Harry B. Smith
The Love Song (1925)

ONLY A MAN
Howard Blankman
By Hex (OB) (1956)

ONLY A PASSING PHASE
Sandy Wilson
Valmouth (OB) (1960)

ONLY A ROSE
Rudolf Friml
Brian Hooker
The Vagabond King (1925)

ONLY A SMILE
Jean Gilbert
Harry B. Smith
The Red Rose (1928)

ONLY ANOTHER BOY AND GIRL
Cole Porter
Seven Lively Arts (1944)

ONLY BOY, THE
Harold Orlob
Irving Caesar
Talk About Girls (1927)

ONLY DANCE I KNOW, THE
Irving Berlin
Mr. President (1962)

ONLY FOR AMERICANS
Irving Berlin
Miss Liberty (1949)

**ONLY GAME THAT I WOULD PLAY,
THE**
H. Maurice Jacquet
William Brady
The Silver Swan (1929)

ONLY IF YOU'RE IN LOVE
Johnny Mercer
Top Banana (1951)

ONLY LOVE
Jerry Herman
Madame Aphrodite (OB) (1961)

ONLY LOVE
John Kander
Fred Ebb
Zorbá (1968)

ONLY MORE!
Lionel Bart
La Strada (1969)

ONLY ONE
Sigmund Romberg
Harry B. Smith
Princess Flavia (1925)

ONLY ONE
Frank Grey
McElbert Moore and Frank Grey
The Matinee Girl (1926)

ONLY ONE, THE
Johann Strauss II, adapted by Oscar
 Straus
Clare Kummer
Three Waltzes (1937)

ONLY ONE, THE
Lee Pockriss
Anne Croswell
Tovarich (1963)

ONLY ONE FOR ME, THE
Lewis E. Gensler
B. G. DeSylva
Captain Jinks (1925)

ONLY ONE FOR ME, THE
Harry Akst
Benny Davis
Artists and Models (1927)

ONLY RAINBOWS
Moose Charlap
Norman Gimbel
The Conquering Hero (1961)

ONLY TIME WILL TELL
Harold Rome
Destry Rides Again (1959)

OO, HOW I LOVE YOU
Harold Orlob
Irving Caesar
Talk About Girls (1927)

OOF DAH MAN, THE
C. Luckey Roberts
Alex C. Rogers
My Magnolia (1926)

OOH, DO YOU LOVE YOU!
Charles Strouse
Lee Adams
(It's a Bird, It's a Plane) It's Superman
 (1966)

OOH, I'M THINKING
Ray Henderson
B. G. DeSylva and Lew Brown
Strike Me Pink (1933)

OOH, MAYBE IT'S YOU
Irving Berlin
Ziegfeld Follies (1927)

OOH, MY FEET
Frank Loesser
The Most Happy Fella (1956)

OOH, OOH, OOH, WHAT YOU DO TO
ME
Walter Kent
Kim Gannon
Seventeen (1951)

OOH! THAT KISS
Harry Warren
Mort Dixon and Joe Young
The Laugh Parade (1931)

OOH! WHAT YOU SAID
Hoagy Carmichael
Johnny Mercer
Walk With Music (1940)

OOM-PAH-PAH
Lionel Bart
Oliver! (1963)

OOOO-EEEE
Paul Nassau and Oscar Brand
The Education of Hyman Kaplan
 (1968)

OPEN A NEW WINDOW
Jerry Herman
Mame (1966)

OPEN AND SHUT IDEA
Emile Berté and Maury Rubens
J. Keirn Brennan
Music in May (1929)

OPEN BOOK
Joseph Meyer
Edward Eliscu
Lady Fingers (1929)

OPEN THAT DOOR
J. C. Johnson
Change Your Luck (1930)

OPEN THE GATES OF MADRID
Morris Hamilton
Grace Henry
Earl Carroll's Vanities (1926)

OPEN THE WINDOW
Norman Campbell
Donald Campbell and Normal Campbell
Anne of Green Gables (OB) (1971)

OPEN UP YOUR HEART
Vincent Youmans
Billy Rose and Edward Eliscu
Great Day! (1929)

OPEN YOUR EYES
Burton Lane
Alan Jay Lerner
Royal Wedding (F) (1951)

OPEN YOUR WINDOW
Emile Berté and Maury Rubens
J. Keirn Brennan
Music in May (1929)

OPENING FOR A PRINCESS, AN
Mary Rodgers
Marshall Barer
Once Upon a Mattress (OB) (1959)

OPENING FOR EVERYBODY, AN
Jay Gorney
Jean and Walter Kerr
Touch and Go (1949)

OPENING NIGHT
Lee Wainer
Robert Sour
Sing for Your Supper (1939)

OPERA STAR
Hal Jordan
Jerry Douglas
Rondelay (OB) (1969)

OPPORTUNITY!
Gordon Duffy
Harry M. Haldane
Happy Town (1959)

OPPOSITE SEX, THE
Michael Cleary
Arthur Swanstrom
Sea Legs (1937)

OPPOSITES
Jimmy Van Heusen
Sammy Cahn
Skyscraper (1965)

OR WHAT HAVE YOU?
Morris Hamilton
Grace Henry
The Little Show (1929)

ORANGE BLOSSOM HOME
Raymond Hubbell
Anne Caldwell
Three Cheers (1928)

ORANGE BLOSSOMS
Jean Schwartz
Clifford Grey and William Cary Duncan
Sunny Days (1928)

ORANGE GROVE IN CALIFORNIA, AN
Irving Berlin
Music Box Revue (1923)

ORANGES
Milton Susskind
Paul Porter and Benjamin Hapgood Burt
Florida Girl (1925)

ORCHIDS
Donald Heywood
Black Rhythm (1936)

ORCHIDS IN THE MOONLIGHT
Vincent Youmans
Edward Eliscu and Gus Kahn
Flying Down to Rio (F) (1933)

ORDINARY COUPLE, AN
Richard Rodgers
Oscar Hammerstein II
The Sound of Music (1959)

ORDINARY GUY
Harold Rome
Sing Out the News (1938)

ORDINARY PEOPLE
Richard Adler
Kwamina (1961)

ORE FROM A GOLD MINE
Duke Ellington
John Latouche
Beggar's Holiday (1946)

ORIENTAL MEMORIES
Alfred Goodman, Maury Rubens, and
  J. Fred Coots
Clifford Grey
Artists and Models (1925)

ORIENTAL MOON
Jerome Kern
Oscar Hammerstein II
Sweet Adeline (1929)

ORIENTAL NIGHTS
Mann Holiner
Alberta Nichols
Gay Paree (1926)

ORIGINAL SIN
Don McAfee
Nancy Leeds
Great Scot! (OB) (1965)

ORPHAN IN THE STORM
Harvey Schmidt
Tom Jones
Celebration (1969)

ORTHODOX FOOL, AN
Richard Rodgers
No Strings (1962)

OTHER FELLOW'S GIRL, THE
Percy Wenrich
Raymond Peck
Castles in the Air (1926)

OTHER GENERATION, THE
Richard Rodgers
Oscar Hammerstein II
Flower Drum Song (1958)

OTHER HALF OF ME, THE
Jack Lawrence and Stan Freeman
I Had a Ball (1964)

OTHER HANDS, OTHER HEARTS
Harold Rome
Fanny (1954)

OTHER ONE, THE
Arthur Siegel
June Carroll
New Faces (1962)

OTHER SIDE OF THE TRACKS, THE
Cy Coleman
Carolyn Leigh
Little Me (1962)

OTHER SIDE OF THE WALL, THE
Bruce Montgomery
The Amorous Flea (OB) (1964)

OUI, OUI
Alberta Nichols
Mann Holiner
Angela (1928)

OUR ANCIENT LIBERTIES
Kurt Weill
Maxwell Anderson
Knickerbocker Holiday (1938)

OUR BRIDAL NIGHT
Sigmund Romberg
Dorothy Donnelly
My Princess (1927)

OUR BUSINESS IS NEWS
Eddie Stuart
Harvey Lasker
Old Bucks and New Wings (OB)
  (1962)

OUR CHILD
C. Luckey Roberts
Alex C. Rogers
My Magnolia (1926)

OUR CHILDREN
Charles Strouse
Lee Adams
All American (1962)

OUR CROWN
Cole Porter
Jubilee (1935)

OUR FIRST KISS
Sammy Fain
Jack Yellen
George White's Scandals (1939)

OUR HOME
Richard Lewine
Ted Fetter
The Girl from Wyoming (OB) (1938)

OUR JIMMY
Bill and Patti Jacob
Jimmy (1969)

OUR LANGUAGE OF LOVE
Marguerite Monnot
Julian More, David Heneker, and
    Monte Norman
Irma La Douce (1960)

OUR LAST WALTZ TOGETHER
Oscar Straus
Clare Kummer
Three Waltzes (1937)

OUR LITTLE CAPTAIN
George Gershwin
Ira Gershwin
Tip-Toes (1925)

OUR LITTLE KINGDOM
Rudolf Friml
Otto Harbach and Oscar Hammer-
    stein II
The Wild Rose (1926)

OUR LITTLE LADY UPSTAIRS
Sigmund Romberg
Irving Caesar
Melody (1933)

OUR LITTLE SECRET
Burt Bacharach
Hal David
Promises, Promises (1968)

OUR LOVE HAS FLOWN AWAY
Rick Besoyan
The Student Gypsy (OB) (1963)

OUR OWN WAY OF GOING ALONG
George M. Cohan
The Mery Malones (1927)

OUR SONG
Jerome Kern
Dorothy Fields
When You're in Love (F) (1937)

OUR SONG
Maria Grever
Raymond Leveen
Viva O'Brien (1941)

OUR STATE FAIR
Richard Rodgers
Oscar Hammerstein II
State Fair (F) (1945)

OUR TOWN
James Shelton
The Straw Hat Revue (1939)

OUR WEDDING DAY
Irving Berlin
As Thousands Cheer (1933)

OURS
Cole Porter
Red, Hot and Blue! (1936)

OUSING CHA-CHA, THE
C. Jackson and James Hatch
Fly Blackbird (OB) (1962)

OUT FOR NO GOOD
Philip Charig
Dan Shapiro and Milton Pascal
Follow the Girls (1944)

OUT IN THE OPEN AIR
Burton Lane
Howard Dietz
Three's a Crowd (1930)

OUT IN THE SUN
Franz Lehár
Edward Eliscu
Frederika (1937)

OUT OF BREATH
Everett Miller
Johnny Mercer
The Garrick Gaieties (1930)

OUT OF BREATH
Julian Slade
Dorothy Reynolds and Julian Slade
Salad Days (OB) (1958)

OUT OF LUCK WITH LUCK
George Harwell
What a Killing (OB) (1961)

OUT OF MY DREAMS
Richard Rodgers
Oscar Hammerstein II
Oklahoma! (1943)

OUT OF SIGHT, OUT OF MIND
John Mundy
Edward Eager
The Liar (1950)

OUT OF SIGHT, OUT OF MIND
Sol Berkowitz
James Lipton
Nowhere to Go but Up (1962)

OUT OF THE BLUE
Jerome Kern
Oscar Hammerstein II
Sweet Adeline (1929)

OUT OF THE CLEAR BLUE SKY
Vernon Duke
Ogden Nash
Two's Company (1952)

OUT OF A CLEAR BLUE SKY
Harold Arlen
Ted Koehler
Earl Carroll's Vanities (1930)

OUT OF THE WAY
Sigmund Romberg (developed by Don Walker)
Leo Robin
The Girl in Pink Tights (1954)

OUT OF THIS WORLD
Harold Arlen
Johnny Mercer
Out of This World (F) (1945)

OUT OF TOWN
Earl Wilson, Jr.
A Day in the Life of Just About Everyone (OB) (1971)

OUT OF TOWN BUYERS
Albert Von Tilzer
Neville Fleeson
Bye Bye, Bonnie (1927)

OUT ON THE LOOSE
Harry Tierney
Joseph McCarthy
Rio Rita (1927)

OUT TO LAUNCH
Joseph Raposo
Erich Segal
Sing Muse! (OB) (1961)

OUT WHERE THE BLUES BEGIN
Jimmy McHugh
Dorothy Fields
Hello Daddy (1928)

OUTDOOR MAN FOR MY INDOOR SPORTS, AN
Ray Henderson
B. G. DeSylva and Lew Brown
Hold Everything! (1928)

OUTRACING LIGHT
Wally Harper
Paul Zakrzewski
Sensations (OB) (1970)

OUTSIDE LOOKING IN
Harry Archer
Edward Eliscu
Sweet and Low (1930)

OUTSIDE OF THAT I LOVE YOU
Irving Berlin
Louisiana Purchase (1940)

OVER A GARDEN WALL
Con Conrad
William B. Friedlander
Mercenary Mary (1925)

OVER AND OVER
Hugh Martin
Make a Wish (1951)

OVER AND OVER
Jerry Herman
I Feel Wonderful (OB) (1954)

OVER AND OVER AGAIN
Richard Rodgers
Lorenz Hart
Jumbo (1935)

OVER FORTY
Robert Holton
June Carroll
Hi, Paisano! (OB) (1961)

OVER HERE
J. Fred Coots
Arthur Swanstrom and Benny Davis
Sons o' Fun (1929)

OVER HERE
Arthur Schwartz
Howard Dietz
Jennie (1963)

OVER IN EUROPE
Kurt Weill
Paul Green
Johnny Johnson (1936)

OVER THE GARDEN WALL
Robert Hood Bowers
Francis DeWitt
Oh, Ernest! (1927)

OVER THE RAINBOW*
Harold Arlen
E. Y. Harburg
The Wizard of Oz (F) (1939)

OVER THE RIVER AND INTO THE WOODS
Jack Holmes
New Faces (1962)

OVERFLOW
George Gershwin
DuBose Heyward
Porgy and Bess (1935)

OVERNIGHT
Louis Alter
Billy Rose and Charlotte Kent
Sweet and Low (1930)

OVERSPEND
Richard Lewine
Arnold B. Horwitt
The Girls Against the Boys (1959)

OXFORD BAGS
Philip Braham
Arthur Wimperis
Charlot's Revue (1926)

OXFORD DAYS
Alfred Goodman
Clifford Grey
Sky High (1925)

OYEZ, OYEZ, OYEZ
George Gershwin
Ira Gershwin
Let 'Em Eat Cake (1933)

OZARKS ARE CALLING ME HOME, THE
Cole Porter
Red, Hot and Blue! (1936)

PABLO
Sigmund Romberg
Irving Caesar
Nina Rosa (1930)

PACK UP YOUR BLUES AND SMILE
Peter de Rose and Albert Von Tilzer
Jo Trent
Yes, Yes, Yvette (1927)

———
*Academy Award Winner

PACK UP YOUR SINS AND GO TO THE
DEVIL
Irving Berlin
Music Box Revue (1922)

PADDY MacNEIL AND HIS AUTOMO-
BILE
Noël Coward
The Girl Who Came to Supper (1963)

PADLOCK YOUR BLUES
Ray Perkins
Max and Nathaniel Lief
The Greenwich Village Follies (1928)

PADUCAH
Shelley Mowell
Mike Stewart
Shoestring Revue (OB) (1955)

PAGEANT SONG
Norman Campbell
Donald Campbell and Norman Camp-
bell
Anne of Green Gables (OB) (1971)

PAINT A RAINBOW
Ervin Drake
What Makes Sammy Run? (1964)

PAINT ME A RAINBOW
Sam Pottle
Tom Whedon
All Kinds of Giants (OB) (1961)

PAINTING A VANITIES GIRL
Ernie Golden
Earl Carroll's Vanities (1928)

PAJAMA GAME, THE
Richard Adler and Jerry Ross
The Pajama Game (1954)

PAL JOEY
Richard Rodgers
Lorenz Hart
Pal Joey (1940)

PALACE OF DREAMS
Albert Sirmay and Arthur Schwartz
Arthur Swanstrom
Princess Charming (1930)

PALE VENETIAN MOON, THE
Jerome Kern
Anne Caldwell
The Bunch and Judy (1922)

PALM BEACH BABY
Herman Hupfeld
A la Carte (1927)

PALM BEACH WALK
Walter G. Samuels
Morrie Ryskind
Ned Wayburn's Gambols (1929)

PALOMINO PAL
John Kander
Fred Ebb
Flora, the Red Menace (1965)

PALS OF THE PENTAGON
Harold Rome
Alive and Kicking (1950)

PANACHE
Jule Styne
E. Y. Harburg
Darling of the Day (1968)

PANASSOCIATIVE
Susan Hulsman Bingham
Myrna Lamb
Mod Donna (OB) (1970)

PANIC
Elmer Bernstein
Carolyn Leigh
How Now, Dow Jones (1967)

PANIC IN PANAMA
Harry Ruby
Bert Kalmar
High Kickers (1941)

PANIC'S ON, THE
Albert Sirmay and Arthur Schwartz
Arthur Swanstrom
Princess Charming (1930)

PANISSE AND SON
Harold Rome
Fanny (1954)

PANSIES ON PARADE
Porter Grainger
Fast and Furious (1931)

PANSY
Maceo Pinkard
Pansy (1929)

PANTALETTES
Carl Millöcker (revised by Theo Mack-
    eben)
Rowland Leigh
The Dubarry (1932)

PAPA LIKES A HOT PAPOOSE
Jay Gorney
E. Y. Harburg
Earl Carroll's Sketch Book (1929)

PAPA-DE-DA-DA
Spencer Williams, Clarence Todd,
    and Clarence Williams
Blackbirds (1930)

PAPA, LET'S DO IT AGAIN
Johnny Brandon
Cindy (OB) (1964)

PAPA LEWIS, MAMA GREEN
Harold Rome
Pins and Needles (OB) (1937)

PAPA, WON'T YOU DANCE WITH ME?
Jule Styne
Sammy Cahn
High Button Shoes (1947)

PAPA'S GOT A JOB
Ned Lehak
Robert Sour
Sing for Your Supper (1939)

PAPA'S RETURN
Ann Ronell
Count Me In (1942)

PAPER MATCHES
Alyn Heim
Malcolm L. LaPrade
Will the Mail Train Run Tonight?
    (OB) (1964)

PAPER OF GOLD
Eaton Magoon, Jr.
13 Daughters (1961)

PAPER TIGER
Earl Wilson, Jr.
*A Day in the Life of Just About Every-
    one* (OB) (1971)

PAPERS, THE
Harry Ruby
Bert Kalmar
Top Speed (1929)

PARADE IN TOWN, A
Stephen Sondheim
Anyone Can Whistle (1964)

PARADE NIGHT
Will Irwin
Norman Zeno
The Show Is On (1936)

**PARADE OF THE CHRISTMAS DIN-
NER**
C. Luckey Roberts
Alex C. Rogers
My Magnolia (1926)

PARADE OF THE WOODEN SOLDIERS
Leon Jessel
Chauve-Souris (1922)

PARADISE STOLEN
Sigmund Romberg
Rowland Leigh
My Romance (1948)

PARDON ME, SIR
Irving Burgie
Ballad for Bimshire (OB) (1963)

PARDON ME WHILE I DANCE
John Jennings
Riverwind (OB) (1962)

PARDON MY ENGLISH
George Gershwin
Ira Gershwin
Pardon My English (1933)

PARDON OUR FRENCH
Victor Young
Edward Heyman
Pardon Our French (1950)

PAREE
Johann Strauss II, adapted by Oscar
  Straus
Clare Kummer
Three Waltzes (1937)

PAREE HAS THE FEVER NOW
Vincent Valentini
Parisiana (1928)

PAREE, WHAT DID YOU DO TO ME?
Cole Porter
Fifty Million Frenchmen (1929)

PARIS
E. Ray Goetz and Louis Alter
Paris (1928)

PARIS, FRANCE
Hugh Martin
Make a Wish (1951)

PARIS GOWN
Jule Styne
Bob Hilliard
Hazel Flagg (1953)

PARIS GREEN
Vincent Valentini
Parisiana (1928)

PARIS IS A LONELY TOWN
Harold Arlen
E. Y. Harburg
Gay Purr-ee (F) (1961)

PARIS LOVES LOVERS
Cole Porter
Silk Stockings (1955)

PARIS ORIGINAL
Frank Loesser
*How to Succeed in Business without
  Really Trying* (1961)

PARIS SINGS AGAIN
Paul Durand
Harry Graham
Yours Is my Heart (1946)

PARIS TAUGHT ME 'ZIS
Abel Baer
Sam Lewis and Joe Young
Lady Do (1927)

PARIS WAKES UP AND SMILES
Irving Berlin
Miss Liberty (1949)

PARISIAN PIERROT
Noël Coward
Charlot's Revue (1924)

PARISIANA ROSES
Vincent Valentini
Parisiana (1928)

PARISIANS, THE
Frederick Loewe
Alan Jay Lerner
Gigi (F) (1958)

PARK
Lance Mulcahy
Paul Cherry
Park (1970)

PARK AVENUE STRUT
Phil Baker and Maury Rubens
Moe Jaffe and Harold Atteridge
Pleasure Bound (1929)

PARK AVENUE'S GOING TO TOWN
Edgar Fairchild
Milton Pascal
The Illustrators' Show (1936)

PARKING METER LIKE ME, A
Menachem Zur
Herbert Appleman
Unfair to Goliath (OB) (1970)

PARNASSE
Claude Leveilee
Gladys Shelley
Gogo Loves You (OB) (1964)

PART OF THE CROWD
Maury Laws
Jules Bass
Month of Sundays (OB) (1968)

PARTNERS
Jordan Ramin
Frank H. Stanton and Murray Semos
Look Where I'm At! (OB) (1971)

PARTY GETS GOING, THE
Richard Rodgers
Oscar Hammerstein II
Pipe Dream (1955)

PARTY SONG
Tommy Wolf
Fran Landesman
The Nervous Set (1959)

PARTY TALK
Sammy Fain
Marilyn and Alan Bergman
Something More! (1964)

PARTY THAT WE'RE GONNA HAVE TOMORROW NIGHT, THE
Richard Rodgers
Oscar Hammerstein II
Pipe Dream (1955)

PARTY'S ON THE HOUSE, THE
David Heneker
Half a Sixpence (1965)

PARTY'S OVER, THE
Jule Styne
Betty Comden and Adolph Green
Bells Are Ringing (1956)

PARTY'S OVER NOW, THE
Noël Coward
Set to Music (1939)

PASS THAT PEACE PIPE
Roger Edens, Hugh Martin, and Ralph Blane
Good News (F) (1947)

PASS THE FOOTBALL
Leonard Bernstein
Betty Comden and Adolph Green
Wonderful Town (1953)

PASSATELLA (THE DRINKING GAME)
Armando Trovaioli
Pietro Garinei and Sandro Giovannini
Rugantino (1964)

PASSENGER'S ALWAYS RIGHT, THE
Noël Coward
Sail Away (1961)

PASSIN' THROUGH
Robert Rosenblum
Robert Rosenblum, Howard Schuman
Up Eden (OB) (1968)

PASSING OF TIME, THE
Al Carmines
Maria Irene Fornes
Promenade (OB) (1969)

PAST MY PRIME
Gene de Paul
Johnny Mercer
Li'l Abner (1956)

PATIENCE
Norman Dean
Autumn's Here (OB) (1966)

PATIENCE AND GENTLENESS
Richard Freitas
Morty Neff and George Mysels
The Difficult Woman (OB) (1962)

PATIENTLY SMILING
Franz Lehár
Harry Graham
Yours Is My Heart (1946)

PATSY
Steve Allen
Sophie (1963)

PAY DAY
C. Luckey Roberts
Alex C. Rogers
My Magnolia (1926)

PAY DAY
Sigmund Romberg
Irving Caesar
Nina Rosa (1930)

PAY DAY PAULINE
Vincent Youmans
Otto Harbach
No, No, Nanette (1925)

PAY HEED
Vernon Duke
John Latouche
Cabin in the Sky (1940)

PAY, PAY, PAY
Bill Mahoney
My Wife and I (OB) (1966)

PAYADOR
Sigmund Romberg
Irving Caesar
Nina Rosa (1930)

PAYDAY
Arthur Schwartz
Dorothy Fields
A Tree Grows in Brooklyn
(1951)

PAYING OFF
Dave Stamper
Fred Herendeen
Orchids Preferred (1937)

PEACE, BROTHER
Jimmy Van Heusen
Eddie De Lange
Swingin' the Dream (1939)

PEACE COME TO EVERY HEART
John Morris
Gerald Freedman
A Time for Singing (1966)

PEACE LOVE AND GOOD DAMN
Ron Steward and Neal Tate
Ron Steward
Sambo (OB) (1969)

PEACH ON THE BEACH
Vincent Youmans
Otto Harbach
No, No, Nanette (1925)

PEANUT SONG
Al Carmines
Rosalyn Drexler
Home Movies (OB) (1964)

PEANUTS AND KISSES
Robert Russell Bennett
Owen Murphy and Robert A. Simon
Hold Your Horses (1933)

PEAR TREE QUINTET
Richard Hill and John Hawkins
Nevill Coghill
Canterbury Tales (1969)

PEARL OF BROADWAY
Jerome Kern
Bert Kalmar and Harry Ruby
Lucky (1927)

PEARLS
Galt MacDermot
John Guare
Two Gentlemen of Verona (1971)

PEBBLE WALTZ
Paul Klein
Fred Ebb
Morning Sun (OB) (1963)

PECULIAR STATE OF AFFAIRS
Ernest G. Schweikert
Frank Reardon
Rumple (1957)

PEDRO, ICHABOD
George Lessner
Miriam Battista and Russell Maloney
Sleepy Hollow (1948)

PEEPIN' TOMMY
Vincent Valentini
Parisiana (1928)

PENALTY OF LOVE, THE
Porter Grainger
Donald Heywood
Hot Rhythm (1930)

PENNY CANDY
Arthur Siegel
June Carroll
New Faces (1952)

PENNY FOR YOUR THOUGHTS, A
Vernon Duke
E. Y. Harburg
Walk a Little Faster (1932)

PENNY FRIEND, THE
William Roy
The Penny Friend (OB) (1966)

PENNY PLAIN, TWOPENCE COLORED
Robert Wright and George Forrest
Kean (1961)

PENTS-UN-WRECKUM
Al Carmines
Rosalyn Drexler
Home Movies (OB) (1964)

PEOPLE
Jule Styne
Bob Merrill
Funny Girl (1964)

PEOPLE IN LOVE
William Roy
Maggie (1953)

PEOPLE IN THE STREET, THE
Earl Wilson, Jr.
*A Day in the Life of Just About Every-
   one* (OB) (1971)

PEOPLE OF TASTE
Martha Caples
Nancy Hamilton
New Faces (1934)

PEOPLE WATCHERS
Bob Merrill
Henry, Sweet Henry (1967)

PEOPLE WHO ARE NICE
Jimmy Van Heusen
Sammy Cahn
Walking Happy (1966)

PEOPLE WILL SAY WE'RE IN LOVE
Richard Rodgers
Oscar Hammerstein II
Oklahoma! (1943)

PEOPLE'S CHOICE, THE
Norman Martin
Fred Ebb
Put It in Writing (OB) (1963)

PEP
Sigmund Romberg
Arthur Wimperis
Louie the 14th (1925)

PEPPER AND SALT
Alma Sanders
Monte Carlo
Mystery Moon (1930)

PERCOLATIN'
J. C. Johnson
Change Your Luck (1930)

PERCUSSION
Don Elliott
James Costigan
The Beast in Me (1963)

PERCY WITH PERSEVERANCE
Edward Ward
George Waggoner
Tattle Tales (1933)

PERENNIAL DEBUTANTES
Cole Porter
Red, Hot and Blue! (1936)

PERFECT EVENING, A
Glenn Paxton
Robert Goldman and George Weiss
First Impressions (1959)

PERFECT MAN
Stefan Kanfer, Jess J. Korman, and Jo-
   seph Grayhon
I Want You (OB) (1961)

PERFECT YOUNG LADIES
Sandy Wilson
The Boy Friend (1954)

PERFECTION
Lee Pockriss
Anne Croswell
Ernest in Love (OB) (1960)

PERFECTLY CHARMING VISIT, A
Philip Springer
Joan Javits
Hotel Passionato (OB) (1965)

PERFECTLY LOVELY COUPLE
Richard Rodgers
Stephen Sondheim
Do I Hear a Waltz? (1965)

PERFECTLY MARVELOUS
John Kander
Fred Ebb
Cabaret (1966)

PERFUME OF LOVE, THE*
Cole Porter
Silk Stockings (1955)

PERISH THE BAUBLES
Robert Kessler
Lola Permagent
O Marry Me! (OB) (1961)

PERNAMBUCO
Frank Loesser
Where's Charley? (1948)

PERSIAN WAY OF LIFE, THE
Don Walker
George Marion, Jr.
Allah Be Praised (1944)

PERSONAL HEAVEN
Eugene and Ralph Berton
Two for Tonight (OB) (1939)

PERSONALITY
George M. Cohan
Billie (1928)

PERSONALLY YOURS
Michael H. Cleary
Max and Nathaniel Lief
Hey Nonny Nonny! (1932)

PERSPIRATION
Lee Wainer
John Latouche
Sing for Your Supper (1939)

PERSUASION, THE
Frederick Loewe
Alan Jay Lerner
Camelot (1960)

PET ME, POPPA
Frank Loesser
Guys and Dolls (F) (1955)

PETECA!
Heitor Villa-Lobos
Robert Wright and George Forrest
Magdalena (1948)

PETER PAN
Carroll Gibbons
Billy Rose and James Dyrenforth
Crazy Quilt (1931)

PETER, PETER
Leonard Bernstein
Peter Pan (1950)

PETER'S DENIAL
Andrew Lloyd Webber
Tim Rice
Jesus Christ Superstar (1971)

PETITE BELLE LILY
Coleridge-Taylor Perkinson
Errol Hill
Man Better Man (OB) (1969)

PETTICOAT HIGH
Harold Arlen
Johnny Mercer
Saratoga (1959)

PETTY CRIME
Bob Goodman
Wild and Wonderful (1971)

PFFFT!
Jerry Bock
Sheldon Harnick
The Body Beautiful (1958)

PHIL THE FIDDLER
Richard Lewine
Arnold B. Horwitt
Make Mine Manhattan (1948)

———
*Dropped from New York production

PHILOLOGICAL WALTZ
Donald Swann
Michael Flanders
At the Drop of a Hat (1959)

PHILOSOPHY
Carl Friberg
Hal Hackady
New Faces (1968)

PHOOEY
Don Tucker
Red, White and Maddox (1969)

PHYSICAL FITNESS
Charles Strouse
Lee Adams
All American (1962)

PIANO LESSON
Meredith Willson
The Music Man (1957)

PICCANINNY PIE
Harold Orlob
Hairpin Harmony (1943)

PICCOLINO, THE
Irving Berlin
Top Hat (F) (1935)

PICK 'EM UP AND LAY 'EM DOWN
Werner Janssen
Mann Holiner and J. Keirn Brennan
Boom-Boom (1929)

PICK-ME-UP!
Gordon Duffy
Harry M. Haldane
Happy Town (1959)

PICK-POCKET TANGO
Albert Hague
Dorothy Fields
Redhead (1959)

PICK YOURSELF A FLOWER
Claibe Richardson
Kenward Elmslie
The Grass Harp (1971)

PICK YOURSELF UP
Jerome Kern
Dorothy Fields
Swing Time (F) (1936)

PICKALITTLE
Meredith Willson
The Music Man (1957)

PICKIN' COTTON
Ray Henderson
B. G. DeSylva and Lew Brown
George White's Scandals (1928)

PICNIC, THE
Norman Campbell
Donald Campbell and Norman Campbell
Anne of Green Gables (OB) (1971)

PICKPOCKET, THE
Helen Miller
Eve Merriam
Inner City (1971)

PICKWICKIANS, THE
Cyril Ornadel
Leslie Bricusse
Pickwick (1965)

PICTURE OF HAPPINESS, THE
Jerry Bock
Sheldon Harnick
Tenderloin (1960)

PICTURE OF ME WITHOUT YOU, A
Cole Porter
Jubilee (1935)

PIDDLE, TWIDDLE, AND RESOLVE
Sherman Edwards
1776 (1969)

PIE EYED PIPER
Sammy Fain
Irving Kahal
Everybody's Welcome (1931)

PIE IN THE SKY
Michael H. Cleary
Max and Nathaniel Lief
Shoot the Works (1931)

PIÈCE DE RÉSISTANCE
Heitor Villa-Lobos
Robert Wright and George Forrest
Magdalena (1948)

PIECE OF A GIRL, A
Vernon Duke
Howard Dietz
Jackpot (1944)

PIED PIPER
Mike Brandt, Michael Knight, and
    Robert J. Lowery
Exchange (OB) (1970)

PIERRE
Alma Sanders
Monte Carlo
Oh! Oh! Nurse (1925)

PIGTAILS AND FRECKLES
Irving Berlin
Mr. President (1962)

PILATE AND CHRIST
Andrew Lloyd Webber
Tim Rice
Jesus Christ Superstar (1971)

PILATE'S DREAM
Andrew Lloyd Webber
Tim Rice
Jesus Christ Superstar (1971)

PILGRIM FATHERS, THE
Serge Walter
Agnes Morgan
The Grand Street Follies (1929)

PILGRIM'S PROCESSION
Leonard Bernstein
Richard Wilbur
Candide (1956)

PILL A DAY, A
Jerome Kern
Anne Caldwell
The City Chap (1925)

PILL PARADE
Jay Thompson
From A to Z (1960)

PILLAR TO POST
Bob Merrill
Henry, Sweet Henry (1967)

PILLOW FOR HIS ROYAL HEAD, A
Fred Spielman and Arthur Gershwin
Stanley Adams
A Lady Says Yes (1945)

PIN CUSHION, A
Maury Rubens
Clifford Grey
The Great Temptations (1926)

PINCHING MYSELF
Alexander Hill
Hummin' Sam (1933)

PINE CONES AND HOLLY BERRIES
Meredith Willson
Here's Love (1963)

PINPIPI'S SOB OF LOVE
Sandy Wilson
Valmouth (OB) (1960)

PIONEERS
Stan Harte, Jr.
Walt Whitman
Leaves of Grass (OB) (1971)

PIPE DREAMING
Cole Porter
Around the World (1946)

PIPES OF PAN AMERICANA
Gerald Marks
Irving Caesar
My Dear Public (1943)

PIPES OF PANSY*
Richard Rodgers
Lorenz Hart
She's My Baby (1928)

PIRAEUS, MY LOVE
Manos Hadjidakis
Joe Darion
Illya Darling (1967)

———
*Dropped from New York production

PIRATE JENNY
Kurt Weill
Marc Blitzstein
The Threepenny Opera (OB) (1954)

PIRATE SONG, THE
Leonard Bernstein
Peter Pan (1950)

PIRATE SONG
Mark Charlap
Carolyn Leigh
Peter Pan (1954)

PIRATE'S SONG, THE
Edward Earle
Yvonne Tarr
The Decameron (OB) (1961)

PISCEAN, THE
Ron Steward and Neal Tate
Ron Steward
Sambo (OB) (1969)

PISTACHIO
Mark Lawrence
Small Wonder (1948)

PITTER PATTER
Hugo Peretti, Luigi Creatore, and
    George David Weiss
Maggie Flynn (1968)

PITTSBURGH
Arthur Schwartz
Howard Dietz
Inside U.S.A. (1948)

PITY THE SUNSET
Harold Arlen
E. Y. Harburg
Jamaica (1957)

PIZARRO WAS A VERY NARROW
MAN
Sigmund Romberg
Irving Caesar
Nina Rosa (1930)

PLACE IN THE COUNTRY
George Gershwin
Ira Gershwin
Treasure Girl (1928)

PLACES, EVERYBODY
Arthur Schwartz
Dorothy Fields
Stars in Your Eyes (1939)

PLAIN WE LIVE
Albert Hague
Arnold B. Horwitt
Plain and Fancy (1955)

PLAN IT BY THE PLANETS
Heitor Villa-Lobos
Robert Wright and George Forrest
Magdalena (1948)

PLANK, THE
Leonard Bernstein
Peter Pan (1950)

PLANT A RADISH
Harvey Schmidt
Tom Jones
The Fantasticks (OB) (1960)

PLANT YOU NOW, DIG YOU LATER
Richard Rodgers
Lorenz Hart
Pal Joey (1940)

PLANTATION IN PHILADELPHIA
Morton Gould
Dorothy Fields
Arms and the Girl (1950)

PLASTIC ALLIGATOR, THE
Meredith Willson
Here's Love (1963)

PLASTIC SURGERY
Frank Grey
Earle Crooker and McElbert Moore
Happy (1927)

PLAY A SIMPLE MELODY
Irving Berlin
Watch Your Step (1914)

PLAY BALL WITH THE LORD
Stanley Lebowsky
Fred Tobias
Gantry (1970)

PLAY BOY
Richard Rodgers
Lorenz Hart
Heads Up! (1929)

PLAY GYPSIES, DANCE GYPSIES
Emmerich Kalman
Harry B. Smith
Countess Maritza (1926)

PLAY IS THE BUNK, THE
Max Rich
Jack Scholl
Keep Moving (1934)

PLAY ME A BAGPIPE TUNE
Seymour Furth and Lee Edwards
R. F. Carroll
Bringing Up Father (1925)

PLAY ME A NEW TUNE
J. Fred Coots and Maury Rubens
Clifford Grey
Mayflowers (1925)

PLAY ME AN OLD TIME TWO-STEP
Sam Morrison
Dolph Singer
Summer Wives (1936)

PLAY, ORCHESTRA, PLAY!
Noël Coward
Tonight at 8:30 (Shadow Play) (1936)

PLAY THE GAME
Vincent Youmans
Billy Rose and Edward Eliscu
Great Day! (1929)

PLAY US A POLKA, DOT
Jerome Kern
Oscar Hammerstein II
Sweet Adeline (1929)

PLAYBOY'S WORK IS NEVER DONE, A
Robert Rosenblum
Robert Rosenblum and Howard Schuman
Up Eden (OB) (1968)

PLAYGROUND IN THE SKY
James F. Hanley
Eddie Dowling
Sidewalks of New York (1927)

PLAYING CROQUET
Rick Besoyan
Little Mary Sunshine (OB) (1959)

PLAYTHINGS OF LOVE
Emil Gerstenberger
Howard Johnson
The Lace Petticoat (1927)

PLAZA 6–9423
Harold Rome
Sing Out the News (1938)

PLEASANT BEACH HOUSE
Bob Merrill
Take Me Along (1959)

PLEASE DON'T MAKE ME BE GOOD*
Cole Porter
Fifty Million Frenchmen (1929)

PLEASE GOD
Bill Mahoney
My Wife and I (OB) (1966)

PLEASE LET ME READ
Joseph Raposo
Erich Segal
Sing Muse! (OB) (1961)

PLEASE LET ME TELL YOU
Frank Loesser
The Most Happy Fella (1956)

PLEASE STAY
John Kander
Fred Ebb
The Happy Time (1968)

PLEASE, TEACHER
J. Fred Coots
Clifford Grey
June Days (1925)

———
*Dropped from New York production

PLEASURE AND PRIVILEGE
Jerry Bock
Sheldon Harnick
The Rothschilds (1970)

PLEASURE'S ABOUT TO BE MINE, THE
Elmer Bernstein
Carolyn Leigh
How Now, Dow Jones (1967)

PLENTY BAMBINI
Frank Loesser
The Most Happy Fella (1956)

PLENTY OF PENNSYLVANIA
Albert Hague
Arnold B. Horwitt
Plain and Fancy (1955)

PLOT AND COUNTERPLOT
Robert Swerdlow
Love Me, Love My Children (OB) (1971)

PLOT TO CATCH A MAN IN, A
John Mundy
Edward Eager
The Liar (1950)

PLUMED KNIGHT, THE
Oscar Brand
How to Steal an Election (OB) (1968)

PLUNDERING OF THE TOWN, THE
Jimmy Van Heusen
Johnny Burke
Carnival in Flanders (1953)

PO, PO, PO
Manos Hadjidakis
Joe Darion
Illya Darling (1967)

POCKETFUL OF DREAMS
Harold Rome
Michael Todd's Peep Show (1950)

POETRY AND ALL THAT JAZZ
Leon Pober
Bud Freeman
Beg, Borrow or Steal (1960)

POETRY OF MOTION, THE
George Gershwin
B. G. DeSylva and Ira Gershwin
Tell Me More (1925)

POKER-POLKA, THE
Victor Young
Edward Heyman
Pardon Our French (1950)

POKER POLKA
Harvey Schmidt
Tom Jones
110 in the Shade (1963)

POLAR BEAR STRUT, THE
Arthur Schwartz
Theodore Goodwin
The Grand Street Follies (OB) (1926)

POLICE!
Francis Thorne
Arnold Weinstein
Fortuna (OB) (1962)

POLICEMAN'S BALL, THE
Irving Berlin
Miss Liberty (1949)

POLITICS
Robert Emmett Dolan
Johnny Mercer
Texas, Li'l Darlin' (1949)

POLITICS AND POKER
Jerry Bock
Sheldon Harnick
Fiorello (1959)

POLKA, THE
Harold Arlen
Johnny Mercer
Saratoga (1959)

POLKA DOT, THE
Henry Sullivan
Clifford Orr
John Murray Anderson's Almanac (1929)

POLLY
Philip Charig
Irving Caesar
Polly (1929)

POLLY OF HOLLYWOOD
Will Morrisey
Edmund Joseph
Polly of Hollywood (1927)

POLLYANNA
Robert Hood Bowers
Francis DeWitt
Oh, Ernest! (1927)

POLLY'S SONG
Kurt Weill
Marc Blitzstein
The Threepenny Opera (OB) (1954)

POMPANOLA
Ray Henderson
B. G. DeSylva
Three Cheers (1928)

PONCHO DE PANTHER FROM BRAZIL
Georges Bizet
Oscar Hammerstein II
Carmen Jones (1943)

PONIES ON PARADE
Clarence Gaskill
Earl Carroll's Vanities (1925)

PO' LIL' BLACK CHILE
Frank Harling
Laurence Stallings
Deep River (1926)

POOL OF LOVE
Winthrop Cortelyou
Derick Wulff
Kiss Me (1927)

POOR
Jacques Urbont
Bruce Geller
All in Love (OB) (1961)

POOR APACHE, THE
Richard Rodgers

Lorenz Hart
Love Me Tonight (F) (1932)

POOR AS A CHURCH MOUSE
Vernon Duke
Howard Dietz
Sadie Thompson (1944)

POOR BABY
Stephen Sondheim
Company (1970)

POOR BUTTERFLY
Raymond Hubbell
John Golden
The Big Show (1916)

POOR ISABEL
Richard Freitas
Morty Neff and George Mysels
The Difficult Woman (OB) (1962)

POOR JERUSALEM
Andrew Lloyd Webber
Tim Rice
Jesus Christ Superstar (1971)

POOR JOE
Richard Rodgers
Oscar Hammerstein II
Allegro (1947)

POOR LITTLE BOY
Robert Larimer
King of the Whole Damn World! (OB)
 (1962)

POOR LITTLE DOORSTEP BABY
Michael H. Cleary
Max and Nathaniel Lief
Shoot the Works (1931)

POOR LITTLE HOLLYWOOD STAR
Cy Coleman
Carolyn Leigh
Little Me (1962)

POOR LITTLE MARIE
James F. Hanley
Gene Buck
No Foolin' (1926)

POOR LITTLE ME
Harry Revel
Arnold B. Horwitt
Are You With It? (1945)

POOR LITTLE PERSON
Bob Merrill
Henry, Sweet Henry (1967)

POOR LITTLE PIERRETTE
Sandy Wilson
The Boy Friend (1954)

POOR LITTLE RICH GIRL
Noël Coward
Charlot's Revue (1926)

POOR LITTLE, SHY LITTLE, DEMURE LITTLE ME
Harry Revel
Mack Gordon
Smiling Faces (1932)

POOR MAN
George Lessner
Miriam Battista and Russell Maloney
Sleepy Hollow (1948)

POOR MAN, A
Al Carmines
Maria Irene Fornes
Promenade (OB) (1969)

POOR MAN AT PARTING, A
Mel Marvin
Ted Berger
Shoemaker's Holiday (OB) (1967)

POOR PIERROT
Harry Archer
Harlan Thompson
Merry-Merry (1925)

POOR PIERROT
Jerome Kern
Otto Harbach
The Cat and the Fiddle (1931)

POOR PORGY
Sylvan Green
Frederick Herendeen
Provincetown Follies (OB) (1935)

POMPADOUR
Sigmund Romberg
Irving Caesar
Melody (1933)

POPPA KNOWS BEST
Richard Rodgers
Martin Charnin
Two by Two (1970)

POPPY THE DREAM GIRL
Seymour Furth and Lee Edward
R. F. Carroll
Bringing Up Father (1925)

PORE JUD IS DAID
Richard Rodgers
Oscar Hammerstein II
Oklahoma! (1943)

PORGY
Jimmy McHugh
Dorothy Fields
Blackbirds (1928)

PORTEROLOGY
Porter Grainger and Freddie Johnson
Lucky Sambo (1925)

PORTOFINO
Louis Bellson and Will Irwin
Richard Ney
Portofino (1958)

POSTAGE STAMP PRINCIPALITY
Harold Karr
Matt Dubey
Happy Hunting (1956)

POSTERITY IS JUST AROUND THE CORNER
George Gershwin
Ira Gershwin
Of Thee I Sing (1931)

POT OF MYRTLE, A
Cy Young
That Hat! (OB) (1964)

POTTAWATOMIE
Richard Rodgers
Lorenz Hart
Too Many Girls (1939)

POVERTY PROGRAM
Helen Miller
Eve Merriam
Inner City (1971)

POVERTY ROW OR LUXURY LANE
Gus Edwards
Howard Johnson
Broadway Sho-Window (1936)

POW! BAM! ZONK!
Charles Strouse
Lee Adams
(It's a Bird, It's a Plane) It's Superman
(1966)

POW-WOW POLKA
Jule Styne
Betty Comden and Adolph Green
Peter Pan (1954)

POWDER PUFF
J. Fred Coots and Maury Rubens
Clifford Grey and McElbert Moore
A Night in Paris (1926)

POWER
Wally Harper
Paul Zakrzewski
Sensations (OB) (1970)

POWER OF NEGATIVE THINKING, THE
Bud McCreery
The Littlest Revue (OB) (1956)

POWER STRONGER THAN WILL, A
Al Carmines
Rosalyn Drexler
Home Movies (OB) (1964)

POX UPON THE TRAITOR'S BROW, A
Milton Schafer
Ira Levin
Drat! The Cat! (1965)

P** P* B**** B** D******
Donald Swann
Michael Swann
At the Drop of Another Hat (1959)

PRACTICAL
William Roy
Maggie (1953)

PRACTISING UP ON YOU
Philip Charig
Howard Dietz
Three's a Crowd (1930)

PRAIRIE BLUES
Russell Tarbox
Charles O. Locke
Hello, Paris (1930)

PRAYER
Jerome Kern
Oscar Hammerstein II
Music in the Air (1932)

PRAYER
Sigmund Romberg
Rowland Leigh
My Romance (1948)

PRAYER
Buster Davis
Steven Vinaver
Diversions (OB) (1958)

PREHISTORIC COMPLAINT
Donald Swann
Michael Flanders
At the Drop of Another Hat (1966)

PRELUDE
Michael Valenti
John Lewin
Blood Red Roses (1970)

PRELUDIUM
Richard Rodgers
Oscar Hammerstein II
The Sound of Music (1959)

PREMEDITATED LUCK
Francis Thorne
Arnold Weinstein
Fortuna (OB) (1962)

PREPARE YE THE WAY OF THE LORD
Stephen Schwartz
Godspell (OB) (1971)

PREPOSTEROUS
Ernest Gold
Anne Croswell
I'm Solomon (1968)

PRESENTATION, THE
Jerry Blatt
Jerry Blatt and Lonnie Burstein
Have I Got One for You (OB) (1968)

PRESENTING CLARA SPENCER
Leon Pober
Bud Freeman
Beg, Borrow or Steal (1960)

PRESIDENT'S DAUGHTER, THE
Murray Rumshinsky
Jacob Jacobs
The President's Daughter (1970)

PRETTY AS A PICTURE
Harold Arlen
E. Y. Harburg
Bloomer Girl (1944)

PRETTY FLOWER
Ron Steward and Neal Tate
Ron Steward
Sambo (OB) (1969)

PRETTY GIRL
Morris Hamilton
Grace Henry
Earl Carroll's Vanities (1928)

PRETTY GIRL IS LIKE A MELODY, A
Irving Berlin
Ziegfeld Follies (1919)

PRETTY KITTY
George Kleinsinger
Joe Darion
Shinbone Alley (1957)

PRETTY LITTLE PICTURE
Stephen Sondheim
*A Funny Thing Happened on the Way
  to the Forum* (1962)

PRETTY LITTLE SO-AND-SO
Edgar Fairchild

Arthur Schwartz
The New Yorkers (1927)

PRETTY LITTLE STRANGER
Charles Rosoff
Leo Robin
Judy (1927)

PRETTY, PETITE AND SWEET
Harry Archer
Walter O'Keefe
Just a Minute (1928)

PRETTY TO WALK WITH
Harold Arlen
E. Y. Harburg
Jamaica (1957)

PRIAM'S LITTLE CONGAI
Will Irwin
Agnes Morgan
The Grand Street Follies (1929)

PRICE IN MY WORK
George Harwell
What a Killing (OB) (1961)

PRIGIO DON'T KNOW
Lehman Engel
Agnes Morgan
A Hero Is Born (1937)

PRIM AND PROPER
Skip Redwine and Larry Frank
*Frank Merriwell, or Honor Chal-
  lenged* (1971)

PRIMA DONNA
Claude Leveilee
Gladys Shelley
Gogo Loves You (OB) (1964)

PRINCE CHARMING
Sigmund Romberg
Dorothy Donnelly
My Princess (1927)

PRINCE CHARMING
Walter Kollo
Harry B. Smith
Three Little Girls (1930)

PRINCE CHARMING
Harden Church
Edward Heyman
Caviar (1934)

PRINCE IS MAD, THE
George Fischoff
Verna Tomasson
The Prince and the Pauper (OB) (1963)

PRINCELY SCHEME, A
Mark Charlap
Carolyn Leigh
Peter Pan (1954)

PRINCES AND PRINCESSES
Noël Coward
Tonight at 8:30 (Family Album) (1936)

PRINCE'S FAREWELL, THE
Cy Coleman
Carolyn Leigh
Little Me (1962)

PRINCES' STREET
Don McAfee
Nancy Leeds
Great Scot! (OB) (1965)

PRINCESS OF DOLLAR PRINCESSES
Leo Fall
George Grossmith, Jr.
The Dollar Princess (1909)

PRINCESS OF PURE DELIGHT, THE
Kurt Weill
Ira Gershwin
Lady in the Dark (1941)

PRINCIPLE OF THE THING, THE
Bill Mahoney
My Wife and I (OB) (1966)

PRIORITIES
Lou Cooper
Roslyn Harvey
Of V We Sing (1942)

PRISMS
Carl Friberg
Hal Hackady
New Faces (1968)

PRISONERS IN NIGGERTOWN
Galt MacDermot
Gerome Ragni and James Rado
Hair (1968)

PRISONER'S LULLABY
Edwin Greenberg
Pilgrim's Progress (OB) (1962)

PRIVATE HUNTING GROUND
Norman Dean
Autumn's Here (OB) (1966)

PROBABLY
C. C. Courtney and Ragan Courtney
Earl of Ruston (1971)

PROBABLY IN LOVE
Jack Urbont
Bruce Geller
Livin' the Life (OB) (1957)

PROBLEM
Alan Friedman
Dennis Marks
Fallout (OB) (1959)

PROCESSION
Coleridge-Taylor Perkinson
Errol Hill
Man Better Man (OB) (1969)

PROGRESS
Kurt Weill
Alan Jay Lerner
Love Life (1948)

PROGRESS
Robert Waldman
Alfred Uhry
Here's Where I Belong (1968)

PROGRESS IS THE ROOT OF ALL EVIL
Gene de Paul
Johnny Mercer
Li'l Abner (1956)

PROLOGUE
Arthur Schwartz
Howard Dietz
The Show Is On (1936)

PROLOGUE
Leonard Bernstein
Stephen Sondheim
West Side Story (1957)

PROMENADE, A
Frederick Loewe
Earle Crooker
Great Lady (1938)

PROMENADE THE ESPLANADE
Jean Schwartz
Alfred Bryan
A Night in Spain (1927)

PROMENADE WALK AT THE BEACH, THE
Alfred Goodman, Maury Rubens, and J. Fred Coots
Clifford Grey
Artists and Models (1925)

PROMISE ME A ROSE
Bob Merrill
Take Me Along (1959)

PROMISE NOT TO STAND ME UP AGAIN
Albert Von Tilzer
Neville Fleeson
Bye Bye, Bonnie (1927)

PROMISE OF WHAT I COULD BE, THE
Stanley Lebowsky
Fred Tobias
Gantry (1970)

PROMISE YOUR KISSES
Con Conrad
Gus Kahn
Kitty's Kisses (1926)

PROMISES, PROMISES
Burt Bacharach
Hal David
Promises, Promises (1968)

PROPER DUE
Robert Kessler
Lola Permagent
O Marry Me! (OB) (1961)

PROPER GENTLEMAN, A
David Heneker
Half a Sixpence (1965)

PROPINQUITY
Sonny Burke
Paul Francis Webster and Ray Golden
Alive and Kicking (1950)

PROPOSAL DUET
Laurence Rosenthal
James Lipton
Sherry! (1967)

PROUD OF YOU
John Green
George Marion, Jr.
Beat the Band (1942)

PROVE I'M REALLY HERE
Lor Crane
John B. Kuntz
Whispers on the Wind (OB) (1970)

PRUDENCE, HAVE FAITH
Alyn Heim
Malcolm L. LaPrade
Will the Mail Train Run Tonight? (OB) (1964)

PSALM, THE
Mitch Leigh
Joe Darion
Man of La Mancha (1965)

PSALM OF JEHOSHAPHAT, THE
Deed Meyer
Stones of Jehoshaphat (OB) (1963)

PSYCHIATRY SONG, THE
Kurt Weill
Paul Green
Johnny Johnson (1936)

PTOLEMY
Ervin Drake
Her First Roman (1968)

PUBLIC ENEMY NUMBER ONE
Cole Porter
Anything Goes (1934)

PUBLIC ENEMY NO. 1
Harold Rome
Pins and Needles (OB) (1937)

PUDDLES
Mike Brandt, Michael Knight, and
  Robert J. Lowery
Exchange (OB) (1970)

PUKA PUKA PANTS
Eaton Magoon, Jr.
13 Daughters (1961)

PULITZER PRIZE, THE*
Irving Berlin
Miss Liberty (1949)

PULL THE BOAT FOR ELI
Richard Lewine
Ted Fetter
Naughty-Naught (OB) (1937)

PULL YOURSELF TOGETHER
Philip Charig and Richard Myers
Leo Robin
Allez-Oop (1927)

PULVERIZE THE KAISER
Robert Waldman
Alfred Uhry
Here's Where I Belong (1968)

PUNCH AND JUDY MAN
Harry Warren
Mort Dixon and Joe Young
The Laugh Parade (1931)

PUNS
Gerald Alters
Herbert Hartig
Wet Paint (OB) (1965)

PUPPET DREAM
Meyer Kupferman
Paul Goodman
Jonah (OB) (1966)

PURE IN HEART, THE
Skip Redwine and Larry Frank
Frank Merriwell, or Honor Challenged (1971)

PUREFOY'S LAMENT
Milton Schafer
Ira Levin
Drat! The Cat! (1965)

PURPLE ROSE
Vernon Duke
Ogden Nash
Two's Company (1952)

PURLIE
Gary Geld
Peter Udell
Purlie (1970)

PURSUIT
Marian Grudeff and Raymond Jessel
Baker Street (1965)

PURTY LITTLE THING, A
Philip Broughton
Will B. Johnstone
Nine-Fifteen Revue (1930)

PUSH A BUTTON IN A HUTTON
Jay Gorney
Barry Trivers
Heaven on Earth (1948)

PUSH AROUND
Richard Rodgers
Lorenz Hart
Betsy (1926)

PUSH DE BUTTON
Harold Arlen
E. Y. Harburg
Jamaica (1957)

PUSSY CAT SONG
Al Carmines
Rosalyn Drexler
Home Movies (OB) (1964)

---

*Dropped from New York production

PUSSY FOOT, THE
Leroy Anderson
Joan Ford, Walter and Jean Kerr
Goldilocks (1958)

PUT A CURSE ON YOU
Melvin Van Peebles
Ain't Supposed to Die a Natural Death (1971)

PUT 'EM BACK
Gene de Paul
Johnny Mercer
Li'l Abner (1956)

PUT HIM AWAY
Richard Rodgers
Martin Charnin
Two by Two (1970)

PUT IT AWAY TILL SPRING
Peter Nolan
Joshua Titzell
The Garrick Gaieties (1930)

PUT IT IN THE BOOK
Leslie Bricusse and Anthony Newley
The Roar of the Greasepaint - The Smell of the Crowd (1965)

PUT IT IN WRITING
Alan Kohan
Put It in Writing (OB) (1963)

PUT ME TO THE TEST
Jerome Kern
Ira Gershwin
Cover Girl (F) (1944)

PUT ON A HAPPY FACE
Charles Strouse
Lee Adams
Bye Bye Birdie (1960)

PUT ON YOUR SUNDAY CLOTHES
Jerry Herman
Hello, Dolly! (1964)

PUT YOUR HEART IN A SONG
Ray Henderson
Ted Koehler
Say When (1934)

PUT YOUR MIND RIGHT ON IT
Jimmy Johnson
Perry Bradford
Messin' Around (1929)

PUT YOUR TROUBLES IN A CANDY BOX
Edward Kunneke
Clifford Grey
Mayflowers (1925)

PUTTIN' ON THE RITZ
Irving Berlin
Puttin' on the Ritz (F) (1929)

PUTTING ON THE RITZ
Ray Henderson
B. G. DeSylva
Three Cheers (1928)

PUTTY IN YOUR HANDS
Laurence Rosenthal
James Lipton
Sherry! (1967)

PUZZLEMENT, A
Richard Rodgers
Oscar Hammerstein II
The King and I (1951)

QUALIFICATIONS
Porter Grainger
Yeah Man (1932)

QUARREL FOR THREE
Duke Ellington
John Latouche
Beggar's Holiday (1946)

QUARREL-TET
Moose Charlap
Norman Gimbel
Whoop-Up (1958)

QUARTET EROTICA
Harold Arlen
Ira Gershwin and E. Y. Harburg
Life Begins at 8:40 (1934)

QUARTET FINALE
Leonard Bernstein
Richard Wilbur
Candide (1956)

QUEEN ELIZABETH
Richard Rodgers
Lorenz Hart
The Garrick Gaieties (1926)

QUEEN ESTHER
George Kleinsinger
Beatrice Goldsmith
Of V We Sing (1942)

QUEEN FOR A DAY
Richard Adler and Jerry Ross
John Murray Anderson's Almanac
   (1953)

QUEEN OF MY HEART
Rudolf Friml
P. G. Wodehouse and Clifford
Grey
The Three Musketeers (1928)

QUEEN OF SPAIN
Harvey Schmidt
Tom Jones
Shoestring Revue (OB) (1957)

QUEEN OF TERRE HAUTE, THE*
Cole Porter
Fifty Million Frenchmen (1929)

QUEEN OF THE BURLESQUE WHEEL
Steve Allen
Sophie (1963)

QUEENIE'S BALLYHOO (C'MON,
FOLKS)
Jerome Kern
Oscar Hammerstein II
Show Boat (1927)

QUEER LITTLE INSECT
George Kleinsinger
Joe Darion
Shinbone Alley (1957)

QUELLE HEURE EST-IL?
Claude Leveilee
Gladys Shelley
Gogo Loves You (OB) (1964)

QUELQUE CHOSE*
Cole Porter
Paris (1928)

QUERIDA
Maury Rubens
Clifford Grey
The Great Temptations (1926)

QUESTION OF GAIT, A
Lehman Engel
Thomas Burke
A Hero Is Born (1937)

QUEUE AT DRURY LANE
Robert Wright and George Forrest
Kean (1961)

QUICK HENRY, THE FLIT
Harry Revel
Mack Gordon
Smiling Faces (1932)

QUICKLY
Jacques Urbont
Bruce Geller
All in Love (OB) (1961)

QUIET
Leonard Bernstein
Richard Wilbur
Candide (1956)

QUIET
Mary Rodgers
Marshall Barer
Once Upon a Mattress (OB) (1959)

QUIET COUNTRY
Kenn Long and Jim Crozier
Kenn Long
Touch (OB) (1970)

QUIET GIRL, A
Leonard Bernstein
Betty Comden and Adolph Green
Wonderful Town (1953)

_____
*Dropped from New York production

QUIET LAND, A
Robert Wright and George Forrest
(based on Rachmaninoff)
Anya (1965)

QUIET LIFE, A
Johnny Burke
Donnybrook! (1961)

QUIET NIGHT
Richard Rodgers
Lorenz Hart
On Your Toes (1936)

QUIET STREET
George Kleinsinger
Joe Darion
Shinbone Alley (1957)

QUIET THING, A
John Kander
Fred Ebb
Flora, the Red Menace (1965)

QUIT KIDDIN'
Raymond Hubbell
Anne Caldwell
Yours Truly (1927)

QUITE SUDDENLY
G. Wood
F. Jasmine Addams (OB) (1971)

QUITTIN' TIME
John Rox
All in Fun (1940)

QUITTIN' TIME
Nancy Ford
Gretchen Cryer
Now Is the Time for All Good Men
  (OB) (1967)

RABBIT SONG
Armand Vecsey
P. G. Wodehouse
The Nightingale (1927)

RACE, THE
George Harwell
What a Killing (OB) (1961)

RACE IS OVER, THE
Joseph Meyer and James F. Hanley
B. G. DeSylva
Big Boy (1925)

RACIN' FORM
Harold Arlen
Johnny Mercer
St. Louis Woman (1946)

RACING WITH THE CLOCK
Richard Adler and Jerry Ross
The Pajama Game (1954)

RACKETY-COO
Rudolf Friml
Otto Harbach
Katinka (1915)

RADIO CITY, I LOVE YOU
Lee Wainer
June Carroll
New Jaces (1943)

RADZIWILL
Ralph Benatzky
Meet My Sister (1930)

RAFESVILLE, U.S.A.
Leon Pober
Bud Freeman
Beg, Borrow or Steal (1960)

RAFFLES
Vernon Duke
Al Dubin
Keep Off the Grass (1940)

RAG, A BONE, A HANK OF HAIR, A
George Harwell
What a Killing (OB) (1961)

RAG OFFEN THE BUSH
Gene de Paul
Johnny Mercer
Li'l Abner (1956)

RAGGEDY-ANN
Jerome Kern
Anne Caldwell
The Stepping Stones (1923)

RAGS
Deed Meyer
'Toinette (1961)

RAGS AND TATTERS
Richard Rodgers
Lorenz Hart
Simple Simon (1930)

RAGTIME ROMEO
James Mundy
John Latouche
The Vamp (1955)

RAH, RAH, RAH
Sam Stept
Irving Caesar and Herb Magidson
George White's Music Hall Varieties
  (1932)

RAHADLAKUM
Robert Wright and George Forrest
  (based on Alexander Borodin)
Kismet (1953)

RAIN IN SPAIN, THE
Frederick Loewe
Alan Jay Lerner
My Fair Lady (1956)

RAIN ON THE ROOF
Stephen Sondheim
Follies (1971)

RAIN ON THE SEA
Irving Caesar and Sam Lerner
Gerald Marks
My Dear Public (1934)

RAIN OR SHINE
Milton Ager
Jack Yellen
Rain or Shine (1928)

RAIN SONG, THE
Harvey Schmidt
Tom Jones
110 in the Shade (1963)

RAIN YOUR LOVE ON ME
Nancy Ford
Gretchen Cryer
Now Is the Time for All Good Men
  (OB) (1967)

RAINBOW
Harold Levey
Zelda Sears
Rainbow Rose (1926)

RAINBOW OF GIRLS
Irving Berlin
Ziegfeld Follies (1927)

RAINBOW OF YOUR SMILE, THE
Percy Wenrich
Raymond Peck
Castles in the Air (1926)

RAINING IN MY HEART
Jim Wise
George Haimsohn and Robin Miller
Dames at Sea (OB) (1968)

RAINY DAY, A
Arthur Schwartz
Howard Dietz
Flying Colors (1932)

RAINY NIGHT IN RIO, A
Arthur Schwartz
Leo Robin
The Time, the Place, and the Girl (F)
  (1946)

RAISE THE DUST
Joseph Meyer
Edward Eliscu
Lady Fingers (1929)

RAISING CAIN
Robert Waldman
Alfred Uhry
Here's Where I Belong (1968)

**RAKISH YOUNG MAN WITH THE
WHISKERS**
Harold Arlen
E. Y. Harburg
Bloomer Girl (1944)

RALLY ROUND ME
Vincent Youmans
Ring Lardner
Smiles (1930)

RANCHO MEXICANO
Tatanacho
The Garrick Gaieties (1925)

RANG-TANG
Ford Dabney
Jo Trent
Rang-Tang (1927)

RANGER'S SONG, THE
Sigmund Romberg
Harry B. Smith
The Love Call (1927)

RANGERS' SONG, THE
Harry Tierney
Joseph McCarthy
Rio Rita (1927)

RAP TAP ON WOOD
Cole Porter
Born to Dance (F) (1936)

RAQUEL
George Whiting and Joe Burke
Earl Carroll's Vanities (1928)

RAT-TAT-TAT-TAT
Jule Styne
Bob Merrill
Funny Girl (1964)

RAUNCHY
Harvey Schmidt
Tom Jones
110 in the Shade (1963)

RAVING BEAUTY
Hugh Martin and Ralph Blane
Best Foot Forward (OB) (1963)

RAZZ-ME-TAZZ-JAZZ
Kenneth Gaburo
Seyril Schochen
The Tiger Rag (OB) (1961)

REACH OUT
Claibe Richardson
Kenward Elmslie
The Grass Harp (1971)

REACHING FOR THE MOON
Harry Ruby
Bert Kalmar
Top Speed (1929)

REACHING, TOUCHING
Kenn Long and Jim Crozier
Kenn Long
Touch (OB) (1970)

READ WHAT THE PAPERS SAY
Ray Henderson
B. G. DeSylva and Lew Brown
George White's Scandals (1925)

READIN', WRITIN' AND RYTHMATIC
Leo Edwards
Herman Timberg
You'll See Stars (1942)

READING, WRITING AND A LITTLE BIT OF RHYTHM
Jimmy McHugh
Al Dubin
The Streets of Paris (1939)

READY CASH
Sammy Fain
Dan Shapiro
Ankles Aweigh (1955)

REAL AMERICAN FOLK SONG, THE
George Gershwin
Ira Gershwin
Ladies First (1918)

REAL AMERICAN TUNE, A
Ray Henderson
B. G. DeSylva and Lew Brown
George White's Scandals (1928)

REAL LIVE GIRL
Cy Coleman
Carolyn Leigh
Little Me (1962)

REAL ME, THE
Charles Strouse
Lee Adams
All American (1962)

REAL RICH LADIES
Jay Thompson
Double Entry (OB) (1961)

REAL THING, THE
Mary Rodgers
Marshall Barer
The Mad Show (OB) (1966)

REALLY AND TRULY
Jean Schwartz
Clifford Grey and William Cary Duncan
Sunny Days (1928)

REASON TO MARRY
Robert Holton
June Carroll
Hi, Paisano! (OB) (1961)

RECIPE FOR HUSBANDRY, THE
Mel Marvin
Ted Berger
Shoemaker's Holiday (OB) (1967)

RECIPROCITY
Walter Kent
Kim Gannon
Seventeen (1951)

RECKLESS
Jerome Kern
Oscar Hammerstein II
Reckless (F) (1935)

RED BALL EXPRESS, THE
Harold Rome
Call Me Mister (1946)

RED BARON, THE
Clark Gesner
You're a Good Man, Charlie Brown
(OB) (1967)

RED-BLOODED AMERICAN BOY
Jack Lawrence and Stan Freeman
I Had a Ball (1964)

RED BLUES
Cole Porter
Silk Stockings (1955)

RED COLLAR JOB
Louis Bellson and Will Irwin
Richard Ney
Portofino (1958)

RED HEADED WOMAN, A
George Gershwin
Ira Gershwin
Porgy and Bess (1935)

RED, HOT AND BLUE
Cole Porter
Red, Hot and Blue! (1936)

RED HOT AND BLUE RHYTHM
J. Fred Coots
Arthur Swanstrom and Benny Davis
Sons o' Guns (1929)

RED HOT CHICAGO
Ray Henderson
B. G. DeSylva and Lew Brown
Flying High (1930)

RED HOT MAMA
Steve Allen
Sophie (1963)

RED HOT TRUMPET
Richard Rodgers
Lorenz Hart
Spring Is Here (1929)

RED LETTER DAY
Ernest G. Schweikert
Frank Reardon
Rumple (1957)

RED RIVER
Alma Sanders
Monte Carlo
The Houseboat on the Styx (1928)

RED, WHITE AND MADDOX KAZOO MARCH
Don Tucker
Red, White and Maddox (1969)

RED WINE
Rudolf Friml
P. G. Wodehouse and Clifford Grey
The Three Musketeers (1928)

REDECORATE
Abraham Ellstein
Walter Bullock
Great to Be Alive (1950)

REFLECTIONS
Hal Jordan
Jerry Douglas
Rondelay (OB) (1969)

REFLECTIONS
Robert Swerdlow
Love Me, Love My Children (OB) (1971)

REFORM
Jerry Bock
Sheldon Harnick
Tenderloin (1960)

REGAL ROMP, THE
Alberta Nichols
Mann Holiner
Angela (1928)

REGARDEZ-MOI
Sigmund Romberg
Oscar Hammerstein II
East Wind (1931)

REGENCY RAKES
Noël Coward
Conversation Piece (1934)

REGIMENT LOVES THE GIRLS, THE
Edward Kunneke
Clifford Grey
Mayflowers (1925)

REGIMENTAL BAND
Sigmund Romberg
Arthur Wimperis
Louie the 14th (1925)

REGIMENTAL SONG
Rudolf Friml
Brian Hooker
The White Eagle (1927)

REJOICE
Gary William Friedman

Will Holt
The Me Nobody Knows (OB) (1970)

REIDOF'S
Hal Jordan
Jerry Douglas
Rondelay (OB) (1969)

RELATIVELY SIMPLE AFFAIR, A
Jerry Bock
Sheldon Harnick
The Body Beautiful (1958)

RELAX
Harold Rome
Wish You Were Here (1952)

RELAX AND ENJOY IT
Clay Warnick
Edward Eager
Dream with Music (1944)

RELIGION IN MY FEET
J. C. Johnson
Change Your Luck (1930)

RELUCTANT CANNIBAL, THE
Donald Swann
Michael Flanders
At the Drop of a Hat (1959)

REMARKABLE
Stefan Kanfer, Jess J. Korman, and Joseph Grayhon
I Want You (OB) (1961)

REMARKABLE FELLOW
Victor Young
Stella Unger
Seventh Heaven (1955)

REMARKABLE PEOPLE WE
John Green
Edward Heyman
Here Goes the Bride (1931)

REMEMBER HIM
Alyn Heim
Malcolm L. LaPrade
Will the Mail Train Run Tonight? (OB) (1964)

REMEMBER ME (LOVE SONG)
Edward Kunneke (based on Offen-
  bach)
Harry B. Smith
The Love Song (1925)

REMEMBER ME SMILING
Robert Rosenblum
Robert Rosenblum and Howard Schu-
  man
Up Eden (OB) (1968)

REMEMBER, REMEMBER
Frank Fields
Armand Aulicino
The Shoemaker and the Peddler (OB)
  (1960)

REMEMBER THAT I CARE
Kurt Weill
Langston Hughes
Street Scene (1947)

REMEMBER THE DANCING
David Baker
David Craig
Copper and Brass (1957)

REMEMBER THE NIGHT
Frederico Valerio
Elizabeth Miele
Hit the Trail (1954)

REMEMBER WHEN I HATED YOU?
Al Carmines
Rosalyn Drexler
Home Movies (OB) (1964)

REMEMBERING YOU
J. Fred Coots
Clifford Grey
June Days (1925)

REMEMB'RING
Vivian and Rosetta Duncan
Topsy and Eva (1924)

REMIND ME
Jerome Kern
Dorothy Fields
One Night in the Tropics (F) (1940)

RENDEZVOUS
Sigmund Romberg
Irving Caesar
Melody (1933)

RENDEZVOUS TIME IN PARIS
Jimmy McHugh
Al Dubin
The Streets of Paris (1939)

RENITA RENATA
Emil Gerstenberger and Carle Carl-
  ton
Howard Johnson
The Lace Petticoat (1927)

REQUIEM
Ron Dante and Gene Allan
Billy (1969)

RESCUE, THE
John Clifton
John Clifton and Ben Tarver
Man with a Load of Mischief (OB)
  (1966)

RESPECTABILITY
Harold Rome
Destry Rides Again (1959)

REST ROOM ROSE
Richard Rodgers
Lorenz Hart
Crazy Quilt (1931)

RESTLESS
Ray Henderson
B. G. DeSylva and Lew Brown
Strike Me Pink (1933)

RESTLESS
Joan Edwards and Lyn Duddy
Tickets Please (1950)

RESTLESS HEART
Harold Rome
Fanny (1954)

REUBEN
Harry Archer
Harlan Thompson
Twinkle Twinkle (1926)

REVENGE
John Kander
James Goldman, John Kander, and
    William Goldman
A Family Affair (1962)

REVENGE
Charles Strouse
Lee Adams
(It's a Bird, It's a Plane) It's Superman
    (1966)

REVIEWING THE SITUATION
Lionel Bart
Oliver! (1963)

REVIVAL, THE
Peter Link
C. C. Courtney and Ragan Courtney
Earl of Ruston (1971)

REVIVAL DAY
Will Irwin
Malcolm McComb
Sweet and Low (1930)

RHAPSODY
Morgan Lewis
Nancy Hamilton
One for the Money (1939)

RHAPSODY OF LOVE
H. Maurice Jacquet
Preston Sturges
The Well of Romance (1930)

RHODE ISLAND IS FAMOUS FOR YOU
Arthur Schwartz
Howard Dietz
Inside U.S.A. (1948)

RHUMBA JUMPS, THE
Hoagy Carmichael
Johnny Mercer
Walk With Music (1940)

RHYME FOR ANGELA, A
Kurt Weill
Ira Gershwin
The Firebrand of Florence (1945)

RHYMES HAVE I
Robert Wright and George Forrest
    (based on Alexander Borodin)
Kismet (1953)

RHYTHM
Richard Rodgers
Lorenz Hart
The Show Is On (1936)

RHYTHM FEET
J. C. Johnson
Change Your Luck (1930)

RHYTHM IN MY HAIR
Will Irwin
Norman Zeno
Fools Rush In (1934)

RHYTHM IS A RACKET
Eubie Blake
J. Milton Reddie and Cecil Mack
Swing It (1937)

**RHYTHM IS RED AN' WHITE AN'
BLUE, THE**
Al Moss
David Greggory
Tis of Thee (1940)

RHYTHM OF AMERICA
Eubie Blake
Noble Sissle
Shuffle Along (1952)

RHYTHM OF LIFE
Cy Coleman
Dorothy Fields
Sweet Charity (1966)

RHYTHM OF THE DAY
Owen Murphy
Donald Lindley
Earl Carroll's Vanities (1925)

RHYTHM OF THE DAY
Richard Rodgers
Lorenz Hart
Dancing Lady (F) (1933)

RHYTHM OF THE WAVES
Vincent Rose
Charles and Harry Tobias
Earl Carroll's Sketch Book (1929)

RIBBONS AND BOWS
Irving Berlin
Ziegfeld Follies (1927)

RIBBONS DOWN MY BACK
Jerry Herman
Hello, Dolly! (1964)

RIBBONS I WILL GIVE THEE
Mel Marvin
Ted Berger
Shoemaker's Holiday (OB) (1967)

RIBLAH'S LAMENT
Deed Meyer
Stones of Jehoshaphat (OB) (1963)

RICH, THE
Marc Blitzstein
The Cradle Will Rock (1938)

RICH, THE
Bob Merrill
Carnival (1961)

RICH BUTTERFLY
Richard Lewine
Arnold B. Horwitt
The Girls Against the Boys (1959)

RICH IS
Larry Grossman
Hal Hackady
Minnie's Boys (1970)

RICH MAN! POOR MAN!
Richard Rodgers
Lorenz Hart
Spring Is Here (1929)

RICH MAN'S FRUG
Cy Coleman
Dorothy Fields
Sweet Charity (1966)

RICH OR POOR
Kay Swift
Paul James
Fine and Dandy (1930)

RICH, RICH, RICH
Mary Rodgers
Martin Charnin
Hot Spot (1963)

RIDDLE ME THIS
Lewis E. Gensler
E. Y. Harburg
Ballyhoo (1932)

RIDDLE OF YOU, THE
Robert Larimer
King of the Whole Damn World! (OB)
   (1962)

RIDDLE SONG, THE
Helen Miller
Eve Merriam
Inner City (1971)

RIDE, COWBOY, RIDE
Richard Lewine
Ted Fetter
The Girl from Wyoming (OB) (1938)

RIDE 'EM, COWBOY
Robert Emmett Dolan
Johnny Mercer
Texas, Li'l Darlin' (1949)

RIDIN' HIGH
Cole Porter
Red, Hot and Blue! (1936)

RIDIN' ON THE BREEZE
Jerome Moross
John Latouche
Ballet Ballads (1948)

RIDIN' ON THE MOON
Harold Arlen
Johnny Mercer
St. Louis Woman (1946)

RIDING HABIT
Arthur Schwartz
Howard Dietz
Flying Colors (1932)

RIFF SONG, THE
Sigmund Romberg
Otto Harbach and Oscar Hammerstein II
The Desert Song (1926)

RIGHT ABOUT HERE
Arthur Siegel
New Faces (1968)

RIGHT AS THE RAIN
Harold Arlen
E. Y. Harburg
Bloomer Girl (1944)

RIGHT AT THE START OF IT
Arthur Schwartz
Howard Dietz
Three's a Crowd (1930)

RIGHT FINGER OF MY LEFT HAND, THE
Albert Hague
Dorothy Fields
Redhead (1959)

RIGHT GIRL, THE
Stephen Sondheim
Follies (1971)

RIGHT GIRLS
John Kander
James Goldman, John Kander, and William Goldman
A Family Affair (1962)

RIGHT HAND MAN
Stan Freeman and Franklin Underwood
Lovely Ladies, Kind Gentlemen (1970)

RIGHT MAN, THE
Maury Rubens and Sam Timberg
Moe Jaffe
Broadway Nights (1929)

RIGHT MAN, THE
Oscar Brand
How to Steal an Election (OB) (1968)

RIGHT OUT OF HEAVEN
Harry Tierney
Joseph McCarthy
Cross My Heart (1928)

RIGHT ROMANCE, THE
Jerome Kern
Leo Robin
Centennial Summer (F) (1946)

RIGHT THIS WAY
Bradford Greene
Marianne Brown Waters
Right This Way (1938)

RIGHT WAY
C. Jackson and James Hatch
Fly Blackbird (OB) (1962)

RIGO'S LAST LULLABY
Evelyn Adler
Tales of Rigo (1927)

RIN-TIN-TIN
Sigmund Romberg
Arthur Wimperis
Louie the 14th (1925)

RING A DING A DING DONG BELL
George Gershwin
Ira Gershwin
Strike Up the Band (1930)

RING IRON
Earl Robinson
Waldo Salt
Sandhog (OB) (1954)

RING ON THE FINGER
Harold Rome
Destry Rides Again (1959)

RING OUT THE BELLS
Burton Lane
Alan Jay Lerner
On a Clear Day You Can See Forever (1965)

RING THE BELL
Jimmy Van Heusen
Johnny Burke
Carnival in Flanders (1953)

RINGALEVIO
Richard Lewine
Arnold B. Horwitt
Make Mine Manhattan (1948)

RINKA TINKA MAN
Lew Kesler
June Sillman
Who's Who (1938)

RIO RITA
Harry Tierney
Joseph McCarthy
Rio Rita (1927)

RIP VAN WINKLE
Sigmund Romberg
Dorothy Fields
Up in Central Park (1945)

RISE AND SHINE
Vincent Youmans
B. G. DeSylva
Take a Chance (1932)

RISING STAR
Franz Lehár
Edward Eliscu
Frederika (1937)

RITA CHEETA
Joseph Martinez Kookoolis and Scott
  Fagan
Scott Fagan
Soon (1971)

RITZ ROLL AND ROCK
Cole Porter
Silk Stockings (F) (1957)

RIVER BANK, THE
Moose Charlap
Norman Gimbel
The Conquering Hero (1961)

RIVER SONG
Harry Tierney
Joseph McCarthy
Rio Rita (1927)

RIVER SONG, THE
Richard Addinsell
Clemence Dane
Come of Age (1934)

RIVER SONG
Heitor Villa-Lobos
Robert Wright and George Forrest
Magdalena (1948)

RIVERS OF TEARS
Harold Rome
The Zulu and the Zayda (1965)

RIVERS TO THE SOUTH
C. Jackson and James Hatch
Fly Blackbird (OB) (1962)

RIVERSIDE BUS
Con Conrad
J. P. McEvoy
Americana (1926)

RIVERSIDE DRIVE
Bill and Patti Jacob
Jimmy (1969)

RIVERWIND
John Jennings
Riverwind (OB) (1962)

RIVIERA
Rudolf Friml
Otto Harbach and Oscar Hammer-
  stein II
The Wild Rose (1926)

RIVIERA
Sandy Wilson
The Boy Friend (1954)

ROAD OF DREAMS
Pat Thayer
Donovan Parsons and Clifford Grey
Mayflowers (1925)

ROAD TO HAMPTON
David Baker
Will Holt
Come Summer (1969)

ROAD TO HAPPINESS, THE
Carl Millöcker (revised by Theo Mack-
eben)
Rowland Leigh
The Dubarry (1932)

ROAD TO HOME, THE
Vincent Youmans
Edward Heyman
Through the Years (1932)

ROAD TO PARADISE, THE
Sigmund Romberg
Rida Johnson Young
Maytime (1971)

ROAD TOUR, THE
Charles Strouse
Lee Adams
Golden Boy (1964)

ROAD YOU DIDN'T TAKE, THE
Stephen Sondheim
Follies (1971)

ROARING TWENTIES STRIKE BACK,
THE
Harold Rome
Bless You All (1950)

ROBBERS' MARCH
Frederic Norton
Oscar Asche
Chu Chin Chow (1906)

ROBBERY, THE
Frank Fields
Armand Aulicino
The Shoemaker and the Peddler (OB)
(1960)

ROBERT, ALVIN, WENDELL AND JO
JO
Gary William Friedman
Will Holt
The Me Nobody Knows (OB) (1970)

ROBERT THE ROUÉ
Jimmy McHugh
Al Dubin
The Streets of Paris (1939)

ROBINSON CRUSOE
Alec Wilder
Arnold Sundgaard
Kittiwake Island (OB) (1960)

ROCHELLE HUDSON TANGO, THE
Claibe Richardson
Paul Rosner
Shoestring Revue (OB) (1957)

ROCK ISLAND
Meredith Willson
The Music Man (1957)

ROCK, ROCK, ROCK
Jimmy McHugh
Harold Adamson
As the Girls Go (1948)

ROCKIN'
David Baker
Will Holt
Come Summer (1969)

ROCKIN' IN RHYTHM
Harold Arlen
Ted Koehler
Earl Carroll's Vanities (1932)

RODEO
William S. Fischer
Maxine Klein
Kiss Now (OB) (1971)

ROLL ALONG, SADIE
Vernon Duke
Ogden Nash
Two's Company (1952)

ROLL CALL IN THE MORNING, THE
Alma Sanders
Monte Carlo
The Houseboat on the Styx (1928)

ROLL 'EM
Gerald Marks
Sam Lerner
Hold It! (1948)

ROLL JORDAN
Eubie Blake
Andy Razaf
Blackbirds (1930)

ROLL OF THE DRUM
Jean Gilbert
Harry B. Smith
The Red Rose (1928)

ROLL OUT THE HOSE, BOYS
Sigmund Romberg (developed by
   Don Walker)
Leo Robin
The Girl in Pink Tights (1954)

ROLL OUT THE MORNING
Joseph Martinez Kookoolis and Scott
   Fagan
Scott Fagan
Soon (1971)

ROLL UP THE RIBBONS
Harvey Schmidt
Tom Jones
I Do! I Do! (1966)

ROLL YER SOCKS UP
Bob Merrill
New Girl in Town (1957)

ROLLER SKATE RAG, THE
Jule Styne
Bob Merrill
Funny Girl (F) (1968)

ROLLIN' IN GOLD
Robert Emmett Dolan
Johnny Mercer
Foxy (1964)

ROLLING STONE
Coleman Dowell
The Tattooed Countess (OB) (1961)

ROMA
Armando Trovaioli
Pietro Garinei and Sandro Giovannini
Rugantino (1964)

ROMANCE
Sigmund Romberg
Otto Harbach and Oscar Hammer-
   stein II
The Desert Song (1926)

ROMANCE
Sigmund Romberg
Harry B. Smith
Cherry Blossoms (1927)

ROMANCE
Rudolf Friml
Rowland Leigh and John Shubert
Music Hath Charms (1934)

ROMANCE
Rick Besoyan
The Student Gypsy (OB) (1963)

ROMANCE!
John Clifton
John Clifton and Ben Tarver
Man with a Load of Mischief (OB)
   (1966)

ROMANCE AND MUSKETEER
Kurt Weill
Maxwell Anderson
Knickerbocker Holiday (1938)

ROMANCE IS CALLING
Edward A. Horan
Frederick Herendeen
All the King's Horses (1934)

ROMANTIC ATMOSPHERE, A
Jerry Bock
Sheldon Harnick
She Loves Me (1963)

ROMANY
Arthur Schwartz
Henry Myers
The New Yorkers (1927)

ROME
Milton Schafer
Ronny Graham
Bravo Giovanni (1962)

RONDELAY
Hal Jordan
Jerry Douglas
Rondelay (OB) (1969)

ROOF SPACE
Marian Grudeff and Raymond Jessel
Baker Street (1965)

ROOM ENOUGH FOR ME
Ray Henderson
B. G. DeSylva and Lew Brown
George White's Scandals (1925)

ROOM IN BLOOMSBURY, A
Sandy Wilson
The Boy Friend (1954)

ROOM IN MY HEART
Sammy Fain
Paul Francis Webster
Christine (1960)

ROOM WITH A BATH, A
Max Ewing
Agnes Morgan
The Grand Street Follies (1929)

ROOM WITH A VIEW, A
Noël Coward
This Year of Grace (1928)

ROOM WITHOUT WINDOWS, A
Ervin Drake
What Makes Sammy Run? (1964)

ROOSTER AND THE HEN, THE
Menachem Zur
Herbert Appleman
Unfair to Goliath (OB) (1970)

ROOTLESS
Leon Pober
Bud Freeman
Beg, Borrow or Steal (1960)

ROSABELLA
Frank Loesser
The Most Happy Fella (1956)

ROSALIE
Cole Porter
Rosalie (F) (1937)

ROSE ARIA, THE
Emil Gerstenberger and Carle Carlton

Howard Johnson
The Lace Petticoat (1927)

ROSE IN THE HEATHER
Franz Lehár
Edward Eliscu
Frederika (1937)

ROSE IS A ROSE, A
Harold Rome
Bless You All (1950)

ROSE LOVEJOY OF PARADISE ALLEY
Harold Rome
Destry Rides Again (1959)

ROSE MARIE
Rudolf Friml
Otto Harbach and Oscar Hammerstein II
Rose Marie (1924)

ROSE OF ARIZONA
Richard Rodgers
Lorenz Hart
The Garrick Gaieties (1926)

ROSE OF DELIGHT
Jerome Kern
Anne Caldwell and Otto Harbach
Criss-Cross (1926)

ROSE OF IRAN
Winthrop Cortelyou
Derick Wulff
Kiss Me (1927)

ROSE OF THE WORLD
Victor Herbert
Glen MacDonough
The Rose of Algeria (1909)

ROSE OF THE WORLD
Morris Hamilton
Grace Henry
Earl Carroll's Vanities (1928)

ROSE OF WASHINGTON SQUARE
James F. Hanley
Ballard MacDonald
Ziegfeld Midnight Frolic (1920)

ROSES OF RED
G. Romilli
Fioretta (1929)

ROSE'S TURN
Jule Styne
Stephen Sondheim
Gypsy (1959)

ROSES UNDERSTAND
George M. Cohan
The Merry Malones (1927)

ROSE-TIME
Ray Henderson
B. G. DeSylva and Lew Brown
George White's Scandals (1925)

ROSEMARY
Frank Loesser
*How to Succeed in Business without
    Really Trying* (1961)

ROSIE
Charles Strouse
Lee Adams
Bye Bye Birdie (1960)

ROSITA RODRIGUEZ; SERENADE
Al Carmines
Maria Irene Fornes
Promenade (OB) (1969)

ROTHSCHILD AND SONS
Jerry Bock
Sheldon Harnick
The Rothschilds (1970)

ROTISSERIE, THE
Alfred Goodman, Maury Rubens, and
    J. Fred Coots
Clifford Grey
Artists and Models (1925)

ROUGH TIMES
Moose Charlap
Norman Gimbel
The Conquering Hero (1961)

ROULETTE
Ida Hoyt Chamberlain
Enchanted Isle (1927)

ROUND AND ROUND
Harvey Schmidt
Tom Jones
The Fantasticks (OB) (1960)

ROUNDABOUT
Vernon Duke
Ogden Nash
Two's Company (1952)

ROUST-ABOUT
Jimmy Johnson
Perry Bradford
Messin' Around (1929)

ROUSTABOUT'S SONG
Milton Ager and Owen Murphy
Jack Yellen
Rain or Shine (1928)

ROYAL BANGKOK ACADEMY, THE
Richard Rodgers
Oscar Hammerstein II
The King and I (1951)

RUB A DUB DUB
Helen Miller
Eve Merriam
Inner City (1971)

RUB-A-DUB YOUR RABBIT'S FOOT
Frank Marcus and Bernard Maltin
Bamboola (1929)

RUB YOUR LAMP
Cole Porter
Let's Face It! (1941)

RUGANTINO IN THE STOCKS
Armando Trovaioli
Pietro Garinei and Sandro Giovannini
Rugantino (1964)

RUE DE LA PAIX
Walter Donaldson
Ballard MacDonald
Sweetheart Time (1926)

RULES AND REGULATIONS
Duke Ellington
Marshall Barer and Fred Tobias
Pousse-Café (1966)

RUMBA RHYTHM
Jimmy Johnson
Stella Unger
Earl Carroll's Vanities (1930)

RUMBOLA
James P. Johnson
Flournoy Miller
Sugar Hill (1931)

RUMSON
Frederick Loewe
Alan Jay Lerner
Paint Your Wagon (1951)

RUN FOR YOUR LIFE
Jimmy Van Heusen
Sammy Cahn
Skyscraper (1965)

RUN, INDIAN, RUN
Victor Ziskin
Joan Javits
Young Abe Lincoln (1961)

RUN, RUN, RUN
Jay Livingston and Ray Evans
Let It Ride (1961)

RUN, RUN, RUN CINDERELLA
Robert Emmett Dolan
Johnny Mercer
Foxy (1964)

RUN TO ME, MY LOVE
Allan Roberts
Lester Lee
All for Love (1949)

RUNNIN'
Porter Grainger and Freddie Johnson
Lucky Sambo (1925)

RUNNING DOWN THE SUN
Robert Swerdlow
Love Me, Love My Children (OB)
(1971)

RUSSIAN BLUES
Noël Coward
Charlot's Revue (1926)

RUSTLE OF YOUR BUSTLE, THE
Will Irwin
Norman Zeno
Earl Carroll's Sketch Book (1935)

SABBATH PRAYER
Jerry Bock
Sheldon Harnick
Fiddler on the Roof (1964)

SABRA, THE
Menachem Zur
Herbert Appleman
Unfair to Goliath (OB) (1970)

SABRE SONG, THE
Sigmund Romberg
Otto Harbach and Oscar Hammer-
stein II
The Desert Song (1926)

SACRIFICE
Susan Hulsman Bingham
Myrna Lamb
Mod Donna (OB) (1970)

SACRIFICE, THE
Dov Seltzer
David Paulsen
To Live Another Summer (1971)

SAD WAS THE DAY
Johnny Burke
Donnybrook! (1961)

SADDER-BUT-WISER GIRL, THE
Meredith Willson
The Music Man (1957)

SADIE, SADIE
Jule Styne
Bob Merrill
Funny Girl (1964)

SAFE
Earl Wilson, Jr.
*A Day in the Life of Just About Every-
one* (OB) (1971)

SAFE IN YOUR ARMS
William Heagney
William Heagney and Tom Connell
There You Are (1933)

SAFETY IN NUMBERS
J. Fred Coots
Clifford Grey
June Days (1925)

SAFETY IN NUMBERS
Sandy Wilson
The Boy Friend (1954)

SAGA OF CARMEN, THE
Ray Henderson
Jack Yellen
Ziegfeld Follies (1943)

SAGA OF THE HAGANAH, THE
Walt Smith
Leon Uris
Ari (1971)

SAHARA MOON
Harry Denny and Dave Ringle
Footlights (1927)

SAIL AWAY
Noël Coward
Sail Away (1961)

SAILING
Ed Tyler
Sweet Miani (OB) (1962)

SAILING AT MIDNIGHT
Vernon Duke
Howard Dietz
Sadie Thompson (1944)

SAILOR OF MY DREAMS, THE
Jim Wise
George Haimsohn
Dames at Sea (OB) (1968)

SAILORS OF THE SEA
Steve Allen
Sophie (1963)

SAILOR'S ROUND
Meyer Kupferman
Paul Goodman
Jonah (OB) (1966)

SAINT GENESIUS
Hal Jordan
Jerry Douglas
Rondelay (OB) (1969)

SAINT LAZARE
Aristide Bruant
Kay Swift
Paris '90 (1952)

SALAAMING THE RAJAH
Harry Tierney
Joseph McCarthy
Cross My Heart (1928)

SALAMAGGIS BIRTHDAY
Melvin Van Peebles
Ain't Supposed to Die a Natural Death (1971)

SALES REPROACH
Jerry Herman
Madame Aphrodite (OB) (1961)

SALESMANSHIP
Philip Springer
Carolyn Leigh
Ziegfeld Follies (1957)

SALLEY GARDENS
John Duffy
Rocco Bufano and John Duffy (based on W.B. Yeats)
Horseman, Pass By (OB) (1969)

SALOMEE
Jule Styne
Bob Hilliard
Hazel Flagg (1953)

SALT AIR
Cole Porter
Gay Divorce (1932)

SALTARELLO, THE
Armando Trovaioli
Pietro Garinei and Sandro Giovannini
Rugantino (1964)

SALVATION
Peter Link and C.C. Courtney
Salvation (OB) (1969)

SALZBURG
Jule Styne
Betty Comden and Adolph Green
Bells Are Ringing (1956)

SAM AND DELILAH
George Gershwin
Ira Gershwin
Girl Crazy (1930)

SAMBO WAS A BAD BOY
Ron Steward and Neal Tate
Ron Steward
Sambo (OB) (1969)

SAMBO'S BANJO
Ford Dabney
Jo Trent
Rang-Tang (1927)

SAME OLD LOVE SONGS
Emmerich Kalman
Harry B. Smith
The Circus Princess (1927)

SAME OLD ME, THE
Victor Ziskin
Joan Javits
Young Abe Lincoln (1961)

SAME OLD MOON, THE
Harry Ruby
Bert Kalmar and Otto Harbach
Lucky (1927)

SAME OLD MOON
Henry Sullivan
John Murray Anderson and Clifford
   Orr
John Murray Anderson's Almanac
   (1929)

SAME OLD SOUTH, THE
Jay Gorney
Henry Myers
Meet the People (1940)

SAME SORT OF GIRL
Jerome Kern
Harry B. Smith
The Girl from Utah (1914)

SAMMY AND TOPSY
Ford Dabney
Jo Trent
Rang-Tang (1927)

SAMSON AND DELILAH
James Mundy
John Latouche
The Vamp (1955)

SAN PASQUALE
Armando Trovaioli
Pietro Garinei and Sandro Giovannini
Rugantino (1964)

SAND IN MY EYES
Julian Slade
Dorothy Reynolds and Julian Slade
Salad Days (OB) (1958)

SANDHOG SONG
Earl Robinson
Waldo Salt
Sandhog (OB) (1954)

SANDS OF TIME
Robert Wright and George Forrest
   (based on Alexander Borodin)
Kismet (1953)

SANDWICH FOR TWO
Gerard Calvi
Harold Rome
La Grosse Valise (1965)

SANDWICH MAN, THE
Richard Rodgers
Lorenz Hart
A Connecticut Yankee (1927)

SANDWICH MAN, THE
Hugh Martin and Timothy Gray
High Spirits (1964)

SANS SOUCI
Johnny Mercer
Top Banana (1951)

SANTA BARBARA
Mike Brandt, Michael Knight, and
   Robert J. Lowery
Exchange (OB) (1970)

SANTO DINERO
Richard Stutz
Milton Pascal
Along Fifth Avenue (1949)

SANTO DOMINGO
Charles Gaynor
Lend an Ear (1948)

SARA JANE
Dale F. Menten
Dale F. Menten and Frederick Gaines
The House of Leather (OB) (1970)

SARATOGA
Harold Arlen
Johnny Mercer
Saratoga (1959)

SASCHA'S GOT A GIRL
Irvin Graham
Crazy with the Heat (1941)

SASKATCHEWAN
Clinton Ballard
Carolyn Richter
The Ballad of Johnny Pot (OB) (1971)

SATAN'S LI'L LAMB
Harold Arlen
E. Y. Harburg and Johnny Mercer
Americana (1932)

SATANIC STRUT
Edward Pola
Eddie Brandt
Woof, Woof (1929)

SATELLITE MOON
Donald Swann
Michael Flanders
At the Drop of a Hat (1959)

SATIN AND SILK
Cole Porter
Silk Stockings (1955)

SATURDAY AFTERNOON
Eubie Blake
Noble Sissle
Shuffle Along (1933)

SATURDAY MORNING
David Shire
Richard Maltby, Jr.
The Sap of Life (OB) (1961)

SATURDAY NIGHT AT THE ROSE AND CROWN
Noël Coward
The Girl Who Came to Supper (1963)

SATURDAY NIGHT IN CENTRAL PARK
Richard Lewine
Arnold B. Horwitt
Make Mine Manhattan (1948)

SATURDAY'S CHILD
Baldwin Bergersen
Phyllis McGinley
Small Wonder (1948)

SAUCER SONG, THE
Julian Slade
Dorothy Reynolds and Julian Slade
Salad Days (OB) (1958)

SAVAGE SERENADE
Herman Hupfeld
Murder at the Vanities (1933)

SAVANNAH
Vernon Duke
John Latouche
Cabin in the Sky (1940)

SAVANNAH
Harold Arlen
E. Y. Harburg
Jamaica (1957)

SAVANNAH STOMP
Walter G. Samuels
Morrie Ryskind
Ned Wayburn's Gambols (1929)

SAVANNAH'S WEDDING
Harold Arlen
E.Y. Harburg
Jamaica (1957)

SAVE A KISS
Leroy Anderson
Joan Ford, Walter and Jean Kerr
Goldilocks (1958)

SAVE ME FROM CAESAR
Ervin Drake
Her First Roman (1968)

SAVE THE PEOPLE
Stephen Schwartz
Godspell (OB) (1971)

SAVE THE VILLAGE
Jerry Herman
Parade (OB) (1960)

SAVOIR FAIRE
Claude Leveilee
Gladys Shelley
Gogo Loves You (OB) (1964)

SAY A PRAYER FOR ME TONIGHT
Frederick Loewe
Alan Jay Lerner
Gigi (F) (1958)

SAY, DARLING
Jule Styne
Betty Comden and Adolph Green
Say, Darling (1958)

SAY IT WITH A SABLE
Ray Henderson
B. G. DeSylva and Lew Brown
George White's Scandals (1925)

SAY IT WITH A SOLITAIRE
Jimmy Monaco
Billy Rose and Ballard MacDonald
Harry Delmar's Revels (1927)

SAY IT WITH GIN
Cole Porter
The New Yorkers (1930)

SAY IT WITH GIRLS
Morris Hamilton
Grace Henry
Earl Carroll's Vanities (1928)

SAY IT WITH MUSIC
Irving Berlin
Music Box Revue (1921)

SAY IT WITH YOUR FEET
Thomas (Fats) Waller and Harry
  Brooks
Andy Razaf
Hot Chocolates (1929)

SAY NO MORE
Sol Kaplan
Edward Eliscu
The Banker's Daughter (OB) (1962)

SAY NOT LOVE IS A DREAM
Franz Lehar
Basil Hood
The Count of Luxembourg (1912)

SAY "OUI" CHÉRIE
Vincent Youmans
George Waggner and J. Russel Robin-
  son
What a Widow! (F) (1930)

SAY SO
George Gershwin
P. G. Wodehouse and Ira Gershwin
Rosalie (1928)

SAY THAT YOU LOVE ME
Richard Myers
Leo Robin
Hello, Yourself! (1928)

SAY THE WORD
Burton Lane
Harold Adamson
The Third Little Show (1931)

**SAY THE WORD THAT WILL MAKE
YOU MINE**
Porter Grainger
Donald Heywood
Hot Rhythm (1930)

SAY "UNCLE"
Rick Besoyan
Little Mary Sunshine (OB) (1959)

SAY (WHAT I WANNA HEAR YOU
SAY)
Ray Henderson
Lew Brown
Hot-Cha! (1932)

SAY WHEN
Jesse Greer
Raymond Klages
Say When (1928)

SAY WHEN
Ray Henderson
Ted Koehler
Say When (1934)

SAY YES, LOOK NO
Robert Kessler
Lola Permagent
O Marry Me! (OB) (1961)

SAY YES, SWEETHEART
Emmerich Kalman
Harry B. Smith
Countess Maritza (1926)

SAY YOU'LL STAY
Lee Pockriss
Anne Croswell
Tovarich (1963)

SAY, YOUNG MAN OF MANHATTAN
Vincent Youmans
Harold Adamson and Clifford Grey
Smiles (1930)

SAYS MY HEART
Burton Lane
Frank Loesser
Cocoanut Grove (F) (1938)

SCANDAL
Johann Strauss II, (adapted by Oscar
    Straus)
Clare Kummer
Three Waltzes (1937)

SCARECROWS
Vincent Youmans
Billy Rose and Edward Eliscu
Great Day! (1929)

SCARED
Clinton Ballard
Carolyn Richter
The Ballad of Johnny Pot (OB) (1971)

SCARLET TRIMMINGS
Deed Meyer
She Shall Have Music (OB) (1959)

SCARS, THE
Kurt Weill
Maxwell Anderson
Knickerbocker Holiday (1938)

SCHEHEREZADE
Harold Goldman
The Garrick Gaieties (1930)

SCHOOL DON'T MEAN A DAMN
THING
Voices, Inc.
The Believers (OB) (1968)

SCHRAFFT'S
Richard Lewine
Arnold B. Horwitt
Make Mine Manhattan (1948)

SCHRAFFT'S UNIVERSITY
Henry Sullivan
Edward Eliscu
John Murray Anderson's Almanac
    (1929)

SCHROEDER
Clark Gesner
You're a Good Man, Charlie Brown
    (OB) (1967)

SCHWARTZ
Peter Link and C. C. Courtney
Salvation (OB) (1969)

SCOTCH ARCHER'S SONG
Rudolf Friml
Brian Hooker
The Vagabond King (1925)

SCRATCH MY BACK
Dean Fuller
Marshall Barer
New Faces (1956)

SCREWY LITTLE TUNE
Philip Charig
James Dyrenforth
Nikki (1931)

SCRIMMAGE OF LIFE, THE
Duke Ellington
John Latouche
Beggar's Holiday (1946)

SEA CHANTEY
Cole Porter
Around the World (1946)

SEA FEVER
Donald Swann
Michael Flanders
At the Drop of a Hat (1959)

SEA IS ALL AROUND US, THE
David Baker
Sheldon Harnick
Shoestring Revue (OB) (1955)

SEA LEGS
Lewis E. Gensler
B. G. DeSylva
Captain Jinks (1925)

SEA SONG, THE (BY THE BEAUTIFUL SEA)
Arthur Schwartz
Dorothy Fields
By the Beautiful Sea (1954)

SEA SONG
John Addison
John Cranko
Cranks (1956)

SEAGULL, STARFISH, PEBBLE
Lionel Bart
La Strada (1969)

SEAL IT WITH A KISS
Arthur Schwartz
Edward Heyman
That Girl from Paris (F) (1936)

SEARCH, THE
Kurt Weill
Maxwell Anderson
Lost in the Stars (1949)

SEARCH IS THROUGH, THE
Harold Arlen
Ira Gershwin
The Country Girl (F) (1954)

SEASON ENDED, THE
Michael H. Cleary
Max and Nathaniel Lief
Hey Nonny Nonny! (1932)

SECOND AVENUE AND 12TH STREET RAG
Vernon Duke
Ogden Nash
The Littlest Revue (OB) (1956)

SECOND BEST
Billy Barnes
The Billy Barnes People (1961)

SECOND CAMPAIGN SONG
Don Tucker
Red, White and Maddox (1969)

SECOND-HAND ROSE
James F. Hanley
Grant Clarke
Ziegfeld Follies (1921)

SECOND HONEYMOON, THE
Susan Hulsman Bingham
Myrna Lamb
Mod Donna (OB) (1970)

SECOND TIME IN LOVE
Harry Warren
Jerome Lawrence and Robert E. Lee
Shangri-La (1956)

SECOND VIOLIN, THE
Fritz Kreisler
William LeBaron
Apple Blossoms (1919)

SECRET LIFE, THE
Leon Carr
Earl Shuman
The Secret Life of Walter Mitty (OB) (1964)

SECRET OF MY LIFE, THE
Sigmund Romberg
Irving Caesar
Nina Rosa (1930)

SECRET OF SUCCESS, THE
Lehman Engel
Agnes Morgan
A Hero Is Born (1937)

SECRET SERVICE, THE
Irving Berlin
Mr. President (1962)

SECRET SONG
Baldwin Bergersen
George Marion, Jr.
Allah Be Praised (1944)

SECRETARY IS NOT A TOY, A
Frank Loesser
How to Succeed in Business without Really Trying (1961)

SECURITY
Jule Styne
Sammy Cahn
High Button Shoes (1947)

SEDUCTION
Johnny Brandon
Billy Noname (OB) (1970)

SEDUCTION SECOND DEGREE
Susan Hulsman Bingham
Myrna Lamb
Mod Donna (OB) (1970)

SEE
Robert Swerdlow
Love Me, Love My Children (OB) (1971)

SEE AMERICA FIRST
Cole Porter
Cole Porter and T. Lawrason Riggs
See America First (1916)

SEE EVERYTHING NEW
Nancy Ford

Gretchen Cryer
Now Is the Time for All Good Men (OB) (1967)

SEE NO EVIL
Mitch Leigh
William Alfred and Phyllis Robinson
Cry for Us All (1970)

SEE SEATTLE
Arthur Schwartz
Howard Dietz
Jennie (1963)

SEE THAT YOU'RE BORN IN TEXAS
Cole Porter
Something for the Boys (1943)

SEE THE LIGHT
John Kander
Fred Ebb
70, Girls, 70 (1971)

SEE THE MONKEY
Raymond Scott
Bernard Hanighen
Lute Song (1946)

SEE WHAT IT GETS YOU
Stephen Sondheim
Anyone Can Whistle (1964)

SEE YOURSELVES IN THE MIRROR
Harold Levey
Owen Murphy
The Greenwich Village Follies (1925)

SEED OF GOD, THE
Heitor Villa-Lobos
Robert Wright and George Forrest
Magdalena (1948)

SEEING THINGS
John Kander
Fred Ebb
The Happy Time (1968)

SELF-EXPRESSION
Arthur Schwartz
Henry Myers
The New Yorkers (1927)

SELF MADE MAN
Arthur Schwartz
Dorothy Fields
Stars in Your Eyes (1939)

SELLING A SONG
Dave Stamper
Fred Herendeen
Orchids Preferred (1937)

SELLING SEX
Jerome Moross
Kyle Crichton
Parade (1935)

SEMINARY SONG
Al Carmines
Rosalyn Drexler
Home Movies (OB) (1964)

SENATE IN SESSION
Jay Gorney
Henry Myers
Meet the People (1940)

SENATORIAL ROLL CALL, THE
George Gershwin
Ira Gershwin
Of Thee I Sing (1931)

SENATORS' SONG, THE
Harold Rome
Call Me Mister (1946)

SEND A BOY
Morgan Lewis
Nancy Hamilton
One for the Money (1939)

SEND FOR ME
Richard Rodgers
Lorenz Hart
Simple Simon (1930)

SEND FOR THE MILITIA
Marc Blitzstein
Parade (1935)

SEND ONE ANGEL DOWN
Arthur Schwartz
Albert Stillman
Virginia (1937)

SEND US BACK TO THE KITCHEN
Harry Revel
Arnold B. Horwitt
Are You With It? (1945)

SENSATIONS
Wally Harper
Paul Zakrzewski
Sensations (OB) (1970)

SENSIBLE THING TO DO, THE
Jack Lawrence and Don Walker
Courtin' Time (1951)

SENSITIVITY
Mary Rodgers
Marshall Barer
Once Upon a Mattress (OB) (1959)

SENTIMENTAL ME
Richard Rodgers
Lorenz Hart
The Garrick Gaieties (1925)

SENTIMENTAL MELODY
J. Fred Coots
Arthur Swanstrom and Benny Davis
Sons o' Guns (1929)

SENTIMENTAL SILLY
Henry Souvaine and Jay Gorney
Morrie Ryskind and Howard Dietz
Merry-Go-Round (1927)

SENTIMENTAL WEATHER
Vernon Duke
Ira Gershwin
Ziegfeld Follies (1936)

SEPTEMBER SONG
Kurt Weill
Maxwell Anderson
Knickerbocker Holiday (1938)

SERA SERA JIM
Melvin Van Peebles
Ain't Supposed to Die a Natural Death (1971)

SERENADE
Sigmund Romberg
Dorothy Donnelly
The Student Prince (1924)

SERENADE
Rudolf Friml
Brian Hooker
The Vagabond King (1925)

SERENADE
H. Maurice Jacquet
Preston Sturges
The Well of Romance (1930)

SERENADE CREOLE
Frank Harling
Laurence Stallings
Deep River (1926)

SERENADE FOR YOU
Robert Stolz
Rowland Leigh
Night of Love (1941)

SERENADE OF LOVE
Sigmund Romberg
Irving Caesar
Nina Rosa (1930)

SERENADE TO THE EMPEROR
Ralph Benatzky
Irving Caesar
White Horse Inn (1936)

SERENADE WITH ASIDES
Frank Loesser
Where's Charley? (1948)

SERMON, THE
Frank Loesser
Greenwillow (1960)

SERVICE FOR SERVICE
Robert Wright and George Forrest
Kean (1961)

SET ME FREE
Frederico Valerio
Elizabeth Miele
Hit the Trail (1954)

7 1/2 CENTS
Richard Adler and Jerry Ross
The Pajama Game (1954)

SEVEN DAYS
Edward Kunneke
Clifford Grey
Mayflowers (1925)

SEVEN DEADLY VIRTUES, THE
Frederick Loewe
Alan Jay Lerner
Camelot (1960)

SEVEN MILLION CRUMBS
Frank Loesser
The Most Happy Fella (1956)

SEVEN SEAS, THE
Jane Douglas
Tom O'Malley
Bella, (OB) (1961)

SEVEN SHEEP, FOUR RED SHIRTS AND A BOTTLE OF GIN
Richard Adler
Kwamina (1961)

SEVENTEEN GUN SALUTE, A
Jimmy Van Heusen
Johnny Burke
Carnival in Flanders (1953)

SEVENTEEN SUMMERS
Paul Klein
Fred Ebb
Morning Sun (OB) (1963)

SEVENTH HEAVEN WALTZ
Rick Besoyan
The Student Gypsy (OB) (1963)

70, GIRLS, 70
John Kander
Fred Ebb
70, Girls, 70 (1971)

SEVENTY-SIX TROMBONES
Meredith Willson
The Music Man (1957)

SEVILLA
Ray Henderson
B. G. DeSylva and Lew Brown
George White's Scandals (1926)

SEVILLA
Ned Lehak
Edward Eliscu
The Third Little Show (1931)

SEW THE BUTTONS ON
John Jennings
Riverwind (OB) (1962)

SEW-UP, THE
Walter Marks
Bajour (1964)

SEX APPEAL
Harold Orlob
Irving Caesar
Talk About Girls (1927)

SEX MARCHES ON
Irving Berlin
Louisiana Purchase (1940)

SEXTET
John Clifton
John Clifton and Ben Tarver
Man with a Load of Mischief (OB)
  (1966)

SEZ I
Johnny Burke
Donnybrook! (1961)

SEZ YOU? SEZ I!
Lewis E. Gensler
B. G. DeSylva
Queen High (1926)

SHADE OF THE PALM, THE
Leslie Stuart
Owen Hall
Florodora (1900)

SHADOW OF THE SUN
Helen Miller
Eve Merriam
Inner City (1971)

SHADOWS
Sigmund Romberg
Otto Harbach
Forbidden Melody (1936)

SHADOWS
Paul Hoffert
David Secter
Get Thee to Canterbury (OB) (1969)

SHADOWS ON THE WALL
Harry Revel
Mack Gordon
Fast and Furious (1931)

SHADY DAN
Al Wilson, Charles Weinberg, and
  Ken Macomber
Yeah Man (1932)

SHADY LADY BIRD
Hugh Martin and Ralph Blane
Best Foot Forward (1941)

SHAGANOLA
Sammy Fain
Charles Tobias
Hellzapoppin' (1938)

SHAKE A LEG
Maceo Pinkard
Pansy (1929)

SHAKE, BROTHER
Joseph Meyer and Philip Charig
Leo Robin
Just Fancy (1927)

SHAKE HIGH, SHAKE LOW
Werner Janssen
Mann Holiner and J. Keirn Brennan
Boom-Boom (1929)

SHAKE WELL BEFORE USING
John Green
Edward Heyman
Here Goes the Bride (1931)

SHAKE YOUR DUSTER
C. Luckey Roberts
Alex C. Rogers
My Magnolia (1926)

SHAKE YOUR MUSIC
Al Wilson, Charles Weinberg, and
  Ken Macomber
Yeah Man (1932)

SHAKE YOURSELF OUT OF HERE
Clarence Gaskill
Earl Carroll's Vanities (1925)

SHAKESPEARE LIED
Elmer Bernstein
Carolyn Leigh
How Now, Dow Jones (1967)

SHAKIN' THE SHAKESPEARE
Harry Revel
Mack Gordon
Smiling Faces (1932)

SHAKING HANDS WITH THE WIND
Ron Dante and Gene Allan
Billy (1969)

SHAKING OF THE SHEETS, THE
Mel Marvin
Ted Berger
Shoemaker's Holiday (OB) (1967)

SHAKING THE BLUES AWAY
Mann Holiner
Alberta Nichols
Gay Paree (1926)

SHAKING THE BLUES AWAY
Irving Berlin
Ziegfeld Follies (1927)

SHALL I TAKE MY HEART AND GO?
Leroy Anderson
Joan Ford, Walter and Jean Kerr
Goldilocks (1958)

SHALL I TELL HIM?
Karl Hajos (based on Tchaikovsky)
Harry B. Smith
Natja (1925)

SHALL I TELL YOU WHAT I THINK OF YOU?
Richard Rodgers
Oscar Hammerstein II
The King and I (1951)

SHALL WE DANCE?
George Gershwin
Ira Gershwin
Shall We Dance? (F) (1937)

SHALL WE DANCE?
Richard Rodgers
Oscar Hammerstein II
The King and I (1951)

SHALL WE JOIN THE LADIES
Vivian Ellis
Graham John
By the Way (1925)

SHALL WE SAY FAREWELL?
Jacques Offenbach
E. Y. Harburg
The Happiest Girl in the World (1961)

SHALOM
Jerry Herman
Milk and Honey (1961)

SHANGRI-LA
Harry Warren
Jerome Lawrence and Robert E. Lee
Shangri-La (1956)

SHAPE OF THINGS, THE
Sheldon Harnick
The Littlest Revue (OB) (1956)

SHAUNY O'SHAY
Hugh Martin
Look Ma, I'm Dancin'! (1948)

SHE CALLED ME FELLOW
Stanley Jay Gelber
John Lollos and Don Christopher
Love and Let Love (OB) (1968)

SHE CAME, SHE SAW, SHE CAN CANNED
Burton Lane
E. Y. Harburg
Hold On to Your Hats (1940)

SHE COULD SHAKE THE MARACAS
Richard Rodgers
Lorenz Hart
Too Many Girls (1939)

SHE DESERVES ME
Hal Jordan
Jerry Douglas
Rondelay (OB) (1969)

SHE DIDN'T SAY YES
Jerome Kern
Otto Harbach
The Cat and the Fiddle (1931)

SHE GOT HIM
Sigmund Romberg
Oscar Hammerstein II
Sunny River (1941)

SHE HADDA GO BACK
Meredith Willson
Here's Love (1963)

SHE IS MY IDEAL
Ralph Benatzky
Meet My Sister (1930)

SHE LIKES BASKETBALL
Burt Bacharach
Hal David
Promises, Promises (1968)

SHE LOVES ME
Tom Johnstone
Phil Cook
When You Smile (1925)

SHE LOVES ME
Jerry Bock
Sheldon Harnick
She Loves Me (1963)

SHE LOVES ME NOT
Arthur Schwartz
Edward Heyman
She Loves Me Not (1933)

SHE LOVES ME NOT
David Shire
Richard Maltby, Jr.
The Sap of Life (OB) (1961)

SHE MAKES YOU THINK OF HOME
William Roy
The Penny Friend (OB) (1966)

SHE NEVER TOLD HER LOVE
Hal Hester and Danny Apolinar
Your Own Thing (1968)

SHE OR HER
Moose Charlap
Norman Gimbel
Whoop-Up (1958)

SHE SHALL HAVE MUSIC
Deed Meyer
She Shall Have Music (OB) (1959)

SHE TOUCHED ME
Milton Schafer
Ira Levin
Drat! The Cat! (1965)

SHE WASN'T YOU
Burton Lane
Alan Jay Lerner
On a Clear Day You Can See Forever
(1965)

"SHELL" GAME, A
Rick Besoyan
Little Mary Sunshine (OB) (1959)

SHEPERD SONG, THE
Erich Wolfgang Korngold (based on
Offenbach)
Herbert Baker
Helen Goes to Troy (1944)

SHEPHERD'S SONG
Jerry Herman
Milk and Honey (1961)

SHERMAN'S MARCH TO THE SEA
Dale F. Menten
Dale F. Menten and Frederick Gaines
The House of Leather (OB) (1970)

SHERRY
Laurence Rosenthal
James Lipton
Sherry! (1967)

SHE'S EXCITING
Morton Gould
Dorothy Fields
Arms and the Girl (1950)

SHE'S GONNA COME HOME WITH
ME
Frank Loesser
The Most Happy Fella (1956)

SHE'S GOT EVERYTHING
Dean Fuller
Marshall Barer
New Faces (1956)

SHE'S GOT THE LOT
Marguerite Monnot
Julian More, David Heneker, and
Monte Norman
Irma La Douce (1960)

SHE'S JUST ANOTHER GIRL
Harold Karr
Matt Dubey
Happy Hunting (1956)

SHE'S MY LOVE
Bob Merrill
Carnival (1961)

SHE'S NO LONGER A GYPSY
Charles Strouse
Lee Adams
Applause (1970)

SHE'S NUTS ABOUT ME
Nacio Herb Brown and Richard Whit-
ing
B. G. DeSylva
Take a Chance (1932)

SHE'S ON HER WAY
Jerome Kern
Anne Caldwell and Otto Harbach
Criss-Cross (1926)

SHE'S ROSES
Milton Schafer
Ira Levin
Drat! The Cat! (1965)

SHE'S SUCH A COMFORT TO ME
Arthur Schwartz
Douglas Furber, Max and Nathaniel
Lief, and Donovan Parsons
Wake Up and Dream (1929)

SHE'S TALKING OUT
Leon Carr
Earl Shuman
The Secret Life of Walter Mitty (OB)
(1964)

SHE'S TOO FAR ABOVE ME
David Heneker
Half a Sixpence (1965)

SHH!
Edward Pola
Eddie Brandt
Woof, Woof (1929)

SHIKA, SHIKA
Harold Rome
Fanny (1954)

SHINBONE ALLEY
George Kleinsinger
Joe Darion
Shinbone Alley (1957)

SHINE ON, HARVEST MOON
Nora Bayes and Jack Norworth
Jack Norworth
Ziegfeld Follies (1908)

SHINE ON YOUR SHOES, A
Arthur Schwartz
Howard Dietz
Flying Colors (1932)

SHIP HAS SAILED, THE
Sam Stept
Lew Brown and Charles Tobias
Yokel Boy (1939)

SHIP OF LOVE
Walter G. Samuels
Morrie Ryskind
Ned Wayburn's Gambols (1929)

SHIP WITHOUT A SAIL, A
Richard Rodgers
Lorenz Hart
Heads Up! (1929)

SHIPOOPI
Meredith Willson
The Music Man (1957)

SHIRTS BY THE MILLIONS
George Gershwin
Ira Gershwin
Let 'Em Eat Cake (1933)

SHOEIN' THE MARE
Harold Arlen
Ira Gershwin and E. Y. Harburg
Life Begins at 8:40 (1934)

SHOELESS JOE FROM HANNIBAL, MO.
Richard Adler and Jerry Ross
Damn Yankees (1955)

SHOES
Will Irwin
Norman Zeno
Fools Rush In (1934)

SHOES
Will Irwin
June Carroll
New Faces (1943)

SHOES WITH WINGS ON
Harry Warren
Ira Gershwin
The Barkleys of Broadway (F) (1949)

SHOLOM ALEICHEM
Joseph Rumshinsky
L. Wolfe Gilbert
The Singing Rabbi (1931)

SHOOTIN' THE PISTOL
Clarence Williams
Chris Smith
Bottomland (1927)

SHOOTING STARS
Alma Sanders
Monte Carlo
Oh! Oh! Nurse (1925)

SHOPPING AROUND
Harold Rome
Wish You Were Here (1952)

SHORE LEAVE
Vincent Youmans
Leo Robin and Clifford Grey
Hit the Deck (1927)

SHORE LEAVE
Rudolf Friml
J. Keirn Brennan
Luana (1930)

SHORTEST DAY OF THE YEAR, THE
Richard Rodgers
Lorenz Hart
The Boys from Syracuse (1938)

SHOULD I BE SWEET?
Vincent Youmans
B. G. DeSylva
Take a Chance (1932)

SHOULD I TELL YOU I LOVE YOU?
Cole Porter
Around the World (1946)

SHOUT ON!
Jimmy Johnson
Perry Bradford
Messin' Around (1929)

SHOUTIN' SINNERS
Frank Marcus and Bernard Maltin
Bamboola (1929)

SHOW A LITTLE PEP
Alma Sanders
Monte Carlo
Oh! Oh! Nurse (1925)

SHOW BUSINESS
Irving Berlin
Annie Get Your Gun (1946)

SHOW HIM THE WAY
Stanley Lebowsky
Fred Tobias
Gantry (1970)

SHOW IS ON, THE
Hoagy Carmichael
Ted Fetter
The Show Is On (1936)

SHOW ME
Frederick Loewe
Alan Jay Lerner
My Fair Lady (1956)

SHOW ME
Al Carmines
Rosalyn Drexler
Home Movies (OB) (1964)

SHOW ME THE TOWN*
George Gershwin
Ira Gershwin
Rosalie (1928)

SHOW ME WHERE THE GOOD TIMES ARE
Kenneth Jacobson
Rhoda Roberts
Show Me Where the Good Times Are (OB) (1970)

SHOW OFF
Albert Selden
Small Wonder (1948)

SHOW TRAIN
Jule Styne
Betty Comden and Adolph Green
Two on the Aisle (1951)

SHOW TUNE IN 2/4 TIME†
Jerry Herman
Parade (OB) (1960)

SHOWSTOPPER
Johnny Myers
Wet Paint (OB) (1965)

SHUFFLE
Richard Rodgers
Lorenz Hart
Betsy (1926)

SHUFFLE OFF TO BUFFALO
Harry Warren
Al Dubin
Forty-Second Street (F) (1933)

SHUFFLE YOUR FEET AND ROLL ALONG
Jimmy McHugh
Dorothy Fields
Blackbirds (1928)

SHUFFLING BILL
Raymond Hubbell
Anne Caldwell
Yours Truly (1927)

SHUNNED
Howard Blankman
By Hex (OB) (1956)

SHY
Mary Rodgers
Marshall Barer
Once Upon a Mattress (OB) (1959)

SI, SI, SENOR
Vincent Youmans
Billy Rose and Edward Eliscu
Great Day! (1929)

SIBERIA
Cole Porter
Silk Stockings (1955)

SID, OL' KID
Bob Merrill
Take Me Along (1959)

SIDE BY SIDE BY SIDE
Stephen Sondheim
Company (1970)

SIDE STREET OFF BROADWAY, A
Edgar Fairchild
Henry Myers
The New Yorkers (1927)

SIEGAL MARCHING SONG
John Kander
James Goldman, John Kander, and William Goldman
A Family Affair (1962)

SIESTA
Richard Freitas
Morty Neff and George Mysels
The Difficult Woman (OB) (1962)

SIGH BY NIGHT
Emmerich Kalman
George Marion, Jr.
Marinka (1945)

---

*Dropped from New York production of *Oh Kay!* (1926)
†Rewritten as "It's Today" for *Mame* (1966)

SIGN HERE
John Kander
Fred Ebb
Flora, the Red Menace (1965)

SIGNAL, THE
George Gershwin
Otto Harbach and Oscar Hammer-
stein II
The Song of the Flame (1925)

SIGNORA PANDOLFI
Milton Schafer
Ronny Graham
Bravo Giovanni (1962)

SILENT CAL
Oscar Brand
How to Steal an Election (OB) (1968)

SILHOUETTE
Emmerich Kalman
Harry B. Smith
The Circus Princess (1927)

SILHOUETTES UNDER THE STARS
Charles Tobias, Charles Newman, and
Murray Mencher
Earl Carroll's Sketch Book (1935)

SILK STOCKINGS
Cole Porter
Silk Stockings (1955)

SILVER EARRING
Irving Burgie
Ballad for Bimshire (OB) (1963)

SILVER MOON
Sigmund Romberg
Dorothy Donnelly
My Maryland (1927)

SILVER SAILS
Harden Church
Edward Heyman
Caviar (1934)

SILVER WINGS
Dave Stamper
Gene Buck
Take the Air (1927)

SILVERS THEME
Peter Link
C. C. Courtney and Ragan Courtney
Earl of Ruston (1971)

SILVERY DAYS
Ed Tyler
Sweet Miani (OB) (1962)

SIMON LEGREE
Harold Arlen
E. Y. Harburg
Bloomer Girl (1944)

SIMON ZEALOTS
Andrew Lloyd Webber
Tim Rice
Jesus Christ Superstar (1971)

SIMPATICA
Richard Rodgers
Lorenz Hart
They Met in Argentina (F) (1943)

SIMPLE
Stephen Sondheim
Anyone Can Whistle (1964)

SIMPLE AIN'T EASY
Moose Charlap
Eddie Lawrence
Kelly (1965)

SIMPLE JOYS OF MAIDENHOOD, THE
Frederick Loewe
Alan Jay Lerner
Camelot (1960)

SIMPLE LIFE, A
Nancy Ford
Gretchen Cryer
Now Is the Time for All Good Men
(OB) (1967)

SIMPLE LIFE, THE
Richard Rodgers
Lorenz Hart
The Girl Friend (1926)

SIMPLE LITTLE THINGS
Harvey Schmidt
Tom Jones
110 in the Shade (1963)

SIMPLE SIMON
Helen Miller
Eve Merriam
Inner City (1971)

SIMPLE SPANISH MAID
Jean Schwartz
Alfred Bryan
A Night in Spain (1927)

SIMPLE WIFE, A
Paul Hoffert
David Secter
Get Thee to Canterbury (OB) (1969)

SIMPLE WORD
Stan Freeman and Franklin Underwood
Lovely Ladies, Kind Gentlemen (1970)

SIMPLY HEAVENLY
David Martin
Langson Hughes
Simply Heavenly (1957)

SIMPSON SISTERS, THE
Albert Hague
Dorothy Fields
Redhead (1959)

SINCE EVE
Jerry Herman
I Feel Wonderful (OB) (1954)

SINCE NORA BROUGHT HER ANGORA AROUND
Vincent Valentini
Parisiana (1928)

SINCE THE TIME WE MET
Michael Leonard
Herbert Martin
How to Be a Jewish Mother (1967)

SINCE YOU'RE ALONE
H. Maurice Jacquet
Preston Sturges
The Well of Romance (1930)

SINCERE
Meredith Willson
The Music Man (1957)

SING
Richard Rodgers
Lorenz Hart
Betsy (1926)

SING A LITTLE JINGLE
Harry Warren
Mort Dixon
Crazy Quilt (1931)

SING A LITTLE SONG
Lucien Denni
Helena Evans
Happy Go Lucky (1926)

SING A LITTLE SONG
George Gershwin
Ira Gershwin
Funny Face (1927)

SING A SONG IN THE RAIN
Harry Rosenthal
Douglas Furber and Irving Caesar
Polly (1929)

SING A SONG OF SAMBO
Ron Steward and Neal Tate
Ron Steward
Sambo (OB) (1969)

SING AMERICAN TUNES
Edward Ward
Frank Fay and William Walsh
Tattle Tales (1933)

SING AND DANCE YOUR TROUBLES AWAY
Eubie Blake
Noble Sissle
Shuffle Along (1933)

SING, BROTHERS!
Jack Waller and Joseph Tunbridge
R. P. Weston and Bert Lee
Tell Her the Truth (1932)

SING, DANCE AND SMILE
Philip Charig
Ben Jerome
Yes, Yes, Yvette (1927)

SING FOR YOUR SUPPER
Richard Rodgers
Lorenz Hart
The Boys from Syracuse (1938)

SING HAPPY
John Kander
Fred Ebb
Flora, the Red Menace (1965)

SING, JACQUES, SING
Mimi Stone
William Kaye
Pimpernel! (OB) (1964)

SING ME A SONG WITH SOCIAL SIG-NIFICANCE
Harold Rome
Pins and Needles (OB) (1937)

SING ME NOT A BALLAD
Kurt Weill
Ira Gershwin
The Firebrand of Florence (1945)

SING MUSE
Joseph Raposo
Erich Segal
Sing Muse! (OB) (1961)

SING MY HEART
Harold Arlen
Ted Koehler
Love Affair (F) (1939)

SING OUT IN THE STREETS
Edwin Greenberg
Pilgrim's Progress (OB) (1962)

SING SING FOR SING SING
Cole Porter
The New Yorkers (1930)

SING SOMETHING SIMPLE
Herman Hupfeld
The Second Little Show (1930)

SING SORROW
Earl Robinson
Waldo Salt
Sandhog (OB) (1954)

SING! SOUTH! SING!
Giuseppe Verdi
Charles Friedman
My Darlin' Aïda (1952)

SING THE MERRY
Sammy Fain
E. Y. Harburg
Flahooley (1951)

SING TO ME, GUITAR
Cole Porter
Mexican Hayride (1944)

SINGAPORE SUE
Jim Wise
George Haimsohn
Dames at Sea (OB) (1968)

SINGER AND THE SONG, THE
Willard Straight
David Eddy
The Athenian Touch (OB) (1964)

SINGER'S CAREER, HA! HA!, THE
Percy Wenrich
Raymond Peck
Castles in the Air (1926)

SINGIN' THE BLUES
Jimmy McHugh
Dorothy Fields
Singin' the Blues (1931)

SINGING A LOVE SONG*
Richard Rodgers
Lorenz Hart
Chee-Chee (1928)

SINGING NURSES
Porter Grainger and Freddie Johnson
Lucky Sambo (1925)

---

*Rewritten as "I Still Believe in You" for
Simple Simon (1930)

SINGING TO YOU
Ben Oakland, Margot Millham, and
   Robert A. Simon
Hold Your Horses (1933)

SINGING TREE, THE
Heitor Villa-Lobos
Robert Wright and George Forrest
Magdalena (1948)

SINGING WHEELS
Ruth Cleary Patterson
Fred Heider
Russell Patterson's Sketch Book (OB)
   (1960)

SINGSPIELIA
Rick Besoyan
The Student Gypsy (OB) (1963)

'SIPPI
Jimmy Johnson
Henry Creamer
Keep Shufflin' (1928)

SIR OR MA'AM
Noël Coward
The Girl Who Came to Supper (1963)

SIREN OF THE TROPICS
Vernon Duke
Howard Dietz
Sadie Thompson (1944)

SIREN'S SONG, THE
Jerome Kern
P. G. Wodehouse
Leave It to Jane (1917)

SISTER MINE
Emmerich Kalman
Harry B. Smith
Countess Maritza (1926)

SISTERS UNDER THE SKIN
Frederick Loewe
Earle Crooker
Great Lady (1938)

SISTERS UNDER THE SKIN
Baldwin Bergersen
Sylvia Marks
Of V We Sing (1942)

SIT DOWN, JOHN
Sherman Edwards
1776 (1969)

SIT DOWN SONG, THE
Coleridge-Taylor Perkinson
Ray McIver
God Is a (Guess What?) (OB) (1968)

**SIT DOWN, YOU'RE ROCKIN' THE
BOAT**
Frank Loesser
Guys and Dolls (1950)

SIT IN - WADE IN
Johnny Brandon
Billy Noname (OB) (1970)

SITTING IN THE PARK
Kenn Long and Jim Crozier
Kenn Long
Touch (OB) (1970)

SITTING IN THE SUN
J. Fred Coots
Al Dubin
White Lights (1927)

**SITTING IN THE SUN (JUST WEARING
A SMILE)**
Cliff Friend and George White
George White's Scandals (1929)

SITTING ON YOUR STATUS QUO
Harold Rome
Pins and Needles (OB) (1937)

SITTING OVER THERE
Will Irwin
Norman Zeno
Fools Rush In (1934)

SIX
Charles Strouse
Six (OB) (1971)

SIX BLOCKS FROM THE BRIDGE
Moose Charlap
Eddie Lawrence
Kelly (1965)

SIX LILLIES OF THE VALLEY
Noël Coward
The Girl Who Came to Supper (1963)

SIX MONTHS OUT OF EVERY YEAR
Richard Adler and Jerry Ross
Damn Yankees (1955)

SIX O'CLOCK
Philip Charig
Irving Caesar
Yes, Yes, Yvette (1927)

SIX PALACES
Robert Wright and George Forrest
(based on Rachmaninoff)
Anya (1965)

1617 BROADWAY
Jerry Bock, George Weiss, and Larry
  Holofcener
Mr. Wonderful (1956)

SIXTEENTH SUMMER
Robert Kessler
Martin Charnin
Fallout (OB) (1959)

SIXTY SECOND ROMANCE
Bud Harris
Lawrence Harris
Fools Rush In (1934)

SKIDDLE-DE-SCOW
Jimmy Johnson
Perry Bradford
Messin' Around (1929)

SKIING AT SAKS
Irvin Graham
Who's Who (1938)

SKIN AND BONES
David Baker
Will Holt
Come Summer (1969)

SKINNIN' A CAT
Gary Geld
Peter Udell
Purlie (1970)

SKIP THE BUILD-UP
Sammy Fain
Dan Shapiro
Ankles Aweigh (1955)

SKULL AND BONES
George Gershwin
Ira Gershwin
Treasure Girl (1928)

SKY AND SEA
Oscar Brown, Jr. and Luis Henrique
Joy (OB) (1970)

SKY CITY*
Richard Rodgers
Lorenz Hart
Heads Up! (1929)

SKY GIRL, THE
Jean Schwartz
Alfred Bryan
A Night in Spain (1927)

SKY HIGH
Jimmy Van Heusen
Johnny Burke
Nellie Bly (1946)

SKYSCRAPER BLUES
Gordon Jenkins
Tom Adair
Along Fifth Avenue (1949)

SLAP MY FACE
Alex Fogarty
Edwin Gilbert
New Faces (1936)

SLAP ON THE GREASEPAINT
Berenice Kazounoff
John Latouche
Two for Tonight (OB) (1939)

SLAP THAT BASS
George Gershwin
Ira Gershwin
Shall We Dance (F) (1937)

———
*Dropped from New York production

SLATEY FORK
Walter Cool
Mackey of Appalachia (OB) (1965)

SLAUGHTER ON TENTH AVENUE
Richard Rodgers
On Your Toes (1936)

SLAVES OF BROADWAY
Ray Perkins
Max and Nathaniel Lief
The Greenwich Village Follies (1928)

SLEEP, BABY, DON'T CRY
Baldwin Bergersen
William Archibald
Carib Song (1945)

SLEEP LITTLE MOUSE
Meyer Kupferman
Paul Goodman
Jonah (OB) (1966)

SLEEP, O SLEEP
Sol Kaplan
Edward Eliscu
The Banker's Daughter (OB) (1962)

SLEEP PEACEFUL
Harold Arlen
Johnny Mercer
St. Louis Woman (1946)

SLEEP-TITE
Richard Adler and Jerry Ross
The Pajama Game (1954)

SLEEPIN' BEE, A
Harold Arlen
Harold Arlen and Truman Capote
House of Flowers (1954)

SLEEPY HOLLOW
Norman Dean
Autumn's Here (OB) (1966)

SLEEPYHEAD
Richard Rodgers
Lorenz Hart
The Garrick Gaieties (1926)

SLICE, THE
Jule Styne
Betty Comden and Adolph Green
Hallelujah, Baby! (1967)

SLIDE BOY, SLIDE
Harold Arlen
Harold Arlen and Truman Capote
House of Flowers (1954)

SLIDING DOWN A SILVER CLOUD
Lee David
J. Keirn Brennan
A Night in Venice (1929)

SLIGHT CASE OF ECSTASY, A
Sammy Fain
George Marion, Jr.
Toplitzky of Notre Dame (1946)

SLIGHTLY LESS THAN WONDERFUL
Thomas (Fats) Waller
George Marion, Jr.
Early to Bed (1943)

SLIGHTLY PERFECT
Harry Revel
Arnold B. Horwitt
Are You With It? (1945)

SLIP OF A GIRL, A
Alyn Heim
Malcolm L. LaPrade
Will the Mail Train Run Tonight? (OB) (1964)

SLIPPY SLOPPY SHOES
Gerard Calvi
Harold Rome
La Grosse Valise (1965)

SLOGAN SONG
Johnny Mercer
Top Banana (1951)

SLOTH
Donald Swann
Michael Flanders
At the Drop of Another Hat (1966)

SLOW RIVER
Charles M. Schwab
Henry Myers
The New Yorkers (1927)

SLOW TRAIN
Donald Swann
Michael Flanders
At the Drop of Another Hat (1966)

SLUMBER SONG (GOOD NIGHT)
Richard A. Whiting
Oscar Hammerstein II
Free for All (1931)

SLUMMING ON PARK AVENUE
Irving Berlin
On the Avenue (F) (1937)

SMALL APARTMENT
Deed Meyer
'Toinette (OB) (1961)

SMALL CARTEL, A
Lee Pockriss
Anne Croswell
Tovarich (1963)

SMALL TALK
Richard Adler and Jerry Ross
The Pajama Game (1954)

SMALL TOWN
David Baker
Fred Ebb
Smiling, the Boy Fell Dead (OB)
  (1961)

SMALL WORLD
Jule Styne
Stephen Sondheim
Gypsy (1959)

SMART
Ernest McCarty
Jack Ramer and Ernest McCarty
I Dreamt I Dwelt in Bloomingdale's
  (OB) (1970)

SMART LITTLE GIRLS
Sammy Fain

Jack Yellen
George White's Scandals (1939)

SMART SET
Harry Revel
Mack Gordon
Smiling Faces (1932)

SMART SET
Will Irwin
Paul Peters and George Sklar
Parade (1935)

SMART TO BE SMART
Vernon Duke
E. Y. Harburg
Ziegfeld Follies (1934)

SMELL OF CHRISTMAS, THE
Larry Grossman
Hal Hackady
Minnie's Boys (1970)

SMELLIN' OF VANILLA (BAMBOO CAGE)
Harold Arlen
Harold Arlen and Truman Capote
House of Flowers (1954)

SMEW SONG, THE
Alec Wilder
Arnold Sundgaard
Kittiwake Island (OB) (1960)

SMILE
Donald Heywood
Africana (1927)

SMILE, A KISS, A
Rudolf Friml
Rowland Leigh and John Shubert
Music Hath Charms (1934)

SMILE AT ME
Edward J. Lambert
Smile at Me (1935)

SMILE, DARN YOU, SMILE
Rudolf Friml
Brian Hooker
The White Eagle (1927)

SMILE FOR ME
William Roy
Maggie (1953)

SMILE FOR THE PRESS
Hoagy Carmichael
Johnny Mercer
Walk with Music (1940)

SMILE ON
Milton Susskind
Paul Porter and Benjamin Hapgood
  Burt
Florida Girl (1925)

SMILE, SMILE
Jule Styne
Betty Comden and Adolph Green
Hallelujah, Baby! (1967)

SMILES
Mary Rodgers
Martin Charnin
Hot Spot (1963)

SMOKE GETS IN YOUR EYES
Jerome Kern
Otto Harbach
Roberta (1933)

SMOKIN' REEFERS
Arthur Schwartz
Howard Dietz
Flying Colors (1932)

SMOKY RHYTHM
George Hickman
New Faces (1934)

SNAP INTO IT
Abel Baer
Sam Lewis and Joe Young
Lady Do (1927)

SNAP OUT OF IT
Harry Akst
Benny Davis
Artists and Models (1927)

SNAPPY SHOW IN TOWN
Vincent Youmans
Anne Caldwell
Oh, Please! (1926)

SNOOPY
Clark Gesner
You're a Good Man, Charlie Brown
  (OB) (1967)

SNOWFLAKES AND SWEETHEARTS
Robert Wright and George Forrest
  (based on Rachmaninoff)
Anya (1965)

SO AM I
George Gershwin
Ira Gershwin
Lady, Be Good (1924)

SO ARE YOU!
George Gershwin
Gus Kahn and Ira Gershwin
Show Girl (1929)

SO BEAUTIFUL
Don Elliott
James Costigan
The Beast in Me (1963)

SO DO I
Jean Schwartz
Clifford Grey and William Cary Duncan
Sunny Days (1928)

SO DO I
Vincent Youmans
B. G. DeSylva
Take a Chance (1932)

SO FAR
Richard Rodgers
Oscar Hammerstein II
Allegro (1947)

SO I MARRIED THE GUY
Sam Stept
Herb Magidson
George White's Music Hall Varieties
  (1932)

SO IN LOVE
Cole Porter
Kiss Me, Kate (1948)

SO IT GOES
Jerry Blatt
Jerry Blatt and Lonnie Burstein
Have I Got One for You (OB) (1968)

SO LONESOME
Joe Jordan
Rosamund Johnson
Fast and Furious (1931)

SO LONG AS IT ISN'T SHAKESPEARE
Albert Hague
Marty Brill
Café Crown (1964)

SO LONG, BIG GUY
Charles Strouse
Lee Adams
(It's a Bird, It's a Plane) It's Superman (1966)

SO LONG, DEARIE
Jerry Herman
Hello, Dolly! (1964)

SO LONG, FAREWELL
Richard Rodgers
Oscar Hammerstein II
The Sound of Music (1959)

SO LONG FOR EVER SO LONG
Ray Henderson
Ted Koehler
Say When (1934)

SO LONG, MARY
George M. Cohan
Forty-Five Minutes from Broadway (1906)

SO LONG, YESTERDAY
Stefan Kanfer, Jess J. Korman, and Joseph Grayhon
I Want You (OB) (1961)

SO LOW
Donald Honrath
Nancy Hamilton and June Sillman
New Faces (1934)

SO MUCH THAT I KNOW
Joseph Martinez Kookoolis and Scott Fagan
Scott Fagan
Soon (1971)

SO MUCH TO BE THANKFUL FOR
Alyn Heim
Malcolm L. LaPrade
Will the Mail Train Run Tonight? (OB) (1964)

SO MUCH WORLD
David Baker
Will Holt
Come Summer (1969)

SO NEAR AND YET SO FAR
Cole Porter
You'll Never Get Rich (F) (1941)

SO NONCHALANT
Vernon Duke
E. Y. Harburg
Walk a Little Faster (1932)

SO PROUD
Robert Wright and George Forrest (based on Rachmaninoff)
Anya (1965)

SO RAISE THE BANNER HIGH
Alec Wilder
Arnold Sundgaard
Kittiwake Island (OB) (1960)

SO, SO SOPHIE
Eddie Stuart
Harvey Lasker
Old Bucks and New Wings (OB) (1962)

SO THIS IS MEXICO
Ray Henderson
Lew Brown
Hot-Cha! (1932)

SO WE'LL GO NO MORE A-ROVING
Michael Valenti
Just for Love (OB) (1968)

So What?
George Gershwin
Ira Gershwin
Pardon My English (1933)

So What?
John Kander
Fred Ebb
Cabaret (1966)

So What?
George Fischoff
Carole Bayer
Georgy (1970)

So What? Why Not!
Francis Thorne
Arnold Weinstein
Fortuna (OB) (1962)

So Would I
Milton Ager
Jack Yellen
Rain or Shine (1928)

Soapbox Sillies
Bradford Greene
Marianne Brown Waters
Right This Way (1938)

Social, The
Harold Rome
Destry Rides Again (1959)

Social Director
Harold Rome
Wish You Were Here (1952)

Social Whirl, The
Robert Wright and George Forrest
Kean (1961)

Society Ladder
Harry Ruby
Bert Kalmar
The Five O'Clock Girl (1927)

Sodomy
Galt MacDermot
Gerome Ragni and James Rado
Hair (1968)

Soft in de Moonlight
Frank Harling
Laurence Stallings
Deep River (1926)

Soft Is the Sparrow
Robert Waldman
Alfred Uhry
Here's Where I Belong (1968)

Soft Lights and Sweet Music
Irving Berlin
Face the Music (1932)

Softly, As in a Morning Sunrise
Sigmund Romberg
Oscar Hammerstein II
The New Moon (1928)

Sold
Harry Tierney
Joseph McCarthy
Cross My Heart (1928)

Soldier Boy
Shep Camp
Frank DuPree and Harry B. Smith
Half a Widow (1927)

Soldier of Fortune, A
Jean Gilbert
Harry B. Smith
The Red Rose (1928)

Soldier of Love
Gerald Marks
Irving Caesar
Thumbs Up! (1934)

Soldier Takes Pride in Saluting His Captain, A
John Duffy
Rocco Bufano and John Duffy (based on W.B. Yeats)
Horseman, Pass By (OB) (1969)

Soldiers Anthem
Michael Valenti
John Lewin
Blood Red Roses (1970)

SOLDIERS' MARCH
George Gershwin
Strike Up the Band (1930)

SOLDIERS TRUE
A. Baldwin Sloane
Harry Cort and George E. Stoddard
China Rose (1925)

SOLICITING SUBSCRIPTIONS
Richard Rodgers
Lorenz Hart
The Garrick Gaieties (1925)

SOLILOQUIES
Noël Coward
The Girl Who Came to Supper (1963)

SOLILOQUY
Vincent Youmans
Oscar Hammerstein II
Rainbow (1928)

SOLILOQUY
Richard Rodgers
Oscar Hammerstein II
Carousel (1945)

SOLOMON SONG
Kurt Weill
Marc Blitzstein
The Threepenny Opera (OB) (1954)

SOMBRERO, EL
Cy Coleman
Carolyn Leigh
Wildcat (1960)

SOME ARE BORN GREAT
Stanley Jay Gelber
John Lollos and Don Christopher
Love and Let Love (OB) (1968)

SOME DAY
Rudolf Friml
Brian Hooker
The Vagabond King (1925)

SOME DAY
Ford Dabney

Jo Trent
Rang-Tang (1927)

SOME DAY
Rudi Revil
Kurt Kasznar and Carl Kent
Crazy with the Heat (1941)

SOME DAY I'LL FIND YOU
Noël Coward
Private Lives (1931)

SOME DAY I'M GONNA FLY
Michael Leonard
Herbert Martin
The Yearling (1965)

SOME DAYS EVERYTHING GOES WRONG
Ervin Drake
What Makes Sammy Run? (1964)

SOME ENCHANTED EVENING
Richard Rodgers
Oscar Hammerstein II
South Pacific (1949)

SOME GIRL IS ON YOUR MIND
Jerome Kern
Oscar Hammerstein II
Sweet Adeline (1929)

SOME GIRLS CAN BAKE A PIE
George Gershwin
Ira Gershwin
Of Thee I Sing (1931)

SOME KIND OF MAN
Jule Styne
Sammy Cahn
Look to the Lilies (1970)

SOME LITTLE PEOPLE
Leon Pober
Bud Freeman
Beg, Borrow or Steal (1960)

SOME OTHER DAY
J. Fred Coots
Al Dubin
White Lights (1927)

SOME OTHER TIME
Leonard Bernstein
Betty Comden and Adolph Green
On the Town (1944)

SOME PEOPLE
Jule Styne
Stephen Sondheim
Gypsy (1959)

SOME SAID THEY WERE CRAZY
Earl Robinson
Waldo Salt
Sandhog (OB) (1954)

SOME SORT OF SOMEBODY
Jerome Kern
Elsie Janis
Very Good Eddie (1915)

SOME SUNDAY
Will Holt
That 5 A. M. Jazz (OB) (1964)

SOME SWEET SOMEONE
Herbert Stothart, Bert Kalmar, and
    Harry Ruby
Good Boy (1928)

SOME THINGS
Harold Rome
The Zulu and the Zayda (1965)

**SOME WONDERFUL SORT OF SOME-
ONE**
George Gershwin
Schuyler Greene
Ladies First (1918)

SOMEBODY
Harvey Schmidt
Tom Jones
Celebration (1969)

SOMEBODY ELSE
Raymond Hubbell
Anne Caldwell
Yours Truly (1927)

SOMEBODY FROM SOMEWHERE
George Gershwin

Ira Gershwin
Delicious (F) (1931)

SOMEBODY LIKE ME
Frank Marcus and Bernard Maltin
Bamboola (1929)

SOMEBODY LOVES ME
George Gershwin
B.G. DeSylva and Ballard MacDonald
George White's Scandals (1924)

SOMEBODY OUGHT TO BE TOLD
Sigmund Romberg
Oscar Hammerstein II
May Wine (1935)

SOMEBODY, SOMEWHERE
Frank Loesser
The Most Happy Fella (1956)

**SOMEBODY'S GOING TO THROW A
BIG PARTY**
Cole Porter
Fifty Million Frenchmen (1929)

SOMEDAY, IF WE GROW UP
Norman Curtis
Patricia Taylor Curtis
Walk Down Mah Street! (OB) (1968)

SOMEDAY, MAYBE
Deed Meyer
She Shall Have Music (OB) (1959)

SOMEHOW I COULD NEVER BELIEVE
Kurt Weill
Langston Hughes
Street Scene (1947)

SOMEHOW I'VE ALWAYS KNOWN
Frederico Valerio
Elizabeth Miele
Hit the Trail (1954)

SOMEONE
Alfred Goodman and Maury Rubens
Harry B. Smith
Naughty Riquette (1926)

SOMEONE
Jack Urbont
Bruce Geller
Livin' the Life (OB) (1957)

SOMEONE A LOT LIKE YOU
Jack Holmes
Bill Conklin and Bob Miller
O Say Can You See! (OB) (1962)

SOMEONE AT LAST
Harold Arlen
Ira Gershwin
A Star Is Born (F) (1954)

SOMEONE IN THE KNOW
Ann Ronell
Count Me In (1942)

SOMEONE IS SENDING ME FLOWERS
David Baker
Sheldon Harnick
Shoestring Revue (OB) (1955)

SOMEONE IS WAITING
Stephen Sondheim
Company (1970)

SOMEONE I'VE ALREADY FOUND
Stanley Lebowsky
Fred Tobias
Gantry (1970)

SOMEONE LIKE ME
Ernest Gold
Anne Croswell
I'm Solomon (1968)

SOMEONE LIKE YOU
Alma Sanders
Monte Carlo
The Houseboat on the Styx (1928)

SOMEONE LIKE YOU
Richard Rodgers
Stephen Sondheim
Do I Hear a Waltz? (1965)

SOMEONE LOVES YOU AFTER ALL
Harry Tierney
Joseph McCarthy
Kid Boots (1923)

SOMEONE MUST TRY
John Morris
Gerald Freedman
A Time for Singing (1966)

SOMEONE NEEDS ME
Harvey Schmidt
Tom Jones
I Do! I Do! (1966)

SOMEONE NICE LIKE YOU
Leslie Bricusse and Anthony Newley
Stop the World - I Want to Get Off (1962)

SOMEONE SHOULD TELL THEM*
Richard Rodgers
Lorenz Hart
A Connecticut Yankee (1927)

SOMEONE SUCH AS ME
Francis Thorne
Arnold Weinstein
Fortuna (OB) (1962)

SOMEONE TO ADMIRE, SOMEONE TO ADORE
Serge Walter
Agnes Morgan
The Grand Street Follies (1928)

SOMEONE TO CARE FOR
Duke Ellington
Marshall Barer and Fred Tobias
Pousse-Café (1966)

SOMEONE TO COUNT ON
Deed Meyer
'Toinette (OB) (1961)

SOMEONE TO WATCH OVER ME
George Gershwin
Ira Gershwin
Oh, Kay! (1926)

SOMEONE WAITING
Robert Kessler
Martin Charnin
Fallout (OB) (1959)

---

*Rewritten as "There's So Much More" for
America's Sweetheart (1931)

SOMEONE WOKE UP
Richard Rodgers
Stephen Sondheim
Do I Hear a Waltz? (1965)

SOMEONE YOU KNOW
Victor Ziskin
Joan Javits
Young Abe Lincoln (1961)

SOMETHING BEAUTIFUL
Gary William Friedman
Will Holt
The Me Nobody Knows (OB) (1970)

SOMETHING BIG
Richard Adler
Kwamina (1961)

SOMETHING BIG
Sam Pottle
David Axelrod
New Faces (1968)

SOMETHING DOESN'T HAPPEN
Richard Rodgers
Martin Charnin
Two by Two (1970)

SOMETHING FOR NOTHING
Joseph Meyer and James F. Hanley
B. G. DeSylva
Big Boy (1925)

SOMETHING FOR NOTHING
Claibe Richardson
Kenward Elmslie
The Grass Harp (1971)

SOMETHING FOR THE BOYS
Cole Porter
Something for the Boys (1943)

SOMETHING GOOD
Richard Rodgers
The Sound of Music (F) (1965)

SOMETHING GREATER
Charles Strouse
Lee Adams
Applause (1970)

SOMETHING HAD TO HAPPEN
Jerome Kern
Otto Harbach
Roberta (1933)

SOMETHING HAS HAPPENED
Harvey Schmidt
Tom Jones
I Do! I Do! (1966)

SOMETHING I DREAMED LAST NIGHT
Sammy Fain
Jack Yellen and Herb Magidson
George White's Scandals (1939)

SOMETHING IN HIS EYES
Ernest Gold
Anne Croswell
I'm Solomon (1968)

SOMETHING IN THE AIR OF MAY
Sigmund Romberg
Oscar Hammerstein II
May Wine (1935)

SOMETHING IS COMING TO TEA
Hugh Martin and Timothy Gray
High Spirits (1964)

SOMETHING MORE
Sammy Fain
Marilyn and Alan Bergman
Something More! (1964)

SOMETHING NEW
Howard Blankman
By Hex (OB) (1956)

SOMETHING NEW IS IN MY HEART
Sigmund Romberg
Oscar Hammerstein II
May Wine (1935)

SOMETHING NICE IS GOING TO HAP-PEN
Robert Dahdah
Curley McDimple (OB) (1967)

SOMETHING SEEMS TO TELL ME
Robert Katscher
Irving Caesar
The Wonder Bar (1931)

SOMETHING, SOMEWHERE
Richard Rodgers
Martin Charnin
Two by Two (1970)

SOMETHING SORT OF GRANDISH
Burton Lane
E. Y. Harburg
Finian's Rainbow (1947)

SOMETHING SPANISH IN YOUR EYES
Philip Charig
Irving Caesar
Polly (1929)

SOMETHING SPECIAL
Gordon Duffy
Harry M. Haldane
Happy Town (1959)

SOMETHING SPECIAL
George Fischoff
Carole Bayer
Georgy (1970)

SOMETHING TELLS ME
Henry Souvaine and Jay Gorney
Morrie Ryskind and Howard Dietz
Merry-Go-Round (1927)

SOMETHING TELLS ME
Hugh Martin and Timothy Gray
High Spirits (1964)

SOMETHING TELLS ME I'M IN LOVE
Harold Levey
Owen Murphy
Rainbow Rose (1926)

SOMETHING TO DANCE ABOUT
Irving Berlin
Call Me Madam (1950)

SOMETHING TO LIVE FOR
Joseph Meyer
Edward Eliscu
Lady Fingers (1929)

SOMETHING TO LIVE FOR
Ervin Drake
What Makes Sammy Run? (1964)

SOMETHING TO REMEMBER YOU BY
Arthur Schwartz
Howard Dietz
Three's a Crowd (1930)

SOMETHING TO SING ABOUT
Vincent Youmans
Harold Adamson and Clifford Grey
Smiles (1930)

SOMETHING TO TELL
Maury Rubens and J. Fred Coots
Clifford Grey
The Madcap (1928)

SOMETHING VERY STRANGE
Noël Coward
Sail Away (1961)

SOMETHING WONDERFUL
Richard Rodgers
Oscar Hammerstein II
The King and I (1951)

SOMETHING WONDERFUL CAN HAP-
PEN
Bob Goodman
Wild and Wonderful (1971)

SOMETHING WRONG WITH ME
J. Fred Coots
Clifford Grey
June Days (1925)

SOMETHING YOU LACK
Warburton Guilbert
Nancy Hamilton and June Sillman
New Faces (1934)

SOMETHING YOU NEVER HAD
BEFORE
Arthur Schwartz
Howard Dietz
The Gay Life (1961)

SOMETHING'S ALWAYS HAPPENING ON THE RIVER
Jule Styne
Betty Comden and Adolph Green
Say, Darling (1958)

SOMETHING'S COMING
Leonard Bernstein
Stephen Sondheim
West Side Story (1957)

SOMETHING'S GOING TO HAPPEN TO YOU
James P. Johnson
Flournoy Miller
Sugar Hill (1931)

SOMETHING'S GOT TO GIVE
Johnny Mercer
Daddy Long Legs (F) (1955)

SOMETIMES I WONDER
Frank Fields
Armand Aulicino
The Shoemaker and the Peddler (OB) (1960)

SOMETIMES I'M HAPPY
Vincent Youmans
Irving Caesar
Hit the Deck (1927)

SOMEWHERE
Harry Warren
Jerome Lawrence and Robert E. Lee
Shangri-La (1956)

SOMEWHERE
Leonard Bernstein
Stephen Sondheim
West Side Story (1957)

SOMEWHERE
Rick Besoyan
The Student Gypsy (OB) (1963)

SOMEWHERE IN LOVERS' LAND
Carlton Kelsey and Maury Rubens
Sky High (1925)

SOMEWHERE IN YOUR EYES
John Dooley
Hobo (OB) (1961)

SOMEWHERE THERE'S A LITTLE BLUEBIRD
Charles Gaynor
Show Girl (1961)

SON OF A BILLIONAIRE
George M. Cohan
The Merry Malones (1927)

SON OF AFRICA
Ron Steward and Neal Tate
Ron Steward
Sambo (OB) (1969)

SON OF MAN
Dov Seltzer
David Axelrod
To Live Another Summer (1971)

SON OF THE MA
Marc Blitzstein
Juno (1959)

SON OF THE SUN
Rudolf Friml
J. Keirn Brennan
Luana (1930)

SONG ABOUT LOVE, A
Arthur Schwartz
Henry Myers
The New Yorkers (1927)

SONG FROM SOMEWHERE, A
Robert Wright and George Forrest
(based on Rachmaninoff)
Anya (1965)

SONG IS YOU, THE
Jerome Kern
Oscar Hammerstein II
Music in the Air (1932)

SONG OF A SUMMER NIGHT
Frank Loesser
The Most Happy Fella (1956)

SONG OF GREATER BRITAIN
Michael Valenti
John Lewin
Blood Red Roses (1970)

SONG OF HARLEM
Frank Marcus and Bernard Maltin
Bamboola (1929)

SONG OF LOVE
Sigmund Romberg (based on Schubert)
Dorothy Donnelly
Blossom Time (1921)

SONG OF LOVE
Mary Rodgers
Marshall Barer
Once Upon a Mattress (OB) (1959)

SONG OF MY HEART
Franklin Hauser
Brian Hooker
The O'Flynn (1934)

SONG OF MYSELF
Stan Harte, Jr.
Walt Whitman
Leaves of Grass (OB) (1971)

SONG OF NORWAY, THE
Robert Wright and George Forrest (based on Grieg)
Song of Norway (1944)

SONG OF PATRIOTIC PREJUDICE, A
Donald Swann
Michael Flanders
At the Drop of Another Hat (1966)

SONG OF PRIGIO, THE
Lehman Engel
Agnes Morgan
A Hero Is Born (1937)

SONG OF REPRODUCTION
Donald Swann
Michael Flanders
At the Drop of a Hat (1959)

SONG OF SALLAH SHABETI, THE
Menachem Zur
Herbert Appleman
Unfair to Goliath (OB) (1970)

SONG OF THE BENDS
Earl Robinson
Waldo Salt
Sandhog (OB) (1954)

SONG OF THE BRASS KEY
Sigmund Romberg
Otto Harbach and Oscar Hammerstein II
The Desert Song (1926)

SONG OF THE CLAQUE
Franz Steininger (adapted from Tchaikovsky)
Forman Brown
Music in My Heart (1947)

SONG OF THE COTTON FIELDS
Thomas (Fats) Waller and Harry Brooks
Andy Razaf
Hot Chocolates (1929)

SONG OF THE FAIR DISSENTER LASS
Michael Valenti
John Lewin
Blood Red Roses (1970)

SONG OF THE FLAME
George Gershwin and Herbert Stothart
Otto Harbach and Oscar Hammerstein II
Song of the Flame (1925)

SONG OF THE FOREIGN LEGION
Ray Henderson
B. G. DeSylva and Lew Brown
George White's Scandals (1931)

SONG OF THE GODDESS
Kurt Weill
Paul Green
Johnny Johnson (1936)

SONG OF THE GUNS
Kurt Weill
Paul Green
Johnny Johnson (1936)

SONG OF THE MALCONTENTS
Don Tucker
Red, White and Maddox (1969)

SONG OF THE MASK, THE
James Bredt
Edward Eager
The Happy Hypocrite (OB) (1968)

SONG OF THE MATADORS
Ray Henderson
Lew Brown
Hot-Cha! (1932)

SONG OF THE MOONBEAMS
Vincent Rose
Charles and Harry Tobias
Earl Carroll's Sketch Book (1929)

SONG OF THE OPEN ROAD
Stan Harte, Jr.
Walt Whitman
Leaves of Grass (OB) (1971)

SONG OF THE RIVETER
Arthur Schwartz
Lew Levenson
The Little Show (1929)

SONG OF THE ROUSTABOUTS, THE
Richard Rodgers
Lorenz Hart
Jumbo (1935)

SONG OF THE SARONG
Dorcas Cochran and Charles Rosoff
Earl Carroll's Vanities (1940)

SONG OF THE SETTING SUN
Walter Donaldson
Gus Kahn
Whoopee (1928)

SONG OF THE THIRTEEN COLONIES
Norman Dean
Autumn's Here (OB) (1966)

SONG OF THE TROIKA
Franz Steininger (adapted from Tchaikovsky)
Forman Brown
Music in My Heart (1947)

SONG OF THE VAGABONDS
Rudolf Friml
Brian Hooker
The Vagabond King (1925)

SONG OF THE WEATHER, A
Donald Swann
Michael Flanders
At the Drop of a Hat (1959)

SONG OF THE WITCH
Deed Meyer
Stones of Jehoshaphat (OB) (1963)

SONG OF THE WOODMAN
Harold Arlen
E. Y. Harburg
The Show Is On (1936)

SONG OF THE WOUNDED FRENCH-MAN
Kurt Weill
Paul Green
Johnny Johnson (1936)

SONG OF TWO ISLANDS
John Green
George Marion, Jr.
Beat the Band (1942)

SONG OF VICTORY
Sigmund Romberg
Dorothy Donnelly
My Maryland (1927)

SONG OF WELCOME
Richard Hill and John Hawkins
Nevill Coghill
Canterbury Tales (1969)

SONGS FOR FREE, THE
Sammy Fain
Jack Yellen
George White's Scandals (1939)

SONNY-BOY SLAVE SONG, THE
Coleridge-Taylor Perkinson
Ray McIver
God Is a (Guess What?) (OB) (1968)

SONS
Jerry Bock
Sheldon Harnick
The Rothschilds (1970)

SONS AND DAUGHTERS OF THE SEA
Eubie Blake
J. Milton Reddie and Cecil Mack
Swing It (1937)

SONS OF
Jacques Brel
Eric Blau and Mort Shuman
*Jacques Brel Is Alive and Well and
    Living in Paris* (OB) (1968)

SONS OF FRANCE
Marguerite Monnot
Julian More, David Heneker, and
    Monte Norman
Irma La Douce (1960)

SONS OF GREENTREE
David Baker
Fred Ebb
Smiling, the Boy Fell Dead (OB)
    (1961)

SONS OF THE SEA
Jacques Belasco
Kay Twomey
The Girl from Nantucket (1945)

SOON
George Gershwin
Ira Gershwin
Strike Up the Band (1930)

SOON
Richard Rodgers
Lorenz Hart
Mississippi (F) (1935)

SOON
Walter Marks
Bajour (1964)

SOON
Joseph Martinez Kookoolis and Scott
    Fagan
Scott Fagan
Soon (1971)

SOON IT'S GONNA RAIN
Harvey Schmidt
Tom Jones
The Fantasticks (OB) (1960)

SOON YOU GONNA LEAVE ME, JOE
Frank Loesser
The Most Happy Fella (1956)

SOONER OR LATER
Lionel Bart
La Strada (1969)

SOPHIE
William B. Kernell
Dorothy Donnelly
Hello, Lola (1926)

SOPHIE IN NEW YORK
Steve Allen
Sophie (1963)

SORRY FOR MYSELF
Moose Charlap
Norman Gimbel
Whoop-Up (1958)

SORRY-GRATEFUL
Stephen Sondheim
Company (1970)

**SORRY THAT I STRAYED AWAY
FROM YOU**
Jimmy Johnson
Perry Bradford
Messin' Around (1929)

SORRY WE WON
David Krivoshei
David Paulsen
To Live Another Summer (1971)

SORT O' LONESOME
Herman Hupfeld
A la Carte (1927)

SO'S YOUR OLD MAN
Jerome Kern
Oscar Hammerstein II
Sunny (1925)

SOUL MATES
Alma Sanders
Monte Carlo
The Houseboat on the Styx (1928)

SOUL SAVING SADIE
Joseph Meyer
Billy Rose and Ballard MacDonald
Ziegfeld Follies (1934)

SOULLESS A FAERY DIES
John Duffy
Rocco Bufano and John Duffy (based
  on W.B. Yeats)
Horseman, Pass By (OB) (1969)

SOUND OF MONEY, THE
Harold Rome
I Can Get It for You Wholesale (1962)

SOUND OF MUSIC, THE
Richard Rodgers
Oscar Hammerstein II
The Sound of Music (1959)

SOUND OF THE DRUM, THE
William Heagney
William Heagney and Tom Connell
There You Are (1932)

SOUND OF THE NIGHT
Cy Young
That Hat! (OB) (1964)

SOUNDS
Gary William Friedman
Will Holt
The Me Nobody Knows (OB) (1970)

SOUNDS
Wally Harper
Paul Zakrzewski
Sensations (OB) (1970)

SOUNDS OF SILENCE
Robert Holton
June Carroll
Hi, Paisano! (OB) (1961)

SOUTH AMERICA, TAKE IT AWAY
Harold Rome
Call Me Mister (1946)

SOUTH AMERICAN WAY
Jimmy McHugh
Al Dubin
The Streets of Paris (1939)

SOUTH AMERICAN WAY
Norman Martin
Norman Martin and Fred Ebb
From A to Z (1960)

SOUTH SEA ISLES
George Gershwin
Arthur Jackson
George White's Scandals (1921)

SOUTH WIND IS CALLING
Emil Gerstenberger and Carle Carl-
  ton
Howard Johnson
The Lace Petticoat (1927)

SOUVENIR
Sigmund Romberg
Rowland Leigh
My Romance (1948)

SPANISH LOVE
Sigmund Romberg
Harry B. Smith
The Love Call (1927)

SPANISH MICK, THE
Harry Archer
Harlan Thompson
Merry-Merry (1925)

SPANISH MOON
Tom Johnstone
Phil Cook
When You Smile (1925)

SPANISH PANIC
Mary Rodgers
Marshall Barer
Once Upon a Mattress (OB) (1959)

SPANISH ROSE
Charles Strouse
Lee Adams
Bye Bye Birdie (1960)

SPANISH SHAWL, A
Jean Schwartz
Alfred Bryan
A Night in Spain (1927)

SPARE A LITTLE LOVE
Melville Gideon
Clifford Grey
The Optimists (1928)

SPARE THAT BUILDING
Jimmy Van Heusen
Sammy Cahn
Skyscraper (1965)

SPEAK EASY
Lewis E. Gensler
Owen Murphy and Robert A. Simon
The Gang's All Here (1931)

SPEAK IN SILENCE
Francis Thorne
Arnold Weinstein
Fortuna (OB) (1962)

SPEAK LOW
Kurt Weill
Ogden Nash
One Touch of Venus (1943)

SPEAKING OF LOVE
Vernon Duke
E. Y. Harburg
Walk a Little Faster (1932)

SPEAKING OF PALS
Morton Gould
Betty Comden and Adolph Green
Billion Dollar Baby (1945)

SPEAKING OF YOU
Lewis E. Gensler
Owen Murphy and Robert A. Simon
The Gang's All Here (1931)

SPECIAL ANNOUNCEMENT, A
Leslie Bricusse and Anthony Newley
Stop the World - I Want to Get Off
  (1962)

SPECIAL BULLETIN
Susan Hulsman Bingham
Myrna Lamb
Mod Donna (OB) (1970)

SPECIAL DELIVERY!
Frank Loesser
The Most Happy Fella (1956)

SPECIALLY MADE FOR YOU
Joseph Meyer
William Moll
Jonica (1930)

SPELL OF THOSE HARLEM NIGHTS, THE
Al Wilson, Charles Weinberg, and
  Ken Macomber
Yeah Man (1932)

SPEND IT
C. Luckey Roberts
Alex C. Rogers
My Magnolia (1926)

SPIC AND SPANISH
Richard Rodgers
Lorenz Hart
Too Many Girls (1939)

SPIDER AND THE FLY, THE
Duke Ellington
Marshall Barer and Fred Tobias
Pousse-Café (1966)

SPIDER'S WEB, THE
Milton Schwarzwald
Clifford Grey
The Great Temptations (1926)

SPIEL, THE
James Mundy
John Latouche
The Vamp (1955)

SPINNING SONG
Robert Colby
Robert Colby and Nita Jonas
Half-Past Wednesday (OB) (1962)

SPIRIT OF CAPSULANTI
Sammy Fain
E. Y. Harburg
Flahooley (1951)

SPIRIT OF EDUCATION, THE
Helen Miller
Eve Merriam
Inner City (1971)

SPLENDOR IN THE GRASS
Jacques Urbont
David Newburger
Stag Movie (OB) (1971)

SPORT IS SPORT
Harry Revel
Mack Gordon
Smiling Faces (1932)

SPOSALIZIO
Frank Loesser
The Most Happy Fella (1956)

SPRING
John Mundy
Edward Eager
The Liar (1950)

SPRING AGAIN
Vernon Duke
Ira Gershwin
The Goldwyn Follies (F) (1938)

SPRING BEAUTIES
Al Carmines
Maria Irene Fornes
Promenade (OB) (1969)

SPRING DOTH LET HER COLOURS FLY
Charles Strouse
Lee Adams
The Littlest Revue (OB) (1956)

SPRING FEVER
Harold Arlen
Ira Gershwin and E. Y Harburg
Life Begins at 8:40 (1934)

SPRING HAS SPRUNG
Arthur Schwartz
Dorothy Fields
Excuse My Dust (F) (1951)

SPRING IN AUTUMN
Will Ortman
Gus Kahn and Raymond B. Egan
Holka-Polka (1925)

SPRING IN THE CITY
Paul Nassau and Oscar Brand
The Education of Hyman Kaplan (1968)

SPRING IN VIENNA
Richard Rodgers
Lorenz Hart
I'd Rather Be Right (1937)

SPRING IS HERE
Richard Rodgers
Lorenz Hart
Spring Is Here (1929)

SPRING IS HERE
Jerome Kern
Oscar Hammerstein II
Sweet Adeline (1929)

SPRING IS HERE
Richard Rodgers
Lorenz Hart
I Married an Angel (1938)

SPRING IS IN THE AIR
Henry Souvaine and Jay Gorney
Morrie Ryskind and Howard Dietz
Merry-Go-Round (1927)

SPRING IS IN THE AIR
Gus Edwards
Eugene Conrad
Broadway Sho-Window (1936)

SPRING OF NEXT YEAR, THE
Jerry Herman
Dear World (1969)

SPRING SONG
Warburton Guilbert

Viola Brothers Shore and June Sillman
New Faces (1934)

SPRING TIME OF THE YEAR
Oscar Brand and Paul Nassau
A Joyful Noise (1966)

SPRING TRA LA
Lloyd Waner, Lupin Feine, and Moe Jaffe
A Little Racketeer (1932)

SPRING WILL BE A LITTLE LATE THIS YEAR
Frank Loesser
Christmas Holiday (F) (1944)

SPRINGTIME
Lewis E. Gensler
B. G. DeSylva
Queen High (1926)

SPRINGTIME COMETH, THE
Sammy Fain
E. Y. Harburg
Flahooley (1951)

SPRINGTIME IS IN THE AIR
Johann Strauss I (adapted by Oscar Straus)
Clare Kummer
Three Waltzes (1937)

SQUABBLE SONG, THE
Bill and Patti Jacob
Jimmy (1969)

ST. BRIDGET
Jerry Herman
Mame (1966)

ST. PIERRE
John Kander
Fred Ebb
The Happy Time (1968)

STABILITY
Jerry Bock
Sheldon Harnick
The Rothschilds (1970)

STAG MOVIE
Jacques Urbont
David Newburger
Stag Movie (OB) (1971)

STAGE MANAGERS' CHORUS
Richard Rodgers
Dudley Digges and Lorenz Hart
The Garrick Gaieties (1925)

STAN' UP AND FIGHT
Georges Bizet
Oscar Hammerstein II
Carmen Jones (1943)

STAND AROUND THE BAND
Don Walker
Clay Warnick
Memphis Bound (1945)

STAND BACK
Earl Robinson
Waldo Salt
Sandhog (OB) (1954)

STAND UP AND CHEER
Eddie Stuart
Harvey Lasker
Old Bucks and New Wings (OB) (1962)

STAND UP ON YOUR FEET AND DANCE
Charles M. Schwab
Henry Myers
Bare Facts of 1926 (1926)

STANDING
Peter Link
C. C. Courtney and Ragan Courtney
Earl of Ruston (1971)

STANDING ON THE CORNER
Frank Loesser
The Most Happy Fella (1956)

STAR AND GARTER GIRLS
Lester Lee
Jerry Seelen
Star and Garter (1942)

STAR IN THE TWILIGHT
Karl Hajos (based on Chopin)
Harry B. Smith
White Lilacs (1928)

STAR OF STARS
Philip Charig and Richard Myers
Leo Robin
Allez-Oop (1927)

STAR OF THE NORTH STATE
Sidney Lippman
Sylvia Dee
Barefoot Boy with Cheek (1947)

STAR ON THE MONUMENT, A
Nancy Ford
Gretchen Cryer
Now Is the Time for All Good Men
  (OB) (1967)

STAR TAR
Jim Wise
George Haimsohn and Robin Miller
Dames at Sea (OB) (1968)

STARLIGHT
Albert Von Tilzer
Neville Fleeson
Bye Bye, Bonnie (1927)

STARLIGHT, STARBRIGHT
Helen Miller
Eve Merriam
Inner City (1971)

STARLIT HOUR, THE
Peter de Rose
Mitchell Parrish
Earl Carroll's Vanities (1940)

STARRY SKY
Dimitri Tiomkin
Edward Eliscu
A Little Racketeer (1932)

STARS HAVE BLOWN MY WAY
Tommy Wolf
Fran Landesman
The Nervous Set (1959)

STARS REMAIN, THE
Jay Gorney
Henry Myers
Meet the People (1940)

STARS SEEM SO LOW TONIGHT, THE
Darwin Venneri
Darwin's Theories (OB) (1960)

STARS WITH STRIPES
Max Ewing
Dorothy Sands and Marc Loebell
The Grand Street Follies (OB) (1927)

START DANCING
Jimmy Van Heusen
Johnny Burke
Nellie Bly (1946)

START STOMPIN'
Charles Rosoff
Leo Robin
Judy (1927)

START THE BALL ROLLIN'
David Raksin
June Carroll
If the Shoe Fits (1946)

STARTING AT THE BOTTOM
Kay Swift
Paul James
Fine and Dandy (1930)

STATE OF THE KINGDOM
Sam Pottle
Tom Whedon
All Kinds of Giants (OB) (1961)

STATELY HOMES OF ENGLAND, THE
Noël Coward
Set to Music (1939)

STATION L-O-V-E
Manning Sherwin
Arthur Herzog, Jr.
Bad Habits of 1926 (OB) (1926)

STATISTICS
Helen Miller
Eve Merriam
Inner City (1971)

STATUE, THE
Jacques Brel
Eric Blau and Mort Shuman
*Jacques Brel Is Alive and Well and
    Living in Paris* (OB) (1968)

STAY
Richard Rodgers
Stephen Sondheim
Do I Hear a Waltz? (1965)

STAY AS WE ARE
Arthur Schwartz
Ira Gershwin
Park Avenue (1946)

STAY EAST, YOUNG MAN
Richard Lewine
Ted Fetter
The Girl from Wyoming (OB) (1938)

STAY OUT, SAMMY
Harold Rome
Pins and Needles (OB) (1937)

STAY WELL
Kurt Weill
Maxwell Anderson
Lost in the Stars (1949)

STAY WITH THE HAPPY PEOPLE
Jule Styne
Bob Hilliard
Michael Todd's Peep Show (1950)

STAYING ALIVE
Kenneth Jacobson
Rhoda Roberts
Show Me Where the Good Times Are
    (OB) (1970)

STAYING YOUNG
Bob Merrill
Take Me Along (1959)

STEADY JOB
Dale F. Menten
Dale F. Menten and Frederick Gaines
The House of Leather (OB) (1970)

STEADY, STEADY
Milton Schafer
Ronny Graham
Bravo Giovanni (1962)

STEAM HEAT
Richard Adler and Jerry Ross
The Pajama Game (1954)

STEAM IS ON THE BEAM, THE
John Green
George Marion, Jr.
Beat the Band (1942)

STEAMBOAT
Jack Urbont
Bruce Geller
Livin' the Life (OB) (1957)

STEAMBOAT DAYS
Clarence Williams
Bottomland (1927)

STEAMBOAT WHISTLE, THE
Arthur Schwartz
Howard Dietz
At Home Abroad (1935)

STEP ACROSS THAT LINE
Oscar Brown, Jr.
Buck White (1969)

STEP ON IT
Joseph Meyer
Irving Caesar
Sweetheart Time (1926)

STEP ON THE BLUES
Con Conrad and Will Donaldson
Otto Harbach
Kitty's Kisses (1926)

STEP ON THE GASOLINE
William B. Kernell
Dorothy Donnelly
Hello, Lola (1926)

STEP, STEP SISTERS
Harry Archer
Harlan Thompson
Merry-Merry (1925)

STEP, STEP, STEP
Jack Murray and Joe Brandfon
Half a Widow (1927)

STEP TO PARIS BLUES
Maury Rubens
Clifford Grey
The Madcap (1928)

STEP TO THE REAR
Elmer Bernstein
Carolyn Leigh
How Now, Dow Jones (1967)

STEP UP AND PEP UP THE PARTY
Harry Tierney
Joseph McCarthy
Cross My Heart (1928)

STEPPIN' ALONG
Alexander Hill
Hummin' Sam (1933)

STEPPIN' BABY
Harold Levey
Owen Murphy
Rainbow Rose (1926)

STEPPIN' OUT WITH MY BABY
Irving Berlin
Easter Parade (F) (1948)

STEPS OF THE CAPITOL, THE
Burton Lane
Laffing Room Only (1944)

STEREOPHONIC SOUND
Cole Porter
Silk Stockings (1955)

STETSON
Walter Donaldson
Gus Kahn
Whoopee (1928)

STICK AROUND
Charles Strouse
Lee Adams
Golden Boy (1964)

STICK TO YOUR DANCING, MABEL
Charlotte Kent
The Little Show (1929)

STIFF UPPER LIP
George Gershwin
Ira Gershwin
A Damsel in Distress (F) (1937)

STILL I'D LOVE YOU
Ray Henderson
B. G. DeSylva and Lew Brown
Follow Thru (1929)

STIOCHKET
Murray Rumshinsky
Jacob Jacobs
The President's Daughter (1970)

STOCK REPORT
Norman Martin
Fred Ebb
Put It in Writing (OB) (1963)

STOLEN KISSES
Franz Steininger (adapted from Tchaikovsky)
Forman Brown
Music in My Heart (1947)

STOMACHS AND STOMACHS
John Mundy
Edward Eager
The Liar (1950)

STOMPIN' 'EM DOWN
Alexander Hill
Hummin' Sam (1933)

STONE BRIDGE AT EIGHT, THE
James F. Hanley
Eddie Dowling
Honeymoon Lane (1926)

STONES OF JEHOSHAPHAT, THE
Deed Meyer
Stones of Jehoshaphat (OB) (1963)

STONEWALL MOSKOWITZ MARCH
Richard Rodgers
Irving Caesar
Betsy (1926)

STOP
Porter Grainger and Freddie Johnson
Lucky Sambo (1925)

STOP, GO!
Maury Rubens and J. Fred Coots
Clifford Grey
The Madcap (1928)

STOP HOLDING ME BACK
John Mundy
Edward Eager
The Liar (1950)

STOP THAT DANCING
Burton Lane
Laffing Room Only (1944)

STORE-BOUGHT SUIT
Jerome Moross
John Latouche
The Golden Apple (1954)

STORK DON'T COME AROUND ANY MORE, THE
B. Laidlaw
A Night in Venice (1929)

STORMY LOVE
Franz Lehár
Edward Eliscu
Frederika (1937)

STORY OF A CARROT, THE
Sidney Lippman
Sylvia Dee
Barefoot Boy with Cheek (1947)

STORY OF A HORN, THE
Lee Wainer
Robert Sour
Sing for Your Supper (1939)

STORY OF ALICE, THE
Jerry Bock
Larry Holofcener
Catch a Star! (1955)

STORY OF LUCY AND JESSIE, THE
Stephen Sondheim
Follies (1971)

STORY OF MARIE, THE
Charles Gaynor
Show Girl (1961)

STOUTHEARTED MEN
Sigmund Romberg
Oscar Hammerstein II
The New Moon (1928)

STRAIGHT
Joseph Martinez Kookoolis and Scott Fagan
Scott Fagan
Soon (1971)

STRANGE DUET
Jule Styne
Betty Comden and Adolph Green
Subways Are for Sleeping (1961)

STRANGE MUSIC
Robert Wright and George Forrest (based on Grieg)
Song of Norway (1944)

STRANGE NEW LOOK*
James Shelton
Dance Me a Song (1950)

STRANGE NEW WORLD
Paul Nassau and Oscar Brand
The Education of Hyman Kaplan (1968)

STRANGE THING MYSTIFYING
Andrew Lloyd Webber
Tim Rice
Jesus Christ Superstar (1971)

STRANGE WEATHER
Darwin Venneri
Darwin's Theories (OB) (1960)

STRANGELY
Alfred Brooks
Ira J. Bilowit
Of Mice and Men (OB) (1958)

---

*Dropped from New York production

STRANGER
Bronislaw Kaper
John Latouche
Polonaise (1945)

STRANGER IN PARADISE
Robert Wright and George Forrest
(based on Alexander Borodin)
Kismet (1953)

STRANGER INTERLUDE, A
Maceo Pinkard
Pansy (1929)

STRANGERS
Richard Rodgers
Androcles and the Lion (TV) (1967)

STRAW THAT BROKE THE CAMEL'S BACK, THE
Sammy Fain
Marilyn and Alan Bergman
Something More! (1964)

STRAWBERRIES
Lor Crane
John B. Kuntz
Whispers on the Wind (OB) (1970)

STRAWBERRY DAY
William S. Fischer
Maxine Klein
Kiss Now (OB) (1971)

STRAWBERRY JAM
Sigmund Romberg
Dorothy Donnelly
My Maryland (1927)

STREAMLINED POMPADOUR
Robert Stolz
Rowland Leigh
Night of Love (1941)

STREET, THE
Stefan Kanfer, Jess J. Korman, and Joseph Grayhon
I Want You (OB) (1961)

STREET CRIES (STRAWBERRY WOMAN, CRAB MAN)
George Gershwin

DuBose Heyward
Porgy and Bess (1935)

STREET CRIES
Irving Burgie
Ballad for Bimshire (OB) (1963)

STREET SERMON
Helen Miller
Eve Merriam
Inner City (1971)

STREET SONG
James Bredt
Edward Eager
The Happy Hypocrite (OB) (1968)

STREETS OF NEW YORK, THE (IN OLD NEW YORK)
Victor Herbert
Henry Blossom
The Red Mill (1906)

STREETS OF PARIS, THE
Jimmy McHugh
Al Dubin
The Streets of Paris (1939)

STRICTLY CONFIDENTIAL
Dave Stamper
Fred Herendeen
Orchids Preferred (1937)

STRIKE
J. Fred Coots
Clifford Grey
June Days (1925)

STRIKE!
Frederick Loewe
Alan Jay Lerner
Paint Your Wagon (1951)

STRIKE ME PINK
Ray Henderson
B. G. DeSylva and Lew Brown
Strike Me Pink (1933)

STRIKE UP THE BAND!
George Gershwin
Ira Gershwin
Strike Up the Band (1930)

STRING QUARTET
Paul Nassau
Fallout (OB) (1959)

STROLL ON THE PLAZA 'ANA, A
Cole Porter
Panama Hattie (1940)

STROLLING
Porter Grainger and Freddie Johnson
Lucky Sambo (1925)

STROLLING ON THE LIDO
Lee David and Maury Rubens
J. Keirn Brennan and Moe Jaffe
A Night in Venice (1929)

STROLLING, OR WHAT HAVE YOU?
Jerome Kern
Oscar Hammerstein II
Sunny (1925)

STROLLING THRU THE PARK
Sammy Fain
Charles Tobias
Hellzapoppin' (1938)

STROLLING WITH THE ONE I LOVE THE BEST
Sigmund Romberg
Dorothy Donnelly
My Maryland (1927)

STRONGER SEX, THE
Jimmy Van Heusen
Johnny Buke
Carnival in Flanders (1953)

STRONGEST MAN IN THE WORLD, THE
Charles Strouse
Lee Adams
(It's a Bird, It's a Plane) It's Superman (1966)

STRUTTIN' TIME
C. Luckey Roberts
Alex C. Rogers
My Magnolia (1926)

STUCK WITH EACH OTHER
Lee Pockriss
Anne Croswell
Tovarich (1963)

STUCK-UP
Nancy Ford
Gretchen Cryer
Now Is the Time for All Good Men (OB) (1967)

STUDENT ROBIN HOOD OF PILSEN, THE
Randall Thompson
Perry Ivins
Bad Habits of 1926 (OB) (1926)

STUTTERING SONG
Al Carmines
Rosalyn Drexler
Home Movies (OB) (1964)

SUB-DEBS' FIRST FLING
Dave Stamper
Fred Herendeen
Orchids Preferred (1937)

SUBURBAN RETREAT
David Baker
David Craig
Phoenix '55 (OB) (1955)

SUBWAY DIRECTIONS; RIDE THROUGH THE NIGHT
Jule Styne
Betty Comden and Adolph Green
Subways Are for Sleeping (1961)

SUBWAY DREAM
Helen Miller
Eve Merriam
Inner City (1971)

SUBWAY RAG
Buster Davis
Steven Vinaver
Diversions (OB) (1958)

SUBWAY SONG
Richard Lewine
Arnold B. Horwitt
Make Mine Manhattan (1948)

SUBWAY SUN, THE
Ray Perkins
Max and Nathaniel Lief
The Greenwich Village Follies (1928)

SUBWAYS ARE FOR SLEEPING
Jule Styne
Betty Comden and Adolph Green
Subways Are for Sleeping (1961)

SUCCESS
Jule Styne
Betty Comden and Adolph Green
Do Re Mi (1960)

SUCCESS
Hal Jordan
Jerry Douglas
Rondelay (OB) (1969)

SUCH A BEAUTIFUL WORLD
Sol Kaplan
Edward Eliscu
The Banker's Daughter (OB) (1962)

SUCH A MERRY PARTY
Rick Besoyan
Little Mary Sunshine (OB) (1959)

SUCH A SOCIABLE SORT
Jimmy Van Heusen
Sammy Cahn
Walking Happy (1966)

SUCH STUFF AS DREAMS ARE MADE OF
Sammy Fain
Irving Kahal
Boys and Girls Together (1940)

SUDDEN THRILL, THE
Jimmy Van Heusen
Johnny Burke
Carnival in Flanders (1953)

SUDDENLY
Vernon Duke
E. Y. Harburg and Billy Rose
Ziegfeld Follies (1934)

SUDDENLY IT'S SPRING
Jimmy Van Heusen
Johnny Burke
Lady in the Dark (F) (1944)

SUDDENLY STOP AND THINK
Sam Pottle
Tom Whedon
All Kinds of Giants (OB) (1961)

SUDDENLY YOU'RE A STRANGER
Janet Gari
Toby Garson
Lyle (OB) (1970)

SUE ME
Frank Loesser
Guys and Dolls (1950)

SUGAR BABE
Eubie Blake
Noble Sissle
Shuffle Along (1933)

SUGARFOOT
Vernon Duke
Howard Dietz
Jackpot (1944)

SUICIDE SONG
George Kleinsinger
Joe Darion
Shinbone Alley (1957)

SUITS ME FINE
Hugh Martin
Make a Wish (1951)

SUMMER AFTERNOON
Harold Rome
Wish You Were Here (1952)

SUMMER DAY
Marc Blitzstein
Regina (1949)

SUMMER DRESSES
Harold Rome
Bless You All (1950)

SUMMER IS
Jerry Bock
Sheldon Harnick
The Body Beautiful (1958)

SUMMER IS A-COMIN' IN
Vernon Duke
John Latouche
The Lady Comes Across (1942)

SUMMER IS OVER
John Kander
James Goldman, John Kander, and
    William Goldman
A Family Affair (1962)

SUMMER LOVE
Maury Laws
Jules Bass
Month of Sundays (OB) (1968)

SUMMER NIGHTS
Ford Dabney
Jo Trent
Rang-Tang (1927)

SUMMER NIGHTS
Helen Miller
Eve Merriam
Inner City (1971)

SUMMER ROMANCE, A
Raymond Taylor
Lester Judson
Chic (OB) (1959)

SUMMER, SUMMER
Galt MacDermot
John Guare
Two Gentlemen of Verona (1971)

SUMMER TIME, THE
William B. Kernell
Dorothy Donnelly
Hello, Lola (1926)

SUMMER TIME
Rudolf Friml
P. G. Wodehouse and Clifford Grey
The Three Musketeers (1928)

SUMMERTIME
George Gershwin
DuBose Heyward
Porgy and Bess (1935)

SUMMERTIME IS SUMMERTIME
Walter Kent
Kim Gannon
Seventeen (1951)

SUMMERTIME LOVE
Frank Loesser
Greenwillow (1960)

SUN ABOUT TO RISE, THE
Jerome Kern
Oscar Hammerstein II
Sweet Adeline (1929)

SUN AT MY WINDOW, LOVE AT MY
DOOR
Victor Young
Stella Unger
Seventh Heaven (1955)

SUN IS BEGINNING TO CROW,
THE
Richard Adler
Kwamina (1961)

SUN RISES, THE
Sol Kaplan
Edward Eliscu
The Banker's Daughter (OB) (1962)

SUN WILL SHINE, THE
Arthur Schwartz
Morrie Ryskind
Ned Wayburn's Gambols (1929)

SUN WORSHIP
A. Baldwin Sloane
Harry Cort and George E. Stoddard
China Rose (1925)

SUNDAY
J. Fred Coots
Clifford Grey
The Merry World (1926)

SUNDAY
Richard Rodgers
Oscar Hammerstein II
Flower Drum Song (1958)

SUNDAY AFTERNOON
Harry Archer
Harlan Thompson
Twinkle Twinkle (1926)

SUNDAY IN CICERO FALLS
Harold Arlen
E. Y. Harburg
Bloomer Girl (1944)

SUNDAY IN THE PARK
Harold Rome
Pins and Needles (OB) (1937)

SUNDAY MORNING
Ray Henderson
Ted Koehler
Say When (1934)

SUNDAY MORNING
Johnny Burke
Donnybrook! (1961)

SUNDAY MORNING BREAKFAST
TIME
Cole Porter
Jubilee (1935)

SUNDAY MORNING CHURCHMAN
Richard Lewine
Norman Zeno
Entre-Nous (OB) (1935)

SUNDAY MORNING IN JUNE
Paul McGrane
Neville Fleeson
Who's Who (1938)

SUNDAY NIGHT IN NEW YORK
Charles Tobias, Charles Newman, and
  Murray Mencher
Earl Carroll's Sketch Book (1935)

SUNDOWN SERENADE
C. Luckey Roberts
Alex C. Rogers
My Magnolia (1926)

SUN'LL BE UP IN THE MORNING,
THE
Sammy Fain
Jack Yellen
Boys and Girls Together (1940)

SUNNY
Jerome Kern
Oscar Hammerstein II
Sunny (1925)

SUNNY CALIFORNIA
Burton Lane
Laffing Room Only (1944)

SUNNY DISPOSISH
Philip Charig
Ira Gershwin
Americana (1926)

SUNNY RIVER
Sigmund Romberg
Oscar Hammerstein II
Sunny River (1941)

SUNNY SIDE OF YOU
Frank Grey
Earle Crooker and McElbert Moore
Happy (1927)

SUNNY SIDE UP
Ray Henderson
B. G. DeSylva and Lew Brown
Sunny Side Up (F) (1929)

SUNNY SOUTHERN SMILE
Harry Revel
Mack Gordon
Ziegfeld Follies (1931)

SUNRISE ON SUNSET
Baldwin Bergersen
George Marion, Jr.
Allah Be Praised (1944)

SUNRISE, SUNSET
Jerry Bock
Sheldon Harnick
Fiddler on the Roof (1964)

SUNS THAT DAILY RISE, THE
Meyer Kupferman
Paul Goodman
Jonah (OB) (1966)

SUNSET TREE
Jule Styne
E. Y. Harburg
Darling of the Day (1968)

SUNSHINE
Jerome Kern
Oscar Hammerstein II
Sunny (1925)

SUNSHINE
Jule Styne
Leo Robin
Gentlemen Prefer Blondes (1949)

SUNSHINE
Ann Sternberg
Gertrude Stein
Gertrude Stein's First Reader (OB)
  (1969)

SUNSHINE FACE
Steve Allen
Sophie (1963)

SUNSHINE GIRL
Bob Merrill
New Girl in Town (1957)

SUNSHINE TOMORROW
G. Wood
F. Jasmine Addams (OB) (1971)

SUNUP
Percy Wenrich
Harry Clarke
Who Cares? (1930)

SUPERSATIONAL DAY
Jack Urbont
Bruce Geller
Livin' the Life (OB) (1957)

SUPERSTAR
Andrew Lloyd Webber
Tim Rice
Jesus Christ Superstar (1971)

SUPERSTITION
Max Rich
Jack Scholl
Keep Moving (1934)

SUPPER TIME
Irving Berlin
As Thousands Cheer (1933)

SUPPERTIME
Clark Gesner
You're a Good Man, Charlie Brown
  (OB) (1967)

SUPPLE COUPLE
Thomas (Fats) Waller
George Marion, Jr.
Early to Bed (1943)

SUR LA PLAGE
Sandy Wilson
The Boy Friend (1954)

SURE SIGN YOU REALLY LOVE ME
Harry Denny
Footlights (1927)

SURE THING
Jerome Kern
Ira Gershwin
Cover Girl (F) (1944)

SURPLUS BLUES
Harold Rome
Call Me Mister (1946)

SURPRISE
Jay Livingston and Ray Evans
Oh Captain! (1958)

SURREY WITH THE FRINGE ON TOP,
THE
Richard Rodgers
Oscar Hammerstein II
Oklahoma! (1943)

SURVIVE
Harvey Schmidt
Tom Jones
Celebration (1969)

SUSAN BELLE, THE
Eubie Blake
J. Milton Reddie and Cecil Mack
Swing It (1937)

SUSANNAH'S SQUEAKING SHOES
Muriel Lillie
Arthur Weigall
Charlot's Revue (1926)

SUSAN'S SONG
Kenn Long and Jim Crozier
Kenn Long
Touch (OB) (1970)

SUZIE
Jerome Kern
Anne Caldwell
Criss-Cross (1926)

SUZY IS A GOOD THING
Richard Rodgers
Oscar Hammerstein II
Pipe Dream (1955)

SWALLOWS, THE
Richard Rodgers
Lorenz Hart
She's My Baby (1928)

SWAMPS OF HOME, THE
Mary Rodgers
Marshall Barer
Once Upon a Mattress (OB) (1959)

SWAN, THE
Jule Styne
Bob Merrill
Funny Girl (F) (1968)

SWANEE
George Gershwin
Irving Caesar
Sinbad (1919)

SWANEE MOON
Eubie Blake
Noble Sissle
Shuffle Along (1952)

SWANEE RIVER MELODY
Charles Weinberg
Al Wilson
Americana (1926)

SWAPPING SWEET NOTHINGS WITH YOU
Robert Russell Bennett
Owen Murphy and Robert A. Simon
Hold Your Horses (1933)

SWEAT SONG
Earl Robinson
Waldo Salt
Sandhog (OB) (1954)

SWEEP
Jay Thompson
Double Entry (OB) (1961)

SWEET AND HOT
Harold Arlen
Jack Yellen
You Said It (1931)

SWEET AND LOW-DOWN
George Gershwin
Ira Gershwin
Tip-Toes (1925)

SWEET AS SUGAR CANE
Vincent Youmans
Billy Rose and Edward Eliscu
Great Day! (1929)

SWEET BEGINNING
Leslie Bricusse and Anthony Newley
The Roar of the Greasepaint - The Smell of the Crowd (1965)

SWEET CHARITY
Ruth Cleary Patterson
Les Kramer
Russell Patterson's Sketch Book (OB) (1960)

SWEET CHARITY
Cy Coleman
Dorothy Fields
Sweet Charity (1966)

SWEET DANGER
Robert Wright and George Forrest
Kean (1961)

SWEET EVENING BREEZE
Ford Dabney
Jo Trent
Rang-Tang (1927)

SWEET FOOL
Rudolf Friml
Rowland Leigh and John Shubert
Music Hath Charms (1934)

SWEET GERALDINE
Richard Rodgers
Lorenz Hart
America's Sweetheart (1931)

SWEET HELEN
Erich Wolfgang Korngold (based on
    Offenbach)
Herbert Baker
Helen Goes to Troy (1944)

SWEET HENRY LOVES YOU
Joseph Martinez Kookoolis and Scott
    Fagan
Scott Fagan
Soon (1971)

SWEET LADY
Frank Crumit and Dave Zoob
Howard Johnson
Tangerine (1921)

SWEET LIAR
Herbert Stothart
Irving Caesar
Polly (1929)

SWEET LIAR
Irving Caesar
George White's Music Hall Varieties
    (1932)

SWEET LITTLE BABY O' MINE
J. C. Johnson
Change Your Luck (1930)

SWEET LITTLE STRANGER
Harry Revel
Mack Gordon
Smiling Faces (1932)

SWEET MADNESS
Victor Young
Ned Washington
Murder at the Vanities (1933)

SWEET MELODY OF NIGHT
Erich Korngold
Oscar Hammerstein II
Give Us This Night (F) (1936)

SWEET MEMORIES
Eddie Stuart
Harvey Lasker
Old Bucks and New Wings (OB)
    (1962)

SWEET MEMORY
Goerge Fischoff
Carole Bayer
Georgy (1970)

SWEET MUSIC
Arthur Schwartz
Howard Dietz
The Band Wagon (1931)

SWEET OLD FASHIONED WALTZ
Walter G. Samuels
Morrie Ryskind
Ned Wayburn's Gambols (1929)

SWEET ONE
Lewis E. Gensler
Robert A. Simon
Ups-A-Daisy (1928)

SWEET PETER
Richard Rodgers
Lorenz Hart
Dearest Enemy (1925)

SWEET POPOPPER
C. Luckey Roberts
Alex C. Rogers
My Magnolia (1926)

SWEET SAVANNAH SUE
Thomas (Fats) Waller and Harry
  Brooks
Andy Razaf
Hot Chocolates (1929)

SWEET SIXTY-FIVE
Richard Rodgers
Lorenz Hart
I'd Rather Be Right (1937)

SWEET THURSDAY
Richard Rodgers
Oscar Hammerstein II
Pipe Dream (1955)

SWEET TIME
Will Holt
That 5 A. M. Jazz (OB) (1964)

SWEET WILLIAM
Frederick Loewe
Earle Crooker
Great Lady (1938)

SWEET WILLIAM
David Baker
David Craig
Copper and Brass (1957)

SWEETENHEART
Richard Rodgers
Lorenz Hart
Simple Simon (1930)

SWEETER THAN YOU*
Harry Ruby
Bert Kalmar
Twinkle Twinkle (1926)

SWEETEST OF THE ROSES
Lewis E. Gensler
Robert A. Simon
Ups-A-Daisy (1928)

SWEETEST SOUNDS, THE
Richard Rodgers
No Strings (1962)

SWEETEST THING IN LIFE, THE
Jerome Kern
B. G. DeSylva
Peter Pan (1924)

**SWEETHEART OF OUR STUDENT
CORPS**
Emile Berté and Maury Rubens
J. Keirn Brennan
Music in May (1929)

**SWEETHEART OF YOUR DREAM,
THE**
Percy Wenrich
Raymond Peck
Castles in the Air (1926)

SWEETHEART TIME
Joseph Meyer
Irving Caesar
Sweetheart Time (1926)

SWEETHEARTS
Victor Herbert
Robert B. Smith
Sweethearts (1913)

SWEETHEARTS
Harry Tierney
Joseph McCarthy
Rio Rita (1927)

SWEETHEARTS OF THE TEAM, THE
Richard Rodgers
Lorenz Hart
Too Many Girls (1939)

SWEETNESS
John Dooley
Hobo (OB) (1961)

SWEPT AWAY
Robert Wright and George Forrest
Kean (1961)

SWING!
Leonard Bernstein
Betty Comden and Adolph Green
Wonderful Town (1953)

SWING-A-DING-A-LING
Robert Dahdah
Curley McDimple (OB) (1967)

---

*Also in *Top Speed* (1929)

SWING LOW, SWEET HARRIET
Philip Charig
Dan Shapiro and Milton Pascal
Artists and Models (1943)

SWING SONG
Noël Coward
The Girl Who Came to Supper (1963)

SWING THAT SWING
Cole Porter
Jubilee (1935)

SWING YOUR BAG
Mitch Leigh
William Alfred and Phyllis Robinson
Cry for Us All (1970)

SWING YOUR LADY, MR. HEMINGWAY
Ray Henderson
Jack Yellen
Ziegfeld Follies (1943)

SWING YOUR PROJECTS
Jule Styne
Betty Comden and Adolph Green
Subways Are for Sleeping (1961)

SWING YOUR TAILS
Arthur Schwartz
Howard Dietz
The Second Little Show (1930)

SWINGIN' A DREAM
Jimmy Van Heusen
Eddie De Lange
Swingin' the Dream (1939)

SWINGIN' THE JINX AWAY
Cole Porter
Born to Dance (F) (1936)

SWINGING A DANCE
Oscar Brand and Paul Nassau
A Joyful Noise (1966)

SWINGING ON THE GATE
William B. Kernell
Dorothy Donnelly
Hello, Lola (1926)

SWINGY LITTLE THINGY
Sam H. Stept
Bud Green
Shady Lady (1933)

SWITCHBLADE BESS
Charles Gaynor
Show Girl (1961)

'S WONDERFUL
George Gershwin
Ira Gershwin
Funny Face (1927)

SWOOP OF THE MOOPEM
Al Carmines
Rosalyn Drexler
Home Movies (OB) (1964)

SWORD FOR THE KING, A
Albert Sirmay and Arthur Schwartz
Arthur Swanstrom
Princess Charming (1930)

SWORD, ROSE AND CAPE
Bob Merrill
Carnival (1961)

SYMPATHETIC SOMEONE
Jerome Kern
Anne Caldwell
The City Chap (1925)

SYMPATHY
Rudolf Friml
Otto Harbach
The Firefly (1912)

SYMPATHY
John Dooley
Hobo (OB) (1961)

SYMPHONY
Galt MacDermot
John Guare
Two Gentlemen of Verona (1971)

SYNCOPATIN'
Johnny Brandon
Who's Who, Baby? (OB) (1968)

SYNERGY
Peter Stampfel and Antonia
Operation Sidewinder (1970)

TA RA RA BOOM DE AY
Noël Coward
Bitter Sweet (1929)

TA TA, OL' BEAN*
Manning Sherwin
Edward Eliscu
Nine-Fifteen Revue (1930)

TABLOID PAPERS
Con Conrad
J. P. McEvoy
Americana (1926)

TAFFY
Helen Miller
Eve Merriam
Inner City (1971)

TAILOR MADE BABIES
Frank Marcus and Bernard Maltin
Bamboola (1929)

TAILOR, MOTEL KAMZOIL, THE
Jerry Bock
Sheldon Harnick
Fiddler on the Roof (1964)

TAKE A CHANCE
Jane Douglas
Tom O'Malley
Bella (OB) (1961)

TAKE A CRANK LETTER
Robert Emmett Dolan
Johnny Mercer
Texas, Li'l Darlin' (1949)

TAKE A GOOD LOOK AROUND
Jerry Herman
Madame Aphrodite (OB) (1961)

TAKE A JOB
Jule Styne
Betty Comden and Adolph Green
Do Re Mi (1960)

TAKE A KNIFE
Susan Hulsman Bingham
Myrna Lamb
Mod Donna (OB) (1970)

TAKE A LITTLE BABY HOME WITH YOU
Alfred Goodman, Maury Rubens, and
J. Fred Coots
Clifford Grey
Artists and Models (1925)

TAKE A LITTLE DIP
Milton Susskind
Paul Porter and Benjamin Hapgood
Burt
Florida Girl (1925)

TAKE A LITTLE ONE-STEP†
Vincent Youmans
Zelda Sears
No, No, Nanette (1925)

TAKE A LITTLE SIP
Claibe Richardson
Kenward Elmslie
The Grass Harp (1971)

TAKE A LITTLE STROLL WITH ME
J. Fred Coots and Maury Rubens
Clifford Grey
Mayflowers (1925)

TAKE A PICK
Paul Hoffert
David Secter
Get Thee to Canterbury (OB) (1969)

TAKE A POEM
George Kleinsinger
Norman Corwin
Of V We Sing (1942)

TAKE-A-TOUR, CONGRESSMAN
Helen Miller
Eve Merriam
Inner City (1971)

---

*Also in *Everybody's Welcome* (1931)
†Added to 1971 revival; originally in *Lollipop* (1924)

TAKE A TRIP TO HARLEM
Eubie Blake
Andy Razaf
Blackbirds (1930)

TAKE A WALK WITH ME
Edward Kunneke (based on Offen-
bach)
Harry B. Smith
The Love Song (1925)

TAKE AND TAKE AND TAKE
Richard Rodgers
Lorenz Hart
I'd Rather Be Right (1937)

TAKE BACK YOUR MINK
Frank Loesser
Guys and Dolls (1950)

TAKE 'EM TO THE DOOR BLUES
J. Fred Coots
Clifford Grey
June Days (1925)

TAKE EVERY OPPORTUNITY
Stefan Kanfer, Jess J. Korman, and Jo-
seph Grayhon
I Want You (OB) (1961)

TAKE HIM
Richard Rodgers
Lorenz Hart
Pal Joey (1940)

TAKE HIM TO JAIL
Porter Grainger and Freddie Johnson
Lucky Sambo (1925)

TAKE HOLD THE CRUTCH
Gary William Friedman
Will Holt
The Me Nobody Knows (OB) (1970)

TAKE IT AWAY
Fred Stamer
Gen Genovese
Buttrio Square (1952)

TAKE IT IN YOUR STRIDE*
Irving Berlin
Annie Get Your Gun (1946)

TAKE IT SLOW, JOE
Harold Arlen
E. Y. Harburg
Jamaica (1957)

TAKE KIDS
Jack Urbont
Bruce Geller
Livin' the Life (OB) (1957)

TAKE LOVE EASY
Duke Ellington
John Latouche
Beggar's Holiday (1946)

TAKE ME ALONG
Bob Merrill
Take Me Along (1959)

TAKE ME AWAY
Peter Tinturin
Sidney Clare and Charles Tobias
Earl Carroll's Vanities (1932)

TAKE ME BACK
Sol Berkowitz
James Lipton
Nowhere to Go but Up (1962)

TAKE ME BACK TO MANHATTAN
Cole Porter
The New Yorkers (1930)

TAKE ME BACK TO TEXAS
Jack Holmes
Bill Conklin and Bob Miller
O Say Can You See! (OB) (1962)

**TAKE ME BACK TO TEXAS WITH
YOU**
Hugh Martin
Make a Wish (1951)

TAKE ME FOR A HONEYMOON RIDE
Jerome Kern
Oscar Hammerstein II
Sweet Adeline (1929)

_____

*Dropped from New York production

TAKE MY ADVICE
Erich Wolfgang Korngold (based on Offenbach)
Herbert Baker
Helen Goes to Troy (1944)

TAKE MY HAND IN FRIENDSHIP
Edwin Greenberg
Pilgrim's Progress (OB) (1962)

TAKE MY HEART WITH YOU
Fred Spielman and Arthur Gershwin
Stanley Adams
A Lady Says Yes (1945)

TAKE OFF THE COAT
Harold Rome
Bless You All (1950)

TAKE THE AIR
Dave Stamper
Gene Buck
Take the Air (1927)

TAKE THE MOMENT
Richard Rodgers
Stephen Sondheim
Do I Hear a Waltz? (1965)

TAKE THE STEAMER TO NANTUCKET
Jacques Belasco
Kay Twomey
The Girl from Nantucket (1945)

TAKE THE WORD OF A GENTLEMAN
Jimmy Van Heusen
Johnny Burke
Carnival in Flanders (1953)

TAKE THEM ALL AWAY
Jack Strachey
Charlot's Revue (1926)

TAKE YOUR TIME
Frederico Valerio
Elizabeth Miele
Hit the Trail (1954)

TAKE YOUR TIME AND TAKE YOUR PICK
Albert Hague
Arnold B. Horwitt
Plain and Fancy (1955)

TAKE YOURSELF A TRIP
Alex Fogarty
Edwin Gilbert
You Never Know (1938)

TAKEN BY SURPRISE
Robert Hood Bowers
Francis DeWitt
Oh, Ernest! (1927)

TAKEN FOR A RIDE
Michael H. Cleary
Max and Nathaniel Lief
Shoot the Works (1931)

TAKING A CHANCE ON LOVE
Vernon Duke
John Latouche and Ted Fetter
Cabin in the Sky (1940)

TAKING A WIFE
Sigmund Romberg
Arthur Wimperis
Louie the 14th (1925)

TAKING CARE OF YOU
Walter Marks
Golden Rainbow (1968)

TAKING INVENTORY
Richard Freitas
Morty Neff and George Mysels
The Difficult Woman (OB) (1962)

TAKING NO CHANCES
Kurt Weill
Alan Jay Lerner
Love Life (1948)

TAKING OFF
Philip Charig
James Dyrenforth
Nikki (1931)

TAKING THE CURE
William Dyer
Don Parks and William Dyer
Jo! (OB) (1964)

TALE OF A SHIRT, THE
Irving Berlin
The Cocoanuts (1925)

TALE OF AN OYSTER, THE
Cole Porter
Fifty Million Frenchmen (1929)

TALES OF HOFFMAN, THE
Irving Caesar and A. Segal
Betsy (1926)

TALK
Edward Earle
Yvonne Tarr
The Decameron (OB) (1961)

TALK
Cyril Ornadel
Leslie Bricusse
Pickwick (1965)

TALK ABOUT A BUSY LITTLE HOUSEHOLD
George M. Cohan
The Merry Malones (1927)

TALK ABOUT GIRLS
Stephen Jones
Irving Caesar
Talk About Girls (1927)

TALK TO HIM
Jerry Bock, George Weiss, and Larry Holofcener
Mr. Wonderful (1956)

TALK TO ME
Richard Lewine
Arnold B. Horwitt
Make Mine Manhattan (1948)

TALK TO ME
Julian Stein
Lester Judson
Chic (OB) (1959)

TALK TO ME
Sol Berkowitz
James Lipton
Miss Emily Adam (OB) (1960)

TALK TO ME, BABY
Robert Emmett Dolan
Johnny Mercer
Foxy (1964)

TALK WITH ONE'S CONSCIENCE, A
Deed Meyer
Stones of Jehoshaphat (OB) (1963)

TALK WITH YOUR HEEL AND YOUR TOE
Oscar Levant
Irving Caesar
Ripples (1930)

TALKATIVE TOES
Vernon Duke
Howard Dietz
Three's a Crowd (1930)

TALKIN 'BOUT YOU
Gordon Duffy
Harry M. Haldane
Happy Town (1959)

TALKIN' IN TONGUES
Claibe Richardson
Kenward Elmslie
The Grass Harp (1971)

TALKIN' WITH YOUR FEET
Harry Warren
Jerome Lawrence and Robert E. Lee
Shangri-La (1956)

TALKING TO YOU
Hugh Martin and Timothy Gray
High Spirits (1964)

TALKING TO YOURSELF
Jule Styne
Betty Comden and Adolph Green
Hallelujah, Baby! (1967)

TALL HOPE
Cy Coleman
Carolyn Leigh
Wildcat (1960)

TALLY-HO
Alberta Nichols
Mann Holiner
Angela (1928)

TAMBOREE
Edward A. Horan
Frederick Herendeen
All the King's Horses (1934)

TAMBOURINE
Carl Sigman
Bob Hilliard
Angel in the Wings (1947)

TAMPA
Henry Souvaine and Jay Gorney
Morrie Ryskind and Howard Dietz
Merry-Go-Round (1927)

TAMPICO TAP
Albert Von Tilzer
Neville Fleeson
Bye Bye, Bonnie (1927)

TAMPICO TUNE
Frank Marcus and Bernard Maltin
Bamboola (1929)

TANGLES
Robert Hood Bowers
Francis DeWitt
Oh, Ernest! (1927)

TANGO
Sam Pottle
David Axelrod
New Faces (1968)

TANGO BALLAD
Kurt Weill
Marc Blitzstein
The Threepenny Opera (OB) (1954)

TANGO MELODY
Irving Berlin
The Cocoanuts (1925)

TANZ MIT MIR
Bob Merrill
Carnival (1961)

TAP, TAP, THE
Jesse Greer
Billy Rose and Ballard MacDonald
Padlocks (1927)

TAP THE PLATE
Oscar Brown, Jr.
Buck White (1969)

TAP THE TOE
Joseph Meyer and James F. Hanley
B. G. DeSylva
Big Boy (1925)

TAPPIN' THE BARREL
Victor Young
Joseph Young and Ned Washington
Blackbirds of 1934 (1933)

TAPPIN' THE TOE
J. Fred Coots
Al Dubin
White Lights (1927)

TAPS
Walter Donaldson
Gus Kahn
Whoopee (1928)

TARANTELLA
Mark Charlap
Carolyn Leigh
Peter Pan (1954)

TARANTELLA RHYTHM
Frank D'Armond
Will Morrissey
Saluta (1934)

TARTAR
George Gershwin and Herbert Stothart
Otto Harbach and Oscar Hammerstein II
Song of the Flame (1925)

TARTAR SONG, THE
Richard Rodgers
Lorenz Hart
Chee-Chee (1928)

TARTS AND FLOWERS
Harden Church
Edward Heyman
Caviar (1934)

TASTE
Walter Marks
Golden Rainbow (1968)

TASTE OF THE SEA, A
Henry Sullivan
Earle Crooker
Thumbs Up! (1934)

TATTOOED WOMAN
Coleman Dowell
The Tattooed Countess (OB) (1961)

TAVERN SONG
Sigmund Romberg
Oscar Hammerstein II
The New Moon (1928)

TAX COLLECTOR'S SOLILOQUY, THE
William Klenosky
Utopia! (OB) (1963)

TAXI DRIVERS' LAMENT
Randall Thompson
Agnes Morgan
The Grand Street Follies (OB) (1926)

TEA FOR TWO
Vincent Youmans
Irving Caesar
No, No, Nanette (1925)

TEA IN CHICAGO
James Shelton
Mrs. Patterson (1954)

TEA IN THE RAIN
Nancy Ford
Gretchen Cryer
Now is the Time for All Good Men (OB) (1967)

TEA PARTY
Baldwin Bergersen
William Archibald
The Crystal Heart (1960)

TEA-TEA-TEA
Philip Springer
Joan Javits
Hotel Passionato (OB) (1965)

TEA TIME
Charles M. Schwab
Henry Myers
Bare Facts of 1926 (1926)

TEA TIME TAP
Harry Ruby
Bert Kalmar
The Five O'Clock Girl (1927)

TEACH ME TO DANCE LIKE GRANDMA
Noël Coward
This Year of Grace (1928)

TEACHER, TEACHER
Jerome Kern
Anne Caldwell
She's a Good Fellow (1919)

T.E.A.M. (THE BASEBALL GAME)
Clark Gesner
You're a Good Man, Charlie Brown (OB) (1967)

TEARS
Stan Harte, Jr.
Walt Whitman
Leaves of Grass (OB) (1971)

TEASING MAMA
Jimmy Johnson
Henry Creamer
Keep Shufflin' (1928)

TEE TEEDLE TUM DI DUM
George M. Cohan
The Merry Malones (1927)

TEENY BOPPER
Norman Curtis
Patricia Taylor Curtis
Walk Down Mah Street! (OB) (1968)

TEETER TOTTER TESSIE
Morgan Lewis
Nancy Hamilton
One for the Money (1939)

TELEPHONE GIRLIE
Vincent Youmans
Otto Harbach
No, No, Nanette (1925)

TELEPHONE HOUR, THE
Charles Strouse
Lee Adams
Bye Bye Birdie (1960)

TELEPHONE SONG
John Kander
Fred Ebb
Cabaret (1966)

TELEPHONE TANGO
John Addison
John Cranko
Cranks (1956)

TELL A HANDSOME STRANGER
Rick Besoyan
Little Mary Sunshine (OB) (1959)

TELL HER
Arthur Siegel
June Carroll
New Faces (1956)

TELL HER
John Morris
Gerald Freedman
A Time for Singing (1966)

TELL HER IN THE SPRINGTIME
Irving Berlin
Music Box Revue (1924)

TELL HER THE TRUTH
Jack Waller and Joseph Tunbridge
R. P. Weston and Bert Lee
Tell Her the Truth (1932)

TELL IT TO THE MARINES
Richard Rodgers
Lorenz Hart
Present Arms (1928)

TELL ME AGAIN
Shep Camp
Frank DuPree
Half a Widow (1927)

TELL ME GOODBYE
Paul Klein
Fred Ebb
Morning Sun (OB) (1963)

TELL ME HOW
Frederico Valerio
Elizabeth Miele
Hit the Trail (1954)

TELL ME, LITTLE GYPSY
Irving Berlin
Ziegfeld Follies (1920)

TELL ME MORE!
George Gershwin
B. G. DeSylva and Ira Gershwin
Tell Me More (1925)

TELL ME NOT THAT YOU ARE FORGETTING
Edward Kunneke (based on Offenbach)
Harry B. Smith
The Love Song (1925)

TELL ME, PRETTY MAIDEN
Leslie Stuart
Owen Hall
Florodora (1900)

TELL ME, PRETTY MAIDEN
Harold Rome
Sing Out the News (1938)

TELL ME SOMETHING ABOUT YOURSELF
Michael H. Cleary
Max and Nathaniel Lief
Hey Nonny Nonny! (1932)

TELL ME THE STORY
Morgan Lewis
Nancy Hamilton
Three to Make Ready (1946)

TELL ME THE STORY OF YOUR LIFE
Claude Leveilee
Gladys Shelley
Gogo Loves You (OB) (1964)

TELL ME, WHAT CAN THIS BE?
Ralph Benatzky
Meet My Sister (1930)

TELL ME, WHAT IS LOVE?
Noël Coward
Bitter Sweet (1929)

TELL ME WHO YOU ARE
Lewis E. Gensler
Robert A Simon
Ups-A-Daisy (1928)

TELL THE DOC
George Gershwin
Ira Gershwin
Funny Face (1927)

TELL THE WORLD I'M THROUGH
Harry Ruby
Bert Kalmar
The Five O'Clock Girl (1927)

TEMPERANCE POLKA
David Baker
Fred Ebb
Smiling, the Boy Fell Dead (OB) (1961)

TEMPLE, THE
Andrew Lloyd Webber
Tim Rice
Jesus Christ Superstar (1971)

TEMPT ME NOT
Richard Rodgers
Lorenz Hart
Too Many Girls (1939)

TEMPTATION STRUT, THE
Earl Lindsay and Maury Rubens
Clifford Grey
The Great Temptations (1926)

TEN CENTS A DANCE
Richard Rodgers
Lorenz Hart
Simple Simon (1930)

TEN MINUTES AGO
Richard Rodgers
Oscar Hammerstein II
Cinderella (TV) (1957)

TEN MINUTES IN BED
Ned Lehak
Allen Boretz
Sweet and Low (1930)

TEN O'CLOCK TOWN
Michael Cleary
Arthur Swanstrom
Sea Legs (1937)

TENDER SHEPHERD
Mark Charlap
Carolyn Leigh
Peter Pan (1954)

TENDER SPOT, A
Ervin Drake
What Makes Sammy Run? (1964)

TENNESSEE DAN
Richard Rodgers
Lorenz Hart
America's Sweetheart (1931)

TENNIS
Percy Wenrich
Harry Clarke
Who Cares? (1930)

TENNIS CHAMPS
Richard Rodgers
Lorenz Hart
The Garrick Gaieties (1926)

TENTH AND GREENWICH
Melvin Van Peebles
Ain't Supposed to Die a Natural Death (1971)

TERESA
Robert Holton
June Carroll
Hi, Paisano! (OB) (1961)

TERRIBLY ATTRACTIVE
Arthur Schwartz
Dorothy Fields
Stars in Your Eyes (1939)

TESS'S TORCH SONG
Harold Arlen
Ted Koehler
Up in Arms (F) (1944)

TEST, THE
Kenneth Jacobson
Rhoda Roberts
Show Me Where the Good Times Are
(OB) (1970)

TÊTE-À-TÊTE, A
Cy Young
That Hat! (OB) (1964)

TEXAS, LI'L DARLIN'
Robert Emmett Dolan
Johnny Mercer
Texas, Li'l Darlin' (1949)

TEXAS STOMP
Will Morrisey
Edmund Joseph
Polly of Hollywood (1927)

TEXTILE TROOPS, THE
Max Ewing
Agnes Morgan
The Grand Street Follies (1929)

THANK HEAVEN FOR LITTLE GIRLS
Frederick Loewe
Alan Jay Lerner
Gigi (F) (1958)

THANK YOU
Al Carmines
Maria Irene Fornes
Promenade (OB) (1969)

THANK YOU, DON'T MENTION IT
Harry Revel
Mack Gordon
Smiling Faces (1932)

THANK YOU FOR A LOVELY EVENING
Jimmy McHugh
Dorothy Fields
Have a Heart (F) (1934)

THANK YOU, MA'AM
Duke Ellington
Marshall Barer and Fred Tobias
Pousse-Café (1966)

THANK YOU, MADAM
Jerry Bock
Sheldon Harnick
Shes Loves Me (1963)

THANK YOU, MRS. BUTTERFIELD
Abraham Ellstein
Walter Bullock
Great to Be Alive (1950)

THANK YOU SO MUCH
Richard Rodgers
Stephen Sondheim
Do I Hear a Waltz? (1965)

THANK YOU SONG, THE
Hugo Peretti, Luigi Creatore, and
George David Weiss
Maggie Flynn (1968)

THANK YOU, SOUTH AMERICA
Sammy Fain
Jack Yellen
Sons o' Fun (1941)

THANK YOUR FATHER
Ray Henderson
B. G. DeSylva and Lew Brown
Flying High (1930)

THANK YOUR LUCKY STARS
Arthur Schwartz
Frank Loesser
Thank Your Lucky Stars (F) (1943)

THANKS
Stan Harte, Jr.
Walt Whitman
Leaves of Grass (OB) (1971)

THANKS FOR A DARN NICE TIME
Harry Tierney
Joseph McCarthy
Cross My Heart (1928)

THANKS FOR A LOUSY EVENING
Philip Charig
Dan Shapiro and Milton Pascal
Follow the Girls (1944)

THANKS FOR THE FRANCS
Jimmy McHugh
Al Dubin
The Streets of Paris (1939)

THANKS, SWEET JESUS!
Stanley Lebowsky
Fred Tobias
Gantry (1970)

THANKS TO YOU
Henry Sullivan
Edward Eliscu
A Little Racketeer (1932)

THAT BIG-BELLIED BOTTLE
Don McAfee
Nancy Leeds
Great Scot! (OB) (1965)

THAT CERTAIN FEELING
George Gershwin
Ira Gershwin
Tip-Toes (1925)

THAT CERTAIN PARTY
William B. Kernell
Dorothy Donnelly
Hello, Lola (1926)

THAT CERTAIN THING
Edward Pola
Eddie Brandt
Woof, Woof (1929)

THAT DAY WILL COME
Eddie Stuart
Harvey Lasker
Old Bucks and New Wings (OB) (1962)

THAT DIRTY OLD MAN
Stephen Sondheim
A Funny Thing Happened on the Way to the Forum (1962)

THAT FACE!
Hugh Martin
Make a Wish (1951)

THAT FACE
Lee Pockriss
Anne Croswell
Tovarich (1963)

THAT FELLOW MANUELO
Arthur Schwartz
Howard Dietz
Revenge with Music (1934)

THAT GREAT COME AND GET IT DAY
Burton Lane
E. Y. Harburg
Finian's Rainbow (1947)

THAT GUILTY FEELING
Bill Weeden
David Finkle
I'm Solomon (1968)

THAT LINDY HOP
Eubie Blake
Andy Razaf
Blackbirds (1930)

THAT LITTLE SOMETHING
Jerome Kern
Bert Kalmar and Harry Ruby
Lucky (1927)

THAT LOST BARBERSHOP CHORD
George Gershwin
Ira Gershwin
Americana (1926)

THAT LUCKY FELLOW
Jerome Kern
Oscar Hammerstein II
Very Warm for May (1939)

THAT MAN AND WOMAN THING
Baldwin Bergersen
John Rox
All in Fun (1940)

THAT MAN OVER THERE
Meredith Willson
Here's Love (1963)

THAT MEANS NOTHING TO ME
A. L. Keith and Lee Sterling
Naughty Cinderella (1925)

THAT MISTER MAN OF MINE
Jim Wise
George Haimsohn and Robin Miller
Dames at Sea (OB) (1968)

THAT MOMENT OF MOMENTS
Vernon Duke
Ira Gershwin
Ziegfeld Follies (1936)

**THAT NAUGHTY SHOW FROM GAY
PAREE**
Sigmund Romberg (developed by
   Don Walker)
Leo Robin
The Girl in Pink Tights (1954)

THAT OLD BLACK MAGIC
Harold Arlen
Johnny Mercer
Star Spangled Rhythm (F) (1942)

THAT OLD FAMILAR RING
Bill and Patti Jacob
Jimmy (1969)

THAT OLD TIME CROWD
Moose Charlap
Eddie Lawrence
Kelly (1965)

THAT PRELUDE!
Robert Wright and George Forrest
(based on Rachmaninoff)
Anya (1965)

THAT RHYTHM MAN
Thomas (Fats) Waller and Harry
   Brooks
Andy Razaf
Hot Chocolates (1929)

THAT RUSSIAN WINTER
Irving Berlin
This Is the Army (1942)

THAT SLAVERY IS LOVE
Mitch Leigh
William Alfred and Phyllis Robinson
Cry for Us All (1970)

THAT SOMETHING EXTRA SPECIAL
Jule Styne
E. Y. Harburg
Darling of the Day (1968)

THAT SPECIAL DAY
Don McAfee
Nancy Leeds
Great Scot! (OB) (1965)

THAT TERRIBLE TUNE
Morgan Lewis
Nancy Hamilton
Two for the Show (1940)

THAT TERRIFIC RAINBOW
Richard Rodgers
Lorenz Hart
Pal Joey (1940)

THAT TIRED FEELING
Louis Alter
Harry Ruskin and Leighton K. Brill
Ballyhoo (1930)

THAT WAS YESTERDAY
Jerry Herman
Milk and Honey (1961)

THAT WAS YOUR LIFE
Eddie Stuart
Harvey Lasker
Old Bucks and New Wings (OB)
   (1962)

THAT WEEK IN PARIS
Ben Oakland
Oscar Hammerstein II
The Lady Objects (F) (1938)

THAT WONDERFUL MELODY
Noël Coward
Bitter Sweet (1929)

THAT'LL BE THE DAY
Jacques Offenbach

E. Y. Harburg
The Happiest Girl in the World (1961)

THAT'LL BE THE DAY
Johnny Brandon
Who's Who, Baby? (OB) (1968)

THAT'LL SHOW HIM
Stephen Sondheim
A Funny Thing Happened on the Way to the Forum (1962)

THAT'S A CRIME
Marguerite Monnot
Julian More, David Heneker, and Monte Norman
Irma La Douce (1960)

THAT'S A VERY INTERESTING QUESTION
Galt MacDermot
John Guare
Two Gentlemen of Verona (1971)

THAT'S BROADWAY
Gene Herbert and Teddy Hall
Bright Lights of 1944 (1943)

THAT'S CLASS
Jimmy Van Heusen
Johnny Burke
Nellie Bly (1946)

THAT'S ENTERTAINMENT
Arthur Schwartz
Howard Dietz
The Band Wagon (F) (1953)

THAT'S FINE
Jack Waller and Joseph Tunbridge
R. P. Weston and Bert Lee
Tell Her the Truth (1932)

THAT'S FOR ME
Richard Rodgers
Oscar Hammerstein II
State Fair (F) (1945)

THAT'S FOR SURE
Johnny Mercer
Top Banana (1951)

THAT'S GOOD ENOUGH FOR ME
Elmer Bernstein
Carolyn Leigh
How Now, Dow Jones (1967)

THAT'S GOOD—THAT'S BAD
Mary Rodgers
Martin Charnin
Hot Spot (1963)

THAT'S HER LIFE
Coleman Dowell
The Tattooed Countess (OB) (1961)

THAT'S HIM
Kurt Weill
Ogden Nash
One Touch of Venus (1943)

THAT'S HOW I LOVE THE BLUES
Hugh Martin and Ralph Blane
Best Foot Forward (1941)

THAT'S HOW IT GOES
Arthur Schwartz
Dorothy Fields
A Tree Grows in Brooklyn (1951)

THAT'S HOW IT IS
George Fischoff
Carole Bayer
Georgy (1970)

THAT'S HOW IT STARTS
Bob Merrill
Take Me Along (1959)

THAT'S HOW YOUNG I FEEL
Jerry Herman
Mame (1966)

THAT'S LIFE
Vernon Duke
E. Y. Harburg
Walk a Little Faster (1932)

THAT'S LOVE
Richard Rodgers
Lorenz Hart
Nana (F) (1934)

THAT'S LOVE
Louis Bellson and Will Irwin
Richard Ney
Portofino (1958)

THAT'S MY APPROACH TO LOVE
Harold Orlob
Hairpin Harmony (1943)

THAT'S MY FELLA
Morton Gould
Dorothy Fields
Arms and the Girl (1950)

THAT'S MY MAN
Harold Orlob
Irving Caesar
Talk About Girls (1927)

THAT'S NOT CRICKET
Arthur Schwartz
Howard Dietz
At Home Abroad (1935)

THAT'S RELIGION
Porter Grainger
Yeah Man (1932)

THAT'S RIGHT!
Paul Klein
Fred Ebb
Morning Sun (OB) (1963)

THAT'S RIGHT, MR. SYPH
Mildred Kayden
Frank Gagliano
Paradise Gardens East (OB) (1969)

THAT'S THE IRISH IN HER
Seymour Furth and Lee Edwards
R. F. Carroll
Bringing Up Father (1925)

THAT'S THE LAW
Cyril Ornadel
Leslie Bricusse
Pickwick (1965)

THAT'S THE LIFE FOR ME
Albert Hague
Marty Brill
Café Crown (1964)

THAT'S THE TIME WHEN I MISS YOU
Alexander Fogarty
Seymour Morris
Cape Cod Follies (1929)

THAT'S THE WAY IT HAPPENS
Richard Rodgers
Oscar Hammerstein II
Me and Juliet (1953)

THAT'S WHAT HE DID
George Gershwin
Ira Gershwin
Let 'Em Eat Cake (1933)

**THAT'S WHAT I GOT FOR NOT LIS-
TENING TO MY MOTHER**
Ruth Cleary Patterson
Floria Vestoff
Russell Patterson's Sketch Book (OB)
  (1960)

**THAT'S WHAT I TOLD HIM LAST
NIGHT**
Morton Gould
Dorothy Fields
Arms and the Girl (1950)

THAT'S WHAT I WANT FOR JANIE
Cy Coleman
Carolyn Leigh
Wildcat (1960)

**THAT'S WHAT I'D LIKE FOR CHRIST-
MAS**
Cyril Ornadel
Leslie Bricusse
Pickwick (1965)

THAT'S WHAT IT IS TO BE YOUNG
Leslie Bricusse and Anthony Newley
*The Roar of the Greasepaint—The
  Smell of the Crowd* (1965)

THAT'S WHAT THE PUBLIC WANTS
Stefan Kanfer, Jess J. Korman, and Jo-
  seph Grayhon
I Want You (OB) (1961)

**THAT'S WHAT THE WELL DRESSED
MAN IN HARLEM WILL WEAR**
Irving Berlin
This Is the Army (1942)

THAT'S WHAT YOUNG LADIES DO
John Morris
Gerald Freedman
A Time for Singing (1966)

THAT'S WHAT'S HAPPENING, BABY
Johnny Brandon
Who's Who, Baby? (OB) (1968)

THAT'S WHERE A MAN FITS IN
James Mundy
John Latouche
The Vamp (1955)

THAT'S WHERE WE COME IN
Samuel Pokrass
E. Y. Harburg
Ziegfeld Follies (1934)

THAT'S WHY DARKIES WERE BORN
Ray Henderson
B. G. DeSylva and Lew Brown
George White's Scandals (1931)

THAT'S WHY I WANT TO GO HOME
Alma Sanders
Monte Carlo
Louisiana Lady (1947)

THAT'S WHY I'M HERE TONIGHT
Ruth Cleary Patterson
Les Kramer
Russell Patterson's Sketch Book (OB) (1960)

THAT'S WHY WE MISBEHAVE
Alexander Fogarty
Edith Lois and Urana Clarke
Cape Cod Follies (1929)

THAT'S WHY WE'RE DANCING
Jimmy McHugh
Dorothy Fields
Lew Leslie's International Revue (1930)

THAT'S YOUR FUNERAL
Lionel Bart
Oliver (1963)

THAT'S YOUR THING, BABY
Tom Sankey
The Golden Screw (OB) (1967)

THEATRE IS A LADY, THE
Vernon Duke
Ogden Nash
Two's Company (1952)

THEM AND THEY
Jule Styne
Sammy Cahn
Look to the Lilies (1970)

THEN
Noël Coward
Tonight at 8:30 (Shadow Play) (1936)

THEN CAME THE WAR
Ben Black
The Vanderbilt Revue (1930)

THEN I'LL HAVE TIME FOR YOU
Ray Henderson
B. G. DeSylva and Lew Brown
Follow Thru (1929)

THEN YOU MAY TAKE ME TO THE FAIR
Frederick Loewe
Alan Jay Lerner
Camelot (1960)

THEN YOU WERE NEVER IN LOVE
Burton Lane
E. Y. Harburg
Hold On to Your Hats (1940)

THEN YOU WILL KNOW
Sigmund Romberg
Otto Harbach and Oscar Hammerstein II
The Desert Song (1926)

THERE
Jerry Bock, George Weiss, and Larry Holofcener
Mr. Wonderful (1956)

THERE AIN'T NO COLOR LINE AROUND THE RAINBOW
Irving Caesar
Gerald Marks and Sam Lerner
My Dear Public (1943)

THERE AIN'T NO FLIES ON JESUS
Peter Link and C. C. Courtney
Salvation (OB) (1969)

THERE AIN'T NO FLIES ON ME
Bob Merrill
New Girl in Town (1957)

THERE ARE YANKS (FROM THE BANKS OF THE WABASH)
Vernon Duke
Howard Dietz
Jackpot (1944)

THERE AREN'T MANY LADIES IN THE MILE END ROAD
Johnny Brandon
Who's Who, Baby? (OB) (1968)

THERE BUT FOR YOU GO I
Frederick Loewe
Alan Jay Lerner
Brigadoon (1947)

THERE COMES A TIME
Jerry Herman
Madame Aphrodite (OB) (1961)

THERE COMES A TIME
Jule Styne
Sammy Cahn
Look to the Lillies (1970)

THERE GOES A MAD OLD MAN
Bruce Montgomery
The Amorous Flea (OB) (1964)

THERE GOES MY GAL
Walter Cool
Mackey of Appalachia (OB) (1965)

THERE GOES TIME
Willard Straight
David Eddy
The Athenian Touch (OB) (1964)

THERE HAD TO BE THE WALTZ
Frederick Loewe
Earle Crooker
Great Lady (1938)

THERE HE GOES, MR. PHILEAS FOGG
Cole Porter
Around the World (1946)

THERE I GO DREAMING AGAIN
Ray Henderson
Lew Brown
Hot-Cha! (1932)

THERE I'D BE
Morton Gould
Betty Comden and Adolph Green
Billion Dollar Baby (1945)

THERE IS A CURIOUS PARADOX
Harvey Schmidt
Tom Jones
The Fantasticks (OB) (1960)

THERE IS A GARDEN IN LOVELAND
Karl Hajos (based on Tchaikovsky)
Harry B. Smith
Natja (1925)

THERE IS BEAUTIFUL YOU ARE
John Morris
Gerald Freedman
A Time for Singing (1966)

THERE IS NO DIFFERENCE
Claude Leveilee
Gladys Shelley
Gogo Loves You (OB) (1964)

THERE IS NOTHIN' LIKE A DAME
Richard Rodgers
Oscar Hammerstein II
South Pacific (1949)

THERE IS ONLY ONE PARIS FOR THAT
Marguerite Monnot
Julian More, David Heneker, and Monte Norman
Irma La Douce (1960)

THERE IS ONLY ONE THING TO BE SURE OF
Edward Thomas
Martin Charnin
Ballad for a Firing Squad (OB) (1968)

THERE IS THAT IN ME
Stan Harte, Jr.
Walt Whitman
Leaves of Grass (OB) (1971)

THERE MUST BE SOMEONE FOR
ME
Cole Porter
Mexican Hayride (1944)

THERE MUST BE SOMETHIN' BETTER
THAN LOVE
Morton Gould
Dorothy Fields
Arms and the Girl (1950)

THERE NEVER WAS A TOWN LIKE
PARIS
Mann Holiner
Alberta Nichols
Gay Paree (1926)

THERE NEVER WAS A WOMAN
Leroy Anderson
Joan Ford, Walter and Jean Kerr
Goldilocks (1958)

THERE ONCE WAS A MAN
Richard Adler and Jerry Ross
The Pajama Game (1954)

THERE WAS A LITTLE MAN
Helen Miller
Inner City (1971)

THERE WAS ONCE A LITTLE VIL-
LAGE BY THE SEA
Noël Coward
Conversation Piece (1934)

THERE WILL BE A GIRL
Harry Revel
Mack Gordon
Smiling Faces (1932)

THERE YOU ARE
William Heagney
William Heagney and Tom Connell
There You Are (1932)

THERE YOU GO AGAIN
Alex Ander
Blood (OB) (1971)

THERE'LL ALWAYS BE A LADY FAIR
Cole Porter
Anything Goes (1934)

THERE'LL BE LIFE, LOVE, AND
LAUGHTER
Kurt Weill
Ira Gershwin
The Firebrand of Florence (1945)

THERE'LL BE TROUBLE
Kurt Weill
Langston Hughes
Street Scene (1947)

THERE'LL HAVE TO BE CHANGES
MADE
Giuseppe Verdi
Charles Friedman
My Darlin' Aïda (1952)

THERE'S A BOAT DAT'S LEAVIN'
SOON FOR NEW YORK
George Gershwin
Ira Gershwin
Porgy and Bess (1935)

THERE'S A BOY IN HARLEM
Richard Rodgers
Lorenz Hart
Fools for Scandal (F) (1938)

THERE'S A BROADWAY UP IN
HEAVEN
Gerald Dolin
Edward J. Lambert
Smile at Me (1935)

THERE'S A BUILDING GOING UP
Sammy Fain
Paul Francis Webster and Ray Golden
Alive and Kicking (1950)

THERE'S A CHILL IN THE AIR
Frank D'Armond
Will Morrissey
Saluta (1934)

THERE'S A CIRCUS IN TOWN
Lionel Bart
La Strada (1969)

THERE'S A COACH COMIN' IN
Frederick Loewe
Alan Jay Lerner
Paint Your Wagon (1951)

THERE'S A COMIN' TOGETHER
George Fischoff
Carole Bayer
Georgy (1970)

THERE'S A GIRL
Rick Besoyan
Babes in the Wood (OB) (1964)

THERE'S A GREAT DAY COMING, MANANA
Burton Lane
E. Y. Harburg
Hold On to Your Hats (1940)

THERE'S A HAPPY LAND IN THE SKY
Cole Porter
Something for the Boys (1943)

THERE'S A HILL BEYOND A HILL
Jerome Kern
Oscar Hammerstein II
Music in the Air (1932)

THERE'S A LOT OF THINGS YOU CAN DO WITH TWO (BUT NOT WITH THREE)
Sidney Lippman
Sylvia Dee
Barefoot Boy with Cheek (1947)

THERE'S A MAN IN MY LIFE
Thomas (Fats) Waller
George Marion, Jr.
Early to Bed (1943)

THERE'S A MUDDLE
Robert Hood Bowers
Francis DeWitt
Oh, Ernest! (1927)

THERE'S A RAINBOW ON THE WAY
J. Fred Coots
Arthur Swanstrom and Benny Davis
Sons o' Guns (1929)

THERE'S A SMALL HOTEL
Richard Rodgers
Lorenz Hart
On Your Toes (1936)

THERE'S ALWAYS SOMETHING FISHY ABOUT THE FRENCH
Noël Coward
Conversation Piece (1934)

THERE'S GOIN' TO BE A WEDDING
Nancy Ford
Gretchen Cryer
Now Is the Time for All Good Men (OB) (1967)

THERE'S GOT TO BE LOVE
Walter Cool
Mackey of Appalachia (OB) (1965)

THERE'S GOTTA BE A VILLAIN
Robert Larimer
King of the Whole Damn World! (OB) (1962)

THERE'S GOTTA BE A WEDDING
Jimmy Van Heusen
Eddie De Lange
Swingin' the Dream (1939)

THERE'S GOTTA BE SOMETHING BETTER THAN THIS
Cy Coleman
Dorothy Fields
Sweet Charity (1966)

THERE'S HISTORY TO BE MADE
George Lessner
Miriam Battista and Russell Maloney
Sleepy Hollow (1948)

THERE'S LIFE IN THE OLD FOLKS YET
Rick Besoyan
The Student Gypsy (OB) (1963)

THERE'S LOVE IN THE COUNTRY
Dale F. Menten
Dale F. Menten and Frederick Gaines
The House of Leather (OB) (1970)

THERE'S LOVE IN THE HEART I
HOLD
Emile Berté and Maury Rubens
J. Keirn Brennan
Music in May (1929)

THERE'S MUSIC IN A KISS
Al Sherman, Al Lewis, and Abner Silver
Earl Carroll's Sketch Book (1935)

THERE'S NO GETTING AWAY FROM
YOU
Jimmy McHugh
Harold Adamson
As the Girls Go (1948)

THERE'S NO HOLDING ME
Arthur Schwartz
Ira Gershwin
Park Avenue (1946)

THERE'S NO MAN LIKE A SNOWMAN
Victor Young
Edward Heyman
Pardon Our French (1950)

THERE'S NO PLACE LIKE THE COUN-
TRY
Arthur Jones
Gen Genovese
Buttrio Square (1952)

THERE'S NO REASON IN THE WORLD
Jerry Herman
Milk and Honey (1961)

THERE'S NO ROOM FOR PEOPLE ANY
MORE
Julian Stein
Lester Judson
Chic (OB) (1959)

THERE'S NO SCHOOL LIKE OUR
SCHOOL
Skip Redwine and Larry Frank
*Frank Merriwell, or Honor Chal-
lenged* (1971)

THERE'S NOTHIN' SO BAD FOR A
WOMAN
Richard Rodgers
Oscar Hammerstein II
Carousel (1945)

THERE'S NOTHING LIKE A MODEL T
Jule Styne
Sammy Cahn
High Button Shoes (1947)

THERE'S NOTHING LIKE IT
Abraham Ellstein
Walter Bullock
Great to Be Alive (1950)

THERE'S NOTHING LIKE MARRIAGE
FOR PEOPLE
Arthur Schwartz
Ira Gershwin
Park Avenue (1946)

THERE'S NOTHING LIKE TRAVEL
Jimmy Van Heusen
Johnny Burke
Nellie Bly (1946)

THERE'S NOTHING NEW IN OLD
NEW YORK
Harry Akst
Benny Davis
Artists and Models (1927)

THERE'S NOTHING NEW UNDER THE
SUN
Vivian Ellis
Graham John
By the Way (1925)

THERE'S NOTHING NEW UNDER THE
SUN
Meyer Kupferman
Paul Goodman
Jonah (OB) (1966)

THERE'S NOTHING NICER THAN
PEOPLE
Harold Rome
Wish You Were Here (1952)

THERE'S NOTHING THE MATTER
WITH ME
Ray Henderson
Lew Brown
Hot-Cha! (1932)

THERE'S NOTHING WRONG WITH A
KISS
Oscar Levant
Irving Caesar and Graham John
Ripples (1930)

THERE'S NOTHING WRONG WITH
OUR VALUES
Billy Barnes
The Billy Barnes People (1961)

THERE'S NOWHERE TO GO BUT UP
Kurt Weill
Maxwell Anderson
Knickerbocker Holiday (1938)

THERE'S ROOM ENOUGH FOR US
Gene de Paul
Johnny Mercer
Li'l Abner (1956)

THERE'S ROOM IN MY HOUSE
John Kander
James Goldman, John Kander, and
  William Goldman
A Family Affair (1962)

THERE'S SO MUCH MORE
Richard Rodgers
Lorenz Hart
America's Sweetheart (1931)

THERE'S SOMETHING ABOUT A
HORSE
Jay Livingston and Ray Evans
Let It Ride (1961)

THERE'S SOMETHING ABOUT YOU
Emmerich Kalman
Harry B. Smith
The Circus Princess (1927)

THERE'S SOMETHING ABOUT YOU
Cyril Ornadel
Leslie Bricusse
Pickwick (1965)

THERE'S SOMETHING ABOUT YOU
Jim Wise
George Haimsohn and Robin Miller
Dames at Sea (OB) (1968)

THERE'S SOMETHING SPANISH IN
YOUR EYES
Cliff Friend and George White
George White's Scandals (1929)

THERE'S THE MOON
Richard Hill and John Hawkins
Nevill Coghill
Canterbury Tales (1969)

THERE'S "YES" IN THE AIR
Thomas (Fats) Waller
George Marion, Jr.
Early to Bed (1943)

THERMODYNAMIC DUO
Donald Swann
Michael Flanders
At the Drop of Another Hat (1966)

THESE ACRES
Coleman Dowell
The Tattooed Countess (OB) (1961)

THESE ARE WORTH FIGHTING FOR
Jack Holmes
Bill Conklin and Bob Miller
O Say Can You See! (OB) (1962)

THESE CHARMING PEOPLE
George Gershwin
Ira Gershwin
Tip-Toes (1925)

THESE FOUR WALLS
Stanley Lebowsky
Fred Tobias
Gantry (1970)

THESE THINGS I KNOW ARE TRUE
Jennifer Konecky
Wet Paint (OB) (1965)

THESE TROPICS
Sigmund Romberg
Oscar Hammerstein II
East Wind (1931)

THEY AIN'T DONE RIGHT BY OUR NELL
Cole Porter
Panama Hattie (1940)

THEY ALL FALL IN LOVE
Cole Porter
The Battle of Paris (F) (1929)

THEY ALL LAUGHED
George Gershwin
Ira Gershwin
Shall We Dance (F) (1937)

THEY ALL LOVE ME
William Heagney
William Heagney and Tom Connell
There You Are (1932)

THEY CALL THE WIND MARIA
Frederick Loewe
Alan Jay Lerner
Paint Your Wagon (1951)

THEY CAN'T TAKE THAT AWAY FROM ME
George Gershwin
Ira Gershwin
Shall We Dance (F) (1937)

THEY COULDN'T COMPARE TO YOU
Cole Porter
Out of This World (1950)

THEY DIDN'T BELIEVE ME
Jerome Kern
Herbert Reynolds
The Girl from Utah (1914)

THEY DON'T MAKE 'EM LIKE THAT ANYMORE
Elmer Bernstein
Carolyn Leigh
How Now, Dow Jones (1967)

THEY FALL IN LOVE
George M. Cohan
Billie (1928)

THEY LEARN ABOUT WOMEN FROM ME
Harold Arlen

Jack Yellen
You Said It (1931)

THEY LIKE IKE
Irving Berlin
Call Me Madam (1950)

THEY LOVE ME
Irving Berlin
Mr. President (1962)

THEY NEVER PROVED A THING
Bill and Patti Jacob
Jimmy (1969)

THEY PASS BY SINGING
George Gershwin
DuBose Heyward
Porgy and Bess (1935)

THEY SAY
Lehman Engel
Agnes Morgan
A Hero Is Born (1937)

THEY SAY
Jerry Bock
Sheldon Harnick
The Rothschilds (1970)

THEY SAY IT'S WONDERFUL
Irving Berlin
Annie Get Your Gun (1946)

THEY STILL LOOK GOOD
Con Conrad
William B. Friedlander
Mercenary Mary (1925)

THEY TALK A DIFFERENT LANGUAGE
Robert Emmett Dolan
Johnny Mercer
Texas, Li'l Darlin' (1949)

THEY WERE YOU
Harvey Schmidt
Tom Jones
The Fantasticks (OB) (1960)

THEY WON'T KNOW ME
Harold Rome
Wish You Were Here (1952)

THEY'LL SAY I'VE BEEN DREAMING
Stanley Jay Gelber
John Lollos and Don Christopher
Love and Let Love (OB) (1968)

THEY'RE BLAMING THE CHARLES-TON
Irving Berlin
The Cocoanuts (1925)

THEY'RE EITHER TOO YOUNG OR TOO OLD
Arthur Schwartz
Frank Loesser
Thank Your Lucky Stars (F) (1943)

THEY'RE HOT NOW UP IN ICELAND
Vincent Valentini
Parisiana (1928)

THEY'RE OFF
Alexander Hill
Hummin' Sam (1933)

THEY'VE GOT A LOT TO LEARN
Steve Allen
Sophie (1963)

THEY'VE GOT TO COMPLAIN
Bill Mahoney
My Wife and I (OB) (1966)

THIEF IN THE NIGHT
Arthur Schwartz
Howard Dietz
At Home Abroad (1935)

THIMBLEFUL
William Roy
Maggie (1953)

THINE ALONE
Victor Herbert
Henry Blossom
Eileen (1917)

THINGS
Harold Arlen
Ira Gershwin and E. Y. Harburg
Life Begins at 8:40 (1934)

THINGS AIN'T AS NICE
Walter Cool
Mackey of Appalachia (OB) (1965)

THINGS ARE GOING NICELY
Lor Crane
John B. Kuntz
Whispers on the Wind (OB) (1970)

THINGS ARE GOING WELL TODAY
Arthur Siegel
June Carroll
Shoestring Revue (OB) (1955)

THINGS ARE GONNA HUM THIS SUMMER
Walter Kent
Kim Gannon
Seventeen (1951)

THINGS ARE LOOKING UP
George Gershwin
Ira Gershwin
A Damsel in Distress (F) (1937)

THINGS THAT LOVERS SAY, THE
George Lessner
Miriam Battista and Russell Maloney
Sleepy Hollow (1948)

THINGS THAT WERE MADE FOR LOVE, THE
Peter de Rose
Charles Tobias and Irving Kahal
Pleasure Bound (1929)

THINGS TO REMEMBER
Leslie Bricusse and Anthony Newley
The Roar of the Greasepaint—The Smell of the Crowd (1965)

THINGS WE THINK WE ARE, THE
Ervin Drake
Her First Roman (1968)

THINGS WERE MUCH BETTER IN THE PAST
Janet Gari
Toby Garson
Lyle (OB) (1970)

THINGS YOU WANT, THE
Jerome Kern
Oscar Hammerstein II
High, Wide and Handsome (F) (1937)

THINK
Leon Pober
Bud Freeman
Beg, Borrow or Steal (1960)

THINK BEAUTIFUL
Jack Lawrence and Stan Freeman
I Had a Ball (1964)

THINK BIG RICH
Claibe Richardson
Kenward Elmslie
The Grass Harp (1971)

THINK HOW IT'S GONNA BE
Charles Strouse
Lee Adams
Applause (1970)

THINK IT OVER
Arthur Schwartz
Howard Dietz
Revenge with Music (1934)

THINK MINK
Johnny Brandon
Cindy (OB) (1964)

THINK OF MY REPUTATION
Harry Revel
Mack Gordon
Smiling Faces (1932)

THINK OF SOMETHING ELSE
Jimmy Van Heusen
Sammy Cahn
Walking Happy (1966)

THINK OF THE TIME I SAVE
Richard Adler and Jerry Ross
The Pajama Game (1954)

THINK SPRING
David Baker
Will Holt
Come Summer (1969)

THINKIN'
Richard Rodgers
Oscar Hammerstein II
Pipe Dream (1955)

THINKING
Richard Rodgers
Stephen Sondheim
Do I Hear a Waltz? (1965)

THINKING OF YOU
Con Conrad
Gus Kahn
Kitty's Kisses (1926)

THINKING OF YOU
Harry Ruby
Bert Kalmar
The Five O'Clock Girl (1927)

THINKING OUT LOUD
Harry Akst
Lew Brown
Calling All Stars (1934)

THIRD AVENUE L
Michael Brown
The Littlest Revue (OB) (1956)

THIRD FROM THE END, THE
Charles M. Schwab
Henry Myers
Bare Facts of 1926 (1926)

13 DAUGHTERS
Eaton Magoon, Jr.
13 Daughters (1961)

1348
Edward Earle
Yvonne Tarr
The Decameron (OB) (1961)

13 OLD MAIDS
Eaton Magoon, Jr.
13 Daughters (1961)

THIRTIES, THE
Jule Styne
Betty Comden and Adolph Green
Fade Out—Fade In (1964)

THIRTY-FIVE SUMMERS AGO
Ray Henderson
Jack Yellen
Ziegfeld Follies (1943)

THIS AMAZING LONDON TOWN
Jerry Bock
Sheldon Harnick
The Rothschilds (1970)

THIS CAN'T BE LOVE
Richard Rodgers
Lorenz Hart
The Boys from Syracuse (1938)

THIS CITY IS A KISSER
William S. Fischer
Maxine Klein
Kiss Now (OB) (1971)

THIS CORNUCOPIAN LAND
Mitch Leigh
William Alfred and Phyllis Robinson
Cry for Us All (1970)

THIS COULD GO ON FOR YEARS
George Gershwin
Ira Gershwin
Strike Up the Band (1930)

THIS DECADENT AGE
Alyn Heim
Malcolm L. LaPrade
Will the Mail Train Run Tonight?
(OB) (1964)

THIS DREAM
Leslie Bricusse and Anthony Newley
The Roar of the Greasepaint—The Smell of the Crowd (1965)

THIS FUNNY WORLD
Richard Rodgers
Lorenz Hart
Betsy (1926)

THIS GOES UP
Richard Rodgers
Lorenz Hart
She's My Baby (1928)

THIS GREAT PURPLE BUTTERFLY
John Duffy
Rocco Bufano and John Duffy (based on W.B. Yeats)
Horseman, Pass By (OB) (1969)

THIS HAD BETTER BE LOVE
Jay Gorney
Jean and Walter Kerr
Touch and Go (1949)

THIS HAS NEVER BEEN DONE BEFORE
Jerry Herman
I Feel Wonderful (OB) (1954)

THIS HEAT
Paul Klein
Fred Ebb
Morning Sun (OB) (1963)

THIS HOUSE
Harvey Schmidt
Tom Jones
I Do! I Do! (1966)

THIS IS A DARNED FINE FUNERAL
Charles Gaynor
Show Girl (1961)

THIS IS A DOLLAR BILL
Stefan Kanfer, Jess J. Korman, and Joseph Grayhon
I Want You (OB) (1961)

THIS IS A GREAT COUNTRY
Irving Berlin
Mr. President (1962)

THIS IS A NIGHT CLUB
Clarence Gaskill
Earl Carroll's Vanities (1925)

THIS IS A TOUGH NEIGHBORHOOD
Moose Charlap
Eddie Lawrence
Kelly (1965)

THIS IS ALL VERY NEW TO ME
Albert Hague
Arnold B. Horwitt
Plain and Fancy (1955)

THIS IS AS FAR AS I GO
Burton Lane
Laffing Room Only (1944)

THIS IS DIFFERENT, DEAR
Michael H. Cleary
Max and Nathaniel Lief
Hey Nonny Nonny! (1932)

THIS IS ENGLAND
Mimi Stone
William Kaye
Pimpernel! (OB) (1964)

THIS IS HOW IT FEELS
Richard Rodgers
Oscar Hammerstein II
South Pacific (1949)

THIS IS IT
Arthur Schwartz
Dorothy Fields
Stars in Your Eyes (1939)

THIS IS IT
Ray Henderson
Jack Yellen
Ziegfeld Follies (1943)

THIS IS MY BELOVED
Harry Revel
Arnold B. Horwitt
Are You With It? (1945)

THIS IS MY HOLIDAY
Frederick Loewe
Alan Jay Lerner
The Day Before Spring (1945)

THIS IS MY KIND OF LOVE
Robert Wright and George Forrest
   (based on Rachmaninoff)
Anya (1965)

THIS IS MY NIGHT TO HOWL
Richard Rodgers

Lorenz Hart
A Connecticut Yankee (1943)

THIS IS MY NIGHT TO HOWL
Robert Emmett Dolan
Johnny Mercer
Foxy (1964)

THIS IS MY WEDDING DAY
Abel Baer
Sam Lewis and Joe Young
Lady Do (1927)

THIS IS NEW
Kurt Weill
Ira Gershwin
Lady in the Dark (1941)

THIS IS NOT A SONG
Vernon Duke
E. Y. Harburg and E. Hartman
Ziegfeld Follies (1934)

THIS IS OUR PRIVATE LOVE SONG
Irving Caesar
Sam Lerner
My Dear Public (1943)

THIS IS QUITE A PERFECT NIGHT
Dean Fuller
Marshall Barer
New Faces (1956)

THIS IS SO NICE
Thomas (Fats) Waller
George Marion, Jr.
Early to Bed (1943)

THIS IS SPRING
Jimmy McHugh
Al Dubin
Keep Off the Grass (1940)

THIS IS THE ARMY, MR. JONES
Irving Berlin
This Is the Army (1942)

THIS IS THE DAY
Richard Freitas
Morty Neff and George Mysels
The Difficult Woman (OB) (1962)

THIS IS THE END OF THE STORY
David Raksin
June Carroll
If the Shoe Fits (1946)

THIS IS THE GIRL FOR ME
Norman Dean
Autumn's Here (OB) (1966)

THIS IS THE LIFE
Kurt Weill
Alan Jay Lerner
Love Life (1948)

THIS IS THE LIFE
Charles Strouse
Lee Adams
Golden Boy (1964)

THIS IS THE MISSUS
Ray Henderson
B. G. DeSylva and Lew Brown
George White's Scandals (1931)

THIS IS THE WAY WE GO TO SCHOOL
Helen Miller
Eve Merriam
Inner City (1971)

THIS IS WHAT I CALL LOVE
Harold Karr
Matt Dubey
Happy Hunting (1956)

THIS IS WHERE I CAME IN
Vernon Duke
John Latouche
The Lady Comes Across (1942)

THIS IS WINTER
Jimmy McHugh
Al Dubin
Keep Off the Grass (1940)

THIS ISN'T HEAVEN
Richard Rodgers
State Fair (F) (remake) (1962)

THIS JESUS MUST DIE
Andrew Lloyd Webber
Tim Rice
Jesus Christ Superstar (1971)

THIS KIND OF A GIRL
Arthur Schwartz
Howard Dietz
The Gay Life (1961)

THIS LITTLE YANKEE
Mary Rodgers
Martin Charnin
Hot Spot (1963)

THIS MERRY CHRISTMAS
Morgan Lewis
Nancy Hamilton
Two for the Show (1940)

THIS MUCH I KNOW
Harold Karr
Matt Dubey
Happy Hunting (1956)

THIS NEARLY WAS MINE
Richard Rodgers
Oscar Hammerstein II
South Pacific (1949)

THIS OLD SHIP
Voices, Inc.
The Believers (OB) (1968)

THIS ONE DAY
Claibe Richardson
Kenward Elmslie
The Grass Harp (1971)

THIS PLUM IS TOO RIPE
Harvey Schmidt
Tom Jones
The Fantasticks (OB) (1960)

THIS REALLY ISN'T ME
Glenn Paxton
Robert Goldman and George Weiss
First Impressions (1959)

THIS SAME HEART
Rudolf Friml
Johnny Burke
The Vagabond King (F) (1956)

THIS STATE OF AFFAIRS
Rick Besoyan
Babes in the Wood (OB) (1964)

THIS TIME
Irving Berlin
This Is the Army (1942)

THIS TIME
Stan Freeman and Franklin Underwood
Lovely Ladies, Kind Gentlemen
(1970)

THIS TIME IT'S TRUE LOVE
Noël Coward
The Girl Who Came to Supper (1963)

THIS TIME OF THE YEAR
Burton Lane
E. Y. Harburg
Finian's Ranbow (1947)

THIS TIME THE DREAM'S ON ME
Harold Arlen
Johnny Mercer
Blues in the Night (F) (1941)

THIS TUXEDO IS MINE!
David Baker
David Craig
Phoenix '55 (OB) (1955)

THIS WAS A REAL NICE CLAMBAKE
Richard Rodgers
Oscar Hammerstein II
Carousel (1945)

THIS WAS JUST ANOTHER DAY
Walter Kent
Kim Gannon
Seventeen (1951)

THIS WEEK AMERICANS
Richard Rodgers
Stephen Sondheim
Do I Hear a Waltz? (1965)

THIS WOMAN
Baldwin Bergersen
William Archibald
Carib Song (1945)

THIS WORLD
Gary William Friedman
Will Holt
The Me Nobody Knows (OB) (1970)

THIS WORLD OF CONFUSION
Cy Young
That Hat! (OB) (1964)

THIS YEAR'S KISSES
Irving Berlin
On the Avenue (F) (1937)

THOSE EYES SO TENDER
Jean Gilbert
Harry Graham
Katja (1926)

THOSE MAMMY SINGERS
Gene Lockhart
Bunk of 1926 (1926)

THOSE WERE THE DAYS
Will Holt
That 5 A.M. Jazz (OB) (1964)

THOSE WERE THE GOOD OLD DAYS
Richard Adler and Jerry Ross
Damn Yankees (1955)

**THOU, JULIA, THOU HAS METAMOR-
PHOSED ME**
Galt MacDermot
John Guare
Two Gentlemen of Verona (1971)

**THOU, PROTEUS, THOU HAS META-
MORPHOSED ME**
Galt MacDermot
John Guare
Two Gentlemen of Verona (1971)

THOU SWELL
Richard Rodgers
Lorenz Hart
A Connecticut Yankee (1927)

THOUGH TONGUES MAY WAG
Frederick Loewe
Earle Crooker
Great Lady (1938)

THOUGHT OF YOU, THE
Harold Rome
Fanny (1954)

THOUGHTLESS
Jerry Livingston
Mack David
Bright Lights of 1944 (1943)

THOUSAND ISLANDS SONG
Carl Sigman
Bob Hilliard
Angel in the Wings (1947)

THOUSAND, THOUSAND
Coleridge-Taylor Perkinson
Errol Hill
Man Better Man (OB) (1969)

THOUSAND TIMES, A
Shep Camp
Frank DuPree and Harry B. Smith
Half a Widow (1927)

THOUSANDS OF MILES
Kurt Weill
Maxwell Anderson
Lost in the Stars (1949)

THREE B's, THE
Richard Rodgers
Lorenz Hart
On Your Toes (1936)

THREE B's, THE
Hugh Martin and Ralph Blane
Best Foot Forward (1941)

THREE BEARS, THE
Herbert Stothart, Bert Kalmar, and Harry Ruby
Good Boy (1928)

THREE BOXES OF LONGS, PLEASE
Melvin Van Peebles
Ain't Supposed to Die a Natural Death (1971)

THREE CHEERS FOR THE UNION!
George Gershwin
Ira Gershwin
Strike Up the Band (1930)

THREE COINS IN THE FOUNTAIN*
Jule Styne

Sammy Cahn
Three Coins in the Fountain (F) (1954)

THREE COWARDS CRAVEN
Alyn Heim
Malcolm L. LaPrade
Will the Mail Train Run Tonight? (OB) (1964)

THREE GIRLS IN A BOAT
Frederick Loewe
Alan Jay Lerner
What's Up? (1943)

THREE LETTERS
Jerry Bock
Sheldon Harnick
She Loves Me (1963)

THREE LITTLE COLUMNISTS
Michael H. Cleary
Max and Nathaniel Lief
Hey Nonny Nonny! (1932)

THREE LITTLE DEBUTANTES
Noël Coward
Set to Music (1939)

THREE LITTLE MAIDS
Max Ewing
Agnes Morgan
The Grand Street Follies (OB) (1927)

THREE LITTLE MAIDS
Jimmy McHugh
Al Dubin
The Streets of Paris (1939)

THREE LITTLE MAIDS FROM SCHOOL
Jimmy McHugh
Dorothy Fields
Hello Daddy (1928)

THREE LITTLE QUEENS OF THE SILVER SCREEN
Charles Gaynor
Lend an Ear (1948)

———
*Academy Award Winner

THREE LITTLE WORDS
Bert Kalmar
Harry Ruby
Check and Double Check (F) (1930)

THREE LOVES
Robert Wright and George Forrest
   (based on Grieg)
Song of Norway (1944)

THREE LOVES
Charles Strouse
Mike Stewart
Shoestring Revue (OB) (1955)

THREE MEN ON A DATE
Hugh Martin and Ralph Blane
Best Foot Forward (1941)

THREE MUSKETEERS, THE
Richard Rodgers
Lorenz Hart
The Garrick Gaieties (1925)

THREE OLD LADIES FROM HADES
Mischa and Wesley Portnoff
Donagh MacDonagh
Happy As Larry (1950)

THREE PARADISES
Jay Livingston and Ray Evans
Oh Captain! (1958)

3/4 DRAG
Jerry Blatt
Jerry Blatt and Lonnie Burstein
Have I Got One for You (OB) (1968)

THREE QUARTER TIME
George Gershwin
Ira Gershwin
Pardon My English (1933)

THREE QUESTIONS
David Raksin
June Carroll
If the Shoe Fits (1946)

THREE R'S, THE
Henry Russell and Morry Olsen
Orchids Preferred (1937)

THREE RIDDLES, THE
Ernest Gold
Erich Segal
I'm Solomon (1968)

THREE ROUSING CHEERS
Vernon Duke
John Latouche
The Lady Comes Across (1942)

THREE SHIPS
John Morris
Gerald Freedman
A Time for Singing (1966)

THREE SISTERS WHO ARE NOT SISTERS, THE
Ann Sternberg
Gertrude Stein
Gertrude Stein's First Reader (OB) (1969)

THREE STONES TO STAND ON
Giuseppe Verdi
Charles Friedman
My Darlin' Aïda (1952)

THREE TIMES A DAY
George Gershwin
B. G. DeSylva and Ira Gershwin
Tell Me More (1925)

THREE WHITE FEATHERS
Noël Coward
Set to Music (1939)

THREE'S A CROWD
Franz Steininger (adapted from Tchaikovsky)
Forman Brown
Music in My Heart (1947)

THRILL IS GONE, THE
Ray Henderson
B. G. DeSylva and Lew Brown
George White's Scandals (1931)

THRILL ME
Lewis E. Gensler
E. Y. Harburg
Ballyhoo (1932)

THRILL OF A KISS, THE
Jean Gilbert
Harry B. Smith
The Red Rose (1928)

THROTTLE THROTTLEBOTTOM
George Gershwin
Ira Gershwin
Let 'Em Eat Cake (1933)

THROUGH A THOUSAND DREAMS
Arthur Schwartz
Leo Robin
The Time, the Place and the Girl (F)
  (1946)

THROUGH THE BAMBOO
A. Baldwin Sloane
Harry Cort and George E. Stoddard
China Rose (1925)

THROUGH THE NIGHT
Frank Grey
Earle Crooker and McElbert Moore
Happy (1927)

THROUGH THE YEARS
Vincent Youmans
Edward Heyman
Through the Years (1932)

THROW A PETAL
Eaton Magoon, Jr.
13 Daughters (1961)

THROW IT OUT THE WINDOW
Louis Alter
Harry Ruskin and Leighton K. Brill
Ballyhoo (1930)

THROW ME A ROSE
Emmerich Kalman
P. G. Wodehouse and M. E. Rourke
Miss Springtime (1916)

THROW THE ANCHOR AWAY
Arthur Schwartz
Dorothy Fields
By the Beautiful Sea (1954)

THROW THE HOUSE OUT OF THE WINDOW
Richard Freitas
Morty Neff and George Mysels
The Difficult Woman (OB) (1962)

THROWING A PARTY
Henry Sullivan
Edward Eliscu
A Little Racketeer (1932)

THUMBELINA
Frank Loesser
Hans Christian Andersen (F) (1951)

TICKETS PLEASE
Clay Warnick
Mel Tolkin and Lucille Kallen
Tickets Please (1950)

TICKETYBOO
Ann Ronell
Count Me In (1942)

TICKLE TOE, THE
Louis A. Hirsch
Otto Harbach
Going Up (1917)

TICKLED PINK
Nacio Herb Brown and Richard Whiting
B. G. DeSylva
Take a Chance (1932)

TICKLING THE IVORIES
Irving Berlin
Ziegfeld Follies (1927)

TIDE POOL, THE
Richard Rodgers
Oscar Hammerstein II
Pipe Dream (1955)

TIE YOUR CARES TO A MELODY
Joseph Meyer
William Moll
Jonica (1930)

TIGER, TIGER
Jerry Bock
Sheldon Harnick
The Apple Tree (1966)

TIGER RAG BLUES
Kenneth Gaburo
Seyril Schochen
The Tiger Rag (OB) (1961)

TIL THE BIG FAT MOON FALLS DOWN
Moose Charlap
Norman Gimbel
Whoop-Up (1958)

TILL GOOD LUCK COMES MY WAY
Jerome Kern
Oscar Hammerstein II
Show Boat (1927)

TILL I MET YOU
H. Maurice Jacquet
William Brady and Alonzo Price
The Silver Swan (1929)

TILL THE CLOUDS ROLL BY
Jerome Kern
Jerome Kern, Guy Bolton, and P. G. Wodehouse
Oh, Boy! (1917)

TILL THE REAL THING COMES ALONG
Alberta Nichols
Mann Holiner
Rhapsody in Black (1931)

TILL THEN
Sherman Edwards
1776 (1969)

TILL THERE WAS YOU
Meredith Willson
The Music Man (1957)

TILL TOMORROW
Jerry Bock
Sheldon Harnick
Fiorello (1959)

TILLER, FOSTER, HOFFMAN, HALE AND ALBERTINA RASCH
Henry Sullivan
Henry Myers
John Murray Anderson's Almanac (1929)

TILLIE OF LONGACRE SQUARE
James F. Hanley
Harold Atteridge and Ballard Mac-Donald
Gay Paree (1925)

TIME
Jane Douglas
Tom O'Malley
Bella (OB) (1961)

TIME
Oscar Brown, Jr.
Joy (OB) (1970)

TIME AIN'T VERY LONG
Donald Heywood
Africana (1927)

TIME AND TIDE
Vernon Duke
E. Y. Harburg
Walk a Little Faster (1932)

TIME AND TIDE
Robert Kessler
Lola Permagent
O Marry Me! (OB) (1961)

TIME AND TIME AGAIN
George Gershwin
DuBose Heyward
Porgy and Bess (1935)

TIME AND TIME AGAIN
Leo Edwards
Herman Timberg
You'll See Stars (1942)

TIME AND TIME AGAIN
David Shire
Richard Maltby, Jr.
The Sap of Life (OB) (1961)

TIME FOR JUKIN'
Walter Kent
Lew Brown and Charles Tobias
Yokel Boy (1939)

TIME FOR SINGING, A
John Morris
Gerald Freedman
A Time for Singing (1966)

TIME FOR TEA
Arthur Siegel
June Carroll
New Faces (1952)

TIME IS NOW, THE
Mark Bucci
David Rogers
Vintage '60 (OB) (1960)

TIME IS STANDING STILL
Sigmund Romberg
Oscar Hammerstein II
Sunny River (1941)

TIME MARCHES ON!
Vernon Duke
Ira Gershwin
Ziegfeld Follies (1936)

TIME MARCHES ON
Dale F. Menten
Dale F. Menten and Frederick Gaines
The House of Leather (OB) (1970)

TIME OF MY LIFE, THE
Julian Slade
Dorothy Reynolds and Julian Slade
Salad Days (OB) (1958)

TIME OF YOUR LIFE, THE
William Provost
Peter K. Smith
Crazy with the Heat (1941)

TIME ON MY HANDS
Vincent Youmans
Harold Adamson and Mack Gordon
Smiles (1930)

TIME REMEMBERED
Vernon Duke
Time Remembered (1957)

TIME STANDS STILL
George Lessner

Miriam Battista and Russell Maloney
Sleepy Hollow (1948)

TIME STEP
Paul Klein
Fred Ebb
From A to Z (1960)

TIME TO CALL IT QUITS
Jeanne Bargy
Jeanne Bargy, Frank Gehrecke, and
   Herb Corey
Greenwich Village U.S.A. (OB) (1960)

TIME TO LET GO
Ernest Gold
Anne Croswell
I'm Solomon (1968)

TIME TO SING, THE
Harry Ruby
Bert Kalmar
High Kickers (1941)

TIME WE TALKED
Robert Holton
June Carroll
Hi, Paisano! (OB) (1961)

TIME WILL BE
William Dyer
Don Parks and William Dyer
Jo! (OB) (1964)

TIMES SQUARE DANCE
Sammy Fain
Jack Yellen
Boys and Girls Together (1940)

TIMID FRIEDA
Jacques Brel
Eric Blau and Mort Shuman
*Jacques Brel Is Alive and Well and
   Living in Paris* (OB) (1968)

TIN PAN ALLEY
Cy Coleman
Joseph McCarthy, Jr.
John Murray Anderson's Almanac
   (1953)

TING-A-LING-DEARIE
Rick Besoyan
The Student Gypsy (OB) (1963)

TING-A-LING, THE BELLS'LL RING
Irving Berlin
The Cocoanuts (1925)

TINKLE! TINKLE!
Milton Ager
Jack Yellen
John Murray Anderson's Almanac
  (1929)

TINY ROOM
Hugh Martin
Look Ma, I'm Dancin'! (1948)

TINY, THE CHAMPION
Coleridge-Taylor Perkinson
Errol Hill
Man Better Man (OB) (1969)

TIPPECANOE AND TYLER TOO
Oscar Brand
How to Steal an Election (OB) (1968)

TIP-TOE TAP-TAP
Irving Actman
Jean Herbert
Earl Carroll's Sketch Book (1929)

TIP-TOES
George Gershwin
Ira Gershwin
Tip-Toes (1925)

TIP YOUR HAT
Bradford Greene
Marianne Brown Waters
Right This Way (1938)

TIPPY TIPPY TOES
Cy Coleman
Carolyn Leigh
Wildcat (1960)

TIRED OF THE SOUTH
Gerald Dolin
Edward J. Lambert
Smile at Me (1935)

TIRRALLALLERA
Armando Trovaioli
Pietro Garinei and Sandro Giovannini
Rugantino (1964)

'TIS LOVE
Sigmund Romberg
Harry B. Smith
The Love Call (1927)

TIS OF THEE
Alex North
Alfred Hayes
Tis of Thee (1940)

TITANIA'S PHILOSOPHY
Rick Besoyan
Babes in the Wood (OB) (1964)

TITINA
Leo Daniderff
Bertal-Maubon and E. Ronn
Puzzles of 1925 (1925)

TKAMBUZA
Harold Rome
The Zulu and the Zayda (1965)

T'MORRA, T'MORRA
Harold Arlen
E. Y. Harburg
Bloomer Girl (1944)

TNT
Duke Ellington
John Latouche
Beggar's Holiday (1946)

TO ADJUST IS A MUST
Ernest G. Schweikert
Frank Reardon
Rumple (1957)

TO AN ISLE IN THE WATER
John Duffy
Rocco Bufano and John Duffy (based
  on W.B. Yeats)
Horseman, Pass By (OB) (1969)

TO BATH DERRY-O
Jacques Urbont
Bruce Geller
All in Love (OB) (1961)

TO BE A KING
Sam Pottle
Tom Whedon
To Be a Giant (OB) (1961)

TO BE ALONE WITH YOU
Mark Sandrich, Jr.
Sidney Michaels
Ben Franklin in Paris (1964)

TO BE ARTISTIC
Bob Merrill
Henry, Sweet Henry (1967)

TO BE OR NOT TO BE
Irving Berlin
As Thousands Cheer (1933)

TO BE OR NOT TO BE IN LOVE
Philip Charig
Ray Golden, Danny Shapiro, and Milton Pascal
Catch a Star! (1955)

TO DO A LITTLE GOOD
Jule Styne
Sammy Cahn
Look to the Lilies (1970)

TO DREAM OR NOT TO DREAM
Alyn Heim
Malcolm L. LaPrade
Will the Mail Train Run Tonight? (OB) (1964)

TO EACH HIS DULCINEA
Mitch Leigh
Joe Darion
Man of La Mancha (1965)

TO GET AWAY
Cole Porter
Jubilee (1935)

TO GET OUT OF THIS WORLD ALIVE
Jule Styne
E. Y. Harburg
Darling of the Day (1968)

TO HAVE AND TO HOLD
Richard Rodgers
Oscar Hammerstein II
Allegro (1947)

TO HEAVEN ON THE BRONX EXPRESS
George M. Cohan
The Merry Malones (1927)

TO KEEP MY LOVE ALIVE
Richard Rodgers
Lorenz Hart
A Connecticut Yankee (1943)

TO KNOW YOU IS TO LOVE YOU
Ray Henderson
B. G. DeSylva and Lew Brown
Hold Everything! (1928)

TO LIFE
Jerry Bock
Sheldon Harnick
Fiddler on the Roof (1964)

TO LIVE ANOTHER SUMMER, TO PASS ANOTHER WINTER
Dov Seltzer
David Paulsen
To Live Another Summer (1971)

TO LOOK UPON MY LOVE
Robert Wright and George Forrest
Kean (1961)

TO LOVE IS TO LIVE
Johann Strauss II, adapted by Oscar Straus
Clare Kummer
Three Waltzes (1937)

TO MY WIFE
Harold Rome
Fanny (1954)

TO PROVE MY LOVE
Maria Grever
Raymond Leveen
Viva O'Brien (1941)

TO THE BEAT OF MY HEART
Samuel Pokrass
E. Y. Harburg
Ziegfeld Follies (1934)

To THE DANCE
Richard Myers
Leo Robin
Hello, Yourself! (1928)

To THE GARDEN
Harvey Schmidt
Tom Jones
Celebration (1969)

To THE LAND OF MY OWN RO-
MANCE
Victor Herbert
Harry B. Smith
The Enchantress (1911)

To THE TOP
Oscar Brand and Paul Nassau
A Joyful Noise (1966)

To TOUCH THE SKY
Joseph Martinez Kookoolis and Scott
    Fagan
Scott Fagan
Soon (1971)

To WAR!
Kurt Weill
Maxwell Anderson
Knickerbocker Holiday (1938)

To WHOM IT MAY CONCERN
Frederick Loewe
Earle Crooker
Great Lady (1938)

To WHOM IT MAY CONCERN ME
Galt MacDermot
John Guare
Two Gentlemen of Verona (1971)

TOAD'S LAMENT, THE
Jerry Blatt
Jerry Blatt and Lonnie Burstein
Have I Got One for You (OB) (1968)

TOAST, THE
Hugh Martin
Look Ma, I'm Dancin'! (1948)

TOAST OF THE BOYS AT THE POST,
THE
Vernon Duke
John Latouche
Banjo Eyes (1941)

TOAST TO ALPHA CHOLERA, A
Sidney Lippman
Sylvia Dee
Barefoot Boy with Cheek (1947)

TOAST TO THE BRIDE, A
Johnny Burke
Donnybrook! (1961)

TOAST TO VOLSTEAD, A
Cole Porter
Fifty Million Frenchmen (1929)

TOBACCO BLUES, THE
Mischa and Wesley Portnoff
Donagh MacDonagh
Happy As Larry (1950)

TODAY
Carl Millöcker (revised by Theo Mack-
    eben)
Rowland Leigh
The Dubarry (1932)

TODAY AT YOUR HOUSE, TOMOR-
ROW AT MINE
Jack Lawrence and Don Walker
Courtin' Time (1951)

TODAY I AM A GLAMOUR GIRL
Hoagy Carmichael
Johnny Mercer
Walk with Music (1940)

TODAY I IS SO HAPPY
Baldwin Bergersen
William Archibald
Carib Song (1945)

TODAY I LOVE EV'RYBODY
Harold Arlen
Dorothy Fields
The Farmer Takes a Wife (F) (1953)

TODAY I SAW A ROSE
Albert Hague
Allen Sherman
The Fig Leaves Are Falling (1969)

TODAY IS A DAY FOR A BAND TO PLAY
Milton Schafer
Ira Levin
Drat! The Cat! (1965)

TODAY WILL BE YESTERDAY TO-MORROW
Philip Charig
Dan Shapiro and Milton Pascal
Follow the Girls (1944)

TODAY'S THE DAY
Willard Straight
David Eddy
The Athenian Touch (OB) (1964)

TODDLIN' ALONG
George Gershwin
Ira Gershwin
Nine-Fifteen Revue (1930)

TOGETHER FOREVER
Harvey Schmidt
Tom Jones
I Do! I Do! (1966)

TOGETHER WHEREVER WE GO
Jule Styne
Stephen Sondheim
Gypsy (1959)

TOGETHER WITH MUSIC
Noël Coward
Together with Music (TV) (1955)

TOGETHERNESS
Dickson Hughes and Everett Sloane
From A to Z (1960)

TOGETHERNESS
Mavor Moore
New Faces (1962)

'TOINETTE
Deed Meyer
'Toinette (OB) (1961)

TOKAY
Noël Coward
Bitter Sweet (1929)

TOM, DICK OR HARRY
Cole Porter
Kiss Me, Kate (1948)

TOM, TOM
Helen Miller
Eve Merriam
Inner City (1971)

TOMMY, TOMMY
Jerry Bock
Sheldon Harnick
Tenderloin (1960)

TOMORROW
Rudolf Friml
Brian Hooker
The Vagabond King (1925)

TOMORROW
A. Baldwin Sloane
Harry Cort and George E. Stoddard
China Rose (1925)

TOMORROW*
Con Conrad
William B. Friedlander
Mercenary Mary (1925)

TOMORROW
Cole Porter
Leave It to Me (1938)

TOMORROW
Alex North
Alfred Hayes
Tis of Thee (1940)

TOMORROW BELONGS TO ME
John Kander
Fred Ebb
Cabaret (1966)

TOMORROW IS A LOVELY DAY
Irving Berlin
Louisiana Purchase (1940)

————
*Adapted from Chopin's Nocturne No. 12

TOMORROW IS HERE
David Baker
David Craig
Phoenix '55 (OB) (1955)

TOMORROW IS THE FIRST DAY OF
THE REST OF MY LIFE
Peter Link and C. C. Courtney
Salvation (OB) (1969)

TOMORROW IS THE TIME
Arthur Schwartz
Ira Gershwin
Park Avenue (1946)

TOMORROW MORNING
Harold Rome
Destry Rides Again (1959)

TOMORROW MORNING
John Kander
Fred Ebb
The Happy Time (1968)

TOMORROW MOUNTAIN
Duke Ellington
John Latouche
Beggar's Holiday (1946)

TOMORROW WALTZ, THE
Edwin Greenberg
Pilgrim's Progress (OB) (1962)

TOMORROW WHEN THE WORLD
COMES CRASHING DOWN AROUND
OUR EARS
Philip Springer
Joan Javits
Hotel Passionato (OB) (1965)

TOMORROW WILL BE THE SAME
Lance Mulcahy
Paul Cherry
Park (1970)

TONIGHT
Richard A. Whiting
Oscar Hammerstein II
Free for All (1931)

TONIGHT
George Gershwin
Ira Gershwin
Pardon My English (1933)

TONIGHT
Leonard Bernstein
Stephen Sondheim
West Side Story (1957)

TONIGHT AT EIGHT
Jerry Bock
Sheldon Harnick
She Loves Me (1963)

TONIGHT AT THE MARDI GRAS
Irving Berlin
Louisiana Purchase (1940)

TONIGHT I LOVE YOU MORE*
Cole Porter
Out of This World (1950)

TONIGHT IS OPENING NIGHT
Nacio Herb Brown and Richard Whit-
　ing
B. G. DeSylva
Take a Chance (1932)

TONIGHT MAY NEVER COME AGAIN
Sigmund Romberg
Irving Caesar
Melody (1933)

TONIGHT OR NEVER
Joseph Meyer
William Moll
Jonica (1930)

TONIGHT OR NEVER
Jack Meskill, Raymond Klages, and
　Vincent Rose
Earl Carroll's Vanities (1931)

TONIGHT OR NEVER
Robert Stolz
Rowland Leigh
Night of Love (1941)

―――――
*Dropped from New York production

TONIGHT YOU ARE IN PAREE
Hugh Martin
Make a Wish (1951)

TONIGHT YOU DANCE WITH ME
Hal Jordan
Jerry Douglas
Rondelay (OB) (1969)

TONIGHT'S THE FIGHT
Joseph Raposo
Erich Segal
Sing Muse! (OB) (1961)

TONIGHT'S THE NIGHT
Alex Fogarty
June Sillman
New Faces (1936)

TONIGHT'S THE NIGHT
Johnny Brandon
Cindy (OB) (1964)

TONY, TONY, TONY
Sigmund Romberg
Harry B. Smith
The Love Call (1927)

TONY'S THOUGHTS
Frank Loesser
The Most Happy Fella (1956)

TOO BAD
Alfred Nathan
George Oppenheimer
The Manhatters (1927)

TOO BAD
Cole Porter
Silk Stockings (1955)

TOO CHARMING
Mark Sandrich, Jr.
Sidney Michaels
Ben Franklin in Paris (1964)

TOO CLOSE FOR COMFORT
Jerry Bock, George Weiss, and Larry
  Holofcener
Mr. Wonderful (1956)

TOO DARN HOT
Cole Porter
Kiss Me, Kate (1948)

TOO GOOD FOR THE AVERAGE MAN
Richard Rodgers
Lorenz Hart
On Your Toes (1936)

TOO GOOD TO BE TRUE
Ray Henderson
B. G. DeSylva and Lew Brown
Hold Everything! (1928)

TOO LATE NOW
Burton Lane
Alan Jay Lerner
Royal Wedding (F) (1951)

TOO LITTLE TIME FOR LOVE
Louis Bellson and Will Irwin
Richard Ney
Portofino (1958)

TOO LONG AT THE FAIR
Billy Barnes
The Billy Barnes Revue (1959)

TOO MANY GIRLS
Richard Rodgers
Lorenz Hart
Too Many Girls (1939)

TOO MANY MORNINGS
Stephen Sondheim
Follies (1971)

TOO MANY PEOPLE ALONE*
Harvey Schmidt
Tom Jones
110 in the Shade

TOO MANY QUESTIONS
Paul Nassau
Fallout (OB) (1959)

TOO MANY RINGS AROUND ROSIE
Vincent Youmans
Irving Caesar
No, No, Nanette (1925)

———
*Dropped from New York production

Too Many Tomorrows
Cy Coleman
Dorothy Fields
Sweet Charity (1966)

Too Much Work
Richard Addinsell
Clemence Dane
Come of Age (1934)

Too Nice a Day to Go to School
Sidney Lippman
Sylvia Dee
Barefoot Boy with Cheek (1947)

Too Old
Ray Haney
Alfred Aiken
We're Civilized? (OB) (1962)

Too Old for Love
Coleman Dowell
The Tattooed Countess (OB) (1961)

Too Soon
Harold Rome
I Can Get It for You Wholesale (1962)

Too Tired to Love
William S. Fischer
Maxine Klein
Kiss Now (OB) (1971)

Too, Too Divine
Vernon Duke
E. Y. Harburg
The Garrick Gaieties (1930)

Too Young
Coleman Dowell
The Tattooed Countess (OB) (1961)

Too Young to Live
Richard Lewine
Arnold B. Horwitt
The Girls Against the Boys (1959)

Toodle-oo
Vincent Youmans
Oscar Hammerstein II and William
  Cary Duncan
Mary Jane McKane (1923)

Toodle-oo
Albert Von Tilzer
Neville Fleeson
Bye Bye, Bonnie (1927)

Tooth and Claw
Duke Ellington
John Latouche
Beggar's Holiday (1946)

Top Banana
Johnny Mercer
Top Banana (1951)

Top Hat, White Tie and Tails
Irving Berlin
Top Hat (F) (1935)

Top of the Hill, The
John Kander
Fred Ebb
Zorbá (1968)

Top of the Train
Robert Waldman
Alfred Uhry
Here's Where I Belong (1968)

Topple Down
Edward Pola
Eddie Brandt
Woof, Woof (1929)

Torch Parade
Ray Henderson
Ted Koehler
Say When (1934)

Torch Singer, The (What Do You Think My Heart Is Made Of?)
Henry Sullivan
Earle Crooker
Thumbs Up! (1934)

Torch Song, The
Harry Warren
Mort Dixon and Joe Young
The Laugh Parade (1931)

Torch Song
Irving Berlin
Face the Music (1932)

TORMENTED
Richard Freitas
Morty Neff and George Mysels
The Difficult Woman (OB) (1962)

TOSY AND COSH
Burton Lane
Alan Jay Lerner
On a Clear Day You Can See Forever
(1965)

TOTEM TOM-TOM
Rudolf Friml
Otto Harbach and Oscar Hammerstein II
Rose Marie (1924)

TOUCH AND GO
Buster Davis
Steven Vinaver
Diversions (OB) (1958)

TOUCH AND GO
Elmer Bernstein
Carolyn Leigh
How Now, Dow Jones (1967)

TOUCH KISS
William S. Fischer
Maxine Klein
Kiss Now (OB) (1971)

TOUCH OF PARIS
Mimi Stone
William Kaye
Pimpernel! (OB) (1964)

TOUCH OF YOUR HAND, THE
Jerome Kern
Otto Harbach
Roberta (1933)

TOUCHED IN THE HEAD
Michael Cleary
Arthur Swanstrom
Sea Legs (1937)

**TOUCHING YOUR HAND IS LIKE
TOUCHING YOUR MIND**
Nancy Ford
Gretchen Cryer
The Last Sweet Days of Isaac (OB)
(1970)

TOUJOURS GAI
George Kleinsinger
Joe Darion
Shinbone Alley (1957)

TOUR MUST GO ON, THE
Hugh Martin
Make a Wish (1951)

TOURIST MADRIGAL
Richard B. Chodosh
Barry Alan Grael
The Streets of New York (OB) (1963)

TOWER OF BABBLE
Stephen Schwartz
Godspell (OB) (1971)

TO-WHIT-TO-WHOO
Robert Colby
Robert Colby and Nita Jonas
Half-Past Wednesday (OB) (1962)

TOWN HALL TONIGHT
Richard Rodgers
Lorenz Hart
The Girl Friend (1926)

TOYLAND
Victor Herbert
Glen MacDonough
Babes in Toyland (1903)

TOYLAND
Gene P. Bissell
New Faces (1968)

TRA-LA-LA
George Gershwin
Arthur Francis (Ira Gershwin)
For Goodness Sake (1922)

TRA LA LA
Lehman Engel
Agnes Morgan
A Hero Is Born (1937)

TRA-LA-LA-LA
Elsie Janis and Vincent Scotto
Puzzles of 1925 (1925)

TRADITION
Jerry Bock
Sheldon Harnick
Fiddler on the Roof (1964)

TRAILING A SHOOTING STAR
Albert Sirmay and Arthur Schwartz
Arthur Swanstrom
Princess Charming (1930)

TRAIN, THE
Irving Berlin
Miss Liberty (1949)

TRAIN TIME
Baldwin Bergersen
June Sillman
Who's Who (1938)

TRAIN TO JOHANNESBURG
Kurt Weill
Maxwell Anderson
Lost in the Stars (1949)

TRAIN WITH THE CUSHIONED SEATS, THE
William Roy
Maggie (1953)

TRAMP! TRAMP! TRAMP!
Victor Herbert
Rida Johnson Young
Naughty Marietta (1910)

TRAMPLE YOUR TROUBLES
Jean Schwartz
Clifford Grey and William Cary Duncan
Sunny Days (1928)

TRAMPS OF THE DESERT
Ford Dabney
Jo Trent
Rang-Tang (1927)

TRANSPARENT CRYSTAL MOMENT, A
Nancy Ford
Gretchen Cryer
The Last Sweet Days of Isaac (OB) (1970)

TRANSPORT OF DELIGHT, A
Donald Swann
Michael Flanders
At the Drop of a Hat (1959)

TRAPPED
Susan Hulsman Bingham
Myrna Lamb
Mod Donna (OB) (1970)

TRAVEL THE ROAD OF LOVE
Tommy Wolf
Fran Landesman
The Nervous Set (1959)

TRAVEL, TRAVEL, TRAVEL
Milton Susskind
Paul Porter and Benjamin Hapgood Burt
Florida Girl (1925)

TRAVEL, TRAVEL, TRAVEL
Heitor Villa-Lobos
Robert Wright and George Forrest
Magdalena (1948)

TRAVELIN' MAN
William S. Fischer
Maxine Klein
Kiss Now (OB) (1971)

TRAVELIN' ON
G. Wood
F. Jasmine Addams (OB) (1971)

TRAVELLIN'
J. C. Johnson
Change Your Luck (1930)

TRAVELLING SONG
Kenneth Gaburo
Seyril Schochen
The Tiger Rag (OB) (1961)

TREAT A WOMAN LIKE A DRUM
Emmerich Kalman
George Marion, Jr.
Marinka (1945)

TREAT 'EM ROUGH
Charles M. Schwab
Henry Myers
Bare Facts of 1926 (1926)

TREAT ME ROUGH
George Gershwin
Ira Gershwin
Girl Crazy (1930)

TREE, THE
Gary William Friedman
Will Holt
The Me Nobody Knows (OB) (1970)

TREE AND THE SUN, THE
George Fischoff
Verna Tomasson
The Prince and the Pauper (OB)
(1963)

TREE IN THE PARK, A
Richard Rodgers
Lorenz Hart
Peggy-Ann (1926)

TRIAL BEFORE PILATE
Andrew Lloyd Webber
Tim Rice
Jesus Christ Superstar (1971)

TRIAL SONG, THE
H. Maurice Jacquet
William Brady
The Silver Swan (1929)

TRIANGLE
Charles M. Schwab
Henry Myers
The New Yorkers (1927)

TRIED BY THE CENTRE COURT
Donald Swann
Michael Flanders
At the Drop of a Hat (1959)

TRILOGY
Bud McCreery
Put It in Writing (OB) (1963)

TRINITY
Susan Hulsman Bingham
Myrna Lamb
Mod Donna (OB) (1970)

TRIO
Frederick Loewe
Alan Jay Lerner
Paint Your Wagon (1951)

TRIP
Charles Strouse
Six (OB) (1971)

TRIP DOESN'T CARE AT ALL, A
Philip Kadison
Thomas Howell
Along Fifth Avenue (1949)

TRIP TO THE LIBRARY, A
Jerry Bock
Sheldon Harnick
She Loves Me (1963)

TRIPPING
Kenn Long and Jim Crozier
Kenn Long
Touch (OB) (1970)

TRIPPING THE LIGHT FANTASTIC
Harold Rome
Wish You Were Here (1952)

TROJAN HORSE, THE
Richard Rodgers
Lorenz Hart
Simple Simon (1930)

TROLLEY SONG, THE
Hugh Martin and Ralph Blane
Meet Me in St. Louis (F) (1944)

TROTTIN' TO THE FAIR
Ralph Blane
Three Wishes for Jamie (1952)

TROUBLE
Milton Susskind
Paul Porter and Benjamin Hapgood
Burt
Florida Girl (1925)

TROUBLE
Meredith Willson
The Music Man (1957)

TROUBLE MAN
Kurt Weill
Maxwell Anderson
Lost in the Stars (1949)

TROUBLE WITH ME, THE
Howard Blankman
By Hex (OB) (1956)

TROUBLE WITH WOMEN, THE
Kurt Weill
Ogden Nash
One Touch of Venus (1943)

TROUBLED LADY
George Harwell
What a Killing (OB) (1961)

TROWL THE BOWL
Mel Marvin
Ted Berger
Shoemaker's Holiday (OB) (1967)

TRUCKERS BALL
Donald Heywood
Black Rhythm (1936)

TRUCKIN' IN MY TAILS
Ray Henderson
Jack Yellen
George White's Scandals (1936)

TRUE BLUE
Richard Myers
Leo Robin
Hello, Yourself! (1928)

TRUE HEARTS
Sigmund Romberg
Arthur Wimperis
Louie the 14th (1925)

TRUE LOVE
Joseph Meyer and James F. Hanley
B. G. DeSylva
Big Boy (1925)

TRUE LOVE
Harold Arlen
Johnny Mercer
St. Louis Woman (1946)

TRUE LOVE
Cole Porter
High Society (F) (1956)

TRUE ROMANCE
George Kleinsinger
Joe Darion
Shinbone Alley (1957)

TRUMPETER AND THE LOVER, THE
Vincent Youmans
Edward Heyman
Through the Years (1932)

TRUMPETER, BLOW YOUR GOLDEN HORN
George Gershwin
Ira Gershwin
Of Thee I Sing (1931)

TRUTH
John Mundy
Edward Eager
The Liar (1950)

TRUTH
Moose Charlap
Norman Gimbel
The Conquering Hero (1961)

TRUTH, THE
Cy Coleman
Carolyn Leigh
Little Me (1962)

TRY A TRIO
Jacques Urbont
David Newburger
Stag Movie (OB) (1971)

TRY AGAIN TOMORROW
Richard Rodgers
Lorenz Hart
She's My Baby (1928)

TRY DANCING
Harry Ruby
Bert Kalmar
Top Speed (1929)

TRY HER OUT AT DANCES
Sigmund Romberg
Oscar Hammerstein II
The New Moon (1928)

TRY ME
Jerry Bock
Sheldon Harnick
She Loves Me (1963)

TRY THE SKY
William S. Fischer
Maxine Klein
Kiss Now (OB) (1971)

TRY TO FORGET
Jerome Kern
Otto Harbach
The Cat and the Fiddle (1931)

TRY TO LOVE ME JUST AS I AM
Jule Styne
Betty Comden and Adolph Green
Say, Darling (1958)

TRY TO MAKE THE BEST OF IT
Janet Gari
Toby Garson
Lyle (OB) (1970)

TRY TO REMEMBER
Harvey Schmidt
Tom Jones
The Fantasticks (OB) (1960)

TSCHAIKOWSKY
Kurt Weill
Ira Gershwin
Lady in the Dark (1941)

TSING-LA-LA
Erich Wolfgang Korngold (based on
  Offenbach)
Herbert Baker
Helen Goes to Troy (1944)

TU SAIS
Serge Walter
Agnes Morgan
The Grand Street Follies (1928)

TULIP TIME
Dave Stamper
Gene Buck
Ziegfeld Follies (1919)

TURKEY LURKEY TIME
Burt Bacharach
Hal David
Promises, Promises (1968)

TURN BACK, O MAN
Stephen Schwartz
Godspell (OB) (1971)

TURN ME LOOSE ON BROADWAY
Vernon Duke
Ogden Nash
Two's Company (1952)

TURN MY LITTLE MILLWHEEL
Paul Delmet
Kay Swift
Paris '90 (1952)

TURN ON THE CHARM
Emmerich Kalman
George Marion, Jr.
Marinka (1945)

TURN ON THE HEAT
Ray Henderson
B. G. DeSylva and Lew Brown
Sunny Side Up (F) (1929)

TURN OUT THE LIGHT
Nacio Herb Brown and Richard Whit-
  ing
B. G. DeSylva
Take a Chance (1932)

TURN TO ME
Joseph Meyer
Edward Eliscu
Lady Fingers (1929)

TUROOLA
Ed Tyler
Sweet Miani (OB) (1962)

TURTLE SONG
Harold Arlen
Harold Arlen and Truman Capote
House of Flowers (1954)

'TWAS NOT SO LONG AGO
Jerome Kern
Oscar Hammerstein II
Sweet Adeline (1929)

TWEEDLEDEE FOR PRESIDENT
George Gershwin
Ira Gershwin
Let 'Em Eat Cake (1933)

TWEET TWEET
Ray Henderson
B. G. DeSylva and Lew Brown
George White's Scandals (1926)

TWELVE DAYS TO CHRISTMAS
Jerry Bock
Sheldon Harnick
She Loves Me (1963)

TWELVE O'CLOCK AND ALL IS WELL
Philip Charig
Dan Shapiro and Milton Pascal
Follow the Girls (1944)

TWELVE O'CLOCK SONG
Deed Meyer
She Shall Have Music (OB) (1959)

TWELVE ROOFTOPS LEAPING
Helen Miller
Eve Merriam
Inner City (1971)

TWENTIETH CENTURY BLUES*
Noël Coward
Cavalcade (F) (1932)

28 MEN
Earl Robinson
Waldo Salt
Sandhog (OB) (1954)

TWENTY-EIGHT MEN
Stan Harte, Jr.
Walt Whitman
Leaves of Grass (OB) (1971)

TWENTY TONS OF T.N.T.
Donald Swann
Michael Flanders
At the Drop of Another Hat (1966)

TWENTY YEARS
Stan Harte, Jr.
Walt Whitman
Leaves of Grass (OB) (1971)

TWENTY YEARS AGO
Ray Henderson
B. G. DeSylva and Lew Brown
George White's Scandals (1926)

TWICE SHY
Donald Swann
Michael Flanders
At the Drop of Another Hat (1966)

TWILIGHT
Morris Hamilton
Grace Henry
Earl Carroll's Vanities (1926)

TWILIGHT SONG
C. Jackson and James Hatch
Fly Blackbird (OB) (1962)

TWILIGHT VOICES
Sigmund Romberg
Harry B. Smith
Princess Flavia (1925)

'TWILL NEVER BE THE SAME
John Mundy
Edward Eager
The Liar (1950)

TWIN SOLILOQUIES
Richard Rodgers
Oscar Hammerstein II
South Pacific (1949)

TWINKLE IN YOUR EYE, A
Richard Rodgers
Lorenz Hart
I Married an Angel (1938)

---

*Originally in London stage production

TWINKLE TWINKLE
Harry Archer
Harlan Thompson
Twinkle Twinkle (1926)

TWINS
Earl Robinson
Waldo Salt
Sandhog (OB) (1954)

TWIST MY ARM
Sammy Fain
Paul Webster
Catch a Star! (1955)

TWO A DAY
Jerry Herman
Parade (OB) (1960)

TWO-A-DAY FOR KEITH
Richard Rodgers
Lorenz Hart
On Your Toes (1936)

TWO A DAY ON THE MILKY WAY
Dean Fuller
Marshall Barer
Ziegfeld Follies (1957)

TWO BOYS
Ray Henderson
B. G. DeSylva
Three Cheers (1928)

TWO BY TWO
David Baker
Fred Ebb
Smiling, the Boy Fell Dead (OB) (1961)

TWO BY TWO
Richard Rodgers
Martin Charnin
Two by Two (1970)

TWO-FACED WOMAN
Arthur Schwartz
Howard Dietz
Flying Colors (1932)

TWO FACES IN THE DARK
Albert Hague
Dorothy Fields
Redhead (1959)

TWO FALLS TO A FINISH
Al Carmines
Rosalyn Drexler
Home Movies (OB) (1964)

TWO FEET IN TWO-FOUR TIME
Harold Arlen
Irving Caesar
George White's Music Hall Varieties (1932)

TWO FELLOWS AND A GIRL
Con Conrad
Gus Kahn
Kitty's Kisses (1926)

TWO GENTLEMEN OF VERONA
Galt MacDermot
John Guare
Two Gentlemen of Verona (1971)

TWO GET TOGETHER
Will Irwin
Norman Zeno
Fools Rush In (1934)

TWO GROWN-UP PEOPLE AT PLAY
Earl Wilson, Jr.
A Day in the Life of Just About Everyone (OB) (1971)

TWO IN A TAXI
Jimmy McHugh
Howard Dietz
Keep Off the Grass (1940)

TWO IS COMPANY
Winthrop Cortelyou
Derick Wulff
Kiss Me (1927)

TWO LADIES
John Kander
Fred Ebb
Cabaret (1966)

TWO LADIES AND A MAN
Sigmund Romberg
Otto Harbach
Forbidden Melody (1936)

TWO LADIES IN DE SHADE OF DE BA-
NANA TREE
Harold Arlen
Harold Arlen and Truman Capote
House of Flowers (1954)

TWO LITTLE ANGELS
Al Carmines
Maria Irene Fornes
Promenade (OB) (1969)

TWO LITTLE BLUEBIRDS
Jerome Kern
Oscar Hammerstein II
Sunny (1925)

TWO LITTLE LOVE BEES
Heinrich Reinhardt
Harry B. and Robert B. Smith
The Spring Maid (1910)

TWO LITTLE PUSSYCATS
Leon Carr
Earl Shuman
The Secret Life of Walter Mitty (OB)
   (1964)

TWO LITTLE SHIPS
Armand Vecsey
P. G. Wodehouse
The Nightingale (1927)

TWO LITTLE STARS
Frank Harling
Laurence Stallings
Deep River (1926)

TWO LOST SOULS
Richard Adler and Jerry Ross
Damn Yankees (1955)

TWO LOVING ARMS
Joseph Meyer and Philip Charig
Leo Robin
Just Fancy (1927)

TWO OF US, THE
George M. Cohan
Billie (1928)

TWO PERFECT LOVERS
Burton Lane
Samuel Lerner
Artists and Models (1930)

TWO STRINGS TO A BOW
Michael Valenti
Just for Love (OB) (1968)

2,000 MILES
Tom Sankey
The Golden Screw (OB) (1967)

TWO UNFORTUNATE ORPHANS
Richard Rodgers
Lorenz Hart
America's Sweetheart (1931)

TWO YEARS IN THE MAKING
Leroy Anderson
Joan Ford, Walter and Jean Kerr
Goldilocks (1958)

TYPICAL SELF-MADE AMERICAN, A
George Gershwin
Ira Gershwin
Strike Up the Band (1930)

TYPICALLY ENGLISH
Leslie Bricusse and Anthony Newley
Stop the World—I Want to Get Off
   (1962)

TYPISCHE DEUTSCHE
Leslie Bricusse and Anthony Newley
Stop the World—I Want to Get Off
   (1962) .

UGG-A-WUGG
Jule Styne
Betty Comden and Adolph Green
Peter Pan (1954)

UGLY DUCKLING, THE
Frank Loesser
Hans Christian Andersen (F) (1951)

UH-HUH, OH, YEAH!
Jerry Bock
Sheldon Harnick
The Body Beautiful (1958)

UH-OH!
Lee Pockriss
Anne Croswell
Tovarich (1963)

UKULELE LORELEI
George Gershwin
B. G. DeSylva and Ira Gershwin
Tell Me More (1925)

ULTERIOR MOTIVE
Richard Freitas
Morty Neff and George Mysels
The Difficult Woman (OB) (1962)

ULTIVAC
Sol Berkowitz
James Lipton
Miss Emily Adam (OB) (1960)

UN, DEUX, TROIS
Deed Meyer
'Toinette (OB) (1961)

UNACCUSTOMED AS I AM
Max Ewing
Agnes Morgan
The Grand Street Follies (OB) (1927)

UNACCUSTOMED AS I AM
Vernon Duke
E. Y. Harburg
Walk a Little Faster (1932)

UNAFRAID
John Kander
Fred Ebb
Flora, the Red Menace (1965)

UNCLE SAM RAG, THE
Albert Hague
Dorothy Fields
Redhead (1959)

UNCLE SAM'S LULLABY
Sam Stept
Lew Brown and Charles Tobias
Yokel Boy (1939)

UNDECIDED BLUES, THE
Elsie Janis
Puzzles of 1925 (1925)

UNDER A SPELL
Louis Bellson and Will Irwin
Richard Ney
Portofino (1958)

UNDER A TREE
Alec Wilder
Arnold Sundgaard
Kittiwake Island (OB) (1960)

UNDER MY SKIN
Harry Archer
Will B. Johnstone
Entre-Nous (OB) (1935)

UNDER MY UMBRELLA
Alma Sanders
Monte Carlo
Oh! Oh! Nurse (1925)

UNDER THE BAMBOO TREE
Robert Cole
Sally in Our Alley (1902)

UNDER THE CLOCK AT THE ASTOR
Manning Sherwin
Ned Wever
Crazy Quilt (1931)

UNDER THE MIDSUMMER MOON
Shep Camp
Harry B. Smith
Half a Widow (1927)

UNDER THE SLEEPING VOLCANO
Jay Gorney
Jean and Walter Kerr
Touch and Go (1949)

UNDER THE SUN
Oscar Brown, Jr.
Joy (OB) (1970)

UNDER THE TREE
Harvey Schmidt
Tom Jones
Celebration (1969)

UNDER YOUR SPELL
Arthur Schwartz
Howard Dietz
Under Your Spell (F) (1936)

UNDERNEATH IT ALL
Larry Grossman
Hal Hackady
Minnie's Boys (1970)

UNDERSTAND IT
Mike Brandt, Michael Knight, and
    Robert J. Lowery
Exchange (OB) (1970)

UNEXPECTEDLY
Sol Kaplan
Edward Eliscu
The Banker's Daughter (OB)
(1962)

UNFAIR
Jerry Bock
Sheldon Harnick
Fiorello (1959)

UNFORTUNATE ROSE
Vincent Valentini
Parisiana (1928)

UNGRATEFUL
Richard Freitas
Morty Neff and George Mysels
The Difficult Woman (OB) (1962)

UNICEF SONG
Sammy Fain
Paul Francis Webster
Christine (1960)

UNION LABEL
Jay Gorney
Henry Myers
Meet the People (1940)

UNION SQUARE
George Gershwin
Ira Gershwin
Let 'Em Eat Cake (1933)

UNMISTAKABLE SIGN
David Baker
David Craig
Copper and Brass (1957)

UNNECESSARY TOWN
Gene de Paul
Johnny Mercer
Li'l Abner (1956)

UNOFFICIAL SPOKESMAN, THE
George Gershwin
Ira Gershwin
Strike Up the Band (1930)

UNREQUITED LOVE
Al Carmines
Maria Irene Fornes
Promenade (OB) (1969)

UNREQUITED LOVE MARCH
Ronny Graham
Wet Paint (OB) (1965)

UNSEEN BUDS
Stan Harte, Jr.
Walt Whitman
Leaves of Grass (OB) (1971)

UNTALENTED RELATIVE, THE
Arthur Siegel
Joey Carter and Richard Maury
New Faces (1962)

UNTIL TODAY
Oscar Brand and Paul Nassau
A Joyful Noise (1966)

UNTIL YOU GET SOMEBODY ELSE
Walter Donaldson
Gus Kahn
Whoopee (1928)

UNTO YOUR HEART
Emile Berté and Maury Rubens
J. Keirn Brennan
Music in May (1929)

UNTOGETHER CINDERELLA
Ron Steward and Neal Tate
Ron Steward
Sambo (OB) (1969)

UP AMONG THE CHIMNEY POTS
Kay Swift
Paul James
Nine-Fifteen Revue (1930)

UP AND AT 'EM! ON TO VICT'RY
George Gershwin
Ira Gershwin
Let 'Em Eat Cake (1933)

UP AND DOWN
Wally Harper
Paul Zakrzewski
Sensations (OB) (1970)

UP CHICKAMAUGA HILL
Kurt Weill
Paul Green
Johnny Johnson (1936)

UP FROM THE GUTTER
Sigmund Romberg
Dorothy Fields
Up in Central Park (1945)

UP IN THE CLOUDS
Harry Ruby
Bert Kalmar
The Five O'Clock Girl (1927)

UP IN THE ELEVATED RAILWAY
Sigmund Romberg (developed by Don Walker)
Leo Robin
The Girl in Pink Tights (1954)

UP ON HIGH
Alfred Nathan
George Oppenheimer
The Manhatters (1927)

UP WHERE THE PEOPLE ARE
Meredith Willson
The Unsinkable Molly Brown (1960)

UP WITH THE LARK
Jerome Kern
Leo Robin
Centennial Summer (F) (1946)

UPON A MOONLIGHT NIGHT IN MAY
Franz Lehár
Harry Graham
Yours Is My Heart (1946)

UPS-A-DAISY
Lewis E. Gensler
Robert A. Simon
Ups-A-Daisy (1928)

UPSTAIRS
Burt Bacharach
Hal David
Promises, Promises (1968)

UPSTAIRS-DOWNSTAIRS
Lor Crane
John B. Kuntz
Whispers on the Wind (OB) (1970)

URBAN RENEWAL
Helen Miller
Eve Merriam
Inner City (1971)

URITI
Milton Schafer
Ronny Graham
Bravo Giovanni (1962)

US ON A BUS
Vee Lawnhurst
Tot Seymour
Summer Wives (1936)

US TWO
Jack Holmes
Bill Conklin and Bob Miller
O Say Can You See! (OB) (1962)

USE YOUR IMAGINATION
Cole Porter
Out of This World (1950)

USE YOUR NOGGIN
Jimmy Van Heusen
Sammy Cahn
Walking Happy (1966)

USEFUL PHRASES
Noël Coward
Sail Away (1961)

USELESS SONG
Kurt Weill
Marc Blitzstein
The Threepenny Opera (OB) (1954)

USHER FROM THE MEZZANINE, THE
Jule Styne
Betty Comden and Adolph Green
Fade Out—Fade In (1964)

VACATION IN THE STORE
Gordon Jenkins
Tom Adair
Along Fifth Avenue (1949)

VAGABOND SONG, THE
Alex Fry
Lyon Phelps
Do You Know the Milky Way? (1961)

VALENCIA
José Padilla
Clifford Grey
The Great Temptations (1926)

VALMOUTH
Sandy Wilson
Valmouth (OB) (1960)

VALSE ANGLAISE
John Addison
John Cranko
Cranks (1956)

VALSE MILIEU
Marguerite Monnot
Julian More, David Heneker, and
Monte Norman
Irma La Douce (1960)

VAMP YOUR MEN
Sigmund Romberg
Arthur Wimperis
Louie the 14th (1925)

VAMPS, THE
James Mundy
John Latouche
The Vamp (1955)

VAN BUREN
Oscar Brand
How to Steal an Election (OB) (1968)

VANITEASER
Michael Cleary and Paul Jones
Earl Carroll's Vanities (1928)

VARSITY DRAG, THE
Ray Henderson
B. G. DeSylva and Lew Brown
Good News (1927)

VE VOULDN'T GONTO DO IT
Kurt Weill
Maxwell Anderson
Knickerbocker Holiday (1938)

VEDI LA VITA
Frank Fields
Armand Aulicino
The Shoemaker and the Peddler (OB)
(1960)

VELASQUEZ
Noël Coward
This Year of Grace (1928)

VEN I VALSE
Bob Merrill
New Girl in Town (1957)

VENDOR'S CALLS
Frederick Loewe
Alan Jay Lerner
Brigadoon (1947)

VENDOR'S SONG
Irving Burgie
Ballad for Bimshire (OB) (1963)

VENETIAN WEDDING MOON
Al Goodman, J. Fred Coots, and
Maury Rubens
Clifford Grey
Gay Paree (1925)

VENEZIA AND HER THREE LOVERS
Victor Young
Edward Heyman
Pardon Our French (1950)

VENGEANCE
Alyn Heim
Malcolm L. LaPrade
Will the Mail Train Run Tonight?
(OB) (1964)

VENICE
Cole Porter
The New Yorkers (1930)

VERANDAH WALTZ, THE
Mitch Leigh
William Alfred and Phyllis Robinson
Cry for Us All (1970)

VERONICA TAKES OVER
Jack Holmes
Bill Conklin and Bob Miller
O Say Can You See! (OB) (1962)

VERY
Cyril Ornadel
Leslie Bricusse
Pickwick (1965)

VERY FULL AND PRODUCTIVE DAY, A
William Roy
The Penny Friend (OB) (1966)

VERY MUCH IN LOVE
Rick Besoyan
The Student Gypsy (OB) (1963)

VERY NECESSARY YOU, THE
Jimmy Van Heusen
Johnny Burke
Carnival in Flanders (1953)

VERY NEXT MAN, THE
Jerry Bock
Sheldon Harnick
Fiorello (1959)

VERY NICE MAN, A
Bob Merrill
Carnival (1961)

VERY PROPER TOWN, A
Jay Livingston and Ray Evans
Oh Captain! (1958)

VERY SOFT SHOES
Mary Rodgers
Marshall Barer
Once Upon a Mattress (OB) (1959)

VERY SPECIAL DAY, A
Richard Rodgers
Oscar Hammerstein II
Me and Juliet (1953)

VERY, VERY, VERY
Kurt Weill
Ogden Nash
One Touch of Venus (1943)

VESPER BELL
Rudolf Friml
P. G. Wodehouse and Clifford Grey
The Three Musketeers (1928)

VICTIM OF THE VOODOO DRUMS
Victor Young
Joseph Young and Ned Washington
Blackbirds (1934)

VICTORIA TRIO
Paul Nassau
Fallout (OB) (1959)

VIENNA GOSSIP
Johann Strauss I, adapted by Oscar
  Straus
Three Waltzes (1937)

VIENNESE
Ladislas Kun
The Garrick Gaieties (1926)

VILIA
Franz Lehár
Adrian Ross
The Merry Widow (1907)

VILLAIN ALWAYS GETS IT, THE
Sammy Fain
Dan Shapiro
Ankles Aweigh (1955)

VILLAINY
Alyn Heim
Malcolm L. LaPrade
Will the Mail Train Run Tonight?
  (OB) (1964)

VIOLETS
Edward Kunneke (based on Offen-
bach)
Harry B. Smith
The Love Song (1925)

V. I. P.
Jule Styne
Betty Comden and Adolph Green
Do Re Mi (1960)

VIEW FROM MY WINDOW, THE
Earl Wilson, Jr.
*A Day in the Life of Just About Every-
one* (OB) (1971)

VINEYARDS OF MANHATTAN, THE
Arthur Schwartz
Agnes Morgan
The Grand Street Follies (1929)

VIOLINS FROM NOWHERE
Sammy Fain
Herb Magidson
Michael Todd's Peep Show (1950)

VIRGIN OF VELEZ-JERMANO, THE
Robert Rosenblum
Robert Rosenblum and Howard Schu-
man
Up Eden (OB) (1968)

VIRGIN POLKA, THE
John Dooley
Hobo (OB) (1961)

VIRGINIA
George Gershwin
B. G. DeSylva
Sweet Little Devil (1924)

VIRGINIA
Vincent Youmans
Oscar Hammerstein II
Rainbow (1928)

VIRGINIA
Arthur Schwartz
Albert Stillman
Virginia (1937)

VIRGINS WRAPPED IN CELLOPHANE
John Jacob Loeb
Paul Francis Webster
Murder at the Vanities (1933)

VIRTUE ARRIVEDERCI
Milton Schafer
Ronny Graham
Bravo Giovanni (1962)

VISION OF THE FUTURE, A
Joseph Rumshinsky
L. Wolfe Gilbert
The Singing Rabbi (1931)

VISION SONG
Raymond Scott
Bernard Hanighen
Lute Song (1946)

VISIT PANAMA
Cole Porter
Panama Hattie (1940)

VISITING HOURS
Earl Wilson, Jr.
*A Day in the Life of Just About Every-
one* (OB) (1971)

VISITORS ASHORE
Warburton Guilbert
Everett Marcy and Nancy Hamilton
New Faces (1934)

VITE, VITE, VITE
Cole Porter
Leave it to Me (1938)

VIVA FOR GENEVA
Harold Arlen
E. Y. Harburg
Hooray for What! (1937)

VIVA VITAMINS
Fred Spielman and Arthur Gershwin
Stanley Adams
A Lady Says Yes (1945)

VIVE LA DIFFÉRENCE
John Kander
Fred Ebb
Zorbá (1968)

VIVE LA VIRTUE
Jacques Offenbach
E. Y. Harburg
The Happiest Girl in the World (1961)

VIVE LA YOU
Rudolf Friml
Johnny Burke
The Vagabond King (F) (1956)

VIVIENNE
Cole Porter
Paris (1928)

VODKA
George Gershwin and Herbert Stothart
Otto Harbach and Oscar Hammerstein II
Song of the Flame (1925)

VODKA, VODKA!
Robert Wright and George Forrest
(based on Rachmaninoff)
Anya (1965)

VOICE OF GOD, THE
Edwin Greenberg
Pilgrim's Progress (OB) (1962)

VOICE OF THE CITY, THE
Herbert Stothart, Bert Kalmar, and
Harry Ruby
Good Boy (1928)

VOICE OF THE HIGH SIERRAS
Ida Hoyt Chamberlain
Enchanted Isle (1927)

VOODOO
Johnny Brandon
Who's Who, Baby? (OB) (1968)

VOODOO OF THE ZULU ISLE
J. Fred Coots and Maury Rubens
Clifford Grey and McElbert Moore
A Night in Paris (1926)

VOTE FOR LINCOLN
Victor Ziskin
Joan Javits
Young Abe Lincoln (1961)

WABASH 4-7473
G. Wood
Bruce Kirby
Shoestring Revue (OB) (1955)

WADDYA SAY—WE STEAL AWAY
James F. Hanley
Eddie Dowling
Honeymoon Lane (1926)

WADE IN THE WATER
Vernon Duke
John Latouche
Cabin in the Sky (OB) (1964)

WAH-WAH
Martin Broones
Ballard MacDonald
Rufus Lemaire's Affairs (1927)

WAIT
Joseph Martinez Kookoolis and Scott
Fagan
Scott Fagan
Soon (1971)

WAIT FOR ME
Bob Goodman
Wild and Wonderful (1971)

WAIT FOR THE HAPPY ENDING
Milton Ager
Jack Yellen
John Murray Anderson's Almanac
(1929)

WAIT FOR TOMORROW
Bronislaw Kaper (based on Chopin)
John Latouche
Polonaise (1945)

WAIT 'TIL WE'RE SIXTY-FIVE
Burton Lane
Alan Jay Lerner
On a Clear Day You Can See Forever
(1965)

WAIT TILL THE COWS COME HOME
Ivan Caryll
Anne Caldwell
Jack O'Lantern (1917)

WAIT TILL TOMORROW
Jerome Kern
P. G. Wodehouse
Leave It to Jane (1917)

WAIT TILL YOU SEE ME IN THE MORNING
Hoagy Carmichael
Johnny Mercer
Walk with Music (1940)

WAIT TILL YOU SEE HER
Richard Rodgers
Lorenz Hart
By Jupiter (1942)

WAITERS
Emmerich Kalman
Harry B. Smith
The Circus Princess (1927)

WAITIN'
Harold Arlen
Harold Arlen and Truman Capote
House of Flowers (1954)

WAITIN' FOR MY DEARIE
Frederick Loewe
Alan Jay Lerner
Brigadoon (1947)

WAITIN' FOR THE EVENING TRAIN
Arthur Schwartz
Howard Dietz
Jennie (1963)

WAITING ALL THE TIME FOR YOU
Frank Grey
McElbert Moore and Frank Grey
The Matinee Girl (1926)

WAITING FOR THE GIRLS UPSTAIRS
Stephen Sondheim
Follies (1971)

WAITING FOR THE MEN
Earl Robinson
Waldo Salt
Sandhog (OB) (1954)

WAITING FOR THE TRAIN
George Gershwin
Ira Gershwin
Tip-Toes (1925)

WAITING FOR THE WHISTLE TO BLOW
Eubie Blake
Noble Sissle
Shuffle Along (1933)

WAITING FOR YOU
Vincent Youmans
Otto Harbach
No, No, Nanette (1925)

WAITING IN A QUEUE
Noël Coward
This Year of Grace (1928)

WAITING, WAITING
Jule Styne
Betty Comden and Adolph Green
Do Re Mi (1960)

WAKE ME UP A STAR
Michael Cleary
Arthur Swanstrom
Sea Legs (1937)

WAKE UP
C. Jackson and James Hatch
Fly Blackbird (OB) (1962)

WAKE UP AND DREAM
Cole Porter
Wake Up and Dream (1929)

WAKE UP, SLEEPY MOON
Max Rich
Jack Scholl
Keep Moving (1934)

WAKING UP SUN
Robert Waldman
Alfred Uhry
Here's Where I Belong (1968)

WALK AWAY
Elmer Bernstein
Carolyn Leigh
How Now, Dow Jones (1967)

WALK DOWN MY STREET
Norman Curtis
Patricia Taylor Curtis
Walk Down Mah Street! (OB) (1968)

WALK HIM UP THE STAIRS
Gary Geld
Peter Udell
Purlie (1970)

WALK INTO HEAVEN
Claibe Richardson
Kenward Elmslie
The Grass Harp (1971)

WALK LIKE A SAILOR
Sammy Fain
Dan Shapiro
Ankles Aweigh (1955)

WALK, LORDY, WALK
Norman Curtis
Patricia Taylor Curtis
Walk Down Mah Street! (OB) (1968)

WALK ON HOME
Jim Turner
Doug Dyer
Blood (OB) (1971)

WALK SWEET
Harry Warren
Jerome Lawrence and Robert E. Lee
Shangri-La (1956)

WALK TOGETHER, CHILDREN
J. C. Johnson
Change Your Luck (1930)

WALKER WALK, THE
Bill and Patti Jacob
Jimmy (1969)

WALKIN' ALONG MINDIN' MY BUSI-NESS
Burton Lane
E. Y. Harburg
Hold On to Your Hats (1940)

WALKIN' IN THE RAIN
Steven Metcalf
Fred Bluth
Drat! (OB) (1971)

WALKIN' ON AIR
Harry Revel
Mack Gordon
Fast and Furious (1931)

WALKIN' THE TRACK
Con Conrad
Gus Kahn
Kitty's Kisses (1926)

WALKING AWAY WHISTLING
Frank Loesser
Greenwillow (1960)

WALKING DOGS AROUND
Ray Henderson
B. G. DeSylva and Lew Brown
George White's Scandals (1926)

WALKING DOWN THE ROAD
Alan Kohan and William Angelos
Put It in Writing (OB) (1963)

WALKING HAPPY
Jimmy Van Heusen
Sammy Cahn
Walking Happy (1966)

WALKING HOME WITH ANGELINE
George Gershwin
Brian Hooker
Our Nell (1922)

WALKING HOME WITH JOSIE
Jerome Kern
Anne Caldwell
The City Chap (1925)

WALKING IN SPACE
Galt MacDermot
Gerome Ragni and James Rado
Hair (1968)

WALKING THE DECK
Frank D'Armond
Will Morrissey
Saluta (1934)

WALKING THE DOG*
George Gershwin
Shall We Dance (F) (1937)

WALKING WITH PENINNAH
Leon Carr
Earl Shuman
The Secret Life of Walter Mitty (OB) (1964)

WALL STREET
Jim Wise
George Haimsohn and Robin Miller
Dames at Sea (OB) (1968)

WALL STREET REEL
Arthur Siegel
Jim Fuerst
New Faces (1962)

WALL STREET ZOO
Lucien Denni
Helena Evans
Happy Go Lucky (1926)

WALLA WALLA BOOLA, THE
Noël Coward
The Girl Who Came to Supper (1963)

WALTER MITTY MARCH, THE
Leon Carr
Earl Shuman
The Secret Life of Walter Mitty (OB) (1964)

WALTZ AT MAXIM'S (SHE IS NOT THINKING of ME)
Frederick Loewe
Alan Jay Lerner
Gigi (F) (1958)

WALTZ DOWN THE AISLE†
Cole Porter
Anything Goes (1934)

WALTZ ETERNAL
Robert Wright and George Forrest (based on Grieg)
Song of Norway (1944)

WALTZ FOR A BALL
Richard Rodgers
Cinderella (TV) (1957)

WALTZ FOR TWO BALLOONS, A
Earl Wilson, Jr.
A Day in the Life of Just About Everyone (OB) (1971)

WALTZ I HEARD IN A DREAM, THE
Kay Swift
Paris '90 (1952)

WALTZ IN SWINGTIME, THE
Jerome Kern
Dorothy Fields
Swing Time (F) (1936)

WALTZ OF LOVE, THE
Richard Fall
Irving Caesar
White Horse Inn (1936)

WALTZ THAT BROUGHT YOU BACK TO ME, THE
Carmen Lombardo
Irving Caesar
George White's Music Hall Varieties (1932)

WALTZ WAS BORN IN VIENNA, A
Frederick Loewe
Earle Crooker
The Illustrators' Show (1936)

WALTZ WITH ME
Walter Kollo
Harry B. Smith
Three Little Girls (1930)

WALTZING IN THE MOONLIGHT
Harry Ruby
Bert Kalmar
High Kickers (1941)

WANAPOO BAY
Rudolf Friml
J. Keirn Brennan
Luana (1930)

---

*Instrumental, later published as "Promenade"

†Dropped from New York production

WANDER AWAY
Herbert Stothart
Otto Harbach and Oscar Hammerstein II
Song of the Flame (1925)

WANDERING IN DREAMLAND
Martin Broones
Ballard MacDonald
Rufus Lemaire's Affairs (1927)

WAND'RIN' STAR
Frederick Loewe
Alan Jay Lerner
Paint Your Wagon (1951)

WANDR'ING HEART
Arthur Schwartz
Howard Dietz
Revenge with Music (1934)

WANT TO GET RETARDED?
Norman Curtis
Patricia Taylor Curtis
Walk Down Mah Street! (OB) (1968)

WANTA, HOPE TO FEEL AT HOME
Alfred Brooks
Ira J. Bilowit
Of Mice and Men (OB) (1958)

WANTING THINGS
Burt Bacharach
Hal David
Promises, Promises (1968)

WANTING YOU
Will Morrisey
Edmund Joseph
Polly of Hollywood (1927)

WANTING YOU
Sigmund Romberg
Oscar Hammerstein II
The New Moon (1928)

WAR AND REBELLION
Coleridge-Taylor Perkinson
Errol Hill
Man Better Man (OB) (1969)

WAR BABIES
Gary William Friedman
Will Holt
The Me Nobody Knows (OB) (1970)

WAR IS GOOD BUSINESS
Wally Harper
Paul Zakrzewski
Sensations (OB) (1970)

WAR IS WAR
Richard Rodgers
Lorenz Hart
Dearest Enemy (1925)

WARM ALL OVER
Frank Loesser
The Most Happy Fella (1956)

WARM BREEZES AT TWILIGHT
Ed Tyler
Sweet Miani (OB) (1962)

WAS I?
Chick Endor
Charles Farrell
Ziegfeld Follies (1931)

WAS I WAZIR?
Robert Wright and George Forrest
(based on Alexander Borodin)
Kismet (1953)

WAS SHE PRETTIER THAN I?
Hugh Martin and Timothy Gray
High Spirits (1964)

WAS THAT ME TALKING
Robert Rosenblum
Robert Rosenblum and Howard Schuman
Up Eden (OB) (1968)

WASHED AWAY
Nancy Ford
Gretchen Cryer
Now Is the Time for All Good Men (OB) (1967)

WASHINGTON SQUARE
Clay Warnick
Mel Tolkin and Lucille Kallen
Tickets Please (1950)

WASHINGTON SQUARE DANCE
Irving Berlin
Call Me Madam (1950)

WASHINGTON TWIST, THE
Irving Berlin
Mr. President (1962)

WASN'T IT A SIMPLY LOVELY WED-
DING?
Glenn Paxton
Robert Goldman and George Weiss
First Impressions (1959)

WASN'T IT BEAUTIFUL WHILE IT
LASTED?
Ray Henderson
B. G. DeSylva and Lew Brown
Flying High (1930)

WASN'T IT GREAT?*
Richard Rodgers
Lorenz Hart
She's My Baby (1928)

WASN'T IT NICE?
Rudolf Friml
Irving Caesar
No Foolin' (1926)

WASTING AWAY
J. C. Johnson
Change Your Luck (1930)

WATCH MY BABY WALK
Peter de Rose
Jo Trent
Earl Carroll's Vanities (1928)

WATCH MY DUST
Jule Styne
Betty Comden and Adolph Green
Hallelujah, Baby! (1967)

WATCH OUT FOR CLAGGART/WORK
Ron Dante and Gene Allan
Billy (1969)

WATCH THE BIRDIES
Emil Gerstenberger and Carle Carl-
ton
Howard Johnson
The Lace Petticoat (1927)

WATCHING
Kenn Long and Jim Crozier
Kenn Long
Touch (OB) (1970)

WATCHING THE BIG PARADE GO BY
David Shire
Richard Maltby, Jr.
The Sap of Life (OB) (1961)

WATCHING THE CLOUDS ROLL BY
Harry Ruby
Bert Kalmar
Animal Crackers (1928)

WATER MOVIN' SLOW
Baldwin Bergersen
William Archibald
Carib Song (1945)

WATER UNDER THE BRIDGE
Vernon Duke
E. Y. Harburg
Ziegfeld Follies (1934)

WATER WEARS DOWN THE STONE,
THE
Harold Rome
The Zulu and the Zayda (1965)

WATERWORKS MADRIGAL, THE
Coleman Dowell
The Tattooed Countess (OB) (1961)

WAVE A HAND
Stanley Lebowsky
Fred Tobias
Gantry (1970)

WAY BACK IN 1939 A.D.
Hoagy Carmichael
Johnny Mercer
Walk with Music (1940)

---

*Dropped from New York production

WAY DOWN BLUES
George Kleinsinger
Joe Darion
Shinbone Alley (1957)

WAY DOWN IN LIL' OLD TEXAS
Jane Douglas
Tom O'Malley
Bella (OB) (1961)

WAY DOWN TOWN
James F. Hanley
Eddie Dowling
Sidewalks of New York (1927)

WAY IT MIGHT HAVE BEEN, THE
Hugh Martin
Look Ma, I'm Dancin'! (1948)

WAY MY ANCESTORS WENT, THE
Ann Ronell
Count Me In (1942)

WAY OUT IN RAINBOW LAND
Alma Sanders
Monte Carlo
Oh! Oh! Nurse (1925)

WAY OUT WEST
Richard Rodgers
Lorenz Hart
Babes in Arms (1937)

WAY OUT WEST IN JERSEY
Kurt Weill
Ogden Nash
One Touch of Venus (1943)

WAY OUT WEST WHERE THE EAST BEGINS
Burton Lane
E. Y. Harburg
Hold On to Your Hats (1940)

WAY THINGS ARE, THE
Harold Rome
I Can Get It for You Wholesale (1962)

WAY UP NORTH IN DIXIE
Philip Charig
Dan Shapiro and Milton Pascal
Artists and Models (1943)

WAY YOU LOOK TONIGHT, THE*
Jerome Kern
Dorothy Fields
Swing Time (F) (1936)

WAYSIDE FLOWER
Sigmund Romberg
Arthur Wimperis
Louie the 14th (1925)

WAYSIDE INN
John Clifton
John Clifton and Ben Tarver
Man with a Load of Mischief (OB) (1966)

WE
Albert Hague
Allen Sherman
The Fig Leaves Are Falling (1969)

WE ARE CUT IN TWAIN
Kurt Weill
Maxwell Anderson
Knickerbocker Holiday (1938)

WE ARE FRIENDS
Walter Cool
Mackey of Appalachia (OB) (1965)

WE ARE THE SHOW GIRLS
Morris Hamilton
Grace Henry
Earl Carroll's Vanities (1926)

WE ARE THE WAITERS
Clarence Gaskill
Earl Carroll's Vanities (1925)

WE ARE THE WHORES
Susan Hulsman Bingham
Myrna Lamb
Mod Donna (OB) (1970)

WE ARE WHAT WE ARE
Robert Waldman
Alfred Uhry
Here's Where I Belong (1968)

———
*Academy Award Winner

WE BELIEVE
Lehman Engel
Agnes Morgan
A Hero Is Born (1937)

WE BELONG
Janet Gari
Toby Garson
Lyle (OB) (1970)

WE BELONG TOGETHER
Jerome Kern
Oscar Hammerstein II
Music in the Air (1932)

WE BESEECH THEE
Stephen Schwartz
Godspell (OB) (1971)

WE CAME IN CHAINS
Oscar Brown, Jr.
Buck White (1969)

WE CAME TOGETHER
Jacques Urbont
David Newburger
Stag Movie (OB) (1971)

WE CAN ALL GIVE LOVE
Stanley Lebowsky
Fred Tobias
Gantry (1970)

WE CAN BE PROUD
Marc Blitzstein
Juno (1959)

WE CLEARLY REQUESTED
Norman Campbell
Donald Campbell and Norman Campbell
Anne of Green Gables (OB) (1971)

WE DESERVE EACH OTHER
Richard Rodgers
Oscar Hammerstein II
Me and Juliet (1953)

WE DID IT BEFORE
Charlie Tobias and Cliff Friend
Banjo Eyes (1941)

WE DIDN'T ASK TO BE BORN
Ernest McCarty
Jack Ramer and Ernest McCarty
I Dreamt I Dwelt in Bloomingdale's (OB) (1970)

WE DON'T MATTER AT ALL
Charles Strouse
Lee Adams
(It's a Bird, It's a Plane) It's Superman (1966)

WE DON'T UNDERSTAND OUR CHILDREN
Julian Slade
Dorothy Reynolds and Julian Slade
Salad Days (OB) (1958)

WE DRINK TO YOU, J. H. BRODY
Cole Porter
Leave It to Me (1938)

WE FEEL OUR MAN IS DEFINITELY YOU
Sidney Lippman
Sylvia Dee
Barefoot Boy with Cheek (1947)

WE GON' JUMP UP
Irving Burgie
Ballad for Bimshire (OB) (1963)

WE GOT A FUTURE
Alfred Brooks
Ira J. Bilowit
Of Mice and Men (OB) (1958)

WE GOT LOVE
Jeanne Bargy
Jeanne Bargy, Frank Gehrecke, and Herb Corey
Greenwich Village U.S.A. (OB) (1960)

WE GOT TROUBLES
Walter Cool
Mackey of Appalachia (OB) (1965)

WE GOT US
Walter Marks
Golden Rainbow (1968)

WE HAD TO REHEARSE
Arthur Schwartz
Albert Stillman
Virginia (1937)

WE HAVE A DATE
Lou Cooper
Roslyn Harvey
Of V We Sing (1942)

WE HAVE NEVER MET
Cy Young
That Hat! (OB) (1964)

WE HAVEN'T GOT A POT TO COOK IN
Jimmy McHugh
Al Dubin
The Streets of Paris (1939)

WE HOPE TO MAKE A HIT
Seymour Furth and Lee Edwards
R. F. Carroll
Bringing Up Father (1925)

WE INCORPORATED
Frank D'Armond
Will Morrissey
Saluta (1934)

WE KISS IN A SHADOW
Richard Rodgers
Oscar Hammerstein II
The King and I (1951)

WE KNOW RENO
John Green
Edward Heyman
Here Goes the Bride (1931)

WE KNOW WHAT YOU WANT AND
WE GOT IT
Ruth Cleary Patterson
Floria Vestoff
Russell Patterson's Sketch Book (OB)
  (1960)

WE KNOW WHERE WE'VE BEEN
Maury Laws
Jules Bass
Month of Sundays (OB) (1968)

WE LOVE TO GO TO WORK
Muriel Pollock
Max and Nathaniel Lief and Harold
  Atteridge
Pleasure Bound (1929)

WE LOVE YOU, CONRAD!
Charles Strouse
Lee Adams
Bye Bye Birdie (1960)

WE LOVES YA, JIMEY
Albert Hague
Dorothy Fields
Redhead (1959)

WE MAKE A PROMISE
Johnny Brandon
Billy Noname (OB) (1970)

WE MAKE THE SHOW
Carlton Kelsey and Maury Rubens
Clifford Grey
Sky High (1925)

WE MAKIN' DOUGH YOU SO AND SO
RAG, THE
Sol Berkowitz
James Lipton
Nowhere to Go but Up (1962)

WE MIGHT PLAY TIDDLE DE WINKS
Richard Myers
Leo Robin
Hello, Yourself! (1928)

WE NEED A LITTLE CHRISTMAS
Jerry Herman
Mame (1966)

WE NEED HIM
Charles Strouse
Lee Adams
(It's a Bird, It's a Plane) It's Superman
  (1966)

WE NEVER SLEEP
Oscar Levant
Irving Caesar and Graham John
Ripples (1930)

WE OF ME, THE
G. Wood
F. Jasmine Addams (OB) (1971)

WE OPEN IN VENICE
Cole Porter
Kiss Me, Kate (1948)

WE PIRATES FROM WEEHAWKEN
Richard Rodgers
Lorenz Hart
Peggy-Ann (1926)

WE PRIZE MOST THE THINGS WE MISS
Ralph Benatzky
Irving Caesar
White Horse Inn (1936)

WE SAID WE WOULDN'T LOOK BACK
Julian Slade
Dorothy Reynolds and Julian Slade
Salad Days (OB) (1958)

WE SAIL THE SEAS
Mark Sandrich, Jr.
Sidney Michaels
Ben Franklin in Paris (1964)

WE SAW EVERYBODY THERE
Philip Springer
Joan Javits
Hotel Passionato (OB) (1965)

WE SAW THE SEA
Irving Berlin
Follow the Fleet (F) (1936)

WE SHALL MEET IN THE GREAT HEREAFTER
Nancy Ford
Gretchen Cryer
Now Is the Time for All Good Men (OB) (1967)

WE SHALL MEET TO PART, NO NEVER
Harold Arlen
Johnny Mercer
St. Louis Woman (1946)

WE SHOULD CARE
Irving Berlin
The Cocoanuts (1925)

WE SING AMERICA
Harold Rome
Pins and Needles (OB) (1937)

WE SPEAK THE SAME LANGUAGE
Charles Strouse
Lee Adams
All American (1962)

WE TWO
Emmerich Kalman and Herbert Stothart
Otto Harbach and Oscar Hammerstein II
Golden Dawn (1927)

WE TWO
Murray Rumshinsky
Jacob Jacobs
The President's Daughter (1970)

WE WANT OUR BREAKFAST
Harold Levey
Owen Murphy
Rainbow Rose (1926)

WE WANT YOU*
Harry Ruby
Bert Kalmar
The Five O'Clock Girl (1927)

WE WERE A WOW
Harry Archer
Harlan Thompson
Merry-Merry (1925)

WE WERE BORN BY CHANCE
Kenneth Gaburo
Seyril Schochen
The Tiger Rag (OB) (1961)

WE WERE DANCING
Noël Coward
Tonight at 8:30 (We Were Dancing) (1936)

———
*Also in *Top Speed* (1929)

WE WERE SO YOUNG
Jerome Kern
Oscar Hammerstein II
Sweet Adeline (F) (1934)

WE WON'T CHARLESTON
Harry Ruby
Bert Kalmar
The Ramblers (1926)

WE WON'T DISCUSS IT
Milton Schafer
Ronny Graham
Bravo Giovanni (1962)

WE WON'T FORGET TO WRITE
Oscar Brand and Paul Nassau
A Joyful Noise (1966)

WE WON'T LET IT HAPPEN HERE
Sammy Fain
Charles Tobias
Hellzapoppin' (1938)

WE WON'T TAKE IT BACK
Arthur Schwartz
Howard Dietz
Inside U.S.A. (1948)

WEAKER SEX, THE
Lewis E. Gensler
B. G. DeSylva
Queen High (1926)

WEAKER SEX, THE
Alberta Nichols
Mann Holiner
Angela (1928)

WEALTH
Jerry Bock
Sheldon Harnick
The Apple Tree (1966)

WEAR YOUR SUNDAY SMILE
Charles Rosoff
Leo Robin
Judy (1927)

WEARING OF THE BLUE
David Baker

David Craig
Copper and Brass (1957)

WEARY FEET
Donald Heywood
Africana (1927)

WEARY NEAR TO DYIN'
Bob Merrill
Henry, Sweet Henry (1967)

WEATHERBEE'S DRUG STORE
Walter Kent
Kim Gannon
Seventeen (1951)

WE'D RATHER BE RIGHT
Harold Rome
Arthur Kramer
Pins and Needles (OB) (1937)

WE'D RATHER DANCE THAN EAT
Dave Stamper
Gene Buck
Take the Air (1927)

WEDDING, THE
Jerry Herman
Milk and Honey (1961)

WEDDING, THE
John Kander
James Goldman, John Kander, and
    William Goldman
A Family Affair (1962)

WEDDING, THE
Duke Ellington
Marshall Barer and Fred Tobias
Pousse-Café (1966)

WEDDING! A WEDDING!, A
William Dyer
Don Parks and William Dyer
Jo! (OB) (1964)

WEDDING BELLS
Kay Swift
Paul James
Fine and Dandy (1930)

WEDDING BELLS RING ON, THE
Vincent Youmans
Billy Rose and Edward Eliscu
Great Day! (1929)

WEDDING CELEBRATION, THE
Deed Meyer
Stones of Jehoshaphat (OB) (1963)

WEDDING CHIMES
Seymour Furth and Lee Edwards
R. F. Carroll
Bringing Up Father (1925)

WEDDING DANCE
Jerry Bock
Sheldon Harnick
Fiddler on the Roof (1964)

WEDDING IN THE PARK
Jay Gorney
Barry Trivers
Heaven on Earth (1948)

WEDDING IN THE SPRING
Jerome Kern
Johnny Mercer
You Were Never Lovelier (F) (1942)

WEDDING KNELL, THE
Jerome Kern
Oscar Hammerstein II
Sunny (1925)

WEDDING OF THE YEAR
Ervin Drake
What Makes Sammy Run? (1964)

WEDDING-OF-THE-YEAR BLUES
Harold Karr
Matt Dubey
Happy Hunting (1956)

WEDDING PARADE, THE
Joseph Meyer
William Moll
Jonica (1930)

WEDDING SONG
Kurt Weill
Marc Blitzstein
The Threepenny Opera (OB) (1954)

WEDDING SONG, THE
Michael Leonard
Herbert Martin
How to Be a Jewish Mother (1967)

WEDGEWOOD MAID
Al Goodman, Maury Rubens, and J. Fred Coots
Clifford Grey
Gay Paree (1925)

WEEP NO MORE
Gordon Jenkins
Tom Adair
Along Fifth Avenue (1949)

WEEP NO MORE, MY BABY
John Green
Edward Heyman
Murder at the Vanities (1933)

WELCOME
Mary Rodgers
Martin Charnin
Hot Spot (1963)

WELCOME
Arthur Schwartz
Howard Dietz
Jennie (1963)

WELCOME HINGES
Harold Arlen
E. Y. Harburg
Bloomer Girl (1944)

WELCOME HOME
Joseph Meyer and James F. Hanley
B. G. DeSylva
Big Boy (1925)

WELCOME HOME
Winthrop Cortelyou
Derick Wulff
Kiss Me (1927)

WELCOME HOME
Harold Rome
Fanny (1954)

WELCOME HOME
Richard Adler
Kwamina (1961)

WELCOME HOME
Rick Besoyan
The Student Gypsy (OB) (1963)

WELCOME HOME AGAIN
Victor Ziskin
Joan Javits
Young Abe Lincoln (1961)

WELCOME, LITTLE ONE
Lor Crane
John B. Kuntz
Whispers on the Wind (OB) (1970)

WELCOME, MR. GOLDEN!
Murray Rumshinsky
Jacob Jacobs
The President's Daughter (1970)

WELCOME ON THE LANDING STAGE
Ralph Benatzky
Irving Caesar
White Horse Inn (1936)

WELCOME SONG
Sammy Fain
Paul Francis Webster
Christine (1960)

WELCOME SONG
Irving Burgie
Ballad for Bimshire (OB) (1963)

WELCOME TO JERRY
Cole Porter
Panama Hattie (1940)

WELCOME TO POOTZIE VAN DOYLE
Noël Coward
The Girl Who Came to Supper (1963)

WELCOME TO SLUDGEPOOL
Leslie Bricusse and Anthony Newley
Stop the World—I Want to Get Off
  (1962)

WELCOME TO SUNVALE
Leslie Bricusse and Anthony Newley
Stop the World—I Want to Get Off
  (1962)

WELCOME TO THE QUEEN
Rudolf Friml
P. G. Wodehouse and Clifford Grey
The Three Musketeers (1928)

WELCOME TO THE THEATER
Charles Strouse
Lee Adams
Applause (1970)

WE'LL ALWAYS STAY IN LOVE
Darwin Venneri
Darwin's Theories (OB) (1960)

WE'LL BE THE SAME
Richard Rodgers
Lorenz Hart
America's Sweetheart (1931)

WE'LL BE THERE
J. Fred Coots
Arthur Swanstrom and Benny Davis
Sons o' Guns (1929)

**WE'LL BUILD A BRAND NEW BAM-
BOO BUNGALOW**
A. Baldwin Sloane
Harry Cort and George E. Stoddard
China Rose (1925)

WE'LL FIND A WAY
Joseph Raposo
Erich Segal
Sing Muse! (OB) (1961)

WE'LL GET ALONG
Muriel Pollock
Max and Nathaniel Lief and Harold
  Atteridge
Pleasure Bound (1929)

WE'LL GO AWAY TOGETHER
Kurt Weill
Langston Hughes
Street Scene (1947)

WE'LL HAVE A NEW HOME IN THE
MORNING
Willard Robison
J. Russel Robinson and Gene Buck
Take the Air (1927)

WE'LL HAVE OUR GOOD DAYS
Harry Tierney
Joseph McCarthy
Cross My Heart (1928)

WE'LL JUST BE TWO COMMUTERS
Harry Archer
Walter O'Keefe
Just a Minute (1928)

WE'LL LIVE ALL OVER AGAIN
Vernon Duke
John Latouche
Cabin in the Sky (OB) (1964)

WE'LL SUFFER TOGETHER
Philip Springer
Joan Javits
Hotel Passionato (OB) (1965)

WE'LL SWING IT THROUGH
Lee Wainer
John Lund
New Faces (1943)

WELL, DID YOU EVAH!*
Cole Porter
Du Barry Was a Lady (1939)

WELL IT AIN'T
Mary Rodgers
Larry Siegel and Stan Hart
The Mad Show (OB) (1966)

WELL KNOWN FACT, A
Harvey Schmidt
Tom Jones
I Do! I Do! (1966)

WELL OF ROMANCE, THE
H. Maurice Jacquet
Preston Sturges
The Well of Romance (1930)

WELL, WELL!
Lee Wainer
June Carroll
New Faces (1943)

WELL, YOU SEE
John Green
Edward Heyman
Here Goes the Bride (1931)

WELLS FARGO WAGON
Meredith Willson
The Music Man (1957)

WENDY
Jule Styne
Betty Comden and Adolph Green
Peter Pan (1954)

WE'RE A COUPLE OF SALESMEN
Eubie Blake
Noble Sissle
Shuffle Along (1933)

WE'RE A HOME
Robert Waldman
Alfred Uhry
Here's Where I Belong (1968)

WE'RE ABOUT TO START BIG RE-
HEARSIN'
Cole Porter
Red, Hot and Blue! (1936)

WE'RE ALIVE
Marc Blitzstein
Juno (1959)

WE'RE ALL IN THE SAME BOAT
Sigmund Romberg (developed by
    Don Walker)
Leo Robin
The Girl in Pink Tights (1954)

WE'RE BETTING ON YOU
Robert Kessler
Martin Charnin
Fallout (OB) (1959)

_____
*Also in film *High Society* (1956)

WE'RE CALLING ON MR. BROOKS
Ray Henderson
B. G. DeSylva and Lew Brown
Hold Everything! (1928)

WE'RE CIVILIZED
Ray Haney
Alfred Aiken
We're Civilized? (OB) (1962)

WE'RE FOR LOVE
Ralph Blane
Three Wishes for Jamie (1952)

WE'RE GOING AWAY
Gene Lockhart
Bunk of 1926 (1926)

WE'RE GOING TO BALANCE THE BUDGET
Richard Rodgers
Lorenz Hart
I'd Rather Be Right (1937)

WE'RE GOING TO MAKE BOOM-BOOM
Werner Janssen
Mann Holiner and J. Keirn Brennan
Boom-Boom (1929)

WE'RE GONNA BE ALL RIGHT
Richard Rodgers
Stephen Sondheim
Do I Hear a Waltz? (1965)

WE'RE GONNA HAVE A WEDDING
Don McAfee
Nancy Leeds
Great Scot! (OB) (1965)

WE'RE GONNA TURN ON FREEDOM
Johnny Brandon
Billy Noname (OB) (1970)

WE'RE GONNA WIN
Oscar Brand
How to Steal an Election (OB) (1968)

WE'RE HAVING A BABY
Vernon Duke
Harold Adamson
Banjo Eyes (1941)

WE'RE HAVING A PARTY
Walter Cool
Mackey of Appalachia (OB) (1965)

WE'RE HAVING OUR FLING
Jerry Livingston
Mack David
Bright Lights of 1944 (1943)

WE'RE HERE
J. C. Johnson
Change Your Luck (1930)

WE'RE HOME
Bob Merrill
Take Me Along (1959)

WE'RE JUMPING INTO SOMETHING
Blanche Merrill
Puzzles of 1925 (1925)

WE'RE LOOKING FOR A PIANO
Julian Slade
Dorothy Reynolds and Julian Slade
Salad Days (OB) (1958)

WE'RE NOT CHILDREN
Jay Livingston and Ray Evans
Oh Captain! (1958)

WE'RE OFF
Richard Lewine
Ted Fetter
The Fireman's Flame (OB) (1937)

WE'RE OFF TO FEATHERMORE
Cole Porter
Jubilee (1935)

WE'RE OFF TO SEE THE WIZARD
Harold Arlen
E. Y. Harburg
The Wizard of Oz (F) (1939)

WE'RE ON THE MAP
Harry Ruby
Bert Kalmar
Twinkle Twinkle (1926)

WE'RE SHARIN' SHARON
Stanley Lebowsky
Fred Tobias
Gantry (1970)

WE'RE STILL ON THE MAP
Ann Ronell
Count Me In (1942)

WE'RE THE BERRIES
Eubie Blake
Andy Razaf
Blackbirds (1930)

WE'RE THE GIRLS YOU CAN'T FORGET
James F. Hanley
Eddie Dowling
Sidewalks of New York (1927)

WE'RE TODAY
Norman Curtis
Patricia Taylor Curtis
Walk Down Mah Street! (OB) (1968)

WERE THINE THAT SPECIAL FACE
Cole Porter
Kiss Me, Kate (1948)

WERE THIS TO PROVE A FEATHER IN MY HAT
Alec Wilder
Arnold Sundgaard
Kittiwake Island (OB) (1960)

WEST POINT SONG
Sigmund Romberg
P. G. Wodehouse
Rosalie (1928)

WEST WIND
Vincent Youmans
J. Russel Robinson
Song of the West (F) (1930)

WEST WIND
Kurt Weill
Ogden Nash
One Touch of Venus (1943)

WESTERN PEOPLE FUNNY
Richard Rodgers
Oscar Hammerstein II
The King and I (1951)

WESTWARD HO!
Dorcas Cochran and Charles Rosoff
Earl Carroll's Vanities (1940)

WE'VE DECIDED TO STAY
Harry Warren
Jerome Lawrence and Robert E. Lee
Shangri-La (1956)

WE'VE GOT A FEELING IN OUR BONES
William Klenosky
Utopia! (OB) (1963)

WE'VE GOT HIM
George M. Cohan
The Merry Malones (1927)

WE'VE GOT THE SONG
Harold Rome
Sing Out the News (1938)

WE'VE HAD A GRAND OLD TIME
George M. Cohan
The Merry Malones (1927)

WE'VE JUST BEGUN
Harold Rome
Harold Rome and Charles Friedman
Pins and Needles (OB) (1937)

WHA'D YOU COME TO COLLEGE FOR?
Harold Arlen
Jack Yellen
You Said It (1931)

WHADDAYA SAY, KID
Clinton Ballard
Carolyn Richter
The Ballad of Johnny Pot (OB) (1971)

WHAT A BLESSING
Frank Loesser
Greenwillow (1960)

WHAT A BORE
Jerry Blatt
Jerry Blatt and Lonnie Burstein
Have I Got One for You (OB) (1968)

WHAT A CASE I'VE GOT ON YOU
Arthur Schwartz
Howard Dietz
The Second Little Show (1930)

WHAT A CHARMING COUPLE
Arthur Schwartz
Howard Dietz
The Gay Life (1961)

WHAT A COUNTRY!
Charles Strouse
Lee Adams
All American (1962)

WHAT A CRAZY WAY TO SPEND SUNDAY
Cole Porter
Mexican Hayride (1944)

WHAT A CURIOUS GIRL
Philip Springer
Joan Javits
Hotel Passionato (OB) (1965)

WHAT A DAY!
Abraham Ellstein
Walter Bullock
Great to Be Alive (1950)

WHAT A DAY FOR A WONDERFUL DAY
Jordan Ramin
Frank H. Stanton and Murray Semos
Look Where I'm At! (OB) (1971)

WHAT A DAY FOR ME
Mimi Stone
William Kaye
Pimpernel! (OB) (1964)

WHAT A DELIGHTFUL
Sammy Fain
Paul Francis Webster and Ray Golden
Alive and Kicking (1950)

WHAT A GIRL
Werner Janssen
Mann Holiner and J. Keirn Brennan
Boom-Boom (1929)

WHAT A GIRL
Richard Rodgers
Lorenz Hart
Spring Is Here (1929)

WHAT A GOOD DAY IS SATURDAY
John Morris
Gerald Freedman
A Time for Singing (1966)

WHAT A GREAT PAIR WE'LL BE
Cole Porter
Red, Hot and Blue! (1936)

WHAT A HAPPY DAY
Michael Leonard
Herbert Martin
The Yearling (1965)

WHAT A JAMBOREE
Ida Hoyt Chamberlain
Enchanted Isle (1927)

WHAT A KILLING
George Harwell
What a Killing (OB) (1961)

WHAT A LIFE!
Harry Archer
Harlan Thompson
Merry-Merry (1925)

WHAT A LIFE
Richard Freitas
Morty Neff and George Mysels
The Difficult Woman (OB) (1962)

WHAT A LIFE
Mel Marvin
Ted Berger
Shoemaker's Holiday (OB) (1967)

WHAT A LONG COLD WINTER!
William Dyer
Don Parks and William Dyer
Jo! (OB) (1964)

WHAT A LOVELY DAY FOR A WEDDING
Richard Rodgers
Oscar Hammerstein II
Allegro (1947)

WHAT A LOVELY DREAM
Francis Thorne
Arnold Weinstein
Fortuna (OB) (1962)

WHAT A LOVELY NIGHT
Frank Grey
Earle Crooker and McElbert Moore
Happy (1927)

WHAT A MAN!
Leslie Bricusse and Anthony Newley
*The Roar of the Greasepaint—The
  Smell of the Crowd* (1965)

WHAT A MAN
Lionel Bart
La Strada (1969)

WHAT A NICE IDEA
Galt MacDermot
John Guare
Two Gentlemen of Verona (1971)

WHAT A NICE MUNICIPAL PARK
Cole Porter
Jubilee (1935)

WHAT A NIGHT!
Philip Springer
Joan Javits
Hotel Passionato (OB) (1965)

**WHAT A NIGHT THIS IS GOING TO
BE**
Marian Grudeff and Raymond Jessel
Baker Street (1965)

WHAT A PARTY
John Morris
Gerald Freedman
A Time for Singing (1966)

WHAT A PIECE OF WORK IS MAN
Galt MacDermot
Gerome Ragni and James Rado
Hair (1968)

WHAT A PRETTY BABY YOU ARE
Leo Edwards
Herman Timberg
You'll See Stars (1942)

WHAT A SHAME
Don McAfee
Nancy Leeds
Great Scot! (OB) (1965)

WHAT A SONG CAN DO
Bernie Wayne and Lee Morris
Catch a Star! (1955)

WHAT A WASTE
Leonard Bernstein
Betty Comden and Adolph Green
Wonderful Town (1953)

WHAT A WEDDING
Johnny Brandon
Cindy (OB) (1964)

**WHAT A WHALE OF A DIFFERENCE
A WOMAN CAN MAKE**
Charles Rosoff
Leo Robin
Judy (1927)

WHAT A WONDERFUL WORLD
Arthur Schwartz
Howard Dietz
At Home Abroad (1935)

WHAT A WORLD THIS WOULD BE
Ray Henderson
B. G. DeSylva and Lew Brown
George White's Scandals (1925)

WHAT-A-YA-SAY
Harold Orlob
Hairpin Harmony (1943)

WHAT ABOUT ME
Clinton Ballard
Carolyn Richter
The Ballad of Johnny Pot (OB) (1971)

**WHAT ABRAHAM LINCOLN ONCE
SAID**
Menachem Zur
Herbert Appleman
Unfair to Goliath (OB) (1970)

WHAT AM I HANGIN' AROUND FOR?
William Klenosky
Utopia! (OB) (1963)

WHAT AM I TO DO?
Cole Porter
The Man Who Came to Dinner (1939)

WHAT AMERICA MEANS TO ME
Don Tucker
Red, White and Maddox (1969)

WHAT ARE THE BASIC THINGS?
Dov Seltzer
Lillian Burstein
To Live Another Summer (1971)

WHAT ARE THEY DOING TO US NOW?
Harold Rome
I Can Get It for You Wholesale (1962)

WHAT ARE WE DOING IN EGYPT?
Ervin Drake
Her First Roman (1968)

WHAT ARE WE GONNA DO TO-NIGHT?
Leon Pober
Bud Freeman
Beg, Borrow or Steal (1960)

WHAT ARE WE HERE FOR?
George Gershwin
Ira Gershwin
Treasure Girl (1928)

WHAT ARE YOU DOING THE REST OF YOUR LIFE
Burton Lane
Ted Koehler
Hollywood Canteen (F) (1944)

WHAT ARE YOU GOING TO DO ABOUT LOVE?
Dave Stamper
Fred Herendeen
Orchids Preferred (1937)

WHAT ARE YOU RUNNING FROM, MISTER?
Jordan Ramin
Frank H. Stanton and Murray Semos
Look Where I'm At! (OB) (1971)

WHAT CAN I GIVE YOU?
Phillip Broughton
Will B. Johnstone
Entre-Nous (OB) (1935)

WHAT CAN IT BE?
Jacques Urbont
Bruce Geller
All in Love (OB) (1961)

WHAT CAN THEY SEE IN DANCING?
Vivian Ellis
Graham John
By the Way (1925)

WHAT CAN YOU DO WITH A MAN?
Richard Rodgers
Lorenz Hart
The Boys from Syracuse (1938)

WHAT CAN YOU SAY IN A LOVE SONG?
Harold Arlen
Ira Gershwin and E. Y. Harburg
Life Begins at 8:40 (1934)

WHAT CARE I?
Sigmund Romberg
Harry B. Smith
Princess Flavia (1925)

WHAT CARE WE?
Ben Schwartz
Tales of Rigo (1927)

WHAT CAUSES THAT?
George Gershwin
Ira Gershwin
Treasure Girl (1928)

WHAT CHANCE HAVE I?
Irving Berlin
Louisiana Purchase (1940)

WHAT COULD I DO?
Werner Janssen
Mann Holiner and J. Keirn Brennan
Boom-Boom (1929)

WHAT COULD I DO, BUT FALL IN LOVE WITH YOU?
Alma Sanders

Monte Carlo
Mystery Moon (1930)

WHAT DID DELLA WEAR?
Arthur Schwartz
Agnes Morgan and Albert Carroll
The Grand Street Follies (1929)

WHAT DID I EVER SEE IN HIM?
Charles Strouse
Lee Adams
Bye Bye Birdie (1960)

**WHAT DID I HAVE THAT I DON'T
HAVE**
Burton Lane
Alan Jay Lerner
On a Clear Day You Can See Forever
  (1965)

WHAT DID WILLIAM TELL?
Philip Charig and Richard Myers
Leo Robin
Allez-Oop (1927)

WHAT DIFFERENCE DOES IT MAKE?
Constance Shepard
McElbert Moore and Frank Grey
The Matinee Girl (1926)

WHAT DO I DO NOW?
Earl Wilson, Jr.
*A Day in the Life of Just About Every-
one* (OB) (1971)

WHAT DO I DO NOW?
Claibe Richardson
Kenward Elmslie
The Grass Harp (1971)

WHAT DO I KNOW?
Ralph Blane
Three Wishes for Jamie (1952)

WHAT DO I KNOW?
Hal Hester and Danny Apolinar
Your Own Thing (1968)

WHAT DO I WANT WITH LOVE?
Eubie Blake
J. Milton Reddie and Cecil Mack
Swing It (1937)

WHAT DO I WANT WITH LOVE?
Sandy Wilson
Valmouth (OB) (1960)

WHAT DO SIMPLE FOLK DO?
Frederick Loewe
Alan Jay Lerner
Camelot (1960)

WHAT DO THE NEIGHBORS SAY?
Harold Orlob
Hairpin Harmony (1943)

WHAT DO THEY CARE?
Edwin Greenberg
Pilgrim's Progress (OB) (1962)

WHAT DO WE CARE?
Harold Arlen
Jack Yellen
You Said It (1931)

WHAT DO WE CARE?
George Kleinsinger
Joe Darion
Shinbone Alley (1957)

WHAT DO WE CARE IF IT RAINS
Mel Marvin
Ted Berger
Shoemaker's Holiday (OB) (1967)

WHAT DO WE DO? WE FLY!
Richard Rodgers
Stephen Sondheim
Do I Hear a Waltz? (1965)

**WHAT DO WE HAVE TO HOLD ON
TO?**
Billy Barnes
The Billy Barnes People (1961)

WHAT DO WOMEN WANT
Richard Hill and John Hawkins
Nevill Coghill
Canterbury Tales (1969)

WHAT DO YOU DO SUNDAY, MARY?
Stephen Jones
Irving Caesar
Poppy (1923)

WHAT DO YOU SAY
Don Elliott
James Costigan
The Beast in Me (1963)

WHAT DO YOU THINK ABOUT MEN?
Cole Porter
Out of This World (1950)

WHAT DO YOU THINK I AM?
Hugh Martin and Ralph Blane
Best Foot Forward (1941)

WHAT DO YOU WANT WITH MONEY?
Richard Rodgers
Lorenz Hart
Hallelujah, I'm a Bum (F) (1933)

WHAT DOES A LOVER PACK?
Galt MacDermot
John Guare
Two Gentlemen of Verona (1971)

WHAT DOES HE LOOK LIKE?
Irving Berlin
This Is the Army (1942)

WHAT DOES HE WANT OF ME
Mitch Leigh
Joe Darion
Man of La Mancha (1965)

WHAT DOES IT MEAN?
Philip Charig and Richard Myers
Leo Robin
Allez-Oop (1927)

WHAT DOES THAT DREAM MEAN?
Harold Karr
Matt Dubey
New Faces (1956)

WHAT D'YA SAY?
Jesse Greer
Raymond Kages
The Circus Princess (1927)

WHAT D'YA SAY
Henry Souvaine and Jay Gorney
Morrie Ryskind and Howard Dietz
Merry-Go-Round (1927)

WHAT D'YA SAY?
Ray Henderson
B. G. DeSylva and Lew Brown
George White's Scandals (1928)

WHAT EVERY LITTLE GIRL SHOULD KNOW
Arthur Schwartz
Henry Myers
The Little Show (1929)

WHAT EVERY OLD GIRL SHOULD KNOW
Harry Warren
Jerome Lawrence and Robert E. Lee
Shangri-La (1956)

WHAT EVERY WOMAN KNOWS
William Roy
Maggie (1953)

WHAT GOOD DOES IT DO
Harold Arlen
E. Y. Harburg
Jamaica (1957)

WHAT GOOD IS LOVE?
Harold Rome
Pins and Needles (OB) (1937)

WHAT GOOD WOULD THE MOON BE?
Kurt Weill
Langston Hughes
Street Scene (1947)

WHAT GREAT BIG EYES YOU HAVE
Henry Sullivan
Edward Eliscu
A Little Racketeer (1932)

WHAT GREAT MEN CANNOT DO
R. P. Weston
Bert Lee
Naughty Riquette (1926)

WHAT HAPPENED?
Vernon Duke
Howard Dietz
Jackpot (1944)

WHAT HAPPENED TO ME TONIGHT?
Richard Adler
Kwamina (1961)

WHAT HAPPENS TO LIFE
Gary William Friedman
Will Holt
The Me Nobody Knows (OB) (1970)

WHAT HAS HAPPENED?
Rich Besoyan
Little Mary Sunshine (OB) (1959)

WHAT HAS HE GOT?
Vernon Duke
Ted Fetter
The Show Is On (1936)

WHAT HAS MADE THE MOVIES?
Maury Rubens
Clifford Grey
The Madcap (1928)

WHAT HAVE I DONE?
J. C. Johnson
Change Your Luck (1930)

WHAT HAVE I DONE?
James P. Johnson
Flournoy Miller
Sugar Hill (1931)

WHAT HAVE YOU DONE TO ME?
Lewis E. Gensler
Owen Murphy and Robert A. Simon
The Gang's All Here (1931)

WHAT HAVE YOU GOT TO HAVE?
Lewis E. Gensler
E. Y. Harburg
Ballyhoo (1932)

WHAT HO, MRS. BRISKET
Noël Coward
The Girl Who Came to Supper (1963)

WHAT I MEAN TO SAY
Moose Charlap
Norman Gimbel
Whoop-Up (1958)

WHAT I SAY GOES
John Kander
James Goldman, John Kander, and
  William Goldman
A Family Affair (1962)

WHAT I WAS WARNED ABOUT
Hugh Martin
Make a Wish (1951)

WHAT IN THE WORLD DID YOU WANT?
Hugh Martin and Timothy Gray
High Spirits (1964)

WHAT IS A FRIEND?
Oscar Brown, Jr. and Luis Henrique
Joy (OB) (1970)

WHAT IS A FRIEND FOR?
Harold Arlen
Harold Arlen and Truman Capote
House of Flowers (1954)

WHAT IS A MAN?*
Richard Rodgers
Lorenz Hart
Pal Joey (1940)

WHAT IS A WOMAN
Willard Straight
David Eddy
The Athenian Touch (OB) (1964)

WHAT IS A WOMAN?
Harvey Schmidt
Tom Jones
I Do! I Do! (1966)

WHAT IS GOOD FOR DEPRESSIONS
Kenneth Gaburo
Seyril Schochen
The Tiger Rag (OB) (1961)

WHAT IS IT?
Richard Rodgers
Lorenz Hart
The Girl Friend (1926)

———
*Originally written as "Love is My Friend"

WHAT IS LOVE?
Howard Blankman
By Hex (OB) (1956)

WHAT IS LOVE?
Michael Valenti
Just for Love (OB) (1968)

WHAT IS THAT TUNE?
Cole Porter
You Never Know (1938)

WHAT IS THE GOOD?
Lew Kesler
Clifford Grey
Ned Wayburn's Gambols (1929)

WHAT IS THE STARS?
Marc Blitzstein
Juno (1959)

WHAT IS THERE TO SAY?
Vernon Duke
E. Y. Harburg
Ziegfeld Follies (1934)

WHAT IS THERE TO SING ABOUT?
Charles Strouse
Six (OB) (1971)

WHAT IS THIS FEELING IN THE AIR?
Jule Styne
Betty Comden and Adolph Green
Subways Are for Sleeping (1961)

WHAT IS THIS SENSATION?
Philip Springer
Joan Javits
Hotel Passionato (OB) (1965)

WHAT IS THIS THING CALLED LOVE?
Cole Porter
Wake Up and Dream (1929)

WHAT IS YOUR NAME?
Robert Holton
June Carroll
Hi, Paisano! (OB) (1961)

WHAT I'VE ALWAYS WANTED
Charles Strouse
Lee Adams
(It's a Bird, It's a Plane) It's Superman (1966)

WHAT KIND OF BABY
Menachem Zur
Herbert Appleman
Unfair to Goliath (OB) (1970)

WHAT KIND OF FOOL AM I?
Leslie Bricusse and Anthony Newley
Stop the World—I Want to Get Off (1962)

WHAT KIND OF LIFE IS THAT?
Norman Martin
Fred Ebb
Put It in Writing (OB) (1963)

WHAT KIND OF PARENTS
Wally Harper
Paul Zakrzewski
Sensations (OB) (1970)

WHAT MAKES A MARRIAGE MERRY
Jule Styne
E. Y. Harburg
Darling of the Day (1968)

WHAT MAKES IT HAPPEN
Jimmy Van Heusen
Sammy Cahn
Walking Happy (1966)

WHAT MAKES ME LOVE HIM
Jerry Bock
Sheldon Harnick
The Apple Tree (1966)

WHAT MAKES YOU SO WONDERFUL
Herbert Stothart, Bert Kalmar, and Harry Ruby
Good Boy (1928)

WHAT MIGHT HAVE BEEN
Edward Thomas
Martin Charnin
Ballad for a Firing Squad (OB) (1968)

WHAT MORE CAN A GENERAL DO?
George Gershwin
Ira Gershwin
Let 'Em Eat Cake (1933)

WHAT MORE DO I NEED?
Murray Rumshinsky
Jacob Jacobs
The President's Daughter (1970)

WHAT NEXT?
Charles Zwar
Alan Melville
From A to Z (1960)

WHAT—NO DIXIE?
Victor Young
Joseph Young and Ned Washington
Blackbirds of 1934 (1933)

WHAT SHADOWS WE ARE
Norman Curtis
Patricia Taylor Curtis
Walk Down Mah Street! (OB) (1968)

WHAT SHALL I BELIEVE IN NOW?
Voices, Inc.
The Believers (OB) (1968)

WHAT SHALL I DO?
Cole Porter
You Never Know (1938)

WHAT SORT OF WEDDING IS THIS?
George Gershwin
Ira Gershwin
Pardon My English (1933)

WHAT STYLE!
John Clifton
John Clifton and Ben Tarver
Man with a Load of Mischief (OB)
(1966)

WHAT TAKES MY FANCY
Cy Coleman
Carolyn Leigh
Wildcat (1960)

WHAT THE HELL
George Kleinsinger
Joe Darion
Shinbone Alley (1957)

WHAT THEN?
Edward Thomas
Martin Charnin
Ballad for a Firing Squad (OB) (1968)

WHAT THEN?
John Duffy
Rocco Bufano and John Duffy (based
on W.B. Yeats)
Horseman, Pass By (OB) (1969)

WHAT THIS PARTY NEEDS
Harold Rome
Harold Rome and Arthur Kramer
Pins and Needles (OB) (1937)

WHAT TO DO?
Robert Larimer
King of the Whole Damn World! (OB)
(1962)

WHAT WE PICK UP
Alfred Nathan
George Oppenheimer
The Manhatters (1927)

**WHAT WILL BECOME OF OUR EN-
GLAND?**
Cole Porter
Gay Divorce (1932)

WHAT WILL IT BE?
Marc Blitzstein
Regina (1949)

WHAT WILL THE FUTURE SAY?
Erich Wolfgang Korngold (based on
Offenbach)
Herbert Baker
Helen Goes to Troy (1944)

WHAT WOULD I CARE
Harry Ruby
Bert Kalmar
Top Speed (1929)

**WHAT WOULD WE DO WITHOUT
YOU**
Stephen Sondheim
Company (1970)

WHAT WOULD YOU DO?
John Kander
Fred Ebb
Cabaret (1966)

WHAT WOULD YOU DO?
Murray Rumshinsky
Jacob Jacobs
The President's Daughter (1970)

WHAT YOU ARE
Hal Jordan
Jerry Douglas
Rondelay (OB) (1969)

WHAT YOU WANT WITH BESS?
George Gershwin
DuBose Heyward
Porgy and Bess (1935)

WHATEVER BECAME OF OLD TEMPLE
Mark Sandrich, Jr.
Sidney Michaels
Ben Franklin in Paris (1964)

WHATEVER THAT MAY BE
Jacques Offenbach
E. Y. Harburg
The Happiest Girl in the World (1961)

WHAT'LL THEY THINK OF NEXT?
Hoagy Carmichael
Johnny Mercer
Walk with Music (1940)

WHAT'S A GIRL SUPPOSED TO DO?
Robert Stolz
Robert Sour
Mr. Strauss Goes to Boston (1945)

WHAT'S A GUY LIKE YOU DOIN' IN A PLACE LIKE THIS?
Nancy Ford
Gretchen Cryer
Now Is the Time for All Good Men (OB) (1967)

WHAT'S A KISS AMONG FRIENDS?
Vincent Youmans
Leo Robin and Clifford Grey
Hit the Deck (1927)

WHAT'S A MAMA FOR?
Robert Larimer
King of the Whole Damn World! (OB) (1962)

WHAT'S A NICE GIRL LIKE HER
Galt MacDermot
John Guare
Two Gentlemen of Verona (1971)

WHAT'S A SAILOR GOT?
Jacques Belasco
Kay Twomey
The Girl from Nantucket (1945)

WHAT'S A SHOW?
Shelley Mowell
Mike Stewart
Shoestring Revue (OB) (1957)

WHAT'S BECOME OF THE BOWERY?
Vincent Valentini
Parisiana (1928)

WHAT'S COOKING?
Norman Martin
Fred Ebb
Put It in Writing (OB) (1963)

WHAT'S GOIN' ON HERE?
Frederick Loewe
Alan Jay Lerner
Paint Your Wagon (1951)

WHAT'S GOING ON INSIDE?
Lionel Bart
La Strada (1969)

WHAT'S GONNA BE TOMORROW
Albert Hague
Marty Brill
Café Crown (1964)

WHAT'S GONNA HAPPEN TO ME?
Joseph Martinez Kookoolis and Scott Fagan
Scott Fagan
Soon (1971)

WHAT'S GOOD ABOUT GOOD NIGHT?
Jerome Kern
Dorothy Fields
The Joy of Living (F) (1938)

WHAT'S GOOD ABOUT GOODBYE?
Harold Arlen
Leo Robin
Casbah (F) (1948)

WHAT'S GOOD FOR GENERAL BULL-MOOSE
Gene de Paul
Johnny Mercer
Li'l Abner (1956)

WHAT'S HE LIKE?
Jacques Belasco
Kay Twomey
The Girl from Nantucket (1945)

WHAT'S IN A NAME
John Mundy
Edward Eager
The Liar (1950)

WHAT'S IN A NAME?
Darwin Venneri
Darwin's Theories (OB) (1960)

WHAT'S IN IT FOR ME?
Harold Rome
I Can Get It for You Wholesale ((1962)

WHAT'S IN IT FOR YOU?
Jerry Bock
Sheldon Harnick
Tenderloin (1960)

WHAT'S IN STORE FOR YOU
Leon DeCosta
Kosher Kitty Kelly (1925)

WHAT'S IN THE AIR
Nancy Ford
Gretchen Cryer
Now Is the Time for All Good Men
  (OB) (1967)

WHAT'S KEEPING MY PRINCE CHARMING?
Alberta Nichols
Mann Holiner
Rhapsody in Black (1931)

WHAT'S MINE IS THINE
Al Moss
Alfred Hayes
Tis of Thee (1940)

WHAT'S MINE IS YOURS
Vernon Duke
Howard Dietz
Jackpot (1944)

WHAT'S MY MAN GONNA BE LIKE?
Cole Porter
The Vanderbilt Revue (1930)

WHAT'S NEW AT THE ZOO?
Jule Styne
Betty Comden and Adolph Green
Do Re Mi (1960)

WHAT'S NEW IN NEW YORK
Baldwin Bergersen
George Marion, Jr.
Allah Be Praised (1944)

WHAT'S THE BUZZ?
Andrew Lloyd Webber
Tim Rice
Jesus Christ Superstar (1971)

WHAT'S THE DIFFERENCE
John Green
Edward Heyman
Here Goes the Bride (1931)

WHAT'S THE FUN OF BEING KING?
Robert Colby
Robert Colby and Nita Jonas
Half-Past Wednesday (OB) (1962)

WHAT'S THE MATTER WITH BUFFALO?
Albert Hague
Marty Brill
Café Crown (1964)

WHAT'S THE MATTER WITH OUR CITY?
Jay Gorney
Barry Trivers
Heaven on Earth (1948)

WHAT'S THE NAME OF WHAT'S-HIS-NAME?
Robert Colby
Robert Colby and Nita Jonas
Half-Past Wednesday (OB) (1962)

WHAT'S THE REASON?
Maury Rubens
Harold Atteridge
The Greenwich Village Follies (1928)

WHAT'S THE USE?
Leonard Bernstein
Richard Wilbur
Candide (1956)

WHAT'S THE USE OF TALKING?
Richard Rodgers
Lorenz Hart
The Garrick Gaieties (1926)

WHAT'S THE USE OF WOND'RIN'?
Richard Rodgers
Oscar Hammerstein II
Carousel (1945)

WHAT'S THE YOUNGER GENERATION COMING TO?
David Raksin
June Carroll
If the Shoe Fits (1946)

WHAT'S TO LOSE
Tommy Wolf
Fran Landesman
The Nervous Set (1959)

WHAT'S WRONG WITH ME?
Edward Earle
Yvonne Tarr
The Decameron (OB) (1961)

WHAT'S WRONG WITH ME?
Richard Adler
Kwamina (1961)

WHEELS
Morris Hamilton
Grace Henry
Earl Carroll's Vanities (1928)

WHEELS OF STEEL
Kay Swift
Paul James
Fine and Dandy (1930)

WHEN
Manning Sherwin
Arthur Herzog, Jr.
Bad Habits of 1926 (OB) (1926)

WHEN
Cliff Friend
Lew Brown
Piggy (1927)

WHEN
Harold Rome
Bless You All (1950)

WHEN A BLACK MAN'S BLUE
George A. Little, Art Sizemore, and Ed G. Nelson
Brown Buddies (1930)

WHEN A FELLA NEEDS A FRIEND
Sol Berkowitz
James Lipton
Nowhere to Go but Up (1962)

WHEN A FELLOW MEETS A FLAPPER ON BROADWAY
Philip Charig
Irving Caesar
Polly (1929)

WHEN A GIRL FORGETS TO SCREAM
Sigmund Romberg
Otto Harbach
Forbidden Melody (1936)

WHEN A GOOD MAN TAKES TO DRINK
Harry Revel
Arnold B. Horwitt
Are You With It? (1945)

WHEN A HICK CHICK MEETS A CITY SLICKER
Jacques Belasco
Burt Milton
The Girl from Nantucket (1945)

WHEN A MAID WEARS PURPLE
STOCKINGS
Mel Marvin
Ted Berger
Shoemaker's Holiday (OB) (1967)

WHEN A PANSY WAS A FLOWER
Will Irwin
Billy Rose and Malcolm McComb
Sweet and Low (1930)

WHEN A ROBIN LEAVES CHICAGO
Alec Wilder
Arnold Sundgaard
Kittiwake Island (OB) (1960)

WHEN A WOMAN HAS A BABY
Kurt Weill
Langston Hughes
Street Scene (1947)

WHEN AM I GOING TO MEET YOUR
MOTHER?
Richard Adler and Jerry Ross
John Murray Anderson's Almanac
(1953)

WHEN DID I FALL IN LOVE?
Jerry Bock
Sheldon Harnick
Fiorello (1959)

WHEN DO WE DANCE?
George Gershwin
Ira Gershwin
Tip-Toes (1925)

WHEN DOES THIS FEELING GO
AWAY?
Hugh Martin
Make a Wish (1951)

WHEN EVERYTHING IS HUNKY-
DORY
Niclas Kempner
Graham John
The Street Singer (1929)

WHEN FOREIGN PRINCES COME TO
VISIT US
Noël Coward
The Girl Who Came to Supper (1963)

WHEN GEMINI MEETS CAPRICORN
Harold Rome
I Can Get It For You Wholesale (1962)

WHEN GENTLEMEN GREW WHISK-
ERS AND LADIES GREW OLD
Charles Rosoff
Leo Robin
Judy (1927)

WHEN HE LOOKS AT ME
John Morris
Gerald Freedman
A Time for Singing (1966)

WHEN HEARTS ARE YOUNG
Sigmund Romberg and Alfred Good-
man
Cyrus Wood
The Lady in Ermine (1922)

WHEN I AM FREE TO LOVE
Sigmund Romberg (developed by
Don Walker)
Leo Robin
The Girl in Pink Tights (1954)

WHEN I DANCE WITH THE PERSON I
LOVE
Mark Sandrich, Jr.
Sidney Michaels
Ben Franklin in Paris (1964)

WHEN I DRINK WITH MY LOVE
Baldwin Bergersen
William Archibald
The Crystal Heart (OB) (1960)

WHEN I FALL IN LOVE
Albert Selden
Small Wonder (1948)

WHEN I FELL IN LOVE
Jerome Kern
Anne Caldwell
The City Chap (1925)

WHEN I GO ON THE STAGE
Richard Rodgers
Lorenz Hart
She's My Baby (1928)

WHEN I GROW TOO OLD TO DREAM
Sigmund Romberg
Oscar Hammerstein II
The Night Is Young (F) (1935)

WHEN I GROW UP (THE G-MAN SONG)
Harold Rome
Pins and Needles (OB) (1937)

WHEN I LOVE AGAIN
Jerry Herman
I Feel Wonderful (OB) (1954)

WHEN I LOVE, I LOVE
Ray Henderson
B. G. DeSylva and Lew Brown
Hold Everything! (1928)

WHEN I MAKE A MILLION FOR YOU
Lucien Denni
Helena Evans
Happy Go Lucky (1926)

WHEN I MARCH WITH APRIL IN MAY
Clarence Williams
Spencer Williams
Bottomland (1927)

WHEN I MARRY MR. SNOW
Richard Rodgers
Oscar Hammerstein II
Carousel (1945)

WHEN I TAKE YOU ALL TO LONDON
Sigmund Romberg
Harry B. Smith
The Love Call (1927)

WHEN I WALK WITH YOU
Duke Ellington
John Latouche
Beggar's Holiday (1946)

WHEN I WAS A CHILD
Earl Wilson, Jr.
A Day in the Life of Just About Everyone (OB) (1971)

WHEN I WAS A GIRL LIKE YOU
Sigmund Romberg
Dorothy Donnelly
My Princess (1927)

WHEN I WAS A LITTLE CUCKOO
Cole Porter
Seven Lively Arts (1944)

WHEN I WAS YOUNG
Jule Styne
Sammy Cahn
Look to the Lilies (1970)

WHEN I'M ALONE
Don Elliott
James Costigan
The Beast in Me (1963)

WHEN I'M BEING BORN AGAIN
Burton Lane
Alan Jay Lerner
On a Clear Day You Can See Forever (1965)

WHEN I'M IN A QUIET MOOD
David Martin
Langston Hughes
Simply Heavenly (1957)

WHEN I'M IN LOVE
Steve Allen
Sophie (1963)

WHEN I'M IN PAREE
Maurice Yvain
Max and Nathaniel Lief
Luckee Girl (1928)

WHEN I'M LOOKING AT YOU
Herbert Stothart
Clifford Grey
The Rogue Song (F) (1930)

WHEN I'M NOT NEAR THE GIRL I LOVE
Burton Lane
E. Y. Harburg
Finian's Rainbow (1947)

WHEN IT DRIES
Richard Rodgers
Martin Charnin
Two by Two (1970)

WHEN IT GETS DARK
Seymour Furth and Lee Edwards
R. F. Carroll
Bringing Up Father (1925)

WHEN IT'S ALL SAID AND DONE
Cole Porter
Leave It to Me (1938)

WHEN IT'S CACTUS TIME IN ARIZONA
George Gershwin
Ira Gershwin
Girl Crazy (1930)

WHEN LOVE BECKONED (IN FIFTY-SECOND STREET)
Cole Porter
Du Barry Was a Lady (1939)

WHEN LOVE COMES SWINGIN' ALONG
Ray Henderson
Ted Koehler
Say When (1934)

WHEN LOVE COMES YOUR WAY
Cole Porter
Jubilee (1935)

WHEN LOVE IS NEAR
Will Ortman
Gus Kahn and Raymond B. Egan
Holka-Polka (1925)

WHEN LOVERS FALL IN LOVE
Hal Jordan
Jerry Douglas
Rondelay (OB) (1969)

WHEN LOVE'S IN THE AIR
Jean Gilbert
Harry Graham
Katja (1926)

WHEN MCGREGOR SINGS OFF KEY
Sammy Fain
Charles Tobias
Hellzapoppin' (1938)

WHEN ME, MOWGLI, LOVE
Cole Porter
Jubilee (1935)

WHEN MOSES SPAKE TO GOLDSTEIN
Menachem Zur
Herbert Appleman
Unfair to Goliath (OB) (1970)

WHEN MY BABY GOES TO TOWN
Cole Porter
Something for the Boys (1943)

WHEN MY DREAMS COME TRUE*
Irving Berlin
The Cocoanuts (F) (1929)

WHEN MY EYES MEET YOURS
Arthur Brander
The Seventh Heart (1927)

WHEN MY LITTLE SHIP COMES IN
Frank Grey
McElbert Moore and Frank Grey
The Matinee Girl (1926)

WHEN MY MAN RETURNS
George Moustaki
David Paulsen
To Live Another Summer (1971)

WHEN MY VIOLIN IS CALLING
Edward Kunneke (based on Offen-
  bach)
Harry B. Smith
The Love Song (1925)

WHEN ONE DEEMS A LADY SWEET
Alec Wilder
Arnold Sundgaard
Kittiwake Island (OB) (1960)

WHEN OPPORTUNITY KNOCKS
Richard Lewine
Ted Fetter
Entre-Nous (OB) (1935)

---

*Added to the film version

WHEN SHE WALKS IN THE ROOM
Sigmund Romberg
Dorothy Fields
Up in Central Park (1945)

WHEN SOMEONE YOU LOVE LOVES YOU
Charles Gaynor
Lend an Ear (1948)

WHEN THE BABY COMES
John Morris
Gerald Freedman
A Time for Singing (1966)

WHEN THE BLUEBIRDS FLY ALL OVER THE WORLD
Jack Holmes
Bill Conklin and Bob Miller
O Say Can You See! (OB) (1962)

WHEN THE BO-TREE BLOSSOMS AGAIN
Jerome Kern
Bert Kalmar and Harry Ruby
Lucky (1927)

WHEN THE BOYS COME HOME
Harold Arlen
E. Y. Harburg
Bloomer Girl (1944)

WHEN THE CHILDREN ARE ASLEEP
Richard Rodgers
Oscar Hammerstein II
Carousel (1945)

WHEN THE DEBBIES GO BY
George Gershwin
B. G. DeSylva and Ira Gershwin
Tell Me More (1925)

WHEN THE DUCHESS IS AWAY
Kurt Weill
Ira Gershwin
The Firebrand of Florence (1945)

WHEN THE HURDY GURDY PLAYS
Harold Levey
Owen Murphy
Rainbow Rose (1926)

WHEN THE IDLE POOR BECOME THE IDLE RICH
Burton Lane
E. Y. Harburg
Finian's Rainbow (1947)

WHEN THE KIDS GET MARRIED
Harvey Schmidt
Tom Jones
I Do! I Do! (1966)

WHEN THE NYLONS BLOOM AGAIN
Thomas (Fats) Waller
George Marion, Jr.
Early to Bed (1934)

WHEN THE PARTY GIVES A PARTY
Sigmund Romberg
Dorothy Fields
Up in Central Park (1945)

WHEN THE SHAKER PLAYS A COCK-TAIL TUNE
James F. Hanley
Gene Buck
No Foolin' (1926)

WHEN THE SHEETS COME BACK FROM THE LAUNDRY
Abraham Ellstein
Walter Bullock
Great to Be Alive (1950)

WHEN THE SPRING IS IN THE AIR
Jerome Kern
Oscar Hammerstein II
Music in the Air (1932)

WHEN THE SUN KISSED THE ROSE GOODBYE
Gitz Rice
Paul Porter
Nic-Nax (1926)

WHEN THE SUN MEETS THE MOON IN FINALE-LAND
Charles M. Schwab
Henry Myers
The Garrick Gaieties (1930)

WHEN THE TALL MAN TALKS
Moose Charlap
Norman Gimbel
Whoop-Up (1958)

WHEN THE TIME IS RIGHT
Gordon Duffy
Harry M. Haldane
Happy Town (1959)

WHEN THE WINGS OF THE WIND
TAKE ME HOME
Ruth Cleary Patterson
Les Kramer
Russell Patterson's Sketch Book (OB)
(1960)

WHEN THINGS ARE BRIGHT AND
ROSY
Harry Ruby
Bert Kalmar
Animal Crackers (1928)

WHEN TIME TAKES YOUR HAND
Bruce Montgomery
The Amorous Flea (OB) (1964)

WHEN TOMORROW COMES
Kenneth Jacobson
Rhoda Roberts
Show Me Where the Good Times Are
(OB) (1970)

WHEN WE GET OUR DIVORCE
Jerome Kern
Oscar Hammerstein II
Sunny (1925)

WHEN WE MEET AGAIN
Harold Rome
Call Me Mister (1946)

WHEN WE'RE BRIDE AND GROOM
Harry Archer
Harlan Thompson
Twinkle Twinkle (1926)

WHEN WE'RE IN LOVE*
Richard Lewine
Ted Fetter
Naughty-Naught (OB) (1946)

WHEN WILL I LEARN
Paul Nassau and Oscar Brand
The Education of Hyman Kaplan
(1968)

WHEN YOU ARE CLOSE TO ME
Alma Sanders
Monte Carlo
Louisiana Lady (1947)

WHEN YOU ARE YOUNG
Sigmund Romberg
Oscar Hammerstein II
East Wind (1931)

WHEN YOU CARRY YOUR OWN SUIT-
CASE
Steve Allen
Sophie (1963)

WHEN YOU GET TO CONGRESS
Albert Von Tilzer
Neville Fleeson
Bye Bye, Bonnie (1927)

WHEN YOU GO DOWN BY MISS JEN-
NY'S
Duke Ellington
John Latouche
Beggar's Holiday (1946)

WHEN YOU GROW UP
Giuseppe Verdi
Charles Friedman
My Darlin' Aïda (1952)

WHEN YOU HEAR THE WIND
Eaton Magoon, Jr.
13 Daughters (1961)

WHEN YOU LIVE ON AN ISLAND
Vernon Duke
Howard Dietz
Sadie Thompson (1944)

WHEN YOU LOOK IN YOUR LOOKING
GLASS
Paul Mann and Stephen Weiss
Sam Lewis
Hellzapoppin' (1938)

---

*Added to 1946 revival

WHEN YOU LOVE ONLY ONE
Arthur Schwartz
Howard Dietz
Revenge with Music (1934)

WHEN YOU SAY NO TO LOVE
Vincent Valentini
Parisiana (1928)

WHEN YOU SMILE
Tom Johnstone
Phil Cook
When You Smile (1925)

WHEN YOU WANT ME
Noël Coward
Sail Away (1961)

WHEN YOU WRITE A GREEK
COMEDY
Willard Straight
David Eddy
The Athenian Touch (OB) (1966)

WHEN YOUR BOY BECOMES A MAN
Richard A. Whiting
Oscar Hammerstein II
Free for All (1931)

WHEN YOUR LOVER SAYS GOODBYE
André Previn
Alan Jay Lerner
Coco (1969)

WHEN YOU'RE AWAY
Victor Herbert
Henry Blossom
The Only Girl (1914)

WHEN YOU'RE DANCING THE
WALTZ
Richard Rodgers
Lorenz Hart
Dancing Pirate (F) (1936)

WHEN YOU'RE FAR AWAY FROM
NEW YORK TOWN
Arthur Schwartz
Howard Dietz
Jennie (1963)

WHEN YOU'RE IN THE ROOM
Ben Oakland
Oscar Hammerstein II
The Lady Objects (F) (1938)

WHEN YOU'RE YOUNG AND IN LOVE
Hal Hester and Danny Apolinar
Your Own Thing (1968)

WHEN YUBA PLAYS THE RUMBA ON
HIS TUBA
Herman Hupfeld
The Third Little Show (1931)

WHENEVER I DREAM
Con Conrad
Gus Kahn
Kitty's Kisses (1926)

WHERE?
Marc Blitzstein
Juno (1959)

WHERE AM I GOING?
Cy Coleman
Dorothy Fields
Sweet Charity (1966)

WHERE ARE THE BLOSSOMS
Paul Hoffert
David Secter
Get Thee to Canterbury (OB) (1969)

WHERE ARE THE GIRLS OF YESTER-
DAY
Richard Hill and John Hawkins
Nevill Coghill
Canterbury Tales (1969)

WHERE ARE THE MEN?
Cole Porter
Anything Goes (1934)

WHERE ARE THE SNOWS
Harvey Schmidt
Tom Jones
I Do! I Do! (1966)

WHERE ARE THEY?
Jerry Bock
Sheldon Harnick
The Body Beautiful (1958)

WHERE ARE YOUR CHILDREN?
Billy Barnes
The Billy Barnes Revue (1959)

WHERE CAN HE BE?
Arthur Schwartz
Howard Dietz
The Band Wagon (1931)

WHERE CAN I GO FROM YOU?
Baldwin Bergersen
Virginia Faulkner
All in Fun (1940)

WHERE CAN THE BABY BE?
Richard Rodgers
Lorenz Hart
She's My Baby (1928)

WHERE CAN THE RICH AND POOR
BE FRIENDS?
Richard B. Chodosh
Barry Alan Grael
The Streets of New York (OB) (1963)

WHERE CAN YOU TAKE A GIRL?
Burt Bacharach
Hal David
Promises, Promises (1968)

WHERE DID IT GO?
Harvey Schmidt
Tom Jones
Celebration (1969)

WHERE DID THE NIGHT GO?
Harold Rome
Wish You Were Here (1952)

WHERE DID THE SUMMER GO TO?
Norman Campbell
Donald Campbell and Norman Campbell
Anne of Green Gables (OB) (1971)

WHERE DID WE GO? OUT
Richard Lewine
Arnold B. Horwitt
The Girls Against the Boys (1959)

WHERE DO I GO?
Galt MacDermot
Gerome Ragni and James Rado
Hair (1968)

WHERE DO I GO FROM HERE?*
Jerry Bock
Sheldon Harnick
Fiorello (1959)

WHERE DO I GO FROM HERE?
Voices, Inc.
The Believers (OB) (1968)

WHERE DO YOU GET YOUR GREENS?
Morgan Lewis
Nancy Hamilton
Two for the Show (1940)

WHERE DO YOU TRAVEL?
Hugh Martin and Ralph Blane
Best Foot Forward (1941)

WHERE DOES A MAN BEGIN?
Don McAfee
Nancy Leeds
Great Scot! (OB) (1965)

"WHERE HAS MY HUBBY GONE"
BLUES
Vincent Youmans
Irving Caesar
No, No, Nanette (1925)

WHERE HAS TOM GONE
John Addison
John Cranko
Cranks (1956)

WHERE HAVE I BEEN?
Robert Waldman
Alfred Uhry
Here's Where I Belong (1968)

WHERE HAVE WE MET BEFORE?
Vernon Duke
E. Y. Harburg
Walk a Little Faster (1932)

—————
*Dropped from New York production

WHERE HAVE YOU BEEN?
Cole Porter
The New Yorkers (1930)

WHERE HAVE YOU BEEN ALL MY LIFE?
Philip Charig and Richard Myers
Leo Robin
Allez-Oop (1927)

WHERE IS HE?
Arthur Siegel
June Carroll
New Faces (1968)

WHERE IS LOVE?
Erich Wolfgang Korngold (based on Offenbach)
Herbert Baker
Helen Goes to Troy (1944)

WHERE IS LOVE?
Lionel Bart
Oliver! (1963)

WHERE IS MATTHEW GOING?
Norman Campbell
Donald Campbell and Norman Campbell
Anne of Green Gables (OB) (1971)

WHERE IS THAT RAINBOW?
Don McAfee
Nancy Leeds
Great Scot! (OB) (1965)

WHERE IS THAT SOMEONE FOR ME?
Victor Young
Stella Unger
Seventh Heaven (1955)

WHERE IS THE CLOWN?
Billy Barnes
The Billy Barnes People (1961)

WHERE IS THE KNIGHT FOR ME?
Mel Marvin
Ted Berger
Shoemaker's Holiday (OB) (1967)

WHERE IS THE LIFE THAT LATE I LED?
Cole Porter
Kiss Me, Kate (1948)

WHERE IS THE MAN FOR ME?
Steven Metcalf
Fred Bluth
Drat! (OB) (1971)

WHERE IS THE MAN I MARRIED?
Hugh Martin and Timothy Gray
High Spirits (1964)

WHERE IS THE TRIBE FOR ME?
Walter Marks
Bajour (1964)

WHERE IS THE WALTZ
Alonzo Levister
Paul Nassau
New Faces (1968)

WHERE LOVE GROWS
Jean Gilbert
Harry B. Smith
The Red Rose (1928)

WHERE, OH WHERE
Cole Porter
Out of This World (1950)

WHERE, OH WHERE CAN I FIND LOVE?
Jesse Greer
Stanley Adams
Shady Lady (1933)

WHERE OR WHEN
Richard Rodgers
Lorenz Hart
Babes in Arms (1937)

WHERE SHALL I FIND HIM?
Noël Coward
Sail Away (1961)

WHERE SHALL I GO?
Voices, Inc.
The Believers (OB) (1968)

WHERE THE HUDSON RIVER FLOWS
Richard Rodgers
Lorenz Hart
Dearest Enemy (1925)

WHERE THE MORNING GLORIES TWINE
Martin Broones
Ballard MacDonald
Rufus Lemaire's Affairs (1927)

WHERE THE TREES ARE GREEN WITH PARROTS
Sandy Wilson
Valmouth (OB) (1960)

WHERE WAS I
Jimmy Van Heusen
Sammy Cahn
Walking Happy (1966)

WHERE WAS I WHEN THEY PASSED OUT LUCK?
Larry Grossman
Hal Hackady
Minnie's Boys (1970)

WHERE WE CAN BE IN LOVE
Leon DeCosta
Kosher Kitty Kelly (1925)

WHERE WERE YOU—WHERE WAS I?
George M. Cohan
Billie (1928)

WHERE WOULD YOU BE WITHOUT ME?
Leslie Bricusse and Anthony Newley
The Roar of the Greasepaint - The Smell of the Crowd (1965)

WHERE WOULD YOU GET YOUR COAT?
Cole Porter
Fifty Million Frenchmen (1929)

WHERE YOU ARE
Philip Charig
Dan Shapiro and Milton Pascal
Follow the Girls (1944)

WHERE YOU ARE
Raymond Scott
Bernard Hanighen
Lute Song (1946)

WHERE YOU ARE
Arthur Schwartz
Howard Dietz
Jennie (1963)

WHERE YOU GO I GO
George Gershwin
Ira Gershwin
Pardon My English (1933)

WHERE YOU LEAD
Rudolf Friml
J. Keirn Brennan
Luana (1930)

WHERE YOUR NAME IS CARVED WITH MINE
Ray Henderson
B. G. DeSylva and Lew Brown
George White's Scandals (1928)

WHEREAS
Bob Merrill
Henry, Sweet Henry (1967)

WHERE'D MARILLA COME FROM?
Norman Campbell
Donald Campbell and Norman Campbell
Anne of Green Gables (OB) (1971)

WHEREFORE ART THOU, JULIET
Charlotte Kent
The Illustrators' Show (1936)

WHERE'S CHARLEY?
Frank Loesser
Where's Charley? (1948)

WHERE'S MY HAPPY ENDING?
Harry Revel
Mack Gordon and Harold Adamson
Fast and Furious (1931)

WHERE'S MY SHOE?
Jerry Bock
Sheldon Harnick
She Loves Me (1963)

WHERE'S MY WIFE?
Frederick Loewe
Alan Jay Lerner
The Day Before Spring (1945)

WHERE'S NORTH?
Galt MacDermot
John Guare
Two Gentlemen of Verona (1971)

WHERE'S THAT RAINBOW?
Richard Rodgers
Lorenz Hart
Peggy-Ann (1926)

WHERE'S THE BOY? HERE'S THE GIRL!
George Gershwin
Ira Gershwin
Treasure Girl (1928)

WHERE'S THE BOY I SAVED FOR A RAINY DAY?
Baldwin Bergersen
John Rox
All in Fun (1940)

WHEREVER I MAY GO
Frederico Valerio
Elizabeth Miele
Hit the Trail (1954)

WHEREVER THEY FLY THE FLAG OF OLD ENGLAND
Cole Porter
Around the World (1946)

WHEREVER YOU ARE
James F. Hanley
Eddie Dowling
Sidewalks of New York (1927)

WHICH?*
Cole Porter
Paris (1928)

WHICH DOOR
Jerry Bock
Sheldon Harnick
The Apple Tree (1966)

WHICH SHALL IT BE?
Frank Grey
Ethelberta Hasbrook
Happy (1927)

WHICH WAY?
Charles Strouse
Lee Adams
All American (1962)

WHICH WITCH?
Charles Zwar
Allan Melville
John Murray Anderson's Almanac (1953)

WHICHAWAY'D THEY GO
Robert Emmett Dolan
Johnny Mercer
Texas, Li'l Darlin' (1949)

WHILE THE CITY SLEEPS
Charles Strouse
Lee Adams
Golden Boy (1964)

WHILE THERE'S A SONG TO SING
Franz Steininger (adapted from Tchaikovsky)
Forman Brown
Music in My Heart (1947)

WHILE YOU ARE YOUNG
Harold Arlen
Jack Yellen
You Said It (1931)

WHILE YOU LOVE ME
Johann Strauss
Desmond Carter
The Great Waltz (1934)

WHILING MY TIME AWAY
Henry Sullivan
Edward Eliscu
A Little Racketeer (1932)

WHIP, THE
Emmerich Kalman and Herbert Stothart

---

*Dropped from New York production

Otto Harbach and Oscar Hammerstein II
Golden Dawn (1927)

WHIP-POOR-WILL
Jerome Kern
B. G. DeSylva
Sally (1920)

WHIRLED INTO HAPPINESS
Carlton Kelsey and Maury Rubens
Clifford Grey
Sky High (1925)

WHISKEY BUG
Jack Urbont
Bruce Geller
Livin' the Life (OB) (1957)

WHISPERING SONG, THE
Leon DeCosta
The Blonde Sinner (1926)

WHISPERING TREES
Maury Rubens and J. Fred Coots
Herbert Reynolds
The Merry World (1926)

WHISPERS ON THE WIND
Lor Crane
John B. Kuntz
Whispers on the Wind (OB) (1970)

WHISTLE
Harry Ruby
Bert Kalmar
Twinkle Twinkle (1926)

WHISTLE AWAY YOUR BLUES
Richard Myers
Leo Robin
The Greenwich Village Follies (1925)

WHISTLE WHILE YOU WORK, BOYS
Walter Kollo
Harry B. Smith
Three Little Girls (1930)

WHISTLE WORKS, A
Rick Besoyan
The Student Gypsy (OB) (1963)

WHISTLES
Joyce Stanton
Patrick Fox
Blood (OB) (1971)

WHISTLING BOY, THE
Jerome Kern
Dorothy Fields
When You're in Love (F) (1937)

WHISTLING FOR A KISS
Richard Myers
E. Y. Harburg and Johnny Mercer
Americana (1932)

WHITE BOYS
Galt MacDermot
Gerome Ragni and James Rado
Hair (1968)

WHITE CHRISTMAS*
Irving Berlin
Holiday Inn (F) (1942)

WHITE HEAT
Arthur Schwartz
Howard Dietz
The Band Wagon (1931)

WHITE HORSE INN
Ralph Benatzky
Irving Caesar
White Horse Inn (1936)

WHITE IS THE DOVE
Buster Davis
Steven Vinaver
Diversions (OB) (1958)

WHITE LIGHTS
J. Fred Coots
Al Dubin
White Lights (1927)

WHITE LIGHTS WERE COMING
Maury Rubens and Sam Timberg
Moe Jaffe
Broadway Nights (1929)

___
*Academy Award Winner

WHITE LILACS
Karl Hajos (based on Chopin)
Harry B. Smith
White Lilacs (1928)

WHITE SLAVERY FANDANGO, THE
Jay Thompson
Double Entry (OB) (1961)

WHITE WITCH OF JAMAICA, THE
Arthur Siegel
June Carroll
New Faces (1956)

WHITHER THOU GOEST
Oscar Brand and Paul Nassau
A Joyful Noise (1966)

WHIZZIN' AWAY ALONG DE TRACK
Georges Bizet
Oscar Hammerstein II
Carmen Jones (1943)

WHO?
Jerome Kern
Oscar Hammerstein II
Sunny (1925)

WHO AM I?
Emmerich Kalman
Harry B. Smith
Countess Maritza (1926)

WHO AM I?
Leonard Bernstein
Peter Pan (1950)

WHO AM I?
Johnny Brandon
Cindy (OB) (1964)

WHO AM I THAT YOU SHOULD CARE FOR ME?*
Vincent Youmans
Gus Kahn
Rainbow (1928)

WHO AM I THINKING OF?
A. Baldwin Sloane
Harry Cort and George E. Stoddard
China Rose (1925)

WHO AM I, WHO ARE YOU, WHO ARE WE?
William Roy
The Penny Friend (OB) (1966)

WHO ARE WE KIDDING?
Steve Allen
Sophie (1963)

WHO ARE YOU?†
Richard Rodgers
Lorenz Hart
The Boys from Syracuse (F) (1940)

WHO ARE YOU?
Deed Meyer
She Shall Have Music (OB) (1959)

WHO ARE YOU NOW?
Jule Styne
Bob Merrill
Funny Girl (1964)

WHO BITES THE HOLE IN SCHWEITZER CHEESE?
Alma Sanders
Monte Carlo
Oh! Oh! Nurse (1925)

WHO CAN? YOU CAN!
Arthur Schwartz
Howard Dietz
The Gay Life (1961)

WHO CAN I TURN TO (WHEN NOBODY NEEDS ME)
Leslie Bricusse and Anthony Newley
The Roar of the Greasepaint - The Smell of the Crowd (1965)

WHO CAN TELL**
Fritz Kreisler
William LeBaron
Apple Blossoms (1919)

---

*Dropped from New York production
†Added to film version
**Same melody as "Stars in My Eyes" from film *The King Steps Out* (1936) (lyrics by Dorothy Fields)

WHO CARES?
Haydn Wood, Joseph Tunbridge, and
 Jack Waller
Dion Titheradge
Artists and Models (1930)

WHO CARES?
Percy Wenrich
Harry Clarke
Who Cares? (1930)

WHO CARES?
George Gershwin
Ira Gershwin
Of Thee I Sing (1931)

WHO COMMITTED THE MURDER?
Richard Myers
Edward Heyman
Murder at the Vanities (1933)

WHO DID? YOU DID
Harry Ruby
Bert Kalmar
The Five O'Clock Girl (1927)

WHO DO YOU LOVE, I HOPE
Irving Berlin
Annie Get Your Gun (1964)

WHO DO YOU THINK YOU ARE?
Sidney Lippman
Sylvia Dee
Barefoot Boy with Cheek (1947)

WHO DOES SHE THINK SHE IS?
Jordan Ramin
Frank H. Stanton and Murray Semos
Look Where I'm At! (OB) (1971)

WHO DONE IT?
Abraham Ellstein
Walter Bullock
Great to Be Alive (1950)

WHO FILLS THE BILL
Sammy Fain
Marilyn and Alan Bergman
Something More! (1964)

WHO GIVES A HEY?
Mel Marvin
Ted Berger
Shoemaker's Holiday (OB) (1967)

WHO GIVES A SOU?
Hugh Martin
Make a Wish (1951)

WHO HIT ME?
Charles Gaynor
Lend an Ear (1948)

WHO IS IT ALWAYS THERE?
John Addison
John Cranko
Cranks (1956)

WHO IS GENERAL STAFF?
Ann Ronell
Count Me In (1942)

WHO IS SAMUEL COOPER?
Kurt Weill
Alan Jay Lerner
Love Life (1948)

WHO IS SYLVIA?
Galt MacDermot
John Guare
Two Gentlemen of Verona (1971)

WHO IS THE BRAVEST?
Jule Styne
Bob Hillard
Hazel Flagg (1953)

WHO IS THE LUCKY GIRL TO BE?
George Gershwin
Ira Gershwin
Of Thee I Sing (1931)

WHO KILLED NOBODY
Helen Miller
Eve Merriam
Inner City (1971)

WHO KNOWS?
Robert Stolz
Robert Sour
Mr. Strauss Goes to Boston (1945)

WHO KNOWS?
Harold Rome
I Can Get It for You Wholesale (1962)

WHO KNOWS BETTER THAN I
Maury Laws
Jules Bass
Month of Sundays (OB) (1968)

WHO KNOWS WHAT MIGHT HAVE BEEN?
Jule Styne
Betty Comden and Adolph Green
Subways Are for Sleeping (1961)

WHO MAKES SUCH A MIRACLE
Stan Harte, Jr.
Walt Whitman
Leaves of Grass (OB) (1971)

WHO NEEDS IT?
Deed Meyer
She Shall Have Music (OB) (1959)

WHO PUT OUT THE LIGHT THAT LIT THE CANDLE . . .
John Dooley
Hobo (OB) (1961)

WHO SAID THERE IS NO SANTA CLAUS?
Sammy Fain
E. Y. Harburg
Flahooley (1951)

WHO STARTED THE RHUMBA?
Vernon Duke
John Latouche
Banjo Eyes (1941)

WHO TAUGHT HER EVERYTHING?
Jule Styne
Bob Merrill
Funny Girl (1964)

WHO TO LOVE IF NOT A STRANGER
Mitch Leigh
William Alfred and Phyllis Robinson
Cry for Us All (1970)

WHO WALKS LIKE A SCARECROW
Norman Dean
Autumn's Here (OB) (1966)

WHO WANTS TO BE A MILLIONAIRE?
Cole Porter
High Society (F) (1956)

WHO WANTS TO LOVE SPANISH LADIES?
Vincent Youmans
Oscar Hammerstein II
Rainbow (1928)

WHO WAS CHASING PAUL REVERE?
Joseph Meyer and James F. Hanley
B. G. DeSylva
Big Boy (1925)

WHO? WHERE? WHAT?
Robert Colby
Robert Colby and Nita Jonas
Half-Past Wednesday (OB) (1962)

(WHO, WHO, WHO, WHO) WHO IS SHE?
Jerry Bock
Sheldon Harnick
The Apple Tree (1966)

WHO WILL BUY?
Lionel Bart
Oliver! (1963)

WHO WILL I BE?
Ernest McCarty
Jack Ramer and Ernest McCarty
I Dreamt I Dwelt in Bloomingdale's (OB) (1970)

WHO WOULD HAVE DREAMED?
Cole Porter
Panama Hattie (1940)

WHO WOULDN'T?
Vincent Valentini
Parisiana (1928)

WHO? YOU?
Lewis E. Gensler
B. G. DeSylva
Queen High (1926)

WHOA, EMMA!
Edward Kunneke
Clifford Grey
Mayflowers (1925)

WHOA, GAL
Ida Hoyt Chamberlain
Enchanted Isle (1927)

WHO'D BELIEVE
Kenneth Jacobson
Rhoda Roberts
Show Me Where the Good Times Are
(OB) (1970)

WHOEVER YOU ARE
Burt Bacharach
Hal David
Promises, Promises (1968)

WHOLE WORLD LOVES, THE
Sigmund Romberg
Irving Caesar
Melody (1933)

WHO'LL BUY?
Kurt Weill
Maxwell Anderson
Lost in the Stars (1949)

WHO'LL MEND A BROKEN HEART?
Lewis E. Gensler
B. G. DeSylva
Queen High (1926)

WHOOP-TI-AY
Frederick Loewe
Alan Jay Lerner
Paint Your Wagon (1951)

WHOOPIN' AND A-HOLLERIN'
Robert Emmett Dolan
Johnny Mercer
Texas, Li'l Darlin' (1949)

WHOOPSIE*
Richard Rodgers
Lorenz Hart
She's My Baby (1928)

WHOOSHIN' THROUGH MY FLESH
Claibe Richardson
Kenward Elmslie
The Grass Harp (1971)

**WHO'S BEEN LISTENING TO MY
HEART?**
Harry Ruby
Bert Kalmar
Animal Crackers (1928)

WHO'S BEEN SITTING IN MY CHAIR?
Leroy Anderson
Joan Ford, Walter and Jean Kerr
Goldilocks (1958)

WHO'S DOING WHAT TO ERWIN?
Jay Livingston and Ray Evans
Let It Ride (1961)

WHO'S GOIN' TO GET YOU?
Milton Ager
Jack Yellen
Rain or Shine (1928)

WHO'S GONNA BE the WINNER?
Morton Gould
Betty Comden and Adolph Green
Billion Dollar Baby (1945)

WHO'S GOT THE PAIN?
Richard Adler and Jerry Ross
Damn Yankees (1955)

WHO'S PERFECT?
Robert Larimer
King of the Whole Damn World! (OB)
(1962)

WHO'S PERFECT FOR YOU?
Robert Larimer
King of the Whole Damn World! (OB)
(1962)

WHO'S THAT GIRL?
Charles Strouse
Lee Adams
Applause (1970)

---

*Dropped from New York production

WHO'S THAT WOMAN?
Stephen Sondheim
Follies (1971)

WHO'S THE BOY?
Ray Perkins
Max and Nathaniel Lief
The Greenwich Village Follies (1928)

WHO'S THE FOOL?
C. Jackson and James Hatch
Fly Blackbird (OB) (1962)

WHO'S THE GREATEST——?
George Gershwin
Ira Gershwin
Let 'Em Eat Cake (1933)

WHO'S WHO?
Walter Donaldson
Ballard MacDonald
Sweetheart Time (1926)

WHO'S WHO
Baldwin Bergersen
June Sillman
Who's Who (1938)

WHO'S WHO
John Addison
John Cranko
Cranks (1956)

WHOSE BABY ARE YOU?
Jerome Kern
Anne Caldwell
The Night Boat (1920)

WHOSIS-WHATSIS, THE
Ray Henderson
B. G. DeSylva and Lew Brown
George White's Scandals (1925)

WHY?
J. Fred Coots
Arthur Swanstrom and Benny Davis
Sons o' Guns (1929)

WHY?
Don Elliott
James Costigan
The Beast in Me (1963)

WHY?
Paul Klein
Fred Ebb
Morning Sun (OB) (1963)

WHY AIN'T I HOME?
Vincent Youmans
Ring Lardner
Smiles (1930)

WHY AIN'T WE FREE?
Giuseppe Verdi
Charles Friedman
My Darlin' Aïda (1952)

WHY AM I A HIT WITH THE LADIES?
Irving Berlin
The Cocoanuts (1925)

WHY AND BECAUSE
Lor Crane
John B. Kuntz
Whispers on the Wind (OB) (1970)

WHY ARE THEY FOLLOWING ME?
Carlton Kelsey and Maury Rubens
Clifford Grey
Sky High (1925)

WHY ARE WE HERE?
William Klenosky
Utopia! (OB) (1963)

WHY BE AFRAID TO DANCE?
Harold Rome
Fanny (1954)

WHY CAN'T HE SEE?
Jule Styne
Sammy Cahn
Look to the Lilies (1970)

WHY CAN'T I?
Richard Rodgers
Lorenz Hart
Spring Is Here (1929)

WHY CAN'T I SPEAK?
John Kander
Fred Ebb
Zorbá (1968)

WHY CAN'T I WALK AWAY?
Hugo Peretti, Luigi Creatore, and
  George David Weiss
Maggie Flynn (1968)

WHY CAN'T IT HAPPEN AGAIN?
Michel Emer
Sammy Gallup
All For Love (1949)

WHY CAN'T IT HAPPEN TO ME?
Maury Rubens
Clifford Grey
The Madcap (1928)

WHY CAN'T THE ENGLISH?
Frederick Loewe
Alan Jay Lerner
My Fair Lady (1956)

**WHY CAN'T THIS NIGHT LAST
FOREVER?**
Frederick Loewe
Earle Crooker
Great Lady (1938)

WHY CAN'T YOU BEHAVE?
Cole Porter
Kiss Me, Kate (1948)

WHY CAN'T WE BE UNHAPPY?
Jeanne Bargy
Jeanne Bargy, Frank Gehrecke, and
  Herb Corey
Greenwich Village U.S.A. (OB) (1960)

WHY COULDN'T WE INCORPORATE?
Alma Sanders
Monte Carlo
Mystery Moon (1930)

WHY DID I CHOOSE YOU?
Michael Leonard
Herbert Martin
The Yearling (1965)

WHY DID WE MARRY SOLDIERS?
Sigmund Romberg
Otto Harbach and Oscar Hammer-
  stein II
The Desert Song (1926)

WHY DID YOU DO IT?
Arthur Schwartz
Howard Dietz
Between the Devil (1937)

**WHY DID YOU KISS MY HEART
AWAKE?**
Franz Lehár
Edward Eliscu
Frederika (1937)

WHY DIDN'T YOU TELL ME
Edward Pola
Eddie Brandt
Woof, Woof (1929)

WHY DO I?
Richard Rodgers
Lorenz Hart
The Girl Friend (1926)

WHY DO I LOVE YOU?
George Gershwin
B. G. DeSylva and Ira Gershwin
Tell Me More (1925)

WHY DO I LOVE YOU?
Jerome Kern
Oscar Hammerstein II
Show Boat (1927)

**WHY DO THE WRONG PEOPLE
TRAVEL?**
Noël Coward
Sail Away (1961)

**WHY DO THEY MAKE 'EM SO
BEAUTIFUL?**
A. Baldwin Sloane
Harry Cort and George E. Stoddard
China Rose (1925)

**WHY DO THEY SAY THEY'RE THE
FAIR SEX?**
Ann Ronell
Count Me In (1942)

WHY DO YA ROLL THOSE EYES?
Philip Charig
Morrie Ryskind
Americana (1926)

WHY DO YOU SUPPOSE?*
Richard Rodgers
Lorenz Hart
Heads Up! (1929)

WHY DO YOU TEASE ME?
Muriel Pollock
Max and Nathaniel Lief and Harold
  Atteridge
Pleasure Bound (1929)

WHY DOES IT HAVE TO BE YOU?
James Mundy
John Latouche
The Vamp (1955)

**WHY DOES THE WHOLE DAMN
WORLD ADORE ME?**
Laurence Rosenthal
James Lipton
Sherry! (1967)

WHY DON'T WE?
Maury Rubens and Sam Timberg
Moe Jaffe
Broadway Nights (1929)

WHY DON'T WE SWITCH?
George Fischoff
Verna Tomasson
The Prince and the Pauper (OB)
  (1963)

WHY DON'T YOU BELIEVE ME?
Mike Brandt, Michael Knight, and
  Robert J. Lowery
Exchange (OB) (1970)

WHY FIGHT THIS?
Johnny Mercer
Saratoga (1959)

WHY GO ANYWHERE AT ALL?
Arthur Schwartz
Howard Dietz
The Gay Life (1961)

WHY GROW OLD?
Bill Mahoney
My Wife and I (OB) (1966)

WHY HER?
David Baker
David Craig
Copper and Brass (1957)

WHY IS LOVE?
J. Fred Coots
Clifford Grey
June Days (1925)

**WHY IS THE WORLD SO CHANGED
TODAY?**
Emmerich Kalman
Harry B. Smith
Countess Maritza (1926)

WHY MARRY THEM?
Cole Porter
Gay Divorce (1932)

WHY ME?
Richard Rodgers
Martin Charnin
Two by Two (1970)

**WHY MUST WE ALWAYS BE DREAM-
ING?**
Sigmund Romberg
P. G. Wodehouse
Rosalie (1928)

WHY NOT?
Al Carmines
Maria Irene Fornes
Promenade (OB) (1969)

WHY NOT FOR MARRIAGE
Louis Bellson and Will Irwin
Richard Ney
Portofino (1958)

WHY NOT KATIE?
Albert Hague
Arnold B. Horwitt
Plain and Fancy (1955)

WHY SHOULD I WAKE UP?
John Kander

———
*Originally written as "How Was I to
Know" for *She's My Baby* (1928)

Fred Ebb
Cabaret (1966)

WHY SHOULDN'T I?
Cole Porter
Jubilee (1935)

WHY SHOULDN'T I?
Deed Meyer
'Toinette (OB) (1961)

WHY SHOULDN'T I HAVE YOU?
Cole Porter
Fifty Million Frenchmen (1929)

WHY SPEAK OF MONEY?
George Gershwin
Ira Gershwin
Let 'Em Eat Cake (1933)

WHY TRY HARD TO BE GOOD?
Alfred Brooks
Ira J. Billowit
Of Mice and Men (OB) (1958)

WHY WAS I BORN?
Jerome Kern
Oscar Hammerstein II
Sweet Adeline (1929)

WHY WAS I BORN ON A FARM?
George Lessner
Miriam Battista and Russell Maloney
Sleepy Hollow (1948)

WHY WIVES
Jacques Urbont
Bruce Geller
All in Love (OB) (1961)

WHY WOULD ANYONE WANT TO GET MARRIED?
John Morris
Gerald Freedman
A Time for Singing (1966)

WHY WOULDN'T I DO?
Ivor Novello
Ivor Novello, Desmond Carter
Wake Up and Dream (1929)

WICKED MAN, A
Lee Pockriss
Anne Croswell
Ernest in Love (OB) (1960)

WICKED, UNWHOLESOME, EXPENSIVE
John Rox
Fools Rush In (1934)

WIDE-AWAKE MORNING
Frank Fields
Armand Aulicino
The Shoemaker and the Peddler (OB) (1960)

WIDE OPEN SPACES, THE
Frederico Valerio
Elizabeth Miele
Hit the Trail (1954)

WIDE PANTS WILLIE
James F. Hanley
Harold Atteridge and Henry Creamer
Gay Paree (1925)

WILD ABOUT MUSIC
Maurice Yvain
Max and Nathaniel Lief
Luckee Girl (1928)

WILD AND RECKLESS
Milton Schafer
Ira Levin
Drat! The Cat! (1965)

WILD AND WONDERFUL
Bob Goodman
Wild and Wonderful (1971)

WILD AND WOOLY WEST, THE
Dave Stamper
Gene Buck
Take the Air (1927)

WILD BIRDS CALLING
David Baker
Will Holt
Come Summer (1969)

WILD JUSTICE, THE
Kurt Weill
Maxwell Anderson
Lost in the Stars (1949)

WILD ROSE
Jerome Kern
Clifford Grey
Sally (1920)

WILD ROSE, THE
Rudolf Friml
Otto Harbach and Oscar Hammerstein II
The Wild Rose (1926)

WILDCAT
Cy Coleman
Carolyn Leigh
Wildcat (1960)

WILDCATS
Richard Rodgers
Oscar Hammerstein II
Allegro (1947)

WILDFLOWER
Vincent Youmans and Herbert Stothart
Otto Harbach and Oscar Hammerstein II
Wildflower (1923)

WILDFLOWERS
Ann Sternberg
Gertrude Stein
Gertrude Stein's First Reader (OB) (1969)

WILKES-BARRE, PA.
Lee Pockriss
Anne Croswell
Tovarich (1963)

WILL HE EVER KNOW?
Stanley Jay Gelber
John Lollos and Don Christopher
Love and Let Love (OB) (1968)

WILL HE LIKE ME?
Jerry Bock
Sheldon Harnick
She Loves Me (1963)

WILL I EVER TELL YOU
Meredith Willson
The Music Man (1957)

WILL YOU MARRY ME?
Richard Rodgers
Oscar Hammerstein II
Pipe Dream (1955)

WILL YOU MARRY ME TOMORROW, MARIA?
Jerome Kern
Oscar Hammerstein II
High, Wide and Handsome (F) (1937)

WILL YOU REMEMBER?
Sigmund Romberg
Rida Johnson Young
Maytime (1917)

WILL YOU REMEMBER? WILL YOU FORGET?
Lewis E. Gensler
Robert A. Simon and Clifford Grey
Ups-A-Daisy (1928)

WILL YOU REMEMBER ME?
Kurt Weill
Maxwell Anderson
Knickerbocker Holiday (1938)

WILL YOU THINK OF ME TOMORROW?
Bill and Patti Jacob
Jimmy (1969)

WILLA
Leon Carr
Earl Shuman
The Secret Life of Walter Mitty (OB) (1964)

WILLIAM McKINLEY HIGH
Albert Selden
Burt Shevelove
Small Wonder (1948)

WILLIE'S LITTLE WHISTLE
Will Irwin
Norman Zeno
Fools Rush In (1934)

WILLING AND EAGER
Richard Rodgers
State Fair (F) (remake) (1962)

WILLKOMMEN
John Kander
Fred Ebb
Cabaret (1966)

WILLOW TREE
Raymond Scott
Bernard Hanighen
Lute Song (1946)

WILLOW, WILLOW, WILLOW
Robert Wright and George Forrest
Kean (1961)

WIMMEN'S WAYS
Oscar Brown, Jr.
Joy (OB) (1970)

WINDCHILD
Gary Graham
Touch (OB) (1970)

WINDFLOWERS
Jerome Moross
John Latouche
The Golden Apple (1954)

WINDOW CLEANERS, THE
Harry Ruby
Bert Kalmar
The Greenwich Village Follies (1925)

WINDOWS
Eugene and Ralph Berton
Two for Tonight (OB) (1939)

WINGED VICTORY
David Rose
Winged Victory (1943)

WINGS OF THE MORNING
William Heagney
William Heagney and Tom Connell
There You Are (1932)

WINO WILL
Helen Miller

Eve Merriam
Inner City (1971)

WINONA
Rudolf Friml
Brian Hooker
The White Eagle (1927)

WINTER AND SPRING
Rudolf Friml
Edward Eliscu
Nine-Fifteen Revue (1930)

WINTER AND SUMMER
Harvey Schmidt
Tom Jones
Celebration (1969)

WINTER IN CENTRAL PARK
Jerome Kern
Oscar Hammerstein II
Sweet Adeline (1929)

WINTER NIGHTS
Helen Miller
Eve Merriam
Inner City (1971)

WINTERGREEN FOR PRESIDENT
George Gershwin
Ira Gershwin
Of Thee I Sing (1931)

WINTER'S HERE
Skip Redwine and Larry Frank
Frank Merriwell, or Honor Challenged (1971)

WISDOM
Helen Miller
Eve Merriam
Inner City (1971)

WISH
Ernest G. Schweikert
Frank Reardon
Rumple (1957)

WISH I MAY
Hugh Martin and Ralph Blane
Best Foot Forward (OB) (1963)

WISH ME LUCK
Jay Gorney
Jean and Walter Kerr
Touch and Go (1949)

WISH THEM WELL
Richard Rodgers
Oscar Hammerstein II
Allegro (1947)

WISH YOU WERE HERE
Harold Rome
Wish You Were Here (1952)

WISHA WURRA
Johnny Burke
Donnybrook! (1961)

WISHING SONG
John Jennings
Riverwind (OB) (1962)

WISHY WASHY WOMAN
Robert Rosenblum
Robert Rosenblum and Howard Schu-
man
Up Eden (OB) (1968)

WITCH SONG
Ray Haney
Alfred Aiken
We're Civilized? (OB) (1962)

WITCHES' BREW
Jule Styne
Betty Comden and Adolph Green
Hallelujah, Baby! (1967)

WITH A LITTLE BIT OF LUCK
Frederick Loewe
Alan Jay Lerner
My Fair Lady (1956)

WITH A SNAP OF MY FINGER
Stan Freeman and Franklin Underwood
Lovely Ladies, Kind Gentlemen
(1970)

WITH A SONG IN MY HEART
Richard Rodgers
Lorenz Hart
Spring Is Here (1929)

WITH A SWORD IN MY BUCKLE
George Fischoff
Verna Tomasson
The Prince and the Pauper (OB)
(1963)

WITH A TWIST OF THE WRIST
Irvin Graham
Crazy with the Heat (1941)

WITH A WAVE OF MY WAND
David Raksin
June Carroll
If the Shoe Fits (1946)

WITH ALL MY HEART
Johann Strauss
Desmond Carter
The Great Waltz (1934)

WITH MY HEAD IN THE CLOUDS
Irving Berlin
This Is the Army (1942)

WITH SO LITTLE TO BE SURE OF
Stephen Sondheim
Anyone Can Whistle (1964)

WITH THE DAWN
Sigmund Romberg
Irving Caesar
Nina Rosa (1930)

WITH THIS RING
Laurence Rosenthal
James Lipton
Sherry! (1967)

WITH YOU
Steve Allen
Sophie (1963)

WITH YOU, WITH ME
Richard Lewine
Entre-Nous (OB) (1927)

WITH YOUR HAND IN MY HAND
Ernest Gold
Anne Croswell
I'm Solomon (1968)

WITHOUT A CARESS
Fred Spielman and Arthur Gershwin
Stanley Adams
A Lady Says Yes (1945)

WITHOUT A MOTHER
Murray Rumshinsky
Jacob Jacobs
The President's Daughter (1970)

WITHOUT A SHADOW OF A DOUBT
Ord Hamilton
Artists and Models (1930)

WITHOUT A SONG
Vincent Youmans
Billy Rose and Edward Eliscu
Great Day! (1929)

WITHOUT A SPONSOR
Harold Orlob
Hairpin Harmony (1943)

WITHOUT A STITCH
Mischa and Wesley Portnoff
Donagh MacDonagh
Happy As Larry (1950)

WITHOUT LOVE
Ray Henderson
B. G. DeSylva and Lew Brown
Flying High (1930)

WITHOUT LOVE
Cole Porter
Silk Stockings (1955)

WITHOUT ME
John Kander
Fred Ebb
The Happy Time (1968)

WITHOUT YOU
Robert Stolz
Rowland Leigh
Night of Love (1941)

WITHOUT YOU
Frederick Loewe
Alan Jay Lerner
My Fair Lady (1956)

WITHOUT YOU I'M NOTHING
Jerry Bock, George Weiss, and Larry
    Holofcener
Mr. Wonderful (1956)

WITHOUT YOUR LOVE
Carl Millöcker (revised by Theo Mack-
    eben)
Rowland Leigh
The Dubarry (1932)

WOE IS ME
Lehman Engel
Agnes Morgan
A Hero Is Born (1937)

WOLF TIME
Sammy Fain
George Marion, Jr.
Toplitzky of Notre Dame (1946)

WOMAN
Edward Kunneke
Clifford Grey
Mayflowers (1925)

WOMAN, A
Mimi Stone
William Kaye
Pimpernel! (OB) (1964)

WOMAN AGAINST THE WORLD
Clay Warnick
Edward Eager
Dream with Music (1944)

WOMAN FOR THE MAN, THE
Charles Strouse
Lee Adams
(It's a Bird, It's a Plane) It's Superman
    (1966)

WOMAN I WAS BEFORE, THE
Sammy Fain
Paul Francis Webster
Christine (1960)

WOMAN IN HIS ROOM, THE
Frank Loesser
Where's Charley? (1948)

WOMAN IN LOVE, A
Frank Loesser
Guys and Dolls (F) (1955)

WOMAN IN LOVE
Bob Merrill
Henry, Sweet Henry (1967)

WOMAN IS A RASCAL
Baldwin Bergersen
William Archibald
Carib Song (1945)

WOMAN IS A SOMETIME THING, A
George Gershwin
DuBose Heyward
Porgy and Bess (1935)

WOMAN IS A WOMAN IS A WOMAN, A
Rick Besoyan
The Student Gypsy (OB) (1963)

WOMAN IS HOW SHE LOVES, A
André Previn
Alan Jay Lerner
Coco (1969)

WOMAN IS JUST A FEMALE, A
Earl Wilson, Jr.
A Day in the Life of Just About Every-one (OB) (1971)

WOMAN MAKES THE MAN
Claude Leveilee
Gladys Shelley
Gogo Loves You (OB) (1964)

WOMAN MUST NEVER GROW OLD, A
John Jennings
Riverwind (OB) (1962)

WOMAN MUST THINK OF THESE THINGS, A
John Jennings
Riverwind (OB) (1962)

WOMAN OF THE YEAR, THE
Ann Ronell
Count Me In (1942)

WOMAN TO LADY
George Gershwin
DuBose Heyward
Porgy and Bess (1935)

WOMAN WAITS FOR ME, A
Stan Harte, Jr.
Walt Whitman
Leaves of Grass (OB) (1971)

WOMAN WHO LIVED UP THERE, THE
Kurt Weill
Langston Hughes
Street Scene (1947)

WOMAN WOULDN'T BE A WOMAN, A
George Kleinsinger
Joe Darion
Shinbone Alley (1957)

WOMAN'S MUCH BETTER OFF ALONE, A
Coleman Dowell
The Tattooed Countess (OB) (1961)

WOMAN'S PREROGATIVE, A
Harold Arlen
Johnny Mercer
St. Louis Woman (1946)

WOMAN'S TOUCH, THE
George Gershwin
Ira Gershwin
Oh, Kay! (1926)

WOMEN
Franz Lehár
Adrian Ross
The Merry Widow (1907)

WOMEN
Richard Rodgers
Lorenz Hart
Jumbo (1935)

WOMEN!
Edward Earle
Yvonne Tarr
The Decameron (OB) (1961)

WOMEN
David Baker
Will Holt
Come Summer (1969)

WOMEN SIMPLE
Jacques Urbont
Bruce Geller
All in Love (OB) (1961)

WOMEN WEAVING
Heitor Villa-Lobos
Robert Wright and George Forrest
Magdalena (1948)

WOMEN, WOMEN, WOMEN
Duke Ellington
John Latouche
Beggar's Holiday (1946)

WOMEN'S CLUB BLUES
Kurt Weill
Alan Jay Lerner
Love Life (1948)

WOMEN'S LIBERATION
Murray Rumshinsky
Jacob Jacobs
The President's Daughter (1970)

WOMEN'S WORK
Lehman Engel
Edward Eager
The Liar (1950)

WOMEN'S WORK IS NEVER DONE
Herbert Stothart
Otto Harbach and Oscar Hammerstein II
Song of the Flame (1925)

WOMPOM, THE
Donald Swann
Michael Flanders
At the Drop of a Hat (1959)

WONDER, A
John Clifton
John Clifton and Ben Tarver
Man with a Load of Mischief (OB) (1966)

WONDER OF THE KINGDOM
Mel Marvin
Ted Berger
Shoemaker's Holiday (OB) (1967)

WONDER WHERE MY HEART IS
Deed Meyer
She Shall Have Music (OB) (1959)

WONDER WHY
Philip Charig
James Dyrenforth
Nikki (1931)

WONDERFUL COPENHAGEN
Frank Loesser
Hans Christian Andersen (F) (1951)

WONDERFUL DAY LIKE TODAY, A
Leslie Bricusse and Anthony Newley
The Roar of the Greasepaint—The Smell of the Crowd (1965)

WONDERFUL GIRLS
Al Goodman and J. Fred Coots
Clifford Grey
Gay Paree (1925)

WONDERFUL GOOD
Howard Blankman
By Hex (OB) (1956)

WONDERFUL MACHINE, THE
David Baker
Fred Ebb
Smiling, the Boy Fell Dead (OB) (1961)

WONDERFUL, MARVELOUS YOU
Moose Charlap
Norman Gimbel
The Conquering Hero (1961)

WONDERFUL MUSIC
Harvey Schmidt
Tom Jones
110 in the Shade (1963)

WONDERFUL PARTY
John Kander
James Goldman, John Kander, and William Goldman
A Family Affair (1962)

WONDERFUL RHYTHM
Tom Johnstone
Phil Cook
When You Smile (1925)

WONDERFUL WAY OF LIFE, A
Ruth Cleary Patterson
Les Kramer and Florida Vestoff
Russell Patterson's Sketch Book (OB) (1960)

WONDERFUL YESTERDAY
Tom Johnstone
Phil Cook
When You Smile (1925)

WONDERING
Mike Brandt, Michael Knight, and Robert J. Lowery
Exchange (OB) (1970)

WONDERING WHO
Alexander Fogarty
George Fitch
Cape Cod Follies (1929)

WONDRIN'
Norman Campbell
Donald Campbell and Norman Campbell
Anne of Green Gables (OB) (1971)

WON'T I DO?
Edward Pola
Eddie Brandt
Woof, Woof (1929)

WON'T YOU CHARLESTON WITH ME?
Sandy Wilson
The Boy Friend (1954)

WON'T YOU COME ACROSS?
Rudolf Friml
Otto Harbach, Oscar Hammerstein II
The Wild Rose (1926)

WON'T YOU COME TO THE PARTY?
William Roy
The Penny Friend (OB) (1966)

WON'T YOU MARRY ME?
Sigmund Romberg
Dorothy Donnelly
My Maryland (1927)

WON'T YOU MARRY ME?
Moose Charlap
Norman Gimbel
The Conquering Hero (1961)

WON'T YOU TELL ME
Charles M. Schwab
Henry Myers
Bare Facts of 1926 (1926)

WON'T YOU TELL ME WHY?
Jack Waller and Joseph Tunbridge
R. P. Weston and Bert Lee
Tell Her the Truth (1932)

WOODEN WEDDING
Kurt Weill
Ogden Nash
One Touch of Venus (1943)

WOOF
Will Irwin
Norman Zeno
The Show Is On (1936)

WORD A DAY, A
Johnny Mercer
Top Banana (1951)

WORDS, THE
Norman Campbell
Donald Campbell and Norman Campbell
Anne of Green Gables (OB) (1971)

WORDS, MUSIC, CASH
Karl Hajos (based on Chopin)
Harry B. Smith
White Lilacs (1928)

WORDS WILL PAY MY WAY
Maury Laws
Jules Bass
Month of Sundays (OB) (1968)

WORDS WITHOUT MUSIC
Vernon Duke
Ira Gershwin
Ziegfeld Follies (1936)

WORDS, WORDS, WORDS
Walter Marks
Bajour (1964)

WORK ALIKE
Frank Grey
Earle Crooker
The Little Show (1929)

WORK SONG
Earl Robinson
Waldo Salt
Sandhog (OB) (1954)

WORKER AND THE SHIRKER, THE
Susan Hulsman Bingham
Myrna Lamb
Mod Donna (OB) (1970)

WORKOUT
Charles Strouse
Lee Adams
Golden Boy (1964)

WORLD BELONGS TO THE YOUNG, THE
André Previn
Alan Jay Lerner
Coco (1969)

WORLD IS BEAUTIFUL TODAY, THE
Jule Styne
Bob Hilliard
Hazal Flagg (1953)

WORLD IS COMIN' TO A START, THE
Gary Geld
Peter Udell
Purlie (1970)

WORLD IS FULL OF VILLAINS, THE
Kurt Weill
Ira Gershwin
The Firebrand of Florence (1945)

WORLD IS IN MY ARMS, THE
Burton Lane
E. Y. Harburg
Hold On to Your Hats (1940)

WORLD IS MEAN, THE
Kurt Weill
Marc Blitzstein
The Threepenny Opera (OB) (1954)

WORLD IS MINE, THE*
George Gershwin
Ira Gershwin
Funny Face (1927)

WORLD IS YOUR BALLOON, THE
Sammy Fain
E. Y. Harburg
Flahooley (1951)

WORLD OF DREAMS
Victor Herbert
Edward Eliscu
Nine-Fifteen Revue (1930)

WORLD OUTSIDE, THE
Harry Warren
Jerome Lawrence and Robert E. Lee
Shangri-La (1956)

WORLD, TAKE ME BACK†
Jerry Herman
Hello, Dolly! (1964)

WORLD TO WIN, A
David Baker
Fred Ebb
Smiling, the Boy Fell Dead (OB) (1961)

WORLD TODAY, THE
William Roy
The Penny Friend (OB) (1966)

WORLD WEARY
Noël Coward
This Year of Grace (1928)

---

*Dropped from New York production; subsequently in *Nine-Fifteen Revue* (1930) as "Toddlin' Along"
†Added in 1970.

WORLDS APART
Jerry Bock
Sheldon Harnick
Man in the Moon (1963)

WOULD-JA?
Manning Sherwin
Arthur Herzog, Jr.
Bad Habits of 1926 (OB) (1926)

WOULD'JA FOR A BIG RED APPLE?
Henry Souvaine
Everett Miller and Johnny Mercer
Americana (1932)

WOULD THAT I
Mel Marvin
Ted Berger
Shoemaker's Holiday (OB) (1967)

WOULD YOU BE SO KINDLY
Burton Lane
E. Y. Harburg
Hold On to Your Hats (1940)

WOULD YOU LET ME KNOW?
John Addison
John Cranko
Cranks (1956)

WOULD YOU LIKE TO TAKE A WALK*
Harry Warren
Mort Dixon and Billy Rose
Sweet and Low (1930)

WOULDN'T IT BE LOVERLY?
Frederick Loewe
Alan Jay Lerner
My Fair Lady (1956)

WOULDN'T THAT BE WONDERFUL
Herman Hupfeld
Hey Nonny Nonny! (1932)

WOULDN'T YOU LIKE TO BE ON BROADWAY?
Kurt Weill
Langston Hughes
Street Scene (1947)

WOW-OOH-WOLF
Cole Porter
Seven Lively Arts (1944)

WRAP ME IN YOUR SERAPE
Maria Grever
Raymond Leveen
Viva O'Brien (1941)

WRAPPED IN A RIBBON AND TIED IN A BOW
Kurt Weill
Langston Hughes
Street Scene (1947)

WRAPPED UP IN YOU
Ben Oakland
Jack Murray and Barry Trivers
Ziegfeld Follies (1931)

WRATH OF ACHILLES, THE
Joseph Raposo
Erich Segal
Sing Muse! (OB) (1961)

WRECK OF A MAC, THE
Marguerite Monnot
Julian More, David Heneker, and Monte Norman
Irma La Douce (1960)

WRITE HIM A CHALLENGE
Stanley Jay Gelber
John Lollos and Don Christopher
Love and Let Love (OB) (1968)

WRITTEN IN YOUR HAND
Sigmund Romberg
Rowland Leigh
My Romance (1948)

WRONG!
Jimmy Van Heusen
Sammy Cahn
Skyscraper (1965)

WRONG NOTE RAG
Leonard Bernstein
Betty Comden and Adolph Green
Wonderful Town (1953)

___
*Also in *Crazy Quilt* (1931)

WUNDERBAR
Cole Porter
Kiss Me, Kate (1948)

XANADU
Gerard Calvi
Harold Rome
La Grosse Valise (1965)

#X9RL220
Jerry Powell
Michael McWhinney
New Faces (1968)

YA CHARA
Manos Hadjidakis
Joe Darion
Illya Darling (1967)

YAHOO STEP, THE*
Charles Gaynor
Lend an Ear (1948)

YALLER
Charles M. Schwab
Henry Myers
Three's a Crowd (1930)

YAMA-YAMA MAN, THE
Karl Hoschna
George Collin Davis
Three Twins (1908)

YANKEE DOLLAR
Harold Arlen
E. Y. Harburg
Jamaica (1957)

YANKEE DOODLE BOY, THE
George M. Cohan
Little Johnny Jones (1904)

YANKEE FATHER IN THE YANKEE HOME, THE
George M. Cohan
The Merry Malones (1927)

YANKEE STAY
Ray Haney
Alfred Aiken
We're Civilized? (OB) (1962)

YANKYULA
Rudolf Friml
J. Keirn Brennan
Luana (1930)

YASNI KOZKOLAI
Noël Coward
The Girl Who Came to Supper (1963)

Y'ASSOU
John Kander
Fred Ebb
Zorbá (1968)

YATATA, YATATA, YATATA
Richard Rodgers
Oscar Hammerstein II
Allegro (1947)

Y'CAN'T WIN
Gordon Duffy
Harry M. Haldane
Happy Town (1959)

YE LUNCHTIME FOLLIES
Richard Rodgers
Lorenz Hart
A Connecticut Yankee (1943)

YEAR IS A DAY, A
Baldwin Bergersen
William Archibald
The Crystal Heart (OB) (1960)

YEARS BEFORE US, THE
Frank Loesser
Where's Charley? (1948)

YEEMY YEEMY
James Mundy
John Latouche
The Vamp (1955)

YELLOW DRUM
Claibe Richardson
Kenward Elmslie
The Grass Harp (1971)

---

*Also in *Show Girl* (1961)

YER MY FRIEND, AINTCHA?
Bob Merrill
New Girl in Town (1957)

YERUSHALIAM
Walt Smith
Leon Uris
Ari (1971)

YES
John Kander
Fred Ebb
70, Girls, 70 (1971)

YES AND NO
Sigmund Romberg
Harry B. Smith
Princess Flavia (1925)

YES, AUNT
Baldwin Bergersen
William Archibald
The Crystal Heart (OB) (1960)

YES, I KNOW THAT I'M ALIVE
Nancy Ford
Gretchen Cryer
The Last Sweet Days of Isaac (OB)
(1970)

YES, I LOVE YOU HONEY
Jerry Livingston
Mack David
Bright Lights of 1944 (1943)

YES, MY HEART
Bob Merrill
Carnival (1961)

YES OR NO
Edward Kunneke (based on Offen-
bach)
Harry B. Smith
The Love Song (1925)

YES, SIR, I'VE MADE A DATE
Lee Wainer
J. B. Rosenberg
New Faces (1943)

YES, YES, YES
Cole Porter
You Never Know (1938)

YES, YES, YVETTE
Philip Charig
Irving Caesar
Yes, Yes, Yvette (1927)

YESTERDAY I LOVED YOU
Mary Rodgers
Marshall Barer
Once Upon a Mattress (OB) (1959)

**YESTERDAY WAS SUCH A LOVELY
DAY**
Irving Burgie
Ballad for Bimshire (OB) (1963)

YESTERDAYS
Jerome Kern
Otto Harbach
Roberta (1933)

YIP AHOY
Harold Rome
Sing Out the News (1938)

YOO-HOO BLUES, THE
Morgan Lewis
Nancy Hamilton
One for the Money (1939)

YOU
Albert Sirmay and Arthur Schwartz
Arthur Swanstrom
Princess Charming (1930)

YOU
Richard Rodgers
Martin Charnin
Two by Two (1970)

YOU AIN'T GOT NO SAVOIR FAIRE
Richard Rodgers
Lorenz Hart
America's Sweetheart (1931)

YOU AIN'T NO ASTRONAUT
Melvin Van Peebles
*Ain't Supposed to Die a Natural
Death* (1971)

YOU AIN'T SO HOT
Jerome Moross
Paul Peters and George Sklar
Parade (1935)

YOU ALWAYS LOVE THE SAME GIRL
Richard Rodgers
Lorenz Hart
A Connecticut Yankee (1943)

YOU ALWAYS TALK OF FRIENDSHIP
Alma Sanders
Monte Carlo
Mystery Moon (1930)

YOU AND I
Steven Metcalf
Fred Bluth
Drat! (OB) (1971)

YOU AND I ARE PASSERSBY
Jean Gilbert
Harry B. Smith
The Red Rose (1928)

YOU AND I COULD BE JUST LIKE THAT
Henry Sullivan
Edward Eliscu
A Little Racketeer (1932)

YOU AND I KNOW
Arthur Schwartz
Albert Stillman and Laurence Stallings
Virginia (1937)

YOU AND I, LOVE
John Kander
Fred Ebb
70, Girls, 70 (1971)

YOU AND I LOVE YOU AND ME
Albert Von Tilzer
Neville Fleeson
Bye Bye, Bonnie (1927)

YOU AND THE NIGHT AND THE MUSIC
Arthur Schwartz
Howard Dietz
Revenge with Music (1934)

YOU AND YOUR KISS
Jerome Kern
Dorothy Fields
One Night in the Tropics (F) (1940)

YOU APPEAL TO ME
Sigmund Romberg
Harry B. Smith
The Love Call (1927)

YOU ARE
Clark Gesner
New Faces (1968)

YOU ARE ALL I'VE WANTED
Sigmund Romberg
Otto Harbach
Forbidden Melody (1936)

YOU ARE BEAUTIFUL
Richard Rodgers
Oscar Hammerstein II
Flower Drum Song (1958)

YOU ARE FOR LOVING
Hugh Martin and Ralph Blane
Best Foot Forward (OB) (1963)

YOU ARE FREE
Victor Jacobi
William LeBaron
Apple Blossoms (1919)

YOU ARE LOVE
Jerome Kern
Oscar Hammerstein II
Show Boat (1927)

YOU ARE MY DARLIN' BRIDE
Giuseppe Verdi
Charles Friedman
My Darlin' Aida (1952)

YOU ARE MY DAY DREAM
Cliff Friend and George White
George White's Scandals (1929)

YOU ARE MY DOWNFALL
Sammy Fain
George Marion, Jr.
Toplitzky of Notre Dame (1946)

YOU ARE MY SONGS
Johann Strauss
Desmond Carter
The Great Waltz (1934)

YOU ARE MY WOMAN
Sigmund Romberg
Oscar Hammerstein II
East Wind (1931)

YOU ARE NEVER AWAY
Richard Rodgers
Oscar Hammerstein II
Allegro (1947)

YOU ARE NOT REAL
Jerry Bock
Sheldon Harnick
The Apple Tree (1966)

YOU ARE ROMANCE
Philip Charig
Dan Shapiro and Milton Pascal
Artists and Models (1943)

YOU ARE SIXTEEN
Richard Rodgers
Oscar Hammerstein II
The Sound of Music (1959)

YOU ARE SO FAIR
Richard Rodgers
Lorenz Hart
Babes in Arms (1937)

YOU ARE THE SONG
Sigmund Romberg
Irving Caesar
Melody (1933)

YOU ARE TOO BEAUTIFUL
Richard Rodgers
Lorenz Hart
Hallelujah, I'm a Bum (F) (1933)

YOU ARE WOMAN
Jule Styne
Bob Merrill
Funny Girl (1964)

YOU ARE YOU
George Gershwin and Herbert Sto-
thart
Otto Harbach and Oscar Hammer-
stein II
Song of the Flame (1925)

YOU ARE YOU
John Kander
Fred Ebb
Flora, the Red Menace (1965)

YOU BEAUTIFUL SO AND SO
Ted Snyder
Billy Rose
Earl Carroll's Sketch Book (1929)

YOU BECOME ME
William Roy
Maggie (1953)

YOU BURN ME UP
Jean Gilbert
Harry B. Smith
Marching By (1932)

YOU CAME ALONG
Joseph Meyer and Philip Charig
Leo Robin
Just Fancy (1927)

YOU CAN DANCE
Victor Ziskin
Joan Javits
Young Abe Lincoln (1961)

**YOU CAN DANCE WITH ANY GIRL
AT ALL**
Vincent Youmans
Irving Caesar
No, No, Nanette (1925)

YOU CAN DO NO WRONG
Cole Porter
The Pirate (F) (1948)

YOU CAN HANG YOUR HAT HERE
Ray Haney
Alfred Aiken
We're Civilized? (OB) (1962)

YOU CAN HAVE HIM
Irving Berlin
Miss Liberty (1949)

YOU CAN MAKE MY LIFE A BED OF ROSES
Ray Henderson
Lew Brown
Hot-Cha! (1932)

YOU CAN NEVER TELL
Niclas Kempner
Graham John
The Street Singer (1929)

YOU CAN REACH THE SUN
Bob Goodman
Wild and Wonderful (1971)

YOU CAN TRUST ME
Ervin Drake
What Makes Sammy Run? (1964)

YOU CAN'T BRUSH ME OFF
Irving Berlin
Louisiana Purchase (1940)

YOU CAN'T EYE A SHY BABY
Abel Baer
Sam Lewis and Joe Young
Lady Do (1927)

YOU CAN'T FOOL THE PEOPLE
George Kleinsinger
Alfred Hayes
Of V We Sing (1942)

YOU CAN'T FOOL YOUR DREAMS
Richard Rodgers
Lorenz Hart
Poor Little Ritz Girl (1920)

YOU CAN'T GET A MAN WITH A GUN
Irving Berlin
Annie Get Your Gun (1946)

YOU CAN'T GET UP BEFORE NOON WITHOUT BEING A SQUARE
Melvin Van Peebles
Ain't Supposed to Die a Natural Death (1971)

YOU CAN'T MAKE LOVE
Lee Pockriss
Anne Croswell
Ernest in Love (OB) (1960)

YOU CAN'T MISS IT
Albert Hague
Arnold B. Horwitt
Plain and Fancy (1955)

YOU CAN'T OVERDO A GOOD THING
Joseph Meyer
Floyd Huddleston
Shuffle Along (1952)

YOU CAN'T PUT CATSUP ON THE MOON
Sammy Fain
Irving Kahal
Boys and Girls Together (1940)

YOU CAN'T STOP ME FROM LOVING YOU
Alberta Nichols
Mann Holiner
Rhapsody in Black (1931)

YOU CAN'T TAKE IT WITH YOU
Joan Edwards and Lyn Duddy
Tickets Please (1950)

YOU CAN'T WALK BACK FROM AN AEROPLANE
Irving Bibo and William B. Friedlander
Footlights (1927)

YOU CLICK WITH ME
Bradford Greene
Marianne Brown Waters
Right This Way (1938)

YOU COULD DRIVE A PERSON CRAZY
Stephen Sondheim
Company (1970)

YOU COULDN'T BE CUTER
Jerome Kern
Dorothy Fields
The Joy of Living (F) (1938)

YOU COULDN'T BLAME ME FOR THAT
Harry Ruby
Bert Kalmar
Top Speed (1929)

YOU DESERVE ME
Jack Lawrence and Stan Freeman
I Had a Ball (1964)

YOU DEVIL YOU
Stefan Kanfer, Jess J. Korman, and Joseph Grayhon
I Want You (OB) (1961)

YOU DID IT
Frederick Loewe
Alan Jay Lerner
My Fair Lady (1956)

YOU DO SOMETHING TO ME
Cole Porter
Fifty Million Frenchmen (1929)

YOU DON'T DANCE
Philip Charig
Dan Shapiro and Milton Pascal
Follow the Girls (1944)

YOU DON'T HAVE TO DO IT FOR ME
Larry Grossman
Hal Hackady
Minnie's Boys (1970)

YOU DON'T KNOW
Meredith Willson
Here's Love (1963)

YOU DON'T KNOW HIM
Jay Livingston and Ray Evans
Oh Captain! (1958)

YOU DON'T KNOW PAREE
Cole Porter
Fifty Million Frenchmen (1929)

YOU DON'T LOOK FOR LOVE
Eubie Blake
Noble Sissle
Shuffle Along (1933)

YOU DON'T REMIND ME*
Cole Porter
Out of This World (1950)

YOU DON'T TELL ME
Richard Rodgers
No Strings (1962)

YOU-DON'T-WANT-TO-PLAY-WITH-ME BLUES, THE
Sandy Wilson
The Boy Friend (1954)

YOU FORGOT YOUR GLOVES
Ned Lehak
Edward Eliscu
The Third Little Show (1931)

YOU FOUND ME AND I FOUND YOU
Jerome Kern
P. G. Wodehouse
Oh, Lady! Lady!! (1918)

YOU GAY DOG YOU!
Philip Springer
Joan Javits
Hotel Passionato (OB) (1965)

YOU GOTTA BE HOLDIN' OUT FIVE DOLLARS ON ME
Melvin Van Peebles
Ain't Supposed to Die a Natural Death (1971)

YOU GOTTA GET A GIMMICK
Jule Styne
Stephen Sondheim
Gypsy (1959)

YOU GOTTA HAVE A DESTINATION
William Klenosky
Utopia! (OB) (1963)

YOU GOTTA KEEP SAYING "NO"
Harry Revel
Arnold B. Horwitt
Are You With It? (1945)

YOU HAVE CAST YOUR SHADOW ON THE SEA
Richard Rodgers
Lorenz Hart
The Boys from Syracuse (1938)

YOU HAVE EVERYTHING
Arthur Schwartz
Howard Dietz
Between the Devil (1937)

---

*Dropped from New York production

YOU HAVE GOT TO HAVE A RUDDER
ON THE ARK
Richard Rodgers
Martin Charnin
Two by Two (1970)

YOU HAVE ME—I HAVE YOU
Harold Levey
Owen Murphy
The Greenwich Village Follies (1925)

YOU HAVE MY HEART
Frank D'Armond
Will Morrissey
Saluta (1934)

YOU HAVE TO DO WHAT YOU DO DO
Kurt Weill
Ira Gershwin
The Firebrand of Florence (1945)

YOU HAVEN'T CHANGED AT ALL
Frederick Loewe
Alan Jay Lerner
The Day Before Spring (1945)

YOU HAVEN'T LIVED UNTIL YOU'VE
PLAYED THE PALACE
Charles Gaynor
Show Girl (1961)

YOU HELP ME
Ervin Drake
What Makes Sammy Run? (1964)

YOU I LIKE
Jerry Herman
Madame Aphrodite (OB) (1961)

YOU IN YOUR ROOM; I IN MINE
Winthrop Cortelyou
Derick Wulff
Kiss Me (1927)

YOU IRRITATE ME SO
Cole Porter
Let's Face It! (1941)

YOU KISSED ME
Morton Gould
Dorothy Fields
Arms and the Girl (1950)

YOU KNOW, I KNOW
Harry Archer
Harlan Thompson
Twinkle Twinkle (1926)

YOU KNOW, OH LORD
Baldwin Bergersen
William Archibald
Carib Song (1945)

YOU LOOK LIKE ME
Al Carmines
Rosalyn Drexler
Home Movies (OB) (1964)

YOU LOST YOUR OPPORTUNITY
Charles M. Schwab
Henry Myers
The Garrick Gaieties (1930)

YOU LOVE ME
Herman Hupfeld
Murder at the Vanities (1933)

YOU LOVE ME
Lee Pockriss
Anne Croswell
Tovarich (1963)

YOU MADE IT POSSIBLE, DEAR
Eddie Stuart
Harvey Lasker
Old Bucks and New Wings (OB)
(1962)

YOU MAY BE THE SOMEONE
Norman Dean
Autumn's Here (OB) (1966)

YOU MAY HAVE PLANTED MANY A
LILY
Alma Sanders
Monte Carlo
Oh! Oh! Nurse (1925)

YOU MIGHT AS WELL PRETEND
Morgan Lewis
Edward Eliscu and Ted Fetter
The Third Little Show (1931)

You Must Be Born with It
Irving Berlin
Face the Music (1932)

You Must Come Over Blues
Lewis E. Gensler
B. G. DeSylva and Ira Gershwin
Captain Jinks (1925)

You Mustn't Be Discouraged
Jule Styne
Betty Comden and Adolph Green
Fade Out—Fade In (1964)

You Mustn't Kick It Around
Richard Rodgers
Lorenz Hart
Pal Joey (1940)

You Need a Hobby
Irving Berlin
Mr. President (1962)

You Never Can Tell
Mary Rodgers
Steven Vinaver
The Mad Show (OB) (1966)

You Never Knew about Me
Jerome Kern
P. G. Wodehouse
Oh, Boy! (1917)

You Never Know
Cole Porter
You Never Know (1938)

You Never Know What Comes Next
Robert Stolz
Robert Sour
Mr. Strauss Goes to Boston (1945)

You Never Know What Hit You
Harold Rome
Bless You All (1950)

You Never Met a Feller Like Me
Cyril Ornadel
Leslie Bricusse
Pickwick (1965)

You Never Miss the Water
Norman Dean
Autumn's Here (OB) (1966)

You Never Really Know
Voices, Inc.
The Believers (OB) (1968)

You Never Saw That Before
Jimmy Van Heusen
Johnny Burke
Nellie Bly (1946)

You Never Say Yes
Richard Rodgers
Lorenz Hart
Spring Is Here (1929)

You or No One
Harold Arlen
Johnny Mercer
Saratoga (1959)

You, or Nobody!
Irving Caesar
Yes, Yes, Yvette! (1927)

You Poor Thing
Marc Blitzstein
Juno (1959)

You Remind Me of My Mother
George M. Cohan
Little Nellie Kelly (1922)

You Remind Me of You
Larry Grossman
Hal Hackady
Minnie's Boys (1970)

You Said It
Harold Arlen
Jack Yellen
You Said It (1931)

You Said It
Cole Porter
Panama Hattie (1940)

YOU SAID SOMETHING
Jerome Kern
Jerome Kern and P. G. Wodehouse
Have a Heart (1917)

YOU SAY THE NICEST THINGS, BABY
Jimmy McHugh
Harold Adamson
As the Girls Go (1948)

YOU SAY—THEY SAY
Stan Freeman and Franklin Underwood
Lovely Ladies, Kind Gentlemen (1970)

YOU SAY YOU CARE
Jule Styne
Leo Robin
Gentlemen Prefer Blondes (1949)

YOU SET MY HEART TO MUSIC
Eaton Magoon, Jr.
13 Daughters (1961)

YOU SHOULD BE SET TO MUSIC
Irvin Graham
Crazy with the Heat (1941)

YOU SHOULD KNOW
J. C. Johnson
Change Your Luck (1930)

YOU SHOULD SEE YOURSELF
Cy Coleman
Dorothy Fields
Sweet Charity (1966)

YOU SMILED AT ME
Harry Ruby
Bert Kalmar
The Ramblers (1926)

YOU STILL LOVE ME
C. C. Courtney
C. C. Courtney and Ragan Courtney
Earl of Ruston (1971)

YOU SWEET SO AND SO
Philip Charig and Joseph Meyer
Ira Gershwin
Sweet and Low (1930)

YOU TAKE PARIS
Coleman Dowell
The Tattooed Countess (OB) (1961)

YOU TALK JUST LIKE MY MAW
Georges Bizet
Oscar Hammerstein II
Carmen Jones (1943)

YOU TOLD ME THAT YOU LOVED ME,
BUT YOU NEVER TOLD ME WHY
Gene Lockhart
Bunk of 1926 (1926)

YOU TOO CAN BE A PUPPET
Sammy Fain
E. Y. Harburg
Flahooley (1951)

YOU TOOK ADVANTAGE OF ME
Richard Rodgers
Lorenz Hart
Present Arms (1928)

YOU TOOK ME BY SURPRISE
Vernon Duke
John Latouche
The Lady Comes Across (1942)

YOU TOOK POSSESSION OF ME
Gerald Marks
Sam Lerner
Hold It! (1948)

YOU TREACHEROUS MEN
Jerry Bock
Sheldon Harnick
Man in the Moon (1963)

YOU WAIT AND WAIT AND WAIT
Sigmund Romberg
Oscar Hammerstein II
May Wine (1935)

YOU WALKED OUT
David Baker
David Craig
Copper and Brass (1957)

YOU WANT TO MOURN
Earl Robinson
Waldo Salt
Sandhog (OB) (1954)

You Wanted Me, I Wanted You
Harold Arlen
Ted Koehler
Nine-Fifteen Revue (1930)

You Wash and I'll Dry
Frederick Loewe
Alan Jay Lerner
What's Up? (1943)

You Were Dead, You Know
Leonard Bernstein
John Latouche and Richard Wilbur
Candide (1956)

You Were Meant for Me
Eubie Blake
Noble Sissle
Charlot's Revue (1924)

You Were Never Lovelier
Jerome Kern
Johnny Mercer
You Were Never Lovelier (F) (1942)

You Were There
Noël Coward
Tonight at 8:30 (Shadow Play) (1936)

You Will Never Be Lonely
Arthur Schwartz
Howard Dietz
The Gay Life (1961)

You Will Never Know
Vincent Youmans
Paul James
Nine-Fifteen Revue (1930)

You Will Remember Vienna
Sigmund Romberg
Oscar Hammerstein II
Viennese Nights (F) (1930)

You Will, Won't You?
Jerome Kern
Anne Caldwell and Otto Harbach
Criss-Cross (1926)

You Wonder How These Things Begin
Harvey Schmidt
Tom Jones
The Fantasticks (OB) (1960)

You Won't Say No
Tom Sankey
The Golden Screw (OB) (1967)

You Wouldn't Fool Me, Would You?
Ray Henderson
B. G. DeSylva and Lew Brown
Follow Thru (1929)

You'd Be Amazed
John Clifton
John Clifton and Ben Tarver
Man with a Load of Mischief (OB) (1966)

You'd Be Hard to Replace
Harry Warren
Ira Gershwin
The Barkleys of Broadway (F) (1949)

You'd Be So Nice to Come Home To
Cole Porter
Something to Shout About (F) (1942)

You'd Be Surprised
Irving Berlin
Ziegfeld Follies (1919)

You'd Better Dance
Jerry Livingston
Mack David
Bright Lights of 1944 (1943)

You'd Better Go Now
Irvin Graham
Bickley Reichner
New Faces (1936)

You'd Better Love Me
Hugh Martin and Timothy Gray
High Spirits (1964)

YOU'D LIKE NEBRASKA
Mary Rodgers
Martin Charnin
Hot Spot (1963)

YOU'LL DO
Harold Arlen
Jack Yellen
You Said It (1931)

YOU'LL FIND MICE
Helen Miller
Eve Merriam
Inner City (1971)

YOU'LL HAVE TO GUESS
Karl Hajos (based on Tschaikovsky)
Harry B. Smith
Natja (1925)

YOU'LL KILL 'EM
Harry Archer
Walter O'Keefe
Just a Minute (1928)

YOU'LL KNOW THAT IT'S ME
Philip Charig
Dan Shapiro and Milton Pascal
Artists and Models (1943)

YOU'LL MAKE AN ELEGANT BUTLER
Joan Javits and Philip Springer
Tovarich (1963)

YOU'LL NEVER GET AWAY FROM ME
Jule Styne
Stephen Sondheim
Gypsy (1959)

YOU'LL NEVER KNOW
Lewis E. Gensler
B. G. DeSylva
Queen High (1926)

YOU'LL NEVER WALK ALONE
Richard Rodgers
Oscar Hammerstein II
Carousel (1945)

YOU'LL THINK OF SOMEONE
Burt Bacharach
Hal David
Promises, Promises (1968)

YOUNG AND FOOLISH
Albert Hague
Arnold B. Horwitt
Plain and Fancy (1955)

YOUNG BLACK JOE
Roger Wolfe Kahn
Irving Caesar
Americana (1928)

YOUNG ENOUGH TO DREAM
Ron Steward and Neal Tate
Ron Steward
Sambo (OB) (1969)

YOUNG IDEAS
Charles Tobias, Charles Newman, and
　Murray Mencher
Earl Carroll's Sketch Book (1935)

YOUNG MAN'S FANCY, A
Milton Ager
John Murray Anderson and Jack Yellen
What's in a Name? (1922)

YOUNG PEOPLE
Frank Loesser
The Most Happy Fella (1956)

YOUNG PEOPLE THINK ABOUT LOVE
Kurt Weill
Maxwell Anderson
Knickerbocker Holiday (1938)

YOUNG PRETTY GIRL LIKE YOU, A
Burt Bacharach
Hal David
Promises, Promises (1968)

YOUNGER SET, THE
James F. Hanley
Eddie Dowling
Sidewalks of New York (1927)

YOUNGER SET, THE
J. Fred Coots
Arthur Swanstrom and Benny Davis
Sons o' Guns (1929)

YOUNGER THAN SPRINGTIME
Richard Rodgers
Oscar Hammerstein II
South Pacific (1949)

YOUNGEST PRESIDENT, THE
Robert Kessler
Martin Charnin
Put It in Writing (OB) (1963)

YOUR BROADWAY AND MINE
Maury Rubens
Moe Jaffe
Broadway Nights (1929)

YOUR COUNTRY NEEDS YOU
Edward Kunneke (based on Offen-
bach)
Harry B. Smith
The Love Song (1925)

YOUR DISPOSITION IS MINE
Jimmy McHugh
Dorothy Fields
Hello Daddy (1928)

YOUR DREAM (IS THE SAME AS MY DREAM)
Jerome Kern
Oscar Hammerstein II and Otto Har-
bach
One Night in the Tropics (F) (1940)

YOUR EYES
Rudolf Friml
P. G. Wodehouse and Clifford Grey
The Three Musketeers (1928)

YOUR FACE IS SO FAMILIAR
Alex Fogarty
Edwin Gilbert
New Faces (1936)

YOUR FACE IS YOUR FORTUNE
Jerry Livingston
Mack David
Bright Lights of 1944 (1943)

YOUR FATAL FASCINATION
Jacques Belasco
Kay Twomey
The Girl from Nantucket (1945)

YOUR GOOD MORNING
Jerry Herman
Parade (OB) (1960)

YOUR HAND IN MINE
Jerry Herman
Parade (OB) (1960)

YOUR LAND AND MY LAND
Sigmund Romberg
Dorothy Donnelly
My Maryland (1927)

YOUR LOVE I CRAVE
Jimmy Johnson
Perry Bradford
Messin' Around (1929)

YOUR MOTHER'S SON-IN-LAW
Alberta Nichols
Mann Holiner
Blackbirds of 1934 (1933)

YOUR NAME MAY BE PARIS
Joseph Raposo
Erich Segal
Sing Muse! (OB) (1961)

YOUR PRINCE WAS NOT SO CHARM-ING
Harden Church
Edward Heyman
Caviar (1934)

YOUR SMILES, YOUR TEARS
Sigmund Romberg
Irving Caesar
Nina Rosa (1930)

YOUR TYPE IS COMING BACK
Sam H. Stept
Bud Green
Shady Lady (1933)

YOU'RE A BAD INFLUENCE ON ME
Cole Porter
Red, Hot and Blue! (1936)

YOU'RE A BUILDER-UPPER
Harold Arlen

Ira Gershwin and E. Y. Harburg
Life Begins at 8:40 (1934)

YOU'RE A GOOD MAN, CHARLIE BROWN
Clark Gesner
You're a Good Man, Charlie Brown
  (OB) (1967)

YOU'RE A GRAND OLD FLAG
George M. Cohan
George Washington, Jr. (1906)

YOU'RE A LIAR
Cy Coleman
Carolyn Leigh
Wildcat (1960)

YOU'RE A LONG, LONG WAY FROM AMERICA
Noël Coward
Sail Away (1961)

YOU'RE A MAGICIAN
Gerald Dolin
Edward J. Lambert
Smile at Me (1935)

YOU'RE A MAN
Rick Besoyan
The Student Gypsy (OB) (1963)

YOU'RE A QUEER ONE, JULIE JORDAN
Richard Rodgers
Oscar Hammerstein II
Carousel (1945)

YOU'RE A STRANGER IN THIS NEIGHBORHOOD
Albert Hague
Marty Brill
Café Crown (1964)

YOU'RE A WONDERFUL GIRL
Shep Camp
Frank DuPree and Harry B. Smith
Half a Widow (1927)

YOU'RE ALL THE WORLD TO ME
Harold Levey
Owen Murphy
Rainbow Rose (1926)

YOU'RE ALL THE WORLD TO ME
Edward Pola
Eddie Brandt
Woof, Woof (1929)

YOU'RE ALL THE WORLD TO ME
Burton Lane
Alan Jay Lerner
Royal Wedding (F) (1951)

YOU'RE ALWAYS IN MY ARMS
Harry Tierney
Joseph McCarthy
Rio Rita (F) (1929)

YOU'RE AN OLD SMOOTHIE
Nacio Herb Brown and Richard Whiting
B. G. DeSylva
Take a Chance (1932)

YOU'RE AS ENGLISH AS
Richard Adler
Kwamina (1961)

YOU'RE ASKING ME
Edward A. Horan
Frederick Herendeen
All the King's Horses (1934)

YOU'RE COLOSSAL
James Mundy
John Latouche
The Vamp (1955)

YOU'RE DEAD!
Jimmy Van Heusen
Johnny Burke
Carnival in Flanders (1953)

YOU'RE DELICIOUS
Don Elliott
James Costigan
The Beast in Me (1963)

YOU'RE DEVASTATING
Jerome Kern
Otto Harbach
Roberta (1933)

YOU'RE DREAMING
Robert Swerdlow
Love Me, Love My Children (OB)
(1971)

YOU'RE EASY TO DANCE WITH
Irving Berlin
Holiday Inn (F) (1942)

YOU'RE EVERYWHERE
Vincent Youmans
Edward Heyman
Through the Years (1932)

YOU'RE FALSE
Giuseppe Verdi
Charles Friedman
My Darlin' Aïda (1952)

YOU'RE FAR FROM WONDERFUL
Vernon Duke
Ogden Nash
The Littlest Revue (OB) (1956)

YOU'RE FAR TOO NEAR ME
Kurt Weill
Ira Gershwin
The Firebrand of Florence (1945)

YOU'RE GONNA DANCE WITH ME, WILLIE
Jule Styne
Bob Hilliard
Hazel Flagg (1953)

YOU'RE GONNA LOVE TOMORROW
Stephen Sondheim
Follies (1971)

YOU'RE HERE AND I'M HERE
Jerome Kern
Harry B. Smith
The Marriage Market (1914)

YOU'RE IN LOVE
Franz Lehar
Adrian Ross
Gypsy Love (1911)

YOU'RE IN LOVE
Cole Porter
Gay Divorce (1932)

YOU'RE IN LOVE
Joseph Raposo
Erich Segal
Sing Muse! (OB) (1961)

YOU'RE IN PARIS
Mark Sandrich, Jr.
Sidney Michaels
Ben Franklin in Paris (1964)

YOU'RE JUST IN LOVE
Irving Berlin
Call Me Madam (1950)

YOU'RE LAUGHING AT ME
Irving Berlin
On the Avenue (F) (1937)

YOU'RE LIKE
Ray Haney
Alfred Aiken
We're Civilized? (OB) (1962)

YOU'RE LONELY AND I'M LONELY
Irving Berlin
Louisiana Purchase (1940)

YOU'RE LUCKY
Hugh Martin and Ralph Blane
Best Foot Forward (OB) (1963)

YOU'RE LUCKY TO ME
Eubie Blake
Andy Razaf
Blackbirds (1930)

YOU'RE MINE, ALL MINE
Fred Stamer
Gen Genovese
Buttrio Square (1952)

YOU'RE MOMMA'S
Robert Waldman
Alfred Uhry
Here's Where I Belong (1968)

YOU'RE MORE THAN A NAME AND
ADDRESS
Fred Spielman and Arthur Gershwin
Stanley Adams
A Lady Says Yes (1945)

YOU'RE MUSICAL
Lionel Bart
La Strada (1969)

YOU'RE MY EVERYTHING
Harry Warren
Mort Dixon and Joe Young
The Laugh Parade (1931)

YOU'RE MY GIRL
Jule Styne
Sammy Cahn
High Button Shoes (1947)

YOU'RE MY HAPPINESS
Kenneth Jacobson
Rhoda Roberts
Show Me Where the Good Times Are
   (OB) (1970)

YOU'RE MY MAN
Robert Kessler
Martin Charnin
Fallout (OB) (1959)

YOU'RE MY RELAXATION
Charles Schwab
Robert Sour
New Faces (1934)

YOU'RE NEARER
Richard Rodgers
Lorenz Hart
Too Many Girls (F) (1940)

YOU'RE NO GOOD
Ervin Drake
What Makes Sammy Run? (1964)

YOU'RE NOT
Leon Carr
Earl Shuman
The Secret Life of Walter Mitty (OB)
   (1964)

YOU'RE NOT ALONE
Jacques Brel
Eric Blau and Mort Shuman
*Jacques Brel Is Alive and Well and
   Living in Paris* (OB) (1968)

YOU'RE NOT FOOLIN' ME
Harvey Schmidt
Tom Jones
110 in the Shade (1963)

YOU'RE NOT PRETTY BUT YOU'RE
MINE
Burton Lane
E. Y. Harburg
Americana (1932)

YOU'RE NOT THE ONE
Jesse Greer
Stanley Adams
Shady Lady (1933)

YOU'RE NOT THE TYPE
Arthur Schwartz
Howard Dietz
The Gay Life (1961)

YOU'RE NOTHING
Buster Davis
Steven Vinaver
Diversions (OB) (1958)

YOU'RE ON MY MIND
Harry Ruby
Bert Kalmar
High Kickers (1941)

YOU'RE PERF
Philip Charig
Dan Shapiro and Milton Pascal
Follow the Girls (1944)

YOU'RE PERFECT
Joseph Meyer
Edward Eliscu
Lady Fingers (1929)

YOU'RE RIGHT, YOU'RE RIGHT
Jimmy Van Heusen
Sammy Cahn
Walking Happy (1966)

You're Sensational
Cole Porter
High Society (F) (1956)

You're So Beautiful That——
Johnny Mercer
Top Banana (1951)

You're So Lovely and I'm So Lonely
Richard Rodgers
Lorenz Hart
Something Gay (1935)

You're So Much a Part of Me
Richard Adler and Jerry Ross
John Murray Anderson's Almanac (1953)

You're So Near (So Near and Yet So Far)
Jay Gorney
Barry Trivers
Heaven on Earth (1948)

You're So Nice to Remember*
David Rose
Winged Victory (1943)

You're So Right for Me
Jay Livingston and Ray Evans
Oh Captain! (1958)

You're the Better Half of Me
Jimmy McHugh
Dorothy Fields
The Vanderbilt Revue (1930)

You're the Cats
Richard Rodgers
Lorenz Hart
The Hot Heiress (F) (1931)

You're the Cream in My Coffee
Ray Henderson
B. G. DeSylva and Lew Brown
Hold Everything! (1928)

You're the Cure for What Ails Me
Harold Arlen
E. Y. Harburg
The Singing Kid (F) (1935)

You're the Fairest Flower
Rick Besoyan
Little Mary Sunshine (OB) (1959)

You're the Fellow the Fortune Teller Told Me About
Lucien Denni
Helena Evans
Happy Go Lucky (1926)

You're the First Cup of Coffee
Jay Gorney
Barry Trivers
Heaven on Earth (1948)

You're the Lord of Any Manor
Fred Spielman and Arthur Gershwin
Stanley Adams
A Lady Says Yes (1945)

You're the Most Impossible Person
Deed Meyer
'Toinette (OB) (1961)

You're the One
Harry Archer
Harlan Thompson
Merry-Merry (1925)

You're the One
Vincent Youmans
J. Russel Robinson and George Waggner
What a Widow! (F) (1930)

You're the One I'm For
Clark Gesner
New Faces (1968)

You're the Only One
Clarence Williams
Len Gray
Bottomland (1927)

You're the Only One
Don McAfee
Nancy Leeds
Great Scot! (OB) (1965)

---

*Dropped from New York production

YOU'RE THE REASON
Harold Orlob
Hairpin Harmony (1968)

YOU'RE THE SUNRISE*
Arthur Schwartz
Howard Dietz
The Second Little Show (1930)

YOU'RE THE SWEET BEGINNING
Robert Colby
Robert Colby and Nita Jonas
Half-Past Wednesday (OB) (1962)

YOU'RE THE TOP
Cole Porter
Anything Goes (1934)

YOU'RE TOO SMART
Walter Cool
Mackey of Appalachia (OB) (1965)

YOU'RE WHAT I NEED
Richard Rodgers
Lorenz Hart
She's My Baby (1928)

YOU'RE WONDERFUL
Buster Davis
Steven Vinaver
Diversions (OB) (1958)

YOURS, ALL YOURS
Moose Charlap
Norman Gimbel
The Conquering Hero (1961)

YOURS IS MY HEART ALONE
Franz Lehár
Harry Graham
Yours Is My Heart (1946)

YOURS SINCERELY
Richard Rodgers
Lorenz Hart
Spring Is Here (1929)

YOURS, YOURS, YOURS
Sherman Edwards
1776 (1969)

YOUTH OF THE HEART, THE
Donald Swann
Sydney Carter
At the Drop of a Hat (1959)

YOU'VE BROKEN A FINE WOMAN'S HEART
Stan Freeman and Franklin Underwood
Lovely Ladies, Kind Gentlemen (1970)

YOU'VE COME HOME
Cy Coleman
Carolyn Leigh
Wildcat (1960)

YOU'VE GOT A HOLD ON ME
Frederick Loewe
Alan Jay Lerner
What's Up? (1943)

YOU'VE GOT A LEASE ON MY HEART
Sammy Fain
Irving Kahal
Everybody's Welcome (1931)

YOU'VE GOT A WAY WITH YOU
Richard Myers
Leo Robin
Hello, Yourself! (1928)

YOU'VE GOT IT ALL
Ann Ronell
Count Me In (1942)

YOU'VE GOT ME UP A TREE
Alberta Nichols
Mann Holiner
Angela (1928)

YOU'VE GOT POSSIBILITIES
Charles Strouse
Lee Adams
(It's a Bird, It's a Plane) It's Superman (1966)

YOU'VE GOT SOMETHING
Cole Porter
Red, Hot and Blue! (1936)

---

*Dropped from New York production

You've Got Something to Say
Leon Pober
Bud Freeman
Beg, Borrow or Steal (1960)

You've Got Something to Sing About
Al Moss
Alfred Hayes
Tis of Thee (1940)

You've Got that Kind of a Face
George Lessner
Miriam Battista and Russell Maloney
Sleepy Hollow (1948)

You've Got That Thing
Cole Porter
Fifty Million Frenchmen (1929)

You've Got the Devil in Your Bones
William Klenosky
Utopia! (OB) (1963)

You've Got to Appease with a Strip Tease
Toby Sacher
Lewis Allen
Of V We Sing (1942)

You've Got to Be a Lady
Steve Allen
Sophie (1963)

You've Got to Be a Little Crazy
Sigmund Romberg (developed by Don Walker)
Leo Robin
The Girl in Pink Tights (1954)

You've Got to Dance
Elsie Janis
Puzzles of 1925 (1925)

You've Got to Have Heart
Richard Adler and Jerry Ross
Damn Yankees (1955)

You've Got to Have Koo Wah
Eubie Blake
Noble Sissle
Shuffle Along (1933)

You've Got to Know Just How to Make Love
Alma Sanders
Monte Carlo
The Houseboat on the Styx (1928)

You've Got to Pick a Pocket or Two
Lionel Bart
Oliver! (1963)

You've Got to Sell Yourself
Henry Sullivan
Edward Eliscu
A Little Racketeer (1932)

You've Got to Surrender
Richard Rodgers
Lorenz Hart
Heads Up! (1929)

You've Got What Gets Me
George Gershwin
Ira Gershwin
Girl Crazy (F) (1932)

You've Got What I Need
Charles Strouse
Lee Adams
(It's a Bird, It's a Plane) It's Superman (1966)

You've Made Me Happy Today
Niclas Kempner
Graham John
The Street Singer (1929)

You've Never Been Loved
Sammy Stept
Dan Shapiro
Michael Todd's Peep Show (1950)

You've Stolen My Heart
John Mundy
Edward Eager
The Liar (1950)

Yucatana
Maria Grever
Raymond Leveen
Viva O'Brien (1941)

YULETIDE, PARK AVENUE
Harold Rome
Call Me Mister (1946)

YUM TICKY-TICKY
Bob Merrill
Carnival (1961)

YVONNE
Clarence Gaskill
Earl Carroll's Vanities (1925)

ZEBEKIKO
Manos Hadjidakis
Joe Darion
Illya Darling (1967)

ZEN IS WHEN
Leon Pober
Bud Freeman
Beg, Borrow or Steal (1960)

ZIGEUNER
Noël Coward
Bitter Sweet (1929)

ZIM ZAM ZEE
Richard Lewine
Ted Fetter
Naughty-Naught (OB) (1937)

ZING, WENT THE STRINGS OF MY HEART
James F. Hanley
Thumbs Up! (1934)

ZIP
Lucien Denni
Helena Evans
Happy Go Lucky (1926)

ZIP
Richard Rodgers
Lorenz Hart
Pal Joey (1940)

ZITA
Ben Schwartz
Tales of Rigo (1927)

ZULU LOVE SONG
Harold Rome
The Zulu and the Zayda (1965)

Productions

Productions

A LA CARTE
August 17, 1927 (46 perfs.)
Music and lyrics by Herman Hupfeld
  Hors d'Oeuvres
  Give Trouble the Air (Music by
    Louis Alter; lyrics by Leo Robin)
  Palm Beach Baby
  Baby's Blue
  Never Again (Music and lyrics by
    Norman Gregg)
  Kangaroo (Music by James P. John-
    son; lyrics by Henry Creamer)
  Sort o' Lonesome
  The Calinda

AFRICANA
July 11, 1927 (72 perfs)
Music and lyrics by Donald Heywood
  Weary Feet
  The Old-Fashioned Cakewalk
  Time Ain't Very Long
  Smile
  Clorinda
  The Africana Stomp
  I'm Comin', Virginia (Lyrics by Will
    Marion Cook and Donald Hey-
    wood)

AIN'T SUPPOSED TO DIE A NATURAL DEATH
October 20, 1971 (325 perfs)
Music and lyrics by Melvin Van Pee-
bles
  Just Don't Make No Sense
  Coolest Place in Town
  You Can't Get Up Before Noon
    without Being a Square
  Mirror, Mirror on the Wall
  Come Raising Your Leg on Me
  You Gotta Be Holdin' Out Five Dol-
    lars on Me
  Sera Sera Jim
  Catch That on the Corner
  The Dozens
  Funky Girl on Motherless Broad-
    way
  Tenth and Greenwich
  Heh Heh Good Mornin' Sunshine
  You Ain't No Astronaut
  Three Boxes of Longs, Please
  Lily Has Done the Zampoughi Ev-
    ery Time I Pulled Her Coattail
  I Got the Blood
  Salamaggis Birthday
  Come on Feet, Do Your Thing
  Put a Curse on You
Cast album: A & M

ALIVE AND KICKING
January 17, 1950 (46 perfs)
  Alive and Kicking (Music by Hal
    Borne; lyrics by Ray Golden and
    Sid Kuller)
  Pals of the Pentagon (Music and lyr-
    ics by Harold Rome)
  What a Delightful (Music by Sammy
    Fain; lyrics by Paul Francis Web-
    ster and Ray Golden)
  Abou Ben Adhem (Music and lyrics
    by Ray Golden)
  Cry, Baby, Cry (Music and lyrics by
    Harold Rome)
  One Word Led to Another (Music
    by Hal Borne; lyrics by Ray
    Golden)
  Love, It Hurts So Good (Music and
    lyrics by Harold Rome)
  There's a Building Going Up (Music

by Sammy Fain; lyrics by Paul Francis Webster and Ray Golden)
Propinquity (Music by Sonny Burke; lyrics by Paul Francis Webster and Ray Golden)
I'm All Yours (Music by Leo Schumer; lyrics by Mike Stuart)
One! Two! Three! (Music by Sonny Burke; lyrics by Paul Francis Webster and Ray Golden)
French with Tears (Music and lyrics by Harold Rome)

ALL AMERICAN
March 19, 1962 (80 perfs)
Music by Charles Strouse
Lyrics by Lee Adams
  Melt Us!
  What a Country!
  Our Children
  Animal Attraction
  We Speak the Same Language
  I Can Teach Them
  It's Fun to Think
  Once Upon a Time
  Nightlife
  I've Just Seen Her
  Physical Fitness
  The Fight Song
  I Couldn't Have Done It Alone
  If I Were You
  Have a Dream
  I'm Fascinating
  The Real Me
  Which Way?
  It's Up to Me
Cast album: Columbia
Vocal selection

ALL FOR LOVE
January 22, 1949 (121 perfs)
Music by Allan Roberts
Lyrics by Lester Lee
  All for Love
  My Baby's Bored
  The Big Four (Music and lyrics by Peter Howard Weiss)
  Why Can't It Happen Again? (Music by Michel Emer; lyrics by Sammy Gallup)
  My Heart's in the Middle of July
  It's a Living

Run to Me, My Love
No Time for Nothin' but Love
Dreamer with a Penny
The Farrell Girl
Oh, How Unfortunate You Mortals Be

ALL IN FUN
December 27, 1940 (3 perfs)
Music by Baldwin Bergersen
  It's All in Fun (Lyrics by S. K. Russel)
  Where Can I Go from You? (Lyrics by Virginia Faulkner)
  Love and I (Lyrics by Irvin Graham and June Sillman)
  April in Harrisburg (Lyrics by Virginia Faulkner)
  That Man and Woman Thing (Lyrics by John Rox)
  It's a Big, Wide, Wonderful World (Music and lyrics by John Rox)
  How Did It Get So Late So Early? (Music by Will Irwin; lyrics by June Sillman)
  Where's the Boy I Saved for a Rainy Day? (Lyrics by John Rox)
  My Memories Started with You (Lyrics by June Sillman)
  Macumba (Lyrics by June Sillman)
  Quittin' Time (Music and lyrics by John Rox)

ALL IN LOVE* (OB)
November 10, 1961 (141 perfs)
Music by Jacques Urbont
Lyrics by Bruce Geller
  To Bath Derry-O
  Poor
  What Can It Be?
  Odds
  I Love a Fool
  A More Than Ordinary Glorious Vocabulary
  Women Simple
  The Lady Was Made to Be Loved
  The Good Old Ways
  Honour
  I Found Him

———

*Based on Sheridan's *The Rivals*

Day Dreams
Don't Ask Me
Why Wives
Quickly
All in Love
Cast album: Mercury

ALL KINDS OF GIANTS (OB)
December 18, 1961 (16 perfs)
Music by Sam Pottle
Lyrics by Tom Whedon
State of the Kingdom
My Prince
Paint Me a Rainbow
Logic!
If I Were Only Someone
To Be a King
Suddenly Stop and Think
My Star
All Kinds of Giants
Friends
Here We Are
Be Yourself

ALL THE KING'S HORSES
January 30, 1934 (120 perfs)
Music by Edward A. Horan
Lyrics by Frederick Herendeen
Fame Is a Phoney
Tamboree
The Hair of the Heir
You're Asking Me
Evening Star
I Found a Song
Langenstein in Spring
Charming
I've Gone Nuts Over You
Mamazelle Papazelle
Romance Is Calling

ALLAH BE PRAISED
April 20, 1944 (20 perfs)
Music by Don Walker and Baldwin
Bergersen
Lyrics by George Marion, Jr.
The Persian Way of Life (Music by
Don Walker)
Allah Be Praised (Music by Don
Walker)
What's New in New York (Music by
Baldwin Bergersen)
Leaf in the Wind (Music by Baldwin
Bergersen)

Katinka to Eva to Frances (Music by
Don Walker)
Let's Go Too Far (Music by Don
Walker)
Getting Oriental Over You (Music
by Don Walker)
Secret Song (Music by Baldwin
Bergersen)
Sunrise on Sunset (Music by Bald-
win Bergersen)

ALLEGRO
October 10, 1947 (315 perfs)
Music by Richard Rodgers
Lyrics by Oscar Hammerstein II
Joseph Taylor, Jr.
I Know It Can Happen Again
One Foot, Other Foot
Poor Joe
A Fellow Needs a Girl
A Darn Nice Campus
Wildcats
So Far
You Are Never Away
What a Lovely Day for a Wedding
It May be a Good Idea
To Have and to Hold
Wish Them Well
Money Isn't Ev'rything
Yatata, Yatata, Yatata
The Gentleman is a Dope
Allegro
Come Home
Cast Album: RCA
Vocal score

ALLEZ-OOP
August 2, 1927 (120 perfs)
Music by Philip Charig and Richard
Myers
Lyrics by Leo Robin
What Does It Mean?
Hoof, Hoof
Where Have You Been All My
Life?
A Kiss with a Kick
Pull Yourself Together
Doin' the Gorilla
Star of Stars
Blow Hot and Heavy
In the Heart of Spain
What Did William Tell?

ALONG FIFTH AVENUE
January 13, 1949 (180 perfs)

Fifth Avenue (Music by Gordon Jenkins; lyrics by Tom Adair)

The Best Time of Day (Music by Gordon Jenkins; lyrics by Tom Adair)

If This Is Glamour! (Music by Richard Stutz; lyrics by Rick French)

Skyscraper Blues (Music by Gordon Jenkins; lyrics by Tom Adair)

I Love Love in New York (Music by Gordon Jenkins; lyrics by Tom Adair)

The Fugitive from Fifth Avenue (Music by Richard Stutz; lyrics by Nat Hiken)

Santo Dinero (Music by Richard Stutz; lyrics by Milton Pascal)

In the Lobby (Music by Gordon Jenkins; lyrics by Tom Adair)

Weep No More (Music by Gordon Jenkins; lyrics by Tom Adair)

Chant d'Amour (Music by Gordon Jenkins; lyrics by Nat Hiken)

Vacation in the Store (Music by Gordon Jenkins; lyrics by Tom Adair)

Call It Applefritters (Music by Richard Stutz; lyrics by Milton Pascal)

A Trip Doesn't Care at All (Music by Philip Kadison; lyrics by Thomas Howell)

AMERICANA (1926)
July 26, 1926 (224 perfs)

American Revue Girls (Music by Con Conrad; Lyrics by J. P. McEvoy)

Sunny Disposish (Music by Philip Charig; lyrics by Ira Gershwin)

Kosher Kleagle (Music by Philip Charig; lyrics by J. P. McEvoy)

That Lost Barbershop Chord (Music by George Gershwin; lyrics by Ira Gershwin)

Blowin' the Blues Away (Music by Philip Charig; lyrics by Ira Gershwin)

Dreaming (Music by Con Conrad and Henry Souvaine; lyrics by J. P. McEvoy)

Riverside Bus (Music by Con Conrad; lyrics by J. P. McEvoy)

Tabloid Papers (Music by Con Conrad; lyrics by J. P. McEvoy)

Why Do Ya Roll Those Eyes? (Music by Philip Charig; lyrics by Morrie Ryskind)

Swanee River Melody (Music by Charles Weinberg; lyrics by Al Wilson)

AMERICANA (1928)
October 30, 1928 (12 perfs)
Music by Roger Wolfe Kahn
Lyrics by Irving Caesar

Life As a Twosome* (Music by Joseph Meyer and Roger Wolfe Kahn)

Jazz City (Music by Henry Souvaine; lyrics by J. P. McEvoy)

The Ameri-can-can

No Place Like Home

Young Black Joe

Hot Pants

AMERICANA (1932)
October 5, 1932 (76 perfs)

Would'ja for a Big Red Apple (Music by Henry Souvaine; lyrics by Everett Miller and Johnny Mercer)

Whistling for a Kiss (Music by Richard Myers; lyrics by E. Y. Harburg and Johnny Mercer)

Satan's Li'l Lamb (Music by Harold Arlen; lyrics by E. Y. Harburg and Johnny Mercer)

You're Not Pretty but You're Mine (Music by Burton Lane; lyrics by E. Y. Harburg)

Brother, Can You Spare a Dime? (Music by Jay Gorney; lyrics by E. Y. Harburg)

Let Me Match My Private Life with Yours (Music by Vernon Duke; lyrics by E. Y. Harburg)

Five Minutes of Spring (Music by Jay Gorney; lyrics by E. Y. Harburg)

Get That Sun into You (Music by Richard Myers; lyrics by E. Y. Harburg)

---

*Also in *Here's Howe* (1928)

AMERICA'S SWEETHEART
February 10, 1931 (135 perfs)
Music by Richard Rodgers
Lyrics by Lorenz Hart
  Mr. Dolan Is Passing Through
  In Californ-i-a
  My Sweet
  I've Got Five Dollars
  Sweet Geraldine
  There's So Much More
  We'll Be the Same
  How About It?
  Innocent Chorus Girls of Yesterday
  A Lady Must Live
  You Ain't Got No Savoir Faire
  Two Unfortunate Orphans
  I Want a Man
  Tennessee Dan

AMOROUS FLEA, THE* (OB)
February 17, 1964 (93 perfs)
Music and lyrics by Bruce Montgomery
  All about Me
  Learning Love
  There Goes a Mad Old Man
  Dialogue on Dalliance
  March of the Vigilant Vassals
  Lessons on Life
  Man Is a Man's Best Friend
  The Other Side of the Wall
  Closeness Begets Closeness
  It's a Stretchy Day
  When Time Takes Your Hand
  The Amorous Flea

ANGEL IN THE WINGS
December 11, 1947 (308 perfs)
Music by Carl Sigman
Lyrics by Bob Hilliard
  Long Green Blues
  Holler Blue Murder
  Breezy
  Civilization
  Tambourine
  If It Were Easy to Do
  Thousand Islands Song
  The Big Brass Band from Brazil

ANGELA
December 3, 1928 (40 perfs)
Music by Alberta Nichols

Lyrics by Mann Holiner
  The Weaker Sex
  Love Is Like That
  Don't Forget Your Etiquette
  The Baron, the Duchess, and the Count
  The Regal Romp
  Tally-Ho
  I Can't Believe It's True
  Bundle of Love
  Maybe So
  You've Got Me Up a Tree
  Bearing Silver Platters
  Oui, Oui

ANIMAL CRACKERS
October 23, 1928 (191 perfs)
Music by Harry Ruby
Lyrics by Bert Kalmar
  News
  Hooray for Captain Spalding!
  Who's Been Listening to My Heart?
  The Long Island Low Down
  Go Places and Do Things
  Watching the Clouds Roll By
  When Things Are Bright and Rosy
  Cool Off
  Musketeers

ANKLES AWEIGH
April 18, 1955 (176 perfs)
Music by Sammy Fain
Lyrics by Dan Shapiro
  Italy
  Old Fashioned Mothers
  Skip the Build-Up
  Nothing At All
  Walk Like a Sailor
  Headin' for the Bottom
  Nothing Can Replace a Man
  Here's to Dear Old Us
  His and Hers
  La Fiesta
  Ready Cash
  Kiss Me and Kill Me with Love
  Honeymoon
  The Villain Always Gets It
  The Code
  Eleven O'Clock Song
Cast Album: Decca

---

*Based on Molière's The School for Wives

ANNE OF GREEN GABLES *(OB)
December 21, 1971 (16 perfs)
Music by Norman Campbell
Lyrics by Donald Campbell and Norman Campbell
Great Workers for the Cause
Where Is Matthew Going?
Gee, I'm Glad I'm No One Else but Me
We Clearly Requested
The Facts
Where'd Marilla Come From?
Humble Pie
Oh, Mrs. Lynde
Avonlea, We Love Thee
Wondrin'
Did You Hear?
Ice Cream
The Picnic
Where Did the Summer Go To?
Kindred Spirits
Open the Window
The Words
I'll Show Him
General Store
Pageant Song
If It Hadn't Been For Me
Anne of Green Gables

ANNIE GET YOUR GUN
May 16, 1946 (1,147 perfs)
Music and lyrics by Irving Berlin
Buffalo Bill
I'm a Bad, Bad Man
Doin' What Comes Naturally
The Girl That I Marry
You Can't Get a Man with a Gun
Show Business
They Say It's Wonderful
Moonshine Lullaby
I'll Share It All with You
My Defenses Are Down
I'm an Indian Too
I Got Lost in His Arms
Who Do You Love, I Hope
I Got the Sun in the Morning
Anything You Can Do
Take It in Your Stride†
An Old-fashioned Wedding**
Cast Album: Decca
Vocal score

ANYA††
November 29, 1965 (16 performances)
Music and lyrics by Robert Wright and George Forrest (based on Rachmaninoff)
Anya
A Song from Somewhere
Vodka, Vodka!
So Proud
Homeward
Snowflakes and Sweethearts
On That Day
Six Palaces
Hand in Hand
This Is My Kind of Love
That Prelude!
A Quiet Land
Here Tonight, Tomorrow Where?
Leben Sie Wohl
If This Is Goodbye
Little Hands
All Hail the Empress
Cast album: United Artists

ANYONE CAN WHISTLE
April 4, 1964 (9 perfs)
Music and lyrics by Stephen Sondheim
I'm Like the Bluebird
Me and My Town
Miracle Song
Simple
A-1 March
Come Play wiz Me
Anyone Can Whistle
A Parade in Town
Everybody Says Don't
I've Got You to Lean On
See What It Gets You
With So Little to Be Sure Of
Cast Album: Columbia
Vocal score

---

*Based on novel by L. M. Montgomery
†Dropped from New York production
**Added to 1966 revival
††Based on *Anastasia*, by Marcelle Maurette and Guy Bolton

ANYTHING GOES
November 21, 1934 (420 perfs)
Music and lyrics by Cole Porter
  I Get a Kick Out of You
  Bon Voyage
  All through the Night
  There'll Always Be a Lady Fair
  Where Are the Men?
  You're the Top
  Anything Goes
  Public Enemy Number One
  Blow, Gabriel, Blow
  Be Like the Bluebird
  Buddy, Beware
  The Gypsy in Me
  Waltz down the Aisle*
Album: (1962 Off-Broadway cast) Epic
Vocal Score

APPLAUSE†
March 30, 1970 (896 perfs)
Music by Charles Strouse
Lyrics by Lee Adams
  Backstage Babble
  Think How It's Gonna Be
  But Alive
  The Best Night of My Life
  Who's That Girl?
  Applause
  Hurry Back
  Fasten Your Seat Belts
  Welcome to the Theater
  Inner Thoughts
  Good Friends
  She's No Longer a Gypsy
  One of a Kind
  One Hallowe'en
  Something Greater
Cast album: ABC-Paramount
Vocal score
Vocal selection

APPLE TREE, THE
October 18, 1966 (463 perfs)
Music by Jerry Bock
Lyrics by Sheldon Harnick
Part I—The Diary of Adam and Eve**
  Here in Eden
  Feelings
  Eve
  Friends

  The Apple Tree (Forbidden Fruit)
  Beautiful, Beautiful World
  It's a Fish
  Go to Sleep Whatever You Are
  What Makes Me Love Him
Part II—The Lady or the Tiger††
  I'll Tell You a Truth
  Make Way
  Forbidden Love (in Gaul)
  I've Got What You Want
  Tiger, Tiger
  Which Door
Part III—Passionella***
  Oh, to Be a Movie Star
  Gorgeous
  (Who, Who, Who, Who) Who Is She?
  Wealth
  You Are Not Real
  George L.
Cast album: Columbia
Vocal score
Vocal selection

ARE YOU WITH IT?
November 10, 1945 (264 perfs)
Music by Harry Revel
Lyrics by Arnold B. Horwitt
  Five More Minutes in Bed
  Nutmeg Insurance
  Slightly Perfect
  When a Good Man Takes to Drink
  Poor Little Me
  Are You With It?
  This Is My Beloved
  Send Us Back to the Kitchen
  Here I Go Again
  You Gotta Keep Saying "No"
  Just Beyond the Rainbow
  In Our Cozy Little Cottage of To-morrow

---

*Dropped from New York production
†Based on the film *All About Eve* and the original story by Mary Orr
**Based on *The Diary of Adam and Eve* by Mark Twain
††Based on *The Lady or the Tiger* by Frank Stockton
***Based on *Passionella* by Jules Feiffer

ARI*
January 15, 1971 (19 perfs)
Music by Walt Smith
Lyrics by Leon Uris
  Children's Lament
  Yerushaliam
  The Saga of the Haganah
  Give Me One Good Reason
  Dov's Nightmare
  Karen's Lullaby
  Aphrodite
  My Galilee
  The Lord Helps Those Who Help
    Themselves
  The Alphabet Song
  My Brother's Keeper
  The Exodus
  He'll Never Be Mine
  One Flag
  I See What I Choose to See
  Ari's Promise

ARMS AND THE GIRL†
February 2, 1950 (134 perfs)
Music by Morton Gould
Lyrics by Dorothy Fields
  A Girl with a Flame
  That's What I Told Him Last Night
  I Like It Here
  That's My Fella
  A Cow and a Plough and a Frau
  Nothin' for Nothin'
  He Will Tonight
  Plantation in Philadelphia
  You Kissed Me
  Don't Talk
  I'll Never Learn
  There Must Be Somethin' Better
    than Love
  She's Exciting
  Mister Washington! Uncle George
Cast album: Decca

AROUND THE WORLD**
May 31, 1946 (74 perfs)
Music and lyrics by Cole Porter
  Look What I Found
  There He Goes, Mr. Phileas Fogg
  Meerahlah
  Sea Chantey
  Should I Tell You I Love You?
  Pipe Dreaming
  If You Smile at Me
  Wherever They Fly the Flag of Old
    England
  The Marine's Hymn

ARTISTS AND MODELS (1925)
June 24, 1925 (411 perfs)
Music by Alfred Goodman, Maury Rubens, and J. Fred Coots
Lyrics by Clifford Grey
  The Maid of the Milky Way
  Let Me Dance
  Cellini's Dream
  Take a Little Baby Home with You
  Mothers of the World
  Follow Your Star
  The Magic Garden of Love
  The Rotisserie
  The Promenade Walk at the Beach
  Oriental Memories
  Lucita
  Flexatone

ARTISTS AND MODELS (1927)
November 15, 1927 (151 perfs)
  Here Am I—Broken Hearted (Music by Ray Henderson; lyrics by B. G. DeSylva and Lew Brown)
  Oh, Peggy (Music by Harry Akst; lyrics by Benny Davis)
  The Only One for Me (Music by Harry Akst; lyrics by Benny Davis)
  Is Everybody Happy Now? (Music by Maury Rubens; lyrics by Jack Osterman and Ted Lewis)
  The Call of Broadway (Music by Maury Rubens; lyrics by Jack Osterman and Ted Lewis)
  The Lobster Crawl (Music by Harry Akst; lyrics by Benny Davis)
  There's Nothing New in Old New York (Music by Harry Akst; lyrics by Benny Davis)
  Snap Out of It (Music by Harry Akst; lyrics by Benny Davis)

---

*Based on the novel *Exodus* by Leon Uris
†Based on play, *The Pursuit of Happiness* by Lawrence Langner and Armina Marshall
**Based on the novel by Jules Verne

ARTISTS AND MODELS (1930)
June 10, 1930 (55 perfs)
My Real Ideal (Music by Burton Lane; lyrics by Samuel Lerner)
Without a Shadow of a Doubt (Music and lyrics by Ord Hamilton)
Who Cares? (Music by Haydn Wood, Joseph Tunbridge, and Jack Waller; lyrics by Dion Titheradge)
Two Perfect Lovers (Music by Burton Lane; lyrics by Samuel Lerner)

ARTISTS AND MODELS (1943)
November 5, 1942 (27 perfs)
Music by Philip Charig
Lyrics by Dan Shapiro and Milton Pascal
Way Up North in Dixie
Swing Low, Sweet Harriet
You'll Know That It's Me
How'ja Like to Take Me Home
My Heart Is on a Binge
You Are Romance
Blowing the Top

AS THE GIRLS GO
November 13, 1948 (420 perfs)
Music by Jimmy McHugh
Lyrics by Harold Adamson
As the Girls Go
Nobody's Heart but Mine
Brighten Up and Be a Little Sunbeam
Rock, Rock, Rock
It's More Fun Than a Picnic
American Cannes
You Say the Nicest Things, Baby
I've Got the President's Ear
Holiday in the Country
There's No Getting Away from You
I Got Lucky in the Rain
Father's Day
It Takes a Woman to Take a Man

AS THOUSANDS CHEER
September 30, 1933 (400 perfs)
Music and lyrics by Irving Berlin
How's Chances?
Heat Wave
Majestic Sails at Midnight
Lonely Heart
The Funnies
To Be or Not to Be
Easter Parade
Supper Time
Our Wedding Day
I've Got Harlem on My Mind
Not for All the Rice in China

AT HOME ABROAD
September 19, 1935 (198 perfs)
Music by Arthur Schwartz
Lyrics by Howard Dietz
Get Away from It All
That's Not Cricket
Hottentot Potentate
Farewell, My Lovely
The Lady with the Tap
Thief in the Night
O Leo
Love Is a Dancing Thing
What a Wonderful World
The Steamboat Whistle
Get Yourself a Geisha
Got a Bran' New Suit

AT THE DROP OF A HAT
October 8, 1959 (215 perfs)
Music by Donald Swann
Lyrics by Michael Flanders
A Transport of Delight
Song of Reproduction
The Hog Beneath the Skin
The Youth of the Heart (Lyrics by Sydney Carter)
The Wompom
Sea Fever
A Gnu
Judgement of Paris
Philological Waltz
Satellite Moon
A Happy Song
A Song of the Weather
The Reluctant Cannibal
In the Bath
Design for Living
Tried by the Centre Court
Misalliance
Kokoraki
Madeira, M'Dear?
The Hippopotamus
Cast album: Angel

AT THE DROP OF ANOTHER HAT
December 27, 1966 (105 perfs)
Music by Donald Swann
Lyrics by Michael Flanders
  The Gas Man Cometh
  From Our Bestiary
  P** P* B**** B** D******
  Bilbo's Song
  Slow Train
  Thermodynamic Duo
  Sloth
  In the Desert
  Los Olivados
  Motor Perpetuo
  A Song of Patriotic Prejudice
  All Gall
  Horoscope
  Armadillo Idyll
  Twenty Tons of T.N.T.
  Ill Wind
  Food for Thought
  Prehistoric Complaint
  Twice Shy
Cast album: Angel

ATHENIAN TOUCH, THE (OB)
January 14, 1964 (1 perf)
Music by Willard Straight
Lyrics by David Eddy
  There Goes Time
  Today's the Day
  No Garlic Tonight
  Have a Little Sooth on Me
  Harmony, Sweet Harmony
  The Singer and the Song
  When You Write a Greek Comedy
  What Is a Woman
  Eleleu!
  Look Away
  Love, You Are So Difficult
  A Lady of Leisure
  An Awkward Little Boy
  An Agent's Blood
  Lysistrata
  All We Need to Know
Cast album: Broadway East

AUTUMN'S HERE* (OB)
October 25, 1966 (80 perfs)
Music and lyrics by Norman Dean
  Sleepy Hollow

  Boy, Do I Hate Horse Races
  Me and My Horse
  Autumn's Here
  Song of the Thirteen Colonies
  Patience
  For the Harvest Safely Gathered
  Who Walks Like a Scarecrow
  This Is the Girl for Me
  Do You Think I'm Pretty?
  Fine Words and Fancy Phrases
  Private Hunting Ground
  It's a Long Road Home
  Brom and Katrina
  Dark New England Night
  Dutch Country Table
  You Never Miss the Water
  Any Day Now
  You May Be the Someone
  Beware As You Ride through the
    Hollow

BABES IN ARMS
April 14, 1937 (289 perfs)
Music by Richard Rodgers
Lyrics by Lorenz Hart
  Where or When
  Babes in Arms
  I Wish I Were in Love Again
  All Dark People
  Way Out West
  My Funny Valentine
  Johnny One Note
  Imagine
  All at Once
  The Lady Is a Tramp
  You Are So Fair
Album: (Studio cast) Columbia
Vocal score

BABES IN THE WOOD† (OB)
December 28, 1964 (45 perfs)
Music and lyrics by Rick Besoyan

---

*Based on Washington Irving's *Legend of Sleepy Hollow.*
†Adapted from Shakespeare's *A Midsummer Night's Dream*

This State of Affairs
Titania's Philosophy
A Lover Waits
The Gossip Song
I'm Not for You
Mother
Old Fashioned Girl
Love Is Lovely
Babes in the Wood
Anyone Can Make a Mistake
Cavorting
There's a Girl
Little Tear
Helena's Solution
Helena
Midsummer Night
Moon Madness
The Alphabet Song

BAD HABITS OF 1926 (OB)
April 30, 1926 (19 perfs)
Music by Manning Sherwin
Lyrics by Arthur Herzog, Jr.
Are We Downhearted?
When
Gone Away Blues
Station L-O-V-E
Would-ja?
Cinderella of Our Block
Funeral of Charleston
Manhattan Transfer
Chorus Girl Blues
Geisha Girl
Let Me Be Myself
The Student Robin Hood of Pilsen
(Music by Randall Thompson; lyrics by Perry Ivins)
Keep Your Shirt On
The Lifeguards

BAJOUR*
November 23, 1964 (218 perfs)
Music and lyrics by Walter Marks
Move Over, New York
Where Is the Tribe for Me?
Love-Line
Words, Words, Words
Mean
Must It Be Love?
Bajour
Soon
I Can

Living Simply
Honest Man
Guarantees
Love Is a Chance
The Sew-Up
Cast album: Columbia
Vocal selection

BAKER STREET†
February 16, 1965 (313 perfs)
Music and lyrics by Marian Grudeff
and Raymond Jessel
It's So Simple
I'm in London Again
Leave It to Us, Gov
Letters
Cold Clear World
Finding Words for Spring
What a Night This Is Going to Be
London Underworld
I Shall Miss You
Roof Space
A Married Man
I'd Do It Again
Pursuit
Jewelry
Cast album: MGM

BALLAD FOR A FIRING SQUAD (OB)
December 11, 1968 (7 perfs)
Music by Edward Thomas
Lyrics by Martin Charnin
Ballad for a Firing Squad
Is This a Fact?
There Is Only One Thing to Be Sure Of
How Young You Were Tonight
I'm Saving Myself for a Soldier
Everyone Has Something to Hide
Fritzie
The Choice Is Yours
Maman
Not Now, Not Here
I Did Not Sleep Last Night
Hello Yank
I Don't See Him Very Much Anymore

---

*Based on stories by Joseph Mitchell
†Adapted from stories by Sir Arthur Conan Doyle

What Then?
What Might Have Been

BALLAD FOR BIMSHIRE (OB)
October 15, 1963 (74 perfs)
Music and lyrics by Irving Burgie
  Ballad for Bimshire
  Street Cries
  Fore Day Noon in the Mornin'
  Lately I've Been Feeling So Strange
  Deep in My Heart
  Have You Got Charm?
  Hail Britannia
  Welcome Song
  Belle Plain
  I'm a Dandy
  Silver Earring
  My Love Will Come By
  Chicken's a Popular Bird
  Pardon Me, Sir
  Yesterday Was Such a Lovely
    Day
  The Master Plan
  Chant
  Vendor's Song
  We Gon' Jump Up
Cast album: London

BALLAD OF JOHNNY POT, THE (OB)
April 26, 1971 (16 perfs)
Music by Clinton Ballard
Lyrics by Carolyn Richter
  The Ballad of Johnny Pot
  Johnny's Creed
  Hard Hat Stetsons
  The Letter
  Discarded Blues
  Whaddaya Say, Kid
  Crazy
  Head Down the Road
  A Carol
  Lonely Is the Life
  What About Me
  Have Some Pot
  Scared
  How Wonderful It Is
  Like It
  Dance of Distraction
  Saskatchewan
  Little Sparrows
  Find My Way Alone

BALLET BALLADS
May 18, 1948 (69 perfs)
Music by Jerome Moross
Lyrics by John Latouche
  Ridin' on the Breeze
  I've Got Me
  My Yellow Flower

BALLYHOO (1930)
December 22, 1930 (68 perfs)
Music by Louis Alter
Lyrics by Harry Ruskin and Leighton
K. Brill
  How I Could Go for You
  That Tired Feeling
  No Wonder I'm Blue (Lyrics by Os-
    car Hammerstein II)
  Throw It Out the Window
  Blow Hot—Blow Cold
  If I Were You
  I'm One of God's Children (Lyrics
    by Oscar Hammerstein II and
    Harry Ruskin)
  Good Girls Love Bad Men

BALLYHOO (1932)
September 6, 1932 (94 perfs)
Music by Lewis E. Gensler
Lyrics by E. Y. Harburg
  Falling Off the Wagon
  Thrill Me
  Old-Fashioned Wedding
  How Do You Do It?
  Man About Yonkers
  Ballyhujah
  Love, Nuts and Noodles
  Riddle Me This
  What Have You Got to Have?

BAMBOOLA
June 26, 1929 (27 perfs)
Music and lyrics by Frank Marcus and
Bernard Maltin
  Evenin'
  Ace of Spades
  Dixie Vagabond
  Rub-a-Dub Your Rabbit's Foot
  Bamboola
  Somebody Like Me
  Tailor Made Babies
  African Whoopee
  Tampico Tune

Song of Harlem
Shoutin' Sinners
Anna
Hot Patootie Wedding Night

BAND WAGON, THE
June 3, 1931 (260 perfs)
Music by Arthur Schwartz
Lyrics by Howard Dietz
  It Better Be Good
  Sweet Music
  High and Low
  Hoops
  Confession
  New Sun in the Sky
  Miserable with You
  I Love Louisa
  Dancing in the Dark
  Where Can He Be?
  White Heat
  The Beggar Waltz
Album: (Studio cast) Columbia
Added to film version: (1953)
  That's Entertainment
Cast album: MGM

BANJO EYES*
December 25, 1941 (126 perfs)
Music by Vernon Duke
Lyrics by John Latouche
  The Greeting Cards
  I'll Take the City
  The Toast of the Boys at the Post
  I've Got to Hand It to You
  A Nickel to My Name
  Who Started the Rhumba?
  It Could Only Happen in the Movies (Lyrics by Harold Adamson)
  Make with the Feet (Lyrics by Harold Adamson)
  We're Having a Baby (Lyrics by Harold Adamson)
  Banjo Eyes
  We Did It Before (Music and lyrics by Charlie Tobias and Cliff Friend)
  Not a Care in the World†

BANKER'S DAUGHTER, THE** (OB)**
January 22, 1962 (68 perfs)
Music by Sol Kaplan
Lyrics by Edward Eliscu

One More Day
Gentlemens' Understanding
Such a Beautiful World
Genteel
In a Brownstone Mansion
Both Ends Against the Middle
The Sun Rises
Father's Daughter
Say No More
More Than One More Day
Nero, Caesar, Napoleon
Head in the Stars
Sleep, O Sleep
Unexpectedly
A Carriage for Alida
It's So Heart-warming

BARE FACTS OF 1926
July 16, 1926 (107 perfs)
Music by Charles M. Schwab
Lyrics by Henry Myers
  Won't You Tell Me
  Stand Up on Your Feet and Dance
  Treat 'Em Rough
  The Third from the End
  Cradle Song
  Nice Girl
  Tea Time

BAREFOOT BOY WITH CHEEK††
April 3, 1947 (108 perfs)
Music by Sidney Lippman
Lyrics by Sylvia Dee
  A Toast to Alpha Cholera
  We Feel Our Man Is Definitely You
  The Legendary Eino Fflliikkiin-nenn
  Too Nice a Day to Go to School
  I Knew I'd Know
  I'll Turn a Little Cog
  Who Do You Think You Are?
  Everything Leads Right Back to Love

---

*Based on the play *Three Men on a Horse* by John Cecil Holm and George Abbott
†Also in Off-broadway revival of *Cabin in the Sky* (1964)
**Based on Boucicault's *Streets of New York*
††Based on the Max Shulman novel

Little Yetta's Gonna Get a Man
Alice in Boogieland
After Graduation
There's a Lot of Things You Can Do
  with Two (But Not with Three)
The Story of a Carrot
Star of the North State
It Couldn't Be Done (But We Did It)

BEAST IN ME, THE*
May 16, 1963 (4 perfs)
Music by Don Elliott
Lyrics by James Costigan
  Percussion
  So Beautiful
  You're Delicious
  I Owe Ohio
  Go, Go, Go
  Eat Your Breakfast
  Eat Your Nice Lily, Unicorn
  Bacchanale
  Calypso Kitty
  Glorious Cheese
  Why?
  J'Ai
  What Do You Say
  When I'm Alone
  Hallelujah

BEAT THE BAND
October 14, 1942 (68 perfs)
Music by John Green
Lyrics by George Marion, Jr.
  Down Through the Agents
  Free, Cute and Size Fourteen
  Song of Two Islands
  Keep It Casual
  Proud of You
  Break It Up
  Let's Comb Beaches
  The Hula Girl
  America Loves a Band
  The Afternoon of a Phoney
  Men
  The Steam Is on the Beam
  I'm Physical, You're Cultured
  Ev'ry Other Heartbeat
  The Four Freedoms—Calypso

BEG, BORROW OR STEAL
February 10, 1960 (5 perfs)
Music by Leon Pober

Lyrics by Bud Freeman
  Some Little People
  Rootless
  What Are We Gonna Do To-
    night?
  Poetry and All That Jazz
  Don't Stand Too Close to the Pic-
    ture
  Beg, Borrow or Steal
  No One Knows Me
  Zen Is When
  Clara
  You've Got Something to Say
  Presenting Clara Spencer
  I Can't Stop Talking
  It's All in Your Mind
  In Time
  Think
  Little People
  Rafesville, U.S.A.
  Let's Be Strangers Again
Cast album: Commentary

BEGGAR'S HOLIDAY†
December 26, 1946 (111 perfs)
Music by Duke Ellington
Lyrics by John Latouche
  When You Go Down by Miss Jen-
    ny's
  I've Got Me
  TNT
  Take Love Easy
  I Wanna Be Bad
  When I Walk with You
  The Scrimmage of Life
  Ore From a Gold Mine
  Tooth and Claw
  Maybe I Should Change My Ways
  On the Wrong Side of the Railroad
    Tracks
  Tomorrow Mountain
  Girls Want a Hero
  Lullaby for Junior
  Quarrel for Three

------

*Based on *Fables for Our Time* by James
Thurber
†Based on *The Beggar's Opera* by John
Gay

Brown Penny*
Women, Women, Women
The Hunted

BELIEVERS, THE (OB)
May 9, 1968 (295 perfs)
Music and lyrics by Voices, Inc.
  African Sequence
  Believers' Chants
  Believers' Laments
  This Old Ship
  Where Shall I Go?
  What Shall I Believe in Now?
  I Just Got in the City
  City Blues
  You Never Really Know
  Early One Morning Blues
  Daily Buzz
  Childrens' Games
  School Don't Mean a Damn Thing
  I'm Gonna Do My Things
  Where Do I Go from Here?
  Burn This Town
  Learn to Love
Cast album: RCA

BELLA (OB)
November 16, 1961 (6 perfs)
Music by Jane Douglas
Lyrics by Tom O'Malley
  On the Seashore by the Sea
  It Isn't the Same
  All About Evelyn
  Could Be
  Time
  The Seven Seas
  Hand in Hand
  Love Doesn't Grow on Trees
  I'm Happy
  My Card
  Kiss Me
  Madame from Paree
  Big, Big
  Take a Chance
  Way Down in Lil' Old Texas
  For Love or Money

BELLS ARE RINGING
November 29, 1956 (924 perfs)
Music by Jule Styne
Lyrics by Betty Comden and Adolph
Green

Bells Are Ringing
It's a Perfect Relationship
On My Own
It's a Simple Little System
Is It a Crime?
Hello, Hello There
I Met a Girl
Long Before I Knew You
Mu-Cha-Cha
Just in Time
Drop That Name
The Party's Over
Salzburg
The Midas Touch
I'm Going Back
Independent
Cast album: Columbia
Vocal score

BEN FRANKLIN IN PARIS
October 27, 1964 (215 perfs)
Music by Mark Sandrich, Jr.
Lyrics by Sidney Michaels
  We Sail the Seas
  I Invented Myself
  Too Charming
  Whatever Became of Old Temple
  Half the Battle
  A Balloon Is Ascending
  To Be Alone with You
  You're in Paris
  How Laughable It Is
  Hic Haec Hoc
  God Bless the Human Elbow
  When I Dance With the Person I
    Love
  Diane Is
  Look for Small Pleasures
  I Love the Ladies
Cast album: Capitol
Vocal selection

BEST FOOT FORWARD
October 1, 1941 (326 perfs)
Music and lyrics by Hugh Martin and
Ralph Blane
  Don't Sell the Night Short
  Three Men on a Date
  That's How I Love the Blues

_____
*Lyric based on poem by W. B. Yeats

The Three B's
Ev'ry Time
The Guy Who Brought Me
I Know You by Heart
Shady Lady Bird
Buckle Down, Winsocki
My First Promise
What Do You Think I Am?
Just a Little Joint with a Juke Box
Where Do You Travel?
I'd Gladly Trade
Added to 1963 Off-Broadway production: (224 perfs)
Wish I May
Hollywood Story
Alive and Kicking
You're Lucky
Raving Beauty
You Are for Loving
Album: (Off-Broadway cast) Cadence

BETSY
December 28, 1926 (39 perfs)
Music by Richard Rodgers
Lyrics by Lorenz Hart
The Kitzel Engagement
My Missus
Stonewall Moskowitz March (Lyrics by Irving Caesar)
One of Us Should Be Two
Sing
In Our Parlor on the Third Floor Back
This Funny World
The Tales of Hoffman (Music and lyrics by Irving Caesar and A. Segal)
Follow On
Push Around
Bugle Blow
Cradle of the Deep
If I Were You
Blue Skies (Music and lyrics by Irving Berlin)
Leave It to Levy (Music and lyrics by Irving Caesar)
Birds on High
Shuffle
Come and Tell Me*

BETWEEN THE DEVIL
December 22, 1937 (93 perfs)
Music by Arthur Schwartz
Lyrics by Howard Dietz
I See Your Face Before Me
The Night Before the Morning After
I've Made Up My Mind
Don't Go Away, Monsieur
Experience
Five O'Clock
Triplets
Fly By Night
You Have Everything
Bye-Bye Butterfly Lover
Celina Couldn't Say "No"
Front Page News
Why Did You Do It?
By Myself
The Gendarme
I'm Against Rhythm

BIG BOY
January 7, 1925 (48 perfs)
Music by Joseph Meyer and James F. Hanley
Lyrics by B. G. DeSylva
As Long As I've Got My Mammy
Born and Bred in Old Kentucky
Hello, Tucky
Lackawanna
Who Was Chasing Paul Revere
The Dance from Down Yonder
Welcome Home
Lead 'Em On
The Day I Rode Half Fare
True Love
Tap the Toe
Cookies and Bookies
The Race Is Over
Come On and Play
Something for Nothing

BILLIE†
October 1, 1928 (112 perfs)
Music and lyrics by George M. Cohan
New York

---

*Dropped from New York production
†Based on Cohan's play *Broadway Jones*

Come to St. Thomas's
Happy
Billie
Go Home Ev'ry Once in a While
Friends
The Cause of the Situation
Ev'ry Boy in Town's My Sweet-
heart
They Fall in Love
Where Were You—Where Was I?
The Jones' Family Friends
I'm a One Girl Man
Personality
Bluff
The Two of Us

BILLION DOLLAR BABY
December 21, 1945 (219 perfs)
Music by Morton Gould
Lyrics by Betty Comden and Adolph
Green
   Million Dollar Smile
   Who's Gonna Be the Winner?
   Dreams Come True
   Charleston
   Broadway Blossom
   Speaking of Pals
   There I'd Be
   One Track Mind
   Bad Timing
   A Lovely Girl
   Havin' a Time
   Faithless
   I'm Sure of Your Love
   A Life with Rocky

BILLY*
March 22, 1969 (1 perf)
Music and lyrics by Ron Dante and
Gene Allan
   Molly
   Chanty
   Watch Out for Claggart/Work
   Shaking Hands with the Wind
   Billy
   It Ain't Us Who Make the Wars
   The Bridge to Nowhere
   The Night and the Sea
   In the Arms of a Stranger
   The Fiddlers' Green
   My Captain
   Requiem

BILLY BARNES PEOPLE, THE
June 13, 1961 (7 perfs)
Music and lyrics by Billy Barnes
   If It Wasn't for People
   There's Nothing Wrong With Our
    Values
   Don't Bother
   Damn-Alot
   What Do We Have to Hold on To?
   I Like You
   Before and After
   Let's Get Drunk
   It's Not Easy
   The Matinee
   The End?
   Second Best
   Dolls
   Where Is the Clown?
   Marital Infidelity

BILLY BARNES REVUE, THE
June 9, 1959 (199 perfs including Off-
Broadway run)
Music and lyrics by Billy Barnes
   Do a Revue
   Where Are Your Children?
   Foolin' Ourselves
   Las Vegas
   Too Long at the Fair
   Listen to the Beat!
   City of the Angels
   Blocks
   One of Those Days

BILLY NONAME (OB)
March 2, 1970 (48 perfs)
Music and lyrics by Johnny Brandon
   King Joe
   Seduction
   Billy Noname
   Boychild
   A Different Drummer
   Look through the Window
   It's Our Time Now
   Hello World
   At the End of the Day
   I Want to Live
   Manchild

---

*Suggested by Herman Melville's *Billy Budd.*

Color Me White
We're Gonna Turn On Freedom
Mother Earth
Sit In—Wade In
Movin'
The Dream
Black Boy
Burn, Baby, Burn
We Make a Promise
Get Your Slice of Cake

BITTER SWEET
November 5, 1929 (159 perfs)
Music and lyrics by Noël Coward
That Wonderful Melody
The Call of Life
If You Could Only Come with Me
I'll See You Again
Tell Me, What Is Love?
The Last Dance
Life in the Morning
Ladies of the Town
If Love Were All
Evermore and a Day
Dear Little Café
Tokay
Bonne Nuit, Merci
Kiss Me
Ta Ra Ra Boom De Ay
Alas, the Time Is Past
Green Carnations
Zigeuner
Album: (studio cast) Angel
Vocal score

BLACK RHYTHM
December 19, 1936 (6 perfs)
Music and lyrics by Donald Heywood
Truckers Ball
Bow Down, Sinners
Orchids
Here 'Tis
Black Rhythm
Doin' the Toledo
Emaline

BLACKBERRIES OF 1932
April 4, 1932 (24 perfs)
Music and lyrics by Donald Heywood
The Answer Is No
Blackberries

Brown Sugar
First Thing in the Morning
Harlem Mania
Love Me More—Love Me Less (Music by Tom Peluso; lyrics by Ben Bernard)

BLACKBIRDS OF 1928
May 9, 1928 (518 perfs)
Music by Jimmy McHugh
Lyrics by Dorothy Fields
Digga Digga Do
I Can't Give You Anything But Love*
Bandanna Babies
Porgy
Magnolia's Wedding Day
Doin' the New Low-Down
Here Comes My Blackbird
Dixie
Baby!†
Shuffle Your Feet and Roll Along
Studio album: (special cast) Columbia

BLACKBIRDS OF 1930
October 22, 1930 (57 perfs)
Music by Eubie Blake
Lyrics by Andy Razaf
Roll Jordan
Cabin Door
Memories of You
Mozambique
Green Pastures (Lyrics by Will Morrissey and Andy Razaf)
You're Lucky to Me
Papa-De-Da-Da (Music and lyrics by Spencer Williams, Clarence Todd, and Clarence Williams)
My Handy Man Ain't Handy No More
Take a Trip to Harlem
We're the Berries
That Lindy Hop
Dianna Lee

BLACKBIRDS OF 1934
December 2, 1933 (25 perfs)
I'm Walkin' the Chalk Line (Music

---

*Dropped from "Harry Delmar's Revels" (1927)
†Dropped from New York Production

by Alberta Nichols; lyrics by
Mann Holiner)

I Just Couldn't Take It, Baby (Music
by Alberta Nichols; lyrics by
Mann Holiner)

A Hundred Years from Today (Music by Victor Young; lyrics by Joseph Young and Ned Washington)

Your Mother's Son-in-Law (Music
by Alberta Nichols; lyrics by
Mann Holiner)

Tappin' the Barrel (Music by Victor
Young; lyrics by Joseph Young
and Ned Washington)

Victim of the Voodoo Drums (Music
by Victor Young; lyrics by Joseph
Young and Ned Washington)

Doin' the Shim Sham (Music by Alberta Nichols; lyrics by Mann Holiner)

Let Me Be Born Again (Music by
Victor Young; lyrics by Joseph
Young, and Ned Washington)

What—No Dixie? (Music by Victor
Young; lyrics by Joseph Young
and Ned Washington)

BLESS YOU ALL
December 14, 1950 (84 perfs)
Music and lyrics by Harold Rome
  Bless You All
  Do You Know a Better Way to Make
  a Living?
  Don't Wanna Write about the South
  I Can Hear It Now
  When
  Little Things Meant So Much to Me
  A Rose Is a Rose
  Love Letter to Manhattan
  Summer Dresses
  Take Off the Coat
  The Desert Flame
  You Never Know What Hit You
  The Roaring Twenties Strike Back

BLONDE SINNER, THE
July 14, 1926 (173 perfs)
Music and lyrics by Leon DeCosta
  Don't You Cheat
  Oh, What a Playmate You Could
  Make
  If You Said What You Thought

Man Is a Mistake
The Whispering Song
Lips
Bye-Bye Babe

BLOOD (OB)
March 7, 1971 (14 perfs)
  Baby Rue (Music by Patrick Fox;
  lyrics by Avra Petrides)
  High Lonesome (Music by Horald
  Griffiths; lyrics by Doug Dyer)
  Hard Time War Time (Music and
  lyrics by the Blood Company)
  Hear the Guns (Music by Margaret
  Dorn, Elizabeth Howard and
  Tom Willis; lyrics by Doug Dyer)
  Lullaby (Music and lyrics by Patrick
  Fox)
  Cold Steel (Music by Horald
  Griffiths; lyrics by Doug Dyer)
  Every Father (Music by Linda
  Swenson and Patrick Fox; lyrics
  by Doug Dyer and Horald
  Griffiths)
  I Had a Son (Music and lyrics by
  Mary Boylan)
  There You Go Again (Music and lyrics by Alex Ander)
  Father, Father (Music and lyrics by
  Patrick Fox)
  Gas Can (Music by Patrick Fox; lyrics by Doug Dyer)
  Nobody's Fault (Music and lyrics by
  Alex Ander)
  I Dreamt About My Home (Music
  by Linda Swenson; lyrics by Doug
  Dyer)
  Madness Murder (Music by Margaret Dorn; lyrics by Doug Dyer)
  Whistles (Music by Joyce Stanton;
  lyrics by Patrick Fox)
  I Woke Up Today (Music and lyrics
  by Christopher Cox)
  Four Thousand Years (Music by Patrick Fox; lyrics by Doug Dyer)
  Walk On Home (Music by Jim
  Turner; lyrics by Doug Dyer)
  Heebie-Jeebie Furies (Music by Jim
  Turner; lyrics by Doug Dyer)
  Don't Call Us (Music by Jim Turner;
  lyrics by Mary Boylan)
  Before You Knew I Loved You (Mu-

sic by Maggie Hyatt; lyrics by Doug Dyer)
Destruction (Music by Jim Turner; lyrics by Doug Dyer)
Monkey in a Tree (Music by David Cohen; lyrics by Horald Griffiths)
Minute by Minute (Music by Patrick Fox; lyrics by Doug Dyer)
Love Came to Me (Music by Doug Dyer, Patrick Fox and the Blood Company; lyrics by Doug Dyer)
New Snow (Music by Margaret Dorn; lyrics by Doug Dyer)
Just a Little Bit (Music and lyrics by Horald Griffiths)
Hail to the Blood (Music and lyrics by Horald Griffiths)

BLOOD RED ROSES
March 22, 1970 (1 perf)
Music by Michael Valenti
Lyrics by John Lewin
    The Cream of English Youth
    A Garden in the Sun
    In the Country Where I Come From
    Black Dog Rum
    How Fucked up Things Are
    The English Rose
    O Rock Eternal
    Soldiers Anthem
    Prelude
    Blood Red Roses
    The Fourth Light Dragoons
    Song of Greater Britain
    Song of the Fair Dissenter Lass

BLOOMER GIRL
October 5, 1944 (654 perfs)
Music by Harold Arlen
Lyrics by E. Y. Harburg
    When the Boys Come Home
    Evelina
    Welcome Hinges
    Farmer's Daughter
    It Was Good Enough for Grandma
    The Eagle and Me
    Right as the Rain
    T'morra, T'morra
    Rakish Young Man With the Whiskers
    Pretty as a Picture

Sunday in Cicero Falls
I Got a Song
Simon Legree
I Never Was Born
Man For Sale
Cast album: Decca

BODY BEAUTIFUL, THE
January 23, 1958 (60 perfs)
Music by Jerry Bock
Lyrics by Sheldon Harnick
    Where Are They?
    The Body Beautiful
    Pffft!
    Fair Warning
    Leave Well Enough Alone
    Blonde Blues
    Uh-huh, Oh, Yeah!
    All of These and More
    Nobility
    Summer Is
    The Honeymoon Is Over
    Just My Luck
    The Art of Conversation
    Gloria
    A Relatively Simple Affair
Vocal selection

BOOM-BOOM*
January 28, 1929 (72 perfs)
Music by Werner Janssen
Lyrics by Mann Holiner and J. Keirn Brennan
    What Could I Do?
    On Top
    Be That Way
    Shake High, Shake Low
    Nina
    What a Girl
    Just a Big-Hearted Man
    He's Just My Ideal
    Pick 'Em Up and Lay 'Em Down
    Messin' Round
    We're Going to Make Boom-Boom
    Blow the Blues Away

BOTTOMLAND
June 27, 1927 (21 perfs)
Music by Clarence Williams

----

*Based on the play *Mlle Ma Mère* by Louis Verneuil

Steamboat Days (Lyrics by Clarence Williams)

Shootin' the Pistol (Lyrics by Chris Smith)

Bottomland (Lyrics by Jo Trent)

You're the Only One (Lyrics by Len Gray)

Come On Home (Music and lyrics by Donald Heywood)

Dancing Girl (Lyrics by Spencer Williams)

Any Time (Lyrics by Joe Jordan)

When I March with April in May (Lyrics by Spencer Williams)

BOY FRIEND, THE
September 30, 1954 (485 perfs)
Music and lyrics by Sandy Wilson
Perfect Young Ladies
The Boy Friend
Won't You Charleston with Me?
Fancy Forgetting
I Could Be Happy with You
Sur La Plage
A Room in Bloomsbury
You-Don't-Want-to-Play-With-Me Blues, The
Safety in Numbers
Riviera
It's Never Too Late to Fall in Love
Poor Little Pierrette
Cast album: RCA
Vocal score
Vocal selection

BOYS AND GIRLS TOGETHER
October 1, 1940 (191 perfs)
Music by Sammy Fain
Lyrics by Irving Kahal and Jack Yellen
Liable to Catch On
Such Stuff As Dreams Are Made Of (Lyrics by Irving Kahal)
I Want to Live (Lyrics by Jack Yellen)
Times Square Dance (Lyrics by Jack Yellen)
You Can't Put Catsup on the Moon (Lyrics by Irving Kahal)
The Sun'll Be Up in the Morning (Lyrics by Jack Yellen)
The Latin in Me

BOYS FROM SYRACUSE, THE*
November 23, 1938 (235 perfs)
Music by Richard Rodgers
Lyrics by Lorenz Hart
I Had Twins
Dear Old Syracuse
What Can You Do with a Man?
Falling in Love with Love
The Shortest Day of the Year
This Can't Be Love
Let Antipholus In
Ladies of the Evening
He and She
You Have Cast Your Shadow on the Sea
Come with Me
Big Brother
Sing for Your Supper
Oh, Diogenes
Album: (Studio cast) Columbia
Vocal score
Vocal selection
Added to film version: (1940)
Who Are You?

BRAVO GIOVANNI†
May 19, 1962 (76 perfs)
Music by Milton Schafer
Lyrics by Ronny Graham
Rome
Uriti
Breachy's Law
I'm All I've Got
The Argument
Signora Pandolfi
The Kangaroo
If I Were the Man
Steady, Steady
We Won't Discuss It
Ah! Camminare
Virtue Arrivederci
Bravo, Giovanni
One Little World Apart
Jump In
Miranda
Cast album: Columbia
Vocal selection

---

*Based on William Shakespeare's *A Comedy of Errors*
†Adapted from the novel by Howard Shaw

BRIGADOON
March 13, 1947 (581 perfs)
Music by Frederick Loewe
Lyrics by Alan Jay Lerner
  Once in the Highlands
  Brigadoon
  Vendors' Calls
  Down on MacConnachy Square
  Waitin' for My Dearie
  I'll Go Home with Bonnie Jean
  The Heather on the Hill
  The Love of My Life
  Jeannie's Packin' Up
  Come to Me, Bend to Me
  Almost Like Being in Love
  The Chase
  There but for You Go I
  My Mother's Wedding Day
  From This Day On
Cast album: RCA
Vocal score
Vocal selection

BRIGHT LIGHTS OF 1944
September 16, 1943 (4 perfs)
Music by Jerry Livingston
Lyrics by Mack David
  Haven't We Met Before?
  You'd Better Dance
  Thoughtless
  Don't Forget the Girl from Punxsutawney
  That's Broadway (Music and lyrics by Gene Herbert and Teddy Hall)
  We're Having Our Fling
  Back Bay Beat
  Your Face Is Your Fortune
  Yes, I Love You Honey
  A Lick, and a Riff, and a Slow Bounce

BRINGING UP FATHER*
March 30, 1925 (24 perfs)
Music by Seymour Furth and Lee Edwards
Lyrics by R. F. Carroll
  An Angel Without Wings
  That's the Irish in Her
  When It Gets Dark
  We Hope to Make a Hit
  Play Me a Bagpipe Tune
  The Girls of New York

  The Gainesboro Glide
  The Merry Go Round
  Moonlight
  A Lady Bred in the Purple
  Poppy the Dream Girl
  My Lady's Fan
  Wedding Chimes

BROADWAY NIGHTS
July 15, 1929 (40 perfs)
Music by Maury Rubens and Sam Timberg
Lyrics by Moe Jaffe
  Why Don't We?
  Hotsy Totsy Hats
  The Right Man
  White Lights Were Coming
  Arabian Nights
  Come Hit Your Baby
  Your Broadway and Mine (Music by Maury Rubens)
  Heart of a Rose
  Baby-Doll Dance (Music by Maury Rubens and Phil Svigals; lyrics by J. Keirn Brennan and Moe Jaffe)

BROADWAY SHO-WINDOW
April 12, 1936 (24 perfs)
  Hitch Your Wagon to a Star (Music by Richard Lewine; lyrics by Ted Fetter)
  Poverty Row or Luxury Lane (Music by Gus Edwards; lyrics by Howard Johnson)
  Spring Is in the Air (Music by Gus Edwards; lyrics by Eugene Conrad)

BROWN BUDDIES
October 7, 1930 (111 perfs)
  Give Me a Man Like That (Music and lyrics by George A. Little and Art Sizemore)
  When a Black Man's Blue (Music and lyrics by George A. Little, Art Sizemore, and Ed G. Nelson)
  Missouri (Music and lyrics by Nat Reed)

—————
*Based on the cartoons by George McManus

I Hate Myself (for Falling in Love with You) (Music and lyrics by Abner Silver and Dave Oppenheim)

Happy (Music by Nat Reed; lyrics by Bob Joffe)

Don't Leave Your Little Blackbird Blue (Music and lyrics by Joe Jordan, Porter Grainger, and Shelton Brooks)

Darky Rhythm (Music by Peter Tinturin; lyrics by Joe Young)

Dancin' 'Way Your Sin (Music and lyrics by J.C. Johnson)

Betty Lou (Music by Joe Jordan; lyrics by Rosamond Johnson)

BUCK WHITE*
December 2, 1969 (7 perfs)
Music and lyrics by Oscar Brown, Jr.
Honey Man Song
Money, Money, Money
Nobody Does My Thing
Step Across That Line
H. N. I. C.
Beautiful Allelujah Days
Tap the Plate
Big Time Buck White Chant
Better Far
We Came in Chains
Black Balloons
Look at Them
Mighty Whitey
Get Down

BUNK OF 1926
February 16, 1926 (104 perfs)
Music and lyrics by Gene Lockhart
Bunk
You Told Me That You Loved Me, but You Never Told Me Why
Monte, the Model
Those Mammy Singers
A Modest Little Thing
Cuddle Up
We're Going Away
The Milky Way
Chatter
How Very Long Ago
Do You Do the Charleston?

BUTTRIO SQUARE
October 14, 1952 (7 perfs)
Music by Fred Stamer
Lyrics by Gen Genovese
Every Day Is a Holiday
Let's Make It Forever
I'll Tell the World
There's No Place Like the Country (Music by Arthur Jones)
Take It Away
Get Me Out
I'm Gonna Be a Pop
One Is a Lonely Number
Love Swept Like a Storm
I Keep Telling Myself (Music by Arthur Jones)
More and More
You're Mine, All Mine

BY HEX (OB)
June 18, 1956 (40 perfs)
Music and lyrics by Howard Blankman
Market Day
Shunned
Ferhuddled and Ferhexed
Wonderful Good
What Is Love?
I Can Learn
Only a Man
An Amishman
I Have Lived
I Know My Love
The Trouble with Me
Something New
It Takes Time

BY JUPITER†
June 2, 1942 (427 perfs)
Music by Richard Rodgers
Lyrics by Lorenz Hart
For Jupiter and Greece
Jupiter Forbid
Life With Father
Nobody's Heart

---

*Based on the play, *Big Time Buck White* by Joseph Dolan Tuotti
†Based on the play *The Warrior's Husband* by Julian F. Thompson

The Gateway of the Temple of Minerva
Here's a Hand
No, Mother, No
The Boy I Left Behind Me
Ev'rything I've Got
Bottoms Up
Careless Rhapsody
Wait Till You See Her
Now That I've Got My Strength
Cast album: (1967 Off-Broadway cast) RCA

BY THE BEAUTIFUL SEA
April 8, 1954 (270 perfs)
Music by Arthur Schwartz
Lyrics by Dorothy Fields
Mona From Arizona
The Sea Song (By the Beautiful Sea)
Old Enough to Love
Coney Island Boat
Alone Too Long
Happy Habit
Good Time Charlie
I'd Rather Wake Up by Myself
Hooray for George the Third
Hang Up!
More Love Than Your Love
Throw the Anchor Away
Cast album: Capitol

BY THE WAY
December 28, 1925 (176 perfs)
Music by Vivian Ellis
Lyrics by Graham John
By the Way
Shall We Join the Ladies
What Can They See in Dancing?
My Castle in Spain (Music and lyrics by Isham Jones)
The Beauty of Bath
Gather Roses While You May
In the Same Way I Love You (Music by H. M. Tennent; lyrics by Eric Little)
I Know Someone Loves Me
High Street, Africa
Hum a Little Tune
No One's Ever Kissed Me
Nippy
There's Nothing New Under the Sun

BYE BYE BIRDIE
April 14, 1960 (607 perfs)
Music by Charles Strouse
Lyrics by Lee Adams
An English Teacher
The Telephone Hour
How Lovely to Be a Woman
We Love You, Conrad!
Put On a Happy Face
Normal American Boy
One Boy
Honestly Sincere
Hymn for a Sunday Evening
One Last Kiss
What Did I Ever See in Him?
A Lot of Livin' To Do
Kids
Baby, Talk to Me
Spanish Rose
Rosie
Cast album: Columbia
Vocal score
Vocal selection

BYE BYE, BONNIE
January 13, 1927 (125 perfs)
Music by Albert Von Tilzer
Lyrics by Neville Fleeson
Have You Used Soft Soap?
Promise Not to Stand Me Up Again
Love Is Like a Blushing Rose
Out of Town Buyers
You and I Love You and Me
Just Cross the River from Queens
Bye Bye, Bonnie
I Like to Make It Cozy
Toodle-Oo
When You Get to Congress
In My Arms Again
Lovin' off My Mind
Look in Your Engagement Book
Starlight
Tampico Tap

CABARET*
November 20, 1966 (1,166 perfs)
Music by John Kander
Lyrics by Fred Ebb

---

*Based on John Van Druten's play, *I Am a Camera*

Willkommen
So What?
Don't Tell Mama
Telephone Song
Perfectly Marvelous
Two Ladies
It Couldn't Please Me More
Tomorrow Belongs to Me
Why Should I Wake Up?
The Money Song
Married
Meeskite
If You Could See Her
What Would You Do?
Cabaret
Cast album: Columbia
Vocal score
Vocal selection
Added to film version: (1972)
Mein Herr
Maybe This Time
Money

CABIN IN THE SKY
October 25, 1940 (156 perfs)
Music by Vernon Duke
Lyrics by John Latouche
The General's Song
Pay Heed
Taking a Chance on Love (Lyrics by
John Latouche and Ted Fetter)
Cabin in the Sky
Do What You Wanna Do
My Old Virginia Home (On the
River Nile)
Love Me Tomorrow
Love Turned the Light Out
Honey in the Honeycomb
Savannah
Added to film version (1943):
Happiness Is a Thing Called Joe
(Music by Harold Arlen; lyrics by
E. Y. Harburg)
Added to 1964 Off-Broadway produc-
tion: (47 perfs)
Wade in the Water
Make Way
The Man Upstairs
We'll Live All Over Again
Not So Bad to Be Good
Living It Up (Lyrics by Vernon
Duke)

Not a Care in the World*
Gospel: Great Day
Album: (Off-Broadway cast) Capitol

CAFÉ CROWN†
April 17, 1964 (3 perfs)
Music by Albert Hague
Lyrics by Marty Brill
You're a Stranger in This Neighbor-
hood
What's the Matter with Buffalo?
All Those Years
Au Revoir Poland—Hello New York
Make the Most of Spring
So Long As It Isn't Shakespeare
A Lifetime Love
I'm Gonna Move
A Mother's Heart
On This Wedding Day
What's Gonna Be Tomorrow
A Man Must Have Something to
Live For
That's the Life for Me
Magical Things in Life

CALL ME MADAM
October 12, 1950 (644 perfs)
Music and lyrics by Irving Berlin
Mrs. Sally Adams
Hostess with the Mostes' on the Ball
Washington Square Dance
Lichtenburg
Can You Use Any Money Today?
Marrying for Love
The Ocarina
It's a Lovely Day Today
The Best Thing for You
Something to Dance About
Once Upon a Time Today
They Like Ike
You're Just in Love
Cast albums: RCA (Dinah Shore);
Decca (Ethel Merman and studio
cast)
Vocal score

CALL ME MISTER
April 18, 1946 (734 perfs)
Music and lyrics by Harold Rome

---

*Previously used in *Banjo Eyes* (1941)
†Based on the play by Hy Kraft

Goin' Home Train
Along with Me
Surplus Blues
The Drug Store Song
The Red Ball Express
Military Life
Call Me Mister
Yuletide, Park Avenue
When We Meet Again
The Face on the Dime
A Home of Our Own
His Old Man
South America, Take it Away
The Senators' Song

CALLING ALL STARS
December 13, 1934 (36 perfs)
Music by Harry Akst
Lyrics by Lew Brown
Calling All Stars
Thinking Out Loud
I've Nothing to Offer
If It's Love
I Don't Want to Be President
I'd Like to Dunk You in My Coffee
I'm Stepping out of the Picture
He Just Beats a Tom-Tom
My Old Hoss
Just Mention Joe

CAMELOT*
December 3, 1960 (873 perfs)
Music by Frederick Loewe
Lyrics by Alan Jay Lerner
I Wonder What the King Is Doing
  Tonight
The Simple Joys of Maidenhood
Camelot
Follow Me
C'est Moi
The Lusty Month of May
Then You May Take Me to the Fair
How to Handle a Woman
The Jousts
Before I Gaze at You Again
If Ever I Would Leave You
The Seven Deadly Virtues
What Do Simple Folk Do?
The Persuasion
Fie On Goodness
I Loved You Once in Silence
Guenevere

Cast album: Columbia
Vocal score
Vocal selection

CAN-CAN
May 7, 1953 (892 perfs)
Music and lyrics by Cole Porter
Maidens Typical of France
Never Give Anything Away
C'est Magnifique
Come Along with Me
Live and Let Live
I Am in Love
If You Loved Me Truly
Montmart'
Allez-Vous En
Never, Never Be an Artist
It's All Right with Me
Every Man Is a Stupid Man
I Love Paris
Can-Can
Cast album: Capitol
Vocal score
Vocal selection

CANDIDE†
December 1, 1956 (73 perfs)
Music by Leonard Bernstein
The Best of All Possible Worlds
  (Lyrics by Richard Wilbur)
Oh, Happy We (Lyrics by Richard
  Wilbur)
It Must Be So (Lyrics by Richard
  Wilbur)
Lisbon Sequence (Lyrics by Leon-
  ard Bernstein)
It Must Be Me (Lyrics by Richard
  Wilbur)
Glitter and Be Gay (Lyrics by Rich-
  ard Wilbur)
You Were Dead, You Know (Lyrics
  by John Latouche and Richard
  Wilbur)
Pilgrims' Procession (Lyrics by
  Richard Wilbur)
My Love (Lyrics by John Latouche
  and Richard Wilbur)

---

*Based on *The Once and Future King* by T.
H. White
†Based on Voltaire's satire

I Am Easily Assimilated (Lyrics by Leonard Bernstein)
Quartet Finale (Lyrics by Richard Wilbur)
Quiet (Lyrics by Richard Wilbur)
Eldorado (Lyrics by Lillian Hellman)
Bon Voyage (Lyrics by Richard Wilbur)
What's the Use? (Lyrics by Richard Wilbur)
Gavotte (Lyrics by Dorothy Parker)
Make Our Garden Grow (Lyrics by Richard Wilbur)
Cast album: Columbia
Vocal score

CANTERBURY TALES*
February 3, 1969 (121 perfs)
Music by Richard Hill and John Hawkins
Lyrics by Nevill Coghill
  Song of Welcome
  Good Night Hymn
  Canterbury Day
  I Have a Noble Cock
  Darling, Let Me Teach You How to Kiss
  There's the Moon
  It Depends on What You're At
  Love Will Conquer All
  Beer Is Best
  Come On and Marry Me Honey
  Where Are the Girls of Yesterday
  Hymen, Hymen
  If She Has Never Loved Before
  I'll Give My Love a Ring
  Pear Tree Quintet
  I Am All A-Blaze
  What Do Women Want
  April Song
Cast album: Capitol
Vocal selection

CAPE COD FOLLIES
September 18, 1929 (29 perfs)
Music by Alexander Fogarty
  Clutching at Shadows (Lyrics by Seymour Morris)
  That's Why We Misbehave (Lyrics by Edith Lois and Urana Clarke)
  That's the Time When I Miss You
  (Lyrics by Seymour Morris)
  Wondering Who (Lyrics by George Fitch)
  Looking at Life through a Rainbow (Music by Kenneth Burton; lyrics by Walter Craig)

CAPTAIN JINKS†
September 8, 1925 (167 perfs)
Music by Lewis E. Gensler
Lyrics by B. G. DeSylva
  Ain't Love Wonderful?
  Fond of You
  I Do
  Kiki
  New Love
  The Only One for Me
  Sea Legs
  You Must Come Over Blues (Lyrics by B. G. DeSylva and Ira Gershwin)

CARIB SONG
September 27, 1945 (36 perfs)
Music by Baldwin Bergersen
Lyrics by William Archibald
  Go Sit by the Body
  This Woman
  Water Movin' Slow
  Basket, Make a Basket
  Woman Is a Rascal
  A Girl She Can't Remain
  Market Song
  Sleep, Baby, Don't Cry
  Today I Is So Happy
  Can't Stop the Sea
  You Know, Oh Lord
  Go Down to the River (Washer Woman)
  Oh, Lonely One

CARMEN JONES**
December 2, 1943 (502 perfs)
Music by Georges Bizet
Lyrics by Oscar Hammerstein II

---

*Based on a translation from Geoffrey Chaucer
†Based on play Captain Jinks of the Horse Marines by Clyde Fitch
**Based on Meilhac and Halevy's adaptation of Prosper Merimee's Carmen.

Lif' 'Em Up and Put 'Em Down
Honey Gal o' Mine
Good Luck
Dat's Love
You Talk Just Like My Maw
Carmen Jones Is Goin' to Jail
Dere's a Café on de Corner
Beat Out Dat Rhythm on a Drum
Stan' Up and Fight
Whizzin' Away Along de Track
Dis Flower
If You Would Only Come Away
De Cards Don't Lie
Dat Ol' Boy
Poncho de Panther from Brazil
My Joe
Get Yer Program for de Big Fight
Dat's Our Man
Cast album: Decca
Vocal selection

CARNIVAL*
April 13, 1961 (719 perfs)
Music and lyrics by Bob Merrill
Direct From Vienna
A Very Nice Man
I've Got to Find a Reason
Mira
Sword, Rose and Cape
Humming
Yes, My Heart
Everybody Likes You
Magic, Magic
Tanz Mit Mir
Yum Ticky-Ticky
The Rich
Beautiful Candy
Her Face
Grand Imperial Cirque de Paris
I Hate Him
Carnival Theme (Love Makes the World Go Round)
Always Always You
She's My Love
Cast album: MGM
Vocal selection

CARNIVAL IN FLANDERS†
September 8, 1953 (6 perfs)
Music by Jimmy Van Heusen
Lyrics by Johnny Burke
Ring the Bell

The Very Necessary You
It's a Fine Old Institution
I'm One of Your Admirers
The Plundering of the Town
The Stronger Sex
The Sudden Thrill
It's an Old Spanish Custom
A Seventeen Gun Salute
You're Dead!
Here's That Rainy Day
Take the Word of a Gentleman
A Moment of Your Love
How Far Can a Lady Go?

CAROUSEL**
April 19, 1945 (890 perfs)
Music by Richard Rodgers
Lyrics by Oscar Hammerstein II
Carousel Waltz
You're a Queer One, Julie Jordan
When I Marry Mr. Snow
If I Loved You
June is Bustin' Out All Over
When the Children Are Asleep
Blow High, Blow Low
Soliloquy
This Was a Real Nice Clambake
Geraniums in the Winder
There's Nothin' So Bad for a Woman
What's the Use of Wond'rin'
You'll Never Walk Alone
The Highest Judge of All
Cast album: Decca
Vocal score
Vocal selection

CASTLES IN THE AIR
September 6, 1926 (160 perfs)
Music by Percy Wenrich
Lyrics by Raymond Peck
I Don't Blame 'Em
Love's Refrain

---

*Based on the film *Lili,* based in turn on Paul Gallico's story *The Seven Souls of Clement O'Reilly*
†Based on the French film *La Kermesse Héroique*
**Based on the play *Liliom* by Ferenc Molnár, as adapted by Benjamin F. Glazer

Lantern of Love
The Singer's Career, Ha! Ha!
The Other Fellow's Girl
If You Are in Love with a Girl
The Sweetheart of Your Dream
I Would Like to Fondle You
The Rainbow of Your Smile
Baby
Latavia
Land of Romance
My Lips, My Love, My Soul
The Latavian Chant
Girls and the Gimmies
Love Rules the World

CAT AND THE FIDDLE, THE
October 15, 1931 (395 perfs.)
Music by Jerome Kern
Lyrics by Otto Harbach
She Didn't Say "Yes"
The Night Was Made for Love
I Watch the Love Parade
The Breeze Kissed Your Hair
One Moment Alone
Try to Forget
Poor Pierrot
A New Love Is Old
Ha! Cha! Cha!
Album: (Studio cast) Epic
Vocal score

CATCH A STAR!
September 6, 1955 (23 perfs)
Catch a Star! (Music by Sammy Fain; lyrics by Paul Webster)
Everybody Wants to Be in Show Business (Music and lyrics by Ray Golden, Bud Burtson, and Philip Charig)
A Little Traveling Music (Music by Hal Borne; lyrics by Paul Webster and Ray Golden)
One Hour Ahead of the Posse (Music by Philip Charig; lyrics by Ray Golden and Dave Ormont)
Las Vegas (Music and lyrics by Ray Golden, Sy Kleinman, and Lee Adams)
To Be or Not to Be in Love (Music by Philip Charig; lyrics by Ray Golden, Danny Shapiro, and Milton Pascal)

The Story of Alice (Music by Jerry Bock; lyrics by Larry Holofcener)
What a Song Can Do (Music and lyrics by Bernie Wayne and Lee Morris)
Carnival in Court (Music by Jay Navarre; lyrics by Ray Golden and I. A. L. Diamond)
Twist My Arm (Music by Sammy Fain; lyrics by Paul Webster)
Foreign Cars (Music and lyrics by Norman Martin)
New Hollywood Plots (Music by Sammy Fain; lyrics by Paul Webster)
Gruntled (Music and lyrics by Ray Golden, Sy Kleinman, and Philip Charig)
Fly, Little Heart (Music by Jerry Bock; lyrics by Larry Holofcener)
Bachelor Hoedown (Music by Jerry Bock; lyrics by Larry Holofcener)
Boffola (Music by Philip Charig; lyrics by Danny Shapiro, Milton Pascal, and Ray Golden)

CAVIAR
June 7, 1934 (20 perfs)
Music by Harden Church
Lyrics by Edward Heyman
One in a Million
Dream Kingdom
Here's to You
My Heart's an Open Book
Silver Sails
Nightwind
Tarts and Flowers
Prince Charming
Gypsy
I Feel Sorta——
Your Prince Was Not So Charming
Haywire (Music by Edward Heyman)

CELEBRATION
January 22, 1969 (109 perfs)
Music by Harvey Schmidt
Lyrics by Tom Jones
Celebration
Orphan in the Storm
Survive
Somebody

Bored
My Garden
Where Did It Go?
Love Song
To the Garden
I'm Glad To See You've Got What You Want
It's You Who Makes Me Young
Not My Problem
Fifty Million Years Ago
Under the Tree
Winter and Summer
Cast album: Capitol
Vocal score
Vocal selection

CHANGE YOUR LUCK
June 6, 1930 (17 perfs)
Music and lyrics by J. C. Johnson
  Sweet Little Baby o' Mine
  Can't Be Bothered Now
  Ain't Puttin' Out Nothin'
  Religion in My Feet
  You Should Know
  Wasting Away
  Walk Together, Children
  Honesty
  Mr. Mummy Man
  My Regular Man
  I'm Honest
  We're Here
  Open That Door
  Change Your Luck
  Percolatin'
  Travellin'
  What Have I Done?
  Rhythm Feet

CHARLOT'S REVUE OF 1926
November 10, 1925 (138 perfs)
  How D'You Do (Music by Philip Braham; lyrics by Eric Blore and Dion Titheradge)
  Let's All Go Raving Mad (Music by Philip Braham; lyrics by Hugh E. Wright)
  Gigolette (Music by Franz Lehár; lyrics by Irving Caesar)
  Russian Blues (Music and lyrics by Noël Coward)
  Take Them All Away (Music and lyrics by Jack Strachey)

Poor Little Rich Girl (Music and lyrics by Noël Coward)
Susannah's Squeaking Shoes (Music by Muriel Lillie; lyrics by Arthur Weigall)
Oxford Bags (Music by Philip Braham; lyrics by Arthur Wimperis)
March with Me! (Music by Ivor Novello; lyrics by Douglas Furber)
A Cup of Coffee, a Sandwich and You (Music by Joseph Meyer; lyrics by Billy Rose and Al Dubin)
The Fox Has Left His Lair (Music by Peggy Connor; lyrics by Douglas Furber)
Carrie (Music and lyrics by Noël Coward)

CHEE-CHEE*
September 25, 1928 (31 perfs)
Music by Richard Rodgers
Lyrics by Lorenz Hart
  I Must Love You†
  Dear, Oh Dear
  Moon of My Delight
  Better Be Good to Me
  The Tartar Song
  Singing a Love Song**

CHERRY BLOSSOMS††
March 28, 1927 (56 perfs)
Music by Sigmund Romberg
Lyrics by Harry B. Smith
  I'll Peek-a-boo You
  Legend Song
  If You Know What I Think
  Feast of the Lanterns
  Cigarette Song
  Happy Rickshaw Man
  Japanese Serenade
  I Want to Be There
  Romance

---

*Adapted from novel *The Son of the Grand Eunuch* by Charles Petit
†Rewritten as "Send for Me" in *Simple Simon* (1930)
**Rewritten as "I Still Believe in You" in *Simple Simon* (1930)
††Based on play *The Willow Tree* by Benrimo and Harrison Rhodes

CHIC (OB)
May 19, 1959 (6 perfs)
Lyrics by Lester Judson
  Chic (Music by Julian Stein)
  Flattery (Music by Edward C. Redding)
  The Mouse (Music by Edward C. Redding; lyrics by Lester Judson and Edward C. Redding)
  Charity (Music by Murray Grand; lyrics by Lester Judson and Robin Miller)
  Julie Is Mine (Music by Raymond Taylor)
  Mediocrity (Music by Murray Grand)
  Talk to Me (Music by Julian Stein)
  The Angry Young Men (Music by Julian Stein)
  East Side Story (Music by Julian Stein)
  A Summer Romance (Music by Raymond Taylor)
  There's No Room for People Any More (Music by Julian Stein)
  The Happy Years (Music by Raymond Taylor)

CHINA ROSE
January 19, 1925 (96 perfs)
Music by A. Baldwin Sloane
Lyrics by Harry Cort and George E. Stoddard
  Sun Worship
  Soldiers True
  Maiden Fair
  Chinese Potentate
  We'll Build a Brand New Bamboo Bungalow
  I'm High, I'm Low
  China Rose
  I'm All Alone
  Who Am I Thinking Of?
  I Like the Girls
  Through the Bamboo
  Chinese Lantern Man
  Home
  China Bogie Man
  Just a Kiss
  Hail the Bridegroom
  Tomorrow
  Great White Way in China

  I'm No Butterfly
  Calling You My Own
  Why Do They Make 'Em so Beautiful?
  Happy Bride

CHRISTINE*
May 7, 1960 (12 perfs)
Music by Sammy Fain
Lyrics by Paul Francis Webster
  Welcome Song
  My Indian Family
  A Doctor's Soliloquy
  UNICEF Song
  My Little Lost Girl
  I'm Just a Little Sparrow
  How to Pick a Man a Wife
  The Lovely Girls of Akbarabad
  Room in My Heart
  I Never Meant to Fall in Love
  Freedom Can Be a Most Uncomfortable Thing
  Ireland Was Never Like This
  He Loves Her
  Christine
  I Love Him
  Kathakali
  Bharatha Natyan
  The Woman I Was Before
Cast album: Columbia

CINDY (OB)
March 19, 1964 (428 perfs)
Music and lyrics by Johnny Brandon
  Once Upon a Time
  Let's Pretend
  Is There Something to What He Said?
  Papa, Let's Do It Again
  A Genuine Feminine Girl
  Cindy
  Think Mink
  Tonight's the Night
  Who Am I?
  If You've Got It, You've Got It
  The Life That I Planned for Him
  If It's Love

_____
*Adapted from *My Indian Family* by Hilda Wernher

Got the World in the Palm of My
Hand
Call Me Lucky
Laugh It Up
What a Wedding
Cast album: ABC-Paramount

CIRCUS PRINCESS, THE
April 25, 1927 (192 perfs)
Music by Emmerich Kalman
Lyrics by Harry B. Smith
But Who Cares?
Silhouette
Bravo, Bravo
There's Something About You
Dear Eyes That Haunt Me
Same Old Love Songs
I Dare to Speak of Love to You
Girls, I Am True to All of You
Joy Bells
The Hussars' Song
Like You
I Like the Boys
What D'Ya Say? (Music by Jesse
Greer; lyrics by Raymond Klages)
Guarded
Waiters
I'll Be Waiting
Vocal score

CITY CHAP, THE*
October 26, 1925 (72 perfs)
Music by Jerome Kern
Lyrics by Anne Caldwell
Like the Nymphs of Spring
The Go-Getter
Journey's End (Lyrics by P. G.
Wodehouse)
Sympathetic Someone
The City Chap
He Is the Type
If You Are As Good As You Look
The Fountain of Youth
A Pill a Day
Walking Home with Josie
Bubbles of Bliss
No One Knows
When I Fell in Love

Coco
December 18, 1969 (332 perfs)
Music by André Previn
Lyrics by Alan Jay Lerner

But That's the Way You Are
The World Belongs to the Young
Let's Go Home
Mademoiselle Cliché de Paris
On the Corner of the Rue Cambon
The Money Rings Out Like Free-
dom
A Brand New Dress
A Woman Is How She Loves
Gabrielle
Coco
Fiasco
When Your Lover Says Goodbye
Ohrbach's, Bloomingdale's, Best
and Saks
Always Mademoiselle
Cast album: ABC-Paramount
Vocal selection

COCOANUTS, THE
December 8, 1925 (375 perfs)
Music and lyrics by Irving Berlin
The Guests
The Bellhops
Family Reputation
Lucky Boy
Why Am I a Hit with the Ladies?
A Little Bungalow
Florida By the Sea
The Monkey Doodle-Doo
Five o'Clock Tea
They're Blaming the Charleston
We Should Care
Minstrel Days
Tango Melody
The Tale of a Shirt
Ting-A-Ling, the Bells'll Ring
Added to film version: (1929)
When My Dreams Come True

COLETTE† (OB)
May 6, 1970 (101 perfs)
Music by Harvey Schmidt
Lyrics by Tom Jones
The Bouilloux Girls

---

*Adapted from the play *The Fortune
Hunter* by Winchell Smith
†Based on *Earthly Paradise*, Robert
Phelps' collection of Colette's autobio-
graphical writings

Femme du Monde
Earthly Paradise
Cast album: MIO International

COME OF AGE
January 12, 1934 (35 perfs)
Music by Richard Addinsell
Lyrics by Clemence Dane
I Came to Your Room
I Come Out of a Dream
I'm Afraid of the Dark
The River Song
Too Much Work

COME ON STRONG
(Play with one song)
October 4, 1962 (36 perfs)
Music by Jimmy Van Heusen
Lyrics by Sammy Cahn
Come On Strong

COME SUMMER
March 18, 1969 (7 perfs)
Music by David Baker
Lyrics by Will Holt
Good Time Charlie
Think Spring
Wild Birds Calling
Goodbye, My Bachelor
Fine, Thank You, Fine
Road to Hampton
Come Summer
Let Me Be
Feather in My Shoe
The Loggers' Song
Jude's Holler
Faucett Falls Fancy
Rockin'
Skin and Bones
Moonglade
Women
No
So Much World

COMPANY
April 26, 1970 (690 perfs)
Music and lyrics by Stephen Sondheim
Company
The Little Things You Do Together
Sorry-Grateful
You Could Drive a Person Crazy
Have I Got a Girl for You

Someone Is Waiting
Another Hundred People
Getting Married Today
Side by Side by Side
What Would We Do without You
Poor Baby
Barcelona
The Ladies Who Lunch
Being Alive
Cast album: Columbia
Vocal score
Vocal selection

CONNECTICUT YANKEE, A*
November 3, 1927 (418 perfs)
Music by Richard Rodgers
Lyrics by Lorenz Hart
A Ladies' Home Companion
My Heart Stood Still
Thou Swell
At the Round Table
On a Desert Island with Thee
Nothing's Wrong
I Blush†
Someone Should Tell Them**
I Feel at Home with You
The Sandwich Men
Evelyn, What Do You Say?
Added to 1943 production: (135 perfs)
This Is My Night to Howl
To Keep My Love Alive
Ye Lunchtime Follies
Can't You Do a Friend a Favor?
You Always Love the Same Girl
The Camelot Samba

CONQUERING HERO, THE††
January 16, 1961 (8 perfs)
Music by Moose Charlap
Lyrics by Norman Gimbel
Girls! Girls!
Five Shots of Whiskey
Hail, the Conquering Hero!
Must Be Given to You
Wonderful, Marvelous You

---

*Based on the Mark Twain novel
†Dropped from New York production
**Rewritten as "There's So Much More"
for *America's Sweetheart* (1931)
††Based on *Hail, the Conquering Hero* by
Preston Sturges

Truth
Won't You Marry Me?
The River Bank
Only Rainbows
The Campaign
One Mother Each
I'm Beautiful
Rough Times
Yours, All Yours

CONVERSATION PIECE
October 23, 1934 (55 perfs)
Music and lyrics by Noël Coward
I'll Follow My Secret Heart
Regency Rakes
Charming, Charming
Dear Little Soldiers
There's Always Something Fishy
    About the French
English Lesson
There Was Once a Little Village by
    the Sea
Nevermore
Album: (Special Cast) Columbia
Vocal score

COPPER AND BRASS
October 17, 1957 (36 perfs)
Music by David Baker
Lyrics by David Craig
Career Guidance
Wearing of the Blue
I Need All the Help I Can Get
Cool Combo Mambo
You Walked Out
Cool Credo
Bringing Up Daughter
Don't Look Now
Baby's Baby
Call the Police
Unmistakable Sign
Why Her?
Me and Love
Remember the Dancing
Sweet William
Little Woman

COUNT ME IN
October 8, 1942 (61 perfs)
Music and lyrics by Ann Ronell
All Out Bugle Call
The Way My Ancestors Went

Someone in the Know
On Leave for Love
You've Got It All
Why Do They Say They're the Fair
    Sex?
We're Still on the Map
Ticketyboo
Who Is General Staff?
The Woman of the Year
Papa's Return

COUNTESS MARITZA
September 18, 1926 (321 perfs)
Music by Emmerich Kalman
Lyrics by Harry B. Smith
Dear Home of Mine, Goodbye
Hola, Follow, Follow Me
In the Days Gone By
Make Up Your Mind
The Music Thrills Me
Sister Mine
The One I'm Looking For
Play Gypsies, Dance Gypsies
Say Yes, Sweetheart
Don't Tempt Me
Love Has Found My Heart (Melody
    revised by Alfred Goodman)
I'll Keep On Dreaming
Who Am I?
Why Is the World So Changed To-
    day?
Brown-Eyed Girl
Vocal score

COURTIN' TIME*
June 14, 1951 (37 perfs)
Music and lyrics by Jack Lawrence
and Don Walker
Today at Your House, Tomorrow at
    Mine
Fixin' for a Long Cold Winter
Araminto to Herself
An Old-Fashioned Glimmer in Your
    Eye
Goodbye, Dear Friend
I Do! He Doesn't!
Golden Moment
Johnny Ride the Sky

---

*Based on the play *The Farmer's Wife* by
Eden Phillpotts

The Sensible Thing to Do
Masculinity
Maine Will Remember the Maine
Heart in Hand

CRADLE WILL ROCK, THE
January 3, 1938 (108 perfs)
Music and lyrics by Marc Blitzstein
Croon-Spoon
Honolulu
Gus and Sadie Love Song
Nickel under the Foot
The Cradle Will Rock
Joe Worker
Art for Art's ake
Doctor and Ella
Drugstore Scene
The Freedom of the Press
Leaflets
The Rich
Cast album: (1964 revival) MGM

CRANKS
November 26, 1956 (40 perfs)
Music by John Addison
Lyrics by John Cranko
Who's Who
Adrift
Where Has Tom Gone?
Cold Comfort
Who Is It Always There?
Chiromancy
New Blue
Valse Anglaise
Don't Let Him Know You
Sea Song
Telephone Tango
I'm the Boy You Should Say "Yes"
To
Metamorphosis
Would You Let Me Know?
Dirge
Arthur, Son of Martha
Goodnight
Cast album: HMV

CRAZY WITH THE HEAT
January 14, 1941 (99 perfs)
With a Twist of the Wrist (Music and lyrics by Irvin Graham)
Sascha's Got a Girl (Music and lyrics by Irvin Graham)

Some Day (Music by Rudi Revil; lyrics by Kurt Kasznar and Carl Kent)
The Time of Your Life (Music by William Provost; lyrics by Peter K. Smith)
Crazy with the Heat (Music by Rudi Revil; lyrics by Irvin Graham)
You Should Be Set to Music (Music and lyrics by Irvin Graham)

CRAZY QUILT
May 19, 1931 (67 perfs)
Sing a Little Jingle (Music by Harry Warren; lyrics by Mort Dixon)
I Found a Million Dollar Baby (Music by Harry Warren; lyrics by Billy Rose and Mort Dixon)
I Want to Do a Number with the Boys (Music by Rowland Wilson; lyrics by Ned Wever)
Under the Clock at the Astor (Music by Manning Sherwin; lyrics by Ned Wever)
In the Merry Month of Maybe (Music by Harry Warren; lyrics by Ira Gershwin and Billy Rose)
Kept in Suspense (Music by Carroll Gibbons; lyrics by Billy Rose and James Dyrenforth)
Crazy Quilt (Music by Harry Warren; lyrics by Bud Green)
Would You Like to Take a Walk? (Music by Harry Warren; lyrics by Billy Rose and Mort Dixon)
Peter Pan (Music by Carroll Gibbons; lyrics by Billy Rose and James Dyrenforth)
Rest Room Rose (Music by Richard Rodgers; lyrics by Lorenz Hart)

CRISS-CROSS
Octobber 12, 1926 (210 perfs)
Music by Jerome Kern
Lyrics by Anne Caldwell and Otto Harbach
Cinderella Girl
She's On Her Way
Flap-a-Doodle
Bread and Butter
In Araby with You
Kiss a Four Leaf Clover

Rose of Delight
You Will, Won't You?
Suzie (Lyrics by Anne Caldwell)
The Ali Baba Babies

CROSS MY HEART
September 17, 1928 (64 perfs)
Music by Harry Tierney
Lyrics by Joseph McCarthy
Step Up and Pep Up the Party
Sold
Dream Sweetheart
Salaaming the Raja
Right Out of Heaven
Hot Sands
In the Gardens of Noor-Ed-Deen
Lady Whippoorwill
Come Along, Sunshine
We'll Have Our Good Days
Thanks for a Darn Nice Time

CRY FOR US ALL*
April 8, 1970 (9 perfs)
Music by Mitch Leigh
Lyrics by William Alfred and Phyllis
Robinson
See No Evil
The End of My Race
How Are You Since?
The Mayor's Chair
The Cruelty Man
The Verandah Waltz
Home Free All
The Broken Heart, or the Wages of
Sin
The Confessional
Who to Love If Not a Stranger
Cry for Us All
Swing Your Bag
Call in to Her
That Slavery Is Love
I Lost It
Aggie, Oh Aggie
The Leg of the Duck
This Cornucopian Land
Cast album: Project Three

CRYSTAL HEART, THE (OB)
February 15, 1960 (8 perfs)
Music by Baldwin Bergersen
Lyrics by William Archibald
A Year Is a Day

A Monkey When He Loves
Handsome Husbands
Yes, Aunt
A Girl with a Ribbon
I Must Paint
I Wanted to See the World
Fireflies
How Strange the Silence
When I Drink with My Love
Desperate
Lovely Island
Bluebird
Agnes and Me
Madam, I Beg You!
My Heart Won't Learn
Tea Party
Lovely Bridesmaids
It Took Them
D-o-g

CURLEY MCDIMPLE (OB)
November 22, 1967 (931 perfs)
Music and lyrics by Robert Dahdah
A Cup of Coffee
I Try
Curley McDimple
Love is the Loveliest Love Song
Are There Any More Rosie
O'Gradys?
Dancing in the Rain
At the Playland Jamboree
I've Got a Little Secret
The Meanest Man in Town
Something Nice is Going to Happen
Swing-a-Ding-a-Ling
Hi de hi de hi, Hi de hi de ho
Dwarf's Song
Vocal selection

DAMES AT SEA (OB)
December 20, 1968 (575 perfs)
Music by Jim Wise
Lyrics by George Haimsohn and
Robin Miller
Wall Street
It's You
Broadway Baby
That Mister Man of Mine

___
*Based on William Alfred's play *Hogan's
Goat*

Choo-Choo Honeymoon
The Sailor of My Dreams (Lyrics by George Haimsohn)
Singapore Sue (Lyrics by George Haimsohn)
Good Times Are Here to Stay (Lyrics by George Haimsohn)
Dames at Sea
The Beguine
Raining in My Heart
There's Something About You
The Echo Waltz (Lyrics by George Haimsohn)
Star Tar
Let's Have a Simple Wedding
Cast album: Columbia
Vocal selection

DAMN YANKEES*
May 5, 1955 (1,019 perfs)
Music and lyrics by Richard Adler and Jerry Ross
Six Months Out of Every Year
Goodbye, Old Girl
You've Got to Have Heart
Shoeless Joe from Hannibal, Mo.
A Little Brains—a Little Talent
A Man Doesn't Know
Who's Got the Pain?
The Game
Near to You
Those Were the Good Old Days
Two Lost Souls
Cast album: RCA
Vocal score
Vocal selection

DANCE ME A SONG
January 20, 1950 (35 perfs)
Music and lyrics by James Shelton
It's the Weather
I'm the Girl
Love
One Is a Lonely Number (Music by Albert Hague; lyrics by Maurice Valency)
My Little Dog Has Ego (Music and lyrics by Herman Hupfeld)
Lilac Wine
Matilda

Dance Me a Song
Strange New Look†

DARLING OF THE DAY**
January 27, 1968 (32 perfs)
Music by Jule Styne
Lyrics by E. Y. Harburg
Mad for Art
He's a Genius
To Get Out Of This World Alive
It's Enough To Make a Lady Fall In Love
A Gentleman's Gentleman
Double Soliloquy
Let's See What Happens
Panache
I've Got a Rainbow Working for Me
Money, Money, Money
That Something Extra Special
What Makes a Marriage Merry
Not on Your Nellie
Sunset Tree
Butler in The Abbey
Cast album: RCA

DARWIN'S THEORIES (OB)
October 19, 1960 (2 perfs)
Music and lyrics by Darwin Venneri
I Know How You Wonder
Love Is Strange
Love Me Little
What's In a Name?
The Stars Seem So Low Tonight
Carried Away
Strange Weather
We'll Always Stay in Love

DAY BEFORE SPRING, THE
November 22, 1945 (167 perfs)
Music by Frederick Loewe
Lyrics by Alan Jay Lerner
The Day Before Spring
God's Green World
You Haven't Changed At All
My Love Is a Married Man
Friends to the End

---

*Based on the novel *The Year the Yankees Lost the Pennant* by Douglass Wallop
†Dropped from New York production
**Based on Arnold Bennett's *Buried Alive*

A Jug of Wine
I Love You This Morning
Where's My Wife?
This Is My Holiday

DAY IN THE LIFE OF JUST ABOUT EV-
ERYONE, A (OB)
March 9, 1971 (7 perfs)
Music and lyrics by Earl Wilson, Jr.
  If I Could Live My Life Again
  The View from My Window
  A Brief Dissertation on the Rele-
    vancy of a Liberal Education in a
    Contemporary Society
  Fare Thee Well
  A Waltz for Two Balloons
  Safe
  When I Was a Child
  Give Us This Day
  Goin' Home
  Out of Town
  Merrill, Lynch, Pierce, Fenner and
    Clyde
  Everybody Loves a Single Girl
  Two Grown-up People at Play
  What Do I Do Now?
  Got to Be a Woman Now
  He's Beginning to Look a Lot Like
    Me
  A Woman Is Just a Female
  Faces without Names
  Paper Tiger
  The People in the Street
  Visiting Hours
  The Man I Could Have Been
  Isn't That What Makes Life Worth-
    while?

DEAR WORLD*
February 6,1969 (132 perfs)
Music and lyrics by Jerry Herman
  The Spring of Next Year
  Each Tomorrow Morning
  I Don't Want to Know
  I've Never Said I Love You
  Garbage
  Dear World
  Kiss Her Now
  And I Was Beautiful
  One Person
Cast album: Columbia
Vocal selection

DEAREST ENEMY
September 18, 1925 (286 perfs)
Music by Richard Rodgers
Lyrics by Lorenz Hart
  Heigh-Ho, Lackaday!
  War is War
  I Beg Your Pardon
  Cheerio
  Full Blown Roses
  The Hermits
  Here in My Arms
  Gavotte
  I'd Like to Hide It
  Where the Hudson River Flows
  Bye and Bye
  Old Enough to Love
  Sweet Peter
  Here's a Kiss

DECAMERON, THE† (OB)
April 12, 1961 (39 perfs)
Music by Edward Earle
Lyrics by Yvonne Tarr
  1348
  Talk
  Deceive Me
  Ballad of Tancred
  Golden Goblet
  What's Wrong with Me?
  Women!
  Love Is Paradise
  I Know, I Know
  Cuckold's Delight
  Barnabo
  The Pirate's Song
  Nightingale
  Come, Sweet Love

DEEP HARLEM
January 7, 1929 (8 perfs)
Music by Joe Jordan
Lyrics by Homer Tutt and Henry
Creamer
  Deep Harlem
  Mexican Blues
  I Shall Love You

---

*Based on *The Madwoman of Chaillot* by
Jean Giraudoux, as adapted by Maurice Va-
lency.
†Based on the Love Tales of Boccaccio

Deliver
Kentucky

DEEP RIVER
October 4, 1926 (32 perfs)
Music by Frank Harling
Lyrics by Laurence Stallings
  Ashes and Fire
  Cherokee Rose
  De Old Clay Road
  Dis Is de Day
  Love Lasts a Day
  Po' Lil' Black Chile
  Serenade Creole
  Soft in de Moonlight
  Two Little Stars

DESERT SONG, THE
November 30, 1926 (471 perfs)
Music by Sigmund Romberg
Lyrics by Otto Harbach and Oscar
Hammerstein II
  The Riff Song
  Margot
  I'll Be a Buoyant Girl
  Why Did We Marry Soldiers?
  French Marching Song
  Romance
  Then You Will Know
  I Want a Kiss
  "It"
  The Desert Song
  Song of the Brass Key
  One Good Man Gone Wrong
  Let Love Go
  One Flower Grows Alone in Your
    Garden
  One Alone
  The Sabre Song
  Farewell
  Let's Have a Love Affair
Album: (Studio cast) Columbia
Vocal score

DESTRY RIDES AGAIN*
April 23, 1959 (473 perfs)
Music and lyrics by Harold Rome
  Bottleneck
  Ladies
  Hoop-de-Dingle
  Tomorrow Morning
  Ballad of the Gun
  The Social

I Know Your Kind
I Hate Him
Rose Lovejoy of Paradise Alley
Anyone Would Love You
Once Knew a Fella
Every Once in a While
Fair Warning
Are You Ready, Gyp Watson?
Not Guilty
Only Time Will Tell
Respectability
Ring on the Finger
I Say Hello
Cast album: Decca
Vocal score

DIFFICULT WOMAN, THE (OB)
April 25, 1962 (3 perfs)
Music by Richard Freitas
Lyrics by Morty Neff and George My-
sels
  Grandioso
  Ulterior Motive
  Siesta
  One in My Position
  Malumba
  The Hangman's Plea
  Ungrateful
  Poor Isabel
  Milonga
  What a Life
  Bull Blood and Brandy
  Patience and Gentleness
  Tormented
  Taking Inventory
  I Won't Take No for an Answer
  This Is the Day
  Throw the House out of the Win-
    dow

DIVERSIONS (OB)
November 7, 1958 (85 perfs)
Music by Buster Davis
Lyrics by Steven Vinaver
  You're Nothing
  Touch and Go
  Subway Rag
  Here Comes the Ballad
  White Is the Dove
  Prayer

---

*Based on the film

You're Wonderful
He Follows Me Around

Do I Hear a Waltz?*
March 18, 1965 (220 perfs)
Music by Richard Rodgers
Lyrics by Stephen Sondheim
Someone Woke Up
This Week Americans
What Do We Do? We Fly!
Someone Like You
Bargaining
Here We Are Again
Thinking
No Understand
Take the Moment
Moon in My Window
We're Gonna Be All Right
Do I Hear a Waltz?
Stay
Perfectly Lovely Couple
Thank You So Much
Cast album: Columbia
Vocal score
Vocal selection

Do Re Mi
December 26, 1960 (400 perfs)
Music by Jule Styne
Lyrics by Betty Comden and Adolph
Green
Waiting, Waiting
All You Need Is a Quarter
Take a Job
The Juke Box Hop
It's Legitimate
I Know about Love
Cry Like the Wind
Ambition
Success
Fireworks
What's New at the Zoo?
Asking for You
The Late, Late Show
Adventure
Make Someone Happy
V. I. P.
All of My Life
Cast album: RCA
Vocal score
Vocal selection

Do You Know the Milky Way?
October 16, 1961 (16 perfs)
Music by Alex Fry
Lyrics by Lyon Phelps
Do You Know the Milky Way?
The Child's Song
The Vagabond Song

Donnybrook!†
May 18, 1961 (68 perfs)
Music and lyrics by Johnny Burke
Sez I
The Day the Snow Is Meltin'
Sad Was the Day
Donnybrook
Ellen Roe
Sunday Morning
The Loveable Irish
I Wouldn't Bet One Penny
He Makes Me Feel I'm Lovely
I Have My Own Way
A Toast to the Bride
Wisha Wurra
A Quiet Life
Mr. Flynn
Dee-lightful Is the Word
For My Own
Cast album: Kapp

Double Entry (ob)
February 20, 1961 (56 perfs)
Music and lyrics by Jay Thompson
Sweep
Kinda Sorta Doin' Nothing
Real Rich Ladies
The Oldest Trick in the World
Dear Madame Scarlatina
The Fortune
The White Slavery Fandango
All the Young Men

Drat! (ob)
October 18, 1971 (1 perf)
Music by Steven Metcalf
Lyrics by Fred Bluth
Little Fairies
Early Bird Eddy

---

*Based on the play *The Time of the Cuckoo*
by Arthur Laurents
†Based on film *The Quiet Man*

Walkin' in the Rain
Friday, Friday
My Geranium
Kick It Around
You and I
Where Is the Man for Me?
Frightened of the Dark
Desperation Quintet
Drat!
Has Anyone Seen My Daddy
Lean on Me
Bye and Bye
The Chase

DRAT! THE CAT!
October 10, 1965 (8 perfs)
Music by Milton Schafer
Lyrics by Ira Levin
    Drat! The Cat!
    My Son, Uphold the Law
    Holmes and Watson
    She Touched Me
    Wild and Reckless
    She's Roses
    Dancing with Alice
    Purefoy's Lament
    A Pox Upon the Traitor's Brow
    Deep in Your Heart
    Let's Go
    It's Your Fault
    Today Is a Day for a Band to
        Play
    I Like Him
    Justice Triumphant
Vocal selection

DREAM WITH MUSIC
May 18, 1944 (28 perfs)
Music by Clay Warnick
Lyrics by Edward Eager
    Be Glad You're Alive
    I'm Afraid I'm in Love
    Baby, Don't Count on Me
    Give, Sinbad, Give
    I'll Take the Solo
    Love at Second Sight
    Relax and Enjoy It
    Come with Me
    Battle of the Genie
    Mr. and Mrs. Wrong
    The Lion and the Lamb
    Mouse Meets Girl

The Moon Song
Woman Against the World

DUBARRY, THE
November 22, 1932 (87 perfs)
Music by Carl Millöcker (revised by
    Theo Mackeben)
Lyrics by Rowland Leigh
    Today
    On the Stage
    Without Your Love
    If I Am Dreaming
    Happy Little Jeanne
    Pantalettes
    Dance for the Gentlemen
    I Give My Heart
    Beauty
    The Road to Happiness
    Ga-Ga
    The Dubarry

DU BARRY WAS A LADY
December 6, 1939 (408 perfs)
Music and lyrics by Cole Porter
    Ev'ry Day a Holiday
    It Ain't Etiquette
    When Love Beckoned (in Fifty-
        Second Street)
    Come On In
    Mesdames and Messieurs
    But In the Morning, No!
    Do I Love You?
    Du Barry Was a Lady
    Give Him the Oo-La-La
    Well, Did You Evah!*
    It Was Written in the Stars
    L'Après-Midi d'un Boeuf
    Katie Went to Haiti
    Friendship

DUCHESS MISBEHAVES, THE
February 13, 1946 (5 perfs)
Music by Frank Black
Lyrics by Gladys Shelley
    Art
    My Only Romance
    Broadminded
    I Hate Myself in the Morning
    Men

------
*Also used in film *High Society* (1958)

Couldn't Be More in Love
Ole Ole
Katie Did in Madrid
Morning in Madrid
Lost
The Honeymoon Is Over
Fair Weather Friends
The Nightmare

EARL CARROLL'S SKETCH BOOK (1929)
July 1, 1929 (400 perfs)

Legs, Legs, Legs (Music by Jay Gorney; lyrics by E. Y. Harburg)
For Someone I Love (Music by Ted Snyder; lyrics by Benny Davis)
Song of the Moonbeams (Music by Vincent Rose; lyrics by Charles and Harry Tobias)
Kinda Cute (Music by Jay Gorney; lyrics by E. Y. Harburg)
Fascinating You (Music and lyrics by Benee Russell, Vincent Rose, Charles and Harry Tobias)
Like Me Less, Love Me More (Music by Jay Gorney; lyrics by E. Y. Harburg)
Crashing the Golden Gate (Music by Jay Gorney and Phil Cohan; lyrics by E. Y. Harburg)
Rhythm of the Waves (Music by Vincent Rose; lyrics by Charles and Harry Tobias)
You Beautiful So and So (Music by Ted Snyder; lyrics by Billy Rose)
Don't Hang Your Dreams on a Rainbow (Music by Arnold Johnson; lyrics by Irving Kahal)
Tip-Toe Tap-Tap (Music by Irving Actman; lyrics by Jean Herbert)
Papa Likes a Hot Papoose (Music by Jay Gorney; lyrics by E. Y. Harburg)
My Sunny South (Music and lyrics by Abner Silver)

EARL CARROLL'S SKETCH BOOK (1935)
June 4, 1935 (207 perfs)

Let's Swing It (Music and lyrics by Charles Tobias, Charles Newman, and Murray Mencher)
Anna Louise of Louisiana (Music by Will Irwin; lyrics by Norman Zeno)
At Last (Music by Henry Tobias; lyrics by Charles Tobias and Sam Lewis)
Gringola (Music and lyrics by Charles Tobias, Charles Newman, and Murray Mencher)
There's Music in a Kiss (Music and lyrics by Al Sherman, Al Lewis, and Abner Silver)
Young Ideas (Music and lyrics by Charles Tobias, Charles Newman, and Murray Mencher)
Let the Man Who Makes the Gun (Music by Gerald Marks; lyrics by Raymond B. Egan)
The Rustle of Your Bustle (Music by Will Irwin; lyrics by Norman Zeno)
Silhouettes under the Stars (Music and lyrics by Charles Tobias, Charles Newman, and Murray Mencher)
Mardi Gras Day in New Orleans (Music by Will Irwin; lyrics by Norman Zeno)
Sunday Night in New York (Music and lyrics by Charles Tobias, Charles Newman, and Murray Mencher)

EARL CARROLL'S VANITIES (1925)
July 6, 1925 (390 perfs)
Music and lyrics by Clarence Gaskill

We Are the Waiters
Beautiful Ladies of the Night
This Is a Night Club
The Chow Mein Girls
A Kiss in the Moonlight
I Thank You
Ponies on Parade
Dorothy
At the Gate of Roses
Rhythm of the Day (Music by Owen Murphy; lyrics by Donald Lindley)
Yvonne
Shake Yourself Out of Here

EARL CARROLL'S VANITIES (1926)
August 24, 1926 (303 perfs)
Music by Morris Hamilton
Lyrics by Grace Henry
  Open the Gates of Madrid
  Cool 'Em Off
  We Are the Show Girls
  Natacha (Music and lyrics by Berton Braley, M.de Jari, and Alex James)
  Adorable (Music and lyrics by Tom Ford and Ray Wynburn)
  Climbing Up the Ladder of Love (Music by Jesse Greer; lyrics by Raymond Klages)
  The Lament of Shakespeare
  All Is Vanity
  Twilight
  Hugs and Kisses (Music by Louis Alter; lyrics by Raymond Klages)
  The Chinese Idol (Music and lyrics by Berton Braley, M.de Jari, and Alex James)
  Alabama Stomp (Music by James P. Johnson; lyrics by Henry Creamer)
  Broadway to Madrid

EARL CARROLL'S VANITIES (1928)
August 6, 1928 (203 perfs)
Music by Morris Hamilton
Lyrics by Grace Henry
  Say It with Girls
  Pretty Girl
  Rose of the World
  Flutterby Baby
  Wheels
  Vaniteaser (Music and lyrics by Michael Cleary and Paul Jones)
  Getting the Beautiful Girls (Music by Michael Cleary; lyrics by Ned Washington)
  Raquel (Music and lyrics by George Whiting and Joe Burke)
  My Arms Are Open (Music by Michael Cleary; lyrics by Ned Washington)
  Blue Shadows (Music by Louis Alter; lyrics by Raymond Klages)
  Oh, How That Man Can Love (Music and lyrics by Lillian Roth and Herb Magidson)
  Watch My Baby Walk (Music by Peter de Rose; lyrics by Jo Trent)
  Once in a Lifetime (Music by Jesse Greer; lyrics by Raymond Klages)
  Painting a Vanities Girl (Music and lyrics by Ernie Golden)
  I'm Flyin' High (Music and lyrics by Abner Silver, Jack Le Soir, and Roy Doll)

EARL CARROLL'S VANITIES (1930)
July 1, 1930 (215 perfs)
  Knee Deep in June (Music by Jay Gorney; lyrics by E. Y. Harburg)
  One Love (Music by Harold Arlen; lyrics by Ted Koehler)
  Hittin' the Bottle (Music by Harold Arlen; lyrics by Ted Koehler)
  The March of Time (Music by Harold Arlen; lyrics by Ted Koehler)
  Love Boats (Music by Jay Gorney; lyrics by E.Y.Harburg)
  I Came to Life (Music by Jay Gorney; lyrics by E. Y. Harburg)
  Rumba Rhythm (Music by Jimmy Johnson; lyrics by Stella Unger)
  Out of a Clear Blue Sky (Music by Harold Arlen; lyrics by Ted Koehler)
  Going Up (Music by Jay Gorney; lyrics by E. Y. Harburg)

EARL CARROLL'S VANITIES (1931)
August 27, 1931 (278 perfs)
Music by Burton Lane
Lyrics by Harold Adamson
  It's Great to Be in Love (Music and lyrics by Cliff Friend)
  Have a Heart
  Going to Town with Me
  Tonight or Never (Music and lyrics by Jack Meskill, Raymond Klages, and Vincent Rose)
  The Mahoneyphone
  Love Came into My Heart
  I'm Back in Circulation Again (Music by Michael H. Cleary; lyrics by Max and Nathaniel Lief)
  Heigh Ho, the Gang's All Here

EARL CARROLL'S VANITIES (1932)
September 27, 1932 (87 perfs)
  My Darling (Music by Richard My-

ers; lyrics by Edward Heyman)

Along Came Love (Music by Henry Tobias; lyrics by Charles Tobias and Haven Gillespie)

Love Is My Inspiration (Music by André Renaud; lyrics by Ted Koehler)

I've Got a Right to Sing the Blues (Music by Harold Arlen; lyrics by Ted Koehler)

Take Me Away (Music by Peter Tinturin; lyrics by Sidney Clare and Charles Tobias)

Forsaken (Music by Richard Myers; lyrics by Edward Heyman)

Rockin' in Rhythm (Music by Harold Arlen; lyrics by Ted Koehler)

EARL CARROLL'S VANITIES (1940)

January 13, 1940 (25 perfs)

Music and lyrics by Dorcas Cochran and Charles Rosoff

The Lady Has Oomph

Angel (Music by Peter de Rose; lyrics by Mitchell Parrish)

Charming

The Starlit Hour (Music by Peter de Rose; lyrics by Mitchell Parrish)

Westward Ho!

Can the Can-Can

I Want My Mama (Music by Jararaca and Vincent Paiva; lyrics by Al Stillman)

Song of the Sarong

EARL OF RUSTON

May 5, 1971 (5 perfs)

Music by Peter Link

Lyrics by C. C. Courtney and Ragan Courtney

Just Your Old Friend

Earl Is Crazy

Guitar Song

Easy to Be Lonely

Standing

Probably (Music by C. C. and Ragan Courtney)

Mama, Earl Done Ate the Tooth Paste Again (Music by C. C. and Ragan Courtney)

Silvers Theme

Mama, Mama, Mama

I've Been Sent Back to the First Grade (Music by C. C. Courtney)

The Revival

My Name Is Leda Pearl (Music by C. C. Courtney)

Insane Poontang (Music by C. C. and Ragan Courtney)

You Still Love Me (Music by C. C. Courtney)

Earl Was Ahead

EARLY TO BED

June 17, 1943 (380 perfs)

Music by Thomas (Fats) Waller

Lyrics by George Marion, Jr.

A Girl Who Doesn't Ripple When She Bends

There's a Man in My Life

Me and My Old World Charm

Supple Couple

Slightly Less Than Wonderful

This Is So Nice

The Ladies Who Sing with a Band

There's "Yes" in the Air

Get Away, Young Man

Long Time No Song

Early to Bed

When the Nylons Bloom Again

EAST WIND

October 27, 1931 (23 perfs)

Music by Sigmund Romberg

Lyrics by Oscar Hammerstein II

It's a Wonderful World

East Wind

I Saw Your Eyes

These Tropics

Are You Love?

You Are My Woman

Minnie

Embrace Me

The Americans Are Coming

I'd Be a Fool

Regardez-Moi

When You Are Young

EDUCATION OF H*Y*M*A*N K*A*P*L*A*N, THE*

April 4, 1968 (28 perfs)

---

*Based on the stories by Leo Rosten

Music and lyrics by Paul Nassau and Oscar Brand
  Strange New World
  OOOO-EEEE
  A Dedicated Teacher
  Lieben Dich
  Loving You
  The Day I Met Your Father
  Anything Is Possible
  Spring in the City
  Old Fashioned Husband
  Julius Caesar
  I Never Felt Better In My Life
  When Will I Learn
  All American

ENCHANTED ISLE
September 19, 1927 (32 perfs)
Music and lyrics by Ida Hoyt Chamberlain
  Hacienda Garden
  Enchanted Castle
  Jazz
  Business Is Business
  Whoa, Gal
  Julianne
  Close in Your Arms
  California
  Dream Girl
  Enchanted Isle
  Abandon
  Cowboy Potentate
  Love Thought Garden
  What a Jamboree
  Voice of the High Sierras
  Dream Boat
  Roulette
  Down to the Sea
  Could I Forget?

ENTRE-NOUS (OB)
December 30, 1935 (47 perfs)
Music by Richard Lewine
Lyrics by Will B. Johnstone
  Entre-Nous
  Let's Go High Hat
  I'll See You Home (Music by Harry Archer)
  Let's Get Married or Something (Lyric by Ted Fetter)
  With You, With Me (Music and lyrics by Richard Lewine)

Kick in the Pants (Music by Harry Archer)
  Sunday Morning Churchman (Lyrics by Norman Zeno)
  Under My Skin (Music by Harry Archer)
  What Can I Give You? (Music by Phillip Broughton)
  A. J. (Music by Harry Archer)
  Am I? (Music by Harry Archer)
  When Opportunity Knocks (Lyrics by Ted Fetter)

ERNEST IN LOVE* (OB)
May 4, 1960 (111 perfs)
Music by Lee Pockriss
Lyrics by Anne Croswell
  Come Raise Your Cup
  How Do You Find the Words?
  The Hat
  Mr. Bunbury
  Perfection
  A Handbag Is Not a Proper Mother
  A Wicked Man
  Metaphorically Speaking
  You Can't Make Love
  Lost
  My Very First Impression
  The Muffin Song
  My Eternal Devotion
Cast album: Columbia

EVERYBODY'S WELCOME†
October 13, 1931 (139 perfs)
  One in a Million (Music by Harry Revel; lyrics by Mack Gordon)
  All Wrapped Up In You (Music by Harry Revel; lyrics by Mack Gordon and Harold Adamson)
  Pie Eyed Piper (Music by Sammy Fain; lyrics by Irving Kahal)
  Ta Ta, Old Bean (Music by Manning Sherwin; lyrics by Edward Eliscu)
  As Time Goes By (Music and lyrics by Herman Hupfeld)**
  Even As You and I (Music by

---

*Based on play *The Importance of Being Earnest* by Oscar Wilde
†Based on play *Up Pops the Devil* by Albert Hackett and Frances Goodrich

**Also in film *Casablanca* (1942)

Sammy Fain; lyrics by Irving Kahal)

Feather in a Breeze (Music by Sammy Fain; lyrics by Irving Kahal)

You've Got a Lease on My Heart (Music by Sammy Fain; lyrics by Irving Kahal)

Nature Played a Dirty Trick on You (Music by Manning Sherwin; lyrics by Arthur Lippmann and Milton Pascal)

I Shot the Works (Music by Manning Sherwin; lyrics by Arthur Lippmann and Milton Pascal)

Is Rhythm Necessary? (Music by Sammy Fain; lyrics by Irving Kahal)

EXCHANGE (OB)
February 8, 1970 (1 perf)
Music and lyrics by Mike Brandt, Michael Knight, and Robert J. Lowery
All Over My Mind
If You Listen to My Song
Anthem
If I Had the Answers
Why Don't You Believe Me?
Wondering
A Madrigal
Never Ever Land
Dancing Through Lifetimes
The Flower Song
Carrion Train
Come on Train
L. A. Incident
Santa Barbara
Puddles
Flying Somehow
Mumble Nothing
Understand It
King
Pied Piper
Coonskin Cap
Maybe Tomorrow
I Can Make It

FADE OUT—FADE IN
May 26, 1964 (271 perfs)
Music by Jule Styne
Lyrics by Betty Comden and Adolph Green

The Thirties
It's Good to Be Back Home
Fear
Call Me Savage
The Usher from the Mezzanine
I'm with You
My Fortune Is My Face
Lila Tremaine
Go Home Train
Close Harmony
You Mustn't Be Discouraged
The Dangerous Age
The Fiddler and the Fighter
Fade Out—Fade In
Cast album: ABC-Paramount
Vocal selection

F. JASMINE ADDAMS* (OB)
October 27, 1971 (6 perfs)
Music and lyrics by G. Wood
How About You and Me
If I Had a . . . . . .
Miss Pinhead
Baby, That's Love
Did I Make a Good Impression?
Good As Anybody
The We of Me
Travelin' On
Sunshine Tomorrow
F. Jasmine Addams
How Sweet Is Peach Ice Cream
Do Me a Favor
Another Day
Quite Suddenly

FACE THE MUSIC
February 17, 1932 (165 perfs)
Music and lyrics by Irving Berlin
Lunching at the Automat
Let's Have Another Cup of Coffee
Torch Song
You Must Be Born With It
On a Roof in Manhattan
My Beautiful Rhinestone Girl
Soft Lights and Sweet Music
I Say It's Spinach
Drinking Song

---

*Based on *The Member of the Wedding*, Carson McCullers' dramatization of her own novel.

Dear Old Crinoline Days
I Don't Want to Be Married
Manhattan Madness

FALLOUT (OB)
May 20, 1959 (31 perfs)
Music by Robert Kessler
Lyrics by Martin Charnin
We're Betting on You
String Quartet (Music and lyrics by Paul Nassau)
Sixteenth Summer
Someone Waiting
The Victoria Trio (Music and lyrics by Paul Nassau)
I Think I'd Like to Fall in Love (Music and lyrics by Martin Charnin)
Clandestine
Music Hath'nt
Look
Too Many Questions (Music and lyrics by Paul Nassau)
Problem (Music by Alan Friedman; lyrics by Dennis Marks)
You're My Man
Individuals (Music by Jerry Alters; lyrics by Herb Hartig)
Oh Say, Can You See?
Love Is (Music and lyrics by Martin Charnin)

FAMILY AFFAIR, A
January 27, 1962 (65 perfs)
Music by John Kander
Lyrics by James Goldman, John Kander, and William Goldman
Anything for You
Beautiful
My Son, the Lawyer
Every Girl Wants to Get Married
Right Girls
Kalua Bay
There's Room in My House
Siegal Marching Song
Harmony
Now, Morris
Wonderful Party
Revenge
Summer Is Over
I'm Worse Than Anybody
What I Say Goes
The Wedding

Cast album: United Artists
Vocal selection

FANNY*
November 4, 1954 (888 perfs)
Music and lyrics by Harold Rome
Never Too Late for Love
Cold Cream Jar Song
Octopus Song
Restless Heart
Why Be Afraid to Dance?
Shika Shika
Welcome Home
I Like You
I Have to Tell You
Fanny
Panisse and Son
Birthday Song
To My Wife
The Thought of You
Love is a Very Light Thing
Other Hands, Other Hearts
Be Kind to Your Parents
Cast album: RCA
Vocal score
Vocal selection

FANTASTICKS, THE (OB)†

May 3, 1960**
Music by Harvey Schmidt
Lyrics by Tom Jones
Try to Remember
Much More
Metaphor
Never Say No
It Depends on What You Pay
You Wonder How These Things Begin
Soon It's Gonna Rain
Happy Ending
This Plum Is Too Ripe
I Can See It
Plant a Radish
Round and Round
There Is a Curious Paradox
They Were You
Cast album: MGM

---

*Based on the trilogy by Marcel Pagnol
†Suggested by *Les Romantiques* by Edmond Rostand.
**Still running December 31, 1972.

Vocal score
Vocal selection

FAST AND FURIOUS
September 15, 1931 (6 perfs)
Music by Harry Revel
Lyrics by Mack Gordon
  Fast and Furious
  Walkin' on Air
  So Lonesome (Music by Joe Jordan;
    lyrics by Rosamond Johnson)
  Frowns
  Doing the Dumbbell
  Shadows on the Wall
  Where's My Happy Ending? (Lyrics
    by Mack Gordon and Harold
    Adamson)
  Hot, Hot Mama (Music and lyrics by
    Porter Grainger)
  Boomerang (Music by Joe Jordan;
    lyrics by Rosamond Johnson)
  Pansies on Parade (Music and lyrics
    by Porter Grainger)
  Hot Feet
  Let's Raise Hell (Music and lyrics by
    Porter Grainger)

FIDDLER ON THE ROOF*
September 22, 1964† (3,242 perfs)
Music by Jerry Bock
Lyrics by Sheldon Harnick
  Tradition
  Matchmaker, Matchmaker
  If I Were a Rich Man
  Sabbath Prayer
  To Life
  Miracle of Miracles
  The Tailor, Motel Kamzoil
  Sunrise, Sunset
  Wedding Dance
  Now I Have Everything
  Do You Love Me?
  I Just Heard
  Far from the Home I Love
  Anatevka
  Epilogue
Cast album: RCA
Vocal score
Vocal selection

FIFTY MILLION FRENCHMEN
November 27, 1929 (254 perfs)
Music and lyrics by Cole Porter

  A Toast to Volstead
  You Do Something to Me
  The American Express
  You've Got That Thing
  Find Me a Primitive Man
  Where Would You Get Your Coat?
  Do You Want to See Paris?
  At Longchamps Today
  The Happy Heaven of Harlem
  Why Shouldn't I Have You?
  Somebody's Going to Throw a Big
    Party
  It Isn't Done
  I'm in Love
  The Tale of an Oyster
  Paree, What Did You Do to Me?
  You Don't Know Paree
  I'm Unlucky at Gambling
  Let's Step Out
  The Boy Friend Back Home
  I Worship You**
  Please Don't Make Me Be Good**
  The Queen of Terre Haute**

FIG LEAVES ARE FALLING, THE
January 2, 1969 (4 perfs)
Music by Albert Hague
Lyrics by Allen Sherman
  All Is Well in Larchmont
  Lillian
  Like Yours
  All of My Laughter
  Give Me a Cause
  Today I Saw a Rose
  We
  For Our Sake
  Light One Candle
  Oh, Boy
  The Fig Leaves Are Falling
  For the Rest of My Life
  I Like It
  Old Fashioned Song
  Did I Ever Really Live?

FINE AND DANDY
September 23, 1930 (246 perfs)
Music by Kay Swift

---

*Based on stories by Sholom Aleichem
†Longest run in Broadway history
**Dropped from New York production

Lyrics by Paul James
 Rich or Poor
 Fine and Dandy
 Wheels of Steel
 Starting at the Bottom
 Can This Be Love?
 I'll Hit a New High
 Let's Go Eat Worms in the Garden
 The Jig Hop
 Nobody Breaks My Heart
 Wedding Bells

FINIAN'S RAINBOW

January 10, 1947 (725 perfs)
Music by Burton Lane
Lyrics by E. Y. Harburg
 This Time of the Year
 How Are Things in Glocca Morra?
 If This Isn't Love
 Look to the Rainbow
 Old Devil Moon
 Something Sort of Grandish
 Necessity
 When the Idle Poor Become the
  Idle Rich
 The Begat
 When I'm Not Near the Girl I Love
 That Great Come and Get It Day
Cast album: Columbia
Vocal score
Vocal selection

FIORELLO!*

November 23, 1959 (795 perfs)
Music by Jerry Bock
Lyrics by Sheldon Harnick
 On the Side of the Angels
 Politics and Poker
 Unfair
 Marie's Law
 The Name's LaGuardia
 The Bum Won
 I Love a Cop
 Till Tomorrow
 Home Again
 When Did I Fall in Love?
 Gentleman Jimmy
 Little Tin Box
 The Very Next Man
 Where Do I Go from Here?†
Cast album: Capitol
Vocal selection

FIORETTA

February 5, 1929 (111 perfs)
 Dream Boat (Music by George
  Bagby; lyrics by Grace Henry and
  Jo Trent)
 Fioretta (Music and lyrics by G.
  Romilli)
 Blade of Mine (Music by George
  Bagby; lyrics by Grace Henry)
 Alone with You (Music by G.
  Romilli; lyrics by Grace Henry
  and Jo Trent)
 Roses of Red (Music and lyrics by G.
  Romilli)
 Carissima (Music by G. Romilli; lyr-
  ics by Grace Henry)

FIREBRAND OF FLORENCE, THE**

March 22, 1945 (43 perfs)
Music by Kurt Weill
Lyrics by Ira Gershwin
 One Man's Death Is Another Man's
  Living
 Come to Florence
 My Lords and Ladies
 There'll Be Life, Love, and Laugh-
  ter
 You're Far Too Near Me
 Alessandro the Wise
 I am Happy Here
 Sing Me Not a Ballad
 When the Duchess Is Away
 I Know Where There's a Cozy Nook
 The Nighttime Is No Time for
  Thinking
 Dizzily, Busily
 The Little Naked Boy
 My Dear Benvenuto
 Just in Case
 A Rhyme for Angela
 The World is Full of Villains
 You Have to Do What You Do
  Do
 Love Is My Enemy
 Come to Paris

---

*Pulitzer Prize Winner
†Dropped from New York production
**Based on play *The Firebrand*, by Edwin
Justus Mayer

FIREMAN'S FLAME, THE (OB)
October 9, 1937 (204 perfs)
Music by Richard Lewine
Lyrics by Ted Fetter
  Hose Boys
  The Fireman's Flame
  Fire Belles' Gallop
  Doin' the Waltz
  We're Off
  Do My Eyes Deceive Me?
  Mother Isn't Getting Any Younger
  It's a Lovely Night on the Hudson
    River
  I Like the Nose on Your Face
Vocal score

FIRST IMPRESSIONS*
March 19, 1959 (84 perfs)
Music by Glenn Paxton
Lyrics by Robert Goldman and
George Weiss
  Five Daughters
  I'm Me
  Have You Heard the News?
  A Perfect Evening
  As Long As There's a Mother
  Love Will Find Out the Way
  A Gentleman Never Falls Wildly In
    Love
  Fragrant Flower
  I Feel Sorry for the Girl
  I Suddenly Find It Agreeable
  This Really Isn't Me
  Wasn't It a Simply Lovely Wed-
    ding?
  A House in Town
  The Heart Has Won the Game
  Let's Fetch the Carriage
Cast album: Columbia

FIVE O'CLOCK GIRL, THE
October 10, 1927 (280 perfs)
Music by Harry Ruby
Lyrics by Bert Kalmar
  I'm One Little Party
  We Want You†
  Thinking of You
  Happy Go Lucky
  Up in the Clouds
  Any Little Thing
  Following in Father's Footsteps
  Lonesome Romeos

Tea Time Tap
Who Did? You Did
Society Ladder
Tell the World I'm Through

FLAHOOLEY
May 14, 1951 (40 perfs)
Music by Sammy Fain
Lyrics by E. Y. Harburg
  You Too Can Be a Puppet
  Here's to Your Illusions
  B. G. Bigelow, Inc.
  Najla's Song
  Who Said There Is No Santa
    Claus?
  Flahooley
  The World Is Your Balloon
  He's Only Wonderful
  Arabian for "Get Happy"
  Jump, Little Chillun
  Spirit of Capsulanti
  Happy Hunting
  The Springtime Cometh
  Sing the Merry
Cast album: Capitol

FLORA, THE RED MENACE**
May 11, 1965 (87 perfs)
Music by John Kander
Lyrics by Fred Ebb
  Unafraid
  All I Need Is One Good Break
  Not Every Day of the Week
  Sign Here
  The Flame
  Palomino Pal
  A Quiet Thing
  Hello, Waves
  Dear Love
  Express Yourself
  Knock, Knock
  Sing Happy
  You Are You
Cast album: RCA

---

*Based on the novel *Pride and Prejudice*
by Jane Austen
†Also in *Top Speed* (1929)
**Based on the novel *Love Is Just Around
the Corner* by Lester Atwell

FLORIDA GIRL
November 2, 1925 (40 perfs)
Music by Milton Susskind
Lyrics by Paul Porter and Benjamin
Hapgood Burt
  Travel, Travel, Travel
  Oranges
  Lady of My Heart
  Smile On
  Into Society
  Daphne
  Take a Little Dip
  Oh, You!
  Trouble
  Chinky China Charleston
  As a Troubador

FLOWER DRUM SONG*
December 1, 1958 (600 perfs)
Music by Richard Rodgers
Lyrics by Oscar Hammerstein II
  You Are Beautiful
  A Hundred Million Miracles
  I Enjoy Being a Girl
  I Am Going to Like It Here
  Like a God
  Chop Suey
  Don't Marry Me
  Grant Avenue
  Love, Look Away
  Fan Tan Fannie
  Gliding through My Memoree
  The Other Generation
  Sunday
  My Best Love†
Cast album: Columbia
Vocal score
Vocal selection

FLY BLACKBIRD (OB)
February 5, 1962 (127 perfs)
Music and lyrics by C. Jackson and
James Hatch
  Everything Comes to Those Who
    Wait
  Now
  Big Betty's Song
  I'm Sick of the Whole Damn Prob-
    lem
  Who's the Fool?
  Couldn't We
  Right Way

The Ousing Cha-Cha
Natchitoches, Louisiana
Fly Blackbird
The Gong Song
Rivers to the South
Lilac Tree
Twilight Song
The Love Elixir
Mister Boy
Old White Tom
Wake Up
Cast album: Mercury

FLYING COLORS
September 15, 1932 (188 perfs)
Music by Arthur Schwartz
Lyrics by Howard Dietz
  Two-Faced Woman
  A Rainy Day
  Mother Told Me So
  A Shine on Your Shoes
  Alone Together
  Louisiana Hayride
  Mein Kleine Akrobat
  Smokin' Reefers
  Fatal Fascination
  It Was Never Like This
  Day After Day
  All's Well
  Riding Habit
  My Heart Is Part of You

FLYING HIGH
March 3, 1930 (357 perfs)
Music by Ray Henderson
Lyrics by B. G. DeSylva and Lew
Brown
  I'll Know Him
  Wasn't It Beautiful While It
    Lasted?
  Air Minded
  The First Time for Me
  Flying High
  Thank Your Father
  Happy Landing
  Good for You—Bad for Me
  Red Hot Chicago
  Without Love

―――――――
*Based on the novel by C. Y. Lee
†Dropped from New York production

Mrs. Krause's Blue-Eyed Baby Boy
I'll Get My Man

FOLLIES
April 4, 1971 (522 perfs)
Music and lyrics by Stephen Sond-
heim
Beautiful Girls
Don't Look at Me
Waiting for the Girls Upstairs
Rain on the Roof
Ah, Paris!
Broadway Baby
The Road You Didn't Take
Bolero d'Amour
In Buddy's Eyes
Who's That Woman?
I'm Still Here
Too Many Mornings
The Right Girl
One More Kiss
Could I Leave You?
Loveland
You're Gonna Love Tomorrow
Love Will See Us Through
The God-Why-Don't-You-Love-Me
Blues
Losing My Mind
The Story of Lucy and Jessie
Live, Laugh, Love
Cast album: Capitol
Vocal selection
Vocal score

FOLLOW THE GIRLS
April 8, 1944 (882 perfs)
Music by Philip Charig
Lyrics by Dan Shapiro and Milton Pas-
cal
At the Spotlight Canteen
You Don't Dance
Thanks for a Lousy Evening
You're Perf
Twelve O'Clock and All Is Well
Out for No Good
Where You Are
Follow the Girls
John Paul Jones
I Wanna Get Married
Today Will Be Yesterday Tomorrow
I'm Gonna Hang My Hat

FOLLOW THRU
January 9, 1929 (403 perfs)
Music by Ray Henderson
Lyrics by B. G. DeSylva and Lew
Brown
The Daring Gibson Girl
The 1908 Life
It's a Great Sport
My Lucky Star
Button Up Your Overcoat
You Wouldn't Fool Me, Would You?
He's a Man's Man
Then I'll Have Time for You
I Want to Be Bad
Married Men and Single Men
No More You
I Could Give Up Anything but You
Follow Thru
Still I'd Love You

FOOLS RUSH IN
December 25, 1934 (14 perfs)
Music by Will Irwin
Lyrics by Norman Zeno
I Want to Dance
Napoleon
Jim Dandy
Sitting Over There
Love, Come Take Me
Shoes
New Sensation
Rhythm in My Hair
Willie's Little Whistle
Two Get Together
Ghost Town
I'm So in Love
Building Up to a Let-Down (Lyrics
by Norman Zeno and Lee Brody)
Ca, c'est Sixth Avenue (Music and
lyrics by Lee Brody and Richard
Jones)
Sixty Second Romance (Music by
Bud Harris; lyrics by Lawrence
Harris)
Let's Hold Hands (Music by Richard
Lewine; lyrics by June Sillman)
Wicked, Unwholesome, Expensive
(Music and lyrics by John Rox)

FOOTLIGHTS
August 19, 1927 (43 perfs)
Sure Sign You Really Love Me (Mu-
sic and lyrics by Harry Denny)

Just When I Thought I Had You All to Myself (Music and lyrics by Harry Denny and Joe Fletcher)
Footlight Walk (Music and lyrics by Harry Denny)
You Can't Walk Back from an Aeroplane (Music and lyrics by Irving Bibo and William B. Friedlander)
Gypsy Sweetheart (Music and lyrics by Irving Kahal, Francis Wheeler, and Ted Snyder)
I Adore You (Music and lyrics by Ballard MacDonald, Sam Coslow, and René Mercier)
Sahara Moon (Music and lyrics by Harry Denny and Dave Ringle)

FORBIDDEN MELODY
November 2, 1936 (32 perfs)
Music by Sigmund Romberg
Lyrics by Otto Harbach
Bucharest
Lady in the Window
Just Hello
Moonlight and Violins
Two Ladies and a Man
You Are All I've Wanted
How Could a Fellow Want More?
No Use Pretending
Hear the Gypsies Playing
Shadows
When a Girl Forgets to Scream
Blame It All on the Night

FORTUNA (OB)
January 3, 1962 (5 perfs)
Music by Francis Thorne
Lyrics by Arnold Weinstein
A Deal
Someone Such As Me
Checking the Facts
Call Him Papa
In My Heart
So What? Why Not!
The Ice House Fire
O Stomach of Mine, We Eat!
Police!
Angelica
Speak in Silence
Premeditated Luck
What a Lovely Dream
Million Goes to Million

FOXY*
February 16, 1964 (72 perfs)
Music by Robert Emmett Dolan
Lyrics by Johnny Mercer
Many Ways to Skin a Cat
Rollin' in Gold
My Weight in Gold
Money Isn't Everything
Larceny and Love
Ebenezer McAfee III
Talk to Me, Baby
This Is My Night to Howl
Bon Vivant
It's Easy When You Know How
Run, Run, Run Cinderella
I'm Way Ahead of the Game
A Case of Rape
In Loving Memory

FRANK MERRIWELL, OR HONOR CHALLENGED†
April 24, 1971 (1 perf)
Music and lyrics by Skip Redwine and Larry Frank
There's No School Like Our School
Howdy, Mr. Sunshine
Prim and Proper
Inza
Look for the Happiness Ahead
I'd Be Crazy to Be Crazy Over You
Now It's Fall
The Fallin'-Out-of-Love Rag
Frank, Frank, Frank
In Real Life
The Broadway of My Heart
Winter's Here
The Pure in Heart
Don't Turn His Picture to the Wall
Manuel Your Friend

FREDERIKA
February 4, 1937 (95 perfs)
Music by Franz Lehár
Lyrics by Edward Eliscu
Out in the Sun
I Asked My Heart
Rising Star
One

---

*Suggested by Ben Jonson's *Volpone*
†Based on *Frank Merriwell's School Days* by Burt L. Standish (Gilbert Patten)

Rose in the Heather
Stormy Love
A Kiss to Remind You
Jealousy Begins at Home
Why Did You Kiss My Heart
Awake?
The Bane of Man
Vocal score

FREE FOR ALL
September 8, 1931 (15 perfs)
Music by Richard A. Whiting
Lyrics by Oscar Hammerstein II
I Love Him, the Rat
Free For All
The Girl Next Door
Living in Sin
Just Eighteen
Not That I Care
Slumber Song (Good Night)
When Your Boy Becomes a
Man
Tonight
Nevada Moonlight

FROM A TO Z
April 20, 1960 (21 perfs)
Best Gold (Music and lyrics by Jerry
Herman)
Pill Parade (Music and lyrics by Jay
Thompson)
Togetherness (Music and lyrics by
Dickson Hughes and Everett
Sloane)
Balloons (Music and lyrics by Jack
Holmes)
Hire a Guy (Music by Mary Rodgers;
lyrics by Marshall Barer)
I Said to Love (Music by Paul Klein;
lyrics by Fred Ebb)
Charlie (Music and lyrics by Fred
Ebb and Norman Martin)
Grand Jury Jump (Music by Paul
Klein; lyrics by Fred Ebb)
South American Way (Music by
Norman Martin; lyrics by Nor-
man Martin and Fred Ebb)
Time Step (Music by Paul Klein; lyr-
ics by Fred Ebb)
Countermelody (Music by Mary
Rodgers and Jay Thompson; lyrics
by Marshall Barer)

Four for the Road (Music by Paul
Klein; lyrics by Lee Goldsmith
and Fred Ebb)
What Next? (Music by Charles
Zwar; lyrics by Alan Melville)

FUNNY FACE
November 22, 1927 (244 perfs)
Music by George Gershwin
Lyrics by Ira Gershwin
Birthday Party
Once
Funny Face
High Hat
'S Wonderful
Let's Kiss and Make Up
In the Swim
He Loves and She Loves
Tell the Doc
My One and Only
Sing a Little Song
The Babbitt and the Bromide
Dance Alone with You*
The World Is Mine†
Cast album: (English production)
Monmouth-Evergreen

FUNNY GIRL
March 26, 1964 (1348 perfs)
Music by Jule Styne
Lyrics by Bob Merrill
If a Girl Isn't Pretty
I'm the Greatest Star
Cornet Man
Who Taught Her Everything?
His Love Makes Me Beautiful
I Want to Be Seen With You To-
night
Henry Street
People
You Are Woman
Don't Rain on My Parade
Sadie, Sadie
Find Yourself a Man
Rat-Tat-Tat-Tat

---

*Dropped from New York production; re-
written as "Ev'rybody Knows I Love Somebody" for *Rosalie* (1928)
†Dropped from New York production;
subsequently in *Nine-Fifteen Revue* (1930)
under title "Toddlin' Along."

Who Are You Now?
The Music That Makes Me Dance
Cast album: Capitol
Vocal score
Vocal selection

FUNNY THING HAPPENED ON THE WAY TO THE FORUM, A
May 8, 1962 (964 perfs)
Music and lyrics by Stephen Sondheim
Comedy Tonight
Love, I Hear
Free
The House of Marcus Lycus
Lovely
Pretty Little Picture
Everybody Ought to Have a Maid
I'm Calm
Impossible
Bring Me My Bride
That Dirty Old Man
That'll Show Him
Funeral Sequence
Love Is in the Air*
Cast album: Capitol
Vocal score
Vocal selection

GANG'S ALL HERE, THE
February 18, 1931 (23 perfs)
Music by Lewis E. Gensler
Lyrics by Owen Murphy and Robert A. Simon
What Have You Done to Me?
The Gang's All Here
Dumb Girl
Gypsy Rose
Baby Wanna Go Bye-Bye
Adorable Julie
Husband, Lover, and Wife
Speaking of You
By Special Permission of the Copyright Owners, I Love You
The Moon, the Wind and the Sea
It Always Takes Two
How Can I Get Rid of Those Blues?
Speak Easy

GANTRY†
February 14, 1970 (1 perf)
Music by Stanley Lebowsky
Lyrics by Fred Tobias
Wave a Hand
He Was There
Play Ball with the Lord
Katie Jonas
Thanks, Sweet Jesus!
Someone I've Already Found
He's Never Too Busy
We're Sharin' Sharon
We Can All Give Love
Foresight
These Four Walls
Show Him the Way
The Promise of What I Could Be

GARRICK GAIETIES, THE (First Edition)
May 17, 1925 (211 perfs)
Music by Richard Rodgers
Lyrics by Lorenz Hart
Soliciting Subscriptions
Gilding the Guild
Butcher, Baker, Candlestick-Maker (Music by Mana-Zucca; lyrics by Benjamin M. Kaye)
An Old-Fashioned Girl (Lyrics by Edith Meiser)
April Fool
Stage Managers' Chorus (Lyrics by Dudley Digges and Lorenz Hart)
The Joy Spreader
Rancho Mexicano (Music and Lyrics by Tatanacho)
Ladies of the Box Office
Manhattan
The Three Musketeers
Do You Love Me?
On with the Dance
Black and White
Sentimental Me

GARRICK GAIETIES, THE (Second Edition)
May 10, 1926 (174 perfs)

---

*Dropped from New York production
†Based on the novel *Elmer Gantry* by Sinclair Lewis

Music by Richard Rodgers
Lyrics by Lorenz Hart
  Mountain Greenery
  Keys to Heaven
  Sleepyhead
  Rose of Arizona
  Viennese (Music by Ladislas Kun)
  What's the Use of Talking?
  Idles of the King
  Queen Elizabeth
  Gigolo
  Four Little Song Pluggers
  Tennis Champs
  Allez-Oop

GARRICK GAIETIES, THE (Third Edition)
June 4, 1930 (155 perfs)
  Ankle Up the Altar with Me (Music by Richard Myers; lyrics by Edward Eliscu)
  You Lost Your Opportunity (Music by Charles M. Schwab; lyrics by Henry Myers)
  Do Tell (Music by Charles M. Schwab; lyrics by Henry Myers)
  Lazy Levee Loungers (Music and lyrics by Willard Robison)
  Out of Breath (Music by Everett Miller; lyrics by Johnny Mercer)
  I Am Only Human After All (Music by Vernon Duke; lyrics by Ira Gershwin and E. Y. Harburg)
  Just a Sister (Music and lyrics by Thomas McKnight)
  I'm Grover (Music by Vernon Duke; lyrics by Newman Levy)
  Johnny Wanamaker (Music by Kay Swift; lyrics by Paul James)
  Beauty (Music by Ned Lehak; lyrics by Allen Boretz)
  Put It Away Till Spring (Music by Peter Nolan; lyrics by Joshua Titzell)
  I've Got It Again (Music by Ned Lehak; lyrics by Allen Boretz)
  Scheherezade (Music and lyrics by Harold Goldman)
  Too, Too Divine (Music by Vernon Duke; lyrics by E. Y. Harburg)
  When the Sun Meets the Moon in

Finale-Land (Music by Charles M. Schwab; lyrics by Henry Myers)

GAY DIVORCE
November 29, 1932 (248 perfs)
Music and lyrics by Cole Porter
  After You
  Why Marry Them?
  Salt Air
  I Still Love the Red, White and Blue
  Night and Day
  How's Your Romance?
  What Will Become of Our England?
  I've Got You on My Mind
  Mr. and Missus Fitch
  You're in Love
Added to film: (The Gay Divorcee—1934)
  The Continental (Music by Con Conrad; lyrics by Herb Magidson)

GAY LIFE, THE*
November 18, 1961 (113 perfs)
Music by Arthur Schwartz
Lyrics by Howard Dietz
  What a Charming Couple
  Why Go Anywhere At All?
  Bring Your Darling Daughter
  Now I'm Ready for a Frau
  Magic Moment
  Who Can? You Can!
  Oh, Mein Liebchen
  The Label on the Bottle
  This Kind of a Girl
  The Bloom Is off the Rose
  I'm Glad I'm Single
  Something You Never Had Before
  You Will Never Be Lonely
  You're Not the Type
  Come A-Wandering with Me
  I Never Had a Chance
  I Wouldn't Marry You
  For the First Time
Cast album: Capitol

GAY PAREE
August 18, 1925 (190 perfs)
  Wide Pants Willie (Music by James F. Hanley; lyrics by Harold Atteridge and Henry Creamer)

_____

*Suggested by Arthur Schnitzler's *Anatole*

Tillie of Longacre Square (Music by James F. Hanley; lyrics by Harold Atteridge and Ballard Mac-Donald)

My Sugar Plum (Music by Joseph Meyer and J. Fred Coots; lyrics by B. G. DeSylva)

Give Me the Rain (Music by Maury Rubens; lyrics by Lester Allen and Henry Creamer)

Bamboo Babies (Music by Joseph Meyer and James F. Hanley; lyrics by Ballard MacDonald)

Venetian Wedding Moon (Music by Al Goodman, J. Fred Coots, and Maury Rubens; lyrics by Clifford Grey)

I Was Meant for Someone (Music by James F. Hanley; lyrics by Ballard MacDonald)

Wedgewood Maid (Music by Al Goodman, Maury Rubens, and J. Fred Coots; lyrics by Clifford Grey)

Wonderful Girls (Music by Al Goodman, and J. Fred Coots; lyrics by Clifford Grey)

Every Girl Must Have a Little Bull (Music by Al Goodman and J. Fred Coots; lyrics by Clifford Grey)

Baby's Baby Grand (Music by Al Goodman and J. Fred Coots; lyrics by Clifford Grey)

GAY PAREE
November 9, 1926 (175 perfs)
Music by Mann Holiner
Lyrics by Alberta Nichols
College Days
Fine Feathers
Bad Little Boy with Dancing Legs
Broken Rhythm
Kandahar Isle
Oriental Nights
Shaking the Blues Away
There Never Was a Town Like Paris
Do That Doo-Da (Music by Maury Rubens; lyrics by J. Keirn Brennan)
"Je t'Aime" Means I Love You (Music and lyrics by Powers Gouraud)

GENTLEMEN PREFER BLONDES*
December 8, 1949 (740 perfs)
Music by Jule Styne
Lyrics by Leo Robin
It's High Time
Bye Bye Baby
A Little Girl from Little Rock
Just a Kiss Apart
I Love What I'm Doing
It's Delightful Down in Chile
You Say You Care
I'm A'Tingle, I'm A'Glow
Sunshine
Diamonds Are a Girl's Best Friend
Mamie Is Mimi
Homesick Blues
Gentlemen Prefer Blondes
Keeping Cool with Coolidge
Cast album: Columbia
Vocal score

GEORGE M!
April 10, 1968 (435 perfs)
Music and lyrics by George M. Cohan (score consisting of more than 30 previously produced songs by Cohan with revisions by Mary Cohan)

GEORGE WHITE'S MUSIC HALL VARIETIES
November 22, 1932 (71 perfs)
Birds of a Feather (Music by Carmen Lombardo; lyrics by Irving Caesar)
So I Married the Guy (Music by Sam Stept; lyrics by Herb Magidson)
The Waltz That Brought You Back to Me (Music by Carmen Lombardo; lyrics by Irving Caesar)
Sweet Liar (Music and lyrics by Irving Caesar)
Cabin in the Cotton (Music by Harold Arlen; lyrics by Irving Caesar and George White)
Two Feet in Two-Four Time (Music by Harold Arlen; lyrics by Irving Caesar)
Rah, Rah, Rah (Music by Sam Stept; lyrics by Irving Caesar and Herb Magidson)

---

*Based on the novel by Anita Loos

Oh, Lady (Music by Sam Stept; lyrics by Herb Magidson)

Hold Me Closer (Music and lyrics by Max Rich, Frank Littau, and Jack Scholl)

A Bottle and a Bird (Music and lyrics by Irving Caesar)

Let's Turn Out the Lights and Go to Sleep (Music and lyrics by Herman Hupfeld)

GEORGE WHITE'S SCANDALS (1925)
June 22, 1925 (169 perfs)
Music by Ray Henderson
Lyrics by B. G. DeSylva and Lew Brown

Read What the Papers Say
Rose-Time
Fly, Butterfly
I Want a Lovable Baby
Say It with a Sable
Even As You and I
Room Enough for Me
The Girl of Tomorrow
The Whosis-Whatsis
What a World This Would Be
Give Us the Charleston
Beware of the Girl with the Fan

GEORGE WHITE'S SCANDALS (1926)
June 14, 1926 (424 perfs)
Music by Ray Henderson
Lyrics by B. G. DeSylva and Lew Brown

Lucky Day
Tweet Tweet
Lady Fair
Walking Dogs Around
Black Bottom
The Birth of the Blues
Sevilla
David and Lenore
The Girl Is You and the Boy Is Me
My Jewels
Twenty Years Ago

GEORGE WHITE'S SCANDALS (1928)
July 2, 1928 (230 perfs)
Music by Ray Henderson
Lyrics by B. G. DeSylva and Lew Brown

I'm on the Crest of a Wave
An Old Fashioned Girl

Pickin' Cotton
A Real American Tune
Where Your Name Is Carved with Mine
What D'Ya Say?

GEORGE WHITE'S SCANDALS (1929)
September 23, 1929 (161 perfs)
Music and lyrics by Cliff Friend and George White

Bigger and Better than Ever
Sitting in the Sun (Just Wearing a Smile)
Bottoms Up
You Are My Day Dream
Drop Your Kerchief
Love Birds
18 Days Ago
Is Izzy Azzy Woz?
There's Something Spanish in Your Eyes

GEORGE WHITE'S SCANDALS (1931)
September 14, 1931 (202 perfs)
Music by Ray Henderson
Lyrics by B. G. DeSylva and Lew Brown

Life Is Just a Bowl of Cherries
Beginning of Love
The Thrill Is Gone
This Is the Missus
Ladies and Gentlemen, That's Love
That's Why Darkies Were Born
Song of the Foreign Legion
Here It Is
My Song
Back from Hollywood
The Good Old Days

GEORGE WHITE'S SCANDALS (1936)
December 25, 1935 (110 perfs)
Music by Ray Henderson
Lyrics by Jack Yellen

Life Begins at Sweet Sixteen
Boondoggling
Cigarette
I Like It With Music
Truckin' in My Tails
May I Have My Gloves?
I'm the Fellow Who Loves You
Models
I've Got to Get Hot

Anything Can Happen (Lyrics by Jack Yellen and Ballard Mac-Donald)

GEORGE WHITE'S SCANDALS (1939)
August 28, 1939 (120 perfs)
Music by Sammy Fain
Lyrics by Jack Yellen
Are You Havin' Any Fun?
Smart Little Girls
Our First Kiss
The Mexiconga (Lyrics by Jack Yellen and Herb Magidson)
Good Night, My Beautiful
Something I Dreamed Last Night (Lyrics by Jack Yellen and Herb Magidson)
In Waikiki
The Songs for Free

GEORGY*
February 26, 1970 (4 perfs)
Music by George Fischoff
Lyrics by Carole Bayer
Howdjadoo
Make It Happen Now
Ol' Pease Puddin'
Just for the Ride
So What?
Georgy
A Baby
That's How It Is
There's a Comin' Together
Something Special
Half of Me
Gettin' Back to Me
Sweet Memory
Life's a Holiday

GERTRUDE STEIN'S FIRST READER
(OB)
December 15, 1969 (40 perfs)
Music by Ann Sternberg
Lyrics by Gertrude Stein
Sunshine
Wildflowers
A Dog
The Blackberry Vine
Big Bird
The Three Sisters Who Are Not Sisters
Be Very Careful

New World
Jenny
How They Do, Do
In a Garden
Cast album: Polydor

GET THEE TO CANTERBURY† (OB)
January 25, 1969 (20 perfs)
Music by Paul Hoffert
Lyrics by David Secter
Get Thee to Canterbury
The Journey
Take a Pick
Death Beware
Buy My Pardons
Dreams
Canter Banter
Day of Judgement
Ballad of Sir Topaz
Bottom's Up
A Simple Wife
Shadows
Alison Dear
Where are the Blossoms
On the Relative Merits of Education and Experience
Everybody Gets It in the End

GIRL CRAZY
October 14, 1930 (272 perfs)
Music by George Gershwin
Lyrics by Ira Gershwin
The Lonesome Cowboy
Bidin' My Time
Could You Use Me?
Broncho Busters
Barbary Coast
Embraceable You
Sam and Delilah
I Got Rhythm
Land of the Gay Caballero
But Not for Me
Treat Me Rough
Boy! What Love Has Done to Me!
When It's Cactus Time in Arizona

---

*Based on the novel by Margaret Forster and the screen play by Margaret Forster and Peter Nichols
†Adapted from Chaucer's The Canterbury Tales

Added to film version (1932):
You've Got What Gets Me
Album: (Studio cast) Columbia
Vocal score

GIRL FRIEND, THE
March 17, 1926 (301 perfs)
Music by Richard Rodgers
Lyrics by Lorenz Hart
Hey! Hey!
The Simple Life
The Girl Friend
Good-bye, Lenny!
The Blue Room
Cabarets
Why Do I?
The Damsel Who Done All the Dirt
He's a Winner
Town Hall Tonight
Good Fellow, Mine
Creole Crooning Song
I'd Like to Take You Home
What Is It?

GIRL FROM NANTUCKET, THE
November 8, 1945 (12 perfs)
Music by Jacques Belasco
Lyrics by Kay Twomey
I Want to See More of You
Take the Steamer to Nantucket
What's He Like?
What's a Sailor Got?
Magnificent Failure (Music and lyrics by Hughie Prince and Dick Rogers)
When a Hick Chick Meets a City Slicker (Lyrics by Burt Milton)
Your Fatal Fascination
Let's Do and Say We Didn't (Music and lyrics by Hughie Prince and Dick Rogers)
Nothing Matters
Sons of the Sea
Isn't It a Lovely View?
From Morning Till Night
I Love That Boy
Hammock in the Blue
Boukra Fill Mish Mish

GIRL FROM WYOMING, THE (OB)
October 29, 1938 (86 perfs)
Music by Richard Lewine

Lyrics by Ted Fetter
Boston in the Spring
Ride, Cowboy, Ride
Hats Off
Manuelo
The Dying Cowboy
Lullaby of the Plain
Our Home
Stay East, Young Man
Kickin' the Corn Around

GIRL IN PINK TIGHTS, THE
March 5, 1954 (115 perfs)
Music by Sigmund Romberg (developed by Don Walker)
Lyrics by Leo Robin
That Naughty Show from Gay Paree
Lost in Loveliness
I Promised Their Mothers
Up in the Elevated Railway
In Paris and in Love
You've Got to Be a Little Crazy
When I Am Free to Love
Out of the Way
Roll Out the Hose, Boys
My Heart Won't Say Goodbye
We're All in the Same Boat
Love Is the Funniest Thing
The Cardinal's Guard Are We
Cast album: Columbia

GIRL WHO CAME TO SUPPER, THE*
December 8, 1963 (112 perfs)
Music and lyrics by Noël Coward
Swing Song
Yasni Kozkolai
My Family Tree
I've Been Invited to a Party
When Foreign Princes Come to Visit Us
Sir or Ma'am
Soliloquies
Lonely
London Is a Little Bit of All Right
What Ho, Mrs. Brisket
Don't Take Our Charlie for the Army

———

*Based on the play *The Sleeping Prince* by Terence Rattigan

Saturday Night at the Rose and Crown
Coronation Chorale
How Do You Do, Middle Age?
Here and Now
Curt, Clear and Concise
Welcome to Pootzie Van Doyle
The Coconut Girl
Paddy MacNeil and His Automobile
Six Lillies of the Valley
The Walla Walla Boola
This Time It's True Love
I'll Remember Her
Cast album: Columbia

GIRLS AGAINST THE BOYS, THE
November 2, 1959 (16 perfs)
Music by Richard Lewine
Lyrics by Arnold B. Horwitt
The Girls Against the Boys
Rich Butterfly
I Gotta Have You
Lolita
Where Did We Go? Out
Too Young to Live
Overspend
Girls and Boys
Old Fashioned Girl
Nobody Else But You (Music by Albert Hague)

GIRLS OF SUMMER
(Play with one song)
November 19, 1956 (56 perfs)
Music and lyrics by Stephen Sondheim
Girls of Summer

GOD IS A (GUESS WHAT?) (OB)
December 17, 1968 (32 perfs)
Music by Coleridge-Taylor Perkinson
Lyrics by Ray McIver
A Mighty Fortress
The Lynch-Him Song
The Sonny-Boy Slave Song
The Black-Black Song
The Golden Rule Song
God Will Take Care
The Darkies Song
The Sit Down Song
The Lyncher's Prayer

GODSPELL* (OB)
May 17, 1971†
Music and lyrics by Stephen Schwartz
Tower of Babble
Prepare Ye the Way of the Lord
Save the People
Day by Day
Learn Your Lessons Well
Bless the Lord
All for the Best
All Good Gifts
Light of the World
Turn Back, O Man
Alas for You
By My Side (Music by Peggy Gordon; lyrics by Jay Hamburger)
We Beseech Thee
On the Willows
Cast album: Bell
Vocal selection

GOGO LOVES YOU (OB)
October 9, 1964 (2 perfs)
Music by Claude Leveilee
Lyrics by Gladys Shelley
Parnasse
Prima Donna
Bazoom
He Can, I Can
Gogo
There Is No Difference
Keep in Touch
My Uncle's Mistress
Happy Love Affair
Tell Me the Story of Your Life
Woman Makes the Man
Life Is Lovely
College of L'Amour
Savoir Faire
Quelle Heure Est-Il?

GOLDEN APPLE, THE
April 20, 1954 (173 perfs)**
Music by Jerome Moross
Lyrics by John Latouche
Nothing Ever Happens in Angel's Roost

---

*Based on the Gospel according to St. Matthew
†Still running December 31, 1971
**Includes original OB run

My Love Is on the Way
It Was a Glad Adventure
Come Along, Boys
It's the Going Home Together
Helen Is Always Willing
Introducin' Mr. Paris
Lazy Afternoon
My Picture in the Papers
Windflowers
Store-bought Suit
Goona-Goona
Doomed, Doomed, Doomed
Circe, Circe
Cast album: Elektra

GOLDEN BOY*
October 20, 1964 (569 perfs)
Music by Charles Strouse
Lyrics by Lee Adams
  Workout
  Night Song
  Everything's Great
  Gimme Some
  Stick Around
  Don't Forget 127th Street
  Lorna's Here
  The Road Tour
  This Is the Life
  Golden Boy
  While the City Sleeps
  Colorful
  I Want To Be with You
  No More
  Can't You See It?
  The Fight
Cast album: Capitol
Vocal selection

GOLDEN DAWN
November 30, 1927 (184 perfs)
Music by Emmerich Kalman and Herbert Stothart
Lyrics by Otto Harbach and Oscar Hammerstein II
  The Whip
  We Two
  Here in the Dark
  My Bwanna
  Consolation
  Africa
  Dawn (Music by Robert Stolz and Herbert Stothart)

Jungle Shadows
Mulunghu Tabu
It's Always the Way

GOLDEN RAINBOW†
February 4, 1968 (385 perfs)
Music and lyrics by Walter Marks
  Golden Rainbow
  We Got Us
  He Needs Me Now
  Kid
  For Once in Your Life
  Taking Care of You
  I've Got To Be Me
  Taste
  Desert Moon
  All in Fun
  It's You Again
  How Could I Be So Wrong
Cast album: Columbia
Vocal selection

GOLDEN SCREW, THE (OB)
January 27, 1967 (40 perfs)
Music and lyrics by Tom Sankey
  New Evaline
  2000 Miles
  Jesus Come Down
  You Won't Say No
  The Beautiful People
  I Heard My Mother Crying
  I Can't Make It Anymore
  Can I Touch You?
  That's Your Thing, Baby
  I Can't Remember
  Bottom End of Bleecker Street
  Flippin' Out
  Little White Dog

GOLDILOCKS
October 11, 1958 (161 perfs)
Music by Leroy Anderson
Lyrics by Joan Ford, Walter and Jean Kerr
  Lazy Moon
  Give the Little Lady a Great Big Hand

---

*Based on the play by Clifford Odets
†Based on the play *A Hole in the Head* by Arnold Schulman

Save a Kiss
No One'll Ever Love You
Who's Been Sitting in My Chair?
There Never Was a Woman
The Pussy Foot
Lady in Waiting
The Beast in You
Shall I Take My Heart and Go?
I Can't Be in Love
Bad Companions
I Never Know When
Two Years in the Making
Heart of Stone
Cast album: Columbia

GOOD BOY
September 5, 1928 (253 perfs)
Music and lyrics by Herbert Stothart,
Bert Kalmar, and Harry Ruby
What Makes You So Wonderful
Good Boy
The Voice of the City
Manhattan Walk
Some Sweet Someone
I Have My Moments
I Wanna Be Loved By You
The Three Bears
Oh, What a Man
Good Boy Wedding March
Nina

GOOD NEWS
September 6, 1927 (551 perfs)
Music by Ray Henderson
Lyrics by B. G. DeSylva and Lew
Brown
A Ladies' Man
Flaming Youth
Happy Days
Just Imagine
The Best Things in Life Are Free
On the Campus
The Varsity Drag
Baby! What?
Lucky in Love
A Girl of the Pi Beta Phi
In the Meantime
Good News
Added to film version: (1947)
The French Lesson (Music by Roger
Edens; lyrics by Betty Comden
and Adolph Green)

Pass That Peace Pipe (Music and
lyrics by Roger Edens, Hugh Martin, and Ralph Blane)
Soundtrack album: MGM

GRAND STREET FOLLIES, THE (1926) (OB)
June 15, 1926 (55 perfs)
Fixed for Life (Music by Randall
Thompson; lyrics by Agnes Mor-
gan)
Little Igloo for Two (Music by Ar-
thur Schwartz; lyrics by Agnes
Morgan)
The Boosters' Song of the Far North
(Music by Randall Thompson; lyr-
ics by Agnes Morgan)
Aurory Bory Alice (Music by Lily
Hyland; lyrics by Agnes Morgan)
Taxi Drivers' Lament (Music by
Randall Thompson; lyrics by
Agnes Morgan)
The Discontented Bandits (Music
by Lily Hyland; lyrics by Agnes
Morgan)
Beatrice Lillie Ballad (Music by
Randall Thompson; lyrics by
Agnes Morgan)
My Icy Floe (Music by Randall
Thompson; lyrics by Agnes Mor-
gan)
If You Know What I Mean (Music by
Arthur Schwartz; lyrics by Theo-
dore Goodwin and Albert Carroll)
The Polar Bear Strut (Music by Ar-
thur Schwartz; lyrics by Theo-
dore Goodwin)
Northern Blues (Music by Walter
(Gustave) Haenschen; lyrics by
Robert A. Simon)

GRAND STREET FOLLIES, THE (1927) (OB)
May 19, 1927 (148 perfs)
Music by Max Ewing
Lyrics by Agnes Morgan
Stars with Stripes (Lyrics by Doro-
thy Sands and Marc Loebell)
La Prisonnière (Lyrics by Albert
Carroll)
Three Little Maids
Don't Ask Her Another

If You Haven't Got "It"
A Bedtime Story
The Naughty Nineties
Unaccustomed As I Am
The Banquet

GRAND STREET FOLLIES, THE (1928)
May 28, 1928 (144 perfs)
Music by Max Ewing and Serge Walter
Lyrics by Agnes Morgan
  Command to Love (Music by Serge Walter)
  Tu Sais (Music by Serge Walter)
  Just a Little Love Song (Music and lyrics by Max Ewing)
  Someone to Admire, Someone to Adore (Music by Serge Walter)
  The Briny Blues (Music by Serge Walter)
  Husky, Dusky Annabelle (Music by Max Ewing)
  Hey, Nonny, Hey (Music by Max Ewing)

GRAND STREET FOLLIES, THE (1929)
May 1, 1929 (85 perfs)
Lyrics by Agnes Morgan
  The Amoeba's Lament (Music by Arthur Schwartz)
  The Double Standard (Music by Arthur Schwartz)
  The Vineyards of Manhattan (Music by Arthur Schwartz)
  Priam's Little Congai (Music by Will Irwin)
  I've Got You on My Mind (Music and lyrics by Max Ewing)
  British Maidens (Music by Max Ewing)
  A Room with a Bath (Music by Max Ewing)
  The Girl I Might Have Been (Music and lyrics by Max Ewing)
  I Need You So (Music by Arthur Schwartz; lyrics by David Goldberg and Howard Dietz)
  Don't Do It (Music by Arthur Schwartz)
  I Love You and I Like You (Music by Arthur Schwartz; lyrics by Max and Nathaniel Lief)

The Pilgrim Fathers (Music by Serge Walter)
The Textile Troops (Music by Max Ewing)
What Did Della Wear? (Music by Arthur Schwartz; lyrics by Agnes Morgan and Albert Carroll)
My Dynamo (Music by Arthur Schwartz)
I'll Never Forget (Music by Max Ewing; lyrics by Albert Carroll)

GRASS HARP, THE*
November 2, 1971 (7 perfs)
Music by Claibe Richardson
Lyrics by Kenward Elmslie
  Dropsy Cure Weather
  This One Day
  Think Big Rich
  If There's Love Enough
  Yellow Drum
  Marry with Me
  I'll Always Be in Love
  Floozies
  Call Me Babylove
  Walk into Heaven
  Hang a Little Moolah on the Washline
  Talkin' in Tongues
  Whooshin' through My Flesh
  Something for Nothing
  Indian Blues
  Take a Little Sip
  What Do I Do Now?
  Pick Yourself a Flower
  Reach Out
Cast album: Painted Smiles

GREAT DAY!
October 17, 1929 (36 perfs)
Music by Vincent Youmans
Lyrics by Billy Rose and Edward Eliscu
  Does It Pay to Be a Lady?
  I Like What You Like
  Happy Because I'm in Love
  Great Day!
  One Love

———
*Based on the novel and play by Truman Capote

Si, Si, Señor
Open Up Your Heart
The Wedding Bells Ring On
More Than You Know
Play the Game
Help Us Tonight
Sweet As Sugar Cane
Without a Song
Scarecrows

GREAT LADY

December 1, 1938 (20 perfs)
Music by Frederick Loewe
Lyrics by Earle Crooker
A Promenade
Sweet William
I Have Room in My Heart
Why Can't This Night Last
  Forever?
May I Suggest Romance?
In the Carefree Realm of Fancy
To Whom It May Concern
Though Tongues May Wag
Keep Your Hand on Your Heart
And So Will You
The Little Corporal
Sisters under the Skin
There Had to Be the Waltz
I Never Saw a King Before
Madame Is at Home

GREAT MAGOO, THE

(Play with one song)
December 2, 1932 (11 perfs)
Music by Harold Arlen
Lyrics by Billy Rose and E. Y. Harburg
It's Only a Paper Moon*

GREAT SCOT! (OB)

November 10, 1965 (38 perfs)
Music by Don McAfee
Lyrics by Nancy Leeds
You're The Only One
Great Scot!
I'll Find a Dream Somewhere
He's Not for Me
That Special Day
Brandy in Your Champagne
I'm Gonna Have a Baby
Original Sin
I'll Still Love Jean
Where Is That Rainbow?

Princes' Street
Happy New Year
That Big-Bellied Bottle
He Knows Where to Find Me
Where Does a Man Begin?
What A Shame
I Left a Dream Somewhere
We're Gonna Have a Wedding

GREAT TEMPTATIONS, THE

May 18, 1926 (197 perfs)
Music by Maury Rubens
Lyrics by Clifford Grey
Never Say the World Was Made to
  Cry
Any Step
The Spider's Web (Music by Milton
  Schwarzwald)
A Pin Cushion
The Temptation Strut (Music by
  Earl Lindsday and Maury Ru-
  bens)
The Guards of Fantasy
Querida
Valencia (Music by José Padilla)
A Garden of Memories
The Chevalier of the Highway
Dancing Town
Beauty Is Vanity
The Atlantic City Girl

GREAT TO BE ALIVE

March 23, 1950 (52 perfs)
Music by Abraham Ellstein
Lyrics by Walter Bullock
When the Sheets Come Back from
  the Laundry
It's a Long Time Till Tomorrow
Headin' for a Weddin'
Redecorate
What a Day!
Call It Love
There's Nothing Like It
Dreams Ago
From This Day On
Who Done It?
Blue Day
Thank You, Mrs. Butterfield

---

*Also in film Take A Chance (1933)

GREAT WALTZ, THE
September 22, 1934 (347 perfs)
Music by Johann Strauss
Lyrics by Desmond Carter
  Morning
  Look Before You Leap
  You Are My Songs
  Love Will Find You
  On Love Alone
  Like a Star in the Sky
  With All My Heart
  Night
  Love's Never Lost
  For We Love You Still
  While You Love Me
  Love and War
  Danube So Blue
Vocal score

GREENWICH VILLAGE FOLLIES, THE (1925)
December 24, 1925 (180 perfs)
Music by Harold Levey
Lyrics by Owen Murphy
  You Have Me—I Have You
  The Lady of the Snow
  Life Is Like a Toy Balloon
  See Yourselves in the Mirror
  Whistle Away Your Blues (Music by Richard Myers; lyrics by Leo Robin)
  The Window Cleaners (Music by Harry Ruby; lyrics by Bert Kalmar)
  Go South (Music by Richard Myers; lyrics by Owen Murphy)
  The Life of the Party (Music by Richard Myers; lyrics by Harry Ruskin)

GREENWICH VILLAGE FOLLIES, THE (1928)
April 9, 1928 (128 perfs)
Music by Ray Perkins
Lyrics by Max and Nathaniel Lief
  Padlock Your Blues
  Golden Gate
  What's the Reason? (Music by Maury Rubens; lyrics by Harold Atteridge)
  Slaves of Broadway
  Get Your Man
  The Subway Sun
  Who's the Boy?
  Down at the Village
  High, High Up in the Clouds (Music by Maury Rubens)

GREENWICH VILLAGE U.S.A. (OB)
September 28, 1960 (87 perfs)
Music by Jeanne Bargy
Lyrics by Jeanne Bargy, Frank Gehrecke, and Herb Corey
  Greenwich Village U.S.A.
  How Can Anyone So Sweet
  Happy Guy
  Why Can't We Be Unhappy?
  Love's Melody
  We Got Love
  Time to Call It Quits
  Baby, You Bore Me
  Love Me
  Mulhaney's Song
Cast album: 20th Century

GREENWILLOW*
March 8, 1960 (95 perfs)
Music and lyrics by Frank Loesser
  A Day Borrowed from Heaven
  The Music of Home
  Dorrie's Wish
  Gideon Briggs, I Love You
  Summertime Love
  Walking Away Whistling
  The Sermon
  Greenwillow Christmas
  Could've Been a Ring
  Never Will I Marry
  Faraway Boy
  Clang Dang the Bell
  What a Blessing
  He Died Good
Cast album: RCA

GUYS AND DOLLS†
November 24, 1950 (1,200 perfs)
Music and lyrics by Frank Loesser
  Fugue for Tinhorns
  Follow the Fold
  The Oldest Established

---

*Based on the novel by B. J. Chute
†Based on the Damon Runyon story *The Idyll of Miss Sarah Brown*

I'll Know
A Bushel and a Peck
Adelaide's Lament
Guys and Dolls
If I Were a Bell
My Time of Day
I've Never Been in Love Before
Take Back Your Mink
More I Cannot Wish You
Luck Be a Lady
Sue Me
Sit Down, You're Rockin' the Boat
Cast album: Decca
Vocal selection
Vocal Score
Added to film version: (1955)
A Woman in Love
Pet Me, Poppa
Adelaide

GYPSY*
May 21, 1959 (702 perfs)
Music by Jule Styne
Lyrics by Stephen Sondheim
Let Me Entertain You
Some People
Small World
Mr. Goldstone
Little Lamb
You'll Never Get Away From Me
Broadway
If Momma Was Married
All I Need Is the Girl
Everything's Coming Up Roses
Together Wherever We Go
You Gotta Get a Gimmick
Mamma's Talkin' Soft†
Rose's Turn
Cast album: Columbia
Vocal score
Vocal selection

HAIR
April 29, 1968 (1,742 perfs)
Music by Galt MacDermot
Lyrics by Gerome Ragni and James
Rado
Aquarius
Donna
Hashish
Sodomy
Colored Spade

Manchester
Ain't Got No
I Believe in Love
Air
Initials
I Got Life
Going Down
Hair
My Conviction
Easy to be Hard
Hung
Don't Put It Down
Frank Mills
Hare Krishna
Where Do I Go?
Electric Blues
Black Boys
White Boys
Walking in Space
Abie Baby
Prisoners in Niggertown
What a Piece of Work Is Man
Good Morning Starshine
The Bed
The Flesh Failures
Cast album: RCA
Vocal selection

HAIRPIN HARMONY
October 1, 1943 (3 perfs)
Music and lyrics by Harold Orlob
Hairpin Harmony
What-a-Ya-Say
You're the Reason
I'm Tickled Pink
I'm a Butter Hoarder
Without a Sponsor
I Can Be Like Grandpa
That's My Approach to Love
What Do the Neighbors Say?
Piccaninny Pie

HALF A SIXPENCE**
April 25, 1965 (512 perfs)
Music and lyrics by David Heneker
All in the Cause of Economy

---

*Suggested by the memoirs of Gypsy Rose
Lee
†Dropped from New York production
**Based on H. G. Wells' *Kipps*

Half a Sixpence
Money to Burn
A Proper Gentleman
She's Too Far Above Me
If the Rain's Got to Fall
The Old Military Canal
Long Ago
Flash Bang Wallop
I Know What I Am
The Party's on the House
Cast album: RCA
Vocal score
Vocal selection

HALF A WIDOW
September 12, 1927 (16 perfs)
Music by Shep Camp
Lyrics by Frank DuPree and Harry B.
Smith
  Let's Laugh and Be Merry
  Under the Midsummer Moon (Lyrics by Harry B. Smith)
  It's Great to Be a Doughboy (Lyrics by Frank DuPree)
  Longing for You (Lyrics by Frank DuPree)
  I Wonder If She Will Remember
  Step, Step, Step (Music and lyrics by Jack Murray and Joe Brandfon)
  Tell Me Again (Lyrics by Frank DuPree)
  A Thousand Times
  Soldier Boy
  You're a Wonderful Girl
  I'm Through with War
  France Will Not Forget (Music and lyrics by Geoffrey O'Hara and Gordon Johnstone)

HALF-PAST WEDNESDAY (OB)
April 6, 1962 (2 perfs)
Music by Robert Colby
Lyrics by Robert Colby and Nita Jonas
  Give 'Em a Lollipop
  I've Got a Goose
  What's the Fun of Being King
  You're the Sweet Beginning
  Who? Where? What?
  Spinning Song
  Jumpin' Jehosephat
  If You Did It Once
  How Lovely, How Lovely

Ladies in Waiting
Grandfathers
To-Whit-To-Whoo
What's the Name of What's-His-Name?
If-If-If-If
Companionship
I Know a Secret
Cast album: Columbia

HALLELUJAH, BABY!
April 26, 1967 (293 perfs)
Music by Jule Styne
Lyrics by Betty Comden and Adolph
Green
  Back in the Kitchen
  My Own Morning
  The Slice
  Farewell, Farewell
  Feet Do Yo' Stuff
  Watch My Dust
  Smile, Smile
  Witches' Brew
  I Wanted to Change Him
  Being Good Isn't Good Enough
  Talking to Yourself
  Hallelujah, Baby
  Not Mine
  I Don't Know Where She Got It
  Now's the Time
Cast album: Columbia
Vocal selection

**HAPPIEST GIRL IN THE WORLD,
THE***
April 3, 1961 (97 perfs)
Music by Jacques Offenbach
Lyrics by E. Y. Harburg
  The Olympics
  Cheers for the Hero
  The Glory That Is Greece
  The Happiest Girl in the World
  The Greek Marine
  Shall We Say Farewell?
  Never Be-Devil the Devil
  Whatever That May Be
  Eureka
  Vive la Virtue
  Adrift on a Star

---

*With a bow to Aristophanes and Bulfinch

That'll Be the Day
How Soon, Oh Moon
Love-Sick Serenade
Five Minutes of Spring
Never Trust a Virgin
Cast album: Columbia

HAPPY
December 5, 1927 (82 perfs)
Music by Frank Grey
Lyrics by Earle Crooker and McElbert Moore
  Plastic Surgery
  Check Your Troubles
  Through the Night
  Sunny Side of You
  Lorelei
  If You'll Put Up with Me
  Happy
  Here's to You, Jack
  One Good Friend
  Hitting on High
  Blacksheep
  Which Shall It Be? (Lyrics by Ethelberta Hasbrook)
  What a Lovely Night
  Mad About You

HAPPY AS LARRY
January 6, 1950 (3 perfs)
Music by Mischa and Wesley Portnoff
Lyrics by Donagh MacDonagh
  No One Loves Me
  Without a Stitch
  Now and Then
  October
  Mrs. Larry, Tell Me This
  A Cup of Tea
  He's with My Johnny
  And So He Died
  Three Old Ladies from Hades
  It's Pleasant and Delightful
  The Dirty Dog
  The Flatulent Ballad
  The Loyalist Wife
  Oh, Mrs. Larry
  Give the Doctor the Best in the House
  Double Murder, Double Death
  He's a Bold Rogue
  I Remember Her
  The Tobacco Blues

HAPPY BIRTHDAY
(Play with one song)
October 31, 1946 (564 perfs)
Music by Richard Rodgers
Lyrics by Oscar Hammerstein II
  I Haven't Got a Worry in the World

HAPPY GO LUCKY
September 30, 1926 (52 perfs)
Music by Lucien Denni
Lyrics by Helena Evans
  Sing a Little Song
  Free, Free, Free
  Love Thoughts
  How Are You, Lady Love?
  When I Make a Million for You
  Happy Melody
  Choose Your Flowers
  It's In, It's Out
  Zip
  It's Wonderful
  Happy Go Lucky
  In Vaudeville
  Wall Street Zoo
  You're the Fellow the Fortune Teller Told Me All About

HAPPY HUNTING
December 6, 1956 (412 perfs)
Music by Harold Karr
Lyrics by Matt Dubey
  Postage Stamp Principality
  Don't Tell Me
  Gee, but It's Good to Be Here
  Mutual Admiration Society
  For Love or Money
  It's Like a Beautiful Woman
  Wedding-of-the-Year Blues
  Mr. Livingstone
  If'n
  This Is What I Call Love
  A New-Fangled Tango
  She's Just Another Girl
  The Game of Love
  Happy Hunting
  I'm a Funny Dame
  This Much I Know
  Just Another Guy
  Everyone Who's "Who's Who"
Cast album: RCA

HAPPY HYPOCRITE, THE* (OB)
September 5, 1968 (17 perfs)
Music by James Bredt
Lyrics by Edward Eager
  Street Song
  Deep in Me
  The Amorous Arrow
  Echo Song
  Miss Mere
  Mornings at Seven
  The Song of the Mask
  Almost Too Good to Be True
  Don't Take Sides
  Hell Hath No Fury
  I Must Smile
  Once, Only Once
  The Face of Love

HAPPY TIME, THE†
January 18, 1968 (286 perfs)
Music by John Kander
Lyrics by Fred Ebb
  The Happy Time
  He's Back
  Catch My Garter
  Tomorrow Morning
  Please Stay
  I Don't Remember You
  St. Pierre
  Without Me
  Among My Yesterdays
  The Life of the Party
  Seeing Things
  A Certain Girl
  Being Alive
Cast album: RCA
Vocal selection

HAPPY TOWN
October 7, 1959 (5 perfs)
Music by Gordon Duffy
Lyrics by Harry M. Haldane
  It Isn't Easy
  Celebration!
  Something Special
  The Legend of Black-Eyed Susan
    Grey
  Opportunity!
  As Busy As Anyone Can Be
  Heaven Protect Me!
  I Feel Like a Brother to You
  Hoedown!

I Am What I Am!
The Beat of a Heart
Mean
When the Time Is Right
Pick-Me-Up!
I'm Stuck with Love
Nothing in Common
Talkin' 'bout You
Y' Can't Win

HARRY DELMAR'S REVELS
November 28, 1927 (114 perfs)
  I Love a Man in Uniform (Music by
    Jimmy Monaco; lyrics by Billy
    Rose and Ballard MacDonald)
  My Rainbow (Music by Jeanne
    Hackett; lyrics by Lester Lee)
  Say It with a Solitaire (Music by
    Jimmy Monaco; lyrics by Billy
    Rose and Ballard MacDonald)
  If You Have Troubles Laugh Them
    Away (Music and lyrics by Lester
    Lee)
  Irresistible You (Music by Jimmy
    Monaco; lyrics by Billy Rose and
    Ballard MacDonald)

HAVE I GOT ONE FOR YOU (OB)
January 7, 1968 (1 perf)
Music by Jerry Blatt
Lyrics by Jerry Blatt and Lonnie Bur-
stein
  The Toad's Lament
  Chapter One
  Fly Away
  It's Comin' True
  Have I Got a Girl for You
  Imagine Me
  Ode to Marcello
  Livin' in a Hole
  The Chicken Song
  I Should Stay
  My Dream Is Through
  What a Bore
  A Nice Girl Like You
  So It Goes

---

*Based on the short story by Max Beer-
bohm
†Based on the play by Samuel Taylor and
the book by Robert L. Fontaine

The Getaway Quintet
¾ Drag
The Presentation
Cast album: ABC-Paramount

HAZEL FLAGG*
February 11, 1953 (190 perfs)
Music by Jule Styne
Lyrics by Bob Hilliard
A Little More Heart
The World Is Beautiful Today
I'm Glad I'm Leaving
Hello, Hazel
Paris Gown
Every Street's a Boulevard in Old New York
How Do You Speak to an Angel?
I Feel Like I'm Gonna Live Forever
You're Gonna Dance with Me, Willie
Who Is the Bravest?
Salomee
Autograph Chant
Laura De Maupassant
Cast album: RCA

HEADS UP!
November 11, 1929 (144 perfs)
Music by Richard Rodgers
Lyrics by Lorenz Hart
You've Got to Surrender
Play Boy
Mother Grows Younger
Why Do You Suppose?†
Me for You
Ongsay and Anceday
It Must Be Heaven
My Man Is On the Make
The Lass Who Loved a Sailor
A Ship without a Sail
Knees
I Can Do Wonders with You**
Sky City**

HEAVEN ON EARTH
September 16, 1948 (12 perfs)
Music by Jay Gorney
Lyrics by Barry Trivers
In the Back of a Hack
Anything Can Happen
You're So Near (So Near and Yet So Far)

Don't Forget to Dream
Bench in the Park
The Letter
Push a Button in a Hutton
Home Is Where the Heart Is
Apple Jack
Wedding in the Park
Heaven on Earth
What's the Matter with Our City?
You're the First Cup of Coffee
Gift Number
Musical Tour of the City

HELEN GOES TO TROY
April 24, 1944 (96 perfs)
Music by Erich Wolfgang Korngold (based on Offenbach)
Lyrics by Herbert Baker
Come to the Sacrifice
Where Is Love?
Tsing-la-la
Take My Advice
The Shepherd Song
The Judgement of Paris
What Will the Future Say?
Extra! Extra!
Sweet Helen
Love at Last
Bring on the Concubines
If Menelaus Only Knew It
Is It a Dream?
A Little Chat
Advice to Husbands
Come with Me

HELLO DADDY
December 26, 1928 (196 perfs)
Music by Jimmy McHugh
Lyrics by Dorothy Fields
Three Little Maids from School
I Want Plenty of You
Futuristic Rhythm
Let's Sit and Talk about You
Your Disposition Is Mine
In a Great Big Way

---

*Based on the film *Nothing Sacred* by Ben Hecht
†Originally written as "How Was I To Know?" for *She's My Baby* (1928)
**Dropped from New York production

Maybe Means Yes
As Long As We're in Love
Out Where the Blues Begin

HELLO, DOLLY!*
January 16, 1964 (2,844 perfs)
Music and lyrics by Jerry Herman
I Put My Hand In
It Takes a Woman
Put on Your Sunday Clothes
Ribbons Down My Back
Motherhood
Dancing
Before the Parade Passes By
Elegance
Hello, Dolly!
It Only Takes a Moment
So Long, Dearie
Love, Look in My Window†
World, Take Me Back†
Cast album: RCA
Vocal score
Vocal selection

HELLO, LOLA**
January 12, 1926 (47 perfs)
Music by William B. Kernell
Lyrics by Dorothy Donnelly
Bread and Butter and Sugar
The Summer Time
My Brother Willie
My Baby Talk Lady
Hello, Cousin Lola
Five Foot-Two
Step on the Gasoline
Swinging on the Gate
That Certain Party
In the Dark
I Know Something
Little Boy Blue
Keep It Up
Sophie
Don't Stop

HELLO, PARIS††
November 15, 1930 (33 perfs)
Deep Paradise (Music by Russell Tarbox; lyrics by Charles O. Locke)
Gotta Have Hips Now (Music by Russell Tarbox; lyrics by Charles O. Locke)

Every Bit of You (Music and lyrics by Kenneth Friede and Adrian Samish)
I Stumbled over You (Music by Maury Rubens; lyrics by Henry Dagand)
Prairie Blues (Music by Russell Tarbox; lyrics by Charles O. Locke)
I'll Admit (Music by Maury Rubens; lyrics by Henry Dagand)

HELLO, YOURSELF!
October 30, 1928 (87 perfs)
Music by Richard Myers
Lyrics by Leo Robin
We Might Play Tiddle de Winks
Hello, Yourself
You've Got a Way with You
He Man
Say That You Love Me
True Blue
Daily Dozen
I Want the World to Know
Jericho
To the Dance

HELLZAPOPPIN'
September 22, 1938 (1,404 perfs)
Music by Sammy Fain
Lyrics by Charles Tobias
Hellzapoppin'
Fuddle-Dee-Duddle
Strolling thru the Park
Abe Lincoln (Music and lyrics by Earl Robinson and Alfred Hayes)
Shaganola
It's Time to Say "Aloha"
When You Look in Your Looking Glass (Music by Paul Mann and Stephen Weiss; lyrics by Sam Lewis)
Blow a Balloon up to the Moon
Boomps-a-Daisy (Music and lyrics by Annette Mills)

---

*Suggested by Thornton Wilder's *The Matchmaker*
†Added in 1970.
**Based on the novel and play *Seventeen* by Booth Tarkington
††Based on Homer Croy's novel *They Had to See Paris*

We Won't Let It Happen Here
When McGregor Sings Off Key

HENRY, SWEET HENRY*
October 23, 1967 (80 perfs)
Music and lyrics by Bob Merrill
Academic Fugue
In Some Little World
Pillar to Post
Here I Am
Whereas
I Wonder How It Is To Dance with a Boy
Nobody Steps on Kafritz
Henry, Sweet Henry
Woman in Love
People Watchers
Weary Near to Dyin'
Poor Little Person
I'm Blue Too
To Be Artistic
Forever
Do You Ever Go to Boston
Cast album: ABC-Paramount

HER FIRST ROMAN†
October 20, 1968 (17 perfs)
Music and lyrics by Ervin Drake
What Are We Doing in Egypt?
Hail Sphinx
Save Me from Caesar
Many Young Men from Now
Ptolemy
Kind Old Gentleman
Her First Roman
Magic Carpet
The Things We Think We Are
I Cannot Make Him Jealous
The Dangerous Age
In Vino Veritas
Caesar Is Wrong
Just for Today

HERE GOES THE BRIDE
November 3, 1931 (7 perfs)
Music by John Green
Lyrics by Edward Heyman
The Inside Story
Remarkable People We
My Sweetheart 'Tis of Thee
Shake Well Before Using
We Know Reno

Well, You See
What's the Difference
One Second of Sex
Hello, My Lover, Goodbye
It's My Nature
It Means So Little to You (Music by Richard Myers)
Music in My Fingers (Music by Richard Myers)
Ohhh! Ahhh!

HERE'S HOWE
May 1, 1928 (71 perfs)
Music by Joseph Meyer and Roger Wolfe Kahn
Lyrics by Irving Caesar
Beauty in the Movies
Life As a Twosome**
Crazy Rhythm
Imagination
I'd Rather Dance Here Than Hereafter
Here's Howe
Boston Post Road
On My Mind a New Love

HERE'S LOVE††
October 3, 1963 (334 perfs)
Music & lyrics by Meredith Willson
The Big Clown Balloons
Arm in Arm
You Don't Know
The Plastic Alligator
The Bugle
Here's Love
My Wish
Pine Cones and Holly Berries
Look, Little Girl
Expect Things to Happen
She Hadda Go Back
That Man Over There
My State
Nothing in Common
Cast album: Columbia
Vocal selection

---

*Based on Nora Johnson's novel *The World of Henry Orient*
†Based on George Bernard Shaw's *Caesar and Cleopatra*
**Also in *Americana*, 2nd edition (1928)
††Based on the film *Miracle on 34th Street*

HERE'S WHERE I BELONG*
March 3, 1968 (1 perf)
Music by Robert Waldman
Lyrics by Alfred Uhry
  We Are What We Are
  Cal Gets By
  Raising Cain
  Soft Is the Sparrow
  Where Have I Been?
  No Time
  Progress
  Good Boy
  Act Like a Lady
  Top of the Train
  Waking Up Sun
  Pulverize the Kaiser
  You're Momma's
  Here's Where I Belong
  We're a Home

HERO IS BORN, A
October 1, 1937 (50 perfs)
Music by Lehman Engel
Lyrics by Agnes Morgan
  Tra La La
  Matters Culinary
  Fiddle Dee Dee
  Music in the Air
  Magic Gifts
  A Question of Gait (Lyrics by
    Thomas Burke)
  Woe Is Me
  Off to Gluckstein
  Keeping Prigio Company
  The Secret of Success
  We Believe
  A Love-Lorn Maid
  They Say
  The Best Dance of All
  The Song of Prigio
  Hurray for Life
  Prigio Don't Know
  The Last Word

HEY NONNY NONNY!
June 6, 1932 (32 perfs)
Music by Michael H. Cleary
Lyrics by Max and Nathaniel Lief
  Personally Yours
  Tell Me Something about Yourself
  This Is Different, Dear
  Manhattan Lullaby

  Three Little Columnists
  On My Nude Ranch with You
  I Didn't Know That It Was Loaded
  Minsky's Metropolitan Grand Op-
    era
  The Season Ended
  Hey Nonny Nonny (Music by Will
    Irwin; lyrics by Ogden Nash)
  Be a Little Lackadaisical (Music and
    lyrics by Herman Hupfeld)
  Lady in Waiting (Music by Alberta
    Nichols; lyrics by Mann Holiner)
  I'm Really Not That Way (Music by
    Will Irwin; lyrics by Malcolm
    McComb)
  Wouldn't That Be Wonderful (Mu-
    sic and lyrics by Herman Hup-
    feld)
  In Those Good Old Horsecar Days
    (Music by Will Irwin; lyrics by
    Malcolm McComb)
  Let's Go Lovin' (Music and lyrics by
    Herman Hupfeld)

HI, PAISANO! (OB)
September 30, 1961 (3 perfs)
Music by Robert Holton
Lyrics by June Carroll
  What Is Your Name?
  Cubes and Abstracts
  Dino Repetti
  Office under the Sky
  Hi, Paisano
  Time We Talked
  Dino's in Love
  Faith
  Sounds of Silence
  Girl He Adores
  It Happens Every Day
  Born in America
  Teresa
  Carousel
  Reason to Marry
  Dozen Husbands
  Over Forty
  I Know What He's Up To
  Let Me Drown

------

*Based on the novel *East of Eden* by John
Steinbeck

HIGH BUTTON SHOES
October 9, 1947 (727 perfs)
Music by Jule Styne
Lyrics by Sammy Cahn
  He Tried to Make a Dollar
  Can't You Just See Yourself?
  There's Nothing Like a Model T
  Next to Texas, I Love You
  Security
  Bird Watcher's Song
  Get Away for a Day in the Country
  Papa, Won't You Dance With Me?
  On a Sunday by the Sea
  You're My Girl
  I Still Get Jealous
  Nobody Ever Died for Dear Old
    Rutgers
Cast album: Camden

HIGH KICKERS
October 31, 1941 (171 perfs)
Music by Harry Ruby
Lyrics by Bert Kalmar
  My Sweetheart Mamie
  Didn't Your Mother Tell You Nothing?
  You're On My Mind
  Panic in Panama
  The Girls
  The Time to Sing
  I've Got Something
  Cigarettes
  Waltzing in the Moonlight

HIGH SPIRITS*
April 7, 1964 (375 perfs)
Music and lyrics by Hugh Martin and
Timothy Gray
  Was She Prettier Than I?
  The Bicycle Song
  You'd Better Love Me
  Where Is the Man I Married?
  The Sandwich Man
  Go Into Your Trance
  Forever and a Day
  Something Tells Me
  I Know Your Heart
  Faster Than Sound
  If I Gave You
  Talking to You
  Home Sweet Heaven
  Something Is Coming to Tea

  The Exorcism
  What in the World Did You Want?
Cast album: ABC-Paramount
Vocal selection

HIGHER AND HIGHER
April 4, 1940 (108 perfs)
Music by Richard Rodgers
Lyrics by Lorenz Hart
  A Barking Baby Never Bites
  From Another World
  Mornings at Seven
  Nothing but You
  Disgustingly Rich
  Blue Monday
  Ev'ry Sunday Afternoon
  Lovely Day for a Murder
  How's Your Health
  It Never Entered My Mind
  I'm Afraid

HIT THE DECK†
April 25, 1927 (352 perfs)
Music by Vincent Youmans
Lyrics by Leo Robin and Clifford Grey
  Join the Navy
  What's a Kiss Among Friends?
  The Harbor of My Heart
  Shore Leave
  Lucky Bird
  Loo Loo
  Nothing Could Be Sweeter**
  Sometimes I'm Happy (Lyrics by Irving Caesar)
  Hallelujah!
  If He'll Come Back to Me
Written for film version: (1929)
  Keepin' Myself for You (Lyrics by
    Sidney Clare)

HIT THE TRAIL
December 2, 1954 (4 perfs)
Music by Frederico Valerio
Lyrics by Elizabeth Miele
  On with the Show

---

*Based on the play *Blithe Spirit* by Noël
Coward
†Based on play *Shore Leave* by Hubert Osborne
**Later published as "Why, Oh Why?"

Mr. Right
Dynamic
Blue Sierras
No! No! No!
The Wide Open Spaces
Gold Cannot Buy
Remember the Night
Tell Me How
It Was Destiny
Just a Wonderful Time
Nevada Hoe Down
New Look Feeling
Set Me Free
Somehow I've Always Known
My Fatal Charm
Men Are a Pain in the Neck
Wherever I May Go
Take Your Time
Happy Birthday

HOBO (OB)
April 10, 1961 (32 perfs)
Music and lyrics by John Dooley
Nuthin' for Nuthin'
Jonah's Wail
Sympathy
The Virgin Polka
Cindy
Julie
From the Moment
Bleecker Street
Sweetness
On the Day When the World Goes
  Boom
Somewhere in Your Eyes
I Hate You
Good or Nothing
Little Birds
Who Put Out the Light That Lit the
  Candle . . .

HOLD EVERYTHING!
October 10, 1928 (413 perfs)
Music by Ray Henderson
Lyrics by B. G. DeSylva and Lew
Brown
We're Calling on Mr. Brooks
An Outdoor Man for My Indoor
  Sports
Footwork
You're the Cream in My Coffee
When I Love, I Love

Too Good to Be True
To Know You Is to Love You
Don't Hold Everything
For Sweet Charity's Sake
Genealogy
Oh, Gosh
It's All Over but the Shoutin'

HOLD IT!
May 5, 1948 (46 perfs)
Music by Gerald Marks
Lyrics by Sam Lerner
Heaven Sent
Buck in the Bank
Always You
About Face
Fundamental Character
Hold It!
Nevermore
Roll 'Em
It Was So Nice Having You
Down the Well
You Took Possession of Me
Friendly Enemy

HOLD ON TO YOUR HATS
September 11, 1940 (158 perfs)
Music by Burton Lane
Lyrics by E. Y. Harburg
Way Out West Where the East Be-
  gins
Hold On to Your Hats
Walkin' Along Mindin' My Business
The World Is in My Arms
Would You Be So Kindly
Life Was Pie for the Pioneer
Don't Let It Get You Down
There's a Great Day Coming,
  Manana
Then You Were Never in Love
Down on the Dude Ranch
She Came, She Saw, She Can
  Canned
Old Timer

HOLD YOUR HORSES
September 25, 1933 (88 perfs)
Music by Robert Russell Bennett
Lyrics by Owen Murphy and Robert
A. Simon
Good Evening, Mr. Man in the
  Moon

Galloping through the Park
Hold Your Horses
Peanuts and Kisses
High Shoes
Singing to You (Music and lyrics by
    Ben Oakland, Margot Millham,
    and Robert A. Simon)
If I Love Again (Music by Ben Oak-
    land; lyrics by J. P. Murray)
I Guess I Love You
Happy Little Weekend
Old Man Subway
Do You?
I'd Like to Take You Home to Meet
    My Mother
Swapping Sweet Nothings with You

HOLKA-POLKA
October 14, 1925 (21 perfs)
Music by Will Ortman
Lyrics by Gus Kahn and Raymond B.
Egan
    Home of My Heart
    When Love Is Near
    In a Little While
    Holka-Polka
    The Highway's Call
    Spring in Autumn

HOME MOVIES (OB)
May 11, 1964 (72 perfs)
Music by Al Carmines
Lyrics by Rosalyn Drexler
    A Mania
    Peanut Song
    Pents-un-Wreckum
    Swoop of the Moopem
    Birdies
    A Power Stronger Than Will
    Equipment Song
    You Look Like Me
    Remember When I Hated You?
    Once You've Seen Everything
    Darkness Song
    Show Me
    My Number Is Eleven
    Boasting Song
    I Know You Sell It
    Here They Come Now
    Lower the Boom
    Chocolate Turkey
    Daisies

Do Not Bruise the Fruit
Stuttering Song
Pussy Cat Song
Seminary Song
I'm Gwine Lie Down
Two Falls to a Finish

HONEYMOON LANE
September 20, 1926 (353 perfs)
Music by James F. Hanley
Lyrics by Eddie Dowling
    Little White House
    Dreams for Sale
    On to Hollywood
    Waddya Say—We Steal Away
    Head Over Heels in Love
    A Little Smile, a Little Sigh
    The Stone Bridge at Eight
    Half a Moon (Lyrics by Eddie Dowl-
        ing and Herbert Reynolds)
    Little Old New Hampshire
    Mary Dear
    Jersey Walk
    Gee, but I'd Like to Be Bad

HOORAY FOR WHAT!
December 1, 1937 (200 perfs)
Music by Harold Arlen
Lyrics by E. Y. Harburg
    Hooray for What!
    God's Country
    I've Gone Romantic on You
    Moanin' in the Mornin'
    Viva for Geneva
    Life's a Dance
    Napoleon's a Pastry
    Down with Love
    A Fashion Girl
    The Night of the Embassy Ball
    In the Shade of the New Apple Tree

HORSEMAN, PASS BY* (OB)
January 15, 1969 (37 perfs)
Music by John Duffy
Lyrics by Rocco Bufano and John
Duffy (based on W. B. Yeats)
    What Then?
    This Great Purple Butterfly

———
*Based on the writings of William Butler
Yeats

Brown Penny
A Soldier Takes Pride in Saluting
His Captain
Before the World Was Made
Last Confession
Mad As the Mist and Snow
Crazy Jane on the Day of Judge-
ment
Her Anxiety
Salley Gardens
Soulless a Faery Dies
To an Isle in the Water
Consolation

HOT-CHA!
March 8, 1932 (119 perfs)
Music by Ray Henderson
Lyrics by Lew Brown
You Can Make My Life a Bed of
Roses
So This Is Mexico
Conchita
I Want Another Portion of That
Say (What I Wanna Hear You Say)
José, Can't You See!
Fiesta
I Make Up for That in Other Ways
There I Go Dreaming Again
There's Nothing the Matter with
Me
Song of the Matadors

HOT CHOCOLATES
June 29, 1929 (228 perfs)
Music by Thomas (Fats) Waller and
Harry Brooks
Lyrics by Andy Razaf
Song of the Cotton Fields
Sweet Savannah Sue
Say It with Your Feet
Ain't Misbehavin'
Goddess of Rain
Dixie Cinderella
Black and Blue
That Rhythm Man
Can't We Get Together
Off Time

HOT RHYTHM
August 21, 1930 (73 perfs)
Music by Porter Grainger
Lyrics by Donald Heywood

Say the Word That Will Make You
Mine
The Penalty of Love
Hot Rhythm
Loving You the Way I Do (Music by
Eubie Blake; lyrics by Jack Scholl
and Will Morrissey)

HOT SPOT
April 19, 1963 (43 perfs)
Music by Mary Rodgers
Lyrics by Martin Charnin
Don't Laugh
Welcome
This Little Yankee
Smiles
A Little Trouble
You'd Like Nebraska
Hey, Love
I Had Two Dregs
Rich, Rich, Rich
That's Good—That's Bad
I Think the World of You
Gabie
A Matter of Time
Big Meeting Tonight
A Far, Far Better Way

HOTEL PASSIONATO (OB)
October 22, 1965 (11 perfs)
Music by Philip Springer
Lyrics by Joan Javits
Not Getting Any Younger
What a Curious Girl
We'll Suffer Together
A Perfectly Charming Visit
You Gay Dog You!
Hotel Passionato
Don't!
What Is This Sensation?
Tea-Tea-Tea
Hot Water Bottles
Good-Good-Good
Tomorrow When the World Comes
Crashing Down around Our Ears
Marry Me
What a Night!
We Saw Everybody There

HOUSE OF FLOWERS
December 30, 1954 (165 perfs)
Music by Harold Arlen

Lyrics by Harold Arlen and Truman
Capote
  Waitin'
  One Man Ain't Quite Enough
  A Sleepin' Bee
  Smellin' of Vanilla (Bamboo Cage)
  House of Flowers
  Two Ladies in de Shade of de Ba-
    nana Tree
  What Is a Friend For?
  Slide Boy, Slide
  I'm Gonna Leave Off Wearing My
    Shoes
  Has I Let You Down
  I Never Has Seen Snow
  Turtle Song
  Don't Like Goodbyes
  Mardi Gras
Cast album: Columbia
Vocal selection

HOUSE OF LEATHER, THE (OB)
March 18, 1970 (1 perf)
Music by Dale F. Menten
Lyrics by Dale F. Menten and Freder-
ick Gaines
  House of Leather Theme
  Sara Jane
  Graduates of Mrs. Grimm's Learn-
    ing
  Do You Recall the House of
    Leather?
  Copper's Creed
  Here I Am
  Mrs. Grimm
  Time Marches On
  Children's Song (Recess with Mrs.
    Grimm)
  Steady Job
  Imagine You're Alive
  Dixie Prelude (Civil War)
  Armies of the Right
  God Is Black
  I'd Give Her to the World of Dia-
    monds
  There's Love in the Country
  Now It's Gone, Gone, Gone
  Sherman's March to the Sea
  Death and Reality
Cast album: Capitol

HOUSEBOAT ON THE STYX, THE*
December 25, 1928 (103 perfs)
Music by Alma Sanders
Lyrics by Monte Carlo
  Ode to the Styx
  The Houseboat on the Styx
  The Roll Call in the Morning
  Cleopatra, We're Fond of You
  The Fountain of Youth
  My Heaven
  Club Song
  Back in the Days of Long Ago
  An Irate Pirate Am I
  Red River
  Soul Mates
  Hell's Finest
  Men of Hades
  You've Got to Know Just How to
    Make Love
  Someone Like You

HOW NOW, DOW JONES
December 7, 1967 (220 perfs)
Music by Elmer Bernstein
Lyrics by Carolyn Leigh
  A-B-C
  They Don't Make 'Em Like That
    Anymore
  Live a Little
  The Pleasure's About to Be Mine
  A Little Investigation
  Walk Away
  Goodbye, Failure, Goodbye
  Step to the Rear
  Shakespeare Lied
  Big Trouble
  Credo
  One of Those Moments
  He's Here!
  Panic
  Touch and Go
  That's Good Enough for Me
Cast album: RCA

HOW TO BE A JEWISH MOTHER†
December 28, 1967 (21 perfs)
Music by Michael Leonard
Lyrics by Herbert Martin

---

*Based on the story by John Kendrick
Bangs
†Based on the book by Dan Greenburg

Once the Man You Laughed At
Laugh a Little
Since the Time We Met
The Wedding Song
Child You Are

HOW TO STEAL AN ELECTION (OB)
October 13, 1968 (89 perfs)
Music and lyrics by Oscar Brand
The Plumed Knight
Clay and Frelinghuysen
Get on the Raft with Taft
Silent Cal
Nobody's Listening
The Right Man
How to Steal an Election
Van Buren
Tippecanoe and Tyler Too
Charisma
Lincoln and Soda
Lincoln and Liberty
Grant
Law and Order
Lucky Lindy
Down among the Grass Roots
Get Out the Vote
Mr. Might've Been
We're Gonna Win
More of the Same
Cast album: RCA

HOW TO SUCCEED IN BUSINESS WITHOUT REALLY TRYING*†
October 14, 1961 (1,095 perfs)
Music and lyrics by Frank Loesser
How To
Happy to Keep His Dinner Warm
Coffee Break
The Company Way
A Secretary Is Not a Toy
Been a Long Day
Grand Old Ivy
Paris Original
Rosemary
Cinderella, Darling
Love from a Heart of Gold
I Believe in You
Brotherhood of Man
Cast album: RCA
Vocal score
Vocal selection

HUMMIN' SAM
April 8, 1933 (1 perf)
Music and lyrics by Alexander Hill
Steppin' Along
Harlem Dan
How the First Song Was Born
They're Off
Pinching Myself
Change Your Mind about Me
If I Didn't Have You
In the Stretch
Jubilee
A Little Bit of Quicksilver
Answer My Heart
Stompin' 'Em Down
I'll Be True, but I'll Be Blue
Jitters
Fifteen Minutes a Day
Ain'tcha Glad You Got Music?
Dancing, and I Mean Dancing

I CAN GET IT FOR YOU WHOLESALE**
March 22, 1962 (300 perfs)
Music and lyrics by Harold Rome
I'm Not a Well Man
The Way Things Are
When Gemini Meets Capricorn
Momma, Momma
The Sound of Money
The Family Way
Too Soon
Who Knows?
Have I Told You Lately?
Ballad of the Garment Trade
A Gift Today
Miss Marmelstein
A Funny Thing Happened
What's in It For Me?
What Are They Doing to Us Now?
Eat a Little Something
Cast album: Columbia
Vocal score
Vocal selection

---

*Adapted from the book by Shepherd Mead
†Pulitzer Prize Winner
**Based on the novel by Jerome Weidman

I Do! I Do!*
December 5, 1966 (560 perfs)
Music by Harvey Schmidt
Lyrics by Tom Jones
  All the Dearly Beloved
  Together Forever
  I Do! I Do!
  Good Night
  I Love My Wife
  Something Has Happened
  My Cup Runneth Over
  Love Isn't Everything
  Nobody's Perfect
  A Well Known Fact
  Flaming Agnes
  The Honeymoon Is Over
  Where Are the Snows
  When the Kids Get Married
  The Father of the Bride
  What Is a Woman
  Someone Needs Me
  Roll Up the Ribbons
  This House
Cast album: RCA
Vocal score
Vocal selection

**I Dreamt I Dwelt in Blooming-
dale's (OB)**
February 12, 1970 (5 perfs)
Music by Ernest McCarty
Lyrics by Jack Ramer and Ernest
McCarty
  Ballad of Dry Dock Country
  Makin' Believe
  Who Will I Be?
  I Dreamt I Dwelt in Bloomingdale's
  We Didn't Ask to Be Born
  Any Spare Change?
  Brown Paper Bag
  Naomi
  Smart

I Feel Wonderful (OB)
October 18, 1954 (49 perfs)
Music and lyrics by Jerry Herman
  When I Love Again
  It's Christmas Today
  Over and Over
  I Feel Wonderful
  Lonesome in New York
  This Has Never Been Done Before

Dior, Dior
Jailhouse Blues
Since Eve

I Had a Ball
December 15, 1964 (184 perfs)
Music and lyrics by Jack Lawrence
and Stan Freeman
  Coney Island, U.S.A.
  The Other Half of Me
  Red-Blooded American Boy
  I Got Everything I Want
  Freud
  Think Beautiful
  Addie's at It Again
  Faith
  Can It Be Possible?
  The Neighborhood Song
  The Affluent Society
  Boys, Boys, Boys
  Fickle Finger of Fate
  I Had a Ball
  Almost
  You Deserve Me
Cast album: Mercury
Vocal selection

I Married an Angel
May 11, 1938 (338 perfs)
Music by Richard Rodgers
Lyrics by Lorenz Hart
  Did You Ever Get Stung?
  I Married an Angel
  The Modiste
  I'll Tell the Man in the Street
  How to Win Friends and Influence
    People
  Spring Is Here
  Angel Without Wings
  A Twinkle in Your Eye
  At the Roxy Music Hall

I Want You (OB)
September 14, 1961 (4 perfs)
Music and lyrics by Stefan Kanfer, Jess
J. Korman, and Joseph Grayhon
  My Daddy Was Right
  I Want You

---

*Based on Jan de Hartog's play *The Four-
poster*

This Is a Dollar Bill
Perfect Man
The Farewells
Remarkable
That's What the Public Wants
Ain't It Funny
So Long, Yesterday
You Devil You
Loyal American
The Street
Hong Kong Gong
Take Every Opportunity

I'D RATHER BE RIGHT
November 2, 1937 (290 perfs)
Music by Richard Rodgers
Lyrics by Lorenz Hart
A Homogeneous Cabinet
Have You Met Miss Jones?
Take and Take and Take
Spring in Vienna
A Little Bit of Constitutional Fun
Sweet Sixty-Five
We're Going to Balance the
   Budget
Labor Is the Thing
I'd Rather Be Right
Off the Record
A Baby Bond
Ev'rybody Loves You*

IF THE SHOE FITS
December 5, 1946 (20 perfs)
Music by David Raksin
Lyrics by June Carroll
Start the Ball Rollin'
I Wish
In the Morning
Come and Bring Your Instruments
Night After Night
Every Eve
With a Wave of My Wand
Am I a Man or a Mouse?
I'm Not Myself Tonight
Three Questions
If the Shoe Fits
What's the Younger Generation
   Coming to?
Have You Seen the Countess
   Cindy?
I Took Another Look
This Is the End of the Story

I Want to Go Back to the Bottom of
   the Garden
My Business Man

ILLUSTRATORS' SHOW, THE
January 22, 1936 (5 perfs)
I Want to Play with the Girls (Music
   by Edgar Fairchild; lyrics by Mil-
   ton Pascal)
Let's Talk about the Weather (Mu-
   sic and lyrics by Charlotte Kent)
I've Walked in the Moonlight (Mu-
   sic by Edgar Fairchild; lyrics by
   Milton Pascal)
Park Avenue's Going to Town (Mu-
   sic by Edgar Fairchild; lyrics by
   Milton Pascal)
Bang, the Bell Rang! (Music by Ir-
   ving Actman; lyrics by Frank
   Loesser)
A Waltz Was Born in Vienna (Music
   by Frederick Loewe; lyrics by
   Earle Crooker)
I'm You (Music by Irving Actman;
   lyrics by Frank Loesser)
Just for Tonight (Music and lyrics by
   Charlotte Kent)
Give Me the Wild Trumpets (Music
   by Irving Actman; lyrics by Frank
   Loesser)
Hello, Ma (Music by Michael H.
   Cleary; lyrics by Max and Nathan-
   iel Lief)
I Love a Polka So (Music by Berenice
   Kazounoff; lyrics by Carl Randall)
Wherefore Art Thou, Juliet (Music
   and lyrics by Charlotte Kent)

ILLYA DARLING†
April 11, 1967 (320 perfs)
Music by Manos Hadjidakis
Lyrics by Joe Darion
Po, Po, Po
Zebekiko
Piraeus, My Love
Golden Land
Love, Love, Love
I Think She Needs Me

———
*Dropped from New York production
†Based on the film *Never on Sunday*

I'll Never Lay Down Any More
After Love
Birthday Song
Medea Tango
Illya Darling
Dear Mr. Schubert
The Lesson
Never on Sunday
Ya Chara
Cast album: United Artists

I'M SOLOMON*
April 23, 1968 (7 perfs)
Music by Ernest Gold
Lyrics by Anne Croswell
  David and Bathsheba
  Hail the Son of David
  Preposterous
  Have You Heard?
  The Citation
  In Love with a Fool
  Someone Like Me
  In Someone Else's Sandals
  The Three Riddles (Lyrics by Erich Segal)
  Once in 2.7 Years
  Have You Ever Been Alone with a King Before? (Music by Bill Weeden; lyrics by David Finkle)
  Time to Let Go
  Lord I Am But a Little Child
  Something in His Eyes
  That Guilty Feeling (Music by Bill Weeden; lyrics by David Finkle)
  With Your Hand in My Hand

INNER CITY†
December 19, 1971 (97 perfs)
Music by Helen Miller
Lyrics by Eve Merriam
  Fee Fi Fo Fum
  Now I Lay Me
  Locks
  I Had a Little Teevee
  Hushabye Baby
  My Mother Said
  Diddle Diddle Dumpling
  Rub a Dub Dub
  You'll Find Mice
  Ding Dong Bell
  The Brave Old City of New York
  Urban Renewal

The Nub of the Nation
Mary, Mary
City Life
One Misty, Moisty Morning
Jack Be Nimble
If Wishes Were Horses
One Man
Deep in the Night
Statistics
Twelve Rooftops Leaping
Take-a-Tour, Congressman
Simple Simon
Poverty Program
One, Two
Tom, Tom
Hickety, Pickety
Half Alive
This Is the Way We Go to School
The Spirit of Education
Little Jack Horner
Subway Dream
Christmas Is Coming
I'm Sorry Says the Machine
Jeremiah Obadiah
Riddle Song
Shadow of the Sun
Boys and Girls Come Out to Play
Summer Nights
Lucy Locket
Winter Nights
Wisdom
The Hooker
Wino Will
Man in the Doorway
Starlight, Starbright
The Cow Jumped over the Moon
The Dealer
Taffy
Numbers
The Pickpocket
Law and Order
Kindness
As I Went Over
There Was a Little Man
Who Killed Nobody
It's My Belief

---

*Based on the play *King Solomon and the Cobbler* by Sammy Gronemann
†Based on Eve Merriam's book *The Inner City Mother Goose*

Street Sermon
The Great If
On This Rock
Cast album: RCA

INSIDE U.S.A
April 30, 1948 (399 perfs)
Music by Arthur Schwartz
Lyrics by Howard Dietz
Inside U.S.A.
Pittsburgh
Blue Grass
Haunted Heart
First Prize at the Fair
At the Mardi Gras
My Gal Is Mine Once More
We Won't Take It Back
Rhode Island Is Famous for You

IRMA LA DOUCE
September 29, 1960 (527 perfs)
Music by Marguerite Monnot
Lyrics by Julian More, David
Heneker, and Monte Norman
Valse Milieu
Sons of France
The Bridge of Caulaincourt
Our Language of Love
She's Got the Lot
Dis-donc, Dis-donc
Le Grisbi Is le Root of le Evil in Man
The Wreck of a Mec
That's a Crime
From a Prison Cell
Irma La Douce
There is Only One Paris for That
But
Christmas Child
Cast album: Columbia

**(IT'S A BIRD, IT'S A PLANE)
IT'S SUPERMAN***
March 29, 1966 (129 perfs)
Music by Charles Strouse
Lyrics by Lee Adams
Doing Good
We Need Him
It's Superman
We Don't Matter at All
Revenge
The Woman for the Man
You've Got Possibilities

What I've Always Wanted
Everything's Easy When You Know
How
It's Super Nice
So Long, Big Guy
The Strongest Man in the World
Ooh, Do You Love You!
You've Got What I Need
I'm Not Finished Yet
Pow! Bam! Zonk!
Cast album: Columbia
Vocal selection

JACKPOT
January 13, 1944 (67 perfs)
Music by Vernon Duke
Lyrics by Howard Dietz
The Last Long Mile
Blind Date
I Kissed My Girl Goodbye
A Piece of a Girl
My Top Sergeant
Sugarfoot
What Happened?
He's Good for Nothing but Me
What's Mine Is Yours
It Was Nice Knowing You
Nobody Ever Pins Me Up
I've Got a One Track Mind
There Are Yanks (from the Banks of
the Wabash)

**JACQUES BREL IS ALIVE AND WELL
AND LIVING IN PARIS (OB)**
January 22, 1968 (1,847 perfs)
Music by Jacques Brel
English lyrics by Eric Blau and Mort
Shuman
Marathon
Alone
Madeleine
I Loved
Mathilde
Bachelor's Dance
Timid Frieda
My Death
Girls and Dogs
Jackie
The Statue

_____
*Based on the comic strip "Superman"

Desperate Ones
Sons Of
Amsterdam
The Bulls
Old Folks
Marieke
Brussels
Fannette
Funeral Tango
The Middle Class
You're Not Alone
Next
Carousel
If We Only Have Love
Cast album: Columbia
Vocal selection

JAMAICA
October 31, 1957 (558 perfs)
Music by Harold Arlen
Lyrics by E. Y. Harburg
Savannah
Savannah's Wedding
Pretty to Walk With
Push de Button
Incompatibility
Little Biscuit
Cocoanut Sweet
Pity the Sunset
Take It Slow, Joe
Yankee Dollar
Monkey in the Mango Tree
Ain't It the Truth
What Good Does It Do
Leave the Atom Alone
Napoleon
For Every Fish
I Don't Think I'll End It All Today
Cast album: RCA
Vocal selection

JENNIE*
October 17, 1963 (82 perfs)
Music by Arthur Schwartz
Lyrics by Howard Dietz
Waitin' for the Evening Train
When You're Far Away from New
 York Town
I Still Look at You That Way
For Better or Worse
Born Again
Over Here

Before I Kiss the World Goodbye
Where You Are
The Jig
See Seattle
High Is Better Than Low
The Night May Be Dark
I Believe in Takin' a Chance
Welcome
Lonely Nights
Cast album: RCA

JESUS CHRIST SUPERSTAR
October 12, 1971†
Music by Andrew Lloyd Webber
Lyrics by Tim Rice
Heaven on Their Minds
What's the Buzz?
Strange Thing Mystifying
Everything's Alright
This Jesus Must Die
Hosanna
Simon Zealots
Poor Jerusalem
Pilate's Dream
The Temple
I Don't Know How to Love Him
Damned for All Time
The Last Supper
Gethsemane
The Arrest
Peter's Denial
Pilate and Christ
King Herod's Song
Could We Start Again, Please
Judas' Death
Trial Before Pilate
Superstar
The Crucifixion
John 19:41
Cast album: Decca

JIMMY**
October 23, 1969 (84 perfs)
Music and lyrics by Bill and Patti
Jacob

---

*Suggested by *Laurette* by Marguerite
Courtney
†Still running December 31, 1972
**Based on Gene Fowler's novel *Beau
James*

Will You Think of Me Tomorrow?
The Little Woman
The Darlin' of New York
Five Lovely Ladies
Oh, Gee!
That Old Familiar Ring
The Walker Walk
I Only Wanna Laugh
They Never Proved a Thing
Riverside Drive
The Squabble Song
One in a Million
It's a Nice Place to Visit
The Charmin' Son-of-a-Bitch
Jimmy
Our Jimmy
Life Is a One-Way Street
Cast album: RCA
Vocal selection

Jo!* (OB)

February 12, 1964 (63 perfs)
Music by William Dyer
Lyrics by Don Parks and William Dyer
Harmony, Mass.
Deep in the Bosom of the Family
Hurry Home
Let's Be Elegant or Die!
Castles in the Air
Time Will Be
What a Long Cold Winter!
Afraid to Fall in Love
A Wedding! A Wedding!
I Like
Genius Burns
If You Can Find a True Love
Nice As Any Man Can Be
More Than Friends
Taking the Cure

JOHN MURRAY ANDERSON'S ALMANAC (1929)

August 14, 1929 (69 perfs)
The Almanac Covers (Music by Henry Sullivan; lyrics by Edward Eliscu)
The Polka Dot (Music by Henry Sullivan; lyrics by Clifford Orr)
Tinkle! Tinkle! (Music by Milton Ager; lyrics by Jack Yellen)
I Can't Remember the Words (Music by Milton Ager and Henry Cabot Lodge; lyrics by Jack Yellen)
Wait for the Happy Ending (Music by Milton Ager; lyrics by Jack Yellen)
I May Be Wrong (but I Think You're Wonderful) (Music by Henry Sullivan; lyrics by Harry Ruskin)
The Nightingale Song (Music by Milton Ager; lyrics by Jack Yellen)
Schrafft's University (Music by Henry Sullivan; lyrics by Edward Eliscu)
The New Yorker (Music by Milton Ager; lyrics by Jack Yellen)
Same Old Moon (Music by Henry Sullivan; lyrics by John Murray Anderson and Clifford Orr)
Educate Your Feet (Music by Milton Ager; lyrics by Jack Yellen)
Getting into the Talkies (Music by Milton Ager; lyrics by Jack Yellen)
Tiller, Foster, Hoffman, Hale and Albertina Rasch (Music by Henry Sullivan; lyrics by Henry Myers)
Builders of Dreams (Music by Henry Sullivan; lyrics by John Murray Anderson)

JOHN MURRAY ANDERSON'S ALMANAC (1953)

December 10, 1953 (227 perfs)
Music and lyrics by Richard Adler and Jerry Ross
Harlequinade
Queen for a Day
You're So Much a Part of Me
I Dare to Dream (Music by Michael Grace and Carl Tucker; lyrics by Sammy Gallup)
Nightingale, Bring Me a Rose (Music by Henry Sullivan; lyrics by John Murray Anderson)
My Love is a Wanderer (Music and lyrics by Bart Howard)
Tin Pan Alley (Music by Cy Coleman; lyrics by Joseph McCarthy, Jr.)

---

*Based on the novel *Little Women* by Louisa May Alcott

Merry Little Minuet (Music and lyrics by Sheldon Harnick)
Hope You Come Back
If Every Month Were June (Music by Henry Sullivan; lyrics by John Murray Anderson)
Which Witch? (Music by Charles Zwar; lyrics by Allan Melville)
Fini
Acorn in the Meadow
When Am I Going to Meet Your Mother?
The Earth and the Sky (Music and lyrics by John Rox)

JOHNNY JOHNSON
November 19, 1936 (68 perfs)
Music by Kurt Weill
Lyrics by Paul Green
Over in Europe
Democracy's Call
Up Chickamauga Hill
Johnny's Melody
Aggie's Sewing Machine Song
O, Heart of Love
Captain Valentine's Tango
Song of the Goddess
Song of the Wounded Frenchman
Cowboy Song (Oh, the Rio Grande)
Song of the Guns
Mon Ami, My Friend
The Allied High Command
In Times of Tumult and War
Johnny's Arrest and Homecoming
How Sweetly Friendship Binds
The Psychiatry Song
Hymn to Peace
Johnny's Song (Listen to My Song)*
Cast album: Heliodor

JONAH (OB)
February 15, 1966 (24 perfs)
Music by Meyer Kupferman
Lyrics by Paul Goodman
Leviathan
Hey, What's This?
Sailor's Round
Evocation
Jonah's Melodrama
I'll Carry You an Inch
Puppet Dream
Sleep Little Mouse

I Cried for My Troubles
My God, Why Hast Thou Forsaken Me?
Forty Days
There's Nothing New under the Sun
Miserere
Day After Day
The Suns That Daily Rise
I Am a Little Worm

JONICA
April 7, 1930 (40 perfs)
Music by Joseph Meyer
Lyrics by William Moll
The Night It Happened
Au Revoir
Tonight or Never
One Step Nearer the Moon
I Want Someone (Music and lyrics by William B. Friedlander)
Tie Your Cares to a Melody
Specially Made for You
Beautiful Girls
March of the Rice and Old Shoes
A Million Good Reasons
If You Were the Apple
Here in My Heart
The Wedding Parade

JOY (OB)
January 27, 1970 (205 perfs)
Music and lyrics by Oscar Brown, Jr.
Time
Under the Sun
Wimmen's Ways
Funny Feelin' (Music and lyrics by Oscar Brown, Jr. and Luis Henrique)
If I Only Had (Music and lyrics by Oscar Brown, Jr. and Charles Aznavour)
What Is a Friend? (Music and lyrics by Oscar Brown, Jr. and Luis Henrique)
Much As I Love You (Music and lyrics by Oscar Brown, Jr. and Luis Henrique)

_____
*Later published as "To Love You and to Lose You," with lyrics by Edward Heyman

Sky and Sea (Music and lyrics by Oscar Brown, Jr. and Johnny Alf)

Afro Blue (Music and lyrics by Oscar Brown, Jr. and Mongo Santamaria)

Mother Africa's Day (Music and lyrics by Oscar Brown, Jr. and Sivuca)

A New Generation (Music and lyrics by Oscar Brown, Jr. and Luis Henrique)

Brown Baby

Funky World

Nothing but a Fool (Music and lyrics by Oscar Brown, Jr. and Luis Henrique)

Flowing to the Sea

Brother, Where Are You?

Cast album: RCA

JOYFUL NOISE, A*
December 15, 1966 (12 perfs)
Music and lyrics by Oscar Brand and Paul Nassau
  Longtime Travelin'
  A Joyful Noise
  I'm Ready
  Spring Time of the Year
  I Like to Look My Best
  No Talent
  Not Me
  Until Today
  Swinging a Dance
  To the Top
  I Love Nashville
  Whither Thou Goest
  We Won't Forget to Write
  Ballad Maker
  Barefoot Gal
  Fool's Gold
  The Big Guitar
  Love Was
  I Say Yes
  Lord, You Sure Know How to Make a New Day
Vocal selection

JUBILEE
October 12, 1935 (169 perfs)
Music and lyrics by Cole Porter
  Why Shouldn't I?

  The Kling-Kling Bird on the Divi-Divi Tree
  We're Off to Feathermore
  When Love Comes Your Way
  What a Nice Municipal Park
  When Me, Mowgli, Love
  Gather Ye Autographs While Ye May
  Begin the Beguine
  My Most Intimate Friend
  A Picture of Me without You
  Everybod-ee Who's Anybod-ee
  Sunday Morning Breakfast Time
  Mr. and Mrs. Smith
  Gay Little Wives
  Me and Marie
  Just One of Those Things
  Our Crown
  Swing That Swing
  My Loulou
  Good Morning, Miss Standing
  To Get Away

JUDY
February 8, 1927 (104 perfs)
Music by Charles Rosoff
Lyrics by Leo Robin
  Hobohemia
  Hard to Get Along With
  Looking for a Thrill
  Cinderella
  Pretty Little Stranger
  One Baby
  Wear Your Sunday Smile
  What a Whale of a Difference a Woman Can Make
  Judy, Who D'Ya Love?
  When Gentlemen Grew Whiskers and Ladies Grew Old
  The Curfew Shall Not Ring Tonight
  Start Stompin'

JUMBO
November 16, 1935 (233 perfs)
Music by Richard Rodgers
Lyrics by Lorenz Hart
  Over and Over Again
  The Circus Is on Parade

---

*Based on Borden Deal's novel *The Innocent Breed*

The Most Beautiful Girl in the World
Laugh
My Romance
Little Girl Blue
The Song of the Roustabouts
Women
Memories of Madison Square Garden
Diavalo
The Circus Wedding
Album: (Film version) Columbia

JUNE DAYS*
August 6, 1925 (85 perfs)
Music by J. Fred Coots
Lyrics by Clifford Grey
  Something Wrong with Me
  Remembering You
  Lucky
  June Days (Music by Stephen Jones; lyrics by Clifford Grey and Cyrus Wood)
  A Busy Evening
  All I Want Is Love (Music by Hal Dyson; lyrics by James Kendis)
  Strike
  Charming Women
  Anytime, Anywhere, Anyhow (Music by Richard Rodgers; lyrics by Lorenz Hart)
  How Do You Doodle Do?
  Naughty Little Step
  Girls Dream of One Thing
  Safety in Numbers
  Please, Teacher
  Take 'em to the Door Blues
  Why is Love?

JUNE MOON†
(Play with songs)
October 9, 1929 (273 perfs)
Music and lyrics by Ring Lardner
  Montana Moon
  Life Is a Game
  June Moon
  Give Our Child a Name

JUNO**
March 9, 1959 (16 perfs)
Music and lyrics by Marc Blitzstein
  We're Alive

I Wish It So
Son of the Ma
We Can Be Proud
Daarlin' Man
One Kind Word
Old Sayin's
What Is the Stars?
You Poor Thing
My True Heart
On a Day Like This
Bird Upon the Tree
Music in the House
It's Not Irish
The Liffey Waltz
Johnny
For Love
Where?
Cast album: Columbia

JUST A MINUTE
October 8, 1928 (80 perfs)
Music by Harry Archer
Lyrics by Walter O'Keefe
  You'll Kill 'Em
  Doggone
  We'll Just Be Two Commuters
  Anything Your Heart Desires
  Coming Out of the Garden
  I've Got a Cookie Jar but No Cookies
  The Break-Me-Down
  Pretty, Petite and Sweet
  I'm Ninety-eight Pounds of Sweetness
  Heigh-Ho Cheerio
  Just a Minute

JUST FANCY††
October 11, 1927 (79 perfs)
Music by Joseph Meyer and Philip Charig
Lyrics by Leo Robin

---

*Based on play The Charm School by Alice Duer Miller
†Based on Lardner's short story Some Like 'Em Cold
**Based on the play Juno and the Paycock by Sean O'Casey
††Based on the play Just Suppose by A.E. Thomas

Ain't Love Grand
Shake, Brother!
Memories
Dressed Up for Your Sunday Beau
Two Loving Arms
Humpty-Dumpty
Naughty Boy
Mi Chiquita
I'm a Highway Gentleman
Coo-Coo
You Came Along

JUST FOR LOVE (OB)
October 17, 1968 (6 perfs)
Music and lyrics by Michael Valenti
Just for Love
One and Twenty
Mary Ann
Come Live with Me
A Birthday
Two Strings to a Bow
Did Not
What Is Love?
Jenny Kissed Me
Echo
Bella
Man Is for Woman Made
So We'll Go No More A-Roving

KATJA
October 18, 1926 (113 perfs)
Music by Jean Gilbert
Lyrics by Harry Graham
When Love's in the Air
Cruel Chief
Dance with You
All the World Love's a Lover
Just for Tonight (Music by Maury
Rubens; lyrics by Clifford Grey)
I Fell Head over Heels in Love
Congratulations
If You Cared
Those Eyes So Tender
Night Birds
Leander
In Jail
Oh, Woe Is Me

KEAN*
November 2, 1961 (92 perfs)
Music and lyrics by Robert Wright and
George Forrest

Penny Plain, Twopence Colored
Man and Shadow
Mayfair Affair
Sweet Danger
Queue at Drury Lane
King of London
To Look upon My Love
Let's Improvise
Elena
The Social Whirl
The Fog and the Grog
Civilized People
Service for Service
Willow, Willow, Willow
Chime In!
Swept Away
Domesticity
Clown of London
Apology
Cast album: Columbia

KEEP IT CLEAN
June 24, 1929 (16 perfs)
Just a Little Blue for You (Music and
lyrics by James F. Hanley)
Broadway Mammy (Music and lyr-
ics by Clarence Gaskill and
Jimmy Duffy)
Doin' the Hot-cha-cha (Music and
lyrics by Lester Lee)
I See You but What Do You See in
Me? (Music and lyrics by Lester
Lee)
All I Need Is Someone Like You
(Music by Harry Archer; lyrics by
Charles Tobias)
Let Me Hold You in My Arms (Mu-
sic and lyrics by Clarence Gaskill)

KEEP MOVING
August 23, 1934 (21 perfs)
Music by Max Rich
Lyrics by Jack Scholl
The Play Is the Bunk
Wake Up, Sleepy Moon
Command to Love (Music by Henry
Sullivan)
Midtown

———

*From a comedy by Jean-Paul Sartre,
based on the play by Alexandre Dumas

Hot-Cha Chiquita
Superstition
Lovely, Lovely Day (Music by Max Rich and Billy Taylor)
Now Is the Time
Isn't It a Funny Thing?

KEEP OFF THE GRASS
May 23, 1940 (44 perfs)
Music by Jimmy McHugh
Lyrics by Al Dubin
The Cabby's Serenade
This Is Spring
Crazy As a Loon
I'll Applaud You with My Feet
A Fugitive from Esquire (Lyrics by Howard Dietz)
Two in a Taxi (Lyrics by Howard Dietz)
The Old Park Bench (Lyrics by Howard Dietz)
A Latin Tune, a Manhattan Moon and You
Clear Out of This World
Look Out for My Heart
Old Jitterbug
Raffles (Music by Vernon Duke)
This Is Winter

KEEP SHUFFLIN'
February 27, 1928 (104 perfs)
Teasing Mama (Music by Jimmy Johnson; lyrics by Henry Creamer)
Chocolate Bar (Music by Thomas (Fats) Waller; lyrics by Andy Razaf)
Labor Day Parade (Music by Clarence Todd; lyrics by Andy Razaf)
Give Me the Sunshine (Music by Jimmy Johnson; lyrics by Henry Creamer and Con Conrad)
Leg It (Music by Clarence Todd; lyrics by Henry Creamer and Con Conrad)
'Sippi (Music by Jimmy Johnson; lyrics by Henry Creamer)
How Jazz Was Born (Music by Thomas (Fats) Waller; lyrics by Andy Razaf)
Keep Shufflin' (Music by Thomas (Fats) Waller; lyrics by Andy Razaf)
Everybody's Happy in Jimtown (Music by Thomas (Fats) Waller; lyrics by Andy Razaf)
Dusky Love (Music by Will Vodery; lyrics by Henry Creamer)
Charlie, My Back Door Man (Music by Clarence Todd; lyrics by Henry Creamer and Con Conrad)
On the Levee (Music by Jimmy Johnson; lyrics by Henry Creamer)

KELLY
February 6, 1965 (1 perf)
Music by Moose Charlap
Lyrics by Eddie Lawrence
Ode to the Bridge
Six Blocks from the Bridge
That Old Time Crowd
Simple Ain't Easy
I'm Gonna Walk Right Up to Her
A Moment Ago
This Is a Tough Neighborhood
Never Go There Anymore
Life Can Be Beautiful
Everyone Here Loves Kelly
Ballad to a Brute
Heavyweight Champ of the World
Me and the Elements

KING AND I, THE*
March 29, 1951 (1,246 perfs)
Music by Richard Rodgers
Lyrics by Oscar Hammerstein II
I Whistle a Happy Tune
My Lord and Master
Hello, Young Lovers
March of the Royal Siamese Children
A Puzzlement
The Royal Bangkok Academy
Getting to Know You
We Kiss in a Shadow
Shall I Tell You What I Think of You?
Something Wonderful

_____
*Based on the novel *Anna and the King of Siam* by Margaret Landon

Western People Funny
I Have Dreamed
The King's Song
Shall We Dance?
Cast album: Decca
Vocal score
Vocal selection

KING OF THE WHOLE DAMN WORLD! (OB)

April 12, 1962 (43 perfs)
Music and lyrics by Robert Larimer
What to Do?
Grasshop Song
Poor Little Boy
The Night Gondolfi Got Married
King of the World
Who's Perfect?
Little Dog Blue
March You Off in Style
The Riddle of You
How Do They Ever Grow Up?
What's a Mama For?
Don't Tear Up the Horse
Slips
Who's Perfect for You?
Far Rockaway
There's Gotta Be a Villain

KISMET*

December 3, 1953 (583 perfs)
Music and lyrics by Robert Wright and George Forrest (based on Alexander Borodin)
Sands of Time
Rhymes Have I
Fate
Bazaar of the Caravans
Not Since Nineveh
Baubles, Bangles and Beads
Stranger in Paradise
He's in Love!
Gesticulate
Night of My Nights
Was I Wazir?
Rahadlakum
And This Is My Beloved
The Olive Tree
Cast album: Columbia
Vocal score
Vocal selection

KISS ME

July 18, 1927 (28 perfs)
Music by Winthrop Cortelyou
Lyrics by Derick Wulff
Kiss Me
I Have Something Nice for You
Arab Maid with Midnight Eyes
You in Your Room; I in Mine
Two Is Company
Rose of Iran
Welcome Home
If You'll Always Say Yes
Pool of Love
Always Another Girl

KISS ME, KATE†

December 30, 1948 (1,077 perfs)
Music and lyrics by Cole Porter
Another Op'nin', Another Show
Why Can't You Behave
Wunderbar
So In Love
We Open in Venice
Tom, Dick or Harry
I've Come to Wive It Wealthily in Padua
I Hate Men
Were Thine That Special Face
I Sing of Love
Too Darn Hot
Where Is the Life That Late I Led?
Always True to You in My Fashion
Bianca
Brush Up Your Shakespeare
I Am Ashamed That Women Are So Simple
Kiss Me, Kate
Cast album: Columbia
Vocal score
Vocal selection

KISS NOW (OB)

April 20, 1971 (3 perfs)
Music by William S. Fischer
Lyrics by Maxine Klein
This City Is a Kisser
Travelin' Man
The June Taylor

---

*Based on the play by Edward Knoblock
†Based on *The Taming of the Shrew* by William Shakespeare

Too Tired to Love
Try the Sky
Death Dance
No Touch Mine
Strawberry Day
Touch Kiss
Rodeo
French Thing Tango
Kabuki Rock
Kiss Now

KITTIWAKE ISLAND (OB)
October 12, 1960 (7 perfs)
Music by Alec Wilder
Lyrics by Arnold Sundgaard
Were This to Prove a Feather in My
    Hat
It Doesn't Look Deserted
Can This Be a Toe Print?
Good Morning, Dr. Puffin
I'd Gladly Walk to Alaska
The Smew Song
Never Try Too Hard
Under a Tree
I Delight in the Sight of My Lydia
The Bard
Robinson Crusoe
Nothing Is Working Quite Right
Don't Give Up the Hunt, Dr. Puffin
If Love's Like a Lark
When One Deems a Lady Sweet
When a Robin Leaves Chicago
So Raise the Banner High
Oceanography and Old Astronomy
It's So Easy to Say
Hail, the Mythic Smew

KITTY'S KISSES
May 6, 1926 (170 perfs)
Music by Con Conrad
Lyrics by Gus Kahn
Walkin' the Track
Choo Choo Love
Kitty's Kisses
I Love to Dance
Thinking of You
Two Fellows and a Girl
I'm in Love (Lyrics by Gus Kahn
    and Otto Harbach)
Promise Your Kisses
Early in the Morning
I Don't Want Him

Needles
Whenever I Dream
Bounce Me
Step on the Blues (Music by Con
    Conrad and Will Donaldson; lyr-
    ics by Otto Harbach)

KNICKERBOCKER HOLIDAY
October 19, 1938 (168 perfs)
Music by Kurt Weill
Lyrics by Maxwell Anderson
Clickety-clack
It's a Law
There's Nowhere to Go but Up
It Never Was You
How Can You Tell an American?
Will You Remember Me?
One Touch of Alchemy
The One Indispensable Man
Young People Think About Love
September Song
Ballad of the Robbers
We are Cut in Twain
To War!
Our Ancient Liberties
Romance and Musketeer
The Scars
Dirge for a Soldier
Ve Vouldn't Gonto Do It
Vocal score

KOSHER KITTY KELLY
June 15, 1925 (105 perfs)
Music and lyrics by Leon DeCosta
Dancing Toes
Kosher Kitty Kelly
What's in Store for You
I'll Cuddle Up to You
I Want to Dance with You
Where We can Be in Love

KWAMINA
October 23, 1961 (32 perfs)
Music and lyrics by Richard Adler
The Cocoa Bean Song
Welcome Home
The Sun Is Beginning to Crow
Did You Hear That?
You're As English As
Seven Sheep, Four Red Shirts and a
    Bottle of Gin

Nothing More to Look Forward To
What's Wrong with Me?
Something Big
Ordinary People
Mammy Traders
A Man Can Have No Choice
What Happened to Me Tonight?
One Wife
Another Time, Another Place
Fetish
Cast album: Capitol

LA GROSSE VALISE
December 14, 1965 (7 perfs)
Music by Gerard Calvi
Lyrics by Harold Rome
  La Grosse Valise
  A Big One
  C'est Defendu
  Hamburg Waltz
  Happy Song
  For You
  Sandwich for Two
  La Java
  Xanadu
  Slippy Sloppy Shoes
  Delilah Done Me Wrong
  Hawaii

LA STRADA*
December 14, 1969 (1 perf)
Music and lyrics by Lionel Bart
  Seagull, Starfish, Pebble
  The Great Zampano
  What's Going on Inside?
  Belonging
  I Don't Like You
  There's a Circus in Town
  You're Musical
  Only More!
  What a Man
  Everything Needs Something
  Sooner or Later

LACE PETTICOAT, THE
January 4, 1927 (15 perfs)
Music by Emil Gerstenberger and
  Carle Carlton
Lyrics by Howard Johnson
  Watch the Birdies
  Renita Renata
  South Wind Is Calling

The Boy in the Blue Uniform
Engagement Ring
Dear, Dear Departed
Little Lace Petticoat (Lyrics by
  Carle Carlton)
Have You Forgotten?
The Rose Aria
The Heart Is Free
Playthings of Love (Music by Emil
  Gerstenberger)
The Girl That I Adore (Music by
  Emil Gerstenberger; lyrics by
  Carle Carlton)

LADY COMES ACROSS, THE
January 9, 1942 (3 perfs)
Music by Vernon Duke
Lyrics by John Latouche
  Three Rousing Cheers
  You Took Me By Surprise
  Hit the Ramp
  February (Music and lyrics by
    Danny Shapiro, Jerry Seelen, and
    Lester Lee)
  Eenie, Meenie, Minee, Mo
  This Is Where I Came In
  Summer Is A-Comin' In

LADY DO
April 18, 1927 (56 perfs)
Music by Abel Baer
Lyrics by Sam Lewis and Joe Young
  Buddy Rose
  Live Today
  Paris Taught Me 'Zis
  On Double Fifth Avenue
  You Can't Eye a Shy Baby
  O Sole Mi—Whose Soul Are You?
  Lady Do
  Little Miss Small Town
  Snap Into It
  Blah! But Not Blue
  In the Long Run
  In My Castle in Sorrento
  Dreamy Montmartre
  This Is My Wedding Day
  Jiggle Your Feet

---

*Based on the Federico Fellini film

LADY FINGERS*
January 31, 1929 (132 perfs)
Music by Joseph Meyer
Lyrics by Edward Eliscu
   I Want You All to Myself
   Let Me Weep on Your Shoulder
   Open Book
   Something to Live For
   Sing† (Music by Richard Rodgers;
      lyrics by Lorenz Hart)
   Ga-Ga!
   My Wedding
   You're Perfect
   I Love You More Than Yesterday
      (Music by Richard Rodgers; lyrics
      by Lorenz Hart)
   Follow Master
   Turn to Me
   Raise the Dust

LADY IN THE DARK
January 23, 1941 (467 perfs)
Music by Kurt Weill
Lyrics by Ira Gershwin
   Oh, Fabulous One
   Huxley
   One Life to Live
   Girl of the Moment
   Mapleton High Choral
   This Is New
   The Princess of Pure Delight
   The Greatest Show on Earth
   The Best Years of His Life
   Tschaikowsky
   Jenny (The Saga of)
   My Ship
Vocal Score
Album: RCA
Added to film version: (1944)
   Suddenly, It's Spring (Music by
      Jimmy Van Heusen; lyrics by
      Johnny Burke)

LADY SAYS YES, A
January 10, 1945 (87 perfs)
Music by Fred Spielman and Arthur
   Gershwin
Lyrics by Stanley Adams
   Viva Vitamins
   You're the Lord of Any Manor
   Take My Heart with You

   Without a Caress
   I Wonder Why You Wander
   I Don't Care What They Say About
      Me
   A Hop, a Skip, a Jump, a Look
   A Pillow for His Royal Head
   Don't Wake Them Up Too Soon
   You're More Than a Name and Ad-
      dress
   It's the Girl Everytime, It's the Girl

LAFFING ROOM ONLY
December 23, 1944 (232 perfs)
Music and lyrics by Burton Lane
   Hooray for Anywhere
   Go Down to Boston Harbor
   Stop That Dancing
   This Is As Far As I Go
   Feudin' and Fightin' (Lyrics by Al
      Dubin and Burton Lane)
   Got That Good Time Feelin'
   Gotta Get Joy (Lyrics by Al Dubin
      and Burton Lane)
   Sunny California
   The Steps of the Capitol

LAST SWEET DAYS OF ISAAC, THE (OB)
January 26, 1970 (485 perfs)
Music by Nancy Ford
Lyrics by Gretchen Cryer
   The Last Sweet Days of Isaac
   A Transparent Crystal Moment
   My Most Important Moments Go
      By
   Love You Came to Me
   I Want to Walk to San Francisco
   Touching Your Hand Is Like Touch-
      ing Your Mind
   Yes, I Know That I'm Alive
Cast album: RCA

LAUGH PARADE, THE
November 2, 1931 (231 perfs)
Music by Harry Warren
Lyrics by Mort Dixon and Joe Young
   Punch and Judy Man

---

*Based on the play *Easy Come, Easy Go* by
Owen Davis
†Originally in *Betsy* (1926)

The Laugh Parade
Got to Go to Town
Ooh! That Kiss
The Torch Song
Excuse for Song and Dance
You're My Everything
Love Me Forever

LEAVE IT TO ME*
November 9, 1938 (307 perfs)
Music and lyrics by Cole Porter
How Do You Spell Ambassador?
We Drink to You, J. H. Brody
Vite, Vite, Vite
I'm Taking the Steps to Russia
Get Out of Town
When It's All Said and Done
Most Gentlemen Don't Like Love
Comrade Alonzo
From Now On
I Want to Go Home
My Heart Belongs to Daddy
Tomorrow
Far Far Away
From the U.S.A. to the U.S.S.R.

LEAVES OF GRASS† (OB)
September 12, 1971 (49 perfs)
Music by Stan Harte, Jr.
Come, Said My Soul
There Is That in Me
Song of the Open Road
Give Me
Who Makes Much of a Miracle
Tears
Twenty-eight Men
A Woman Waits for Me
As Adam
Do You Suppose
Enough
Dirge for Two Veterans
How Solemn
Oh, Captain, My Captain
Pioneers
Song of Myself
Excelsior
In the Prison
Twenty Years
Unseen Buds
Goodbye, My Fancy
Thanks
I Hear America Singing

LEND AN EAR
December 16, 1948 (460 perfs)
Music and lyrics by Charles Gaynor
After Hours
Give Your Heart a Chance to Sing
Neurotic You and Psychopathic Me
I'm Not in Love
Friday Dancing Class
Ballade
When Someone You Love Loves You
The Gladiola Girl—introducing:
(a) Join Us in a Cup of Tea**
(b) Where Is the She for Me?
(c) I'll Be True to You
(d) Doin' the Old Yahoo Step**
(e) A Little Game of Tennis
(f) In Our Teeny Little Weeny Nest
Santo Domingo
I'm On the Lookout
Three Little Queens of the Silver Screen
Molly O'Reilly
Who Hit Me?

LET 'EM EAT CAKE
October 21, 1933 (90 perfs)
Music by George Gershwin
Lyrics by Ira Gershwin
Tweedledee for President
Union Square
Shirts by the Millions
Comes the Revolution
Mine
Climb Up the Social Ladder
Cloistered from the Noisy City
What More Can a General Do?
On and On and On
Double Dummy Drill
Let 'Em Eat Cake
Blue, Blue, Blue
Who's the Greatest——?
No Comprenez, No Capish, No Versteh!
Why Speak of Money?
No Better Way to Start a Case

---

*Based on the play *Clear All Wires* by Samuel and Bella Spewack
†Based on Walt Whitman's *Leaves of Grass*
**Also in *Show Girl* (1961)

Up and at 'Em! On to Vict'ry
Oyez, Oyez, Oyez
That's What He Did
I Know a Foul Ball
Throttle Throttlebottom
A Hell of a Hole
Let 'Em Eat Caviar
Hanging Throttlebottom in the
  Morning

LET IT RIDE!*
October 12, 1961 (68 perfs)
Music and lyrics by Jay Livingston and
Ray Evans
  Run, Run, Run
  The Nicest Thing
  Hey, Jimmy, Joe, John, Jim, Jack
  Broads Ain't People
  Let It Ride
  I'll Learn Ya
  Love Let Me Know
  Happy Birthday
  Everything Beautiful
  Who's Doing What to Erwin?
  I Wouldn't Have Had To
  There's Something About a Horse
  He Needs You
  Just an Honest Mistake
  His Own Little Island
  If Flutterby Wins
Cast album: RCA

LET'S FACE IT!†
October 29, 1941 (547 perfs)
Music and lyrics by Cole Porter
  Milk, Milk, Milk
  A Lady Needs a Rest
  Jerry, My Soldier Boy
  Let's Face It
  Farming
  Ev'rything I love
  Ace in the Hole
  You Irritate Me So
  Rub Your Lamp
  I've Got Some Unfinished Business
    With You
  Let's Not Talk about Love
  A Little Rumba Numba
  I Hate You, Darling
  Melody in Four F (Music and lyrics
    by Sylvia Fine and Max Liebman)
  Get Yourself a Girl

LEW LESLIE'S INTERNATIONAL REVUE
February 25, 1930 (95 perfs)
Music by Jimmy McHugh
Lyrics by Dorothy Fields
  Make Up Your Mind
  That's Why We're Dancing
  On the Sunny Side of the Street
  Big Papoose Is on the Loose
  Exactly Like You
  The Margineers
  Gypsy Love
  Keys to Your Heart
  Cinderella Brown
  International Rhythm

LIAR, THE
May 18, 1950 (12 perfs)
Music by John Mundy
Lyrics by Edward Eager
  The Ladies' Opinion
  You've Stolen My Heart
  The Liar's Song
  Truth
  Lack-a-Day
  Stop Holding Me Back
  What's In a Name?
  Women's Work (Music by Lehman
    Engel)
  Spring
  Stomach and Stomachs
  A Jewel of a Duel
  Out of Sight, Out of Mind
  A Plot to Catch a Man In
  'Twill Never Be the Same

LIFE BEGINS AT 8:40
August 27, 1934 (237 perfs)
Music by Harold Arlen
Lyrics by Ira Gershwin and E.Y. Harburg
  Spring Fever
  You're a Builder Upper
  My Paramount-Publix-Roxy Rose
  Shoein' the Mare
  Quartet Erotica

---

*Based on play Three Men On a Horse by
John Cecil Holm and George Abbott
†Based on play The Cradle Snatchers by
Norma Mitchell and Russell Medcraft

Fun to Be Fooled
C'est la Vie
What Can You Say in a Love Song?
Let's Take a Walk around the Block
Things
All the Elks and Masons
I Couldn't Hold My Man
It Was Long Ago

LI'L ABNER*
November 15, 1956 (693 perfs)
Music by Gene de Paul
Lyrics by Johnny Mercer
  It's a Typical Day
  If I Had My Druthers
  Jubilation T. Cornpone
  Rag Offen the Bush
  Namely You
  What's Good for General Bullmoose
  There's Room Enough for Us
  Unnecessary Town
  The Country's in the Very Best of
    Hands
  Oh, Happy Day
  Past My Prime
  Love in a Home
  Progress is the Root of All Evil
  Put 'Em Back
  The Matrimonial Stomp
Cast album: Columbia
Vocal score
Vocal selection

LITTLE MARY SUNSHINE (OB)
November 18, 1959 (1,143 perfs)
Music and lyrics by Rick Besoyan
  The Forest Rangers
  Little Mary Sunshine
  Look for a Sky of Blue
  You're the Fairest Flower
  In Izzenschnooken on the Lovely
    Essenzook Zee
  Playing Croquet
  How Do You Do?
  Tell a Handsome Stranger
  Once in a Blue Moon
  Colorado Love Call
  Every Little Nothing
  What Has Happened?
  Such a Merry Party
  Say "Uncle"
  Me, a Big Heap Indian

Naughty, Naughty Nancy
Mata Hari
Do You Ever Dream of Vienna?
A "Shell" Game
Coo Coo
Cast album: Capitol
Vocal score
Vocal selection

LITTLE ME†
November 17, 1962 (257 perfs)
Music by Cy Coleman
Lyrics by Carolyn Leigh
  The Truth
  The Other Side of the Tracks
  Birthday Party
  I Love You
  Deep Down Inside
  Be a Performer!
  Dimples
  Boom—Boom
  I've Got Your Number
  Real Live Girl
  Poor Little Hollywood Star
  Little Me
  The Prince's Farewell
  Here's to Us
Cast album: RCA
Vocal selection

LITTLE RACKETEER, A
January 18, 1932 (32 perfs)
Music by Henry Sullivan
Lyrics by Edward Eliscu
  Night Club Nights
  Thanks to You
  Dou, Dou
  Blow, Gabriel
  Mr. Moon (Music and lyrics by
    Lloyd Waner, Lupin Feine, and
    Moe Jaffe)
  Throwing a Party
  You and I Could Be Just Like That
  I'll Ballyhoo You (Music by Dimitri
    Tiomkin)
  Danger If I Love You
  I Have a Run in My Stocking

---

*Based on characters created by Al Capp
†Based on the novel by Patrick Dennis

You've Got to Sell Yourself
Spring Tra La (Music and lyrics by Lloyd Waner, Lupin Feine, and Moe Jaffe)
What Great Big Eyes You Have
Starry Sky (Music by Dimitri Tiomkin)
Here's to Night
Whiling My Time Away

LITTLE SHOW, THE (FIRST EDITION)
April 30, 1929 (321 perfs)
Man About Town (Music by Arthur Schwartz; lyrics by Howard Dietz)
Get Up on a New Routine (Music by Arthur Schwartz; lyrics by Howard Dietz)
Caught in the Rain (Music by Henry Sullivan; lyrics by Howard Dietz)
Or What Have You? (Music by Morris Hamilton; lyrics by Grace Henry)
I've Made a Habit of You (Music by Arthur Schwartz; lyrics by Howard Dietz)
Can't We Be Friends? (Music by Kay Swift; lyrics by Paul James)
Little Old New York (Music by Arthur Schwartz; lyrics by Howard Dietz)
Song of the Riveter (Music by Arthur Schwartz; lyrics by Lew Levenson)
What Every Little Girl Should Know (Music by Arthur Schwartz; lyrics by Henry Myers)
Hut in Hoboken (Music and lyrics by Herman Hupfeld)
Stick to Your Dancing, Mabel (Music and lyrics by Charlotte Kent)
I Guess I'll Have to Change My Plan (Music by Arthur Schwartz; lyrics by Howard Dietz)
Work Alike (Music by Frank Grey; lyrics by Earle Crooker)
Moanin' Low (Music by Ralph Rainger; lyrics by Howard Dietz)

LITTLEST REVUE, THE (OB)
May 22, 1956 (32 perfs)
Music by Vernon Duke

Lyrics by Ogden Nash
Good Little Girls (Lyrics by Sammy Cahn)
Second Avenue and 12th Street Rag
The Shape of Things (Music and lyrics by Sheldon Harnick)
Madly in Love
Born Too Late
Summer Is A-Comin' In* (Lyrics by John Latouche)
A Little Love, a Little Money
Third Avenue L (Music and lyrics by Michael Brown)
Fly Now, Pay Later
You're Far from Wonderful
I Lost the Rhythm (Music and lyrics by Charles Strouse)
Spring Doth Let Her Colours Fly (Music by Charles Strouse; lyrics by Lee Adams)
Love Is Still in Town
I'm Glad I'm Not a Man
The Power of Negative Thinking (Music and lyrics by Bud McCreery)
Cast album: Epic

LIVIN' THE LIFE (OB)
April 27, 1957 (25 perfs)
Music by Jack Urbont
Lyrics by Bruce Geller
Someone
Whiskey Bug
Livin' the Life
Steamboat
Take Kids
Probably in Love
Don't Tell Me
All of 'Em Say
Late Love
Ain't It a Shame
Supersational Day
MacDougal's Cave

LOOK MA, I'M DANCIN'!
January 29, 1948 (188 perfs)
Music and lyrics by Hugh Martin
Gotta Dance
Shauny O'Shay

*Previously in *The Lady Comes Across* (1942)

The Toast
I'm Tired of Texas
Tiny Room
The Little Boy Blues
The New Look
Horrible, Horrible Love
If You'll Be Mine
I'm Not So Bright
I'm the First Girl
The Way It Might Have Been
Cast album: Decca

LOOK TO THE LILIES*
March 29, 1970 (25 perfs)
Music by Jule Styne
Lyrics by Sammy Cahn
  Gott Iss Gut
  First Class Number One Bum
  Himmlisher Vater
  Follow the Lamb
  Don't Talk about God
  When I Was Young
  Meet My Seester
  One Little Brick at a Time
  To Do a Little Good
  There Comes a Time
  Why Can't He See?
  I'd Sure Like to Give It a Shot
  Them and They
  Does It Really Matter?
  Look to the Lilies
  I Admire You Very Much, Mr.
    Schmidt
  Some Kind of Man
  Casamagordo, New Mexico
  I, Yes Me, That's Who
Vocal selection

LOOK WHERE I'M AT!† (OB)
March 5, 1971 (1 perf)
Music by Jordan Ramin
Lyrics by Frank H. Stanton and Murray Semos
  What a Day for a Wonderful Day
  Animals
  What Are You Running from, Mister?
  Partners
  What Does She Think She Is?
  Look Where I'm At!
  Never, Never Leave Me
  Money Isn't Everything, But. . .

Company of Men
The Me I Want to Be
Little Sparrow
Euphoria

LOST IN THE STARS*
October 30, 1949 (273 perfs)
Music by Kurt Weill
Lyrics by Maxwell Anderson
  The Hills of Ixopo
  Thousands of Miles
  Train to Johannesburg
  The Search
  The Little Gray House
  Who'll Buy?
  Trouble Man
  Murder in Parkwold
  Fear
  Lost in the Stars
  The Wild Justice
  O Tixo, Tixo, Help Me
  Stay Well
  Cry, the Beloved Country
  Big Mole
  A Bird of Passage
Cast album: Decca
Vocal score

LOUIE THE 14TH
March 3, 1925 (319 perfs)
Music by Sigmund Romberg
Lyrics by Arthur Wimperis
  Market Day
  Homeland
  Wayside Flower
  Regimental Band
  Taking a Wife
  The Little Blue Pig
  Pep
  Edelweiss (Lyrics by Clifford Grey)
  Rin-tin-tin
  Follow the Rajah
  I'm Harold, I'm Harold
  Moon Flower

---

*Based on William E. Barrett's novel *Lilies of the Field*
†Adapted from Thorne Smith's novel, *Rain in the Doorway*
**Based on the novel *Cry, the Beloved Country* by Alan Paton

Vamp Your Men
True Hearts
Little Peach

LOUISIANA LADY*
June 2, 1947 (4 perfs)
Music by Alma Sanders
Lyrics by Monte Carlo
Gold, Women and Laughter
That's Why I Want to Go Home
Men about Town
Just a Bit Naïve
The Cuckoo-Cheena
I Want to Live—I Want to Love
The Night Was All to Blame
Beware of Lips That Say "Chérie"
Louisiana's Holiday
It's Mardi Gras
No, No, Mamselle
When You Are Close to Me
No One Cares for Dreams
Mammy's Little Baby

LOUISIANA PURCHASE
May 28, 1940 (444 perfs)
Music and lyrics by Irving Berlin
Sex Marches On
Louisiana Purchase
Tomorrow Is a Lovely Day
Outside of That I Love You
You're Lonely and I'm Lonely
Tonight at the Mardi Gras
Latins Know How
What Chance Have I?
The Lord Done Fixed Up My Soul
Fools Fall in Love
Old Man's Darling—Young Man's Slave
You Can't Brush Me Off

LOVE AND LET LOVE† (OB)
January 3, 1968 (14 perfs)
Music by Stanley Jay Gelber
Lyrics by John Lollos and Don Christopher
I've Got a Pain
If She Could Only Feel the Same
The Dancing Rogue
Will He Ever Know?
I Like It
Man Is Made for Woman
Epistle of Love

Love Lesson
I'll Smile
I Will Have Him
Write Him a Challenge
She Called Me Fellow
They'll Say I've Been Dreaming
How Do I Know You're Not Mad, Sir?
I Found My Twin
Some Are Born Great

LOVE CALL, THE**
October 24, 1927 (81 perfs)
Music by Sigmund Romberg
Lyrics by Harry B. Smith
Tony, Tony, Tony
'Tis Love
When I Take You All to London
Bonita
Eyes That Love
If That's What You Want
The Ranger's Song
The Lark
Good Pals
I Am Captured
Hear the Trumpet Call
I Live, I Die for You
You Appeal to Me
Fiesta
Spanish Love

LOVE LIFE
October 7, 1948 (252 perfs)
Music by Kurt Weill
Lyrics by Alan Jay Lerner
Who Is Samuel Cooper?
My Name Is Samuel Cooper
Here I'll Stay
Progress
I Remember It Well
Green-Up Time
Economics
Mother's Getting Nervous
My Kind of Night

---

*Based on play *Creoles* by Samuel Shipman and Kenneth Perkins
†Based on William Shakespeare's *Twelfth Night*
**Based on the play *Arizona,* by Augustus Thomas

Women's Club Blues
Love Song
I'm Your Man
Ho, Billy O!
Is It Him or Is It Me?
This Is the Life
Minstrel Parade
Madame Zuzu
Taking No Chances
Mr. Right

LOVE ME, LOVE MY CHILDREN (OB)
November 3, 1971 (187 perfs)
Music and lyrics by Robert Swerdlow
Don't Twist My Mind
Reflections
See
Fat City
Leave the World Behind
Don't Be a Miracle
Face to Face
Journey Home
Critics
Let Me Down Walking in the
World
North American Shmear
Gingerbread Girl
Plot and Counterplot
Do the Least You Can
You're Dreaming
Running Down the Sun
Love Me, Love Me Children
Cast album: United Artists

LOVE SONG, THE*
January 13, 1925 (167 perfs)
Music by Edward Kunneke (based on
Offenbach)
Lyrics by Harry B. Smith
Tell Me Not That You Are Forget-
ting
All Aboard for Paris
Love Is Not for a Day
Love Will Find You Some Day
Your Country Needs You
Fair Land of Dreaming
Take a Walk with Me
Remember Me (Love Song)
A Farmer's Life
When My Violin Is Calling
Only a Dream
Military Men I Love

Yes or No
Violets

LOVELY LADIES, KIND GENTLEMEN†
December 28, 1970 (16 perfs)
Music and lyrics by Stan Freeman and
Franklin Underwood
With a Snap of My Finger
Right Hand Man
Find Your Own Cricket
One Side of World
Geisha
You Say—They Say
This Time
Simple Word
Garden Guaracha
If It's Good Enough for Lady Astor
Chaya
Call Me Back
Lovely Ladies, Kind Gentlemen
You've Broken a Fine Woman's
Heart
One More for the Last One
Vocal selection

LOVELY LADY
December 29, 1927 (164 perfs)
Music by Dave Stamper and Harold
Levey
Lyrics by Cyrus Wood
Bad Luck, I'll Laugh at You
The Lost Step
Boy Friends
Make Believe You're Happy
Lovely Lady (Lyrics by Harry A.
Steinberg and Eddie Ward)
Breakfast in Bed
Lingerie
At the Barbecue (Lyrics by Harry A.
Steinberg and Eddie Ward)

LUANA**
September 17, 1930 (21 perfs)
Music by Rudolf Friml
Lyrics by J. Keirn Brennan

---

*Based on the life and music of Offenbach
†Based on Vern J. Sneider's book *The Tea-
house of the August Moon* and the play by
John Patrick
**Based on play, *The Bird of Paradise* by
Richard Walton Tully

Hoku Loa
Luana
Aloha
My Bird of Paradise
Shore Leave
Son of the Sun
By Welawela
Yankyula
Where You Lead
Magic Spell of Love
Drums of Kane
In the Clouds
Wanapoo Bay

LUCKEE GIRL*
September 15, 1928 (81 perfs)
Music by Maurice Yvain
Lyrics by Max and Nathaniel Lief
A Flat in Montmartre
If You'd Be Happy, Don't Fall in Love
When I'm in Paree
I Love You So
Hold Your Man
A Good Old Egg
I'll Take You to the Country
Facts of Life
Wild About Music
Chiffon
I Hate You
Come On and Make Whoopee (Music by Werner Janssen; lyrics by Mann Holiner)
Friends and Lovers
Bad Girl

LUCKY
March 22, 1927 (71 perfs)
Cingalese Girls (Music by Harry Ruby; lyrics by Bert Kalmar and Otto Harbach)
The Same Old Moon (Music by Harry Ruby; lyrics by Bert Kalmar and Otto Harbach)
When the Bo-Tree Blossoms Again (Music by Jerome Kern; lyrics by Bert Kalmar and Harry Ruby)
Lucky (Music by Jerome Kern; lyrics by Bert Kalmar and Harry Ruby)
That Little Something (Music by

Jerome Kern; lyrics by Bert Kalmar and Harry Ruby)
Dancing the Devil Away (Music by Harry Ruby; lyrics by Bert Kalmar and Otto Harbach)
Pearl of Broadway (Music by Jerome Kern; lyrics by Bert Kalmar and Harry Ruby)

LUCKY SAMBO
June 6, 1925 (9 perfs)
Music and lyrics by Porter Grainger and Freddie Johnson
Happy
Stop
June
Don't Forget Bandanna Days
Anybody's Man Will Be My Man
Aunt Jemima
Coal Oil
Charley from That Charleston Dancin' School
If You Can't Bring It, You've Got to Send It
Strolling
Dreary, Dreary, Rainy Days
Take Him to Jail
Always on the Job
Singing Nurses
Dandy Dan
Porterology
Love Me While You're Gone
Keep A-Diggin'
Runnin'
Midnight Cabaret
Havin' a Wonderful Time
Not So Long Ago
Alexander's Ragtime Wedding Day

LUTE SONG
February 6, 1946 (142 perfs)
Music by Raymond Scott
Lyrics by Bernard Hanighen
Mountain High, Valley Low
See the Monkey
Where You Are
Willow Tree
Vision Song

*Based on French play *Un Bon Garçon* by André Barde and Maurice Yvain

Chinese Market Place
Bitter Harvest
The Lute Song
Cast album: Decca

LYLE (OB)
March 20, 1970 (4 perfs)
Music by Janet Gari
Lyrics by Toby Garson
  Always Leave 'Em Wanting More
  I Can't Believe It's Real
  Generation Gap
  I Belong
  Me, Me, Me
  Alternate Parking
  Try to Make the Best of It
  Loretta
  Look at Me
  Crocodiles Cry
  On the Road
  Lyle's Turn
  Suddenly You're a Stranger
  Everybody Wants to Be Remembered
  Lyle
  Things Were Much Better in the Past
  We Belong

MACKEY OF APPALACHIA (OB)
October 6, 1965 (48 perfs)
Music and lyrics by Walter Cool
  Mackey of Appalachia
  Judging Song
  I Wonder Why
  Love Me Too
  You're Too Smart
  There Goes My Gal
  Love Will Come Your Way
  It's Sad to Be Lonesome
  Slatey Fork
  How We Would Like Our Man
  Lonely Voice
  My Love, My Love
  Blue and Troubled
  My Little Girl
  We're Having a Party
  Go Up to the Mountain
  There's Got to Be Love
  We Got Troubles
  Gotta Pay
  Only a Day Dream

Things Ain't As Nice
Everybody Loves a Tree
We Are Friends

MAD SHOW, THE (OB)*
January 9, 1966 (871 perfs)
Music by Mary Rodgers
Lyrics by Marshall Barer, Larry Siegel, and Steven Vinaver
  You Never Can Tell (Lyrics by Steven Vinaver)
  Eccch (Lyrics by Marshall Barer)
  The Real Thing (Lyrics by Marshall Barer)
  Well It Ain't (Lyrics by Larry Siegel and Stan Hart)
  Misery Is (Lyrics by Marshall Barer)
  Hate Song (Lyrics by Steven Vinaver)
  Looking for Someone (Lyrics by Marshall Barer)
  The Gift of Maggie (and Others) (Lyrics by Marshall Barer)
  The Boy From (Lyrics by Esteban Ria Nido)
Cast album: Columbia

MADAME APHRODITE (OB)
December 29, 1961 (13 perfs)
Music and lyrics by Jerry Herman
  I Don't Mind
  Sales Reproach
  Beat the World
  Miss Euclid Avenue
  Beautiful
  You I Like
  And a Drop of Lavendar Oil
  The Girls Who Sit and Wait
  Afferdytie
  There Comes a Time
  Only Love
  Take a Good Look Around

MADCAP, THE
January 31, 1928 (103 perfs)
Music by Maury Rubens
Lyrics by Clifford Grey
  Buy Your Way
  Old Enough to Marry

---

*Based on *MAD* Magazine

Birdies
What Has Made the Movies?
Honeymooning Blues
My Best Pal
Why Can't It Happen to Me?
Odle-De-O
Me, the Moonlight and Me
Honey, Be My Honey-Bee (Music by Maury Rubens and J. Fred Coots)
Step to Paris Blues
Something to Tell (Music by Maury Rubens and J. Fred Coots)
Stop, Go! (Music by Maury Rubens and J. Fred Coots)

MAGDALENA
September 20, 1948 (88 perfs)
Music by Heitor Villa-Lobos
Lyrics by Robert Wright and George Forrest
Women Weaving
Peteca!
The Omen Bird
My Bus and I
The Emerald
The Civilized People
Food for Thought
Come to Colombia
Plan It by the Planets
Bon Soir, Paris
Travel, Travel, Travel
Magdalena
The Broken Pianolita
Greeting
River Song
The Forbidden Orchid
The Singing Tree
Lost
Freedom
Pièce de Résistance
The Broken Bus
The Seed of God

MAGGIE*
February 18, 1953 (5 perfs.)
Music and lyrics by William Roy
I Never Laughed in My Life
Long and Weary Wait
Thimbleful
He's the Man
What Every Woman Knows

Any Afternoon about Five
Smile for Me
You Become Me
It's Only Thirty Years
The New Me
The Train with the Cushioned Seats
People in Love
Practical
Charm
Fun in the Country

MAGGIE FLYNN
October 23, 1968 (81 perfs)
Music and lyrics by Hugo Peretti, Luigi Creatore, and George David Weiss
Never Gonna Make Me Fight
It's a Nice Cold Morning
I Wouldn't Have You Any Other Way
Learn How to Laugh
Maggie Flynn
The Thank You Song
Look Around Your Little World
I Won't Let It Happen Again
How About a Ball?
Pitter Patter
Why Can't I Walk Away?
Mr. Clown
Don't You Think It's Very Nice?
Cast album: RCA
Vocal selection

MAKE A WISH†
April 18, 1951 (102 perfs)
Music and lyrics by Hugh Martin
The Tour Must Go On
I Wanna Be Good'n Bad
What I Was Warned About
Who Gives a Sou?
Tonight You Are in Paree
When Does This Feeling Go Away?
Suits Me Fine
Paris, France
That Face!
Make a Wish

---

*Based on *What Every Woman Knows,* by Sir James M. Barrie
†Based on the play *The Good Fairy* by Ferenc Molnár

I'll Never Make a Frenchman out of
You
Over and Over
Take Me Back to Texas with You

MAKE MINE MANHATTAN
January 15, 1948 (429 perfs)
Music by Richard Lewine
Lyrics by Arnold B. Horwitt
  Anything Can Happen in New York
  Phil the Fiddler
  Movie House in Manhattan
  Talk to Me
  Schrafft's
  I Don't Know Her Name
  The Good Old Days (Lyrics by Arnold B. Horwitt and Ted Fetter)
  Saturday Night in Central Park
  Ringalevio
  Noises in the Street (Lyrics by Peter Barry, David Greggory, and Arnold B. Horwitt)
  I Fell in Love with You
  My Brudder and Me
  Gentleman Friend
  Subway Song
  Glad to Be Back

MAMBA'S DAUGHTERS
(Play with one song)
January 3, 1939 (162 perfs)
  Lonesome Walls (Music by Jerome Kern; lyrics by DuBose Heyward)

MAME*
May 24, 1966 (1,508 perfs)
Music and lyrics by Jerry Herman
  St. Bridget
  It's Today
  Open a New Window
  The Man in the Moon
  My Best Girl
  We Need a Little Christmas
  The Fox Hunt
  Mame
  Bosom Buddies
  Gooch's Song
  That's How Young I Feel
  If He Walked into My Life
Cast album: Columbia
Vocal score
Vocal selection

MAN BETTER MAN (OB)
July 2, 1969 (32 perfs)
Music by Coleridge-Taylor Perkinson
Lyrics by Errol Hill
  Procession
  Tiny, the Champion
  I Love Petite Belle
  One Day, One Day, Congotay
  One, Two, Three
  Man Better Man
  Petite Belle Lily
  Thousand, Thousand
  Me Alone
  Girl in the Coffee
  Colie Gone
  War and Rebellion
  Beautiful Heaven
  Briscoe, the Hero

MAN IN THE MOON
April 11, 1963 (7 perfs)
Music by Jerry Bock
Lyrics by Sheldon Harnick
  Look Where I Am
  Itch to Be Rich
  Worlds Apart
  You Treacherous Men
  Ain't You Never Been Afraid?
Cast album: Golden

MAN OF LA MANCHA†
November 22, 1965 (2,329 perfs**)
Music by Mitch Leigh
Lyrics by Joe Darion
  Man of La Mancha
  It's All the Same
  Dulcinea
  I'm Only Thinking of Him
  I Really Like Him
  What Does He Want of Me
  Little Bird, Little Bird
  Barber's Song
  Golden Helmet
  To Each His Dulcinea
  The Impossible Dream (The Quest)

---

*Based on the novel *Auntie Mame* by Patrick Dennis and the play by Jerome Lawrence and Robert E. Lee
†Suggested by the life and works of Miguel de Cervantes y Saavedra
**Includes original OB run

The Combat
Knight of the Woeful Countenance
Aldonza
The Knight of the Mirrors
A Little Gossip
The Psalm
Cast album: Kapp
Vocal score
Vocal selection

MAN WHO CAME TO DINNER, THE
(Play with one song)
October 16, 1939 (739 perfs)
Music and lyrics by Cole Porter
　What Am I to Do?

MAN WITH A LOAD OF MISCHIEF*
(OB)
November 6, 1966 (240 perfs)
Music by John Clifton
Lyrics by John Clifton and Ben Tarver
　Wayside Inn
　The Rescue
　Goodbye, My Sweet
　Romance!
　Lover Lost
　Once You've Had a Little Taste
　Hulla-Baloo-Balay
　You'd Be Amazed
　A Friend Like You
　Masquerade
　Man with a Load of Mischief
　What Style!
　A Wonder
　Make Way for My Lady!
　Forget
　Any Other Way
　Little Rag Doll
　Sextet
Cast album: Kapp

MANHATTAN MARY
September 26, 1927 (264 perfs)
Music by Ray Henderson
Lyrics by B. G. DeSylva and Lew Brown
　Broadway
　Hudson Duster
　The Five-Step
　Nothing but Love
　It Won't Be Long Now
　Memories

My Blue Bird's Home Again
Dawn
Manhattan Mary

MANHATTERS, THE
August 3, 1927 (77 perfs)
Music by Alfred Nathan
Lyrics by George Oppenheimer
　Off to See New York
　Up on High
　What We Pick Up
　Love's Old Sweet Song
　I Don't Want a Song at Twilight
　Close Your Eyes
　Too Bad
　Every Animal Has Its Mate
　Nigger Heaven Blues

MARCHING BY
March 3, 1932 (12 perfs)
　I Love You, My Darling (Music by Jean Gilbert; lyrics by George Hirst and Edward Eliscu)
　Let Fate Decide (Music by Maury Rubens; lyrics by Harry B. Smith)
　It Might Have Been (Music and lyrics by Gus Arnheim, George Waggner, and Neil Moret)
　I've Gotta Keep My Eye on You (Music by Harry Revel; lyrics by Mack Gordon)
　Marching By (Music by Gus Edwards; lyrics by Harry Clark and Guy Robertson)
　Here We Are in Love (Music by Jean Gilbert; lyrics by Harry B. Smith)
　All's Fair in Love and War (Music by Jean Gilbert; lyrics by Harry B. Smith)
　You Burn Me Up (Music by Jean Gilbert; lyrics by Harry B. Smith)

MARINKA
July 18, 1945 (165 perfs)
Music by Emmerich Kalman
Lyrics by George Marion, Jr.
　One Touch of Vienna
　My Prince Came Riding

---

*Based on the play by Ashley Dukes

Cab Song
If I Never Waltz Again
Turn on the Charm
I Admit
One Last Love Song
Old Man Danube
Sigh by Night
Treat a Woman Like a Drum

MATINEE GIRL, THE
February 1, 1926 (25 perfs)
Music by Frank Grey
Lyrics by McElbert Moore and Frank
Grey
  At the Matinee
  Mash Notes (Music by Frank Grey
    and McElbert Moore)
  Joy Ride (Music by Frank Grey and
    McElbert Moore)
  The One You Love
  When My Little Ship Comes In
  Jumping Jack
  Like-a-Me, Like-a-You (Music by
    Frank Grey and McElbert Moore)
  Only One
  His Spanish Guitar
  Holding Hands
  Havanola Roll
  What Difference Does It Make?
    (Music by Constance Shepard)
  Waiting All the Time for You
  A Little Bit of Spanish
  The Biggest Thing in My Life
  Do I Dear, I Do (Music and lyrics by
    McElbert Moore)

MAYFLOWERS
November 24, 1925 (81 perfs)
Music by Edward Kunneke
Lyrics by Clifford Grey
  Whoa, Emma!
  Road of Dreams (Music by Pat
    Thayer; lyrics by Donovan Par-
    sons and Clifford Grey)
  How Do You Do?
  The Grecian Bend
  Play Me a New Tune (Music by J.
    Fred Coots and Maury Rubens)
  Foolish Wives
  Take a Little Stroll with Me (Music
    by J. Fred Coots and Maury Ru-
    bens)

Seven Days
Oh! Sam (Music by J. Fred Coots and
  Maury Rubens)
Mayflower (Music by J. Fred Coots,
  Maury Rubens, and Pat Thayer)
The Regiment Loves the Girls
Good Night Ladies
Woman
Put Your Troubles in a Candy Box
  (Music by J. Fred Coots)

MAY WINE*
December 5, 1935 (213 perfs.)
Music by Sigmund Romberg
Lyrics by Oscar Hammerstein II
  Something in the Air of May
  A Chanson in the Prater
  A Doll Fantasy
  You Wait and Wait and Wait
  I Built a Dream One Day
  Dance, My Darlings
  Always Be a Gentleman
  Somebody Ought to Be Told
  Something New Is in My Heart
  Just Once around the Clock

ME AND JULIET
May 28, 1953 (358 perfs)
Music by Richard Rodgers
Lyrics by Oscar Hammerstein II
  A Very Special Day
  That's the Way It Happens
  Marriage Type Love
  Keep It Gay
  The Big Black Giant
  No Other Love
  It's Me
  Intermission Talk
  It Feels Good
  The Baby You Love
  We Deserve Each Other
  I'm Your Girl
Cast album: RCA
Vocal score
Vocal selection

_____
*Based on a story by Wallace Smith and
Eric von Stroheim

ME NOBODY KNOWS, THE (OB)
May 18, 1970 (587 perfs*)
Music by Gary William Friedman
Lyrics by Will Holt
  Dream Babies
  Light Sings
  This World
  Numbers
  What Happens to Life
  Take Hold the Crutch
  Flying Milk and Runaway Plates
  I Love What the Girls Have
  How I Feel
  If I Had a Million Dollars
  Fugue for Four Girls
  Rejoice
  Sounds
  The Tree
  Robert, Alvin, Wendell and Jo Jo
  Jail-Life Walk
  Something Beautiful
  Black
  The Horse
  Let Me Come In
  War Babies
Cast album: Atlantic
Vocal selection

MEET MY SISTER
December 30, 1930 (165 perfs)
Music and lyrics by Ralph Benatzky
  Love Has Faded Away
  Five Thousand Francs
  Tell Me, What Can This Be?
  Always In My Heart
  Radziwill
  Look and Love Is Here
  The Devil May Care
  I Gotta Have My Moments
  It's Money - It's Fame - It's Love
  I Like You
  Friendship
  She Is My Ideal
  Birds in the Spring

MEET THE PEOPLE
December 25, 1940 (160 perfs)
Music by Jay Gorney
Lyrics by Henry Myers
  Meet the People
  Senate in Session
  The Stars Remain

Union Label
The Bill of Rights
American Plan
Let's Steal a Tune from Offenbach
A Fellow and a Girl (Lyrics by Edward Eliscu)
The Same Old South
No Lookin' Back (Lyrics by Henry Myers and Edward Eliscu)
In Chichicastenango

MELODY
February 14, 1933 (80 perfs)
Music by Sigmund Romberg
Lyrics by Irving Caesar
  Melody
  Our Little Lady Upstairs
  I'd Write a Song
  Good Friends Surround Me
  On to Africa!
  You Are the Song
  In My Garden
  Rendezvous
  Pompadour
  Never Had an Education
  The Whole World Loves
  Give Me a Roll on a Drum
  Tonight May Never Come Again
Vocal score

MEMPHIS BOUND
May 24, 1945 (36 perfs)
Music by Don Walker
Lyrics by Clay Warnick
  Big Old River
  Stand around the Band
  Old Love and Brand New Love
  Growing Pains
(Remainder of score adaptation of Gilbert and Sullivan's *H.M.S. Pinafore*)

MERCENARY MARY
April 13, 1925 (136 perfs)
Music by Con Conrad
Lyrics by William B. Friedlander
  Over a Garden Wall
  Just You and I and the Baby
  Charleston Mad

―――――
*Including original OB run

Honey, I'm in Love with You
They Still Look Good
Tomorrow*
Come On Along
Mercenary Mary
Beautiful Baby
Chaste Woman
Cherchez la Femme
Everything's Going to Be All
    Right

MERRY-GO-ROUND
May 31, 1927 (135 perfs)
Music by Henry Souvaine and Jay
Gorney
Lyrics by Morrie Ryskind and Howard
Dietz
    Gabriel
    Sentimental Silly
    Let's Be Happy Now
    If Love Should Come to Me
    New York Town
    Cider Ella
    Tampa
    Spring Is in the Air
    Something Tells Me
    Hogan's Alley
    What D'Ya Say
    I've Got a Yes Girl

MERRY MALONES, THE
September 26, 1927 (216 perfs)
Music and lyrics by George M. Cohan
    Talk About a Busy Little Household
    Like the Wandering Minstrel
    Son of a Billionaire
    Molly Malone
    Honor of the Family
    A Feeling in Your Heart
    To Heaven on the Bronx Express
    A Night of Masquerade
    Behind the Mask
    We've Had a Grand Old Time
    Charming
    We've Got Him
    A Busy Little Center
    Our Own Way of Going Along
    The Easter Sunday Parade
    Roses Understand
    Gip-Gip
    God Is Good to the Irish
    Blue Skies, Gray Skies

Like a Little Ladylike Lady Like
    You
Tee Teedle Tum Di Dum
The Yankee Father in the Yankee
    Home

MERRY-MERRY
September 24, 1925 (197 perfs)
Music by Harry Archer
Lyrics by Harlan Thompson
    It Must Be Love
    What a Life!
    Every Little Note
    We Were a Wow
    My Own
    Little Girl
    I Was Blue
    The Spanish Mick
    Oh, Wasn't It Lovely?
    Step, Step Sisters
    Poor Pierrot
    You're the One

MERRY WORLD, THE†
June 8, 1926 (85 perfs)
    Deauville (Music and lyrics by Her-
        man Hupfeld)
    Don't Fall in Love with Me (Music
        and lyrics by Herman Hupfeld)
    Golden Gates of Happiness (Music
        by J. Fred Coots; lyrics by Clifford
        Grey)
    Whispering Trees (Music by Maury
        Rubens and J. Fred Coots; lyrics
        by Herbert Reynolds)
    I Fell Head Over Heels in Love
        (Music by Pat Thayer; lyrics by
        Donovan Parsons)
    Dancing Jim (Music by Marc An-
        thony; lyrics by Donovan Parsons)
    Sunday (Music by J. Fred Coots; lyr-
        ics by Clifford Grey)

MESSIN' AROUND
April 22, 1929 (33 perfs)
Music by Jimmy Johnson
Lyrics by Perry Bradford

---

*Adapted from Chopin's Nocturne No. 12
†Retitled *Passions of 1926*

Harlem Town
Skiddle-de-Scow
Get Away from That Window
Your Love I Crave
Shout On!
I Don't Love Nobody but You
Roust-about
Mississippi
Sorry That I Strayed Away from You
Put Your Mind Right on It
Messin' Around
I Need You

MEXICAN HAYRIDE
January 28, 1944 (481 perfs)
Music and lyrics by Cole Porter
Sing to Me, Guitar
The Good-Will Movement
I Love You
There Must Be Someone for Me
Carlotta
Girls
What a Crazy Way to Spend Sunday
Abracadabra
Count Your Blessings
Cast album: Decca

MICHAEL TODD'S PEEP SHOW
June 28, 1950 (278 perfs)
The Model Hasn't Changed (Music and lyrics by Harold Rome)
You've Never Been Loved (Music by Sammy Stept; lyrics by Dan Shapiro)
Got What It Takes (Music by Sammy Stept; lyrics by Dan Shapiro)
I Hate a Parade (Music and lyrics by Harold Rome)
Blue Night (Music and lyrics by Bhumibol-Chakraband and N. Tong Yai)
Stay with the Happy People (Music by Jule Styne; lyrics by Bob Hilliard)
Violins from Nowhere (Music by Sammy Fain; lyrics by Herb Magidson)
Pocketful of Dreams (Music and lyrics by Harold Rome)
Gimme the Shimmy (Music and lyrics by Harold Rome)

MILK AND HONEY
October 10, 1961 (543 perfs)
Music and lyrics by Jerry Herman
Shepherd's Song
Shalom
Independence Day Hora
Milk and Honey
There's No Reason in the World
Chin Up, Ladies
That Was Yesterday
Let's Not Waste a Moment
The Wedding
Like a Young Man
I Will Follow You
Hymn to Hymie
As Simple As That
Cast album: RCA
Vocal score
Vocal selection

MINNIE'S BOYS
March 26, 1970 (76 perfs)
Music by Larry Grossman
Lyrics by Hal Hackady
Five Growing Boys
Rich Is
More Precious Far
Four Nightingales
Underneath It All
Mama, a Rainbow
You Don't Have to Do It for Me
If You Wind Me Up
Where Was I When They Passed Out Luck?
The Smell of Christmas
You Remind Me of You
Minnie's Boys
Be Happy
Cast album: Project 3
Vocal selection

MISS EMILY ADAM (OB)
March 29, 1960 (21 perfs)
Music by Sol Berkowitz
Lyrics by James Lipton
Home
Oh, the Shame
Name: Emily Adam
All Aboard
Obedian March
It's Positively You
Once Upon a Time

Talk to Me
Love Is
Ultivac
Fun ·
Dear Old Friend
According to Plotnik
I'm Your Valentine
At the Ball
Homeward

MISS LIBERTY
July 15, 1949 (308 perfs)
Music and lyrics by Irving Berlin
  Extra, Extra!
  I'd Like My Picture Took
  The Most Expensive Statue in the
    World
  A Little Fish in a Big Pond
  Let's Take an Old-Fashioned Walk
  Homework
  Paris Wakes Up and Smiles
  Only for Americans
  Just One Way to Say I Love You
  Miss Liberty
  The Train
  You Can Have Him
  The Policeman's Ball
  Follow the Leader Jig
  Me an' My Bundle
  Falling Out of Love Can Be Fun
  Give Me Your Tired, Your Poor
    (Lyrics by Emma Lazarus)
  Honorable Profession of the Fourth
    Estate, The*
  Pulitzer Prize, The*
Cast album: Columbia

MOD DONNA (OB)
April 24, 1970 (48 perfs)
Music by Susan Hulsman Bingham
Lyrics by Myrna Lamb
  Trapped
  Earthworms
  The Incorporation
  Invitation
  All the Way Down
  The Deal
  Liberia
  The Morning After
  Charlie's Plaint
  Creon
  The Worker and the Shirker

Food Is Love
First Act Crisis
Astrociggy
Hollow
Seduction Second Degree
Panassociative
Earth Dance
Trinity
Special Bulletin
Take a Knife
The Second Honeymoon
Jeff's Plaints
Incantation
Beautiful Man
Sacrifice
Now!
We Are the Whores

MONTH OF SUNDAYS† (OB)
September 16, 1968 (8 perfs)
Music by Maury Laws
Lyrics by Jules Bass
  How Far Can You Follow
  I Won't Worry
  Communicate
  Part of the Crowd
  We Know Where We've Been
  Summer Love
  Who Knows Better Than I
  Words Will Pay My Way
  Elbow Room
  My First Girl
  Flower, I Don't Need You Anymore
  It's Out of My Hands

MORNING SUN (OB)**
October 6, 1963 (9 perfs)
Music by Paul Klein
Lyrics by Fred Ebb
  Morning Sun
  This Heat
  Tell Me Goodbye
  New Boy in Town
  Good As Anybody
  Mr. Chigger
  Pebble Waltz
  Follow Him

---

*Dropped from New York production
†Based on the play, *The Great Git-Away*
by Romeo Muller
**Based on a story by Mary Deasy

Missouri Mule
Seventeen Summers
It's a Lie
My Sister-in-Law
Why?
That's Right!
For Once in My Life
All the Pretty Little Horses
I Seen It with My Very Own Eyes

MOST HAPPY FELLA, THE*
May 3, 1956 (676 perfs)
Music and lyrics by Frank Loesser
Ooh, My Feet
I Know How It Is
Seven Million Crumbs
The Letter
Somebody, Somewhere
The Most Happy Fella
Standing on the Corner
Joey, Joey, Joey
Soon You Gonna Leave Me, Joe
Rosabella
Abbondanza
Plenty Bambini
Sposalizio
Special Delivery!
Benvenuta
Aren't You Glad?
Don't Cry
Fresno Beauties (Cold and Dead)
Love and Kindness
Happy to Make Your Acquaintance
I Don't Like This Dame
Big "D"
How Beautiful the Days
Young People
Warm All Over
I Like Everybody
I Love Him
Like a Woman Loves a Man
My Heart Is So Full of You
Mama, Mama
Goodbye, Darlin'
Song of a Summer Night
Please Let Me Tell You
Tony's Thoughts
She's Gonna Come Home with Me
I Made a Fist
Cast album: Columbia
Vocal score
Vocal selection

MR. PRESIDENT
October 20, 1962 (265 perfs)
Music and lyrics by Irving Berlin
Let's Go Back to the Waltz
In Our Hide-Away
The First Lady
Meat and Potatoes
I've Got to Be Around
The Secret Service
It Gets Lonely in the White House
Is He the Only Man in the World?
They Love Me
Pigtails and Freckles
Don't Be Afraid of Romance
Laugh It Up
Empty Pockets Filled with Love
Glad to Be Home
You Need a Hobby
The Washington Twist
The Only Dance I Know
I'm Gonna Get Him
This Is a Great Country
Cast album: Columbia

MR. STRAUSS GOES TO BOSTON
September 6, 1945 (12 perfs)
Music by Robert Stolz
Lyrics by Robert Sour
Can Anyone See?
For the Sake of Art
Laughing Waltz (Adaptation of Johann Strauss melody)
Mr. Strauss Goes to Boston
Down with Sin
Who Knows?
Midnight Waltz (Adaptation of Johann Strauss melody)
Into the Night
Going Back Home
You Never Know What Comes Next
What's a Girl Supposed to Do?
The Grand and Glorious Fourth

MR. WONDERFUL
March 22, 1956 (383 perfs)
Music and lyrics by Jerry Bock, George Weiss, and Larry Holofcener

---

*Based on the play *They Knew What They Wanted* by Sidney Howard

1617 Broadway
Without You I'm Nothing
Jacques D'Iraq
Ethel, Baby
Mr. Wonderful
Charlie Welch
Big Time
Talk to Him
Too Close for Comfort
There
I've Been Too Busy
Cast album: Decca
Vocal selection

MRS. PATTERSON
December 1, 1954 (101 perfs)
Music and lyrics by James Shelton
Mrs. Patterson
If I Was a Boy
Be Good, Be Good, Be Good
My Daddy Is a Dandy
I Wish I Was a Bumble Bee
Tea in Chicago
Cast album: RCA

MURDER AT THE VANITIES
September 8, 1933 (298 perfs)
Music by Richard Myers
Lyrics by Edward Heyman
Sweet Madness (Music by Victor
Young; lyrics by Ned Washington)
Weep No More, My Baby (Music by
John Green)
Me for You Forever
Who Committed the Murder?
Savage Serenade (Music and lyrics
by Herman Hupfeld)
Virgins Wrapped in Cellophane
(Music by John Jacob Loeb; lyrics
by Paul Francis Webster)
You Love Me (Music and lyrics by
Herman Hupfeld)
Dust in Your Eyes (Music and lyrics
by Irving and Lionel Newman)

MURDER IN THE OLD RED BARN (OB)
(Play with two songs)
February 1, 1936 (251 perfs)
Music by Richard Lewine
Lyrics by John Latouche
Not on Your Tintype
Don't Turn Us out of the House

MUSIC HATH CHARMS
December 29, 1934 (25 perfs)
Music by Rudolf Friml
Lyrics by Rowland Leigh and John
Shubert
Gondolier Song
Maria
Lovey-Dovey
It's Three O'Clock
Romance
Love Is Only What You Make It
Let Me Be Free
Sweet Fool
Cavaliers
Ladies, Beware
Exquisite Moment
My Palace of Dreams
It Happened
A Smile, a Kiss
It's You I Want to Love Tonight

MUSIC IN MAY
April 1, 1929 (80 perfs)
Music by Emile Berté and Maury Rubens
Lyrics by J. Keirn Brennan
Open Your Window
The Glory of Spring
Sweetheart of Our Student Corps
Open and Shut Idea
I Found a Friend
Unto Your Heart
High, High, High
There's Love in the Heart I Hold
I'd Like to Love Them All
I'm in Love
No Other Love
For the Papa
Lips That Laugh at Love

MUSIC IN MY HEART
October 2, 1947 (124 perfs)
Music by Franz Steininger (adapted
from Tchaikovsky)
Lyrics by Forman Brown
Natuscha
Love Is a Game for Soldiers
Stolen Kisses
No! No! No!
While There's a Song to Sing
The Balalaika Serenade
Am I Enchanted?

Gossip
Once Upon a Time
Three's a Crowd
Song of the Troika
The Ballerina's Story
Song of the Claque
Love Song
Love Is the Sovereign of My
   Heart

MUSIC IN THE AIR
November 8, 1932 (342 perfs)
Music by Jerome Kern
Lyrics by Oscar Hammerstein II
   Melodies of May*
   I've Told Every Little Star
   Prayer
   There's a Hill Beyond a Hill
   And Love Was Born
   I'm Coming Home
   I'm Alone
   I Am So Eager
   One More Dance
   Night Flies By
   When the Spring Is in the Air
   In Egern on the Tegern See
   The Song Is You
   We Belong Together
Album: (Studio cast) RCA
Vocal score

MUSIC MAN, THE
December 19, 1957 (1,375 perfs)
Music and lyrics by Meredith Willson
   Rock Island
   Iowa Stubborn
   Trouble
   Piano Lesson
   Goodnight My Someone
   Seventy-Six Trombones
   Sincere
   The Sadder-but-Wiser Girl
   Pickalittle
   Marian the Librarian
   My White Knight
   Wells Fargo Wagon
   It's You
   Shipoopi
   Lida Rose
   Will I Ever Tell You
   Gary, Indiana
   Till There Was You

Cast album: Capitol
Vocal score
Vocal selection

MY DARLIN' AÏDA
October 27, 1952 (89 perfs)
Music by Giuseppe Verdi†
Lyrics by Charles Friedman
   My Darlin' Aïda
   Love Is Trouble
   Me and Lee
   March On for Tennessee
   Why Ain't We Free?
   Knights of the White Cross
   Homecoming
   When You Grow Up
   King Cotton
   Gotta Live Free
   Sing! South! Sing!
   I Want to Pray
   Alone
   Three Stones to Stand On
   You're False
   There'll Have to Be Changes
      Made
   Away
   Land of Mine
   I Don't Want You
   You Are My Darlin' Bride
   Oh, Sky, Goodbye

MY DEAR PUBLIC
September 9, 1943 (45 perfs)
   Feet on the Sidewalk (Head in the
      Sky) (Music and lyrics by Sam
      Lerner and Gerald Marks)
   My Spies Tell Me (You Love No-
      body but Me) (Music by Gerald
      Marks; lyrics by Irving Caesar and
      Sam Lerner)
   This Is Our Private Love Song (Mu-
      sic by Irving Caesar; lyrics by Sam
      Lerner)
   There Ain't No Color Line around
      the Rainbow (Music by Irving
      Caesar; lyrics by Gerald Marks
      and Sam Lerner)

---

*Choral setting of Beethovan Piano Sonata
Op. 2 No. 3
†Music adapted by Hans Spialek

Pipes of Pan Americana (Music by Gerald Marks; lyrics by Irving Caesar)

Love Is Such a Cheat (Music and lyrics by Irving Caesar, Gerald Marks, and Irma Hollander)

I Love to Sing the Words (Music by Irving Caesar; lyrics by Gerald Marks and Sam Lerner)

Rain on the Sea (Music by Irving Caesar and Sam Lerner; lyrics by Gerald Marks)

Now That I'm Free (Music by Irving Caesar; lyrics by Irma Hollander)

MY FAIR LADY*
March 15, 1956 (2,717 perfs)
Music by Frederick Loewe
Lyrics by Alan Jay Lerner
Why Can't the English?
Wouldn't It Be Loverly?
With a Little Bit of Luck
I'm an Ordinary Man
Just You Wait
The Rain in Spain
I Could Have Danced All Night
Ascot Gavotte
On the Street Where You Live
Embassy Waltz
You Did It
Show Me
Get Me to the Church on Time
A Hymn to Him
Without You
I've Grown Accustomed to Her Face
Cast album: Columbia
Vocal score
Vocal selection

MY MAGNOLIA
July 8, 1926 (4 perfs)
Music by C. Luckey Roberts
Lyrics by Alex C. Rogers
At Your Service
Baby Mine
Shake Your Duster
Pay Day
My Magnolia
Hard Times
Spend It
Laugh Your Blues Away

Gallopin' Dominoes
Headin' South
Merry Christmas
Struttin' Time
Our Child
Gee Chee
Sundown Serenade
Parade of the Christmas Dinner
Baby Wants
The Oof Dah Man
Sweet Popopper

MY MARYLAND†
September 12, 1927 (312 perfs)
Music by Sigmund Romberg
Lyrics by Dorothy Donnelly
Strolling with the One I Love the Best
Mr. Cupid
Won't You Marry Me?
Your Land and My Land
Silver Moon
The Mocking Bird
Strawberry Jam
Mexico
Old John Barleycorn
Song of Victory
Ker-choo!
Boys in Gray
Mother
Bonnie Blue Flag
Hail Stonewall Jackson

MY PRINCESS
October 6, 1927 (20 perfs)
Music by Sigmund Romberg
Lyrics by Dorothy Donnelly
Gigolo
I Wonder Why
Follow the Sun to the South
When I Was a Girl Like You
Here's How
Dear Girls, Goodbye
Eviva
Our Bridal Night
My Mimosa

---

*Based on the play *Pygmalion* by George Bernard Shaw
†Based on the play *Barbara Frietchie* by Clyde Fitch

Prince Charming
My Passion Flower

MY ROMANCE*
November 29, 1948 (95 perfs)
Music by Sigmund Romberg
Lyrics by Rowland Leigh
  Souvenir
  1898
  Debutante
  Written in Your Hand
  Millefleurs
  Love and Laughter
  From Now Onward
  Little Emmaline
  Desire
  If Only
  Bella Donna
  Paradise Stolen
  In Love with Romance
  Prayer

MY WIFE AND I (OB)
October 10, 1966 (14 perfs)
Music and lyrics by Bill Mahoney
  Confusion
  Busy, Busy Day
  They've Got to Complain
  My Wife and I
  Pay, Pay, Pay
  I've Got a Problem
  It's Pouring
  I'll Come By
  Dad Got Girls
  Baltimore
  The Principle of the Thing
  Please God
  I Really Love You
  I'll Try to Smile
  Family Tree
  Why Grow Old?

MYSTERY MOON
June 23, 1930 (1 perf)
Music by Alma Sanders
Lyrics by Monte Carlo
  Pepper and Salt
  Mechanical Man
  You Always Talk of Friendship
  One Night in the Rain
  What Could I Do, but Fall in Love
    with You?

It's All O.K.
Mystery Moon
Why Couldn't We Incorporate?
Milkmaids of Broadway
Clean Out the Corner

NATJA
February 16, 1925 (32 perfs)
Music by Karl Hajos (based on Tchai-
  kovsky)
Lyrics by Harry B. Smith
  Honor and Glory
  Comrade, You Have a Chance
    Here
  I Hear Love Call Me
  Beside the Star of Glory
  You'll Have to Guess
  The Magic of Moonlight and Love
  Shall I Tell Him?
  March On
  Eyes That Haunt Me
  There Is a Garden in Loveland

NAUGHTY CINDERELLA
November 9, 1925 (121 perfs)
  Nothing but "Yes" in My Eyes (Mu-
    sic and lyrics by E. Ray Goetz)
  J'Ai Deux Amants (Music by Andre
    Messager; lyrics by Sacha Guitry)
  Do I Love You? (Music by Henri
    Christine and E. Ray Goetz; lyrics
    by E. Ray Goetz)
  That Means Nothing to Me (Music
    and lyrics by A. L. Keith and Lee
    Sterling)
  Mia Luna (Music by Puccini (not
    Giacomo); lyrics by E. Ray Goetz)

NAUGHTY-NAUGHT (OB)
January 23, 1937 (173 perfs)
Music by Richard Lewine
Lyrics by Ted Fetter
  Goodbye Girls, Hello Yale
  Naughty-Naught
  Love Makes the World Go Round
  Coney by the Sea
  Zim Zam Zee
  Pull the Boat for Eli

---

*Based on play *Romance* by Edward Sheldon

When We're in Love*
Vocal score

NAUGHTY RIQUETTE
September 13, 1926 (88 perfs)
Lyrics by Harry B. Smith
Naughty Riquette (Music by Maury Rubens and Kendall Burgess)
I May (Music by Maury Rubens and Kendall Burgess)
Make Believe You're Mine (Music by Oscar Straus)
In Armenia (Music by Oscar Straus)
Someone (Music by Alfred Goodman and Maury Rubens)
What Great Men Cannot Do (Music by R. P. Weston; lyrics by Bert Lee)

NED WAYBURN'S GAMBOLS
January 15, 1929 (31 perfs)
Music by Walter G. Samuels
Lyrics by Morrie Ryskind
Crescent Moon
The Church around the Corner
I Bring My Girls Along
Little Dream That's Coming True
Palm Beach Walk
Savannah Stomp
Sweet Old Fashioned Waltz
The Sun Will Shine (Music by Arthur Schwartz)
Ship of Love
In the Days Gone By
Gypsy Days (Music by Arthur Schwartz)
What Is the Good (Music by Lew Kesler; lyrics by Clifford Grey)

NELLIE BLY
January 21, 1946 (16 perfs)
Music by Jimmy Van Heusen
Lyrics by Johnny Burke
There's Nothing Like Travel
All Around the World
Fogarty the Great
That's Class
Nellie Bly
May the Best Man Win
How About a Date?
You Never Saw That Before
Sky High

No News Today
Just My Luck
Aladdin's Daughter
Start Dancing
Harmony

NERVOUS SET, THE
May 12, 1959 (23 perfs)
Music by Tommy Wolf
Lyrics by Fran Landesman
Man, We're Beat
New York
What's to Lose
Stars Have Blown My Way
Fun Life
How Do You Like Your Love?
Party Song
Night People
I've Got a Lot to Learn about Life
The Ballad of the Sad Young Men
A Country Gentleman
Max the Millionaire
Travel the Road of Love
Laugh, I Thought I'd Die
Cast album: Columbia

NEVER TOO LATE
(Play with one song)
November 27, 1962 (1,007 perfs)
Music by Jerry Bock
Lyrics by Sheldon Harnick
Never Too Late Cha-Cha

NEW FACES OF 1934
March 15, 1934 (148 perfs)
New Faces (Music by Martha Caples; lyrics by Nancy Hamilton)
Something You Lack (Music by Warburton Guilbert; lyrics by Nancy Hamilton and June Sillman)
Visitors Ashore (Music by Warburton Guilbert; lyrics by Everett Marcy and Nancy Hamilton)
Lamplight (Music and lyrics by James Shelton)
Music in My Heart (Music by Warburton Guilbert; lyrics by June Sillman)

---

*Added to 1946 revival

My Last Affair (Music and lyrics by Haven Johnson)

Smoky Rhythm (Music and lyrics by George Hickman)

The Gutter Song (Music and lyrics by James Shelton)

You're My Relaxation (Music by Charles Schwab; lyrics by Robert Sour)

Modern Madrigal (Music by Warburton Guilbert; lyrics by Viola Brothers Shore and June Sillman)

'Cause You Won't Play House (Music by Morgan Lewis; lyrics by E. Y. Harburg)

People of Taste (Music by Martha Caples; lyrics by Nancy Hamilton)

So Low (Music by Donald Honrath; lyrics by Nancy Hamilton and June Sillman)

He Loves Me (Music by Cliff Allen; lyrics by Nancy Hamilton)

Spring Song (Music by Warburton Guilbert; lyrics by Viola Brothers Shore and June Sillman)

On the Other Hand (Music by Martha Caples; lyrics by Nancy Hamilton)

NEW FACES OF 1936
May 19, 1936 (193 perfs)

New Faces (Music by Alex Fogarty; lyrics by Edwin Gilbert)

Slap My Face (Music by Alex Fogarty; lyrics by Edwin Gilbert)

Tonight's the Night (Music by Alex Fogarty; lyrics by June Sillman)

Chi-Chi (Music by Irvin Graham; lyrics by June Sillman)

Miss Mimsey (Music and lyrics by Irvin Graham)

My Love Is Young (Music by Irvin Graham; lyrics by Bickley Reichner)

Lottie of the Literati (Music by Alex Fogarty; lyrics by Edwin Gilbert)

Love Is a Dancer (Music by Muriel Pollock; lyrics by Jean Sothern)

You'd Better Go Now (Music by Irvin Graham; lyrics by Bickley Reichner)

Your Face Is So Familiar (Music by Alex Fogarty; lyrics by Edwin Gilbert)

NEW FACES OF 1943
December 22, 1942 (94 perfs)

We'll Swing it Through (Music by Lee Wainer; lyrics by John Lund)

Animals Are Nice (Music by Lee Wainer; lyrics by J. B. Rosenberg)

Love, Are You Raising Your Head? (Music by Lee Wainer; lyrics by June Carroll)

Yes, Sir, I've Made a Date (Music by Lee Wainer; lyrics by J. B. Rosenberg)

Radio City, I Love You (Music by Lee Wainer; lyrics by June Carroll)

Land of Rockefellera (Music by Lee Wainer; lyrics by John Lund)

Shoes (Music by Will Irwin; lyrics by June Carroll)

Back to Bundling (Music by Lee Wainer; lyrics by Dorothy Sachs)

Hey, Gal! (Music by Will Irwin; lyrics by June Carroll)

Well, Well! (Music by Lee Wainer; lyrics by June Carroll)

NEW FACES OF 1952
May 16, 1952 (365 perfs)

Lucky Pierre (Music and lyrics by Ronny Graham)

Guess Who I Saw Today? (Music by Murray Grand; lyrics by Elisse Boyd)

Love Is a Simple Thing (Music by Arthur Siegel; lyrics by June Carroll)

Boston Beguine (Music and lyrics by Sheldon Harnick)

Nanty Puts Her Hair Up (Music by Arthur Siegel; lyrics by Herbert Farjeon)

Time for Tea (Music by Arthur Siegel; lyrics by June Carroll)

Bal Petit Bal (Music and lyrics by Francis Lemarque)

Don't Fall Asleep (Music and lyrics by Ronny Graham)

Lizzie Borden (Music and lyrics by Michael Brown)

I'm In Love with Miss Logan (Music and lyrics by Ronny Graham)

Penny Candy (Music by Arthur Siegel; lyrics by June Carroll)

Convention Bound (Music and lyrics by Ronny Graham)

Monotonous (Music by Arthur Siegel; lyrics by June Carroll)

He Takes Me Off His Income Tax (Music by Arthur Siegel; lyrics by June Carroll)

Cast album: RCA

NEW FACES OF 1956

June 14, 1956 (220 perfs)

And He Flipped (Music and lyrics by John Rox)

April in Fairbanks (Music and lyrics by Murray Grand)

What Does That Dream Mean? (Music by Harold Karr; lyrics by Matt Dubey)

Tell Her (Music by Arthur Siegel; lyrics by June Carroll)

Hurry (Music by Murray Grand; lyrics by Murray Grand and Elisse Boyd)

A Doll's House (Music by Arthur Siegel; lyrics by June Carroll)

Isn't She Lovely? (Music by Dean Fuller; lyrics by Marshall Barer)

Don't Wait Till It's Too Late to See Paris (Music by Arthur Siegel; lyrics by June Carroll)

Scratch My Back (Music by Dean Fuller; lyrics by Marshall Barer)

Boy Most Likely to Succeed (Music by Arthur Siegel; lyrics by June Carroll)

The Broken Kimona (Music by Robert Stringer; lyrics by Richard Maury)

This Is Quite a Perfect Night (Music by Dean Fuller; lyrics by Marshall Barer)

The White Witch of Jamaica (Music by Arthur Siegel; lyrics by June Carroll)

The Greatest Invention (Music and lyrics by Matt Dubey, Harold Karr, and Sid Silvers)

Mustapha Abdullah Abu Ben Al Raajid (Music by Dean Fuller; lyrics by Marshall Barer)

She's Got Everything (Music by Dean Fuller; lyrics by Marshall Barer)

One Perfect Moment (Music and lyrics by Marshall Barer, Dean Fuller, and Leslie Julian-Jones)

Girls 'n Girls 'n Girls (Music and lyrics by Irvin Graham)

Cast album: RCA

NEW FACES OF 1962

February 1, 1962 (28 perfs)

Moral Rearmament (Music and lyrics by Jack Holmes)

In the Morning (Music and lyrics by Ronny Graham)

Happiness (Music by Marie Gordon; lyrics by David Rogers)

Togetherness (Music and lyrics by Mavor Moore)

A Moment of Truth (Music and lyrics by Jack Holmes)

I Want You To Be the First To Know (Music by Arthur Siegel; lyrics by June Carroll)

A.B.C.'s (Music by Mark Bucci; lyrics by David Rogers)

It Depends On How You Look at Things (Music by Arthur Siegel; lyrics by June Carroll)

Freedomland (Music and lyrics by Jack Holmes)

Over the River and into the Woods (Music and lyrics by Jack Holmes)

Johnny Mishuga (Music by Mark Bucci; lyrics by David Rogers and Mark Bucci)

Collective Beauty (Music by William Roy; lyrics by Michael McWhinney)

The Other One (Music by Arthur Siegel; lyrics by June Carroll)

The Untalented Relative (Music by Arthur Siegel; lyrics by Joey Carter and Richard Maury)

Love Is Good for You (Music by Arthur Siegel; lyrics by June Carroll)

Wall Street Reel (Music by Arthur Siegel; lyrics by Jim Fuerst)

NEW FACES OF 1968
May 2, 1968 (52 perfs)
  By the Sea (Music and lyrics by Clark Gesner)
  Where Is the Waltz? (Music by Alonzo Levister; lyrics by Paul Nassau)
  A New Waltz (Music by Fred Hellerman; lyrics by Fran Minkoff)
  The Girl in the Mirror (Music by Fred Hellerman; lyrics by Fran Minkoff)
  Something Big (Music by Sam Pottle; lyrics by David Axelrod)
  Love in a New Tempo (Music and lyrics by Ronny Graham)
  Hungry (Music and lyrics by Murray Grand)
  Luncheon Ballad (Music by Jerry Powell; lyrics by Michael McWhinney)
  You're the One I'm For (Music and lyrics by Clark Gesner)
  Where Is Me? (Music by Arthur Siegel; lyrics by June Carroll)
  Right About Here (Music and lyrics by Arthur Siegel)
  Toyland (Music and lyrics by Gene P. Bissell)
  Hullabaloo at Thebes (Music and lyrics by Ronny Graham)
  #X9RL220 (Music by Jerry Powell; lyrics by Michael McWhinney)
  You Are (Music and lyrics by Clark Gesner)
  Evil (Music and lyrics by Sydney Shaw)
  Prisms (Music by Carl Friberg; lyrics by Hal Hackady)
  Tango (Music by Sam Pottle; lyrics by David Axelrod)
  Cymbals and Tambourines (Music and lyrics by Arthur Siegel)
  Philosophy (Music by Carl Friberg; lyrics by Hal Hackady)
  Das Chicago Song (Music by Michael Cohen; lyrics by Tony Geiss)
  Missed America (Music and lyrics by Kenny Solms and Gail Parent)
  Die Zusammenfugung (Music by Sam Pottle; lyrics by David Axelrod)
  The Girl of the Minute (Music by David Shire; lyrics by Richard Maltby, Jr.)
Cast album: Warner Bros.

NEW GIRL IN TOWN*
May 14, 1957 (431 perfs)
Music and lyrics by Bob Merrill
  Roll Yer Socks Up
  Anna Lilla
  Sunshine Girl
  On the Farm
  Flings
  It's Good to Be Alive
  Look at 'Er
  Yer My Friend, Aintcha?
  Did You Close Your Eyes?
  At the Check Apron Ball
  There Ain't No Flies on Me
  Ven I Valse
  If That Was Love
  Chess and Checkers
Cast album: RCA

NEW MOON, THE
September 19, 1928 (509 perfs)
Music by Sigmund Romberg
Lyrics by Oscar Hammerstein II
  Marianne
  The Girl on the Prow
  Gorgeous Alexander
  An Interrupted Love Song
  Tavern Song
  Softly, As in a Morning Sunrise
  Stouthearted Men
  One Kiss
  Ladies of the Jury
  Wanting You
  Funny Little Sailor Man
  Lover, Come Back to Me
  Love Is Quite a Simple Thing
  Try Her Out at Dances
Album: (Studio cast) Capitol
Vocal score

_____
*Based on the play *Anna Christie* by Eugene O'Neill

NEW YORKERS, THE
March 10, 1927 (52 perfs)
Lyrics by Henry Myers
99 Per Cent Pure (Music by Arthur Schwartz)
Burn 'Em Up (Music by Edgar Fairchild)
Triangle (Music by Charles M. Schwab)
I Can't Get into the Quota (Music by Arthur Schwartz)
Nothing Left but Dreams (Music by Edgar Fairchild)
Slow River (Music by Charles M. Schwab)
Self-Expression (Music by Arthur Schwartz)
Here Comes the Prince of Wales (Music by Arthur Schwartz)
Pretty Little So-and-So (Music by Edgar Fairchild)
A Song About Love (Music by Arthur Schwartz)
A Side Street Off Broadway (Music by Edgar Fairchild)
Floating thru the Air (Music by Arthur Schwartz)
Romany (Music by Arthur Schwartz)

NEW YORKERS, THE
December 8, 1930 (168 perfs)
Music and lyrics by Cole Porter
Go Into Your Dance
Where Have You Been?
Say It with Gin
Venice
Love for Sale
I'm Getting Myself Ready for You
The Great Indoors
Let's Fly Away
Sing Sing for Sing Sing
Take Me Back to Manhattan
I Happen to Like New York
Just One of Those Things*

NIC-NAX OF 1926
August 2, 1926 (13 perfs)
Music by Gitz Rice
Broads of Broadway (Lyrics by Paul Porter)
When the Sun Kissed the Rose Goodbye (Lyrics by Paul Porter)
I Have Forgotten You Almost (Lyrics by Anna Fitziu)
For a Girl Like You (Lyrics by Joe Goodwin)
Everything Is High Yellow Now (Lyrics by Paul Porter)
Burma Moon (Lyrics by Paul Porter)

NIGHT IN PARIS, A
January 5, 1926 (335 perfs)
In Chinatown in Frisco (Music by Maurice Yvain; lyrics by Clifford Grey and McElbert Moore)
Louisiana (Music by J. Fred Coots and Maury Rubens; lyrics by McElbert Moore)
Powder Puff (Music by J. Fred Coots and Maury Rubens; lyrics by Clifford Grey and McElbert Moore)
Voodoo of the Zulu Isle (Music by J. Fred Coots and Maury Rubens; lyrics by Clifford Grey and McElbert Moore)
Bobbed Haired Baby (Music by J. Fred Coots and Maury Rubens; lyrics by McElbert Moore)
The Black Mask (Temptation) (Music by J. J. Shubert Jr.; lyrics by Clifford Grey and McElbert Moore)
The Nile (Music and lyrics by Xaver Leroux)
Amy (Music by Roy Webb; lyrics by F. Coulon)

NIGHT IN SPAIN, A
May 3, 1927 (174 perfs)
Music by Jean Schwartz
Lyrics by Alfred Bryan
Argentine
International Vamp
De-dum-dum
The Sky Girl
Promenade the Esplanade
My Rose of Spain

_____
*Dropped from New York production; title re-used for new song in *Jubilee* (1935)

Hot, Hot Honey
Simple Spanish Maid
The Curfew Walk
Bambazoola
A Million Eyes
A Spanish Shawl

NIGHT IN VENICE, A
May 21, 1929 (175 perfs)
Strolling on the Lido (Music by Lee David and Maury Rubens; lyrics by J. Keirn Brennan and Moe Jaffe)
I'm for You (Music by Lee David; lyrics by J. Keirn Brennan)
Loose Ankles (Music and lyrics by Moe Jaffe, Clay Boland, and Maury Rubens)
One Night of Love (Music by Maury Rubens; lyrics by J. Keirn Brennan)
Sliding Down a Silver Cloud (Music by Lee David; lyrics by J. Keirn Brennan)
The Stork Don't Come Around Any More (Music and lyrics by B. Laidlaw)

NIGHT OF LOVE
January 7, 1941 (7 perfs)
Music by Robert Stolz
Lyrics by Rowland Leigh
My Loved One
Chiquitin Trio
I'm Thinking of Love
The One Man I Need
Tonight or Never
Serenade for You
Without You
Loosen Up
Streamlined Pompadour

NIGHTINGALE, THE
January 3, 1927 (96 perfs)
Music by Armand Vecsey
Lyrics by P. G. Wodehouse
Breakfast in Bed
Josephine (Lyrics by Clifford Grey)
May Moon
Once in September (Lyrics by Clifford Grey)
Two Little Ships

Homeland
Another One Gone Wrong
Love Like Yours Is Rare Indeed
Rabbit Song

NIKKI
September 29, 1931 (40 perfs)
Music by Philip Charig
Lyrics by James Dyrenforth
Screwy Little Tune
Taking Off
Wonder Why
On Account of I Love You
Now I Know
My Heart Is Calling
The Ghost of Little Egypt

NINA ROSA
September 20, 1930 (129 perfs)
Music by Sigmund Romberg
Lyrics by Irving Caesar
Pay Day
Pablo
Nina Rosa
With the Dawn
Payador
The Secret of My Life
Your Smiles, Your Tears
Serenade of Love
Pizarro Was a Very Narrow Man
A Kiss I Must Refuse You
Latigo
A Gaucho Love Song
My First Love, My Last Love (Lyrics by Irving Caesar and Otto Harbach)
Vocal score

NINE-FIFTEEN REVUE
February 11, 1930 (7 perfs)
Up Among the Chimney Pots (Music by Kay Swift; lyrics by Paul James)
Toddlin' Along (Music by George Gershwin; lyrics by Ira Gershwin)
World of Dreams (Music by Victor Herbert; lyrics by Edward Eliscu)
Ta Ta, Ol' Bean (Music by Manning Sherwin; lyrics by Edward Eliscu)
Knock on Wood (Music by Richard Myers; lyrics by Edward Eliscu)
Get Happy (Music by Harold Arlen; lyrics by Ted Koehler)

Winter and Spring (Music by Rudolf Friml; lyrics by Edward Eliscu)

Boudoir Dolls (Music by Ned Lehak; lyrics by Edward Eliscu)

Breakfast Dance (Music by Ralph Rainger; lyrics by Edward Eliscu)

How Would a City Girl Know? (Music by Kay Swift; lyrics by Paul James)

A Purty Little Thing (Music by Philip Broughton; lyrics by Will B. Johnstone)

Gotta Find a Way to Do It (Music by Roger Wolfe Kahn; lyrics by Paul James)

You Will Never Know (Music by Vincent Youmans; lyrics by Paul James)

Gee It's So Good, It's Too Bad (Music by Harold Arlen; lyrics by Ted Koehler)

You Wanted Me, I Wanted You (Music by Harold Arlen; lyrics by Ted Koehler)

No Foolin'
June 24, 1926 (108 perfs)
Music by James F. Hanley
Lyrics by Gene Buck
Honey, Be Mine
No Foolin'
Florida, the Moon and You (Music by Rudolf Friml)
Every Little Thing You Do
Wasn't It Nice? (Music by Rudolf Friml; lyrics by Irving Caesar)
Nize Baby (Lyrics by Ballard Mac-Donald)
Don't Do the Charleston
Poor Little Marie
When the Shaker Plays a Cocktail Tune

No, No, Nanette*
September 16, 1925 (321 perfs)
Music by Vincent Youmans
The Call of the Sea (Lyrics by Otto Harbach)
Too Many Rings Around Rosie (Lyrics by Irving Caesar)
Waiting for You (Lyrics by Otto Harbach)

I Want to Be Happy (Lyrics by Irving Caesar)

No, No, Nanette (Lyrics by Otto Harbach)

Peach on the Beach (Lyrics by Otto Harbach)

My Doctor (Lyrics by Otto Harbach)

Fight Over Me (Lyrics by Otto Harbach)

Tea for Two (Lyrics by Irving Caesar)

You Can Dance with Any Girl At All (Lyrics by Irving Caesar)

Telephone Girlie (Lyrics by Otto Harbach)

"Where Has My Hubby Gone" Blues (Lyrics by Irving Caesar)

Pay Day Pauline (Lyrics by Otto Harbach)

I've Confessed to the Breeze† (Lyrics by Otto Harbach)

Take a Little One-Step† (Lyrics by Zelda Sears)

Cast album (1971 revival): Columbia

No Strings
March 15, 1962 (580 perfs)
Music and lyrics by Richard Rodgers
The Sweetest Sounds
How Sad
Loads of Love
The Man Who Has Everything
Be My Host
La La La
You Don't Tell Me
Love Makes the World Go
Nobody Told Me
Look No Further
Maine
An Orthodox Fool
Eager Beaver
No Strings
Cast album: Capitol
Vocal score
Vocal selection

---

*Based on play *My Lady Friends* by Emil Nyitray and Frank Mandel
†Added to 1971 revival

NOW IS THE TIME FOR ALL GOOD MEN (OB)
September 26, 1967 (111 perfs)
Music by Nancy Ford
Lyrics by Gretchen Cryer
　We Shall Meet in the Great Here-
　　after
　Quittin' Time
　What's in the Air
　Keep 'Em Busy, Keep 'Em Quiet
　Tea in the Rain
　What's a Guy Like You Doin' in a
　　Place Like This?
　Halloween Hayride
　See Everything New
　All Alone
　He Could Show Me
　Washed Away
　Stuck-Up
　My Holiday
　On My Own
　It Was Good Enough for Grandpa
　A Simple Life
　A Star on the Monument
　Rain Your Love on Me
　There's Going to Be a Wedding
Cast album: Columbia

NOWHERE TO GO BUT UP
November 10, 1962 (9 perfs)
Music by Sol Berkowitz
Lyrics by James Lipton
　Ain't You Ashamed?
　The We Makin' Dough You So and
　　So Rag
　Live a Little
　Mr. Baiello
　When a Fella Needs a Friend
　The Odds and Ends of Love
　Nowhere to Go but Up
　Take Me Back
　I Love You for That
　Baby, Baby
　Out of Sight, Out of Mind
　Follow the Leader Septet
　Dear Mom

O MARRY ME!* (OB)
October 27, 1961 (21 perfs)
Music by Robert Kessler
Lyrics by Lola Pergament
　I Love Everything That's Old

Time and Tide
The Kind of Man
Ale House Song
Proper Due
Be a Lover
Perish the Baubles
The Meeting
Fashions
Say Yes, Look No
Let's All Be Exactly and Precisely
　What We Are
The Braggart Song
O Marry Me!
Betrayed
Motherly Love
Morality

O SAY CAN YOU SEE! (OB)
October 8, 1962 (32 perfs)
Music by Jack Holmes
Lyrics by Bill Conklin and Bob Miller
　The Freedom Choo Choo Is Leav-
　　ing Today
　Dreamboat from Dreamland
　Dogface Jive
　Us Two
　Take Me Back to Texas
　Doughnuts for Defense
　Canteen Serenade
　These Are Worth Fighting For
　Someone a Lot Like You
　Veronica Takes Over
　Buy Bonds, Buster, Buy Bonds
　Chico-Chico Chico-Layo
　Flim Flam Flooey
　When the Bluebirds Fly All Over
　　the World
　Just the Way You Are
　My G. I. Joey
　O Say Can You See!
Cast album: Grenville

OF MICE AND MEN† (OB)
December 4, 1958 (37 perfs)
Music by Alfred Brooks
Lyrics by Ira J. Bilowit
　Nice House We Got Here

———
*Based on Oliver Goldsmith's *She Stoops to
Conquer*
†Based on John Steinbeck's play

No Ketchup
We Got a Future
Buckin' Barley
Curley's Wife
Wanta, Hope to Feel at Home
Lemme Tell Ya
Just Someone to Talk To
Dudin' Up
Nice Fella
Why Try Hard to Be Good?
Never Do a Bad Thing
Is There Some Place for Me?
A Guy, A Guy, A Guy
Strangely
Candy's Lament

OF THEE I SING*
December 26, 1931 (441 perfs)
Music by George Gershwin
Lyrics by Ira Gershwin
Wintergreen for President
Who Is the Lucky Girl to Be?
The Dimple on My Knee
Because, Because
Never Was There a Girl So Fair
Some Girls Can Bake a Pie
Love Is Sweeping the Country
Of Thee I Sing
Here's a Kiss for Cinderella
I Was the Most Beautiful Blossom
Who Cares?
Garçon, S'il Vous Plaît
The Illegitimate Daughter
The Senatorial Roll Call
Jilted
I'm about to Be a Mother (Who Could Ask for Anything More?)
Posterity Is Just around the Corner
Trumpeter, Blow Your Golden Horn
Cast album: (1952 revival) Capitol
Vocal score

OF V WE SING
Feburary 11, 1942 (76 perfs)
You Can't Fool the People (Music by George Kleinsinger; lyrics by Alfred Hayes)
Sisters under the Skin (Music by Baldwin Bergersen; lyrics by Sylvia Marks)
Don't Sing Solo (Music by George Kleinsinger; lyrics by Roslyn Harvey)
Freedom Road (Music by Toby Sacher; lyrics by Lewis Allen)
Brooklyn Cantata (Music by George Kleinsinger; lyrics by Mike Stratton)
Take a Poem (Music by George Kleinsinger; lyrics by Norman Corwin)
Priorities (Music by Lou Cooper; lyrics by Roslyn Harvey)
Queen Esther (Music by George Kleinsinger; lyrics by Beatrice Goldsmith)
Gertie the Stool Pigeon's Daughter (Music by Ned Lehak; lyrics by Joe Darion)
You've Got to Appease with a Strip Tease (Music by Toby Sacher; lyrics by Lewis Allen)
We Have a Date (Music by Lou Cooper; lyrics by Roslyn Harvey)
Juke Box (Music by Alex North; lyrics by Alfred Hayes)
Of V We Sing (Music by Lou Cooper; lyrics by Arthur Zipser)

O'FLYNN, THE
December 27, 1934 (11 perfs)
Music by Franklin Hauser
A Lovely Lady (Lyrics by Russell Janney)
Child of Erin (Lyrics by Russell Janney)
Song of My Heart (Lyrics by Brian Hooker)
The Man I Love Is Here (Lyrics by Brian Hooker)

OH CAPTAIN!†
February 4, 1958 (192 perfs)
Music and lyrics by Jay Livingston and Ray Evans
A Very Proper Town
Life Does a Man a Favor
Captain Henry St. James

---

*Pulitzer Prize Winner
†Based on the film *The Captain's Paradise*

Three Paradises
Surprise
Hey, Madame
Femininity
It's Never Quite the Same
We're Not Children
Give It All You Got
Love Is Hell
Keep It Simple
The Morning Music of Montmartre
You Don't Know Him
I've Been There and I'm Back
Double Standard
You're So Right for Me
All the Time
Cast album: Columbia

OH, ERNEST!*
May 9, 1927 (56 perfs)
Music by Robert Hood Bowers
Lyrics by Francis DeWitt
  On the Beach
  Taken by Surprise
  Ancestry
  Cupid's College
  Didoes
  Over the Garden Wall
  Cecily
  Let's Pretend
  Pollyanna
  Don't Scold
  Give Me Someone
  Little Stranger
  He Knows Where the Rose Is in
    Bloom
  Tangles
  There's a Muddle
  Never Trouble Trouble

OH, KAY!
November 8, 1926 (256 perfs)
Music by George Gershwin
Lyrics by Ira Gershwin
  The Womans' Touch
  Don't Ask!
  Dear Little Girl
  Maybe
  Clap Yo' Hands
  Bride and Groom
  Do Do Do
  Someone to Watch over Me
  Fidgety Feet

Heaven on Earth (Lyrics by Ira
  Gershwin and Howard Dietz)
Oh, Kay (Lyrics by Ira Gershwin
  and Howard Dietz)
Show Me the Town†
Album: (Studio cast) Columbia

OH! OH! NURSE
December 7, 1925 (32 perfs)
Music by Alma Sanders
Lyrics by Monte Carlo
  Show a Little Pep
  Love Will Keep Us Young
  You May Have Planted Many a Lily
  Way Out in Rainbow Land
  Cleopatra
  Who Bites the Hole in Schweitzer
    Cheese?
  Keep a Kiss for Me
  Pierre
  My Lady Love
  I'll Give the World to You
  No Hearts for Sale
  Is It Any Wonder?
  Butter and Egg Baby
  Newlywed Express
  Under My Umbrella
  No, I Won't
  Shooting Stars

OH, PLEASE!
December 17, 1926 (75 perfs)
Music by Vincent Youmans
Lyrics by Anne Caldwell
  Homely but Clean
  Snappy Show in Town
  Like He Loves Me
  Nicodemus
  I'd Steal a Star
  I Know That You Know
  I'm Waiting for a Wonderful Girl
  Love Me
  I Can't Be Happy
  The Girls of the Old Brigade

---

*Based on Oscar Wilde's play *The Impor-
tance of Being Earnest*
†Dropped from New York production;
used in *Rosalie* (1928)

OKLAHOMA!*
March 31, 1943 (2,212 perfs)
Music by Richard Rodgers
Lyrics by Oscar Hammerstein II
  Oh, What a Beautiful Mornin'
  The Surrey with the Fringe on Top
  Kansas City
  I Cain't Say No
  Many a New Day
  It's a Scandal! It's an Outrage!
  People Will Say We're in Love
  Pore Jud Is Daid
  Lonely Room
  Out of My Dreams
  The Farmer and the Cowman
  All er Nothin'
  Oklahoma
  Boys and Girls Like You and Me†
Cast album: Decca
Vocal score
Vocal selection

OLD BUCKS AND NEW WINGS (OB)
November 5, 1962 (8 perfs)
Music by Eddie Stuart
Lyrics by Harvey Lasker
  Our Business Is News
  Get the News
  So, So Sophie
  That Was Your Life
  Keith's, Pantages and Loews
  That Day Will Come
  Sweet Memories
  You Made It Possible, Dear
  It Could Be Calais
  Stand Up and Cheer
  Let's Bring Back Showbusiness

OLIVER!**
January 6, 1963 (774 perfs)
Music and lyrics by Lionel Bart
  Food, Glorious Food
  Oliver!
  I Shall Scream
  Boy for Sale
  That's Your Funeral
  Where is Love?
  Consider Yourself
  You've Got to Pick a Pocket or Two
  It's a Fine Life
  Be Back Soon
  Oom-Pah-Pah

  My Name
  As Long As He Needs Me
  I'd Do Anything
  Who Will Buy?
  Reviewing the Situation
Cast album: RCA
Vocal score
Vocal selection

ON A CLEAR DAY YOU CAN SEE FOREVER
October 17, 1965 (280 perfs)
Music by Burton Lane
Lyrics by Alan Jay Lerner
  Hurry! It's Lovely Up Here
  Ring Out the Bells
  Tosy and Cosh
  On a Clear Day You Can See
    Forever
  On the S.S. Bernard Cohn
  Don't Tamper with My Sister
  She Wasn't You
  Melinda
  When I'm Being Born Again
  What Did I Have That I Don't Have
  Wait 'Til We're Sixty-Five
  Come Back to Me
Cast album: RCA
Vocal score
Vocal selection
Added to film version: (1969)
  Go to Sleep
  Love with All the Trimmings
Soundtrack album: Columbia

ON THE TOWN
December 28, 1944 (463 perfs)
Music by Leonard Bernstein
Lyrics by Betty Comden and Adolph Green
  I Feel Like I'm Not Out of Bed Yet
  New York, New York
  Come Up to My Place
  Carried Away
  Lonely Town
  Lucky to Be Me

_____
*Based on the play *Green Grow the Lilacs* by Lynn Riggs
†Dropped from New York Production
**Based on Charles Dickens' *Oliver Twist*

Some Other Time
I Can Cook Too (Lyrics by Leonard Bernstein, Betty Comden, and Adolph Green)

ON YOUR TOES
April 11, 1936 (315 perfs)
Music by Richard Rodgers
Lyrics by Lorenz Hart
Two-a-Day for Keith
The Three B's
It's Got to Be Love
Too Good for the Average Man
There's a Small Hotel
The Heart Is Quicker Than the Eye
La Princesse Zenobia (ballet)
Quiet Night
Glad to Be Unhappy
On Your Toes
Slaughter on Tenth Avenue (ballet)
Album: (Studio cast) Columbia

ONCE UPON A MATTRESS*
May 11, 1959 (460 perfs†)
Music by Mary Rodgers
Lyrics by Marshall Barer
Many Moons Ago
An Opening for a Princess
In a Little While
Shy
The Minstrel
The Jester and I
Sensitivity
The Swamps of Home
Normandy
Spanish Panic
Song of Love
Quiet
Happily Ever After
Man to Man Talk
Very Soft Shoes
Yesterday I Loved You
Lullaby
Cast album: Kapp
Vocal score
Vocal selection

ONE FOR THE MONEY
February 4, 1939 (132 perfs)
Music by Morgan Lewis
Lyrics by Nancy Hamilton
I Only Know

Rhapsody
Teeter Totter Tessie
Send a Boy
A Little Bit Delighted with the Weather
Once Upon a Time
The Yoo-Hoo Blues
Kiss Me and We'll Both Go Home

110 IN THE SHADE**
October 24, 1963 (330 perfs)
Music by Harvey Schmidt
Lyrics by Tom Jones
Another Hot Day
Lizzie's Coming Home
Love, Don't Turn Away
Poker Polka
Hungry Men
The Rain Song
You're Not Foolin' Me
Raunchy
A Man and a Woman
Old Maid
Everything Beautiful Happens at Night
Melisande
Simple Little Things
Little Red Hat
Is It Really Me?
Wonderful Music
Too Many People Alone††
Cast album: RCA
Vocal score
Vocal selection

ONE TOUCH OF VENUS
October 7, 1943 (567 perfs)
Music by Kurt Weill
Lyrics by Ogden Nash
New Art Is True Art
One Touch of Venus
How Much I Love You
West Wind
Way Out West in Jersey
I'm a Stranger Here Myself

---

*Based on fairy tale *The Princess and the Pea*
†Includes initial OB run
**Based on the play *The Rainmaker* by N. Richard Nash
††Dropped from New York production

Foolish Heart
The Trouble with Women
Speak Low
Dr. Crippen
Very, Very, Very
Catch Hatch
That's Him
Wooden Wedding
Cast album: Decca

OPERATION SIDEWINDER
March 12, 1970 (52 perfs)
  Catch Me (Music and lyrics by Sam Shepard)
  Alien Song (Music and lyrics by Sam Shepard)
  Euphoria (Music and lyrics by Robin Remaily)
  Don't Leave Me Dangling in the Dust (Music and lyrics by Robin Remaily)
  Synergy (Music and lyrics by Peter Stampfel and Antonia)
  Bad Karma (Music and lyrics by Peter Stampfel and Antonia)
  Generalonely (Music and lyrics by Steve Weber)
  Do It Girl (Music and lyrics by Peter Stampfel and Antonia)
  Float Me Down Your Pipeline (Music and lyrics by Antonia)
  I Disremember Quite Well (Music and lyrics by Antonia)
  Hathor (Music and lyrics by Peter Stampfel)
  C.I.A. Man (Music and lyrics by Tuli Kupferberg, Peter Stampfel, and Antonia)

OPTIMISTS, THE
January 30, 1928 (24 perfs)
Music by Melville Gideon
  Amapu (Lyrics by Edward Knoblock)
  I Promise I'll Be Practically True to You (Lyrics by Clifford Grey)
  If I Gave You a Rose (Lyrics by Granville English)
  Little Lacquer Lady (Lyrics by Clifford Seyler)
  Spare a Little Love (Lyrics by Clifford Grey)

ORCHIDS PREFERRED
May 11, 1937 (7 perfs)
Music by Dave Stamper
Lyrics by Fred Herendeen
  I'm Leaving the Bad Girls for Good
  Selling a Song
  Sub-Debs' First Fling
  The Dying Swan
  The Three R's (Music and lyrics by Henry Russell and Morry Olsen)
  A Million Dollars
  Eddy-Mac
  Boy, Girl, Moon
  Strictly Confidential
  Minsky
  My Lady's Hand
  Man About Town
  Paying Off
  The Echo of a Song
  What Are You Going to Do About Love?

OUT OF THIS WORLD*
December 21, 1950 (157 perfs)
Music and lyrics by Cole Porter
  I Jupiter, I Rex
  Use Your Imagination
  Hail, Hail, Hail
  I Got Beauty
  Where, Oh Where
  I Am Loved
  They Couldn't Compare to You
  I Sleep Easier Now
  Climb Up the Mountain
  No Lover for Me
  Cherry Pies Ought to Be You
  Hark to the Song of the Night
  Nobody's Chasing Me
  From This Moment On†
  You Don't Remind Me†
  What Do You Think About Men?
  Tonight I Love You More†
Cast album: Columbia

PADLOCKS OF 1927
July 5, 1927 (95 perfs)
  Hot Heels (Music by Lee David; lyrics by Billy Rose and Ballard MacDonald)

---

*Based on the Amphitryon legend
†Dropped from New York production

If I Had a Lover (Music by Henry Tobias; lyrics by Billy Rose and Ballard MacDonald)
The Tap, Tap (Music by Jesse Greer; lyrics by Billy Rose and Ballard MacDonald)

PAINT YOUR WAGON
November 12, 1951 (289 perfs)
Music by Frederick Loewe
Lyrics by Alan Jay Lerner
  I'm On My Way
  Rumson
  What's Goin' On Here?
  I Talk to the Trees
  They Call the Wind Maria
  I Still See Elisa
  How Can I Wait?
  Trio
  In Between
  Whoop-Ti-Ay
  Carino Mio
  There's a Coach Comin' In
  Hand Me Down That Can o' Beans
  Another Autumn
  Movin'
  All for Him
  Wand'rin' Star
  Strike!
Cast album: RCA
Vocal score
Vocal selection
Added to film version (1969):
Music by André Previn
  The First Thing You Know
  A Million Miles Away behind the Door
  The Gospel of No Name City
  The Best Things in Life Are Dirty
  Gold Fever
Soundtrack album: ABC-Paramount

PAJAMA GAME, THE*
May 13, 1954 (1,063 perfs)
Music and lyrics by Richard Adler and Jerry Ross
  The Pajama Game
  Racing with the Clock
  A New Town is a Blue Town
  I'm Not at All in Love
  I'll Never Be Jealous Again
  Hey There

  Her Is
  Sleep-Tite
  Once a Year Day
  Small Talk
  There Once Was a Man
  Steam Heat
  Think of the Time I Save
  Hernando's Hideaway
  7½ Cents
Cast album: Columbia
Vocal score
Vocal selection

PAL JOEY†
December 25, 1940 (374 perfs)
Music by Richard Rodgers
Lyrics by Lorenz Hart
  You Mustn't Kick It Around
  I Could Write a Book
  Chicago
  That Terrific Rainbow
  Love Is My Friend**
  Happy Hunting Horn
  Bewitched, Bothered and Bewildered
  Pal Joey
  The Flower Garden of My Heart
  Zip
  Plant You Now, Dig You Later
  In Our Little Den of Iniquity
  Do It the Hard Way
  Take Him
Album: (Studio cast) Columbia
Vocal score
Vocal selection

PANAMA HATTIE
October 30, 1940 (501 perfs)
Music and lyrics by Cole Porter
  Join It Right Away
  Visit Panama
  American Family
  My Mother Would Love You
  I've Still Got My Health
  Fresh As a Daisy

---

*Based on the novel *7½ Cents* by Richard Bissell
†Based on stories by John O'Hara
**Lyric rewritten as "What Is a Man?" after New York opening

Welcome to Jerry
Let's Be Buddies
I'm Throwing a Ball Tonight
I Detest a Fiesta
Who Would Have Dreamed
Make It Another Old-Fashioned,
   Please
All I've Got to Get Now Is My Man
You Said It
God Bless the Women
A Stroll on the Plaza 'ana
They Ain't Done Right By Our Nell

PANSY
May 14, 1929 (3 perfs)
Music and lyrics by Maceo Pinkard
   It's Commencement Day
   Breakin' the Rhythm
   Pansy
   Campus Walk
   I'd Be Happy
   Gettin' Together
   Shake a Leg
   If the Blues Don't Get You
   A Stranger Interlude
   A Bouquet of Fond Memories

PARADE (1935)
May 20, 1935 (40 perfs)
Music by Jerome Moross
Lyrics by Paul Peters and George
Sklar
   On Parade
   I'm Telling You, Louie
   I'm an International Orphan
   Smart Set (Music by Will Irwin)
   Life Could Be So Beautiful
   Send for the Militia (Music and lyr-
      ics by Marc Blitzstein)
   You Ain't So Hot
   Boys in Blue
   Fear in My Heart
   My Feet Are Firmly Planted on the
      Ground (Lyrics by Emanuel
      Eisenberg)
   Marry the Family (Lyrics by Mi-
      chael Blankfort)
   Selling Sex (Lyrics by Kyle Crich-
      ton)
   Bon Voyage (Lyrics by Kyle Crich-
      ton)
   Join Our Ranks

PARADE (OB)
January 20, 1960 (95 perfs)
Music and lyrics by Jerry Herman
   Show Tune in 2/4 Time*
   Save the Village
   Your Hand in Mine
   Confession to a Park Avenue
      Mother (I'm In Love with a West
      Side Girl)
   Two a Day
   Just Plain Folks
   The Antique Man
   The Next Time I Love
   Your Good Morning
   Maria in Spats
   Another Candle
   Jolly Theatrical Season
Cast album: Kapp

PARADISE GARDENS EAST (OB)
March 10, 1969 (16 perfs)
Music by Mildred Kayden
Lyrics by Frank Gagliano
   Harmony
   The Beat of the City
   I'll Bet You're a Cat Girl
   Gussy and the Beautiful People
   Look at My Sister
   Black and Blue Pumps
   That's Right, Mr. Syph
   The Incinerator Hour

PARDON MY ENGLISH
January 20, 1933 (46 perfs.)
Music by George Gershwin
Lyrics by Ira Gershwin
   Three Quarter Time
   Lorelei
   Pardon My English
   Dancing in the Streets
   So What?
   Isn't It a Pity?
   My Cousin in Milwaukee
   Hail the Happy Couple
   The Dresden Northwest Mounted
   Luckiest Man in the World
   What Sort of Wedding Is This?
   Tonight

_____
*Rewritten as "It's Today" for *Mame*
(1966)

Where You Go I Go
I've Got to Be There
He's Not Himself

PARDON OUR FRENCH
September 27, 1950 (100 perfs)
Music by Victor Young
Lyrics by Edward Heyman
Pardon Our French
There's No Man Like a Snowman
I Ought to Know More About You
Venezia and Her Three Lovers
A Face in the Crowd
I'm Gonna Make a Fool out of April
The Flower Song
Dolly from the Follies Bergère
The Poker-Polka

PARIS
October 8, 1928 (195 perfs)
Music and lyrics by Cole Porter
The Land of Going to Be (Music and
lyrics by E. Ray Goetz and Walter
Kollo)
Paris (Music and lyrics by E. Ray Go-
etz and Louis Alter)
Babes in the Wood
Don't Look at Me That Way
Let's Fall in Love
Vivienne
Heaven Hop
Quelque Chose*
Which?*
Let's Misbehave*

PARIS '90
March 4, 1952 (87 perfs)
Music and lyrics by Kay Swift
Turn My Little Millwheel (Music by
Paul Delmet)
Lend Me a Bob Till Monday
Calliope
Saint Lazare (Music by Aristide Bru-
ant)
Madame Arthur (Music by Yvette
Guilbert)
The Waltz I Heard in a Dream
Cast album: Columbia

PARISIANA
February 9, 1928 (28 perfs)
Music and lyrics by Vincent Valentini

Keep on Dancing
When You Say No to Love
Keep It Under Your Hat
Who Wouldn't
Since Nora Brought Her Angora
Around
Parisiana Roses
What's Become of the Bowery?
The Ghost of Old Black Joe
Paris Green
In a Gondola with You
Golliwog
Unfortunate Rose
They're Hot Now Up in Iceland
Peepin' Tommy
Paree Has the Fever Now

PARK
April 22, 1970 (5 perfs)
Music by Lance Mulcahy
Lyrics by Paul Cherry
All the Little Things in the World
Are Waiting
Hello Is the Way Things Begin
Bein' a Kid
Elizabeth
He Talks to Me
Tomorrow Will Be the Same
One Man
Park
I Want It Just to Happen
I Can See
Compromise
Jamie
I'd Marry You Again

PARK AVENUE
November 4, 1946 (72 perfs)
Music by Arthur Schwartz
Lyrics by Ira Gershwin
Tomorrow Is the Time
For the Life of Me
The Dew Was on the Rose
Don't Be a Woman If You Can
Nevada
There's No Holding Me
There's Nothing Like Marriage for
People
Hope for the Best
My Son-in-Law

―――――

*Dropped from New York production

The Land of Opportunitee
Goodbye to All That
Stay As We Are

PEGGY-ANN*

December 27, 1926 (333 perfs)
Music by Richard Rodgers
Lyrics by Lorenz Hart
Hello
A Tree in the Park
Howdy Broadway
A Little Birdie Told Me So
Charming, Charming
Where's That Rainbow?
We Pirates from Weehawken
In His Arms
Chuck It!
I'm So Humble
Havana
Maybe It's Me
Give This Little Girl a Hand

PENNY FRIEND, THE† (OB)

December 26, 1966 (32 perfs)
Music and lyrics by William Roy
The Penny Friend
She Makes You Think of Home
Who Am I, Who Are You, Who Are
We?
Mrs. Bodie
I Am Going to Dance
Feet
The Great Unknown
How Doth the Apple Butterfly
The Diagnostician
Won't You Come to the Party
The Grand Parade
A Very Full and Productive Day
The World Today

PETER PAN**

April 24, 1950 (321 perfs)
Music and lyrics by Leonard Bernstein
Who Am I?
My House
Peter, Peter
The Pirate Song
The Plank
Never Land
Cast album: Columbia
Vocal selection

PETER PAN**

October 20, 1954 (152 perfs)
Tender Shepherd (Music by Mark Charlap; lyrics by Carolyn Leigh)
I've Gotta Crow (Music by Mark Charlap; lyrics by Carolyn Leigh)
Never Never Land (Music by Jule Styne; lyrics by Betty Comden and Adolph Green)
I'm Flying (Music by Mark Charlap; lyrics by Carolyn Leigh)
Pirate Song (Music by Mark Charlap; lyrics by Carolyn Leigh)
A Princely Scheme (Music by Mark Charlap; lyrics by Carolyn Leigh)
Indians (Music by Mark Charlap; lyrics by Carolyn Leigh)
Wendy (Music by Jule Styne; lyrics by Betty Comden and Adolph Green)
I Won't Grow Up (Music by Mark Charlap; lyrics by Carolyn Leigh)
Mysterious Lady (Music by Jule Styne; lyrics by Betty Comden and Adolph Green)
Ugg-a-Wugg (Music by Jule Styne; lyrics by Betty Comden and Adolph Green)
Pow-Wow Polka (Music by Jule Styne; lyrics by Betty Comden and Adolph Green)
Captain Hook's Waltz (Music by Jule Styne; lyrics by Betty Comden and Adolph Green)
Distant Melody (Music by Jule Styne; lyrics by Betty Comden and Adolph Green)
Captain Hook's Tango (Music by Mark Charlap; lyrics by Carolyn Leigh)
Tarantella (Music by Mark Charlap; lyrics by Carolyn Leigh)
Cast album: RCA
Vocal score

---

*Suggested by the 1910 musical comedy *Tillie's Nightmare* by Edgar Smith and A. Baldwin Sloane
†Based on the play *A Kiss for Cinderella* by Sir James M. Barrie
**Based on the play by Sir James M. Barrie

PETTICOAT FEVER
(Play with one song)
March 4, 1935 (137 perfs)
Music by Frederick Loewe
Lyrics by Irene Alexander
  Love Tiptoed through My Heart

PHOENIX '55 (OB)
April 23, 1955 (97 perfs)
Music by David Baker
Lyrics by David Craig
  It Says Here
  Tomorrow Is Here
  All Around the World
  Never Wait for Love
  Down to the Sea
  This Tuxedo Is Mine!
  Just Him
  A Funny Heart
  Suburban Retreat

PICKWICK*
October 4, 1965 (56 perfs)
Music by Cyril Ornadel
Lyrics by Leslie Bricusse
  I Like the Company of Men
  That's What I'd Like for Christmas
  The Pickwickians
  A Bit of a Character
  There's Something About You
  A Gentleman's Gentleman
  You Never Met a Feller Like
    Me
  I'll Never Be Lonely Again
  Fizkin and Pickwick
  Very
  If I Ruled the World
  Talk
  That's the Law
  Damages
Cast album: Philips

PIGGY
January 11, 1927 (83 perfs)
Music by Cliff Friend
Lyrics by Lew Brown
  I Need a Little Bit, You Need a Lit-
    tle Bit
  I Wanna Go Voom Voom
  It Just Had to Happen
  Didn't It
  Oh, Baby

A Little Change of Atmosphere
It's Easy to Say Hello
The Music of a Rippling Stream
When
Let's Stroll Along and Sing a Song of
  Love
Ding, Dong, Dell

PILGRIM'S PROGRESS (OB)
March 20, 1962 (8 perfs)
Music and lyrics by Edwin Greenberg
  The Ballad of Bedford Gaol
  A + B = C
  Giza-on-the-Nile
  Blackest of Tresses
  Capital of the World
  Husband of Mine
  Take My Hand in Friendship
  The Voice of God
  What Do They Care?
  I'm Feeling Better All the Time
  Prisoner's Lullaby
  The Girls Who Sell Orangeade
  The Tomorrow Waltz
  My Daughter, My Angel
  Sing Out in the Streets

PIMPERNEL!† (OB)
January 7, 1964 (3 perfs)
Music by Mimi Stone
Lyrics by William Kaye
  This Is England
  Dangerous Game
  A la Pimpernel
  Le Croissant
  Touch of Paris
  Everything's Just Divine
  A Woman
  Le Bon Mot
  As If I Weren't There
  Liberty, Equality, Fraternity
  Love of Long Ago
  What a Day for Me
  I'm Seeing Things
  Sing, Jacques, Sing
  Nose Ahead

---

*Based on Charles Dickens' *Pickwick Papers*
†Based on the novel *The Scarlet Pimpernel* by Baroness Orczy

PINS AND NEEDLES (OB)
November 27, 1937 (1,108 perfs)
Music and lyrics by Harold Rome
First Impression (Lyrics by Harold Rome and Charles Friedman)
Sing Me a Song with Social Significance
Public Enemy No. 1
We'd Rather Be Right (Lyrics by Arthur Kramer)
Sunday in the Park
Nobody Makes a Pass at Me
Economics I
Men Awake
It's Not Cricket to Picket
Chain Store Daisy
What Good Is Love?
One Big Union for Two
Four Little Angels of Peace
Doin' the Reactionary
We've Just Begun (Lyrics by Harold Rome and Charles Friedman)
Added during run:
Papa Lewis, Mama Green
I've Got the Nerve to Be in Love
It's Better with a Union Man
Sitting on Your Status Quo
Mene, Mene, Tekel
Back to Work
Brittania Waives the Rules (Music by Berenice Kazounoff; lyrics by Arnold B. Horwitt and John Latouche)
Oh, Give Me the Good Old Days
When I Grow Up (The G-Man Song)
Stay Out, Sammy
We Sing America
What This Party Needs (Lyrics by Harold Rome and Arthur Kramer)
Lorelei on the Rocks (Music by Berenice Kazounoff; lyrics by John Latouche)
Album (Studio Cast): Columbia
Vocal score
Vocal selection

PIPE DREAM*
November 30, 1955 (246 perfs)
Music by Richard Rodgers
Lyrics by Oscar Hammerstein II

All Kinds of People
The Tide Pool
Ev'rybody's Got a Home but Me
A Lopsided Bus
Bums' Opera
The Man I Used to Be
Sweet Thursday
Suzy Is a Good Thing
All at Once You Love Her
The Happiest House on the Block
The Party That We're Gonna Have Tomorrow Night
The Party Gets Going
I Am a Witch
Will You Marry Me?
Thinkin'
How Long?
The Next Time It Happens
Cast album: RCA
Vocal score

PLAIN AND FANCY
January 27, 1955 (461 perfs)
Music by Albert Hague
Lyrics by Arnold B. Horwitt
You Can't Miss It
It Wonders Me
Plenty of Pennsylvania
Young and Foolish
Why Not Katie?
It's a Helluva Way to Run a Love Affair
This Is All Very New to Me
Plain We Live
How Do You Raise a Barn?
Follow Your Heart
City Mouse, Country Mouse
I'll Show Him!
Take Your Time and Take Your Pick
Cast album: Capitol
Vocal score

PLEASURE BOUND
February 18, 1929 (136 perfs)
Music by Muriel Pollock
Lyrics by Max and Nathaniel Lief and Harold Atteridge

———

*Based on the novel *Sweet Thursday* by John Steinbeck

We Love to Go to Work

Just Suppose (Music by Phil Baker and Maury Rubens; lyrics by Sid Silvers and Moe Jaffe)

We'll Get Along

Park Avenue Strut (Music by Phil Baker and Maury Rubens; lyrics by Moe Jaffe and Harold Atteridge)

Cross Word Puzzles

My Melody Man (Music by Peter de Rose; lyrics by Charles Tobias and Henry Clare)

The Things That Were Made for Love (Music by Peter de Rose; lyrics by Charles Tobias and Irving Kahal)

Why Do You Tease Me?

POLLY*

January 8, 1929 (15 perfs)
Music by Philip Charig
Lyrics by Irving Caesar
  Lots of Time for Sue
  On with the Dance
  Little Bo-Peep
  When a Fellow Meets a Flapper on Broadway
  Sing a Song in the Rain (Music by Harry Rosenthal; lyrics by Douglas Furber and Irving Caesar)
  Comme ci, Comme ça
  Nobody Wants Me
  Polly
  Sweet Liar (Music by Herbert Stothart)
  Heel and Toe
  Life Is Love
  Something Spanish in Your Eyes

POLLY OF HOLLYWOOD

February 21, 1927 (24 perfs)
Music by Will Morrisey
Lyrics by Edmund Joseph
  Midnight Daddy
  Company Manners
  Polly of Hollywood
  Texas Stomp
  Wanting You
  New Kind of Rhythm

POLONAISE

October 6, 1945 (113 perfs)
Music by Bronislaw Kaper (based on Chopin)
Lyrics by John Latouche
  Laughing Bells
  O Heart of My Country
  Stranger (Music by Bronislaw Kaper)
  Au Revoir, Soldier (Music by Bronislaw Kaper)
  Meadowlark
  Hay, Hay, Hay (Music by Bronislaw Kaper)
  Moonlight Soliloquy
  Just for Tonight
  Exchange for Lovers
  An Imperial Conference
  Now I Know Your Face by Heart
  I Wonder As I Wander
  The Next Time I Care (Music by Bronislaw Kaper)
  Wait for Tomorrow
Album: (Studio cast) Camden

PORGY AND BESS†

October 10, 1935 (124 perfs)
Music by George Gershwin
Lyrics by DuBose Heyward and Ira Gershwin
  Summertime
  A Woman Is a Sometime Thing
  They Pass By Singing
  Crap Game Fugue
  Gone, Gone, Gone!
  Overflow
  My Man's Gone Now
  Leavin' fo' de Promis' Lan'
  It Take a Long Pull to Get There (All above lyrics by DuBose Heyward)
  I Got Plenty o' Nuttin' (Lyrics by DuBose Heyward and Ira Gershwin)
  Woman to Lady (Lyrics by DuBose Heyward)

---

*Based on David Belasco's play *Polly with a Past*

†Based on play *Porgy* by DuBose and Dorothy Heyward

Bess, You Is My Woman Now (Lyrics by DuBose Heyward and Ira Gershwin)
Oh, I Can't Sit Down (Lyrics by Ira Gershwin)
It Ain't Necessarily So (Lyrics by Ira Gershwin)
What You Want with Bess? (Lyrics by DuBose Heyward)
Time and Time Again (Lyrics by DuBose Heyward)
Street Cries (Strawberry Woman, Crab Man) (Lyrics by DuBose Heyward)
I Loves You, Porgy (Lyrics by DuBose Heyward and Ira Gershwin)
Oh, de Lawd Shake de Heaven (Lyrics by DuBose Heyward)
A Red Headed Woman (Lyrics by Ira Gershwin)
Oh, Doctor Jesus (Lyrics by DuBose Heyward and Ira Gershwin)
Clara, Don't You Be Downhearted (Lyrics by DuBose Heyward)
There's a Boat Dat's Leavin' Soon for New York (Lyrics by Ira Gershwin)
Oh, Bess, Oh Where's My Bess (Lyrics by Ira Gershwin)
I'm On My Way (Lyrics by DuBose Heyward)
Three-record album: (Studio Cast)
Odyssey
Vocal Score
Vocal selection

PORTOFINO
February 21, 1958 (3 perfs)
Music by Louis Bellson and Will Irwin
Lyrics by Richard Ney
  Come Along ·
  No Wedding Bells for Me
  Red-Collar Job
  Here I Come
  New Dreams for Old
  A Dream for Angela
  Isn't It Wonderful
  Under a Spell
  That's Love
  Too Little Time for Love
  It Might Be Love

Morning Prayer
The Grand Prix of Portofino
Portofino
I'm in League with the Devil
Why Not for Marriage

POUSSE-CAFÉ
March 18, 1966 (3 perfs)
Music by Duke Ellington
Lyrics by Marshall Barer and Fred Tobias
  The Spider and the Fly
  Rules and Regulations
  Follow Me Up The Stairs
  Goodbye Charlie
  C'est Comme ça
  Thank You, Ma'am
  The Eleventh Commandment
  Someone to Care For
  The Wedding
  Let's
  The Good Old Days
  Easy to Take
  Old World Charm

PRESENT ARMS
April 26, 1928 (155 perfs)
Music by Richard Rodgers
Lyrics by Lorenz Hart
  Tell It to the Marines
  You Took Advantage of Me
  Do I Hear You Saying "I Love You"?
  A Kiss for Cinderella
  Is It the Uniform?
  Crazy Elbows
  Down by the Sea
  I'm a Fool, Little One
  Blue Ocean Blues
  Hawaii
  Kohala, Welcome

PRESIDENT'S DAUGHTER, THE
November 3, 1970 (72 perfs)
Music by Murray Rumshinsky
Lyrics by Jacob Jacobs
  Women's Liberation
  The President's Daughter
  I Have What You Want!
  A Lesson in Yiddish
  Everything Is Possible in Life
  Welcome, Mr. Golden!

Stiochket
Without a Mother
Love at Golden Years
If Only I Could Be a Kid Again
An Old Man Shouldn't Be Born
We Two
What More Do I Need?
What Would You Do?

PRINCE AND THE PAUPER, THE* (OB)
October 12, 1963 (158 perfs)
Music by George Fischoff
Lyrics by Verna Tomasson
  Garbage Court Round
  In a Story Book
  I've Been a-Begging
  Why Don't We Switch?
  Do This, Do That
  The Prince Is Mad
  Oh, Pity the Man
  With a Sword in My Buckle
  Ev'rybody Needs Somebody to
    Love
  The Tree and the Sun
  King Foo-Foo the First
  Coronation Song
Cast album: London

PRINCESS CHARMING
October 13, 1930 (56 perfs)
Music by Albert Sirmay and Arthur
  Schwartz
Lyrics by Arthur Swanstrom
  Leave It All to Your Faithful Am-
    bassador
  Palace of Dreams
  The Panic's On
  Trailing a Shooting Star
  A Sword for the King
  I'll Be There
  One for All
  You
  It's a Wonderful Thing for a King
  I Love Love (Music by Robert Em-
    mett Dolan; lyrics by Walter
    O'Keefe)
  I'll Never Leave You
  Happiness and Joy to the King

PRINCESS FLAVIA†
November 2, 1925 (152 perfs)
Music by Sigmund Romberg

Lyrics by Harry B. Smith
  Yes or No
  On, Comrades
  Marionettes
  What Care I?
  Convent Bells Are Ringing
  I Dare Not Love You
  By This Token
  Dance With Me
  Twilight Voices
  Only One
  I Love Them All
  In Ruritania

PRIVATE LIVES
(Play with one song)
January 27, 1931 (256 perfs)
Music and lyrics by Noël Coward
  Some Day I'll Find You

PROMENADE (OB)
June 4, 1969 (259 perfs)
Music by Al Carmines
Lyrics by Maria Irene Fornes
  Dig, Dig, Dig
  Unrequited Love
  Isn't That Clear?
  Don't Eat It
  Four
  Chicken Is He
  A Flower
  Rosita Rodriguez; Serenade
  Après Vous I
  Bliss
  The Moment Has Passed
  Thank You
  The Clothes Make the Man
  The Cigarette Song
  Two Little Angels
  The Passing of Time
  Capricious and Fickle
  Crown Me
  Mr. Phelps
  Madeline
  Spring Beauties
  A Poor Man
  Why Not?

---

*Based on the story by Mark Twain
†Based on novel *The Prisoner of Zenda* by
Anthony Hope

The Finger Song
Little Fool
Czardas
The Laughing Song
A Mother's Love
Listen, I Feel
I Saw a Man
All Is Well in the City
Cast album: RCA
Vocal selection

PROMISES, PROMISES*
December 1, 1968 (1,281 perfs)
Music by Burt Bacharach
Lyrics by Hal David
  Half As Big As Life
  Upstairs
  You'll Think of Someone
  Our Little Secret
  She Likes Basketball
  Knowing When to Leave
  Where Can You Take a Girl?
  Wanting Things
  Turkey Lurkey Time
  A Fact Can Be a Beautiful Thing
  Whoever You Are
  A Young Pretty Girl Like You
  I'll Never Fall in Love Again
  Promises, Promises
Cast album: United Artists
Vocal score
Vocal selection

PROVINCETOWN FOLLIES (OB)
November 3, 1935 (63 perfs)
  Poor Porgy (Music by Sylvan Green;
    lyrics by Frederick Herendeen)
  New Words for an Old Love Song
    (Music by Dave Stamper; lyrics by
    Frederick Herendeen)

PURLIE†
March 15, 1970 (688 perfs)
Music by Gary Geld
Lyrics by Peter Udell
  Walk Him up the Stairs
  New Fangled Preacher Man
  Skinnin' a Cat
  Purlie
  The Harder They Fall
  Charlie's Songs
  Big Fish, Little Fish

I Got Love
Great White Father
Down Home
First Thing Monday Mornin'
He Can Do It
The World Is Comin' to a Start
Cast album: Ampex
Vocal selection

PUT IT IN WRITING (OB)
May 13, 1963 (24 perfs)
  Literary Cocktail Party (Music and
    lyrics by Bud McCreery)
  I Hope You're Happy (Music by
    Norman Martin; lyrics by Fred
    Ebb)
  Trilogy (Music and lyrics by Bud
    McCreery)
  Give 'Em a Kiss (Music and lyrics by
    G. Wood)
  The Ayes of Texas (Music by Nor-
    man Martin; lyrics by Fred Ebb)
  Daisy (Music and lyrics by G. Wood)
  The People's Choice (Music by Nor-
    man Martin; lyrics by Fred Ebb)
  What's Cooking? (Music by Norman
    Martin; lyrics by Fred Ebb)
  The Youngest President (Music by
    Robert Kessler; lyrics by Martin
    Charnin)
  Emmy Lou (Music by Norman Mar-
    tin; lyrics by Fred Ebb)
  Stock Report (Music by Norman
    Martin; lyrics by Fred Ebb)
  Arty (Music by James Wise; lyrics by
    David Bimonte)
  What Kind of Life Is That? (Music
    by Norman Martin; lyrics by Fred
    Ebb)
  Put It in Writing (Music and lyrics
    by Alan Kohan)
  Walking down the Road (Music and
    lyrics by Alan Kohan and William
    Angelos)

---

*Based on the screenplay *The Apartment*
by Billy Wilder and I. A. L. Diamond
†Based on the play *Purlie Victorious* by
Ossie Davis

PUZZLES OF 1925
February 2, 1925 (104 perfs)
  The Undecided Blues (Music and lyrics by Elsie Janis)
  Titina (Music by Leo Daniderff; lyrics by Bertal-Maubon and E. Ronn)
  Tra-la-la-la (Music and lyrics by Elsie Janis and Vincent Scotto)
  You've Got to Dance (Music and lyrics by Elsie Janis)
  Je Vous Aime (Music and lyrics by Arthur L. Beiner)
  We're Jumping into Something (Music and lyrics by Blanche Merrill)
  Doo-Dab (Music by Harry Ruby; lyrics by Bert Kalmar)

QUEEN HIGH
September 8, 1926 (367 perfs)
Music by Lewis E. Gensler
Lyrics by B. G. DeSylva
  It Pays to Advertise
  Everything Will Happen for the Best
  You'll Never Know
  Don't Forget (Music by James F. Hanley)
  Who? You!
  The Weaker Sex
  Cross Your Heart
  Sez You? Sez I!
  Beautiful Baby (Music by James F. Hanley)
  Who'll Mend a Broken Heart?
  Gentlemen Prefer Blondes
  Springtime

RAIN OR SHINE
February 9, 1928 (360 perfs)
Music by Milton Ager
Lyrics by Jack Yellen
  Glad Tidings
  Circus Days
  So Would I
  Add a Little Wiggle
  Rain or Shine
  Oh, Baby! (Music and lyrics by Owen Murphy)
  Roustabout's Song (Music by Milton Ager and Owen Murphy)

Hey, Rube
Falling Star
Feelin' Good (Music by Owen Murphy)
Forever and Ever
Who's Goin' to Get You?
Breakfast with You

RAINBOW
November 21, 1928 (29 perfs)
Music by Vincent Youmans
Lyrics by Oscar Hammerstein II
  On the Golden Trail
  My Mother Told Me Not to Trust a Soldier
  Virginia
  I Want a Man
  Soliloquy
  I Like You As You Are
  The One Girl
  Let Me Give All My Love to Thee
  Diamond in the Rough
  Who Wants to Love Spanish Ladies?
  Hay! Straw!
  The Bride Was Dressed in White
  Added to film version: (retitled *Song of the West*) (1930)
  West Wind (Lyrics by J. Russel Robinson)

RAINBOW ROSE
March 16, 1926 (55 perfs)
Music by Harold Levey
Lyrics by Owen Murphy
  We Want Our Breakfast
  Steppin' Baby
  You're All the World to Me
  Jealous
  First, Last, and Only
  Something Tells Me I'm in Love
  Going Over the Bumps
  If You Were Someone Else
  When the Hurdy Gurdy Plays
  Dreams
  Let's Run Away and Get Married
  Rainbow (Lyrics by Zelda Sears)

RAMBLERS, THE
September 20, 1926 (291 perfs)
Music by Harry Ruby
Lyrics by Bert Kalmar
  Like You Do

Oh! How We Love Our Alma Mater
Just One Kiss
All Alone Monday
Any Little Tune
California Skies
You Smiled at Me
We Won't Charleston
The Movie Ball

RANG-TANG
July 12, 1927 (119 perfs)
Music by Ford Dabney
Lyrics by Jo Trent
Everybody Shout
Sammy and Topsy
Brown
Sambo's Banjo
Some Day
Come to Africa
Jungle Rose
Monkey Land
Sweet Evening Breeze
Summer Nights
Tramps of the Desert
Harlem
Rang-Tang

RED, HOT AND BLUE!
October 29, 1936 (183 perfs)
Music and lyrics by Cole Porter
At Ye Olde Coffee Shoppe in
Cheyenne
It's a Great Life
Perennial Debutantes
Ours
Down in the Depths, on the 90th
Floor
Carry On
You've Got Something
It's De-Lovely
A Little Skipper from Heaven
Above
Five Hundred Million
Ridin' High
We're About to Start Big Rehearsin'
Hymn to Hymen
What a Great Pair We'll Be
The Ozarks Are Calling Me Home
Red, Hot and Blue
You're a Bad Influence on Me
Goodbye, Little Dream, Goodbye*
Vocal score

RED ROBE, THE†
December 25, 1928 (167 perfs)
Music by Jean Gilbert
Lyrics by Harry B. Smith
Roll of the Drum
I'll Love Them All to Death
King of the Sword (Music by Robert
Stolz and Maury Rubens; lyrics by
J. Keirn Brennan)
Only a Smile
Joy or Strife
Home o' Mine
Believe in Me (Music by Arthur
Schwartz)
I've Got It (Music by Alberta Nichols; lyrics by Mann Holiner)
Where Love Grows
The Thrill of a Kiss
How the Girls Adore Me
Laugh at Life (Music by Maury Rubens; lyrics by J. Delany Dunn)
A Soldier of Fortune
I Plead, Dear Heart
You and I Are Passersby

RED, WHITE AND MADDOX
January 26, 1969 (41 perfs)
Music and lyrics by Don Tucker
What America Means to Me
Givers and Getters
Jubilee Joe
Ballad of a Redneck
First Campaign Song
Hoe Down
Phooey
Second Campaign Song
God Is an American
Hip-Hooray for Washington
City Life
Song of the Malcontents
The General's Song
Little Mary Sue
Billy Joe Ju
The Impeachment Waltz
Red, White and Maddox Kazoo
March

*Dropped from New York production
†Based on the novel, *Under the Red Robe*
by Stanley Weyman

REDHEAD
February 5, 1959 (452 perfs)
Music by Albert Hague
Lyrics by Dorothy Fields
  The Simpson Sisters
  The Right Finger of My Left Hand
  Just for Once
  Merely Marvelous
  The Uncle Sam Rag
  Erbie Fitch's Twitch
  My Girl Is Just Enough Woman for
    Me
  Behave Yourself
  Look Who's in Love
  Two Faces in the Dark
  I'm Back in Circulation
  We Loves Ya, Jimey
  Pick-Pocket Tango
  I'll Try
Cast album: RCA
Vocal score

REGINA*
October 31, 1949 (56 perfs)
Music and lyrics by Marc Blitzstein
  Summer Day
  Chinkypin
  The Best Things of All
  Greedy Girl
  What Will It Be?
  Blues
Cast album: Columbia

REVENGE WITH MUSIC†
November 28, 1934 (158 perfs)
Music by Arthur Schwartz
Lyrics by Howard Dietz
  Flamenco
  When You Love Only One
  Never Marry a Dancer
  If There Is Someone Lovelier Than
    You
  In the Noonday Sun
  That Fellow Manuelo
  Think It Over
  Maria
  My Father Said
  You and the Night and the Music
  Once-in-a-While
  In the Middle of the Night
  Wandr'ing Heart

RHAPSODY IN BLACK
May 4, 1931 (80 perfs)
Music by Alberta Nichols
Lyrics by Mann Holiner
  What's Keeping My Prince Charm-
    ing?
  Eccentricity
  Till the Real Thing Comes Along
    (Lyrics by Mann Holiner and
    Sammy Cahn)
  You Can't Stop Me from Loving You
  Harlem Moon

RIGHT THIS WAY
January 5, 1938 (14 perfs)
Music by Sammy Fain
Lyrics by Irving Kahal
  I Love the Way We Fell in Love
  Doughnuts and Coffee
  It's Great to Be Home Again
  He Can Dance
  I Can Dream, Can't I?
  Soapbox Sillies (Music by Bradford
    Greene; lyrics by Marianne
    Brown Waters)
  Don't Listen to Your Heart (Music
    by Bradford Greene; lyrics by Ma-
    rianne Brown Waters)
  Tip Your Hat (Music by Bradford
    Greene; lyrics by Marianne
    Brown Waters)
  You Click with Me (Music by Brad-
    ford Greene; lyrics by Marianne
    Brown Waters)
  I'll Be Seeing You
  Right This Way (Music by Bradford
    Greene; lyrics by Marianne
    Brown Waters)

RIO RITA
February 2, 1927 (504 perfs)
Music by Harry Tierney
Lyrics by Joseph McCarthy
  The Best Little Lover in Town
  Sweethearts
  River Song

---

*Based on the play The Little Foxes by Lil-
lian Hellman
†Based on novel The Three-Cornered Hat
by Pedro de Alarcon

Are You There?
Rio Rita
The Rangers' Song
The Kinkajou
If You're In Love, You'll Waltz
Out on the Loose
I Can Speak Espagnol
Following the Sun Around
Vocal score
Added to film version: (1929)
You're Always in My Arms
Added to film version: (1942)
Long Before You Came Along (Music by Harold Arlen; lyrics by E. Y. Harburg)

RIPPLES
February 11, 1930 (55 perfs)
Music by Oscar Levant
Lyrics by Irving Caesar and Graham John
Gentlemen of the Press
Barefoot Girl
Is It Love? (Lyrics by Irving Caesar)
We Never Sleep
I Take after Rip
Babykins
I'm Afraid (Music by Albert Sirmay)
There's Nothing Wrong with a Kiss
Girls of Long Ago
Talk with Your Heel and Your Toe (Lyrics by Irving Caesar)
I'm a Little Bit Fonder of You (Music and lyrics by Irving Caesar)
Anything May Happen Any Day (Music by Jerome Kern; lyrics by Graham John)

RIVERWIND (OB)
December 12, 1962 (443 perfs)
Music and lyrics by John Jennings
I Cannot Tell Her So
I Want a Surprise
Riverwind
American Family Plan
Wishing Song
Pardon Me While I Dance
Sew the Buttons On
Almost, But Not Quite
A Woman Must Think of These Things
Laughing Face

A Woman Must Never Grow Old
I'd Forgotten How Beautiful She Could Be
Cast album: London

THE ROAR OF THE GREASEPAINT - THE SMELL OF THE CROWD
May 16, 1965 (232 perfs)
Music and lyrics by Leslie Bricusse and Anthony Newley
The Beautiful Land
A Wonderful Day Like Today
It Isn't Enough
Things to Remember
Put It in the Book
This Dream
Where Would You Be without Me?
Look at That Face
My First Love Song
The Joker
Who Can I Turn To (When Nobody Needs Me)
Funny Funeral
That's What It Is to Be Young
What a Man!
Feeling Good
Nothing Can Stop Me Now!
My Way
Sweet Beginning
Cast album: RCA
Vocal selection

ROBERTA*
November 18, 1933 (295 perfs)
Music by Jerome Kern
Lyrics by Otto Harbach
Alpha, Beta, Pi
You're Devastating
Let's Begin
Yesterdays
Something Had to Happen
The Touch of Your Hand
I'll Be Hard to Handle (Lyrics by Bernard Dougall)
Hot Spot
Smoke Gets in Your Eyes
Don't Ask Me Not to Sing
Album: (Studio cast) Columbia

---

*Based on the novel *Gowns by Roberta* by Alice Duer Miller

Vocal score
Added to film version (1935)
  I Won't Dance (Lyrics by Dorothy
  Fields, Oscar Hammerstein II,
  Otto Harbach, and Jimmy
  McHugh)
  Lovely to Look At (Lyrics by Doro-
  thy Fields and Jimmy McHugh)

RONDELAY* (OB)
November 5, 1969 (11 perfs)
Music by Hal Jordan
Lyrics by Jerry Douglas
  Rondelay
  Lovers of the Lamplight
  One Hundred Virgins
  Angel Face
  Tonight You Dance with Me
  Easy
  The First Kiss
  Afterward
  She Deserves Me
  Closer
  Honor
  The Answer
  Failure
  Success
  The Days of My Youth
  I've Got a Surprise for You
  Reidhof's
  Champagne
  Dessert
  Masquerade
  When Lovers Fall in Love
  What You Are
  A Castle in India
  Back to Nature
  Saint Genesius
  Opera Star
  Not So Young Love
  Auf Wiedersehen
  Gusto
  Happy Ending
  I'll Show You the World To-
  night
  Reflections
  Before Breakfast
  Give and Take

ROSALIE
January 10, 1928 (335 perfs)
  Show Me the Town (Music by

George Gershwin; lyrics by Ira
  Gershwin)
  Hussars March (Music by Sigmund
  Romberg; lyrics by P. G. Wode-
  house)
  Say So (Music by George Gershwin;
  lyrics by P.G. Wodehouse and Ira
  Gershwin)
  Let Me Be a Friend to You (Music
  by George Gershwin; lyrics by Ira
  Gershwin)
  West Point Song (Music by Sigmund
  Romberg; lyrics by P.G. Wode-
  house)
  Oh Gee! Oh Joy! (Music by George
  Gershwin; lyrics by Ira Gershwin
  and P.G. Wodehouse)
  New York Serenade (Music by
  George Gershwin; lyrics by Ira
  Gershwin and P. G. Wodehouse)
  Ev'rybody Knows I Love Some-
  body† (Music by George Gersh-
  win; lyrics by Ira Gershwin)
  How Long Has This Been Going
  On? (Music by George Gershwin;
  lyrics by Ira Gershwin)
  Why Must We Always Be Dream-
  ing? (Music by Sigmund Rom-
  berg; lyrics by P. G. Wode-
  house)
  Beautiful Gypsy** (Music by
  George Gershwin; lyrics by Ira
  Gershwin)

ROTHSCHILDS, THE††
October 19, 1970 (505 perfs)
Music by Jerry Bock
Lyrics by Sheldon Harnick
  Pleasure and Privilege
  One Room
  He Tossed a Coin
  Sons
  Everything
  Rothschild and Sons
  Allons

---

*Based on Arthur Schnitzler's *La Ronde*
†Same music as "Dance Alone With You"
from *Funny Face*
**Dropped from New York production
††Based on the book by Frederic Morton

Give England Strength
This Amazing London Town
They Say
I'm in Love! I'm in Love!
In My Own Lifetime
Have You Ever Seen a Prettier Little Congress?
Stability
Bonds
Cast album: Columbia
Vocal selection

RUFUS LEMAIRE'S AFFAIRS
March 28, 1927 (56 perfs)
Music by Martin Broones
Lyrics by Ballard MacDonald
Wah-Wah
Wandering in Dreamland
I Can't Get Over a Girl Like You (Lyrics by Harry Ruskin)
Bring Back Those Minstrel Days
Mexico
Land of Broken Dreams
Where the Morning Glories Twine
Dancing by Moonlight

RUGANTINO
February 6, 1964 (28 perfs)
Music by Armando Trovaioli
Lyrics by Pietro Garinei and Sandro Giovannini
(Lyric translation by Edward Eager)
The Game of Morra
Rugantino in the Stocks
A House Is Not the Same without a Woman
Nothing to Do
Just Look!
The Saltarello
Tirrallallera
The Headsman and I
Ciumachella
Lantern Night
Roma
I'm Happy
Just Stay Alive
San Pasquale
Passatella (The Drinking Game)
It's Quick and Easy
Boy and Man
Cast album: Warner Bros.

RUMPLE
November 6, 1957 (45 perfs)
Music by Ernest G. Schweikert
Lyrics by Frank Reardon
It's You for Me
In Times Like These
Red Letter Day
The First Time I Spoke of You
Oblivia
Peculiar State of Affairs
How Do You Say Goodbye?
Gentlemen of the Press
To Adjust Is a Must
Coax Me
All Dressed Up
Wish

RUSSELL PATTERSON'S SKETCH BOOK (OB)
February 16, 1960 (3 perfs)
Music by Ruth Cleary Patterson
We Know What You Want and We Got It (Lyrics by Floria Vestoff)
That's Why I'm Here Tonight (Lyrics by Les Kramer)
Dancing to the Rhythm of the Raindrops (Lyrics by Gladys Shelley)
I Want to Take 'Em Off for Norman Rockwell (Lyrics by Les Kramer)
May in Manhattan (Lyrics by Tom Romano)
La Calinda (Lyrics by Gladys Shelley)
Singing Wheels (Lyrics by Fred Heider)
That's What I Got for Not Listening to My Mother (Lyrics by Floria Vestoff)
Let's Not Get Married (Lyrics by George Blake and Les Kramer)
My First Love (Lyrics by Fred Heider)
Sweet Charity (Lyrics by Les Kramer)
When the Wings of the Wind Take Me Home (Lyrics by Les Kramer)
A Wonderful Way of Life (Lyrics by Les Kramer and Floria Vestoff)

SADIE THOMPSON*
November 16, 1944 (60 perfs)
Music by Vernon Duke
Lyrics by Howard Dietz
  Barrel of Beads
  Fisherman's Wharf
  When You Live on an Island
  Poor As a Church Mouse
  The Love I Long For
  Garden in the Sky
  Siren of the Tropics
  Life's a Funny Present from Some-
    one
  Born All Over Again
  Sailing at Midnight

SAIL AWAY
October 3, 1961 (167 perfs)
Music and lyrics by Noël Coward
  Come to Me
  Sail Away
  Where Shall I Find Him?
  Beatnik Love Affair
  Later Than Spring
  The Passenger's Always Right
  Useful Phrases
  Go Slow, Johnny
  You're a Long, Long Way from
    America
  Something Very Strange
  The Little Ones' ABC
  Don't Turn Away from Love
  When You Want Me
  Why Do the Wrong People Travel?
Cast album: Capitol
Vocal selection

ST. LOUIS WOMAN†
March 30, 1946 (113 perfs)
Music by Harold Arlen
Lyrics by Johnny Mercer
  L'il Augie Is a Natural Man
  Any Place I Hang My Hat Is Home
  I Feel My Luck Comin' Down
  True Love
  Legalize My Name
  Cake Walk Your Lady
  Come Rain or Come Shine
  Chinquapin Bush
  We Shall Meet to Part, No Never
  Lullaby
  Sleep Peaceful

  Leavin' Time
  A Woman's Prerogative
  Ridin' on the Moon
  Least That's My Opinion
  Racin' Form
  Come On, L'il Augie
  I Wonder What Became of Me**
Cast album: Capitol

SALAD DAYS (OB)
November 10, 1958 (80 perfs)
Music by Julian Slade
Lyrics by Dorothy Reynolds and
Julian Slade
  The Dons Chorus
  We Said We Wouldn't Look Back
  Find Yourself Something to Do
  I Sit in the Sun
  Oh, Look at Me!
  Hush-Hush
  Out of Breath
  Cleopatra
  Sand in My Eyes
  It's Easy to Sing
  Let's Take a Stroll through London
  We're Looking for a Piano
  The Saucer Song
  The Time of My Life
  We Don't Understand Our Chil-
    dren
Album: (British cast) London
Vocal score

SALUTA
August 28, 1934 (40 perfs)
Music by Frank D'Armond
Lyrics by Will Morrissey
  Black Horse Tavern
  Just Say the Word (Lyrics by Milton
    Berle)
  Walking the Deck
  I'll Produce for You
  Night
  Help the Seamen

---

*Based on the play *Rain* by John Colton
(based, in turn, on the short story "Miss
Thompson" by W. Somerset Maugham)
†Based on the novel *God Sends Sunday* by
Arna Bontemps
**Dropped from New York production

You Have My Heart
Tarantella Rhythm
Mi! Mi!
We Incorporated
There's a Chill in the Air
The Great Dictator and Me

SALVATION (OB)
September 24, 1969 (239 perfs)
Music and lyrics by Peter Link and
C. C. Courtney
Salvation
In Between
1001
Honest Confession Is Good for the
Soul
Ballin'
Let the Moment Slip By
Gina
If You Let Me Make Love to You
Then Why Can't I Touch You
There Ain't No Flies on Jesus
Deadalus
Deuteronomy XVII Verse 2
For Ever
Footloose Youth and Fancy Free
Schwartz
Let's Get Lost in Now
Back to Genesis
Tomorrow Is the First Day of the
Rest of My Life
Cast album: Capitol
Vocal selection

SAMBO (OB)
December 12, 1969 (37 perfs)
Music by Ron Steward and Neal Tate
Lyrics by Ron Steward
Sing a Song of Sambo
Hey Boy
I Am Child
Young Enough to Dream
Mama Always Said
Baddest Mammyjammy
Sambo Was a Bad Boy
Pretty Flower
I Could Dig You
Do You Care Too Much?
Be Black
Let's Go Down
Astrology
The Eternal Virgin

Boy Blue
The Piscean
Aries
Untogether Cinderella
Peace Love and Good Damn
Come On Home
Black Man
Get an Education
Ask and You Shall Receive
Son of Africa

SANDHOG* (OB)
November 29, 1954 (48 perfs)
Music by Earl Robinson
Lyrics by Waldo Salt
Come Down
Some Said They Were Crazy
Sing Sorrow
Hey Joe
Johnny's Cursing Song
Come and Be Married
Johnny O
Good Old Days
Song of the Bends
By the Glenside
High Air
Work Song
28 Men
Sandhog Song
Sweat Song
Fugue on a Hot Afternoon in a
Small Flat
Twins
Katie O'Sullivan
Ring Iron
You Want to Mourn
Ma, Ma, Where's My Dad?
Waiting for the Men
Greathead Shield
Stand Back
Oh, Oh, Oh, O'Sullivan
Cast album: Vanguard

SAP OF LIFE, THE (OB)
October 2, 1961 (49 perfs)
Music by David Shire
Lyrics by Richard Maltby, Jr.
Saturday Morning

_____
*Based on Theodore Dreiser's short story,
St. Columbia and the River

Farewell, Family
Charmed Life
Fill Up Your Life with Sunshine
Good Morning
Watching the Big Parade Go
  By
The Love of Your Life
A Hero's Love
Children Have It Easy
She Loves Me Not
Mind Over Matter
Time and Time Again

SARATOGA*
December 7, 1959 (80 perfs)
Music by Harold Arlen
Lyrics by Johnny Mercer
  I'll Be Respectable
  One Step - Two Step
  Gettin' a Man (Music and lyrics by
    Johnny Mercer)
  Petticoat High
  Why Fight This? (Music and lyrics
    by Johnny Mercer)
  A Game of Poker
  Love Held Lightly
  The Gamblers
  Saratoga
  The Gossip Song
  Countin' Our Chickens
  You or No One
  The Cure
  The Men Who Run the Country
    (Music and lyrics by Johnny Mer-
    cer)
  The Man in My Life
  The Polka
  Goose Never Be a Peacock
  Dog Eat Dog
Cast album: RCA
Vocal selection

SAY, DARLING†
April 3, 1958 (332 perfs)
Music by Jule Styne
Lyrics by Betty Comden and Adolph
Green
  Try to Love Me Just As I Am
  It's Doom
  The Husking Bee
  It's the Second Time You Meet That
    Matters

Chief of Love
Say, Darling
The Carnival Song
Dance Only with Me
Something's Always Happening on
  the River
Cast album: RCA

SAY WHEN
June 26, 1928 (15 perfs)
Music by Jesse Greer
Lyrics by Raymond Klages
  My One Girl (Music and lyrics by
    Frank E. Harling)
  How About It?
  No Room in My Heart (Music by
    Ray Perkins; lyrics by Max and
    Nathaniel Lief)
  Cheerio (Lyrics by James J.
    Walker**)
  One Step to Heaven
  In My Love Boat (Music by Ray Per-
    kins; lyrics by Max and Nathaniel
    Lief)
  Say When
  Give Me a Night (Music and lyrics
    by Frank E. Harling)

SAY WHEN
November 8, 1934 (76 perfs)
Music by Ray Henderson
Lyrics by Ted Koehler
  When Love Comes Swingin'
    Along
  Declaration Day
  It Must Have Been the Night
  Say When
  Don't Tell Me It's Bad
  Sunday Morning
  Isn't It June?
  Put Your Heart in a Song
  So Long for Ever So Long
  Torch Parade
  Let's Take Advantage of Now

---

*Based on the novel *Saratoga Trunk* by
Edna Ferber
†Based on the book by Richard Bissell
**Mayor of New York City

SEA LEGS
May 18, 1937 (15 perfs)
Music by Michael Cleary
Lyrics by Arthur Swanstrom
  Off on a Weekend Cruise
  The Opposite Sex
  Infatuation
  A Dark Stranger
  Looks Like Love Is Here to Stay
  Ten O'Clock Town
  Chasing Henry
  Catalina
  Touched in the Head
  Wake Me Up a Star

SECOND LITTLE SHOW, THE
September 2, 1930 (63 perfs)
Music by Arthur Schwartz
Lyrics by Howard Dietz
  New New York
  Swing Your Tails
  Foolish Face
  My Heart Begins to Thump!
    Thump! (Music by Morgan Lewis;
    lyrics by Ted Fetter)
  What a Case I've Got on You
  Good Clean Sport
  Lucky Seven
  My Intuition
  I Started on a Shoestring
  Sing Something Simple (Music and
    lyrics by Herman Hupfeld)
  You're the Sunrise

SECRET LIFE OF WALTER MITTY, THE *(OB)
October 26, 1964 (96 perfs)
Music by Leon Carr
Lyrics by Earl Shuman
  The Secret Life
  The Walter Mitty March
  Now That I Am Forty
  Walking with Peninnah
  Drip, Drop, Tapoketa
  Aggie
  Don't Forget
  Marriage Is for Old Folks
  Hello, I Love You, Goodbye
  Willa
  Confidence
  Two Little Pussycats
  Fan the Flame

  She's Talking Out
  You're Not
  Lonely Ones
Cast album: Columbia

SENSATIONS† (OB)
October 25, 1970 (16 perfs)
Music by Wally Harper; lyrics by Paul
Zakrzewski
  Lonely Children
  Sensations
  Good Little Boy
  The Beginning
  What Kind of Parents
  Power
  Up and Down
  Friar's Tune
  Oh, My Age
  Outracing Light
  War Is Good Business
  The Kill
  Lying Here
  Middle Class Revolution
  I'll Stay, I'll Go
  I Cannot Wait
  Sounds
  No Place for Me
  Morning Sun
  In Nomine Dei
Cast album: Mercury

SET TO MUSIC
January 18, 1939 (129 perfs)
Music and lyrics by Noël Coward
  Three Little Debutantes
  Mad About the Boy
  The Stately Homes of England
  I'm So Weary of It All
  Children of the Ritz
  Three White Feathers
  Midnight Matinee
  Never Again
  I Went to a Marvelous Party
  The Party's Over Now

---

*Based on the short story by James
Thurber
†Suggested by William Shakespeare's
Romeo and Juliet

SEVEN LIVELY ARTS
December 7, 1944 (183 perfs)
Music and lyrics by Cole Porter
  Big Town
  Is It the Girl?
  Only Another Boy and Girl
  Wow-Ooh-Wolf
  Drink
  When I Was a Little Cuckoo
  Frahngee-Pahnee
  Dancin' to a Jungle Drum
  Ev'ry Time We Say Goodbye
  Hence It Don't Make Sense
  The Band Started Swinging a Song
  The Big Parade

SEVENTEEN*
June 21, 1951 (180 perfs)
Music by Walter Kent
Lyrics by Kim Gannon
  Weatherbee's Drug Store
  This Was Just Another Day
  Things Are Gonna Hum This Summer
  How Do You Do, Miss Pratt
  Summertime Is Summertime
  Reciprocity
  Ode to Lola
  A Headache and a Heartache
  Ooh, Ooh, Ooh, What You Do to Me
  Hoosier Way
  I Could Get Married Today
  After All, It's Spring
Cast album: RCA

1776
March 16, 1969 (1,217 perfs)
Music and lyrics by Sherman Edwards
  Sit Down, John
  Piddle, Twiddle and Resolve
  Till Then
  The Lees of Old Virginia
  But, Mr. Adams
  Yours, Yours, Yours
  He Plays the Violin
  Momma Look Sharp
  Cool, Cool, Considerate Men
  The Egg
  Molasses to Rum
  Is Anybody There?
Cast album: Columbia
Vocal selection

SEVENTH HEART, THE
(Play with music)
May 2, 1927 (8 perfs)
Music and lyrics by Arthur Brander
  I Wonder If Love Is a Dream
  Cinema Blues
  For I'm in Love
  When My Eyes Meet Yours

SEVENTH HEAVEN†
May 26, 1955 (44 perfs)
Music by Victor Young
Lyrics by Stella Unger
  C'est la Vie
  Where Is That Someone for Me?
  Camille, Colette, Fifi
  A Man with a Dream
  Remarkable Fellow
  If It's a Dream
  Happy Little Crook
  Sun at My Window, Love at My Door
  A "Miss You" Kiss
  Love, Love, Love
  Love Sneaks Up on You
Cast album: Decca

70, GIRLS, 70**
April 15, 1971 (36 perfs)
Music by John Kander
Lyrics by Fred Ebb
  Old Folks
  Home
  Broadway, My Street
  Coffee in a Cardboard Cup
  You and I, Love
  Do We?
  Hit It, Lorraine
  See the Light
  Boom Ditty Boom
  Believe
  Go Visit
  70, Girls, 70
  The Elephant Song
  Yes
Cast album: Columbia
Vocal selection

_____
*Based on the novel by Booth Tarkington
†Based on the play by Austin Strong
**Based on the film *Make Mine Mink*

SHADY LADY
July 5, 1933 (30 perfs)

You're Not the One (Music by Jesse Greer; lyrics by Stanley Adams)

Live, Laugh and Love (Music by Sam H. Stept; lyrics by Bud Green)

Isn't It Swell to Dream (Music by Sam H. Stept; lyrics by Bud Green)

I'll Betcha That I'll Getcha (Music by Jesse Greer; lyrics by Stanley Adams)

Swingy Little Thingy (Music by Sam H. Stept; lyrics by Stanley Adams)

Everything but My Man (Music and lyrics by Serge Walter)

Isn't It Remarkable (Music by Jesse Greer; lyrics by Stanley Adams)

Any Way the Wind Blows (Music by Sam H. Stept; lyrics by Bud Green)

Your Type is Coming Back (Music by Sam H. Stept; lyrics by Bud Green)

One Heart (Music by Sam H. Stept; lyrics by Bud Green)

Hiya Sucker (Music by Jesse Greer; lyrics by Stanley Adams)

Get Hot Foot (Music by Sam H. Stept; lyrics by Bud Green)

Where, Oh Where Can I Find Love? (Music by Jesse Greer; lyrics by Stanley Adams)

SHANGRI-LA*
June 13, 1956 (21 perfs)
Music by Harry Warren
Lyrics by Jerome Lawrence and Robert E. Lee

Om Mani Padme Hum
Lost Horizon
The Man I Never Met
Every Time You Danced with Me
The World Outside
I'm Just a Little Bit Confused
The Beetle Race
Somewhere
What Every Old Girl Should Know
Second Time in Love
Talkin' with Your Feet
Walk Sweet
Love Is What I Never Knew
We've Decided to Stay
Shangri-La

SHE LOVES ME†
April 23, 1963 (301 perfs)
Music by Jerry Bock
Lyrics by Sheldon Harnick

Good Morning, Good Day
Thank You, Madam
Days Gone By
No More Candy
Three Letters
Tonight at Eight
I Don't Know His Name
Goodbye, Georg
Will He Like Me?
Ilona
I Resolve
A Romantic Atmosphere
Dear Friend
Try Me
Where's My Shoe?
Ice Cream
She Loves Me
A Trip to the Library
Grand Knowing You
Twelve Days to Christmas

Cast album: MGM
Vocal selection

SHE LOVES ME NOT
(Play with two songs)
November 20, 1933 (360 perfs)
Music by Arthur Schwartz
Lyrics by Edward Heyman

After All, You're All I'm After
She Loves Me Not

SHE SHALL HAVE MUSIC (OB)
January 22, 1959 (54 perfs)
Music and lyrics by Deed Meyer

No True Love
Here's What a Mistress Ought to Be
Scarlet Trimmings

---

*Based on novel *Lost Horizon* by James Hilton
†Based on the play *Parfumerie* by Miklos Laslo and the film *The Shop Around the Corner*

Someday, Maybe
Moi
Wonder Where My Heart Is
Twelve O'Clock Song
Who Are You?
Basic
Maud, the Bawd
She Shall Have Music
I Live to Love
One Sweet Moment
Blind Man's Buff
Who Needs It?
If I Am to Marry You

SHERRY!*
March 27, 1967 (65 perfs)
Music by Laurence Rosenthal
Lyrics by James Lipton
  In the Very Next Moment
  Why Does the Whole Damn World
    Adore Me?
  Maggie's Date
  Maybe It's Time for Me
  How Can You Kiss Those Times
    Goodbye
  With This Ring
  Sherry
  Au Revoir
  Proposal Duet
  Listen, Cosette
  Christmas Eve Broadcast
  Putty in Your Hands
  Imagine That
  Marry the Girl Myself
  Harriet Sedley
Vocal selection

SHE'S MY BABY
January 3, 1928 (71 perfs)
Music by Richard Rodgers
Lyrics by Lorenz Hart
  This Goes Up
  My Lucky Star
  You're What I Need
  Here She Comes
  The Swallows
  When I Go on the Stage
  Try Again Tomorrow
  Camera Shoot
  Where Can the Baby Be?
  I Need Some Cooling Off
  A Little House in Soho

A Baby's Best Friend
Whoopsie†
Wasn't It Great?†
How Was I to Know†**
Pipes of Pansy†

SHINBONE ALLEY††
April 13, 1957 (49 perfs)
Music by George Kleinsinger
Lyrics by Joe Darion
  What Do We Care?
  Toujours Gai
  Queer Little Insect
  Big Bill
  True Romance
  The Lightning Bug Song
  I Gotta Be
  Flotsam and Jetsam
  Come to Mee-ow
  Suicide Song
  Shinbone Alley
  The Moth Song
  A Woman Wouldn't Be a Woman
  The Lullaby
  What the Hell
  Pretty Kitty
  Way Down Blues
  The Lady Bug Song
  Be a Pussycat
  Quiet Street

SHOEMAKER AND THE PEDDLER, THE* (OB)**
October 14, 1960 (43 perfs)
Music by Frank Fields
Lyrics by Armand Aulicino
  Headlines
  Ah, Hum; Oh, Hum
  Vedi la Vita
  Wide-Awake Morning
  Fish Song
  Childhood Lullaby
  Naughty Bird Tarantella

---

*Based on *The Man Who Came to Dinner*
by George S. Kaufman and Moss Hart
†Dropped from New York production
**Rewritten as "Why Do You Suppose?"
for *Heads Up* (1929)
††Based on *archy and mehitabel* stories by
Don Marquis
***Based on the Sacco and Vanzetti case

The Robbery
Is This the Way?
Sometimes I Wonder
Remember, Remember
Mio Fratello
The Nightmare
The Letter
Goodbye, My City
Guilty!

SHOEMAKER'S HOLIDAY*(OB)
March 2, 1967 (6 perfs)
Music by Mel Marvin
Lyrics by Ted Berger
Cold's the Wind
What Do We Care If It Rains
A Poor Man at Parting
Who Gives a Hey
Where Is the Knight for Me?
When a Maid Wears Purple Stockings
Down a Down Down Derry
Gather Ye Rose Buds
Ribbons I Will Give Thee
My Lovely Lad
Trowl the Bowl
The Wonder of the Kingdom
The Recipe for Husbandry
The Shaking of the Sheets
Would That I
Everythin' Is Tinglin'
What a Life

SHOESTRING REVUE (1955) (OB)
February 28, 1955 (100 perfs)
Man's Inhumanity (Music by Charles Strouse; Lyrics by Mike Stewart)
Inevitably Me (Music and lyrics by Ken Welch)
Someone is Sending Me Flowers (Music by David Baker; lyrics by Sheldon Harnick)
Garbage (Music and lyrics by Sheldon Harnick)
Paducah (Music by Shelley Mowell; lyrics by Mike Stewart)
Kings and Queens (Music by Arthur Siegel; lyrics by June Carroll)
Wabash 4–7473 (Music by G. Wood; lyrics by Bruce Kirby
Medea in Disneyland (Music by Lloyd Norlin; lyrics by Sheldon Harnick)
Entire History of the World in Two Minutes and Thirty-two Seconds (Music by Charles Strouse; lyrics by Mike Stewart)
New to Me (Music by Ken Welch; lyrics by Bud McCreery)
A Million Windows and I (Music by Alec Wilder; lyrics by Norman Gimbel)
Three Loves (Music by Charles Strouse; lyrics by Mike Stewart)
Things Are Going Well Today (Music by Arthur Siegel; lyrics by June Carroll)
The Sea Is All Around Us (Music by David Baker; lyrics by Sheldon Harnick)
Cast album: Offbeat

SHOESTRING REVUE (1957) (OB)
November 5, 1956 (110 perfs)
For Critics Only (Music by Shelley Mowell; lyrics by Mike Stewart)
What's a Show? (Music by Shelley Mowell; lyrics by Mike Stewart)
Queen of Spain (Music by Harvey Schmidt; lyrics by Tom Jones)
At Twenty-Two (Music by Harvey Schmidt; lyrics by Tom Jones)
Love Is a Feeling (Music by Moose Charlap; lyrics by Norman Gimbel)
The Rochelle Hudson Tango (Music by Claibe Richardson; lyrics by Paul Rosner)
Don't Say You Like Tchaikowsky (Music by Claibe Richardson; lyrics by Paul Rosner)
Lament on Fifth Avenue (Music by Claibe Richardson; lyrics by Paul Rosner)
Best Loved Girls (Music by David Baker; lyrics by Sheldon Harnick)
Always One Day More (Music by Philip Springer; lyrics by Carolyn Leigh)

———
*Based on the Elizabethan comedy by Thomas Dekker

Can You See a Girl Like Me in the Role? (Music by William Howe; lyrics by Max Showalter)
Family Trouble (Music by Leopold Antelme; lyrics by Anthony Chalmers)
Cast album: Offbeat

SHOOT THE WORKS
July 21, 1931 (87 perfs)
Music by Michael H. Cleary
Lyrics by Max and Nathaniel Lief
It's in the Stars
Taken for a Ride
I Want to Chisel In on Your Heart
How Can the Night Be Good?
Pie in the Sky
Poor Little Doorstep Baby
The First Lady of the Land
Do What You Like (Music by Philip Charig; words by Leo Robin)
Hot Moonlight (Music by Jay Gorney; lyrics by E. Y. Harburg)
How's Your Uncle? (Music by Jimmy McHugh; lyrics by Dorothy Fields)
Muchacha (Music by Vernon Duke and Jay Gorney; lyrics by E. Y. Harburg)
Begging for Love (Music and lyrics by Irving Berlin)
Let's Go Out in the Open Air (Music and lyrics by Ann Ronell)
My Heart's a Banjo (Music by Jay Gorney; lyrics by E. Y. Harburg)

SHOW BOAT*
December 27, 1927 (572 perfs)
Music by Jerome Kern
Lyrics by Oscar Hammerstein II
Make Believe
Ol' Man River
Can't Help Lovin' Dat Man
Life Upon the Wicked Stage
Till Good Luck Comes My Way
I Might Fall Back on You
Queenie's Ballyhoo (C'mon, Folks)
You Are Love
Why Do I Love You?
In Dahomey
Bill (Lyrics by P. G. Wodehouse and Oscar Hammerstein II)

Hey, Fellah!
Dance Away the Night†
Nobody Else But Me**
Added to film version: (1936)
I Have the Room Above
Gallivantin' Around
Ah Still Suits Me
Album: (Lincoln Center Cast) RCA
Vocal score
Vocal selection

SHOW GIRL
July 2, 1929 (111 perfs)
Music by George Gershwin
Lyrics by Gus Kahn and Ira Gershwin
Happy Birthday
My Sunday Fella
How Could I Forget?
Lolita
Do What You Do!
One Man
So Are You!
I Must Be Home by Twelve O'Clock
Black and White
Harlem Serenade
Home Blues††
Follow the Minstrel Band
Liza (All the Clouds'll Roll Away)
Feeling Sentimental***

SHOW GIRL
January 12, 1961 (100 perfs)
Music and lyrics by Charles Gaynor
The Girl in the Show
Calypso Pete
The Girl Who Lives in Montparnasse
Join Us in a Cup of Tea†††
This Is a Darned Fine Funeral
The Yahoo Step†††
Switchblade Bess
You Haven't Lived Until You've Played the Palace
Somewhere There's a Little Bluebird

*Based on the novel by Edna Ferber
†Added to London production (1928)
**Added to 1946 revival
††Based on slow theme from *An American in Paris*
***Dropped from New York production
†††Also in *Lend an Ear* (1948)

The Story of Marie
My Kind of Love
Cast album: Roulette

SHOW IS ON, THE
December 25, 1936 (237 perfs)
Prologue (Music by Arthur Schwartz; lyrics by Howard Dietz)
The Show Is On (Music by Hoagy Carmichael; lyrics by Ted Fetter)
Now (Music by Vernon Duke; lyrics by Ted Fetter)
Rhythm (Music by Richard Rodgers; lyrics by Lorenz Hart)
What Has He Got? (Music by Vernon Duke, lyrics by Ted Fetter)
Song of the Woodman (Music by Harold Arlen; lyrics by E. Y. Harburg)
Casanova (Music by Vernon Duke; lyrics by Ted Fetter)
Long As You've Got Your Health (Music by Will Irwin; lyrics by E. Y. Harburg and Norman Zeno)
Buy Yourself a Balloon (Music and lyrics by Herman Hupfeld)
Parade Night (Music by Will Irwin; lyrics by Norman Zeno)
By Strauss (Music by George Gershwin; lyrics by Ira Gershwin)
Woof (Music by Will Irwin; lyrics by Norman Zeno)
Little Old Lady (Music by Hoagy Carmichael; lyrics by Stanley Adams)
Josephine Waters (Music by Harold Arlen; lyrics by E. Y. Harburg)
Epilogue (Music by Vernon Duke; lyrics by Ted Fetter)

SHOW ME WHERE THE GOOD TIMES ARE* (OB)
March 5, 1970 (29 perfs)
Music by Kenneth Jacobson
Lyrics by Rhoda Roberts
How Do I Feel?
He's Wonderful
Look Up
Show Me Where the Good Times Are

You're My Happiness
Café Royale Rag Time
Staying Alive
One Big Happy Family
Follow Your Heart
Look Who's Throwing a Party
When Tomorrow Comes
The Test
I'm Not Getting Any Younger
Who'd Believe

SHUFFLE ALONG OF 1933
December 26, 1932 (17 perfs)
Music by Eubie Blake
Lyrics by Noble Sissle
Labor Day Parade
Sing and Dance Your Troubles Away
You Don't Look for Love
Bandanna Ways
Keep Your Chin Up
Breakin' 'Em In
In the Land of Sunny Sunflowers
Sugar Babe
Chickens Come Home to Roost
Waiting for the Whistle to Blow
Saturday Afternoon
Here 'Tis
Lonesome Man
Falling in Love
We're a Couple of Salesmen
Dusting Around
Arabian Moon
If It's Any News to You
You've Got to Have Koo Wah

SHUFFLE ALONG OF 1952
May 8, 1952 (4 perfs)
Music by Eubie Blake
Lyrics by Noble Sissle
Falling
City Called Heaven
Bitten by Love (Music by Joseph Meyer; lyrics by Floyd Huddleston)
Bongo-Boola
Swanee Moon
Rhythm of America

---

*Based on Molière's *The Imaginary Invalid*

It's the Gown That Makes the Gal That Makes the Guy (Lyrics by Joan Javits)

You Can't Overdo a Good Thing (Music by Joseph Meyer; lyrics by Floyd Huddleston)

My Day (Music by Joseph Meyer; lyrics by Floyd Huddleston)

Give It Love (Music by Joseph Meyer; lyrics by Floyd Huddleston)

Farewell with Love

SIDEWALKS OF NEW YORK
October 3, 1927 (112 perfs)
Music by James F. Hanley
Lyrics by Eddie Dowling
The Younger Set
Way Down Town
Wherever You Are
Nothing Can Ever Happen in New York
Little Bum
Oh, for the Life of a Cowboy
Playground in the Sky
We're the Girls You Can't Forget
Headin' for Harlem
Just a Little Smile from You
Goldfish Glide

SILK STOCKINGS*
February 24, 1955 (477 perfs)
Music and lyrics by Cole Porter
Paris Loves Lovers
Stereophonic Sound
It's a Chemical Reaction
All of You
Too Bad
Satin and Silk
Without Love
As On through the Seasons We Sail
Josephine
Siberia
Silk Stockings
Red Blues
Perfume of Love, The†
Cast album: RCA
Vocal selection
Added to film version: (1957)
Fated to be Mated
Ritz Roll and Rock
Sound track album: MGM

SILVER SWAN, THE
November 27, 1929 (21 perfs)
Music by H. Maurice Jacquet
Lyrics by William Brady
The Only Game That I Would Play
A la Viennese
I Like the Military Man
The Trial Song
The Brave Deserve the Fair
Till I Met You (Lyrics by William Brady and Alonzo Price)
Cigarette
Love Letters
Merry-Go-Round
The Lonely Road
I Love You, I Adore You

SIMPLE SIMON
February 18, 1930 (135 perfs)
Music by Richard Rodgers
Lyrics by Lorenz Hart
Coney Island
Don't Tell Your Folks
Magic Music
I Still Believe in You
Send for Me
Dull and Gay
Sweetenheart
Hunting the Fox
Mocking Bird
I Love the Woods
On With the Dance
I Can Do Wonders with You
Ten Cents a Dance
In Your Chapeau
The Trojan Horse
Rags and Tatters
Cottage in the Country
Dancing on the Ceiling†
He Was Too Good to Me†

SIMPLY HEAVENLY
May 21, 1957 (62 perfs**)
Music by David Martin
Lyrics by Langston Hughes
Simply Heavenly

---

*Based on the film *Ninotchka*
†Dropped from New York production
**Not including original OB run

Let Me Take You for a Ride
Broken String Blues
Did You Ever Hear the Blues?
I'm Gonna Be John Henry
When I'm in a Quiet Mood
Look for the Morning Star
Let's Ball Awhile
The Men in My Life
Good Old Girl
Cast album: Columbia

SING FOR YOUR SUPPER
April 24, 1939 (60 perfs)
Music by Lee Wainer
Lyrics by Robert Sour
  At Long Last
  Her Pop's a Cop (Music by Ned
    Lehak; lyrics by Irving Crane and
    Phil Conwit)
  Opening Night
  Bonnie Banks
  How Can We Swing It?
  Oh Boy, Can We Deduct
  Imagine My Finding You Here (Mu-
    sic by Ned Lehak)
  Papa's Got a Job (Music by Ned
    Lehak)
  Lucky
  Legitimate (Lyrics by John
    Latouche)
  The Story of a Horn
  Perspiration (Lyrics by John
    Latouche)
  Leaning on a Shovel (Lyrics by John
    Latouche)
  Ballad for Americans (Music by Earl
    Robinson; lyrics by John
    Latouche)

SING MUSE! (OB)
December 6, 1961 (39 perfs)
Music by Joseph Raposo
Lyrics by Erich Segal
  Helen Quit Your Yellin'
  Out to Launch
  I Am a Travelling Poet
  O Pallas Athene
  Your Name May Be Paris
  Sing Muse
  You're in Love
  The Wrath of Achilles
  No Champagne

Please Let Me Read
Business Is Bad
In Our Own Little Salon
Fame!
We'll Find a Way
Tonight's the Fight
I'm to Blame

SING OUT THE NEWS
September 24, 1938 (105 perfs)
Music and lyrics by Harold Rome
  How Long Can Love Keep Laugh-
    ing?
  Ordinary Guy
  One of These Fine Days
  Tell Me, Pretty Maiden
  Plaza 6-9423
  My Heart Is Unemployed
  Yip Ahoy
  Entre-Nous
  We've Got the Song

SINGIN' THE BLUES
(Play with two songs)
September 16, 1931 (45 perfs)
Music by Jimmy McHugh
Lyrics by Dorothy Fields
  It's the Darndest Thing
  Singin' the Blues

SINGING RABBI, THE
September 10, 1931 (4 perfs)
Music by Joseph Rumshinsky
Lyrics by L. Wolfe Gilbert
  Sholom Aleichem
  Hear O Israel
  A Vision of the Future

SIX (OB)
April 12, 1971 (8 perfs)
Music and lyrics by Charles Strouse
  What Is There to Sing About?
  The Garden
  Love Song
  Six
  Coming Attractions
  The Invisible Man
  The Critic
  Trip
  The Beginning
  The Dream

SKY HIGH
March 2, 1925 (217 perfs)
Music by Carlton Kelsey and Maury Rubens
Lyrics by Clifford Grey
  Hello, the Little Birds Have Flown
  The Best Songs of All
  Oxford Days (Music by Alfred Goodman)
  Give Your Heart in June-Time (Music by Victor Herbert; lyrics by Clifford Grey and Harold Atteridge)
  Find a Good Time
  Why Are They Following Me?
  Somewhere in Lovers' Land
  We Make the Show
  The Letter Song
  Man o' My Dreams (Music by Alfred Goodman)
  Let It Rain (Music and lyrics by James Kendis and Hal Dyson)
  Whirled into Happiness

SKYSCRAPER*
November 13, 1965 (248 perfs)
Music by Jimmy Van Heusen
Lyrics by Sammy Cahn
  Occasional Flight of Fancy
  Run for Your Life
  Local 403
  Opposites
  Just the Crust
  Everybody Has a Right to Be Wrong
  Wrong!
  More Than One Way
  Haute Couture
  Don't Worry
  I'll Only Miss Her When I Think of Her
  Spare That Building
Cast album: Capitol

SLEEPY HOLLOW†
June 3, 1948 (12 perfs)
Music by George Lessner
Lyrics by Miriam Battista and Russell Maloney
  Time Stands Still
  I Still Have to Learn
  Ask Me Again

  Never Let Her Go
  There's History to Be Made
  Here and Now
  Why Was I Born on a Farm?
  If
  My Lucky Lover
  A Musical Lesson
  You've Got That Kind of a Face
  I'm Lost (Lyrics by Ruth Aarons)
  Good Night
  The Englishman's Head
  Pedro, Ichabod
  Poor Man
  The Things That Lovers Say
  Ichabod
  The Gray Goose

SMALL WONDER
September 15, 1948 (134 perfs)
  Count Your Blessings (Music by Baldwin Bergersen; lyrics by Phyllis McGinley)
  The Commuters' Song (Music by Baldwin Bergersen; lyrics by Phyllis McGinley)
  Ballad for Billionaires (Music by Albert Selden; lyrics by Burt Shevelove)
  No Time (Music by Baldwin Bergersen; lyrics by Phyllis McGinley)
  Flaming Youth (Music by Albert Selden; lyrics by Burt Shevelove)
  Show Off (Music and lyrics by Albert Selden)
  Badaroma (Music by Albert Selden; lyrics by Burt Shevelove)
  Nobody Told Me (Music by Baldwin Bergersen; lyrics by Phyllis McGinley)
  Pistachio (Music and lyrics by Mark Lawrence)
  When I Fall in Love (Music and lyrics by Albert Selden)
  Saturday's Child (Music by Baldwin Bergersen; lyrics by Phyllis McGinley)
  William McKinley High (Music by

---

*Based on Elmer Rice's *Dream Girl*
†Based on *The Legend of Sleepy Hollow* by Washington Irving

Albert Selden; lyrics by Burt
Shevelove)
From A to Z (Music by Albert Sel-
den; lyrics by Burt Shevelove)
Just an Ordinary Guy (Music by Al-
bert Selden; lyrics by Phyllis
McGinley and Burt Sheve-
love)

SMILE AT ME
August 23, 1935 (27 perfs)
Music by Gerald Dolin
Lyrics by Edward J. Lambert
Here and There
Fiesta in Madrid
Smile at Me (Music by Edward J.
Lambert)
Tired of the South
Goona Goona
There's a Broadway Up in Heaven
I'm Dreaming While We're Danc-
ing
You're a Magician
Calcutta
Caribbeana
I Love to Flutter

SMILES
November 18, 1930 (63 perfs)
Music by Vincent Youmans
Lyrics by Harold Adamson and Clif-
ford Grey
The Bowery
Say, Young Man of Manhattan
Rally Round Me (Lyrics by Ring
Lardner)
Hotcha Ma Chotch
Time on My Hands (Lyrics by Har-
old Adamson and Mack Gordon)
Be Good to Me (Lyrics by Ring
Lardner)
Clever, Those Chinese
Anyway, We've Had Fun (Lyrics by
Ring Lardner)
Something to Sing About
Here's a Day to Be Happy
If I Were You, Love (Lyrics by Ring
Lardner)
I'm Glad I Waited
La Marseilles
Why Ain't I Home? (Lyrics by Ring
Lardner)

Dancing Wedding
Carry on, Keep Smiling

SMILING FACES
August 30, 1932 (31 perfs)
Music by Harry Revel
Lyrics by Mack Gordon
Sport Is Sport
I've Fallen Out of Love
Sweet Little Stranger
Shakin' the Shakespeare
Thank You, Don't Mention It
Smart Set
Poor Little, Shy Little, Demure Lit-
tle Me
There Will Be a Girl
Think of My Reputation
Quick Henry, the Flit
Can't Get Rid of Me
In a Little Stucco in the Sticks
I Stumbled over You and Fell in
Love
Old Spanish Custom

SMILING, THE BOY FELL DEAD (OB)
April 19, 1961 (22 perfs)
Music by David Baker
Lyrics by Fred Ebb
Sons of Greentree
Let's Evolve
The ABC's of Success
If I Felt Any Younger Today
More Than Ever Now
I've Got a Wonderful Future
Small Town
Heredity—Environment
The Gatsby Bridge March
A World to Win
The Wonderful Machine
Temperance Polka
Daydreams
Dear Old Dad
Me and Dorothea
Two by Two

SOCIAL REGISTER, THE
(Play with one song)
November 9, 1931 (97 perfs)
Music by Lou Alter
Lyrics by Ira Gershwin
The Key to My Heart

SOMETHING FOR THE BOYS
January 7, 1943 (422 perfs)
Music and lyrics by Cole Porter
    See That You're Born in Texas
    When My Baby Goes to Town
    Something for the Boys
    Could It Be You?
    Hey, Good-Lookin'
    He's a Right Guy
    The Leader of a Big-Time Band
    I'm in Love with a Soldier Boy
    By the Mississinewah
    There's a Happy Land in the Sky

SOMETHING GAY
(Play with one song)
April 29, 1935 (72 perfs)
Music by Richard Rodgers
Lyrics by Lorenz Hart
    You Are So Lovely and I'm So
        Lonely

SOMETHING MORE!*
November 10, 1964 (15 perfs)
Music by Sammy Fain
Lyrics by Marilyn and Alan Bergman
    Something More
    Who Fills the Bill
    The Straw That Broke the Camel's
        Back
    Better All the Time
    Don't Make a Move
    No Questions
    Church of My Choice
    Jaded, Degraded Am I
    I've Got Nothin' to Do
    Party Talk
    In No Time at All
    The Master of the Greatest Art of
        All
    Grazie Per Niente
    I Feel Like New Year's Eve
    One Long Last Look
    Ode to a Key
    Bravo, Bravo, Novelisto
    Life Is Too Short
    Mineola
    Come Sta

SONG OF NORWAY
August 21, 1944 (860 perfs)
Music and lyrics by Robert Wright and

George Forrest (based on Grieg)
    The Legend
    Hill of Dreams
    Freddy and His Fiddle
    Now
    Strange Music
    Midsummer's Eve
    March of the Trollgers
    Hymn of Betrothal
    Bon Vivant
    Three Loves
    Down Your Tea
    Nordraak's Farewell
    Chocolate Pas de Trois
    Waltz Eternal
    I Love You
    At Christmastime
    The Song of Norway
Cast album: Decca
Vocal score
Vocal selection

SONG OF THE FLAME
December 30, 1925 (194 perfs)
Music by George Gershwin and Her-
    bert Stothart
Lyrics by Otto Harbach and Oscar
Hammerstein II
    Far Away
    Song of the Flame
    Cossack Love Song (Don't Forget
        Me)
    Tartar
    Vodka
    You Are You
    The Signal (Music by George Gersh-
        win)
    Midnight Bells (Music by George
        Gershwin)
    Women's Work Is Never Done (Mu-
        sic by Herbert Stothart)
    Great Big Bear (Music by Herbert
        Stothart)
    Wander Away (Music by Herbert
        Stothart)

---

*Based on the novel *Portofino P. T. A.* by
Gerald Green

Sons o' Fun
December 1, 1941 (742 perfs)
Music by Sammy Fain
Lyrics by Jack Yellen
  It's a New Kind of Thing
  Happy in Love
  Thank You, South America
  It's a Mighty Fine Country We
    Have Here
  Manuelo
  Let's Say Goodnight with a Dance

Sons o' Guns
November 26, 1929 (295 perfs)
Music by J. Fred Coots
Lyrics by Arthur Swanstrom and
Benny Davis
  The Younger Set
  May I Say I Love You?
  I'm That Way Over You
  We'll Be There
  The Can-Canola
  Why?
  Cross Your Fingers
  Red Hot and Blue Rhythm
  Over Here
  It's You I Love
  Let's Merge
  Sentimental Melody
  There's a Rainbow on the Way

Soon
January 12, 1971 (3 perfs)
Music by Joseph Martinez Kookoolis
  and Scott Fagan
Lyrics by Scott Fagan
  Let the World Begin Again
  In Your Hands
  I See the Light/Gentle Sighs
  Roll Out the Morning
  Everybody's Running
  Henry Is Where It's At
  Music, Music
  Glad to Know Ya
  Rita Cheeta
  To Touch the Sky
  Marketing, Marketing
  Sweet Henry Loves You
  One More Time
  Straight
  Wait
  Faces, Names and Places

  Annie's Thing
  Doing the High
  Soon
  Country Store Living
  What's Gonna Happen to Me?
  On the Charts
  Molecules
  So Much That I Know
  Child of Sympathy
  Frustration
  It Won't Be Long

Sophie*
April 15, 1963 (8 perfs)
Music and lyrics by Steve Allen
  Red Hot Mama
  Sunshine Face
  Mr. Henry Jones
  Sophie in New York
  Patsy
  I'll Show Them All
  Hold On to Your Hats
  Fast Cars and Fightin' Women
  Queen of the Burlesque Wheel
  When You Carry Your Own Suit-
    case
  When I'm in Love
  Sailors of the Sea
  I Want the Kind of a Fella
  Who Are We Kidding
  Don't Look Back
  I'd Know It
  You've Got to Be a Lady
  I Love You Today
  With You
  I've Got 'Em Standing in Line
  They've Got a Lot to Learn

Sound of Music, The†
November 16, 1959 (1,443 perfs)
Music by Richard Rodgers
Lyrics by Oscar Hammerstein II
  Preludium
  The Sound of Music
  Maria
  My Favorite Things
  Do-Re-Mi
  You Are Sixteen

—————
*Based on the life of Sophie Tucker
†Suggested by *The Trapp Family Singers*
by Maria Augusta Trapp

The Lonely Goatherd
How Can Love Survive?
So Long, Farewell
Climb Ev'ry Mountain
No Way to Stop It
An Ordinary Couple
Edelweiss
Cast album: Columbia
Vocal score
Vocal selection
Added to film version (1965),
Lyrics by Richard Rodgers:
  I Have Confidence in Me
  Something Good
Cast album: RCA

SOUTH PACIFIC*†
April 7, 1949 (1,925 perfs)
Music by Richard Rodgers
Lyrics by Oscar Hammerstein II
  Dites-moi Pourquoi
  A Cockeyed Optimist
  Twin Soliloquies
  Some Enchanted Evening
  Bloody Mary
  There Is Nothin' Like a Dame
  Bali Ha'i
  I'm Gonna Wash That Man Right
    Outa My Hair
  I'm in Love With a Wonderful Guy
  Younger Than Springtime
  This Is How It Feels
  Happy Talk
  Honey Bun
  Carefully Taught
  This Nearly Was Mine
  My Girl Back Home**
Cast album: Columbia
Vocal score
Vocal selection

SPRING IS HERE
March 11, 1929 (104 perfs)
Music by Richard Rodgers
Lyrics by Lorenz Hart
  Spring Is Here
  Yours Sincerely
  You Never Say Yes
  With a Song in My Heart
  Baby's Awake Now
  Red Hot Trumpet
  What a Girl

Rich Man! Poor Man!
Why Can't I?

STAG MOVIE (OB)
January 3, 1971 (88 perfs)
Music by Jacques Urbont
Lyrics by David Newburger
  Stag Movie
  Looking at the Sun
  I Want More Out of Life Than This
  Grocery Boy
  Splendor in the Grass
  It's So Good
  Get in Line
  Try a Trio
  Get Your Rocks off Rock
  We Came Together

STAR AND GARTER
June 24, 1942 (605 perfs)
  Star and Garter Girls (Music by
    Lester Lee; lyrics by Jerry Seelen)
  Les Sylphides avec La Bumpe (Mu-
    sic and lyrics by Irving Gordon,
    Alan Roberts, and Jerome Brai-
    nin)
  Bunny, Bunny, Bunny (Music and
    lyrics by Harold Rome)
  For a Quarter (Music by Lester Lee;
    lyrics by Jerry Seelen)
  The Harem (Music and lyrics by Ir-
    ving Gordon, Alan Roberts, and
    Jerome Brainin)
  I Don't Get It (Music by Doris
    Tauber; lyrics by Sis Wilner)
  Brazilian Nuts (Music by Dorival
    Caymmi; lyrics by Al Stillman)

STARS IN YOUR EYES
February 9, 1939 (127 perfs)
Music by Arthur Schwartz
Lyrics by Dorothy Fields
  Places, Everybody
  One Brief Moment
  This Is It

---

*Adapted from *Tales of the South Pacific*
by James A. Michener
†Pulitzer Prize Winner
**Dropped from New York production;
used in film version (1958)

All the Time
Self Made Man
Okay for Sound
The Lady Needs a Change
Terribly Attractive
Just a Little Bit More
As of Today
He's Goin' Home
I'll Pay the Check
Never a Dull Moment
It's All Yours

STONES OF JEHOSHAPHAT (OB)
December 17, 1963 (6 perfs)
Music and lyrics by Deed Meyer
A Man Who Speaks for Himself
The Psalm of Jehoshaphat
Riblah's Lament
A Talk with One's Conscience
The Stones of Jehoshaphat
I Could Go with the Wind
Song of the Witch
The Jester's Tale
The Wedding Celebration
Beauteous Is the Bride
Look Through the Moongate
Jehoshaphat Makes Up His Mind
Long Live the Greedy

STOP THE WORLD—I WANT TO GET OFF
October 3, 1962 (556 perfs)
Music and lyrics by Leslie Bricusse
and Anthony Newley
The A.B.C. Song
I Want to Be Rich
Typically English
A Special Announcement
Lumbered
Welcome to Sludgepool
Gonna Build a Mountain
Glorious Russian
Meilinki Meilchick
Family Fugue
Typische Deutsche
Nag! Nag! Nag!
All American
Once In a Lifetime
Mumbo Jumbo
Welcome to Sunvale
Someone Nice Like You

What Kind of Fool Am I?
Cast album: London
Vocal selection

STRAW HAT REVUE, THE
September 29, 1939 (75 perfs)
Crashing Thru (Music and lyrics by Sylvia Fine)
Four Young People (Music and lyrics by James Shelton)
Anatole of Paris (Music and lyrics by Sylvia Fine)
The Great Chandelier (Music and lyrics by Sylvia Fine)
Our Town (Music and lyrics by James Shelton)

STREET SCENE*
January 9, 1947 (148 perfs)
Music by Kurt Weill
Lyrics by Langston Hughes
Ain't It Awful, the Heat?
I Got a Marble and a Star
Get a Load of That
When a Woman Has a Baby
Somehow I Never Could Believe
Ice Cream
Let Things Be Like They Always Was
Wrapped in a Ribbon and Tied in a Bow
Lonely House
Wouldn't You Like to Be on Broadway?
What Good Would the Moon Be?
Moon-Faced, Starry-Eyed
Remember That I Care
Catch Me If You Can
There'll Be Trouble
A Boy Like You
We'll Go Away Together
The Woman Who Lived Up There
Lullaby
I Loved Her, Too
Don't Forget the Lilac Bush
Cast album: Columbia
Vocal score

---

*Based on Elmer Rice's play

STREET SINGER, THE
September 17, 1929 (189 perfs)
Music by Niclas Kempner
Lyrics by Graham John
  You Can Never Tell
  I Am
  When Everything Is Hunky-Dory
  The Girl That I'll Adore
  You've Made Me Happy Today!
  Oh, Theobold, Oh, Elmer
  From Now On (Music by Richard
    Myers; lyrics by Edward Eliscu)
  Knocking on Wood

STREETS OF NEW YORK, THE* (OB)
October 29, 1963 (84 perfs)
Music by Richard B. Chodosh
Lyrics by Barry Alan Grael
  Tourist Madrigal
  He'll Come to Me Crawling
  If I May
  Aren't You Warm?
  Where Can the Rich and Poor Be
    Friends?
  California
  Christmas Carol
  Laugh After Laugh
  Arms for the Love of Me
  Close Your Eyes
  Love Wins Again

STREETS OF PARIS, THE
June 19, 1939 (274 perfs)
Music by Jimmy McHugh
Lyrics by Al Dubin
  The Streets of Paris
  Thanks for the Francs
  Danger in the Dark
  Three Little Maids
  Is It Possible?
  Rendezvous Time in Paris
  South American Way
  History Is Made at Night (Music and
    lyrics by Harold Rome)
  We Haven't Got a Pot to Cook In
  Robert the Roué
  Doin' the Chamberlain
  Reading, Writing and a Little Bit of
    Rhythm
  The French Have a Word for It (Mu-
    sic and lyrics by Harold Rome)

STRIKE ME PINK
March 4, 1933 (105 perfs)
Music by Ray Henderson
Lyrics by B. G. DeSylva and Lew
Brown
  It's Great to Be Alive
  Strike Me Pink
  Home to Harlem
  Love and Rhythm
  Let's Call It a Day
  Restless
  Ooh, I'm Thinking
  I Hate to Think That You'll Grow
    Old, Baby
  Hollywood, Park Avenue and
    Broadway
  On Any Street

STRIKE UP THE BAND
January 14, 1930 (191 perfs)
Music by George Gershwin
Lyrics by Ira Gershwin
  I Mean to Say
  A Typical Self-Made American
  Soon
  The Unofficial Spokesman
  Three Cheers for the Union!
  This Could Go on for Years
  If I Became the President
  Hangin' Around with You
  Strike Up the Band!
  Military Dancing Drill
  Mademoiselle in New Rochelle
  I've Got a Crush on You†
  How About a Boy Like Me?
  I Want to Be a War Bride
  Soldiers' March (*Instrumental*)
  Ring a Ding a Ding Dong Bell
Vocal score

STUDENT GYPSY, THE (OB)
September 30, 1963 (16 perfs)
Music and lyrics by Rick Besoyan
  Welcome Home
  Singspielia
  Romance
  Somewhere

---

*Based on the play by Dion Boucicault
†Also in *Treasure Girl* (1928)

It's a Wonderful Day to Do Nothing
The Gypsy Life
The Grenadiers' Marching Song
Greetings
Kiss Me
Ting-a-Ling-Dearie
Merry May
Seventh Heaven Waltz
You're a Man
A Whistle Works
Gypsy of Love
Our Love Has Flown Away
A Woman Is a Woman Is a
  Woman
Very Much in Love
My Life Is Yours
There's Life in the Old Folks Yet
The Drinking Song

SUBWAYS ARE FOR SLEEPING*
December 27, 1961 (205 perfs)
Music by Jule Styne
Lyrics by Betty Comden and Adolph
Green
  Subways Are for Sleeping
  Girls Like Me
  Subway Directions; Ride through
    the Night
  I'm Just Taking My Time
  I Was a Shoo-In
  Who Knows What Might Have
    Been?
  Strange Duet
  Swing Your Projects
  I Said It and I'm Glad
  Be a Santa
  How Can You Describe a Face?
  I Just Can't Wait
  Comes Once in a Lifetime
  What Is This Feeling in the Air?
Cast album: Columbia

SUGAR HILL
December 25, 1931 (11 perfs)
Music by James P. Johnson
Lyrics by Flournoy Miller
  Noisy Neighbors
  I Love You, Honey
  Hanging Around Yo' Door
  Hot Harlem
  Boston
  What Have I Done?

Hot Rhythm
Fooling Around with Love
Rumbola
Something's Going to Happen to
  You
Moving Day

SUMMER WIVES
April 13, 1936 (8 perfs)
Music by Sam Morrison
Lyrics by Dolph Singer
  Lowen-Green Country Club, I Love
    You
  The Chatterbox
  Mickey
  I Wrote a Song for You (Lyrics by
    Dolph Singer and William Dun-
    ham)
  Play Me an Old Time Two-Step
  My Love Carries On
  Us on a Bus (Music by Vee Lawn-
    hurst; lyrics by Tot Seymour)

SUNNY
September 22, 1925 (517 perfs)
Music by Jerome Kern
Lyrics by Oscar Hammerstein II
  Sunny
  Who?
  So's Your Old Man
  Let's Say Good Night Till It's Morn-
    ing
  D'Ye Love Me?
  The Wedding Knell
  Two Little Bluebirds
  When We Get Our Divorce
  Sunshine
  Strolling, or What Have You?
  Magnolia in the Woods
  Dream a Dream†
Cast album: (British production) Stan-
  yan
Vocal score
Added to film version: (1930)
  I Was Alone (Lyrics by Oscar Ham-
    merstein II and Otto Harbach)

---

*Suggested by the book by Edmund G.
Love
†Dropped from New York production

SUNNY DAYS
February 8, 1928 (101 perfs)
Music by Jean Schwartz
Lyrics by Clifford Grey and William Cary Duncan
A Belle, a Beau and a Boutonnière
One Sunny Day
Ginette
I'll Be Smiling
Really and Truly
I've Got to Be Good
Hang Your Hat on the Moon
So Do I
Orange Blossoms
Trample Your Troubles

SUNNY RIVER
December 4, 1941 (36 perfs)
Music by Sigmund Romberg
Lyrics by Oscar Hammerstein II
My Girl and I
Call It a Dream
It Can Happen to Anyone
The Butterflies and Bees
Along the Winding Road
Bundling
Can You Sing?
Making Conversation
Let Me Live Today
Bow-Legged Sal
Sunny River
The Duello
She Got Him
Time Is Standing Still

SWEET ADELINE
September 2, 1929 (234 perfs)
Music by Jerome Kern
Lyrics by Oscar Hammerstein II
Play Us a Polka, Dot
'Twas Not So Long Ago
My Husband's First Wife
Here Am I
First Mate Martin
Spring Is Here
Out of the Blue
Naughty Boy
Oriental Moon
Mollie O'Donahue
Why Was I Born?
Winter in Central Park
The Sun About to Rise
Some Girl Is On Your Mind
Don't Ever Leave Me
Take Me for a Honeymoon Ride
Added to film version: (1935)
We Were So Young
Lonely Feet

SWEET AND LOW
November 17, 1930 (184 perfs)
Mr. Jessel (Music and lyrics by Charlotte Kent)
Dancing with Tears in Their Eyes (Music by Will Irwin; lyrics by Billy Rose and Mort Dixon)
Outside Looking In (Music by Harry Archer; lyrics by Edward Eliscu)
Cheerful Little Earful (Music by Harry Warren; lyrics by Ira Gershwin and Billy Rose)
Ten Minutes in Bed (Music by Ned Lehak; lyrics by Allen Boretz)
When a Pansy Was a Flower (Music by Will Irwin; lyrics by Billy Rose and Malcolm McComb)
Would You Like to Take a Walk?* (Music by Harry Warren; lyrics by Mort Dixon and Billy Rose)
Revival Day (Music by Will Irwin; lyrics by Malcolm McComb)
For I'm in Love Again (Music by Mischa Spoliansky; lyrics by Billy Rose and Mort Dixon)
I Knew Him Before He Was Spanish (Music by Dana Suesse; lyrics by Billy Rose and Ballard MacDonald)
Overnight (Music by Louis Alter; lyrics by Billy Rose and Charlotte Kent)
You Sweet So and So (Music by Philip Charig and Joseph Meyer; lyrics by Ira Gershwin)

SWEET CHARITY†
January 29, 1966 (608 perfs)
Music by Cy Coleman
Lyrics by Dorothy Fields

---

*Also in *Crazy Quilt* (1931)
†Based on the screenplay *Nights of Cabiria* by Federico Fellini, Tullio Pinelli, and Ennio Flaiano.

You Should See Yourself
Big Spender
Charity's Soliloquy
Rich Man's Frug
If My Friends Could See Me Now
Too Many Tomorrows
There's Gotta Be Something Better
  Than This
I'm the Bravest Individual
Rhythm of Life
Baby Dream Your Dream
Sweet Charity
Where Am I Going
I'm a Brass Band
I Love to Cry At Weddings
Cast album: Columbia
Vocal selection
Added to film version: (1970)
  My Personal Property
  It's a Nice Face
Soundtrack album: Decca

SWEET MIANI (OB)
September 25, 1962 (22 perfs)
Music and lyrics by Ed Tyler
  Middle of the Sea
  Legend of the Islands
  Black Pearls
  Going Native
  A Honey to Love
  Sailing
  Not Tabu
  Maluan Moon
  Canticle to the Wind
  Homesick in Our Hearts
  Just Sit Back and Relax
  Forever and Always
  Turoola
  Miani
  Silvery Days
  Code of the Licensed Pilot
  Warm Breezes at Twilight
  Far Away Island

SWEETHEART TIME*
January 19, 1926 (145 perfs)
  Marian (Music by Walter Donald-
    son; lyrics by Ballard MacDonald)
  Step on It (Music by Joseph Meyer;
    lyrics by Irving Caesar)
  I Know That I Love You (Music by

Harry Ruby; lyrics by Bert Kal-
  mar)
Sweetheart Time (Music by Joseph
  Meyer; lyrics by Irving Caesar)
A Girl in Your Arms (Music by Jay
  Gorney; lyrics by Irving Caesar)
One Way Street (Music by Walter
  Donaldson; lyrics by Ballard Mac-
  Donald)
At the Party (Music by Harry Ruby;
  lyrics by Bert Kalmar)
Who's Who? (Music by Walter Don-
  aldson; lyrics by Ballard Mac-
  Donald)
Rue de la Paix (Music by Walter
  Donaldson; lyrics by Ballard Mac-
  Donald)
Cocktail Melody (Music by Walter
  Donaldson; lyrics by Ballard Mac-
  Donald)

SWING IT
July 22, 1937 (60 perfs)
Music by Eubie Blake
Lyrics by J. Milton Reddie and Cecil
Mack
  The Susan Belle
  What Do I Want with Love?
  It's the Youth in Me
  Ain't We Got Love
  Old Time Swing
  Shine
  Green and Blue
  By the Sweat of Your Brow
  Captain, Mate and Crew
  Sons and Daughters of the Sea
  Huggin' and Muggin'
  Rhythm Is a Racket

SWINGIN' THE DREAM†
November 29, 1939 (13 perfs)
Music by Jimmy Van Heusen
Lyrics by Eddie De Lange
  Peace, Brother
  There's Gotta Be a Wedding
  Swingin' a Dream

---

*Based on play *Never Say Die* by W. H.
Post and William Collier
†Based on William Shakespeare's *A Mid-
summer Night's Dream*

Moonland
Love's a Riddle
Darn That Dream

TAKE A CHANCE
November 26, 1932 (243 perfs)
Music by Nacio Herb Brown and Richard Whiting
Lyrics by B. G. DeSylva
    The Life of the Party
    Should I Be Sweet? (Music by Vincent Youmans)
    So Do I (Music by Vincent Youmans)
    I Got Religion (Music by Vincent Youmans)
    She's Nuts about Me
    Tickled Pink
    Turn Out the Light
    Charity
    Oh, How I Long to Belong to You (Music by Vincent Youmans)
    Rise and Shine (Music by Vincent Youmans)
    Tonight Is Opening Night
    You're an Old Smoothie
    Eadie Was a Lady
    My Lover* (Music by Vincent Youmans; lyrics by B. G. DeSylva)
    I Want to Be with You* (Music by Vincent Youmans; lyrics by B. G. DeSylva)

TAKE ME ALONG†
October 22, 1959 (448 perfs)
Music and lyrics by Bob Merrill
    Oh, Please
    I Would Die
    Sid, Ol' Kid
    Staying Young
    I Get Embarrassed
    We're Home
    Take Me Along
    For Sweet Charity
    Pleasant Beach House
    That's How It Starts
    Promise Me a Rose
    Little Green Snake
    Nine O'Clock
    But Yours
Cast album: RCA

TAKE THE AIR
November 22, 1927 (296 perfs)
Music by Dave Stamper
Lyrics by Gene Buck
    All Aboard for Times Square
    Silver Wings
    The Wild and Wooly West
    Carmela
    Carmen Has Nothing on Me
    Maybe I'll Baby You
    We'll Have a New Home in the Morning (Music by Willard Robison; lyrics by J. Russel Robinson and Gene Buck)
    Take the Air
    On a Pony for Two (Music by James F. Hanley)
    Lullaby
    We'd Rather Dance Than Eat
    Japanese Moon
    Ham and Eggs in the Morning (Music by Con Conrad and Abner Silver; lyrics by Al Dubin)

TALES OF RIGO
(Play with songs)
May 30, 1927 (8 perfs)
Music and lyrics by Ben Schwartz
    I'll Tell You All Someday
    In Romany
    What Care We?
    Little Princess
    Zita
    Rigo's Last Lullaby (Music and lyrics by Evelyn Adler)

TALK ABOUT GIRLS
June 14, 1927 (15 perfs)
Music by Harold Orlob
Lyrics by Irving Caesar
    In Central Park
    Come to Lower Falls
    The Only Boy
    Oo, How I Love You
    Home Town
    Talk About Girls (Music by Stephen Jones)

---

*Dropped from New York production
†Based on the play *Ah, Wilderness* by Eugene O'Neill

A Lonely Girl
Maybe I Will
In Twos
Sex Appeal
That's My Man
Nineteen Twenty-Seven
One Boy's Enough for Me

TATTLE TALES
June 1, 1933 (28 perfs)
  I'll Take an Option on You (Music
    by Ralph Rainger; lyrics by Leo
    Robin)
  Harlem Lullaby (Music and lyrics by
    Willard Robison)
  Hang Up Your Hat on Broadway
    (Music by Edward Ward; lyrics by
    George Waggner, Grossman and
    Sylvester)
  Percy with Perseverance (Music by
    Edward Ward; lyrics by George
    Waggner)
  The First Spring Day (Music by
    Howard Jackson; lyrics by Ed-
    ward Eliscu)
  Jig Saw Jamboree (Music by Eddie
    Bienbryer; lyrics by William
    Walsh)
  Sing American Tunes (Music by Ed-
    ward Ward; lyrics by Frank Fay
    and William Walsh)
  Another Case of the Blues (Music by
    Richard Myers; lyrics by Johnny
    Mercer)
  Just a Sentimental Tune (Music by
    Louis Alter; lyrics by Max and Na-
    thaniel Lief)

TATTOOED COUNTESS, THE* (OB)
April 3, 1961 (4 perfs)
Music and lyrics by Coleman Dowell
  Home Town Girl
  You Take Paris
  These Acres
  The Brushing Stone
  Advice
  Fin de Sickle
  The Waterworks Madrigal
  How She Glows
  High Up
  Rolling Stone
  Dusters, Goggles and Hats

Je M'en Fiche
Gossip
Tattooed Woman
Too Old for Love
That's Her Life
Autumn
A Woman's Much Better Off
  Alone
Too Young
I Can Take It
Got to Find My Way

TELL HER THE TRUTH†
October 28, 1932 (11 perfs)
Music by Jack Waller and Joseph Tun-
bridge
Lyrics by R. P. Weston and Bert Lee
  Hoch, Caroline!
  Happy the Day
  Won't You Tell Me Why?
  Sing, Brothers!
  That's Fine
  Tell Her the Truth
  Horrortorio

TELL ME MORE**
April 13, 1925 (100 perfs)
Music by George Gershwin
Lyrics by B. G. DeSylva and Ira Gersh-
win
  Tell Me More!
  Mr. and Mrs. Sipkin
  When the Debbies Go By
  Three Times a Day
  Why Do I Love You?
  How Can I Win You Now?
  Kickin' the Clouds Away
  Love Is in the Air
  My Fair Lady
  In Sardinia
  Baby!
  The Poetry of Motion
  Ukulele Lorelei

---

*Based on Carl Van Vechten's novel
†Based on the play *Nothing But the Truth*
by James Montgomery, from a novel by
Frederick Isham
**Out-of-town title: *My Fair Lady*

TENDERLOIN*
October 17, 1960 (216 perfs)
Music by Jerry Bock
Lyrics by Sheldon Harnick
  Bless This Land
  Little Old New York
  Dr. Brock
  Artificial Flowers
  What's in It for You?
  Reform
  Tommy, Tommy
  The Picture of Happiness
  Dear Friend
  The Army of the Just
  How the Money Changes Hands
  Good Clean Fun
  My Miss Mary
  My Gentle Young Johnny
  I Wonder What It's Like†
  Lovely Laurie†
Cast album: Capitol
Vocal selection

TEXAS, LI'L DARLIN'
November 25, 1949 (293 perfs)
Music by Robert Emmett Dolan
Lyrics by Johnny Mercer
  Whoopin' and a-Hollerin'
  Texas, Li'l Darlin'
  They Talk a Different Language
  A Month of Sundays
  Down in the Valley
  Hootin' Owl Trail
  The Big Movie Show in the
    Sky
  Horseshoes Are Lucky
  Love Me, Love My Dog
  Take a Crank Letter
  Politics
  Ride 'Em, Cowboy
  Affable, Balding Me
  Whichaway'd They Go
  It's Great to Be Alive
Cast album: Decca

THAT 5 A.M. JAZZ (OB)
October 19, 1964 (94 perfs)
Music and lyrics by Will Holt
  Some Sunday
  Campaign Song
  Gonna Get a Woman
  The Happy Daze Saloon

The All-American Two-Step
Sweet Time
Nuevo Laredo
Those Were the Days

THAT HAT! (OB)
September 23, 1964 (1 perf)
Music and lyrics by Cy Young
  Exposition
  Italian Straw Hat
  My Husband
  Do a Little Exercise
  Draw Me a Circle
  It's All Off
  Sound of the Night
  I Love a Man
  A Tête-à-Tête
  The Apology
  My, It's Been Grand
  We Have Never Met
  Give Me a Pinch
  A Pot of Myrtle
  This World of Confusion

THERE YOU ARE
May 16, 1932 (8 perfs)
Music by William Heagney
Lyrics by William Heagney and Tom
Connell
  Haunting Refrain
  There You Are
  Lover's Holiday
  They All Love Me
  Aces Up
  Safe in Your Arms
  Love Lives On
  More and More
  The Sound of the Drum
  Wings of the Morning
  The Love Potion
  Just a Little Penthouse and
    You
  Carolita
  Legend of the Mission Bells

---

*Based on the novel by Samuel Hopkins
Adams
†Dropped from New York production
**Adapted from *An Italian Straw Hat* by
Eugene Labiche and Marc-Michel

THIRD LITTLE SHOW, THE
June 1, 1931 (136 perfs)
I'll Putcha Pitcha in the Paper (Music by Michael H. Cleary; lyrics by Max and Nathaniel Lief)
Say the Word (Music by Burton Lane; lyrics by Harold Adamson)
Mad Dogs and Englishmen (Music and lyrics by Noël Coward)
Falling in Love (Music by Henry Sullivan; lyrics by Earle Crooker)
Going, Going, Gone! (Music by Henry Sullivan; lyrics by Edward Eliscu)
You Forgot Your Gloves (Music by Ned Lehak; lyrics by Edward Eliscu)
I've Lost My Heart (Music by Morris Hamilton; lyrics by Grace Henry)
When Yuba Plays the Rumba on His Tuba (Music and lyrics by Herman Hupfeld)
Sevilla (Music by Ned Lehak; lyrics by Edward Eliscu)
African Shrieks (Music by Ned Lehak; lyrics by Edward Eliscu)
You Might as Well Pretend (Music by Morgan Lewis; lyrics by Edward Eliscu and Ted Fetter)
Little Geezer (Music by Michael H. Cleary; lyrics by Max and Nathaniel Lief and Dave Oppenheim)
Le Five O'Clock (Music by Will Irwin; lyrics by Carl Randall)
Cinema Lorelei (Music by Ned Lehak; lyrics by Edward Eliscu)
Any Little Fish* (Music and lyrics by Noël Coward)

13 DAUGHTERS
March 2, 1961 (28 perfs)
Music and lyrics by Eaton Magoon, Jr.
Kuli Kuli
House on the Hill
13 Daughters
Paper of Gold
Let-a-Go Your Heart
Alphabet Song
Throw a Petal
When You Hear the Wind
Ka Wahine Akamai
You Set My Heart to Music
13 Old Maids
Nothing Man Cannot Do

Hoomalimali
My Pleasure
Puka Puka Pants
My Hawaii
Hiiaka
Cast album: Mahalo

THIS IS THE ARMY
July 4, 1942 (113 perfs)
Music and lyrics by Irving Berlin
This Is the Army, Mr. Jones
I'm Getting Tired So I Can Sleep
My Sergeant and I Are Buddies
I Left My Heart at the Stage Door Canteen
The Army's Made a Man Out of Me
That Russian Winter
That's What the Well Dressed Man in Harlem Will Wear
American Eagles
With My Head in the Clouds
Aryans under the Skin
How About a Cheer for the Navy
What Does He Look Like?
This Time
Oh, How I Hate to Get Up in the Morning†
Cast album: Decca

THIS YEAR OF GRACE
November 7, 1928 (157 perfs)
Music and lyrics by Noël Coward
Waiting in a Queue
Mary Make Believe
Lorelei
A Room with a View
Teach Me to Dance Like Grandma
The Lido Beach
Little Women
English Lido
Mother's Complaint
Britannia Rules the Waves
Dance, Little Lady
Chauve Souris
World Weary
Velasquez
Caballero
Vocal score

---

*Dropped from New York production
†First introduced in *Yip, Yip, Yaphank* (1918)

THREE CHEERS
October 15, 1928 (210 perfs)
Music by Ray Henderson
Lyrics by B. G. DeSylva
  The Americans Are Here
  Lady Luck
  Maybe This Is Love
  It's an Old Spanish Custom
  Pompanola
  Because You're Beautiful
  Bobby and Me
  My Silver Tree (Music by Raymond
    Hubbell; lyrics by Anne Caldwell)
  Gee, It's Great to Be Alive
  Putting On the Ritz
  Two Boys
  Let's All Sing the Lard Song (Music
    by Leslie Sarony; lyrics by Anne
    Caldwell)
  Orange Blossom Home (Music by
    Raymond Hubbell; lyrics by Anne
    Caldwell)
  Happy Hoboes

THREE LITTLE GIRLS
April 14, 1930 (104 perfs)
Music by Walter Kollo
Lyrics by Harry B. Smith
  Love's Happy Dream
  Whistle While You Work, Boys
  Letter Song
  Annette
  I'll Tell You
  Cottage in the Country
  Doll Song
  Waltz with Me
  Love Comes Once in a Lifetime
    (Music by Harold Stern and Harry
    Perella; lyrics by Stella Unger)
  Prince Charming

THREE MUSKETEERS, THE*
March 13, 1928 (318 perfs)
Music by Rudolf Friml
Lyrics by P. G. Wodehouse and
Clifford Grey
  Summer Time
  All for One and One for All
  The "He" for Me
  Heart of Mine
  Vesper Bell
  Dreams

March of the Musketeers
The Colonel and the Major
Love Is the Sun
Your Eyes
Welcome to the Queen
Red Wine
Ma Belle
A Kiss Before I Go
My Sword
Queen of My Heart
Ev'ry Little While

THREE TO MAKE READY
March 7, 1946 (323 perfs)
Music by Morgan Lewis
Lyrics by Nancy Hamilton
  It's a Nice Night for It
  Tell Me the Story
  The Old Soft Shoe
  Barnaby Beach
  Kenosha Canoe
  If It's Love
  A Lovely Lazy Kind of Day
  And Why Not I?
  Oh, You're a Wonderful Person

THREE WALTZES
December 25, 1937 (122 perfs)
Lyrics by Clare Kummer
  Springtime Is in the Air (Music by
    Johann Strauss I, adapted by Os-
    car Straus)
  My Heart Controls My Head (Music
    by Johann Strauss I, adapted by
    Oscar Straus)
  Vienna Gossip (Music by Johann
    Strauss I, adapted by Oscar
    Straus)
  Do You Recall? (Music by Johann
    Strauss I, adapted by Oscar
    Straus)
  To Love Is to Live (Music by Johann
    Strauss II, adapted by Oscar
    Straus)
  The Only One (Music by Johann
    Strauss II, adapted by Oscar
    Straus)
  Paree (Music by Johann Strauss II,
    adapted by Oscar Straus)

---

*Based on the novel by Alexandre Dumas

I'll Can-Can All Day (Music by Johann Strauss II, adapted by Oscar Straus)

Scandal (Music by Johann Strauss II, adapted by Oscar Straus)

The History of Three Generations of Chorus Girls (Music by Oscar Straus)

Our Last Waltz Together (Music by Oscar Straus)

I Sometimes Wonder (Music by Oscar Straus)

The Days of Old (Music by Oscar Straus)

THREE WISHES FOR JAMIE
March 21, 1952 (94 perfs)
Music and lyrics by Ralph Blane
  The Girl That I Court in My Mind
  My Home's a Highway
  We're for Love
  My Heart's Darlin'
  Goin' on a Hayride
  Love Has Nothing to Do with Looks (Lyrics by Charles Lederer)
  I'll Sing You a Song
  It Must Be Spring
  The Army Mule Song
  What Do I Know?
  It's a Wishing World
  April Face
  Trottin' to the Fair
Cast album: Capitol

THREEPENNY OPERA, THE * (OB)
March 10, 1954 (95 perfs)
September 20, 1955 (2,611 perfs)
Music by Kurt Weill
Lyrics by Marc Blitzstein
  Mack the Knife
  Morning Anthem
  Instead-Of Song
  The Bide-a-Wee in Soho
  Wedding Song
  Army Song
  Love Song
  Ballad of Dependency
  The World Is Mean
  Polly's Song
  Pirate Jenny
  Tango Ballad
  Ballad of the Easy Life

  Barbara Song
  Jealousy Duet
  How to Survive
  Useless Song
  Solomon Song
  Call from the Grave
  Death Message
  The Mounted Messenger
Cast album: MGM
Vocal score

THREE'S A CROWD
October 15, 1930 (272 perfs.)
  Practising Up on You (Music by Philip Charig; lyrics by Howard Dietz)
  Something to Remember You By (Music by Arthur Schwartz; lyrics by Howard Dietz)
  Out in the Open Air (Music by Burton Lane; lyrics by Howard Dietz)
  Je t'Aime (Music by Arthur Schwartz; lyrics by Howard Dietz)
  Talkative Toes (Music by Vernon Duke; lyrics by Howard Dietz)
  All the King's Horses (Music and lyrics by Alec Wilder, Eddie Brandt, and Howard Dietz)
  Body and Soul (Music by John Green; lyrics by Edward Heyman, Robert Sour, and Frank Eyton)
  The Moment I Saw You (Music by Arthur Schwartz; lyrics by Howard Dietz)
  Forget All Your Books (Music by Burton Lane; lyrics by Howard Dietz)
  Yaller (Music by Charles M. Schwab; lyrics by Henry Myers)
  Night After Night (Music by Arthur Schwartz; lyrics by Howard Dietz)
  Right at the Start of It (Music by Arthur Schwartz; lyrics by Howard Dietz)

---

*Original Broadway version, with lyrics by Gifford Cochran and Jerrold Krimsky, opened April 13, 1933 (12 perfs)

THROUGH THE YEARS*
January 28, 1932 (20 perfs)
Music by Vincent Youmans
Lyrics by Edward Heyman
  Kathleen, Mine
  Kinda Like You
  I'll Come Back to You
  How Happy Is the Bride
  It's Every Girl's Ambition
  Through the Years
  The Trumpeter and the Lover
  You're Everywhere
  The Road to Home
  Drums in My Heart

THUMBS UP!
December 27, 1934 (156 perfs)
  Beautiful Night (Music and lyrics by
    Ballard MacDonald, Karl Stark,
    and James F. Hanley)
  Zing, Went the Strings of My Heart
    (Music and lyrics by James F.
    Hanley)
  Lily Belle May June (Music by
    Henry Sullivan; lyrics by Earle
    Crooker)
  Flamenco (Music by Henry Sul-
    livan; lyrics by Earle Crooker)
  Eileen Avourneen (Music by Henry
    Sullivan; lyrics by John Murray
    Anderson)
  The Torch Singer (What Do You
    Think My Heart Is Made Of?)
    (Music by Henry Sullivan; lyrics
    by Earle Crooker)
  My Arab Complex (Music by Henry
    Sullivan; lyrics by Ballard Mac-
    Donald)
  Soldier of Love (Music by Gerald
    Marks; lyrics by Irving Caesar)
  Color Blind (Music by Henry Sul-
    livan; lyrics by Earle Crooker)
  Continental Honeymoon (Music by
    James F. Hanley; lyrics by Ballard
    MacDonald and James F. Hanley)
  A Taste of the Sea (Music by Henry
    Sullivan; lyrics by Earle Crooker)
  Merrily We Waltz Along (Music by
    Henry Sullivan; lyrics by Earle
    Crooker)
  I've Gotta See a Man about His
    Daughter (Music and lyrics by

Jean Herbert, Karl Stark, and
    James F. Hanley)
  Autumn in New York (Music and
    lyrics by Vernon Duke)

TICKETS PLEASE
April 27, 1950 (245 perfs)
Music and lyrics by Joan Edwards and
Lyn Duddy
  Tickets Please (Music by Clay War-
    nick; lyrics by Mel Tolkin and Lu-
    cille Kallen)
  Washington Square (Music by Clay
    Warnick; lyrics by Mel Tolkin and
    Lucille Kallen)
  Darn it, Baby, That's Love
  Restless
  You Can't Take it with You
  Back at the Palace (Music by Clay
    Warnick; lyrics by Mel Tolkin and
    Lucille Kallen)
  The Moment I Looked in Your Eyes
  Maha Roger (Music by Clay War-
    nick; lyrics by Mel Tolkin and Lu-
    cille Kallen)

TIGER RAG, THE (OB)
February 16, 1961 (14 perfs)
Music by Kenneth Gaburo
Lyrics by Seyril Schochen
  We Were Born By Chance
  Cheerio, Old Boys
  Flirtation Waltz
  Honeysuckle Vine
  Travelling Song
  Razz-Me-Tazz-Jazz
  Tiger Rag Blues
  What Is Good for Depressions
  Apache
  Irish Washerwoman's Lament
  My Father Was a Peculiar Man

TIME FOR SINGING, A†
May 21, 1966 (41 perfs)
Music by John Morris
Lyrics by Gerald Freedman

---

*Based on play Smilin' Through by Allan
Langdon Martin and Jane Cowl
†Based on Richard Llewellyn's novel How
Green Was My Valley

Come You Men
How Green Was My Valley
Old Long John
Here Come Your Men
What a Good Day Is Saturday
Peace Come to Every Heart
Someone Must Try
Oh, How I Adore Your Name
That's What Young Ladies Do
When He Looks at Me
Far from Home
I Wonder If
What a Party
Let Me Love You
Why Would Anyone Want to Get
  Married
A Time for Singing
When the Baby Comes
I'm Always Wrong
There Is Beautiful You Are
Three Ships
Tell Her
And the Mountains Sing Back
Gone in Sorrow
Cast album: Warner Bros.

TIME REMEMBERED
(Play with two songs)
November 12, 1957 (247 perfs)
Music and lyrics by Vernon Duke
  Ages Ago
  Time Remembered

TIP-TOES
December 28, 1925 (192 perfs)
Music by George Gershwin
Lyrics by Ira Gershwin
  Waiting for the Train
  Nice Baby! (Come to Papa!)
  Looking for a Boy
  Lady Luck
  When Do We Dance?
  These Charming People
  That Certain Feeling
  Sweet and Low-Down
  Our Little Captain
  Harbor of Dreams
  Nightie-Night
  Tip-Toes
  It's a Great Little World
Album: (original British Cast) Mon-
  mouth-Evergreen

TIS OF THEE
October 26, 1940 (1 perf)
  You've Got Something to Sing
    About (Music by Al Moss; lyrics by
    Alfred Hayes)
  Lupe (Music by Alex North; lyrics
    by Alfred Hayes)
  What's Mine Is Thine (Music by Al
    Moss; lyrics by Alfred Hayes)
  Brooklyn Cantata (Music by George
    Kleinsinger; lyrics by Mike Strat-
    ton)
  After Tonight (Music by Al Moss;
    lyrics by Alfred Hayes)
  Noises in the Street* (Music by
    Richard Lewine; lyrics by David
    Greggory and Peter Barry)
  Tis of Thee (Music by Alex North;
    lyrics by Alfred Hayes)
  The Lady (Music by Elsie Peters;
    lyrics by Alfred Hayes)
  The Rhythm Is Red an' White an'
    Blue (Music by Al Moss; lyrics by
    David Greggory)
  Tomorrow (Music by Alex North;
    lyrics by Alfred Hayes)

TO LIVE ANOTHER SUMMER
October 21, 1971 (173 perfs)
Music by Dov Seltzer
Lyrics by David Paulsen
  Son of Man (Lyrics by David Axel-
    rod)
  The Sacrifice
  What Are the Basic Things? (Lyrics
    by Lillian Burstein)
  The Grove of Eucalyptus (Music by
    Naomi Shemer; lyrics by George
    Sherman)
  The Boy with the Fiddle (Music by
    Alexander Argov)
  Can You Hear My Voice? (Music by
    Samuel Kraus; lyrics by George
    Sherman)
  Mediteranee
  When My Man Returns (Music by
    George Moustaki)

-----
*Rewritten for *Make Mine Manhatten*
(1948)

Better Days
To Live Another Summer, to Pass
    Another Winter
Noah's Ark (Music by Naomi
    Shemer)
Don't Destroy the World
Give Shalom and Sabbath to Jerusa-
    lem
Sorry We Won (Music by David
    Krivoshei)
I'm Alive (Music by David Krivo-
    shei)
Give Me a Star (Music by David
    Krivoshei)
Cast album: Buddah
Vocal selection

'TOINETTE* (OB)
November 20, 1961 (31 perfs)
Music and lyrics by Deed Meyer
    Rags
    Bonjour
    Come On Outside and Get Some
        Air
    Why Shouldn't I?
    A Father Speaks
    A Lullaby
    Honest Honore
    Someone to Count On
    Un, Deux, Trois
    Fly Away
    'Toinette
    Madly in Love with You Am I
    Beat, Little Pulse
    Even a Doctor Can Make a
        Mistake
    Dr. Iatro
    Small Apartment
    You're the Most Impossible Person

TONIGHT AT 8:30
November 24, 1936 (118 perfs)
Music and lyrics by Noël Coward

WE WERE DANCING
    We Were Dancing

SHADOW PLAY
    Then
    You Were There
    Play, Orchestra, Play!

RED PEPPERS
    Has Anybody Seen Our Ship?
    Men about Town

FAMILY ALBUM
    Here's a Toast
    Princes and Princesses
    Let's Play a Tune on the Music
        Box
    Hearts and Flowers

TOO MANY GIRLS
October 18, 1939 (249 perfs)
Music by Richard Rodgers
Lyrics by Lorenz Hart
    Heroes in the Fall
    Tempt Me Not
    My Prince
    Pottawatomie
    'Cause We Got Cake
    Love Never Went to College
    Spic and Spanish
    I Like to Recognize the Tune
    Look Out
    The Sweethearts of the Team
    She Could Shake the Maracas
    I Didn't Know What Time It Was
    Too Many Girls
    Give It Back to the Indians
    Added to film version: (1940)
    You're Nearer

TOP BANANA
November 1, 1951 (350 perfs)
Music and lyrics by Johnny Mercer
    The Man of the Year This Week
    You're So Beautiful that——
    Top Banana
    Elevator Song
    Hail to MacCracken's
    Only If You're in Love
    My Home Is in My Shoes
    I Fought Every Step of the Way
    O.K. for T.V.
    Slogan Song
    Meet Miss Blendo
    Sans Souci
    A Dog Is a Man's Best Friend
    That's for Sure

_____
*Based on Molière's *Le Malade Imaginaire*

A Word a Day
Be My Guest
Cast album: Capitol

TOP SPEED
December 25, 1929 (102 perfs)
Music by Harry Ruby
Lyrics by Bert Kalmar
In the Summer
The Papers
Try Dancing
I Like to Be Liked
Keep Your Undershirt On
We Want You
Goodness Gracious
I'll Know and She'll Know
What Would I Care
Dizzy Feet
On the Border Line
Hot and Bothered
Sweeter Than You*
Reaching for the Moon
You Couldn't Blame Me for That
Fireworks

TOPLITZKY OF NOTRE DAME
December 26, 1946 (60 perfs)
Music by Sammy Fain
Lyrics by George Marion, Jr.
Let Us Gather at the Goal Line
Baby, Let's Face It
I Wanna Go to City College
Love Is a Random Thing
Common Sense
A Slight Case of Ecstasy
Wolf Time
McInerney's Farm
You Are My Downfall
All American Man

TOUCH (OB)
November 8, 1970 (422 perfs)
Music by Kenn Long and Jim Crozier
Lyrics by Kenn Long
Declaration
Windchild (Music and lyrics by Gary Graham)
City Song
Sitting in the Park
I Don't Care
Goodbyes
Come to the Road

Reaching, Touching
Guiness, Woman
Susan's Song
Maxine!
Quiet Country
Tripping
Garden Song
Watching
Hasseltown
Confrontation Song
Alphagenesis
Cast album: Ampex

TOUCH AND GO
October 13, 1949 (176 perfs)
Music by Jay Gorney
Lyrics by Jean and Walter Kerr
An Opening for Everybody
This Had Better Be Love
American Primitive
Highbrow, Lowbrow
Easy Does It
Be a Mess
Broadway Love Song
It'll Be All Right in a Hundred Years
Wish Me Luck
Under the Sleeping Volcano
Men of the Water-Mark
Mr. Brown, Miss Dupree
Miss Platt Selects Mate

TOVARICH†
March 18, 1963 (264 perfs)
Music by Lee Pockriss
Lyrics by Anne Croswell
Nitchevo
I Go to Bed
You'll Make an Elegant Butler (Music and lyrics by Joan Javits and Philip Springer)
Stuck with Each Other
Say You'll Stay
You Love Me
That Face
Wilkes-Barre, Pa.
No! No! No!
A Small Cartel

---

*Also in *Twinkle Twinkle* (1926)
†Based on the comedy by Jacques Deval

It Used to Be
Kukla Katusha
Make a Friend
The Only One
Uh-Oh!
Managed
I Know the Feeling
All for You
Grade Polonaise
Cast album: Capitol

TREASURE GIRL
November 8, 1928 (68 perfs)
Music by George Gershwin
Lyrics by Ira Gershwin
  Skull and Bones
  I've Got a Crush on You*
  Oh, So Nice
  According to Mr. Grimes
  Place in the Country
  K-ra-zy for You
  I Don't Think I'll Fall in Love
    Today
  Got a Rainbow
  Feeling I'm Falling
  What Are We Here For?
  Where's the Boy? Here's the
    Girl!
  What Causes That?

TREE GROWS IN BROOKLYN, A†
April 19, 1951 (270 perfs)
Music by Arthur Schwartz
Lyrics by Dorothy Fields
  Payday
  Mine 'Til Monday
  Make the Man Love Me
  I'm Like a New Broom
  Look Who's Dancing
  Love Is the Reason
  If You Haven't Got a Sweetheart
  I'll Buy You a Star
  That's How It Goes
  He Had Refinement
  Growing Pains
  Is That My Prince?
  Don't Be Afraid
Cast album: Columbia

TWIGS
(Play with one song)
November 14, 1971 (289 perfs)

Music and lyrics by Stephen Sondheim
  Hollywood and Vine

TWINKLE TWINKLE
November 16, 1926 (167 perfs)
Music by Harry Archer
Lyrics by Harlan Thompson
  You Know, I Know
  Get a Load of This
  We're on the Map (Music by
    Harry Ruby; lyrics by Bert Kal-
    mar)
  Reuben
  Twinkle Twinkle
  Hustle, Bustle
  Sweeter Than You** (Music by
    Harry Ruby; lyrics by Bert Kal-
    mar)
  Crime
  Sunday Afternoon
  Whistle (Music by Harry Ruby; lyr-
    ics by Bert Kalmar)
  I Hate to Talk About Myself
  When We're Bride and Groom

TWO BY TWO††
November 10, 1970 (343 perfs)
Music by Richard Rodgers
Lyrics by Martin Charnin
  Why Me?
  Put Him Away
  The Gitka's Song
  Something, Somewhere
  You Have Got to Have a Rudder on
    the Ark
  Something Doesn't Happen
  An Old Man
  Ninety Again!
  Two by Two
  I Do Not Know a Day I Did Not
    Love You
  When It Dries
  You
  The Golden Ram

---

*Also in *Strike Up the Band* (1930)
†Based on the novel by Betty Smith
**Also in *Top Speed* (1929)
††Based on the play *The Flowering Peach*
by Clifford Odets

Poppa Knows Best
As Far As I'm Concerned
Hey, Girlie
The Covenant
Cast album: Columbia
Vocal score
Vocal selection

TWO FOR THE SHOW
February 8, 1940 (124 perfs)
Music by Morgan Lewis
Lyrics by Nancy Hamilton
Calypso Joe
This Merry Christmas
That Terrible Tune
The All-Girl Band
Where Do You Get Your Greens?
At Last It's Love
Fool for Luck
How High the Moon
A House with a Little Red Barn

TWO FOR TONIGHT (OB)
December 28, 1939 (30 perfs)
Slap on the Greasepaint (Music by Berenice Kazounoff; lyrics by John Latouche)
Personal Heaven (Music and lyrics by Eugene and Ralph Berton)
Could You Use a New Friend? (Music and lyrics by Eugene and Ralph Berton)
Call of the Wild (Music by Berenice Kazounoff; lyrics by Sylvia Marks)
Masquerade (Music and lyrics by Charles Herbert)
Windows (Music and lyrics by Eugene and Ralph Berton)
Nursery (Music and lyrics by Charles Herbert)
Five O'Clock (Music by Bernie Wayne; lyrics by Ben Raleigh)
Dancing Alone (Music and lyrics by Ralph and Eugene Berton)
Blues (Music and lyrics by John Latouche)
Home Is Where You Hang Your Hat (Music by Berenice Kazounoff; lyrics by John Latouche)
Blasé (Music by Berenice Kazounoff; lyrics by John Latouche)

TWO GENTLEMEN OF VERONA*
December 1, 1971†
Music by Galt MacDermot
Lyrics by John Guare
Summer, Summer
I Love My Father
That's a Very Interesting Question
I'd Like to Be a Rose
Thou, Julia, Thou Has Metamorphosed Me
Symphony
I Am Not Interested in Love
Love, Is That You?
Thou, Proteus, Thou Has Metamorphosed Me
What Does a Lover Pack?
Pearls
Two Gentlemen of Verona
Follow the Rainbow
Where's North?
Bring All the Boys Back Home
Love's Revenge
To Whom It May Concern Me
Night Letter
Calla Lily Lady
Land of Betrayal
Hot Lover
What a Nice Idea
Who Is Sylvia?
Love Me
Eglamour
Kidnapped
Mansion
What's a Nice Girl Like Her
Don't Have the Baby
Milkmaid
Love Has Driven Me Sane
Cast album: ABC/Dunhill

TWO ON THE AISLE
July 19, 1951 (279 perfs)
Music by Jule Styne
Lyrics by Betty Comden and Adolph Green
Show Train
Here She Comes Now
If You Hadn't, but You Did

---

*Based on the play by William Shakespeare
†Still running December 31, 1972|

Catch Our Act at the Met
Everlasting
Give a Little, Get a Little
How Will He Know?
Hold Me—Hold Me—Hold Me
Cast album: Decca

TWO'S COMPANY
December 15, 1952 (91 perfs)
Music by Vernon Duke
Lyrics by Ogden Nash
  The Theatre Is a Lady
  Turn Me Loose on Broadway
  It Just Occurred to Me (Lyrics by
    Sammy Cahn)
  Baby Couldn't Dance
  A Man's Home (Music and lyrics by
    Sheldon Harnick)
  Roundabout
  Roll Along, Sadie
  Out of the Clear Blue Sky
  Esther (Lyrics by Sammy Cahn)
  Haunted Hot Spot
  Purple Rose
  Just Like a Man
Cast album: RCA

UNDER THE COUNTER
October 3, 1947 (27 perfs)
Music by Manning Sherwin
Lyrics by Harold Purcell
  Everywhere
  No One's Tried to Kiss Me
  The Moment I Saw You
  Let's Get Back to Glamour
  Ai Yi Yi

UNFAIR TO GOLIATH (OB)
January 25, 1970 (73 perfs)
Music by Menachem Zur
Lyrics by Herbert Appleman
  The Danger of Peace Is Over
  In the Reign of Chaim
  What Kind of Baby
  A Parking Meter Like Me
  The Sabra
  The Famous Rabbi
  When Moses Spake to Goldstein
  The Rooster and the Hen
  What Abraham Lincoln Once Said
  The Song of Sallah Shabeti

UNSINKABLE MOLLY BROWN, THE
November 3, 1960 (532 perfs)
Music and lyrics by Meredith Willson
  I Ain't Down Yet
  Belly Up to the Bar, Boys
  I've A'ready Started In
  I'll Never Say No
  My Own Brass Bed
  The Denver Police
  Beautiful People of Denver
  Are You Sure?
  Happy Birthday, Mrs. J. J. Brown
  Bon Jour
  If I Knew
  Chick-a-Pen
  Keep-A-Hoppin'
  Up Where the People Are
  Dolce Far Niente
Cast album: Capitol
Vocal score
Vocal selection

UP EDEN (OB)
November 27, 1968 (8 perfs)
Music by Robert Rosenblum
Lyrics by Robert Rosenblum and
Howard Schuman
  Haven't You Wondered
  Wishy Washy Woman
  Hannibal's Comin'
  Homesick
  Let Me Show You the World
  Remember Me Smiling
  Passin' Through
  A Playboy's Work Is Never Done
  Nothing Ever Happens Till 2 A.M.
  Was That Me Talking?
  The Virgin of Velez-Jermano
  A Little More Like You
  No More Edens

UP IN CENTRAL PARK
January 27, 1945 (504 perfs)
Music by Sigmund Romberg
Lyrics by Dorothy Fields
  Up from the Gutter
  Carousel in the Park
  It Doesn't Cost You Anything to
    Dream
  Boss Tweed
  When She Walks in the Room
  Currier and Ives

Close as Pages in a Book
Rip Van Winkle
The Fireman's Bride
When the Party Gives a Party
The Big Back Yard
April Snow
The Birds and the Bees
Cast album: Decca

UPS-A-DAISY
October 8, 1928 (40 perfs)
Music by Lewis E. Gensler
Lyrics by Robert A. Simon
  Ups-A-Daisy
  Great Little Guy
  Oh, How Happy We'll Be (Lyrics by
    Robert A. Simon and Clifford
    Grey)
  I've Got a Baby
  Tell Me Who You Are
  Will You Remember? Will You For-
    get? (Lyrics by Robert A. Simon
    and Clifford Grey)
  Oh, How I Miss You Blues (Lyrics by
    Robert A. Simon and Clifford
    Grey)
  Sweet One
  Sweetest of the Roses
  Hot
  I Can't Believe It's True*

UTOPIA! (OB)
May 6, 1963 (11 perfs)
Music and lyrics by William Klenosky
  Why Are We Here?
  The Ballad of Utopia
  April in Siberia
  We've Got a Feeling in Our Bones
  You've Got the Devil in Your Eyes
  I Work for Pravda
  The Tax Collector's Soliloquy
  You Gotta Have a Destination
  The National Anthem of Utopia
  The Masses Are Asses
  What Am I Hangin' Around For?
  I Can't Pretend
  All You Need Is a Little Love

VAGABOND KING, THE†
September 21, 1925 (511 perfs)
Music by Rudolf Friml
Lyrics by Brian Hooker

Love for Sale
Drinking Song
Song of the Vagabonds
Some Day
Only a Rose
Hunting
Scotch Archer's Song
Tomorrow
Nocturne
Serenade
Huguette Waltz
Love Me Tonight
Album (Studio Cast): Decca
Vocal Score
Vocal selection
Written for 1930 film version:
  If I Were King (Music and lyrics by
    Newell Chase, Leo Robin, and
    Sam Coslow)
Written for 1956 film version:
Music by Rudolf Friml; lyrics by
Johnny Burke
  This Same Heart
  Vive la You
  Bon Jour

VALMOUTH** (OB)
October 6, 1960 (14 perfs)
Music and lyrics by Sandy Wilson
  Valmouth
  Magic Fingers
  Mustapha
  I Loved a Man
  All the Girls Were Pretty
  What Do I Want with Love?
  Just Once More
  Lady of the Manor
  Big Best Shoes
  Niri-Esther
  Cry of the Peacock
  Little Girl Baby
  The Cathedral of Clemenza
  Only a Passing Phase
  Where the Trees Are Green with
    Parrots
  My Talking Day

---

*Dropped from New York production
†Based on play *If I Were King* by Justin
Huntly McCarthy
**Based on the novel by Ronald Firbank

I Will Miss You
Pinpipi's Sob of Love
Cast album: PYE

VAMP, THE
November 10, 1955 (60 perfs)
Music by James Mundy
Lyrics by John Latouche
  The Spiel
  The Flickers
  Keep Your Nose to the Grindstone
  That's Where a Man Fits In
  I've Always Loved You
  You're Colossal
  Fan Club Chant
  Have You Met Delilah?
  Yeemy Yeemy
  The Vamps
  Four Little Misfits
  Samson and Delilah
  Why Does It Have to Be You?
  Ragtime Romeo
  I'm Everybody's Baby
  The Impossible She

VANDERBILT REVUE, THE
November 5, 1930 (13 perfs)
Music by Jimmy McHugh
Lyrics by Dorothy Fields
  Button Up Your Heart
  Cut In
  Blue Again
  Ex-Gigolo (Music by Mario Braggi-
    otti; lyrics by E. Y. Harburg)
  Then Came the War (Music and lyr-
    ics by Ben Black)
  I'm from Granada (Music by Mario
    Braggiotti; lyrics by David Sid-
    ney)
  What's My Man Gonna Be Like?
    (Music and lyrics by Cole Porter)
  Better Not Try It (Music and lyrics
    by Michael H. Cleary, Herb Mag-
    idson, and Ned Washington)
  I Give Myself Away (Music by
    Jacques Fray; lyrics by Edward
    Eliscu)
  You're the Better Half of Me
  Half Way to Heaven (Music by
    Mario Braggiotti; lyrics by David
    Sidney)

VERY WARM FOR MAY
November 17, 1939 (59 perfs)
Music by Jerome Kern
Lyrics by Oscar Hammerstein II
  All the Things You Are
  Heaven in My Arms (Music in My
    Heart)
  That Lucky Fellow
  In the Heart of the Dark
  All in Fun
  In Other Words, Seventeen

VINTAGE '60 (OB)
September 12, 1960 (8 perfs)
  The Time Is Now (Music by Mark
    Bucci; lyrics by David Rogers)
  All American (Music by David
    Baker; lyrics by Sheldon Harnick)
  Down in the Streets (Music and lyr-
    ics by Tommy Garlock and Alan
    Jeffreys)
  Do It in Two (Music and lyrics by
    Jack Wilson and Alan Jeffreys)
  Dublin Town (Music and lyrics by
    Fred Ebb, Paul Klein, and Lee
    Goldsmith)
  Forget Me (Music by David Baker;
    lyrics by Sheldon Harnick)
  Afraid of Love (Music and lyrics
    by Alice Clark and David
    Morton)

VIRGINIA
September 2, 1937 (60 perfs)
Music by Arthur Schwartz
Lyrics by Albert Stillman
  Virginia
  We Had to Rehearse
  An Old Flame Never Dies (Lyrics
    by Albert Stillman and Laurence
    Stallings)
  Send One Angel Down
  My Bridal Gown (Lyrics by Albert
    Stillman and Laurence Stallings)
  Good and Lucky
  It's Our Duty to the King
  If You Were Someone Else
  Goodbye, Jonah
  My Heart Is Dancing
  Meet Me at the Fair
  You and I Know (Lyrics by Albert
    Stillman and Laurence Stallings)

Fee-Fie-Fo-Fum
I'll Be Sittin' in de Lap o' de
   Lord

VIVA O'BRIEN
October 9, 1941 (20 perfs)
Music by Maria Grever
Lyrics by Raymond Leveen
   Mozambamba
   Don José O'Brien
   Mood of the Moment
   Mexican Bad Men
   Carinito
   Broken-Hearted Romeo
   Wrap Me in Your Serape
   Yucatana
   Our Song
   El Matador Terrifico
   How Long?
   To Prove My Love

WAKE UP AND DREAM
December 30, 1929 (136 perfs)
Music and lyrics by Cole Porter
   Wake Up and Dream
   She's Such a Comfort to Me (Music
      by Arthur Schwartz; lyrics by
      Douglas Furber, Max and Na-
      thaniel Lief, and Donovan Par-
      sons)
   I Loved Him but He Didn't Love
      Me
   More Incredible Happenings (Mu-
      sic and lyrics by Ronald Jeans)
   Fancy Our Meeting (Music by Jo-
      seph Meyer and Philip Charig;
      lyrics by Douglas Furber)
   The Banjo That Man Joe Plays
   I'm a Gigolo
   Agua Sincopada
   Looking at You
   What Is This Thing Called Love?
   I Dream of a Girl in a Shawl
   I Want to Be Raided by You
   Why Wouldn't I Do? (Music by Ivor
      Novello; lyrics by Ivor Novello
      and Desmond Carter)

WALK A LITTLE FASTER
December 7, 1932 (119 perfs)
Music by Vernon Duke
Lyrics by E. Y. Harburg

That's Life
Unaccustomed As I Am
Off Again, On Again
April in Paris
A Penny for Your Thoughts
Where Have We Met Before?
Frisco Fanny (Music by Henry Sul-
   livan; lyrics by Earl Crooker)
So Nonchalant
Time and Tide
Mayfair (Music by William Waliter;
   lyrics by Rowland Leigh)
Speaking of Love
End of a Perfect Night

WALK DOWN MAH STREET! (OB)
June 12, 1968 (135 perfs)
Music by Norman Curtis
Lyrics by Patricia Taylor Curtis
   We're Today
   Walk Down My Street
   If You Want to Get Ahead
   Just One More Time
   I'm Just a Statistic
   Someday, If We Grow Up
   What Shadows We Are
   Want to Get Retarded?
   Teeny Bopper
   Flower Child
   For Four Hundred Years
   Don't Have to Take It Any More
   Lonely Girl
   Clean Up Your Own Backyard
   Walk, Lordy, Walk

WALK WITH MUSIC
June 4, 1940 (55 perfs)
Music by Hoagy Carmichael
Lyrics by Johnny Mercer
   Greetings, Gates
   Today I Am a Glamour Girl
   Even If I Say It Myself
   I Walk with Music
   Ooh! What You Said
   Everything Happens to Me
   Wait Till You See Me in the Morn-
      ing
   Break It Up, Cinderella
   Smile for the Press
   Friend of the Family
   Way Back in 1939 A.D.
   How Nice for Me

The Rhumba Jumps
What'll They Think of Next?

WALKING HAPPY*
November 26, 1966 (161 perfs)
Music by Jimmy Van Heusen
Lyrics by Sammy Cahn
    Think of Something Else
    Where Was I
    How D'ya Talk to A Girl
    Clog and Grog
    If I Be Your Best Chance
    A Joyful Thing
    What Makes It Happen
    Use Your Noggin
    You're Right, You're Right
    I'll Make a Man of the Man
    Walking Happy
    I Don't Think I'm in Love
    Such a Sociable Sort
    It Might As Well Be Her
    People Who Are Nice
Cast album: Capitol
Vocal selection

WELL OF ROMANCE, THE
November 7, 1930 (8 perfs)
Music by H. Maurice Jacquet
Lyrics by Preston Sturges
    At Lovetime
    The Well of Romance
    Be Oh So Careful, Ann
    Hail the King
    Dream of Dreams
    Since You're Alone
    How Can You Tell?
    I'll Never Complain
    Fare Thee Well
    One Night
    Rhapsody of Love
    For You and for Me
    Serenade

WE'RE CIVILIZED? (OB)
November 8, 1962 (22 perfs)
Music by Ray Haney
Lyrics by Alfred Aiken
    Brewing the Love Potion
    Too Old
    J. B. Pictures, Inc
    Everything Is Wonderful
    Me Atahualpa

No Place to Go
Lullaby Wind
I Like
You Can Hang Your Hat Here
You're Like
Witch Song
Mother Nature
Bad If He Does, Worse If He Don't
Muted
Yankee Stay
We're Civilized

WEST SIDE STORY
September 26, 1957 (732 perfs; return
    engagement 249 perfs)
Music by Leonard Bernstein
Lyrics by Stephen Sondheim
    Prologue
    Jet Song
    Something's Coming
    Maria
    Tonight
    America
    Cool
    One Hand, One Heart
    Tonight
    I Feel Pretty
    Somewhere
    Gee, Officer Krupke!
    A Boy Like That
    I Have a Love
Cast album: Columbia
Vocal score
Vocal selection

WET PAINT (OB)
April 12, 1965 (16 perfs)
    Concert Encore (Music and lyrics
        by Sheldon Harnick)
    Neville (Music and lyrics by Tony
        Geiss)
    Cantata (Music by Gerald Alters;
        lyrics by Herbert Hartig)
    Cream in My Coffee (Music by Ed
        Scott; lyrics by Anne Croswell)
    Love Affair (Music by Bob Kessler;
        lyrics by Martin Charnin)
    Unrequited Love March (Music and

---

*Based on Harold Brighouse's play *Hobson's Choice*

lyrics by Ronny Graham)
Puns (Music by Gerald Alters; lyrics by Herbert Hartig)
I Know He'll Understand (Music and lyrics by Johnny Myers)
Canary (Music by Stan Davis; lyrics by Giles O'Connor)
Showstopper (Music and lyrics by Johnny Myers)
These Things I Know Are True (Music and lyrics by Jennifer Konecky)

WHAT A KILLING (OB)
March 27, 1961 (1 perf)
Music and lyrics by George Harwell
  The Chicago That I Know
  The Customer Is Always Right
  Troubled Lady
  Look at What It's Done
  I'm a Positive Guy
  Out of Luck with Luck
  Laughing Out Loud
  Here I Come
  Nobody Cheats Big Mike
  Fools Come and Fools Go
  The Race
  A Rag, a Bone, a Hank of Hair
  Face the Facts
  Oh, How I Love You
  Price in My Work
  Lennie
  What a Killing

WHAT MAKES SAMMY RUN?*
February 27, 1964 (540 perfs)
Music and lyrics by Ervin Drake
  A New Pair of Shoes
  You Help Me
  A Tender Spot
  Lites—Camera—Platitude
  My Hometown
  Monsoon
  I See Something
  Maybe Some Other Time
  You Can Trust Me
  A Room without Windows
  Kiss Me No Kisses
  I Feel Humble
  Something to Live For
  Paint a Rainbow

You're No Good
The Friendliest Thing
Wedding of the Year
Some Days Everything Goes Wrong
Cast album: Columbia

WHAT'S UP?
November 11, 1943 (63 perfs)
Music by Frederick Loewe
Lyrics by Alan Jay Lerner
  Miss Langley's School for Girls
  From the Chimney to the Cellar
  You've Got a Hold on Me
  A Girl Is Like a Book
  Joshua
  Three Girls in a Boat
  How Fly Times
  My Last Love
  You Wash and I'll Dry
  The Ill-Tempered Clavichord

WHEN YOU SMILE
October 25, 1925 (49 perfs)
Music by Tom Johnstone
Lyrics by Phil Cook
  Spanish Moon
  Naughty Eyes
  One Little Girl
  Let's Have a Good Time
  Gee, We Get Along
  When You Smile
  All Work and No Play
  Keep Them Guessing
  Keep Building Your Castles
  Let's Dance and Make Up
  Wonderful Rhythm
  June
  Oh, What a Girl
  Wonderful Yesterday
  Buy an Extra
  She Loves Me

WHERE'S CHARLEY?†
October 11, 1948 (792 perfs)
Music and lyrics by Frank Loesser
  The Years Before Us
  Better Get Out of Here

---

*Based on the novel by Budd Schulberg
†Based on the play *Charley's Aunt* by Brandon Thomas

The New Ashmolean Marching So-
ciety and Students' Conservatory
Band
My Darling, My Darling
Make a Miracle
Serenade with Asides
Lovelier Than Ever
The Woman in His Room
Pernambuco
Where's Charley?
Once in Love with Amy
The Gossips
At the Red Rose Cotillion
British cast album: Monmouth-Ever-
green
Vocal score
Vocal selection

WHISPERS ON THE WIND (OB)
June 3, 1970 (9 perfs)
Music by Lor Crane
Lyrics by John B. Kuntz
Whispers on the Wind
Welcome, Little One
Midwestern Summer
Why and Because
Children's Games
Miss Cadwallader
Upstairs-Downstairs
Strawberries
Is There a City?
Carmen Viscenzo
Neighbors
Apples and Raisins
Things Are Going Nicely
It Won't Be Long
Prove I'm Really Here

WHITE EAGLE, THE*
December 26, 1927 (48 perfs)
Music by Rudolf Friml
Lyrics by Brian Hooker
Dance, Dance, Dance
Regimental Song
Alone (My Lover)
Gather the Rose
Bad Man Number
Give Me One Hour
Winona
Smile, Darn You, Smile
My Heaven with You

Indian Lullaby
A Home for You

WHITE HORSE INN
October 1, 1936 (223 perfs)
Music by Ralph Benatzky
Lyrics by Irving Caesar
Arrival of Tourists
Leave It to Katarina (Music by Jara
Benes)
I Cannot Live without Your Love
White Horse Inn
Blue Eyes (Music by Robert Stolz)
Market Day in the Village
Goodbye, Au Revoir, Auf Wieder-
sehn† (Music by Eric Coates)
High Up on the Hills
I Would Love to Have You Love Me
(Music by Irving Caesar, Sammy
Lerner, and Gerald Marks)
Welcome on the Landing Stage
In a Little Swiss Chalet (Music by
Will Irwin; lyrics by Norman
Zeno)
Serenade to the Emperor
We Prize Most the Things We Miss
The Waltz of Love (Music by Rich-
ard Fall)
Album: (Studio cast) Angel

WHITE LILACS
September 10, 1928 (138 perfs)
Music by Karl Hajos (based on Chopin)
Lyrics by Harry B. Smith
The Music Call
Adorable You
Words, Music, Cash
I Love Love
White Lilacs
Far Away and Long Ago
Star in the Twilight
Melodies within My Heart
Know When to Smile
Castle of Love
I Love You and I Adore You

---

*Based on the play *The Squaw Man* by Ed-
win Milton Royle
†Adapted from Coates' *Knightsbridge
March*

WHITE LIGHTS
October 11, 1927 (31 perfs)
Music by J. Fred Coots
Lyrics by Al Dubin
  Some Other Day
  Tappin' the Toe
  Deceiving Blue Bird
  Don't Throw Me Down
  White Lights
  I'll Keep On Dreaming of You
  Eyeful of You
  Sitting in the Sun
  Better Times Are Coming (Music by
    Jimmie Steiger; lyrics by Dolph
    Singer)

WHO CARES?
July 8, 1930 (32 perfs)
Music by Percy Wenrich
Lyrics by Harry Clarke
  Believe It or Not
  Tennis
  Dance of the Fan
  Who Cares?
  Broadway
  Sunup
  Dixieland
  The Hunt

WHOOPEE*
December 4, 1928 (379 perfs)
Music by Walter Donaldson
Lyrics by Gus Kahn
  It's a Beautiful Day Today
  Here's to the Girl of My Heart
  I'm Bringing a Red, Red Rose
  Gypsy Joe
  Makin' Whoopee
  Go Get 'Im
  Until You Get Somebody Else
  Taps
  Come West, Little Girl, Come
    West
  Love Me or Leave Me
  Song of the Setting Sun
  Stetson
  Hallowe'en Whoopee Ball

WHOOP-UP†
December 22, 1958 (56 perfs)
Music by Moose Charlap
Lyrics by Norman Gimbel

  Glenda's Place
  When the Tall Man Talks
  Nobody Throw Those Bull
  Love Eyes
  Men
  Never Before
  Caress Me, Possess Me, Perfume
  Flattery
  The Girl in His Arms
  The Best of What the Country's Got
  I Wash My Hands
  Quarrel-tet
  Sorry for Myself
  Til the Big Fat Moon Falls Down
  What I Mean to Say
  Montana
  She or Her
Cast album: MGM

WHO'S WHO
March 1, 1938 (23 perfs)
  Who's Who (Music by Baldwin
    Bergersen; lyrics by June Sillman)
  Skiing at Saks (Music and lyrics by
    Irvin Graham)
  Croupier (Music by Baldwin Berg-
    ersen; lyrics by June Sillman)
  Rinka Tinka Man (Music by Lew
    Kesler; lyrics by June Sillman)
  Sunday Morning in June (Music by
    Paul McGrane; lyrics by Neville
    Fleeson)
  I Dance Alone (Music and lyrics by
    James Shelton)
  I Must Waltz (Music by Baldwin
    Bergersen; lyrics by Irvin Gra-
    ham)
  Dusky Debutante (Music by Bald-
    win Bergersen; lyrics by June Sill-
    man)
  The Girl with the Paint on Her Face
    (Music and lyrics by Irvin Gra-
    ham)
  Train Time (Music by Baldwin
    Bergersen; lyrics by June Sillman)
  I Must Have a Dinner Coat (Music

*Based on the play *The Nervous Wreck* by
Owen Davis
†Based on *Stay Away, Joe* by Dan Cush-
man

and lyrics by James Shelton)
It's You I Want (Music by Paul McGrane; lyrics by Al Stillman)
Let Your Hair Down with a Bang (Music by Baldwin Bergersen; lyrics by June Sillman)

WHO'S WHO, BABY? (OB)
January 29, 1968 (16 perfs)
Music and lyrics by Johnny Brandon
Island of Happiness
That'll Be the Day
Come-Along-a-Me, Babe
Nothin's Gonna Change
There Aren't Many Ladies in the Mile End Road
Syncopatin'
Voodoo
How Do You Stop Loving Someone?
Drums
Feminine-inity
That's What's Happening, Baby
Me
Nobody to Cry To

WILD AND WONDERFUL
December 7, 1971 (1 perf)
Music and lyrics by Bob Goodman
Wild and Wonderful
My First Moment
I Spy
Desmond's Dilemma
The Moment Is Now
Something Wonderful Can Happen
Chances
Jenny
Fallen Angels
Petty Crime
Come a Little Closer
Is This My Town?
You Can Reach the Sun
A Different Kind of World
Wait for Me

WILD ROSE, THE
October 20, 1926 (61 perfs)
Music by Rudolf Friml
Lyrics by Otto Harbach and Oscar Hammerstein II
Riviera
Lovely Lady

Brown Eyes
Love Me, Don't You?
It Was Fate
The Wild Rose
Lady of the Rose
One Golden Hour
Our Little Kingdom
Won't You Come Across?
The Coronation

WILDCAT
December 16, 1960 (172 perfs)
Music by Cy Coleman
Lyrics by Carolyn Leigh
I Hear
Hey, Look Me Over
Wildcat
You've Come Home
That's What I Want for Janie
What Takes My Fancy
You're a Liar
One Day We Dance
Give a Little Whistle
Tall Hope
Tippy Tippy Toes
El Sombrero
Corduroy Road
Cast album: RCA
Vocal score
Vocal selection

WILL THE MAIL TRAIN RUN TO-NIGHT? (OB)
January 9, 1964 (8 perfs)
Music by Alyn Heim
Lyrics by Malcolm L. LaPrade
So Much to Be Thankful For
Dearer to Me
Nature's Serenade
Honeymoon Choo-choo
Hickory, Dickory
Comes the Dawn
Paper Matches
To Dream or Not to Dream
Prudence, Have Faith
Villainy
Three Cowards Craven
Vengeance
This Decadent Age
Heroism
A Slip of a Girl
Remember Him

I'll Walk Alone
The Fall of Valor
Age of Miracles
Bitter Tears
No Sacrifice

WINGED VICTORY
November 20, 1943 (212 perfs)
Music and lyrics by David Rose
  My Dream Book of Memories
  Winged Victory
  You're So Nice to Remember*

WISH YOU WERE HERE†
June 25, 1952 (598 perfs)
Music and lyrics by Harold Rome
  Camp Karefree
  There's Nothing Nicer Than People
  Social Director
  Shopping Around
  Bright College Days
  Mix and Mingle
  Could Be
  Tripping the Light Fantastic
  Where Did the Night Go?
  Certain Individuals
  They Won't Know Me
  Summer Afternoon
  Don José of Far Rockaway
  Everybody Loves Somebody
  Wish You Were Here
  Relax
  Flattery
  Glimpse of Love*
Cast album: RCA
Vocal score
Vocal selection

WONDER BAR, THE
March 17, 1931 (86 perfs)
Music by Robert Katscher
Lyrics by Irving Caesar
  Good Evening, Friends
  I'm Falling in Love
  Elizabeth
  Ma Mère (Music by Harry Warren;
    lyrics by Al Jolson and Irving Cae-
    sar)
  Oh, Donna Clara (Music by J. Pe-
    tersburski)
  Something Seems to Tell Me

WONDERFUL TOWN**
February 25, 1953 (559 perfs)
Music by Leonard Bernstein
Lyrics by Betty Comden and Adolph
Green
  Christopher Street
  Ohio
  One Hundred Easy Ways
  What a Waste
  A Little Bit in Love
  Pass the Football
  Conversation Piece
  A Quiet Girl
  Conga!
  My Darlin' Eileen
  Swing!
  It's Love
  Wrong Note Rag
Cast album: Decca

WOOF, WOOF
December 25, 1929 (45 perfs)
Music and lyrics by Edward Pola and
Eddie Brandt
  I Like It
  I'll Take Care of You
  That Certain Thing
  I Mean What I Say
  You're All the World to Me
  A Girl Like You
  Fair Weather
  Shh!
  Satanic Strut
  Topple Down
  Won't I Do?
  Why Didn't You Tell Me
  Lay Your Bets

YEAH MAN
May 26, 1932 (2 perfs)
Music and lyrics by Al Wilson, Charles
Weinberg, and Ken Macomber
  Mississippi Joys

---

*Dropped from New York production
†Based on the play *Having Wonderful
Time* by Arthur Kober
**Based on the play *My Sister Eileen* by
Joseph Fields and Jerome Chodorov and
the stories by Ruth McKenney.

Gotta Get de Boat Loaded
Dancing Fool
That's Religion (Music and lyrics by Porter Grainger)
At the Barbecue
I'm Always Happy When I'm in Your Arms
I've Got What It Takes
Crazy Idea of Love
Qualifications (Music and lyrics by Porter Grainger)
Come to Harlem
The Spell of Those Harlem Nights
Baby, I Could Do It for You
Shady Dan
Give Me Your Love
Shake Your Music

YEARLING, THE*
December 10, 1965 (3 perfs)
Music by Michael Leonard
Lyrics by Herbert Martin
Let Him Kick Up His Heels
Boy Talk
Bear Hunt
Some Day I'm Gonna Fly
Lonely Clearing
Everything in the World I Love
I'm All Smiles
The Kind of Man a Woman Needs
What a Happy Day
Ain't He a Joy?
Why Did I Choose You?
One Promise
Nothing More
Everything Beautiful
Vocal selection

YES, YES, YVETTE
October 3, 1927 (40 perfs)
Pack Up Your Blues and Smile (Music by Peter de Rose and Albert Von Tilzer; lyrics by Jo Trent)
My Lady (Music and lyrics by Frank Crumit and Ben Jerome)
Yes, Yes, Yvette (Music by Philip Charig; lyrics by Irving Caesar)
How'd You Like To (Music by Stephen Jones; lyrics by Irving Caesar)
Six O'Clock (Music by Philip Charig; lyrics by Irving Caesar)

Sing, Dance and Smile (Music by Philip Charig; lyrics by Ben Jerome)
Do You Love as I Love? (Music by Joseph Meyer; lyrics by Irving Caesar)
You, or Nobody! (Music and lyrics by Irving Caesar)

YOKEL BOY
July 6, 1939 (208 perfs)
Music by Sam Stept
Lyrics by Lew Brown and Charles Tobias
A Boy Named Lem
I Know I'm Nobody
For the Sake of Lexington
Comes Love
It's Me Again
Let's Make Memories Tonight
Time for Jukin' (Music by Walter Kent)
Uncle Sam's Lullaby
Hollywood and Vine
Catherine the Great
The Ship Has Sailed
I Can't Afford to Dream

YOU NEVER KNOW†
September 21, 1938 (78 perfs)
Music and lyrics by Cole Porter
I Am Gaston
Au Revoir, Cher Baron
By Candlelight (Music by Robert Katscher; lyrics by Rowland Leigh)
Maria
You Never Know
Ladies Room (Music by Alex Fogarty; lyrics by Edwin Gilbert)
What Is That Tune?
For No Rhyme or Reason
From Alpha to Omega
Don't Let It Get You Down
What Shall I Do? (Lyrics by Rowland Leigh)

---

*Based on the novel by Marjorie Kinnan Rawlings
†Based on play *Candle Light* by Siegfried Geyer

Let's Put It to Music (Music by Alex Fogarty and Edwin Gilbert)
At Long Last Love
Take Yourself a Trip (Music by Alex Fogarty; lyrics by Edwin Gilbert)
Yes, Yes, Yes
Gendarme (Music by Robert Katscher; lyrics by Rowland Leigh)
No (You Can't Have My Heart) (Music and lyrics by Dana Suesse)
Good Evening, Princess

YOU SAID IT
January 19, 1931 (192 perfs)
Music by Harold Arlen
Lyrics by Jack Yellen
Wha'd You Come to College For?
You Said It
They Learn About Women from Me
While You Are Young
It's Different with Me
Learn to Croon
Sweet and Hot
If He Really Loves Me
What Do We Care?
You'll Do

YOU'LL SEE STARS
December 29, 1942 (4 perfs)
Music by Leo Edwards
Lyrics by Herman Timberg
Future Stars
Time and Time Again
All You Have to Do Is Stand There
Dancing on a Rainbow
Betcha I Make Good
What a Pretty Baby You Are
Readin', Writin' and Rythmatic

YOUNG ABE LINCOLN
April 25, 1961 (27 perfs)
Music by Victor Ziskin
Lyrics by Joan Javits
The Same Old Me
Cheer Up!
You Can Dance
Someone You Know
I Want to Be a Little Frog in a Little Pond
Don't P-P-Point Them Guns at Me
The Captain Lincoln March

Run, Indian, Run
Welcome Home Again
Vote for Lincoln
Frontier Politics
Cast album: Golden

YOUR OWN THING* (OB)
January 13, 1968 (937) perfs)
Music and lyrics by Hal Hester and Danny Apolinar
No One's Perfect, Dear
The Flowers
I'm Me! (I'm Not Afraid)
Baby! Baby!
Come Away, Death
I'm On My Way to the Top
She Never Told Her Love
Be Gentle
What Do I Know?
The Now Generation
The Middle Years
When You're Young and in Love
Hunca Munca
Don't Leave Me
Do Your Own Thing
Cast album: RCA
Vocal selection

YOU'RE A GOOD MAN, CHARLIE BROWN† (OB)
March 7, 1967 (1,597 perfs)
Music and lyrics by Clark Gesner
You're a Good Man, Charlie Brown
Schroeder
Snoopy
My Blanket and Me
Kite
Dr. Lucy (The Doctor Is In)
Book Report
The Red Baron
T. E. A. M. (The Baseball Game)
Little Known Facts
Suppertime
Happiness
Cast album: MGM
Vocal selection

---

*Suggested by William Shakespeare's *Twelfth Night*
†Based on the comic strip *Peanuts* by Charles M. Schulz

YOURS IS MY HEART*
September 5, 1946 (36 perfs)
Music by Franz Lehár
Lyrics by Harry Graham
  Goodbye, Paree
  Free As the Air
  Chinese Melody
  Patiently Smiling
  A Cup of China Tea
  Upon a Moonlight Night in
    May
  Love, What Has Given You
    This Magic Power?
  Men of China
  Chingo-Pingo
  Yours Is My Heart Alone
  Paris Sings Again (Music by Paul
    Durand)
  Ma Petite Chérie

YOURS TRULY
January 25, 1927 (127 perfs)
Music by Raymond Hubbell
Lyrics by Anne Caldwell
  Follow the Guide
  Mayfair
  Shuffling Bill
  Look at the World and Smile
  Somebody Else
  The Gunman
  Lotus Flower
  Quit Kiddin'
  Mary Has a Little Fair
  Don' Shake My Tree
  I Want a Pal
  Dawn of Dreams

ZIEGFELD FOLLIES (1927)
August 16, 1927 (168 perfs)
Music and lyrics by Irving Berlin
  Ribbons and Bows
  Shaking the Blues Away
  Ooh, Maybe It's You
  Rainbow of Girls
  It All Belongs to Me
  It's Up to the Band
  Jimmy
  Learn to Sing a Love
    Song
  Tickling the Ivories
  Jungle Jingle

ZIEGFELD FOLLIES (1931)
July 1, 1931 (165 perfs)
  Bring On the Follies Girls (
    Dave Stamper; lyrics l
    Buck)
  Help Yourself to Happine
    by Harry Revel; lyrics l
    Richman and Mack Gor
  Sunny Southern Smile (N
    Harry Revel; lyrics by M
    don)
  Half-Caste Woman (Music
    ics by Noël Coward)
  Broadway Reverie (Music
    Stamper; lyrics by Gene
  Was I? (Music by Chick Ei
    ics by Charles Farrell)
  Cigarettes, Cigars! (Music l
    Revel; lyrics by Mack G
  Do the New York (Music
    Oakland; lyrics by Jack
    and Barry Trivers)
  Mailu (Music by Jay Gorn
    by E. Y. Harburg)
  Changing of the Guards (l
    Ben Oakland; lyrics by J
    ray and Barry Trivers)
  Here We Are in Love (Mus
    Oakland; lyrics by Jack
    and Barry Trivers)
  Wrapped Up in You (Musi
    Oakland; lyrics by Jack
    and Barry Trivers)

ZIEGFELD FOLLIES (1934)
January 4, 1934 (182 perfs)
Music by Vernon Duke
Lyrics by E. Y. Harburg
  Smart to Be Smart
  That's Where We Come I
    by Samuel Pokrass)
  Soul Saving Sadie (Music b
    Meyer; lyrics by Billy l
    Ballard MacDonald)
  Water Under the Bridge
  Barefoot Boy (Music by J
    Hanley; lyrics by Chris 1
  I Like the Likes of You
  What Is There to Say?

———
*Also known as *The Land of Sm*

To the Beat of My Heart (Music by Samuel Pokrass)

Countess Dubinsky (Music by Joseph Meyer; lyrics by Billy Rose and Ballard MacDonald)

Suddenly (Lyrics by E. Y. Harburg and Billy Rose)

Moon About Town (Music by Dana Suesse)

This Is Not a Song (Lyrics by E. Y. Harburg and E. Hartman)

ZIEGFELD FOLLIES (1936)
January 30, 1936 (227 perfs.)
Music by Vernon Duke
Lyrics by Ira Gershwin
Time Marches On!
He Hasn't a Thing Except Me
My Red-Letter Day
Island in the West Indies
Words Without Music
The Economic Situation
Fancy, Fancy
Maharanee
The Gazooka
That Moment of Moments
Sentimental Weather
Five A.M.
I Can't Get Started
Modernistic Moe
Dancing to Our Score (Lyrics by Ira Gershwin and Billy Rose)

ZIEGFELD FOLLIES (1943)
April 14, 1943 (553 perfs)
Music by Ray Henderson
Lyrics by Jack Yellen
Thirty-Five Summers Ago
This Is It
Love Songs Are Made in the Night
Come Up and Have a Cup of Coffee
The Saga of Carmen
Swing Your Lady, Mr. Hemingway
Back to the Farm (Music and lyrics by Bud Burtson)
Hindu Serenade
The Micromaniac (Music and lyrics by Harold Rome)
Hold That Smile

ZIEGFELD FOLLIES (1957)
March 1, 1957 (123 perfs)
Bring On the Girls (Music and lyrics by Richard Myers and Jack Lawrence)
If You Got Music (Music by Colin Romoff; lyrics by David Rogers)
Mangoes (Music and lyrics by Dee Libbey and Sid Wayne)
I Don't Wanna Rock (Music by Colin Romoff; lyrics by David Rogers)
Intoxication (Music by Dean Fuller; lyrics by Marshall Barer)
Music for Madame (Music and lyrics by Jack Lawrence and Richard Myers)
Two a Day on the Milky Way (Music by Dean Fuller; lyrics by Marshall Barer)
Salesmanship (Music by Philip Springer; lyrics by Carolyn Leigh)
Honorable Mambo (Music by Dean Fuller; lyrics by Marshall Barer)
The Lover in Me (Music by Philip Springer; lyrics by Carolyn Leigh)
Miss Follies of 192– (Music and lyrics by Herman Hupfeld)
Make Me (Music and lyrics by Tony Velone, Larry Spier, and Uhpio Minucci)
Element of Doubt, An (Music by Sammy Fain; lyrics by Howard Dietz)
My Late, Late Lady (Music by Dean Fuller; lyrics by Marshall Barer)
Miss Follies (Music by Colin Romoff; lyrics by David Rogers)

ZORBÁ*
November 17, 1968 (305 perfs)
Music by John Kander
Lyrics by Fred Ebb
Life Is
The First Time
The Top of the Hill
No Boom Boom
Vive la Différence

---

*Adapted from *Zorbá the Greek* by Nikos Kazantzakis

The Butterfly
Goodbye, Canavaro
Grandpapa
Only Love
Y'assou
Why Can't I Speak?
The Crow
Happy Birthday
I Am Free
Cast album: Capitol
Vocal selection

ZULU AND THE ZAYDA, THE*
November 10, 1965 (179 perfs)
Music and lyrics by Harold Rome

Tkambuza
Crocodile Wife
Good to Be Alive
The Water Wears Down the Stone
Rivers of Tears
Like the Breeze Blows
Oisgetzaychnet
Some Things
Zulu Love Song
L'Chayim
Cold, Cold Room
Cast album: Columbia
Vocal selection

_____

*Based on a story by Dan Jacobson

Chronological List of Productions

Chronological List of Productions

1925
Big Boy
The Love Song
China Rose
Puzzles of 1925
Natja
Sky High
Louie the 14th
Bringing up Father
Tell Me More
Mercenary Mary
The Garrick Gaieties
Lucky Sambo
Kosher Kitty Kelly
George White's Scandals
Artists and Models
Earl Carroll's Vanities
June Days
Gay Paree
Smile at Me
Captain Jinks
No, No, Nanette
Dearest Enemy
The Vagabond King
Sunny
Merry-Merry
When You Smile
Holka-Polka
The City Chap
Princess Flavia
Florida Girl
Naughty Cinderella
Charlot's Revue
Mayflowers
Oh! Oh! Nurse
The Cocoanuts
The Greenwich Village Follies
Tip-Toes

1925 continued
By the Way
Song of the Flame

1926
A Night in Paris
Hello, Lola
Sweetheart Time
The Matinee Girl
Bunk of 1926
Rainbow Rose
The Girl Friend
Bad Habits of 1926 (OB)
Kitty's Kisses
The Garrick Gaieties (2nd ed.)
The Great Temptations
The Merry World
George White's Scandals
The Grand Street Follies of 1926 (OB)
No Foolin'
My Magnolia
The Blonde Sinner
Bare Facts of 1926
Americana
Nic-Nax of 1926
Earl Carroll's Vanities
Castles in the Air
Queen High
Naughty Riquette
Countess Maritza
The Ramblers
Honeymoon Lane
Happy Go Lucky
Deep River
Criss-Cross
Katja
The Wild Rose
Oh, Kay!
Gay Paree

1926 continued
Twinkle, Twinkle
The Desert Song
Oh, Please!
Peggy-Ann
Betsy

1927
The Nightingale
The Lace Petticoat
Piggy
Bye Bye, Bonnie
Yours Truly
Rio Rita
Judy
Polly of Hollywood
The New Yorkers
Lucky
Rufus Lemaire's Affairs
Cherry Blossoms
Lady Do
Hit the Deck
The Circus Princess
The Seventh Heart
A Night in Spain
Oh, Ernest!
The Grand Street Follies of 1927 (OB)
Tales of Rigo
Merry-Go-Round
Talk About Girls
Bottomland
Padlocks of 1927
Africana
Rang-Tang
Kiss Me
Allez-Oop
The Manhatters
Ziegfeld Follies
A la Carte
Footlights
Good News
Half a Widow
My Maryland
Enchanted Isle
The Merry Malones
Manhattan Mary
Sidewalks of New York
Yes, Yes, Yvette
My Princess
The Five O'Clock Girl
White Lights
Just Fancy

1927 continued
The Love Call
A Connecticut Yankee
Artists and Models
Funny Face
Take the Air
Harry Delmar's Revels
Golden Dawn
Happy
The White Eagle
Show Boat
Lovely Lady

1928
She's My Baby
Rosalie
The Optimists
The Madcap
Sunny Days
Rain or Shine
Parisiana
Keep Shufflin'
The Three Musketeers
The Greenwich Village Follies
Present Arms
Here's Howe
Blackbirds of 1928
The Grand Street Follies of 1928
Say When
George White's Scandals
Earl Carroll's Vanities
Good Boy
White Lilacs
Luckee Girl
Cross My Heart
The New Moon
Chee-Chee
Billie
Just a Minute
Paris
Ups-A-Daisy
Hold Everything!
Three Cheers
Animal Crackers
Americana (2nd ed.)
Hello, Yourself!
This Year of Grace
Treasure Girl
Rainbow
Angela
Whoopee
The Houseboat on the Styx

1928 continued
The Red Robe
Hello Daddy

1929
Deep Harlem
Polly
Follow Thru
Ned Wayburn's Gambols
Boom-Boom
Lady Fingers
Fioretta
Pleasure Bound
Spring is Here
Music in May
Messin' Around
The Little Show
The Grand Street Follies of 1929
Pansy
A Night in Venice
Keep It Clean
Bamboola
Hot Chocolates
Earl Carroll's Sketch Book
Show Girl
Broadway Nights
John Murray Anderson's Almanac
Sweet Adeline
The Street Singer
Cape Cod Follies
George White's Scandals
June Moon
Great Day!
Bitter Sweet
Heads Up!
Sons o' Guns
Fifty Million Frenchmen
The Silver Swan
Top Speed
Woof, Woof
Wake Up and Dream

1930
Strike Up the Band
Nine-Fifteen Revue
Ripples
Simple Simon
Lew Leslie's International Revue
Flying High
Jonica
Three Little Girls
The Garrick Gaieties (3rd ed.)

1930 continued
Change Your Luck
Artists and Models
Mystery Moon
Earl Carroll's Vanities
Who Cares?
Hot Rhythm
The Second Little Show
Luana
Nina Rosa
Fine and Dandy
Brown Buddies
Princess Charming
Girl Crazy
Three's a Crowd
Blackbirds of 1930
The Vanderbilt Revue
The Well of Romance
Hello, Paris
Sweet and Low
Smiles
The New Yorkers
Ballyhoo
Meet My Sister

1931
You Said It
Private Lives
America's Sweetheart
The Gang's All Here
The Wonder Bar
Rhapsody in Black
Crazy Quilt
The Third Little Show
The Band Wagon
Ziegfeld Follies
Shoot the Works
Earl Carroll's Vanities
Free for All
The Singing Rabbi
George White's Scandals
Fast and Furious
Singin' The Blues
Nikki
Everybody's Welcome
The Cat and the Fiddle
East Wind
The Laugh Parade
Here Goes the Bride
The Social Register
Sugar Hill
Of Thee I Sing

1932
A Little Racketeer
Through the Years
Face the Music
Marching By
Hot-Cha!
Blackberries of 1932
There You Are
Yeah Man
Hey Nonny Nonny!
Smiling Faces
Ballyhoo of '32
Flying Colors
Earl Carroll's Vanities
Americana (3rd ed.)
Tell Her the Truth
Music in the Air
The Dubarry
George White's Music Hall Varieties
Take a Chance
Gay Divorce
The Great Magoo
Walk a Little Faster
Shuffle Along of 1933

1933
Pardon My English
Melody
Strike Me Pink
Hummin' Sam
Tattle Tales
Shady Lady
Murder at the Vanities
Hold Your Horses
As Thousands Cheer
Let 'Em Eat Cake
Roberta
She Loves Me Not
Blackbirds of 1934

1934
Ziegfeld Follies
Come of Age
All The King's Horses
New Faces of 1934
Caviar
Keep Moving
Life Begins at 8:40
Saluta
The Great Waltz
Conversation Piece
Say When

1934 continued
Anything Goes
Revenge with Music
Calling All Stars
Fools Rush In
Thumbs Up!
The O'Flynn
Music Hath Charms

1935
Petticoat Fever
Something Gay
Parade
Earl Carroll's Sketch Book
Smile at Me
At Home Abroad
Porgy and Bess
Jubilee
Provincetown Follies (OB)
Jumbo
May Wine
George White's Scandals
Entre-Nous (OB)

1936
The Illustrators' Show
Ziegfeld Follies
Murder in the Old Red Barn (OB)
On Your Toes
Broadway Sho-Window
Summer Wives
New Faces of 1936
White Horse Inn
Red, Hot and Blue!
Forbidden Melody
Johnny Johnson
Tonight at 8:30
Black Rhythm
The Show Is On

1937
Naughty-Naught (OB)
Frederika
Babes in Arms
Orchids Preferred
Sea Legs
Swing It
Virginia
A Hero Is Born
The Fireman's Flame (OB)
I'd Rather Be Right
Pins and Needles (OB)

1937 continued
Hooray for What!
Between the Devil
Three Waltzes

1938
The Cradle Will Rock
Right This Way
Who's Who
I Married an Angel
The Two Bouquets
You Never Know
Hellzapoppin'
Sing Out the News
Knickerbocker Holiday
The Girl from Wyoming (OB)
Leave It to Me
The Boys from Syracuse
Great Lady

1939
Mamba's Daughters
Set to Music
One for the Money
Stars in Your Eyes
Sing for Your Supper
The Streets of Paris
Yokel Boy
George White's Scandals
The Straw Hat Revue
The Man Who Came to Dinner
Too Many Girls
Very Warm for May
Swingin' the Dream
Du Barry Was a Lady
Two for Tonight (OB)

1940
Earl Carroll's Vanities
Two for the Show
Higher and Higher
Keep off the Grass
Louisiana Purchase
Walk with Music
Hold On to Your Hats
Boys and Girls Together
Cabin in the Sky
Tis of Thee
Panama Hattie
Pal Joey
Meet the People
All in Fun

1941
Night of Love
Crazy with the Heat
Lady in the Dark
Best Foot Forward
Viva O'Brien
Let's Face It!
High Kickers
Sons o' Fun
Sunny River
Banjo Eyes

1942
The Lady Comes Across
Of V We Sing
By Jupiter
Star and Garter
This Is the Army
Count Me In
Beat the Band
New Faces of 1943
You'll See Stars

1943
Something for the Boys
Oklahoma!
Ziegfeld Follies
Early to Bed
My Dear Public
Bright Lights of 1944
Hairpin Harmony
One Touch of Venus
Artists and Models
What's Up
A Connecticut Yankee (revival)
Winged Victory
Carmen Jones

1944
Jackpot
Mexican Hayride
Follow the Girls
Allah Be Praised
Helen Goes to Troy
Dream with Music
Song of Norway
Bloomer Girl
Sadie Thompson
Seven Lively Arts
Laffing Room Only
On the Town

1945
A Lady Says Yes
Up in Central Park
The Firebrand of Florence
Carousel
Memphis Bound
Marinka
Mr. Strauss Goes to Boston
Carib Song
Polonaise
The Girl from Nantucket
Are You With It?
The Day Before Spring
Billion Dollar Baby

1946
Nellie Bly
Lute Song
The Duchess Misbehaves
Three to Make Ready
St. Louis Woman
Call Me Mister
Annie Get Your Gun
Around the World
Yours Is My Heart
Happy Birthday
Park Avenue
If the Shoe Fits
Beggar's Holiday
Toplitzky of Notre Dame

1947
Street Scene
Finian's Rainbow
Brigadoon
Barefoot Boy with Cheek
Louisiana Lady
Music in My Heart
Under the Counter
High Button Shoes
Allegro
Angel in the Wings

1948
Make Mine Manhattan
Look Ma, I'm Dancing!
Inside U.S.A.
Hold It!
Ballet Ballads
Sleepy Hollow
Small Wonder
Heaven on Earth

1948 continued
Magdalena
Love Life
Where's Charley?
My Romance
As the Girls Go
Lend an Ear
Kiss Me, Kate

1949
Along Fifth Avenue
All for Love
South Pacific
Miss Liberty
Touch and Go
Lost in the Stars
Regina
Texas, Li'l Darlin'
Gentlemen Prefer Blondes

1950
Happy As Larry
Alive and Kicking
Dance Me a Song
Arms and the Girl
Great to Be Alive
Peter Pan
Tickets Please
The Liar
Michael Todd's Peep Show
Pardon Our French
Call Me Madam
Guys and Dolls
Bless You All
Out of This World

1951
The King and I
Make a Wish
A Tree Grows in Brooklyn
Flahooley
Courtin' Time
Seventeen
Two on the Aisle
Top Banana
Paint Your Wagon

1952
Paris '90
Three Wishes for Jamie
Shuffle Along of 1952
New Faces of 1952

1952 continued
Wish You Were Here
Buttrio Square
My Darlin' Aïda
Two's Company

1953
Hazel Flagg
Maggie
Wonderful Town
Can-Can
Me and Juliet
Carnival in Flanders
Kismet
John Murray Anderson's Almanac

1954
The Girl in Pink Tights
The Threepenny Opera (OB)
By the Beautiful Sea
The Golden Apple
The Pajama Game
The Boy Friend
I Feel Wonderful (OB)
Peter Pan
Fanny
Sandhog (OB)
Mrs. Patterson
Hit the Trail
House of Flowers

1955
Plain and Fancy
Silk Stockings
Shoestring Revue (OB)
Ankles Aweigh
Phoenix '55 (OB)
Damn Yankees
Seventh Heaven
Catch a Star
The Vamp
Pipe Dream

1956
My Fair Lady
Mr. Wonderful
The Most Happy Fella
The Littlest Revue (OB)
Shangri-La
New Faces of 1956
By Hex (OB)
Shoestring Revue (OB)

1956 continued
Li'l Abner
Girls of Summer
Cranks
Bells Are Ringing
Candide
Happy Hunting

1957
Ziegfeld Follies
Shinbone Alley
Livin' the Life (OB)
New Girl in Town
Simply Heavenly
West Side Story
Copper and Brass
Jamaica
Rumple
Time Remembered
The Music Man

1958
The Body Beautiful
Oh Captain!
Portofino
Say, Darling
Goldilocks
Diversions (OB)
Salad Days (OB)
Flower Drum Song
Of Mice and Men (OB)
Whoop-Up

1959
She Shall Have Music (OB)
Redhead
Juno
First Impressions
Destry Rides Again
Once Upon a Mattress (OB)
The Nervous Set
Chic (OB)
Fallout (OB)
Gypsy
The Billy Barnes Revue
Happy Town
At the Drop of a Hat
Take Me Along
The Girls Against the Boys
The Sound of Music
Little Mary Sunshine (OB)

1959 continued
Fiorello!
Saratoga

1960
Parade (OB)
Beg, Borrow or Steal
The Crystal Heart (OB)
Russell Patterson's Sketch Book
    (OB)
Greenwillow
Miss Emily Adam (OB)
Bye Bye Birdie
From A to Z
Christine
The Fantasticks (OB)
Ernest in Love (OB)
Vintage '60 (OB)
Greenwich Village U.S.A. (OB)
Irma La Douce
Valmouth (OB)
Kittiwake Island (OB)
The Shoemaker and the Peddler
    (OB)
Tenderloin
Darwin's Theories (OB)
The Unsinkable Molly Brown
Camelot
Wildcat
Do Re Mi

1961
The Conquering Hero
Show Girl
The Tiger Rag (OB)
Double Entry (OB)
13 Daughters
What a Killing (OB)
The Happiest Girl in the World
The Tattooed Countess (OB)
Hobo (OB)
The Decameron (OB)
Carnival
Smiling, the Boy Fell Dead (OB)
Young Abe Lincoln
Donnybrook!
The Billy Barnes People
I Want You (OB)
Hi, Paisano! (OB)
The Sap of Life (OB)
Sail Away
Milk and Honey

1961 continued
Let It Ride!
How to Succeed in Business without
    Really Trying
Do You Know the Milky Way?
Kwamina
O Marry Me! (OB)
Kean
All in Love (OB)
Bella (OB)
The Gay Life
'Toinette (OB)
Sing Muse! (OB)
All Kinds of Giants (OB)
Subways Are for Sleeping
Madame Aphrodite (OB)

1962
Fortuna (OB)
The Banker's Daughter (OB)
A Family Affair
New Faces of 1962
Fly Blackbird (OB)
No Strings
All American
Pilgrim's Progress (OB)
I Can Get It for You Wholesale
Half-Past Wednesday (OB)
King of the Whole Damn World! (OB)
The Difficult Woman (OB)
A Funny Thing Happened on the Way
    to the Forum
Bravo Giovanni
Sweet Miani (OB)
Stop the World—I Want to Get Off
Come on Strong
O Say Can You See! (OB)
Mr. President
Old Bucks and New Wings (OB)
We're Civilized? (OB)
Nowhere to Go but Up
Little Me
Never Too Late
Riverwind (OB)

1963
Oliver!
Tovarich
Man in the Moon
Sophie
Hot Spot
She Loves Me

1963 continued
Utopia! (OB)
Put It in Writing (OB)
The Beast in Me
The Student Gypsy (OB)
Here's Love
Morning Sun (OB)
The Prince and the Pauper (OB)
Ballad for Bimshire (OB)
Jennie
110 in the Shade
The Streets of New York (OB)
The Girl Who Came to Supper
Stones of Jehoshaphat (OB)

1964
Pimpernel! (OB)
Will the Mail Train Run Tonight?
   (OB)
The Athenian Touch (OB)
Hello, Dolly!
The Amorous Flea (OB)
Rugantino
Jo! (OB)
Foxy
What Makes Sammy Run?
Cindy (OB)
Funny Girl
Anyone Can Whistle
High Spirits
Café Crown
Home Movies (OB)
Fade Out—Fade In
Fiddler on the Roof
That Hat! (OB)
Gogo Loves You (OB)
That 5 A.M. Jazz (OB)
Golden Boy
The Secret Life of Walter Mitty (OB)
Ben Franklin in Paris
Something More!
Bajour
I Had a Ball
Babes in the Wood (OB)

1965
Kelly
Baker Street
Do I Hear a Waltz?
Wet Paint (OB)
Half a Sixpence
Flora, the Red Menace

1965 continued
The Roar of the Greasepaint—The
   Smell of the Crowd
Pickwick
Mackey of Appalachia (OB)
Drat! The Cat!
On a Clear Day You Can See Forever
Hotel Passionato (OB)
The Zulu and the Zayda
Great Scot! (OB)
Skyscraper
Man of La Mancha
Anya
The Yearling
La Grosse Valise

1966
The Mad Show (OB)
Sweet Charity
Jonah (OB)
Pousse-Café
(It's a Bird, It's a Plane) It's Superman
A Time for Singing
Mame
My Wife and I (OB)
The Apple Tree
Autumn's Here (OB)
Man with a Load of Mischief (OB)
Cabaret
Walking Happy
I Do! I Do!
A Joyful Noise
The Penny Friend (OB)
At the Drop of Another Hat

1967
The Golden Screw (OB)
Shoemaker's Holiday (OB)
You're a Good Man, Charlie Brown
   (OB)
Sherry!
Illya Darling
People Is the Thing the World Is Full-
   est of (OB)
Hallelujah, Baby!
Now Is the Time for All Good Men
   (OB)
Henry, Sweet Henry
Curley McDimple (OB)
How Now, Dow Jones
How to Be a Jewish Mother

1968
Love and Let Love (OB)
Have I Got One for You (OB)
Your Own Thing (OB)
The Happy Time
Jacques Brel Is Alive and Well and
 Living in Paris (OB)
Who's Who, Baby? (OB)
Darling of the Day
Golden Rainbow
Here's Where I Belong
The Education of Hyman Kaplan
I'm Solomon
Hair
New Faces of 1968
George M!
The Believers (OB)
Walk Down Mah Street! (OB)
The Happy Hypocrite (OB)
Month of Sundays (OB)
How to Steal an Election (OB)
Just for Love (OB)
Her First Roman
Maggie Flynn
Zorbá
Up Eden (OB)
Promises, Promises
Ballad for a Firing Squad (OB)
God Is a (Guess What?) (OB)
Dames at Sea (OB)

1969
The Fig Leaves Are Falling
Horseman, Pass By (OB)
Celebration
Get Thee to Canterbury (OB)
Red, White and Maddox
Canterbury Tales
Dear World
Paradise Gardens East (OB)
1776
Come Summer
Billy (OB)
Promenade (OB)
Man Better Man (OB)
Salvation (OB)
Jimmy
Rondelay (OB)
Buck White
Sambo (OB)
La Strada

1969 continued
Gertrude Stein's First Reader (OB)
Coco

1970
Unfair to Goliath (OB)
The Last Sweet Days of Isaac (OB)
Joy (OB)
Exchange (OB)
I Dreamt I Dwelt in Bloomingdale's
 (OB)
Gantry
Georgy
Billy Noname (OB)
Show Me Where the Good Times Are
 (OB)
Operation Sidewinder
Purlie
The House of Leather (OB)
Lyle (OB)
Blood Red Roses
Minnie's Boys
Look to the Lilies
Applause
Cry for Us All
Park
Mod Donna (OB)
Company
Colette (OB)
The Me Nobody Knows (OB)
Whispers on the Wind (OB)
The Rothschilds
Sensations (OB)
Touch (OB)
The President's Daughter
Two by Two
Lovely Ladies, Kind Gentlemen

1971
Stag Movie (OB)
Soon
Ari
Look Where I'm At! (OB)
Blood (OB)
A Day in the Life of Just About Every-
 one (OB)
Follies
Six (OB)
70, Girls, 70
Kiss Now (OB)
Frank Merriwell, or Honor Chal-
 lenged

1971 continued
The Ballad of Johnny Pot (OB)
Earl of Ruston
Godspell (OB)
Leaves of Grass (OB)
Jesus Christ Superstar
Drat! (OB)
Ain't Supposed to Die a Natural Death
To Live Another Summer

1971 continued
F. Jasmine Addams (OB)
The Grass Harp
Love Me, Love My Children (OB)
Twigs
Two Gentlemen of Verona
Wild and Wonderful
Inner City
Anne of Green Gables (OB)

Index of Composers and Lyricists

Index of Composers and Lyricists